The Memoirs of
General William Tecumseh Sherman

THE COMPLETE ANNOTATED EDITION

William Tecumseh Sherman

Brady-Handy Collection, Library of Congress,
Prints & Photographs Division, LC-DIG-cwpbh-04445

The Memoirs of General William Tecumseh Sherman

THE COMPLETE ANNOTATED EDITION

William T. Sherman

EDITED BY John F. Marszalek

with Louie P. Gallo and David S. Nolen

THE BELKNAP PRESS OF
HARVARD UNIVERSITY PRESS
Cambridge, Massachusetts
London, England
2025

First printing

Printed in the United States of America

EU GPSR Authorised Representative LOGOS EUROPE,
9 rue Nicolas Poussin, 17000, LA ROCHELLE, France
E-mail: Contact@logoseurope.eu

Library of Congress Cataloging-in-Publication Data

Names: Sherman, William Tecumseh, 1854–1863 author | Marszalek, John F., 1939– editor | Gallo, Louie P. annotator | Nolen, David S. annotator
Title: The memoirs of General William Tecumseh Sherman : the complete annotated edition / William T. Sherman ; edited by John F. Marszalek, with Louie P. Gallo and David S. Nolen.
Description: Complete annotated edition, Second edition. | Cambridge, Massachusetts ; London, England : The Belknap Press of Harvard University Press, 2025. | Includes index.
Identifiers: LCCN 2024061584 (print) | LCCN 2024061585 (ebook) | ISBN 9780674988354 volumes 1–2 hardback | ISBN 9780674301856 epub | ISBN 9780674301863 pdf
Subjects: LCSH: Sherman, William Tecumseh, 1854–1863 | United States. Army—Biography | Generals—United States—Biography | United States—History—Civil War, 1861–1865—Personal narratives | United States—History—Civil War, 1861–1865—Campaigns | LCGFT: Autobiographies
Classification: LCC E467.1.S55 S52 2025 (print) | LCC E467.1.S55 (ebook) | DDC 973.7/81—dc23/eng/20250319
LC record available at https://lccn.loc.gov/2024061584
LC ebook record available at https://lccn.loc.gov/2024061585

In Memory of

DR. AARON S. CRAWFORD

CONTENTS

VOLUME II

PREFACE

It is only natural that those who edited *The Personal Memoirs of Ulysses S. Grant: The Complete Annotated Edition* should undertake the same task for the memoirs of General William T. Sherman. Grant and Sherman, after all, were close friends and Sherman himself would provide his own annotations to Grant's *Memoirs.* Sherman's personal copies of Ulysses S. Grant's *Memoirs,* featuring his own handwritten annotations, were sold at auction on May 14, 2024, by Fleischer Auctions. It is hard now to grasp the immense popularity of these two generals whose remembrances were later published. In fact, during his lifetime Sherman remained one of the most notable figures of the American Civil War.

Sherman's *Memoirs* have been republished in many editions, but none are as well done as this edition. We are indebted to Dr. John F. Marszalek, Louie P. Gallo, and David S. Nolen, who have provided extensive annotations that illuminate Sherman's narrative and add substantive academic value to Sherman scholarship. We are also indebted to the Ulysses S. Grant Presidential Library, the Mississippi State University Libraries, and Mississippi State University, as well as its current president, Dr. Mark E. Keenum. Without their institutional and academic support, this project would not have been possible.

People from my generation remember seeing in our public libraries the books in green binding with gilded stars on their spines in imitation of the shoulder straps of the military leaders who provided their thoughts on the Civil War. How fortunate that annotated versions of both Grant's and Sherman's memoirs are now available to us all.

Frank J. Williams
Former Chief Justice of the Rhode Island Supreme Court
President-Emeritus of the Ulysses S. Grant Association

INTRODUCTION

In the years after the Civil War, the generals and common soldiers who had fought in the immense internecine conflict that the United States had endured reflected on their wartime experiences. Newspapers, magazines, books, and remembrances began to appear, revealing each side's perception of what transpired during the struggle. In its "Battles and Leaders" series, published between 1884 and 1887, *Century Magazine* gave officers from the North and the South a chance to promote their stories. Most impactful, however, was the publication of memoirs by important Civil War leaders. To this day, Ulysses S. Grant's *Memoirs,* published posthumously in 1885, are considered to be some of the best of the genre, but they are hardly alone. In 1875, while Grant was still president of the United States, William Tecumseh Sherman, Grant's closest friend and the commanding general of the U.S. Army at the time, published his own account of the Civil War. His *Memoirs* were some of the earliest—and most controversial—remembrances of the war.

William T. Sherman emerged from the Civil War both admired and detested. Northerners saw him as a hero. Southerners saw him as a civil-society-wrecking ogre who did not understand how gentlemen properly fought each other in civilized warfare. Today historians rank him as one of the great leaders of the war, pointing out the significance of his March to the Sea and his campaign through the Carolinas, and how he moved warfare from the old-fashioned professional army mode to the destructive, psychological methodology that includes civilians in the conflict between the armies. Consequently, what Sherman wrote in his memoirs about the way he fought the war resulted in one of the most debated books of the late nineteenth century.

At first Sherman was hesitant to publish his memoirs. He thought instead of using his own papers, and those that he could obtain through the War Department, to tell his descendants the story that he wanted them to know. He started to write about his role in the conflict around 1868, but at the urging of friends he began to formally write his memoirs in 1873. In early January 1875 he corresponded with historian and diplomat George Bancroft, indicating that he was writing about his own view of the conflict.[1] A week later he wrote a letter to a Cincinnati publishing house, Robert Clarke and Company, telling them how much he admired the good work they had done on several earlier books and inquiring whether the company would be interested in publishing his book. He told them that his memoirs were more "personal than historical," that he had the manuscript ready but wanted to make some changes and then publish it immediately rather than posthumously. The owner of the company responded the next day, saying that he would publish Sherman's book at the company's expense with Sherman receiving the "usual author's 10 per cent" royalty.[2]

Sherman was pleased with Clarke's response. He wrote to his eldest son, Thomas, whose opinion he greatly respected, that he was ready to move forward. "It may involve me in some controversies," he noted, "but these I can abide by absolute silence." He admonished his son, "Don't say a word of this for I want to keep quiet till it is all ready." Sherman expected that his brother John would "be surprised and maybe alarmed" to learn that he had decided to publish his memoirs. He then decided to entertain deals from other publishers, including D. Appleton and Company in New York, which also offered to publish the book. Appleton agreed to do the two-volume work and pay him a royalty of 40 cents for each volume sold. Sherman said that, in turn, he would pay $2,000 for the "stereotype plates" so he would "absolutely" own the work. And he wanted it out in three months. He was clearly pleased with how quickly this arrangement was being made.[3]

Although Sherman had decided to publish his memoirs with D. Appleton and Company, he still reached out to a variety of people for their approval. He told Bancroft that he was worried about his work and admitted, "I would rather fight Shiloh over again and hear the bones of the dead & living crunching under the Artillery wheels than attempt to describe it in words." He also wrote to relatives like William Scott in New York City, and to Co-

[1] Edward Caudill and Paul Ashdown, *Sherman's March in Myth and Memory* (Lanham, MD: Rowan and Littlefield, 2006), 29–30; WTS to George Bancroft, Jan. 4, 1875, George Bancroft Papers, Massachusetts Historical Society.

[2] WTS to Robert Clarke and Company, Jan. 10, 1875, T. W. Norris Collection, Bancroft Library; Robert Clarke to WTS, Jan. 11, 1875, WTS Papers, Library of Congress.

[3] WTS to Thomas Sherman, Jan. 16, 1875, Sherman Family Papers, University of Notre Dame Archives; WTS to John Sherman, Jan. 23, 1875, in *The Sherman Letters: Correspondence between General Sherman and Senator Sherman from 1837 to 1891,* ed. Rachel Sherman Thorndike (New York: Da Capo, 1969), 343.

lumbia University historian John W. Draper. He got the advice of his wife Ellen, who told friends that she would send them a copy when the memoirs were released; Sherman made the same promise to some of his closest friends.[4]

On May 15, 1875, the big day arrived. Appleton informed Sherman that his *Memoirs* had been published. The company had received orders for over 5,000 copies, and another 5,000 would be coming out in a second printing. There were even rumors of a Berlin company printing the *Memoirs* in German. The volumes were bound in blue with gold lettering, some twenty-four chapters and 814 pages. The original two-volume set sold for $5.50. Sherman could not have been more pleased, although he worried about not receiving any royalties from the German edition. He had not been aware that foreign books were not covered by an international copyright.[5]

Sherman's *Memoirs* were an immediate sensation. The text of the first edition included nothing about his early life, instead jumping directly into the story of Sherman's military career at the beginning of the Mexican-American War. The bulk of the text focused on Sherman's experiences during the Civil War, concluding with a chapter in which he offered his take on what the American military should have learned from the war. It was all presented in Sherman's forthright style, and he included unvarnished assessments of fellow officers and subordinates.

Initial newspaper reviews were favorable. The *New York Times* printed "copious extracts" from the *Memoirs* in its pages throughout May 1875.[6] The public rushed to purchase copies, and important figures eventually weighed in on the work's quality. Adam Badeau, one of Ulysses S. Grant's military aides and a historian of the Civil War, called the *Memoirs* "among the very highest contributions to military annals—in all time." Future president and Civil War veteran James A. Garfield praised Sherman, saying that Sherman "tells frankly where he felt himself aggrieved and is equally plain in his

[4] WTS to Bancroft, Jan. 4, 1875, George Bancroft Papers, Massachusetts Historical Society; WTS to William Scott, Jan. 23, 1875, WTS, Missouri Historical Society; WTS to John W. Draper, Jan. 23, 1875, John W. Draper Family Papers, Library of Congress; Samuel H. Byers, *Twenty Years in Europe: A Consul-General's Memories of Noted People, with Letters from General W. T. Sherman* (Chicago: Rand, McNally, 1900), 104–106; WTS to W. Appleton, May 15, 1875, and W. Appleton to WTS, May 15, 1875, WTS Collection, State Historical Society of Iowa.

[5] W. Appleton to WTS, May 15, 1875, WTS Collection, State Historical Society of Iowa.

[6] "Gen. Sherman's Memoirs: Recollections of an Intensely Active Man and a Great General," *New York Times,* May 11, 1875; "New Publications: Gen. Sherman's Memoirs," *New York Times,* May 12, 1875.

opinion of the faults of those with whom he served. This may not have been discreet but it is a fair and truthful picture of his own mind and for that I love him." Others were more critical. Joseph "Fighting Joe" Hooker thought Sherman had been unfairly critical of certain generals, and proclaimed, "I had rather be among those maligned by the *Memoirs* than among those commended." Newspaper reporter Franc B. Wilkie, an old press enemy of Sherman's, carefully insisted that he had always been fair to the general and that he believed that Sherman's *Memoirs* were too critical of war reporters.[7]

Sherman felt hurt and surprised by the criticism he received, but he tried hard not to let the words get to him. He told his son Tom there was a "good deal of comment just now but you must not be uneasy—I have plenty of proof on all contested points." When old friend Admiral David D. Porter sent along some papers in support of something Sherman had said in his *Memoirs,* Sherman jokingly responded, "I do not think I will have to call on you for the Torpedo boat to blow up the Critics."[8]

All this debate quickly settled into what some readers considered unfair attacks on "political generals": men with no military training or experience who joined the army and held important positions because of their political connections. These men did not let any slights they read in the *Memoirs* go unanswered. For example, former postmaster general Montgomery Blair tried to defend his brother, General Frank Blair, against Sherman's critiques. Sherman responded bluntly, "After you have read the Memoirs please write me wherein I have manifested a want of respect or kindness for your brother."[9]

The greatest critic was one of Sherman's former subordinates, William Sooy Smith, who expressed outrage at Sherman's criticism of his performance during the Meridian Campaign in 1864. Smith kept writing to Sherman demanding that his former commander rewrite the Meridian section because that account was completely wrong. He told Sherman that if he did not make

[7] Adam Badeau to WTS, May 20, 1875, WTS Papers, Library of Congress; James A. Garfield, June 22, 1875, diary entry, in *The Diary of James A. Garfield,* ed. Harry James Brown and Frederick D. Williams (East Lansing: Michigan State University Press, 1983), 3:103; John Sherman to WTS, Dec. 19, 1875, WTS Papers, Library of Congress; "Sherman's Memoirs: Major Gen. Hooker Severely Criticises Them," *New York Times,* May 28, 1875, 1; Franc B. Wilkie to WTS, May 22, 1875, WTS Papers, Library of Congress.

[8] WTS to Thomas Sherman, May 24, 1875, Sherman Family Papers, University of Notre Dame Archives; WTS to D. D. Porter, May 31, 1875, David D. Porter Family Papers, Library of Congress.

[9] WTS to Montgomery Blair, May 27, 1875, Blair Family Papers, Library of Congress.

corrections, Sherman "would own [the] inaccuracies" and Smith would then "assume that they are intentional." Smith wrote letter after letter, insisting that he had not done the terrible things Sherman accused him of. He said, "I will never rest until the wrong statements . . . are fully and fairly corrected." For his part, Sherman insisted that he would not change anything because he knew he was right. "You seem to think that I should not have written 'my memoirs,' but 'yours.' I saw events from my own standpoint, not yours," Sherman said. He also expressed willingness to have General J. D. Webster of Chicago arbitrate the dispute, but nothing was ever settled between Smith and Sherman.[10]

Such comments for and against Sherman's account continued appearing regularly. Francis E. Spinner, treasurer of the United States from 1861 to 1875, said he loved the *Memoirs* so much that it was the first book he had read in some twenty years. The famous Comte de Paris, who wrote his own history of the Civil War, said that after reading the *Memoirs,* "the reader feels as if he had a long and familiar talk with the great leader of the great March."[11]

Sherman's confidence in his account of the war was particularly evident when he emceed the annual meeting of the Society of the Army of the Tennessee. Having heard a great deal of criticism of his *Memoirs,* he came prepared to talk to his old comrades forthrightly. "We ain't sorry for what we have done, and don't intend to apologize for it," he insisted. The next day when it was time to respond to a variety of toasts, Sherman was given the task of discussing the March to the Sea. At first he gave a restrained explanation, but then quickly turned to talking about his *Memoirs.* "I have no apology to make or excuses to offer," he said. "I advise the living witnesses now to testify before the great tribunal of the world—at least those who do not fear the critics—that the whole truth may be manifest." He summed up his speech by saying, "In conclusion, whether the army that marched to the sea was fortunate or not in its leader, I regret that some one of the recent better Generals had not stood in my shoes then; and still more that they are not in my shoes now." The audience erupted in "prolonged applause."[12]

[10] William Sooy Smith to WTS, July 2, 9, 1875; WTS to J. D. Webster, July 11, 1875, WTS Papers, Library of Congress.

[11] F. E. Spinner to WTS, June, 28, 1875; Comte de Paris to WTS, Oct. 14, 1875, WTS Papers, Library of Congress.

[12] *Report of the Proceedings of the Society of the Army of the Tennessee, at the 9th Annual Meeting,* Sept. 29–30, 1875 (Cincinnati: Society of the Army of the Tennessee, 1877), 388, 404, 406.

All this was mild compared to what followed. Henry Van Ness Boynton, who had been an officer in the Army of the Cumberland and a great admirer of its commander, General George H. Thomas, was outraged at what Sherman wrote about Thomas. Sherman refused to accept the criticism. "I may have committed errors, I surely have made some omissions, and prudence would have dictated more," he conceded, but ultimately he denied that he had unfairly attacked Thomas or others. Boynton then began to write reviews critical of the Sherman *Memoirs.* He compiled the many critiques he had written for his local newspaper, the *Cincinnati Gazette,* into a book, published as *Sherman's Historical Raid: The Memoirs in the Light of the Record.* In the book's preface he claimed that Sherman's *Memoirs* were "intensely egotistical, unreliable, and cruelly unjust to nearly all his distinguished associates," including Grant. And to make sure that nobody missed the point, Boynton had his book bound in blue with gold lettering, just like Sherman's *Memoirs.*[13]

At first Sherman tried to ignore Boynton, but then he began to suspect that his old enemy, Secretary of War William W. Belknap, was behind Boynton's criticism. So, Sherman asked his friends to counter Boynton's critiques. For example, General Jacob D. Cox composed an extended defense of Sherman and attacked Boynton. With Sherman's guidance, Charles W. Moulton, Sherman's brother-in-law, wrote a pamphlet defending the *Memoirs.* But eventually Sherman decided that he needed to publish an amended version of the *Memoirs* to quiet the criticism, and he considered publishing a second edition. Meanwhile the Appleton company tried to keep Sherman calm, telling him that "no one who writes a book ever can hope to escape a certain amount of 'unpleasant criticism,' while few find so much praise." Sherman paid no attention to the Appleton editors and continued to fret. He said, "I want to get this matter of the Memoirs off my mind if possible, for it annoys me excessively." Lamenting the whole state of the debate, he wrote, "If we few can't agree I don't see how the General Public will."[14]

Several critics, including Boynton, claimed that the real problem with the *Memoirs* was that Sherman did not give Ulysses S. Grant adequate credit, especially with regard to the planning of the now-famous March to the Sea. It became increasingly clear that Grant was the only person who could solve the

[13] *Report of the Proceedings,* 406; Draper to WTS, Nov. 15, 1875, and WTS to Charles W. Moulton, Nov. 1 and Dec. 18, 1875, WTS Papers, New York Public Library; WTS to Samuel M. Bowman, Dec. 2, 1875, Special Collections, Northwestern University.

[14] Appleton to WTS, Oct. 5, 1875, WTS Papers, Library of Congress; WTS to Bowman, Jan. 19, 25, 1875, Special Collections, Northwestern University.

imbroglio. Sherman knew that if Grant took his side, the whole controversy would soon be over. Slowly the pendulum moved in that direction. While attending the annual meeting of the Society of the Army of the Cumberland, Sherman met with Grant and New York senator Roscoe Conkling, at which time Grant indicated that he had found nothing to criticize in Sherman's *Memoirs.* Sherman asked Conkling to verify what Grant had said, so that Sherman could use his words to defend his *Memoirs.* Conkling did not feel comfortable asking Grant to do this, though, so the controversy continued.[15]

The issue culminated in a surprising way. Grant and James A. Garfield met on January 16, 1876, and Grant once again praised Sherman's *Memoirs.* He said he had read Sherman's *Memoirs* more carefully than he had read any book since he had become president, and that he "had taken a pencil and paper for the purpose of making notes and criticisms, but when he had finished it there was really nothing to dispute." Two days later, Grant and Sherman had dinner together, and Grant promised Sherman a letter supporting the *Memoirs.* Sherman wrote to Grant the next day to make sure the general would follow up on his promise.[16]

Grant responded with a ringing endorsement of the *Memoirs* that fit Sherman's purpose: "I will repeat that I do not believe a more correct history can be given of the events recorded by you in the 'Memoirs' . . . The mistakes, in my judgement, are entirely in speculations." And so, for the moment, the controversy died.[17]

However, the dispute over the accuracy of the *Memoirs* was reignited when a reporter for the *Cleveland Leader* interviewed Sherman in 1880. The old general again attacked Boynton. "You could hire him to do anything for money," Sherman said, adding that "for a thousand dollars" Boynton would "slander his own mother." In response, Boynton insisted that Sherman had been misquoted, but Sherman dismissed the suggestion. "This is a hard thing to say of any man," he wrote to Boynton, "but I believe it of you." Boynton then demanded Sherman be court-martialed, while Sherman requested a civil trial instead. John Sherman told his brother to ignore Boynton, stating that

[15] Roscoe Conkling to WTS, Oct. 15, 1875, and WTS to Conkling, Nov. 1, 1875, WTS Papers, Library of Congress.

[16] James A. Garfield, Jan. 16, 1876, diary entry, *Diary of James A. Garfield,* 3:216–217; WTS to Conkling, Jan. 18, 1876, Conkling Papers, Library of Congress; WTS to USG, Jan. 19, 1876, *PUSG,* 27:20–21*n.*

[17] USG to WTS, Jan. 29, 1876, *PUSG,* 27:16–21.

people considered him "a liar and a libeler." Nothing came of either legal action, but once again the *Memoirs* were in the news.[18]

In reaction to all the controversy, Sherman finally decided to publish a second edition of his *Memoirs.* Out of respect for Grant, whose *Memoirs* were published posthumously in 1885, Sherman waited to release the second edition of his own *Memoirs.* Beginning in 1886 he worked with Moulton to revise the text, adding a new first chapter dealing with his early life, a new final chapter covering his time after the war, about fifty minor changes to the text, and two appendixes containing reports, letters, and comments related to criticism and praise of the first edition. Concluding that he had been factual the first time around, Sherman left the substance of the work unchanged in the second edition. As he put it, "Of omissions there are plenty, but of willful perversion of facts, none."[19]

There have been numerous republications of the *Memoirs* since the late 1800s; all are based on the second edition, but they are not uniformly annotated. A variety of publishers, such as Charles L. Webster and D. Appleton, and historians, such as William McFeely, Charles Royster, B. H. Liddle Hart, and Michael Fellman, have written new introductions and provided some annotations. The proliferation of editions is testament that Sherman's text has retained high stature over the years among both historians and popular readers. Historians, sometimes critically and other times unquestioningly, have mined the *Memoirs* for Sherman's unique perspectives and reflections on the events that he played such a large part in. One historian pointed out, "It would be difficult to exaggerate the influence of [Sherman's *Memoirs*] on both popular and professional conceptions of the Civil War."[20]

This new, extensively annotated edition of Sherman's *Memoirs* aims to present the modern reader with the clearest contextualization possible of Sherman's important words.

To this day, scholars and casual readers remain captivated by Sherman's perspectives on the Civil War. Years after their entry into the forum of public

[18] Henry Van Ness Boynton to WTS, Jan. 16, 1876, WTS Papers, Library of Congress; Laura Mammina, Lesley J. Gordon, and Megan L. Bever, eds., *American Discord: The Republic and Its People in the Civil War Era* (Baton Rouge: LSU Press, 2020); John Sherman to WTS, Dec. 10, 1875, *PUSG,* 27:20n.

[19] James L. McDonough, *William Tecumseh Sherman: In The Service of My Country—A Life* (New York: W. W. Norton, 2016), 710–711.

[20] Albert Castel, "Prevaricating through Georgia: Sherman's *Memoirs* as a Source on the Atlanta Campaign," *Civil War History* 12, no. 1 (1994): 48.

opinion, Sherman's arguments about what happened and his assessments of his own and others' efforts remain controversial. This new annotated edition, which presents Sherman's thoughts in his own words with additional information about their context, ensures that Sherman's *Memoirs* will remain accessible and relevant to a modern audience for years to come.

John F. Marszalek

EDITORIAL PROCEDURE

This edition of *The Memoirs of General William Tecumseh Sherman* is the first comprehensively annotated edition of the text. Using a procedure similar to the one used in *The Personal Memoirs of Ulysses S. Grant: The Complete Annotated Edition,* edited by John F. Marszalek, David S. Nolen, and Louie P. Gallo (Cambridge, MA: Belknap Press of Harvard University Press, 2017), the editors provide contextual annotations of Sherman's text in order to make it more accessible for both casual readers and researchers.

To that end, they do not add explanatory text for data the general reader can easily find in other places. They only interject with their own words when it is necessary to clarify Sherman's narrative; for example, if Sherman's account includes a factual error, the editors provide an annotation to correct it. The text and punctuation are those of the second published edition from 1886, but the editors make note of any textual changes made by Sherman and correct acknowledged errata and other typographical errors.

The text presented here is in one volume, although both the first and second editions were published in two volumes. The editors chose to use the text of the second edition because it was the last edition that Sherman personally amended. In that edition, Sherman added a new first chapter related to his early life, a new last chapter about his postwar experiences, and an appendix for each volume. To show the motivation for some of Sherman's changes in the second edition, the editors provide annotations that cross-reference the appendix.

The editors attempt to identify every person Sherman mentions in the *Memoirs* the first time they appear. Such notes include full name, birth and death years in parentheses, relevant biographical details, and their relevant military experience. Any special relationship to Sherman is also noted, as are unusual or outstanding facts about the individual. A lack of parenthetical dates or a question mark in place of a date indicates that the editors found no reliable information for that individual's date of birth or death. Where the editors could find birth or death dates only in sources that were difficult to verify, they designated those dates with a "c." for "circa." Where the text of the *Memoirs* mentions or quotes Sherman correspondence, the editors relied heavily on *The War of the Rebellion: A Compilation of the Official Records of the Union and Confederate Armies,* 128 vols. (Washington, DC: GPO, 1880–1901) and *The Papers of Ulysses S. Grant,* 32 vols., ed. John Y. Simon and John F. Marszalek (Carbondale: Southern Illinois University Press, 1967–2012); both of these sources include significant portions of Sherman's Civil War correspondence. However, no sources or annotations are provided when Sherman gives the name / date of his own correspondence or when he provides the entire text of a letter, dispatch, order, or report. The editors also rely on George W. Cullum's *Biographical Register of the Officers and Graduates of the U.S. Military Academy at West Point, N.Y.*, 3rd ed. (Boston: Houghton, Mifflin and Company, 1891).

Some charts and tables contained errors of addition in the original editions; the editors have silently corrected those errors for this edition. Images that were included in the nineteenth-century editions have been omitted from this edition. The original maps in the *Memoirs* do not provide clear renderings of the terrain and do not reference modern landmarks; therefore, the editors have not included them in the text. Instead the editors provide references to the relevant maps in George B. Davis et al., *Official Military Atlas of the Civil War* (New York: Fairfax Press, 1983). Sherman's original spellings of place-names are retained. Named places that still exist and are readily identifiable are not annotated. Places that no longer exist or whose names have changed or are now unknown are annotated to explain their relative location. Distances between locations are measured by straight-line mileage (as the crow flies).

TABLES

ABBREVIATIONS

Art.	Artillery
Brig.	Brigade
Capt.	Captain
Cav.	Cavalry
Co.	Company
Col.	Colonel
CWHC	John H. Eicher and David J. Eicher, *Civil War High Commands* (Stanford, CA: Stanford University Press, 2001)
Dept.	Department
Dist.	District
Div.	Division
Gen.	General
Gov.	Governor
GPO	Government Printing Office
Inf.	Infantry
OR	*The War of the Rebellion: A Compilation of the Official Records of the Union and Confederate Armies,* 128 vols. (Washington, DC: GPO, 1880–1901)
ORN	*Official Records of the Union and Confederate Navies in the War of the Rebellion,* 30 vols. (Washington, DC: GPO, 1894–1922)
Pres.	President
PUSG	*The Papers of Ulysses S. Grant,* 32 vols., ed. John Y. Simon and John F. Marszalek (Carbondale: Southern Illinois University Press, 1967–2012)
USG	Ulysses S. Grant
USMA	United States Military Academy, West Point, NY
USMA	George W. Cullum, *Biographical Register of the Officers and Graduates of the U.S. Military Academy at West Point, N.Y.*, 3rd ed. (Boston: Houghton, Mifflin and Company, 1891)
WTS	William T. Sherman

The Memoirs of

General William Tecumseh Sherman

THE COMPLETE ANNOTATED EDITION

The Memoirs of William T. Sherman

GENERAL W. T. SHERMAN

TO

HIS COMRADES IN ARMS,

VOLUNTEERS AND REGULARS.

Nearly ten years have passed since the close of the civil war in America, and yet no satisfactory history thereof is accessible to the public; nor should any be attempted until the Government has published, and placed within the reach of students, the abundant materials that are buried in the War Department at Washington. These are in process of compilation; but, at the rate of progress for the past ten years, it is probable that a new century will come before they are published and circulated, with full indexes to enable the historian to make a judicious selection of materials.

What is now offered is not designed as a history of the war, or even as a complete account of all the incidents in which the writer bore a part, but merely his recollection of events, corrected by a reference to his own memoranda, which may assist the future historian when he comes to describe the whole, and account for the motives and reasons which influenced some of the actors in the grand drama of war.

I trust a perusal of these pages will prove interesting to the survivors, who have manifested so often their intense love of the "cause" which moved a nation to vindicate its own authority; and, equally so, to the rising generation, who therefrom may learn that a country and government such as ours are worth fighting for, and dying for, if need be.

If successful in this, I shall feel amply repaid for departing from the usage of military men, who seldom attempt to publish their own deeds, but rest content with simply contributing by their acts to the honor and glory of their country.

WILLIAM T. SHERMAN,
General.

St. Louis, Missouri, *January* 21, 1875.

Preface to the Second Edition.

Another ten years have passed since I ventured to publish my Memoirs, and, being once more at leisure, I have revised them in the light of the many criticisms public and private.[1]

My habit has been to note in pencil the suggestions of critics, and to examine the substance of their differences; for critics must differ from the author, to manifest their superiority.

Where I have found material error I have corrected; and I have added two chapters, one at the beginning, another at the end, both of the most general character, and an appendix.

I wish my friends and enemies to understand that I disclaim the character of historian, but assume to be a witness on the stand before the great tribunal of history, to assist some future Napier,[2] Alison,[3] or Hume[4] to comprehend the feelings and thoughts of the actors in the grand conflicts of the recent past, and thereby to lessen his labors in the compilation necessary for the future benefit of mankind.

In this free country every man is at perfect liberty to publish his own thoughts and impressions, and any witness who may differ from me should publish his own version of facts in the truthful narration of which he is inter-

[1] See Appendix to Volume I and II.

[2] From 1828 to 1840, Sir William Francis Patrick Napier (1786–1860), a British solider and historian, published the six-volume *History of the War in the Peninsula and the South of France from the Year 1807 to the Year 1814*. He also published *The Conquest of Scinde* in 1845. "Sir William Napier," *Morning Post* (London, England), Feb. 15, 1860, 5.

[3] From 1833 to 1843, Sir Archibald Alison (1792–1867), a Scottish historian, published the ten-volume edition of *History of Europe from the Commencement of the French Revolution in 1789 to the Restoration of the Bourbons in 1815*. "Death of Archibald Alison," *Glasgow Herald*, May 24, 1867, 4.

[4] David Hume (1711–1776), a Scottish historian, published the *Treatise on Human Nature* and multiple volumes of the *History of England*. Thomas B. Shaw, *A History of English Literature*, 4th ed. (London: John Murray, 1868), 355.

ested. I am publishing my own memoirs, not *theirs,* and we all know that no three honest witnesses of a simple brawl can agree on all the details. How much more likely will be the difference in a great battle covering a vast space of broken ground, when each division, brigade, regiment, and even company, naturally and honestly believes that it was the focus of the whole affair! Each of them won the battle. None ever lost. That was the fate of the old man who unhappily commanded.

In this edition I give the best maps which I believe have ever been prepared, compiled by General O. M. Poe,[5] from personal knowledge and official surveys, and what I chiefly aim to establish is the true *cause* of the *results* which are already known to the whole world;[6] and it may be a relief to many to know that I shall publish no other, but, like the player at cards, will "stand;" not that I have accomplished perfection, but because I can do no better with the cards in hand. Of omissions there are plenty, but of wilful perversion of facts, none.

In the preface to the first edition, in 1875, I used these words: "Nearly ten years have passed since the close of the civil war in America, and yet no satisfactory history thereof is accessible to the public; nor should any be attempted until the Government has published, and placed within the reach of students, the abundant materials that are buried in the War Department at Washington. These are in process of compilation; but, at the rate of progress for the past ten years, it is probable that a new century will come before they are published and circulated, with full indexes to enable the historian to make a judicious selection of materials."

Another decade is past, and I am in possession of all these publications, my last being Volume XI, Part 3, Series 1, the last date in which is August 30, 1862. I am afraid that if I assume again the character of prophet, I must extend the time deep into the next century, and pray meanwhile that the official records of the war, "Union and Confederate," may approach completion before the "next war," or rather that we, as a people, may be spared another war until the last one is officially recorded. Meantime the rising generation must be content with memoirs and histories compiled from the best sources available.

[5] Orlando M. Poe (1832–1895) graduated from the USMA in 1856 and was appointed as an engineer in the Military Div. of the Mississippi in 1863. *CWHC,* 432.

[6] Because the original maps in the *Memoirs* are not clear and thus are not helpful to the reader, we have not included them in the text. Instead we provide references to the relevant maps in George B. Davis et al., *Official Military Atlas of the Civil War* (New York: Fairfax Press, 1983).

In this sense I offer mine as to the events of which I was an eye-witness and participant, or for which I was responsible.

W. T. SHERMAN,
General (retired).

St. Louis, Missouri, *March 30, 1885.*

Volume I

I

From 1820 to the Mexican War.

1820–1846.

According to Cothren, in his "History of Ancient Woodbury, Connecticut,"[1] the Sherman family came from Dedham, Essex County, England. The first recorded name is of Edmond Sherman, with his three sons, Edmond, Samuel, and John, who were at Boston before 1636; and further it is distinctly recorded that Hon. Samuel Sherman, *Rev. John,* his brother, and Captain John, his first cousin, arrived from Dedham, Essex County, England, in 1634.[2] Samuel afterward married Sarah Mitchell, who had come (in the same ship) from England, and finally settled at Stratford, Connecticut.[3] The other two (Johns) located at Watertown, Massachusetts.

Note: This chapter was not included in the first edition (1875) of WTS's *Memoirs.* It was added to the second edition (1886) as the new opening chapter.

[1] William Cothren (1819–1898) published the first volume of his *History of Ancient Woodbury, Connecticut, from the First Indian Deed in 1659 to 1872,* in 1854. Two more volumes were published in 1872 and 1879. J. A. Spalding, *Illustrated Popular Biography of Connecticut* (Hartford, CT: Case, Lockwood, and Brainard, 1891), 99.

[2] Edmund Sherman (1572–1641) immigrated with his family to Wethersfield, CT, in 1635. Edmund Sherman (Jr.) (1599–1673) settled with his family in Watertown, MA. He later returned to England, where he died. Samuel Sherman (1618–1700) immigrated with his family to Wethersfield, CT, later moving to Stratford, CT. John Sherman (1613–1685) graduated from Trinity College, Cambridge, in 1633. While serving as a minister, he lived in various places throughout New England, including Wethersfield, Milford, and Watertown, CT. John Sherman (1612–c. 1691) immigrated to Watertown, MA, around 1636. Frank D. Sherman, *The Ancestry of James Morgan Sherman and His Descendants* (New York: Privately printed, 1915), 6–7; Thomas T. Sherman, *Sherman Genealogy Including Families of Essex, Suffolk and Norfolk, England* (Madison: University of Wisconsin, 1920), 105, 108.

[3] Sarah Mitchell (c. 1621–1665) was born in Halifax, Yorkshire County, England, and immigrated to New England with her family in 1636. She married Samuel Sherman around 1640. Based on the historical record, Samuel's family traveled aboard the ship *Elizabeth* and Sarah's family traveled on the ship *James.* Henry Bond and Horatio Gates Jones, *Genealogies of the*

From Captain John Sherman are descended Roger Sherman, the signer of the Declaration of Independence, Hon. William M. Evarts, the Messrs. Hoar, of Massachusetts, and many others of national fame.[4] Our own family are descended from the Hon. Samuel Sherman and his son, the Rev. John, who was born in 1650–'51; then another John, born in 1687; then Judge Daniel, born in 1721;[5] then Taylor Sherman, our grandfather, who was born in 1758. Taylor Sherman was a lawyer and judge in Norwalk, Connecticut, where he resided until his death, May 4, 1815; leaving a widow,

---

Families and Descendants of the Early Settlers of Watertown, Massachusetts, Including Waltham and Weston (Boston: Little, Brown and Co., 1855), 934; Henry R. Stiles, *Families of Ancient Wethersfield, Connecticut, Consisting of Volume II of The History of Ancient Wethersfield* (Westminster: Heritage Books, 2007), 504.

[4] Roger Sherman (1721–1793) was born in Newton, MA, and moved to Connecticut in 1743. He served as a delegate to the First Continental Congress in 1774 and was on the committee that drafted the Declaration of Independence. He served as a member of the Constitutional Convention of 1787, the U.S. House of Representatives, and the U.S. Senate. William M. Evarts (1818–1901) defended Henry Ward Beecher in the controversial *Tilton v. Beecher* trial in 1875. He also served as U.S. attorney general from 1868 to 1869, secretary of state from 1877 to 1881, and U.S. senator from New York from 1885 to 1891. The Hoar family (including Samuel, George, Ebenezer, and Sherman Hoar) were prominent in American politics. Francis S. Drake, *Dictionary of American Biography* (Boston: Houghton, Osgood and Co., 1879), 823; Roger K. Newman, ed., *The Yale Biographical Dictionary of American Law* (New Haven, CT: Yale University Press, 2009), 190; Henry S. Nourse, *The Hoar Family in America and Its English Ancestry: A Compilation from Collections Made by the Hon. George Frisbie Hoar* (Boston: David Clapp and Sons, Printers, 1899).

[5] John Sherman (1650–1730) was born in Stratford, CT, and was a deacon in the Congregational Church. He served as speaker of the Connecticut Assembly from 1711 to 1712. John Sherman (1687–1727) was from Woodbury, CT. In 1714 he married Emma Preston, and together they had seven children. Daniel Sherman (1721–1799) was born in Woodbury, CT, and married Mindwell Taylor in 1741. He was a member of the Connecticut Committee of Safety and the General Assembly. Sherman, *Sherman Genealogy,* 134, 148–149; Gertrude B. Darwin, *Lineage Book: National Society of the Daughters of the American Revolution* (Harrisburg, PA: Telegraph Printing, 1910), 30:79; Hewson L. Peake, *A Standard History of Erie Country, Ohio: An Authentic Narrative of the Past, with Particular Attention to the Modern Era in the Commercial, Industrial, Civic and Social Development—A Chronicle of the People with Family Lineage and Memoirs* (Chicago: Lewis, 1916), 30:603.

Betsey Stoddard Sherman,[6] and three children, Charles R. (our father), Daniel, and Betsey.[7]

When the State of Connecticut, in 1786, ceded to the United States her claim to the western part of her public domain, as defined by her Royal Charter, she reserved a large district in what is now northern Ohio, a portion of which (five hundred thousand acres) composed the "Fire-Land District," which was set apart to indemnify the parties who had lost property in Connecticut by the raids of Generals Arnold, Tryon, and others during the latter part of the Revolutionary War.[8]

[6]Taylor Sherman (1758–1815) was born in Woodbury, CT. He married Elizabeth Stoddard in 1787 and was a member of the Connecticut General Assembly from 1794 to 1796, a judge of probate for the District of Norwalk from 1802 to 1815, and a collector of internal revenue for the Second District of Connecticut. Elizabeth Stoddard Sherman (1767–1848) was born in Woodbury. After her husband's death, she moved to Lancaster, OH, with her son, Charles, and later died in Mansfield, OH. *A Biographical Record of Fairfield County, Ohio* (New York: S. J. Clarke, 1902), 143–144; Norwalk Historical and Memorial Library Association, *Norwalk after Two Hundred and Fifty Years: An Account of the Celebration of the 250th Anniversary of the Charter of the Town, 1651–September 11th–1901* (South Norwalk: C. A. Freeman, 1901), 280.

[7]Charles R. Sherman (1788–1829) was born in Norwalk, CT. He studied law at Dartmouth College and was admitted to the bar in 1810. He moved to Lancaster, OH, in 1811. In 1813 he was appointed by Pres. James Madison to serve as the collector of internal revenue for the Third District of Ohio. In 1823 he was elected by the legislature to serve as a judge on the Supreme Court of Ohio. Daniel Sherman (1790–1864) was born in Norwalk, CT, and moved to Ohio, where he married Abby Guthrie. After Abby's death in 1820, Daniel married Laura Hubbell in 1824. Elizabeth Sherman (1791–1851) married Judge Jacob Parker in Lancaster, OH, in 1820. They had three children together. *A Biographical Record of Fairfield County, Ohio,* 145; Sherman, *Sherman Genealogy,* 254–55.

[8]Benedict Arnold (1741–1801) was born in Norwich, CT. He served as a general in the Continental Army during the Revolutionary War. While in command at West Point, he plotted with British major John André to give up the critical fort on the Hudson River. After his plot was discovered, he defected to the British Army in 1780 and served as an officer until the war's end. He died in London in 1801. William Tryon (1729–1788) was born in Surrey, England. He was a British Army officer and served as a colonel during the Seven Years' War. After the war he became lieutenant governor and then royal governor of North Carolina from 1765 to 1771 and then of New York from 1771 to 1780. During the American Revolutionary War, Tryon was awarded the rank of major general of the British Provincials. Joyce Lee Malcolm, *The Tragedy of Benedict Arnold: An American Life* (New York: Pegasus, 2018); William S. Powell, ed., *Dictionary of North Carolina Biography,* vol. 6, *T–Z* (Chapel Hill: University of

Our grandfather, Judge Taylor Sherman, was one of the commissioners appointed by the State of Connecticut to quiet the Indian title, and to survey and subdivide this Fire-Land District, which includes the present counties of Huron and Erie.[9] In his capacity as commissioner he made several trips to Ohio in the early part of this century, and it is supposed that he then contracted the disease which proved fatal. For his labor and losses he received a title to two sections of land, which fact was probably the prime cause of the migration of our family to the West. My father received a good education, and was admitted to the bar at Norwalk, Connecticut, where, in 1810, he, at twenty years of age, married Mary Hoyt, also of Norwalk,[10] and at once migrated to Ohio, leaving his wife (my mother) for a time. His first purpose was to settle at Zanesville, Ohio, but he finally chose Lancaster, Fairfield County, where he at once engaged in the practice of his profession. In 1811 he returned to Norwalk, where, meantime, was born Charles Taylor Sherman, the eldest of the family, who with his mother was carried to Ohio on horseback.[11]

Judge Taylor Sherman's family remained in Norwalk till 1815, when his death led to the emigration of the remainder of the family, viz., of Uncle Daniel Sherman, who settled at Monroeville, Ohio, as a farmer, where he lived and died quite recently, leaving children and grandchildren; and an aunt, Betsey, who married Judge Parker,[12] of Mansfield, and died in 1851,

---

North Carolina Press, 1996), s.v. "Tyron, William (1729–27 Jan. 1788)"; Spencer Tucker, ed., *500 Great Military Leaders* (Santa Barbara: ABC-CLIO, 2015), vol. 1, s.v. "Arnold, Benedict."

[9] Taylor Sherman went to the area in 1805 to facilitate the removal of Native Americans from the land. John F. Marszalek, *Sherman: A Soldier's Passion for Order* (New York: Free Press, 1993), 2.

[10] Mary Hoyt (1787–1852) was born in Norwalk, CT, and received her education from the Poughkeepsie, NY, Female Seminary. She died in Mansfield, OH. *A Biographical Record of Fairfield County, Ohio,* 144; Sherman, *Sherman Genealogy,* 318.

[11] Charles T. Sherman (1811–1879) graduated with a law degree from Ohio University in 1830. He served as the U.S district court judge in the Northern District of Ohio from 1867 to 1872. The Sherman family moved to Lancaster, OH, in April 1812. Lynn Hoogenboom, *William Tecumseh Sherman: The Fight to Preserve the Union* (New York: Rosen, 2004), 17; Sherman, *Sherman Genealogy,* 318, 388.

[12] Jacob Parker (1791–1857) was elected by the Ohio legislature as the presiding judge of the Ohio Court of Common Pleas for Richland County for 1841 to 1848. Sherman, *Sherman Genealogy,* 255.

leaving children and grandchildren; also Grandmother Elizabeth Stoddard Sherman, who resided with her daughter, Mrs. Betsey Parker, in Mansfield until her death, August 1, 1848.

Thus my father, Charles R. Sherman, became finally established at Lancaster, Ohio, as a lawyer, with his own family in the year 1811, and continued there till the time of his death, in 1829. I have no doubt that he was in the first instance attracted to Lancaster by the natural beauty of its scenery, and the charms of its already established society. He continued in the practice of his profession, which in those days was no sinecure, for the ordinary circuit was made on horseback, and embraced Marietta, Cincinnati, and Detroit. Hardly was the family established there when the War of 1812 caused great alarm and distress in all Ohio. The English captured Detroit and the shores of Lake Erie down to the Maumee River; while the Indians still occupied the greater part of the State. Nearly every man had to be somewhat of a soldier, but I think my father was only a commissary;[13] still, he seems to have caught a fancy for the great chief of the Shawnees, "Tecumseh."[14]

Perry's victory on Lake Erie was the turning-point of the Western campaign,[15] and General Harrison's victory over the British and Indians at the river Thames in Canada ended the war in the West, and restored peace and tranquillity to the exposed settlers of Ohio.[16] My father at once resumed his practice at the bar, and was soon recognized as an able and successful lawyer. When, in 1816, my brother James was born, he insisted on engrafting the Indian name "Tecumseh" on the usual family list. My mother had already named her first son after her own brother *Charles;* and insisted on the second son taking the name of her other brother James, and when I

[13] Charles R. Sherman served as major for the 1st Regiment, 1st Brig., 3rd Div., Ohio Militia. Sherman, *Sherman Genealogy,* 318.

[14] Tecumseh (1768–1813) was most likely born in a village near present-day Piqua, OH. He was a Shawnee leader who fought against the United States during the War of 1812. He died at the Battle of the Thames in Upper Canada. Marszalek, *Sherman,* 4; Spencer Tucker, ed., *The Encyclopedia of the War of 1812* (Santa Barbara: ABC-CLIO, 2012), s.v. "Tecumseh."

[15] Oliver Hazard Perry (1785–1919) was born in South Kingston, RI. On Sept. 10, 1813, Perry's American fleet defeated British forces under the command of Robert Barclay at the Battle of Lake Erie. Tucker, *Encyclopedia of the War of 1812,* s.v. "Perry, Oliver Hazard."

[16] William Henry Harrison (1773–1841) defeated the British and Native American forces at the Battle of the Thames on Oct. 5, 1813. He was later elected president of the United States in 1841. Tucker, *Encyclopedia of the War of 1812,* s.v. "Harrison, William Henry."

came along, on the 8th of February, 1820, mother having no more brothers, my father succeeded in his original purpose, and named me William *Tecumseh*.[17]

The family rapidly increased till it embraced six boys and five girls, all of whom attained maturity and married; of these six are still living.[18]

In the year 1821 a vacancy occurred in the Supreme Court of Ohio, and I find this petition:

SOMERSET, OHIO, *July* 6, 1821.

May it please your Excellency:

We ask leave to recommend to your Excellency's favorable notice Charles R. Sherman, Esq., of Lancaster, as a man possessing in an eminent degree those qualifications so much to be desired in a Judge of the Supreme Court.

From a long acquaintance with Mr. Sherman, we are happy to be able to state to your Excellency that our minds are led to the conclusion that that gentleman possesses a disposition noble and generous, a mind discriminating, comprehensive, and combining a heart pure, benevolent and humane. Manners dignified, mild, and complaisant, and a firmness not to be shaken and of unquestioned integrity.

But Mr. Sherman's character cannot be unknown to your Excellency, and on that acquaintance without further comment we might safely rest his pretensions.

[17] Mary had a brother named Charles Hoyt (1791–1869) and two brothers named James: the first born in 1777, who died prior to 1806, and the second named James Isaac (1782–1858). David Webster Hoyt, *A Genealogical History of the Hoyt, Haight, and Hight Families* (Boston: Henry Hoyt, 1871), 425. For scholarly discussion on the origin of WTS's name, see Carl R. Schenker Jr., "My Father . . . Named Me William Tecumseh: Rebutting the Charge That General Sherman Lied about His Name," *Ohio History* 111 (2008): 55–79.

[18] Sherman's siblings included: Charles T. Sherman (1811–1879), Mary Elizabeth Reese (1812–1900), James Sherman (1814–1864), Amelia McComb (1816–1862), Julia Ann Willock (1818–1842), Lampson Parker Sherman (1821–1900), John Sherman (1823–1900), Susan Denman Bartley (1825–1876), Hoyt Sherman (1827–1904), and Frances Beecher Moulton (1829–c. 1889). Sherman, *Sherman Genealogy,* 319–326; William T. Sherman, *Sherman's Civil War: Selected Correspondence of William T. Sherman, 1860–1865,* ed. Brooks D. Simpson and Jean V. Berlin (Chapel Hill: University of North Carolina Press, 1999), 94*n,* 101*n.*

We think we hazard little in assuring your Excellency that his appointment would give almost universal satisfaction to the citizens of Perry County.

With great consideration, we have the honor to be

Your Excellency's most obedient humble servants,

Charles A. Hood,
George Treat,[19]
Peter Dittoe,
P. Odlin,
J. B. Orten,
T. Beckwith,[20]
William P. Dorst,[21]
John Murray,
Jacob Moins,[22]
B. Eaton,
Daniel Griggs,
Henry Dittoe,
Nicholas Mccarty.

His Excellency Ethan A. Brown,
Governor of Ohio, Columbus.

He was soon after appointed a Judge of the Supreme Court, and served in that capacity to the day of his death.

[19] Most likely George Trout (1762–1829), who served as one of the first associate judges of Perry County. He assisted in the creation of the new county seat and donated the land for the county courthouse in Somerset. A. A. Graham, *History of Fairfield and Perry Counties, Ohio* (Chicago: W. H. Beers, 1883), 2:571.

[20] Most likely John Beckwith (1791–1880), who was appointed clerk by the associate judges of Perry County, OH, for the years 1818–1828, 1832–1839, and 1848–1857. *A Centennial Biographical History of the City of Columbus and Franklin County Ohio* (Chicago: Lewis, 1901), 66; Graham, *History of Fairfield and Perry Counties,* 2:46–47.

[21] William P. Darst (1797–1875) was the clerk of court for Perry County, OH, from 1828 to 1832. "Brevities," *Portsmouth Daily Times* (Portsmouth, OH), Nov. 20, 1875, 3; Sandford C. Gladden, *The Durst and Darst Families of America with Discussions of Some Forty Related Families* (self-pub., 1969), 292; Graham, *History of Fairfield and Perry Counties,* 2:47, 56, 268.

[22] Most likely Jacob Mains (1794–1888), who served as an appraiser for Reading Township, OH, in 1819. Graham, *History of Fairfield and Perry Counties,* 2:263, 268; "Died," *Weekly Jeffersonian* (Findlay, OH), Mar. 22, 1888, 8.

My memory extends back to about 1827, and I recall him, returning home on horseback, when all the boys used to run and contend for the privilege of riding his horse from the front door back to the stable. On one occasion, I was the first, and being mounted rode to the stable; but "Old Dick" was impatient because the stable-door was not opened promptly, so he started for the barn of our neighbor Mr. King;[23] there, also, no one was in waiting to open the gate, and, after a reasonable time, "Dick" started back for home somewhat in a hurry, and threw me among a pile of stones, in front of preacher Wright's house,[24] where I was picked up apparently a dead boy; but my time was not yet, and I recovered, though the scars remain to this day.

The year 1829 was a sad one to our family. We were then ten children, my eldest brother Charles absent at the State University, Athens, Ohio; my next brother, James, in a store at Cincinnati; and the rest were at home, at school. Father was away on the circuit. One day Jane Sturgeon[25] came to the school, called us out, and when we reached home all was lamentation: news had come that father was ill unto death, at Lebanon, a hundred miles away. Mother started at once, by coach, but met the news of his death about Washington, and returned home. He had ridden on horseback from Cincinnati to Lebanon to hold court, during a hot day in June. On the next day he took his seat on the bench, opened court in the forenoon, but in the afternoon, after recess, was seized with a severe chill and had to adjourn the court. The best medical aid was called in, and for three days with apparent success, but the fever then assumed a more dangerous type, and he gradually yielded to it, dying on the sixth day, viz., June 24, 1829.

My brother James had been summoned from Cincinnati, and was present at his bedside, as was also Henry Stoddard, Esq., of Dayton, Ohio, our cousin.[26] Mr. Stoddard once told me that the cause of my father's death was

[23] Possibly William or Christian King. The King family arrived in Lancaster, OH, around the turn of the nineteenth century. C .M. L. Wiseman, *Centennial History of Lancaster, Ohio, and Lancaster People, 1898* (self-pub., 1898), 32–33, 84.

[24] John Wright (1776–1854) organized the Rush Creek Presbyterian Church near Lancaster, OH, and became the church's first minister in 1806, serving as minister until 1832. Wiseman, *Centennial History*, 45, 200.

[25] Jane Sturgeon (c. 1812–1888) was a neighbor and close friend of the Sherman family. Stanley P. Hirshon, *The White Tecumseh: A Biography of William T. Sherman* (New York: John Wiley, 1997), 6.

[26] Henry Stoddard (1788–1869) was admitted to the bar in 1812; in 1816 he moved to Dayton, OH, where he practiced as a circuit lawyer until 1844. Cothren, *History of Ancient Woodbury, Connecticut*, 2:1555–1557.

cholera; but at that time, 1829, there was no Asiatic cholera in the United States, and the family attributed his death to exposure to the hot sun of June, and a consequent fever, "typhoid."

From the resolutions of the bench, bar, and public generally, now in my possession, his death was universally deplored; more especially by his neighbors in Lancaster, and by the Society of Freemasons, of which he was the High-Priest of Arch Chapter No. 11.

His death left the family very poor, but friends rose up with proffers of generous care and assistance; for all the neighbors knew that mother could not maintain so large a family without help. My eldest brother, Charles, had nearly completed his education at the university at Athens, and concluded to go to his uncle, Judge Parker, at Mansfield, Ohio, to study law. My eldest sister, Elizabeth, soon after married William J. Reese, Esq.;[27] James was already in a store at Cincinnati; and, with the exception of the three youngest children, the rest of us were scattered. I fell to the charge of the Hon. Thomas Ewing, who took me to his family, and ever after treated me as his own son.[28]

I continued at the Academy in Lancaster, which was the best in the place; indeed, as good a school as any in Ohio.[29] We studied all the common branches of knowledge, including Latin, Greek, and French. At first the school was kept by Mr. Parsons;[30] he was succeeded by Mr. Brown, and he by two brothers, Samuel and Mark How. These were all excellent teachers, and we made good progress, first at the old academy and afterward at a new school-house, built by Samuel How, in the orchard of Hugh Boyle, Esq.[31]

[27] William J. Reese (1804–1883) married Mary Elizabeth Sherman in 1829. John Sherman, *Recollections of Forty Years in the House, Senate, and Cabinet: An Autobiography* (Chicago: Werner Co., 1895), 1:23–24.

[28] Thomas Ewing (1789–1871) served as a U.S senator, secretary of the treasury under Pres. William Henry Harrison, and first secretary of the interior under Pres. Zachary Taylor. According to WTS's brother John, Ewing was a long-standing family friend who offered to adopt WTS. *Memorial of Thomas Ewing of Ohio* (New York: Catholic Publication Society, 1878), 18–19, 24, 27; Sherman, *Recollections*, 29.

[29] The Lancaster Academy was built in 1820 and promoted by Thomas Ewing and Charles R. Sherman. Both WTS and his brother John attended the school. Wiseman, *Centennial History*, 132–133.

[30] Most likely Joel S. Parsons (1801–1840), who taught at the public school on Walnut Street. Wiseman, *Centennial History*, 148–149.

[31] Samuel Howe (1807–1877) and Mark Howe ran the Lancaster Academy and oversaw its successor, Howe's Academy, from approximately 1830 to 1846. Hugh Boyle (1773–1848) became Lancaster's clerk of the Court of Common Pleas in 1803 and held that position for thirty

Time passed with us as with boys generally. Mr. Ewing was in the United States Senate, and I was notified to prepare for West Point, of which institution we had little knowledge, except that it was very strict, and that the army was its natural consequence. In 1834 I was large for my age, and the construction of canals was the rage in Ohio. A canal was projected to connect with the great Ohio Canal at Carroll (eight miles above Lancaster), down the valley of the Hock Hocking to Athens (forty-four miles), and thence to the Ohio River by slack water.[32]

Preacher Carpenter, of Lancaster, was appointed to make the preliminary surveys,[33] and selected the necessary working party out of the boys of the town. From our school were chosen——Wilson, Emanuel Geisy,[34] William King,[35] and myself. Geisy and I were the rod-men. We worked during that fall and next spring, marking two experimental lines, and for our work we each received a silver half-dollar for each day's actual work, the first money any of us had ever earned.

In June, 1835, one of our school-fellows, William Irvin,[36] was appointed a cadet to West Point, and, as it required sixteen years of age for admission, I had to wait another year. During the autumn of 1835 and spring of 1836 I devoted myself chiefly to mathematics and French, which were known to be the chief requisites for admission to West Point.

---

years. George L. Davis, *Samuel Davis, of Oxford, Mass., and Joseph Davis of Dudley, Mass., and Their Descendants* (North Andover, MA: George Davis, 1884), 314–316; Wiseman, *Centennial History,* 28–30, 132–134.

[32]The Hocking Canal extended from Carroll, OH, to Athens, OH. The section of the Hocking Canal that went through Lancaster was called the Lancaster Lateral. Ohio State Archaeological and Historical Society, *History of the Ohio Canals* (Columbus, OH: Press of Fred J. Heer, 1905), 40.

[33]Samuel Carpenter (1794–1870) was employed as an engineer in charge of public works in Fairfield County, OH, in 1816. Later in life he became a minister of the "old Regular Baptists," and assisted in the construction of the Ohio Canal. Seymour Carpenter, *Genealogical Notes of the Carpenter Family* (Springfield: Illinois State Journal, 1907), 216–218.

[34]Emanuel Giesy (c. 1819–1880) was the son of John U. Giesy, owner of a local bakery and tavern. Wiseman, *Centennial History,* 326.

[35]WTS once described William King, one of his childhood best friends, as "the worst rascal in town." Marszalek, *Sherman,* 5, 13.

[36]William Irvin (1819–1852), a relative of WTS, graduated from the USMA in 1839 and became a lieutenant colonel in the 2nd Ohio Reg. during the Mexican-American War. *USMA,* 2:13; Marszalek, *Sherman,* 23.

Some time in the spring of 1836 I received through Mr. Ewing, then at Washington, from the Secretary of War, Mr. Poinsett,[37] the letter of appointment as a cadet, with a list of the articles of clothing necessary to be taken along, all of which were liberally provided by Mrs. Ewing;[38] and with orders to report to Mr. Ewing, at Washington, by a certain date, I left Lancaster about the 20th of May in the stage-coach for Zanesville. There we transferred to the coaches of the Great National Road, the highway of travel from the West to the East. The stages generally travelled in gangs of from one to six coaches, each drawn by four good horses, carrying nine passengers inside and three or four outside.

In about three days, travelling day and night, we reached Frederick, Maryland. There we were told that we could take rail-cars to Baltimore, and thence to Washington; but there was also a two-horse hack ready to start for Washington direct. Not having full faith in the novel and dangerous railroad, I stuck to the coach, and in the night reached Gadsby's Hotel in Washington City.[39]

The next morning I hunted up Mr. Ewing, and found him boarding with a mess of Senators at Mrs. Hill's, corner of Third and C Streets, and transferred my trunk to the same place.[40] I spent a week in Washington, and think I saw more of the place in that time than I ever have since in the many years of residence there. General Jackson was President, and was at the zenith of his

[37] Lewis Cass (1782–1866), not Joel Poinsett (1779–1851), was the secretary of war in the spring of 1836. William G. Bell, *Secretaries of War and Secretaries of the Army: Portraits and Biographical Sketches* (Washington, DC: Center of Military History, United States Army, 1982), s.vv. "Lewis Cass," "Joel Roberts Poinsett."

[38] Maria Willis Boyle Ewing (1801–1864) married Thomas Ewing in 1820. Marszalek, *Sherman,* 8–12; Harvey Scott, *A Complete History of Fairfield County, Ohio, 1795–1876* (Columbus, OH: Siebert and Lilley, 1877), 171–172.

[39] Gadsby's Hotel, also known as "The National Hotel," was built in 1826 by John Gadsby at the intersection of Pennsylvania Avenue and 6th Street NW. Prominent politicians, such as Abraham Lincoln and Andrew Jackson, were patrons of the hotel. The building was closed in 1921 and demolished in 1942. Thomas J. Carrier, *Images of America: Washington, D.C., a Historical Walking Tour* (Charleston, SC: Arcadia, 1999), 44.

[40] Maria Hamilton-Hill (c. 1797–1881) was from Maryland and married Henry V. Hill in April 1816. Her son, Bennett H. Hill, graduated from the USMA in 1837. Hellen W. Brown, *Index of Marriage Licenses, Prince George's County, Maryland, 1777–1886* (Baltimore: Clearfield, 1995), 98; *USMA,* 1:676; Maria L. H. Kelley and Inez B. Cherault, *Hamilton Family of Charles County Maryland* (Houston: Standard, 1930), 31; *Memorial of Thomas Ewing of Ohio,* 68.

fame.[41] I recall looking at him a full hour, one morning, through the wood railing on Pennsylvania Avenue, as he paced up and down the gravel walk on the north front of the White House. He wore a cap and an overcoat so full that his form seemed smaller than I had expected. I also recall the appearance of Postmaster-General Amos Kendall, of Vice-President Van Buren, Messrs. Calhoun, Webster, Clay, Cass, Silas Wright, etc.[42]

In due time I took my departure for West Point with Cadets Belt and Bronaugh. These were appointed cadets as from Ohio, although neither had ever seen that State. But in those days there were fewer applicants from Ohio than now, and near the close of the term the vacancies unasked for were usually filled from applicants on the spot. Neither of these parties, however, graduated, so the State of Ohio lost nothing.[43] We went to Baltimore by rail, there

[41] Andrew Jackson (1767–1845) served as U.S. president from 1829 to 1837. Spencer Tucker, ed., *Almanac of American Military History,* vol. 1, *1000–1830* (Santa Barbara: ABC-CLIO, 2013), s.v. "Andrew Jackson (1767–1845)."

[42] The national figures WTS lists here are as follows: Amos Kendall (1789–1869), who served as postmaster general under Andrew Jackson and Martin Van Buren from 1835 to 1840; Martin Van Buren (1782–1862), who served as U.S. vice president from 1833 to 1837 and then as U.S. president from 1837 to 1841; John C. Calhoun (1782–1850), who (among other offices he held) represented South Carolina in the U.S. Senate in 1832–1843 and 1845–1850; Daniel Webster (1782–1852), who represented Massachusetts in the U.S. Senate in 1827–1841 and 1845–1850 and was the Whig presidential candidate in 1836; Henry Clay (1777–1852), who (among other offices he held) represented Kentucky in the U.S. Senate in 1806–1807, 1810–1811, and 1831–1842; and Silas Wright (1795–1847), who represented New York in the U.S. Senate from 1833 to 1844. Mark R. Cheathem, *Andrew Jackson and the Rise of the Democrats: A Reference Guide* (Santa Barbara: ABC-CLIO, 2015), 251; Spencer Tucker, ed., *The Encyclopedia of the Mexican-American War: A Political, Social, and Military History,* vol. 1, *A–L* (Santa Barbara: ABC-CLIO, 2013), s.vv. "Calhoun, John Caldwell," "Clay, Henry," "Van Buren, Martin," "Webster, Daniel"; *Biographical Directory of the United States Congress, 1774–2005, the Continental Congress, September 5, 1774, to October 21, 1788 and the Congress of the United States from the First through the One Hundred Eighth Congresses, March 4, 1789, to January 3, 2005, Inclusive,* House Document No. 108-222 (Washington, DC: GPO, 2005), 2204.

[43] Both William Spriggs Belt (listed as an Ohio appointee) and William Bronaugh (listed as an appointee from Washington, DC) entered the USMA in 1836. Neither of them appeared in the 1837 roster of cadets. *List of Cadets, United States Military Academy, West Point, New York, from Its Origin till June 30, 1937* (West Point, NY: USMA Printing Office, 1937), 12, 19; *Official Register of the Officers and Cadets of the U.S. Military Academy, West Point, New York. June, 1837* (New York: USMA Printing Office, 1837), 14–17.

took a boat up to Havre de Grace, then the rail to Wilmington, Delaware, and up the Delaware in a boat to Philadelphia. I staid over in Philadelphia one day at the old Mansion House, to visit the family of my brother-in-law, Mr. Reese. I found his father a fine sample of the old merchant gentleman, in a good house in Arch Street, with his accomplished daughters, who had been to Ohio, and whom I had seen there.[44] From Philadelphia we took boat to Bordentown, rail to Amboy, and boat again to New York City, stopping at the American Hotel.[45] I staid a week in New York City, visiting my uncle, Charles Hoyt, at his beautiful place on Brooklyn Heights, and my uncle James, then living in White Street. My friend William Scott was there, the young husband of my cousin, Louise Hoyt; a neatly-dressed young fellow, who looked on me as an untamed animal just caught in the far West—"fit food for gunpowder," and good for nothing else.[46]

About June 12th I embarked in the steamer Cornelius Vanderbilt for West Point; registered in the office of Lieutenant C. F. Smith, Adjutant of the Military Academy,[47] as a new cadet of the class of 1836, and at once became installed as the "plebe" of my fellow-townsman, William Irvin, then entering his Third Class.

Colonel R. E. De Russy was Superintendent; Major John Fowle, Sixth United States Infantry, Commandant. The principal Professors were: Mahan,

[44] WTS likely referred here to the Mansion House Hotel on S. 3rd Street. Jacob Reese (c. 1765–c. 1844) lived in a home at 399 Arch Street during the time referenced by WTS. A. M'Elroy, *Philadelphia Directory for 1837: Containing the Names of the Inhabitants, Their Occupations, Places of Business, and Dwelling-Houses; Also a List of the Streets, Lanes and Wharves; the City Officers, Public Institutions, and Banks, besides Other Useful Information* (Philadelphia: Rackliff and Jones, 1837), 182.

[45] WTS most likely traveled through Perth Amboy, NJ. The American Hotel was adjacent to City Hall Park, located at Barclay Street and Broadway. John Hayward, *A Gazetteer of the United States of America* (Hartford, CT: Case, Tiffany, and Co., 1853), 491; Robert J. Vandewater, *The Tourist or Pocket Manual for Travellers on the Hudson River, the Western Canal, and Stage Road* (New York: J. and J. Harper, 1830), 10; John P. Wall and Harold E. Pickersgill, *History of Middlesex County, New Jersey, 1664–1920* (New York: Lewis Historical, 1921), 2:377.

[46] William Scott (1803–1889) and Louise Hoyt Scott (1810–1858) were married in 1830. Fred Q. Bowman, *10,000 Vital Records of Eastern New York, 1777–1834* (Baltimore: Genealogical, 1987), entry 7655.

[47] Charles F. Smith (1807–1862) was the adjutant of the USMA from 1831 to 1838. *USMA*, 1:353–354.

Engineering; Bartlett, Natural Philosophy; Bailey, Chemistry; Church, Mathematics; Weir, Drawing; and Berard, French.[48]

The routine of military training and of instruction was then fully established, and has remained almost the same ever since. To give a mere outline would swell this to an inconvenient size, and I therefore merely state that I went through the regular course of four years, graduating in June, 1840, number six in a class of forty-three. These forty-three were all that remained of more than one hundred which originally constituted the class.[49] At the Academy I was not considered a good soldier, for at no time was I selected for any office, but remained a private throughout the whole four years. Then, as now, neatness in dress and form, with a strict conformity to the rules, were the qualifications required for office, and I suppose I was found not to excel in any of these. In studies I always held a respectable reputation with the professors, and generally ranked among the best, especially in drawing, chemistry, mathematics, and natural philosophy.[50] My average demerits, per annum, were about one hundred and fifty, which reduced my final class standing from number four to six.[51]

[48] René E. De Russy (1792–1865) served as superintendent of the USMA from 1833 to 1838. John Fowle (1789–1838) was commandant of cadets from 1833 until he was killed by a boiler explosion while aboard the steamer *Moselle* near Cincinnati, OH, on April 24, 1838. Dennis H. Mahan (1802–1871) served as professor of engineering from 1832 to 1871. William H. C. Bartlett (1804–1893) taught natural and experimental philosophy from 1834 to 1871. Jacob W. Bailey (1811–1857) taught chemistry, mineralogy, and geology from 1834 to 1857. Albert E. Church (1807–1878) taught mathematics in the years 1828–1831 and 1833–1878. Robert W. Weir (1803–1889) taught drawing from 1834 to 1876. Claudius Berard (1786–1848) served as the first teacher of French at the USMA from 1815 to 1848. *USMA,* 1:29–30, 36, 38–39, 110, 319–320, 364–365, 404–405, 501. "Genealogy," *Boston Evening Transcript,* June 8, 1898, 11.

[49] WTS was one of the seventy-six cadets from the fourth class who completed their first year and participated in the general examination in June 1837. Ultimately, he finished sixth out of forty-two in his graduating class in 1840. *Official Register of the Officers and Cadets of the U.S. Military Academy, West Point, New York. June, 1837* (New York: USMA Printing Office, 1837), 14–17. *Official Register . . . 1840,* 9–10.

[50] In his final year at the USMA, WTS ranked seventh in engineering, seventh in ethics, twelfth in infantry tactics, eighth in artillery, and fourth in chemistry, mineralogy, and geology. *Official Register . . . 1840,* 9–10.

[51] Over the course of his four years at the USMA, WTS received a total of 380 demerits. He never finished higher than sixth overall in his class in any of his years at the USMA. *Official Register . . . 1837,* 14, 22; *Official Register . . . 1838,* 11, 22; *Official Register . . . 1839,* 8, 22; *Official Register . . . 1840,* 9, 24.

In June, 1840, after the final examination, the class graduated and we received our diplomas. Meantime, Major Delafield, United States Engineers, had become Superintendent; Major C. F. Smith, Commandant of Cadets;[52] but the corps of professors and assistants remained almost unchanged during our whole term. We were all granted the usual furlough of three months, and parted for our homes, there to await assignment to our respective corps and regiments. In due season I was appointed and commissioned second-lieutenant, Third Artillery, and ordered to report at Governor's Island, New York Harbor, at the end of September. I spent my furlough mostly at Lancaster and Mansfield, Ohio; toward the close of September returned to New York, reported to Major Justin Dimock, commanding the recruiting rendezvous at Governor's Island,[53] and was assigned to command a company of recruits preparing for service in Florida. Early in October this company was detailed, as one of four, to embark in a sailing-vessel for Savannah, Georgia, under command of Captain and Brevet Major Penrose.[54] We embarked and sailed, reaching Savannah about the middle of October, where we transferred to a small steamer and proceeded by the inland route to St. Augustine, Florida. We reached St. Augustine at the same time with the Eighth Infantry, commanded by Colonel and Brevet Brigadier-General William J. Worth.[55] At that time General Zachary Taylor was in chief command in Florida, and had his headquarters at Tampa Bay.[56] My regiment, the Third Artillery, occupied the posts along the Atlantic coast of Florida, from St. Augustine south to Key Biscayne, and my own company, A, was at Fort Pierce, Indian River.

[52] Richard Delafield (1798–1873) served as superintendent of the USMA from 1838 to 1845 and from 1856 to 1861. Smith served as commandant of cadets from 1838 to 1842. *USMA,* 1:181–185, 354.

[53] Justin Dimick (1800–1871) graduated from the USMA in 1819 and fought in the Mexican-American War and the Civil War, and served as the governor of the Soldiers' Home in Washington, DC, in 1864–1865. *CWHC,* 210.

[54] James W. Penrose (1808–1849) graduated from the USMA in 1828 and fought in the Black Hawk, Seminole, and Mexican-American Wars. *USMA,* 1:419.

[55] William J. Worth (1794–1849) was promoted to colonel in July 1838 and was brevetted brigadier general in Mar. 1842. *USMA,* 1:28–29.

[56] Zachary Taylor (1784–1850) was placed in command of the Department of Florida in May 1838. He later rose to fame in the Mexican-American War and served as the twelfth president of the United States. K. Jack Bauer, *Zachary Taylor: Soldier, Planter, Statesman of the Old Southwest* (Baton Rouge: LSU Press, 1993), 5, 9, 59; Joseph Fry, *A Life of Gen. Zachary Taylor* (Philadelphia: Grigg, Elliot and Co, 1848), 58, 188; Tucker, *Encyclopedia of the Mexican-American War,* vol. 1, s.v. "Taylor, Zachary."

At St. Augustine I was detached from the company of recruits, which was designed for the Second Infantry, and was ordered to join my proper company at Fort Pierce. Colonel William Gates commanded the regiment, with Lieutenant William Austine Brown as adjutant of the regiment.[57] Lieutenant Bragg commanded the post of St. Augustine with his own company, E, and G (Garner's), then commanded by Lieutenant Judd.[58] In a few days I embarked in the little steamer William Gaston down the coast, stopping one day at New Smyrna, held by John R. Vinton's company (B), with which was serving Lieutenant William H. Shover.[59]

In due season we arrived off the bar of Indian River and anchored. A whaleboat came off with a crew of four men, steered by a character of some note, known as the Pilot Ashlock.[60] I transferred self and baggage to this boat, and, with the mails, was carried through the surf over the bar, into the mouth of Indian River Inlet. It was then dark; we transferred to a smaller boat, and the same crew pulled us up through a channel in the middle of Mangrove Islands, the roosting-place of thousands of pelicans and birds that rose in clouds and circled above our heads. The water below was alive with fish, whose course through it could be seen by the phosphoric wake; and Ashlock told me many a tale of the Indian war then in progress, and of his adventures in hunting and fishing, which he described as the best in the world. About two miles from the

[57] William Gates (1788–1868) graduated from the USMA in 1806 and was promoted to colonel in Oct. 1845. William A. Brown (1815–1904) graduated from the USMA in 1838 and served in the Second Seminole War. He was garrisoned at Fort Pickens, FL, in 1842 and at Fort Moultrie from 1842 to 1846. *USMA,* 1:717; *CWHC,* 251.

[58] Braxton Bragg (1817–1876) graduated from the USMA in 1837 and later served as a major general in the Confederate Army during the Civil War. Hezekiah Garner (1790–1841) was promoted to captain in July 1838. He died while stationed in Picolata, FL. Henry Judd (1819–1892) graduated from the USMA in 1839 and was promoted to first lieutenant for his service during the Second Seminole War in 1841. He fought in the Mexican-American War, and served as general superintendent of volunteer recruiting services during the Civil War. *USMA,* 1:747–748; *CWHC,* 140–141; Charles K. Gardner, *A Dictionary of All Officers, Who Have Been Commissioned or Have Been Appointed and Served, in the Army of the United States* (New York: G. P. Putnam, 1853), s.v. "Hezekiah Garner."

[59] John R. Vinton (1801–1847) was killed by artillery fire during the Mexican-American War. William H. Shover (1814–1850) graduated from the USMA in 1838 and served as a first lieutenant throughout the Seminole Wars. *USMA,* 1:159–160, 703.

[60] Hugh Ashlock (c. 1805–1841) was a private in the Mounted Florida Volunteers. *Florida Militia Muster Rolls, Seminole Indian Wars* (St. Augustine: Florida Department of Military Affairs, 1837), 7:64.

bar, we emerged into the lagoon, a broad expanse of shallow water that lies parallel with the coast, separated from it by a narrow strip of sand, backed by a continuous series of islands and promontories, covered with a dense growth of mangrove and saw-palmetto. Pulling across this lagoon, in about three more miles we approached the lights of Fort Pierce. Reaching a small wharf, we landed, and were met by the officers of the post, Lieutenants George Taylor and Edward J. Steptoe, and Assistant-Surgeon James Simons.[61] Taking the mail-bag, we walked up a steep sand-bluff on which the fort was situated, and across the parade-ground to the officers' quarters. These were six or seven log-houses, thatched with palmetto-leaves, built on high posts, with a porch in front, facing the water. The men's quarters were also of logs forming the two sides of a rectangle, open toward the water; the intervals and flanks were closed with log stockades. I was assigned to one of these rooms, and at once began service with my company, A, then commanded by Lieutenant Taylor.

The season was hardly yet come for active operations against the Indians, so that the officers were naturally attracted to Ashlock, who was the best fisherman I ever saw. He soon initiated us into the mysteries of shark-spearing, trolling for red-fish, and taking the sheep's-head and mullet. These abounded so that we could at any time catch an unlimited quantity at pleasure. The companies also owned nets for catching green turtles. These nets had meshes about a foot square, were set across channels in the lagoon, the ends secured to stakes driven into the mud, the lower line sunk with lead or stone weights and the upper line floated with cork. We usually visited these nets twice a day, and found from one to six green turtles entangled in the meshes. Disengaging them, they were carried to pens, made with stakes stuck in the mud, where they were fed with mangrove-leaves, and our cooks had at all times an ample supply of the best of green turtles. They were so cheap and common that the soldiers regarded it as an imposition when compelled to eat green turtle steaks, instead of poor Florida beef, or the usual barrelled mess-pork. I do not recall in my whole experience a spot on earth where fish, oysters, and green turtles so abound as at Fort Pierce, Florida.

[61] George W. Taylor (c. 1816–1853) graduated from the USMA in 1837 and fought in the Second and Third Seminole Wars. Edward J. Steptoe (1815–1865) graduated from the USMA in 1837 and fought in the Second and Third Seminole Wars and the Mexican-American War. James Simons (c. 1807–1883) served as an assistant surgeon in the U.S. Army from 1839 to 1856. He served in the Second Seminole War, Mexican-American War, and the Civil War. *USMA,* 1:679, 689; Guy V. Henry, *Military Record of Civilian Appointments in the United States Army* (New York: Carlton, 1869), 1:112.

In November, Major Childs arrived with Lieutenant Van Vliet[62] and a detachment of recruits to fill our two companies, and preparations were at once begun for active operations in the field. At that time the Indians in the Peninsula of Florida were scattered, and the war consisted in hunting up and securing the small fragments, to be sent to join the others of their tribe of Seminoles already established in the Indian Territory west of Arkansas. Our expeditions were mostly made in boats in the lagoons extending from the "Haul-over," near two hundred miles above the fort, down to Jupiter Inlet, about fifty miles below, and in the many streams which emptied therein.[63] Many such expeditions were made during that winter, with more or less success, in which we succeeded in picking up small parties of men, women, and children. On one occasion, near the "Haul-over," when I was not present, the expedition was more successful. It struck a party of nearly fifty Indians, killed several warriors, and captured others. In this expedition my classmate, Lieutenant Van Vliet, who was an excellent shot, killed a warrior who was running at full speed among trees, and one of the sergeants of our company (Broderick) was said to have dispatched three warriors, and it was reported that he took the scalp of one and brought it in to the fort as a trophy. Broderick was so elated that, on reaching the post, he had to celebrate his victory by a big drunk.

There was at the time a poor, weakly soldier of our company whose wife cooked for our mess. She was somewhat of a flirt, and rather fond of admiration. Sergeant Broderick was attracted to her, and hung around the mess-house more than the husband fancied; so he reported the matter to Lieutenant Taylor, who reproved Broderick for his behavior. A few days afterward the husband again appealed to his commanding officer (Taylor), who exclaimed: "Haven't you got a musket? Can't you defend your own family?" Very soon after a shot was heard down by the mess-house, and it transpired that the husband had actually shot Broderick, inflicting a wound which proved mortal. The law and army regulations required that the man should

[62]Thomas Childs (1796–1853) graduated from the USMA in 1814 and fought in the War of 1812, the Seminole Wars, and the Mexican-American War. Stewart Van Vliet (1815–1901), a lifelong friend of WTS, graduated from the USMA in 1840. He served as a quartermaster in the U.S. Army during the Civil War and reached the rank of colonel in 1872. *USMA,* 1:116–117; *CWHC,* 543.

[63]The Haul Over Canal, located approximately one hundred miles north of Fort Pierce, connected the Indian River with the Mosquito Lagoon. The distance between Fort Pierce and Jupiter Inlet was approximately thirty-five miles. George B. Davis et al., *Official Military Atlas of the Civil War* (New York: Fairfax Press, 1983), plate 146, maps 1 and 2.

be sent to the nearest civil court, which was at St. Augustine; accordingly, the prisoner and necessary witnesses were sent up by the next monthly steamer. Among the latter were lieutenant Taylor and the pilot Ashlock.

After they had been gone about a month, the sentinel on the roof-top of our quarters reported the smoke of a steamer approaching the bar, and, as I was acting quartermaster, I took a boat and pulled down to get the mail. I reached the log-hut in which the pilots lived, and saw them start with their boat across the bar, board the steamer, and then return. Ashlock was at his old post at the steering-oar, with two ladies, who soon came to the landing, having passed through a very heavy surf, and I was presented to one as *Mrs. Ashlock,* and the other as her sister, a very pretty little Minorcan girl of about fourteen years of age.[64] Mrs. Ashlock herself was probably eighteen or twenty years old, and a very handsome woman. I was hurriedly informed that the murder trial was in progress at St. Augustine; that Ashlock had given his testimony, and had availed himself of the chance to take a wife to share with him the solitude of his desolate hut on the beach at Indian River. He had brought ashore his wife, her sister, and their chests, with the mail, and had orders to return immediately to the steamer (Gaston or Harney)[65] to bring ashore some soldiers belonging to another company, E (Braggs), which had been ordered from St. Augustine to Fort Pierce. Ashlock left his wife and her sister standing on the beach near the pilot-hut, and started back with his whale-boat across the bar. I also took the mail and started up to the fort, and had hardly reached the wharf when I observed another boat following me. As soon as this reached the wharf the men reported that Ashlock and all his crew, with the exception of one man, had been drowned a few minutes after I had left the beach. They said his surf-boat had reached the steamer, had taken on board a load of soldiers, some eight or ten, and had started back through the surf, when on the bar a heavy breaker upset the boat, and all were lost except the boy who pulled the bow-oar, who clung to the rope or painter, hauled himself to the upset boat, held on, drifted with it outside the breakers, and was finally beached near a mile down the coast.[66] They reported also that

[64] Carmeta Canovas Ashlock (c. 1823–?) married Hugh Ashlock during the murder trial in 1841. Her sister was Julia Canovas (c. 1827–?). W. Fletcher Johnson, *Life of William Tecumseh Sherman* (Philadelphia: Edgewood, 1891), 42.

[65] The ship in question was the *William Gaston.* B. Homan, ed., *Army and Navy Chronicle,* no. 47 (Washington, DC: T. Barnard, 1841), 12:372.

[66] Contemporary reports indicated that during the initial incident, on Oct. 25, 1841, eleven people drowned, including Ashlock, a boy, two men, and seven U.S. Army soldiers. Three

the steamer had got up anchor, run in as close to the bar as she could, paused awhile, and then had started down the coast.

I instantly took a fresh crew of soldiers and returned to the bar; there sat poor Mrs. Ashlock on her chest of clothes, a weeping widow, who had seen her husband perish amid sharks and waves; she clung to the hope that the steamer had picked him up, but, strange to say, he could not swim, although he had been employed on the water all his life.

Her sister was more demonstrative, and wailed as one lost to all hope and life. She appealed to us all to do miracles to save the struggling men in the waves, though two hours had already passed, and to have gone out then among those heavy breakers, with an inexperienced crew, would have been worse than suicide. All I could do was to reorganize the guard at the beach, take the two desolate females up to the fort, and give them the use of my own quarters. Very soon their anguish was quieted, and they began to look for the return of their steamer with Ashlock and his rescued crew. The next day I went again to the beach with Lieutenant Ord,[67] and we found that one or two bodies had been washed ashore, torn all to pieces by the sharks, which literally swarmed the inlet at every new tide. In a few days the weather moderated, and the steamer returned from the south, but the surf was so high that she anchored a mile off. I went out myself, in the whale or surf boat, over that terrible bar with a crew of soldiers, boarded the steamer, and learned that none other of Ashlock's crew except the one before mentioned had been saved; but, on the contrary, the captain of the steamer had sent one of his own boats to their rescue,[68] which was likewise upset in the surf, and, out of the three men in her, one had drifted back outside the breakers, clinging to the upturned boat, and was picked up. This sad and fatal catastrophe made us all *afraid* of that bar, and in returning to the shore I adopted the more prudent course of beaching the boat below the inlet, which insured us a good ducking, but was attended with less risk to life.

I had to return to the fort and bear to Mrs. Ashlock the absolute truth, that her husband was lost forever.

---

more men died while attempting to rescue the victims. Homan, *Army and Navy Chronicle,* no. 47, 12:372.

[67] Edward O. C. Ord (1818–1883) graduated from the USMA in 1839. He was WTS's first roommate at the academy, in 1836. *CWHC,* 409–410; Steven E. Woodworth, *Sherman: Lessons in Leadership* (New York: Palgrave MacMillan, 2009), 10.

[68] A man identified as "Captain Henry" was captain of the *William Gaston.* Homan, *Army and Navy Chronicle,* no. 47, 12:372.

Meantime her sister had entirely recovered her equilibrium, and being the guest of the officers, who were extremely courteous to her, she did not lament so loudly the calamity that saved them a long life of banishment on the beach of Indian River. By the first opportunity they were sent back to St. Augustine, the possessors of all of Ashlock's worldly goods and effects, consisting of a good rifle, several cast-nets, hand-lines, etc., etc., besides some three hundred dollars in money, which was due him by the quartermaster for his services as pilot. I afterward saw these ladies at St. Augustine, and years afterward the younger one came to Charleston, South Carolina, the wife of the somewhat famous Captain Thistle, agent for the United States for live-oak in Florida, who was noted as the first of the troublesome class of inventors of modern artillery. He was the inventor of a gun that "did not recoil at all," or "if anything it recoiled a little forward."[69]

One day, in the summer of 1841, the sentinel on the house-top at Fort Pierce called out, "Indians! Indians!" Everybody sprang to his gun, the companies formed promptly on the parade-ground, and soon were reported as approaching the post, from the pine-woods in rear, four Indians on horseback. They rode straight up to the gateway, dismounted, and came in. They were conducted by the officer of the day to the commanding officer, Major Childs, who sat on the porch in front of his own room. After the usual pause, one of them, a black man named Joe, who spoke English, said they had been sent in by Coacoochee (Wild Cat), one of the most noted of the Seminole chiefs, to see the big chief of the post.[70] He gradually unwrapped a piece of paper, which was passed over to Major Childs, who read it, and it was in the nature of a "Safe Guard" for "Wild Cat" to come into Fort Pierce to receive provisions

[69] Hezekiah L. Thistle married Julia Canovas in St. John's County, FL, in Aug. 1844. On June 17, 1840, the Congressional Committee on Military Affairs considered a petition by Thistle to adopt his wrought-iron cannon. Thistle suggested that his cannon would be $756 cheaper than the brass cannons that were being used by the military at the time. *Public Documents Printed by Order of the Senate of the United States, during the First Session of the Twenty-Sixth Congress,* vol. 8, document no. 561 (Washington, DC: Blair and Rives, 1840).

[70] Coacoochee (c. 1810–1857) was the son of Seminole leader Emathla (also known as King Phillip) and the nephew of Seminole leader Micco Nuppa. He became the second most prominent Seminole leader in Florida during the Seminole Wars. He was captured in May 1841 and removed to a reservation. In 1849 he left for Mexico, where he later died. James Parins, *Encyclopedia of American Indian Removal* (Santa Barbara: Greenwood, 2011), 1:51–53; Susan A. Miller, *Coacoochee's Bones* (Lawrence: University Press of Kansas, 2003), 22–23; J. T. Sprague, *The Origin, Progress, and Conclusion of the Florida War* (New York: Appleton, 1848), 277, 324.

and assistance while collecting his tribe, with the purpose of emigrating to their reservation west of Arkansas. The paper was signed by General Worth, who had succeeded General Taylor, at Tampa Bay, in command of all the troops in Florida.[71] Major Childs inquired, "Where is Coacoochee?" and was answered, "Close by," when Joe explained that he had been sent in by his chief to see if the paper was all right. Major Childs said it was "all right," and that Coacoochee ought to come in himself. Joe offered to go out and bring him in, when Major Childs ordered me to take eight or ten mounted men and go out to escort him in. Detailing ten men to saddle up, and taking Joe and one Indian boy along on their own ponies, I started out under their guidance.

We continued to ride five or six miles, when I began to suspect treachery, of which I had heard so much in former years, and had been specially cautioned against by the older officers; but Joe always answered, "Only a little way." At last we approached one of those close hammocks, so well known in Florida, standing like an island in the interminable pine-forest, with a pond of water near it. On its edge I noticed a few Indians loitering, which Joe pointed out as *the place.* Apprehensive of treachery, I halted the guard, gave orders to the sergeant to watch me closely, and rode forward alone with the two Indian guides. As we neared the hammock, about a dozen Indian warriors rose up and waited for us. When in their midst I inquired for the chief, Coacoochee. He approached my horse and, slapping his breast, said, "Me Coacoochee." He was a very handsome young Indian warrior, not more than twenty-five years old, but in his then dress could hardly be distinguished from the rest. I then explained to him, through Joe, that I had been sent by my "chief" to escort him into the fort. He wanted me to get down and "talk." I told him that I had no "talk" in me, but that, on his reaching the post, he could talk as much as he pleased with the "big chief," Major Childs. They all seemed to be indifferent, and in no hurry; and I noticed that all their guns were leaning against a tree. I beckoned to the sergeant, who advanced rapidly with his escort, and told him to secure the rifles, which he proceeded to do. Coacoochee pretended to be very angry, but I explained to him that his warriors were tired and mine were not, and that the soldiers would carry the guns on their horses. I told him I would provide him a horse to ride, and the sooner he was ready the better for all. He then stripped, washed himself in the pond, and began to dress in all his Indian finery, which consisted of buck-

[71]Taylor was succeeded by W. R. Armistead in May 1840. Worth relieved Armistead in May 1841. Harry G. Cutler, *History of Florida: Past and Present, Historical and Biographical* (Chicago: Lewis, 1923), 1:50.

skin leggins, moccasins, and several shirts. He then began to put on vests, one after another, and one of them had the marks of a bullet, just above the pocket, with the stain of blood. In the pocket was a one-dollar Tallahassee Bank note, and the rascal had the impudence to ask me to give him silver coin for that dollar. He had evidently killed the wearer, and was disappointed because the pocket contained a paper dollar instead of one in silver. In due time he was dressed with turban and ostrich-feathers, and mounted the horse reserved for him, and thus we rode back together to Fort Pierce. Major Childs and all the officers received him on the porch, and there we had a regular "talk." Coacoochee "was tired of the war." "His people were scattered and it would take a 'moon' to collect them for emigration," and he "wanted rations for that time," etc., etc.

All this was agreed to, and a month was allowed for him to get ready with his whole band (numbering some one hundred and fifty or one hundred and sixty) to migrate. The "talk" then ceased, and Coacoochee and his envoys proceeded to get regularly drunk, which was easily done by the agency of commissary whiskey. They staid at Fort Pierce during the night, and the next day departed. Several times during the month there came into the post two or more of these same Indians, always to beg for something to eat or drink, and after a full month Coacoochee and about twenty of his warriors came in with several ponies, but with none of their women or children. Major Childs had not from the beginning the least faith in his sincerity; had made up his mind to seize the whole party and compel them to emigrate. He arranged for the usual council, and instructed Lieutenant Taylor to invite Coacoochee and his uncle (who was held to be a principal chief)[72] to his room to take some good brandy, instead of the common commissary whiskey. At a signal agreed on I was to go to the quarters of Company A, to dispatch the first-sergeant and another man to Lieutenant Taylor's room, there to seize the two chiefs and secure them; and with the company I was to enter Major Childs's room and secure the remainder of the party. Meantime Lieutenant Van Vliet was ordered to go to the quarters of his company, F, and at the same signal to march rapidly to the rear of the officers' quarters, so as to catch any who might attempt to escape by the open windows to the rear.

All resulted exactly as prearranged, and in a few minutes the whole party was in irons. At first they claimed that we had acted treacherously, but very soon they admitted that for a month Coacoochee had been quietly removing

[72] Some sources identify this man as a brother of Coacoochee's father Emathla, possibly known as Tuskinia or Micco. Miller, *Coacoochee's Bones,* 43; Sprague, *Florida War,* 277.

his women and children toward Lake Okeechobee and the Everglades; and that this visit to our post was to have been their last. It so happened that almost at the instant of our seizing these Indians a vessel arrived off the bar with reënforcements from St. Augustine. These were brought up to Fort Pierce, and we marched that night and next day rapidly, some fifty miles, to Lake Okeechobee, in hopes to capture the balance of the tribe, especially the families, but they had taken the alarm and escaped. Coacoochee and his warriors were sent by Major Childs in a schooner to New Orleans *en route* to their reservation, but General Worth recalled them to Tampa Bay, and by sending out Coacoochee himself the women and children came in voluntarily, and then all were shipped to their destination. This was a heavy loss to the Seminoles, but there still remained in the Peninsula a few hundred warriors with their families scattered into very small parcels, who were concealed in the most inaccessible hammocks and swamps. These had no difficulty in finding plenty of food anywhere and everywhere. Deer and wild turkey were abundant, and as for fish there was no end to them. Indeed, Florida was the Indian's paradise, was of little value to us, and it was a great pity to remove the Seminoles at all, for we could have collected there all the Choctaws, Creeks, Cherokees, and Chickasaws, in addition to the Seminoles. They would have thrived in the Peninsula, whereas they now occupy lands that are very valuable, which are coveted by their white neighbors on all sides, while the Peninsula, of Florida still remains with a population less than should make a good State.

During that and preceding years General W. S. Harney had penetrated and crossed through the Everglades, capturing and hanging Chekika and his band, and had brought in many prisoners, who were also shipped West.[73] We at Fort Pierce made several other excursions to Jupiter, Lake Worth, Lauderdale, and into the Everglades, picking up here and there a family, so that it was absurd any longer to call it a "war." These excursions, however, possessed

[73] William S. Harney (1800–1889) joined the U.S. Army as a second lieutenant in 1818. He was promoted to lieutenant colonel of the 2nd Dragoons in 1836 and was transferred to Florida to fight in the Seminole Wars. In Dec. 1840, Harney and his troops killed the Seminole leader Chekika (also spelled "Chakaika"), taking thirty-six Native Americans captive. Harney hanged Chakaika's corpse from a nearby tree and hanged at least two other prisoners. Michael L. Nunnally, *American Indian Wars: A Chronology of Confrontations between Native Peoples and Settlers and the United States Military, 1500s–1901* (Jefferson, NC: McFarland, 2007), 84; William Sturtevant, "Chakaika and the 'Spanish Indians': Documentary Sources Compared with Seminole Tradition," *Tequesta* 13 (1953): 52–54; Tucker, *Encyclopedia of the Mexican-American War,* s.v. "Harney, William Selby."

to us a peculiar charm, for the fragrance of the air, the abundance of game and fish, and just enough of adventure, gave to life a relish. I had just returned to Lauderdale from one of these scouts with Lieutenants Rankin, Ord, George H. Thomas, Field, Van Vliet, and others, when I received notice of my promotion to be first-lieutenant of Company G, which occurred November 30, 1841, and I was ordered to return to Fort Pierce, turn over the public property for which I was accountable to Lieutenant H. S. Burton, and then to join my new company at St. Augustine.[74]

I reached St. Augustine before Christmas, and was assigned to command a detachment of twenty men stationed at Picolata, on the St. John's River, eighteen miles distant.[75] At St. Augustine were still the headquarters of the regiment, Colonel William Gates, with Company E, Lieutenant Bragg, and Company G, Lieutenant H. B. Judd. The only buildings at Picolata were the one occupied by my detachment, which had been built for a hospital, and the dwelling of a family named Williams, with whom I boarded.[76] On the other hand, St. Augustine had many pleasant families, among whom was prominent that of United States Judge Bronson.[77] I was half my time in St. Augustine or on the road, and remember the old place with pleasure. In February we received

[74] James L. Rankin (1817–1845) graduated from the USMA in 1839 and was promoted to first lieutenant, 3rd U.S. Art., in Apr. 1840. He was killed after being thrown from his horse while on garrison duty in Savannah, GA. George H. Thomas (1816–1870) graduated from the USMA in 1840 and joined the 3rd U.S. Art. in Florida. He served in the Mexican-American War as a brevet major, and became a major general during the Civil War. Horace B. Field (1818–1853) graduated from the USMA in 1840 and joined the 3rd U.S. Art. in Florida soon after graduation. In 1853, Field and approximately 200 other people aboard the steamer *San Francisco* died when the ship sank during a storm. Henry S. Burton (1818–1869) graduated from the USMA in 1839 and fought in the Seminole Wars and the Mexican-American War, and was later brevetted brigadier general for his actions during the Civil War. *USMA,* 1:747; 2:33–34, 43–44; James G. Wilson and John Fiske, eds., *Appletons' Cyclopedia of American Biography* (New York: D. Appleton., 1888), vol. 1, s.v. "Burton, Henry S."

[75] Picolata, FL, was a former Spanish settlement that was eighteen miles due west of St. Augustine. James M. Denham and Canter Brown Jr., eds., *Cracker Times and Pioneer Lives* (Columbia: University of South Carolina Press, 2000), 102.

[76] WTS most likely referred here to the family of John Lee and Martha Williams. The family moved to Picolata, FL, by way of St. Augustine, in 1834. Denham and Brown, *Cracker Times,* 102–103.

[77] Isaac H. Bronson (1802–1855) was admitted to the bar in 1822. He was elected to the U.S. House of Representatives in 1836 and was appointed U.S. judge for the eastern district of Florida in 1840, a position he held for the remainder of his life. Joseph Anderson and Anna L.

orders transferring the whole regiment to the Gulf posts, and our company, G, was ordered to escort Colonel Gates and his family across to the Suwanee River, *en route* for Pensacola. The company, with the colonel and his family, reached Picolata (where my detachment joined), and we embarked in a steamboat for Pilatka. Here Lieutenant Judd discovered that he had forgotten something and had to return to St. Augustine, so that I commanded the company on the march, having with me Second-Lieutenant George B. Ayres.[78] Our first march was to Fort Russell, then Micanopy, Wacahoota, and Wacasassee, all which posts were garrisoned by the Second or Seventh Infantry.[79] At Wacasassee we met General Worth and his staff, *en route* for Pilatka. Lieutenant Judd overtook us about the Suwanee, where we embarked on a small boat for Cedar Keys, and there took a larger one for Pensacola, where the colonel and his family landed, and our company proceeded on in the same vessel to our post—Fort Morgan, Mobile Point.

This fort had not been occupied by troops for many years, was very dirty, and we found little or no stores there. Major Ogden, of the engineers, occupied a house outside the fort.[80] I was quartermaster and commissary, and, taking advantage of one of the engineer schooners engaged in bringing materials for the fort, I went up to Mobile city, and, through the agency of Messrs. Deshon, Taylor, and Myers, merchants,[81] procured all essentials for the troops, and re-

---

Ward, eds., *The Town and City of Waterbury, Connecticut, from the Aboriginal Period to the Year Eighteen Hundred and Ninety-Five* (New Haven, CT: Price and Lee, 1896), 3:826.

[78] George W. Ayres (1821–1846) graduated from the USMA in 1841 and served as a second lieutenant during the Second Seminole War. He was killed in the Mexican-American War during the Battle of Molino del Rey in Sept. 1847. *USMA,* 2:74.

[79] Fort Russell was located along the east side of Orange Lake and approximately thirty miles southwest of Palatka, FL. Wacahoota was located ten miles west of Micanopy, FL, and Wacasassee was located twenty miles west of Wacahoota. Benson J. Lossing, *A Pictorial History of the United States: For Schools and Families* (New York: Mason Brothers, 1860), 312 (map); Davis et al., *Official Military Atlas,* plate 146, maps 1 and 2.

[80] Cornelius A. Ogden (1799–1856) graduated from the USMA in 1819 and was promoted to first lieutenant in the U.S. Army Corps of Engineers in July 1824. He served as the superintending engineer of the construction of Fort Morgan during the years 1825–1834 and 1841–1847. *USMA,* 1:206.

[81] Charles Deshon (c. 1816–1879) had a business partnership with Taylor and Myers that sold various supplies to the military. In Mar. 1849, Deshon and Myers signed a petition for the state legislature to provide Mobile a banking facility. *Alabama Planter (The Weekly Herald and Tribune),* Mar. 19, 1849, 127; Clive Webb, *Fight against Fear: Southern Jews and Black Civil Rights* (Athens: University of Georgia Press, 2001), 6; Twenty-Eighth Congress, First Session,

turned to the post. In the course of a week or ten days arrived another company, H, commanded by Lieutenant James Ketchum, with Lieutenants Rankin and Sewall L. Fish, and an assistant surgeon (Wells). Ketchum became the commanding officer, and Lieutenant Rankin quartermaster.[82] We proceeded to put the post in as good order as possible; had regular guard-mounting and parades, but little drill. We found magnificent fishing with the seine on the outer beach, and sometimes in a single haul we would take ten or fifteen barrels of the best kind of fish, embracing pompinos, red-fish, snappers, etc.

We remained there till June, when the regiment was ordered to exchange from the Gulf posts to those on the Atlantic, extending from Savannah to North Carolina. The brig Wetumpka was chartered, and our company (G) embarked and sailed to Pensacola, where we took on board another company (D) (Burke's), commanded by Lieutenant H. S. Burton, with Colonel Gates, the regimental headquarters, and some families.[83] From Pensacola we sailed for Charleston, South Carolina. The weather was hot, the winds light, and we made a long passage; but at last reached Charleston Harbor, disembarked, and took post in Fort Moultrie.

Soon after two other companies arrived, Bragg's (B) and Keyes's[84] (K). The two former companies were already quartered inside of Fort Moultrie,

---

United States Congressional Serial Set 447, The Late Florida Squadron- Expenditures, June 14, 1844, Report 582 (Washington, DC: GPO, 1844), 3:17.

[82] James Ketchum (1818–1846) graduated from the USMA in 1838 and fought in the Second Seminole War. He resigned from the U.S. Army in Apr. 1844. Sewall L. Fremont (1816–1886) graduated from the USMA in 1841. He changed his last name from Fish to Fremont soon after graduation. He served in the Seminole Wars and the Mexican-American War. Sewall was one of the few survivors of the wreck of the steamer *San Francisco* in Dec. 1853. John B. Wells (d. 1853) became an assistant surgeon in Feb. 1834 and major surgeon in Oct. 1846. He served in the Mexican-American War. William K. Bixby and William H. Samson, eds., *Letters of Zachary Taylor: From the Battle-Fields of the Mexican War* (Rochester, NY: Genesee, 1908), 2*n;* Harvey E. Brown, comp., *The Medical Department of the United States Army from 1775–1873* (Washington, DC: Surgeon General's Office, 1873), 177; *USMA,* 1:702; 2:81; *Sixteenth Annual Reunion of the Association of the Graduates of the United States Military Academy at West Point, New York, June 12th, 1885* (East Saginaw, MI: Evening News, 1885), 118.

[83] Martin J. Burke (1816–1847) attended the USMA from 1832 to 1836 and was stationed at Fort Moultrie, SC, from 1842 to 1845. He later died while serving in the Mexican-American War. *USMA,* 1:649.

[84] Erasmus D. Keyes (1810–1895) graduated from the USMA in 1832 and served in the Second and Third Seminole Wars, the Mexican-American War, and the Civil War. *USMA,* 1:510–511.

and these latter were placed in gun-sheds, outside, which were altered into barracks. We remained at Fort Moultrie nearly five years, until the Mexican War scattered us forever. Our life there was of strict garrison duty, with plenty of leisure for hunting and social entertainments. We soon formed many and most pleasant acquaintances in the city of Charleston; and it so happened that many of the families resided at Sullivan's Island in the summer season, where we could reciprocate the hospitalities extended to us in the winter.

During the summer of 1843, having been continuously on duty for three years, I applied for and received a leave of absence for three months, which I spent mostly in Ohio. In November I started to return to my post at Charleston by way of New Orleans; took the stage to Chillicothe, Ohio, November 16th, having Henry Stanberry, Esq., and wife, as travelling companions.[85] We continued by stage next day to Portsmouth, Ohio.

At Portsmouth Mr. Stanberry took a boat up the river, and I one down to Cincinnati. There I found my brothers Lampson and Hoyt employed in the "Gazette" printing-office, and spent much time with them and Charles Anderson, Esq., visiting his brother Larz,[86] Mr. Longworth, some of his artist

[85] Henry Stanbery (1803–1881) graduated from Washington College in 1819. After he passed the bar in 1824, he was invited to practice law with Thomas Ewing in Lancaster, OH. He was married to Frances E. Beecher for eleven years until she died in 1840. He married Cecelia K. Bond (c. 1820–1881) in 1841. In 1846 Stanbery was elected attorney general of Ohio, and later Pres. Andrew Johnson appointed him U.S. attorney general. Wilson and Fiske, eds., *Appletons' Cyclopedia of American Biography,* vol. 5, s.v. "Stanbery, Henry"; George I. Reed, Emilius O. Randall, and Charles T. Grece, eds., *Bench and Bar of Ohio: A Compendium of History and Biography* (Chicago: Century, 1897), 1:85; Andrew Johnson, *The Papers of Andrew Johnson,* ed. Paul H. Bergeron (Knoxville: University of Tennessee Press, 1997), 14:50.

[86] Charles Anderson (1814–1890) graduated from Miami University in 1833 and was elected to the Ohio Senate in 1844. At the start of the Civil War, he became a colonel of the 93rd Ohio Volunteers. He was elected lieutenant governor of Ohio in 1863 and finished the unexpired term of the deceased governor John Brough. Larz Anderson (1803–1878) graduated from Harvard College in 1822. During his life, he was involved in developing railroads and libraries in Cincinnati, OH. He married Catherine Longworth, the daughter of Cincinnati businessman Nicholas Longworth. Richard F. Miller, ed., *States at War: A Reference Guide for Ohio in the Civil War* (Lebanon, NH: University Press of New England, 2015), 5:350*n;* Daniel Ryan, *A History of Ohio with Biographical Sketches of Her Governors and the Ordinance of 1787* (Columbus, OH: A. H. Smythe, 1888), s.v. "Charles Anderson"; William A. Taylor, *Centennial History of Columbus and Franklin County, Ohio* (Chicago: S. J. Clarke, 1909), 1:324.

friends,[87] and especially Miss Sallie Carneal, then quite a belle, and noted for her fine voice.[88]

On the 20th I took passage on the steamboat Manhattan for St. Louis; reached Louisville, where Dr. Conrad,[89] of the army, joined me, and in the Manhattan we continued on to St. Louis, with a mixed crowd. We reached the Mississippi at Cairo the 23d, and St. Louis, Friday, November 24, 1843. At St. Louis we called on Colonel S. W. Kearney and Major Cooper, his adjutant-general, and found my classmate, Lieutenant McNutt, of the ordnance, stationed at the arsenal;[90] also Mr. Deas, an artist, and Pacificus Ord, who was

[87] Nicholas Longworth (1783–1863) in 1804 moved to Cincinnati, where he studied law until 1819. Later he became the largest landowner in the area and one of the wealthiest people in the United States. Longworth was a notable patron of the arts. He supported multiple artists, including sculptor Hiram Powers (1805–1873) and painters Robert S. Duncanson (1821–1872) and William H. Powell (1823–1879). When WTS was in the Cincinnati area in Nov. 1843, Longworth was a patron of artists Lily M. Spencer (c. 1822–1902) and James H. Beard (1811–1893). Charles Cist, *Sketches and Statistics of Cincinnati in 1851* (Cincinnati: W. H. Moore, 1851), 333–334; *Harper's Weekly: A Journal of Civilization,* Mar. 7, 1863, 145–146; Abby S. Schwartz, "Nicholas Longworth: Art Patron of Cincinnati," *Queen City Heritage,* 46 (Spring 1988), 17, 20–27.

[88] Sallie Carneal-Burke (1821–1850) was the daughter of Thomas Davis Carneal of Kentucky. She was a notable musician and singer based out of Cincinnati. She married Glendy Burke, a wealthy merchant from New Orleans. E. F. Ellet, *Queens of American Society* (New York: Charles Scribner, 1867), 426; "Obituary," *New Orleans Commercial Bulletin,* Aug. 17, 1850, 2.

[89] James N. Conrad attended to the sick and wounded at Fort Russell in Key Biscayne, FL, during the years 1840–1841. *Army and Navy Chronicle,* Feb. 14, 1839, no. 7 (Washington, DC: A. B. Claxton and Co., 1839), 8:108; Joan Blank, *Key Biscayne: A History of Miami's Tropical Island and the Cape Florida Lighthouse* (Sarasota, FL: Pineapple, 1996), 47.

[90] Stephen W. Kearney (1794–1848) joined the U.S. Army during the War of 1812. Over the following three decades, Kearney spent his time leading dragoon expeditions along the American western frontier to establish military posts. In 1843 he led an expedition along the Santa Fe Trail, which connected to St. Louis via the Missouri River. He was promoted to brigadier general during the Mexican-American War and later served as the civil governor of California in 1847 and governor of Mexico City during Apr. and June 1848. Samuel Cooper (1798–1876) graduated from the USMA in 1815 and was brevetted captain in 1836. He was appointed adjutant general of the U.S. Army in 1852 and resigned from that position to serve as adjutant general of the Confederate Army in 1861. John McNutt (1819–1881) graduated from the USMA in 1840 and was appointed captain in 1854 and lieutenant colonel in 1874. He served as an

studying law.[91] I spent a week at St. Louis, visiting the arsenal, Jefferson Barracks, and most places of interest, and then became impressed with its great future. It then contained about forty thousand people, and my notes describe thirty-six good steamboats receiving and discharging cargo at the levee.

I took passage December 4th in the steamer John Aull for New Orleans. As we passed Cairo the snow was falling, and the country was wintery and devoid of verdure. Gradually, however, as we proceeded south, the green color came; grass and trees showed the change of latitude, and when in the course of a week we had reached New Orleans, the roses were in full bloom, the sugar-cane just ripe, and a tropical air prevalent. We reached New Orleans December 11, 1843, where I spent about a week visiting the barracks, then occupied by the Seventh Infantry; the theatres, hotels, and all the usual places of interest of that day.

On the 16th of December I continued on to Mobile in the steamer Fashion by way of Lake Pontchartrain; saw there most of my personal friends, Mr. and Mrs. Bull, Judge Bragg and his brother Dunbar,[92] Deshon, Taylor, and Myers,

---

ordnance officer at the Battle of Port Royal and as chief of ordnance, Department of Kansas, from 1861 to 1865. Paul A. Hutton and Durwood Ball, eds., *Soldiers West: Biographies from the Military Frontier,* 2nd ed. (Norman: University of Oklahoma Press, 2009), 43–55, 58, 61; Richard F. Miller, ed., *States at War: A Reference Guide for Pennsylvania in the Civil War* (Hanover, NH: University Press of New England, 2014), 3:306*n;* Secretary of the Association, *Twelfth Annual Reunion of the Association of the Graduates of the U.S. Military Academy, at West Point, New York, June 9, 1881* (East Saginaw: E. W. Lyon, 1881), 45.

[91] Charles Deas (1818–1867) was unable to obtain an appointment to the USMA and instead studied art at the National Academy of Design in New York City. He moved to St. Louis in 1841 and opened an art studio. He continued to create art until 1849, when he was admitted to an asylum due to "melancholia." Pacificus Ord (1816–1900) moved to California in 1849. His brother was E. O. C. Ord, WTS's roommate at the USMA. Pacificus practiced law and later became a judge on the Supreme Court of California. Lawrence O. Christensen et al., *Dictionary of Missouri Biography* (Columbia: University of Missouri Press, 1999), 236; Henry D. Barrows and Luther A. Ingersoll, eds., *A Memorial and Biographical History of the Coast Counties of Central California* (Chicago: Lewis, 1893), 74; J. M. Guinn, *Historical and Biographical Record of Southern California: Containing a History of Southern California from Its Earliest Settlement to the Opening Year of the Twentieth Century* (Chicago: Chapman, 1902), 253.

[92] Possibly Alfred and Mary Bull. John Bragg (1806–1878) graduated from the University of North Carolina in 1824 and served in the North Carolina House of Commons from 1830 to 1834. He later moved to Mobile, AL, and served as a Superior Court judge from 1842 to 1851 and in the U.S. House of Representatives from 1851 to 1853. Dunbar Bragg (1821–1882) moved to Freestone County, TX, in 1850 and served as the treasurer of the county from 1877 to 1882.

etc., and on the 19th of December took passage in the steamboat Bourbon for Montgomery, Alabama, by way of the Alabama River. We reached Montgomery at noon, December 23d, and took cars at 1 P. M. for Franklin, forty miles, which we reached at 7 P. M., thence stages for Griffin, Georgia, *via* La Grange and Greenville. This took the whole night of the 23d and the day of the 24th. At Griffin we took cars for Macon, and thence to Savannah, which we reached Christmas-night, finding Lieutenants Ridgley[93] and Ketchum at tea, where we were soon joined by Rankin and Beckwith.[94]

On the 26th I took the boat for Charleston, reaching my post, and reported for duty Wednesday morning, December 27, 1843.

I had hardly got back to my post when, on the 21st of January, 1844, I received from Lieutenant R. P. Hammond, at Marietta, Georgia, an intimation that Colonel Churchill, Inspector-General of the Army, had applied for me to assist him in taking depositions in upper Georgia and Alabama;[95] concerning certain losses by volunteers in Florida of horses and equipments by reason of the failure of the United States to provide sufficient forage, and for which Congress had made an appropriation. On the 4th of February the order came from the Adjutant-General in Washington for me to proceed to Marietta, Georgia, and report to Inspector-General Churchill. I was delayed till the 14th of February by reason of being on a court-martial, when I was duly relieved and started by rail to Augusta, Georgia, and as far as Madison, where I took the mail-coach, reaching Marietta on the 17th. There I reported

---

John and Dunbar were brothers of Confederate general Braxton Bragg. Jan Onofrio, ed., *Alabama Biographical Dictionary* (St. Clair Shores, MI: Somerset, 1998), s.v. "Bragg, John"; John H. Treat, *The Treat Family: A Genealogy of Trott, Tratt, and Treat for Fifteen Generations, and Four Hundred and Fifty Years in England and America* (Salem, MA: Salem Press, 1893), 444.

[93] Randolph Ridgely (1814–1846) graduated from the USMA in 1837 and was stationed in Augusta, GA, at various times during 1843–1845. He died during the Mexican-American War after he fell from his horse. *USMA,* 1:693.

[94] Edward G. Beckwith (1818–1881) graduated from the USMA in 1838 and authored *Report of Exploration of a Route for the Pacific Railroad* in 1855. He was brevetted brigadier general for his service in the U.S. Army during the Civil War. *CWHC,* 125.

[95] Richard P. Hammond (1820–1891) graduated from the USMA in 1841 and served as assistant to the inspector general in Georgia, Alabama, and Florida from 1843 to 1845. He fought in the Mexican-American War and reached the rank of brevet major in 1847. He resigned from the U.S. Army in 1851. Sylvester Churchill (1783–1862) was a part owner and publisher of the *Vermont Republican,* a Democratic-Republican Party newspaper, from 1808 to 1812. He joined the U.S. Army in 1812 and remained in the military until his death in 1862. Franklin H. Churchill, *Sketch of the Life of Bvt. Brig. Gen. Sylvester Churchill* (New York: Willis McDonald, 1888), 7, 10, 13; *USMA,* 2:84–85.

for duty to Colonel Churchill, who was already engaged on his work, assisted by Lieutenant R. P. Hammond, Third Artillery, and a citizen named Stockton. The colonel had his family with him, consisting of Mrs. Churchill, Mary, now Mrs. Professor Baird, and Charles Churchill, then a boy of about fifteen years of age.[96]

We all lived in a tavern, and had an office convenient. The duty consisted in taking individual depositions of the officers and men who had composed two regiments and a battalion of mounted volunteers that had served in Florida. An oath was administered to each man by Colonel Churchill, who then turned the claimant over to one of us to take down and record his deposition according to certain forms, which enabled them to be consolidated and tabulated. We remained in Marietta about six weeks, during which time I repeatedly rode to *Kenesaw Mountain,* and over the very ground where afterward, in 1864, we had some hard battles.

After closing our business at Marietta the colonel ordered us to transfer our operations to Bellefonte, Alabama.[97] As he proposed to take his family and party by the stage, Hammond lent me his riding-horse, which I rode to Allatoona[98] and the Etowah River. Hearing of certain large Indian mounds near the way, I turned to one side to visit them, stopping a couple of days with Colonel Lewis Tumlin, on whose plantation these mounds were. We struck up such an acquaintance that we corresponded for some years, and as I passed his plantation during the war, in 1864, I inquired for him, but he was not at home.[99] From Tumlin's I rode to Rome, and by way of Wills Valley over

[96] Lucy Hunter-Churchill (1786–1862) married Sylvester Churchill in Aug. 1812. She traveled with her husband throughout the United States as he attended to his duties as inspector general. Mary H. Churchill (1821–1891) married Spencer F. Baird (1823–1887) in Aug. 1846. Charles Churchill (1825-?) married Alice Dow in 1868. Churchill, *Sketch of the Life of Bvt. Brig. Gen. Sylvester Churchill,* 7, 8–9, 60–62; Gardner A. Churchill, Nathaniel W. Churchill, and George M. Bodge, eds., *The Churchill Family in America* (Family of Gardner Churchill, 1904), 99.

[97] Bellefonte, AL, is a ghost town in Jackson County near Hollywood. Bellefonte was the county seat from 1821 to 1859. Virginia O. Foscue, *Place Names in Alabama* (Tuscaloosa: University of Alabama Press, 1989), 15.

[98] Allatoona, GA, now covered by Lake Allatoona, was located approximately forty-eight miles upstream from Rome, GA. The area was flooded after a dam was built at the base of the Etowah River in 1949. *Environmental Impact Statement: Allatoona Dam and Lake, Georgia, Flood Control and Power* (Mobile: Mobile District Corps of Engineers, 1973), 1, 5.

[99] The Native American mounds in question are located on the Etowah River near Cartersville, GA. Lewis Tumlin (c. 1811–1875) volunteered to forcibly remove Native Americans from the area, and eventually became a large landowner. He served in the Georgia General As-

Sand Mountain and the Raccoon Range to the Tennessee River at Bellefonte, Alabama. We all assembled there in March, and continued our work for nearly two months, when, having completed the business, Colonel Churchill, with his family, went North by way of Nashville; Hammond, Stockton, and I returning South on horseback, by Rome, Allatoona, Marietta, Atlanta, and Madison, Georgia. Stockton stopped at Marietta, where he resided. Hammond took the cars at Madison, and I rode alone to Augusta, Georgia, where I left the horse and returned to Charleston and Fort Moultrie by rail.

Thus by a mere accident I was enabled to traverse on horseback the very ground where in after-years I had to conduct vast armies and fight great battles. That the knowledge thus acquired was of infinite use to me, and consequently to the Government, I have always felt and stated.

During the autumn of 1844, a difficulty arose among the officers of Company B, Third Artillery (John R. Vinton's), garrisoning Augusta Arsenal,[100] and I was sent up from Fort Moultrie as a sort of peace-maker. After staying there some months, certain transfers of officers were made, which reconciled the difficulty, and I returned to my post, Fort Moultrie.[101] During that winter, 1844–'45, I was visiting at the plantation of Mr. Poyas, on the east branch of the Cooper, about fifty miles from Fort Moultrie, hunting deer with his son James, and Lieutenant John F. Reynolds, Third Artillery.[102] We had taken our stands, and a deer came out of the swamp near that of Mr. James Poyas, who fired, broke the leg of the deer, which turned back into the swamp and came out again above mine. I could follow his course by the cry of the hounds,

---

sembly at various times throughout his life and was a sheriff of Cass County, GA. George M. Battey, *A History of Rome and Floyd County, State of Georgia* (Atlanta: Webb and Vary, 1922), 1:104; "Death of Lewis Tumlin," *Atlanta Constitution* (Atlanta, GA), June 3, 1875, 2.

[100] The arsenal in Augusta, GA, was constructed in 1829. It was one hundred feet long by thirty feet wide. It was closed in 1955, and the site is now part of Augusta University. Joseph M. Lee III, *Images of America: Augusta, a Postcard History* (Charleston, SC: Arcadia, 2000), 124 (caption).

[101] Vinton's command was significantly reduced in Oct. 1844, which made it difficult to operate the arsenal. Richard S. Barry, "Fort Macon: Its History," *North Carolina Historical Review,* 27, no. 2 (Apr. 1950):166–167.

[102] WTS most likely referred here to James Poyas (1790–1872) and James B. Poyas (c. 1819–c. 1882). John F. Reynolds (1820–1863) graduated from the USMA in 1841 and was stationed at Fort Moultrie as a second lieutenant from 1843 to 1845. He fought in the Mexican-American War and reached the rank of brevet major. He was eventually promoted to major general of volunteers for his actions during the Civil War. He was killed while leading a charge during the Battle of Gettysburg in July 1863. City of Charleston, *Year Book–1881* (Charleston, SC: News and Courier Book Presses, 1881), 118; *USMA,* 2:90–91.

which were in close pursuit. Hastily mounting my horse, I struck across the pine-woods to head the deer off, and when at full career my horse leaped a fallen log and his fore-foot caught one of those hard, unyielding pineknots that brought him with violence to the ground. I got up as quick as possible, and found my right arm out of place at the shoulder, caused by the weight of the double-barrelled gun.

Seeing Reynolds at some distance, I called out lustily and brought him to me. He soon mended the bridle and saddle, which had been broken by the fall, helped me on my horse, and we followed the course of the hounds. At first my arm did not pain me much, but it soon began to ache so that it was almost unendurable. In about three miles we came to a negro hut, where I got off and rested till Reynolds could overtake Poyas and bring him back. They came at last, but by that time the arm was so swollen and painful that I could not ride. They rigged up an old gig belonging to the negro, in which I was carried six miles to the plantation of Mr. Poyas, Sr. A neighboring physician was sent for, who tried the usual methods of setting the arm, but without success; each time making the operation more painful. At last he sent off, got a set of double pulleys and cords, with which he succeeded in extending the muscles and in getting the bone into place. I then returned to Fort Moultrie, but being disabled, applied for a short leave and went North.

I started January 25, 1845; went to Washington, Baltimore, and Lancaster, Ohio, whence I went to Mansfield, and thence back by Newark to Wheeling, Cumberland, Baltimore, Philadelphia, and New York, whence I sailed back for Charleston on the ship Sullivan, reaching Fort Moultrie March 9, 1845.

About that time (March 1, 1845) Congress had, by a joint resolution, provided for the annexation of Texas, then an independent Republic, subject to certain conditions requiring the acceptance of the Republic of Texas to be final and conclusive.[103] We all expected war as a matter of course. At that time General Zachary Taylor had assembled a couple of regiments of infantry and one of dragoons at Fort Jessup, Louisiana,[104] and had orders to extend military protection to Texas against the Indians, or a "foreign enemy," the moment the

[103] Texas was eventually admitted as a state on Dec. 29, 1845. For the full text of "No. 97 Joint Resolution for the Annexation of Texas, March 1, 1845," and other joint resolutions related to the annexation of Texas, see Hunter Miller, ed., *Treaties and Other International Acts of the United States of America,* documents 80–121, 1836–1846 (Washington, DC: GPO, 1934), 1:689–739.

[104] Fort Jessup was built in 1822, twenty-two miles west of Natchitoches, LA. Its original garrison was established and commanded by Colonel Zachary Taylor. It served as an outpost between the United States and Texas for most of its existence. The fort was abandoned in 1846

terms of annexation were accepted. He received notice of such acceptance July 7th, and forthwith proceeded to remove his troops to Corpus Christi, Texas, where, during the summer and fall of 1845, was assembled that force with which, in the spring of 1846, was begun the Mexican War.

Some time during that summer came to Fort Moultrie orders for sending Company E, Third Artillery, Lieutenant Bragg, to New Orleans, there to receive a battery of field-guns, and thence to the camp of General Taylor at Corpus Christi. This was the first company of our regiment sent to the seat of war, and it embarked on the brig Hayne. This was the only company that left Fort Moultrie till after I was detached for recruiting service on the 1st of May, 1846.

Inasmuch as Charleston afterward became famous, as the spot where began our civil war, a general description of it, as it was in 1846, will not be out of place.

The city lies on a long peninsula between the Ashley and Cooper Rivers—a low, level peninsula of sand. Meeting Street is its Broadway, with King Street, next west and parallel, the street of shops and small stores. These streets are crossed at right angles by many others, of which Broad Street was the principal; and the intersection of Meeting and Broad was the heart of the city, marked by the Guard-House[105] and St. Michael's Episcopal Church. The Custom-House, Post-Office,[106] etc., were at the foot of Broad Street, near the wharves of the Cooper River front. At the extremity of the peninsula was a drive, open to the bay, and faced by some of the handsomest houses of the city, called the "Battery." Looking down the bay on the right, was James Island, an irregular triangle of about seven miles, the whole island in cultivation with sea-island cotton. At the lower end was Fort Johnson,[107] then simply the station of

---

after the annexation of Texas. The site of the fort is now a state park. Tucker, ed., *Encyclopedia of the Mexican-American War,* s.v. "Fort Jesup."

[105] The original guard house was constructed in 1769 and torn down in 1838. On the site the city constructed a police station, which was subsequently demolished in 1886 after an earthquake damaged the structure. W. H. Capes, *Charleston, Post Office and Courthouse Renovation: Final Environmental Impact Statement* (Charleston, SC: General Service Administration, 1981), 44–45.

[106] The post office in Charleston was destroyed by the 1886 earthquake, and in 1896 a new building was constructed at the southwest corner of Meeting and Broad Streets. Capes, *Charleston, Post Office and Courthouse Renovation,* 45.

[107] Fort Johnson was built in 1708 and was located on the northeast section of James Island. A second fort was added to the site in 1759 and a third in 1793. The Confederate Army used the

Captain Bowman, United States Engineers, engaged in building Fort Sumter.[108] This fort (Sumter) was erected on an artificial island nearly in mid-channel, made by dumping rocks, mostly brought as ballast in cotton-ships from the North. As the rock reached the surface it was levelled, and made the foundation of Fort Sumter. In 1846 this fort was barely above the water. Still farther out beyond James Island, and separated from it by a wide space of salt marsh with crooked channels, was Morris Island, composed of the sand-dunes thrown up by the wind and the sea, backed with the salt marsh. On this was the lighthouse,[109] but no people.

On the left, looking down the bay from the Battery of Charleston, was, first, Castle Pinckney, a round brick fort, of two tiers of guns, one in embrasure, the other in barbette, built on a marsh island, which was not garrisoned. Farther down the bay a point of the mainland reached the bay, where there was a group of houses, called Mount Pleasant; and at the extremity of the bay, distant six miles, was Sullivan's Island, presenting a smooth sand-beach to the sea, with the line of sand-hills or dunes thrown up by the waves and winds, and the usual backing of marsh and crooked salt-water channels.

At the shoulder of this island was Fort Moultrie, an irregular fort, without ditch or counterscarp, with a brick scarp wall about twelve feet high, which could be scaled anywhere, and this was surmounted by an earth parapet capable of mounting about forty twenty-four and thirty-two pounder smooth-bore iron guns. Inside the fort were three two-story brick barracks, sufficient to quarter the officers and men of two companies of artillery.

At sea was the usual "bar," changing slightly from year to year, but generally the main ship-channel came from the south, parallel to Morris Island, till

---

fort during the initial bombardment of Fort Sumter at the start of the Civil War. Carolyn A. Bonstelle and Geordie Buxton, *Images of America: James Island* (Charleston, SC: Arcadia, 2008), 17 (caption).

[108] Alexander H. Bowman (1803–1865) graduated from the USMA in 1825 and was an assistant professor of geography, history, and ethics at the USMA. He superintended the construction of Fort Sumter and the repairs of defensive fortifications in Charleston Harbor during the years 1838–1853. He later served as the superintendent of the USMA from 1861 to 1864. *USMA,* 2:341–342.

[109] The first Morris Island lighthouse was constructed in 1767. A new 102-foot tower was built in its place in 1838. The tower was destroyed at the start of the Civil War in 1861 and then replaced in 1876. It was eventually decommissioned in 1962 due to erosion along the shoreline. The tower still stands today. Margie W. Clary and Kim McDermott, *Images of America: Southern Carolina Lighthouses* (Charleston, SC: Arcadia, 2008), 9–11, 15, 28.

it was well up to Fort Moultrie, where it curved, passing close to Fort Sumter and up to the wharves of the city, which were built mostly along the Cooper River front.

Charleston was then a proud, aristocratic city, and assumed a leadership in the public opinion of the South far out of proportion to her population, wealth, or commerce. On more than one occasion previously, the inhabitants had almost inaugurated civil war, by their assertion and professed belief that each State had, in the original compact of government, reserved to itself the right to withdraw from the Union at its own option, whenever the people supposed they had sufficient cause. We used to discuss these things at our own mess-tables, vehemently and sometimes quite angrily; but I am sure that I never feared it would go further than it had already gone in the winter of 1832–'33, when the attempt at "nullification" was promptly suppressed by Pres. Jackson's famous declaration, "The Union must and shall be preserved!" and by the judicious management of General Scott.[110]

Still, civil war was to be; and, now that it has come and gone, we can rest secure in the knowledge that as the chief cause, slavery, has been eradicated forever, it is not likely to come again.

[110] In 1832, South Carolina declared that federal protective tariffs were unconstitutional. The Nullification Crisis ended with a compromise spearheaded by U.S. senators Henry Clay and John C. Calhoun. Winfield Scott (1786–1866) entered the U.S. Army in 1808 and reached the rank of brigadier general for his actions during the War of 1812. In 1829 he was placed in charge of the Eastern Division. He later led the U.S. Army in their capture of Mexico City during the Mexican-American War. He was also instrumental in preparing the United States for war against the Confederate Army in 1861. Kevin M. Gannon, "The South Carolina Nullification Crisis, 1828–1833: A Historiographical Overview," in *The Age of Andrew Jackson,* ed. Brian D. McKnight and James S. Humphreys (Kent, OH: Kent State University Press, 2011), 51–53; Spencer Tucker et al., eds., *The Encyclopedia of North American Indian Wars, 1607–1890* (Santa Barbara: ABC-CLIO, 2011), vol. 1, s.v. "Scott, Winfield."

2

Early Recollections of California.

1846–1848.

IN THE SPRING OF 1846 I was a first-lieutenant of Company G, Third Artillery, stationed at Fort Moultrie, South Carolina. The company was commanded by Captain Robert Anderson;[1] Henry B. Judd was the senior first-lieutenant, and I was the junior first-lieutenant, and George B. Ayres the second-lieutenant. Colonel William Gates commanded the post and regiment, with First-Lieutenant William Austine as his adjutant. Two other companies were at the post, viz., Martin Burke's and E. D. Keyes's, and among the officers were T. W. Sherman, Morris Miller, H. B. Field, William Churchill, Joseph Stewart, and Surgeon McLaren.[2]

The country now known as Texas had been recently acquired, and war with Mexico was threatening. One of our companies (Bragg's), with George H.

[1] Robert Anderson (1805–1871) graduated from the USMA in 1825 and was stationed at Fort Moultrie from 1845 to 1846. He was brevetted major for his actions during the Mexican-American War and later commanded U.S. troops during the defense of Fort Sumter in Apr. 1861. *USMA,* 1:347–349.

[2] Thomas W. Sherman (1813–1879) graduated from the USMA in 1836 and was promoted to captain in May 1846. He was not closely related to WTS. Morris S. Miller (1814–1870) graduated from the USMA in 1834. William Churchill (1819–1847) graduated from the USMA in 1840 and was stationed at Fort Moultrie, SC, from 1843 to 1845. He reached the rank of captain for his actions during the Mexican-American War in Mar. 1847, but died seven months later. Joseph Stewart (c. 1822–1904) graduated from the USMA in 1842 and fought in the Mexican-American War as a first lieutenant. Adam N. McLaren (1805–1874) graduated from Columbia College and joined the U.S. Army as an assistant surgeon in 1833. He was stationed at Fort Moultrie, SC, from 1844 to 1846 and served in the Mexican-American War. *USMA,* 1:572–573, 642–643; 2:30, 127–128; James L. McDonough, *William Tecumseh Sherman: In the Service of My Country* (New York: W. W. Norton, 2016), 88; *The Transactions of the American Medical Association, Instituted 1847* (Philadelphia: Collins, 1877), 28:629–631.

Thomas, John F. Reynolds, and Frank Thomas,[3] had gone the year previous and was at that time with General Taylor's army at Corpus Christi, Texas.

In that year (1846) I received the regular detail for recruiting service, with orders to report to the general superintendent at Governor's Island, New York; and accordingly left Fort Moultrie in the latter part of April, and reported to the superintendent, Colonel R. B. Mason, First Dragoons,[4] at New York, on the 1st day of May. I was assigned to the Pittsburg rendezvous, whither I proceeded and relieved Lieutenant Scott.[5] Early in May I took up my quarters at the St. Charles Hotel,[6] and entered upon the discharge of my duties. There was a regular recruiting-station already established, with a sergeant, corporal, and two or three men, with a citizen physician, Dr. McDowell,[7] to examine the recruits. The threatening war with Mexico made a demand for recruits, and I received authority to open another sub-rendezvous at Zanesville, Ohio, whither I took the sergeant and established him. This was very handy to me, as my home was at Lancaster, Ohio, only thirty-six miles off, so that I was thus enabled to visit my friends there quite often.

[3] Francis J. Thomas (c. 1824–1861) graduated from the USMA in 1844 and served in the Mexican-American War. He joined the Confederate Army at the start of the Civil War and was killed at the First Battle of Bull Run. *USMA,* 2:195–196.

[4] Richard B. Mason (1797–1850) joined the U.S. Army as a second lieutenant in 1817. After serving in the Mexican-American War, he briefly served as the civil and military governor for California in 1846 and 1847. *The National Cyclopædia of American Biography, Being the History of the United States* (New York: James T. White, 1897), vol. 7, s.v. "Mason, Richard Barnes."

[5] Henry L. Scott (1814–1886), the son-in-law of notable U.S. Army general Winfield Scott, graduated from the USMA in 1833 and served as his father-in-law's aide-de-camp and chief of staff during the Mexican-American War. *USMA,* 1:565–566.

[6] The St. Charles Hotel was located on Wood St. in downtown Pittsburgh. Today the building (now known as Lawrence Hall) is owned by Point Park University. Len Barcousky, *Civil War Pittsburgh: Forge of the Union* (Charleston, SC: History Press, 2013); George Prior, "Advertising Directory," appendix to *United States Commercial Register, Containing Sketches of the Lives of Distinguished Merchants, Manufacturers, and Artisans* (New York: John Belcher, 1851), 12.

[7] Andrew N. McDowell (d. 1849), a notable physician, treated author Charles Dickens for an illness during his visit to Pittsburgh in 1842. *Biographical Annals of Franklin County, Pennsylvania, Containing Records of Representative Families, Including Many of the Early Settlers, and Biographical Sketches of Prominent Citizens* (Chicago: Genealogical Publishing Co., 1905), 99; Raymond Walters, *Stephen Foster: Youth's Golden Gleam, A Sketch of His Life and Background in Cincinnati, 1846–1850* (Princeton, NJ: Princeton University Press, 1936), 124.

In the latter part of May, when at Wheeling, Virginia,[8] on my way back from Zanesville to Pittsburg, I heard the first news of the battle of Palo Alto and Resaca de la Palma, which occurred on the 8th and 9th of May, and, in common with everybody else, felt intensely excited. That I should be on recruiting service, when my comrades were actually fighting, was intolerable, and I hurried on to my post, Pittsburg. At that time the railroad did not extend west of the Alleghanies, and all journeys were made by stage-coaches. In this instance I traveled from Zanesville to Wheeling, thence to Washington (Pennsylvania), and thence to Pittsburg by stage-coach. On reaching Pittsburg I found many private letters; one from Ord, then a first-lieutenant in Company F, Third Artillery, at Fort McHenry, Baltimore, saying that his company had just received orders for California, and asking me to apply for it. Without committing myself to that project, I wrote to the Adjutant-General, R. Jones,[9] at Washington, D. C., asking him to consider me as an applicant for any active service, and saying that I would willingly forego the recruiting detail, which I well knew plenty of others would jump at. Impatient to approach the scene of active operations, without authority (and I suppose wrongfully), I left my corporal in charge of the rendezvous, and took all the recruits I had made, about twenty-five, in a steamboat to Cincinnati, and turned them over to Major N. C. McCrea, commanding at Newport Barracks.[10] I then reported in Cincinnati, to the superintendent of the Western recruiting service, Colonel Fanning, an old officer with one arm, who inquired by what authority I had come away from my post.[11] I argued that I took it for granted he wanted all the recruits he could get to forward to

[8] Wheeling officially became a city in West Virginia when the state was admitted into the Union during the Civil War in June 1863. Richard O. Curry, *A House Divided: A Study of Statehood Politics and the Copperhead Movement in West Virginia* (Pittsburgh: University of Pittsburgh Press, 1964), 46.

[9] Roger Jones (1788–1852) joined the U.S. Marines as a second lieutenant in 1809 and eventually obtained the rank of major general. Charles B. Davenport, *Naval Officers, Their Heredity and Development* (Washington, DC: Carnegie Institution of Washington, 1919), 110–111.

[10] Nathaniel C. Macrae (1805–1878) graduated from the USMA in 1826 and commanded Newport Barracks in Newport, KY, from 1841 to 1852. The barracks were constructed in 1803 and the U.S. military used the facility continuously until after the Civil War. The site was flooded multiple times in the 1880s, rendering it unsuitable for use. The former site is now the location of James Taylor Park. *USMA,* 1:380–381; Robert D. Webster, *A Brief History of Northern Kentucky* (Lexington: University of Kentucky Press, 2019), 93–94.

[11] Alexander C. W. Fanning (1788–1846) graduated from the USMA in 1812 and fought in the War of 1812 as a first lieutenant. He lost his arm during the Battle of York in 1813. He went

the army at Brownsville, Texas; and did not know but that he might want me to go along. Instead of appreciating my volunteer zeal, he cursed and swore at me for leaving my post without orders, and told me to go back to Pittsburg. I then asked for an order that would entitle me to transportation back, which at first he emphatically refused, but at last he gave the order, and I returned to Pittsburg, all the way by stage, stopping again at Lancaster, where I attended the wedding of my schoolmate Mike Effinger, and also visited my sub-rendezvous at Zanesville. R. S. Ewell, of my class, arrived to open a cavalry rendezvous, but, finding my depot there, he went on to Columbus, Ohio. Tom Jordan afterward was ordered to Zanesville, to take charge of that rendezvous, under the general War Department orders increasing the number of recruiting-stations.[12] I reached Pittsburg late in June, and found the order relieving me from recruiting service, and detailing my classmate H. B. Field to my place. I was assigned to Company F, then under orders for California. By private letters from Lieutenant Ord, I heard that the company had already started from Fort McHenry for Governor's Island, New York Harbor, to take passage for California in a naval transport. I worked all that night, made up my accounts current, and turned over the balance of cash to the citizen physician, Dr. McDowell; and also closed my clothing and property returns, leaving blank receipts with the same gentleman for Field's signature, when he should get there, to be forwarded to the Department at Washington, and the duplicates to me. These I did not receive for more than a year. I remember that I got my orders about 8 P. M. one night, and took passage in the boat for Brownsville, the next morning traveled by stage from Brownsville to Cumberland, Maryland, and thence by cars to Baltimore, Philadelphia, and New York, in a great hurry lest the ship might sail without me. I found Company

---

on to serve as the superintendent of recruiting in the Western Department from May to Aug. 1846. *USMA,* 1:108–109.

[12] Michael Effinger (1819–1890) graduated from Miami University in Ohio and the University of Pennsylvania. He married Elmira Caitlin on June 23, 1846. WTS and Effinger remained friends throughout the rest of their lives. Richard S. Ewell (1817–1872) graduated from the USMA in 1840. In 1846 he began recruiting services, but he was soon transferred to fight in the Mexican-American War. He resigned from the U.S. Army in May 1861 to join the Confederate Army. Thomas Jordan (1819–1895), one of WTS's roommates, graduated from the USMA in 1840 and served during the Second and Third Seminole Wars and the Mexican-American War. He resigned from the U.S. Army in May 1861 to join the Confederate Army. *USMA,* 2:40–41, 58–59; Charles B. Galbreath, *History of Ohio* (Chicago: American Historical Society, 1925), 5:156.

F at Governor's Island, Captain C. Q. Tompkins in command, Lieutenant E. O. C. Ord senior first-lieutenant, myself junior first-lieutenant, Lucien Loeser and Charles Minor the second-lieutenants.[13]

The company had been filled up to one hundred privates, twelve non-commissioned officers, and one ordnance sergeant (Layton), making one hundred and thirteen enlisted men and five officers.[14] Dr. James L. Ord had been employed as acting assistant surgeon to accompany the expedition, and Lieutenant H. W. Halleck, of the engineers, was also to go along.[15] The United States store-ship Lexington was then preparing at the Navy-Yard, Brooklyn, to carry us around Cape Horn to California. She was receiving on board the necessary stores for the long voyage, and for service after our arrival there. Lieutenant-Commander Theodorus Bailey was in command of the

[13] Christopher Q. Tompkins (1813–1877) graduated from the USMA in 1836 and served in the Second Seminole War. He resigned from the U.S. Army in 1847, and later joined a West Virginia Confederate militia as a colonel. Lucien Loeser (1818–1897) graduated from the USMA in 1842 and was stationed at Fort McHenry, MD, when he was promoted to second lieutenant in May 1845. After his transfer to California, he served in the Mexican-American War. He resigned from the military in Dec. 1858. Colville J. Minor (1824–1847) graduated from the USMA in 1846 and died a noncombat death in Monterey, CA, in Aug. 1847. WTS attributed his death to the "filthiness" of the city. *USMA,* 1:648–649; 2:134, 272; 4:59. John F. Marszalek, *Sherman: A Soldier's Passion for Order* (New York: Free Press, 1993), 66–67; *Official Army Register for 1848* (Washington, DC: C. Alexander, 1848), 52.

[14] Co. F, Third Art., had ten noncommissioned officers: Charles Layton, John E. Noble, James H. Carson, Harvey Maxim, Lewis Curman, Patrick Hand, Richard H. Bell, Patrick Reid, Henry A. Hoffman, and Owen Leavy. There were 131 names on the company's muster roll, but sources point to the actual number being 112 or 113 enlisted men and five officers. The remaining recruits arrived later. Charles Layton (c. 1811–1855) was born in England and served in the British Army. He later served as the first lighthouse keeper at Point Pinos, CA, and was shot and killed in 1855 while attempting to capture Mexican outlaw Anastacio Garcia. Hubert H. Bancroft, *History of California, 1846–1848* (San Francisco: History, 1886), 3:709, 5:519*n.* William B. Secrest, *California Feuds: Vengeance, Vendettas and Violence on the Old West Coast* (Sanger, CA: Quill Driver Books, 2005), 16–17.

[15] James L. Ord (c. 1823–1898), a brother of Edward O. C. Ord, graduated from Jefferson Medical College in 1846 and was the acting assistant surgeon in the U.S. Army in July 1846. Henry W. Halleck (1815–1872) graduated from the USMA in 1839 and was promoted to first lieutenant in 1845. He served in the Mexican-American War and was a major general and the general-in-chief of Union forces during the Civil War. *USMA,* 1:733–734; W. Thornton Parker, ed., *Records of the Association of Acting Assistant Surgeons of the United States Army, A.D. 1891* (Salem, MA: Salem Press, 1891), 68–70.

vessel, Lieutenant William H. Macomb executive officer, and Passed-Midshipmen Muse, Spotts, and J. W. A. Nicholson, were the watch-officers; Wilson purser, and Abernethy surgeon.[16] The latter was caterer of the mess, and we all made an advance of cash for him to lay in the necessary mess-stores. To enable us to prepare for so long a voyage and for an indefinite sojourn in that far-off country, the War Department had authorized us to draw six months' pay in advance, which sum of money we invested in surplus clothing and such other things as seemed to us necessary. At last the ship was ready, and was towed down abreast of Fort Columbus,[17] where we were conveyed on board, and on the 14th of July, 1846, we were towed to sea by a steam-tug, and cast off. Colonel R. B. Mason, still superintendent of the general recruiting service, accompanied us down the bay and out to sea, returning with the tug. A few other friends were of the party, but at last they left us, and we were alone upon the sea, and the sailors were busy with the sails and ropes. The Lexington was an old ship, changed from a sloop-of-war

[16] Theodorus Bailey (1805–1877) became a midshipman in the U.S. Navy in 1818 and was promoted through the ranks, reaching captain in 1855. During the Civil War he served on various ships in both the East and West Blockade Squadrons and commanded the East Gulf Blockade Squadron from 1862 to 1864. He was promoted to rear admiral in July 1866 and retired on Oct. 10, 1866. William H. Macomb (1818–1872) joined the U.S. Navy in 1834 and became a lieutenant in 1847. He was appointed commander in 1862 for his actions during the Civil War. William B. Muse (1816–1883) joined the U.S. Navy in 1836 and retired in 1852. James H. Spotts (c. 1822–1882) attended the Naval School of Philadelphia and was promoted to commander during the Civil War and to rear admiral in 1881. James W. A. Nicholson (c. 1820–1887) became a passed midshipman in 1844 and was with the Pacific Squadron from 1846 to 1847. Joseph Wilson was born in Massachusetts. John J. Abernethy (1805–1879) graduated from the College of Physicians and Surgeons in New York City in 1828. He joined the U.S. Navy as an assistant surgeon in 1837 and served in the Mexican-American War and the Civil War. *CWHC,* 112; "Death of Lieutenant Muse," *Baltimore American and Commercial Advertiser,* Apr. 19, 1883, 4; Lewis R. Hamersly, *The Records of Living Officers of the U.S. Navy and Marine Corps,* 4th ed. (Philadelphia: L. R. Hamersly, 1890), 434–435, 446; *Obituary Record of Graduates of Yale College, Deceased during the Academical Year Ending in June 1880, Presented at the Meeting of the Alumni, June 30, 1880,* 386; *Register of All Officers and Agents, Civil, Military, and Naval, in the Service of the United States, on the Thirtieth September, 1847* (Washington, DC: J. and G. S. Gideon, 1847), 219, 222.

[17] Originally completed in 1801, Fort Jay was renamed Fort Columbus around 1807 and renamed Fort Jay again in Jan. 1904. Barbara A. Yocum, *Fort Jay: Historic Structure Report, Governors Island National Monument, National Parks of New York Harbor, New York, New York* (Lowell, MA: Historic Architecture Program, 2006), 128.

to a store-ship, with an after-cabin, a "ward-room," and "between-decks." In the cabin were Captains Bailey and Tompkins, with whom messed the purser, Wilson. In the ward-room were all the other officers, two in each state-room; and Minor, being an extra lieutenant, had to sleep in a hammock slung in the ward-room. Ord[18] and I roomed together; Halleck and Loeser and the others were scattered about. The men were arranged in bunks "between-decks," one set along the sides of the ship, and another, double tier, amidships. The crew were slung in hammocks well forward. Of these there were about fifty. We at once subdivided the company into four squads, under the four lieutenants of the company, and arranged with the naval officers that our men should serve on deck by squads, after the manner of their watches; that the sailors should do all the work aloft, and the soldiers on deck.

On fair days we drilled our men at the manual, and generally kept them employed as much as possible, giving great attention to the police and cleanliness of their dress and bunks; and so successful were we in this, that, though the voyage lasted nearly two hundred days, every man was able to leave the ship and march up the hill to the fort at Monterey, California,[19] carrying his own knapsack and equipments.

The voyage from New York to Rio Janeiro was without accident or any thing to vary the usual monotony. We soon settled down to the humdrum of a long voyage, reading some, not much; playing games, but never gambling; and chiefly engaged in eating our meals regularly. In crossing the equator we had the usual visit of Neptune and his wife, who, with a large razor and a bucket of soapsuds, came over the sides and shaved some of the greenhorns; but naval etiquette exempted the officers, and Neptune was not permitted to come aft of the mizzen-mast.[20] At last, after sixty days of absolute monotony, the island of Raza, off Rio Janeiro, was descried, and we slowly entered the harbor, passing a fort on our right hand, from which came a hail, in the Por-

[18] WTS was referring to Edward O. C. Ord. Marszalek, *Sherman,* 55.

[19] Fort Mervine, constructed in 1846 and originally named Fort Stockton, was located along the coast in Monterey, CA. In 1904 it was renamed the Presidio of Monterey. The site is still used by the military today. Harold E. Raugh Jr., *Images of America: Presidio of Monterey* (Charleston, SC: Arcadia, 2004), 7; Robert B. Roberts, *Encyclopedia of Historic Forts: The Military, Pioneer, and Trading Posts of the United States* (New York: Macmillan, 1988), 78–80.

[20] The "crossing the line" ceremony, a centuries-old ritual traditionally observed by sailors from many nations, is performed when a ship crosses the equator. Simon J. Bronner, *Crossing the Line: Violence, Play, and Drama in Naval Equator Traditions* (Amsterdam: Amsterdam University Press, 2006), 6–8.

tuguese language, from a huge speaking-trumpet, and our officer of the deck answered back in gibberish, according to a well-understood custom of the place.[21] Sugar-loaf Mountain, on the south of the entrance, is very remarkable and well named; is almost conical, with a slight lean. The man-of-war anchorage is about five miles inside the heads, directly in front of the city of Rio Janeiro. Words will not describe the beauty of this perfect harbor, nor the delightful feeling after a long voyage of its fragrant airs, and the entire contrast between all things there and what we had left in New York.

We found the United States frigate Columbia anchored there, and after the Lexington was properly moored, nearly all the officers went on shore for sight-seeing and enjoyment. We landed at a wharf opposite which was a famous French restaurant, Farroux, and after ordering supper we all proceeded to the Rua da Ouvador, where most of the shops were, especially those for making feather flowers, as much to see the pretty girls as the flowers which they so skillfully made; thence we went to the theatre, where, besides some opera, we witnessed the audience and saw the Emperor Dom Pedro, and his Empress, the daughter of the King of Sicily.[22] After the theatre, we went back to the restaurant, where we had an excellent[23] supper, with fruits of every variety and excellence, such as we had never seen before, or even knew the names of. Supper being over, we called for the bill, and it was rendered in French, with Brazilian currency. It footed up some twenty-six thousand reis. The figures alarmed us, so we all put on the waiters' plate various coins in gold, which he took to the counter and returned the change, making the total

[21] Soldiers stationed at Fort Santa Cruz called out to ships entering the harbor of Rio de Janeiro at night, and the expectation was that the ship's occupants would identify the port of departure, name, and nationality of the ship in the reply, whether they understood Portuguese or not. Joseph Blunt, *The Shipmaster's Assistant and Commercial Digest* (New York: Harper, 1848), 567.

[22] Dom Pedro II (1825–1891) was born in Rio de Janeiro, Brazil, and became emperor in 1840. In the first edition of the memoirs (1875), WTS misidentified Dom Pedro's wife, Teresa Christina (1822–1889), as the daughter of "Louis Philippe of France." WTS corrected the mistake in the second edition. Her actual father was Francis I, who was king of Naples and Sicily from 1825 to 1830. Teresa married Pedro II in 1843 and they had four children. During the American Civil War, Pedro declared Brazil neutral but also allowed Confederate ships to seek refuge in the country's ports. He was one of the longest reigning emperors of his time until he was overthrown by a coup in 1889. Anne Commire, ed., *Women in World History* (Waterford, CT: Yorkin, 2000), 7:704; Thomas M. Leonard, ed., *Encyclopedia of U.S.–Latin American Relations* (Los Angeles: CQ Press, 2012), s.v. "Pedro II, Emperor Dom."

[23] In the first edition of the memoirs (1875), the text read "elegant" instead of "excellent."

about sixteen dollars. The millreis is about a dollar, but being a paper-money was at a discount, so as only to be worth about fifty-six cents in coin.

The Lexington remained in Rio about a week, during which we visited the Palace, a few miles in the country,[24] also the Botanic Gardens, a place of infinite interest, with its specimens of tropical fruits, spices, etc., etc., and indeed every place of note. The thing I best recall is a visit Halleck and I made to the *Corcovado,* a high mountain whence the water is conveyed for the supply of the city. We started to take a walk, and passed along the aqueduct, which approaches the city by a series of arches; thence up the point of the hill to a place known as the *Madre,* or fountain, to which all the water that drips from the leaves is conducted by tile gutters, and is carried to the city by an open stone aqueduct.

Here we found Mr. Henry A. Wise, of Virginia, the United States minister to Brazil, and a Dr. Garnett, United States Navy, his intended son-in-law.[25] We had a very interesting conversation, in which Mr. Wise enlarged on the fact that Rio was supplied from the "dews of heaven," for in the dry season the water[26] comes from the mists and fogs which hang around the *Corcovado,* drips from the leaves of the trees, and is conducted to the *Madre* fountain by miles of tile gutters. Halleck and I continued our ascent of the mountain, catching from points of the way magnificent views of the scenery round about Rio Janeiro. We reached near the summit what was called the emperor's coffee-plantation, where we saw coffee-berries in their various stages, and the scaffolds on which the berries were dried before being cleaned. The coffee-tree reminded me of the red haw-tree of Ohio, and the berries were some-

[24] The Imperial Palace at Petropolis, approximately twenty miles north of Rio de Janeiro, was constructed in the 1840s as a summer residence for the emperor and his family. Colin M. MacLachlan, *A History of Modern Brazil: The Past against the Future* (Wilmington, DE: Scholarly Resources, 2003), 17.

[25] Henry Alexander Wise (1806–1876) graduated from Washington College in 1825. He represented Virginia in the U.S. Congress from 1833 to 1844, served as the U.S. minister to Brazil from 1844 to 1847, and as governor of Virginia from 1856 to 1860. He fought as a brigadier general in the Confederate Army during the Civil War. Alexander Y. P. Garnett (1820–1888) graduated from the University of Pennsylvania in 1841 and was an assistant surgeon in the U.S. Navy. In 1846 he was stationed at the Navy Yard in Washington, DC. *CWHC,* 576–577; Howard A. Kelly and Walter L. Burrage, *American Medical Biographies* (Baltimore: Norman and Remington, 1920), s.v. "Garnett, Alexander Yelverton Peyton."

[26] In the first edition of the memoirs (1875), the text read, "for it rarely rains there, and the water . . ."

what like those of the same tree, two grains of coffee being inclosed in one berry. These were dried and cleaned of the husk by hand or by machinery. A short, steep ascent from this place carried us to the summit, from which is beheld one of the most picturesque views on earth. The Organ Mountains to the west and north, the ocean to the east, the city of Rio with its red-tiled houses at our feet, and the entire harbor like a map spread out, with innumerable bright valleys, make up a landscape that cannot be described by mere words. This spot is universally visited by strangers, and has often been described. After enjoying it immeasurably, we returned to the city by another route, tired but amply repaid by our long walk.

In due time all had been done that was requisite, and the Lexington put to sea and resumed her voyage. In October we approached Cape Horn, the first land descried was Staten Island, white with snow,[27] and the ship seemed to be aiming for the channel to its west, straits of Le Maire, but her course was changed and we passed around to the east. In time we saw Cape Horn; an island rounded like an oven, after which it takes its name (*Ornos*) oven. Here we experienced very rough weather, buffeting about under storm stay-sails, and spending nearly a month before the wind favored our passage and enabled the course of the ship to be changed for Valparaiso. One day we sailed parallel with a French sloop-of-war, and it was sublime to watch the two ships rising and falling in those long deep swells of the ocean. All the time we were followed by the usual large flocks of Cape-pigeons and albatrosses of every color. The former resembled the common barn-pigeon exactly, but are in fact gulls of beautiful and varied colors, mostly dove-color.[28] We caught many with fishing-lines baited with pork. We also took in the same way many albatrosses. The white ones are very large, and their down is equal to that of the swan. At last Cape Horn and its swelling seas were left behind, and we reached Valparaiso in about sixty days from Rio. We anchored in the open roadstead, and spent there about ten days, visiting all the usual places of interest, its foretop, main-top, mizzen-top, etc. Halleck and Ord went up to Santiago, the capital of Chili, some sixty miles inland, but I did not go. Valparaiso did not

[27] Staten Island, now known as Isla de los Estados, was visited by Dutch sailors in 1616. They named the island after the States General of the Netherlands. Juan Federico Ponce and Marilén Fernández, *Climatic and Environmental History of Isla de los Estados, Argentina* (Dordrecht: Springer, 2014), 3.

[28] WTS referred to the cape petrel or pintado petrel, commonly called cape pigeons in the nineteenth century. John Richardson et al., *The Museum of Natural History* (Glasgow: William Mackenzie, n.d.), 1:427.

impress me favorably at all. Seen from the sea, it looked like a long string of houses along the narrow beach, surmounted with red banks of earth, with little verdure, and no trees at all. Northward the space widened out somewhat, and gave room for a plaza, but the mass of houses in that quarter were poor. We were there in November, corresponding to our early spring, and we enjoyed the large strawberries which abounded. The Independence frigate, Commodore Shubrick, came in while we were there, having overtaken us, bound also for California. We met there also the sloop-of-war Levant, from California, and from the officers heard of many of the events that had transpired about the time the navy, under Commodore Sloat, had taken possession of the country.[29]

All the necessary supplies being renewed in Valparaiso, the voyage was resumed. For nearly forty days we had uninterrupted favorable winds, being in the "trades," and, having settled down to sailor habits, time passed without notice. We had brought with us all the books we could find in New York about California, and had read them over and over again: Wilkes's "Exploring Expedition;" Dana's "Two Years before the Mast;" and Forbes's "Account of the Missions."[30] It was generally understood we were bound for Monterey, then the capital of Upper California.[31] We knew, of course, that General Kearney was *en route* for the same country overland; that Fremont was there with his exploring party; that the navy had already taken possession, and that a regiment of volunteers, Stevenson's, was to follow us from New York;[32] but

[29] William B. Shubrick (1790–1874) briefly attended Harvard University before becoming a midshipman in 1806. He served in the War of 1812 and was promoted to master commandant in 1820 and captain in 1831. He retired as a rear admiral in 1861 and was a pallbearer for Pres. Abraham Lincoln. John D. Sloat (1781–1867) became a midshipman in 1800 and resigned his position in May 1801. He obtained the rank of captain in 1837. On July 7, 1846, Sloat captured Monterey, CA, and officially claimed California in the name of the U.S. government. *CWHC,* 487, 491; John W. Dwinelle, *The Colonial History of the City of San Francisco . . .* (San Francisco: Towne and Bacon, 1866), 115.

[30] WTS most likely referred here to Charles Wilkes's *Narrative of the United States Exploring Expedition during the Years 1838, 1839, 1840, 1841, 1842* (1845); Richard H. Dana Jr.'s *Two Years before the Mast* (1840); and Alexander Forbes's *California: A History of Upper and Lower California* (1839),which included a chapter titled "Account of the Missionary Establishments."

[31] Upper California, also known as Alta California, was a Mexican territory at the time. Its southern border spanned the Rio Grande and reached as far north as the Oregon Territory. Harr Wagner and Mark Keppel, *California History* (San Francisco: Harr Wagner, 1922), 79, 202.

[32] John C. Frémont (1813–1890) graduated from Charleston College in 1836 and led two expeditions into the Rocky Mountains in 1842 and 1844. He was appointed governor of Cali-

nevertheless we were impatient to reach our destination. About the middle of January the ship began to approach the California coast, of which the captain was duly cautious, because the English and Spanish charts differed some fifteen miles in the longitude, and on all the charts a current of two miles an hour was indicated northward along the coast. At last land was made one morning, and here occurred one of those accidents so provoking after a long and tedious voyage. Macomb, the master and regular navigator, had made the correct observations, but Nicholson during the night, by an observation on the north star, put the ship some twenty miles farther south than was the case by the regular reckoning, so that Captain Bailey gave directions to alter the course of the ship more to the north, and to follow the coast up, and to keep a good lookout for Point Pinos that marks the location of Monterey Bay. The usual north wind slackened, so that when noon allowed Macomb to get a good observation, it was found that we were north of Año Nuevo, the northern headland of Monterey Bay. The ship was put about, but little by little arose one of those southeast storms so common on the coast in winter, and we buffeted about for several days, cursing that unfortunate observation on the north star, for, on first sighting the coast, had we turned for Monterey, instead of away to the north, we would have been snugly anchored before the storm. But the southeaster abated, and the usual northwest wind came out again, and we sailed steadily down into the roadstead of Monterey Bay. This is shaped somewhat like a fish-hook, the barb being the harbor, the point being Point Pinos, the southern headland. Slowly the land came out of the water, the high mountains about Santa Cruz, the low beach of the Salinas, and the strongly-marked ridge terminating in the sea in a point of dark pine-trees. Then the line of whitewashed houses of adobe, backed by the groves of dark oaks, resembling old apple-trees; and then we saw two vessels anchored close to the town. One was a small merchant-brig and another a large ship apparently dismasted. At last we saw a boat coming out to meet us, and when it came alongside, we were surprised to find Lieutenant Henry Wise, master

---

fornia in 1846 and served in that position until he was court-martialed for insubordination the following year. Jonathan D. Stevenson (1800–1894) served as the private secretary to New York governor and future vice president Daniel D. Tompkins. When the Mexican-American War began, Pres. James K. Polk chose Stevenson to take a volunteer regiment of 769 men to California. The first part of the regiment arrived in San Francisco on Mar. 6, 1847, and the remainder arrived on Apr. 18. His regiment was mustered out of service in Aug. 1848. *CWHC,* 243–244; Rounsevelle Wildman, *Overland Monthly, January–June, 1895* (San Francisco: Overland Monthly, 1895), 25:120–121.

of the Independence frigate,[33] that we had left at Valparaiso. Wise had come off to pilot us to our anchorage. While giving orders to the man at the wheel, he, in his peculiar fluent style, told to us, gathered about him, that the Independence had sailed from Valparaiso a week after us and had been in Monterey a week; that the Californians had broken out into an insurrection; that the naval fleet under Commodore Stockton[34] was all down the coast about San Diego; that General Kearney had reached the country, but had had a severe battle at San Pascual, and had been worsted, losing several officers and men, himself and others wounded;[35] that war was then going on at Los Angeles; that the whole country was full of guerrillas, and that recently at Yerba Buena the alcalde, Lieutenant Bartlett, United States Navy, while out after cattle, had been lassoed, etc., etc.[36] Indeed, in the short space of time

[33] Henry A. Wise (1819–1869) joined the U.S. Navy as a midshipman in 1834 and fought in the Mexican-American War. In 1862 he was promoted to lieutenant commander and served as the assistant chief of the Bureau of Ordnance in the U.S. Navy. Jennings C. Wise, *Colonel John Wise of England and Virginia (1617–1695): His Ancestors and Descendants* (Richmond, VA: Bell Book and Stationery, 1918), 143.

[34] Robert F. Stockton (1795–1866) was a student at Princeton University at the start of the War of 1812. He joined the U.S. Navy as a midshipman in 1812 and was commissioned lieutenant in 1814. He left the navy in 1825 and rejoined in 1838. In 1846 he organized a battalion in Monterey, CA, and established an American government in the territory. He retired from the U.S. Navy in 1850 and later represented New Jersey in the U.S. Senate from 1851 to 1853. Mary T. Scudder, *Naval Officers: Their Heredity and Development* (Washington, DC: Carnegie Institution of Washington, 1919), 203–204.

[35] The Battle of San Pasqual took place near Escondido, CA, just north of San Diego, on Dec. 6, 1846. Each side had approximately one hundred cavalry soldiers. The Mexican Army killed approximately eighteen U.S. soldiers and wounded fifteen others while suffering only twelve casualties. Capt. H. S. Turner took command after Kearny was wounded during the battle. Owen C. Coy, *The Battle of San Pasqual: A Report of the California Historical Survey Commission with Special Reference to Its Location* (Sacramento: California State Printing Office, 1921), 3, 8.

[36] Washington A. Bartlett (1816–1865) joined the U.S. Navy in 1833 as a midshipman and was promoted to lieutenant in 1844. During the Mexican-American War, he was appointed first alcalde of San Francisco. In Dec. 1846, while traveling to San Jose, Bartlett and six others were captured by Mexican forces. On Jan. 8, 1847, Bartlett was freed. "Gleanings," *The Yonkers Statesman* (Yonkers, NY), Feb. 16, 1865, 3; James D. Hart, *A Companion to California* (Berkeley: University of California Press, 1987), s.v. "Yerba, Buena"; J. P. Munro-Fraser, *History of Contra Costa County, California* (San Francisco: W. A. Slocum, 1882), 524–527; *National Cyclopædia of American Biography*, vol. 8, s.v. "Bartlett, Washington Allen."

that Wise was piloting our ship in, he told us more news than we could have learned on shore in a week, and, being unfamiliar with the great distances, we imagined that we should have to debark and begin fighting at once. Swords were brought out, guns oiled and made ready, and every thing was in a bustle when the old Lexington dropped her anchor on January 26, 1847, in Monterey Bay, after a voyage of one hundred and ninety-eight days from New York. Every thing on shore looked bright and beautiful, the hills covered with grass and flowers, the live-oaks so serene and homelike, and the low adobe houses, with red-tiled roofs and whitened walls, contrasted well with the dark pine-trees behind, making a decidedly good impression upon us who had come so far to spy out the land. Nothing could be more peaceful in its looks than Monterey in January, 1847. We had already made the acquaintance of Commodore Shubrick and the officers of the Independence in Valparaiso, so that we again met as old friends. Immediate preparations were made for landing, and, as I was quartermaster and commissary, I had plenty to do. There was a small wharf and an adobe custom-house in possession of the navy; also a barrack of two stories, occupied by some marines, commanded by Lieutenant Maddox; and on a hill to the west of the town had been built a two-story block-house of hewed logs occupied by a guard of sailors under command of Lieutenant Baldwin, United States Navy.[37] Not a single modern wagon or cart was to be had in Monterey, nothing but the old Mexican cart with wooden wheels, drawn by two or three pairs of oxen, yoked by the horns. A man named Tom Cole had two or more of these, and he came into immediate requisition. The United States consul, and most prominent man there at the time, was Thomas O. Larkin, who had a store and a pretty good two-story house occupied by his family.[38] It was soon determined that our

[37] William A. T. Maddox (1814–1889) joined the U.S. Marine Corps as a second lieutenant in 1837 and was brevetted captain for his actions during the Battle of Santa Clara in 1847. Charles H. Baldwin (1822–1888) joined the U.S. Navy in 1839 as a midshipman. After attending the Naval Academy in 1844–1845, he was promoted to passed midshipman and transferred to the West Coast to serve during the Mexican-American War. *National Cyclopædia of American Biography,* vol. 4, s.v. "Baldwin, Charles H."; Navy Department, *Dictionary of American Navy Fighting Ships* (Washington, DC: Navy Department, 1969), vol. 4, s.v. "Maddox."

[38] Thomas O. Larkin (1802–1858) moved to California in 1830 and opened his first store in Monterey in July 1834. Soon after, he built his house, which was one of the first two-story buildings in Monterey. In 1844 he became the first person to officially serve as U.S. consul for California. Harlan Hague and David J. Langum, *Thomas O. Larkin: A Life of Patriotism and Profit in Old California* (Norman: University of Oklahoma Press, 1990), 13, 19, 41, 47, 97–99.

company was to land and encamp on the hill at the block-house, and we were also to have possession of the warehouse, or custom-house, for storage. The company was landed on the wharf, and we all marched in full dress with knapsacks and arms, to the hill and relieved the guard under Lieutenant Baldwin. Tents and camp-equipage were hauled up, and soon the camp was established. I remained in a room at the custom-house, where I could superintend the landing of the stores and their proper distribution. I had brought out from New York twenty thousand dollars commissary funds, and eight thousand dollars quartermaster funds, and as the ship contained about six months' supply of provisions, also a saw-mill, grist-mill, and almost every thing needed, we were soon established comfortably. We found the people of Monterey a mixed set of Americans, native Mexicans, and Indians, about one thousand all told. They were kind and pleasant, and seemed to have nothing to do, except such as owned ranches in the country for the rearing of horses and cattle. Horses could be bought at any price from four dollars up to sixteen, but no horse was ever valued above a doubloon or Mexican ounce (sixteen dollars). Cattle cost eight dollars fifty cents for the best, and this made beef net about two cents a pound, but at that time nobody bought beef by the pound, but by the carcass.

Game of all kinds—elk, deer, wild geese, and ducks—was abundant; but coffee, sugar, and small stores, were rare and costly.

There were some half-dozen shops or stores, but their shelves were empty. The people were very fond of riding, dancing, and of shows of any kind. The young fellows took great delight in showing off their horsemanship, and would dash along, picking up a half-dollar from the ground, stop their horses in full career and turn about on the space of a bullock's hide, and their skill with the lasso was certainly wonderful. At full speed they could cast their lasso about the horns of a bull, or so throw it as to catch any particular foot. These fellows would work all day on horseback in driving cattle or catching wild-horses for a mere nothing, but all the money offered would not have hired one of them to walk a mile. The girls were very fond of dancing, and they did dance gracefully and well. Every Sunday, regularly, we had a *baile,* or dance, and sometimes interspersed through the week.

I remember very well, soon after our arrival, that we were all invited to witness a play called "Adam and Eve." Eve was personated by a pretty young girl known as Dolores Gomez, who, however, was dressed very unlike Eve, for she was covered with a petticoat and spangles. Adam was personated by her brother——, the same who has since become somewhat famous as the person on whom is founded the McGarrahan claim.[39] God Almighty was personated, and heaven's occupants seemed very human. Yet the play was pretty, interesting, and elicited universal applause. All the month of February we were by day preparing for our long stay in the country, and at night making the most of the balls and parties of the most primitive kind, picking up a smattering of Spanish, and extending our acquaintance with the people and the *costumbres del pais.* I can well recall that Ord and I, impatient to look inland, got permission and started for the Mission of San Juan Bautista. Mounted on horses, and with our carbines, we took the road by El Toro, quite a prominent hill, around which passes the road to the south, following the Salinas or Monterey River.[40] After about twenty miles over a sandy country covered with oak-bushes and scrub, we entered quite a pretty valley in which there was a ranch at the foot of the Toro. Resting there a while and getting some information, we again started in the direction of a mountain to the north of the Salinas, called the Gavillano.[41] It was quite dark when we reached the Salinas River, which we attempted to pass at several points, but found it full of water, and the quicksands were bad. Hearing the bark of a dog, we changed our course in that direction, and, on hailing, were answered by voices which directed us where to cross. Our knowledge of the language was limited, but we managed to understand, and to flounder through the

[39] Dolores Gomez was active in the California theater scene during this period. In Oct. 1847, she portrayed Fitama in the play *Morayma* based on the history of civil wars in Granada. Vicente P. Gomez lived in Monterey and worked as a clerk in the governor's office. The "McGarrahan claim" was a disputed land claim regarding a quicksilver mine near New Idria, CA. Gomez had claimed ownership of the land and then sold a portion of it to Pacificus Ord. Gomez and Ord then conferred ownership to William McGarrahan of San Francisco, but Gomez and McGarrahan's rights to the land were never confirmed. Minnette A. Ker, "The History of the Theatre in California in the Nineteenth Century" (master's thesis, University of California, 1922), 3–4; Robert J. Parker, "William McGarrahan's 'Panoche Grande Claim,'" *Pacific Historical Review,* no. 3 (Sept. 1936), 5:213; James Wilson, *A Pamphlet Relating to the Claim of Señor Don José Y. Limantour* (San Francisco: Whitton and Towne, 1853), 26.

[40] During the early nineteenth century, multiple names were used for the Salinas River. It was labeled "Monterey River" up until 1850. Erwin G. Gudde, *California Place Names: The Origin and Etymology of Current Geographical Names* (Berkeley: University of California Press, 1969), 209, 277–278.

[41] WTS most likely refers here to the Gabilan mountain range located in the Salinas River Valley. *Annual Report of the State Board of Horticulture of the State of California for 1892* (Sacramento: State Office, 1892), 170.

sand and water, and reached a small adobe-house on the banks of the Salinas, where we spent the night. The house was a single room, without floor or glass; only a rude door, and window with bars. Not a particle of food but meat, yet the man and woman entertained us with the language of lords, put themselves, their house, and every thing, at our "disposition," and made little barefoot children dance for our entertainment. We made our supper of beef, and slept on a bullock's hide on the dirt-floor. In the morning we crossed the Salinas Plain, about fifteen miles of level ground, taking a shot occasionally at wild-geese, which abounded there, and entering the well-wooded valley that comes out from the foot of the Gavillano. We had cruised about all day, and it was almost dark when we reached the house of a Señor Gomez, father of those who at Monterey had performed the parts of Adam and Eve.[42] His house was a two-story adobe, and had a fence in front. It was situated well up among the foot-hills of the Gavillano, and could not be seen until within a few yards. We hitched our horses to the fence and went in just as Gomez was about to sit down to a tempting supper of stewed hare and tortillas. We were officers and caballeros and could not be ignored. After turning our horses to grass, at his invitation we joined him at supper. The allowance, though ample for one, was rather short for three, and I thought the Spanish grandiloquent politeness of Gomez, who was fat and old, was not over-cordial. However, down we sat, and I was helped to a dish of rabbit, with what I thought to be an abundant sauce of tomato. Taking a good mouthful, I felt as though I had taken liquid fire; the tomato was *chile colorado,* or red pepper, of the purest kind. It nearly killed me, and I saw Gomez's eyes twinkle, for he saw that his share of supper was increased. I contented myself with bits of the meat, and an abundant supply of tortillas. Ord was better case-hardened, and stood it better. We staid at Gomez's that night, sleeping, as all did, on the ground, and the next morning we crossed the hill by the bridle-path to the old Mission of San Juan Bautista. The Mission was in a beautiful valley, very level, and bounded on all sides by hills. The plain was covered with wild-grasses and mustard, and had abundant water. Cattle and horses were seen in all

[42] Joaquín Gomez was from Guadalajara, Jalisco, Mexico, and moved to California in the 1830s to work as a customs officer in Monterey. He later received two land grants and established his ranch near Natividad, CA, approximately thirty miles from Monterey. His adobe home was frequented by many people traveling through the area, and it was also the site of the Battle of Natividad during the Mexican-American War in Nov. 1846. Due to debt, Gomez lost his home and ranch in 1848. Marjorie Pierce, *East of the Gabilans: The Ranches, the Towns, the People—Yesterday and Today* (Santa Cruz: Western Tanager Press, 1976), 75–78.

directions, and it was manifest that the priests who first occupied the country were good judges of land. It was Sunday, and all the people, about a hundred, had come to church from the country round about. Ord was somewhat of a Catholic, and entered the church with his clanking spurs and kneeled down, attracting the attention of all, for he had on the uniform of an American officer. As soon as church was out, all rushed to the various sports. I saw the priest, with his gray robes tucked up, playing at billiards,[43] others were cock-fighting, and some at horse-racing. My horse had become lame, and I resolved to buy another. As soon as it was known that I wanted a horse, several came for me, and displayed their horses by dashing past and hauling them up short. There was a fine black stallion that attracted my notice, and, after trying him myself, I concluded a purchase. I left with the seller my own lame horse, which he was to bring to me at Monterey, when I was to pay him ten dollars for the other. The Mission of San Juan bore the marks of high prosperity at a former period, and had a good pear-orchard just under the plateau where stood the church. After spending the day, Ord and I returned to Monterey, about thirty-five miles, by a shorter route. Thus passed the month of February, and, though there were no mails or regular expresses, we heard occasionally from Yerba Buena and Sutter's Fort to the north, and from the army and navy about Los Angeles at the south. We also knew that a quarrel had grown up at Los Angeles, between General Kearney, Colonel Fremont, and Commodore Stockton, as to the right to control affairs in California. Kearney had with him only the fragments of the two companies of dragoons, which had come across from New Mexico with him, and had been handled very roughly by Don Andreas Pico, at San Pascual, in which engagement Captains Moore and Johnson, and Lieutenant Hammond, were killed, and Kearney himself wounded.[44] There remained with him Colonel Swords,

[43] José Antonio Ánzar (c. 1792–1874) moved to California in 1831 and from 1832 to 1854 served as the last Franciscan priest of the Mission of San Juan Bautista. James D. Hart, *A Companion to California* (Berkeley: University of California Press, 1987), 16; *The Overland Monthly: January–June 1915* (San Francisco: Overland Monthly, 1915), 65:502–503.

[44] Andres Pico (1810–1876) was the lessee of the San Fernando mission and owner of the San José Mission. He served as a captain in the Mexican Army at the start of the Mexican-American War. After the war, he was elected to the state assembly in 1851 and the state senate in 1860–1861. Benjamin D. Moore (1810–1846) fought in the Black Hawk War as a first lieutenant. He had reached the rank of captain in the U.S. 1st Dragoons by 1846. Abraham R. Johnston (1815–1846) graduated from the USMA in 1835 and was brevetted second lieutenant in the 1st Dragoons. He was promoted to captain in May 1846 and served as aide-de-camp to General Stephen W.

quartermaster; Captain H. S. Turner, First Dragoons; Captains Emory and Warner, Topographical Engineers; Assistant Surgeon Griffin, and Lieutenant J. W. Davidson.[45] Fremont had marched down from the north with a battalion of volunteers; Commodore Stockton had marched up from San Diego to Los Angeles, with General Kearney, his dragoons, and a battalion of sailors and marines, and was soon joined there by Fremont, and they jointly received the surrender of the insurgents under Andreas Pico.[46] We also knew that General R. B. Mason had been ordered to California; that Colonel John D. Stevenson was coming out to California with a regiment of New York Volunteers; that Commodore Shubrick had orders also from the Navy Department to control matters afloat; that General Kearney, by virtue of his rank, had the right to control all the land-forces in the service of the United States; and that Fremont claimed the same right by virtue of a letter he had received from Colonel Benton, then a Senator, and a man of great influence

---

Kearney. Thomas C. Hammond (1819–1846) graduated from the USMA in 1842 and was brevetted second lieutenant in July 1842. *USMA,* 1:611–612, 2:147–148; A. S. C. Forbes, *California Missions and Landmarks: El Camino Real* (Los Angeles: n.p., 1925), 331–332; M. J. Moore, "Sketch of Captain Benjamin Daviess Moore," *Annual Publication of the Historical Society of Southern California and of the Pioneers of Los Angeles County,* no. 6 (Los Angeles: George Rice, 1904), 1:10–11.

[45] Thomas Swords (1806–1886) graduated from the USMA in 1829 and reached the rank of major and quartermaster of the Army of the West in Apr. 1846. Henry S. Turner (1811–1881) graduated from the USMA in 1834 and was promoted to captain in 1838. He was brevetted major for his actions during the Battle of San Pasqual. He resigned in 1848 and later represented Missouri in the U.S. House of Representatives from 1859 to 1861. William H. Emory (1811–1887) graduated from the USMA in 1831 but resigned from the U.S. Army in 1836. He was recommissioned in 1838 as a first lieutenant in the topographical engineers and fought in the Mexican-American War. William H. Warner (1812–1849) graduated from the USMA in 1836 and was brevetted captain for his actions at the Battle of San Pasqual. John S. Griffin (1816–1898) graduated from the University of Pennsylvania with a medical degree in 1837 and entered the U.S. Army as an assistant surgeon in 1840. He achieved the rank of captain in 1846 and served in the West until 1853. John W. Davidson (1824–1881) graduated from the USMA in 1845 and was a second lieutenant of the U.S. 1st Dragoons during the Battle of San Pasqual. H. D. Barrows, "Memorial Sketch of Dr. John S. Griffin," *Annual Publication of the Historical Society of Southern California and Pioneer Register, Los Angeles* 4, no. 2 (1898): 183–185; *USMA,* 1:498–499, 578–579, 635; *CWHC,* 199–200, 520–521.

[46] Frémont and Pico signed the Treaty of Campo de Cahuenga on Jan. 13, 1847, effectively ending hostilities in California. Charles Epting, *Victorian Los Angeles: From Pio Pico to Angels Flight* (Charleston, SC: History Press, 2015), 25.

with Polk's Administration.[47] So that among the younger officers the query was very natural, "Who the devil is Governor of California?" One day I was on board the Independence frigate, dining with the ward-room officers, when a war-vessel was reported in the offing, which in due time was made out to be the Cyane, Captain DuPont.[48] After dinner, we were all on deck, to watch the new arrival, the ships meanwhile exchanging signals, which were interpreted that General Kearney was on board. As the Cyane approached, a boat was sent to meet her, with Commodore Shubrick's flag-officer, Lieutenant Lewis,[49] to carry the usual messages, and to invite General Kearney to come on board the Independence as the guest of Commodore Shubrick. Quite a number of officers were on deck, among them Lieutenants Wise, Montgomery Lewis, William Chapman, and others, noted wits and wags of the navy.[50] In due time the Cyane anchored close by, and our boat was seen returning with a stranger in the stern-sheets, clothed in army-blue. As the boat came nearer, we saw that it was General Kearney with an old dragoon coat

[47] Thomas Hart Benton (1782–1858) attended the University of North Carolina before he and his family relocated to Tennessee. He later moved to Missouri, which he represented for thirty years in the U.S. Senate. He worked directly with Pres. James K. Polk on the Oregon boundary dispute in 1846. David J. Brewer, ed., *The World's Best Orations from the Earliest Period to the Present Time* (St. Louis: Ferd P. Kaiser, 1899), 2:409–410.

[48] Samuel F. Du Pont (1803–1865) became a midshipman in 1815 and was a captain at the Philadelphia Navy Yard by 1855. He died in June 1865 of bronchial pneumonia. *CWHC,* 218–219.

[49] Henry H. Lewis joined the U.S. Navy in May 1828. He was stationed at the Naval School at Norfolk, VA, as a midshipman in 1835. *Register of All Officers and Agents, Civil, Military, and Naval, in the Service of the United States, on the Thirteenth September 1835 . . .* (Washington, DC: Blair and Rives, 1835), 137; *Register of the Commissioned and Warrant Officers of the Navy of the United States, Including Officers of the Marine Corps, and Others, for the Year 1848* (Washington, DC: C. Alexander, 1848), 42.

[50] Montgomery Lewis (c. 1813–1857) joined the U.S. Navy as a midshipman in 1828 and was promoted to lieutenant in Feb. 1841. George W. Chapman (d. 1853) became a midshipman in 1832 and was promoted to lieutenant in Apr. 1847. *Register of the Commissioned and Warrant Officers of the Navy of the United States, Including Officers of the Marine Corps, and Others, for the Year 1847* (Washington, DC: C. Alexander, 1847), 40; *Register of the Commissioned and Warrant Officers of the Navy of the United States, Including Officers of the Marine Corps, and Others for the Year 1854* (Washington, DC: Robert Armstrong, 1854), 32, 102; Charles Steedman, *Memoirs and Correspondence of Charles Steedman: Rear Admiral, United States Navy, with His Autobiography and Private Journals, 1811–1890,* ed. Amos L. Mason (Cambridge: Riverside, 1912), 116.

on, and an army-cap, to which the general had added the broad *visor,* cut from a full-dress hat, to shade his face and eyes against the glaring sun of the Gila region.[51] Chapman exclaimed: "Fellows, the problem is solved; there is the grand-vizier (visor) by G——d! *He* is Governor of California."

All hands received the general with great heartiness, and he soon passed out of our sight into the commodore's cabin. Between Commodore Shubrick and General Kearney existed from that time forward the greatest harmony and good feeling, and no further trouble existed as to the controlling power on the Pacific coast. General Kearney had dispatched from San Diego his quartermaster, Colonel Swords, to the Sandwich Islands,[52] to purchase clothing and stores for his men, and had come up to Monterey, bringing with him Turner and Warner, leaving Emory and the company of dragoons below. He was delighted to find a full strong company of artillery, subject to his orders, well supplied with clothing and money in all respects, and, much to the disgust of our Captain Tompkins, he took half of his company clothing and part of the money held by me for the relief of his worn-out and almost naked dragoons left behind at Los Angeles. In a few days he moved on shore, took up his quarters at Larkin's house, and established his headquarters, with Captain Turner as his adjutant-general. One day Turner and Warner were at my tent, and, seeing a store-box full of socks, drawers, and calico shirts, of which I had laid in a three years' supply, and of which they had none, made known to me their wants, and I told them to help themselves, which Turner and Warner did. The latter, however, insisted on paying me the cost, and from that date to this Turner and I have been close friends. Warner, poor fellow, was afterward killed by Indians.[53] Things gradually came into shape, a semi-monthly courier line was established from Yerba Buena to San Diego, and we were thus enabled to keep pace with events throughout the country. In March Stevenson's regiment arrived. Colonel Mason also arrived by sea

[51]The Gila region encompassed the Baja Peninsula and the adjacent western coast of Mexico. Bancroft, *History of the Pacific States of North America,* 10:498–499.

[52]The Hawaiian Island chain was designated the "Sandwich Islands" in 1778 by Capt. James Cook. English speakers primarily referred to the islands by that name until the passage of the first Hawaiian constitution in 1840, when the native name "Hawaii" became the official name. Russell Clement, "From Cook to the 1840 Constitution: The Name Change from Sandwich to Hawaiian Islands," *Hawaiian Journal of History* 14 (1980):50–58.

[53]On Sept. 26, 1849, William H. Warner was killed by Native Americans while surveying land in the Sierra Nevada. *The Centennial of the United States Military Academy at West Point, New York, 1802–1902* (Washington, DC: GPO, 1904), 1:560.

from Callao in the store-ship Erie, and P. St. George Cooke's battalion of Mormons reached San Luis Rey. A. J. Smith and George Stoneman were with him, and were assigned to the company of dragoons at Los Angeles.[54] All these troops and the navy regarded General Kearney as the rightful commander, though Fremont still remained at Los Angeles, styling himself as Governor, issuing orders and holding his battalion of California Volunteers in apparent defiance of General Kearney. Colonel Mason and Major Turner were sent down by sea with a paymaster, with muster-rolls and orders to muster this battalion into the service of the United States, to pay and then to muster them out; but on their reaching Los Angeles Fremont would not consent to it, and the controversy became so angry that a challenge was believed to have passed between Mason and Fremont, but the duel never came about. Turner rode up by land in four or five days, and Fremont, becoming alarmed, followed him, as we supposed, to overtake him, but he did not succeed. On Fremont's arrival at Monterey, he camped in a tent about a mile out of town and called on General Kearney, and it was reported that the latter threatened him very severely and ordered him back to Los Angeles immediately, to disband his volunteers, and to cease the exercise of authority of any kind in the country. Feeling a natural curiosity to see Fremont, who was then quite famous by reason of his recent explorations and the still more recent conflicts with Kearney and Mason, I rode out to his camp, and found him in a conical tent with one Captain Owens, who was a mountaineer, trapper, etc., but originally from Zanesville, Ohio.[55] I spent an hour or so with Fremont in his tent, took some tea with him, and left, without being much impressed with

[54] Philip St. George Cooke (1809–1895) graduated from the USMA in 1827 and was promoted to first lieutenant of the U.S. 1st Dragoons in 1833. In 1846 he took command of the Mormon Volunteers and oversaw their march west. In Feb. 1847, he was brevetted lieutenant colonel for his conduct in California. Andrew J. Smith (1815–1897) graduated from the USMA in 1838 and was promoted to captain in Feb. 1847. George Stoneman (1822–1894) graduated from the USMA in 1846 and was a second lieutenant in the U.S. 1st Dragoons during the Mexican-American War. He later served as the governor of California from 1883 to 1888. *CWHC,* 183–184, 492–493, 514; Spencer Tucker, ed., *The Encyclopedia of the Mexican-American War* (Santa Barbara: ABC-CLIO, 2012), vol. 2, s.vv. "Cooke, Philip St. George," "Mormon Battalion."

[55] Most likely Richard L. Owings (1812–1902), commonly known as Dick Owens, who accompanied Frémont on his third expedition to the American West. He served as captain of Co. A of the California Battalion of Mounted Riflemen during the Mexican-American War. Harvey L. Carter, "The Divergent Paths of Frémont's 'Three Marshalls,'" *New Mexico Historical Review,* 48, no. 1 (Winter 1973):11–15.

him. In due time Colonel Swords returned from the Sandwich Islands and relieved me as quartermaster. Captain William G. Marcy, son of the Secretary of War, had also come out in one of Stevenson's ships as an assistant commissary of subsistence, and was stationed at Monterey and relieved me as commissary,[56] so that I reverted to the condition of a company-officer. While acting as a staff-officer I had lived at the custom-house in Monterey, but when relieved I took a tent in line with the other company-officers on the hill, where we had a mess.

Stevenson's regiment reached San Francisco Bay early in March, 1847. Three companies were stationed at the Presidio under Major James A. Hardie; one company (Brackett's) at Sonoma; three, under Colonel Stevenson, at Monterey; and three, under Lieutenant-Colonel Burton, at Santa Barbara.[57] One day I was down at the headquarters at Larkin's house, when General Kearney remarked to me that he was going down to Los Angeles in the ship Lexington, and wanted me to go along as his aide. Of course this was most agreeable to me. Two of Stevenson's companies, with the headquarters and the colonel, were to go also. They embarked, and early in May we sailed for San Pedro. Before embarking, the United States line-of-battle-ship Columbus had reached the coast from China with Commodore Biddle, whose rank gave him the supreme command of the navy on the coast.[58] He was busy in calling in—

[56] William G. Marcy (1818–1896) was made captain in the commissary department with the 1st Regiment of New York Volunteers in 1846. He arrived in San Francisco on Mar. 20, 1847, and relived WTS around this time. His father, William L. Marcy (1786–1857), served as a U.S. senator from 1831 to 1833 and as governor of New York from 1833 to 1838. He served as Pres. James K. Polk's secretary of war from 1845 to 1849, and as Pres. Franklin Pierce's secretary of state from 1853 to 1857. Bailey Millard, *History of the San Francisco Bay Region* (Chicago: American Historical Society, 1924), 2:338.

[57] James A. Hardie (1823–1876) graduated from the USMA in 1843 and was promoted to major in the 1st New York Inf. in 1846. John E. Brackett (d. 1855) graduated from the USMA in 1832. He resigned in 1833 but rejoined the U.S. Army as a captain of the 1st New York Volunteers in Aug. 1846. He later served as a California State House Representative in 1849–1850. Henry Burton commanded companies A, B, and D. Francis D. Clark, *The First Regiment of New York Volunteers Commanded by Colonel Jonathan D. Stevenson, in the Mexican War* (New York: George S. Evans, 1882), 20; *USMA*, 1:513–514; *CWHC*, 279.

[58] James Biddle (1783–1848) entered the U.S. Navy as a midshipman in 1800. Soon after, he was captured and held prisoner in Tripoli for two years. He was promoted to a lieutenant upon his release in 1807 and became a master commandant during the War of 1812. He was later placed in command of the Naval Asylum in Philadelphia from 1838 to 1842. J. F. Loubat, *The Medallic History of the United States of America, 1776–1876* (self-pub., 1878), 1:249–250.

"lassoing"—from the land-service the various naval officers who under Stockton had been doing all sorts of military and civil service on shore. Knowing that I was to go down the coast with General Kearney, he sent for me and handed me two unsealed parcels addressed to Lieutenant Wilson, United States Navy, and Major Gillespie, United States Marines, at Los Angeles.[59] These were written orders pretty much in these words: "On receipt of this order you will repair at once on board the United States ship Lexington at San Pedro, and on reaching Monterey you will report to the undersigned—JAMES BIDDLE." Of course, I executed my part to the letter, and these officers were duly "lassooed." We sailed down the coast with a fair wind, and anchored inside the kelp, abreast of Johnson's house. Messages were forthwith dispatched up to Los Angeles, twenty miles off, and preparations for horses made for us to ride up. We landed, and, as Kearney held to my arm in ascending the steep path up the bluff, he remarked to himself, rather than to me, that it was strange that Fremont did not want to return north by the Lexington on account of sea-sickness, but preferred to go by land over five hundred miles. The younger officers had been discussing what the general would do with Fremont, who was supposed to be in a state of mutiny. Some thought he would be tried and shot, some that he would be carried back *in irons;* and all agreed that if any one else than Fremont had put on such airs, and had acted as he had done, Kearney would have shown him no mercy, for he was regarded as the strictest sort of a disciplinarian. We had a pleasant ride across the plain which lies between the sea-shore and Los Angeles, which we reached in about three hours, the infantry following on foot. We found Colonel P. St. George Cooke living at the house of a Mr. Pryor,[60] and the company of dragoons, with A. J. Smith, Davidson, Stoneman, and Dr. Griffin, quartered in an adobe-house close by. Fremont held his court in the only two-story frame-house in the place. After some time spent at Pryor's house, General Kearney ordered me to call on Fremont to notify him of his arrival, and that

[59] Archibald H. Gillespie (1810–1873) joined the U.S. Marine Corps in 1832 and joined Frémont's forces in California in June 1846. He fought in numerous battles during the Mexican-American War and was brevetted major for his actions. *Dictionary of American Naval Fighting Ships* (Washington, DC: Navy Department, 1968), vol. 3, s.v. "Gillespie."

[60] Nathaniel M. Pryor (1789–1850) arrived in California around 1828. He was a silversmith in Los Angeles and eventually built a house and vineyard on the Palos Verdes peninsula. *The Overland Monthly,* 2nd series, Jan.–June 1889 (San Francisco: Bacon, 1889), 13:230; Charles A. Tuttle, *Reports of Cases Determined in the Supreme Court of the State of California* (San Francisco: Bancroft-Whitney, 1906), 30:391.

he desired to see him. I walked round to the house which had been pointed out to me as his, inquired of a man at the door if the colonel was in, was answered "Yes," and was conducted to a large room on the second floor, where very soon Fremont came in, and I delivered my message. As I was on the point of leaving, he inquired where I was going to, and I answered that I was going back to Pryor's house, where the general was, when he remarked that if I would wait a moment he would go along. Of course I waited, and he soon joined me, dressed much as a Californian, with the peculiar high, broad-brimmed hat, with a fancy cord, and we walked together back to Pryor's, where I left him with General Kearney. We spent several days very pleasantly at Los Angeles, then, as now, the chief *pueblo* of the south, famous for its grapes, fruits, and wines. There was a hill close to the town, from which we had a perfect view of the place. The surrounding country is level, utterly devoid of trees, except the willows and cotton-woods that line the Los Angeles Creek and the *acequias,* or ditches, which lead from it. The space of ground cultivated in vineyards seemed about five miles by one, embracing the town. Every house had its inclosure of vineyard, which resembled a miniature orchard, the vines being very old, ranged in rows, trimmed very close, with irrigating ditches so arranged that a stream of water could be diverted between each row of vines. The Los Angeles and San Gabriel Rivers are fed by melting snows from a range of mountains to the east,[61] and the quantity of cultivated land depends upon the amount of water. This did not seem to be very large; but the San Gabriel River, close by, was represented to contain a larger volume of water, affording the means of greatly enlarging the space for cultivation. The climate was so moderate that oranges, figs, pomegranates, etc., were generally to be found in every yard or inclosure.

At the time of our visit, General Kearney was making his preparations to return overland to the United States, and he arranged to secure a volunteer escort out of the battalion of Mormons that was then stationed at San Luis Rey, under Colonel Cooke and a Major Hunt.[62] This battalion was only en-

[61] WTS was referring to the San Bernardino Mountains. *Index to Executive Documents Printed by Order of the Senate of the United States during the First Session of the Thirty-First Congress, 1849–50,* document 47 (Washington, DC: William M. Belt, 1850), 10:124.

[62] Jefferson Hunt (1803–1879) converted to Mormonism in 1834 and was a captain of Co. A of the Mormon Battalion during the Mexican-American War. LeRoy R. Hafen and Ann W. Hafen, eds., *Journals of Forty-Niners: Salt Lake to Los Angeles* (Lincoln: University of Nebraska Press, 1954), 59–60.

listed for one year, and the time for their discharge was approaching, and it was generally understood that the majority of the men wanted to be discharged so as to join the Mormons who had halted at Salt Lake, but a lieutenant and about forty men volunteered to return to Missouri as the escort of General Kearney.[63] These were mounted on mules and horses, and I was appointed to conduct them to Monterey by land. Leaving the party at Los Angeles to follow by sea in the Lexington, I started with the Mormon detachment and traveled by land. We averaged about thirty miles a day, stopped one day at Santa Barbara, where I saw Colonel Burton, and so on by the usually traveled road to Monterey, reaching it in about fifteen days, arriving some days in advance of the Lexington. This gave me the best kind of an opportunity for seeing the country, which was very sparsely populated indeed, except by a few families at the various Missions. We had no wheeled vehicles, but packed our food and clothing on mules driven ahead, and we slept on the ground in the open air, the rainy season having passed. Fremont followed me by land in a few days, and, by the end of May, General Kearney was all ready at Monterey to take his departure, leaving to succeed him in command Colonel R. B. Mason, First Dragoons. Our Captain (Tompkins), too, had become discontented at his separation from his family, tendered his resignation to General Kearney, and availed himself of a sailing-vessel bound for Callao to reach the East. Colonel Mason selected me as his adjutant-general; and on the very last day of May General Kearney, with his Mormon escort, with Colonel Cooke, Colonel Swords (quartermaster), Captain Turner, and a naval officer, Captain Radford,[64] took his departure for the East overland, leaving us in full possession of California and its fate. Fremont also left California with General Kearney, and with him departed all cause of confusion and disorder in the country. From that time forth no one could dispute the authority of Colonel Mason as in command of all the United States forces on shore, while the senior naval officer had a like control afloat. This was Commodore James Biddle, who had reached the station from China in the Columbus, and he in turn was succeeded by Commodore T. Ap Catesby Jones

[63] In June 1847, Kearny selected twelve men from the Mormon Battalion, three from each company, including Sergeant Nathaniel V. Jones, John Binley, and J. C. Quigley, to escort him on his trip to Fort Leavenworth, KS. Bancroft, *History of California,* 5:453*n.*

[64] William Radford (c. 1808–1890) became a passed midshipman in 1825. During the Civil War he served in the North Atlantic and was promoted to rear admiral in 1866. He retired in 1870. *CWHC,* 443.

in the line-of-battle-ship Ohio. At that time Monterey was our headquarters, and the naval commander for a time remained there, but subsequently San Francisco Bay became the chief naval rendezvous.[65]

Colonel R. B. Mason, First Dragoons, was an officer of great experience, of stern character, deemed by some harsh and severe, but in all my intercourse with him he was kind and agreeable. He had a large fund of good sense, and, during our long period of service together, I enjoyed his unlimited confidence. He had been in his day a splendid shot and hunter, and often entertained me with characteristic anecdotes of Taylor, Twiggs, Worth, Harney, Martin Scott, etc., etc., who were then in Mexico, gaining a national fame.[66] California had settled down to a condition of absolute repose, and we naturally repined at our fate in being so remote from the war in Mexico, where our comrades were reaping large honors. Mason dwelt in a house not far from the Custom-House, with Captain Lanman, United States Navy; I had a small adobe-house back of Larkin's. Halleck and Dr. Murray had a small log-house not far off.[67] The company of artillery was still on the hill, under the command of Lieutenant Ord, engaged in building a fort whereon to mount the guns we had brought out in the Lexington, and also in constructing quar-

[65] Thomas ap C. Jones (1790–1858) was appointed midshipman in 1805 and was promoted to commander in 1820. He served as inspector and superintendent of ordnance for the U.S. Navy and was in command of the Pacific Squadron for the years 1841–1844 and 1847–1850. He arrived in San Francisco with his command on Nov. 20, 1848. Gene A. Smith, *Thomas ap Catesby Jones: Commodore of Manifest Destiny* (Annapolis: Naval Institute Press, 2000), xix–xx, 134–135.

[66] David E. Twiggs (1790–1862) became a captain in the 8th Inf. in 1812. He served in the War of 1812 and was brevetted major general for his actions during the Battle of Monterey in June 1846 during the Mexican-American War. He defected from the U.S. Army and joined the Confederate Army in 1861. He died from pneumonia in July 1862. Martin Scott (1788–1847) was a member of the "Green Mountain Boys" during the War of 1812. He stayed in the army and was later brevetted lieutenant colonel for his actions during the Battle of Monterey. He was killed during the Battle of Molino del Rey on Sept. 8, 1847. *Collections of the Minnesota Historical Society* (St. Paul: Minnesota Historical Society, 1880), 3:180, 187; *CWHC*, 538.

[67] Joseph Lanman (1811–1874) became a passed midshipman in 1831. He served as a captain in the Atlantic Squadron during the Civil War. Robert Murray (1823–1913) graduated from the University of Pennsylvania in 1845 with a medical degree and served as assistant surgeon in California during the Mexican-American War. He was appointed to surgeon in 1860. *CWHC*, 339; Samuel C. Stanton, ed., *The Military Surgeon: Journal of the Association of Military Surgeons of the United States* (Chicago: Association of Military Surgeons of the United States, 1913), 32:422–424.

ters out of hewn pine-logs for the men. Lieutenant Minor, a very clever young officer, had taken violently sick and died about the time I got back from Los Angeles, leaving Lieutenants Ord and Loeser alone with the company, with Assistant-Surgeon Robert Murray. Captain William G. Marcy was the quartermaster and commissary. Naglee's company of Stevenson's regiment had been mounted and was sent out against the Indians in the San Joaquin Valley, and Shannon's company occupied the barracks.[68] Shortly after General Kearney had gone East, we found an order of his on record, removing one Mr. Nash, the Alcalde of Sonoma, and appointing to his place ex-Governor L. W. Boggs.[69] A letter came to Colonel and Governor Mason from Boggs, whom he had personally known in Missouri, complaining that, though he had been appointed alcalde, the then incumbent (Nash) utterly denied Kearney's right to remove him, because he had been elected by the people under the proclamation of Commodore Sloat, and refused to surrender his office or to account for his acts as alcalde. Such a proclamation had been made by Commodore Sloat shortly after the first occupation of California, announcing that the people were free and enlightened American citizens, entitled to all the rights and privileges as such, and among them the right to elect their own officers, etc. The people of Sonoma town and valley, some forty or fifty immigrants from the United States, and very few native Californians, had elected Mr. Nash, and, as stated, he refused to recognize the right of a mere military commander to eject him and to appoint another to his place. Neither General Kearney nor Mason had much respect for this kind of "buncombe," but assumed the true doctrine that California was yet a

[68] Henry M. Naglee (1815–1886) graduated from the USMA in 1835 and served as captain of Co. D, 1st New York Inf., in Aug. 1846. He was a lieutenant colonel in the U.S. Army during the Civil War. William E. Shannon (c. 1821–1850) was born in Ireland and immigrated to the United States around 1846. He became the captain of Co. "I" of the 1st New York Inf. in 1847. His company arrived in Monterey on Apr. 4, 1847, and garrisoned in San Diego from Dec. 28, 1847, until they were discharged on Sept. 25, 1848. *CWHC,* 403; Clark, *First Regiment of New York Volunteers,* 32, 45; Michael C. O'Laughlin, *Irish Families on the California Trail: Pioneers and 49ers from the Earliest Days Including the Gold Rush and San Francisco* (Kansas City: Irish Genealogical Foundation, 2003), 2:33; David R. Stuart, "The Native Peoples of San Joaquin County: Indian Pioneers, Immigrants, Innovators, Freedom Fighters, and Survivors, Part One," *San Joaquin Historian* (Summer 2016): 15–18.

[69] John H. Nash was elected alcalde of Sonoma in 1846. Lilburn W. Boggs was appointed to replace Nash in Apr. 1847. Hubert Howe Bancroft, *History of the Pacific States of North America* (San Francisco: History, 1886), 5:609–610.

Mexican province, held by right of conquest, that the military commander was held responsible to the country, and that the province should be held *in statu quo* until a treaty of peace. This letter of Boggs was therefore referred to Captain Brackett, whose company was stationed at Sonoma, with orders to notify Nash that Boggs was the rightful alcalde; that he must quietly surrender his office, with the books and records thereof, and that he must account for any moneys received from the sale of town-lots, etc., etc.; and in the event of refusal he (Captain Brackett) must compel him by the use of force.[70] In due time we got Brackett's answer, saying that the little community of Sonoma was in a dangerous state of effervescence caused by his orders; that Nash was backed by most of the Americans there who had come across from Missouri with American ideas; that as he (Brackett) was a volunteer officer, likely to be soon discharged, and as he designed to settle there, he asked in consequence to be excused from the execution of this (to him) unpleasant duty. Such a request, coming to an old soldier like Colonel Mason, aroused his wrath, and he would have proceeded rough-shod against Brackett, who, by-the-way, was a West Point graduate, and ought to have known better; but I suggested to the colonel that, the case being a test one, he had better send me up to Sonoma, and I would settle it quick enough. He then gave me an order to go to Sonoma to carry out the instructions already given to Brackett.

I took one soldier with me, Private Barnes,[71] with four horses, two of which we rode, and the other two we drove ahead. The first day we reached Gilroy's and camped by a stream near three or four adobe-huts known as Gilroy's ranch. The next day we passed Murphy's,[72] San José, and Santa Clara Mission, camping some four miles beyond, where a kind of hole had been dug in the ground for water. The whole of this distance, now so beautifully improved and settled, was then scarcely occupied, except by poor ranches producing horses

[70] Mason issued his orders to Brackett on June 2, 1847. R. B. Mason to J. E. Bracket, June 2, 1847, *Index to Executive Documents,* 300.

[71] In a letter dated Aug. 24, 1847, WTS reported that Private J. R. Barnes had "deserted." *California and New Mexico: Message from the President of the United States, Transmitting Information in Answer to a Resolution of the House of the 31st of December, 1849, on the Subject of California and New Mexico* (Washington, DC: GPO, 1850), 350–351.

[72] John C. Gilroy (1794–1869) married into the family that owned the land of Rancho San Ysidro. He served as both the alcalde and justice of the peace for the district. His settlement would become modern-day Gilroy, CA. WTS may have been referring here to the settlement where the family of Martin Murphy Sr. lived in the 1840s. J. P. Munro-Fraser, *History of Santa Clara County, California* (San Francisco: Alley and Bowen, 1881), 81, 133, 272–275.

and cattle. The *pueblo* of San José was a string of low adobe-houses festooned with red peppers and garlic; and the Mission of Santa Clara was a dilapidated concern, with its church and orchard. The long line of poplar-trees lining the road from San José to Santa Clara bespoke a former period when the priests had ruled the land. Just about dark I was lying on the ground near the well, and my soldier Barnes had watered our horses and picketed them to grass, when we heard a horse crushing his way through the high mustard-bushes which filled the plain, and soon a man came to us to inquire if we had seen a saddle-horse pass up the road. We explained to him what we had heard, and he went off in pursuit of his horse. Before dark he came back unsuccessful, and gave his name as Bidwell, the same gentleman who has since been a member of Congress, who is married to Miss Kennedy, of Washington City, and now lives in princely style at Chico, California.[73]

He explained that he was a surveyor, and had been in the lower country engaged in surveying land; that the horse had escaped him with his saddle-bags containing all his notes and papers, and some six hundred dollars in money, all the money he had earned. He spent the night with us on the ground, and the next morning we left him there to continue the search for his horse, and I afterward heard that he had found his saddle-bags all right, but never recovered the horse. The next day toward night we approached the Mission of San Francisco, and the village of Yerba Buena, tired and weary—the wind as usual blowing a perfect hurricane, and a more desolate region it was impossible to conceive of. Leaving Barnes to work his way into the town as best he could with the tired animals, I took the freshest horse and rode forward. I fell in with Lieutenant Fabius Stanley, United States Navy,[74] and we

[73] John Bidwell (1819–1900) was born in New York and arrived in California in 1841. He served in the Mexican-American War and was elected to the U.S. House of Representatives in 1864. In 1868 he married Annie Kennedy-Bidwell (1839–1918), daughter of Joseph C. G. Kennedy, superintendent of the U.S. Census in 1850 and 1860. John ran for U.S. president as the Prohibition Party candidate in 1892. Annie was a philanthropist later in life and donated thousands of acres of land to the city of Chico, CA, for parks and schools. Marcus Benjamin, *John Bidwell, Pioneer: A Sketch of His Career* (Washington, DC: n.p., 1907), 2, 10, 14–15, 31–32, 46–47; "Mrs. Annie K. Bidwell Dies in City of Chico," *Appeal-Democrat* (Marysville, CA), Mar. 11, 1918, 5.

[74] Fabius M. Stanley (1815–1882) entered the U.S. Navy as a midshipman in 1831 and was promoted to lieutenant in 1841. He served in various naval squadrons around the world. *Dictionary of North Carolina Biography* (Chapel Hill: University of North Carolina Press, 1994), vol. 5, s.v. "Fabius M. Stanley."

rode into Yerba Buena together about an hour before sundown, there being nothing but a path from the Mission into the town, deep and heavy with drift-sand. My horse could hardly drag one foot after the other when we reached the old Hudson Bay Company's house, which was then the store of Howard and Mellus. There I learned where Captain Folsom, the quartermaster, was to be found.[75] He was staying with a family of the name of Grimes, who had a small house back of Howard's store, which must have been near where Sacramento Street now crosses Kearney. Folsom was a classmate of mine, had come out with Stevenson's regiment as quartermaster, and was at the time the chief-quartermaster of the department. His office was in the old custom-house standing at the northwest corner of the Plaza. He had hired two warehouses, the only ones there at the time, of one Liedsdorff, the principal man of Yerba Buena, who also owned the only public-house, or tavern, called the City Hotel, on Kearney Street, at the southeast corner of the Plaza.[76] I stopped with Folsom at Mrs. Grimes's, and he sent my horse, as also the other three when Barnes had got in after dark, to a *corral* where he had a little barley, but no hay. At that time nobody fed a horse, but he was usually turned out to pick such scanty grass as he could find on the side-hills. The few government horses used in town were usually sent out to the Presidio, where the grass was somewhat better. At that time (July, 1847), what is now called San Francisco was called Yerba Buena. A naval officer, Lieutenant Washington A. Bartlett, its first alcalde, had caused it to be surveyed and laid out into blocks and lots, which were being sold at sixteen dollars a lot of fifty

[75] William D. M. Howard (1818–1856) moved to California in 1839. He worked as a sailor on trading ships in the Pacific. His business partner, Henry Mellus (1816–1860), moved to California in 1835. Together, they started the firm Mellus & Howard and later purchased the Hudson's Bay Company house in 1845. Mellus returned East in 1850 but moved back to California and was elected mayor of Los Angeles in 1860. Joseph L. Folsom (1816–1855) graduated from the USMA in 1840 and served as an instructor at the academy in 1844. *USMA,* 2:56; Antonio Maria Osio, *The History of Alta California: A Memoir of Mexican California* (Madison: University of Wisconsin Press, 1996), 330; Frank Soulé, John. H. Gihon, and James Nisbet, *The Annals of San Francisco* (New York: Appleton, 1855), 779–780; Mary F. Williams, *History of the San Francisco Committee of Vigilance of 1851* (Berkeley: University of California Press, 1921), 448.

[76] William A. Leidesdorff (1810–1848) was born in the Danish West Indies and moved to California in 1841. He built a large warehouse and the City Hotel in 1841 and owned a 35,000-acre ranch. He served as U.S. vice-consul to Mexico and as treasurer of San Francisco. Kwando M. Kinshasa, *African American Chronology: Chronologies of the American Mosaic* (Westport, CT: Greenwood Press, 2006), 25.

varas square; the understanding being that no single person could purchase of the alcalde more than one in-lot of fifty varas, and one out-lot of a hundred varas. Folsom, however, had got his clerks, orderlies, etc., to buy lots, and they, for a small consideration, conveyed them to him, so that he was nominally the owner of a good many lots. Lieutenant Halleck had bought one of each kind, and so had Warner. Many naval officers had also invested, and Captain Folsom advised me to buy some, but I felt actually insulted that he should think me such a fool as to pay money for property in such a horrid place as Yerba Buena, especially ridiculing his quarter of the city, then called Happy Valley.[77] At that day Montgomery Street was, as now, the business street, extending from Jackson to Sacramento, the water of the bay leaving barely room for a few houses on its east side, and the public warehouses were on a sandy beach about where the Bank of California now stands, viz., near the intersection of Sansome and California, Streets. Along Montgomery Street were the stores of Howard & Mellus, Frank Ward,[78] Sherman & Ruckel, Ross & Co., and it may be one or two others. Around the Plaza were a few houses, among them the City Hotel and the Custom-House, single-story adobes with tiled roofs, and they were by far the most substantial and best houses in the place. The population was estimated at about four hundred, of whom Kanakas (natives of the Sandwich Islands) formed the bulk. At the foot of Clay Street was a small wharf which small boats could reach at high tide; but the principal landing-place was where some stones had fallen into the water, about where Broadway now intersects Battery Street. On the steep bluff above had been excavated, by the navy, during the year before, a bench, wherein were mounted a couple of navy-guns, styled *the battery,* which, I suppose, gave name to the street. I explained to Folsom the object of my visit, and learned from him that he had no boat in which to send me to Sonoma, and that the only chance to get there was to borrow a boat from the navy. The line-of-battle-ship Columbus was then lying at anchor off the town, and he said if I would get up early the next morning I could go off to her in one of the *market*-boats.

[77] Happy Valley, located in modern-day San Francisco, ran along Mission Street and stretched from 1st to 3rd Streets. J. M. Gunn, *History of the State of California and Biographical Record of Oakland and Environs, Containing Biographies of Well-Known Citizens of the Past and Present* (Los Angeles: Historic Record, 1907), 289.

[78] Frank Ward came to San Francisco around 1848 and set up a store in the city. William Grey, *A Picture of Pioneer Times in California: Illustrated with Anecdotes and Stories Taken from Real Life* (San Francisco: W. M. Hinton, 1881), 102.

Accordingly, I was up bright and early, down at the wharf, found a boat, and went off to the Columbus to see Commodore Biddle. On reaching the ship and stating to the officer of the deck my business, I was shown into the commodore's cabin, and soon made known to him my object. Biddle was a small-sized man, but vivacious in the extreme. He had a perfect contempt for all humbug, and at once entered into the business with extreme alacrity. I was somewhat amused at the importance he attached to the step. He had a chaplain, and a private secretary, in a small room latticed off from his cabin, and he first called on them to go out, and, when we were alone, he enlarged on the folly of Sloat's proclamation, giving the people the right to elect their own officers, and commended Kearney and Mason for nipping that idea in the bud, and keeping the power in their own hands. He then sent for the first lieutenant (Drayton),[79] and inquired if there were among the officers on board any who had ever been in the Upper Bay, and learning that there was a midshipman (Whittaker)[80] he was sent for. It so happened that this midshipman had been on a frolic on shore a few nights before, and was accordingly much frightened when summoned into the commodore's presence, but as soon as he was questioned as to his knowledge of the bay, he was sensibly relieved, and professed to know every thing about it.

Accordingly, the long—boat was ordered with this midshipman and eight sailors, prepared with water and provisions for several days' absence. Biddle then asked me if I knew any of his own officers, and which one of them I would prefer to accompany me. I knew most of them, and we settled down on Louis McLane.[81] He was sent for, and it was settled that McLane and I were to conduct this *important* mission, and the commodore enjoined on us complete secrecy, so as to insure success, and he especially cautioned us against being pumped by his ward-room officers, Chapman, Lewis, Wise, etc., while on board his ship. With this injunction I was dismissed to the ward-room, where

[79] Percival Drayton (1812–1865) was promoted to lieutenant in 1838 and later served in the Civil War. Spencer Tucker, ed., *American Civil War: The Definitive Encyclopedia and Document Collection* (Santa Barbara: ABC-CLIO, 2013), vol. 1, s.v. "Drayton, Percival."

[80] WTS may have referred here to John G. Whitaker, who became a midshipman in Sept. 1841 and resigned in May 1849. Thomas H.S. Hamersly, ed., *General Register of the United States Navy and Marine Corps* (Washington, DC: W. K. Boyle, 1882), 763.

[81] Louis McLane (1819–1905) was promoted to midshipman in Mar. 1835 and lieutenant in Sept. 1847. Lewis R. Hamersly, *List of Officers of the Navy of the United States and of the Marine Corps, from 1775 to 1900* (New York: L. R. Hamersly, 1901), 371; "Louis McLane's Will: Leaves Estate to the Widow and Children," *Baltimore Sun,* Dec. 29, 1905, 9.

I found Chapman, Lewis, and Wise, dreadfully exercised at our profound secrecy. The fact that McLane and I had been closeted with the commodore for an hour, that orders for the boat and stores had been made, that the chaplain and clerk had been sent out of the cabin, etc., etc., all excited their curiosity; but McLane and I kept our secret well. The general impression was, that we had some knowledge about the fate of Captain Montgomery's two sons and the crew that had been lost the year before. In 1846 Captain Montgomery commanded at Yerba Buena, on board the St. Mary sloop-of-war,[82] and he had a detachment of men stationed up at Sonoma. Occasionally a boat was sent up with provisions or intelligence to them. Montgomery had two sons on board his ship, one a midshipman, the other his secretary.[83] Having occasion to send some money up to Sonoma, he sent his two sons with a good boat and crew. The boat started with a strong breeze and a very large sail, was watched from the deck until she was out of sight, and has never been heard of since. There was, of course, much speculation as to their fate, some contending that the boat must have been capsized in San Pablo Bay, and that all were lost; others contending that the crew had murdered the officers for the money, and then escaped; but, so far as I know, not a man of that crew has ever been seen or heard of since.[84] When at last the boat was ready for us, we started, leaving all hands, save the commodore, impressed with the belief that we were going on some errand connected with the loss of the missing boat and crew of the St. Mary. We sailed directly north, up the bay and across San Pablo, reached the mouth of Sonoma Creek about dark, and during the night worked up the creek some twelve miles by means of the tide, to a landing called the *Embarcadero.* To maintain the secrecy which the commodore had enjoined on us,

[82] John B. Montgomery (1794–1873) served on the sloop of war *Portsmouth* (not the *St. Mary*) with his sons in California during the Mexican-American War. He was later promoted to captain in 1853 and briefly served in the Pacific Squadron during the Civil War. *CWHC,* 393; Sophie R. De Meissner, *Old Naval Days: Sketches from the Life of Rear Admiral William Readford, U.S.N.* (New York: Henry Holt, 1920), 164.

[83] William H. Montgomery (1820–1846) held a commission in the U.S. Navy, and his brother John E. Montgomery (1830–1846) served as their father's secretary. Thomas H. Montgomery, *A Genealogical History of the Family of Montgomery, Including the Montgomery Pedigree* (Philadelphia: H. B. Ashmead, 1863), 112.

[84] On Dec. 13, 1846, the USS *Warren* sent a launch boat, with public funds and supplies, from Yerba Buena harbor to Fort Sacramento. The fate of the launch, and its crewmates, was never determined. De Meissner, *Old Naval Days,* 164–165; *The Magazine of American History with Notes and Queries,* pt. 2 (New York: A. S. Barnes, 1878), 422–423.

McLane and I agreed to keep up the delusion by pretending to be on a marketing expedition to pick up chickens, pigs, etc., for the mess of the Columbus, soon to depart for home.

Leaving the midshipman and four sailors to guard the boat, we started on foot with the other four for Sonoma Town, which we soon reached. It was a simple open square, around which were some adobe-houses, that of General Vallejo[85] occupying one side. On another was an unfinished two-story adobe building, occupied as a barrack by Brackett's company. We soon found Captain Brackett, and I told him that I intended to take Nash a prisoner and convey him back to Monterey to answer for his mutinous behavior. I got an old sergeant of his company, whom I had known in the Third Artillery, quietly to ascertain the whereabouts of Nash, who was a bachelor, stopping with the family of a lawyer named Green.[86] The sergeant soon returned, saying that Nash had gone over to Napa, but would be back that evening; so McLane and I went up to a farm of some pretensions, occupied by one Andreas Hoepner, with a pretty Sitka wife, who lived a couple of miles above Sonoma, and we bought of him some chickens, pigs, etc.[87] We then visited Governor Boggs's family and that of General Vallejo, who was then, as now, one of the most prominent and influential natives of California. About dark I learned that Nash had come back, and then, giving Brackett orders to have a cart ready at the corner of the plaza, McLane and I went to the house of Green. Posting an armed sailor on each side of the house, we knocked at the door and walked in. We found Green, Nash, and two women, at supper. I inquired if Nash were in, and was first answered "No," but one of the women soon pointed to him, and he rose. We were armed with pistols, and the family was evidently alarmed. I walked up to him and took his arm, and told him to come along with me. He asked me, "Where?" and I said, "Monterey." "Why?" I would explain that more at leisure. Green put himself between me and the

[85] Mariano G. Vallejo (1808–1890) was born in Monterey, CA, and enrolled in the Mexican military as a cadet. He founded the town of Sonoma in 1835 and established a military outpost near a local mission. Honoria Tuomey, *History of Sonoma County, California* (Chicago: S. J. Clarke, 1926), 2:864.

[86] Henry A. Green served as a county judge for Sonoma. Tuomey, *History of Sonoma County,* 1:368.

[87] Andreas Hoeppner immigrated from Russia to California around 1845. He left his wife, Anna Hoeppner, in 1849 and allegedly died in Chile. Bancroft, *History of California,* 3:786; Tuttle, *Reports of Cases,* 41:620.

door, and demanded, in theatrical style, why I dared arrest a peaceable citizen in his house. I simply pointed to my pistol, and told him to get out of the way, which he did. Nash asked to get some clothing, but I told him he should want for nothing. We passed out, Green following us with loud words, which brought the four sailors to the front-door, when I told him to hush up or I would take him prisoner also. About that time one of the sailors, handling his pistol carelessly, discharged it, and Green disappeared very suddenly. We took Nash to the cart, put him in, and proceeded back to our boat. The next morning we were gone.

Nash being out of the way, Boggs entered on his office, and the right to appoint or remove from civil office was never again questioned in California during the military *régime.* Nash was an old man, and was very much alarmed for his personal safety. He had come across the Plains, and had never yet seen the sea. While on our way down the bay, I explained fully to him the state of things in California, and he admitted he had never looked on it in that light before, and professed a willingness to surrender his office; but, having gone so far, I thought it best to take him to Monterey. On our way down the bay the wind was so strong, as we approached the Columbus, that we had to take refuge behind Yerba Buena Island, then called Goat Island, where we landed, and I killed a gray seal. The next morning, the wind being comparatively light, we got out and worked our way up to the Columbus, where I left my prisoner on board, and went on shore to find Commodore Biddle, who had gone to dine with Frank Ward. I found him there, and committed Nash to his charge, with the request that he would send him down to Monterey, which he did in the sloop-of-war Dale, Captain Selfridge[88] commanding. I then returned to Monterey by land, and, when the Dale arrived, Colonel Mason and I went on board, found poor old Mr. Nash half dead with sea-sickness and fear, lest Colonel Mason would treat him with extreme military rigor. But, on the contrary, the colonel spoke to him kindly, released him as a prisoner on his promise to go back to Sonoma, surrender his office to Boggs, and account to him for his acts while in office.[89] He afterward came on shore,

[88]Thomas O. Selfridge (1804–1902) became a midshipman in the U.S. Navy in 1818 and was a commander in 1847. He was promoted to captain in Sept. 1855 and served in the Civil War and reached the rank of rear admiral in 1866. *CWHC,* 478.

[89]Mason met with Nash on July 21, 1847. He wrote, "Mr. Nash has made me every promise that I could possibly require of him, and seems to be now sensible of the error committed." *Index to Executive Documents,* 9:354.

was provided with clothing and a horse, returned to Sonoma, and I never have seen him since.[90]

Matters and things settled down in Upper California, and all moved along with peace and harmony. The war still continued in Mexico, and the navy authorities resolved to employ their time with the capture of Mazatlan and Guaymas.[91] Lower California had already been occupied by two companies of Stevenson's regiment, under Lieutenant-Colonel Burton, who had taken post at La Paz, and a small party of sailors was on shore at San Josef, near Cape San Lucas, detached from the Lexington, Lieutenant-Commander Bailey. The orders for this occupation were made by General Kearney before he left, in pursuance of instructions from the War Department, merely to subserve a political end, for there were few or no people in Lower California, which is a miserable, wretched, dried-up peninsula. I remember the proclamation made by Burton and Captain Bailey, in taking possession, which was in the usual florid style. Bailey signed his name as the senior naval officer at the station, but, as it was necessary to put it into Spanish to reach the inhabitants of the newly-acquired country, it was interpreted, "El mas antiguo de todos los oficiales de la marina," etc., which, literally, is "the most ancient of all the naval officers," etc., a translation at which we made some fun.[92]

The expedition to Mazatlan was, however, for a different purpose, viz., to get possession of the ports of Mazatlan and Guaymas, as a part of the war against Mexico, and not for permanent conquest.

Commodore Shubrick commanded this expedition, and took Halleck along as his engineer-officer. They captured Mazatlan and Guaymas, and then called on Colonel Mason to send soldiers down to hold possession, but he had none to spare, and it was found impossible to raise other volunteers either in California or Oregon, and the navy held these places by detachments of sailors and marines till the end of the war. Burton also called for reënforcements, and Naglee's company was sent to him from Monterey, and these three companies occupied Lower California at the end of the Mexican

[90] Nash died in the winter of 1848 while accompanying a party of Sonoma miners to Mormon Island. W. F. Wallace, *History of Napa County* (Oakland, CA: Enquirer, 1901), 90.

[91] Guaymas was captured on Oct. 20, 1847, and Mazatlan was captured on Nov. 11. Hunt Janin and Ursula Carlson, *The California Campaigns of the U.S.-Mexico War, 1846–1848* (Jefferson, NC: McFarland, 2015), 187.

[92] Burton and Bailey arrived in Baja California on July 21, 1847. For Kearney's May 30, 1847, orders to Burton, see *Index to Executive Documents*, 293–294. Peter Gerhard, "Baja California in the Mexican War, 1846–1848," *Pacific Historical Review* 14, no. 4 (Dec. 1945): 419.

War. Major Hardie still commanded at San Francisco and above; Company F, Third Artillery, and Shannon's company of volunteers, were at Monterey; Lippett's company at Santa Barbara;[93] Colonel Stevenson, with one company of his regiment, and the company of the First Dragoons, was at Los Angeles; and a company of Mormons, reënlisted out of the Mormon Battalion, garrisoned San Diego—and thus matters went along throughout 1847 into 1848. I had occasion to make several trips to Yerba Buena and back, and in the spring of 1848 Colonel Mason and I went down to Santa Barbara in the sloop-of-war Dale.

I spent much time in hunting deer and bear in the mountains back of the Carmel Mission, and ducks and geese in the plains of the Salinas. As soon as the fall rains set in, the young oats would sprout up, and myriads of ducks, brant, and geese, made their appearance. In a single day, or rather in the evening of one day and the morning of the next, I could load a pack-mule with geese and ducks. They had grown somewhat wild from the increased number of hunters, yet, by marking well the place where a flock lighted, I could, by taking advantage of gullies or the shape of the ground, creep up within range; and, giving one barrel on the ground, and the other as they rose, I have secured as many as nine at one discharge. Colonel Mason on one occasion killed eleven geese by one discharge of small shot. The seasons in California are well marked. About October and November the rains begin, and the whole country, plains and mountains, becomes covered with a bright-green grass, with endless flowers. The intervals between the rains give the finest weather possible. These rains are less frequent in March, and cease altogether in April and May, when gradually the grass dies and the whole aspect of things changes, first to yellow, then to brown, and by midsummer all is burnt up and dry as an ash-heap.

When General Kearney first departed we took his office at Larkin's; but shortly afterward we had a broad stairway constructed to lead from the outside to the upper front porch of the barracks. By cutting a large door through the adobe-wall, we made the upper room in the centre our office; and another side-room, connected with it by a door, was Colonel Mason's private office.

I had a single clerk, a soldier named Baden; and William E. P. Hartnell, citizen, also had a table in the same room.[94] He was the government interpreter,

[93] Francis J. Lippitt (1812–1902) was promoted to captain of the 1st New York Inf. in Aug. 1846. Throughout his life, he authored multiple books on theories of war. *CWHC*, 349.

[94] James C. Baden (1818–1868), in 1847, was a clerk and copyist in the 3rd U.S. Art., Co. F. William E. P. Hartnell (1798–1854) moved to Monterey in 1822 and worked as an entrepreneur and as a government translator for federal and state authorities. Bancroft, *History of California,*

and had charge of the civil archives. After Halleck's return from Mazatlan, he was, by Colonel Mason, made Secretary of State; and he then had charge of the civil archives, including the land-titles, of which Fremont first had possession, but which had reverted to us when he left the country.[95]

I remember one day, in the spring of 1848, that two men, Americans, came into the office and inquired for the Governor. I asked their business, and one answered that they had just come down from Captain Sutter[96] on special business, and they wanted to see Governor Mason *in person*. I took them in to the colonel, and left them together. After some time the colonel came to his door and called to me. I went in, and my attention was directed to a series of papers unfolded on his table, in which lay about half an ounce of *placer*-gold. Mason said to me, "What is that?" I touched it and examined one or two of the larger pieces, and asked, "Is it gold?" Mason asked me if I had ever seen native gold. I answered that, in 1844, I was in Upper Georgia, and there saw some native gold, but it was much finer than this, and that it was in phials, or in transparent quills; but I said that, if this were gold, it could be easily tested, first, by its malleability, and next by acids. I took a piece in my teeth, and the metallic lustre was perfect. I then called to the clerk, Baden, to bring an axe and hatchet from the back-yard. When these were brought, I took the largest piece and beat it out flat, and beyond doubt it was metal, and a pure metal. Still, we attached little importance to the fact, for gold was known to exist at San Fernando, at the south, and yet was not considered of much value.

Colonel Mason then handed me a letter from Captain Sutter, addressed to him, stating that he (Sutter) was engaged in erecting a saw-mill at Coloma, about forty miles up the American Fork, above his fort at New Helvetia,[97] for

---

2:707; Alexandra Kindell and Gordon Morris Bakken, eds., *Encyclopedia of Immigration and Migration in the American West* (Thousand Oaks, CA: Sage, 2006), 1:291–292.

95 Contrary to WTS's assertion, Halleck was appointed secretary of state of California on Aug. 13, 1847, two months before he left for Mazatlan. He returned to Monterey, CA, in June 1848. John F. Marszalek, *Commander of All Lincoln's Armies* (Cambridge, MA: Belknap Press of Harvard University Press, 2004), 55, 57, 60.

96 John A. Sutter (1803–1880) was a German immigrant who moved to California in 1839. The gold discovered on his land marked the beginning of the Gold Rush in California. Mark R. Cheathem and Terry Corps, *Historical Dictionary of the Jacksonian Era and Manifest Destiny*, 2nd ed. (Lanham: Rowman and Littlefield, 2017), s.v. "Sutter, John."

97 New Helvetia was the location of modern-day Sacramento. William L. Willis, *History of Sacramento County, California* (Los Angeles: Historic Record, 1913), 62.

the general benefit of the settlers in that vicinity; that he had incurred considerable expense, and wanted a "preëmption" to the quarter-section of land on which the mill was located, embracing the tail-race in which this particular gold had been found.[98] Mason instructed me to prepare a letter, in answer, for his signature. I wrote off a letter, reciting that California was yet a Mexican province, simply held by us as a conquest; that no laws of the United States yet applied to it, much less the land laws or preëmption laws, which could only apply after a public survey. Therefore it was impossible for the Governor to promise him (Sutter) a title to the land; yet, as there were no settlements within forty miles, he was not likely to be disturbed by trespassers. Colonel Mason signed the letter, handed it to one of the gentlemen who had brought the sample of gold, and they departed.[99]

That gold was the *first* discovered in the Sierra Nevada, which soon revolutionized the whole country, and actually moved the whole civilized world. About this time (May and June, 1848), far more importance was attached to quicksilver. One mine, the New Almaden, twelve miles south of San José, was well known, and was in possession of the agent of a Scotch gentleman named Forbes, who at the time was British consul at Tepic, Mexico.[100] Mr. Forbes came up from San Blas in a small brig, which proved to be a Mexican vessel; the vessel was seized, condemned, and actually sold, but Forbes was wealthy, and bought her in. His title to the quicksilver-mine was, however, never disputed, as he had bought it regularly, before our conquest of the country, from another British subject, also named Forbes, a resident of Santa Clara Mission, who had purchased it of the discoverer, a priest;[101] but

[98] The Pre-Emption Act of 1841 allowed a person to claim up to 160 acres of unused, surveyed public land. It was eventually repealed in 1891. Paul W. Gates and Robert Swenson, *History of Public Land Law Development* (Washington, DC: GPO, 1968), 238, 247.

[99] For Mason's letter to Sutter, dated Mar. 5, 1848, see *Index to Executive Documents,* 466.

[100] Alexander Forbes (c. 1778–1862) partnered with Eustace Barron of Tepic, Mexico, to purchase the claim to the Castillero mine, which they renamed the New Almaden mine. The mine was subsequently sold to the Quicksilver Mining Company because the U.S. Supreme Court decided that Barron, Forbes, and Company did not own the mining rights. Michael Boulland and Arthur L. Boudreault, *New Almaden* (Mount Pleasant, SC: Arcadia, 2006), 12–13.

[101] James A. Forbes Sr. (1805–1881) served as British vice-consul to San Francisco. He managed the New Almaden mine until it was purchased by Barron, Forbes, and Company. Padre José Suárez del Real, the Franciscan administer who sold portions of the mission's property to Forbes, arrived in Monterey in 1833. He left the Santa Clara Mission after he allegedly raped a woman named Vicenta Gutierrez. Boulland and Boudreault, *New Almaden,* 12–13; Rayner

the boundaries of the land attached to the mine were even then in dispute. Other men were in search of quicksilver; and the whole range of mountains near the New Almaden mine was stained with the brilliant red of the sulphuret of mercury (cinnabar). A company composed of T. O. Larkin, J. R. Snyder, and others, among them one John Ricord (who was quite a character), also claimed a valuable mine near by. Ricord was a lawyer from about Buffalo, and by some means had got to the Sandwich Islands, where he became a great favorite of the king, Kamehameha; was his attorney-general, and got into a difficulty with the Rev. Mr. Judd, who was a kind of prime-minister to his majesty. One or the other had to go, and Ricord left for San Francisco, where he arrived while Colonel Mason and I were there on some business connected with the customs.[102] Ricord at once made a dead set at Mason with flattery, and all sorts of spurious arguments, to convince him that our military government was too simple in its forms for the new state of facts, and that he was the man to remodel it. I had heard a good deal to his prejudice, and did all I could to prevent Mason taking him into his confidence. We then started back for Monterey. Ricord was along, and night and day he was harping on his scheme; but he disgusted Colonel Mason with his flattery,

---

Wickersham Kelsey, *The United States Consulate in California* (Oakland: University of California, 1910), 196, 254; Gerald McKevitt, "From Franciscan Mission to Jesuit College: A Troubled Transition at Mission Santa Clara," *Southern California Quarterly* 58, no. 2 (Summer 1976): 248; Deborah A. Miranda, "'Saying the Padre Had Grabbed Her': Rape Is the Weapon, Story Is the Cure," *Intertexts* 14, no. 2 (Fall 2010): 99–109.

[102] Jacob R. Snyder (1812–1878) was the surveyor-general for the middle department of California in 1848. In 1849 he represented Sacramento as a delegate for the First California Constitutional Convention, and he was the president of the Society of California Pioneers in 1854–1855. Kamehameha III (1813–1854) became king of Hawaii in 1825. He established a Declaration of Rights and an Edict of Toleration in 1839 and the first constitution for Hawaii in 1840. During his reign, the United States, Great Britain, and France recognized Hawaii's independence. John Ricord (1812–1861) was appointed attorney general for Kamehameha III in 1844. He resigned from his government positions and moved to California in Aug. 1847. Gerrit Parmele Judd (1803–1873) moved to Honolulu in 1828 and was the secretary of state for foreign affairs for King Kamehameha III in 1844. In May 1847, Judd confronted John Ricord for harassing his fifteen-year-old daughter, who had declined his romantic advances. W. D. Alexander, *A Brief History of the Hawaiian People* (New York: American Book, 1891), 333–337; William R. Garner, *Letters from California* (Berkeley: University of California Press, 1970), 52–53*n;* Howard A. Kelly and Walter L. Burrage, eds., *American Medical Biographies* (Baltimore: Norman and Remington, 1920), s.v. "Judd, Gerrit Parmele"; W. F. Swasey, *The Early Days and Men of California* (Oakland, CA: Pacific Press, 1891), 172–177.

and, on reaching Monterey, he opened what he called a law-office, but there were neither courts nor clients, so necessity forced him to turn his thoughts to something else, and quicksilver became his hobby. In the spring of 1848 an appeal came to our office from San José, which compelled the Governor to go up in person. Lieutenant Loeser and I, with a couple of soldiers, went along. At San José the Governor held some kind of a court, in which Ricord and the alcalde had a warm dispute about a certain mine which Ricord, as a member of the Larkin Company, had opened within the limits claimed by the New Almaden Company. On our way up we had visited the ground, and were therefore better prepared to understand the controversy. We had found at New Almaden Mr. Walkinshaw, a fine Scotch gentleman, the resident agent of Mr. Forbes.[103] He had built in the valley, near a small stream, a few board-houses, and some four or five furnaces for the distillation of the mercury. These were very simple in their structure, being composed of whalers' kettles, set in masonry. These kettles were filled with broken ore about the size of McAdam-stone, mingled with lime. Another kettle, reversed, formed the lid, and the seam was luted with clay. On applying heat, the mercury was volatilized and carried into a chimney-stack, where it condensed and flowed back into a reservoir, and then was led in pipes into another kettle outside. After witnessing this process, we visited the mine itself, which outcropped near the apex of the hill, about a thousand feet above the furnaces. We found wagons hauling the mineral down the hill and returning empty, and in the mines quite a number of Sonora miners were blasting and driving for the beautiful ore (cinnabar). It was then, and is now, a most valuable mine. The adit of the mine was at the apex of the hill, which drooped off to the north. We rode along this hill, and saw where many openings had been begun, but these, proving of little or no value, had been abandoned. Three miles beyond, on the west face of the hill, we came to the opening of the "Larkin Company." There was evidence of a good deal of work, but the mine itself was filled up by what seemed a land-slide. The question involved in the lawsuit before the alcalde at San José was, first, whether the mine was or was not on the land belonging to the New Almaden property; and, next, whether the company had complied with all the conditions of the mining laws of Mexico, which were construed to be still in force in California.

These laws required that any one who discovered a valuable mine on private land should first file with the alcalde, or judge of the district, a notice

[103] Robert Walkinshaw was hired as the superintendent of the New Almaden Mine in 1847. His heirs later became partial owners of the mine. Boulland and Boudreault, *New Almaden*, 93.

and claim for the benefits of such discovery; then the mine was to be opened and followed for a distance of at least one hundred feet within a specified time, and the claimants must take out samples of the mineral and deposit the same with the alcalde, who was then required to inspect *personally* the mine, to see that it fulfilled all the conditions of the law, before he could give a written title. In this case the alcalde had been to the mine and had possession of samples of the ore; but, as the mouth of the mine was closed up, as alleged, from the act of God, by a land-slide, it was contended by Ricord and his associates that it was competent to prove by good witnesses that the mine had been opened into the hill one hundred feet, and that, by no negligence of theirs, it had caved in. It was generally understood that Robert J. Walker, United States Secretary of the Treasury, was then a partner in this mining company;[104] and a vessel, the bark Gray Eagle, was ready at San Francisco to sail for New York with the title-papers on which to base a joint-stock company for speculative uses. I think the alcalde was satisfied that the law had been complied with, that he had given the necessary papers, and, as at that time there was nothing developed to show fraud, the Governor (Mason) did not interfere. At that date there was no public house or tavern in San José where we could stop, so we started toward Santa Cruz and encamped about ten miles out, to the west of the town, where we fell in with another party of explorers, of whom Ruckel, of San Francisco, was the head;[105] and after supper, as we sat around the camp-fire, the conversation turned on quicksilver in general, and the result of the contest in San José in particular. Mason was relating to Ruckel the points and the arguments of Ricord, that the company should not suffer from an act of God, viz., the caving in of the mouth of the mine, when a man named Cash, a fellow who had once been in the quartermaster's employ as a teamster, spoke up: "Governor Mason, did Judge Ricord say that?" "Yes," said the Governor; and then Cash related how he and another man, whose name he gave, had been employed by Ricord to undermine a heavy rock that rested above the mouth of the mine, so that it tumbled down, carrying with it a large quantity of earth, and completely filled it up, as we had seen; "and," said Cash, "it took us three days of the hardest kind of work." This was the act of God, and on the papers procured from the

[104] Robert J. Walker (1801–1869) was a U.S. senator from 1835 to 1845 and U.S. secretary of the treasury from 1845 to 1849. Robert Strobel, *Biographical Directory of the United States Executive Branch, 1777–1989* (Westport, CT: Greenwood Press, 1990), 372.

[105] Joseph S. Ruckel was a prominent trader from San Francisco. He later moved to the Oregon Territory and became a boatman. Bancroft, *History of California*, 5:706.

alcalde at that time, I understand, was built a huge speculation, by which thousands of dollars changed hands in the United States and were lost. This happened long before the celebrated McGarrahan claim, which has produced so much noise, and which still is being prosecuted in the courts and in Congress.[106]

On the next day we crossed over the Santa Cruz Mountains, from which we had sublime views of the scenery, first looking east toward the lower Bay of San Francisco, with the bright plains of Santa Clara and San José, and then to the west upon the ocean, the town of Monterey being visible sixty miles off. If my memory is correct, we beheld from that mountain the firing of a salute from the battery at Monterey, and counted the number of guns from the white puffs of smoke, but could not hear the sound. That night we slept on piles of wheat in a mill at Soquel, near Santa Cruz, and, our supplies being short, I advised that we should make an early start next morning, so as to reach the ranch of Don Juan Antonio Vallejo, a particular friend, who had a large and valuable cattle-ranch on the Pajaro River, about twenty miles on our way to Monterey.[107] Accordingly, we were off by the first light of day, and by nine o'clock we had reached the ranch. It was on a high point of the plateau, overlooking the plain of the Pajaro, on which were grazing numbers of horses and cattle. The house was of adobe, with a long range of adobe-huts occupied by the semi-civilized Indians,[108] who at that time did all the labor of a ranch, the herding and marking of cattle, breaking of horses, and cultivating the little patches of wheat and vegetables which constituted all the farming of that day. Every thing about the house looked deserted, and, seeing a small Indian boy leaning up against a post, I approached him and asked him in Spanish, "Where is the master?" "Gone to the Presidio" (Monterey). "Is anybody in the house?" "No." "Is it locked up?" "Yes." "Is no one about who can get in?" "No." "Have you any meat?" "No." "Any flour or grain?" "No." "Any chickens?" "No." "Any eggs?" "No." "What do you live on?" "*Nada*" (nothing). The utter indifference of this boy, and the tone of his answer

[106] McGarrahan and his heirs continued their litigation until 1900, but without success. Parker, "William McGarrahan's 'Panoche Grande Claim,'" 220.

[107] Juan Antonio Vallejo (1816–1857) was the younger brother of Mariano G. Vallejo. He served in politics during the 1840s. Rose M. Beebe and Robert M. Senkewicz, *Mariano Guadalupe Vallejo* (Norman: University of Oklahoma Press, 2023), 7:328.

[108] The Indigenous peoples living in the Monterey Bay area at that time were part of the Ohlone. For more information on the Ohlone, see Malcolm Margolin, *The Ohlone Way: Indian Life in the San Francisco–Monterey Bay Area* (Berkeley: Heyday, 1978).

"*Nada,*" attracted the attention of Colonel Mason, who had been listening to our conversation, and who knew enough of Spanish to catch the meaning, and he exclaimed with some feeling, "So we get *nada* for our breakfast." I felt mortified, for I had held out the prospect of a splendid breakfast of meat and *tortillas* with rice, chickens, eggs, etc., at the ranch of my friend José Antonio, as a justification for taking the Governor, a man of sixty years of age, more than twenty miles at a full canter for his breakfast. But there was no help for it, and we accordingly went a short distance to a pond, where we unpacked our mules and made a slim breakfast on some scraps of hard bread and a bone of pork that remained in our *alforjas.* This was no uncommon thing in those days, when many a *ranchero* with his eleven leagues of land, his hundreds of horses and thousands of cattle, would receive us with all the grandiloquence of a Spanish lord, and confess that he had nothing in his house to eat except the carcass of a beef hung up, from which the stranger might cut and cook, without money or price, what he needed. That night we slept on Salinas Plain, and the next morning reached Monterey. All the missions and houses at that period were alive with fleas, which the natives looked on as pleasant titillators, but they so tortured me that I always gave them a wide berth, and slept on a saddle-blanket, with the saddle for a pillow and the *serape,* or blanket, for a cover. We never feared rain except in winter. As the spring and summer of 1848 advanced, the reports came faster and faster from the gold-mines at Sutter's saw-mill. Stories reached us of fabulous discoveries, and spread throughout the land. Everybody was talking of "Gold! gold!" until it assumed the character of a fever. Some of our soldiers began to desert; citizens were fitting out trains of wagons and pack-mules to go to the mines. We heard of men earning fifty, five hundred, and thousands of dollars per day, and for a time it seemed as though somebody would reach solid gold. Some of this gold began to come to Yerba Buena in trade, and to disturb the value of merchandise, particularly of mules, horses, tin pans, and articles used in mining. I of course could not escape the infection, and at last convinced Colonel Mason that it was our duty to go up and see with our own eyes, that we might report the truth to our Government. As yet we had no regular mail to any part of the United States, but mails had come to us at long intervals, around Cape Horn, and one or two overland. I well remember the first overland mail. It was brought by Kit Carson[109] in saddle-bags from Taos in New

[109] Christopher "Kit" Carson (1809–1868) was a prominent trapper and traveler. He served as a guide for John C. Frémont during the years 1842–1847 and acted as a courier for the U.S. government from 1846 to 1848. He first arrived in Monterey, CA, with mail, on Nov. 22, 1847.

Mexico. We heard of his arrival at Los Angeles, and waited patiently for his arrival at headquarters. His fame then was at its height, from the publication of Fremont's books,[110] and I was very anxious to see a man who had achieved such feats of daring among the wild animals of the Rocky Mountains, and still wilder Indians of the Plains. At last his arrival was reported at the tavern at Monterey, and I hurried to hunt him up. I cannot express my surprise at beholding a small, stoop-shouldered man, with reddish hair, freckled face, soft blue eyes, and nothing to indicate extraordinary courage or daring. He spoke but little, and answered questions in monosyllables. I asked for his mail, and he picked up his light saddle-bags containing the great overland mail, and we walked together to headquarters, where he delivered his parcel into Colonel Mason's own hands. He spent some days in Monterey, during which time we extracted with difficulty some items of his personal history. He was then by commission a lieutenant in the regiment of Mounted Rifles[111] serving in Mexico under Colonel Sumner,[112] and, as he could not reach his regiment from California, Colonel Mason ordered that for a time he should be assigned to duty with A. J. Smith's company, First Dragoons, at Los Angeles. He remained at Los Angeles some months, and was then sent back to the United States with dispatches, traveling two thousand miles almost alone, in preference to being encumbered by a large party.[113]

Edwin L. Sabin, ed., *Kit Carson Days, 1809–1869: "Adventures in the Path of Empire,"* rev. ed. (Lincoln: University of Nebraska Press, 1995), 2:608, 749.

[110] John C. Frémont's reports of his westward expeditions captured the public's attention. The reports were eventually reprinted as *Narrative of the Exploring Expedition to the Rocky Mountains, in the Year 1842; and to Oregon and North California, in the Years 1843–44 in 1846.* Hampton Sides, *Blood and Thunder: An Epic of the American West* (New York: Doubleday, 2006), 52–53, 61.

[111] Carson was appointed as second lieutenant of the Mounted Rifles in June 1847. Sabin, ed., *Kit Carson Days,* 2:749.

[112] Edwin V. Sumner (c. 1797–1863) joined the U.S. 2nd Inf. as a second lieutenant in 1819. He was promoted to lieutenant colonel in 1848 for his actions during the Mexican-American War. He reached the rank of major general during the Civil War and died from a brief illness in 1863. Lillian C. Buttre, *The American Portrait Gallery with Biographical Sketches* (New York: J. C. Buttre, 1880), s.v. "Edwin Vose Sumner."

[113] In a letter to his brother dated Apr. 10, 1848, WTS wrote, "The time is rapidly approaching when Lieut. Carson, the Kit Carson of Frémont narratives, will start for home. He goes from Los Angeles to Santa Fé, and thence to Saint Louis where he will put his mail in the Post Office . . ." William T. Sherman, *Home Letters of General Sherman,* ed. M. A. DeWolfe Howe (New York: Charles Scribner's Sons, 1909), 111–112.

Toward the close of June, 1848, the gold-fever being at its height, by Colonel Mason's orders I made preparations for his trip to the newly-discovered gold-mines at Sutter's Fort. I selected four good soldiers, with Aaron, Colonel Mason's black servant, and a good outfit of horses and pack-mules, we started by the usually traveled route for Yerba Buena. There Captain Folsom and two citizens joined our party. The first difficulty was to cross the bay to Saucelito. Folsom, as quartermaster, had a sort of scow with a large sail, with which to discharge the cargoes of ships, that could not come within a mile of the shore. It took nearly the whole day to get the old scow up to the only wharf there, and then the water was so shallow that the scow, with its load of horses, would not float at the first high tide, but by infinite labor on the next tide she was got off and safely crossed over to Saucelito. We followed in a more comfortable schooner. Having safely landed our horses and mules, we picked up and rode to San Rafael Mission, stopping with Don Timoteo Murphy.[114] The next day's journey took us to Bodega, where lived a man named Stephen Smith, who had the only steam saw-mill in California. He had a Peruvian wife, and employed a number of absolutely naked Indians in making adobes.[115] We spent a day very pleasantly with him, and learned that he had come to California some years before, at the personal advice of Daniel Webster,[116] who had informed him that sooner or later the United States would be in possession of California, and that in consequence it would become a great country. From Bodega we traveled to Sonoma, by way of Petaluma, and spent a day with General Vallejo. I had been there before, as related, in the business of the alcalde Nash. From Sonoma we crossed over by

[114]Timothy "Don Timoteo" Murphy (1800–1853) worked for commercial firms in Dublin, Ireland, and Lima, Peru, before moving to California in 1828. He served as the alcalde of San Rafael, CA, from 1837 to 1849. Thomas F. Prendergast, *Forgotten Pioneers: Irish Leaders in Early California* (Honolulu: University Press of the Pacific, 2001), 33–40.

[115]Stephen Smith (1787–1855) arrived in San Francisco in 1841. In Aug. 1844, he successfully petitioned for 35,487 acres of land from the governor near Bodega, CA. His wife, Manuela Torres Smith Curtis (1827–1871), was from Piura, Peru. A year after Stephen's death, Manuela married Tyler Curtis. Bancroft, *History of California,* 6:20; *Portraits of Early Sonoma County Settlers* (Sonoma: Sonoma County Genealogical Society, 2016), 4–11.

[116]Daniel Webster (1782–1852) served as a U.S. congressman in the years 1813–1817 and 1823–1827, as U.S. Senator in the years 1827–1841 and 1845–1850, and U.S. secretary of state in the years 1841–1843 and 1850–1852. *Dictionary of American Biography,* 2nd ed., s.v. "Webster, Daniel."

way of Napa, Suisun, and Vaca's ranch, to the Puta.[117] In the rainy season, the plain between the Puta and Sacramento Rivers is impassable, but in July the waters dry up; and we passed without trouble, by the trail for Sutter's *Embarcadero.*[118] We reached the Sacramento River, then full of water, with a deep, clear current. The only means of crossing over was by an Indian dugout canoe. We began by carrying across our packs and saddles, and then our people. When all things were ready, the horses were driven into the water, one being guided ahead by a man in the canoe. Of course, the horses and mules at first refused to take to the water, and it was nearly a day's work to get them across, and even then some of our animals after crossing escaped into the woods and undergrowth that lined the river, but we secured enough of them to reach Sutter's Fort, three miles back from the *embarcadero,* where we encamped at the old slough, or pond, near the fort. On application, Captain Sutter sent some Indians back into the bushes, who recovered and brought in all our animals. At that time there was not the sign of a habitation there or thereabouts, except the fort, and an old adobe-house, east of the fort, known as the hospital. The fort itself was one of adobe-walls, about twenty feet high, rectangular in form, with two-story block-houses at diagonal corners. The entrance was by a large gate, open by day and closed at night, with two iron ship's guns near at hand. Inside there was a large house, with a good shingle-roof, used as a storehouse, and all round the walls were ranged rooms, the fort-wall being the outer wall of the house. The inner wall also was of adobe. These rooms were used by Captain Sutter himself and by his people. He had a blacksmith's shop, carpenter's shop, etc., and other rooms where the women made blankets. Sutter was monarch of all he surveyed, and had authority to inflict punishment even unto death, a power he did not fail to use. He had horses, cattle, and sheep, and of these he gave liberally and without price to all in need. He caused to be driven into our camp a beef and some sheep,

[117] In 1843, Manuel Cabeza Vaca and Juan Felipe Peña built the Peña Adobe on a tract of land given to them by the Mexican government near Putah Creek, also known as Rancho Los Putos. Lyn Wilkerson, *Slow Travels: Exploring America's History Along U.S. Highways, California and Nevada Edition* (Lexington, KY: Lulu, 2010), 22.

[118] Sutter's Embarcadero was a ship landing on the Sacramento River, near the mouth of the American River. Kenneth N. Owens, "River City: Sacramento's Gold Rush Birth and Transfiguration," in *River City and Valley Life: An Environmental History of the Sacramento Region,* ed. Christopher J. Castaneda and Lee M. A. Simpson (Pittsburgh: University of Pittsburgh Press, 2013), 40.

which were slaughtered for our use. Already the gold-mines were beginning to be felt. Many people were then encamped, some going and some coming, all full of gold-stories, and each surpassing the other. We found preparations in progress for celebrating the Fourth of July, then close at hand, and we agreed to remain over to assist on the occasion; of course, being the high officials, we were the honored guests. People came from a great distance to attend this celebration of the Fourth of July, and the tables were laid in the large room inside the storehouse of the fort. A man of some note, named Sinclair,[119] presided, and after a substantial meal and a reasonable supply of *aguardiente* we began the toasts. All that I remember is that Folsom and I spoke for our party; others, Captain Sutter included, made speeches, and before the celebration was over Sutter was enthusiastic,[120] and many others showed the effects of the *aguardiente*. The next day (namely, July 5, 1848) we resumed our journey toward the mines, and, in twenty-five miles of as hot and dusty a ride as possible, we reached Mormon Island.[121] I have heretofore stated that the gold was first found in the tail-race of the saw-mill at Coloma, forty miles above Sutter's Fort, or fifteen above Mormon Island, in the bed of the American Fork of the Sacramento River. It seems that Sutter had employed an American named Marshall, a sort of millwright, to do this work for him, but Marshall afterward claimed that in the matter of the saw-mill they were copartners. At all events, Marshall and the family of Mr. Wimmer[122] were living at Coloma, where the pine-trees afforded the best material for lumber. He had under him four white men, Mormons, who had been discharged from Cooke's battalion, and some Indians.[123] These were engaged in

[119] John Sinclair, from Scotland, was Sutter's farming partner. He also worked as a clerk for the Hudson Bay Company. Myron Angel, *History of Placer County, California* (Oakland, CA: Thompson and West, 1882), 47.

[120] In the first edition of the memoirs (1875), WTS used the word "tight" instead of "enthusiastic."

[121] In 1848, several members of the Mormon Battalion found gold on a small island on the American River near Sutter's Fort. The site is now under Folsom Lake in Folsom, CA. Folsom Historical Society, *Images of America: Folsom, California* (Chicago: Arcadia, 1999), 7.

[122] In the first edition of the memoirs (1875), this portion of WTS's text read, "At all events, Marshall and his family, in the winter of 1847–'48, were living . . ."

[123] James W. Marshall (1812–1885) partnered with John Sutter to establish a sawmill in Coloma, CA, in Aug. 1847. Marshall hired Peter L. Wemer and his family to work at the sawmill. In 1847, Marshall also employed William Scott, James Bargee, Alexander Stephens, James Brown, William Johnson, Henry Bigler, and eight to ten Indigenous people. George F. Parsons,

hewing logs, building a mill-dam, and putting up a saw-mill. Marshall, as the architect, had made the "tub-wheel," and had set it in motion, and had also furnished some of the rude parts of machinery necessary for an ordinary up-and-down saw-mill.

Labor was very scarce, expensive, and had to be economized. The mill was built over a dry channel of the river which was calculated to be the tail-race. After arranging his head-race, dam, and *tub-wheel,* he let on the water to test the goodness of his machinery. It worked very well until it was found that the tail-race did not carry off the water fast enough, so he put his men to work in a rude way to clear out the tail-race. They scratched a kind of ditch down the middle of the dry channel, throwing the coarser stones to one side; then, letting on the water again, it would run with velocity down the channel, washing away the dirt, thus saving labor. This course of action was repeated several times, acting exactly like the long Tom afterward resorted to by the miners. As Marshall himself was working in this ditch, he observed particles of yellow metal which he gathered up in his hand, when it seemed to have suddenly flashed across his mind that it was *gold.* After picking up about an ounce, he hurried down to the fort to report to Captain Sutter his discovery. Captain Sutter himself related to me Marshall's account, saying that, as he sat in his room at the fort one day in February or March, 1848, a knock was heard at his door, and he called out, "Come in." In walked Marshall, who was a half-crazy man at best, but then looked strangely wild. "What is the matter, Marshall?" Marshall inquired if any one was within hearing, and began to peer about the room, and look under the bed, when Sutter, fearing that some calamity had befallen the party up at the saw-mill, and that Marshall was really crazy, began to make his way to the door, demanding of Marshall to explain what was the matter. At last he revealed his discovery, and laid before Captain Sutter the pellicles of gold he had picked up in the ditch. At first, Sutter attached little or no importance to the discovery, and told Marshall to go back to the mill, and say nothing of what he had seen to Mr. Wimmer,[124] or any one else. Yet, as it might add value to the location, he dispatched to our headquarters at Monterey, as I have already related, the two men with a written application for a preëmption to the quarter-section of land at Coloma. Marshall returned to the mill, but could not keep out of his wonderful ditch, and

---

The Life and Adventures of James W. Marshall (Sacramento, CA: James W. Marshall and W. Burke, 1870), 6, 79–81.

[124] In the first edition of the memoirs (1875), WTS wrote "to his family," instead of "to Mr. Wimmer."

by some means the other men employed there learned his secret. They then wanted to gather the gold, and Marshall threatened to shoot them if they attempted it; but these men had sense enough to know that if "placer"-gold existed at Coloma, it would also be found farther down-stream, and they gradually "prospected" until they reached Mormon Island, fifteen miles below, where they discovered one of the richest placers on earth. These men revealed the fact to some other Mormons who were employed by Captain Sutter at a grist-mill he was building still lower down the American Fork, and six miles above his fort. All of them struck for higher wages, to which Sutter yielded, until they asked ten dollars a day, which he refused, and the two mills on which he had spent so much money were never built, and fell into decay.

In my opinion, when the Mormons were driven from Nauvoo, Illinois, in 1844, they cast about for a land where they would not be disturbed again, and fixed on California.[125] In the year 1845 a ship, the Brooklyn, sailed from New York for California, with a colony of Mormons, of which Sam Brannan was the leader, and we found them there on our arrival in January, 1847.[126] When General Kearney, at Fort Leavenworth, was collecting volunteers early in 1846, for the Mexican War, he, through the instrumentality of Captain James Allen, brother to our quartermaster, General Robert Allen, raised the battalion of Mormons at Kanesville, Iowa, now Council Bluffs, on the express understanding that it would facilitate their migration to California.[127] But when the Mormons reached Salt Lake, in 1846, they learned that they had been forestalled by the United States forces in California, and they then determined to settle down where they were. Therefore, when this battalion of

[125] In June 1844, Mormon leader Joseph Smith ordered the destruction of a dissenting Mormon newspaper press. In response, the state of Illinois charged Joseph Smith with conspiracy and put him in jail with his brother Hyrum. On June 27, 1844, while in jail, the Smith brothers were killed by a mob. As a result, the Mormon community, under the leadership of Brigham Young, abandoned Nauvoo and moved out West in 1846. Robert B. Flanders, *Nauvoo: Kingdom on the Mississippi* (Urbana: University of Illinois Press, 1975), 306.

[126] Sam Brannan (1819–1889) joined the Church of Jesus Christ of Latter-day Saints in 1842. He was an elder in the church and was also a newspaper printer. Brannan helped bring 238 church members to California. The group arrived in San Francisco in July 1846. Zoeth S. Eldredge, *The Beginnings of San Francisco* (San Francisco: Zoeth S. Eldredge, 1912), 709*n.*

[127] James Allen (1806–1846) graduated from the USMA in 1829 and commanded the Mormon Battalion of Missouri Volunteers as a lieutenant colonel from July 16, 1846, until his death on Aug. 23, 1846. His younger brother, Robert Allen (c. 1811–1886), graduated from the USMA in 1836 and served as the chief quartermaster of the Pacific Division from 1849 to 1852. *USMA,* 1:442–443, 651–653.

five companies of Mormons (raised by Allen, who died on the way, and was succeeded by Cooke) was discharged at Los Angeles, California, in the early summer of 1847, most of the men went to their people at Salt Lake, with all the money received, as pay from the United States, invested in cattle and breeding-horses; one company reënlisted for another year, and the remainder sought work in the country. As soon as the fame of the gold discovery spread through California, the Mormons naturally turned to Mormon Island, so that in July, 1848, we found about three hundred of them there at work. Sam Brannan was on hand as the high-priest, collecting the tithes. Clark, of Clark's Point, an early pioneer,[128] was there also, and nearly all the Mormons who had come out in the Brooklyn, or who had staid in California after the discharge of their battalion, had collected there.[129] I recall the scene as perfectly to-day as though it were yesterday. In the midst of a broken country, all parched and dried by the hot sun of July, sparsely wooded with live-oaks and straggling pines, lay the valley of the American River, with its bold mountain-stream coming out of the Snowy Mountains to the east. In this valley is a flat, or gravel-bed, which in high water is an island, or is overflown, but at the time of our visit was simply a level gravel-bed of the river. On its edges men were digging, and filling buckets with the finer earth and gravel, which was carried to a machine made like a baby's cradle, open at the foot, and at the head a plate of sheet-iron or zinc, punctured full of holes. On this metallic plate was emptied the earth, and water was then poured on it from buckets, while one man shook the cradle with violent rocking by a handle. On the bottom were nailed cleats of wood. With this rude machine four men could earn from forty to one hundred dollars a day, averaging sixteen dollars, or a gold ounce, per man per day. While the sun blazed down on the heads of the miners with tropical heat, the water was bitter cold, and all hands were either standing in the water or had their clothes wet all the time; yet there were no complaints of rheumatism or cold. We made our camp on a small knoll, a little below the island, and from it could overlook the busy scene. A few bush-huts near by served as stores, boarding-houses, and for sleeping; but all

[128] William S. Clark (c. 1807–1889) moved to San Francisco in 1846 and established a wharf in the bay that was later named Clark's Point. It is now called Rincon Point. In the first edition of the memoirs (1875), the text read "one of the elders" instead of "an early pioneer." "County News," *Ferndale Enterprise* (Ferndale, CA), Nov. 29, 1889, 1; Erwin G. Gudde, *California Gold Camps* (Berkeley: University of California Press, 1975), 391.

[129] In the first edition of the memoirs (1875), WTS wrote "as herein related" instead of "had collected there."

hands slept on the ground, with pine-leaves and blankets for bedding. As soon as the news spread that the Governor was there, persons came to see us, and volunteered all kinds of information, illustrating it by samples of the gold, which was of a uniform kind, "scale-gold," bright and beautiful. A large variety, of every conceivable shape and form, was found in the smaller gulches round about, but the gold in the river-bed was uniformly "scale-gold." I remember that Mr. Clark was in camp, talking to Colonel Mason about matters and things generally, when he inquired, "Governor, what business has Sam Brannan to collect the tithes here?" Clark admitted that Brannan was the head of the Mormon church in California, and he was simply questioning as to Brannan's right, as high-priest, to compel the Mormons to pay him the regular tithes. Colonel Mason answered, "Brannan has a perfect right to collect the tax, if you Mormons are fools enough to pay it." "Then," said Clark, "I for one won't pay it any longer." Colonel Mason added: "This is public land, and the gold is the property of the United States; all of you here are trespassers, but, as the Government is benefited by your getting out the gold, I do not intend to interfere." I understood, afterward, that from that time the payment of the tithes ceased, but Brannan had already collected enough money wherewith to hire Sutter's hospital, and to open a store there, in which he made more money than any merchant in California, during that summer and fall. The understanding was, that the money collected by him as tithes was the foundation of his fortune, which is still very large in San Francisco. That evening we all mingled freely with the miners, and witnessed the process of cleaning up and "panning" out, which is the last process for separating the pure gold from the fine dirt and black sand.

The next day we continued our journey up the valley of the American Fork, stopping at various camps, where mining was in progress; and about noon we reached Coloma, the place where gold had been first discovered. The hills were higher, and the timber of better quality. The river was narrower and bolder, and but few miners were at work there, by reason of Marshall's and Sutter's claim to the site. There stood the saw-mill unfinished, the dam and tail-race just as they were left when the Mormons ceased work. Marshall and Wimmer's family of wife and half a dozen children were there,[130] guarding their supposed treasure; living in a house made of clapboards. Here also we were shown many specimens of gold, of a coarser grain than that found at Mormon Island. The next day we crossed the American River to its north side, and visited many small camps of men, in what were called the "dry diggings." Little pools of water

[130] In the first edition of the memoirs (1875), this portion of WTS's text read, "Marshall and his family of wife and half a dozen tow-head children were there . . ."

stood in the beds of the streams, and these were used to wash the dirt; and there the gold was in every conceivable shape and size, some of the specimens weighing several ounces. Some of these "diggings" were extremely rich, but as a whole they were more precarious in results than at the river. Sometimes a lucky fellow would hit on a "pocket," and collect several thousand dollars in a few days, and then again he would be shifting about from place to place, "prospecting," and spending all he had made. Little stores were being opened at every point, where flour, bacon, etc., were sold; every thing being a dollar a pound, and a meal usually costing three dollars. Nobody paid for a bed, for he slept on the ground, without fear of cold or rain. We spent nearly a week in that region, and were quite bewildered by the fabulous tales of recent discoveries, which at the time were confined to the several forks of the American and Yuba Rivers. All this time our horses had nothing to eat but the sparse grass in that region, and we were forced to work our way down toward the Sacramento Valley, or to see our animals perish. Still we contemplated a visit to the Yuba and Feather Rivers, from which we had heard of more wonderful "diggings;" but met a courier, who announced the arrival of a ship at Monterey, with dispatches of great importance from Mazatlan. We accordingly turned our horses back to Sutter's Fort. Crossing the Sacramento again by swimming our horses, and ferrying their loads in that solitary canoe, we took our back track as far as the Napa, and then turned to Benicia, on Carquinez Straits. We found there a solitary adobe-house, occupied by Mr. Hastings and his family, embracing Dr. Semple, the proprietor of the ferry.[131] This ferry was a ship's-boat, with a latteen-sail, which could carry across at one tide six or eight horses.

It took us several days to cross over, and during that time we got well acquainted with the doctor, who was quite a character. He had come to California from Illinois, and was brother to Senator Semple.[132] He was about

[131] Lansford W. Hastings (1819–1870) moved to California with Robert Semple and others in 1845. In his book *Emigrants' Guide* (1845), Hastings proposed an alternate route for settlers traveling to California along the Oregon Trail known as the "Hastings Cut off," despite never attempting the route himself. This was the route taken by the ill-fated Donner Party in 1846. Robert B. Semple (1806–1854) operated a ferry between Benicia and Martinez, CA, in 1848, and the first one from San Francisco to Oakland in 1850. He was a medical doctor and the president of the state's First Constitutional Convention on Sept. 4, 1849. *California Historical Society Quarterly* (San Francisco: California History Society, 1927), 6:130; James D. Hart, *A Companion to California* (Berkeley: University of California Press, 1987), 159, 209.

[132] James Semple (1798–1866) was a U.S. senator from Illinois from 1843 to 1847. James K. Polk, *The Diary of James K. Polk,* ed. Milo M. Quaife (Chicago: A. C. McClurg, 1910), 1:154*n.*

seven feet high, and very intelligent. When we first reached Monterey, he had a printing-press, which belonged to the United States, having been captured at the custom-house, and had been used to print custom-house blanks. With this Dr. Semple, as editor, published the *Californian,* a small sheet of news, once a week; and it was a curiosity in its line, using two *v*'s for a *w,* and other combinations of letters, made necessary by want of type. After some time he removed to Yerba Buena with his paper, and it grew up to be the *Alta California* of to-day.[133] Foreseeing, as he thought, the growth of a great city somewhere on the Bay of San Francisco, he selected Carquinez Straits as its location, and obtained from General Vallejo a title to a league of land, on condition of building up a city thereon to bear the name of Vallejo's wife. This was Francisca Benicia;[134] accordingly, the new city was named "Francisca." At this time, the town near the mouth of the bay was known universally as Yerba Buena; but that name was not known abroad, although San Francisco was familiar to the whole civilized world. Now, some of the chief men of Yerba Buena, Folsom, Howard, Leidesdorf, and others, knowing the importance of a *name,* saw their danger, and, by some action of the *ayuntamiento,* or town council, changed the name of Yerba Buena to "San Francisco."[135] Dr. Semple was outraged at their changing the name to one so like his of *Francisca,* and he in turn changed his town to the other name of Mrs. Vallejo, viz., "Benicia;" and Benicia it has remained to this day. I am convinced that this little circumstance was big with consequences. That Benicia has the best natural site for a commercial city, I am satisfied; and had half the money and half the labor since bestowed upon San Francisco been expended at Benicia, we should have at this day a city of palaces on the Carquinez Straits. The name of "San Francisco," however, fixed the city where it now is; for every ship in 1848–'49, which cleared from any part of the world, knew the name of San Francisco, but not Yerba Buena or Benicia; and, accordingly, ships consigned to Cali-

[133] Semple began publishing the *Californian* in 1846. The *Daily Alta California* began publication in Jan. 1849. Edward C. Kemble, *A History of California Newspapers, 1846–1858,* ed. Helen Harding Bretnor (Los Gatos, CA: Talisman, 1962), 55–57, 81, 88.

[134] Francisca M. F. Benicia (1815–1891) married Mariano G. Vallejo when she was fifteen years old. They had sixteen children together. Julia Bussinger and Beverly Phelan, *Images of America: Benicia* (Charleston, SC: Arcadia, 2004), 13.

[135] In Jan. 1847, Washington A. Bartlett issued a proclamation to change the name of Yerba Buena to San Francisco. Peter Browning, ed., *San Francisco Yerba Buena: From the Beginning to the Gold Rush, 1769–1849* (Lafayette, CA: Great West Books, 1998), 140; Hart, *A Companion to California,* s.vv. "Yerba Buena," "Bartlett, Washington Allon."

fornia came pouring in with their contents, and were anchored in front of Yerba Buena, the first town. Captains and crews deserted for the gold-mines, and now half the city in front of Montgomery Street is built over the hulks thus abandoned. But Dr. Semple, at that time, was all there was of Benicia; he was captain and crew of his ferry-boat, and managed to pass our party to the south side of Carquinez Straits in about two days.

Thence we proceeded up Amador Valley to Alameda Creek, and so on to the old mission of San José; thence to the *pueblo* of San José, where Folsom and those belonging in Yerba Buena went in that direction, and we continued on to Monterey, our party all the way giving official sanction to the news from the gold-mines, and adding new force to the "fever."

On reaching Monterey, we found dispatches from Commodore Shubrick, at Mazatlan, which gave almost positive assurance that the war with Mexico was over; that hostilities had ceased, and commissioners were arranging the terms of peace at Guadalupe Hidalgo.[136] It was well that this news reached California at that critical time; for so contagious had become the "gold-fever" that everybody was bound to go and try his fortune, and the volunteer regiment of Stevenson's would have deserted *en masse,* had the men not been assured that they would very soon be entitled to an honorable discharge.

Many of our regulars did desert, among them the very men who had escorted us faithfully to the mines and back. Our servants also left us, and nothing less than three hundred dollars a month would hire a man in California; Colonel Mason's black boy, Aaron, alone of all our then servants proving faithful. We were forced to resort to all manner of shifts to live. First, we had a mess with a black fellow we called Bustamente as cook; but he got the fever, and had to go. We next took a soldier, but he deserted, and carried off my double-barreled shot-gun, which I prized very highly. To meet this condition of facts, Colonel Mason ordered that liberal furloughs should be given to the soldiers, and promises to all in turn, and he allowed all the officers to draw their rations in kind. As the actual value of the ration was very large, this enabled us to live. Halleck, Murray, Ord, and I, boarded with Doña Augustias, and turned in our rations as pay for our board.

Some time in September, 1848, the official news of the treaty of peace reached us, and the Mexican War *was* over. This treaty was signed in May, and came to us all the way by land by a courier from Lower California, sent

[136]The Treaty of Guadalupe Hidalgo was signed on Feb. 2, 1848. J. S. S. Eisenhower, *So Far from God: The U.S. War with Mexico, 1846–1848* (New York: Random House, 1989), 383.

from La Paz by Lieutenant-Colonel Burton.[137] On its receipt, orders were at once made for the muster-out of all of Stevenson's regiment, and our military forces were thus reduced to the single company of dragoons at Los Angeles, and the one company of artillery at Monterey.[138] Nearly all business had ceased, except that connected with gold; and, during that fall, Colonel Mason, Captain Warner, and I, made another trip up to Sutter's Fort, going also to the newly-discovered mines on the Stanislaus, called "Sonora," named from the miners of Sonora, Mexico, who had first discovered them. We found there pretty much the same state of facts as before existed at Mormon Island and Coloma, and we daily received intelligence of the opening of still other mines north and south.

But I have passed over a very interesting fact. As soon as we had returned from our first visit to the gold-mines, it became important to send home positive knowledge of this valuable discovery. The means of communication with the United States were very precarious, and I suggested to Colonel Mason that a special courier ought to be sent; that Second-Lieutenant Loeser had been promoted to first-lieutenant, and was entitled to go home. He was accordingly detailed to carry the news. I prepared with great care the letter to the adjutant-general[139] of August 17, 1848, which Colonel Mason modified in a few particulars; and, as it was important to send not only the specimens which had been presented to us along our route of travel, I advised the colonel to allow Captain Folsom to purchase and send to Washington a large sample of the commercial gold in general use, and to pay for the same out of the money in his hands known as the "civil fund," arising from duties collected at the several ports in California. He consented to this, and Captain Folsom bought an oyster-can full at ten dollars the ounce, which was the rate of value at which it was then received at the custom-house. Folsom was instructed further to contract with some vessel to carry the messenger to South America,

[137] The Treaty of Guadalupe was ratified by the U.S. Senate on Mar. 10, 1848; the Mexican Senate ratified it on May 25. On Aug. 7, in a letter to the commanding officer in San Jose, CA, WTS wrote, "Last night by an express from Lower California, was received official intelligence of the ratification of a treaty of peace between the republics of the United States and Mexico." Eisenhower, *So Far from God,* 367; 31st Congress, 1st session, House Executive Document 17 (Washington, DC: GPO, 1850), 633.

[138] For General Mason's orders, see General Order no. 50, War Department, Aug. 7, 1848.

[139] Roger Jones (1788–1852) was a veteran of the War of 1812 and served as the adjutant general of the United States from 1825 to 1852. L. H. Jones, ed., *Captain Roger Jones, of London and Virginia* (Albany, NY: Joel Munsell's Sons, 1891), 72.

where he could take the English steamers as far east as Jamaica, with a conditional charter giving increased payment if the vessel could catch the October steamer. Folsom chartered the bark La Lambayecana, owned and navigated by Henry D. Cooke, who has since been the Governor of the District of Columbia.[140] In due time this vessel reached Monterey, and Lieutenant Loeser, with his report and specimens of gold, embarked and sailed. He reached the South American Continent at Payta, Peru, in time, took the English steamer of October to Panama, and thence went on to Kingston, Jamaica, where he found a sailing-vessel bound for New Orleans. On reaching New Orleans, he telegraphed to the War Department his arrival; but so many delays had occurred that he did not reach Washington in time to have the matter embraced in the President's regular message of 1848, as we had calculated. Still, the President made it the subject of a special message, and thus became "official" what had before only reached the world in a very indefinite shape. Then began that wonderful development, and the great emigration to California, by land and by sea, of 1849 and 1850.

As before narrated, Mason, Warner, and I, made a second visit to the mines in September and October, 1848. As the winter season approached, Colonel Mason returned to Monterey, and I remained for a time at Sutter's Fort. In order to share somewhat in the riches of the land, we formed a partnership in a store at Coloma, in charge of Norman S. Bestor, who had been Warner's clerk.[141] We supplied the necessary money, fifteen hundred dollars (five hundred dollars each), and Bestor carried on the store at Coloma for his share. Out of this investment, each of us realized a profit of about fifteen hundred dollars. Warner also got a regular leave of absence, and contracted with Captain Sutter for surveying and locating the town of Sacramento. He received for this sixteen dollars per day for his services as surveyor; and Sutter paid all the hands engaged in the work. The town was laid off mostly up about the fort, but a few streets were staked off along the river-bank, and one or two leading to it. Captain Sutter always contended, however, that no town could possibly exist on the immediate bank of the river, because the spring freshets rose over the bank, and frequently it was necessary to swim a horse to reach the boat-landing. Nevertheless, from the very beginning the town began to

[140] Henry D. Cooke (1825–1881) was a lawyer, printer, and banker. USG nominated him for governor of the District of Columbia in Feb. 1871. *PUSG,* 23:1*n.*

[141] Norman S. Bestor (c. 1820–1904) moved to California in 1846 as an assistant to Lt. William H. Emory. Clyde Arbuckle, *Clyde Arbuckle's History of San Jose* (San Jose, CA: Smith and McKay, 1985), 57; "Norman Scott Bestor," *Washington Post,* Mar. 10, 1904, 4.

be built on the very river-bank, viz., First, Second, and Third Streets, with J and K Streets leading back. Among the principal merchants and traders of that winter, at Sacramento, were Sam Brannan and Hensley, Reading & Co.[142] For several years the site was annually flooded; but the people have persevered in building the levees, and afterward in raising all the streets, so that Sacramento is now a fine city, the capital of the State, and stands where, in 1848, was nothing but a dense mass of bushes, vines, and submerged land. The old fort has disappeared altogether.

During the fall of 1848, Warner, Ord, and I, camped on the bank of the American River, abreast of the fort, at what was known as the "Old Tan-Yard." I was cook, Ord cleaned up the dishes, and Warner looked after the horses; but Ord was deposed as scullion because he would only wipe the tin plates with a tuft of grass, according to the custom of the country, whereas Warner insisted on having them washed after each meal with hot water. Warner was in consequence promoted to scullion, and Ord became the hostler. We drew our rations in kind from the commissary at San Francisco, who sent them up to us by a boat; and we were thus enabled to dispense a generous hospitality to many a poor devil who otherwise would have had nothing to eat.

The winter of 1848–'49 was a period of intense activity throughout California. The rainy season was unfavorable to the operations of gold-mining, and was very hard upon the thousands of houseless men and women who dwelt in the mountains, and even in the towns. Most of the natives and old inhabitants had returned to their ranches and houses; yet there were not roofs enough in the country to shelter the thousands who had arrived by sea and by land. The news had gone forth to the whole civilized world that gold in fabulous quantities was to be had for the mere digging, and adventurers came pouring in blindly to seek their fortunes, without a thought of house or food. Yerba Buena had been converted into San Francisco. Sacramento City had been laid out, lots were being rapidly sold, and the town was being built up as an entrepot to the mines. Stockton also had been chosen as a convenient point for trading with the lower or southern mines. Captain Sutter was the sole proprietor of the former, and Captain Charles Weber was the owner of the site of Stockton, which was as yet known as "French Camp."[143]

[142] The other members of this firm included William Stone, W. D. Howard, Henry Mellus, and Talbot H. Green. Willis, *History of Sacramento County,* 67.

[143] Charles Weber (1814–1881) was born in Germany and arrived in California in 1841. He obtained a tract of land in the San Joaquin Valley and founded the city of Stockton, CA. George H. Tinkman, *California: Men and Events* (Stockton, CA: Record, 1915), 52*n.*

3

Early Recollections of California—(continued).

1849–1850.

The department headquarters still remained at Monterey, but, with the few soldiers, we had next to nothing to do. In midwinter we heard of the approach of a battalion of the Second Dragoons, under Major Lawrence Pike Graham, with Captains Rucker, Coutts, Campbell, and others, along.[1] So exhausted were they by their long march from Upper Mexico that we had to send relief to meet them as they approached. When this command reached Los Angeles, it was left there as the garrison, and Captain A. J. Smith's company of the First Dragoons was brought up to San Francisco.[2] We were also advised that the Second Infantry, Colonel B. Riley, would be sent out around Cape Horn in sailing-ships; that the Mounted Rifles, under Lieutenant-Colonel Loring, would march overland to Oregon; and that Brigadier-General Persifer F. Smith would come out in chief command on the Pacific coast.[3] It was also

[1] Lawrence P. Graham (1815–1905) and Daniel H. Rucker (1812–1910) were brevetted majors for their actions during the Mexican-American War. Cave J. Couts (1821–1874) graduated from the USMA in 1843 and served in the Mexican-American War as a first lieutenant in the 1st Dragoons. In 1848 he was assigned to frontier duty in California, where he remained for the rest of his life. Reuben P. Campbell (1818–1862) graduated from the USMA in 1840 and was brevetted captain for his actions in the Mexican-American War. He was stationed in California in 1848–1849, and later joined the Confederate Army at the outbreak of the Civil War. He was killed at the Battle of Gaines' Mill. *USMA,* 2:19, 50; *CWHC,* 262, 464.

[2] Acting as Mason's adjutant general, WTS gave A. J. Smith orders to move to San Francisco on Aug. 11, 1848. Executive Documents, "Message from the President of the United States," 31st Congress, 1st session (Washington, DC: William M. Belt, 1850), 613–614, 628.

[3] Bennet C. Riley (1787–1853) was a veteran of the War of 1812 and the Mexican-American War. The 2nd Inf. left St. Louis for New York in Sept. 1848 to set sail for California. William W. Loring (1818–1886) was appointed captain of the Second Mounted Riflemen at the outbreak of the Mexican-American War. He lost his left arm during the Battle of Chapultepec. In May 1849, Loring, along with his Mounted Riflemen regiment, escorted a group of white settlers from Missouri to the Oregon Territory. He later joined the Confederate Army in 1861.

known that a contract had been entered into with parties in New York and New Orleans for a monthly line of steamers from those cities to California, *via* Panama.[4] Lieutenant-Colonel Burton had come up from Lower California, and, as captain of the Third Artillery, he was assigned to command Company F, Third Artillery, at Monterey. Captain Warner remained at Sacramento, surveying; and Halleck, Murray, Ord, and I, boarded with Doña Augustias.[5] The season was unusually rainy and severe, but we passed the time with the usual round of dances and parties. The time fixed for the arrival of the mail-steamer was understood to be about January 1, 1849, but the day came and went without any tidings of her. Orders were given to Captain Burton to announce her arrival by firing a national salute, and each morning we listened for the guns from the fort. The month of January passed, and the greater part of February, too. As was usual, the army officers celebrated the 22d of February with a grand ball, given in the new stone school-house, which Alcalde Walter Colton had built.[6] It was

---

Persifor F. Smith (1798–1858) was promoted to major general during the Mexican-American War, and he took command as the military governor of California on Feb. 26, 1849. William H. Ellison, *A Self-Governing Dominion: California, 1849–1860* (Berkeley: University of California Press, 1950), 15; John C. Fredriksen, ed., *Civil War Almanac* (New York: Facts on File, 2007), s.v. "Loring, William W"; Edward H. Moseley and Paul C. Clark Jr., eds., *The A to Z of the United States–Mexican War* (Lanham, MD: Scarecrow Press, 1997), s.v. "Riley, Bennet"; James K. Polk, *The Diary of James K. Polk, 1845–1849,* ed. Milo M. Quaife (Chicago: A. C. McClurg, 1910), 1:413*n;* Frederick B. Shaw, *One Hundred and Forty Years of Service in Peace and War: History of the Second Infantry, United States Army* (Detroit: Strathmore, 1930), 262–263.

[4]The U.S. Mail Steamship Company, owned by George Law, obtained a contract from the federal government to carry travelers on a biweekly basis from New York and places in the Caribbean to the Panama isthmus. The Pacific Mail Steamship Company, owned by William H. Aspinwall, obtained the contract to carry travelers and mail from Panama to California. F. N. Otis, *History of the Panama Railroad and of the Pacific Mail Steamship Company* (New York: Harper, 1867), 16.

[5]Angustias de la Guerra (1815–1890) married Manuel Jimeno in 1833. Manuel left the family in 1853 and Angustias married James L. Ord in 1856. Rose M. Beebe and Robert M. Senkewicz, *Mariano Guadalupe Vallejo: Life in Spanish, Mexican, and American California* (Norman: University of Oklahoma Press, 2023), s.v. "Angustias de la Guerra (1815–90)."

[6]Although President's Day (George Washington's birthday) was not an official holiday in 1849, it was celebrated by the country's citizens. WTS attended the celebration at Colton Hall, the site of the state's First Constitutional Convention, with Angustias de la Guerra. Walter Colton (1797–1851), the first American alcalde of Monterey, serving from 1846 to 1849, completed work on Colton Hall in 1849. He wrote of the hall, "It is built of white stone, quarried

the largest and best hall then in California. The ball was really a handsome affair, and we kept it up nearly all night. The next morning we were at breakfast: present, Doña Augustias, and Manuelita,[7] Halleck, Murray, and myself. We were dull and stupid enough until a gun from the fort aroused us, then another and another. "The steamer!" exclaimed all, and, without waiting for hats or any thing, off we dashed. I reached the wharf hatless, but the doña sent my cap after me by a servant. The white puffs of smoke hung around the fort, mingled with the dense fog, which hid all the water of the bay, and well out to sea could be seen the black spars of some unknown vessel. At the wharf I found a group of soldiers and a small row-boat, which belonged to a brig at anchor in the bay. Hastily ordering a couple of willing soldiers to get in and take the oars, and Mr. Larkin and Mr. Hartnell asking to go along, we jumped in and pushed off. Steering our boat toward the spars, which loomed up above the fog clear and distinct, in about a mile we came to the black hull of the strange monster, the long-expected and most welcome steamer California. Her wheels were barely moving, for her pilot could not see the shore-line distinctly, though the hills and Point of Pines[8] could be clearly made out over the fog, and occasionally a glimpse of some white walls showed where the town lay. A "Jacob's ladder" was lowered for us from the steamer, and in a minute I scrambled up on deck, followed by Larkin and Hartnell, and we found ourselves in the midst of many old friends. There was Canby, the adjutant-general, who was to take my place; Charley Hoyt, my cousin; General Persifer F. Smith and wife; Gibbs, his aide-de-camp; Major Ogden, of the Engineers, and wife; and, indeed, many old Californians, among them Alfred Robinson, and Frank Ward with his pretty bride.[9] By the

---

from a neighboring hill and which easily takes the shape you desire. The lower apartments are for schools; the hall over them, seventy by thirty feet, is for public assemblies." Anna G. Andresen, *Historic Landmarks of Monterey, California* (self-pub., 1917), 20–22; Rose M. Beebe and Robert Senkewicz, trans. and eds., *Testimonios: Early California through the Eyes of Women, 1815–1848* (Norman: University of Oklahoma Press, 2006), 293; Alissandra Dramov, *Carmel by the Sea: The Early Years (1903–1913)* (Bloomington, IN: AuthorHouse, 2012), 39; Charles R. Schultz, *Forty-Niners: 'Round the Horn* (Columbia: University of South Carolina Press, 1999), 319.

[7] Manuela Jimeno (1833–1851) was the oldest daughter of Angustias de la Guerra and Manuel Jimeno. She died from complications of childbirth in 1851. Beebe and Senkewicz, *Testimonios*, 293.

[8] Point of Pines, also known as Point Pinos, was approximately three miles west of Monterey. George Davidson, *The Discovery of San Francisco Bay* (San Francisco: F. F. Partidge, 1907), 31.

[9] Edward R. S. Canby (1817–1873) graduated from the USMA in 1839. He served in the Mexican-American War and as the adjutant general of the Pacific Division from 1849 to 1851.

time the ship was fairly at anchor we had answered a million of questions about gold and the state of the country; and, learning that the ship was out of fuel, had informed the captain (Marshall) that there was abundance of pine-wood, but no willing hands to cut it;[10] that no man could be hired at less than an ounce of gold a day, unless the soldiers would volunteer to do it for some agreed-upon price. As for coal, there was not a pound in Monterey, or anywhere else in California. Vessels with coal were known to be *en route* around Cape Horn, but none had yet reached California.

The arrival of this steamer was the beginning of a new epoch on the Pacific coast; yet there she lay, helpless, without coal or fuel. The native Californians, who had never seen a steamship, stood for days on the beach looking at her, with the universal exclamation, "*Tan feo!*"—how ugly!—and she was truly ugly when compared with the clean, well-sparred frigates and sloops-of-war that had hitherto been seen on the North Pacific coast. It was first supposed it would take ten days to get wood enough to prosecute her voyage, and therefore all the passengers who could took up their quarters on shore. Major

---

Charles H. Hoyt (1825–1897), the son of WTS's uncle Charles Hoyt, was later brevetted brigadier general for his service in the U.S. Army during the Civil War. Frances Jeanette Bureau (1804–1852) was the daughter of a French New Orleans merchant named Francois Bureau. She married Persifor Smith in 1822. Alfred Gibbs (1823–1868) graduated from the USMA in 1846. After service in the Mexican-American War, he served as Persifor F. Smith's aide-de-camp from 1848 to 1856. Cornelius A. Ogden (1799–1853) graduated from the USMA in 1819 and was promoted to major in the U.S. Army Corps of Engineers in 1838. He married Matilda Seals (1804–1887) in 1824. Alfred Robinson (1806–1895) first arrived in California in 1829 and worked for the Pacific Mail Steamship Company. Henriette Zimmerman-Ward (1821–1849) was the daughter of J. C. Zimmerman. She died suddenly in May 1849. Mary D. Alsworth, *Gleanings from Alta California* (Rancho Cordova, CA: Dean, 1982), 13; Durwood Ball, *Army Regulars on the Western Frontier, 1848–1861* (Norman: University of Oklahoma Press, 2001), 67; *USMA,* 1:206–207, 2:18–20, 288–290; *CWHC,* 307; Joseph S. Harris, *Record of the Smith Family* (Philadelphia: Dalcassian, 1906), 65; David W. Hoyt, *A Genealogical History of the Hoyt, Haight, and Hight Families* (Boston: Providence, 1871), 237; Howard L. Leckey, *The Tenmile Country and Its Pioneer Families* (Waynesburg, PA: Greene County Historical Society, 1997), 355; Alfred Robinson, *Life in California,* ed. Joseph Gaer (San Francisco: William Doxey, 1891), 21.

[10] While anchored in Panama Bay on Jan. 17, 1849, John T. Marshall took command of the steamship *California.* The ship ran out of coal approximately 300 miles before reaching Monterey. Some of the wood on board was used to power the boilers. Jay Monaghan, *Chile, Peru, and the California Gold Rush of 1849* (Berkeley: University of California Press, 2022), 120; James M. Spitze, *Personal Memoranda: The Journal of His Voyage to California* (Berkeley: Friends of the Bancroft Library, University of California, 2007), 36.

Canby relieved me, and took the place I had held so long as adjutant-general of the Department of California. The time seemed most opportune for me to leave the service, as I had several splendid offers of employment and of partnership, and, accordingly, I made my written resignation; but General Smith put his veto upon it, saying that he was to command the Division of the Pacific, while General Riley was to have the Department of California, and Colonel Loring that of Oregon.[11] He wanted me as his adjutant-general, because of my familiarity with the country, and knowledge of its then condition. At the time, he had on his staff Gibbs as aide-de-camp, and Fitzgerald as quartermaster.[12] He also had along with him quite a retinue of servants, hired with a clear contract to serve him for a whole year after reaching California, every one of whom deserted, except a young black fellow named Isaac. Mrs. Smith, a pleasant but delicate Louisiana lady, had a white maid-servant, in whose fidelity she had unbounded confidence; but this girl was married to a perfect stranger, and off before she had even landed in San Francisco. It was, therefore, finally arranged that, on the California, I was to accompany General Smith to San Francisco as his adjutant-general. I accordingly sold some of my horses, and arranged for others to go up by land; and from that time I became fairly enlisted in the military family of General Persifer F. Smith.

I parted with my old commander, Colonel Mason, with sincere regret. To me he had ever been kind and considerate, and, while stern, honest to a fault, he was the very embodiment of the principle of fidelity to the interests of the General Government. He possessed a native strong intellect, and far more knowledge of the principles of civil government and law than he got credit for. In private and public expenditures he was extremely economical, but not penurious. In cases where the officers had to contribute money for parties and entertainments, he always gave a double share, because of his allowance of double rations. During our frequent journeys, I was always caterer, and paid all the bills. In settling with him he required a written statement of the items of account, but never disputed one of them. During our time, California was, as now, full of a bold, enterprising, and speculative set of men,

[11] On June 12, 1849, WTS wrote a resignation letter to Persifor F. Smith in response to not receiving a promotion. He wrote, "Self-respect compels me therefore to quit the profession which in time of war and trouble I have failed to merit . . ." John F. Marszalek, *Sherman: A Soldier's Passion for Order* (New York: Free Press, 1993), 75.

[12] Edward H. Fitzgerald (1815–1860) was brevetted major for his actions during the Mexican-American War and was transferred to the 1st Dragoons in Aug. 1849. Thomas H. S. Hamersly, ed., *Complete Army Register of the United States (1779–1879)* (self-pub., 1880), 438–439.

who were engaged in every sort of game to make money. I know that Colonel Mason was beset by them to use his position to make a fortune for himself and his friends; but he never bought land or town-lots, because, he said, it was his place to hold the public estate for the Government as free and unencumbered by claims as possible; and when I wanted him to stop the public-land sales in San Francisco, San José, etc., he would not; for, although he did not believe the titles given by the alcaldes worth a cent, yet they aided to settle the towns and public lands, and he thought, on the whole, the Government would be benefited thereby. The same thing occurred as to the gold-mines. He never took a title to a town-lot, unless it was one, of no real value, from Alcalde Colton, in Monterey, of which I have never heard since. He did take a share in the store which Warner, Bestor, and I, opened at Coloma, paid his share of the capital, five hundred dollars, and received his share of the profits, fifteen hundred dollars.[13] I think also he took a share in a venture to China with Larkin and others; but, on leaving California, he was glad to sell out without profit or loss. In the stern discharge of his duty he made some bitter enemies, among them Henry M. Naglee, who, in the newspapers of the day, endeavored to damage his fair fame.[14] But, knowing him intimately, I am certain that he is entitled to all praise for having so controlled the affairs of the country that, when his successor arrived, all things were so disposed that a civil form of government was an easy matter of adjustment. Colonel Mason was relieved by General Riley some time in April, and left California in the steamer of the 1st May for Washington and St. Louis, where he died of cholera in the summer of 1850, and his body is buried in Bellefontaine Cemetery.[15] His widow afterward married Major (since General) Don Carlos Buell, and is now living in Kentucky.[16]

[13] The store was in business from the fall of 1848 until the spring of 1849. Marszalek, *Sherman,* 72.

[14] On June 15, 1848, Colonel Mason had Naglee arrested for the execution of two prisoners of war without a trial. Naglee was released after Pres. James K. Polk issued a general pardon to military officers acting during the Mexican-American War. Hunt Janin and Ursula Carlson, *The California Campaigns of the U.S.-Mexican War, 1846–1848* (Jefferson, NC: McFarland, 2015), 130.

[15] In the first edition of the memoirs (1875), WTS incorrectly identified the year of Mason's death as 1849. Bennet Riley relieved Richard Mason on Apr. 13, 1849. Mason later died in St. Louis on July 25, 1850. Ball, *Army Regulars,* 9; Leigh H. Irvine, *A History of the New California* (New York: Lewis, 1905), 1:61.

[16] Margaret Hunter (1821–1881) married Don Carlos Buell in 1851 in St. Louis. She died of cancer in Airlie, KY. Albert Welles, *History of the Buell Family in England* (New York: Society

In overhauling the hold of the steamer California, as she lay at anchor in Monterey Bay, a considerable amount of coal was found under some heavy duplicate machinery. With this, and such wood as had been gathered, she was able to renew her voyage. The usual signal was made, and we all went on board. About the 1st of March we entered the Heads, and anchored off San Francisco, near the United States line-of-battle-ship Ohio, Commodore T. Ap Catesby Jones.[17] As was the universal custom of the day, the crew of the California deserted her; and she lay for months unable to make a trip back to Panama, as was expected of her.[18] As soon as we reached San Francisco, the first thing was to secure an office and a house to live in. The weather was rainy and stormy, and snow even lay on the hills back of the Mission. Captain Folsom, the quartermaster, agreed to surrender for our office the old adobe custom-house, on the upper corner of the plaza, as soon as he could remove his papers and effects down to one of his warehouses on the beach; and he also rented for us as quarters the old Hudson Bay Company house on Montgomery Street, which had been used by Howard & Mellus as a store, and at that very time they were moving their goods into a larger brick building just completed for them. As these changes would take some time, General Smith and Colonel Ogden, with their wives, accepted the hospitality offered by Commodore Jones on board the Ohio. I opened the office at the custom-house, and Gibbs, Fitzgerald, and some others of us, slept in the loft of the Hudson Bay Company house until the lower part was cleared of Howard's store, after which General Smith and the ladies moved in. There we had a general mess, and the efforts at house-keeping were simply ludicrous. One servant after another, whom General Smith had brought from New Orleans, with a solemn promise to stand by him for one whole year, deserted without a word of notice or explanation, and in a few days none remained but little Isaac. The ladies had no maid or attendants; and the general, commanding all the mighty forces of the United States on the Pacific coast, had to scratch to get one good meal a day for his family! He was a gentleman of fine social

Library, 1881), 256; "Burial of the Wife of a War Hero," *Times-Picayune* (New Orleans), Aug. 17, 1881, 6.

[17] Contrary to WTS's claim, Commodore Cornelius Stribling was in command of the *Ohio* in 1849. He relieved Commodore Jones on Aug. 19, 1848. *Dictionary of American Naval Fighting Ships* (Washington, DC: GPO, 1969), s.v. "Ship-of-the-Line *Ohio.*"

[18] The *California* left San Francisco on May 15, 1849, with 365 passengers and thirty-six crew members. Ernest A. Wiltsee, *Gold Rush Steamers of the Pacific* (San Francisco: Grabhorn, 1938), 14.

qualities, genial and gentle, and joked at every thing. Poor Mrs. Smith and Mrs. Ogden did not bear it so philosophically. Gibbs, Fitzgerald, and I, could cruise around and find a meal, which cost three dollars, at some of the many restaurants which had sprung up out of red-wood boards and cotton lining; but the general and ladies could not go out, for ladies were *rara aves* at that day in California. Isaac was cook, chamber-maid, and every thing, thoughtless of himself, and struggling, out of the slimmest means, to compound a breakfast for a large and hungry family. Breakfast would be announced any time between ten and twelve, and dinner according to circumstances. Many a time have I seen General Smith, with a can of preserved meat in his hands, going toward the house, take off his hat on meeting a negro, and, on being asked the reason of his politeness, he would answer that they were the only real gentlemen in California. I confess that the fidelity of Colonel Mason's boy "Aaron," and of General Smith's boy "Isaac," at a time when every white man laughed at promises as something made to be broken, has given me a kindly feeling of respect for the negroes, and makes me hope that they will find an honorable "status" in the jumble of affairs in which we now live. That was a dull, hard winter in San Francisco; the rains were heavy, and the mud fearful.[19] I have seen mules stumble in the street, and drown in the liquid mud! Montgomery Street had been filled up with brush and clay, and I always dreaded to ride on horseback along it, because the mud was so deep that a horse's legs would become entangled in the bushes below, and the rider was likely to be thrown and drowned in the mud. The only sidewalks were made of stepping-stones of empty boxes, and here and there a few planks with barrel-staves nailed on. All the town lay along Montgomery Street, from Sacramento to Jackson, and about the plaza. Gambling was the chief occupation of the people. While they were waiting for the cessation of the rainy season, and for the beginning of spring, all sorts of houses were being put up, but of the most flimsy kind, and all were stores, restaurants, or gambling-saloons. Any room twenty by sixty feet would rent for a thousand dollars a month. I had, as my pay, seventy dollars a month, and no one would even try to hire a servant under three hundred dollars. Had it not been for the fifteen hundred dollars I had made in the store at Coloma, I could not have lived through the winter. About the 1st of April arrived the steamer Oregon; but her captain

[19] It rained a total of forty days in San Francisco from Nov. 1849 through Feb. 1850. Glen Conner, *History of Weather Observations, San Francisco, California, 1844–1948* (Ashville, NC: National Climatic Data Center, 2005), 17 (chart).

(Pearson)[20] knew what was the state of affairs on shore, and ran his steamer alongside the line-of-battle-ship Ohio at Saucelito, and obtained the privilege of leaving his crew on board as "prisoners" until he was ready to return to sea. Then, discharging his passengers and getting coal out of some of the ships which had arrived, he retook his crew out of limbo and carried the first regular mail back to Panama early in April. In regular order arrived the third steamer, the Panama; and, as the vessels were arriving with coal, the California was enabled to hire a crew and get off. From that time forward these three ships constituted the regular line of mail-steamers, which has been kept up ever since. By the steamer Oregon arrived out Major R. P. Hammond, J. M. Williams, James Blair, and others;[21] also the gentlemen who, with Major Ogden, were to compose a joint commission to select the sites for the permanent forts and navy-yard of California. This commission was composed of Majors Ogden, Smith, and Leadbetter, of the army, and Captains Goldsborough, Van Brunt, and Blunt, of the navy.[22] These officers, after a most careful study

[20] Robert H. Pearson (1818–1868) commanded the *Oregon,* the second steamer commissioned by the Pacific Mail Steamship Company. Samuel H. Willey and James M. Spitze, *Personal Memoranda: The Journal of His Voyage to California in 1848–1849* (Berkeley: Friends of the Bancroft Library, University of California, 2007), 36.

[21] James Williams (1814–1858) moved to California with his brothers in 1843. He married Mary Patterson, the daughter of Thomas O. Larkin, in Monterey in 1845. James Blair (1819–1853), the son of prominent politician Francis Preston Blair, took a leave of absence from the U.S. Navy in 1849 and moved to California, where he made a living as a steamboat operator. Within his first year, he amassed a net worth of $60,000. When the *Oregon* arrived in San Francisco, it had approximately 350 passengers onboard, including John W. Geary (1819–1873), the first mayor of San Francisco, and Albert Williams (1809–1893), the founder and first pastor of the First Presbyterian Church in San Francisco. Virginia J. Laas, *Love and Power in the Nineteenth Century* (Fayetteville: University of Arkansas Press, 1998), 2; Timonthy Lemucchi, *The Williams Brothers: Missouri to California by Horseback in 1843* (Pittsburgh: Dorrance, 2020), 1, 59; U.S. Census Office, *Report on the Agencies of Transportation in the United States* (Washington, DC: GPO, 1883), 22; Albert Williams, *A Pioneer Pastorate and Times* (San Francisco: Wallace and Hassett, 1879), 6–9.

[22] John L. Smith (1788–1858) was the senior member of the commission. Danville Leadbetter (1811–1866) graduated from the USMA in 1836, and as a captain he served on the Board of Engineers for fortifications on the Pacific Coast from 1851 to 1853. Louis M. Goldsborough (1805–1877) joined the U.S. Navy at the age of seven and was assigned sea duty at the age of eleven. He served as the superintendent at the U.S. Naval Academy from 1853 to 1857. Gershom J. Van Brunt (1798–1863) entered the U.S. Navy in 1818 and was promoted to commodore in 1846. He retired

of the whole subject, selected Mare Island for the navy-yard, and "Benicia" for the storehouses and arsenals of the army. The Pacific Mail Steamship Company also selected Benicia as their depot. Thus was again revived the old struggle for supremacy of these two points as the site of the future city of the Pacific. Meantime, however, San Francisco had secured the *name.* About six hundred ships were anchored there without crews, and could not get away; and there the city *was,* and *had* to be.

Nevertheless, General Smith, being disinterested and unprejudiced, decided on Benicia as the point where the city ought to be, and where the army headquarters should be. By the Oregon there arrived at San Francisco a man who deserves mention here—Baron Steinberger. He had been a great cattle-dealer in the United States, and boasted that he had helped to break the United States Bank, by being indebted to it five million dollars! At all events, he was a splendid-looking fellow, and brought with him from Washington a letter to General Smith and another for Commodore Jones, to the effect that he was a man of enlarged experience in beef; that the authorities in Washington knew that there existed in California large herds of cattle, which were only valuable for their hides and tallow; that it was of great importance to the Government that this beef should be cured and salted so as to be of use to the army and navy, obviating the necessity of shipping salt-beef around Cape Horn. I know he had such a letter from the Secretary of War, Marcy, to General Smith, for it passed into my custody, and I happened to be in Commodore Jones's cabin when the baron presented the one for him from the Secretary of the Navy.[23] The baron was anxious to pitch in at once, and said that all he needed to start with were salt and barrels. After some inquiries of his purser, the commodore promised to let him have the barrels with their salt, as fast as they were emptied by the crew. Then the baron explained that he could get a nice lot of cattle from Don Timoteo Murphy, at the Mission of San Rafael, on the north side of the bay, but he could not get a boat and crew

---

from the Navy in 1863 and died soon after. Simon F. Blunt (c. 1818–1854) married Ellen Lloyd Key, daughter of famed American poet Francis Scott Key, in 1846. He commanded the Pacific Mail Steamship Company's ship *Winfield Scott* when it wrecked in 1853. *USMA,* 1:630; *CWHC,* 258, 541; Jessie B. Frémont, *The Letters of Jessie Benton Frémont,* ed. Pamela Herr and Mary Lee Spence (Urbana: University of Illinois Press, 1993), 49; Hamersly, *Complete Army Register,* 768; Erwin N. Thompson, *Historic Resource Study: Seacoast Fortifications, San Francisco Harbor . . .* (Denver: U.S. Department of the Interior, 1979), 20.

[23] John Y. Mason (1799–1859) served as U.S. secretary of the navy under Pres. James K. Polk from 1846 to 1849. *Dictionary of American Biography,* 2nd ed., s.v. "Mason, John Young."

to handle them. Under the authority from the Secretary of the Navy, the commodore then promised him the use of a boat and crew, until he (the baron) could find and purchase a suitable one for himself. Then the baron opened the first regular butcher-shop in San Francisco, on the wharf about the foot of Broadway or Pacific Street, where we could buy at twenty-five or fifty cents a pound the best roasts, steaks, and cuts of beef, which had cost him nothing, for he never paid anybody if he could help it, and he soon cleaned poor Don Timoteo out. At first, every boat of his, in coming down from the San Rafael, touched at the Ohio, and left the best beefsteaks and roasts for the commodore, but soon the baron had enough money to dispense with the borrowed boat, and set up for himself, and from this small beginning, step by step, he rose in a few months to be one of the richest and most influential men in San Francisco; but in his wild speculations he was at last caught, and became helplessly bankrupt. He followed General Fremont to St. Louis in 1861, where I saw him, but soon afterward he died a pauper in one of the hospitals. When General Smith had his headquarters in San Francisco, in the spring of 1849, Steinberger gave dinners worthy any baron of old; and when, in after-years, I was a banker there, he used to borrow of me small sums of money in repayment for my share of these feasts; and somewhere among my old packages I hold one of his confidential notes for two hundred dollars, but on the whole I got off easily. I have no doubt that, if this man's history could be written out, it would present phases as wonderful as any of romance; but in my judgment he was a dangerous man, without any true-sense of honor or honesty.[24]

Little by little the rains of that season grew less and less, and the hills once more became green and covered with flowers. It became perfectly evident that no family could live in San Francisco on such a salary as Uncle Sam allowed his most favored officials; so General Smith and Major Ogden concluded to send their families back to the United States, and afterward we men-folks could take to camp and live on our rations. The Second Infantry had arrived, and had been distributed, four companies to Monterey, and the rest somewhat as Stevenson's regiment had been. A. J. Smith's company of dragoons was sent up to Sonoma, whither General Smith had resolved to move our headquarters.

[24] John B. Steinberger (1802–1862) arrived in California in 1849 and obtained a ten-year lease from the government for land in San Francisco between Broad and Pacific Streets. He died of dysentery in St. Louis. John W. Dwinelle, *The Colonial History of the City of San Francisco* (San Francisco: Towne and Bacon, 1866), 261–262; "The Late Baron Steinberger," *Times-Picayune* (New Orleans), Nov. 9, 1862, 4; "Personal," *New York Times,* Oct. 21, 1862, 2.

On the steamer which sailed about May 1st (I think the California), we embarked, the ladies for home and we for Monterey. At Monterey we went on shore, and Colonel Mason, who meantime had been relieved by General Riley, went on board, and the steamer departed for Panama. Of all that party I alone am alive.

General Riley had, with his family, taken the house which Colonel Mason had formerly used, and Major Canby and wife had secured rooms at Alvarado's. Captain Kane was quartermaster, and had his family in the house of a man named Garner, near the redoubt.[25] Burton and Company F were still at the fort; the four companies of the Second Infantry were quartered in the barracks, the same building in which we had had our headquarters; and the company officers were quartered in hired buildings near by. General Smith and his aide, Captain Gibbs, went to Larkin's house, and I was at my old rooms at Doña Augustias. As we intended to go back to San Francisco by land and afterward to travel a good deal, General Smith gave me the necessary authority to fit out the party. There happened to be several trains of horses and mules in town, so I purchased about a dozen horses and mules at two hundred dollars a head, on account of the Quartermaster's Department, and we had them kept under guard in the quartermaster's *corral.*

I remember one night being in the quarters of Lieutenant Alfred Sully, where nearly all the officers of the garrison were assembled, listening to Sully's stories. Lieutenant Derby, "Squibob," was one of the number, as also Fred Steele, "Neighbor" Jones,[26] and others, when, just after "tattoo," the orderly-

[25] Juan Bautista Alvarado (1809–1882) was the Mexican governor of California from 1836 to 1842. In 1845 he was appointed administrator of the Customs House in Monterey. Elias K. Kane (1822–1853) graduated from the USMA in 1841 and served as a quartermaster in California from 1847 to 1852. William R. Garner (1803–1849) was born in England and immigrated to California in 1824. He owned a lumber business and a boardinghouse in Monterey in the late 1840s. He was killed by Indigenous people in 1849. Hubert H. Bancroft, *Chronicles of the Builders of the Commonwealth* (San Francisco: History Company, 1892), 2:171; Robert E. Cowan, "Reviewed Work: *Letters from California,* 1846," *California Historical Society Quarterly* 4, no. 1 (Mar. 1925): 90; *USMA,* 2:107.

[26] Alfred Sully (1820–1879) graduated from the USMA in 1841 and was stationed at Monterey for frontier duty from 1849 to 1852. George H. Derby (1823–1861) graduated from the USMA in 1846. While at the academy, he was given the nickname "Squibob," which he later used as one of his literary pseudonyms. He authored the humorous books *Phoenixiana* (published 1856) and *The Squibob Papers* (published 1865) under the name John Phoenix. He died of illness. Frederick Steele (1819–1868) graduated from the USMA in 1843 and was brevetted captain for his actions during the Mexican-American War. He was stationed in California

sergeants came to report the result of "tattoo" roll-call; one reported five men absent, another eight, and so on, until it became certain that twenty-eight men had deserted; and they were so bold and open in their behavior that it amounted to defiance. They had deliberately slung their knapsacks and started for the gold-mines. Dr. Murray and I were the only ones present who were familiar with the country, and I explained how easy they could all be taken by a party going out at once to Salinas Plain, where the country was so open and level that a rabbit could not cross without being seen; that the deserters could not go to the mines without crossing that plain, and could not reach it before daylight. All agreed that the whole regiment would desert if these men were not brought back. Several officers volunteered on the spot to go after them; and, as the soldiers could not be trusted, it was useless to send any but officers in pursuit. Some one went to report the affair to the adjutant-general, Canby, and he to General Riley. I waited some time, and, as the thing grew cold, I thought it was given up, and went to my room and to bed.

About midnight I was called up and informed that there were seven officers willing to go, but the difficulty was to get horses and saddles. I went down to Larkin's house and got General Smith to consent that we might take the horses I had bought for our trip. It was nearly three o'clock A. M. before we were all mounted and ready. I had a musket which I used for hunting. With this I led off at a canter, followed by the others. About six miles out, by the faint moon, I saw ahead of us in the sandy road some blue coats, and, fearing lest they might resist or escape into the dense bushes which lined the road, I halted and found with me Paymaster Hill, Captain N. H. Davis, and Lieutenant John Hamilton.[27] We waited some time for the others, viz.,

---

from 1848 to 1853. David R. Jones (1825–1863) graduated from the USMA in 1846. After serving in the Mexican-American War, he arrived in California in 1849, where he remained until 1851. He was nicknamed "Neighbor" because of his pleasant demeanor. He joined the Confederate Army at the start of the Civil War and died of natural causes in June 1863. *USMA,* 2:96–98, 183–184, 261–262, 288; Gary W. Gallagher, ed., *The Shenandoah Valley Campaign of 1862* (Chapel Hill: University of North Carolina Press, 2003), 194; George R. Stewart, *John Phoenix, Esq., The Veritable Squibob: A Life of Captain George H. Derby, U.S.A.* (New York: Holt, 1937), 27, 78.

[27] Henry Hill (c. 1816–c. 1866) was promoted to major in Nov. 1847. Nelson H. Davis (1821–1890) graduated from the USMA in 1846 and was brevetted first lieutenant for his actions during the Mexican-American War. He arrived in California in 1849 and remained until 1854. John Hamilton (1823–1900) graduated from the USMA in 1847. He served in the Mexican-American War and was later stationed in Monterey from 1849 to 1851. *USMA,* 2:298–299, 305; *Register of the Army of the United States for 1850* (Washington, DC: C. Alexander, 1850), 7.

Canby, Murray, Gibbs, and Sully, to come up, but as they were not in sight we made a dash up the road and captured six of the deserters, who were Germans, with heavy knapsacks on, trudging along the deep, sandy road. They had not expected pursuit, had not heard our horses, and were accordingly easily taken. Finding myself the senior officer present, I ordered Lieutenant Hamilton to search the men and then to march them back to Monterey, suspecting, as was the fact, that the rest of our party had taken a road that branched off a couple of miles back. Daylight broke as we reached the Salinas River, twelve miles out, and there the trail was broad and fresh leading directly out on the Salinas Plain. This plain is about five miles wide, and then the ground becomes somewhat broken. The trail continued very plain, and I rode on at a gallop to where there was an old adobe-ranch on the left of the road, with the head of a lagoon, or pond, close by. I saw one or two of the soldiers getting water at the pond, and others up near the house. I had the best horse and was considerably ahead, but on looking back could see Hill and Davis coming up behind at a gallop. I motioned to them to hurry forward, and turned my horse across the head of the pond, knowing the ground well, as it was a favorite place for shooting geese and ducks. Approaching the house, I ordered the men who were outside to go in. They did not know me personally, and exchanged glances, but I had my musket cocked, and, as the two had seen Davis and Hill coming up pretty fast, they obeyed. Dismounting, I found the house full of deserters, and there was no escape for them. They naturally supposed that I had a strong party with me, and when I ordered them to "fall in" they obeyed from habit. By the time Hill and Davis came up I had them formed in two ranks, the front rank facing about, and I was taking away their bayonets, pistols, etc. We disarmed them, destroying a musket and several pistols, and, on counting them, we found that we three had taken eighteen, which, added to the six first captured, made twenty-four. We made them sling their knapsacks and begin their homeward march. It was near night when we got back, so that these deserters had traveled nearly forty miles since "tattoo" of the night before. The other party had captured three, so that only one man had escaped. I doubt not this prevented the desertion of the bulk of the Second Infantry that spring, for at that time so demoralizing was the effect of the gold-mines that everybody not in the military service justified desertion, because a soldier, if free, could earn more money in a day than he received per month. Not only did soldiers and sailors desert, but captains and masters of ships actually abandoned their vessels and cargoes to try their luck at the mines. Preachers and professors forgot their creeds and took to trade, and even to keeping gambling-houses. I remember that one of our regular soldiers, named Reese, in deserting stole a favorite double-barreled gun of mine, and when the orderly-sergeant of the company, Carson,[28] was going on furlough, I asked him when he came across Reese to try and get my gun back. When he returned he told me that he had found Reese and offered him a hundred dollars for my gun, but Reese sent me word that he liked the gun, and would not take a hundred dollars for it. Soldiers or sailors who could reach the mines were universally shielded by the miners, so that it was next to useless to attempt their recapture. In due season General Persifer Smith, Gibbs, and I, with some hired packers, started back for San Francisco, and soon after we transferred our headquarters to Sonoma. About this time Major Joseph Hooker arrived from the East—the regular adjutant-general of the division—relieved me, and I became thereafter one of General Smith's regular aides-de-camp.[29]

As there was very little to do, General Smith encouraged us to go into any business that would enable us to make money. R. P. Hammond, James Blair, and I, made a contract to survey for Colonel J. D. Stevenson his newly-projected city of "New York of the Pacific," situated at the month of the San Joaquin River. The contract embraced, also, the making of soundings and the marking out of a channel through Suisun Bay. We hired, in San Francisco, a small metallic boat, with a sail, laid in some stores, and proceeded to the United States ship Ohio, anchored at Saucelito, where we borrowed a sailor-boy and lead-lines with which to sound the channel. We sailed up to Benicia, and, at General Smith's request, we surveyed and marked the line dividing the city of Benicia from the government reserve. We then sounded the bay back and forth, and staked out the best channel up Suisun Bay, from which Blair made out sailing directions. We then made the preliminary surveys of the city of "New York of the Pacific," all of which were duly plotted; and for this work we each received from Stevenson five hundred dollars and ten or fifteen lots. I sold

[28] Possibly James H. Carson (1821–1853), who was a second sergeant in the 3rd Art., Co. F. In 1848 he deserted from the U.S. Army to dig for gold while on furlough. Before his death, he published thirty-three articles in a Stockton newspaper which detailed his experiences in California. Peter Browning, ed., *Bright Gem of the Western Seas: California, 1846–1852* (Lafayette: Great West Books, 1991), xiii–xvi.

[29] Joseph Hooker (1815–1879) graduated from the USMA in 1837 and was the assistant adjutant general of the Pacific Division from 1849 to 1851. He became a major general in the U.S. Army during the Civil War. WTS served as Persifor Smith's aide-de-camp and acting assistant adjutant general of the Pacific Division from Feb. 27, 1849, to Jan. 1, 1850. *USMA,* 1:685–687; 2:27.

enough lots to make up another five hundred dollars, and let the balance go; for the city of "New York of the Pacific" never came to any thing.[30] Indeed, cities at the time were being projected by speculators all round the bay and all over the country.

While we were surveying at "New York of the Pacific," occurred one of those little events that showed the force of the gold-fever. We had a sailor-boy with us, about seventeen years old, who cooked our meals and helped work the boat. On shore, we had the sail spread so as to shelter us against the wind and dew. One morning I awoke about daylight, and looked out to see if our sailor-boy was at work getting breakfast; but he was not at the fire at all. Getting up, I discovered that he had converted a *tule-bolsa* into a sail-boat, and was sailing for the gold-mines. He was astride this *bolsa,* with a small parcel of bread and meat done up in a piece of cloth; another piece of cloth, such as we used for making our signal-stations, he had fixed into a sail; and with a paddle he was directing his precarious craft right out into the broad bay, to follow the general direction of the schooners and boats that he knew were ascending the Sacramento River. He was about a hundred yards from the shore. I jerked up my gun, and hailed him to come back. After a moment's hesitation, he let go his sheet and began to paddle back. This *bolsa* was nothing but a bundle of *tule,* or bullrush, bound together with grass-ropes in the shape of a cigar, about ten feet long and about two feet through the butt. With these the California Indians cross streams of considerable size. When he came ashore, I gave him a good overhauling for attempting to desert, and put him to work getting breakfast. In due time we returned him to his ship, the Ohio.

Subsequently, I made a bargain with Mr. Hartnell to survey his ranch at Cosumnes River, Sacramento Valley. Ord and a young citizen, named Seton, were associated with me in this. I bought of Rodman M. Price[31] a surveyor's compass, chain, etc., and, in San Francisco, a small wagon and harness. Availing ourselves of a schooner, chartered to carry Major Miller[32] and two companies of the Second Infantry from San Francisco to Stockton, we got up to our destina-

[30] The "New York of the Pacific" is now the city of Pittsburg, CA. Mel Scott, *The San Francisco Bay Area: A Metropolis in Perspective* (Berkeley: University of California Press, 1985), 29.

[31] Rodman M. Price (1816–1894) was a purser in the U.S. Navy and was stationed in San Francisco. He was a delegate to the California Constitutional Convention in 1849 and was later elected governor of New Jersey. *A Biographical Congressional Directory, 1774–1903* (Washington, DC: GPO, 1903), s.v. "Price, Rodman M."

[32] Albert S. Miller (1803–1852) graduated from the USMA in 1823 and was promoted to major for his actions during the Mexican-American War. *USMA,* 1:318.

tion at little cost.[33] I recall an occurrence that happened when the schooner was anchored in Carquinez Straits, opposite the soldiers' camp on shore. We were waiting for daylight and a fair wind; the schooner lay anchored at an ebb-tide, and about daylight Ord and I had gone ashore for something. Just as we were pulling off from shore, we heard the loud shouts of the men, and saw them all running down toward the water. Our attention thus drawn, we saw something swimming in the water, and pulled toward it, thinking it a coyote; but we soon recognized a large grizzly bear, swimming directly across the channel. Not having any weapon, we hurriedly pulled for the schooner, calling out, as we neared it, "A bear! a bear!" It so happened that Major Miller was on deck, washing his face and hands. He ran rapidly to the bow of the vessel, took the musket from the hands of the sentinel, and fired at the bear, as he passed but a short distance ahead of the schooner. The bear rose, made a growl or howl, but continued his course. As we scrambled up the port-side to get our guns, the mate, with a crew, happened to have a boat on the starboard-side, and, armed only with a hatchet, they pulled up alongside the bear, and the mate struck him in the head with the hatchet. The bear turned, tried to get into the boat, but the mate struck his claws with repeated blows, and made him let go. After several passes with him, the mate actually killed the bear, got a rope round him, and towed him alongside the schooner, where he was hoisted on deck. The carcass weighed over six hundred pounds. It was found that Major Miller's shot had struck the bear in the lower jaw, and thus disabled him. Had it not been for this, the bear would certainly have upset the boat and drowned all in it. As it was, however, his meat served us a good turn in our trip up to Stockton. At Stockton we disembarked our wagon, provisions, and instruments.

There I bought two fine mules at three hundred dollars each, and we hitched up and started for the Cosumnes River. About twelve miles off was the Mokelumne, a wide, bold stream, with a canoe as a ferry-boat. We took our wagon to pieces, and ferried it and its contents across, and then drove our mules into the water. In crossing, one mule became entangled in the rope of the other, and for a time we thought he was a gone mule; but at last he revived and we hitched up. The mules were both pack-animals; neither had ever before seen a wagon. Young Seton also was about as green, and had never handled a mule. We put on the harness, and began to hitch them in, when one of the mules turned his head, saw the wagon, and started. We held on tight, but the beast did not stop until he had shivered the tongue-pole into a

[33] WTS started a two-month furlough on May 15, 1849, to pursue multiple surveying jobs. Marszalek, *Sherman,* 74.

dozen fragments. The fact was, that Seton had hitched the traces before he had put on the blind-bridle. There was considerable swearing done, but that would not mend the pole. There was no place nearer than Sutter's Fort to repair damages, so we were put to our wits' end. We first sent back a mile or so, and bought a raw-hide. Gathering up the fragments of the pole and cutting the hide into strips, we fished it in the rudest manner. As long as the hide was green, the pole was very shaky; but gradually the sun dried the hide, tightened it, and the pole actually held for about a month. This cost us nearly a day of delay; but, when damages were repaired, we harnessed up again, and reached the crossing of the Cosumnes, where our survey was to begin. The *expediente,* or title-papers, of the ranch described it as containing nine or eleven leagues on the Cosumnes, south side, and between the San Joaquin River and Sierra Nevada Mountains. We began at the place where the road crosses the Cosumnes, and laid down a line four miles south, perpendicular to the general direction of the stream; then, surveying up the stream, we marked each mile so as to admit of a subdivision of one mile by four. The land was dry and very poor, with the exception of here and there some small pieces of bottom-land, the great bulk of the bottom-land occurring on the north side of the stream. We continued the survey up some twenty miles into the hills above the mill of Dailor and Sheldon.[34] It took about a month to make this survey, which, when finished, was duly plotted; and for it we received one-tenth of the land, or two subdivisions. Ord and I took the land, and we paid Seton for his labor in cash. By the sale of my share of the land, subsequently, I realized three thousand dollars. After finishing Hartnell's survey, we crossed over to Dailor's, and did some work for him at five hundred dollars a day for the party. Having finished our work on the Cosumnes, we proceeded to Sacramento, where Captain Sutter employed us to connect the survey of Sacramento City, made by Lieutenant Warner, and that of Sutterville, three miles below,[35] which was then being surveyed by Lieutenant J. W. Davidson, of the First Dragoons. At Sutterville, the plateau of the Sacramento

[34] William Daylor (1810–1850) arrived in California in 1835 and was a cook at Sutter's Fort in 1840. He and Jared D. Sheldon (1813–1851), who arrived in California in 1832, opened a store in present-day Sacramento County, CA, in 1848. Elizabeth Pinkerton, *Elk Grove* (Charleston, SC: Arcadia, 2007), 28; William L. Willis, *History of Sacramento County, California* (Los Angeles: Historic Record, 1913), 332.

[35] Sutterville, CA, was a town established by John Sutter in 1844. It was situated approximately three miles south of modern-day Sacramento. Jocelyn M. Isidro, *Sacramento's Land Park* (Charleston, SC: Arcadia, 2005), 7.

approached quite near the river, and it would have made a better site for a town than the low, submerged land where the city now stands; but it seems to be a law of growth that all natural advantages are disregarded wherever once business chooses a location. Old Sutter's *embarcadero* became Sacramento City, simply because it was the first point used for unloading boats for Sutter's Fort, just as the site for San Francisco was fixed by the use of Yerba Buena as the hide-landing for the Mission of "San Francisco de Asis."

I invested my earnings in this survey in three lots in Sacramento City, on which I made a fair profit by a sale to one McNulty, of Mansfield, Ohio.[36] I only had a two months' leave of absence, during which General Smith, his staff, and a retinue of civil friends, were making a tour of the gold-mines,[37] and hearing that he was *en route* back to his headquarters at Sonoma, I knocked off my work, sold my instruments, and left my wagon and mules with my cousin Charley Hoyt, who had a store in Sacramento, and was on the point of moving up to a ranch, for which he had bargained, on Bear Creek, on which was afterward established Camp "Far West."[38] He afterward sold the mules, wagon, etc., for me, and on the whole I think I cleared, by those two months' work, about six thousand dollars. I then returned to headquarters at Sonoma, in time to attend my fellow aide-de-camp Gibbs through a long and dangerous sickness, during which he was on board a store-ship, guarded by Captain George Johnson, who now resides in San Francisco.[39] General Smith had agreed that on the first good opportunity he would send me to the United States as a bearer of dispatches, but this he could not do until he had made the examination of Oregon, which was also in his com-

[36] Possibly William McNulty (c. 1819–1861), a prominent businessman in Sacramento who later died by suicide. "City Intelligence," *Sacramento Daily Union* (Sacramento, CA), Apr. 1, 1861, 5; "Tuesday Evening . . . April 2," *Sacramento Bee,* Apr. 2, 1861, 4.

[37] Persifor F. Smith started his tour of the gold mines in late June 1849. He brought with him Philip T. Tyson (1799–1877), an experimental geologist who coauthored the book *Geology and Industrial Resources of California* (Baltimore: Wm. Minifie and Co.,1851). "Message from the President of the United States," 31st Congress, 1st session, 719–720; *National Cyclopedia of American Biography* (New York: James T. White, 1906), vol. 1, s.v. "Tyson, Philip Thomas."

[38] Camp "Far West" was located on the north bank of the Bear River in modern-day Wheatland, CA. It was surveyed by George "Squibob" Derby in 1849 and was an active camp until 1852. Wheatland Historical Society, *Images of America: Wheatland* (Charleston, SC: Arcadia, 2009), 8, 118 (map).

[39] George A. Johnson (1824–1903) moved to California in 1849 and later worked as a steamboat operator on the Colorado River. Brenda K. Warneka, *Around Laughlin* (Charleston, SC: Arcadia, 2018), 54.

mand. During the summer of 1849 there continued to pour into California a perfect stream of people. Steamers came, and a line was established from San Francisco to Sacramento, of which the Senator was the pioneer, charging sixteen dollars a passage, and actually coining money. Other boats were built, out of materials which had either come around Cape Horn or were brought from the Sandwich Islands. Wharves were built, houses were springing up as if by magic, and the Bay of San Francisco presented as busy a scene of life as any part of the world. Major Allen, of the Quartermaster's Department, who had come out as chief-quartermaster of the division, was building a large warehouse at Benicia, with a row of quarters, out of lumber at one hundred dollars per thousand feet, and the work was done by men at sixteen dollars a day. I have seen a detailed soldier, who got only his monthly pay of eight dollars a month, and twenty cents a day for extra duty, nailing on weather-boards and shingles, alongside a citizen who was paid sixteen dollars a day. This was a real injustice, made the soldiers discontented, and it was hardly to be wondered at that so many deserted. While the mass of people were busy at gold and in mammoth speculations, a set of busy politicians were at work to secure the prizes of civil government. Gwin and Fremont were there, and T. Butler King, of Georgia, had come out from the East, scheming for office.[40] He staid with us at Sonoma, and was generally regarded as the Government candidate for United States Senator. General Riley as Governor, and Captain Halleck as Secretary of State, had issued a proclamation for the election of a convention to frame a State constitution. In due time the elections were held, and the convention was assembled at Monterey.[41] Dr. Semple was elected president; and Gwin, Sutter,[42] Halleck, Butler King, Sherwood, Gilbert, Shannon, and others, were members.[43] General Smith took no part in this convention, but sent me down to watch the

[40] William M. Gwin (1805–1885) moved to California in 1849 where he served as a U.S. senator from 1850 to 1861. Thomas Butler King (1800–1864) was a U.S. congressman from Georgia. In 1849 he was appointed by Pres. Zachary Taylor to report on the prospects of California becoming a state. *Dictionary of American Biography,* 2nd ed., s.v. "King, Thomas Butler"; *The Encyclopedia Britannica,* 9th ed. (Philadelphia: Maxwell Sommerville, 1891), s.v. "Gwin, William McKendree."

[41] The California Constitutional Convention started on Sept. 1, 1849, and the state's first constitution was signed on Oct. 13. Janin and Carlson, *The California Campaigns,* 19–20.

[42] In the first edition of the memoirs (1875), WTS listed the name "Fremont" in place of "Sutter."

[43] Winfield S. Sherwood (1819–1870) was a lawyer who moved to California in 1849 to participate in the state's formation. Edward Gilbert (1819–1852) was an editor and veteran of the Mexican-American War. In 1850, Gilbert was elected to the U.S. House of Representatives

proceedings, and report to him. The only subject of interest was the slavery question. There were no slaves then in California, save a few who had come out as servants, but the Southern people at that time claimed their share of territory, out of that acquired by the common labors of all sections of the Union in the war with Mexico. Still, in California there was little feeling on the subject. I never heard General Smith, who was a Louisianian, express any opinion about it. Nor did Butler King, of Georgia, ever manifest any particular interest in the matter. A committee was named to draft a constitution, which in due time was reported, with the usual clause, then known as the Wilmot Proviso, excluding slavery; and during the debate which ensued very little opposition was made to this clause, which was finally adopted by a large majority, although the convention was made up in large part of men from our Southern States.[44] This matter of California being a free State, afterward, in the national Congress, gave rise to angry debates, which at one time threatened civil war. The result of the convention was the election of State officers, and of the Legislature which sat in San José in October and November, 1849, and which elected Fremont and Gwin as the first United States Senators in Congress from the Pacific coast.

Shortly after returning from Monterey, I was sent by General Smith up to Sacramento City to instruct Lieutenants Warner and Williamson, of the Engineers, to push their surveys of the Sierra Nevada Mountains, for the purpose of ascertaining the possibility of passing that range by a railroad, a subject that then elicited universal interest.[45] It was generally assumed that such a road could not be made along any of the immigrant roads then in use, and

---

after California was admitted into the Union as a state. He was killed in a duel with Gen. James W. Denver in 1852.

For a list of members of the 1849 California Constitutional Convention, see J. Ross Browne, *Report of the Debates in the Convention of California, on the Formation of the State Constitution, in September and October 1849* (Washington, DC: John T. Towers, 1850), 7; *Biographical Dictionary of the American Congress, 1774–1961* (Washington, DC: GPO, 1961), s.v. "Gilbert, Edward"; William A. Ellis, *Norwich University, 1819–1911: Her History, Her Graduates, Her Roll of Honor* (Montpelier, VT: Capital City Press, 1911), 2:276–277.

[44] The Wilmot Proviso, which called for the prohibition of slavery in newly acquired territories, was originally proposed by U.S. Representative David Wilmot in Aug. 1846. The U.S. Congress never officially passed the proposal. James F. Rhodes, *History of the United States* (Port Washington, NY: Kennikat Press, 1892), 1:89–90; Stacey L. Smith, *Freedom's Frontier: California and the Struggle over Unfree Labor, Emancipation, and Reconstruction* (Chapel Hill: University of North Carolina Press, 2013), 112.

[45] Robert S. Williamson (1825–1882) graduated from the USMA in 1848 and was involved in surveying for the Pacific Division of the U.S. Army from 1848 to 1853. *USMA,* 2:346–347.

Warner's orders were to look farther north up the Feather River, or some one of its tributaries.[46] Warner was engaged in this survey during the summer and fall of 1849, and had explored, to the very end of Goose Lake, the source of Feather River. Then, leaving Williamson with the baggage and part of the men, he took about ten men and a first-rate guide,[47] crossed the summit to the east, and had turned south, having the range of mountains on his right hand, with the intention of regaining his camp by another pass in the mountain. The party was strung out, single file, with wide spaces between, Warner ahead. He had just crossed a small valley and ascended one of the spurs covered with sage-brush and rocks, when a band of Indians rose up and poured in a shower of arrows. The mule turned and ran back to the valley, where Warner fell off dead, punctured by five arrows. The mule also died. The guide, who was next to Warner, was mortally wounded; and one or two men had arrows in their bodies, but recovered.[48] The party gathered about Warner's body, in sight of the Indians, who whooped and yelled, but did not venture away from their cover of rocks. This party of men remained there all day without burying the bodies, and at night, by a wide circuit, passed the mountain, and reached Williamson's camp. The news of Warner's death cast a gloom over all the old Californians, who knew him well. He was a careful, prudent, and honest officer, well qualified for his business, and extremely accurate in all his work. He and I had been intimately associated during our four years together in California, and I felt his loss deeply. The season was then too far advanced to attempt to avenge his death, and it was not until the next spring that a party was sent out to gather up and bury his scattered bones.[49]

[46] Warner was ordered to explore the land from upper Sacramento to the Humboldt River on June 27, 1849. *Report of the Secretary of War, Communicating Information in Relation to the Geology and Topography of California,* 31st Congress, 1st session, pt. 2 (Washington, DC: GPO, 1850), 17.

[47] François "Battitu" Bercier was a trapper who worked with the Hudson Bay Company in the Oregon Territory. *Report of the Secretary of War,* pt. 2, 17.

[48] Warner was killed on Sept. 26, 1849. François "Battitu" Bercier, George Cave, and Henry A. Barling were also hit by arrows. Out of the three men, only Barling survived the attack. Although sources call them the "Goose Lake Indians," Warner and his men were mostly likely killed by Klamath or Modoc warriors. Gary C. Anderson and Laura L. Anderson, eds., *The Army Surveys of Gold Rush California: Reports of Topographical Engineers, 1849–1851* (Norman, OK: Arthur H. Clark, 2015), 26; *Register of the Army of the United States for 1850* (Washington, DC: C. Alexander, 1850), 33; *Report of the Secretary of War,* 31st Congress, 1st session, pt. 2, 20.

[49] In May 1850, a detachment of troops led by Captain Nathaniel Lyon searched for Warner's bones. Hubert H. Bancroft, *History of California, 1860–1890* (San Francisco: History Company, 1890), 458*n*.

As winter approached, the immigrants overland came pouring into California, dusty and worn with their two thousand miles of weary travel across the plains and mountains. Those who arrived in October and November reported thousands still behind them, with oxen perishing, and short of food. Appeals were made for help, and General Smith resolved to attempt relief. Major Rucker, who had come across with Pike Graham's Battalion of Dragoons, had exchanged with Major Fitzgerald, of the Quartermaster's Department, and was detailed to conduct this relief. General Smith ordered him to be supplied with one hundred thousand dollars out of the civil fund, subject to his control, and with this to purchase at Sacramento flour, bacon, etc., and to hire men and mules to send out and meet the immigrants.[50] Major Rucker fulfilled this duty perfectly, sending out pack-trains loaded with food by the many routes by which the immigrants were known to be approaching, went out himself with one of these trains, and remained in the mountains until the last immigrant had got in. No doubt this expedition saved many a life which has since been most useful to the country. I remained at Sacramento a good part of the fall of 1849, recognizing among the immigrants many of my old personal friends—John C. Fall, William King, Sam Stambaugh, Hugh Ewing, Hampton Denman, etc.[51] I got Rucker to give these last two employment along with the train for the relief of the immigrants. They had proposed to begin a ranch on my land on the Cosumnes, but afterward changed their minds, and went out with Rucker.

While I was at Sacramento General Smith had gone on his contemplated trip to Oregon, and promised that he would be back in December, when he would send me home with dispatches. Accordingly, as the winter and rainy

[50] On Dec. 15, 1849, it was reported that Smith allotted $160,000 to Rucker for supplies. Bancroft, *History of California,* 451*n*.

[51] John C. Fall (1810–1894) was a salesman in Lancaster, OH, before moving to California in 1849. Sam Stambaugh (d. 1854) was a salesman and banker from Lancaster, OH. Hugh Ewing (1826–1905) was foster brother and brother-in-law to WTS. After dropping out of the USMA, Ewing moved to California in 1848 and resided there until 1852. Hampton Denman (1829–1906) was from Ohio but ran for governor of Kansas in 1859. He later served as the mayor of Leavenworth, KS, from 1858 to 1859 and 1862. Justin M. Glenn, *The Washingtons: A Family History,* pt. 1 (El Dorado Hills, CA: Savas, 2014), 4:1893; George W. Martin, *Transactions of the Kansas State Historical Society, 1907–1908* (Topeka: State Printing Office, 1908), 10: 238–239; Richard F. Miller, ed., *States at War: A Reference Guide for Ohio in the Civil War* (Lebanon, NH: University Press of New England, 2015), 5:446*n;* C. M. L. Wiseman, *Centennial History of Lancaster, Ohio, and Lancaster People* (self-pub., 1898), 87, 230.

season was at hand, I went to San Francisco, and spent some time at the Presidio, waiting patiently for General Smith's return. About Christmas a vessel arrived from Oregon with the dispatches, and an order for me to deliver them in person to General Winfield Scott, in New York City. General Smith had sent them down, remaining in Oregon for a time. Of course I was all ready, and others of our set were going home by the same conveyance, viz., Rucker, Ord, A. J. Smith—some under orders, and the others on leave. Wanting to see my old friends in Monterey, I arranged for my passage in the steamer of January 1, 1850, paying six hundred dollars for passage to New York, and went down to Monterey by land, Rucker accompanying me. The weather was unusually rainy, and all the plain about Santa Clara was under water; but we reached Monterey in time. I again was welcomed by my friends, Doña Augustias, Manuelita, and the family, and it was resolved that I should take two of the boys home with me and put them at Georgetown College for education, viz., Antonio and Porfirio, thirteen and eleven years old.[52] The doña gave me a bag of gold-dust to pay for their passage and to deposit at the college. On the 2d day of January punctually appeared the steamer Oregon. We were all soon on board and off for home. At that time the steamers touched at San Diego, Acapulco, and Panama. Our passage down the coast was unusually pleasant. Arrived at Panama, we hired mules and rode across to Gorgona, on the Cruces River,[53] where we hired a boat and paddled down to the mouth of the river, off which lay the steamer Crescent City. It usually took four days to cross the isthmus, every passenger taking care of himself, and it was really funny to watch the efforts of women and men unaccustomed to mules. It was an old song to us, and the trip across was easy and interesting. In due time we were rowed off to the Crescent City, rolling back and forth in the swell, and we

[52] Georgetown College was established in 1789 and changed its name to Georgetown University in 1815. Jośe Antonio Jimeno and Porfirio Jimeno (1841–1870) were educated at boarding schools in Boston and New York City and later attended Georgetown University. Alice H. Songe, *American Universities and Colleges: A Dictionary of Name Changes* (Metuchen, NJ: Scarecrow, 1978), s.v. "Georgetown University"; Edwin R. Sweeney, *Cochise: Firsthand Accounts of the Chiricahua Apache Chief* (Norman: University of Oklahoma Press, 2014), 108*n*.

[53] Gorgona was abandoned in 1913 during the construction of the Panama Canal. Ulysses S. Grant, *The Personal Memoirs of Ulysses S. Grant: The Complete Annotated Edition,* ed. John F. Marszalek, David S. Nolen, and Louie P. Gallo (Cambridge, MA: Belknap Press of Harvard University Press, 2017), 135*n*.

scrambled aboard by a "Jacob's ladder" from the stern. Some of the women had to be hoisted aboard by lowering a tub from the end of a boom; fun to us who looked on, but awkward enough to the poor women, especially to a very fat one, who attracted much notice. General Fremont, wife and child (Lillie) were passengers with us down from San Francisco;[54] but Mrs. Fremont not being well, they remained over one trip at Panama.

Senator Gwin was one of our passengers, and went through to New York. We reached New York about the close of January, after a safe and pleasant trip.[55] Our party, composed of Ord, A. J. Smith, and Rucker, with the two boys, Antonio and Porfirio, put up at Delmonico's, on Bowling Green;[56] and, as soon as we had cleaned up somewhat, I took a carriage, went to General Scott's office in Ninth Street, delivered my dispatches, was *ordered* to dine with him next day, and then went forth to hunt up my old friends and relations, the Scotts, Hoyts, etc., etc.

On reaching New York, most of us had rough soldier's clothing, but we soon got a new outfit, and I dined with General Scott's family, Mrs. Scott being present, and also their son-in-law and daughter (Colonel and Mrs. H. L. Scott).[57] The general questioned me pretty closely in regard to things on the Pacific coast, especially the politics, and startled me with the assertion that "our country was on the eve of a terrible civil war." He interested me by anecdotes of my old army comrades in his recent battles around the city of Mexico, and I felt deeply the fact that our country had passed through a foreign war, that my comrades had fought great battles, and yet I had not heard a hostile shot.

[54] Jessie Benton (1824–1902) married John. C. Frémont in 1841. The couple moved to California the following year. Elizabeth B. Frémont (1842–1919) was the only daughter of John and Jessie Frémont. John S. McGroarty, *Los Angeles: From the Mountains to the Sea* (Chicago: American Historical Society, 1921), 3:441–442.

[55] WTS's trip East in 1850 took thirty days to complete. His initial voyage to California in 1846 had taken 198 days. Marszalek, *Sherman,* 77.

[56] Delmonico's was established in 1846 in the Bowling Green section of New York City. It moved to Broadway and Fourteenth Street in 1861. Austin B. Griffin, *American Bankruptcy Reports* (Albany, NY: Matthew Bender, 1919), 43:520.

[57] Maria DeHart Mayo (1789–1862) married Winfield Scott in Mar. 1817. They had seven children together. Their daughter Cornelia (1825–1886) married Henry L. Scott (1814–1886), a graduate of the USMA. Bud Hannings, *The War of 1812: A Complete Chronology with Biographies of 63 General Officers* (Jefferson, NC: McFarland, 2012), s.v. "Scott, Winfield"; *USMA,* 1:565–566; Winfield Scott, *Memoirs of Lieut.-General Winfield Scott,* ed. Timothy D. Johnson (Knoxville: University of Tennessee Press, 2015), 344*n*.

Of course, I thought it the last and only chance in my day, and that my career as a soldier was at an end. After some four or five days spent in New York, I was, by an order of General Scott, sent to Washington, to lay before the Secretary of War (Crawford, of Georgia)[58] the dispatches which I had brought from California. On reaching Washington, I found that Mr. Ewing was Secretary of the Interior,[59] and I at once became a member of his family. The family occupied the house of Mr. Blair, on Pennsylvania Avenue, directly in front of the War Department.[60] I immediately repaired to the War Department, and placed my dispatches in the hands of Mr. Crawford, who questioned me somewhat about California, but seemed little interested in the subject, except so far as it related to slavery and the routes through Texas. I then went to call on the President at the White House. I found Major Bliss, who had been my teacher in mathematics at West Point, and was then General Taylor's son-in-law and private secretary.[61] He took me into the room, now used by the President's private secretaries, where President Taylor was. I had never seen him before, though I had served under him in Florida in 1840–'41, and was most agreeably surprised at his fine personal appearance, and his pleasant, easy manners. He received me with great kindness, told me that Colonel Mason had mentioned my name with praise, and that he would be pleased to do me any act of favor. We were with him nearly an hour, talking about California generally, and of his personal friends, Persifer Smith, Riley, Canby, and others. Although General Scott was generally regarded by the army as the most accomplished soldier of the Mexican War, yet General Taylor had that blunt, honest, and stern character, that endeared him to the masses of

[58] George W. Crawford (1798–1872) was governor of Georgia from 1843 to 1845 and U.S. secretary of war from 1849 to 1850. *Dictionary of United States History,* ed. J. Franklin Jameson (Philadelphia: Historical Publishing, 1908), s.v. "Crawford, George W."

[59] The U.S. Congress created the Department of the Interior on Mar. 3, 1849. Thomas Ewing took office as the first U.S. secretary of the interior on Mar. 8, 1849. He served in that position until July 22, 1850. *The United States Department of the Interior: America's Guardian of Natural Resources* (Washington, DC: U.S. Department of the Interior, 1976), 6, 39.

[60] Francis P. Blair (1791–1876) was a political newspaper editor and an early member of the Republican Party. The Blair House was built in the early nineteenth century and was acquired by Blair after the original owner, Gen. Joseph Lovell, passed away. Mark R. Cheathem, *Andrew Jackson and the Rise of the Democrats: A Reference Guide* (Santa Barbara: ABC-CLIO, 2015), 248; *Records of the Columbia Historical Society* (Washington, DC: Columbia Historical Society, 1908), 2:252.

[61] William W. S. Bliss (1815–1853) graduated from the USMA in 1833 and was an assistant professor of mathematics at the academy from 1834 to 1840. *USMA,* 1:542–545.

the people, and made him President. Bliss, too, had gained a large fame by his marked skill and intelligence as an adjutant-general and military adviser. His manner was very unmilitary, and in his talk he stammered and hesitated, so as to make an unfavorable impression on a stranger; but he was wonderfully accurate and skillful with his pen, and his orders and letters form a model of military precision and clearness.

4

Missouri, Louisiana, and California.

1850–1855.

Having returned from California in January, 1850, with dispatches for the War Department, and having delivered them in person first to General Scott in New York City, and afterward to the Secretary of War (Crawford) in Washington City, I applied for and received a leave of absence for six months. I first visited my mother, then living at Mansfield, Ohio, and returned to Washington, where, on the 1st day of May, 1850, I was married to Miss Ellen Boyle Ewing, daughter of the Hon. Thomas Ewing, Secretary of the Interior.[1] The marriage ceremony was attended by a large and distinguished company, embracing Daniel Webster, Henry Clay, T. H. Benton, President Taylor, and all his cabinet.[2] This occurred at the house of Mr. Ewing, the same now owned and occupied by Mr. F. P. Blair, senior, on Pennsylvania Avenue, opposite the War Department. We made a wedding-tour to Baltimore, New York, Niagara, and Ohio, and returned to Washington by the 1st of July. General Taylor participated in the celebration of the Fourth of July, a very hot

[1]Eleanor Boyle Ewing (1824–1888) became WTS's foster sister in 1829. In a letter to Ellen dated Mar. 29, 1850, WTS wrote, "Let us be married the First of May. I have always rejoiced to see the flowers bloom and nature rub off her gray morose garment for the brighter one of Spring. The day is peculiarly appropriate for we can unite our day of joy with all nature and will have her beauties to cheer us." For personal correspondence between Ellen and WTS, see M. A. DeWolfe Howe, ed., *Home Letters of General Sherman* (New York: Charles Scribner's Sons, 1909). John F. Marszalek, *Sherman: A Soldier's Passion for Order* (New York: Free Press, 1993), 80.

[2]The other members of Taylor's cabinet were Secretary of State John M. Clayton (1796–1856), Secretary of the Treasury William M. Meredith (1799–1873), Sectary of War George W. Crawford (1798–1872), Attorney General Reverdy Johnson (1796–1876), Postmaster General Jacob Collamer (1791–1865), and Secretary of the Navy William B. Preston (1805–1862). See *Biographical Directory of the United States Congress, 1774–2005* (Washington, DC: GPO, 2005).

day, by hearing a long speech from the Hon. Henry S. Foote,[3] at the base of the Washington Monument. Returning from the celebration much heated and fatigued, he partook too freely of his favorite iced milk with cherries, and during that night was seized with a severe colic, which by morning had quite prostrated him. It was said that he sent for his son-in-law, Surgeon Wood, United States Army, stationed in Baltimore,[4] and declined medical assistance from anybody else. Mr. Ewing visited him several times, and was manifestly uneasy and anxious, as was also his son-in-law, Major Bliss, then of the army, and his confidential secretary. He rapidly grew worse, and died in about four days.

At that time there was a high state of political feeling pervading the country, on account of the questions growing out of the new Territories just acquired from Mexico by the war. Congress was in session, and General Taylor's sudden death evidently created great alarm. I was present in the Senate-gallery, and saw the oath of office administered to the Vice-President, Mr. Fillmore, a man of splendid physical proportions and commanding appearance;[5] but on the faces of Senators and people could easily be read the feelings of doubt and uncertainty that prevailed. All knew that a change in the cabinet and general policy was likely to result, but at the time it was supposed that Mr. Fillmore, whose home was in Buffalo, would be less liberal than General Taylor to the politicians of the South, who feared, or pretended to fear, a crusade against slavery; or, as was the political cry of the day, that slavery would be prohibited in the Territories and in the places exclusively under the jurisdiction of the United States. Events, however, proved the contrary.

I attended General Taylor's funeral as a sort of aide-de-camp, at the request of the Adjutant-General of the army, Roger Jones, whose brother, a militia-general, commanded the escort, composed of militia and some regulars. Among the regulars I recall the names of Captains John Sedgwick and W. F. Barry.[6]

[3] Henry S. Foote (1804–1880) served as a U.S. senator from Mississippi from 1847 to 1851 and as governor of Mississippi from 1852 to 1854. He represented Tennessee in the Confederate Congress during the Civil War. *The Mississippi Encyclopedia,* ed. Ted Ownby et. al. (Jackson: University Press of Mississippi, 2017), s.v. "Foote, Henry Stuart."

[4] Robert C. Wood (1799–1869) married Zachary Taylor's daughter, Anne M. Taylor. He was also the brother-in-law of Confederate president Jefferson Davis. *CWHC,* 579.

[5] Millard Fillmore (1800–1874) was sworn in as U.S. president on July 10, 1850. Paul Finkelman, *Millard Fillmore* (New York: Times Books, 2011), 3–4, 72.

[6] Walter Jones (1775–1861), a lawyer based in Washington, DC, was a major general who led the Militia of the District of Columbia during presidential inaugurations and funerals. Roger

Hardly was General Taylor decently buried in the Congressional Cemetery when the political struggle recommenced, and it became manifest that Mr. Fillmore favored the general compromise then known as Henry Clay's "Omnibus Bill," and that a general change of cabinet would at once occur.[7] Webster was to succeed Mr. Clayton as Secretary of State, Corwin to succeed Mr. Meredith as Secretary of the Treasury, and A. H. H. Stuart to succeed Mr. Ewing as Secretary of the Interior. Mr. Ewing, however, was immediately appointed by the Governor of the State to succeed Corwin in the Senate.[8] These changes made it necessary for Mr. Ewing to discontinue house-keeping, and Mr. Corwin took his house and furniture off his hands. I escorted the family out to their home in Lancaster, Ohio; but, before this had occurred, some most interesting debates took place in the Senate, which I regularly attended, and heard Clay, Benton, Foote, King of Alabama, Dayton,[9] and the

---

Jones was the brother of Thomas ap Catesby Jones and not related to Walter. Major John Sedgwick (1813–1864) led a company from the U.S. Flying Art. during Zachary Taylor's funeral. He later reached the rank of major general in 1862 and was killed by enemy sniper fire during the Battle of Spotsylvania Court House. William F. Barry (1818–1879) graduated from the USMA in 1838. He coauthored the 1860 book *Instruction for Field Artillery* and attained the rank of major general in the U.S. Army in 1865. *CWHC,* 199, 477; Roger K. Newman, *The Yale Biographical Dictionary of American Law* (New Haven, CT: Yale University Press, 2009), s.v. "Jones, Walter"; *Obituary Addresses Delivered on the Occasion of the Death of Zachary Taylor, President of the United States* (Washington, DC: William M. Belt, 1850), 99.

[7] On May 8, 1850, Henry Clay submitted a series of bills that addressed the issue of California's statehood and the expansion of slavery within the United States and its territories. The bills became known as the "Compromise of 1850." *Harper's Encyclopedia of United States History,* ed. Benson J. Lossing (New York: Harper and Brothers, 1902), 9:193.

[8] Thomas Corwin (1794–1865) was governor of Ohio from 1840 to 1845 and U.S. senator from Ohio from 1845 to 1850. Alexander H. H. Stuart (1807–1891) was a U.S. congressman from Virginia for the years 1841–1850. Seabury Ford (1801–1855) was elected governor of Ohio in 1848 by a margin of 871 votes. Ford appointed Thomas Ewing Sr. interim senator after Corwin resigned on July 22, 1850. John S. C. Abbott, *The History of the State of Ohio: From the Discovery of the Great Valley to the Present Time* (Detroit: Northwestern, 1875), 764–766; *A Biographical Congressional Dictionary, 1774 to 1903* (Washington, DC: GPO, 1903), s.v. "Ohio"; J. L M. Curry, *A Brief Sketch of George Peabody* (Cambridge: Cambridge University Press, 1898), 105–106; Charles Morris, *Famous Orators of the World and Their Best Orations* (Philadelphia: John C. Winston, 1902), 109.

[9] William L. Dayton (1807–1864) was a U.S. senator from New Jersey from 1842 to 1851. He was the Republican vice-presidential candidate in the 1856 presidential election. David J. Brewer, *The World's Best Orations* (St. Louis: Fred P. Kaiser, 1900), 1676.

many real orators of that day. Mr. Calhoun was in his seat, but he was evidently approaching his end, for he was pale and feeble in the extreme. I heard Mr. Webster's last speech on the floor of the Senate, under circumstances that warrant a description. It was publicly known that he was to leave the Senate, and enter the new cabinet of Mr. Fillmore, as his Secretary of State, and that prior to leaving he was to make a great speech on the "Omnibus Bill." Resolved to hear it, I went up to the Capitol on the day named, an hour or so earlier than usual. The speech was to be delivered in the old Senate-chamber, now used by the Supreme Court.[10] The galleries were much smaller than at present, and I found them full to overflowing, with a dense crowd about the door, struggling to reach the stairs. I could not get near, and then tried the reporters' gallery, but found it equally crowded; so I feared I should lose the only possible opportunity to hear Mr. Webster.

I had only a limited personal acquaintance with any of the Senators, but had met Mr. Corwin quite often at Mr. Ewing's house, and I also knew that he had been extremely friendly to my father in his lifetime; so I ventured to send in to him my card, "W. T. S., First-Lieutenant, Third Artillery." He came to the door promptly, when I said, "Mr. Corwin, I believe Mr. Webster is to speak to-day." His answer was, "Yes, he has the floor at one o'clock." I then added that I was extremely anxious to hear him. "Well," said he, "why don't you go into the gallery?" I explained that it was full, and I had tried every access, but found all jammed with people. "Well," said he, "what do you want of me?" I explained that I would like him to take me on the floor of the Senate; that I had often seen from the gallery persons on the floor, no better entitled to it than I. He then asked in his quizzical way, "Are you a foreign embassador?" "No." "Are you the Governor of a State?" "No." "Are you a member of the other House?" "Certainly not." "Have you ever had a vote of thanks by name?" "No." "Well, these are the only privileged members." I then told him he knew well enough who I was, and that if he chose he could take me in. He then said, "Have you any impudence?" I told him, "A reasonable amount if occasion called for it." "Do you think you could become so interested in my conversation as not to notice the door-keeper?" (pointing to him).[11] I told him that there was not the least doubt of it, if he would tell me one of his

[10] The Old Senate Chamber, north of the Capitol Rotunda, was used by the U.S. Senate from 1819 to 1859. The U.S. Supreme Court occupied the chamber from 1860 to 1935. *The Senate Chamber, 1810–1859* (Washington, DC: GPO, 1978), 5.

[11] Robert Beale (1800–1866) served as the sergeant-at-arms and doorkeeper of the U.S. Senate for the years 1845–1853. J. E. Homans and L. E. Dearborn, eds., *The Cyclopedia of*

funny stories. He then took my arm, and led me a turn in the vestibule, talking about some indifferent matter, but all the time directing my looks to his left hand, toward which he was gesticulating with his right; and thus we approached the door-keeper, who began asking me, "Foreign ambassador? Governor of a State? Member of Congress?" etc.; but I caught Corwin's eye, which said plainly, "Don't mind him, pay attention to me," and in this way we entered the Senate-chamber by a side-door. Once in, Corwin said, "Now you can take care of yourself," and I thanked him cordially. I found a seat close behind Mr. Webster, and near General Scott, and heard the whole of the speech. It was heavy in the extreme, and I confess that I was disappointed and tired long before it was finished. No doubt the speech was full of fact and argument, but it had none of the fire of oratory, or intensity of feeling, that marked all of Mr. Clay's efforts.

Toward the end of July, as before stated, all the family went home to Lancaster. Congress was still in session, and the bill adding four captains to the Commissary Department had not passed, but was reasonably certain to, and I was equally sure of being one of them. At that time my name was on the muster-roll of (Light) Company C, Third Artillery (Bragg's), stationed at Jefferson Barracks, near St. Louis. But, as there was cholera at St. Louis, on application, I was permitted to delay joining my company until September.[12] Early in that month, I proceeded to Cincinnati, and thence by steamboat to St. Louis, and then to Jefferson Barracks, where I reported for duty to Captain and Brevet-Colonel Braxton Bragg, commanding (Light) Company C, Third Artillery. The other officers of the company were First-Lieutenant James A. Hardie, and afterward Hackaliah Brown.[13] New horses had just been purchased for the battery, and we were preparing for work, when the mail brought the

American Biography (New York: Press Association Compilers, 1926), s.v. "Beale, John Forbes"; *The Senate Sergeant at Arms and Doorkeeper* (Washington, DC: U.S. Senate, 2008), 16.

[12] St. Louis experienced a severe cholera outbreak in 1849. The disease persisted throughout the city until 1852. In 1885 the St. Louis Health Department theorized that the disease was brought to the city from New Orleans via ships. George Homan, ed., *A Sanitary Survey of St. Louis* (St. Louis: Concord A. S., 1885), 41.

[13] James A. Hardie (1823–1876) graduated from the USMA in 1843 and was promoted to first lieutenant, 3rd Art., in Mar. 1847. He was garrisoned at Jefferson Barracks, MO, from 1850 to 1851. He later served in the Army of the Potomac during the Civil War and was brevetted major general in Mar. 1865. Hackaliah Brown (1822–1853) graduated from the USMA in 1842 and was brevetted captain for his actions during the Mexican-American War. He served at Jefferson Barracks, MO, from 1851 until his death in 1853. *USMA,* 2:134, 161–165.

orders announcing the passage of the bill increasing the Commissary Department by four captains, to which were promoted Captains Shiras, Blair, Sherman, and Bowen.[14] I was ordered to take post at St. Louis, and to relieve Captain A. J. Smith, First Dragoons, who had been acting in that capacity for some months. My commission bore date September 27, 1850. I proceeded forthwith to the city, relieved Captain Smith, and entered on the discharge of the duties of the office.

Colonel N. S. Clarke, Sixth Infantry, commanded the department; Major D. C. Buell was adjutant-general, and Captain W. S. Hancock was regimental quartermaster;[15] Colonel Thomas Swords was the depot quartermaster, and we had our offices in the same building, on the corner of Washington Avenue and Second. Subsequently Major S. Van Vliet relieved Colonel Swords. I remained at the Planters' House until my family arrived, when we occupied a house on Chouteau Avenue, near Twelfth.[16]

During the spring and summer of 1851, Mr. Ewing and Mr. Henry Stoddard, of Dayton, Ohio, a cousin of my father, were much in St. Louis, on business connected with the estate of Major Amos Stoddard, who was of the old army, as early as the beginning of this century. He was stationed at the village of St. Louis at the time of the Louisiana purchase, and when Lewis and Clarke made their famous expedition across the continent to the Columbia River. Major Stoddard at that early day had purchased a small farm back of the village, of some Spaniard or Frenchman, but, as he was a bach-

[14] Alexander E. Shiras (1812–1875), William B. Blair (1817–1883), and Isaac Bowen (1821–1858), all three of whom were graduates of the USMA, were promoted to captain along with WTS. *USMA,* 1:550–551, 701; 2:125; *Journal of the Executive Proceedings of the Senate of the United States of America, 1848–1852* (Washington, DC: GPO, 1887), 8:256.

[15] Newman S. Clarke (c. 1792–1860), a veteran of the War of 1812 and the Mexican-American War, was brevetted brigadier general in 1847. Winfield Scott Hancock (1824–1886) graduated from the USMA in 1844. He served as regimental quartermaster from June 1848 to Oct. 1849. He was promoted to major general in the U.S. Army during the Civil War and was the Democratic Party's presidential nominee in 1880. *CWHC,* 277–278; Richard E. Turley Jr., Janiece L. Johnson, and LeJean Purcell Carruth, eds., *Mountain Meadows Massacre: Collected Legal Papers* (Norman: University of Oklahoma, 2017), 2:914.

[16] The Planters' House, an upscale hotel located on Fourth Street in downtown St. Louis, opened in 1841 and closed in 1891. WTS traveled to Lancaster, OH, in Mar. 1851 to bring back his wife and newborn daughter, Maria Ewing Sherman (1851–1913), to St. Louis. Candace O'Connor, ed., *Saint Louis: An Informal History of the City and Its People, 1764–1865* (St. Louis: Missouri Historical Society Press, 1991), 325–326; Marszalek, *Sherman,* 87; Thomas T. Sherman, *Sherman Genealogy* (New York: Tobias A. Wright, 1920), 398.

elor, and was killed at Fort Meigs, Ohio, during the War of 1812, the title was for many years lost sight of, and the farm was covered over by other claims and by occupants.[17] As St. Louis began to grow, his brothers and sisters, and their descendants, concluded to look up the property. After much and fruitless litigation, they at last retained Mr. Stoddard, of Dayton, who in turn employed Mr. Ewing, and these, after many years of labor, established the title, and in the summer of 1851 they were put in possession by the United States marshal. The ground was laid off, the city survey extended over it, and the whole was sold in partition. I made some purchases, and acquired an interest, which I have retained more or less ever since.

We continued to reside in St. Louis throughout the year 1851, and in the spring of 1852 I had occasion to visit Fort Leavenworth on duty, partly to inspect a lot of cattle which a Mr. Gordon, of Cass County, had contracted to deliver in New Mexico, to enable Colonel Sumner to attempt his scheme of making the soldiers in New Mexico self-supporting, by raising their own meat, and in a measure their own vegetables. I found Fort Leavenworth then, as now, a most beautiful spot, but in the midst of a wild Indian country. There were no whites settled in what is now the State of Kansas. Weston, in Missouri, was the *great* town, and speculation in town-lots there and thereabout burnt the fingers of some of the army-officers, who wanted to plant their scanty dollars in a fruitful soil. I rode on horseback over to Gordon's farm, saw the cattle, concluded the bargain, and returned by way of Independence, Missouri. At Independence I found F. X. Aubrey, a noted man of that day, who had just made a celebrated ride of six hundred miles in six days.[18] That spring the United States quartermaster, Major L. C. Easton,[19] at Fort Union, New Mexico, had occasion to send some message east by a certain

[17] Amos Stoddard (1762–1813) served as the first Civil Commandant of Upper Louisiana. As a quartermaster, Stoddard oversaw the building of Fort Meigs in 1813. He was wounded when the British Army initially laid siege to the fort. He died from his injuries on May 11, 1813. Junius P. Rodriguez, ed., *The Louisiana Purchase: A Historical and Geographical Encyclopedia* (Santa Barbara: ABC-CLIO, 2002), s.v. "Stoddard, Amos."

[18] Francois X. Aubry (1824–1854) made the ride from Santa Fe, NM, to Independence, MO, in Sept. 1848. Traveling at a rate of 140 miles a day, Aubrey completed the trip in five days and sixteen hours. Michael K. Witzel and Gyvel Young-Witzel, *Legendary Route 66* (St. Paul: Voyageur, 2007), 30.

[19] Langdon C. Easton (1814–1884) graduated from the USMA in 1838 and served as a quartermaster in the U.S. Army until his retirement as an assistant quartermaster general in 1881. *USMA,* 1:710–711.

date, and contracted with Aubrey to carry it to the nearest post-office (then Independence, Missouri), making his compensation conditional on the time consumed. He was supplied with a good horse, and an order on the outgoing trains for an exchange. Though the whole route was infested with hostile Indians, and not a house on it, Aubrey started alone with his rifle. He was fortunate in meeting several outward-bound trains, and thereby made frequent changes of horses, some four or five, and reached Independence in six days, having hardly rested or slept the whole way. Of course, he was extremely fatigued, and said there was an opinion among the wild Indians that if a man "sleeps out his sleep," after such extreme exhaustion, he will never awake; and, accordingly, he instructed his landlord to wake him up after eight hours of sleep. When aroused at last, he saw by the clock that he had been asleep twenty hours, and he was dreadfully angry, threatened to murder his landlord, who protested he had tried in every way to get him up, but found it impossible, and had let him "sleep it out." Aubrey, in describing his sensations to me, said he took it for granted he was a dead man; but in fact he sustained no ill effects, and was off again in a few days. I met him afterward often in California, and always esteemed him one of the best samples of that bold race of men who had grown up on the Plains, along with the Indians, in the service of the fur companies. He was afterward, in 1856, killed by R. C. Weightman,[20] in a bar-room row, at Santa Fé, New Mexico,[21] where he had just arrived from California.

In going from Independence to Fort Leavenworth, I had to swim Milk Creek, and sleep all night in a Shawnee camp. The next day I crossed the Kaw or Kansas River in a ferry-boat, maintained by the blacksmith of the

[20] Richard H. Weightman (1818–1861) was expelled from the USMA in 1837 for stabbing a student. He served in the Mexican-American War and was later an elected delegate from the Territory of New Mexico to the U.S. Congress from 1851 to 1853. On Aug. 18, 1854, Weightman got into an argument with Francois X. Aubry in a Santa Fe bar. At some point during the altercation, Aubry drew his pistol. In response, Weightman stabbed and killed him with a bowie knife. Weightman was acquitted on the grounds of "justifiable homicide." At the outbreak of the Civil War, Weightman enlisted in the Confederate Army and was killed in action in 1861 during the Battle of Wilson's Creek. Michael E. Banasik, ed., *Confederate "Tales of the War" in the Trans-Mississippi* (Iowa City: Press of the Camp Pope Bookshop, 2010), 7:44; Richard Melzer, *Buried Treasures: Famous and Unusual Gravesites in New Mexico History* (Santa Fe: Sunstone, 2007), 147.

[21] In the first edition of the memoirs (1875), WTS misidentified the location of the murder as "Taos, New Mexico."

tribe,[22] and reached the fort in the evening. At that day the whole region was unsettled, where now exist many rich counties, highly cultivated, embracing several cities of from ten to forty thousand inhabitants. From Fort Leavenworth I returned by steamboat to St. Louis.

In the summer of 1852, my family went to Lancaster, Ohio; but I remained at my post. Late in the season, it was rumored that I was to be transferred to New Orleans, and in due time I learned the cause. During a part of the Mexican War, Major Seawell, of the Seventh Infantry, had been acting commissary of subsistence at New Orleans,[23] then the great depot of supplies for the troops in Texas, and of those operating beyond the Rio Grande. Commissaries at that time were allowed to purchase in open market, and were not restricted to advertising and awarding contracts to the lowest bidders. It was reported that Major Seawell had purchased largely of the house of Perry Seawell & Co., Mr. Seawell[24] being a relative of his. When he was relieved in his duties by Major Waggaman, of the regular Commissary Department,[25] the latter found Perry Seawell & Co. so prompt and satisfactory that he continued the patronage; for which there was a good reason, because stores for the use of the troops at remote posts had to be packed in a particular way, to bear transportation in wagons, or even on pack-mules; and this firm had made extraordinary preparations for this exclusive purpose. Some time about 1849, a brother of Major Waggaman, who had been clerk to Captain Casey, commissary of subsistence, at Tampa Bay, Florida, was thrown out of office by the death of the captain, and he naturally applied to his brother in New Orleans for employment;[26] and he, in turn, referred him to his friends,

[22] Paschal Fish (1804–1893), a relative of Tecumseh, operated a tavern about a mile south of the Kansas River near Westport, MO. He maintained multiple ferries along the Kansas River. William E. Connelley, *Doniphan's Expedition* (Kansas City: Bryant and Douglas, 1907), 142–143*n;* Don Green, *Shawnee Heritage I: Shawnee Genealogy and Family History* (self-pub., 2014), 114.

[23] Washington Seawell (1802–1888) graduated from the USMA in 1821 and was on commissary duty in 1847. He was brevetted brigadier general in the U.S. Army during the Civil War. *USMA,* 1:358.

[24] The U.S. Commissary of Subsistence Department contracted Perry Seawell to command a post at Baton Rouge, LA, from 1849 to 1851. *Report of the Secretary of War,* 31st Congress, 1st Session, Executive Document 26 (Washington, DC: GPO, 1850), 37.

[25] George G. Waggaman (1816–1884) graduated from the USMA in 1835 and was promoted to captain in the U.S. Commissary of Subsistence in 1841. He was stationed in New Orleans from 1848 to 1852. *USMA,* 1:609–610.

[26] Floyd Waggaman (1820–1857) served as a purser aboard the USS *Macedonia.* John C. Casey (1809–1856) immigrated to the United States from England as a young child and gradu-

Messrs. Perry Seawell & Co. These first employed him as a clerk, and afterward admitted him as a partner. Thus it resulted, in fact, that Major Waggaman was dealing largely, if not exclusively, with a firm of which his brother was a partner.

One day, as General Twiggs was coming across Lake Pontchartrain, he fell in with one of his old cronies, who was an extensive grocer. This gentleman gradually led the conversation to the downward tendency of the times since he and Twiggs were young, saying that, in former years, all the merchants of New Orleans had a chance at government patronage; but now, in order to sell to the army commissary, one had to take a brother in as a partner. General Twiggs resented this, but the merchant again affirmed it, and gave names. As soon as General Twiggs reached his office, he instructed his adjutant-general, Colonel Bliss—who told me this—to address a categorical note of inquiry to Major Waggaman. The major very frankly stated the facts as they had arisen, and insisted that the firm of Perry Seawell & Co. had enjoyed a large patronage, but deserved it richly by reason of their promptness, fairness, and fidelity. The correspondence was sent to Washington, and the result was, that Major Waggaman was ordered to St. Louis, and I was ordered to New Orleans.[27]

I went down to New Orleans in a steamboat in the month of September, 1852, taking with me a clerk, and, on arrival, assumed the office, in a bank-building facing Lafayette Square, in which were the offices of all the army departments. General D. Twiggs was in command of the department, with Colonel W. W. S. Bliss (son-in-law of General Taylor) as his adjutant-general. Colonel A. C. Myers was quartermaster, Captain John F. Reynolds aide-de-camp, and Colonel A. J. Coffee paymaster. I took rooms at the St. Louis Hotel, kept by a most excellent gentleman, Colonel Mudge.[28]

---

ated from the USMA in 1829. He was on commissary duty in Tampa Bay, FL, in 1848–1849, and served as commissioner for the removal of the Seminole tribe in Florida during the years 1849–1856. *USMA,* 1:426–427; Ainsworth R. Spofford, *Eminent and Representative Men of Virginia and the District of Columbia in the Nineteenth Century* (Madison, WI: Brant and Fuller, 1893), 338.

[27] George G. Waggaman was stationed in St. Louis from 1852 until he resigned from the U.S. Army in 1861. He then worked as a wholesale grocer until his death in 1884. Spofford, *Eminent and Representative Men,* 1:609.

[28] Abraham C. Myers (1811–1889) graduated from the USMA in 1833 and served as chief quartermaster of the U.S. Army until he resigned and joined the Confederate Army in 1861. Andrew J. Coffee (1819–1891) was the grandnephew of Pres. Andrew Jackson and worked as a paymaster and surveyor for the U.S. Army in California. Solomon H. Mudge (c. 1803–1860)

Mr. Perry Seawell came to me in person, soliciting a continuance of the custom which he had theretofore enjoyed; but I told him frankly that a change was necessary, and I never saw or heard of him afterward. I simply purchased in open market, arranged for the proper packing of the stores, and had not the least difficulty in supplying the troops and satisfying the head of the department in Washington.[29]

About Christmas, I had notice that my family, consisting of Mrs. Sherman, two children, and nurse, with my sister Fanny (now Mrs. Moulton, of Cincinnati, Ohio), were *en route* for New Orleans by steam-packet;[30] so I hired a house on Magazine Street, and furnished it. Almost at the moment of their arrival, also came from St. Louis my personal friend Major Turner, with a parcel of documents, which, on examination, proved to be articles of copartnership for a bank in California under the title of "Lucas, Turner & Co.," in which my name was embraced as a partner. Major Turner was, at the time, actually *en route* for New York, to embark for San Francisco, to inaugurate the bank, in the nature of a branch of the firm already existing at St. Louis under the name of "Lucas & Symonds." We discussed the matter very fully, and he left with me the papers for reflection, and went on to New York and California.

Shortly after arrived James H. Lucas, Esq., the principal of the banking-firm in St. Louis, a most honorable and wealthy gentleman.[31] He further ex-

---

operated the St. Louis Hotel under the business of S. H. Mudge and Co. The hotel was located at the intersection of St. Louis and Royal Streets. Zella Armstrong, *Notable Southern Families* (Cambridge, MA: Harvard Press, 1922), 2:95; *USMA,* 1:562; Walter Barlow Stevens, *Centennial History of Missouri: One Hundred Years in the Union, 1820–1921* (Ann Arbor, MI: S. J. Clarke, 1921), 6:545; *Cohen's New Orleans Directory for 1855* (New Orleans: Office of the Picayune, 1855), 258.

[29] George Gibson (1775–1861) served as commissary general of subsistence from 1818 until his death in 1861. Peter D. Skirbunt, *The Illustrated History of American Military Commissaries* (Washington, DC: Defense Commissary Agency, 2008), 1:61.

[30] The children in the Sherman family at that time were Maria Ewing Sherman, nicknamed "Minnie," and Mary Elizabeth Sherman (1852–1925), nicknamed "Lizzie," who was named after WTS's mother. WTS's sister, Frances B. Sherman (1829–1889), married Charles W. Moulton in 1855. William T. Sherman, *Sherman's Civil War: Selected Correspondence of William T. Sherman, 1860–1865,* ed. Brooks D. Simpson and Jean V. Berlin (Chapel Hill: University of North Carolina Press, 2014), 19*n;* Marszalek, *Sherman,* 86, 91; Thomas Townsend Sherman, *Sherman Genealogy* (New York: Tobias A. Wright, 1920), 402–403.

[31] James H. Lucas (1800–1873) served as the first president of the St. Louis Gas Company and as a director of the Boatmen's Savings Institution. He joined the banking business sometime after 1839. Howard Louis Conrad, ed., *Encyclopedia of the History of St. Louis: A Compen-*

plained the full programme of the branch in California; that my name had been included at the instance of Major Turner, who was a man of family and property in St. Louis, unwilling to remain long in San Francisco, and who wanted me to succeed him there. He offered me a very tempting income, with an interest that would accumulate and grow. He also disclosed to me that, in establishing a branch in California, he was influenced by the apparent prosperity of Page, Bacon & Co., and further that he had received the principal data, on which he had founded the scheme, from B. R. Nisbet, who was then a teller in the firm of Page, Bacon & Co., of San Francisco;[32] that he also was to be taken in as a partner, and was fully competent to manage all the details of the business; but, as Nisbet was comparatively young, Mr. Lucas wanted me to reside in San Francisco permanently, as the head of the firm. All these matters were fully discussed, and I agreed to apply for a six months' leave of absence, go to San Francisco, see for myself, and be governed by appearances there. I accordingly, with General Twiggs's approval, applied to the adjutant-general for a six months' leave, which was granted; and Captain John F. Reynolds was named to perform my duties during my absence.

During the stay of my family in New Orleans, we enjoyed the society of the families of General Twiggs, Colonel Myers, and Colonel Bliss, as also of many citizens, among whom was the wife of Mr. Day, sister to my brother-in-law, Judge Bartley.[33] General Twiggs was then one of the oldest officers of the army. His history extended back to the War of 1812, and he had served in early days with General Jackson in Florida and in the Creek campaigns. He had fine powers of description, and often entertained us, at his office, with

---

dium of History and Biography for Ready Reference (St. Louis: Southern History, 1889), 3:1318; Timothy W. Hubbard and Lewis E. Davids, *Banking in Mid-America: A History of Missouri's Banks* (New York: Public Affairs, 1969), 68.

[32] Benjamin R. Nisbet (1827–1890), the son of William Nisbet, moved from Kentucky to California to join the banking industry. Dwight L. Clarke, *William Tecumseh Sherman: Gold Rush Banker* (San Francisco: California Historical Society, 1969), 361*n;* "Obituary," *Arizona Weekly Enterprise* (Florence, AZ), Nov. 22, 1890, 4.

[33] Susannah Bartley (1806–1883) married Sylvanus B. Day (1796–1864) in Apr. 1821 in Richland County, OH. Her brother, Thomas W. Bartley (1812–1885), served in the Ohio Senate and House of Representatives before his appointment to the Ohio Supreme Court in 1851. Margery F. D. Hanson and Richard E. Hanson, *Day unto Day: A Study of the Day Family in America* (Burlington, VT: Queen City, 1978), 19, 46, 114; Charles Lanman, *Biographical Annal of the Civil Government of the United States* (New York: J. M. Morrison, 1887), s.v. "Bartley, Thomas W."

accounts of his experiences in the earlier settlements of the Southwest. Colonel Bliss had been General Taylor's adjutant in the Mexican War, and was universally regarded as one of the most finished and accomplished scholars in the army, and his wife was a most agreeable and accomplished lady.[34]

Late in February, I dispatched my family up to Ohio in the steamboat Tecumseh (Captain Pearce);[35] disposed of my house and furniture; turned over to Major Reynolds the funds, property, and records of the office; and took passage in a small steamer for Nicaragua, *en route* for California. We embarked early in March, and in seven days reached Greytown, where we united with the passengers from New York, and proceeded, by the Nicaragua River and Lake, for the Pacific Ocean.

The river was low, and the little steam canal-boats, four in number, grounded often, so that the passengers had to get into the water, to help them over the bars. In all there were about six hundred passengers, of whom about sixty were women and children. In four days we reached Castillo, where there is a decided fall, passed by a short railway, and above this fall we were transferred to a larger boat, which carried us up the rest of the river, and across the beautiful lake Nicaragua, studded with volcanic islands. Landing at Virgin Bay, we rode on mules across to San Juan del Sur, where lay at anchor the propeller S. S. Lewis (Captain Partridge, I think).[36] Passengers were carried through the surf by natives to small boats, and rowed off to the Lewis. The weather was very hot, and quite a scramble followed for state-rooms, especially for those on deck. I succeeded in reaching the purser's office,[37] got my ticket for a berth in one of the best state-rooms on deck, and, just as I was turning from the window, a lady who was a fellow-passenger from New Orleans, a Mrs. D——, called to me to secure her and her lady-friend berths on deck, saying that those below were unendurable. I spoke to the purser, who, at the moment perplexed by the crowd and clamor, answered: "I must put their names down for the other two

[34] Mary Elizabeth Bliss (1824–1909) was Zachary Taylor's youngest daughter. She married William Bliss shortly after her father was elected president in 1848. Elbert Smith, *President Zachary Taylor: The Hero President* (Ann Arbor: University of Michigan Press, 2011), 156–158.

[35] Possibly C. G. Pearce, of Cincinnati, OH. Mack V. Williams, *Williams' Cincinnati Directory* 19 (1869): 451.

[36] According to contemporary sources, a "Captain Sparrow" was in command of the SS *Lewis* in early 1853. Ernest A. Wiltsee, *Gold Rush Steamers of the Pacific* (San Francisco: Grabhorn Press, 1938), 104.

[37] A "Mr. Grimes" served as the purser for the SS *Lewis* in early 1853. Wiltsee, *Gold Rush Steamers,* 104.

berths of *your* state-room; but, as soon as the confusion is over, I will make some change whereby you shall not suffer." As soon as these two women were assigned to a state-room, they took possession, and I was left out. Their names were recorded as "Captain Sherman and ladies." As soon as things were quieted down I remonstrated with the purser, who at last gave me a lower berth in another and larger state-room on deck, with five others, so that my two ladies had the state-room all to themselves. At every meal the steward would come to me, and say, "Captain Sherman, will you bring your ladies to the table?" and we had the best seats in the ship. This continued throughout the voyage, and I assert that "my ladies" were of the most modest and best-behaved in the ship; but some time after we had reached San Francisco one of our fellow-passengers came to me and inquired if I personally knew Mrs. D——, with flaxen tresses, who sang so sweetly for us, and who had come out under my especial escort. I replied I did not, more than the chance acquaintance of the voyage, and what she herself had told me, viz., that she expected to meet her husband, who lived about Mokelumne Hill. He then informed me that she was a woman of the town. Society in California was then decidedly mixed.

In due season the steamship Lewis got under weigh. She was a wooden ship, long and narrow, bark-rigged, and a propeller; very slow, moving not over eight miles an hour. We stopped at Acapulco, and, in eighteen days, passed in sight of Point Pinos at Monterey, and at the speed we were traveling expected to reach San Francisco at 4 A. M. the next day. The cabin-passengers, as was usual, bought of the steward some champagne and cigars, and we had a sort of ovation for the captain, purser, and surgeon of the ship, who were all very clever fellows, though they had a slow and poor ship.

Late at night all the passengers went to bed, expecting to enter the port at daylight. I did not undress, as I thought the captain could and would run in at night, and I lay down with my clothes on. About 4 A. M. I was awakened by a bump and sort of grating of the vessel, which I thought was our arrival at the wharf in San Francisco; but instantly the ship struck heavily; the engines stopped, and the running to and fro on deck showed that something was wrong. In a moment I was out of my state-room, at the bulwark, holding fast to a stanchion, and looking over the side at the white and seething water caused by her sudden and violent stoppage. The sea was comparatively smooth, the night pitch-dark, and the fog deep and impenetrable; the ship would rise with the swell, and come down with a bump and quiver that was decidedly unpleasant. Soon the passengers were out of their rooms, undressed, calling for help, and praying as though the ship were going to sink immediately. Of course she could not sink, being already on the bottom, and the only question was as to the strength of hull to stand the bumping and straining. Great confusion for a time prevailed, but soon I realized that the captain had taken all proper precautions to secure his boats, of which there were six at the davits. These are the first things that steerage-passengers make for in case of shipwreck, and right over my head I heard the captain's voice say in a low tone, but quite decided: "Let go that falls, or, damn you, I'll blow your head off!" This seemingly harsh language gave me great comfort at the time, and on saying so to the captain afterward, he explained that it was addressed to a passenger who attempted to lower one of the boats. Guards, composed of the crew, were soon posted to prevent any interference with the boats, and the officers circulated among the passengers the report that there was no immediate danger; that, fortunately, the sea was smooth; that we were simply aground, and must quietly await daylight.

They advised the passengers to keep quiet, and the ladies and children to dress and sit at the doors of their state-rooms, there to await the advice and action of the officers of the ship, who were perfectly cool and self-possessed. Meantime the ship was working over a reef—for a time I feared she would break in two; but, as the water gradually rose inside to a level with the sea outside, the ship swung broadside to the swell, and all her keel seemed to rest on the rock or sand. At no time did the sea break over the deck—but the water below drove all the people up to the main-deck and to the promenade-deck, and thus we remained for about three hours, when daylight came; but there was a fog so thick that nothing but water could be seen. The captain caused a boat to be carefully lowered, put in her a trustworthy officer with a boat-compass, and we saw her depart into the fog. During her absence the ship's bell was kept tolling. Then the fires were all out, the ship full of water, and gradually breaking up, wriggling with every swell like a willow basket—the sea all round us full of the floating fragments of her sheeting, twisted and torn into a spongy condition. In less than an hour the boat returned, saying that the beach was quite near, not more than a mile away, and had a good place for landing. All the boats were then carefully lowered, and manned by crews belonging to the ship; a piece of the gangway, on the leeward side, was cut away, and all the women, and a few of the worst-scared men, were lowered into the boats, which pulled for shore. In a comparatively short time the boats returned, took new loads, and the debarkation was afterward carried on quietly and systematically. No baggage was allowed to go on shore except bags or parcels carried in the hands of passengers. At times the fog lifted so that we could see from the wreck the tops of the hills, and the outline of the shore; and I remember sitting on the upper or hurricane deck with the captain, who had his maps and compass before him, and was trying to make out where the ship was. I thought I recognized the outline of the hills below the mission of Dolores, and so stated to him; but he called my attention to the fact that the general line of hills bore northwest, whereas the coast south of San Francisco bears due north and south. He therefore concluded that the ship had overrun her reckoning, and was then to the north of San Francisco. He also explained that, the passage up being longer than usual, viz., eighteen days, the coal was short; that at the time the firemen were using some cut-up spars along with the slack of coal, and that this fuel had made more than usual steam, so that the ship must have glided along faster than reckoned. This proved to be the actual case, for, in fact, the steamship Lewis was wrecked April 9, 1853, on "Duckworth Reef," Baulinas Bay, about eighteen miles above the entrance to San Francisco.

The captain had sent ashore the purser in the first boat, with orders to work his way to the city as soon as possible, to report the loss of his vessel, and to bring back help. I remained on the wreck till among the last of the passengers, managing to get a can of crackers and some sardines out of the submerged pantry, a thing the rest of the passengers did not have, and then I went quietly ashore in one of the boats. The passengers were all on the beach, under a steep bluff; had built fires to dry their clothes, but had seen no human being, and had no idea where they were. Taking along with me a fellow-passenger, a young chap about eighteen years old, I scrambled up the bluff, and walked back toward the hills, in hopes to get a good view of some known object. It was then the month of April, and the hills were covered with the beautiful grasses and flowers of that season of the year. We soon found horse paths and tracks, and following them we came upon a drove of horses grazing at large, some of which had saddle-marks. At about two miles from the beach we found a *corral;* and thence, following one of the strongest-marked paths, in about a mile more we descended into a valley, and, on turning a sharp point, reached a board shanty, with a horse picketed near by. Four men were inside eating a meal. I inquired if any of the Lewis's people had been there; they did not seem to understand what I meant when I explained to them that about three miles from them, and beyond the old *corral,* the steamer Lewis was wrecked, and her passengers were on the beach. I inquired where we were, and they answered, "At Baulinas Creek;" that they were employed at a saw-mill just above, and were engaged in shipping lumber to San Francisco; that a schooner loaded with lumber was then about two miles down the creek, waiting for the tide to get out, and doubtless if we would walk down they would take us on board.

I wrote a few words back to the captain, telling him where he was, and that I would hurry to the city to send him help. My companion and I then went on down the creek, and soon descried the schooner anchored out in the stream. On being hailed, a small boat came in and took us on board. The "captain" willingly agreed for a small sum to carry us down to San Francisco; and, as his whole crew consisted of a small boy about twelve years old, we helped him to get up his anchor and pole the schooner down the creek and out over the bar on a high tide. This must have been about 2 P. M. Once over the bar, the sails were hoisted, and we glided along rapidly with a strong, fair, northwest wind. The fog had lifted, so we could see the shores plainly, and the entrance to the bay. In a couple of hours we were entering the bay, and running "wing-and-wing." Outside the wind was simply the usual strong breeze; but, as it passes through the head of the Golden Gate, it increases, and there, too, we met a strong ebb-tide.

The schooner was loaded with lumber, much of which was on deck, lashed down to ring-bolts with raw-hide thongs. The captain was steering, and I was reclining on the lumber, looking at the familiar shore, as we approached Fort Point, when I heard a sort of cry, and felt the schooner going over. As we got into the throat of the "Heads," the force of the wind, meeting a strong ebb-tide, drove the nose of the schooner under water; she dove like a duck, went over on her side, and began to drift out with the tide. I found myself in the water, mixed up with pieces of plank and ropes; struck out, swam round to the stern, got on the keel, and clambered up on the side. Satisfied that she could not sink, by reason of her cargo, I was not in the least alarmed, but thought two shipwrecks in one day not a good beginning for a new, peaceful career. Nobody was drowned, however; the captain and crew were busy in securing such articles as were liable to float off, and I looked out for some passing boat or vessel to pick us up. We were drifting steadily out to sea, while I was signaling to a boat about three miles off, toward Saucelito, and saw her tack and stand toward us. I was busy watching this sail-boat, when I heard a Yankee's voice, close behind, saying, "This is a nice mess you've got yourselves into," and looking about I saw a man in a small boat, who had seen us upset, and had rowed out to us from a schooner anchored close under the fort. Some explanations were made, and when the sail-boat coming from Saucelito was near enough to be spoken to, and the captain had engaged her to help his schooner, we bade him good-by, and got the man in the small boat to carry us ashore, and land us at the foot of the bluff, just below the fort. Once there, I was at home, and we footed it up to the Presidio. Of the sentinel I inquired who was in command of the post, and was answered,

"Major Merchant." He was not then in, but his adjutant, Lieutenant Gardner, was.[38] I sent my card to him; he came out, and was much surprised to find me covered with sand, and dripping with water, a good specimen of a ship-wrecked mariner. A few words of explanation sufficed; horses were provided, and we rode hastily into the city, reaching the office of the Nicaragua Steamship Company (C. K. Garrison, agent)[39] about dark, just as the purser had arrived, by a totally different route. It was too late to send relief that night, but by daylight next morning two steamers were *en route* for and reached the place of wreck in time to relieve the passengers and bring them, and most of the baggage. I lost my carpet-bag, but saved my trunk. The Lewis went to pieces the night after we got off, and, had there been an average sea during the night of our shipwreck, none of us probably would have escaped. That evening in San Francisco I hunted up Major Turner, whom I found boarding, in company with General E. A. Hitchcock, at a Mrs. Ross's, on Clay Street, near Powell.[40] I took quarters with them, and began to make my studies, with a view to a decision whether it was best to undertake this new and untried scheme of banking, or to return to New Orleans and hold on to what I then had, a good army commission.

At the time of my arrival, San Francisco was on the top wave of speculation and prosperity. Major Turner had rented at six hundred dollars a month the office formerly used and then owned by Adams & Co., on the east side of Montgomery Street, between Sacramento and California Streets.[41] B. R. Nisbet was the active partner, and James Reilly the teller. Already the bank of

[38] Charles S. Merchant (1795–1879), a veteran of the War of 1812, graduated from the USMA in 1814. He commanded the 3rd Art. at the Presidio in San Francisco in 1853 and from 1857 to 1861. William M. Gardner (1824–1901), veteran of the Mexican-American War, graduated from the USMA in 1846. He was stationed in San Francisco from 1849 to 1855. *USMA,* 1:112–113; 2:302–303.

[39] Cornelius K. Garrison (1809–1885), a banker and former steamboat captain, was the agent for the Accessory Transit Company in San Francisco in 1853. That year, he was elected mayor of the city. Randall Gabrielan, *Lost Monmouth County* (Charleston: History Press, 2021), 61; T. J. Stiles, *The Epic Life of Cornelius Vanderbilt* (New York: Vintage, 2009), 225.

[40] Ethan A. Hitchcock (1798–1870) graduated from the USMA in 1817. After the Mexican-American War, he commanded the Pacific Division from 1851 to 1854. *USMA,* 1:167–179.

[41] D. H. Haskell opened Adams and Company after he arrived in San Francisco in Oct. 1849. By 1852 the company was converted into a bank with capital of approximately $2,000,000. For a brief history of banks and bankers of San Francisco from 1848 to 1864, see *Monthly Review: Mercantile Trust Company of California,* no. 1 (San Francisco: Mercantile Trust Company of California, 1924), 13:123–127.

Lucas, Turner & Co. was established, and was engaged in selling bills of exchange, receiving deposits, and loaning money at three per cent. a month.

Page, Bacon & Co., and Adams & Co., were in full blast across the street, in Parrott's new granite building,[42] and other bankers were doing seemingly a prosperous business, among them Wells, Fargo & Co.; Drexel, Sather & Church; Burgoyne & Co.; James King of Wm.; Sanders & Brenham; Davidson & Co.; Palmer, Cook & Co., and others. Turner and I had rooms at Mrs. Ross's, and took our meals at restaurants down-town, mostly at a Frenchman's named Martin, on the southwest corner of Montgomery and California Streets. General Hitchcock, of the army, commanding the Department of California, usually messed with us; also a Captain Mason, and Lieutenant Whiting, of the Engineer Corps.[43] We soon secured a small share of business, and became satisfied there was room for profit. Everybody seemed to be making money fast; the city was being rapidly extended and improved; people paid their three per cent. a month interest without fail, and without deeming it excessive. Turner, Nisbet, and I, daily discussed the prospects, and gradually settled down to the conviction that with two hundred thousand dollars capital, and a credit of fifty thousand dollars in New York, we could build up a business that would help the St. Louis house, and at the same time pay expenses in California, with a reasonable profit. Of course, Turner never designed to remain long in California, and I consented to go back to St. Louis, confer with Mr. Lucas and Captain Simonds,[44] agree upon further details, and then return permanently.

I have no memoranda by me now by which to determine the fact, but think I returned to New York in July, 1853, by the Nicaragua route, and thence

[42] John Parrott (1810–1884) worked as a banker and venture capitalist. He cofounded the Parrott & Company Bank in San Francisco in 1855. Clarke, *Sherman: Gold Rush Banker*, 379.

[43] John S. Mason (1824–1897) graduated from the USMA in 1847 and served in the Mexican-American War. He was later stationed in California on frontier duty from 1848 to 1860. William H. C. Whiting (1824–1865) graduated from the USMA in 1845. As a first lieutenant in the Corps of Engineers, he assisted in the construction of fortifications at the entrance to San Francisco Bay from 1853 to 1855. He joined the Confederate Army at the outbreak of the Civil War and died as a prisoner of war in Mar. 1865. *USMA,* 2:208–209, 311–312.

[44] John Simonds (1800–1860) and James Lucas partnered to establish their own banking firm in St. Louis in 1852. J. Thomas Scharf, *History of Saint Louis City and County* (Philadelphia: Louis H. Everts, 1883), 1407.

to St. Louis by way of Lancaster, Ohio, where my family still was.[45] Mr. Lucas promptly agreed to the terms proposed, and further consented, on the expiration of the lease of the Adams & Co. office, to erect a new banking-house in San Francisco, to cost fifty thousand dollars. I then returned to Lancaster, explained to Mr. Ewing and Mrs. Sherman all the details of our agreement, and, meeting their approval, I sent to the Adjutant-General of the army my letter of resignation, to take effect at the end of the six months' leave, and the resignation was accepted, to take effect September 6, 1853. Being then a citizen, I engaged a passage out to California by the Nicaragua route, in the steamer leaving New York September 20th, for myself and family, and accordingly proceeded to New York, where I had a conference with Mr. Meigs, cashier of the American Exchange Bank, and with Messrs. Wadsworth & Sheldon, bankers, who were our New York correspondents;[46] and on the 20th embarked for San Juan del Norte, with the family, composed of Mrs. Sherman, Lizzie, then less than a year old, and her nurse, Mary Lynch.[47] Our passage down was uneventful, and, on the boats up the Nicaragua River, pretty much the same as before. On reaching Virgin Bay, I engaged a native with three mules to carry us across to the Pacific, and as usual the trip partook of the ludicrous—Mrs. Sherman mounted on a donkey about as large as a Newfoundland dog; Mary Lynch on another, trying to carry Lizzie on a pillow before her, but her mule had a fashion of lying down, which scared her, till I exchanged mules, and my California spurs kept that mule on his legs. I carried Lizzie some time till she was fast asleep, when I got our native man to

[45] WTS left San Francisco for New York on July 16, 1853. Clarke, *Sherman: Gold Rush Banker,* 20.

[46] Henry Meigs Jr. (1809–1887) was a cashier at the Metropolitan Bank in New York City in 1854. He became a member of the New York Stock Exchange in 1858 and served as the stock exchange's president in 1877–1878. He also served as the first mayor of Bayonne, NJ, from 1869 to 1879. In addition to being a banker, Julius Wadsworth (1815–1887) served as the president of the Second Avenue Railroad Company in New York City. His banking partner, James O. Sheldon (1823–1907), became a banker in New York City at age twenty-six. He remained in the business until an illness forced him to move back to his home in Connecticut in 1855. Henry Hall, ed., *America's Successful Men of Affairs* (New York: New York Tribune, 1895), vol. 1, s.v. "James Owen Sheldon"; Henry B. Meigs, *Record of the Descendants of Vincent Meigs* (Baltimore: J. S. Bridges, 1901), 86, 255–256; *Rhodes' Journal of Banking for the Year 1887* (New York: Bradford Rhodes, 1887), 14:760.

[47] Mary Lynch (1820–1877) was an Irish immigrant who worked as a nurse for WTS's family. Clarke, *Sherman: Gold Rush Banker,* 20.

carry her awhile. The child woke up, and, finding herself in the hands of a dark-visaged man, she yelled most lustily till I got her away. At the summit of the pass, there was a clear-running brook, where we rested an hour, and bathed Lizzie in its sweet waters. We then continued to the end of our journey, and, without going to the tavern at San Juan del Sur, we passed directly to the vessel, then at anchor about two miles out. To reach her we engaged a native boat, which had to be kept outside the surf. Mrs. Sherman was first taken in the arms of two stout natives; Mary Lynch, carrying Lizzie, was carried by two others; and I followed, mounted on the back of a strapping fellow, while fifty or a hundred others were running to and fro, cackling like geese.

Mary Lynch got scared at the surf, and began screaming like a fool, when Lizzie became convulsed with fear, and one of the natives rushed to her, caught her out of Mary's arms, and carried her swiftly to Mrs. Sherman, who, by that time, was in the boat, but Lizzie had fainted with fear, and for a long time sobbed as though permanently injured. For years she showed symptoms that made us believe she had never entirely recovered from the effects of the scare. In due time we reached the steamer Sierra Nevada, and got a good state-room. Our passage up the coast was pleasant enough; we reached San Francisco; on the 15th of October, and took quarters at an hotel on Stockton Street, near Broadway.

Major Turner remained till some time in November, when he also departed for the East, leaving me and Nisbet to manage the bank. I endeavored to make myself familiar with the business, but of course Nisbet kept the books, and gave his personal attention to the loans, discounts, and drafts, which yielded the profits. I soon saw, however, that the three per cent. charged as premium on bills of exchange was not all profit, but out of this had to come one and a fourth to one and a half for freight, one and a third for insurance, with some indefinite promise of a return premium; then, the cost of blanks, boxing of the bullion, etc., etc. Indeed, I saw no margin for profit at all. Nisbet, however, who had long been familiar with the business, insisted there was a profit, in the fact that the gold-dust or bullion shipped was more valuable than its cost to us. We, of course, had to remit bullion to meet our bills on New York, and bought crude gold-dust, or bars refined by Kellogg & Humbert or E. Justh & Co., for at that time the United States Mint was not in operation.[48] But, as the reports of our shipments came back from New York, I discovered that I was right, and

[48]The U.S. Mint in San Francisco began its operations in Apr. 1854. Over the next eight months, the mint had a coinage output of approximately $500,000 per month. Benjamin Wright, *Banking in California, 1849–1910* (San Francisco: H. S. Crocker, 1910), 161.

Nisbet was wrong; and, although we could not help selling our checks on New York and St. Louis at the same price as other bankers, I discovered that, at all events, the exchange business in San Francisco was rather a losing business than profitable. The same as to loans. We could loan, at three per cent. a month, all our own money, say two hundred and fifty thousand dollars, and a part of our deposit account. This latter account in California was decidedly uncertain. The balance due depositors would run down to a mere nominal sum on steamer-days, which were the 1st and 15th of each month, and then would increase till the next steamer-day, so that we could not make use of any reasonable part of this balance for loans beyond the next steamer-day; or, in other words, we had an expensive bank, with expensive clerks, and all the machinery for taking care of other people's money for their benefit, without corresponding profit. I also saw that loans were attended with *risk* commensurate with the rate; nevertheless, I could not attempt to reform the rules and customs established by others before me, and had to drift along with the rest toward that Niagara that none foresaw at the time.

Shortly after arriving out in 1853, we looked around for a site for the new bank, and the only place then available on Montgomery Street, the Wall Street of San Francisco, was a lot at the corner of Jackson Street, facing Montgomery, with an alley on the north, belonging to James Lick.[49] The ground was sixty by sixty-two feet, and I had to pay for it thirty-two thousand dollars. I then made a contract with the builders, Keyser & Brown, to erect a three-story brick building, with finished basement, for about fifty thousand dollars. This made eighty-two thousand instead of fifty thousand dollars, but I thought Mr. Lucas could stand it and would approve, which he did, though it resulted in loss to him. After the civil war, he told me he had sold the building for forty thousand dollars, about half its cost, but luckily gold was then at 250, so that he could use the forty thousand dollars gold as the equivalent of one hundred thousand dollars currency. The building was erected; I gave it my personal supervision, and it was strongly and thoroughly built, for I saw it two years ago, when several earthquakes had made no impression on it; still, the choice of site was unfortunate, for the city drifted in the opposite direction, viz., toward Market Street. I then thought that all the heavy business would remain toward the foot of Broadway and Jackson Street, because

[49] James Lick (1796–1876) arrived in San Francisco around 1848 with approximately $30,000 on hand. Because of his investments, Lick soon became one of the wealthiest businessmen in the city. Frederick Seitz, *A Selection of Highlights from the History of the National Academy of Sciences, 1863–2005* (Lanham, MD: University Press of America, 2007), 44–45.

there were the deepest water and best wharves, but in this I made a mistake. Nevertheless, in the spring of 1854, the new bank was finished, and we removed to it, paying rents thereafter to our Mr. Lucas instead of to Adams & Co. A man named Wright, during the same season, built a still finer building just across the street from us; Pioche, Bayerque & Co. were already established on another corner of Jackson Street, and the new Metropolitan Theatre was in progress diagonally opposite us.[50] During the whole of 1854 our business steadily grew, our average deposits going up to half a million, and our sales of exchange and consequent shipment of bullion averaging two hundred thousand dollars per steamer. I signed all bills of exchange, and insisted on Nisbet consulting me on loans and discounts. Spite of every caution, however, we lost occasionally by bad loans, and worse by the steady depreciation of real estate. The city of San Francisco was then extending her streets, sewering them, and planking them, with three-inch lumber. In payment for the lumber and the work of contractors, the city authorities paid scrip in even sums of one hundred, five hundred, one thousand, and five thousand dollars. These formed a favorite collateral for loans at from fifty to sixty cents on the dollar, and no one doubted their ultimate value, either by redemption or by being converted into city bonds. The notes also of H. Meiggs, Neeley Thompson & Co., etc., lumber-dealers, were favorite notes, for they paid their interest promptly, and lodged large margins of these street-improvement warrants as collateral. At that time, Meiggs was a prominent man, lived in style in a large house on Broadway, was a member of the City Council, and owned large saw-mills up the coast about Mendocino.[51] In him Nisbet had unbounded faith, but, for some reason, I feared or mistrusted him, and remember that I cautioned Nisbet not to extend his credit, but to gradually contract his loans. On looking over our bills receivable, then about six hundred thousand dollars, I found Meiggs, as principal or indorser, owed us about eighty thousand dollars—all, however,

[50] Stephen A. Wright opened Miners Bank, one of the first banks in San Francisco, in 1848. He moved into the building situated at the northwest corner of Jackson and Montgomery Streets around 1854. The Metropolitan Theatre was built in the fall of 1853 and remained in operation until it burned down in 1857. It was rebuilt in 1861 and officially closed in 1873. Clarke, *Sherman: Gold Rush Banker,* 6; James R. Smith, *San Francisco's Lost Landmarks* (Sanger, CA: Word Dancer, 2005), 99–101.

[51] Henry "Honest Harry" Meiggs (1811–1877), not to be confused with the Henry Meigs Jr. mentioned earlier in this chapter, was a lumber merchant from New York. He moved to San Francisco in 1849. Samuel C. Upham, *Notes of a Voyage to California via Cape Horn* (self-pub., 1878), 145–146.

secured by city warrants; still, he kept bank accounts elsewhere, and was generally a borrower. I instructed Nisbet to insist on his reducing his line as the notes matured, and, as he found it indelicate to speak to Meiggs, I instructed him to refer him to me; accordingly, when, on the next steamer-day, Meiggs appeared at the counter for a draft on Philadelphia, of about twenty thousand dollars, for which he offered his note and collateral, he was referred to me, and I explained to him that our draft was the same as money; that he could have it for cash, but that we were already in advance to him some seventy-five or eighty thousand dollars, and that instead of increasing the amount I must insist on its reduction. He inquired if I mistrusted his ability, etc. I explained, certainly not, but that our duty was to assist those who did *all* their business with us, and, as our means were necessarily limited, I must restrict him to some reasonable sum, say, twenty-five thousand dollars. Meiggs invited me to go with him to a rich mercantile house on Clay Street, whose partners belonged in Hamburg, and there, in the presence of the principals of the house, he demonstrated, as clearly as a proposition in mathematics, that his business at Mendocino was based on calculations that could not fail. The bill of exchange which he wanted, he said would make the last payment on a propeller already built in Philadelphia, which would be sent to San Francisco, to tow into and out of port the schooners and brigs that were bringing his lumber down the coast. I admitted all he said, but renewed my determination to limit his credit to twenty-five thousand dollars. The Hamburg firm then agreed to accept for him the payment of all his debt to us, except the twenty-five thousand dollars, payable in equal parts for the next three steamer-days. Accordingly, Meiggs went back with me to our bank, wrote his note for twenty-five thousand dollars, and secured it by mortgage on real estate and city warrants, and substituted the three acceptances of the Hamburg firm for the overplus. I surrendered to him all his former notes, except one for which he was indorser. The three acceptances duly matured and were paid; one morning Meiggs and family were missing, and it was discovered they had embarked in a sailing-vessel for South America.[52] This was the beginning of a series of failures in San Francisco, that extended through the next two years. As soon as it was known that Meiggs had fled, the town was full of rumors, and everybody was running to and fro to secure his money. His debts amounted to nearly a million dollars. The Hamburg house which, had been humbugged, were heavy losers and failed, I think. I took possession of Meiggs's dwelling-house and other property for which I held his

[52] Meiggs left San Francisco aboard the steamship *America* in the early morning of Oct. 4, 1854. Upham, *Notes of a Voyage*, 148.

mortgage, and in the city warrants thought I had an overplus; but it transpired that Meiggs, being in the City Council, had issued various quantities of street scrip, which was adjudged a forgery, though, beyond doubt, most of it, if not all, was properly signed, but fraudulently issued. On this city scrip our bank must have lost about ten thousand dollars. Meiggs subsequently turned up in Chili, where again he rose to wealth and has paid much of his San Francisco debts, but none to us. He is now in Peru, living like a prince.[53] With Meiggs fell all the lumber-dealers, and many persons dealing in city scrip. Compared with others, our loss was a trifle. In a short time things in San Francisco resumed their wonted course, and we generally laughed at the escapade of Meiggs, and the cursing of his deluded creditors.

Shortly after our arrival in San Francisco, I rented of a Mr. Marryat, son of the English Captain Marryat, the author,[54] a small frame-house on Stockton Street, near Green, buying of him his furniture, and we removed to it about December 1, 1853. Close by, around on Green Street, a man named Dickey was building two small brick-houses, on ground which he had leased of Nicholson. I bought one of these houses, subject to the ground-rent, and moved into it as soon as finished. Lieutenant T. H. Stevens, of the United States Navy,[55] with his family, rented the other; we lived in this house throughout the year 1854, and up to April 17, 1855.

[53] In late 1854 Meiggs and his family arrived in Chile, where he soon acquired government contracts to build railroads and bridges. He died in Lima, Peru, on Sept. 29, 1877. Upham, *Notes of a Voyage,* 145, 151.

[54] Frank Marryat (1826–1855) moved from England to California in June 1850. His father, Frederick Marryat (1792–1848), served in the British Royal Navy and authored multiple novels detailing maritime life. Oliver Warner, *Captain Marryat: A Rediscovery* (Berkeley: University of California Press, 1953), 16; Peter Wild, Donald A. Barclay, and James H. Maguire, eds., *Different Travellers, Different Eyes: Artists' Narratives of the American West, 1820–1920* (Fort Worth: TCU Press, 2001), 93–94.

[55] Thomas Holdup Stevens Jr. (1819–1896) became a lieutenant in the U.S. Navy in 1849 and commanded several vessels during his naval career. Before his retirement, Stevens attained the rank of rear admiral. Charles Morris, *Men of the Century: An Historical Work, Giving Portraits and Sketches of Eminent Citizens of the United States* (Philadelphia: L. R. Hamersly, 1896), 137.

5

California.

1855–1857.

DURING THE WINTER of 1854–'55, I received frequent intimations in my letters from the St. Louis house, that the bank of Page, Bacon & Co. was in trouble, growing out of their relations to the Ohio & Mississippi Railroad, to the contractors for building which they had made large advances, to secure which they had been compelled to take, as it were, an assignment of the contract itself, and finally to assume all the liabilities of the contractors. Then they had to borrow money in New York, and raise other money from time to time, in the purchase of iron and materials for the road, and to pay the hands. The firm in St. Louis and that in San Francisco were different, having different partners, and the St. Louis house naturally pressed the San Francisco firm to ship largely of "gold-dust," which gave them a great name; also to keep as large a balance as possible in New York to sustain their credit.[1] Mr. Page was a very wealthy man, but his wealth consisted mostly of land and property in St. Louis. He was an old man, and a good one; had been a baker, and knew little of banking as a business.[2] This part of his general business was managed exclusively by his son-in-law, Henry D. Bacon, who was young, handsome, and generally popular.[3] How he was drawn into that affair of the Ohio & Mississippi road I have no means of knowing, except by hearsay. Their business in New York was

[1] For more information on the history of Page, Bacon & Company, see Dwight L. Clarke, *William Tecumseh Sherman: Gold Rush Banker* (San Francisco: California Historical Society, 1969), 420–424.

[2] Daniel D. Page (1790–1896) was elected mayor of St. Louis in 1829. He and Henry D. Bacon founded Page, Bacon, & Co. in 1848. William Hyde and Howard L. Conard, eds., *Encyclopedia of the History of St. Louis: A Compendium of History and Biography for Ready Reference* (New York: Southern History, 1899), vol. 3, s.v. "Page, Daniel D."

[3] Henry D. Bacon (1817–1893) moved to St. Louis in 1835 and married Julia Page, the daughter of Daniel D. Page. Richard Edwards and M. Hopewell, *Edwards's Great West and Her Commercial Metropolis* (St. Louis: Edwards's Monthly, 1860), 132–135.

done through the American Exchange Bank, and through Duncan, Sherman & Co. As we were rival houses, the St. Louis partners removed our account from the American Exchange Bank to the Metropolitan Bank; and, as Wadsworth & Sheldon had failed, I was instructed to deal in time bills, and in European exchange, with Schuchardt & Gebhard, bankers in Nassau Street.

In California the house of Page, Bacon & Co. was composed of the same partners as in St. Louis, with the addition of Henry Haight, Judge Chambers, and young Frank Page.[4] The latter had charge of the "branch" in Sacramento. Haight was the real head-man, but he was too fond of lager-beer to be intrusted with so large a business. Beyond all comparison, Page, Bacon & Co. were the most prominent bankers in California in 1853–'55. Though I had notice of danger in that quarter, from our partners in St. Louis, nobody in California doubted their wealth and stability. They must have had, during that winter, an average deposit account of nearly two million dollars, of which seven hundred thousand dollars was in "certificates of deposit," the most stable of all accounts in a bank. Thousands of miners invested their earnings in such certificates, which they converted into drafts on New York, when they were ready to go home or wanted to send their "pile" to their families. Adams & Co. were next in order, because of their numerous offices scattered throughout the mining country.[5] A gentleman named Haskell[6] had been in charge of Adams & Co. in San Francisco, but in the winter of 1854–'55 some changes were made, and the banking department had been transferred to a magnificent office in Halleck's new Metropolitan Block. James King of Wm.[7] had discontinued business on his own account, and been employed by Adams & Co. as their cashier

[4] Henry Haight (1820–1869) moved to San Francisco in 1850 with David Chambers to help establish Page, Bacon, & Co. Frank Page (c. 1820–c. 1883), the son of Daniel D. Page, managed the firm's Sacramento branch. Peter H. Burnett, *Recollections and Opinions of an Old Pioneer* (New York: D. Appleton, 1880), 373; "Death of an Old Citizen," *San Francisco Examiner,* Mar. 25, 1869, 2.

[5] Adams & Co. was founded in 1849 as a branch of the Boston Express Company. *Monthly Review: Mercantile Trust Company of California,* no. 1 (San Francisco: Mercantile Trust Company of California, 1924), 13:123.

[6] Daniel H. Haskell moved to San Francisco and partnered with Alvin Adams and Isaiah C. Woods to establish Adams & Co. Theodore H. Hittell, *History of California* (San Francisco: N .J. Stones, 1897), 3:445.

[7] James King of William (1822–1856) was a banker and journalist in San Francisco. He earned approximately $1,000 a month as the manager of Adams & Co. John D. Lawson, ed., *American State Trials* (St. Louis: Thomas Law, 1926), 15:97.

and banker, and Isaiah C. Wood[8] had succeeded Haskell in chief control of the express department. Wells, Fargo & Co. were also bankers as well as expressmen, and William J. Pardee[9] was the resident partner.

As the mail-steamer came in on February 17, 1855, according to her custom, she ran close to the Long Wharf (Meiggs's) on North Beach,[10] to throw ashore the express-parcels of news for speedy delivery. Some passenger on deck called to a man of his acquaintance standing on the wharf, that Page & Bacon had failed in New York. The news spread like wild-fire, but soon it was met by the newspaper accounts to the effect that some particular acceptances of Page & Bacon, of St. Louis, in the hands of Duncan, Sherman & Co., in New York, had gone to protest. All who had balances at Page, Bacon & Co.'s, or held certificates of deposit, were more or less alarmed, wanted to secure their money, and a general excitement pervaded the whole community. Word was soon passed round that the matter admitted of explanation, viz., that the two houses were distinct and separate concerns, that every draft of the *California* house had been paid in New York, and would continue to be paid. It was expected that this assertion would quiet the fears of the California creditors, but for the next three days there was a steady "run" on that bank. Page, Bacon & Co. stood the first day's run very well, and, as I afterward learned, paid out about six hundred thousand dollars in gold coin.[11] On the 20th of February Henry Haight came to our bank, to see what help we were willing to give him; but I was out, and Nisbet could not answer positively for the firm. Our condition was then very strong. The deposit account was about six hundred thousand dollars, and we had in our vault about five hundred thousand dollars in coin and bullion, besides an equal amount of good bills receivable. Still I did not like to weaken ourselves to help others; but in a most friendly spirit, that night after bank-hours, I went down to Page, Bacon & Co., and entered their office from the

[8] Isaiah C. Woods (1825–1880) moved to California in 1848. Albert Shumate, *The Notorious I. C. Woods of the Adams Express* (Glendale, CA: Albert H. Clark, 1986), 13, 25.

[9] William J. Pardee (1806–1859) was a member of the firm Lansing & Pardee in Little Falls, NY, before moving to San Francisco. Donald L. Jacobus, ed., *The Pardee Genealogy* (New Haven, CT: New Haven Colony Historical Society, 1927), 362.

[10] Long Wharf, also known as Commercial Street Wharf, was built around 1849 and extended 250 feet out from Montgomery Street. It burned down in 1850 but was rebuilt to extend nearly 2,000 feet into the bay. E. M. North Whitcomb, "Along San Francisco's Front," *Overland Monthly* 72, no. 2 (July–Dec. 1918): 31.

[11] For WTS's contemporary report of the collapse of Page, Bacon & Co., see Clarke, *Sherman: Gold Rush Banker*, 107–118.

rear. I found in the cashier's room Folsom, Parrott, Dewey[12] and Payne,[13] Captain Ritchie,[14] Donohue,[15] and others, citizens and friends of the house, who had been called in for consultation. Passing into the main office, where all the book-keepers, tellers, etc., with gas-lights, were busy writing up the day's work, I found Mr. Page, Henry Haight, and Judge Chambers. I spoke to Haight, saying that I was sorry I had been out when he called at our bank, and had now come to see him in the most friendly spirit. Haight had evidently been drinking, and said abruptly that "all the banks would break," that "no bank could instantly pay all its obligations," etc. I answered he could speak for himself, but not for me; that I had come to offer to buy with cash a fair proportion of his bullion, notes, and bills; but, if they were going to fail, I would not be drawn in. Haight's manner was extremely offensive, but Mr. Page tried to smooth it over, saying they had had a bad day's run, and could not answer for the result till their books were written up.

I passed back again into the room where the before-named gentlemen were discussing some paper which lay before them, and was going to pass out, when Captain Folsom, who was an officer of the army, a class-mate and intimate friend of mine, handed me the paper the contents of which they were discussing. It was very short, and in Henry Haight's handwriting, pretty much in these terms: "We, the undersigned property-holders of San Francisco, having *personally* examined the books, papers, etc., of Page, Bacon & Co., do hereby certify that the house is solvent and able to pay all its debts,"

[12] Squire P. Dewey (1815–1889) was born in Nassau in 1815 and worked as a prominent banker and import-export specialist in San Francisco. A. L. Bancroft, *Contemporary Biography of California's Representative Men* (New York: A. L. Bancroft, 1881), 253–258.

[13] Theodore Payne (1816–1861) moved to San Francisco in late 1849. In 1850 he partnered with Squire P. Dewey to establish an auction house named Theodore Payne & Co. Frank Soulé, John. H. Gihon, and James Nisbet, *The Annals of San Francisco* (New York: D. Appleton, 1855), 799–805.

[14] Archibald A. Ritchie (1806–1856) was a prominent landowner in California during the Gold Rush. He owned Rancho Suisun, an 18,000-acre tract of land in Solano County. Albert Shumate, *Captain A. A. Ritchie, California Pioneer* (San Francisco: Society of California Pioneers, 1991), 13, 49.

[15] Peter Donohue (1822–1885) was born in Scotland and as a young boy moved to New Jersey with his family. He moved west during the Gold Rush and in San Francisco founded a blacksmith shop that later became the Union Iron Works. Donohue also founded the San Francisco Gas Company and the Omnibus Railroad. Richard H. Dillon, *Iron Men: California's Industrious Pioneers, Peter, James, and Michael Donohue* (New York: James Stevenson, 2004), 9, 31, 136.

etc. Haight had drawn up and asked them to sign this paper, with the intention to publish it in the next morning's papers, for effect. While I was talking with Captain Folsom, Haight came into the room to listen. I admitted that the effect of such a publication would surely be good, and would probably stave off immediate demand till their assets could be in part converted or realized; but I naturally inquired of Folsom, "Have you personally examined the accounts, as herein recited, and the assets, enough to warrant your signature to this paper?" for, "thereby you in effect become indorsers." Folsom said they had not, when Haight turned on me rudely and said, "Do you think the affairs of such a house as Page, Bacon & Co. can be critically examined in an hour?" I answered: "These gentlemen can do what they please, but they have twelve hours before the bank will open on the morrow, and if the ledger is written up" (as I believed it was or could be by midnight), "they can (by counting the coin, bullion on hand, and notes or stocks of immediate realization) approximate near enough for them to indorse for the remainder." But Haight pooh-poohed me, and I left. Folsom followed me out, told me he could not afford to imperil all he had, and asked my advice. I explained to him that my partner Nisbet had been educated and trained in that very house of Page, Bacon & Co.; that we kept our books exactly as they did; that every day the ledger was written up, so that from it one could see exactly how much actual money was due the depositors and certificates; and then by counting the money in the vault, estimating the bullion on hand, which, though not actual money, could easily be converted into coin, and supplementing these amounts by "bills receivable," they ought to arrive at an approximate result. After Folsom had left me, John Parrott also stopped and talked with me to the same effect. Next morning I looked out for the notice, but no such notice appeared in the morning papers, and I afterward learned that, on Parrott and Folsom demanding an actual count of the money in the vault, Haight angrily refused unless they would accept his word for it, when one after the other declined to sign his paper.

The run on Page, Bacon & Co. therefore continued throughout the 21st, and I expected all day to get an invitation to close our bank for the next day, February 22, which we could have made a holiday by concerted action; but each banker waited for Page, Bacon & Co. to ask for it, and, no such circular coming, in the then state of feeling no other banker was willing to take the initiative. On the morning of February 22, 1855, everybody was startled by receiving a small slip of paper, delivered at all the houses, on which was printed a short notice that, for "want of coin," Page, Bacon & Co. found it necessary to close their bank for a short time. Of course, we all knew the consequences, and that every other bank in San Francisco would be tried. During the 22d we all kept open, and watched our depositors closely; but the day was generally observed by the people as a holiday, and the firemen paraded the streets of San Francisco in unusual strength. But, on writing up our books that night, we found that our deposit account had diminished about sixty-five thousand dollars. Still, there was no run on us, or any other of the banks, that day; yet, observing little knots of men on the street, discussing the state of the banks generally, and overhearing Haight's expression quoted, that, in case of the failure of Page, Bacon & Co., "all the other banks would break," I deemed it prudent to make ready. For some days we had refused all loans and renewals, and we tried, without success, some of our call-loans; but, like Hotspur's spirits, they would not come.[16]

Our financial condition on that day (February 22, 1855) was: Due depositors and demand certificates, five hundred and twenty thousand dollars; to meet which, we had in the vault—coin, three hundred and eighty thousand dollars; bullion, seventy-five thousand dollars; and bills receivable, about six hundred thousand dollars. Of these, at least one hundred thousand dollars were on demand, with stock collaterals. Therefore, for the extent of our business, we were stronger than the Bank of England, or any bank in New York City.

Before daylight next morning, our door-bell was rung, and I was called down-stairs by E. Casserly, Esq. (an eminent lawyer of the day, since United States Senator),[17] who informed me he had just come up from the office of Adams & Co., to tell me that their affairs were in such condition that they would not open that morning at all; and that this, added to the suspension of Page, Bacon & Co., announced the day before, would surely cause a general run on all the banks. I informed him that I expected as much, and was prepared for it.

In going down to the bank that morning, I found Montgomery Street full; but, punctually to the minute, the bank opened, and in rushed the crowd. As usual, the most noisy and clamorous were men and women who held small

[16] In William Shakespeare's play *King Henry IV,* the character Glendower states, "I can call spirits from the vasty deep." Hotspur, an ally of Glendower, responds, "Why, so can I, or so can any man; But will they come when you do call for them?" William Shakespeare, *King Henry IV (Part I),* ed. Henry Morley (London: Cassell, 1898), 83.

[17] Eugene Casserly (1820–1883) was born in Ireland and immigrated to the United States in 1822. He graduated from Georgetown University and practiced law in California before serving as a U.S. senator from 1869 to 1873. Frank H. Gille, ed., *The Encyclopedia of California* (St. Clair: Somerset, 1999), vol. 1, s.v. "Casserly, Eugene."

certificates; still, others with larger accounts were in the crowd, pushing forward for their balances. All were promptly met and paid. Several gentlemen of my personal acquaintance merely asked my word of honor that their money was safe, and went away; others, who had large balances, and no immediate use for coin, gladly accepted gold-bars, whereby we paid out the seventy-five thousand dollars of bullion, relieving the coin to that amount.

Meantime, rumors from the street came pouring in that Wright & Co. had failed; then Wells, Fargo & Co.; then Palmer, Cook & Co., and indeed all, or nearly all, the banks of the city; and I was told that parties on the street were betting high, first, that we would close our doors at eleven o'clock; then twelve, and so on; but we did not, till the usual hour that night. We had paid every demand, and still had a respectable amount left.

This run on the bank (the only one I ever experienced) presented all the features, serious and comical, usual to such occasions. At our counter happened that identical case, narrated of others, of the Frenchman, who was nearly squeezed to death in getting to the counter, and, when he received his money, did not know what to do with it. "If you got the money, I no want him; but if you no got him, I want it like the devil!"

Toward the close of the day, some of our customers deposited, rather ostentatiously, small amounts, not aggregating more than eight or ten thousand dollars. Book-keepers and tellers were kept at work to write up the books; and these showed: Due depositors and certificates, about one hundred and twenty thousand dollars, for which remained of coin about fifty thousand dollars. I resolved not to sleep until I had collected from those owing the bank a part of their debts; for I was angry with them that they had stood back and allowed the panic to fall on the banks alone. Among these were Captain Folsom, who owed us twenty-five thousand dollars, secured by a mortgage on the American Theatre[18] and Tehama Hotel;[19] James Smiley,[20] contractor for building the Custom-House, who owed us two notes of twenty thousand and

[18]The American Theatre, located on Sansome Street, was one of the first theaters built in San Francisco. It burned down in 1850 but was rebuilt in 1851. Hubert H. Bancroft, *West American History* (New York: Bancroft, 1902), 245*n;* Francis C. Wemyss, *Wemyss' Chronology of the American Stage from 1752 to 1852* (New York: William Taylor, 1852), 179.

[19]Folsom constructed the Tehama Hotel at the corner of Sansome and California Streets around 1850. Bancroft, *West American History,* 189*n*.

[20]James Smiley (d. 1892) arrived in San Francisco in 1849 aboard the ship *Gray Eagle*. *Records of the Families of California Pioneers* (California: State Committee of Genealogical Research, Daughters of the American Revolution, 1927), 2:145.

sixteen thousand dollars, for which we held, as collateral, two acceptances of the collector of the port, Major R. P. Hammond, for twenty thousand dollars each; besides other private parties that I need not name. The acceptances given to Smiley were for work done on the Custom-House, but could not be paid until the work was actually laid in the walls, and certified by Major Tower, United States Engineers;[21] but Smiley had an immense amount of granite, brick, iron, etc., on the ground, in advance of construction, and these acceptances were given him expressly that he might raise money thereon for the payment of such materials.

Therefore, as soon as I got my dinner, I took my saddle-horse, and rode to Captain Folsom's house, where I found him in great pain and distress, mental and physical. He was sitting in a chair, and bathing his head with a sponge. I explained to him the object of my visit, and he said he had expected it, and had already sent his agent, Van Winkle,[22] down-town, with instructions to raise what money he could at any cost; but he did not succeed in raising a cent. So great was the shock to public confidence, that men slept on their money, and would not loan it for ten per cent. a week, on any security whatever—even on mint certificates, which were as good as gold, and only required about ten days to be paid in coin by the United States Mint. I then rode up to Hammond's house, on Rincon Hill, and found him there. I explained to him exactly Smiley's affairs, and only asked him to pay one of his acceptances. He inquired, "Why not both?" I answered that was so much the better; it would put me under still greater obligations. He then agreed to meet me at our bank at 10 P.M. I sent word to others that I demanded them to pay what they could on their paper, and then returned to the bank, to meet Hammond. In due time, he came down with Palmer[23] (of Palmer, Cook & Co.), and there he met Smiley, who was, of course, very anxious to retire his notes. We there discussed the matter fully, when Hammond said, "Sherman, give me up my two acceptances,

[21] Zealous B. Tower (1819–1900) graduated from the USMA in 1841 and was the superintending engineer of San Francisco's Custom House and Appraiser's Store from 1855 to 1858. He obtained the rank of major general for his service in the U.S. Army during the Civil War. *USMA,* 2:59–61, 4:55.

[22] Peter W. Van Winkle (c. 1821–c. 1900) served as J. L. Folsom's attorney and executor for his estate. Hubert H. Bancroft, *Bancroft's California Lawyer and Book of Forms* (San Francisco: H. H. Bancroft, 1860), 749; "Van Winkle's Sanity," *San Francisco Chronicle,* Apr. 3, 1889, 8.

[23] Joseph C. Palmer (1819–1882) was a banker accused of misappropriating bank funds in 1855. Lily Frémont, *The Arizona Diary of Lily Frémont,* ed. Mary L. Spence (Tucson: University of Arizona Press, 1997), 231*n;* Hittell, *History of California,* 4:148.

and I will substitute therefor my check of forty thousand dollars," with "the distinct understanding that, if the money is not needed by you, it shall be returned to me, and the transaction then to remain *statu quo.*" To this there was a general assent. Nisbet handed him his two acceptances, and he handed me his check, signed as collector of the port, on Major J. R. Snyder, United States Treasurer, for forty thousand dollars. I afterward rode out, that night, to Major Snyder's house on North Beach, saw him, and he agreed to meet me at 8 A. M. next day, at the United States Mint, and to pay the check, so that I could have the money before the bank opened. The next morning, as agreed on, we met, and he paid me the check in two sealed bags of gold-coin, each marked twenty thousand dollars, which I had carried to the bank, but never opened them, or even broke the seals.

That morning our bank opened as usual, but there was no appearance of a continuation of the "run;" on the contrary, money began to come back on deposit, so that by night we had a considerable increase, and this went on from day to day, till nearly the old condition of things returned. After about three days, finding I had no use for the money obtained on Hammond's check, I took the identical two bags back to the cashier of the Custom-House, and recovered the two acceptances which had been surrendered as described; and Smiley's two notes were afterward paid in their due course, out of the cash received on those identical acceptances. But, years afterward, on settling with Hammond for the Custom-House contract when completed, there was a difference, and Smiley sued Lucas, Turner & Co. for money had and received for his benefit, being the identical forty thousand dollars herein explained, but he lost his case. Hammond, too, was afterward removed from office, and indicted in part for this transaction. He was tried before the United States Circuit Court, Judge McAlister[24] presiding, for a violation of the sub-Treasury Act, but was acquitted. Our bank, having thus passed so well through the crisis, took at once a first rank; but these bank failures had caused so many mercantile losses, and had led to such an utter downfall in the value of real estate, that everybody lost more or less money by bad debts, by depreciation of stocks and collaterals, that became unsalable, if not worthless.

About this time (viz., February, 1855) I had exchanged my house on Green Street, with Mr. Sloat, for the half of a fifty-vara lot on Harrison Street, between Fremont and First, on which there was a small cottage, and I had contracted for

[24] Matthew H. McAlister (1800–1865) was appointed to the U.S. Circuit Court of California by Pres. Franklin Pierce in 1855. *The National Cyclopedia of American Biography* (New York: James T. White, 1909), vol. 11, s.v. "McAllister, Matthew Hall."

the building of a new frame-house thereon, at six thousand dollars. This house was finished on the 9th of April, and my family moved into it at once.

For some time Mrs. Sherman had been anxious to go home to Lancaster, Ohio, where we had left our daughter Minnie, with her grandparents, and we arranged that S. M. Bowman, Esq., and wife,[25] should move into our new house and board us, viz., Lizzie, Willie[26] with the nurse Biddy,[27] and myself, for a fair consideration. It so happened that two of my personal friends, Messrs. Winters and Cunningham of Marysville, and a young fellow named Eagan, now a captain in the Commissary Department, were going East in the steamer of the middle of April, and that Mr. William H. Aspinwall, of New York, and Mr. Chauncey, of Philadelphia, were also going back; and they all offered to look to the personal comfort of Mrs. Sherman on the voyage.[28] They took passage in the steamer Golden Age (Commodore Watkins),[29] which sailed on April 17, 1855. Their passage down the coast was very pleasant till within a day's distance of Panama, when one bright moonlit night, April 29th, the ship, running at full speed, between the Islands Quibo and Quicara, struck on a

[25] Samuel M. Bowman (1815–1885) moved to San Francisco with his wife Elizabeth A. Bowman (1818–1885) in 1852. He was hired as the counsel and attorney for Lucas, Turner, & Co. *First Fifty Years of Cazenovia Seminary, 1825–1875* (Cazenovia, NY: Nelson and Phillips, 1877), 80–82.

[26] William T. Sherman Jr. (1854–1863) was the third child of WTS and Ellen Boyle Ewing. Thomas T. Sherman, *Sherman Genealogy* (New York: Tobias A. Wright, 1920), 399.

[27] Biddy, WTS's children's nurse at the time, married William Quinn of Donegal in May 1856. Anna McAllister, *Ellen Ewing: Wife of General Sherman* (New York: Benziger, 1936), 145.

[28] WTS may have referred here to Gilbert E. Winters (1823–1867), a lawyer and close friend of Abraham Lincoln who served in the U.S. Army during the Mexican-American War and the Civil War. Francis Cunningham (1799–1861) moved to California in 1852 and operated a mill in Marysville, CA, until his death in 1861. Charles P. Eagan (1841–1919) was born in Ireland and educated in San Francisco. He served in the U.S. Commissary Department during the Civil War and Spanish-American War, attaining the rank of brigadier general. David M. Chauncey (1817–1881) arrived in California in 1849 and was the first county assessor of San Francisco. A. J. Baughman, *History of Morrow County, Ohio* (Chicago: Lewis, 1911), 2:598; Graham A. Cosmas, *An Army for Empire: The United States Army in the Spanish-American War* (College Station: Texas A&M University Press, 1994), 60; "Death of a '49er," *Salt Lake Herald*, July 9, 1881, 7; J. M. Guinn, *History of the State of California* (Chicago: Chapman, 1906), 288–289; William D. Murphy, *Biographical Sketches of the State Officers and Members of the Legislature of the State of New York in 1858* (Albany, NY: J. Munsell, 1858), s.v. "David M. Chauncey."

[29] James T. Watkins (1808–1867) worked for the Pacific Mail Company. Ann C. Hart, *Lone Mountain: The Most Revered of San Francisco's Hills* (San Francisco: Pioneer, 1937), 75.

sunken reef, tore out a streak in her bottom, and at once began to fill with water.[30] Fortunately she did not stick fast, but swung off into deep water, and Commodore Watkins happening to be on deck at the moment, walking with Mr. Aspinwall, learning that the water was rushing in with great rapidity, gave orders for a full head of steam, and turned the vessel's bow straight for the Island Quicara. The water rose rapidly in the hold, the passengers were all assembled, fearful of going down, the fires were out, and the last revolution of the wheels made, when her bow touched gently on the beach, and the vessel's stern sank in deep water. Lines were got out, and the ship held in an upright position, so that the passengers were safe, and but little incommoded. I have often heard Mrs. Sherman tell of the boy Eagan, then about fourteen years old, coming to her state-room, and calling to her not to be afraid, as he was a good swimmer; but on coming out into the cabin, partially dressed, she felt more confidence in the cool manner, bearing, and greater strength of Mr. Winters. There must have been nearly a thousand souls on board at the time, few of whom could have been saved had the steamer gone down in mid-channel, which surely would have resulted, had not Commodore Watkins been on deck, or had he been less prompt in his determination to beach his ship.[31] A sail-boat was dispatched toward Panama, which luckily met the steamer John L. Stephens,[32] just coming out of the bay, loaded with about a thousand passengers bound for San Francisco, and she at once proceeded to the relief of the Golden Age. Her passengers were transferred in small boats to the Stephens, which vessel, with her two thousand people crowded together with hardly standing-room, returned to Panama, whence the passengers for the East proceeded to their destination without further delay. Luckily for Mrs. Sherman, Purser Goddard, an old Ohio friend of ours,[33] was on the Stephens, and most kindly gave up his own room to her, and such lady friends as she included in her party.[34] The Golden Age was afterward partially

[30] Quibo and Quicara Islands, also known as Coiba and Jicaron, are located a few miles off the west coast of Panama. The islands were surveyed by the British Navy in 1848. Alexander G. Findlay, *A Directory for the Navigation of the Pacific Ocean* (London: Trinity House, 1851), 1:219.

[31] There were 795 passengers aboard the *Golden Age* when the accident occurred. "Monthly Record of Current Events," *Harper's New Monthly Magazine* (June to Nov. 1855), 11:258.

[32] The correct name of the ship was the *John L. Stevens.* McAllister, *Ellen Ewing,* 129.

[33] George E. Goddard (c. 1824–1879) served as an official on the *Golden Age* and other vessels. *Belmont Chronicle,* no. 7, Feb. 27, 1879, 19:2.

[34] According to Ellen Sherman, she shared the room with a Mrs. Duncan and her young daughter Lily. McAllister, *Ellen Ewing,* 131.

repaired at Quicara, pumped out, and steamed to Panama, when, after further repairs, she resumed her place in the line. I think she is still in existence, but Commodore Watkins afterward lost his life in China, by falling down a hatchway.[35]

Mrs. Sherman returned in the latter part of November of the same year, when Mr. and Mrs. Bowman, who meantime had bought a lot next to us and erected a house thereon, removed to it, and we thus continued close neighbors and friends until we left the country for good in 1857.

During the summer of 1856, in San Francisco, occurred one of those unhappy events, too common to new countries, in which I became involved in spite of myself.

William Neely Johnson was Governor of California, and resided at Sacramento City;[36] General John E. Wool commanded the Department of California, having succeeded General Hitchcock, and had his headquarters at Benicia;[37] and a Mr. Van Ness was mayor of the city.[38] Politics had become a regular and profitable business, and politicians were more than suspected of being corrupt. It was reported and currently believed that the sheriff (Scannell)[39] had been required to pay the Democratic Central Committee a hundred thousand dollars for his nomination, which was equivalent to an election, for an

[35] The steamer *Golden Age* was eventually sold to the Mitsu-Bishi Steam Navigation Company and rechristened the *Hiroshima-Maru.* Commodore Watkins died in Nagasaki Harbor, Japan, on Nov. 12, 1867. Hart, *Lone Mountain,* 75; Will Lawson, *Pacific Steamers* (Glasgow: Brown, Son, & Ferguson, 1927), 36.

[36] WTS confused William Neely Johnson with his brother J. Neely Johnson (1825–1872), who moved to California in 1849 and served as the governor of the state from 1856 to 1858. H. D. Barrows, "Governors of California," *Southern California Quarterly* (Sept. 1903): 6:35.

[37] John E. Wool (1784–1869) served in the War of 1812, the Mexican-American War, and the Civil War. He commanded the Department of California from 1854 to 1857. *CWHC,* 581; *Transactions of the California State Agricultural Society during the Year 1892* (Sacramento: State Office, 1893), 175.

[38] James Van Ness (1818–1872) was elected mayor of San Francisco in a special election held in May 1855. Van Ness's brief time in office was hindered by scandal and violence. Nancy Taniguchi, *Dirty Deeds: Land, Violence, and the 1856 San Francisco Vigilante Committee* (Norman: University of Oklahoma Press, 2016), 27–31.

[39] David S. Scannell (1820–1893) served as sheriff of San Francisco in 1855–1856. During his term he was accused of corruption related to gambling. Amy Greensberg, *Cause for Alarm: Volunteer Fire Department in the Nineteenth-Century City* (Princeton, NJ: Princeton University Press, 1998), 195*n;* "Short Telegrams," *Daily World* (Pittsburg, KS), Apr. 1, 1893, 1.

office of the nominal salary of twelve thousand dollars a year for four years. In the election all sorts of dishonesty were charged and believed, especially of "ballot-box stuffing," and too generally the better classes avoided the elections and dodged jury-duty, so that the affairs of the city government necessarily passed into the hands of a low set of professional politicians. Among them was a man named James Casey, who edited a small paper, the printing office of which was in a room on the third floor of our banking office.[40] I hardly knew him by sight, and rarely if ever saw his paper; but one day Mr. Sather, of the excellent banking firm of Drexel, Sather & Church,[41] came to me, and called my attention to an article in Casey's paper so full of falsehood and malice, that we construed it as an effort to black-mail the banks generally. At that time we were all laboring to restore confidence, which had been so rudely shaken by the panic, and I went up-stairs, found Casey, and pointed out to him the objectionable nature of his article, told him plainly that I could not tolerate his attempt to print and circulate slanders in our building, and, if he repeated it, I would cause him and his press to be thrown out of the windows. He took the hint and moved to more friendly quarters. I mention this fact, to show my estimate of the man, who became a figure in the drama I am about to describe. James King of Wm., as before explained, was in 1853 a banker on his own account, but some time in 1854 he had closed out his business, and engaged with Adams & Co. as cashier. When this firm failed, he, in common with all the employés, was thrown out of employment, and had to look around for something else. He settled down to the publication of an evening paper, called the *Bulletin,* and, being a man of fine manners and address, he at once constituted himself the champion of society against the public and private characters whom he saw fit to arraign.[42]

As might have been expected, this soon brought him into the usual newspaper war with other editors, and especially with Casey, and epithets *à la*

[40] James P. Casey (1827–1856) was the editor of the *Weekly Sunday Times.* Charles F. Adams, *Murder by the Bay: Historic Homicide in and about the City of San Francisco* (Sanger, CA: Word Dancer, 2005), 10; Taniguchi, *Dirty Deeds,* 38.

[41] Peder Sather (1810–1886), born in Norway, was a prominent banker in California. He donated large sums of money to the University of California at Berkeley. Sterling Dow, *Fifty Years of Sathers* (Berkeley: University of California Press, 1965), 30–31.

[42] The first issue of the *Evening Bulletin* was published on Oct. 8, 1855. Ella S. Cummins, *The Story of the Files: A Review of California Writers and Literature* (San Francisco: World's Fair Commission of California, 1893), 409–410.

"Eatanswill" were soon bandying back and forth between them.[43] One evening of May, 1856, King published, in the *Bulletin,* copies of papers procured from New York, to show that Casey had once been sentenced to the State penitentiary at Sing Sing.[44] Casey took mortal offense, and called at the *Bulletin* office, on the corner of Montgomery and Merchant Streets, where he found King, and violent words passed between them, resulting in Casey giving King notice that he would shoot him on sight.[45] King remained in his office till about 5 or 6 P. M., when he started toward his home on Stockton Street, and, as he neared the corner of Washington, Casey approached him from the opposite direction, called to him, and began firing. King had on a short cloak, and in his breast-pocket a small pistol, which he did not use. One of Casey's shots struck him high up in the breast, from which he reeled, was caught by some passing friend, and carried into the express-office on the corner, where he was laid on the counter, and a surgeon sent for. Casey escaped up Washington Street, went to the City Hall, and delivered himself to the sheriff (Scannell), who conveyed him to jail and locked him in a cell.[46] Meantime, the news spread like wildfire, and all the city was in commotion, for King was very popular. Nisbet, who boarded with us on Harrison Street, had been delayed at the bank later than usual, so that he happened to be near at the time, and, when he came out to dinner, he brought me the news of this affair, and said that there was every appearance of a riot down-town that night. This occurred toward the evening of May 14, 1856.

It so happened that, on the urgent solicitation of Van Winkle and of Governor Johnson, I had only a few days before agreed to accept the commission of major-general of the Second Division of Militia, embracing San Francisco. I had received the commission, but had not as yet formally accepted it, or even put myself in communication with the volunteer companies of the city. Of these, at

[43]The *Eatanswill Gazette* was a fictional, politically charged newspaper in the Charles Dickens book *The Posthumous Papers of the Pickwick Club.* See Dickens, *The Posthumous Papers of The Pickwick Club* (London: Gresham, 1903), 124.

[44]On the morning of May 14, 1856, the *Bulletin* issued an editorial that stated, "The fact that Casey has been an inmate of Sing-Sing prison in New York, is no offence against the laws of this State." Hubert H. Bancroft, *History of the Pacific States of North America: Popular Tribunals* (San Francisco: History Company, 1887), 2:38.

[45]For a contemporary report on the exchange between Casey and King, see *True and Minute History of the Assassination of James King of William at San Francisco, California* (San Francisco: Whitton and Towne, 1856), 5.

[46]In the first edition of the memoirs (1875), the sentence begins with the word "Meantime."

that moment of time, there was a company of artillery with four guns, commanded by a Captain Johns, formerly of the army,[47] and two or three uniformed companies of infantry. After dinner I went down-town to see what was going on; found that King had been removed to a room in the Metropolitan Block; that his life was in great peril; that Casey was safe in jail, and the sheriff had called to his assistance a *posse* of the city police, some citizens, and one of the militia companies. The people were gathered in groups on the streets, and the words "Vigilance Committee" were freely spoken, but I saw no signs of immediate violence. The next morning, I again went to the jail, and found all things quiet, but the militia had withdrawn. I then went to the City Hall, saw the mayor, Van Ness, and some of the city officials, agreed to do what I could to maintain order with such militia as were on hand, and then formally accepted the commission, and took the "oath." In 1851 (when I was not in California) there had been a Vigilance Committee, and it was understood that its organization still existed. All the newspapers took ground in favor of the Vigilance Committee, except the *Herald* (John Nugent, editor),[48] and nearly all the best people favored that means of redress. I could see they were organizing, hiring rendezvous, collecting arms, etc., without concealment. It was soon manifest that the companies of volunteers would go with the "committee," and that the public authorities could not rely on them for aid or defense. Still, there were a good many citizens who contended that, if the civil authorities were properly sustained by the people at large, they could and would execute the law. But the papers inflamed the public mind, and the controversy spread to the country. About the third day after the shooting of King, Governor Johnson telegraphed me that he would be down in the evening boat, and asked me to meet him on arrival for consultation. I got C. K. Garrison to go with me, and we met the Governor and his brother[49] on the wharf, and walked up to the International

[47] Thomas D. Johns (1824–1883) graduated from the USMA in 1848 and resigned from the U.S. Army in 1851. He served as a captain in the California Militia from 1852 to 1860. *USMA,* 2:363.

[48] John Nugent (1829–1880) was born in Ireland and immigrated to the United States as a child. He established the *Herald* in 1849; his opposition to the Vigilance Committee of 1856 led to the collapse of the newspaper. Myles Dungan, *How the Irish Won the West* (New York: Skyhorse, 2011), 274–276.

[49] William Neely Johnson (1826–1885) was a lawyer who also served as state librarian of California. W. J. Davis, *An Illustrated History of Sacramento County, California* (Chicago: Lewis, 1890), 58.

Hotel on Jackson Street, above Montgomery.[50] We discussed the state of affairs fully; and Johnson, on learning that his particular friend, William T. Coleman,[51] was the president of the Vigilance Committee, proposed to go and see him. *En route* we stopped at King's room, ascertained that he was slowly sinking, and could not live long; and then near midnight we walked to the Turnverein Hall, where the committee was known to be sitting in consultation. This hall was on Bush Street, at about the intersection of Stockton. It was all lighted up within, but the door was locked.

The Governor knocked at the door, and on inquiry from inside—"Who's there?"—gave his name. After some delay we were admitted into a sort of vestibule, beyond which was a large hall, and we could hear the suppressed voices of a multitude. We were shown into a bar-room to the right, when the Governor asked to see Coleman. The man left us, went into the main hall, and soon returned with Coleman, who was pale and agitated. After shaking hands all round, the Governor said, "Coleman, what the devil is the matter here?" Coleman said, "Governor, it is time this shooting on our streets should stop." The Governor replied, "I agree with you perfectly, and have come down from Sacramento to assist." Coleman rejoined that "the people were tired of it, and had no faith in the officers of the law." A general conversation then followed, in which it was admitted that King would die, and that Casey *must* be executed; but the manner of execution was the thing to be settled, Coleman contending that the people would do it without trusting the courts or the sheriff. It so happened that at that time Judge Norton was on the bench of the court having jurisdiction, and he was universally recognized as an able and upright man, whom no one could or did mistrust;[52] and it also happened that a grand-jury was then in session. Johnson argued that the time had passed in California for mobs and vigilance committees, and said if Coleman and associates would use their influence to support the law, he (the Governor) would undertake that, as soon as King died, the grand-jury should indict, that Judge Norton would try

[50]The International Hotel opened in 1854 and was relocated to Kearny Street. Fred H. Hackett, ed., *The Industries of San Francisco* (San Francisco: Payot and Upham, 1884), 161; Soulé, Gihon, and Nisbet, *Annals of San Francisco,* 650–651.

[51]William T. Coleman (1824–1893), a San Francisco merchant, was in charge of the Vigilance Committee in 1851 and 1856. G. W. Sullivan, *Early Days in California* (San Francisco: Enterprise, 1888), s.v. "William T. Coleman."

[52]Edward Norton (1807–1872) was elected as Superior Court judge for San Francisco in 1854 and later served on the California Supreme Court. *Catalogue of the Sigma Phi with the Thesaurus* (Printed for the Society, 1891), 30–31.

the murderer, and the whole proceeding should be as speedy as decency would allow. Then Coleman said "the people had no confidence in Scannell, the sheriff," who was, he said, in collusion with the rowdy element of San Francisco. Johnson then offered to be personally responsible that Casey should be safely guarded, and should be forthcoming for trial and execution at the proper time. I remember very well Johnson's assertion that he had no right to make these stipulations, and maybe no power to fulfill them; but he did it to save the city and state from the disgrace of a mob. Coleman disclaimed that the vigilance organization was a "mob," admitted that the proposition of the Governor was fair, and all he or any one should ask; and added, if we would wait awhile, he would submit it to the council, and bring back an answer.

We waited nearly an hour, and could hear the hum of voices in the hall, but no words, when Coleman came back, accompanied by a committee, of which I think the two brothers Arrington,[53] Thomas Smiley the auctioneer,[54] Seymour,[55] Truett,[56] and others, were members.[57] The whole conversation was gone over again, and the Governor's proposition was positively agreed to, with this further condition, that the Vigilance Committee should send into the jail a small force of their own men, to make certain that Casey should not be carried off or allowed to escape.

The Governor, his brother William, Garrison, and I, then went up to the jail, where we found the sheriff and his *posse comitatus* of police and citizens. These were styled the "Law-and-Order party," and some of them took offense that the Governor should have held communication with the "damned

[53] William Arrington (1816–1897) and Nicholas O. Arrington (1822–1898) moved to California in 1849. William was a member of the California Society of Pioneers, and Nicholas's daughter was the famous actress Marie Burroughs. Charles W. Haskins, *Argonauts of California* (New York: Fords, Howard, and Hulbert, 1890), 364; Jo W. Linn, *Drake-Arrington, White-Turner, Linn-Brown, and Two Dozen Related Southern Lines* (Salisbury, NC: J. W. Linn, 1984), 125–126.

[54] Thomas J. L. Smiley (1821–1897) served as the first president of the California Stock and Exchange Board. "Thomas J. L. Smiley Dead," *Sacramento Union* (Sacramento, CA), Apr. 24, 1897, 6; Mary F. Williams, *History of the San Francisco Committee of Vigilance, 1851* (Berkeley: University of California Press, 1921), 450–451.

[55] In 1885, Theodore Hittell, a historian and resident of San Francisco in 1856, refuted WTS's claim about a person named "Seymour" being at the meeting or being on the Vigilance Committee. Hittell, *History of California,* 3:503.

[56] Miers F. Truett (1817–1885) was a defense lawyer for the Vigilance Committee. Clarke, *Sherman: Gold Rush Banker,* 396; "Reaper," *Daily Examiner* (San Francisco), Sept. 29, 1885, 1.

[57] For a roster of the leaders of the Vigilance Committee, see Bancroft, *History . . . : Popular Tribunals,* 2:113.

rebels," and several of them left the jail; but the sheriff seemed to agree with the Governor that what he had done was right and best; and, while we were there, some eight or ten armed men arrived from the Vigilance Committee, and were received by the sheriff (Scannell) as a part of his regular *posse.*

The Governor then, near daylight, went to his hotel, and I to my house for a short sleep. Next day I was at the bank, as usual, when, about noon the Governor called, and asked me to walk with him down-street. He said he had just received a message from the Vigilance Committee to the effect that they were not bound by Coleman's promise not to do any thing till the regular trial by jury should be had, etc. He was with reason furious, and asked me to go with him to Truett's store, over which the Executive Committee was said to be in session. We were admitted to a front-room up-stairs, and heard voices in the back-room. The Governor inquired for Coleman, but he was not forthcoming. Another of the committee, Seymour, met us, denied *in toto* the promise of the night before, and the Governor openly accused him of treachery and falsehood.

The quarrel became public, and the newspapers took it up, both parties turning on the Governor; one, the Vigilantes, denying the promise made by Coleman, their president; and the other, the "Law-and-Order party," refusing any further assistance, because Johnson had stooped to make terms with rebels. At all events, he was powerless, and had to let matters drift to a conclusion.

King died about Friday, May 20th, and the funeral was appointed for the next Sunday. Early on that day the Governor sent for me at my house. I found him on the roof of the International, from which we looked down on the whole city, and more especially the face of Telegraph Hill, which was already covered with a crowd of people, while others were moving toward the jail on Broadway. Parties of armed men, in good order, were marching by platoons in the same direction, and formed in line along Broadway, facing the jail-door. Soon a small party was seen to advance to this door, and knock; a parley ensued, the doors were opened, and Casey was led out. In a few minutes another prisoner was brought out, who, proved to be Cora, a man who had once been tried for killing Richardson, the United States Marshal, when the jury disagreed, and he was awaiting a new trial.[58] These prisoners were

[58] Charles Cora (c. 1813–1856), a known gambler in San Francisco, was arrested for the murder of William H. Richardson (1823–1855) following a dispute outside a theater in Nov. 1855. Richardson was appointed U.S. marshal for the District of Northern California in 1853. Cora's lengthy trial inspired the organization of the Vigilance Committee in 1856. Clarke, *Sherman: Gold Rush Banker,* 386*n*; "Murder of Wm. H. Richardson," *Sonoma County Journal* (Petaluma, CA), Nov. 24, 1855, 2.

placed in carriages, and escorted by the armed force down to the rooms of the Vigilance Committee, through the principal streets of the city. The day was exceedingly beautiful, and the whole proceeding was orderly in the extreme. I was under the impression that Casey and Cora were hanged that same Sunday, but was probably in error; but in a very few days they were hanged by the neck—dead—suspended from beams projecting from the windows of the committee's rooms, without other trial than could be given in secret, and by night.[59]

We all thought the matter had ended there, and accordingly the Governor returned to Sacramento in disgust, and I went about my business. But it soon became manifest that the Vigilance Committee had no intention to surrender the power thus usurped. They took a building on Clay Street, near Front, fortified it, employed guards and armed sentinels, sat in midnight council, issued writs of arrest and banishment, and utterly ignored all authority but their own. A good many men were banished and forced to leave the country, but they were of that class we could well spare.[60] Yankee Sullivan, a prisoner in their custody, committed suicide,[61] and a feeling of general insecurity pervaded the city. Business was deranged; and the *Bulletin,* then under control of Tom King, a brother of James,[62] poured out its abuse on some of our best men, as well as the worst. Governor Johnson, being again appealed to, concluded to go to work regularly, and telegraphed me about the 1st of June to meet him at General Wool's headquarters at Benicia that night. I went up, and we met at the hotel where General Wool was boarding. Johnson had with him his Secretary of State.[63] We discussed the state of the country generally, and I had agreed that if Wool would give us arms and ammunition out of the United States Arsenal at Benicia, and if Commodore Farragut, of the

[59] Cora and Casey were executed on May 22, 1856. For a report on the executions, see "The Fate of the Murderers," *New York Herald,* June 29, 1856, 1.

[60] For a complete list of people banished from California by the Vigilance Committee, see Frank M. Smith, ed., *San Francisco Vigilance Committee of '56* (San Francisco: Barry and Baird, 1883), 82.

[61] Frank A. Murray (1813–1856) was a notable prize fighter known as "Yankee Sullivan." Elliot J. Gorn, *The Manly Art: Bare-Knuckle Prize Fighting in America* (Ithaca, NY: Cornell University Press, 1986), 69–80.

[62] Thomas S. King took control of the *Evening Bulletin* after his brother died in May 1856. Cummins, *The Story of the Files,* 409–410.

[63] David F. Douglass (1821–1872) was appointed California's secretary of state in 1856. Mary J. Ignoffo, *Gold Rush Politics: California's First Legislature* (Cupertino: California History Center, 1999), 104.

navy, commanding the navy-yard on Mare Island, would give us a ship, I would call out volunteers, and, when a sufficient number had responded, I would have the arms come down from Benicia in the ship, arm my men, take possession of a thirty-two-pound-gun battery at the Marine Hospital on Rincon Point, thence command a dispersion of the unlawfully-armed force of the Vigilance Committee, and arrest some of the leaders.

We played cards that night, carrying on a conversation, in which Wool insisted on a proclamation commanding the Vigilance Committee to disperse, etc., and he told us how he had on some occasion, as far back as 1814, suppressed a mutiny on the Northern frontier. I did not understand him to make any distinct promise of assistance that night, but he invited us to accompany him on an inspection of the arsenal the next day, which we did. On handling some rifled muskets in the arsenal storehouse he asked me how they would answer our purpose. I said they were the very things, and that we did not want cartridge boxes or belts, but that I would have the cartridges carried in the breeches-pockets, and the caps in the vestpockets. I knew that there were stored in that arsenal four thousand muskets, for I recognized the boxes which we had carried out in the Lexington around Cape Horn in 1846. Afterward we all met at the quarters of Captain D. R. Jones of the army,[64] and I saw the Secretary of State, D. F. Douglass, Esq., walk out with General Wool in earnest conversation, and this Secretary of State afterward asserted that Wool there and then promised us the arms and ammunition, provided the Governor would make his proclamation for the committee to disperse, and that I should afterward call out the militia, etc. On the way back to the hotel at Benicia, General Wool, Captain Callendar of the arsenal,[65] and I, were walking side by side, and I was telling him (General Wool) that I would also need some ammunition for the thirty-two-pound guns then in position at Rincon Point, when Wool turned to Callendar and inquired, "Did I not order those guns to be brought away?" Callendar said: "Yes, general. I made a requisition on the quartermaster[66] for transportation, but his schooner has been so

[64] David R. Jones (1825–1863) graduated from the USMA in 1842 and served as the acting judge advocate of the Pacific Department from 1854 to 1858. At the start of the Civil War he resigned from the U.S. Army to join the Confederate Army. He died in 1863 of a heart attack. *USMA,* 2:288; *CWHC,* 323–324.

[65] Franklin D. Callender (1821–1883) graduated from the USMA in 1839 and commanded the Benicia Arsenal from 1856 to 1860. *USMA,* 1:743–744.

[66] Robert Allen (c. 1811–1886) graduated from the USMA in 1836 and served as chief quartermaster for the Pacific Division from 1854 to 1861. *USMA,* 1:651–653.

busy that the guns are still there." Then said Wool: "Let them remain; we may have use for them." I therefrom inferred, of course, that it was all agreed to so far as he was concerned.

Soon after we had reached the hotel, we ordered a buggy, and Governor Johnson and I drove to Vallejo, six miles, crossed over to Mare Island, and walked up to the commandant's house, where we found Commodore Farragut and his family. We stated our business fairly, but the commodore answered very frankly that he had no authority, without orders from his department, to take any part in civil broils; he doubted the wisdom of the attempt; said he had no ship available except the John Adams, Captain Boutwell,[67] and that she needed repairs. But he assented at last to the proposition to let the sloop John Adams drop down abreast of the city after certain repairs, to lie off there for *moral effect,* which afterward actually occurred.

We then returned to Benicia, and Wool's first question was, "What luck?" We answered, "Not much," and explained what Commodore Farragut could and would do, and that, instead of having a naval vessel, we would seize and use one of the Pacific Mail Company's steamers, lying at their dock in Benicia, to carry down to San Francisco the arms and munitions when the time came.

As the time was then near at hand for the arrival of the evening boats, we all walked down to the wharf together, where I told Johnson that he could not be too careful; that I had not heard General Wool make a positive promise of assistance. Upon this, Johnson called General Wool to one side, and we three drew together. Johnson said: "General Wool, General Sherman is very particular, and wants to know exactly what you propose to do." Wool answered: "I understand, Governor, that in the first place a writ of *habeas corpus* will be issued commanding the jailers of the Vigilance Committee to produce the body of some one of the prisoners held by them (which, of course, will be refused); that you then issue your proclamation commanding them to disperse, and, failing this, you will call out the militia, and command General Sherman with it to suppress the Vigilance Committee as an unlawful body;" to which the Governor responded, "Yes." "Then," said Wool, "on General Sherman's making his requisition, approved by you, I will order the issue of the necessary arms and ammunition." I remember well that I said, emphatically: "That is all

[67] Edward B. Boutwell joined the U.S. Navy in 1819. He was a friend of WTS's wife Ellen and a strong opponent of the Vigilance Committee. "Commodore Boutwell Announces Himself as a Candidate for Congress," *Richmond Dispatch* (Richmond, VA), June 21, 1870, 4; *Naval Register for 1827* (Washington, DC: Office of the Secretary of the Navy, 1827), 26; Taniguchi, *Dirty Deeds,* 101.

I want.—Now, Governor, you may go ahead." We soon parted; Johnson and Douglas taking the boat to Sacramento, and I to San Francisco.

The Chief-Justice, Terry,[68] came to San Francisco the next day, issued a writ of *habeas corpus* for the body of one Maloney,[69] which writ was resisted, as we expected. The Governor then issued his proclamation, and I published my orders, dated June 4, 1855. The Quartermaster-General of the State, General Kibbe,[70] also came to San Francisco, took an office in the City Hall, engaged several rooms for armories, and soon the men began to enroll into companies. In my general orders calling out the militia, I used the expression, "When a sufficient number of men are enrolled, arms and ammunition will be supplied." Some of the best men of the "Vigilantes" came to me and remonstrated, saying that collision would surely result; that it would be terrible, etc. All I could say in reply was, that it was for them to get out of the way. "Remove your fort; cease your midnight councils; and prevent your armed bodies from patrolling the streets." They inquired where I was to get arms, and I answered that I had them *certain.* But personally I went right along with my business at the bank, conscious that at any moment we might have trouble. Another committee of citizens, a conciliatory body, was formed to prevent collision if possible, and the newspapers boiled over with vehement vituperation. This second committee was composed of such men as Crockett,[71] Ritchie, Thornton,[72] Bailey

[68] David S. Terry (1823–1889) moved to California in 1849 and was appointed to the California Supreme Court in 1856. In 1859 he killed U.S. Senator David Broderick in a duel. Terry was later shot and killed when he attempted to attack U.S. Supreme Court Justice Stephen J. Field. John F. Burns and Richard J. Orsi, eds., *Taming the Elephant: Politics, Government, and Law in Pioneer California* (Berkeley: University of California Press, 2003), 40–41; Jeff Erzin, *Confederate Veterans in Northern California: 101 Biographies* (Jefferson, NC: McFarland, 2020), s.v. "David Smith Terry, Sr."

[69] James "Rube" Maloney was accused of corruption and other crimes by the Vigilance Committee. Eventually Maloney was tried and banished from California by the committee. Hittel, *History of California,* 3:567–569; Smith, *San Francisco Vigilance Committee of '56,* 82.

[70] William Kibbe (1822–1904) moved to California in 1849 and served as the state's quartermaster general from 1852 to 1859. "General Kibbe Dead," *Oakland Tribune,* Jan. 25, 1904, 6; *The State Register and Year Book of Facts for the Year 1859* (San Francisco: Henry G. Langley and Samuel A. Morison, 1859), 192.

[71] Joseph B. Crockett (1808–1884) moved to California in 1852 to practice law and later became chief justice of the California Supreme Court. Bennett H. Young, *A History of Jessamine County, Kentucky, from Its Earliest Settlement to 1898* (Louisville: Courier-Journal, 1898), 230.

[72] James D. Thornton (1823–1902) was a lawyer in San Francisco in the 1850s. He was elected to the California Supreme Court in 1880 and served in that capacity until 1891. Clarke, *Sherman: Gold Rush Banker,* 395*n;* "Judge Thornton Passes Away," *Oakland Tribune,* Sept. 30, 1902, 6.

Peyton,[73] Foote, Donohue, Kelly,[74] and others,[75] a class of the most intelligent and wealthy men of the city, who earnestly and honestly desired to prevent bloodshed. They also came to me, and I told them that our men were enrolling very fast, and that, when I deemed the right moment had come, the Vigilance Committee must disperse, else bloodshed and destruction of property would inevitably follow. They also had discovered that the better men of the Vigilance Committee itself were getting tired of the business, and thought that in the execution of Casey and Cora, and the banishment of a dozen or more rowdies, they had done enough, and were then willing to stop. It was suggested that, if our Law-and-Order party would not arm, by a certain day near at hand the committee would disperse, and some of their leaders would submit to an indictment and trial by a jury of citizens, which they knew would acquit them of crime. One day in the bank a man called me to the counter and said, "If you expect to get arms of General Wool, you will be mistaken, for I was at Benicia yesterday, and heard him say he would not give them." This person was known to me to be a man of truth, and I immediately wrote to General Wool a letter telling him what I had heard, and how any hesitation on his part would compromise me as a man of truth and honor; adding that I did not believe we should ever need the arms, but only the *promise* of them, for "the committee was letting down, and would soon disperse and submit to the law," etc. I further asked him to answer me categorically that very night, by the Stockton boat, which would pass Benicia on its way down about midnight, and I would sit up and wait for his answer. I did wait for his letter, but it did not come, and the next day I got a telegraphic dispatch from Governor Johnson, who, at Sacramento, had also heard of General Wool's "back-down," asking me to meet him again at Benicia that night.[76]

[73] Balie Peyton (1803–1878) was a U.S. congressman from Tennessee from 1833 to 1837. In 1853 he moved to California, where he served as prosecuting attorney for San Francisco until 1859. *National Cyclopedia of American Biography,* vol. 7, s.v. "Peyton, Balie."

[74] There was no person named "Kelly" on the committee. It is possible WTS referred here to Terence Kelly, who had been placed on the Vigilance Committee's "Black List." Smith, *San Francisco Vigilance Committee of '56,* 82.

[75] For a complete list of the committee formed in response to the Vigilance Committee, see Bancroft, *History . . . : Popular Tribunals,* 2:307.

[76] The correspondence between WTS, Johnson, and Wool regarding supplies and ammunition occurred on June 5 and 6, 1856. John F. Marszalek, *Sherman: A Soldier's Passion for Order* (New York: Free Press, 1993), 107, 521*n.*

I went up in the evening boat, and found General Wool's aide-de-camp, Captain Arnold, of the army,[77] on the wharf, with a letter in his hand, which he said was for me. I asked for it, but he said he knew its importance, and preferred we should go to General Wool's room together, and the general could hand it to me in person. We did go right up to General Wool's, who took the sealed parcel and laid it aside, saying that it was literally a copy of one he had sent to Governor Johnson, who would doubtless give me a copy; but I insisted that I had made a written communication, and was entitled to a written answer.

At that moment several gentlemen of the "Conciliation party," who had come up in the same steamer with me, asked for admission and came in. I recall the names of Crockett, Foote, Bailey Peyton, Judge Thornton, Donohue, etc., and the conversation became general, Wool trying to explain away the effect of our misunderstanding, taking good pains not to deny his promise made to me personally *on the wharf*. I renewed my application for the letter addressed to me, then lying on his table. On my statement of the case, Bailey Peyton said, "General Wool, I think General Sherman has a right to a written answer from you, for he is surely compromised." Upon this Wool handed me the letter. I opened and read it, and it denied any promise of arms, but otherwise was extremely evasive and non-committal. I had heard of the arrival at the wharf of the Governor and party, and was expecting them at Wool's room, but, instead of stopping at the hotel where we were, they passed to another hotel on the block above. I went up and found there, in a room on the second floor over the bar-room, Governor Johnson, Chief-Justice Terry, Jones, of Palmer, Cooke & Co., E. D. Baker,[78] Volney E. Howard,[79] and one or two others. All were talking furiously against Wool, denouncing him as a d——d liar, and not sparing the severest terms. I showed the Governor General Wool's letter to me, which he said was in effect the same as the one addressed to and received by him at

[77] Richard Arnold (1828–1882) graduated from the USMA in 1846 and served as General Wool's aide-de-camp from 1851 to 1861. *USMA,* 2:416–417.

[78] Edward D. Baker (1811–1861) was born in London and moved to Illinois, where he was elected to the Illinois House of Representatives in 1837 and the Illinois Senate in 1840. He moved to California in 1852 to practice law. Ted Ballard, *Battle of Ball's Bluff* (Washington, DC: Center of Military History, 2001), 68.

[79] Volney E. Howard (1809–1889) was elected to the U.S. Congress as a representative from Texas. He served as U.S. attorney to the Land Commission of California in the 1850s. Ted Ownby et al., *The Mississippi Encyclopedia* (Jackson: University Press of Mississippi, 2017), s.v. "Howard, Volney E."

Sacramento. He was so offended that he would not even call on General Wool, and said he would never again recognize him as an officer or gentleman. We discussed matters generally, and Judge Terry said that the Vigilance Committee were a set of d——d pork-merchants; that they were getting scared, and that General Wool was in collusion with them to bring the State into contempt, etc. I explained that there were no arms in the State except what General Wool had, or what were in the hands of the Vigilance Committee of San Francisco, and that the part of wisdom for us was to be patient and cautious. About that time Crockett and his associates sent up their cards, but Terry and the more violent of the Governor's followers denounced them as no better than "Vigilantes," and wanted the Governor to refuse even to receive them. I explained that they were not "Vigilantes," that Judge Thornton was a "Law-and-Order" man, was one of the first to respond to the call of the sheriff, and that he went actually to the jail with his one arm the night we expected the first attempt at rescue, etc. Johnson then sent word for them to reduce their business to *writing*. They simply sent in a written request for an audience, and they were then promptly admitted. After some general conversation, the Governor said he was prepared to hear them, when Mr. Crockett rose and made a prepared speech embracing a clear and fair statement of the condition of things in San Francisco, concluding with the assertion of the willingness of the committee to disband and submit to trial after a certain date not very remote. All the time Crockett was speaking, Terry sat with his hat on, drawn over his eyes, and with his feet on a table. As soon as Crockett was through, they were dismissed, and Johnson began to prepare a written answer. This was scratched, altered, and amended, to suit the notions of his counselors, and at last was copied and sent. This answer amounted to little or nothing. Seeing that we were powerless for good, and that violent counsels would prevail under the influence of Terry and others, I sat down at the table, and wrote my resignation, which Johnson accepted in a complimentary note on the spot, and at the same time he appointed to my place General Volney E. Howard, then present, a lawyer who had once been a member of Congress from Texas, and who was expected to drive the d——d pork-merchants into the bay at short notice.[80]

I went soon after to General Wool's room, where I found Crockett and the rest of his party; told them that I was out of the fight, having resigned my commission; that I had neglected business that had been intrusted to me by my St. Louis partners; and that I would thenceforward mind my own business,

[80] WTS resigned from the militia in June 1856. Marszalek, *Sherman,* 521*n.*

and leave public affairs severely alone. We all returned to San Francisco that night by the Stockton boat, and I never afterward had any thing to do with politics in California, perfectly satisfied with that short experience. Johnson and Wool fought out their quarrel of veracity in the newspapers and on paper. But, in my opinion, there is not a shadow of doubt that General Wool did deliberately deceive us; that he had authority to issue arms, and that, had he adhered to his promise, we could have checked the committee before it became a fixed institution, and a part of the common law of California. Major-General Volney E. Howard came to San Francisco soon after; continued the organization of militia which I had begun; succeeded in getting a few arms from the country; but one day the Vigilance Committee sallied from their armories, captured the arms of the "Law-and-Order party," put some of their men into prison, while General Howard, with others, escaped to the country; after which the Vigilance Committee had it all their own way. Subsequently, in July, 1856, they arrested Chief-Justice Terry, and tried him for stabbing one of their constables,[81] but he managed to escape at night, and took refuge on the John Adams. In August, they hanged Hetherington[82] and Brace[83] in broad daylight, without any jury-trial; and, soon after, they quietly disbanded.[84] As they controlled the press, they wrote their own history, and the world generally gives them the credit of having purged San Francisco of rowdies and roughs; but their success has given great stimulus to a dangerous principle, that would at any time justify the mob in seizing all the power of government; and who is to say that the Vigilance Committee may not be composed of the worst, instead of the best, elements of a community? Indeed,

[81] Sterling A. Hopkins (d. 1897), the Vigilance Committee's hangman, was stabbed with a bowie knife by David S. Terry while attempting to arrest James "Rube" Maloney. Hopkins survived the attack. Gertrude Atherton, *California: An Intimate History* (New York: Harper and Brothers, 1914), 208–209; Bancroft, *History . . . : Popular Tribunals*, 2:235–236; "Sterling Hopkins Dead," *Alameda Daily Argus* (Alameda, CA), Mar. 6, 1897, 1.

[82] Joseph Hetherington (c. 1821–1856) was born in England and moved to San Francisco in 1850. He was acquitted of the murder of Dr. Baldwin in 1853. The Vigilance Committee arrested and executed him for killing a Dr. Randal. Smith, *San Francisco Vigilance Committee of '56*, 74–75.

[83] Phillander Brace (c. 1834–1856) was arrested by the Vigilance Committee for the murder of police officer Captain West in 1854. Smith, *San Francisco Vigilance Committee*, 74–75.

[84] Hetherington and Brace were hanged on July 29, 1856. The Vigilance Committee disbanded soon after their political candidates failed to win in the Nov. elections. John S. Hittell, *A History of the City of San Francisco and Incidentally of the State of California* (San Francisco: A. L. Bancroft, 1878), 257–258; Smith, *San Francisco Vigilance Committee of '56*, 83.

in San Francisco, as soon as it was demonstrated that the real power had passed from the City Hall to the committee-room, the same set of bailiffs, constables, and rowdies that had infested the City Hall were found in the employment of the "Vigilantes;" and, after three months' experience, the better class of people became tired of the midnight sessions and left the business and power of the committee in the hands of a court, of which a Sydney man was reported to be the head or chief-justice.[85]

During the winter of 1855–'56, and indeed throughout the year 1856, all kinds of business became unsettled in California. The mines continued to yield about fifty millions of gold a year; but little attention was paid to agriculture or to any business other than that of "mining," and, as the placer-gold was becoming worked out, the miners were restless and uneasy, and were shifting about from place to place, impelled by rumors put afloat for speculative purposes.[86] A great many extensive enterprises by joint-stock companies had been begun, in the way of water-ditches, to bring water from the head of the mountain-streams down to the richer alluvial deposits, and nearly all of these companies became embarrassed or bankrupt. Foreign capital, also, which had been attracted to California by reason of the high rates of interest, was being withdrawn, or was tied up in property which could not be sold; and, although our bank's having withstood the panic gave us great credit, still the community itself was shaken, and loans of money were risky in the extreme. A great many merchants, of the highest name, availed themselves of the extremely liberal bankrupt law to get discharged of their old debts, without sacrificing much, if any, of their stocks of goods on hand, except a lawyer's fee; thus realizing Martin Burke's saying that "many a clever fellow had been ruined by paying his debts."[87] The merchants and business-men of San Francisco did not intend to be ruined by such a course. I raised the rate of exchange from three to three and a half, while others kept on at the old rate; and I labored hard to collect old debts, and strove, in making new loans, to be on the safe side. The

[85] John P. Morrow was listed as the committee's "Judge Associate" in 1856. James O'Meara, *The Vigilance Committee of 1856* (San Francisco: James H. Barry, 1887), 4.

[86] In 1855, San Francisco experienced a decrease of $6 million in gold shipments compared to the previous year. Hittell, *A History of San Francisco,* 226.

[87] Martin Burke (1800–1882) joined the U.S. Army in 1820 and was WTS's senior captain when he was stationed at Fort Moultrie, SC, from 1842 to 1846. On Jan. 31, 1891, WTS mentioned Burke during his final public speech delivered at the Press Club Dinner for H. M. Stanley in New York City. William T. Sherman, "General Sherman's Last Speech: The Old Army," *Century Illustrated Monthly Magazine* (May–Oct. 1891), 189–192.

State and city both denied much of their public debt; in fact, repudiated it; and real estate, which the year before had been first-class security, became utterly unsalable.

The office labor and confinement, and the anxiety attending the business, aggravated my asthma to such an extent that at times it deprived me of sleep, and threatened to become chronic and serious; and I was also conscious that the first and original cause which had induced Mr. Lucas to establish the bank in California had ceased. I so reported to him, and that I really believed that he could use his money more safely and to better advantage in St. Louis. This met his prompt approval, and he instructed me gradually to draw out, preparatory to a removal to New York City. Accordingly, early in April, 1857, I published an advertisement in the San Francisco papers, notifying our customers that, on the 1st day of May, we would discontinue business and remove East, requiring all to withdraw their accounts, and declaring that, if any remained on the 1st day of May, their balances would be transferred to the banking-house of Parrott & Co. Punctually to the day, this was done, and the business of Lucas, Turner & Co., of San Francisco, was discontinued, except the more difficult and disagreeable part of collecting their own moneys and selling the real estate, to which the firm had succeeded by purchase or foreclosure. One of the partners, B. R. Nisbet, assisted by our attorney, S. M. Bowman, Esq., remained behind to close up the business of the bank.

6

California, New York, and Kansas.

1857–1859.

HAVING CLOSED THE BANK at San Francisco on the 1st day of May, 1857, accompanied by my family I embarked in the steamer Sonora for Panama, crossed the isthmus, and sailed to New York, whence we proceeded to Lancaster, Ohio, where Mrs. Sherman and the family stopped, and I went on to St. Louis. I found there that some changes had been made in the parent-house, that Mr. Lucas had bought out his partner, Captain Symonds, and that the firm's name had been changed to that of James H. Lucas & Co.

It had also been arranged that an office or branch was to be established in New York City, of which I was to have charge, on pretty much the same terms and conditions as in the previous San Francisco firm.

Mr. Lucas, Major Turner, and I, agreed to meet in New York, soon after the 4th of July. We met accordingly at the Metropolitan Hotel,[1] selected an office, No. 12 Wall Street, purchased the necessary furniture, and engaged a teller, bookkeeper, and porter. The new firm was to bear the same title of Lucas, Turner & Co., with about the same partners in interest, but the nature of the business was totally different. We opened our office on the 21st of July, 1857, and at once began to receive accounts from the West and from California, but our chief business was as the resident agents of the St. Louis firm of James H. Lucas & Co. Personally I took rooms at No. 100 Prince Street,[2] in which house were also quartered Major J. G. Barnard,[3] and Lieutenant J. B.

[1]The Metropolitan Hotel was located at the corner of Prince and Crosby Streets in New York City. *Illustrated New York: The Metropolis of To-Day* (New York: International, 1888), s.v. "Metropolitan Hotel Stables."

[2]The building at 100 Prince Street was owned by a Mrs. Van Nostrand. William T. Sherman, "The Late Major-General J. B. McPherson," *Hours at Home: A Popular Magazine of Religious and Useful Literature,* no. 6 (Apr. 1866), 2:31.

[3]John G. Barnard (1815–1882) graduated second in his class from the USMA in 1833 and served as the superintendent of the USMA in 1855–1856. *USMA,* 1:530–535.

McPherson,[4] United States Engineers, both of whom afterward attained great fame in the civil war.

My business relations in New York were with the Metropolitan Bank and Bank of America; and with the very wealthy and most respectable firm of Schuchhardt & Gebhard, of Nassau Street.[5] Every thing went along swimmingly till the 21st of August, when all Wall Street was thrown into a spasm by the failure of the Ohio Life and Trust Company, and the panic so resembled that in San Francisco, that, having nothing seemingly at stake, I felt amused. But it soon became a serious matter even to me. Western stocks and securities tumbled to such a figure, that all Western banks that held such securities, and had procured advances thereon, were compelled to pay up or substitute increased collaterals. Our own house was not a borrower in New York at all, but many of our Western correspondents were, and it taxed my time to watch their interests. In September, the panic extended so as to threaten the safety of even some of the New York banks not connected with the West; and the alarm became general, and at last universal.[6]

In the very midst of this panic came the news that the steamer Central America, formerly the George Law, with six hundred passengers and about sixteen hundred thousand dollars of treasure, coming from Aspinwall,[7] had foundered at sea, off the coast of Georgia, and that about sixty of the passengers had been providentially picked up by a Swedish bark, and brought into Savannah. The absolute loss of this treasure went to swell the confusion and panic of the day.

A few days after, I was standing in the vestibule of the Metropolitan Hotel, and heard the captain of the Swedish bark tell his singular story of the rescue

[4] James B. McPherson (1828–1864) graduated first in his class from the USMA in 1853 and was the assistant engineer for the construction and repairs of the defenses of New York Harbor from 1854 to 1857. He reached the rank of major general during the Civil War and was shot and killed during WTS's Atlanta Campaign in 1864. *USMA,* 2:515–519.

[5] Frederick Gebhard partnered with his nephew Frederick Schuchardt to form F. Gebhard & Co. in 1822. Gebhard's son eventually became co-owner of the firm, which settled on the name "Schuhardt & Gebhard." Frank G. Griswold, *The House Flag of the Merchants of New York, 1800–1860* (self-pub., 1926), 34–35.

[6] For more information on The Panic of 1857, see James L. Hutson, *The Panic of 1857 and the Coming of the Civil War* (Baton Rouge: LSU Press, 1987).

[7] Aspinwall, a city in Panama, was founded in 1850. The city was named after William H. Aspinwall, founder of the Pacific Mail Steamship Company. The name of the town was later changed to Colón in honor of Christopher Columbus. *The New International Encyclopedia,* 2nd ed. (New York: Dodd and Mead, 1914), s.v. "Colón."

of these passengers.[8] He was a short, sailor-like-looking man, with a strong German or Swedish accent. He said that he was sailing from some port in Honduras for Sweden, running down the Gulf Stream off Savannah. The weather had been heavy for some days, and, about nightfall, as he paced his deck, he observed a man-of-war hawk[9] circle about his vessel, gradually lowering, until the bird was as it were aiming at him. He jerked out a belaying-pin, struck at the bird, missed it, when the hawk again rose high in the air, and a second time began to descend, contract his circle, and make at him again. The second time he hit the bird, and struck it to the deck. This strange fact made him uneasy, and he thought it betokened danger; he went to the binnacle, saw the course he was steering, and without any particular reason he ordered the steersman to alter the course one point to the east.

After this it became quite dark, and he continued to promenade the deck, and had settled into a drowsy state, when as in a dream he thought he heard voices all round his ship. Waking up, he ran to the side of the ship, saw something struggling in the water, and heard clearly cries for help. Instantly heaving his ship to, and lowering all his boats, he managed to pick up sixty or more persons who were floating about on skylights, doors, spars, and whatever fragments remained of the Central America. Had he not changed the course of his vessel by reason of the mysterious conduct of that man-of-war hawk, not a soul would probably have survived the night. It was stated by the rescued passengers, among whom was Billy Birch,[10] that the Central America had sailed from Aspinwall with the passengers and freight which left San Francisco on the 1st of September, and encountered the gale in the Gulf Stream somewhere off Savannah, in which she sprung a leak, filled rapidly, and went down. The passengers who were saved had clung to doors, skylights, and such floating objects as they could reach, and were thus rescued; all the rest, some five hundred in number, had gone down with the ship.[11]

The panic grew worse and worse, and about the end of September there was a general suspension of the banks of New York, and a money crisis extended all

[8] Anders Johnsen was captain of the *Ellen* in 1857. Walter J. Fraser, *Lowcountry Hurricanes: Three Centuries of Storms at Seas and Ashore* (Athens, GA: University of Georgia Press, 2006), 132.

[9] A "man-of-war hawk" is also known as a "frigatebird." Richard J. King, *Ahab's Rolling Sea: A Natural History of Moby-Dick* (Chicago: University of Chicago Press, 2019), 333.

[10] William "Billy" Birch (1831–1897) gained popularity as a minstrel performer. He founded the San Francisco Minstrels in 1864. James Fisher, *Historical Dictionary of American Theater: Beginnings* (Lanham, MD: Rowman and Littlefield, 2015), s.v "Birch, William [Billy]."

[11] The total number of passengers aboard the *Central America* at the time of the wreck was 572. Of those passengers, only 149 survived. Fraser, *Lowcountry Hurricanes,* 132.

over the country. In New York, Lucas, Turner & Co. had nothing at risk. We had large cash balances in the Metropolitan Bank and in the Bank of America, all safe, and we held, for the account of the St. Louis house, at least two hundred thousand dollars, of St. Louis city and county bonds, and of acceptances falling due right along, none extending beyond ninety days. I was advised from St. Louis that money matters were extremely tight; but I did not dream of any danger in that quarter. I knew well that Mr. Lucas was worth two or three million dollars in the best real estate, and inferred from the large balances to their credit with me that no mere panic could shake his credit; but, early on the morning of October 7th, my cousin, James M. Hoyt,[12] came to me in bed, and read me a paragraph in the morning paper, to the effect that James H. Lucas & Co., of St. Louis, had suspended. I was, of course, surprised, but not sorry; for I had always contended that a man of so much visible wealth as Mr. Lucas should not be engaged in a business subject to such vicissitudes. I hurried down to the office, where I received the same information officially, by telegraph, with instructions to make proper disposition of the affairs of the bank, and to come out to St. Louis, with such assets as would be available there. I transferred the funds belonging to all our correspondents, with lists of outstanding checks, to one or other of our bankers, and with the cash balance of the St. Louis house and their available assets started for St. Louis. I may say with confidence that no man lost a cent by either of the banking-firms of Lucas, Turner & Co., of San Francisco or New York; but, as usual, those who owed us were not always as just.

I reached St. Louis October 17th, and found the partners engaged in liquidating the balances due depositors as fast as collections could be forced; and, as the panic began to subside, this process became quite rapid, and Mr. Lucas, by making a loan in Philadelphia, was enabled to close out all accounts without having made any serious sacrifices. Of course, no person ever lost a cent by him: he has recently died, leaving an estate of eight million dollars. During his lifetime, I had opportunities to know him well, and take much pleasure in bearing testimony to his great worth and personal kindness. On the failure of his bank, he assumed personally all the liabilities, released his partners of all responsibility, and offered to assist me to engage in business, which he supposed was due to me because I had resigned my army commission.

[12] James M. Hoyt (1814–1895), WTS's mother's cousin, was a lawyer and president of the Baptist Home Mission Society of America. "At a Ripe Old Age," *Star Tribune* (Minneapolis), Apr. 22, 1895, 5; "Who Hoyt Is," *Mansfield Daily Shield* (Mansfield, OH), May 22, 1895, 4.

I remained in St. Louis till the 7th of December, 1857, assisting in collecting for the bank, and in controlling all matters which came from the New York and San Francisco branches. B. R. Nisbet was still in San Francisco, but had married a Miss Thornton,[13] and was coming home. There still remained in California a good deal of real estate, and notes, valued at about two hundred thousand dollars in the aggregate; so that, at Mr. Lucas's request, I agreed to go out again, to bring matters, if possible, nearer a final settlement. I accordingly left St. Louis, reached Lancaster, where my family was, on the 10th, staid there till after Christmas, and then went to New York, where I remained till January 5th, when I embarked on the steamer Moses Taylor (Captain McGowan)[14] for Aspinwall; caught the Golden Gate (Captain Whiting)[15] at Panama, January 15, 1858; and reached San Francisco on the 28th of January. I found that Nisbet and wife had gone to St. Louis, and that we had passed each other at sea. He had carried the ledger and books to St. Louis, but left a schedule, notes, etc., in the hands of S. M. Bowman, Esq., who passed them over to me.

On the 30th of January I published a notice of the dissolution of the partnership, and called on all who were still indebted to the firm of Lucas, Turner & Co. to pay up, or the notes would be sold at auction. I also advertised that all the real property, was for sale.

Business had somewhat changed since 1857. Parrott & Co.; Garrison, Fritz & Ralston; Wells, Fargo & Co.; Drexel, Sather & Church, and Tallant & Wilde, were the principal bankers. Property continued almost unsalable, and prices were less than a half of what they had been in 1853—'54. William Blanding, Esq.,[16] had rented my house on Harrison Street; so I occupied a room in the

[13] Bessie F. Thornton married Benjamin Nesbitt on Nov. 5, 1857, in San Francisco. She was the daughter of San Francisco judge A. J. Thornton. "Marriages," *Daily Bee* (San Francisco), Nov. 7, 1857, 3.

[14] John McGowan (1805–1891) served in the U.S. Navy for fifty-three years. He commanded the *Moses Taylor* during its maiden voyage on Jan 5, 1858. The ship arrived in Aspinwall on Jan. 13 at 11:00 P.M. "A Veteran Sailor Dead," *Morning Post* (Camden, NJ), Jan. 20, 1891, 3; "The First Trip of the New Steamship *Moses Taylor*," *U.S. Nautical Magazine*, Jan. 1858, 110–112.

[15] Richard L. Whiting (c. 1818–1861) was hired as a captain by the Pacific Mail Steamship Company in 1851. "From California by Pony Express," *Evening Star* (Washington, DC), Feb. 20, 1861, 3; Richard C. McKay, *South Street: A Maritime History of New York* (New York: Haskell House, 1971), 279.

[16] William Blanding (1818–1888) moved to San Francisco in 1854 and was appointed U.S. district attorney for California the following year. Oscar T. Shuck, ed., *History of the Bench and Bar of California* (Los Angeles: Commercial Printing, 1901), s.v. "William Blanding."

bank, No. 11, and boarded at the Meiggs House, corner of Broadway and Montgomery, which we owned. Having reduced expenses to a minimum, I proceeded, with all possible dispatch, to collect outstanding debts, in some instances making sacrifices and compromises. I made some few sales, and generally aimed to put matters in such a shape that time would bring the best result. Some of our heaviest creditors were John M. Rhodes & Co., of Sacramento and Shasta;[17] Langton & Co., of Downieville;[18] and E. M. Strange of Murphy's. In trying to put these debts in course of settlement, I made some arrangement in Downieville with the law-firm of Spears & Thornton, to collect, by suit, a certain note of Green & Purdy for twelve thousand dollars. Early in April, I learned that Spears had collected three thousand seven hundred dollars in money, had appropriated it to his own use, and had pledged another good note taken in part payment of three thousand and fifty-three dollars. He pretended to be insane. I had to make two visits to Downieville on this business, and there made the acquaintance of Mr. Stewart, now a Senator from Nevada. He was married to a daughter of Governor Foote;[19] was living in a small frame-house on the bar just below the town; and his little daughter[20] was playing about the door in the sand. Stewart was then a lawyer in Downieville, in good practice; afterward, by some lucky stroke, became part owner of a valuable silver-mine in Nevada,[21] and is now accounted a mil-

[17] John M. Rhodes (1817–1908) was a banker and early settler of Yolo County, CA. "Death Claims John Rhodes," *Reno Gazette-Journal,* Aug. 5, 1908, 5; Tom Gregory, *History of Yolo County, California* (Los Angeles: Historic Record, 1913), 378.

[18] Samuel W. Langton (1829–1864), a veteran of the Mexican-American War, founded Langton's Pioneer Express in 1850. His business merged with Wells, Fargo & Co. after his death. "Hoyt's Letter Express," *Philatelic Gazette* 8 (Jan.–Dec. 1918): 223.

[19] William M. Stewart (1825–1909) dropped out of Yale University in 1850 and moved to San Francisco. He married Annie E. Foote (1835–1902), the daughter of Henry S. Foote, on May 31, 1855. Stewart moved to Nevada in 1860 and represented the state as a U.S. senator in the years 1865–1875 and 1887–1905. Russell R. Elliott, *Servant of Power: A Political Biography of Senator William M. Stewart* (Reno: University of Nevada Press, 1983).

[20] Elizabeth "Bessie" Stewart (c. 1855–1936) married Richard Campbell Hooker. She moved to France in 1921. "Mrs. Elizabeth Hooker, Dead at Nice, France," *Richmond Times-Dispatch,* Sept. 5, 1936, 15.

[21] Stewart profited from his investments in the Comstock Lode, a silver and gold mine near Virginia City, NV. From its discovery in 1859 until its decline in 1890, the mine yielded approximately $340 million. Dwight L. Clarke, *William Tecumseh Sherman: Gold Rush Banker* (San Francisco: California Historical Society, 1969), 415; *The Encyclopedia Americana* (New York: Encyclopedia Americana Corporation, 1918), vol. 7, s.v. "Comstock Lode."

lionaire. I managed to save something out of Spears, and more out of his partner Thornton. This affair of Spears ruined him, because his insanity was manifestly feigned.

I remained in San Francisco till July 3d, when, having collected and remitted every cent that I could raise, and got all the property in the best shape possible, hearing from St. Louis that business had revived, and that there was no need of further sacrifice, I put all the papers, with a full letter of instructions, and power of attorney, in the hands of William Blanding, Esq., and took passage on the good steamer Golden Gate, Captain Whiting, for Panama and home. I reached Lancaster on July 28, 1858, and found all the family well. I was then perfectly unhampered, but the serious and greater question remained, what was I to do to support my family, consisting of a wife and four children, all accustomed to more than the average comforts of life?

I remained at Lancaster all of August, 1858, during which time I was discussing with Mr. Ewing and others what to do next. Major Turner and Mr. Lucas, in St. Louis, were willing to do any thing to aid me, but I thought best to keep independent. Mr. Ewing had property at Chauncey, consisting of salt-wells and coal-mines, but for that part of Ohio I had no fancy. Two of his sons, Hugh and T. E., Jr.,[22] had established themselves at Leavenworth, Kansas, where they and their father had bought a good deal of land, some near the town, and some back in the country. Mr. Ewing offered to confide to me the general management of his share of interest, and Hugh and T. E., Jr., offered me an equal copartnership in their law-firm. Accordingly, about the 1st of September, I started for Kansas, stopping a couple of weeks in St. Louis, and reached Leavenworth. I found about two miles below the fort, on the river-bank, where in 1851 was a tangled thicket, quite a handsome and thriving city, growing rapidly in rivalry with Kansas City, and St. Joseph, Missouri. After looking about and consulting with friends, among them my classmate Major Stewart Van Vliet, quartermaster at the fort, I concluded to accept the proposition of Mr. Ewing, and accordingly the firm of Sherman & Ewing was duly announced, and our services to the public offered as attorneys-at-law.

We had an office on Main Street, between Shawnee and Delaware, on the second floor, over the office of Hampton Denman, Esq., mayor of the city. This building was a mere shell, and our office was reached by a stairway on the outside. Although in the course of my military reading I had studied a

[22]Thomas Ewing Jr. (1829–1896), a foster brother of WTS, moved to the Kansas Territory in 1856 and served as the chief justice of the Kansas Supreme Court in 1861–1862. *CWHC,* 230.

few of the ordinary law-books, such as Blackstone, Kent, Starkie,[23] etc., I did not presume to be a lawyer; but our agreement was that Thomas Ewing, Jr., a good and thorough lawyer, should manage all business in the courts, while I gave attention to collections, agencies for houses and lands, and such business as my experience in banking had qualified me for. Yet, as my name was embraced in a law-firm, it seemed to me proper to take out a license. Accordingly, one day when United States Judge Lecompte[24] was in our office, I mentioned the matter to him; he told me to go down to the clerk of his court, and he would give me the license. I inquired what examination I would have to submit to, and he replied, "None at all;" he would admit me on the ground of general intelligence.

During that summer we got our share of the business of the profession, then represented by several eminent law-firms, embracing names that have since flourished in the Senate, and in the higher courts of the country. But the most lucrative single case was given me by my friend Major Van Vliet, who employed me to go to Fort Riley, one hundred and thirty-six miles west of Fort Leavenworth, to superintend the repairs to the military road. For this purpose he supplied me with a four-mule ambulance and driver. The country was then sparsely settled, and quite as many Indians were along the road as white people; still there were embryo towns all along the route, and a few farms sprinkled over the beautiful prairies. On reaching Indianola,[25] near Topeka, I found everybody down with the chills and fever. My own driver became so shaky that I had to act as driver and cook. But in due season I reconnoitred the road, and made contracts for repairing some bridges, and for cutting such parts of the road as needed it. I then returned to Fort Leavenworth, and reported, receiving a fair compensation. On my way up I met Colonel Sumner's column, returning from their summer scout on the plains, and spent the night with the officers,

[23] See James Kent, *Commentaries on American Law;* William Blackstone, *Commentaries on the Laws of England;* and Thomas Starkie, *A Treatise on the Law of Slander and Libel: And Incidentally of Malicious Prosecutions.*

[24] Samuel D. Lecompte (1814–1888) was appointed chief justice of the Kansas Territory in 1854 and was later elected to the Kansas state legislature. Noble L. Prentis, *A History of Kansas* (Topeka: Caroline E. Prentis, 1904), 181; "Samuel D. Lecompte," *Topeka State Journal,* Feb. 7, 1887, 1.

[25] Indianola, KS, was founded in Nov. 1854 by H. D. McMeekin. The town was effectively deserted in the early 1860s with the construction of a railroad depot in a nearby town. James L. King, *History of Shawnee County, Kansas and Representative Citizens* (Chicago: Richmond and Arnold, 1905), 55.

among whom were Captains Sackett,[26] Sturgis,[27] etc. Also at Fort Riley I was cordially received and entertained by some old army-friends, among them Major Sedgwick, Captains Totten,[28] Eli Long,[29] etc.

Mrs. Sherman and children arrived out in November, and we spent the winter very comfortably in the house of Thomas Ewing, Jr., on the corner of Third and Pottawottamie Streets. On the 1st of January, 1859, Daniel McCook, Esq.,[30] was admitted to membership in our firm, which became Sherman, Ewing & McCook. Our business continued to grow, but, as the income hardly sufficed for three such expensive personages, I continued to look about for something more certain and profitable, and during that spring undertook for the Hon. Thomas Ewing, of Ohio, to open a farm on a large tract of land he owned on Indian Creek, forty miles west of Leavenworth, for the benefit of his grand-nephew, Henry Clark, and his grand-niece, Mrs. Walker. These arrived out in the spring, by which time I had caused to be erected a small frame dwelling-house, a barn, and fencing for a hundred acres. This helped to pass away time, but afforded little profit; and on the 11th of June, 1859, I wrote to Major D. C. Buell, assistant adjutant-general, on duty in the War Department with Secretary of War Floyd,[31] inquiring if there was a vacancy among the army paymasters, or any thing in his line that I could obtain. He replied promptly, and sent me the printed programme for a military college about to be organized in Louisiana, and advised me to apply for the superintendent's place, saying

[26] Delos B. Sackett (1822–1885) graduated from the USMA in 1845. A veteran of the Mexican-American War, Sackett was stationed at Fort Riley, KS, in 1857–1858. *USMA,* 2:234–236.

[27] Samuel D. Sturgis (1822–1889) graduated from the USMA in 1846 and was stationed in Kansas from 1855 to 1858. *USMA,* 2:278–280.

[28] James Totten (1818–1871) graduated from the USMA in 1841 and was stationed in Kansas from 1857 to 1860. *USMA,* 2:89–90.

[29] Eli Long (1837–1903) graduated from Frankfort Military Academy in 1855 and was promoted to second lieutenant of the U.S. Army, 1st Cav., in June 1856. *CWHC,* 352.

[30] Daniel McCook Jr. (1834–1864) graduated from Florence College in Alabama in 1858. Upon passing the bar exam, he moved to Leavenworth, KS, and started a law firm with WTS and Thomas Ewing Jr. At the outbreak of the Civil War, McCook was commissioned as captain of the 1st Kansas Inf. He was mortally wounded during the assault on Kennesaw Mountain, GA, on June 27, 1864. *CWHC,* 374.

[31] John B. Floyd (1806–1863) was the governor of Virginia from 1849 to 1852 and U.S. secretary of war from 1857 to 1860. He resigned from his position as secretary of war to join the Confederate Army and died of an undisclosed illness during the Civil War. *CWHC,* 237.

that General G. Mason Graham,[32] the half-brother of my old commanding general, R. B. Mason, was very influential in this matter, and would doubtless befriend me on account of the relations that had existed between General Mason and myself in California. Accordingly, I addressed a letter of application to the Hon. R. C. Wickliffe,[33] Baton Rouge, Louisiana, asking the answer to be sent to me at Lancaster, Ohio, where I proposed to leave my family. But, before leaving this branch of the subject, I must explain a little matter of which I have seen an account in print, complimentary or otherwise of the firm of Sherman, Ewing & McCook, more especially of the senior partner.[34]

One day, as I sat in our office, an Irishman came in and said he had a case and wanted a lawyer. I asked him to sit down and give me the points of his case, all the other members of the firm being out. Our client stated that he had rented a lot of an Irish landlord for five dollars a month; that he had erected thereon a small frame shanty, which was occupied by his family; that he had paid his rent regularly up to a recent period, but to his house he had appended a shed which extended over a part of an adjoining vacant lot belonging to the same landlord, for which he was charged two and a half dollars a month, which he refused to pay. The consequence was, that his landlord had for a few months declined even his five dollars monthly rent until the arrears amounted to about seventeen dollars, for which he was sued. I told him we would undertake his case, of which I took notes, and a fee of five dollars in advance, and in due order I placed the notes in the hands of McCook, and thought no more of it.

A month or so after, our client rushed into the office and said his case had been called at Judge Gardner's (I think),[35] and he wanted his lawyer right

[32] George M. Graham (1807–1891) resigned from the USMA in 1826. He was a delegate for the 1839 Whig Party National Convention and went on to serve in the Mexican-American War. "The Distinguished Dead," *Times-Picayune* (New Orleans), Feb. 1, 1891, 2.

[33] Robert C. Wickliffe (1820–1895), the son of Kentucky governor Charles A. Wickliffe, served as the governor of Louisiana from 1856 to 1860. Miriam G. Reeves, *The Governors of Louisiana* (Gretna, LA: Pelican, 1962), s.v. "Robert Charles Wickliffe (1856–1860)."

[34] In early 1869 the *Leavenworth Daily Commercial* (Kansas) published a newspaper article criticizing WTS's limited experience as a lawyer. The article was widely circulated throughout the country. See "General Sherman's Law Practice," *Burlington Free Press* (Burlington, VT), May 5, 1869, 4.

[35] According to subsequent newspaper reports, the judge was named "Squire Whitney." "Leavenworth Items," *Leavenworth Daily Commercial* (Leavenworth, KS), June 4, 1875, 2.

away. I sent him up to the Circuit Court, Judge Pettit's,[36] for McCook, but he soon returned, saying he could not find McCook, and accordingly I hurried with him up to Judge Gardner's office, intending to ask a continuance, but I found our antagonist there, with his lawyer and witnesses,[37] and Judge Gardner would not grant a continuance, so of necessity I had to act, hoping that at every minute McCook would come. But the trial proceeded regularly to its end; we were beaten, and judgment was entered against our client for the amount claimed, and costs. As soon as the matter was explained to McCook, he said "execution" could not be taken for ten days, and, as our client was poor, and had nothing on which the landlord could levy but his house, McCook advised him to get his neighbors together, to pick up the house, and carry it on to another vacant lot, belonging to a non-resident, so that even the house could not be taken in execution. Thus the grasping landlord, though successful in his judgment, failed in the execution, and our client was abundantly satisfied.

In due time I closed up my business at Leavenworth, and went to Lancaster, Ohio, where, in July, 1859, I received notice from Governor Wickliffe that I had been elected superintendent of the proposed college, and inviting me to come down to Louisiana as early as possible, because they were anxious to put the college into operation by the 1st of January following. For this honorable position I was indebted to Major D. C. Buell and General G. Mason Graham, to whom I have made full and due acknowledgment. During the civil war, it was reported and charged that I owed my position to the personal friendship of Generals Bragg and Beauregard,[38] and that, in taking up

[36] In the first edition of the memoirs (1875), WTS wrote "Pettis's" instead of "Pettit's." John Pettit (1807–1877) served as a U.S. congressman from 1843 to 1847 and U.S. senator from 1853 to 1855 from Indiana. He later served as the chief justice of the Kansas Territory. Alfred T. Andreas, *History of the State of Kansas* (self-pub., 1883), 236; Marcus J. Wright et al., *Analytical Historical Reference* (Philadelphia: National Historical Association, 1906), vol. 3, s.v. "Pettit, John (1807–1877)."

[37] According to subsequent newspaper reports, Lewis Burnes (1811–1879) was the lawyer for the plaintiff in the case. "Leavenworth Items," *Leavenworth Daily Commercial* (Leavenworth, KS), June 4, 1875, 2; *The History of Buchanan County, Missouri* (St. Joseph, MO: Union Historical, 1881), 692–693.

[38] P. G. T. Beauregard (1818–1893) graduated from the USMA in 1838 and served in the Mexican-American War. He resigned from his position as superintendent of the USMA in 1861 to join the Confederate Army. *USMA,* 1:697–698.

arms against the South, I had been guilty of a breach of hospitality and friendship. I was not indebted to General Bragg, because he himself told me that he was not even aware that I was an applicant, and had favored the selection of Major Jenkins,[39] another West Point graduate. General Beauregard had nothing whatever to do with the matter.

[39] Walworth Jenkins (1833–1874) graduated from the USMA in 1853 and was assistant professor of French in 1859–1861 and principal assistant professor of French in 1861 at the USMA. *USMA,* 2:542–543.

7

Louisiana.

1859–1861.

In the autumn of 1859, having made arrangements for my family to remain in Lancaster,[1] I proceeded, *via* Columbus, Cincinnati, and Louisville, to Baton Rouge, Louisiana, where I reported for duty to Governor Wickliffe, who, by virtue of his office, was the president of the Board of Supervisors of the new institution over which I was called to preside. He explained to me the act of the Legislature under which the institution was founded;[2] told me that the building was situated near Alexandria, in the parish of Rapides, and was substantially finished; that the future management would rest with a Board of Supervisors, mostly citizens of Rapides Parish, where also resided the Governor-elect, T. O. Moore, who would soon succeed him in his office as Governor and president *ex officio;*[3] and advised me to go at once to Alexandria, and put myself in communication with Moore and the supervisors. Accordingly I took a boat at Baton Rouge, for the mouth of Red River. The

[1]Ellen Ewing Sherman remained in Lancaster with their five children: Maria, Mary Elizabeth Sherman (1852–1925), William T. Sherman Jr., Thomas E. Sherman (1856–1933), and Eleanor M. Sherman (1859–1915), who was born Sept. 5, shortly before WTS departed for Louisiana. James L. McDonough, *William Tecumseh Sherman: In the Service of My Country—A Life* (New York: W. W. Norton, 2016), 162, 166, 187, 222; Thomas T. Sherman, *Sherman Genealogy* (New York: Tobias A. Wright, 1920), 397–399.

[2]In 1853 a three-man commission successfully lobbied the Louisiana legislature to establish a "seminary of learning." A board of seven trustees, appointed by the governor, oversaw the development and construction of the school. James L. Barnidge, "George Mason Graham: The Father of Louisiana State University," *Louisiana History: The Journal of the Louisiana Historical Association* 10, no. 3 (Summer 1969):226–232.

[3]Thomas O. Moore (1804–1876) moved to Rapides Parish, LA, in 1829. After serving in the Louisiana House of Representatives and the Louisiana Senate, he was elected governor of Louisiana on Jan. 23, 1860. Spencer Tucker and Paul G. Pierpaoli, eds., *American Civil War: A State-by-State Encyclopedia* (Santa Barbara: ABC-CLIO, 2015), vol. 1, s.v. "Moore, Thomas Overton."

river being low, and its navigation precarious, I there took the regular mail-coach, as the more certain conveyance, and continued on toward Alexandria. I found, as a fellow-passenger in the coach, Judge Henry Boyce, of the United States District Court, with whom I had made acquaintance years before, at St. Louis,[4] and, as we neared Alexandria, he proposed that we should stop at Governor Moore's and spend the night. Moore's house and plantation were on Bayou Robert, about eight miles from Alexandria. We found him at home, with his wife[5] and a married daughter,[6] and spent the night there. He sent us forward to Alexandria the next morning, in his own carriage. On arriving at Alexandria,[7] I put up at an inn, or boarding-house, and almost immediately thereafter went about ten miles farther up Bayou Rapides, to the plantation and house of General G. Mason Graham, to whom I looked as the principal man with whom I had to deal. He was a high-toned gentleman, and his whole heart was in the enterprise. He at once put me at ease. We acted together most cordially from that time forth, and it was at his house that all the details of the seminary were arranged. We first visited the college-building together. It was located on an old country place of four hundred acres of pine-land, with numerous springs, and the building was very large and handsome. A carpenter, named James, resided there, and had the general charge of the property; but, as there was not a table, chair, black-board, or any thing on hand, necessary for a beginning, I concluded to quarter myself in one of the rooms of the seminary, and board with an old black woman who cooked for James, so that I might personally push forward the necessary preparations. There was an old rail-fence about the place, and a large pile of boards in front. I immediately engaged four carpenters, and set them at work to make out of these boards mess-tables, benches, black-boards, etc. I also opened a correspondence with the professors-elect, and with all parties of influence in the State, who were interested in our work. At the meeting of the Board of Supervisors, held at Alexandria, August 2, 1859, five professors had been

[4] Henry Boyce (1797–1873) was appointed U.S. attorney for the Western District of Louisiana in 1849 by Pres. Zachary Taylor. He served in that capacity until 1861. *Judges of the United States,* 2nd ed. (Washington, DC: GPO, 1983), s.v. "Boyce, Henry."

[5] Bethia J. Leonard (1815–1880) married Thomas O. Moore in Oct. 1830. Evelyn Ownbey, ed., *What Does America Mean to You?* (self-pub., 1942), vol. 2, s.v. "Moore."

[6] Emma J. Moore (1838–1873) married Bernard F. Hayes in 1859. Four years after Bernard died, Emma married Kosciusko R. Hyams in 1867. Lionel D. Melvin, *Remember Our Melvins and Kin* (Charlotte, NC: H. Eaton, 1988), 209.

[7] WTS arrived in Alexandria, LA, on Nov. 7, 1859. Walter L. Fleming, ed., *General W. T. Sherman as College President* (Cleveland: Arthur H. Clark, 1912), 45–46.

elected: 1. W. T. Sherman, Superintendent, and Professor of Engineering, etc.; 2. Anthony Vallas, Professor of Mathematics, Philosophy, etc.;[8] 3. Francis W. Smith, Professor of Chemistry, etc.;[9] 4. David F. Boyd, Professor of Languages, English and Ancient;[10] 5. E. Berti St. Ange, Professor of French and Modern Languages.[11]

These constituted the Academic Board, while the general supervision remained in the Board of Supervisors, composed of the Governor of the State, the Superintendent of Public Education,[12] and twelve members, nominated by the Governor, and confirmed by the Senate.[13] The institution was bound to educate sixteen beneficiary students, free of any charge for tuition. These had only to pay for their clothing and books, while all others had to pay their entire expenses, including tuition.[14]

Early in November, Profs. Smith, Vallas, St. Ange, and I, met a committee of the Board of Supervisors, composed of T. C. Manning,[15] G. Mason Graham,

[8] Antal "Anthony" Vallas (1809–1869) was born in Hungary and moved to the United States in 1850. Barry Cowan, *Louisiana State University* (Charleston, SC: Arcadia, 2013), 49.

[9] Francis W. Smith (1838–1865) was the youngest professor, and the commandant of cadets, at the Louisiana State Seminary when it opened. He later served as a military secretary for Confederate general Robert E. Lee. Cowan, *Louisiana State University,* 49; Walter L. Fleming, *Louisiana State University, 1860–1896* (Baton Rouge: LSU Press, 1936), 32; Germaine M. Reed, *David French Boyd: Founder of Louisiana State University* (Baton Rouge: LSU Press, 1977), 19, 32.

[10] David F. Boyd (1834–1899) joined the Confederate Army at the start of the Civil War and later returned to the Louisiana State Seminary in 1865 to serve as its superintendent. He was instrumental in changing the academy's name to Louisiana State University. Cowan, *Louisiana State University,* 51.

[11] E. Berté St. Ange served as an officer in the French Navy before he moved to the United States. Reed, *David French Boyd,* 18–19.

[12] William I. Hamilton was the Louisiana state superintendent of public education in 1859. "Report of the Special Joint Committee on Levees to the Legislature of the State of Louisiana," *Documents of the Second Session of the Fourth Legislature of the State of Louisiana* (Baton Rouge: J. M. Taylor, 1859), 83.

[13] For a complete list of the Louisiana State Seminary's board of supervisors, see Benjamin L. Price, "Origins of the Ole War Skule: The Creation of the Louisiana Seminary of Learning and Military Institute," *Louisiana History: The Journal of the Louisiana Historical Association,* 52, no. 1 (Winter 2011):40.

[14] For an in-depth study of the first cadets at the Louisiana State Seminary, see Alison Moore, *Sixty '60s* (Baton Rouge: Ortieb Press, 1984).

[15] Thomas C. Manning (1831–1887) moved to Alexandria, LA, in 1855 to work as a lawyer. He later served as the U.S. minister to Mexico. "Death of Thomas C. Manning," *Stark County Democrat* (Canton, OH), Oct. 13, 1887, 1.

and W. W. Whittington,[16] at General Graham's house, and resolved to open the institution to pupils on the 1st day of January, 1860.[17] We adopted a series of by-laws for the government of the institution, which was styled the "Louisiana Seminary of Learning and Military Academy." This title grew out of the original grant, by the Congress of the United States, of a certain township of public land, to be sold by the State, and dedicated to the use of a "seminary of learning." I do not suppose that Congress designed thereby to fix the name or title; but the subject had so long been debated in Louisiana that the name, though awkward, had become familiar. We appended to it "Military Academy," as explanatory of its general design.

On the 17th of November, 1859, the Governor of the State, Wickliffe, issued officially a general circular, prepared by us, giving public notice that the "Seminary of Learning" would open on the 1st day of January, 1860; containing a description of the locality, and the general regulations for the proposed institution; and authorizing parties to apply for further information to the "Superintendent," at Alexandria, Louisiana.[18]

The Legislature had appropriated for the sixteen beneficiaries at the rate of two hundred and eighty-three dollars per annum, to which we added sixty dollars as tuition for pay cadets; and, though the price was low, we undertook to manage for the first year on that basis.

Promptly to the day, we opened, with about sixty cadets present.[19] Major Smith was the commandant of cadets, and I the superintendent. I had been to New Orleans, where I had bought a supply of mattresses, books, and every thing requisite, and we started very much on the basis of West Point and of the Virginia Military Institute, but without uniforms or muskets; yet with roll-calls, sections, and recitations, we kept as near the standard of West Point as possible.

[16] William W. Whittington (1812–1891) was born in Maryland and moved to Rapides Parish, LA, in 1836 to work as a planter and a lawyer. He served one term in the Louisiana state legislature. *Biographical and Historical Memoirs of Northwest Louisiana* (Nashville, TN: Southern, 1890), s.v. "W. W. Whittington, Sr."

[17] The meeting to establish a code of regulations for the Louisiana State Seminary was held on Nov. 19, 1859. Contrary to WTS's claim, Thomas C. Manning was not present at the meeting. Fleming, *Louisiana State University,* 39.

[18] For more information on the circular signed by Louisiana governor Robert C. Wickliffe, see Fleming, *Louisiana State University,* 40.

[19] The first session of the Louisiana State Seminary started on Jan. 2, 1860, with nineteen students present. More students arrived throughout the session. Fleming, *Louisiana State University,* 28, 45; Moore, *Sixty '60s,* 5.

I kept all the money accounts, and gave general directions to the steward, professors, and cadets. The other professors had their regular classes and recitations. We all lived in rooms in the college-building, except Vallas, who had a family, and rented a house near by. A Creole gentleman, B. Jarreau, Esq., had been elected steward, and he also had his family in a house not far off.[20] The other professors had a mess in a room adjoining the mess-hall. A few more cadets joined in the course of the winter, so that we had in all, during the first term, seventy-three cadets, of whom fifty-nine passed the examination on the 30th of July, 1860. During our first term many defects in the original act of the Legislature were demonstrated, and, by the advice of the Board of Supervisors, I went down to Baton Rouge during the session of the Legislature, to advocate and urge the passage of a new bill, putting the institution on a better footing.[21] Thomas O. Moore was then Governor, Bragg was a member of the Board of Public Works, and Richard Taylor was a Senator.[22] I got well acquainted with all of these, and with some of the leading men of the State, and was always treated with the greatest courtesy and kindness. In conjunction with the proper committee of the Legislature, we prepared a new bill, which was passed and approved on the 7th of March, 1860, by which we were to have a beneficiary cadet for each parish, in all fifty-six, and fifteen thousand dollars annually for their maintenance; also twenty thousand dollars for the general use of the college. During that session we got an appropriation of fifteen thousand dollars for building two professors' houses, for the purchase of philosophical and chemical apparatus, and for the beginning of a college library. The seminary was made a State Arsenal, under the title of State Central Arsenal, and I was allowed five hundred dollars a year as its superintendent.[23] These matters took me several times to Baton Rouge that winter, and I recall an event of some interest, which must have happened in February. At that time my brother,

[20] Joseph B. Jarreau (c. 1806–1878) was the steward and purchasing agent for the Louisiana State Seminary in 1860. He maintained the school grounds while the school was closed during the Civil War. Catherine B. Futch, *The Baillio Family* (self-pub., 1961), 273–274.

[21] WTS traveled to Baton Rouge in mid-Feb. McDonough, *William Tecumseh Sherman,* 229.

[22] Richard Taylor (1826–1879), the son of U.S. president Zachary Taylor, moved to Louisiana to work as a sugar planter and served as a Louisiana state senator. He reached the rank of lieutenant general in the Confederate Army during the Civil War. *CWHC,* 523.

[23] In Jan. 1860 a banking firm in London offered WTS a job with a yearly salary of $7,500. In response, Graham and Gov. Moore offered WTS $5,000 a year to remain as the superintendent of the Louisiana State Seminary. Fleming, *Louisiana State University,* 58–60.

John Sherman, was a candidate, in the national House of Representatives, for Speaker, against Bocock, of Virginia.[24] In the South he was regarded as an "abolitionist," the most horrible of all monsters; and many people of Louisiana looked at me with suspicion, as the brother of the abolitionist, John Sherman, and doubted the propriety of having me at the head of an important State institution.[25] By this time I was pretty well acquainted with many of their prominent men, was generally esteemed by all in authority, and by the people of Rapides Parish especially, who saw that I was devoted to my particular business, and that I gave no heed to the political excitement of the day. But the members of the State Senate and House did not know me so well, and it was natural that they should be suspicions of a Northern man, and the brother of him who was the "abolition" candidate for Speaker of the House.

One evening, at a large dinner-party at Governor Moore's, at which were present several members of the Louisiana Legislature, Taylor, Bragg, and the Attorney-General Hyams,[26] after the ladies had left the table, I noticed at Governor Moore's end quite a lively discussion going on, in which my name was frequently used; at length the Governor called to me, saying: "Colonel Sherman, you can readily understand that, with your brother the abolitionist candidate for Speaker, some of our people wonder that you should be here at the head of an important State institution. Now, you are at my table, and I assure you of my confidence. Won't you speak your mind freely on this question of slavery, that so agitates the land? You are under my roof, and, whatever you say, you have my protection."

[24] Thomas S. Bocock (1815–1891) served in the U.S. House of Representatives from 1847 to 1861. He and John Sherman both lost the election for speaker of the House in 1860 to Representative William Pennington of New Jersey. Bocock was elected to the Confederate Congress at the outbreak of the Civil War and was elected speaker of the Confederate House of Representatives in 1862. Ollinger Crenshaw, "The Speakership Contest of 1859–1860: John Sherman's Election a Cause of Disruption?," *Mississippi Valley Historical Review* 29, no. 3 (Dec. 1942):325; "Death of Hon. Thomas S. Bocock," *Alexandria Gazette* (Alexandria, LA), Aug. 7, 1891, 2.

[25] John Sherman's bid to be speaker of the House was compromised by his endorsement of the antislavery book *The Impending Crisis of the South.* For WTS's correspondence with John Sherman during this time, see Rachel Sherman Thorndike, ed., *The Sherman Letters: Correspondence between General and Senator Sherman from 1837–1891* (New York: Charles Scribner, 1894), 76–109; John F. Marszalek, *Sherman: A Soldier's Passion for Order* (New York: Free Press, 1993), 125.

[26] Henry M. Hyams (1805–1875) moved to Louisiana in 1828. Contrary to WTS's assertion, Hyams was never attorney general. He was elected to the Louisiana Senate and served as lieutenant governor of Louisiana during the Civil War. "Death of Gov. Henry M. Hyams," *People's Vindicator* (Natchitoches, LA), July 3, 1875, 2.

I answered: "Governor Moore, you mistake in calling my brother, John Sherman, an abolitionist. We have been separated since childhood—I in the army, and he pursuing his profession of law in Northern Ohio; and it is possible we may differ in general sentiment, but I deny that he is considered at home an abolitionist; and, although he prefers the free institutions under which he lives to those of slavery which prevail here, he would not of himself take from you by law or force any property whatever, even slaves."

Then said Moore: "Give us your own views of slavery as you see it here and throughout the South."

I answered in effect that "the people of Louisiana were hardly responsible for slavery, as they had inherited it; that I found two distinct conditions of slavery, domestic and field hands. The domestic slaves, employed by the families, were probably better treated than any slaves on earth; but the condition of the field-hands was different, depending more on the temper and disposition of their masters and overseers than were those employed about the house;" and I went on to say that, "were I a citizen of Louisiana, and a member of the Legislature, I would deem it wise to bring the legal condition of the slaves more near the status of human beings under all Christian and civilized governments. In the first place, I argued that, in sales of slaves made by the State, I would forbid the separation of families, letting the father, mother, and children, be sold together to one person, instead of each to the highest bidder. And, again, I would advise the repeal of the statute which enacted a severe penalty for even the owner to teach his slave to read and write, because that actually qualified property and took away a part of its value;[27] illustrating the assertion by the case of Henry Sampson,[28] who had been the slave of Colonel Chambers,[29] of Rapides Parish, who had gone to California as the servant of

[27] In 1830 the Louisiana state legislature made it a crime to teach enslaved people how to read or write. Violators faced up to a year in prison. *Acts Passed at the Second Session of the Ninth Legislature of the State of Louisiana* (Donaldsonville, LA: C. W. Duhy, 1830), 96.

[28] Henry F. Sampson (c. 1824–c. 1868) was born in Maryland and was brought to San Francisco in his early twenties. He worked as a porter at WTS's bank. During the Civil War he was hired to work as a porter for the U.S. Mint. In 1862 he signed a petition that lobbied the city's board of education to fund schools for black students. Rudolph M. Lapp, *Blacks in Gold Rush California* (New Haven, CT: Yale University Press, 1977), 174–176, 220.

[29] Josiah Chambers (1820–1917) was one of the largest enslavers in Rapides Parish, LA. He served in the U.S. Army during the Mexican-American War and joined the Confederate Army at the outbreak of the Civil War. "Mr. Josiah Chambers," *Weekly Town Talk* (Alexandria, LA), Mar. 24, 1917, 4.

an officer of the army, and who was afterward employed by me in the bank at San Francisco. At first he could not write or read, and I could only afford to pay him one hundred dollars a month; but he was taught to read and write by Reilley, our bank-teller, when his services became worth two hundred and fifty dollars a month, which enabled him to buy his own freedom and that of his brother and his family."

What I said was listened to by all with the most profound attention; and, when I was through, some one (I think it was Mr. Hyams) struck the table with his fist, making the glasses jingle, and said, "By God, he is right!" and at once he took up the debate, which went on, for an hour or more, on both sides with ability and fairness. Of course, I was glad to be thus relieved, because at the time all men in Louisiana were dreadfully excited on questions affecting their slaves, who constituted the bulk of their wealth, and without whom they honestly believed that sugar, cotton, and rice, could not possibly be cultivated.[30]

On the 30th and 31st of July, 1860, we had an examination at the seminary, winding up with a ball, and as much publicity as possible to attract general notice; and immediately thereafter we all scattered—the cadets to their homes, and the professors wherever they pleased—all to meet again on the 1st day of the next November. Major Smith and I agreed to meet in New York on a certain day in August, to purchase books, models, etc. I went directly to my family in Lancaster, and after a few days proceeded to Washington, to endeavor to procure from the General Government the necessary muskets and equipments for our cadets by the beginning of the next term.[31] I was in Washington on the 17th day of August, and hunted up my friend Major Buell, of the Adjutant-General's Department, who was on duty with the Secretary of War, Floyd. I had with me a letter of Governor Moore's, authorizing me to act in his name. Major Buell took me into Floyd's room at the War Department, to whom I explained my business, and I was agreeably surprised to meet with such easy success. Although the State of Louisiana had already drawn her full quota of arms, Floyd promptly promised to order my requisition to be filled, and I procured the necessary blanks at the Ordnance-Office,

[30] In reference to the goods produced by enslaved people in the South, the Mississippi Secession Ordinance of 1861 stated, "These products are peculiar to the climate verging on the tropical regions, and by an imperious law of nature, none but the black race can bear exposure to the tropical sun. These products have become necessities of the world, and a blow at slavery is a blow at commerce and civilization." *Journal of the State Convention and Ordinances and Resolutions Adopted in January 1861* (Jackson, MS: E. Barksdale, 1861), 86.

[31] WTS had reached Lancaster by Aug. 12, 1860. Marszalek, *Sherman,* 133, 536*n.*

filled them with two hundred cadet muskets, and all equipments complete, and was assured that all these articles would be shipped to Louisiana in season for our use that fall. These assurances were faithfully carried out.

I then went on to New York, there met Major Smith according to appointment, and together we selected and purchased a good supply of uniforms, clothing, and text-books, as well as a fair number of books of history and fiction, to commence a library.

When this business was completed, I returned to Lancaster, and remained with my family till the time approached for me to return to Louisiana.[32] I again left my family at Lancaster, until assured of the completion of the two buildings designed for the married professors for which I had contracted that spring with Mr. Mills, of Alexandria, and which were well under progress when I left in August. One of these was designed for me and the other for Vallas. Mr. Ewing presented me with a horse, which I took down the river with me, and *en route* I ordered from Grimsley & Co. a full equipment of saddle, bridle, etc., the same that I used in the war, and which I lost with my horse, shot under me at Shiloh.[33]

Reaching Alexandria early in October, I pushed forward the construction of the two buildings, some fences, gates, and all other work, with the object of a more perfect start at the opening of the regular term November 1, 1860.

About this time Dr. Powhatan Clark was elected Assistant Professor of Chemistry, etc., and acted as secretary of the Board of Supervisors, but no other changes were made in our small circle of professors.[34]

November came, and with it nearly if not quite all our first set of cadets, and others, to the number of about one hundred and thirty.[35] We divided

[32] WTS had returned to Lancaster by Aug. 30. He then traveled back to the Louisiana State Seminary in late Oct. Marszalek, *Sherman,* 134.

[33] During the Battle of Shiloh in Apr. 1862, three horses were shot out from under WTS. He lost his saddle and riding equipment after the death of his first horse, which he described as a "beautiful sorrel race mare that was fleet as a deer." William T. Sherman, *Home Letters of General Sherman,* ed. M. A. DeWolfe Howe (New York: Charles Scribner, 1909), 220.

[34] Powhatan Clarke (1835–1917) obtained his medical degree in Paris, France. He moved to Louisiana and served in the Confederate Army during the Civil War. He moved to Baltimore, MD, in 1873 and was a professor of chemistry at Baltimore City College for twenty-five years. "Dr. Powhatan Clark Dies on Long Island," *Baltimore Sun,* Apr. 26, 1917, 6; "Clark," *The Town Talk* (Alexandria, LA), Apr. 26, 1917, 5.

[35] For the Louisiana State Seminary's roll of cadets for Jan.–Dec. 1860, see "General Sherman in Louisiana," *Times-Democrat* (New Orleans, LA), May 31, 1903, 21.

them into two companies, issued arms and clothing, and began a regular system of drills and instruction, as well as the regular recitations. I had moved into my new house, but prudently had not sent for my family, nominally on the ground of waiting until the season was further advanced, but really because of the storm that was lowering heavy on the political horizon. The presidential election was to occur in November, and the nominations had already been made in stormy debates by the usual conventions. Lincoln and Hamlin[36] (to the South utterly unknown) were the nominees of the Republican party, and for the first time both these candidates were from Northern States. The Democratic party divided—one set nominating a ticket at Charleston, and the other at Baltimore.[37] Breckenridge and Lane were the nominees of the Southern or Democratic party;[38] and Bell and Everett, a kind of compromise, mostly in favor in Louisiana.[39] Political excitement was at its very height, and it was constantly asserted that Mr. Lincoln's election would imperil the Union. I purposely kept aloof from politics, would take no part, and remember that on the day of the election in November I was notified that it would be advisable for me to vote for Bell and Everett, but I openly said I would not, and I did not. The election of Mr. Lincoln fell upon us all like a clap of thunder. People

[36]The Republican National Convention was held in Chicago on May 16–18, 1860. Hannibal Hamlin (1809–1891), a lawyer from Maine, served as Pres. Abraham Lincoln's vice president for the 1861–1865 term. U.S. Senator Andrew Johnson replaced Hamlin as Lincoln's vice-presidential candidate during the election of 1864. Hamlin later served in the U.S. Senate from 1869 to 1881. Michael Nelson, *The Presidency: A-Z,* 2nd ed. (London: Routledge Taylor and Francis Group, 1998), s.v. "Hamlin, Hannibal"; Joseph P. Smith, *History of the Republican Party in Ohio* (Chicago: Lewis, 1898), 104–216.

[37]Between Apr. and June 1860, the Democratic Party held a series of conventions in Charleston, SC, Baltimore, MD, and Richmond, VA. Smith, *History of the Republican Party,* 127.

[38]John C. Breckinridge (1821–1875) served as U.S. vice president from 1857 to 1861 and was selected by the southern faction of the Democratic Party as its nominee for president in 1860. Joseph Lane (1801–1881), a U.S. senator from Oregon, was selected as Breckinridge's running mate. Northern Democrats selected U.S. Senator Stephen A. Douglas as their presidential nominee, and Herschel V. Johnson of Georgia as his running mate. J. F. Jameson, *Dictionary of United States History* (Philadelphia: Historical, 1908), s.v. "Lane, Joseph"; William L. Richter, *The A to Z of the Civil War and Reconstruction* (Lanham, MD: Scarecrow Press, 2009), s.v "Breckinridge, John C."; Smith, *History of the Republican Party,* 127.

[39]The Constitutional Union Party nominated John Bell (1796–1869) for president and selected Edward Everett (1794–1865) as his running mate. Richard Conley, *Historical Dictionary of the U.S. Presidency* (Lanham, MD: Rowman and Littlefield, 2016), s.v. "Bell, John."; "Death of Edward Everett," *Berkshires County Eagle* (Pittsfield, MA), Jan. 19, 1865, 1.

saw and felt that the South had threatened so long that, if she quietly submitted, the question of slavery in the Territories was at an end forever. I mingled freely with the members of the Board of Supervisors, and with the people of Rapides Parish generally, keeping aloof from all cliques and parties, and I certainly hoped that the threatened storm would blow over, as had so often occurred before, after similar threats. At our seminary the order of exercises went along with the regularity of the seasons. Once a week, I had the older cadets to practise reading, reciting, and elocution, and noticed that their selections were from Calhoun,[40] Yancey,[41] and other Southern speakers, all treating of the defense of their slaves and their home institutions as the very highest duty of the patriot. Among boys this was to be expected; and among the members of our board, though most of them declaimed against politicians generally, and especially abolitionists, as pests, yet there was a growing feeling that danger was in the wind. I recall the visit of a young gentleman who had been sent from Jackson, by the Governor of Mississippi,[42] to confer with Governor Moore, then on his plantation at Bayou Robert, and who had come over to see our college. He spoke to me openly of secession as a fixed fact, and that its details were only left open for discussion. I also recall the visit of some man who was said to be a high officer in the order of "Knights of the Golden Circle," of the existence of which order I was even ignorant, until explained to me by Major Smith and Dr. Clark.[43] But in November, 1860, no man ever approached me offensively, to ascertain my views, or my proposed course of action in case of secession, and no man in or out of authority ever tried to induce me to take part in steps designed to lead toward disunion. I think my general opinions were well known and understood, viz., that "secession was treason, was *war;*" and that in no event would the North

[40] See John C. Calhoun, *John C. Calhoun: Selected Writings and Speeches,* ed. H. Lee Cheek Jr. (Washington, DC: Regnery, 2003).

[41] William L. Yancey (1814–1863) was a newspaper editor and an outspoken secessionist. William L. Richter, *Historical Dictionary of the Old South,* 2nd ed. (Lanham, MD: Scarecrow Press, 2013), s.v. "Yancey, William L."

[42] John J. Pettus (1813–1867) was governor of Mississippi from 1859 to 1863. Terry L. Jones, ed., *Historical Dictionary of the Civil War,* 2nd ed. (Lanham, MD: Scarecrow Press, 2011), vol. 1, s.v. "Pettus, John James."

[43] Organized in the 1850s, The Knights of the Golden Circle was a society of pro-slavery southerners who advocated for a new country that reached into the "Golden Circle" region of the Caribbean. David C. Keehn, *The Knights of the Golden Circle: Secret Empire, Southern Secession, Civil War* (Baton Rouge: LSU Press, 2013), 1–5.

and West permit the Mississippi River to pass out of their control. But some men at the South actually supposed at the time that the Northwestern States, in case of a disruption of the General Government, would be drawn in self-interest to an alliance with the South. What I now write I do not offer as any thing like a history of the important events of that time, but rather as my memory of them, the effect they had on me personally, and to what extent they influenced my personal conduct.

South Carolina seceded December 20, 1860, and Mississippi soon after.[44] Emissaries came to Louisiana to influence the Governor, Legislature, and people, and it was the common assertion that, if all the Cotton States would follow the lead of South Carolina, it would diminish the chances of civil war, because a bold and determined front would deter the General Government from any measures of coercion. About this time also, viz., early in December, we received Mr. Buchanan's annual message to Congress, in which he publicly announced that the General Government had no constitutional power to "coerce a State."[45] I confess this staggered me, and I feared that the prophecies and assertions of Alison[46] and other European commentators on our form of government were right, and that our Constitution was a mere rope of sand, that would break with the first pressure.

The Legislature of Louisiana met on the 10th of December, and passed an act calling a convention of delegates from the people, to meet at Baton Rouge, on the 8th of January, to take into consideration the state of the Union; and, although it was universally admitted that a large majority of the voters of the State were opposed to secession, disunion, and all the steps of the South Carolinians,

[44] Mississippi seceded from the United States on Jan. 9, 1861. Fred H. Alfriend, *The Life of Jefferson Davis* (Cincinnati: Caxton, 1868), 232.

[45] James Buchanan (1791–1868), U.S. president from 1857 to 1861, delivered his State of the Union Address to Congress on Dec. 3, 1860. James Buchanan, *The Works of James Buchanan: Comprising His Speeches, State Papers, and Private Correspondence,* ed. John B. Moore (New York: Antiquarian, 1960), 11:7–40; "Death of Ex-President Buchanan," *Intelligencer Journal* (Lancaster, PA), June 1, 1868, 2.

[46] Archibald Alison (1792–1867) was an English-born historian and lawyer. In his multi-volume book *History of Europe,* Alison made the assertion, "It is perfectly understood in every part of the Union (U.S.), that the first serious attempt to force emancipation upon the country by a general measure, will be the signal for an immediate separation of the Southern States from the Union." Archibald Alison, *History of Europe* (New York: Harper and Brothers, 1843), 4:448; *The Century Dictionary and Cyclopedia* (New York: Century, 1899), vol. 9, s.v. "Alison, Sir Archibald."

yet we saw that they were powerless, and that the politicians would sweep them along rapidly to the end, prearranged by their leaders in Washington. Before the ordinance of secession was passed, or the convention had assembled, on the faith of a telegraphic dispatch sent by the two Senators, Benjamin[47] and Slidell,[48] from their seats in the United States Senate at Washington, Governor Moore ordered the seizure of all the United States forts at the mouth of the Mississippi and Lake Pontchartrain, and of the United States arsenal at Baton Rouge.[49] The forts had no garrisons, but the arsenal was held by a small company of artillery, commanded by Major Haskins, a most worthy and excellent officer, who had lost an arm in Mexico.[50] I remember well that I was strongly and bitterly impressed by the seizure of the arsenal, which occurred on January 10, 1861.

When I went first to Baton Rouge, in 1859, *en route* to Alexandria, I found Captain Rickett's company of artillery stationed in the arsenal, but soon after there was somewhat of a clamor on the Texas frontier about Brownsville, which induced the War Department to order Rickett's company to that frontier.[51] I remember that Governor Moore remonstrated with the Secretary of War because so much dangerous property, composed of muskets, powder, etc., had been left by the United States unguarded, in a parish where the slave

[47] Judah P. Benjamin (1812–1884) was elected to the U.S. Senate in 1852 and served in that position until Louisiana seceded in 1861. He served as secretary of war and secretary of state for the Confederate government, and fled the country when the Confederacy was defeated in 1865. "Judah P. Benjamin," *Pointe Coupee Banner* (New Roads, LA), May 10, 1884, 2.

[48] John Slidell (1793–1871) graduated from Columbia College in 1810, was elected to the U.S. Senate in 1853, and resigned in 1861. He was appointed Confederate commissioner to France. In Oct. 1861, U.S. naval forces captured Slidell and James M. Mason, the Confederate commissioner to Great Britain, aboard the British ship the RMS *Trent*. The *Trent* Affair created tension between the U.S. and British governments. In Jan. 1862 the U.S. allowed Slidell and Mason to travel to Europe. Tucker and Pierpaoli, *American Civil War*, vol. 1, s.v. "Slidell, John."

[49] For Moore's correspondence with Slidell and Benjamin, and his order to seize U.S. forts and arsenals in Louisiana on Jan. 10, see *OR*, 1:1, 493–496, 53, 610.

[50] Joseph A. Haskin (1818–1874) graduated from the USMA in 1839. He lost his left arm at the Battle of Chapultepec during the Mexican-American War. *USMA*, 1:745–746.

[51] James B. Ricketts (1817–1887) graduated from the USMA in 1839 and was stationed in Baton Rouge as a captain in the U.S. 1st Art. from 1857 to 1859. In Sept. 1859, two months prior to Ricketts's arrival in Texas, Juan N. Cortina, a Mexican rancher who opposed the U.S. military presence in the area, raided Brownsville with a group of seventy men. *USMA*, 2:1–6; Jerry Thompson, *Cortina: Defending the Mexican Name in Texas* (College Station: Texas A&M University Press, 2007), 40–45, 268*n*.

population was as five or six to one of whites; and it was on his official demand that the United States Government ordered Haskins's company to replace Rickett's.[52] This company did not number forty men.[53] In the night of January 9th, about five hundred New Orleans militia, under command of a Colonel Wheat,[54] went up from New Orleans by boat, landed, surrounded the arsenal, and demanded its surrender. Haskins was of course unprepared for such a step, yet he at first resolved to defend the post as he best could with his small force.[55] But Bragg, who was an old army acquaintance of his, had a parley with him, exhibited to him the vastly superior force of his assailants, embracing two field-batteries,[56] and offered to procure for him honorable terms, to march out with drums and colors, and to take unmolested passage in a boat up to St. Louis; alleging, further, that the old Union was at an end, and that a just settlement would be made between the two new fragments for all the property stored in the arsenal. Of course it was Haskins's duty to have defended his post to the death; but up to that time the national authorities in Washington had shown such pusillanimity, that the officers of the army knew not what to do. The result, anyhow, was that Haskins surrendered his post, and at once embarked for St. Louis. The arms and munitions stored in the arsenal were scattered—some to Mississippi, some to New Orleans, some to Shreveport; and to me, at the Central Arsenal, were consigned two thousand muskets, three hundred Jäger rifles, and a large amount of cartridges and ammunition. The invoices were signed by the former ordnance-sergeant, Olodowski, as a captain of ordnance, and I think he continued such on General Bragg's staff

[52] In 1860, there were 15,358 enslaved people living in Rapides Parish, accounting for 61 percent of its population. Hillary McLaughlin-Stonham, *From Slavery to Civil Rights: On the Streetcars of New Orleans, 1830s–Present* (Liverpool: Liverpool University Press, 2020), 30; Terry L. Seip, "Slaves and Free Negroes in Alexandria, 1850–1860," *Louisiana History: The Journal of the Louisiana Historical Association* 10, no. 2 (Spring 1969):150.

[53] Haskin commanded approximately eighty troops in early Jan. 1861. John D. Winters, *The Civil War in Louisiana* (Baton Rouge: LSU Press, 1991), 10.

[54] Chatham R. Wheat (1826–1862) graduated from the University of Nashville in 1845 and served in the Mexican-American War. He moved to New Orleans at the start of the Civil War. Jones, *Historical Dictionary of the Civil War,* s.v. "Wheat, Chatham Roberdeau."

[55] After Haskin was initially compelled to surrender the arsenal, he stated, "I've lost one arm in the defense of my flag and I will lose the other, or even my life if necessary, before I surrender to that lot of ragamuffins on the Boulevard." Jones, *Historical Dictionary,*12.

[56] Braxton Bragg, then an aide for Governor Moore, commanded five companies of men during the capture of the Baton Rouge arsenal. Chester G. Hearn, *The Capture of New Orleans, 1862* (Baton Rouge: LSU Press, 1995), 13–14.

through the whole of the subsequent civil war.[57] These arms, etc., came up to me at Alexandria, with orders from Governor Moore to receipt for and account for them. Thus I was made the receiver of stolen goods, and these goods the property of the United States. This grated hard on my feelings as an ex-army-officer, and on counting the arms I noticed that they were packed in the old familiar boxes, with the "U. S." simply scratched off. General G. Mason Graham had resigned as the chairman of the Executive Committee, and Dr. S. A. Smith, of Alexandria, then a member of the State Senate, had succeeded him as chairman, and acted as head of the Board of Supervisors.[58] At the time I was in most intimate correspondence with all of these parties, and our letters must have been full of politics, but I have only retained copies of a few of the letters, which I will embody in this connection, as they will show, better than by any thing I can now recall, the feelings of parties at that critical period. The seizure of the arsenal at Baton Rouge occurred January 10, 1861, and the secession ordinance was not passed until about the 25th or 26th of the same month. At all events, after the seizure of the arsenal, and before the passage of the ordinance of secession, viz., on the 18th of January, I wrote as follows:

> LOUISIANA STATE SEMINARY OF LEARNING AND MILITARY ACADEMY, *January* 18, 1861.
>
> *Governor* THOMAS O. MOORE, *Baton Rouge, Louisiana.*
>
> SIR: As I occupy a *quasi*-military position under the laws of the State, I deem it proper to acquaint you that I accepted such position when Louisiana was a State in the Union, and when the motto of this seminary was inserted in marble over the main door: "By the liberality of the General Government of the United States. The Union—*esto perpetua.*"

[57] Hippolite Oladowski (1800–1878) was born in Poland and moved to the United States, where he served as the Confederate chief of ordnance in the Army of Tennessee. "Col. Hippolite Oladowski," *Baltimore Sun,* Aug. 22, 1878, 2; "Col. H. Oladowski," *Montgomery Advertiser* (Montgomery, AL), Aug. 20, 1878, 3.

[58] George M. Graham resigned as vice president of the board of directors for the Louisiana State Seminary in Aug. 1860. His replacement, Stokes A. Smith (1815–1872), moved to Louisiana in 1839. Smith was a Confederate surgeon in the Civil War and spent the rest of his life as a physician in Alexandria, LA. James L. Barnidge, "George Mason Graham: The Father of Louisiana State University," *Louisiana History* 10, no. 3 (Summer 1969):233–234; "Two Great Physicians Gone," *Louisiana Democrat* (Alexandria, LA), Dec. 18, 1872, 2.

Recent events foreshadow a great change, and it becomes all men to choose. If Louisiana withdraw from the Federal Union, I prefer to maintain my allegiance to the Constitution as long as a fragment of it survives; and my longer stay here would be wrong in every sense of the word.

In that event, I beg you will send or appoint some authorized agent to take charge of the arms and munitions of war belonging to the State, or advise me what disposition to make of them.

And furthermore, as president of the Board of Supervisors, I beg you to take immediate steps to relieve me as superintendent, the moment the State determines to secede, for on no earthly account will I do any act or think any thought hostile to or in defiance of the old Government of the United States.

With great respect, your obedient servant,

W. T. SHERMAN, *Superintendent.*

[PRIVATE.]

January 18, 1861.

To Governor MOORE.

MY DEAR SIR: I take it for granted that you have been expecting for some days the accompanying paper from me (the above official letter). I have repeatedly and again made known to General Graham and Dr. Smith that, in the event of a severance of the relations hitherto existing between the Confederated States of this Union, I would be forced to choose the old Union. It is barely possible all the States may secede, South and North, that new combinations may result, but this process will be one of time and uncertainty, and I cannot with my opinions await the subsequent development.

I have never been a politician, and therefore undervalue the excited feelings and opinions of present rulers, but I do think, if this people cannot execute a form of government like the present, that a worse one will result.

I will keep the cadets as quiet as possible. They are nervous, but I think the interest of the State requires them here, guarding this property, and acquiring a knowledge which will be useful to your State in after-times.

When I leave, which I now regard as certain, the present professors can manage well enough, to afford you leisure time to find a suitable successor to me. You might order Major Smith to receipt for the arms, and to exercise military command, while the academic exercises could go on under the board. In time, some gentleman will turn up, better qualified than I am, to carry on the seminary to its ultimate point of success. I entertain the kindest feelings toward all, and would leave the State with much regret; only in great events we must choose, one way or the other.

Truly, your friend,

W. T. Sherman

January 19, 1861—*Saturday.*

Dr. S. A. Smith, *President Board of Supervisors, Baton Rouge, Louisiana.*

Dear Sir: I have just finished my quarterly reports to the parents of all the cadets here, or who have been here. All my books of account are written up to date. All bills for the houses, fences, etc., are settled, and nothing now remains but the daily routine of recitations and drills. I have written officially and unofficially to Governor Moore, that with my opinions of the claimed right of seccession, of the seizure of public forts, arsenals, etc., and the ignominious capture of a United States garrison, stationed in your midst, as a guard to the arsenal and for the protection of your own people, it would be highly improper for me longer to remain. No great inconvenience can result to the seminary. I will be the chief loser. I came down two months before my pay commenced. I made sacrifices in Kansas to enable me thus to obey the call of Governor Wickliffe, and you know that last winter I declined a most advantageous offer of employment abroad; and thus far I have received nothing as superintendent of the arsenal, though I went to Washington and New York (at my own expense) on the faith of the five hundred dollars salary promised.

These are all small matters in comparison with those involved in the present state of the country, which will cause sacrifices by millions, instead of by hundreds. The more I think of it, the more I think I should be away, the sooner the better; and therefore I hope you will join with Governor Moore in authorizing me to turn over to Major Smith the military command here, and to the academic board the control of the daily exercises and recitations.

There will be no necessity of your coming up. You can let Major Smith receive the few hundreds of cash I have on hand, and I can meet you on a day certain in New Orleans, when we can settle the bank account. Before I leave, I can pay the steward Jarreau his account for the month, and there would be no necessity for other payments till about the close of March, by which time the board can meet, and elect a treasurer and superintendent also.

At present I have no class, and there will be none ready till about the month of May, when there will be a class in "surveying." Even if you do not elect a superintendent in the mean time, Major Smith could easily teach this class, as he is very familiar with the subject-matter. Indeed, I think you will do well to leave the subject of a new superintendent until one perfectly satisfactory turns up.

There is only one favor I would ask. The seminary has plenty of money in bank. The Legislature will surely appropriate for my salary as superintendent of this arsenal. Would you not let me make my drafts on the State Treasury, send them to you, let the Treasurer note them for payment when the appropriation is made, and then pay them out of the seminary fund? The drafts will be paid in March, and the seminary will lose nothing. This would be just to me; for I actually spent two hundred dollars and more in going to Washington and New York, thereby securing from the United States, in advance, three thousand dollars' worth of the very best arms; and clothing and books, at a clear profit to the seminary of over eight hundred dollars. I may be some time in finding new employment, and will stand in need of this money (five hundred dollars); otherwise I would abandon it.

I will not ask you to put the Board of Supervisors to the trouble of meeting, unless you can get a quorum at Baton Rouge.

With great respect, your friend,

W. T. SHERMAN.

By course of mail, I received the following answer from Governor Moore, the original of which I still possess. It is all in General Bragg's handwriting, with which I am familiar:

EXECUTIVE OFFICE,
BATON ROUGE, LOUISIANA, *January* 23, 1861.

MY DEAR SIR: It is with the deepest regret I acknowledge receipt of your communication of the 18th inst. In the pressure of official business, I can now only request you to transfer to Prof. Smith the arms, munitions, and funds in your hands, whenever you conclude to withdraw from the position you have filled with so much distinction.

You cannot regret more than I do the necessity which deprives us of your services, and you will bear with you the respect, confidence, and admiration, of all who have been associated with you. Very truly, your friend,

THOMAS O. MOORE.

Colonel W. T. SHERMAN, *Superintendent Military Academy, Alexandria.*

I must have received several letters from Bragg, about this time, which have not been preserved; for I find that, on the 1st of February, 1861, I wrote him thus:

SEMINARY OF LEARNING,
ALEXANDRIA, LOUISIANA, *February* 1, 1861.

Colonel BRAXTON BRAGG, *Baton Rouge, Louisiana.*

DEAR SIR: Yours of January 23d and 27th are received. I thank you most kindly, and Governor Moore through you, for the kind manner in which you have met my wishes.

Now that I cannot be compromised by political events, I will so shape my course as best to serve the institution, which has a strong hold on my affections and respect.

The Board of Supervisors will be called for the 9th instant, and I will cooperate with them in their measures to place matters here on a safe and secure basis. I expect to be here two weeks, and will make you full returns of money and property belonging to the State Central Arsenal. All the arms and ammunition are safely stored here. Then I will write you more at length. With sincere respect, your friend,

W. T. SHERMAN.

Major Smith's receipt to me, for the arms and property belonging both to the seminary and to the arsenal, is dated February 19, 1861. I subjoin also, in this connection, copies of one or two papers that may prove of interest:

BATON ROUGE, *January* 28, 1861.

To Major SHERMAN, *Superintendent, Alexandria.*

MY DEAR SIR: Your letter was duly received, and would have been answered ere this time could I have arranged sooner the matter of the five hundred dollars. I shall go from here to New Orleans to-day or tomorrow, and will remain there till Saturday after next, perhaps. I shall expect to meet you there, as indicated in your note to me.

I need not tell you that it is with no ordinary regret that I view your determination to leave us, for really I believe that the success of our institution, now almost assured, is jeopardized thereby. I am sure that we will never have a superintendent with whom I shall have more pleasant relations than those which have existed between yourself and me.

I fully appreciate the motives which have induced you to give up a position presenting so many advantages to yourself, and sincerely hope that you may, in any future enterprise, enjoy the success which your character and ability merit and deserve.

Should you come down on the Rapides (steamer), please look after my wife, who will, I hope, accompany you on said boat, or some other good one.

Colonel Bragg informs me that the necessary orders have been given for the transfer and receipt by Major Smith of the public property.

I herewith transmit a request to the secretary to convene the Board of Supervisors, that they may act as seems best to them in the premises.

In the mean time, Major Smith will command by seniority the cadets, and the Academic Board will be able to conduct the scientific exercises of the institution until the Board of Supervisors can have time to act. Hoping to meet you soon at the St. Charles, I am,

Most truly, your friend and servant, S. A. SMITH

P. S.—Governor Moore desires me to express his profound regret that the State is about to lose one who we all fondly hoped had cast his destinies for weal or for woe among us; and that he is sensible that we lose thereby an officer whom it will be difficult, if not impossible, to replace.

S. A. S.

BATON ROUGE, *February* 11, 1861.

To Major SHERMAN, *Alexandria.*

DEAR SIR: I have been in New Orleans for ten days, and on returning here find two letters from you, also your prompt answer to the resolution of the House of Representatives, for which I am much obliged.

The resolution passed the last day before adjournment. I was purposing to respond, when your welcome reports came to hand. I have arranged to pay you your five hundred dollars.

I will say nothing of general politics, except to give my opinion that there is not to be any war.

In that event, would it not be possible for you to become a citizen of our State? Everyone deplores your determination to leave us. At the same time, your friends feel that you are abandoning a position that might become an object of desire to any one.

I will try to meet you in New Orleans at any time you may indicate; but it would be best for you to stop here, when, if possible, I will accompany you. Should you do so, you will find me just above the State-House, and facing it.

Bring with you a few copies of the "Rules of the Seminary."

Yours truly, S. A. Smith

Louisiana State Seminary of Learning and Military Academy, *February* 14, 1861.

Colonel W. T. Sherman.

Sir: I am instructed by the Board of Supervisors of this institution to present a copy of the resolutions adopted by them at their last meeting:

"*Resolved,* That the thanks of the Board of Supervisors are due, and are hereby tendered, to Colonel William T. Sherman for the able and efficient manner in which he has conducted the affairs of the seminary during the time the institution has been under his control—a period attended with unusual difficulties, requiring on the part of the superintendent to successfully overcome them a high order of administrative talent. And the board further bear willing testimony to the valuable services that Colonel Sherman has rendered them in their efforts to establish an institution of learning in accordance with the beneficent design of the State and Federal Governments; evincing at all times a readiness to adapt himself to the ever-varying requirements of an institution of learning in its infancy, struggling to attain a position of honor and usefulness.

"*Resolved, further,* That, in accepting the resignation of Colonel Sherman as Superintendent of the State Seminary of Learning and Military Academy, we tender to him assurances of our high personal regard, and our sincere regret at the occurrence of causes that render it necessary to part with so esteemed and valued a friend, as well as co-laborer in the cause of education."

Powhatan Clarke, *Secretary to the Board.*

A copy of the resolution of the Academic Board, passed at their session of April 1, 1861:

> "*Resolved,* That in the resignation of the late superintendent, Colonel W. T. Sherman, the Academic Board deem it not improper to express their deep conviction of the loss the institution has sustained in being thus deprived of an able head. They cannot fail to appreciate the manliness of character which has always marked the actions of Colonel Sherman. While he is personally endeared to many of them as a friend, they consider it their high pleasure to tender to him in this resolution their regret on his separation, and their sincere wish for his future welfare."

I have given the above at some length, because, during the civil war, it was in Southern circles asserted that I was guilty of a breach of hospitality in taking up arms against the South.[59] They were manifestly the aggressors, and we could only defend our own by assailing them. Yet, without any knowledge of what the future had in store for me, I took unusual precautions that the institution should not be damaged by my withdrawal. About the 20th of February, having turned over all property, records, and money, on hand, to Major Smith, and taking with me the necessary documents to make the final settlement with Dr. S. A. Smith, at the bank in New Orleans, where the funds of the institution were deposited to my credit, I took passage from Alexandria for that city, and arrived there, I think, on the 23d. Dr. Smith met me, and we went to the bank, where I turned over to him the balance, got him to audit all my accounts, certify that they were correct and just, and that there remained not one cent of balance in my hands. I charged in my account current for my salary up to the end of February, at the rate of four thousand dollars a year, and for the five hundred dollars due me as superintendent of the Central Arsenal, all of which was due and had been fairly earned, and then I stood free and discharged of any and every obligation, honorary or business, that was due by me to the State of Louisiana, or to any corporation or individual in that State.

[59] In Oct. 1861, an article in the *Louisville Daily Courier* criticized WTS's decision to fight against the Confederacy. The article stated, "The very fact of his being an Ohioan will tend to alienate and dishearten all the Kentuckians engaged in the Lincoln cause. No Kentuckian who has a throb of Old Kentucky feeling and pride, will ever go into battle against Southerners under the command of an Ohio chief." "Retirement of Gen. Anderson," *Louisville Daily Courier,* Oct. 18, 1861, 3.

This business occupied two or three days, during which I staid at the St. Louis Hotel. I usually sat at table with Colonel and Mrs. Bragg,[60] and an officer who wore the uniform of the State of Louisiana, and was addressed as captain. Bragg wore a colonel's uniform, and explained to me that he was a colonel in the State service, a colonel of artillery, and that some companies of his regiment garrisoned Forts Jackson and St. Philip, and the arsenal at Baton Rouge.

Beauregard at the time had two sons at the Seminary of Learning.[61] I had given them some of my personal care at the father's request, and, wanting to tell him of their condition and progress, I went to his usual office in the Custom-House Building, and found him in the act of starting for Montgomery, Alabama. Bragg said afterward that Beauregard had been sent for by Jefferson Davis,[62] and that it was rumored that he had been made a brigadier-general, of which fact he seemed jealous, because in the old army Bragg was the senior.[63]

Davis and Stephens[64] had been inaugurated President and Vice-President of the Confederate States of America, February 18, 1860, at Montgomery, and those States only embraced the seven cotton States.[65] I recall a conversation at the tea-table, one evening, at the St. Louis Hotel. When Bragg was speaking of Beauregard's promotion, Mrs. Bragg, turning to me, said, "You know that my husband is not a favorite with the new President." My mind was resting on Mr. Lincoln as the *new* President, and I said I did not know that Bragg had ever met Mr. Lincoln, when Mrs. Bragg said, quite pointedly, "I didn't mean *your* President, but *our* President." I knew that Bragg hated Davis bitterly, and that he had resigned from the army in 1855, or 1856, because Davis, as Secretary of

[60] Eliza B. Ellis (1825–1908) married Braxton Bragg in 1849. Samuel J. Martin, *General Braxton Bragg, C.S.A* (Jefferson, NC: McFarland, 2014), 68; "Mrs. Eliza Bragg Goes to Her Reward," *Nashville Banner,* Sept. 26, 1908, 3.

[61] Rene T. Beauregard (1843–1910) and Henry T. Beauregard (1845–1915) were the only sons of P. G. T. Beauregard. Rene served as a judge after the Civil War, and Henry became a planter and real estate agent. "Judge R. T. Beauregard," *St. Bernard Voice* (Arabi, LA), Dec. 17, 1910, 5; "The Last Roll Call," *Confederate Veteran* 23, no. 1 (Jan. 1915):133.

[62] Jefferson Davis (1808–1889), an enslaver from Mississippi, graduated from the USMA in 1828. He served as the U.S. secretary of war from 1853 to 1857 before he was elected as the first and only president of the Confederate States of America. *USMA,* 1:416.

[63] Beauregard was promoted to brigadier general in the Confederate Army on Mar. 1st, 1861. Bragg was promoted to the same rank six days later. *CWHC,* 123, 141.

[64] Alexander H. Stephens (1812–1883), an enslaver from Georgia, was the vice president of the Confederate States of America from 1861 to 1865. *CWHC,* 508–509.

[65] On Feb. 18, 1861, the Confederacy consisted of South Carolina, Mississippi, Florida, Alabama, Georgia, Louisiana, and Texas. Alfriend, *The Life of Jefferson Davis,* 232.

War, had ordered him, with his battery, from Jefferson Barracks, Missouri, to Fort Smith or Fort Washita, in the Indian country, as Bragg expressed it, "to chase Indians with six-pounders."

I visited the quartermaster, Colonel A. C. Myers, who had resigned from the army, January 28, 1861, and had accepted service under the new *régime.* His office was in the same old room in the Lafayette Square building, which he had in 1853, when I was there a commissary, with the same pictures on the wall, and the letters "U. S." on every thing, including his desk, papers, etc. I asked him if he did not feel funny. "No, not at all. The thing was inevitable, secession was a complete success; there would be no war, but the two Governments would settle all matters of business in a friendly spirit, and each would go on in its allotted sphere, without further confusion." About this date, February 16th, General Twiggs, Myers's father-in-law, had surrendered his entire command, in the Department of Texas, to some State troops, with all the Government property,[66] thus consummating the first serious step in the drama of the conspiracy, which was to form a confederacy of the cotton States, before working upon the other slave or border States, and before the 4th of March, the day for the inauguration of President Lincoln.

I walked the streets of New Orleans, and found business going along as usual. Ships were strung for miles along the lower levee, and steamboats above, all discharging or receiving cargo. The Pelican flag of Louisiana was flying over the Custom-House, Mint, City Hall, and everywhere. At the levee ships carried every flag on earth except that of the United States, and I was told that during a procession on the 22d of February, celebrating their emancipation from the despotism of the United States Government, only one national flag was shown from a house, and that the house of Cuthbert Bullitt,[67] on Lafayette Square. He was commanded to take it down, but he refused, and defended it with his pistol.

The only officer of the army that I can recall, as being there at the time, who was faithful, was Colonel C. L. Kilburn, of the Commissary Department, and he was preparing to escape North.[68]

[66] Twiggs surrendered military posts in Texas that contained over $1,300,000 worth of military supplies. Charles E. Little, ed., *Cyclopedia of Classified Dates* (New York: Funk and Wagnalls, 1900), 192.

[67] Cuthbert Bullitt (1809–1906) was a U.S. marshall in New Orleans before the Civil War and later served as the U.S. collector at the Port of New Orleans. "Col. Bullitt, Oldest Knight Templar, Dead," *Lexington Herald* (Lexington, KY), Aug. 6, 1906, 1.

[68] Charles L. Kilburn (1819–1899) graduated from the USMA in 1842 and was later brevetted brigadier general in the U.S. Army for his actions during the Civil War. *USMA,* 2:129–130.

Everybody regarded the change of Government as final; that Louisiana, by a mere declaration, was a free and independent State, and could enter into any new alliance or combination she chose.

Men were being enlisted and armed, to defend the State, and there was not the least evidence that the national Administration designed to make any effort, by force, to vindicate the national authority. I therefore bade adieu to all my friends, and about the 25th of February took my departure by railroad, for Lancaster, *via* Cairo and Cincinnati.

Before leaving this subject, I will simply record the fate of some of my associates. The seminary was dispersed by the war, and all the professors and cadets took service in the Confederacy, except Vallas, St. Ange, and Cadet Taliaferro.[69] The latter joined a Union regiment, as a lieutenant, after New Orleans was retaken by the United States fleet under Farragut. I think that both Vallas and St. Ange have died in poverty since the war.[70] Major Smith joined the rebel army in Virginia, and was killed in April, 1865, as he was withdrawing his garrison, by night, from the batteries at Drury's Bluff, at the time General Lee began his final retreat from Richmond. Boyd became a captain of engineers on the staff of General Richard Taylor, was captured, and was in jail at Natchez, Mississippi, when I was on my Meridian expedition. He succeeded in getting a letter to me on my arrival at Vicksburg, and, on my way down to New Orleans, I stopped at Natchez, took him along, and enabled him to effect an exchange through General Banks.[71] As soon as the war was over, he returned to Alexandria, and reorganized the old institution, where I visited him in 1867; but, the next winter, the building took fire and burned to the ground. The students, library, apparatus, etc., were transferred to Baton Rouge, where the same institution now is, under the title of the Louisiana University. I have been able to do them

[69] Henry B. Taliaferro (1841–1921) was one of the first cadets at the Louisiana State Seminary. In Jan. 1864 he joined Co. E of the 1st Regiment of Louisiana Cav. for the U.S. Army. Moore, *Sixty '60s,* 61–62.

[70] Contrary to WTS's claim, Vallas continued as a scholar of mathematics and philology after he left the Louisiana State Seminary. He was president of the New Orleans Academy of Sciences at the time of his death in 1869. However, St. Ange was left poor and destitute after the Civil War. See Reed, *David French Boyd,* 85; "Obituary Memoir of Professor Anthony Vallas," *De Bow's Monthly Review* 6, no. 7 (July 1869):835–836.

[71] Nathaniel P. Banks (1816–1894) was the governor of Massachusetts from 1858 to 1861 and was commissioned as a major general of volunteers for the U.S. Army in 1861. "Gen. N. P. Banks Dead," *Boston Globe,* Sept. 1, 1894, 1–2.

many acts of kindness, and am still in correspondence with Colonel Boyd, its president.[72]

General G. Mason Graham is still living on his plantation, on Bayou Rapides, old and much respected.

Dr. S. A. Smith became a surgeon in the rebel army, and at the close of the war was medical director of the trans-Mississippi Department, with General Kirby Smith. I have seen him since the war, at New Orleans, where he died about a year ago.

Dr. Clark was in Washington recently, applying for a place as United States consul abroad. I assisted him, but with no success, and he is now at Baltimore, Maryland.

After the battle of Shiloh, I found among the prisoners Cadet Barrow, fitted him out with some clean clothing, of which he was in need, and from him learned that Cadet Workman was killed in that battle.[73]

Governor Moore's plantation was devastated by General Banks's troops. After the war he appealed to me, and through the Attorney-General, Henry Stanbery, I aided in having his land restored to him, and I think he is now living there.

Bragg, Beauregard, and Taylor, enacted high parts in the succeeding war, and now reside in Louisiana or Texas.[74]

[72] For Boyd's assessment of WTS's time at the Louisiana State Seminary, see D. F. Boyd to WTS, July 17, 1875, in the Appendix to Volume II. Cowan, *Louisiana State University*, 51.

[73] Wylie M. Barrow (1843–1863) joined Co. F of the 4th Louisiana Inf. for the Confederate Army. After being captured and exchanged, he went on to fight for the Confederacy in Tennessee and Georgia. In the first edition of the memoirs (1875), WTS did not identify Barrow by name. WTS was mistaken about the death of John D. Workman, who was killed in Virgina in 1864. Fleming, *Louisiana State University*, 125; "Gen. Lee's Staff," *Times Picayune* (New Orleans), Aug. 30, 1864, 4; Moore, *Sixty '60s*, 66–67, 72.

[74] Bragg spent his postwar years in Louisiana, Alabama, and Texas. Beauregard lived in New Orleans after the Civil War and served as the president of the New Orleans, Jackson, and Mississippi Railroad from 1865 to 1870, president of the New Orleans and Carrollton Street Railroad from 1866 to 1876, and supervisor of the Louisiana lottery. Taylor resided in New Orleans after he was paroled by the U.S. Army in May 1865. *CWHC*, 124, 141; "General Richard Taylor," *Indiana State Sentinel* (Indianapolis), Apr. 16, 1879, 4.

8

Missouri.

APRIL AND MAY, 1861.

DURING THE TIME of these events in Louisiana, I was in constant correspondence with my brother, John Sherman, at Washington; Mr. Ewing, at Lancaster, Ohio; and Major H. S. Turner, at St. Louis. I had managed to maintain my family comfortably at Lancaster, but was extremely anxious about the future. It looked like the end of my career, for I did not suppose that "civil war" could give me an employment that would provide for the family. I thought, and may have said, that the national crisis had been brought about by the politicians, and, as it was upon us, they "might fight it out." Therefore, when I turned North from New Orleans, I felt more disposed to look to St. Louis for a home, and to Major Turner to find me employment, than to the public service.

I left New Orleans about the 1st of March, 1861, by rail to Jackson and Clinton, Mississippi, Jackson, Tennessee, and Columbus, Kentucky, where we took a boat to Cairo, and thence, by rail, to Cincinnati and Lancaster. All the way, I heard, in the cars and boats, warm discussions about politics; to the effect that, if Mr. Lincoln should attempt coercion of the seceded States, the other slave or border States would make common cause, when, it was believed, it would be madness to attempt to reduce them to subjection. In the South, the people were earnest, fierce and angry, and were evidently organizing for action; whereas, in Illinois, Indiana, and Ohio, I saw not the least sign of preparation. It certainly looked to me as though the people of the North would tamely submit to a disruption of the Union, and the orators of the South used, openly and constantly, the expressions that there would be no war, and that a lady's thimble would hold all the blood to be shed.[1] On reaching Lancaster, I found letters from my brother John, inviting me to come

[1] In the months leading up to the Civil War, U.S. Senator James Chesnut of South Carolina attempted to downplay the consequences of secession. He allegedly claimed he could "drink all the blood that secession might cause to be shed." John Harold, *Libby, Andersonville, Flor-*

to Washington, as he wanted to see me; and from Major Turner, at St. Louis, that he was trying to secure for me the office of president of the Fifth Street Railroad, with a salary of twenty-five hundred dollars; that Mr. Lucas and D. A. January[2] held a controlling interest of stock, would vote for me, and the election would occur in March. This suited me exactly, and I answered Turner that I would accept, with thanks. But I also thought it right and proper that I should first go to Washington, to talk with my brother, Senator Sherman.

Mr. Lincoln had just been installed, and the newspapers were filled with rumors of every kind indicative of war; the chief act of interest was that Major Robert Anderson had taken by night into Fort Sumter all the troops garrisoning Charleston Harbor, and that he was determined to defend it against the demands of the State of South Carolina and of the Confederate States. I must have reached Washington about the 10th of March. I found my brother there, just appointed Senator, in place of Mr. Chase, who was in the cabinet,[3] and I have no doubt my opinions, thoughts, and feelings, wrought up by the events in Louisiana, seemed to him gloomy and extravagant. About Washington I saw but few signs of preparation, though the Southern Senators and Representatives were daily sounding their threats on the floors of Congress, and were publicly withdrawing to join the Confederate Congress at Montgomery. Even in the War Department and about the public offices there was open, unconcealed talk, amounting to high-treason.

One day, John Sherman took me with him to see Mr. Lincoln. He walked into the room where the secretary to the President now sits,[4] we found the

---

ence: The Capture, Imprisonment, Escape and Rescue of John Harold (Philadelphia: William B. Selheimer, 1870), 95.

[2] Derrick A. January (1815–1869) moved to St. Louis, MO, in 1837, and became a prominent merchant in the city. "D. A. January," *St. Louis Globe-Democrat,* July 23, 1879, 8; "Died," *St. Louis Post-Dispatch,* July 19, 1879, 4.

[3] Salmon P. Chase (1808–1873) resigned from the U.S. Senate on Mar. 6, 1861, and served as U.S. secretary of the treasury from 1861 to 1864. His Senate replacement, John Sherman, was sworn in on Mar. 23, 1861. Chase later served as chief justice of the U.S. Supreme Court from 1864 to 1873. *CWHC,* 170; John Sherman, *John Sherman's Recollections of Forty Years in the House, Senate, and Cabinet* (Chicago: Werner, 1895), 1:232.

[4] In 1875, Orville Babcock, personal secretary to Pres. Ulysses S. Grant, maintained an office in an anteroom on the second floor of the White House. Ralph Kirshner, *The Class of 1861: Custer, Ames, and Their Classmates after West Point* (Carbondale: Southern Illinois University Press, 1999), 133.

room full of people, and Mr. Lincoln sat at the end of the table, talking with three or four gentlemen, who soon left. John walked up, shook hands, and took a chair near him, holding in his hand some papers referring to minor appointments in the State of Ohio, which formed the subject of conversation. Mr. Lincoln took the papers, said he would refer them to the proper heads of departments, and would be glad to make the appointments asked for, if not already promised. John then turned to me, and said, "Mr. President, this is my brother, Colonel Sherman, who is just up from Louisiana, he may give you some information you want." "Ah!" said Mr. Lincoln, "how are they getting along down there?" I said, "They think they are getting along swimmingly—they are preparing for war." "Oh, well!" said he, "I guess we'll manage to keep house." I was silenced, said no more to him, and we soon left.[5] I was sadly disappointed, and remember that I broke out on John, d—ning the politicians generally, saying, "You have got things in a hell of a fix, and you may get them out as you best can," adding that the country was sleeping on a volcano that might burst forth at any minute, but that I was going to St. Louis to take care of my family, and would have no more to do with it. John begged me to be more patient, but I said I would not; that I had no time to wait, that I was off for St. Louis; and off I went. At Lancaster I found letters from Major Turner, inviting me to St. Louis, as the place in the Fifth Street Railroad was a sure thing, and that Mr. Lucas would rent me a good house on Locust Street, suitable for my family, for six hundred dollars a year.

Mrs. Sherman and I gathered our family and effects together, started for St. Louis March 27th, where we rented of Mr. Lucas the house on Locust Street, between Tenth and Eleventh, and occupied it on the 1st of April. Charles Ewing[6] and John Hunter[7] had formed a law-partnership in St. Louis,

[5]According to John Sherman, WTS did not provide a complete description of their meeting with Lincoln. John wrote, "While Mr. Lincoln did say, in response to his tender, 'I guess we will manage to keep house,' he also expressed a hope, which General Sherman knew to be delusive, that the danger would pass by and that the Union would be restored by a peaceful compromise." John Sherman, *Recollections,* 1:242.

[6]Charles Ewing (1835–1883), WTS's foster brother and brother-in-law, graduated with his law degree from the University of Virginia. *CWHC,* 229.

[7]John A. Hunter (1833–1887) served as a quartermaster for the U.S. Army during the Civil War. He moved back to St. Louis after the war and practiced law until he was appointed chief justice of the Utah Supreme Court in 1879. "Death of Judge John A. Hunter," *St. Louis Globe-Democrat,* June 30, 1887, 6.

and agreed to board with us, taking rooms on the third floor. In the latter part of March, I was duly elected president of the Fifth Street Railroad, and entered on the discharge of my duties April 1, 1861. We had a central office on the corner of Fifth and Locust, and also another up at the stables in Bremen.[8] The road was well stocked and in full operation, and all I had to do was to watch the economical administration of existing affairs, which I endeavored to do with fidelity and zeal. But the whole air was full of wars and rumors of wars. The struggle was going on politically for the border States. Even in Missouri, which was a slave State, it was manifest that the Governor of the State, Claiborne Jackson,[9] and all the leading politicians, were for the South in case of a war. The house on the northwest corner of Fifth and Pine was the rebel headquarters, where the rebel flag was hung publicly,[10] and the crowds about the Planters' House were all more or less rebel. There was also a camp in Lindell's Grove, at the end of Olive Street,[11] under command of General D. M. Frost, a Northern man, a graduate of West Point, in open sympathy with the Southern leaders.[12] This camp was nominally a State camp of instruction, but, beyond doubt, was in the interest of the Southern cause, designed to be used against the national authority in the event of the General Government's attempting to coerce the Southern Confederacy. General William S. Harney was in command of the Department of Missouri, and resided in his own house, on Fourth Street, below Market; and there were five or six companies of United

[8] Bremen, MO, was incorporated as a town in 1850 and annexed by St. Louis in 1855. It is now the location of the Hyde Park neighborhood. *Tax Incentives for the Preservation of Historic Structures: Field Hearing before the Subcommittee on Oversight of the Committee on Ways and Means, House of Representatives* (Washington, DC: GPO, 1979), 158.

[9] Claiborne Jackson (1806–1862) was the Confederate governor of Missouri from 1861 to 1862 and was commissioned as a brigadier general in the Confederate Army. He died of cancer in Little Rock, AR, in Dec. 1862. *CWHC,* 314.

[10] Basil Duke (1836–1916), a future Confederate general and leader of the St. Louis "Minute Men," flew a handmade rebel flag above the Berthold Mansion to provoke Unionists in the city. *CWHC,* 217; "Gen. Basil Duke," *Lexington Herald-Leader* (Lexington, KY), Sept. 17, 1916, 1–2; Louis S. Gerteis, *The Civil War in Missouri: A Military History* (Columbia: University of Missouri Press, 2012), 11.

[11] Rebel forces renamed Lindell Grove "Camp Jackson" in honor of Missouri governor Claiborne Jackson. James Peckham, *Gen. Nathaniel Lyon, and Missouri in 1861* (New York: American News, 1866), 131–132.

[12] Daniel M. Frost (1823–1900) graduated from the USMA in 1844 and was a brigadier general in the Missouri State Militia in 1861. *USMA,* 2:194.

States troops in the arsenal, commanded by Captain N. Lyon;[13] throughout the city, there had been organized, almost exclusively out of the German part of the population, four or five regiments of "Home Guards," with which movement Frank Blair,[14] B. Gratz Brown,[15] John M. Schofield,[16] Clinton B. Fisk,[17] and others, were most active on the part of the national authorities. Frank Blair's brother Montgomery was in the cabinet of Mr. Lincoln at Washington,[18] and to him seemed committed the general management of affairs in Missouri.

The newspapers fanned the public excitement to the highest pitch, and threats of attacking the arsenal on the one hand, and the mob of d—d rebels in Camp Jackson on the other, were bandied about. I tried my best to keep out of the current, and only talked freely with a few men; among them Colonel John O'Fallon, a wealthy gentleman who resided above St. Louis.[19] He daily came down to my office in Bremen, and we walked up and down the pavement by the hour, deploring the sad condition of our country, and

[13] Nathaniel Lyon (1818–1861) graduated from the USMA in 1841 and was promoted to brigadier general of the U.S. Volunteers in May 1861. He was killed at the Battle of Wilson's Creek in Aug. 1861. *CWHC,* 357.

[14] Francis P. Blair Jr. (1821–1875) graduated from Princeton University and moved to Missouri in 1842. He served in the U.S. House of Representatives from 1857 to 1864 and reached the rank of major general in the U.S. Army during the Civil War. He served as a U.S. senator from 1871 to 1873. *CWHC,* 133.

[15] Benjamin G. Brown (1826–1885) was a U.S. senator from 1863 to 1867 and governor of Missouri from 1871 to 1873. In 1872, the Liberal Republican Party selected him as their vice-presidential candidate. "B. Gratz Brown," *Public Ledger* (Memphis, TN), Dec. 15, 1885, 2.

[16] John M. Schofield (1831–1906) graduated from the USMA in 1853 and was promoted to major general in the U.S. Army in Mar. 1869. During the Civil War he was awarded the Medal of Honor for his actions at the Battle of Wilson's Creek. He also served as U.S. secretary of war in 1868–1869. *USMA,* 2:524–526; 4:88; 5:78.

[17] Clinton B. Fisk (1828–1890) joined the Missouri State Militia as a private in May 1861 and was brevetted major general in the U.S. Army in Mar. 1865. After the war he served as U.S. Indian commissioner from 1874 to 1890 and was the Prohibition Party's candidate in the presidential election of 1888. *CWHC,* 235.

[18] Montgomery Blair (1813–1883) graduated from the USMA in 1835 and served as Pres. Lincoln's postmaster general from 1861 to 1864. *USMA,* 1:597–601.

[19] John O'Fallon (1790–1865) was one of the wealthiest people in St. Louis during his lifetime. At the time of his death, he was worth approximately $4,000,000. "Death of John O. Fallon," *Richmond Times-Dispatch* (Richmond, VA), Dec. 21, 1865, 3.

the seeming drift toward dissolution and anarchy. I used also to go down to the arsenal occasionally to see Lyon, Totten, and other of my army acquaintance, and was glad to see them making preparations to defend their post, if not to assume the offensive.

The bombardment of Fort Sumter, which was announced by telegraph, began April 12th, and ended on the 14th. We then knew that the war was actually begun, and though the South was openly, manifestly the aggressor, yet her friends and apologists insisted that she was simply acting on a justifiable defensive, and that in the forcible seizure of the public forts within her limits the people were acting with reasonable prudence and foresight. Yet neither party seemed willing to invade, or cross the border. Davis, who ordered the bombardment of Sumter, knew the temper of his people well, and foresaw that it would precipitate the action of the border States; for almost immediately Virginia, North Carolina, Arkansas, and Tennessee, followed the lead of the cotton States, and conventions were deliberating in Kentucky and Missouri.

On the night of Saturday, April 6th, I received the following dispatch:

WASHINGTON, *April* 6, 1861.

Major W. T. SHERMAN:

Will you accept the chief clerkship of the War Department? We will make you assistant Secretary of War when Congress meets.

M. BLAIR, *Postmaster-General.*

To which I replied by telegraph, Monday morning, "I cannot accept;" and by mail as follows:

OFFICE ST. LOUIS RAILROAD COMPANY,
Monday, April 8, 1861.

Hon. M. BLAIR, *Washington, D. C.:*

I received, about nine o'clock Saturday night, your telegraph dispatch, which I have this moment answered, "I cannot accept."

I have quite a large family, and when I resigned my place in Louisiana, on account of secession, I had no time to lose; and, therefore, after my hasty visit to Washington, where I saw no chance of employment, I came to St. Louis, have accepted a place in this company, have rented a house, and incurred other obligations, so that I am not at liberty to change.

> I thank you for the compliment contained in your offer, and assure you that I wish the Administration all success in its almost impossible task of governing this distracted and anarchical people.
>
> Yours truly, W. T. SHERMAN.

I was afterward told that this letter gave offense, and that some of Mr. Lincoln's cabinet concluded that I too would prove false to the country.

Later in that month, after the capture of Fort Sumter by the Confederate authorities, a Dr. Cornyn[20] came to our house on Locust Street, one night after I had gone to bed, and told me he had been sent by Frank Blair, who was not well, and wanted to see me that night at his house. I dressed and walked over to his house on Washington Avenue, near Fourteenth,[21] and found there, in the front-room, several gentlemen, among whom I recall Henry T. Blow.[22] Blair was in the back-room, closeted with some gentleman, who soon left, and I was called in. He there told me that the Government was mistrustful of General Harney, that a change in the command of the department was to be made; that he held it in his power to appoint a brigadier-general, and put him in command of the department, and he offered me the place. I told him I had once offered my services, and they were declined; that I had made business engagements in St. Louis, which I could not throw off at pleasure; that I had long deliberated on my course of action, and must decline his offer, however tempting and complimentary. He reasoned with me, but I persisted. He told me, in that event, he should appoint Lyon, and he did so.

Finding that even my best friends were uneasy as to my political status, on the 8th of May I addressed the following official letter to the Secretary of War:[23]

[20] Florence M. Cornyn (1829–1863) was a surgeon in the Missouri State Militia during the Civil War. In Aug. 1863, Cornyn was shot and killed by fellow soldier, William Bowen, during an altercation outside of a courtroom in Corinth, MS. "Our Cairo Letter," *Chicago Tribune,* June 16, 1863, 2; "The Shooting of Colonel Cornyn by Lieutenant Colonel Bowen," *New York Daily Herald,* Aug. 15, 1863, 1.

[21] Blair lived at 1129 Washington Avenue in Apr. 1861. William E. Parrish, *Frank Blair: Lincoln's Conservative* (Columbia: University of Missouri Press, 1998), 91.

[22] Henry T. Blow (1817–1875) graduated from St. Louis University and was elected to the Missouri Senate in 1856. In 1861, Pres. Lincoln appointed him minister to Venezuela. A year later, he was elected to the U.S. House of Representatives; he served in that capacity for two terms. "Hon. Henry T. Blow," *St. Louis Globe-Democrat,* Sept. 12, 1875, 2.

[23] Simon Cameron (1799–1889) was a U.S. senator from Pennsylvania in the years 1845–1849 and 1857–1861, and U.S. secretary of war in 1861–1862. *CWHC,* 159.

Office of St. Louis Railroad Company,
May 8, 1861.

Hon. S. Cameron, *Secretary of War, Washington, D. C.*

Dear Sir: I hold myself now, as always, prepared to serve my country in the capacity for which I was trained. I did not and will not volunteer for *three months,* because I cannot throw my family on the cold charity of the world. But for the *three-years* call, made by the President, an officer can prepare his command and do good service.

I will not volunteer as a soldier, because rightfully or wrongfully I feel unwilling to take a mere private's place, and, having for many years lived in California and Louisiana, the men are not well enough acquainted with me to elect me to my appropriate place.

Should my services be needed, the records of the War Department will enable you to designate the station in which I can render most service.

Yours truly, W. T. Sherman.

To this I do not think I received a direct answer; but, on the 14th of the same month, I was appointed colonel of the Thirteenth Regular Infantry.

I remember going to the arsenal on the 9th of May, taking my children with me in the street-cars. Within the arsenal wall were drawn up in parallel lines four regiments of the "Home Guards," and I saw men distributing cartridges to the boxes. I also saw General Lyon running about with his hair in the wind, his pockets full of papers, wild and irregular, but I knew him to be a man of vehement purpose and of determined action. I saw of course that it meant business, but whether for defense or offense I did not know. The next morning I went up to the railroad-office in Bremen, as usual, and heard at every corner of the streets that the "Dutch"[24] were moving on Camp Jackson. People were barricading their houses, and men were running in that direction. I hurried through my business as quickly as I could, and got back to my house on Locust Street by twelve o'clock. Charles Ewing and Hunter were there, and insisted on going out to the camp to see "the fun." I tried to dissuade them, saying that in case of conflict the by-standers were more likely to be killed than the men engaged, but they would go. I felt as much interest as anybody else, but staid at home, took my little son Willie, who was about seven years old, and walked up and down the pavement in front of our house,

[24] Citizens of St. Louis, at the time, referred to German immigrants as the "Dutch." Louis S. Gerteis, *Civil War St. Louis* (Lawrence, KS: University Press of Kansas, 2001), 73.

listening for the sound of musketry or cannon in the direction of Camp Jackson. While so engaged Miss Eliza Dean, who lived opposite us, called me across the street, told me that her brother-in-law, Dr. Scott, was a surgeon in Frost's camp, and she was dreadfully afraid he would be killed.[25] I reasoned with her that General Lyon was a regular officer; that if he had gone out, as reported, to Camp Jackson, he would take with him such a force as would make resistance impossible; but she would not be comforted, saying that the camp was made up of the young men from the first and best families of St. Louis, and that they were proud, and would fight. I explained that young men of the best families did not like to be killed better than ordinary people. Edging gradually up the street, I was in Olive Street just about Twelfth, when I saw a man running from the direction of Camp Jackson at full speed, calling, as he went, "They've surrendered, they've surrendered!" So I turned back and rang the bell at Mrs. Dean's. Eliza came to the door, and I explained what I had heard; but she angrily slammed the door in my face! Evidently she was disappointed to find she was mistaken in her estimate of the rash courage of the best families.

I again turned in the direction of Camp Jackson, my boy Willie with me still. At the head of Olive Street, abreast of Lindell's Grove, I found Frank Blair's regiment in the street, with ranks opened, and the Camp Jackson prisoners inside. A crowd of people was gathered around, calling to the prisoners by name, some hurrahing for Jeff Davis, and others encouraging the troops. Men, women, and children, were in the crowd. I passed along till I found myself inside the grove, where I met Charles Ewing and John Hunter, and we stood looking at the troops on the road, heading toward the city. A band of music was playing at the head, and the column made one or two ineffectual starts, but for some reason was halted. The battalion of regulars was abreast of me, of which Major Rufus Saxton was in command,[26] and I gave him an evening paper, which I had bought of the newsboy on my way out. He was reading from it some piece of news, sitting on his horse, when the column

[25] Elizabeth A. Dean (1829–1916) was sister-in-law of Dr. Joseph T. Scott (1833–1896). Scott married Elizabeth's sister, Isidora Churchill Dean, in 1856. "Dr. Joseph T. Scott," *Times-Democrat* (New Orleans), June 26, 1896, 11; "Scalded, Woman Dies; Case Goes to Grand Jury," *Evening Star* (Washington, DC), Sept. 27, 1916, 2.

[26] Rufus Saxton (1824–1908) graduated from the USMA in 1849 and was a first lieutenant in the U.S. 4th Art. during the engagement at Camp Jackson. In 1862 he received the Medal of Honor for his actions during the defense of Harper's Ferry, VA (now WV). *USMA,* 2:385–386; 4:76; 5:69.

again began to move forward, and he resumed his place at the head of his command. At that part of the road, or street, was an embankment about eight feet high, and a drunken fellow tried to pass over it to the people opposite. One of the regular sergeant file-closers ordered him back, but he attempted to pass through the ranks, when the sergeant barred his progress with his musket "a-port." The drunken man seized his musket, when the sergeant threw him off with violence, and he rolled over and over down the bank. By the time this man had picked himself up and got his hat, which had fallen off, and had again mounted the embankment, the regulars had passed, and the head of Osterhaus's regiment of Home Guards had come up.[27] The man had in his hand a small pistol, which he fired off, and I heard that the ball had struck the leg of one of Osterhaus's staff; the regiment stopped; there was a moment of confusion, when the soldiers of that regiment began to fire over our heads in the grove. I heard the balls cutting the leaves above our heads, and saw several men and women running in all directions, some of whom were wounded. Of course there was a general stampede. Charles Ewing threw Willie on the ground and covered him with his body. Hunter ran behind the hill, and I also threw myself on the ground. The fire ran back from the head of the regiment toward its rear, and as I saw the men reloading their pieces, I jerked Willie up, ran back with him into a gulley which covered us, lay there until I saw that the fire had ceased, and that the column was again moving on, when I took up Willie and started back for home round by way of Market Street. A woman and child were killed outright; two or three men were also killed, and several others were wounded.[28] The great mass of the people on that occasion were simply curious spectators, though men were sprinkled through the crowd calling out, "Hurrah for Jeff Davis!" and others were particularly abusive of the "damned Dutch." Lyon posted a guard in charge of the vacant camp, and marched his prisoners down to the arsenal; some were paroled, and others held, till afterward they were regularly exchanged.[29]

[27] Peter J. Osterhaus (1823–1917) was born in Prussia and immigrated to the U.S. in 1849. In 1861 he was a major in the 2nd Missouri Inf. He was eventually promoted to major general for his actions during the Civil War. *CWHC,* 411.

[28] The fighting between Osterhaus's men and the citizens of St. Louis occurred on May 11, 1861. According to newspaper reports, six people were killed during the exchange. "Saturday's Tragedies," *Glasgow Weekly Times* (Glasgow, MO), May 16, 1861, 2.

[29] For a complete list of the prisoners taken by U.S. forces at Camp Jackson on May 10, and later exchanged in Oct. 1861, see *OR,* II, 1, 553–557.

A very few days after this event, May 14th, I received a dispatch from my brother Charles in Washington, telling me to come on at once; that I had been appointed a colonel of the Thirteenth Regular Infantry, and that I was wanted at Washington immediately.

Of course I could no longer defer action. I saw Mr. Lucas, Major Turner, and other friends and parties connected with the road, who agreed that I should go on. I left my family, because I was under the impression that I would be allowed to enlist my own regiment, which would take some time, and I expected to raise the regiment and organize it at Jefferson Barracks. I repaired to Washington, and there found that the Government was trying to rise to a level with the occasion. Mr. Lincoln had, without the sanction of law, authorized the raising of ten new regiments of regulars, each infantry regiment to be composed of three battalions of eight companies each; and had called for seventy-five thousand State volunteers.[30] Even this call seemed to me utterly inadequate; still it was none of my business. I took the oath of office, and was furnished with a list of officers, appointed to my regiment, which was still incomplete. I reported in person to General Scott, at his office on Seventeenth Street, opposite the War Department, and applied for authority to return West, and raise my regiment at Jefferson Barracks, but the general said my lieutenant-colonel, Burbank,[31] was fully qualified to superintend the enlistment, and that he wanted me there; and he at once dictated an order for me to report to him in person for inspection duty.

Satisfied that I would not be permitted to return to St. Louis, I instructed Mrs. Sherman to pack up, return to Lancaster, and trust to the fate of war.

I also resigned my place as president of the Fifth Street Railroad, to take effect at the end of May, so that in fact I received pay from that road for only two months' service, and then began my new army career.

[30] On Apr. 15, 1861, Lincoln issued a call for 75,000 volunteers to defeat the Confederate Army. James M. McPherson, *Battle Cry of Freedom: The Civil War Era* (Oxford: Oxford University Press, 1988), 274.

[31] Sidney Burbank (1807–1882) graduated from the USMA in 1829 and was a lieutenant colonel in the U.S. 13th Inf. in May 1861. *USMA,* 1:432–433.

9

From the Battle of Bull Run to Paducah—Kentucky and Missouri.

1861–1862.

And now that, in these notes, I have fairly reached the period of the civil war, which ravaged our country from 1861 to 1865—an event involving a conflict of passion, of prejudice, and of arms, that has developed results which, for better or worse, have left their mark on the world's history—I feel that I tread on delicate ground.

I have again and again been invited to write a history of the war, or to record for publication my personal recollections of it, with large offers of money therefor; all of which I have heretofore declined, because the truth is not always palatable, and should not always be told.[1] Many of the actors in the grand drama still live, and they and their friends are quick to controversy, which should be avoided. The great end of peace has been attained, with little or no change in our form of government, and the duty of all good men is to allow the passions of that period to subside, that we may direct our physical and mental labor to repair the waste of war, and to engage in the greater task of continuing our hitherto wonderful national development.

What I now propose to do is merely to group some of my personal recollections about the historic persons and events of the day, prepared not with any view to their publication, but rather for preservation till I am gone; and then to be allowed to follow into oblivion the cords of similar papers, or to be used by some historian who may need them by way of illustration.

I have heretofore recorded how I again came into the military service of the United States as a colonel of the Thirteenth Regular Infantry, a regiment that had no existence at the time, and that, instead of being allowed to enlist

[1] In 1874, after he read WTS's earlier written accounts of the Civil War, university professor John W. Draper encouraged WTS to write his memoirs. John F. Marszalek, *Sherman: A Soldier's Passion for Order* (New York: Free Press, 1993), 461.

the men and instruct them, as expected, I was assigned in Washington City, by an order of Lieutenant-General Winfield Scott, to inspection duty near him on the 20th of June, 1861.

At that time Lieutenant-General Scott commanded the army in chief, with Colonel E. D. Townsend as his adjutant-general,[2] Major G. W. Cullum, United States Engineers,[3] and Major Schuyler Hamilton,[4] as aides-de-camp. The general had an office up-stairs on Seventeenth Street, opposite the War Department, and resided in a house close by, on Pennsylvania Avenue. All fears for the immediate safety of the capital had ceased, and quite a large force of regulars and volunteers had been collected in and about Washington. Brigadier-General J. K. Mansfield commanded in the city,[5] and Brigadier-General Irvin McDowell on the other side of the Potomac, with his head-quarters at Arlington House.[6] His troops extended in a semicircle from Alexandria to above Georgetown. Several forts and redoubts were either built or in progress, and the people were already clamorous for a general forward movement. Another considerable army had also been collected in Pennsylvania under General Patterson, and, at the time I speak of, had moved forward to Hagerstown and Williamsport, on the Potomac River.[7] My brother, John Sherman, was a volunteer aide-de-camp to General Patterson, and,

[2] Edward D. Townsend (1817–1893) graduated from the USMA in 1837 and was Scott's assistant adjutant general and chief of staff from Mar. to Nov. 1861. He was brevetted major general in the U.S. Army in Mar. 1865. *USMA,* 1:673–674.

[3] George W. Cullum (1809–1892) graduated from the USMA in 1833 and was Scott's aide-de-camp in Apr.–Nov. 1861. He authored the book series on USMA graduates titled *Register of the Officers and Graduates of the U.S. Military Academy. USMA,* 1:535–537.

[4] Schuyler Hamilton (1822–1903), the grandson of Alexander Hamilton, graduated from the USMA in 1841. He served as Scott's aide-de-camp and right-hand man in Mar.–Nov. 1861. *USMA,* 2:88–89.

[5] Joseph K. F. Mansfield (1803–1862) graduated from the USMA in 1822 and was in command of the Dept. of Washington and the city of Washington, DC, in Apr.–Oct. 1861. He was shot in the stomach at the Battle of Antietam and died on Sept. 18, 1862. *USMA,* 1:276–278; *CWHC,* 363.

[6] Irvin McDowell (1818–1885) graduated from the USMA in 1838 and was in command of the Dept. of Northeastern Virgina before he participated in the First Battle of Bull Run in July 1861. He was later brevetted major general in the U.S. Army for his actions at the Battle of Cedar Mountain. *USMA,* 1:711–712.

[7] Robert "Granny" Patterson (1792–1881) was born in Ireland and moved to the United States in 1799. He was a major general in the Pennsylvania State Militia when he commanded troops outside of Washington, DC, in Apr. 1861. *CWHC,* 418–419.

toward the end of June, I went up to Hagerstown to see him. I found that army in the very act of moving, and we rode down to Williamsport in a buggy, and were present when the leading division crossed the Potomac River by fording it waist-deep.[8] My friend and classmate, George H. Thomas, was there, in command of a brigade in the leading division.[9] I talked with him a good deal, also with General Cadwalader,[10] and with the staff-officers of General Patterson, viz., Fitz-John Porter,[11] Belger,[12] Beckwith,[13] and others, all of whom seemed encouraged to think that the war was to be short and decisive, and that, as soon as it was demonstrated that the General Government meant in earnest to defend its rights and property, some general compromise would result.

Patterson's army crossed the Potomac River on the 1st or 2d of July, and, as John Sherman was to take his seat as a Senator in the called session of Congress, to meet July 4th, he resigned his place as aide-de-camp, presented me his two horses and equipment, and we returned to Washington together.

The Congress assembled punctually on the 4th of July, and the message of Mr. Lincoln was strong and good: it recognized the fact that civil war was upon us, that compromise of any kind was at an end; and he asked for four hundred thousand men, and four hundred million dollars, wherewith to vindicate the national authority, and to regain possession of the captured forts and other property of the United States.[14]

[8] For John Sherman's account of the event, see *OR,* I, 2, 702–703.

[9] In June 1861, Thomas was in command of the 1st Brigade, 1st Div., Dept. of Pennsylvania. *CWHC,* 527.

[10] George Cadwalader (1806–1879) was a major general in the Pennsylvania State Militia in June 1861. *CWHC,* 158.

[11] Fitz-John Porter (1822–1901) graduated from the USMA in 1845 and was chief of staff for the Dept. of Pennsylvania in June 1861. *USMA,* 2:219–220.

[12] James Belger (1816–1891) was chief quartermaster of the Dept. of Pennsylvania in June 1861. Roger D. Hunt, ed., *Colonels in Blue: U.S. Colored Troops, U.S. Armed Forces, Staff Officers and Special Units* (Jefferson, NC: McFarland, 2002), s.v. "James Belger."

[13] Most likely Amos Beckwith (1825–1894), who graduated from the USMA in 1850 and served as aide-de-camp to Gen. McDowell in 1862. He later served as chief of commissary for WTS during the Atlanta and Carolinas Campaigns. "A Vermont Soldier: A Man who Gave Up His Ambitions So as Best to Serve His Country," *Rutland Daily Herald* (Rutland, VT), Nov. 27, 1894, 3; *CWHC,* 125.

[14] For Pres. Lincoln's address to Congress on July 4, 1861, see Abraham Lincoln, *Abraham Lincoln's Pen and Voice: Being a Complete Compilation of His Letters . . . ,* ed. G.M. Van Buren (Cincinnati: Robert Clarke, 1890), 72–95.

It was also immediately demonstrated that the tone and temper of Congress had changed since the Southern Senators and members had withdrawn, and that we, the military, could now go to work with some definite plans and ideas.

The appearance of the troops about Washington was good, but it was manifest they were far from being soldiers. Their uniforms were as various as the States and cities from which they came; their arms were also of every pattern and calibre; and they were so loaded down with overcoats, haversacks, knapsacks, tents, and baggage, that it took from twenty-five to fifty wagons to move the camp of a regiment from one place to another, and some of the camps had bakeries and cooking establishments that would have done credit to Delmonico.

While I was on duty with General Scott, viz., from June 20th to about June 30th, the general frequently communicated to those about him his opinions and proposed plans. He seemed vexed with the clamors of the press for immediate action, and the continued interference in details by the President, Secretary of War, and Congress. He spoke of organizing a grand army of invasion, of which the regulars were to constitute the "iron column," and seemed to intimate that he himself would take the field in person, though he was at the time very old, very heavy, and very unwieldy. His age must have been about seventy-five years.[15]

At that date, July 4, 1861, the rebels had two armies in front of Washington; the one at Manassas Junction, commanded by General Beauregard, with his advance guard at Fairfax Court- House, and indeed almost in sight of Washington. The other, commanded by General Joe Johnston, was at Winchester, with its advance at Martinsburg and Harper's Ferry;[16] but the advance had fallen back before Patterson, who then occupied Martinsburg and the line of the Baltimore & Ohio Railroad.

The temper of Congress and the people would not permit the slow and methodical preparation desired by General Scott; and the cry of "On to Richmond!" which was shared by the volunteers, most of whom had only engaged

[15]In 1861, Scott was six feet, five inches tall and weighed approximately 300 pounds. Jayne E. Blair, *The Essential Civil War: A Handbook to the Battles, Armies, Navies and Commanders* (Jefferson, NC: McFarland, 2006), 37.

[16]Joseph E. Johnston (1807–1891) graduated from the USMA in 1829 and was a quartermaster general in the U.S. Army before the Civil War. He resigned to join the Confederate Army in late Apr. 1861. He commanded Confederate forces near Harper's Ferry, VA (now WV), from May to July 1861. *USMA,* 1:427–429; *CWHC,* 323.

for ninety days, forced General Scott to hasten his preparations, and to order a general advance about the middle of July. McDowell was to move from the defenses of Washington, and Patterson from Martinsburg. In the organization of McDowell's army into divisions and brigades, Colonel David Hunter was assigned to command the Second Division,[17] and I was ordered to take command of his former brigade, which was composed of five regiments in position in and about Fort Corcoran,[18] and on the ground opposite Georgetown. I assumed command on the 30th of June, and proceeded at once to prepare it for the general advance.[19] My command constituted the Third Brigade of the First Division, which division was commanded by Brigadier-General Daniel Tyler, a graduate of West Point, but who had seen little or no actual service.[20] I applied to General McDowell for some staff-officers, and he gave me, as adjutant-general, Lieutenant Piper, of the Third Artillery,[21] and, as aide-de-camp, Lieutenant McQuesten, a fine young cavalry-officer, fresh from West Point.[22]

I selected for the field the Thirteenth New York, Colonel Quinby; the Sixty-ninth New York, Colonel Corcoran; the Seventy-ninth New York, Colonel Cameron; and the Second Wisconsin, Lieutenant—Colonel Peck.[23] These

[17] David Hunter (1802–1886) graduated from the USMA in 1822 and was a brigadier general, U.S. Volunteers, in July 1861. *USMA,* 1:290–293.

[18] Fort Corcoran was situated due west of Washington, DC, approximately one-half mile from the west bank of the Potomac River. Francs T. Miller and Robert S. Lanier, eds., *The Photographic History of the Civil War: Forts and Artillery* (New York: Review of Reviews, 1911), 5:76, cover photo.

[19] On July 16, 1861, Gen. McDowell issued General Orders No. 17, which established the organization of his army in the Dept. of Northeastern Virgina. *OR,* I, 2, 303–304.

[20] Daniel Tyler (1799–1882) graduated from the USMA in 1819 and resigned from the U.S. Army as a first lieutenant in 1834. He returned to the army and was promoted to brigadier general in the Connecticut State Volunteers in May 1861. *USMA,* 1:222–232.

[21] Alexander Piper (1829–1902) graduated from the USMA in 1851 and was promoted to captain in May 1861. *USMA,* 2:439–440; 5:73.

[22] James F. McQuesten (1835–1864) graduated from the USMA in 1861 and was a second lieutenant in the U.S. 2nd Dragoons in July 1861. He was killed at the Battle of Opequan in Sept. 1864. *USMA,* 2:807–808.

[23] Isaac F. Quinby (1821–1891) graduated from the USMA in 1843 and was a colonel in the U.S. Army in July 1861. Michael Corcoran (1827–1863) was born in Ireland and moved to New York in 1849. He was promoted to colonel in the U.S. Army in Apr. 1861 and was killed in a horse-riding accident in VA in Dec. 1863. James Cameron (1800–1861) was a lawyer and journalist who came out of retirement to fight in the Civil War. Henry W. Peck attended the

were all good, strong, volunteer regiments, pretty well commanded; and I had reason to believe that I had one of the best brigades in the whole army. Captain Ayres's battery of the Third Regular Artillery was also attached to my brigade.[24] The other regiment, the Twenty-ninth New York, Colonel Bennett,[25] was destined to be left behind in charge of the forts and camps during our absence, which was expected to be short. Soon after I had assumed the command, a difficulty arose in the Sixty-ninth, an Irish regiment. This regiment had volunteered in New York, early in April, for ninety days; but, by reason of the difficulty of passing through Baltimore,[26] they had come *via* Annapolis, had been held for duty on the railroad as a guard for nearly a month before they actually reached Washington, and were then mustered in about a month after enrollment. Some of the men claimed that they were entitled to their discharge in ninety days from the time of enrollment, whereas the muster-roll read ninety days from the date of muster-in. One day, Colonel Corcoran explained this matter to me. I advised him to reduce the facts to writing, and that I would submit it to the War Department for an authoritative decision. He did so, and the War Department decided that the muster-roll was the only contract of service, that it would be construed literally; and that the regiment would be held till the expiration of three months from the date of muster-in, viz., to about August 1, 1861. General Scott at the same time wrote one of his characteristic letters to Corcoran, telling him that we were about to engage in battle, and he knew his Irish friends would not leave

---

USMA from 1851 to 1853, but never graduated. He resigned from the U.S. Army on July 29, 1861. He later raised and commanded a company of heavy artillery from Oct. 1863 to June 1865. *USMA,* 2:156–157; *CWHC,* 185; "Death of Col. James Cameron," *Centre Democrat* (Bellefonte, PA), July 25, 1861, 2; Helen M. Bingham, *History of Green County, Wisconsin* (Milwaukee: Burdick and Armitage, 1877), 260–307; *The Wisconsin Blue Book* (Madison: Industrial Commission, 1962), 88.

[24] Romeyn B. Ayres (1825–1888) graduated from the USMA in 1847. In the first edition of the memoirs (1875), WTS identified Ayres's battery as the "Fifth Regular Artillery." Although Ayres was in the 5th Art., he was placed in command of Co. E, 3rd Art. during the First Battle of Bull Run. *USMA,* 2:325–329; *OR,* I, 2, 372–373.

[25] Michael P. Bennett (1825–1901) was colonel of the 28th New York State Militia. Fort Bennett, situated near Fort Corcoran, was named after him. William H. Bennett, "Some Pre-Civil War Irish Militiamen of Brooklyn, New York," *Journal of the American Irish Historical Society* (1922), 21:172, 179–180.

[26] On Apr. 19, 1861, the "Pratt Street Riots" occurred in Baltimore, MD, between Confederate sympathizers and the 6th MA Volunteer Regiment. Spencer C. Tucker, ed., *Almanac of American Military History* (Santa Barbara: ABC-CLIO, 2013), s.v. "April 19, 1861."

him in such a crisis. Corcoran and the officers generally wanted to go to the expected battle, but a good many of the men were not so anxious. In the Second Wisconsin, also, was developed a personal difficulty. The actual colonel was S.P. Coon,[27] a good-hearted gentleman, who knew no more of the military art than a child; whereas his lieutenant-colonel, Peck, had been to West Point, and knew the drill. Preferring that the latter should remain in command of the regiment, I put Colonel Coon on my personal staff, which reconciled the difficulty.

In due season, about July 15th, our division moved forward leaving our camps standing; Keyes's brigade in the lead, then Schenck's, then mine, and Richardson's last. We marched *via* Vienna, Germantown, and Centreville, where all the army, composed of five divisions, seemed to converge.[28] The march demonstrated little save the general laxity of discipline; for with all my personal efforts I could not prevent the men from straggling for water, blackberries, or any thing on the way they fancied.

At Centreville, on the 18th, Richardson's brigade was sent by General Tyler to reconnoitre Blackburn's Ford across Bull Run, and he found it strongly guarded. From our camp, at Centreville, we heard the cannonading, and then a sharp musketry-fire. I received orders from General Tyler to send forward Ayres's battery, and very soon after another order came for me to advance with my whole brigade. We marched the three miles at the double-quick, arrived in time to relieve Richardson's brigade, which was just drawing back from the ford, worsted, and stood for half an hour or so under a fire of artillery, which killed four or five of my men. General Tyler was there in person, giving directions, and soon after he ordered us all back to our camp in Centreville. This reconnoissance had developed a strong force, and had been made without the orders of General McDowell; however, it satisfied us that the enemy was in force on the other side of Bull Run, and had no intention to leave without a serious battle. We lay in camp at Centreville all of the 19th and 20th, and during that night began the movement which resulted in the battle of Bull Run, on July 21st. Of this so much has been written that more would be superfluous; and the reports of the opposing commanders, McDowell and Johnston, are fair and correct.[29] It is now generally admitted

[27] S. Park Coon (1820–1883) was a lawyer and the second attorney general of WI. William S. Coon, ed., *Koon and Coons Families of Eastern New York* (Rutland: Tuttle, 1937), 404.

[28] On July 15, WTS commanded approximately 3,400 troops. Marszalek, *Sherman,* 148.

[29] For McDowell's and Johnston's reports on the First Battle of Bull Run, see *OR,* I, 2, 316–328; I, 2, 470–479.

that it was one of the best-planned battles of the war, but one of the worst-fought. Our men had been told so often at home that all they had to do was to make a bold appearance, and the rebels would run; and nearly all of us for the first time then heard the sound of cannon and muskets in anger, and saw the bloody scenes common to all battles, with which we were soon to be familiar. We had good organization, good men, but no cohesion, no real discipline, no respect for authority, no real knowledge of war. Both armies were fairly defeated, and, whichever had stood fast, the other would have run. Though the North was overwhelmed with mortification and shame, the South really had not much to boast of, for in the three or four hours of fighting their organization was so broken up that they did not and could not follow our army, when it was known to be in a state of disgraceful and causeless flight.[30] It is easy to criticise a battle after it is over, but all now admit that none others, equally raw in war, could have done better than we did at Bull Run; and the lesson of that battle should not be lost on a people like ours.

I insert my official report, as a condensed statement of my share in the battle:

Headquarters Third Brigade, First Division
Fort Corcoran, *July* 25, 1861.

To Captain A. Baird, *Assistant Adjutant-General, First Division*

Sir: I have the honor to submit this my report of the operations of my brigade during the action of the 21st instant. The brigade is composed of the Thirteenth New York Volunteers, Colonel Quinby's Sixty-ninth New York, Colonel Corcoran; Seventy-ninth New York, Colonel Cameron; Second Wisconsin, Lieutenant-Colonel Peck; and Company E, Third Artillery, under command of Captain R. B. Ayres, Fifth Artillery. We left our camp near Centreville, pursuant to orders, at half-past 2 A. M., taking place in your column, next to the brigade of General Schenck, and proceeded as far as the halt, before the enemy's

[30] Confederate Gen. Joseph E. Johnston provided his reason for not pursuing the retreating U.S. Army in his post-battle report. He wrote, "The apparent firmness of the U.S. troops at Centreville, who had not been engaged, which checked our pursuit; the strong forces occupying the works near Georgetown, Arlington and Alexandria; the certainty, too, that General Patterson, if needed, would reach Washington with his army of more than thirty thousand men sooner than we could, and the condition and inadequate means of the Army in ammunition, provisions, and transportation prevented any serious thoughts of advancing against the capital." *OR,* I, 2, 478.

position, near the stone bridge across Bull Run. Here the brigade was deployed in line along the skirt of timber to the right of the Warrenton road, and remained quietly in position till after 10 A. M. The enemy remained very quiet, but about that time we saw a rebel regiment leave its cover in our front, and proceed in double-quick time on the road toward Sudley Springs, by which we knew the columns of Colonels Hunter and Heintzelman were approaching. About the same time we observed in motion a large mass of the enemy, below and on the other side of the stone bridge. I directed Captain Ayres to take position with his battery near our right, and to open fire on this mass; but you had previously detached the two rifle-guns belonging to this battery, and, finding that the smooth-bore guns did not reach the enemy's position, we ceased firing, and I sent a request that you would send to me the thirty-pounder rifle-gun attached to Captain Carlisle's battery. At the same time I shifted the New York Sixty-ninth to the extreme right of the brigade. Thus we remained till we heard the musketry-fire across Bull Run, showing that the head of Colonel Hunter's column was engaged. This firing was brisk, and showed that Hunter was driving before him the enemy, till about noon, when it became certain the enemy had come to a stand, and that our forces on the other side of Bull Run were all engaged, artillery and infantry.

Here you sent me the order to cross over with the whole brigade, to the assistance of Colonel Hunter. Early in the day, when reconnoitring the ground, I had seen a horseman descend from a bluff in our front, cross the stream, and show himself in the open field on this side; and, inferring that we could cross over at the same point, I sent forward a company as skirmishers, and followed with the whole brigade, the New York Sixty-ninth leading.

We found no difficulty in crossing over, and met with no opposition in ascending the steep bluff opposite with our infantry, but it was impassable to the artillery, and I sent word back to Captain Ayres to follow if possible, otherwise to use his discretion. Captain Ayres did not cross Bull Run, but remained on that side, with the rest of your division. His report herewith describes his operations during the remainder of the day. Advancing slowly and cautiously with the head of the column, to give time for the regiments in succession to close up their ranks, we first encountered a party of the enemy retreating along a cluster of pines; Lieutenant-Colonel Haggerty, of the Sixty-ninth, without orders, rode out alone, and endeavored to intercept their retreat. One of the enemy, in full view, at short range, shot Haggerty, and he fell dead from his horse. The Sixty-ninth opened fire on this party, which was returned; but, determined to effect our junction with Hunter's division, I ordered this fire to cease, and we proceeded with caution toward the field where we then plainly saw our forces engaged. Displaying our colors conspicuously at the head of our column, we succeeded in attracting the attention of our friends, and soon formed the brigade in rear of Colonel Porter's. Here I learned that Colonel Hunter was disabled by a severe wound, and that General McDowell was on the field. I sought him out, and received his orders to join in pursuit of the enemy, who was falling back to the left of the road by which the army had approached from Sudley Springs. Placing Colonel Quinby's regiment of rifles in front, in column, by division, I directed the other regiments to follow in line of battle, in the order of the Wisconsin Second, New York Seventy-ninth, and New York Sixty-ninth. Quinby's regiment advanced steadily down the hill and up the ridge, from which he opened fire upon the enemy, who had made another stand on ground very favorable to him, and the regiment continued advancing as the enemy gave way, till the head of the column reached the point near which Rickett's battery was so severely cut up. The other regiments descended the hill in line of battle, under a severe cannonade; and, the ground affording comparative shelter from the enemy's artillery, they changed direction, by the right flank, and followed the road before mentioned. At the point where this road crosses the ridge to our left front, the ground was swept by a most severe fire of artillery, rifles, and musketry, and we saw, in succession, several regiments driven from it; among them the Zouaves and battalion of marines. Before reaching the crest of this hill, the roadway was worn deep enough to afford shelter, and I kept the several regiments in it as long as possible; but when the Wisconsin Second was abreast of the enemy, by order of Major Wadsworth, of General McDowell's staff, I ordered it to leave the roadway, by the left flank, and to attack the enemy.

This regiment ascended to the brow of the hill steadily, received the severe fire of the enemy, returned it with spirit, and advanced, delivering its fire. This regiment is uniformed in gray cloth, almost identical with that of the great bulk of the secession army; and, when the regiment fell into confusion and retreated toward the road, there was a universal cry that they were being fired on by our own men. The regiment rallied again, passed the brow of the hill a second time, but was again repulsed in disorder. By this time the New York Seventy-ninth had closed up, and in like manner it was ordered to cross the brow of the hill, and drive the enemy from cover. It was impossible to get a good view of this ground. In it there was one battery of artillery, which poured an incessant fire upon our advancing column, and the ground was very irregular with small clusters of pines, affording shelter, of which the enemy took good advantage. The fire of rifles and musketry was very severe. The Seventy-ninth, headed by its colonel, Cameron, charged across the hill, and for a short time the contest was severe; they rallied several times under fire, but finally broke, and gained the cover of the hill.

This left the field open to the New York Sixty-ninth, Colonel Corcoran, who, in his turn, led his regiment over the crest, and had in full, open view the ground so severely contested; the fire was very severe, and the roar of cannon, musketry, and rifles, incessant; it was manifest the enemy was here in great force, far superior to us at that point. The Sixty-ninth held the ground for some time, but finally fell back in disorder.

All this time Quinby's regiment occupied another ridge, to our left, overlooking the same field of action, and similarly engaged. Here, about half-past 3 P. M., began the scene of confusion and disorder that characterized the remainder of the day. Up to that time, all had kept their places, and seemed perfectly cool, and used to the shell and shot that fell, comparatively harmless, all around us; but the short exposure to an intense fire of small-arms, at close range, had killed many, wounded more, and had produced disorder in all of the battalions that had attempted to encounter it. Men fell away from their ranks, talking, and in great confusion. Colonel Cameron had been mortally wounded, was carried to an ambulance, and reported dying. Many other officers were reported dead or missing, and many of the wounded were making their way, with more or less assistance, to the buildings used as hospitals, on the ridge to the west. We succeeded in partially reforming the regiments, but it was manifest that they would not stand, and I directed Colonel Corcoran to move along the ridge to the rear, near the position where we had first formed the brigade. General McDowell was there in person, and used all possible efforts to reassure the men. By the active exertions of Colonel Corcoran, we formed an irregular square against the cavalry which were then seen to issue from the position from which we had been driven, and we began our retreat toward the same ford of Bull Run by which we had approached the field of battle. There was no positive order to retreat, although for an hour it had been going on by the operation of the men themselves. The ranks were thin and irregular, and we found a stream of people strung from the hospital across Bull Run, and far toward Centreville. After putting in motion the irregular square in person, I pushed forward to find Captain Ayres's battery at the crossing of Bull Run. I sought it at its last position, before the brigade had crossed over, but it was not there; then passing through the woods, where, in the morning, we had first formed line, we approached the blacksmith's shop, but there found a detachment of the secession cavalry and thence made a circuit, avoiding Cub Run Bridge, into Centreville, where I found General McDowell, and from him understood that it was his purpose to rally the forces, and make a stand at Centreville.

But, about nine o'clock at night, I received from General Tyler, in person, the order to continue the retreat to the Potomac. This retreat was by night, and disorderly in the extreme. The men of different regiments mingled together, and some reached the river at Arlington, some at Long Bridge, and the greater part returned to their former camp, at or near Fort Corcoran. I reached this point at noon the next day, and found a miscellaneous crowd crossing over the aqueduct and ferries. Conceiving this to be demoralizing, I at once commanded the guard to be increased, and all persons attempting to pass over to be stopped. This soon produced its effect; men sought their proper companies and regiments. Comparative order was restored, and all were posted to the best advantage.

I herewith inclose the official report of Captain Kelly, commanding officer of the New York Sixty-ninth; also, fall lists of the killed, wounded, and missing.

Our loss was heavy, and occurred chiefly at the point near where Rickett's battery was destroyed. Lieutenant-Colonel Haggerty was killed about noon, before we had effected a junction with Colonel Hunter's division. Colonel Cameron was mortally wounded leading his regiment in the charge, and Colonel Corcoran has been missing since the cavalry-charge near the building used as a hospital.

For names, rank, etc., of the above, I refer to the lists herewith.

REGIMENTS, ETC.	Killed.	Wounded.	Missing.	Total.
Ayres's Battery	6	3	...	9
New York Thirteenth	11	27	20	58
New York Sixty-ninth	38	59	95	192
New York Seventy-ninth	32	51	115	198
Wisconsin Second	24	65	63	152
	111	205	293	609

Lieutenants Piper and McQuesten, of my personal staff, were under fire all day, and carried orders to and fro with as much coolness as on parade. Lieutenant Bagley, of the New York Sixty-ninth, a volunteer aide, asked leave to serve with his company, during the action, and is among those reported missing. I have intelligence that he is a prisoner, and slightly wounded.

Colonel Coon, of Wisconsin, a volunteer aide, also rendered good service during the day.

W. T. Sherman, *Colonel commanding Brigade.*

This report, which I had not read probably since its date till now, recalls to me vividly the whole scene of the affair at Blackburn's Ford, when for the first time in my life I saw cannon-balls strike men and crash through the trees and saplings above and around us, and realized the always sickening confusion as one approaches a fight from the rear; then the night-march from Centreville, on the Warrenton road, standing for hours wondering what was meant; the deployment along the edge of the field that sloped down to Bull Run, and waiting for Hunter's approach on the other aide from the direction of Sudley Springs, away off to our right; the terrible scare of a poor negro who was caught between our lines; the crossing of Bull Run, and the fear lest we should be fired on by our own men; the killing of Lieutenant-Colonel Haggerty, which occurred in plain sight; and the first scenes of a field strewed with dead men and horses. Yet, at that period of the battle, we were the victors and felt jubilant. At that moment, also, my brigade passed Hunter's division; but Heintzelman's was still ahead of us, and we followed its lead along the road toward Manassas Junction, crossing a small stream and ascending a long hill, at the summit of which the battle was going on. Here my regiments came into action well, but successively, and were driven back, each in its turn. For two hours we continued to dash at the woods on our left front, which were full of rebels; but I was convinced their organization was broken, and that they had simply halted there and taken advantage of these woods as a cover, to reach which we had to pass over the intervening fields about the Henry House,[31] which were clear, open, and gave them a decided advantage. After I had put in each of my regiments, and had them driven back to the cover of the road, I had no idea that we were beaten, but reformed the regiments in line in their proper order, and only wanted a little rest, when I found that my brigade was almost alone, except Syke's regulars, who had formed square against cavalry and were coming back.[32] I then realized that the whole army was "in retreat," and that my own men were individually making back for the stone bridge. Corcoran and I formed the brigade into an irregular square, but it fell to pieces; and, along with a crowd, disorganized but not much scared, the brigade got back to Centreville to our former camps. Corcoran was captured, and held a prisoner for some time; but I got safe to Centreville. I saw General McDowell in Centreville, and understood that several of his divisions had not been engaged at all, that he would reorganize them at Centreville, and there await the enemy. I got my four regiments in parallel lines in a field, the same in which we had camped before the battle, and had lain down to sleep under a tree, when I heard some one asking for me. I called out where I was, when General Tyler in person gave me orders to march back to our camps at Fort Corcoran. I aroused my aides, gave them orders to call up the sleeping men, have each regiment to leave the field by a flank and to take the same road back by which we had come. It was near midnight, and the road was full of troops, wagons, and batteries. We tried to keep our regiments separate, but all became inextricably mixed. Toward morning we reached Vienna, where I slept some hours, and the next day, about noon, we reached Fort Corcoran.

A slow, mizzling rain had set in, and probably a more gloomy day never presented itself. All organization seemed to be at an end; but I and my staff labored hard to collect our men into their proper companies and into their former camps, and, on the 23d of July, I moved the Second Wisconsin and Seventy-ninth New York closer in to Fort Corcoran, and got things in better

[31] The Henry House was located approximately 1,000 yards west of Stone's Bridge on Bull Run Creek. R. M. Johnston, *Bull Run: Its Strategy and Tactics* (Boston: Houghton Mifflin, 1913), 198(map).

[32] George Sykes (1822–1880) graduated from the USMA in 1842 and served in the Mexican-American War. He was a major in the 14th U.S. Inf. during the First Battle of Bull Run. *USMA,* 2:140–143.

order than I had expected. Of course, we took it for granted that the rebels would be on our heels, and we accordingly prepared to defend our posts. By the 25th I had collected all the materials, made my report, and had my brigade about as well governed as any in that army; although most of the ninety-day men, especially the Sixty-ninth, had become extremely tired of the war, and wanted to go home. Some of them were so mutinous, at one time, that I had the battery[33] to unlimber, threatening, if they dared to leave camp without orders, I would open fire on them. Drills and the daily exercises were resumed, and I ordered that at the three principal roll-calls the men should form ranks with belts and muskets, and that they should keep their ranks until I in person had received the reports and had dismissed them. The Sixty-ninth still occupied Fort Corcoran, and one morning, after reveille, when I had just received the report, had dismissed the regiment, and was leaving, I found myself in a crowd of men crossing the drawbridge on their way to a barn close by, where they had their sinks; among them was an officer, who said: "Colonel, I am going to New York today. What can I do for you?" I answered: "How can you go to New York? I do not remember to have signed a leave for you." He said, "No; he did not want a leave. He had engaged to serve three months, and had already served more than that time. If the Government did not intend to pay him, he could afford to lose the money; that he was a lawyer, and had neglected his business long enough, and was then going home." I noticed that a good many of the soldiers had paused about us to listen, and knew that, if this officer could defy me, they also would. So I turned on him sharp, and said: "Captain, this question of your term of service has been submitted to the rightful authority, and the decision has been published in orders. You are a soldier, and must submit to orders till you are properly discharged. If you attempt to leave without orders, it will be mutiny, and I will shoot you like a dog! Go back into the fort *now,* instantly, and don't dare to leave without my consent." I had on an overcoat, and may have had my hand about the breast, for he looked at me hard, paused a moment, and then turned back into the fort. The men scattered, and I returned to the house where I was quartered, close by.

That same day, which must have been about July 26th, I was near the river-bank, looking at a block-house which had been built for the defense of the aqueduct, when I saw a carriage coming by the road that crossed the Potomac River at Georgetown by a ferry. I thought I recognized in the carriage the person of President Lincoln. I hurried across a bend, so as to stand by the

[33] In the 1875 first edition of the memoirs (1875), WTS identified the battery as "Ayres's."

road-side as the carriage passed. I was in uniform, with a sword on, and was recognized by Mr. Lincoln and Mr. Seward,[34] who rode side by side in an open hack. I inquired if they were going to my camps, and Mr. Lincoln said: "Yes; we heard that you had got over the big scare, and we thought we would come over and see the 'boys.'" The roads had been much changed and were rough. I asked if I might give directions to his coachman, he promptly invited me to jump in and to tell the coachman which way to drive. Intending to begin on the right and follow round to the left, I turned the driver into a side-road which led up a very steep hill, and, seeing a soldier, called to him and sent him up hurriedly to announce to the colonel (Bennett, I think) that the President was coming. As we slowly ascended the hill, I discovered that Mr. Lincoln was full of feeling, and wanted to encourage our men. I asked if he intended to speak to them, and he said he would like to. I asked him then to please discourage all cheering, noise, or any sort of confusion; that we had had enough of it before Bull Run to ruin any set of men, and that what we needed were cool, thoughtful, hard-fighting soldiers—no more hurrahing, no more humbug. He took my remarks in the most perfect good-nature. Before we had reached the first camp, I heard the drum beating the "assembly," saw the men running for their tents, and in a few minutes the regiment was in line, arms presented, and then brought to an order and "parade rest!"

Mr. Lincoln stood up in the carriage, and made one of the neatest, best, and most feeling addresses I ever listened to, referring to our late disaster at Bull Run, the high duties that still devolved on us, and the brighter days yet to come. At one or two points the soldiers began to cheer, but he promptly checked them, saying: "Don't cheer, boys. I confess I rather like it myself, but Colonel Sherman here says it is not military; and I guess we had better defer to his opinion." In winding up, he explained that, as President, he was commander-in-chief; that he was resolved that the soldiers should have every thing that the law allowed; and he called on one and all to appeal to him personally in case they were wronged. The effect of this speech was excellent.

We passed along in the same manner to all the camps of my brigade; and Mr. Lincoln complimented me highly for the order, cleanliness, and discipline, that he observed. Indeed, he and Mr. Seward both assured me that it was the first bright moment they had experienced since the battle.

[34] William H. Seward (1801–1872) was the governor of New York from 1839 to 1843 and U.S. secretary of state from 1861 to 1869. He was stabbed in the neck and face by Lewis Paine as part of the conspiracy to assassinate Pres. Lincoln on Apr. 14, 1865. *CWHC*, 479.

At last we reached Fort Corcoran. The carriage could not enter, so I ordered the regiment, without arms, to come outside, and gather about Mr. Lincoln, who would speak to them. He made to them the same feeling address, with more personal allusions, because of their special gallantry in the battle under Corcoran, who was still a prisoner in the hands of the enemy; and he concluded with the same general offer of redress in case of grievance. In the crowd I saw the officer with whom I had had the passage at reveille that morning. His face was pale, and lips compressed. I foresaw a scene, but sat on the front seat of the carriage as quiet as a lamb. This officer forced his way through the crowd to the carriage, and said: "Mr. President, I have a cause of grievance. This morning I went to speak to Colonel Sherman, and he threatened to shoot me." Mr. Lincoln, who was still standing, said, "Threatened to shoot you?" "Yes, sir, he threatened to shoot me." Mr. Lincoln looked at him, then at me, and stooping his tall, spare form toward the officer, said to him in a loud stage-whisper, easily heard for some yards around: "Well, if I were you, and he threatened to shoot, I would not trust him, for I believe he would do it." The officer turned about and disappeared, and the men laughed at him. Soon the carriage drove on, and, as we descended the hill, I explained the facts to the President, who answered, "Of course I didn't know any thing about it, but I thought you knew your own business best." I thanked him for his confidence, and assured him that what he had done would go far to enable me to maintain good discipline, and it did.

By this time the day was well spent. I asked to take my leave, and the President and Mr. Seward drove back to Washington. This spirit of mutiny was common to the whole army, and was not subdued till several regiments or parts of regiments had been ordered to Fort Jefferson, Florida, as punishment.[35]

General McDowell had resumed his headquarters at the Arlington House, and was busily engaged in restoring order to his army, sending off the ninety-days men, and replacing them by regiments which had come under the three-years call. We were all trembling lest we should be held personally accountable for the disastrous result of the battle. General McClellan[36] had been summoned

[35] Fort Jefferson served as a military prison during the war. In 1861, fifty-three prisoners were sent to the fort. By 1865, the fort housed approximately 800 prisoners. Susan L. Hitchcock and Beth W. Byrd, *Dry Tortugas National Park: Cultural Landscape Report* (Atlanta: Cultural Resources Division Southeast Regional Office, 2011) 20; James A. Kushlan and Kirsten Hines, *Dry Tortugas National Park* (Charleston: Arcadia, 2019), 53.

[36] George B. McClellan (1826–1885) graduated from the USMA in 1846 and served in the Mexican-American War. He reached the rank of major general in the U.S. Army on May 14, 1861. *USMA,* 2:250–255.

from the West to Washington, and changes in the subordinate commands were announced almost daily.[37] I remember, as a group of officers were talking in the large room of the Arlington House, used as the adjutant-general's office, one evening, some young officer came in with a list of the new brigadiers just announced at the War Department, which embraced the names of Heintzelman, Keyes, Franklin,[38] Andrew Porter,[39] W. T. Sherman, and others, who had been colonels in the battle, and all of whom had shared the common stampede. Of course, we discredited the truth of the list; and Heintzelman broke out in his nasal voice, "By _____ _____, it's all a lie! Every mother's son of you will be cashiered." We all felt he was right, but, nevertheless, it was true; and we were all announced in general orders as brigadier-generals of volunteers.[40]

General McClellan arrived, and, on assuming command, confirmed McDowell's organization. Instead of coming over the river, as we expected, he took a house in Washington, and only came over from time to time to have a review or inspection.[41]

I had received several new regiments, and had begun two new forts on the hill or plateau, above and farther out than Fort Corcoran; and I organized a system of drills, embracing the evolutions of the line, all of which was new to me, and I had to learn the tactics from books; but I was convinced that we had a long, hard war before us, and made up my mind to begin at the very beginning to prepare for it.

August was passing, and troops were pouring in from all quarters; General McClellan told me he intended to organize an army of a hundred thousand men, with one hundred field-batteries, and I still hoped he would come on our side of the Potomac, pitch his tent, and prepare for real hard work, but his headquarters still remained in a house in Washington City. I then thought, and still think, that was a fatal mistake. His choice as general-in-

[37] Gen. Winfield Scott ordered McClellan to take command of the Army of the Potomac on July 25, 1861. *OR,* I, 2, 763, 766.

[38] William B. Franklin (1823–1878) graduated from the USMA in 1843 and was retroactively promoted to brigadier general of the U.S. Volunteers on May 17, 1861. *USMA,* 2:152–154.

[39] Andrew Porter (1820–1872) entered the USMA in 1836 but resigned the next year. During the First Battle of Bull Run, he was colonel of the 1st Brig., 2nd Div., Army of Northeast Virginia, and was retroactively promoted to brigadier general of the U.S. Volunteers on May 17, 1861. *CWHC,* 434.

[40] For the complete list of the U.S. Army officers promoted to brigadier general after the First Battle of Bull Run, see *Official Army Register for 1861* (Washington, DC: GPO, 1861), 55–56.

[41] McClellan arrived in Washington, DC, on July 27, 1861. *OR,* I, 2, 766.

chief at the time was fully justified by his high reputation in the army and country, and, if he then had any political views or ambition, I surely did not suspect it.

About the middle of August I got a note from Brigadier-General Robert Anderson, asking me to come and see him at his room at Willard's Hotel. I rode over and found him in conversation with several gentlemen, and he explained to me that events in Kentucky were approaching a crisis; that the Legislature was in session, and ready, as soon as properly backed by the General Government, to take open sides for the Union cause; that he was offered the command of the Department of the Cumberland, to embrace Kentucky, Tennessee, etc., and that he wanted help, and that the President had offered to allow him to select out of the new brigadiers four of his own choice. I had been a lieutenant in Captain Anderson's company, at Fort Moultrie, from 1843 to 1846, and he explained that he wanted me as his right hand. He also indicated George H. Thomas, D. C. Buell, and Burnside,[42] as the other three. Of course, I always wanted to go West, and was perfectly willing to go with Anderson, especially in a subordinate capacity. We agreed to call on the President on a subsequent day, to talk with him about it, and we did. It hardly seems probable that Mr. Lincoln should have come to Willard's Hotel to meet us, but my impression is that he did, and that General Anderson had some difficulty in prevailing on him to appoint George H. Thomas, a native of Virginia, to be brigadier-general, because so many Southern officers, had already played false; but I was still more emphatic in my indorsement of him by reason of my talk with him at the time he crossed the Potomac with Patterson's army, when Mr. Lincoln promised to appoint him and to assign him to duty with General Anderson. In this interview with Mr. Lincoln, I also explained to him my extreme desire to serve in a subordinate capacity, and in no event to be left in a superior command.[43] He promised me this with promptness, making the

[42] Ambrose E. Burnside (1824–1881) graduated from the USMA in 1847 and served in the Mexican-American War. In Aug. 1861, he was promoted to brigadier general in the U.S. Volunteers. *USMA,* 2:318.

[43] In a letter to his wife, dated Aug. 19, 1861, WTS stated "I went over to Washington on this business some days ago, saw the President & Gen. Scott, at the table of the latter I met Robert Anderson for the first time. I only had a few words with him, but on Saturday he sent for me to meet him at Willards. There I found Senator Johnson, a Mr. Maynard, and two or three other members of Congress from Kentucky and Tennessee." William T. Sherman, *Sherman's Civil War: Selected Correspondence of William T. Sherman, 1860–1865,* ed. Brooks D. Simpson and Jean V. Berlin (Chapel Hill: University of North Carolina Press, 1999), 132.

jocular remark that his chief trouble was to find places for the too many generals who wanted to be at the head of affairs, to command armies, etc.

The official order is dated—

[Special Order No. 114.]

HEADQUARTERS OF THE ARMY,
WASHINGTON, *August* 24, 1861.

The following assignment is made of the general officers of the volunteer service, whose appointment was announced in General Orders No. 62, from the War Department:

To the Department of the Cumberland, Brigadier-General Robert Anderson commanding:

Brigadier-General W. T. Sherman,
Brigadier-General George H. Thomas.

. . . .

By command of Lieutenant-General Scott:

E. D. TOWNSEND, *Assistant Adjutant-General.*[44]

After some days, I was relieved in command of my brigade and post by Brigadier General Fitz-John Porter, and at once took my departure for Cincinnati, Ohio, *via* Cresson, Pennsylvania, where General Anderson was with his family; and he, Thomas, and I, met by appointment at the house of his brother, Larz Anderson, Esq., in Cincinnati. We were there on the 1st and 2d of September, when several prominent gentlemen of Kentucky met us to discuss the situation, among whom were Jackson,[45] Harlan,[46] Speed,[47] and others. At that

[44] WTS misidentified the order as "Special Order No. 114." The correct order number was "Special Order No. 141." For the complete order, see *OR,* I, 51(I), 455.

[45] James S. Jackson (1823–1862) was a lawyer and U.S. Representative from Kentucky in 1861. He joined the U.S. Army as a colonel of the 3rd Kentucky Cav. in Dec. 1861. *CWHC,* 315.

[46] John M. Harlan (1833–1911), a lawyer, joined the U.S. Army as colonel in the 10th Kentucky Inf. at the start of the Civil War. He later served as an associate justice on the U.S. Supreme Court 1877–1911. *CWHC,* 600.

[47] WTS was most likely referring to James Speed (1812–1887), a Kentucky lawyer appointed U.S. attorney general by Pres. Lincoln in 1864. However, his brother, Joshua F. Speed (1814–1882), Lincoln's best friend, was in the Cincinnati, OH, area on Sept 1, 1861. *CWHC,* 611;

time, William Nelson,[48] an officer of the navy, had been commissioned a brigadier-general of volunteers, and had his camp at Dick Robinson, a few miles beyond the Kentucky River, south of Nicholasville;[49] and Brigadier-General L. H. Rousseau[50] had another camp at Jeffersonville, opposite Louisville. The State Legislature was in session at Frankfort, and was ready to take definite action as soon as General Anderson was prepared, for the State was threatened with invasion from Tennessee, by two forces: one from the direction of Nashville, commanded by Generals Albert Sidney Johnston[51] and Buckner;[52] and the other from the direction of Cumberland Gap, commanded by Generals Crittenden[53] and Zollicoffer.[54] General Anderson saw that he had not force enough to resist these two columns, and concluded to send me

---

Harold Holzer, ed., *Lincoln as I Knew Him: Gossip, Tributes, and Revelations from his Best Friends & Worst Enemies* (Chapel Hill: Algonquin Books, 2009), 40.

[48] William "Bull" Nelson (1824–1862) joined the U.S. Navy as a midshipman in 1840 and was transferred to the U.S. Army on Sept. 16, 1861. He was later shot and killed by fellow U.S. Army general Jefferson C. Davis during an argument at the Galt House in Louisville, KY. *CWHC,* 405.

[49] Camp Dick Robinson, a recruiting station established by Nelson in Aug. 1861, was located approximately fifteen miles from Nicholasville, KY. John E. Kleber, *The Kentucky Encyclopedia* (Lexington: University Press of Kentucky, 1992), s.v. "Camp Dick Robinson"; Thomas H. Parker, *History of the 51st Regiment of P.V. and V.V.* (Philadelphia: King and Baird, 1869), 308–309.

[50] Lovell H. Rousseau (1818–1869) was in command of recruitment at Camp Joe Holt near Louisville, KY. *CWHC,* 463.

[51] Albert S. Johnston (1803–1862) graduated from the USMA in 1826 and resigned from the U.S. Army to join the Confederate Army in May 1861. He took command of the Army of Central Kentucky in Oct. 1861, and was placed in command of the Army of Mississippi on Mar. 29, 1862. He was shot in the leg and died during the Battle of Shiloh on Apr. 6, 1862. *CWHC,* 322.

[52] Simon B. Buckner (1823–1914) graduated from the USMA in 1844 and resigned from the U.S. Army in Mar. 1855. He joined the Confederate Army in Sept 1861 and was placed in command of the 2nd Div., Army of Central Kentucky. *CWHC,* 152.

[53] George B. Crittenden (1812–1880) graduated from the USMA in 1832 and resigned from the U.S. Army in June 1861. He joined the Confederate Army in Aug. and was placed in command of a brigade in the Confederate Army of the Potomac. *CWHC,* 190–191.

[54] Felix K. Zollicoffer (1812–1862) was a U.S. congressman from Tennessee from 1853 to 1859 who joined the Confederate Army as a brigadier general in July 1861. He was shot and killed at the Battle of Mill Springs on Jan. 19, 1862. *CWHC,* 586.

in person for help to Indianapolis and Springfield, to confer with the Governors of Indiana, and Illinois, and to General Fremont, who commanded in St. Louis.

McClellan and Fremont were the two men toward whom the country looked as the great Union leaders, and toward them were streaming the newly-raised regiments of infantry and cavalry, and batteries of artillery; nobody seeming to think of the intervening link covered by Kentucky. While I was to make this tour, Generals Anderson and Thomas were to go to Louisville and initiate the department. None of us had a staff, or any of the machinery for organizing an army, and, indeed, we had no army to organize. Anderson was empowered to raise regiments in Kentucky, and to commission a few brigadier-generals.

At Indianapolis I found Governor Morton[55] and all the State officials busy in equipping and providing for the new regiments, and my object was to divert some of them toward Kentucky; but they were called for as fast as they were mustered in, either for the army of McClellan or Fremont. At Springfield also I found the same general activity and zeal, Governor Yates[56] busy in providing for his men; but these men also had been promised to Fremont. I then went on to St. Louis, where all was seeming activity, bustle, and preparation. Meeting R. M. Renick[57] at the Planters' House (where I stopped), I inquired where I could find General Fremont. Renick said, "What do you want with General Fremont?" I said I had come to see him on business; and he added, "You don't suppose that he will see such as you?" and went on to retail all the scandal of the day: that Fremont was a great potentate, surrounded by sentries and guards; that he had a more showy court than any real king; that he kept senators, governors, and the first citizens, dancing attendance for days and weeks before granting an audience, etc.; that if I expected to see him on business, I would have to make my application in writing, and submit to a close scrutiny by his chief of staff[58] and by his civil surroundings. Of course I laughed at all this, and renewed my simple inquiry as to where was his office, and was

[55] Oliver H. P. T. Morton (1823–1877) was governor of Indiana from 1861 to 1867 and U.S. senator from Indiana from 1867 to 1877. *CWHC,* 400.

[56] Richard Yates (1818–1873) was U.S. congressman (1851–1855), governor (1861–1865), and U.S. senator (1865–1871) from Illinois. *CWHC,* 584.

[57] Robert M. Renick (1813–1875) graduated from the USMA in 1835 and was a real estate agent and broker during the Civil War. *USMA,* 1:594.

[58] Anselm Albert was Gen. John C. Frémont's aide-de-camp from Sept. 1861 to Apr. 1862. *CWHC,* 587.

informed that he resided and had his office at Major Brant's new house on Chouteau Avenue.[59] It was then late in the afternoon, and I concluded to wait till the next morning; but that night I received a dispatch from General Anderson in Louisville to hurry back, as events were pressing, and he needed me.

Accordingly, I rose early next morning before daybreak, got breakfast with the early railroad-passengers, and about sunrise was at the gate of General Fremont's headquarters. A sentinel with drawn sabre paraded up and down in front of the house. I had on my undress uniform indicating my rank, and inquired of the sentinel, "Is General Fremont up?" He answered, "I don't know." Seeing that he was a soldier by his bearing, I spoke in a sharp, emphatic voice, "Then find out." He called for the corporal of the guard, and soon a fine-looking German sergeant came, to whom I addressed the same inquiry. He in turn did not know, and I bade him find out, as I had immediate and important business with the general. The sergeant entered the house by the front-basement door, and after ten or fifteen minutes the main front-door above was slowly opened from the inside, and who should appear but my old San Francisco acquaintance Isaiah C. Woods, whom I had not seen or heard of since his flight to Australia, at the time of the failure of Adams & Co. in 1855![60] He ushered me in hastily, closed the door, and conducted me into the office on the right of the hall. We were glad to meet, after so long and eventful an interval, and mutually inquired after our respective families and special acquaintances. I found that he was a commissioned officer, a major on duty with Fremont, and Major Eaton, now of the Paymaster's Department,[61] was in the same office with him. I explained to them that I had come from

[59] In July 1861, Gen. Frémont rented a three-story mansion owned by the family of Joshua B. Brant (1790–1861) for $6,000 a year and used the residence as his military headquarters. Katharine T. Corbett, *In Her Place: A Guide to St. Louis Women's History* (St. Louis: Missouri Historical Society Press, 1999), 83; Richard Edwards and M. Hopewell, *Edward's Great West and Her Commercial Metropolis* (St. Louis: Edward's Monthly, 1860), s.v. "Colonel Joshua B. Brant"; Jessie Benton Frémont, *The Letters of Jessie Benton Frémont,* ed. Pamela Herr and Mary L. Spence (Urbana: University of Illinois Press, 1993), 238*n*.

[60] Woods secretly traveled to Australia on Aug. 5, 1855, to avoid any consequences related to the failure of Adams & Co. He was the chief of transportation on Frémont's staff in Sept. 1861. Roger D. Hunt, *Colonels in Blue: U.S. Colored Troops, U.S. Armed Forces, Staff Officers and Special Units* (Jefferson, NC: McFarland, 2022), 248; "Departure of Isaiah C. Woods for Australia in the Ship *Audubon,*" *Sydney Morning Herald* (Sydney, Australia), Oct. 26, 1855, 2.

[61] Joseph H. Eaton (1815–1896) graduated from the USMA in 1835 and resigned from the U.S. Army in 1856. He was reappointed as paymaster on June 1, 1861, and was Frémont's military secretary in Sept. 1861. *USMA,* 1:619–620; *CWHC,* 222.

General Anderson, and wanted to confer with General Fremont in person. Woods left me, but soon returned, said the general would see me in a very few minutes, and within ten minutes I was shown across the hall into the large parlor, where General Fremont received me very politely. We had met before, as early as 1847, in California, and I had also seen him several times when he was senator. I then in a rapid manner ran over all the points of interest in General Anderson's new sphere of action, hoped he would spare us from the new levies what troops he could, and generally act in concert with us. He told me that his first business would be to drive the rebel General Price[62] and his army out of Missouri, when he would turn his attention down the Mississippi. He asked my opinion about the various kinds of field-artillery which manufacturers were thrusting on him, especially the then newly-invented James gun,[63] and afterward our conversation took a wide turn about the character of the principal citizens of St. Louis, with whom I was well acquainted.

Telling General Fremont that I had been summoned to Louisville and that I should leave in the first train, viz., at 3 P. M., I took my leave of him. Returning to Wood's office, I found there two more Californians, viz., Messrs. Palmer and Haskell, so I felt that, while Fremont might be suspicious of others, he allowed free ingress to his old California acquaintances.

Returning to the Planters' House, I heard of Beard, another Californian, a Mormon, who had the contract for the line of redoubts which Fremont had ordered to be constructed around the city, before he would take his departure for the interior of the State;[64] and while I stood near the office-counter, I saw old Baron Steinberger, a prince among our early California adventurers, come in and look over the register. I avoided him on purpose, but his presence in St. Louis recalled the maxim, "Where the vultures are, there is a carcass close

[62] Sterling Price (1809–1867) was the governor of Missouri 1853–1857 and a major general in the Missouri State Guard in 1861–1862. He led Confederate troops to victory at the Battle of Wilson's Creek in Aug. 1861. *CWHC*, 440.

[63] Charles T. James (1805–1862), a mechanic and U.S. senator from Rhode Island from 1851 to 1857, was commissioned to develop a new model of rifled field artillery in late 1861. For more information on the weapon's design, see James C. Hazlett, Edwin Olmstead, and M. Hume Parks, *Field Artillery Weapons of the Civil War,* rev. ed. (Urbana: University of Illinois Press, 2004), 147–148; Jo Anne M. Quatannens and Diane B. Boyle, *Senators of the United States: A Historical Bibliography* (Washington, DC: GPO, 1995), s.v. "James, Charles Tillinghast."

[64] E. L. Beard moved to Missouri in 1861 and on Sept. 4, 1861, proposed to build fortifications around St. Louis. Frémont approved the proposal the same day. *Report of the Joint Committee on the Conduct of the War, Part III* (Washington, DC: GPO, 1863), 279.

by;"[65] and I suspected that the profitable contracts of the quartermaster, McKinstry,[66] had drawn to St. Louis some of the most enterprising men of California. I suspect they can account for the fact that, in a very short time, Fremont fell from his high estate in Missouri, by reason of frauds, or supposed frauds, in the administration of the affairs of his command.[67]

I left St. Louis that afternoon and reached Louisville the next morning.[68] I found General Anderson quartered at the Louisville Hotel, and he had taken a dwelling house on——Street as an office. Captain O. D. Greene was his adjutant-general,[69] Lieutenant Throckmorton his aide,[70] and Captain Prime, of the Engineer Corps,[71] was on duty with him. General George H. Thomas had been dispatched to camp Dick Robinson, to relieve Nelson.[72]

The city was full of all sorts of rumors. The Legislature, moved by considerations purely of a political nature, had taken the step, whatever it was, that amounted to an adherence to the Union, instead of joining the already-seceded States. This was universally known to be the signal for action. For it we were utterly unprepared, whereas the rebels were fully prepared. General Sidney Johnston immediately crossed into Kentucky, and advanced as far as Bowling Green, which he began to fortify, and thence dispatched General

[65] The quote is an allusion to Matt. 24:28.

[66] Justus McKinstry (1814–1897) graduated from the USMA in 1838 and was appointed quartermaster of the Dept. of the West on Jan. 10, 1861. He was arrested in St. Louis and court-martialed for neglect and violation of duty related to supply contracts. *USMA,* 1:726–727; Spencer C. Tucker, ed., *American Civil War: The Definitive Encyclopedia and Document Collection* (Santa Barbara: ABC-CLIO, 2013), vol. 1, s.v. "McKinstry, Justus."

[67] For more information on the accusations of fraud against Frémont and McKinstry, see *Report of the Joint Committee on the Conduct of the War, Part III* (Washington, DC: GPO, 1863), 7–279.

[68] Anderson ordered WTS to proceed to Louisville on Sept. 7, 1861. *OR,* I, 52 (1), 190.

[69] Oliver D. Greene (1849–1904) graduated from the USMA in 1854 and became assistant adjutant general for the Dept. of the Cumberland on Sept. 24, 1861. *USMA,* 2:590–91.

[70] Charles B. Throckmorton (1842–1915) graduated from Georgetown University and joined the U.S. Army as a second lieutenant in 1861. He remained in the army until 1894. Frederick A. Virkus, ed., *The Abridged Compendium of American Genealogy* (Chicago: F. A. Virkus, 1926), 319; James Fergusson, *The Personal Observations of a Man of Intelligence: Notes of a Tour in North America in 1861,* ed. Ben Wayne (Lambertville, NJ: True Bill Press, 2009), 95.

[71] Frederick E. Prime (1829–1900) graduated from the USMA in 1850 and joined the Dept. of the Cumberland as an engineer on Aug. 15, 1861. *USMA,* 2:400–401.

[72] Thomas was ordered to Camp Dick Robinson on Aug. 28, 1861. *CWHC,* 527.

Buckner with a division forward toward Louisville; General Zollicoffer, in like manner, entered the State and advanced as far as Somerset.[73] On the day I reached Louisville the excitement ran high. It was known that Columbus, Kentucky, had been occupied, September 7th, by a strong rebel force, under Generals Pillow[74] and Polk,[75] and that General Grant[76] had moved from Cairo and occupied Paducah in force on the 6th. Many of the rebel families expected Buckner to reach Louisville at any moment. That night, General Anderson sent for me, and I found with him Mr. Guthrie, president of the Louisville & Nashville Railroad,[77] who had in his hands a dispatch to the effect that the bridge across the Rolling Fork of Salt Creek, less than thirty miles out, had been burned, and that Buckner's force, *en route* for Louisville, had been detained beyond Green River by a train thrown from the track. We learned afterward that a man named Bird had displaced a rail on purpose to throw the train off the track, and thereby give us time.

Mr. Guthrie explained that in the ravine just beyond Salt Creek were several high and important trestles which, if destroyed, would take months to replace, and General Anderson thought it well worth the effort to save them. Also, on Muldraugh's Hill beyond, was a strong position, which had in former years been used as the site for the State "Camp of Instruction," and we all supposed that General Buckner, who was familiar with the ground, was aiming for a position there, from which to operate on Louisville.

[73] Johnston ordered Buckner to occupy Bowling Green on Sept. 16. Buckner entered the city with 4,500 Confederate troops two days later. Zollicoffer started his raids through Kentucky on Sept. 17. William P. Johnston, *The Life of General Albert Sidney Johnston* (New York: D. Appleton, 1878), 308–310, 355–356.

[74] Gideon J. Pillow (1806–1878) fought in the Mexican-American War and was discharged from the U.S. Army in July 1848. He joined the Confederate Army as a brigadier general on July 9, 1861. *CWHC*, 430.

[75] Leonidas Polk (1806–1864) graduated from the USMA in July 1827 and resigned from the U.S. Army later that year. He joined the Confederate Army as a major general on June 25, 1861, and was mortally wounded by a parrot shell at the Battle of Pine Mountain on June 14, 1864. *CWHC*, 432–433.

[76] Ulysses S. Grant (1822–1885) graduated from the USMA in 1843 and served in the Mexican-American War. His effectiveness as a leading general during the Civil War led to his election as president of the United States. He served as president from 1869 to 1877. *CWHC*, 263–264.

[77] James Guthrie (1792–1869) was a prominent Louisville citizen. He became vice president of the Louisville & Nashville Railroad in 1857 and the company's president in 1860. John E. Kleber et al., *The Encyclopedia of Louisville* (Lexington: University Press of Kentucky, 2001), s.v. "Guthrie, James."

All the troops we had to counteract Buckner were Rousseau's Legion, and a few Home Guards in Louisville. The former were still encamped across the river at Jeffersonville; so General Anderson ordered me to go over, and with them, and such Home Guards as we could collect, make the effort to secure possession of Muldraugh's Hill before Buckner could reach it. I took Captain Prime with me, and crossed over to Rousseau's camp. The long-roll was beaten, and within an hour the men, to the number of about one thousand, were marching for the ferry-boat and for the Nashville depot. Meantime General Anderson had sent to collect some Home Guards, and Mr. Guthrie to get the trains ready. It was after midnight before we began to move. The trains proceeded slowly, and it was daybreak when we reached Lebanon Junction, twenty-six miles out, where we disembarked, and marched to the bridge over Salt River, which we found had been burnt; whether to prevent Buckner coming into Louisville, or us from going out, was not clear. Rousseau's Legion forded the stream and marched up to the State Camp of Instruction, finding the high trestles all secure. The railroad-hands went to work at once to rebuild the bridge. I remained a couple of days at Lebanon Junction, during which General Anderson forwarded two regiments of volunteers that had come to him. Before the bridge was done we advanced the whole camp to the summit of Muldraugh's Hill, just back of Elizabethtown. There I learned definitely that General Buckner had not crossed Green River at all, that General Sidney Johnston was fortifying Bowling Green, and preparing for a systematic advance into Kentucky, of which he was a native, and with whose people and geography he must have been familiar.

As fast as fresh troops reached Louisville, they were sent out to me at Muldraugh's Hill, where I was endeavoring to put them into shape for service, and by the 1st of October I had the equivalent of a division of two brigades preparing to move forward toward Green River.[78] The daily correspondence between General Anderson and myself satisfied me that the worry and harassment at Louisville were exhausting his strength and health, and that he would soon leave. On a telegraphic summons from him, about the 5th of October, I went down to Louisville, when General Anderson said he could not stand the mental torture of his command any longer, and that he must go away, or it would kill him. On the 8th of October he actually published an

[78] WTS had approximately 3,000 troops under his command when he reached Muldraugh's Hill, Kentucky. By Oct. 1, 1861, he had received an additional 1,000 to 2,000 troops. James L. McDonough, *William Tecumseh Sherman: In the Service of My Country—A Life* (New York: W. W. Norton, 2016), 281–282; *OR,* I, 4, 278–279.

order relinquishing the command, and, by reason of my seniority, I had no alternative but to assume command, though much against the grain, and in direct violation of Mr. Lincoln's promise to me.[79] I am certain that, in my earliest communication to the War Department, I renewed the expression of my wish to remain in a subordinate position, and that I received the assurance that Brigadier-General Buell would soon arrive from California, and would be sent to relieve me.

By that time I had become pretty familiar with the geography and the general resources of Kentucky. We had parties all over the State raising regiments and companies; but it was manifest that the young men were generally inclined to the cause of the South, while the older men of property wanted to be let alone—i.e., to remain neutral. As to a forward movement that fall, it was simply impracticable; for we were forced to use divergent lines, leading our columns farther and farther apart; and all I could attempt was to go on and collect force and material at the two points already chosen, viz., Dick Robinson and Elizabethtown. General George H. Thomas still continued to command the former, and on the 12th of October I dispatched Brigadier-General A. McD. McCook[80] to command the latter, which had been moved forward to Nolin Creek, fifty-two miles out of Louisville, toward Bowling Green.[81] Staff-officers began to arrive to relieve us of the constant drudgery which, up to that time, had been forced on General Anderson and myself; and these were all good men. Colonel Thomas Swords, quartermaster, arrived on the 13th; Paymaster Larned[82] on the 14th; and Lieutenant Smyzer, Fifth Artillery, acting ordnance-officer,[83] on the 20th; Captain Symonds was already on

[79] For Anderson's order, see *OR,* I, 4, 297.

[80] Alexander M. McCook (1831–1903) graduated from the USMA in 1852 and was promoted to brigadier general, U.S. Volunteers, on Sept. 3, 1861. WTS ordered him to Nolin Creek on Oct. 12. *USMA,* 2:499–500; 5:77; *OR,* I, 4, 306.

[81] Nolin Creek, now known as the Nolin River, starts in LaRue County, KY, and ends in Edmonson County near Mammoth Cave National Park. George B. Davis et al., *Official Military Atlas of the Civil War* (New York: Fairfax Press, 1983), plate 150; Dan Lee, *Three Rivers: A Kentucky Folk History* (Jefferson, NC: McFarland, 2023), 83.

[82] Benjamin F. Larned (1794–1862) joined the U.S. Army in 1813 and was appointed paymaster general in 1854. He held that position until he died of natural causes in 1862. Richard F. Miller, ed., *States at War: A Reference Guide for Pennsylvania in the Civil War* (Hanover, NH: University Press of New England, 2014), 3:342*n.*

[83] Jacob H. Smyser (1838–1885) graduated from the USMA in 1861 and joined the 5th U.S. Art. as a first lieutenant on May 14, 1861. *USMA,* 2:798–799.

duty as the commissary of subsistence; Captain O. D. Greene was the adjutant-general, and completed a good working staff.

The everlasting worry of citizens complaining of every petty delinquency of a soldier, and forcing themselves forward to discuss politics, made the position of a commanding general no sinecure. I continued to strengthen the two corps forward and their routes of supply; all the time expecting that Sidney Johnston, who was a real general, and who had as correct information of our situation as I had, would unite his force with Zollicoffer, and fall on Thomas at Dick Robinson, or McCook at Nolin. Had he done so in October, 1861, he could have walked into Louisville, and the vital part of the population would have hailed him as a deliverer. Why he did not, was to me a mystery then and is now; for I know that he saw the move, and had his wagons loaded up at one time for a start toward Frankfort, passing between our two camps. Conscious of our weakness, I was unnecessarily unhappy, and doubtless exhibited it too much to those near me; but it did seem to me that the Government at Washington, intent on the larger preparations of Fremont in Missouri and McClellan in Washington, actually ignored us in Kentucky.

About this time, say the middle of October, I received notice, by telegraph, that the Secretary of War, Mr. Cameron (then in St. Louis), would visit me at Louisville, on his way back to Washington. I was delighted to have an opportunity to properly represent the actual state of affairs, and got Mr. Guthrie to go with me across to Jeffersonville, to meet the Secretary of War and escort him to Louisville. The train was behind time, but Mr. Guthrie and I waited till it actually arrived. Mr. Cameron was attended by Adjutant-General Lorenzo Thomas,[84] and six or seven gentlemen who turned out to be newspaper reporters. Mr. Cameron's first inquiry was, when he could start for Cincinnati, saying that, as he had been detained at St. Louis so long, it was important he should hurry on to Washington. I explained that the regular mail-boat would leave very soon—viz., at 12 M.—but I begged him to come over to Louisville; that I wanted to see him on business as important as any in Washington, and hoped he would come and spend at least a day with us. He asked if every thing was not well with us, and I told him far from it; that things were actually bad, as bad as bad could be. This seemed to surprise him, and Mr. Guthrie added his persuasion to mine; when Mr. Cameron, learning that he could leave Louisville by rail *via* Frankfort next morning early, and make the same connections at

[84] Lorenzo Thomas (1804–1875) graduated from the USMA in 1823 and served in the Mexican-American War. He was promoted to adjutant general of the U.S. Army on Aug. 3, 1861. *USMA,* 1:308–310.

Cincinnati, consented to go with us to Louisville, with the distinct understanding that he must leave early the next morning for Washington.

We accordingly all took hacks, crossed the river by the ferry, and drove to the Galt House,[85] where I was then staying. Brigadier-General T. J. Wood[86] had come down from Indianapolis by the same train, and was one of the party. We all proceeded to my room on the first floor of the Galt House, where our excellent landlord, Silas Miller, Esq.,[87] sent us a good lunch and something to drink. Mr. Cameron was not well, and lay on my bed, but joined in the general conversation.[88] He and his party seemed to be full of the particulars of the developments in St. Louis of some of Fremont's extravagant contracts and expenses, which were the occasion of Cameron's trip to St. Louis, and which finally resulted in Fremont's being relieved, first by General Hunter,[89] and after by General H. W. Halleck.

After some general conversation, Mr. Cameron called to me, "Now, General Sherman, tell us of your troubles." I said I preferred not to discuss business with so many strangers present. He said, "They are all friends, all members of my family, and you may speak your mind freely and without restraint." I am sure I stepped to the door, locked it to prevent intrusion, and then fully and fairly represented the state of affairs in Kentucky, especially the situation and numbers of my troops. I complained that the new levies of Ohio and Indiana were diverted East and West, and we got scarcely any thing; that our forces at Nolin and Dick Robinson were powerless for invasion, and only tempting to a general such as we believed Sidney Johnston to be; that, if Johnston chose, he could march to Louisville any day. Cameron exclaimed: "You astonish me! Our informants, the Kentucky Senators and members of Congress, claim that they have in Kentucky plenty of men, and all they want are arms and

[85] The original Galt House Hotel was built in 1835 by Aris Throckmorton; it burned down in 1865. Bryan S. Bush, *A History Lover's Guide to Louisville* (Charleston, SC: History Press, 2021), 44.

[86] Thomas J. Wood (1823–1906) graduated from the USMA in 1845 and served in the Mexican-American War. He was promoted to brigadier general on Oct. 11, 1861. *USMA,* 2:211–213; 5:60.

[87] Silas F. Miller (1822–1902), a steamboat captain, took charge of the Galt House Hotel in the early 1850s. "Funeral of Captain Miller," *Courier-Journal* (Louisville, KY), Feb. 6, 1902, 1–2.

[88] WTS met with Cameron at the Galt House Hotel on Oct. 16, 1861. *OR,* I, 4, 313.

[89] David Hunter (1802–1886) graduated from the USMA in 1822 and served in the Mexican-American War. He was placed in command of the Western Dept. on Nov. 2, 1861, and was transferred to the Dept. of Kansas seven days later. *USMA,* 1:290–293.

money." I then said it was not true; for the young men were arming and going out openly in broad daylight to the rebel camps, provided with good horses and guns by their fathers, who were at best "neutral;" and as to arms, he had, in Washington, promised General Anderson forty thousand of the best Springfield muskets, instead of which we had received only about twelve thousand Belgian muskets, which the Governor of Pennsylvania[90] had refused, as had also the Governor of Ohio,[91] but which had been adjudged good enough for Kentucky. I asserted that volunteer colonels raising regiments in various parts of the State had come to Louisville for arms, and when they saw what I had to offer had scorned to receive them—to confirm the truth of which I appealed to Mr. Guthrie, who said that every word I had spoken was true, and he repeated what I had often heard him say, that no man who owned a slave or a mule in Kentucky could be trusted.

Mr. Cameron appeared alarmed at what was said, and turned to Adjutant-General L. Thomas, to inquire if he knew of any troops available, that had not been already assigned. He mentioned Negley's Pennsylvania Brigade, at Pittsburg, and a couple of other regiments that were then *en route* for St. Louis. Mr. Cameron ordered him to divert these to Louisville, and Thomas made the telegraphic orders on the spot.[92] He further promised, on reaching Washington, to give us more of his time and assistance.

In the general conversation which followed, I remember taking a large map of the United States, and assuming the people of the whole South to be in rebellion, that our task was to subdue them, showed that McClellan was on the left, having a frontage of less than a hundred miles, and Fremont the right, about the same; whereas I, the centre, had from the Big Sandy to Paducah, over three hundred miles of frontier; that McClellan had a hundred thousand men, Fremont sixty thousand, whereas to me had only been allotted about eighteen thousand. I argued that, for the purpose of defense we should have sixty thousand men at once, and for offense, would need two hundred thousand, before we were done. Mr. Cameron, who still lay on the bed, threw up his hands and exclaimed, "Great God! where are they to come from?" I asserted that there were plenty of men at the North, ready and willing to come,

[90] Andrew G. Curtin (1815–1894) was governor of Pennsylvania from 1861 to 1867 and U.S. congressman from Pennsylvania from 1881 to 1887. *CWHC,* 194.

[91] William Dennison Jr. (1815–1882) was governor of Ohio from 1860 to 1862 and U.S. postmaster general from 1864 to 1866. *CWHC,* 206.

[92] James S. Negley (1826–1901) was ordered to Louisville, KY, on Oct. 17, 1861. *CWHC,* 404; *OR,* I, 4, 309.

if he would only accept their services; for it was notorious that regiments had been formed in all the Northwestern States, whose services had been refused by the War Department, on the ground that they would not be needed. We discussed all these matters fully, in the most friendly spirit, and I thought I had aroused Mr. Cameron to a realization of the great war that was before us, and was in fact upon us. I heard him tell General Thomas to make a note of our conversation, that he might attend to my requests on reaching Washington. We all spent the evening together agreeably in conversation, many Union citizens calling to pay their respects, and the next morning early we took the train for Frankfort; Mr. Cameron and party going on to Cincinnati and Washington, and I to Camp Dick Robinson to see General Thomas and the troops there.[93]

I found General Thomas in a tavern, with most of his regiments camped about him. He had sent a small force some miles in advance toward Cumberland Gap, under Brigadier-General Schoepf.[94] Remaining there a couple of days, I returned to Louisville; on the 22d of October, General Negley's brigade arrived in boats from Pittsburg, was sent out to Camp Nolin; and the Thirty-seventh Indiana, Colonel Hazzard,[95] and Second Minnesota, Colonel Van Cleve,[96] also reached Louisville by rail, and were posted at Elizabethtown and Lebanon Junction.[97] These were the same troops which had been ordered by Mr. Cameron when at Louisville, and they were all that I received thereafter, prior to my leaving Kentucky. On reaching Washington, Mr. Cameron called on General Thomas, as he himself afterward told me, to submit his memorandum of events during his absence, and in that memorandum was mentioned my *insane* request for two hundred thousand men.[98] By some newspaper man this was seen and published, and, before I had the least conception

[93] WTS had arrived at Camp Dick Robinson by Oct. 22, 1861. *OR,* I, 4, 316.

[94] Albin F. Schoepf (1822–1886) was born in Poland and immigrated to the United States in 1851. He joined the U.S. Army as a brigadier general on Sept. 30, 1861. *CWHC,* 472.

[95] George W. Hazzard (1825–1862) graduated from the USMA in 1847 and was promoted to colonel of the 37th Indiana Volunteers on Oct. 17, 1861. He was mortally wounded at the Battle of White Oak Swamp on June 30, 1862. *USMA,* 2:308.

[96] Horatio P. Van Cleve (1809–1891) graduated from the USMA in 1831 and took command of the 2nd Minnesota Volunteers on July 22, 1861. *USMA,* 1:487; 4:37.

[97] Negley was ordered to Nolin Creek on Oct. 22, 1861, and Hazzard had reached Elizabethtown by Nov. 12. *OR,* I, 4, 318, 354, 359.

[98] For Thomas's official report on the meeting between WTS and Cameron, see *OR,* I, 4, 313–314.

of it, I was universally published throughout the country as "insane, crazy," etc. Without any knowledge, however, of this fact, I had previously addressed to the Adjutant-General of the army at Washington this letter:

HEADQUARTERS DEPARTMENT OF THE CUMBERLAND,
LOUISVILLE, KENTUCKY, *October* 22, 1861.

To General L. THOMAS, *Adjutant-General, Washington, D. C.*

SIR: On my arrival at Camp Dick Robinson, I found General Thomas had stationed a Kentucky regiment at Rock Castle Hill, beyond a river of the same name, and had sent an Ohio and an Indiana regiment forward in support. He was embarrassed for transportation, and I authorized him to hire teams, and to move his whole force nearer to his advance-guard, so as to support it, as he had information of the approach of Zollicoffer toward London. I have just heard from him, that he had sent forward General Schoepf with Colonel Wolford's cavalry, Colonel Steadman's Ohio regiment, and a battery of artillery, followed on a succeeding day by a Tennessee brigade. He had still two Kentucky regiments, the Thirty-eighth Ohio and another battery of artillery, with which he was to follow yesterday. This force, if concentrated, should be strong enough for the purpose; at all events, it is all he had or I could give him.

I explained to you fully, when here, the supposed position of our adversaries, among which was a force in the valley of Big Sandy, supposed to be advancing on Paris, Kentucky. General Nelson at Maysville was instructed to collect all the men he could, and Colonel Gill's regiment of Ohio Volunteers. Colonel Harris was already in position at Olympian Springs, and a regiment lay at Lexington, which I ordered to his support. This leaves the line of Thomas's operations exposed, but I cannot help it. I explained so fully to yourself and the Secretary of War the condition of things, that I can add nothing new until further developments. You know my views that this great centre of our field is too weak, far too weak, and I have begged and implored till I dare not say more.

Buckner still is beyond Green River. He sent a detachment of his men, variously estimated at from two to four thousand toward Greensburg. General Ward, with about one thousand men, retreated to Campbellsburg, where he called to his assistance some partially-formed regiments to the number of about two thousand. The enemy did not advance, and General Ward was at last dates at Campbellsburg. The officers charged with raising regiments must of necessity be near their homes to collect men, and for this reason are out of position; but at or near Greensburg and Lebanon, I desire to assemble as large a force of the Kentucky Volunteers as possible. This organization is necessarily irregular, but the necessity is so great that I must have them, and therefore have issued to them arms and clothing during the process of formation. This has facilitated their enlistment; but inasmuch as the Legislature has provided money for organizing the Kentucky Volunteers, and intrusted its disbursement to a board of loyal gentlemen, I have endeavored to coöperate with them to hasten the formation of these corps.

The great difficulty is, and has been, that as volunteers offer, we have not arms and clothing to give them. The arms sent us are, as you already know, European muskets of uncouth pattern, which the volunteers will not touch.

General McCook has now three brigades—Johnson's, Wood's, and Rousseau's. Negley's brigade arrived to-day, and will be sent out at once. The Minnesota regiment has also arrived, and will be sent forward. Hazzard's regiment of Indiana troops I have ordered to the mouth of Salt Creek, an important point on the turnpike-road leading to Elizabethtown.

I again repeat that our force here is out of all proportion to the importance of the position. Our defeat would be disastrous to the nation; and to expect of new men, who never bore arms, to do miracles, is not right.

I am, with much respect, yours truly,

W. T. Sherman, *Brigadier-General commanding.*

About this time my attention was drawn to the publication in all the Eastern papers, which of course was copied at the West, of the report that I was "crazy, insane, and mad," that "I had demanded two hundred thousand men for the defense of Kentucky;" and the authority given for this report was stated to be the Secretary of War himself, Mr. Cameron, who never, to my knowledge, took pains to affirm or deny it. My position was therefore simply unbearable, and it is probable I resented the cruel insult with language of intense feeling. Still I received no orders, no reënforcements, not a word of encouragement or relief. About November 1st, General McClellan was appointed commander-in-chief of all the armies in the field, and by telegraph called for a report from me. It is herewith given:

HEADQUARTERS DEPARTMENT OF THE CUMBERLAND,
LOUISVILLE, KENTUCKY, *November* 4, 1861.

General L. THOMAS, *Adjutant-General, Washington, D. C.*

SIR: In compliance with the telegraphic orders of General McClellan, received late last night, I submit this report of the forces in Kentucky, and of their condition.

The tabular statement shows the position of the several regiments. The camp at Nolin is at the present extremity of the Nashville Railroad. This force was thrown forward to meet the advance of Buckner's army, which then fell back to Green River, twenty-three miles beyond. These regiments were substantially without means of transportation, other than the railroad, which is guarded at all dangerous points, yet is liable to interruption at any moment, by the tearing up of a rail by the disaffected inhabitants or a hired enemy. These regiments are composed of good materials, but devoid of company officers of experience, and have been put under thorough drill since being in camp. They are generally well clad, and provided for. Beyond Green River, the enemy has masked his forces, and it is very difficult to ascertain even the approximate numbers. No pains have been spared to ascertain them, but without success, and it is well known that they far outnumber us. Depending, however, on the railroads to their rear for transportation, they have not thus far advanced this side of Green River, except in marauding parties. This is the proper line of advance, but will require a very large force, certainly fifty thousand men, as their railroad facilities south enable them to concentrate at Munfordsville the entire strength of the South. General McCook's command is divided into four brigades, under Generals Wood, R. W. Johnson, Rousseau, and Negley.

General Thomas's line of operations is from Lexington, toward Cumberland Gap and Ford, which are occupied by a force of rebel Tennesseeans, under the command of Zollicoffer. Thomas occupies the position at London, in front of two roads which lead to the fertile part of Kentucky, the one by Richmond, and the other by Crab Orchard, with his reserve at Camp Dick Robinson, eight miles south of the Kentucky River. His provisions and stores go by railroad from Cincinnati to Nicholasville, and thence in wagons to his several regiments. He is forced to hire transportation.

Brigadier-General Nelson is operating by the line from Olympian Springs, east of Paris, on the Covington & Lexington Railroad, toward Prestonburg, in the valley of the Big Sandy where is assembled a force of from twenty-five to thirty-five hundred rebel Kentuckians waiting reënforcements from Virginia. My last report from him was to October 28th, at which time he had Colonel Harris's Ohio Second, nine hundred strong; Colonel Norton's Twenty-first Ohio, one thousand; and Colonel Sill's Thirty-third Ohio, seven hundred and fifty strong; with two irregular Kentucky regiments, Colonels Marshall and Metcalf. These troops were on the road near Hazel Green and West Liberty, advancing toward Prestonburg.

Upon an inspection of the map, you will observe these are all divergent lines, but rendered necessary, from the fact that our enemies choose them as places of refuge from pursuit, where they can receive assistance from neighboring States. Our lines are all too weak, probably with the exception of that to Prestonburg. To strengthen these, I am thrown on the raw levies of Ohio and Indiana, who arrive in detachments, perfectly fresh from the country, and loaded down with baggage, also upon the Kentuckians, who are slowly forming regiments all over the State, at points remote from danger, and whom it will be almost impossible to assemble together. The organization of this latter force is, by the laws of Kentucky, under the control of a military board of citizens, at the capital, Frankfort, and they think they will be enabled to have fifteen regiments toward the middle of this month, but I doubt it, and deem it unsafe to rely on them. There are four regiments forming in the neighborhood of Owensboro', near the mouth of Green River, who are doing good service, also in the neighborhood of Campbellsville, but it is unsafe to rely on troops so suddenly armed and equipped. They are not yet clothed or uniformed. I know well you will think our force too widely distributed, but we are forced to it by the attitude of our enemies, whose force and numbers the country never has and probably never will comprehend.

I am told that my estimate of troops needed for this line, viz., two hundred thousand, has been construed to my prejudice, and therefore leave it for the future. This is the great centre on which our enemies can concentrate whatever force is not employed elsewhere. Detailed statement of present force inclosed with this.

With great respect, your obedient servant,

W. T. Sherman, *Brigadier-General commanding.*

Brigadier-General McCook's Camp, at Nolin, Fifty-Two Miles From Louisville, Kentucky, *November* 4, 1861.

First Brigade (General Rousseau).—Third Kentucky, Colonel Bulkley; Fourth Kentucky, Colonel Whittaker; First Cavalry, Colonel Board; Stone's battery; two companies Nineteenth United States Infantry, and two companies Fifteenth United States Infantry, Captain Gilman.

Second Brigade (General T. J. Wood).—Thirty-eighth Indiana, Colonel Scribner; Thirty-ninth Indiana, Colonel Harrison; Thirtieth Indiana, Colonel Bass; Twenty-ninth Indiana, Colonel Miller.

Third Brigade (General Johnson).—Forty-ninth Ohio, Colonel Gibson; Fifteenth Ohio, Colonel Dickey; Thirty-fourth Illinois, Colonel King; Thirty-second Indiana, Colonel Willach.

Fourth Brigade (General Negley).—Seventy-seventh Pennsylvania, Colonel Hambright; Seventy-eighth Pennsylvania, Colonel Sinnell; Seventy-ninth Pennsylvania, Colonel Stambaugh; Battery _____, Captain Mueller.

Camp Dick Robinson (General G. H. Thomas). _____ Kentucky, Colonel Bramlette; _____ Kentucky, Colonel Fry; _____ Kentucky Cavalry, Colonel Woolford; Fourteenth Ohio, Colonel Steadman; First Artillery, Colonel Barnett; Third Ohio, Colonel Carter; _____ East Tennessee, Colonel Byrd.

Bardstown, Kentucky.—Tenth Indiana, Colonel Manson.

Crab Orchard.—Thirty-third Indiana, Colonel Coburn.

Jeffersonville, Indiana.—Thirty-fourth Indiana, Colonel Steele; Thirty-sixth Indiana, Colonel Grose; First Wisconsin, Colonel Starkweather.

Mouth of Salt River.—Ninth Michigan, Colonel Duffield; Thirty-seventh Indiana, Colonel Hazzard.

Lebanon Junction.—Second Minnesota, Colonel Van Cleve.

Olympian Springs.—Second Ohio, Colonel Harris.

Cynthiana, Kentucky.—Thirty-fifth Ohio, Colonel Vandever.

Nicholasville, Kentucky.—Twenty-first Ohio, Colonel Norton; Thirty-eighth Ohio, Colonel Bradley.

Big Hill.—Seventeenth Ohio, Colonel Connell.

Colesburg.—Twenty-fourth Illinois, Colonel Hecker.

Elizabethtown, Kentucky.—Nineteenth Illinois, Colonel Turchin.
Owensboro' or Henderson.—Thirty-first Indiana, Colonel Cruft; Colonel Edwards, forming Rock Castle; Colonel Boyle, Harrodsburg; Colonel Barney, Irvine; Colonel Hazzard, Burksville; Colonel Haskins, Somerset.

And, in order to conclude this subject, I also add copies of two telegraphic dispatches, sent for General McClellan's use about the same time, which are all the official letters received at his headquarters, as certified by the Adjutant-General, L. Thomas, in a letter of February 1, 1862, in answer to an application of my brother, Senator John Sherman, and on which I was adjudged insane:

LOUISVILLE, *November* 3, 10 P. M.

To General MCCLELLAN, *Washington, D. C.:*

Dispatch just received. We are forced to operate on three lines, all dependent on railroads of doubtful safety, requiring strong guards. From Paris to Prestonburg, three Ohio regiments and some militia—enemy variously reported from thirty-five hundred to seven thousand. From Lexington toward Cumberland Gap, Brigadier-General Thomas, one Indiana and five Ohio regiments, two Kentucky and two Tennessee; hired wagons and badly clad. Zollicoffer, at Cumberland Ford, about seven thousand. Lee reported on the way with Virginia reënforcements. In front of Louisville, fifty-two miles, McCook, with four brigades of about thirteen thousand, with four regiments to guard the railroad, at all times in danger. Enemy along the railroad from Green River to Bowling Green, Nashville, and Clarksville. Buckner, Hardee, Sidney Johnston, Polk, and Pillow, the two former in immediate command, the force as large as they want or can subsist, from twenty-five to thirty thousand. Bowling Green strongly fortified. Our forces too small to do good, and too large to sacrifice.

W. T. SHERMAN, *Brigadier-General.*

HEADQUARTERS DEPARTMENT OF THE CUMBERLAND,
LOUISVILLE, KENTUCKY, *November* 6, 1861.

General L. THOMAS, *Adjutant-General.*

SIR: General McClellan telegraphs me to report to him daily the situation of affairs here. The country is so large that it is impossible to give clear and definite views. Our enemies have a terrible advantage in

the fact that in our midst, in our camps, and along our avenues of travel, they have active partisans, farmers and business-men, who seemingly pursue their usual calling, but are in fact spies. They report all our movements and strength, while we can procure information only by circuitous and unreliable means. I inclose you the copy of an intercepted letter, which is but the type of others. Many men from every part of the State are now enrolled under Buckner—have gone to him—while ours have to be raised in neighborhoods, and cannot be called together except at long notice. These volunteers are being organized under the laws of the State, and the 10th of November is fixed for the time of consolidating them into companies and regiments. Many of them are armed by the United States as home guards, and many by General Anderson and myself, because of the necessity of being armed to guard their camps against internal enemies. Should we be overwhelmed, they would scatter, and their arms and clothing will go to the enemy, furnishing the very material they so much need. We should have here a very large force, sufficient to give confidence to the Union men of the ability to do what should be done—possess ourselves of all the State. But all see and feel we are brought to a standstill, and this produces doubt and alarm. With our present force it would be simple madness to cross Green River, and yet hesitation may be as fatal. In like manner the other columns are in peril, not so much in front as rear, the railroads over which our stores must pass being much exposed. I have the Nashville Railroad guarded by three regiments, yet it is far from being safe; and, the moment actual hostilities commence, these roads will be interrupted, and we will be in a dilemma. To meet this in part I have put a cargo of provisions at the mouth of Salt River, guarded by two regiments. All these detachments weaken the main force, and endanger the whole. Do not conclude, as before, that I exaggerate the facts. They are as stated, and the future looks as dark as possible. It would be better if some man of sanguine mind were here, for I am forced to order according to my convictions.
Yours truly,

W. T. Sherman, *Brigadier-General commanding.*

After the war was over, General Thomas J. Wood, then in command of the district of Vicksburg, prepared a statement addressed to the public, describing the interview with the Secretary of War, which he calls a "Council of War." I did not then deem it necessary to renew a matter which had been swept into oblivion by the war itself; but, as it is evidence by an eye-witness, it is worthy of insertion here.

STATEMENT.

On the 11th of October, 1861, the writer, who had been personally on mustering duty in Indiana, was appointed a brigadier-general of volunteers, and ordered to report to General Sherman, then in command of the Department of the Cumberland, with his headquarters at Louisville, having succeeded General Robert Anderson. When the writer was about leaving Indianapolis to proceed to Louisville, Mr. Cameron, returning from his famous visit of inspection to General Fremont's department, at St. Louis, Missouri, arrived at Indianapolis, and announced his intention to visit General Sherman.

The writer was invited to accompany the party to Louisville. Taking the early morning train from Indianapolis to Louisville on the 16th of October, 1861, the party arrived in Jeffersonville shortly after mid-day. General Sherman met the party in Jeffersonville, and accompanied it to the Galt House, in Louisville, the hotel at which he was stopping.

During the afternoon General Sherman informed the writer that a council of war was to be held immediately in his private room in the hotel, and desired him to be present at the council. General Sherman and the writer proceeded directly to the room. The writer entered the room first, and observed in it Mr. Cameron, Adjutant-General L. Thomas, and some other persons, all of whose names he did not know, but whom he recognized as being of Mr. Cameron's party. The name of one of the party the writer had learned, which he remembers as Wilkinson, or Wilkerson, and who he understood was a writer for the *New York Tribune* newspaper. The Hon. James Guthrie was also in the room, having been invited, on account of his eminent position as a citizen of Kentucky, his high civic reputation, and his well-known devotion to the Union, to meet the Secretary of War in the council. When General Sherman entered the room he closed the door, and turned the key in the lock.

Before entering on the business of the meeting, General Sherman remarked substantially: "Mr. Cameron, we have met here to discuss matters and interchange views which should be known only by persons high in the confidence of the Government. There are persons present whom I do not know, and I desire to know, before opening the business of the council, whether they are persons who may be properly allowed to hear the views which I have to submit to you." Mr. Cameron replied, with some little testiness of manner, that the persons referred to belonged to his party, and there was no objection to their knowing whatever might be communicated to him.

Certainly the legitimate and natural conclusion from this remark of Mr. Cameron's was that whatever views might be submitted by General Sherman would be considered under the protection of the seal of secrecy, and would not be divulged to the public till all apprehension of injurious consequences from such disclosure had passed. And it may be remarked, further, that justice to General Sherman required that if, at any future time, his conclusions as to the amount of force necessary to conduct the operations committed to his charge should be made public, the grounds on which his conclusions were based should be made public at the same time.

Mr. Cameron then asked General Sherman what his plans were. To this General Sherman replied that he had no plans; that no sufficient force had been placed at his disposition with which to devise any plan of operations; that, before a commanding general could project a plan of campaign, he must know what amount of force he would have to operate with.

The general added that he had views which he would be happy to submit for the consideration of the Secretary. Mr. Cameron desired to hear General Sherman's views.

General Sherman began by giving his opinion of the people of Kentucky, and the then condition of the State. He remarked that he believed a very large majority of the people of Kentucky were thoroughly devoted to the Union, and loyal to the Government, and that the Unionists embraced almost all the older and more substantial men in the State; but, unfortunately, there was no organization nor arms among the Union men; that the rebel minority, thoroughly vindictive in its sentiments, was organized and armed (this having been done in advance by their leaders), and, beyond the reach of the Federal forces, overawed and prevented the Union men from organizing; that, in his opinion, if Federal protection were extended throughout the State to the Union men, a large force could be raised for the service of the Government.

General Sherman next presented a *résumé* of the information in his possession as to the number of the rebel troops in Kentucky. Commencing with the force at Columbus, Kentucky, the reports varied, giving the strength from ten to twenty thousand. It was commanded by Lieutenant-General Polk. General Sherman fixed it at the lowest estimate; say, ten thousand. The force at Bowling Green, commanded by General A. S. Johnston, supported by Hardee, Buckner, and others, was variously estimated at from eighteen to thirty thousand. General Sherman estimated this force at the lowest figures given to it by his information—eighteen thousand.

He explained that, for purposes of defense, these two forces ought, owing to the facility with which troops might be transported from one to the other, by the net-work of railroads in Middle and West Tennessee, to be considered almost as one. General Sherman remarked, also, on the facility with which reënforcements could be transported by railroad to Bowling Green, from the other rebellious States.

The third organized body of rebel troops was in Eastern Kentucky, under General Zollicoffer, estimated, according to the most reliable information, at six thousand men. This force threatened a descent, if unrestrained, on the blue-grass region of Kentucky, including the cities of Lexington, and Frankfort, the capital of the State; and if successful in its primary movements, as it would gather head as it advanced, might endanger the safety of Cincinnati.

General Sherman said that the information in his possession indicated an intention, on the part of the rebels, of a general and grand advance toward the Ohio River. He further expressed the opinion that, if such advance should be made, and not checked, the rebel force would be swollen by at least twenty thousand recruits from the disloyalists in Kentucky. His low computation of the organized rebel soldiers then in Kentucky fixed the strength at about thirty-five thousand. Add twenty thousand for reënforcements gained in Kentucky, to say nothing of troops drawn from other rebel States, and the effective rebel force in the State, at a low estimate, would be fifty-five thousand men.

General Sherman explained forcibly how largely the difficulties of suppressing the rebellion would be enhanced, if the rebels should be allowed to plant themselves firmly, with strong fortifications, at commanding points on the Ohio River. It would be facile for them to carry the war thence into the loyal States north of the river.

To resist an advance of the rebels, General Sherman stated that he did not have at that time in Kentucky more than some twelve to fourteen thousand effective men. The bulk of this force was posted at camp Nolin, on the Louisville & Nashville Railway, fifty miles south of Louisville. A part of it was in Eastern Kentucky, under General George H. Thomas, and a very small force was in the lower valley of Green River.

This disposition of the force had been made for the double purpose of watching and checking the rebels, and protecting the raising and organization of troops among the Union men of Kentucky.

Having explained the situation from the defensive point of view, General Sherman proceeded to consider it from the offensive standpoint. The Government had undertaken to suppress the rebellion; the *onus faciendi,* therefore, rested on the Government. The rebellion could never be put down, the authority of the paramount Government asserted, and the union of the States declared perpetual, by force of arms, by maintaining the defensive; to accomplish these grand desiderata, it was absolutely necessary the Government should adopt, and maintain until the rebellion was crushed, the *offensive.*

For the purpose of expelling the rebels from Kentucky, General Sherman said that at least sixty thousand soldiers were necessary. Considering that the means of accomplishment must always be proportioned to the end to be achieved, and bearing in mind the array of rebel force then in Kentucky, every sensible man must admit that the estimate of the force given by General Sherman, for driving the rebels out of the State, and reëstablishing and maintaining the authority of the Government, was a very low one. The truth is that, before the rebels were driven from Kentucky, many more than sixty thousand soldiers were sent into the State.

Ascending from the consideration of the narrow question of the political and military situation in Kentucky, and the extent of force necessary to redeem the State from rebel thraldom, forecasting in his sagacious intellect the grand and daring operations which, three years afterward, he realized in a campaign, taken in its entirety, without a parallel in modern times, General Sherman expressed the opinion that, to carry the war to the Gulf of Mexico, and destroy all armed opposition to the Goverment, in the entire Mississippi Valley, at least two hundred thousand troops were absolutely requisite.

So soon as General Sherman had concluded the expression of his views, Mr. Cameron asked, with much warmth and apparent irritation, "Where do you suppose, General Sherman, all this force is to come from?" General Sherman replied that he did not know; that it was not his duty to raise, organize, and put the necessary military force into the field; that duty pertained to the War Department. His duty was to organize campaigns and command the troops after they had been put into the field.

At this point of the proceedings, General Sherman suggested that it might be agreeable to the Secretary to hear the views of Mr. Guthrie. Thus appealed to, Mr. Guthrie said he did not consider himself, being a civilian, competent to give an opinion as to the extent of force necessary to carry the war to the Gulf of Mexico; but, being well informed of the condition of things in Kentucky, he indorsed fully General Sherman's opinion of the force required to drive the rebels out of the State.

The foregoing is a circumstantial account of the deliberations of the council that were of any importance.

A good deal of desultory conversation followed, on immaterial matters; and some orders were issued by telegraph, by the Secretary of War, for some small reënforcements to be sent to Kentucky immediately, from Pennsylvania and Indiana.

A short time after the council was held—the exact time is not now remembered by the writer—an imperfect narrative of it appeared in the *New York Tribune.* This account announced to the public the conclusions uttered by General Sherman in the council, without giving the reasons on which his conclusions were based. The unfairness of this course to General Sherman needs no comment. All military men were shocked by the gross breach of faith which had been committed.

Th. J. Wood, *Major-General Volunteers.*
Vicksburg, Mississippi, *August* 24, 1866.

Brigadier-General Don Carlos Buell arrived at Louisville about the middle of November, with orders to relieve me, and I was transferred for duty to the Department of the Missouri, and ordered to report in person to Major-General H. W. Halleck at St. Louis. I accompanied General Buell to the camp at Nolin, where he reviewed and inspected the camp and troops under the command of General A. McD. McCook, and on our way back General Buell inspected the regiment of Hazzard at Elizabethtown. I then turned over my command to him, and took my departure for St. Louis.[99]

[99] Buell arrived in Louisville and relieved WTS of his command on Nov. 16, 1861. *OR,* I, 4, 359.

At the time I was so relieved I thought, of course, it was done in fulfillment of Mr. Lincoln's promise to me, and as a necessary result of my repeated demand for the fulfillment of that promise; but I saw and felt, and was of course deeply moved to observe, the manifest belief that there was more or less of truth in the rumor that the cares, perplexities, and anxiety of the situation had unbalanced my judgment and mind. It was, doubtless, an incident common to all civil wars, to which I could only submit with the best grace possible, trusting to the future for an opportunity to redeem my fortune and good name.[100] Of course I could not deny the fact, and had to submit to all its painful consequences for months; and, moreover, I could not hide from myself that many of the officers and soldiers subsequently placed under my command looked at me askance and with suspicion. Indeed, it was not until the following April that the battle of Shiloh gave me personally the chance to redeem my good name.

On reaching St. Louis and reporting to General Halleck, I was received kindly, and was shortly afterward (viz., November 23d) sent up to Sedalia to inspect the camp there, and the troops located along the road back to Jefferson City, and I was ordered to assume command in a certain contingency. I found General Steele at Sedalia with his regiments scattered about loosely; and General Pope[101] at Otterville, twenty miles back, with no concert between them. The rebel general, Sterling Price, had his forces down about Osceola and Warsaw. I advised General Halleck to collect the whole of his men into one camp on the La Mine River, near Georgetown, to put them into brigades and divisions, so as to be ready to be handled, and I gave some preliminary orders looking to that end. But the newspapers kept harping on my insanity and paralyzed my efforts. In spite of myself, they tortured from me some words and acts of imprudence. General Halleck telegraphed me on November 26th: "Unless telegraph-lines are interrupted, make no movement of troops without orders;" and on November 29th: "No forward movement of troops on Osceola will be made; only strong reconnoitring-parties will be sent out in the supposed direction of the enemy; the bulk of the troops being held in position till more reliable information is obtained."[102]

[100] In the first edition of the memoirs (1875), this portion of WTS's text read, "Still, on a review of the only official documents before the War Department at the time, it was cruel for a Secretary of War to give a tacit credence to a rumor which probably started without his wish or intention, yet through his instrumentality."

[101] John Pope (1822–1892) graduated from the USMA in 1842 and served in the Mexican-American War. He was a brigadier general of the U.S. Volunteers in late 1861. *USMA,* 2:126–127; 4:58.

[102] Halleck's order to WTS was dated Nov. 27, 1861. *OR,* I, 8, 382.

About the same time I received the following dispatch:

HEADQUARTERS, ST. LOUIS, MISSOURI,
November 28, 1861.

Brigadier-General SHERMAN, *Sedalia:*

Mrs. Sherman is here. General Halleck is satisfied, from reports of scouts received here, that no attack on Sedalia is intended. You will therefore return to this city, and report your observations on the condition of the troops you have examined. Please telegraph when you will leave.

SCHUYLER HAMILTON, *Brigadier-General and Aide-de-Camp.*[103]

I accordingly returned to St. Louis, where I found Mrs. Sherman, naturally and properly distressed at the continued and reiterated reports of the newspapers of my insanity, and she had come from Lancaster to see me. This recall from Sedalia simply swelled the cry. It was alleged that I was recalled by reason of something foolish I had done at Sedalia, though in fact I had done absolutely nothing, except to recommend what was done immediately thereafter on the advice of Colonel McPherson, on a subsequent inspection. Seeing and realizing that my efforts were useless, I concluded to ask for a twenty days' leave of absence, to accompany Mrs. Sherman to our home in Lancaster, and to allow the storm to blow over somewhat. It also happened to be mid-winter, when nothing was doing; so Mrs. Sherman and I returned to Lancaster, where I was born, and where I supposed I was better known and appreciated.

The newspapers kept up their game as though instigated by malice, and chief among them was the *Cincinnati Commercial,* whose editor, Halsted, was generally believed to be an honorable man.[104] P. B. Ewing, Esq.,[105] being in Cincinnati, saw him and asked him why he, who certainly knew better,

[103] The letter from Hamilton to WTS in the *OR* did not include the sentence "Mrs. Sherman is here." *OR,* I, 8, 391.

[104] Murat Halstead (1829–1908) began his work at the *Cincinnati Commercial* in 1853. On Dec. 11, 1861, the newspaper published an article with the headline "General William T. Sherman Insane." Marszalek, *Sherman,* 164; "Great Editor Is Dead," *Warsaw Daily Times* (Warsaw, IN), July 3, 1908, 1.

[105] Philemon B. Ewing (1820–1896), foster brother of WTS, was admitted to the bar in 1841 and became judge of the common pleas court in the 7th Ohio District in Mar. 1862. Emilius O. Randall and Daniel J. Ryan, *History of Ohio: The Rise and Progress of an American State* (New York: Century, 1915), 6:15.

would reiterate such a damaging slander. He answered, quite cavalierly, that it was one of the news-items of the day, and he had to keep up with the time; but he would be most happy to publish any correction I might make, as though I could deny such a malicious piece of scandal affecting myself. On the 12th of November I had occasion to write to General Halleck,[106] and I have a copy of his letter in answer:

St. Louis, *December* 18, 1861.

Brigadier-General W. T. Sherman, *Lancaster, Ohio.*

My dear General: Yours of the 12th was received a day or two ago, but was mislaid for the moment among private papers, or I should have answered it sooner. The newspaper attacks are certainly shameless and scandalous, but I cannot agree with you, that they have us in their power "to destroy us as they please." I certainly get my share of abuse, but it will not disturb me.

Your movement of the troops was not countermanded by me because I thought it an unwise one in itself, but because I was not then ready for it. I had better information of Price's movements than you had, and I had no apprehension of an attack. I intended to concentrate the forces on that line, but I wished the movement delayed until I could determine on a better position.

After receiving Lieutenant-Colonel McPherson's report, I made precisely the location you had ordered. I was desirous at the time not to prevent the advance of Price by any movement on our part, hoping that he would move on Lexington; but finding that he had determined to remain at Osceola for some time at least, I made the movement you proposed. As you could not know my plans, you and others may have misconstrued the reason of my countermanding your orders. . . .

I hope to see you well enough for duty soon. Our organization goes on slowly, but we will effect it in time. Yours truly,

H. W. Halleck.

And subsequently, in a letter to Hon. Thomas Ewing, in answer to some inquiries involving the same general subject, General Halleck wrote as follows:

[106] WTS wrote to Halleck on Dec. 12, 1861, not Nov. 12. *OR,* I, 8, 819.

St. Louis, *February* 15, 1862.

Hon. Thomas Ewing, *Lancaster, Ohio.*

Dear Sir: Your note of the 13th, and one of this date, from Mr. Sherman, in relation to Brigadier-General Sherman's having being relieved from command in Sedalia, in November last, are just received. General Sherman was not put in command at Sedalia; he was authorized to assume it, and did so for a day or two. He did not know my plans, and his movement of troops did not accord with them. I therefore directed him to leave them as they were, and report here the result of his *inspection,* for which purpose he had been ordered there.

No telegram or dispatch of any kind was sent by me, or by any one with my knowledge or authority, in relation to it. After his return here, I gave him a leave of absence of twenty days, for the benefit of his health. As I was then pressing General McClellan for more officers, I deemed it necessary to explain why I did so. I used these words: "I am satisfied that General Sherman's physical and mental system is so completely broken by labor and care as to render him, for the present, unfit for duty; perhaps a few weeks' rest may restore him." This was the only communication I made on the subject. On no occasion have I ever expressed an opinion that his mind was affected otherwise than by over-exertion; to have said so would have done him the greatest injustice.

After General Sherman returned from his short leave, I found that his health was nearly restored, and I placed him temporarily in command of the camp of instruction, numbering over fifteen thousand men. I then wrote to General McClellan that he would soon be able to again take the field. I gave General Sherman a copy of my letter. This is the total of my correspondence on the subject. As evidence that I have every confidence in General Sherman, I have placed him in command of Western Kentucky—a command only second in importance in this department. As soon as divisions and columns can be organized, I propose to send him into the field where he can render most efficient service. I have seen newspaper squibs charging him with being "crazy," etc. This is the grossest injustice; I do not, however, consider such attacks worthy of notice. The best answer is General Sherman's present position, and the valuable services he is rendering to the country. I have the fullest confidence in him.

Very respectfully, your obedient servant,

H. W. Halleck, *Major-General.*

On returning to St. Louis, on the expiration of my leave of absence,[107] I found that General Halleck was beginning to move his troops: one part, under General U. S. Grant, up the Tennessee River; and another part, under General S. R. Curtis,[108] in the direction of Springfield, Missouri. General Grant was then at Paducah, and General Curtis was under orders for Rolla. I was ordered to take Curtis's place in command of the camp of instruction, at Benton Barracks,[109] on the ground back of North St. Louis, now used as the Fair Grounds, by the following order:

[Special Order No. 87].

HEADQUARTERS DEPARTMENT OF THE MISSOURI,
ST. LOUIS, *December* 23, 1861.

[EXTRACT.]

Brigadier-General W. T. Sherman, United States Volunteers, is hereby assigned to the command of the camp of instruction and post of Benton Barracks. He will have every armed regiment and company in his command ready for service at a moment's warning, and will notify all concerned that, when marching orders are received, it is expected that they will be instantly obeyed; no excuses for delay will be admitted. General Sherman will immediately report to these headquarters what regiments and companies, at Benton Barracks, are ready for the field.

By order of Major-General Halleck,
J. C. KELTEN,[110] *Assistant Adjutant-General.*

I immediately assumed command, and found, in the building constructed for the commanding officer, Brigadier-General Strong, and the family of a captain

[107] WTS retuned to St. Louis by Dec. 23, 1861. Marszalek, *Sherman,* 167.

[108] Samuel R. Curtis (1805–1866) graduated from the USMA in 1831 and served in the Mexican-American War. He was placed in command of the Southwestern District of Missouri on Dec. 26, 1861. *USMA,* 1:491–493.

[109] Benton Barracks was a U.S. Army encampment approximately four miles outside of St. Louis. Robert I. Garden, *History of Scott Township, Mahaska County, Iowa: War Reminiscences* (Oskaloosa, IA: Globe, 1907), 112.

[110] John C. Kelton (1828–1893) graduated from the USMA in 1851 and was the assistant adjutant general of the Dept. of Missouri in Dec. 1861. *USMA,* 2:459–460; 4:82.

of Iowa cavalry, with whom we boarded.[111] Major Curtis, son of General Curtis, was the adjutant-general,[112] but was soon relieved by Captain J. H. Hammond, who was appointed assistant adjutant-general, and assigned to duty with me.[113]

Brigadier-General Hurlbut[114] was also there, and about a dozen regiments of infantry and cavalry. I at once gave all matters pertaining to the post my personal attention, got the regiments in as good order as possible, kept up communication with General Halleck's headquarters by telegraph, and, when orders came for the movement of any regiment or detachment, it moved instantly. The winter was very wet, and the ground badly drained. The quarters had been erected by General Fremont, under contract; they were mere shells, but well arranged for a camp, embracing the Fair Grounds, and some forty acres of flat ground west of it. I instituted drills, and was specially ordered by General Halleck to watch Generals Hurlbut and Strong, and report as to their fitness for their commissions as brigadier-generals. I had known Hurlbut as a young lawyer, in Charleston, South Carolina, before the Mexican War, at which time he took a special interest in military matters, and I found him far above the average in the knowledge of regimental and brigade drill, and so reported. General Strong had been a merchant, and he told me that he never professed to be a soldier, but had been urged on the Secretary of War for the commission of a brigadier-general, with the expectation of becoming quartermaster or commissary-general. He was a good, kind-hearted gentleman, boiling over with patriotism and zeal. I advised him what to read and study, was considerably amused at his receiving instruction from a young lieutenant who knew the company and battalion drill, and could hear him practise in his room the words of command, and tone of voice, "Break from the right, to march to the left!" "Battalion, halt!" "Forward into line!" etc. Of course I made a favorable report in his case. Among the infantry and cavalry colonels

[111] William K. Strong (1805–1867) became a brigadier general in the U.S. Army on Sept. 28, 1861. *CWHC,* 517.

[112] Henry Z. Curtis (1835–1862) was a captain and assistant quartermaster in the U.S. Volunteers in 1861. He was shot and killed on Oct. 6, 1863, in Baxter Springs, KS. James Buckingham and Mary J. Tilton, *The Ancestors of Ebenezer Buckingham* (Chicago: R. R. Donnelley, 1892), 130–131.

[113] John H. Hammond (1833–1890) was promoted to captain in the U.S. Army on Nov. 20, 1861. He became assistant adjutant general in Mar. 1862. *CWHC,* 277.

[114] Stephen A. Hurlbut (1815–1882) was an Illinois legislator who became a brigadier general in the U.S. Army on May 17, 1861. *CWHC,* 311–312.

were some who afterward rose to distinction—David Stuart,[115] Gordon Granger,[116] Bussey,[117] etc., etc.

Though it was mid-winter, General Halleck was pushing his preparations most vigorously, and surely he brought order out of chaos in St. Louis with commendable energy. I remember, one night, sitting in his room, on the second floor of the Planters' House, with him and General Cullum, his chief of staff, talking of things generally, and the subject then was of the much-talked-of "advance," as soon as the season would permit. Most people urged the movement down the Mississippi River; but Generals Polk and Pillow had a large rebel force, with heavy guns in a very strong position, at Columbus, Kentucky, about eighteen miles below Cairo. Commodore Foote[118] had his gunboat fleet at Cairo; and General U. S. Grant, who commanded the district, was collecting a large force at Paducah, Cairo, and Bird's Point. General Halleck had a map on his table, with a large pencil in his hand, and asked, "Where is the rebel line?" Cullum drew the pencil through Bowling Green, Forts Donelson and Henry, and Columbus, Kentucky. "That is their line," said Halleck. "Now, where is the proper place to break it?" And either Cullum or I said, "*Naturally* the centre." Halleck drew a line perpendicular to the other, near its middle, and it coincided nearly with the general course of the Tennessee River; and he said, "That's the true line of operations." This occurred more than a month before General Grant began the movement, and, as he was subject to General Halleck's orders, I have always given Halleck the full credit for that movement, which was skillful, successful, and extremely rich in military results; indeed, it was the first real success on our side in the civil war. The movement up the Tennessee began about the 1st of February,[119]

[115] David Stuart (1816–1868) was a U.S. congressman from Michigan from 1853 to 1855 and later commanded the 2nd Brig., 5th Div, Army of the Tennessee, in Mar. 1862. He was wounded during the Battle of Shiloh on Apr. 6, 1862. *CWHC,* 611.

[116] Gordon Granger (1822–1876) graduated from the USMA in 1845 and served in the Mexican-American War. He was promoted to brigadier general, U.S. Volunteers, on Mar. 26, 1862. *USMA,* 2:237–242.

[117] Cyrus Bussey (1833–1915) was an Iowa legislator who became a colonel in Aug. 1861. He served with WTS in Mississippi during his Jackson Campaign in July 1863. *CWHC,* 156.

[118] Andrew H. Foote (1806–1863) joined the U.S. Navy as a midshipman in 1822 and was promoted to captain on June 29, 1861. He commanded the Mississippi River Squadron from Aug. 1861 to May 1862. *CWHC,* 238–239.

[119] On Jan. 30, 1862, Halleck ordered Grant to prepare his troops to move on Fort Henry. *OR,* I, 7, 121.

and Fort Henry was captured by the joint action of the navy under Commodore Foote, and the land-forces under General Grant, on the 6th of February, 1862. About the same time,[120] General S. R. Curtis had moved forward from Rolla, and, on the 8th of March, defeated the rebels under McCulloch,[121] Van Dorn,[122] and Price, at Pea Ridge.

As soon as Fort Henry fell, General Grant marched straight across to Fort Donelson, on the Cumberland River, invested the place, and, as soon as the gunboats had come round from the Tennessee, and had bombarded the water-front, he assaulted; whereupon Buckner surrendered the garrison of twelve thousand men; Pillow and ex-Secretary of War General Floyd having personally escaped across the river at night, occasioning a good deal of fun and criticism at their expense.

Before the fall of Donelson, but after that of Henry, I received, at Benton Barracks, the following orders:

HEADQUARTERS DEPARTMENT OF THE MISSOURI,
ST. LOUIS, *February* 13, 1862.

Brigadier-General SHERMAN, *Benton Barracks:*

You will immediately repair to Paducah, Kentucky, and assume command of that post. Brigadier-General Hurlbut will accompany you. The command of Benton Barracks will be turned over to General Strong.

H. W. HALLECK, *Major-General.*

I started for Paducah the same day, and think that General Cullum went with me to Cairo; General Halleck's purpose being to push forward the operations up the Tennessee River with unusual vigor. On reaching Paducah, I found this dispatch:

[120]The Confederate Army attacked Curtis's forces at Pea Ridge, AR, on Mar. 6, 1862. For Curtis's report on the battle, see *OR,* I, 8, 191–193.

[121]Benjamin McCulloch (1811–1862) was a major general in the Texas Militia before he joined the Confederate Army as a brigadier general on May 11, 1861. He commanded the 1st Div., Army of the West, during the Battle of Pea Ridge. He was shot in the chest and killed on the second day of the battle. *CWHC,* 376.

[122]Earl Van Dorn (1820–1863) graduated from the USMA in 1842 and served in the Mexican-American War. He resigned from the U.S. Army on Jan. 31, 1861, and joined the Confederate Army as a colonel in Mar. On May 7, 1863, he was shot in the head and killed by Dr. James B. Peters for having an affair with his wife. *CWHC,* 542.

HEADQUARTERS DEPARTMENT OF THE MISSOURI,
ST. LOUIS, *February* 15, 1862.

Brigadier-General SHERMAN, *Paducah, Kentucky:*

Send General Grant every thing you can spare from Paducah and Smithland; also General Hurlbut.

Bowling Green has been evacuated entirely.

H. W. HALLECK, *Major-General.*

The next day brought us news of the surrender of Buckner, and probably at no time during the war did we all feel so heavy a weight raised from our breasts, or so thankful for a most fruitful series of victories. They at once gave Generals Halleck, Grant, and C. F. Smith, great fame. Of course, the rebels let go their whole line, and fell back on Nashville and Island No. Ten,[123] and to the Memphis & Charleston Railroad. Everybody was anxious to help. Boats passed up and down constantly, and very soon arrived the rebel prisoners from Donelson. I saw General Buckner on the boat, he seemed self-sufficient, and thought their loss was not really so serious to their cause as we did.

About this time another force of twenty or twenty-five thousand men was collected on the west bank of the Mississippi, above Cairo, under the command of Major-General John Pope, designed to become the "Army of the Mississippi," and to operate, in conjunction with the navy, down the river against the enemy's left flank, which had held the strong post of Columbus, Kentucky, but which, on the fall of Fort Donelson, had fallen back to New Madrid and Island No. 10.[124]

[123] On Apr. 8, 1862, Foote captured Island No. 10, located approximately forty miles below Columbus, KY, on the Mississippi River. Spencer C. Tucker, *Almanac of American History* (London: Bloomsbury, 2012), s.v. "March 16–April 8, 1862."

[124] In the first edition of the memoirs (1875), this portion of WTS's text read, "From the time I had left Kentucky, General Buell had really made no substantial progress, though strongly reënforced beyond even what I had asked for. General Albert Sidney Johnston had remained at Bowling Green until his line was broken at Henry and Donelson, when he let go Bowling Green and fell back hastily to Nashville; and, on Buell's approach, he did not even tarry there, but continued his retreat southward."

10

Battle of Shiloh.

MARCH AND APRIL, 1862.

By the end of February, 1862, Major-General Halleck commanded all the armies in the valley of the Mississippi, from his headquarters in St. Louis. These were, the Army of the Ohio, Major-General Buell, in Kentucky; the Army of the Tennessee, Major-General Grant, at Forts Henry and Donelson; the Army of the Mississippi, Major-General Pope; and that of General S. R. Curtis, in Southwest Missouri.[1] He posted his chief of staff, General Cullum, at Cairo, and me at Paducah, chiefly to expedite and facilitate the important operations then in progress up the Tennessee and Cumberland Rivers.

Fort Donelson had surrendered[2] to General Grant on the 16th of February, and there must have been a good deal of confusion resulting from the necessary care of the wounded, and disposition of prisoners, common to all such occasions, and there was a real difficulty in communicating between St. Louis and Fort Donelson.

General Buell had also followed up the rebel army, which had retreated hastily from Bowling Green to and through Nashville, a city of so much importance to the South, that it was at one time proposed as its capital. Both Generals Grant and Buell looked to its capture as an event of great importance. On the 21st General Grant sent General Smith with his division to Clarksville, fifty

[1] In the first edition of the memoirs (1875), this portion WTS's text read, "In the middle of February, 1862, Major General Halleck commanded all the armies in the valley of the Mississippi, from his headquarters in St. Louis. These were, the Army of the Ohio, Major General Buell, in Kentucky; the Army of the Tennessee, Major General Grant, at Forts Henry and Donelson; and General S. R. Curtis, in Southwest Missouri."

[2] In the first edition of the memoirs (1875), this portion WTS's text read, "Fort Donelson surrendered . . ."

miles above Donelson, toward Nashville, and on the 27th went himself to Nashville to meet and confer with General Buell, but returned to Donelson the next day.

Meantime, General Halleck at St. Louis must have felt that his armies were getting away from him, and began to send dispatches to me at Paducah, to be forwarded by boat, or by a rickety telegraph-line up to Fort Henry, which lay entirely in a hostile country, and was consequently always out of repair. On the 1st of March I received the following dispatch, and forwarded it to General Grant, both by the telegraph and boat:

St. Louis, *March* 1, 1862.

To General Grant, *Fort Henry:*

Transports will be sent you as soon as possible, to move your column up the Tennessee River. The main object of this expedition will be to destroy the railroad-bridge over Bear Creek, near Eastport, Mississippi; and also the railroad connections at Corinth, Jackson, and Humboldt. It is thought best that these objects be attempted in the order named. Strong detachments of cavalry and light artillery, supported by infantry, may by rapid movements reach these points from the river, without any serious opposition.

Avoid any general engagements with strong forces. It will be better to retreat than to risk a general battle. This should be strongly impressed on the officers sent with expeditions from the river. General C. F. Smith or some very discreet officer should be selected for such commands. Having accomplished these objects, or such of them as may be practicable, you will return to Danville, and move on Paris.

Perhaps the troops sent to Jackson and Humboldt can reach Paris by land as easily as to return to the transports. This must depend on the character of the roads and the position of the enemy. All telegraphic lines which can be reached must be cut. The gunboats will accompany the transports for their protection. Any loyal Tennesseeans who desire it, may be enlisted and supplied with arms. Competent officers should be left to command Forts Henry and Donelson in your absence. I have indicated in general terms the object of this.

H. W. Halleck, *Major-General.*

Again on the 2d:

CAIRO, *March* 2, 1862.

To General GRANT:

General Halleck, February 25th, telegraphs me: "General Grant will send no more forces to Clarksville. General Smith's division will come to Fort Henry, or a point higher up on the Tennessee River; transports will also be collected at Paducah. Two gunboats in Tennessee River with Grant. General Grant will immediately have small garrisons detailed for Forts Henry and Donelson, and all other forces made ready for the field."

From your letter of the 28th, I learn you were at Fort Donelson, and General Smith at Nashville, from which I infer you could not have received orders. Halleck's telegram of last night says: "Who sent Smith's division to Nashville? I ordered it across to the Tennessee, where they are wanted immediately. Order them back. Send all spare transports up Tennessee to General Grant." Evidently the general supposes you to be on the Tennessee. I am sending all the transports I can find for you, reporting to General Sherman for orders to go up the Cumberland for you, or, if you march across to Fort Henry, then to send them up the Tennessee.

G. W. CULLUM,[3] *Brigadier-General.*

On the 4th came this dispatch:

ST. LOUIS, *March* 4, 1862.

To Major-General U. S. GRANT:

You will place Major-General C. F. Smith in command of expedition, and remain yourself at Fort Henry. Why do you not obey my orders to report strength and positions of your command?

H. W. HALLECK, *Major-General.*

Halleck was evidently working himself into a passion, but he was too far from the seat of war to make due allowance for the actual state of facts. General Grant had done so much, that General Halleck should have been patient.

[3] In the first edition of the memoirs (1875), this portion WTS's text incorrectly identified him as "J. W. Cullum."

Meantime, at Paducah, I was busy sending boats in every direction—some under the orders of General Halleck, others of General Cullum; others for General Grant, and still others for General Buell at Nashville; and at the same time I was organizing out of the new troops that were arriving at Paducah a division for myself when allowed to take the field, which I had been promised by General Halleck.[4] His purpose was evidently to operate up the Tennessee River, to break up Bear Creek Bridge and the railroad communications between the Mississippi and Tennessee Rivers, and no doubt he was provoked that Generals Grant and Smith had turned aside to Nashville. In the mean time several of the gunboats, under Captain Phelps, United States Navy,[5] had gone up the Tennessee as far as Florence, and on their return had reported a strong Union feeling among the people along the river. On the 10th of March, having received the necessary orders from General Halleck, I embarked my division at Paducah. It was composed of four brigades. The First, commanded by Colonel S. G. Hicks,[6] was composed of the Fortieth Illinois, Forty-sixth Ohio, and Morton's Indiana Battery, on the boats Sallie List, Golden Gate, J. B. Adams, and Lancaster.

The Second Brigade, Colonel D. Stuart, was composed of the Fifty-fifth Illinois, Seventy-first Ohio, and Fifty-fourth Ohio; embarked on the Hannibal, Universe, Hazel Dell, Cheeseman, and Prairie Rose.

The Third Brigade, Colonel Hildebrand,[7] was composed of the Seventy-seventh Ohio, Fifty-seventh Ohio, and Fifty-third Ohio; embarked on the Poland, Anglo-Saxon, Ohio No. Three, and Continental.

[4] WTS took command of the 5th Div., Army of the Tennessee, on Mar. 1, 1862. *CWHC,* 485.

[5] Seth L. Phelps (1824–1885), a close friend of WTS, became a midshipman in the U.S. Navy in 1841 and served in the Mexican-American War. He was promoted to lieutenant commander on July 16, 1862. Jay Slagle, *Ironclad Captain: Seth Ledyard Phelps and the U.S. Navy, 1841–1864* (Kent, OH: Kent State University Press, 1996), 8, 69, 340, 395; Myron J. Smith Jr., *Civil War Biographies from the Western Waters* (Jefferson, NC: McFarland, 2015), s.v. "Phelps, Seth."

[6] Stephen G. Hicks (1809–1869) served in the Mexican-American War and was wounded at the Battle of Shiloh in Apr. 1862. William H. Perrin, ed., *History of Jefferson County, Illinois* (Chicago: Globe, 1883), 249–250.

[7] Jesse Hildebrand (1800–1863) joined the U.S. Volunteers as a colonel in Oct. 1861 and died from sickness on Apr. 18, 1863. WTS said of Hildebrand, "He is the bravest man I ever knew." Gibson L. Cranmer, ed., *History of the Upper Ohio Valley with Family History and Biographical Sketches* (Madison, WI: Brant and Fuller, 1891), 109–110.

The Fourth Brigade, Colonel Buckland,[8] was composed of the Seventy-second Ohio, Forty-eighth Ohio, and Seventieth Ohio; embarked on the Empress, Baltic, Shenango, and Marengo.

We steamed up to Fort Henry, the river being high and in splendid order. There I reported in person to General C. F. Smith, and by him was ordered a few miles above, to the remains of the burned railroad bridge, to await the rendezvous of the rest of his army. I had my headquarters on the Continental.

Among my colonels I had a strange character—Thomas Worthington, colonel of the Forty-sixth Ohio. He was a graduate of West Point, of the class of 1827; was, therefore, older than General Halleck, General Grant, or myself, and claimed to know more of war than all of us put together. In ascending the river he did not keep his place in the column, but pushed on and reached Savannah a day before the rest of my division. When I reached that place, I found that Worthington had landed his regiment, and was flying about giving orders, as though he were commander-in-chief. I made him get back to his boat, and gave him to understand that he must thereafter keep his place.[9] General C. F. Smith arrived about the 13th of March, with a large fleet of boats, containing Hurlbut's division, Lew. Wallace's division, and that of himself, then commanded by Brigadier-General W. H. L. Wallace.[10]

General Smith sent for me to meet him on his boat, and ordered me to push on under escort of the two gunboats, Lexington and Tyler, commanded by Captains Gwin[11] and Shirk,[12] United States Navy. I was to land at some

[8] Ralph P. Buckland (1812–1892) was the mayor of Fremont, OH, before he joined the U.S. Volunteers as a colonel in Jan. 1862. *CWHC,* 151.

[9] Thomas Worthington Jr. (1807–1884), a veteran of the Mexican-American War, was promoted to colonel of the 46th Ohio Volunteers on Jan. 30, 1862. Later that year, WTS court-martialed him for drunkenness and "conduct unbecoming an officer and a gentleman" after he publicly criticized WTS and other officers for their actions during the Battle of Shiloh. Worthington was tried and convicted. A few years later, however, Pres. Andrew Johnson reviewed the case and granted him an honorable discharge. *USMA,* 1:392–393; James L. McDonough, *William Tecumseh Sherman: In the Service of My Country* (New York: W. W. Norton, 2016), 380.

[10] Lewis Wallace (1827–1905), an Indiana legislator, was in command of the 3rd Div., Army of the Tennessee, in Mar. 1862. William H. L. Wallace (1821–1862), a lawyer, took command of the 2nd Div., Army of the Tennessee, on Apr. 2, 1862. *CWHC,* 551–552.

[11] William Gwin (1832–1863) was appointed midshipman in the U.S. Navy in 1847. Spencer Tucker, ed., *Civil War Naval Encyclopedia* (Santa Barbara: ABC-CLIO, 2011), s.v. "Gwin, William."

[12] James W. Shirk (1832–1873) was appointed midshipman in the U.S. Navy in 1849. Tucker, *Civil War Naval Encyclopedia,* s.v. "Shirk, James W."

point below Eastport, and make a break of the Memphis & Charleston Railroad, between Tuscumbia and Corinth. General Smith was quite unwell, and was suffering from his leg, which was swollen and very sore, from a mere abrasion in stepping into a small boat. This actually mortified, and resulted in his death about a month after, viz., April 25, 1862. He was adjutant of the Military Academy during the early part of my career there, and afterward commandant of cadets. He was a very handsome and soldierly man, of great experience, and at Donelson had acted with so much personal bravery that to him many attributed the success of the assault. I immediately steamed up the Tennessee River, following the two gunboats, and, in passing Pittsburg Landing, was told by Captain Gwin that, on his former trip up the river, he had found a rebel regiment of cavalry posted there, and that it was the usual landing-place for the people about Corinth, distant thirty miles. I sent word back to General Smith that, if we were detained up the river, he ought to post some troops at Pittsburg Landing. We went on up the river cautiously, till we saw Eastport and Chickasaw,[13] both of which were occupied by rebel batteries and a small rebel force of infantry.

We then dropped back quietly to the mouth of Yellow River, a few miles below, whence led a road to Burnsville, a place on the Memphis & Charleston road, where were the company's repair-shops. We at once commenced disembarking the command: first the cavalry, which started at once for Burnsville, with orders to tear up the railroad-track, and burn the depots, shops, etc; and I followed with the infantry and artillery as fast as they were disembarked. It was raining very hard at the time. Daylight found us about six miles out, where we met the cavalry returning. They had made numerous attempts to cross the streams, which had become so swollen that mere brooks covered the whole bottom; and my aide-de-camp, Sanger,[14] whom I had dispatched with the cavalry, reported the loss, by drowning, of several of the men.[15] The rain was pouring in torrents, and reports from the rear came that the river was rising very fast, and that, unless we got back to our boats soon, the bottom would be simply impassable. There was no alternative but to regain our boats; and even

[13] Chickasaw, AL, was located one mile east of Eastport, MS, right across the state line. George B. Davis et al., *Official Military Atlas of the Civil War* (New York: Fairfax Press, 1983), plate 149.

[14] William D. Sanger (c. 1831–1873) attended the USMA from 1848 to 1851 but did not graduate. He was promoted to lieutenant colonel in Feb. 1862. *The Story of the Fifty-Fifth Regiment, Illinois Volunteer Infantry in the Civil War, 1861–1865* (Clinton: W. J. Coulter, 1887), 213–214.

[15] For WTS's report on the incident, see *OR*, I, 10(I), 22–23.

this was so difficult, that we had to unharness the artillery-horses, and drag the guns under water through the bayous, to reach the bank of the river. Once more embarked, I concluded to drop down to Pittsburg Landing, and to make the attempt from there. During the night of the 14th, we dropped down to Pittsburg Landing, where I found Hurlbut's division in boats. Leaving my command there, I steamed down to Savannah, and reported to General Smith in person, who saw in the flooded Tennessee the full truth of my report; and he then instructed me to disembark my own division, and that of General Hurlbut, at Pittsburg Landing; to take positions well back, and to leave room for his whole army; telling me that he would soon come up in person, and move out in force to make the lodgment on the railroad, contemplated by General Halleck's orders.

Lieutenant-Colonel McPherson, of General C. F. Smith's, or rather General Halleck's, staff, returned with me, and on the 16th of March we disembarked and marched out about ten miles toward Corinth, to a place called Monterey or Pea Ridge, where the rebels had a cavalry regiment, which of course decamped on our approach, but from the people we learned that trains were bringing large masses of men from every direction into Corinth. McPherson and I reconnoitred the ground well, and then returned to our boats. On the 18th, Hurlbut disembarked his division and took post about a mile and a half out, near where the roads branched, one leading to Corinth and the other toward Hamburg. On the 19th I disembarked my division, and took post about three miles back, three of the brigades covering the roads to Purdy and Corinth, and the other brigade (Stuart's) temporarily at a place on the Hamburg Road, near Lick Creek Ford, where the Bark Road came into the Hamburg Road.[16] Within a few days, Prentiss's[17] division arrived and camped on my left, and afterward McClernand's[18] and W. H. L. Wallace's divisions, which formed a line to our rear. Lew Wallace's division remained on the north side of Snake Creek, on a road leading from Savannah or Crump's Landing to Purdy.

General C. F. Smith remained back at Savannah, in chief command, and I was only responsible for my own division. I kept pickets well out on the

[16] For a detailed map of troop placements before the Battle of Shiloh, see Davis et al., *Official Military Atlas of the Civil War,* plate 12, map 4.

[17] Benjamin M. Prentiss (1819–1901), a lawyer, joined the U.S. Army as a colonel in Apr. 1861. He commanded the 6th Div., Army of the Tennessee. *CWHC,* 438.

[18] John A. McClernand (1812–1900) was a U.S. congressman from Illinois who joined the U.S. Army as a brigadier general in May 1861. He commanded the 1st Div., Army of the Tennessee. *CWHC,* 372.

roads, and made myself familiar with all the ground inside and outside my lines. My personal staff was composed of Captain J. H. Hammond, assistant adjutant-general; Surgeons Hartshorn and L'Hommedieu; Lieutenant Colonels Hascall and Sanger, inspector-generals; Lieutenants McCoy and John Taylor, aides-de-camp.[19] We were all conscious that the enemy was collecting at Corinth, but in what force we could not know, nor did we know what was going on behind us. On the 17th of March, General U. S. Grant was restored to the command of all the troops up the Tennessee River, by reason of General Smith's extreme illness, and because he had explained to General Halleck satisfactorily his conduct after Donelson; and he too made his headquarters at Savannah, but frequently visited our camps. I always acted on the supposition that we were an invading army; that our purpose was to move forward in force, make a lodgment on the Memphis & Charleston road,[20] and thus repeat the grand tactics of Fort Donelson, by separating the rebels in the interior from those at Memphis and on the Mississippi River. We did not fortify our camps against an attack, because we had no orders to do so, and because such a course would have made our raw men timid.[21] The position was naturally strong, with Snake Creek on our right, a deep, bold stream, with a confluent

[19] John H. Hammond (1833–1890) joined the U.S. Army as an assistant adjutant general in Nov. 1861. Dana W. Hartsthorn (1827–1907) graduated from Harvard Medical School in 1856 and served as a surgeon throughout the war. Stephen S. L'Hommedieu (1841–1883) dropped out of the Kentucky Military Institute then joined the 1st Ohio Volunteer Cav. in Aug. 1861. Milo S. Hascall (1829–1904) graduated from the USMA in 1852 and commanded the 15th Brig., 6th Div., Army of the Ohio. James C. McCoy (1828–1875) remained WTS's aide-de-camp until his death on May 29, 1875. John Taylor (1841–1926) was the oldest surviving member of WTS's staff. Mark A. Brown and A. G. Kreidler, eds., "Items of Interest to Physicians," *Lancet-Clinic* (Jan.–June 1907), 58:641; *USMA,* 2:482, 5:76; *CWHC,* 277, 285–286; William T. Sherman, *Home Letters of General Sherman,* ed. M. A. DeWolfe Howe (New York: Charles Scribner's Sons, 1909), 220*n;* T. B. Marshall, *History of the Eighty-Third Ohio Volunteer Infantry: The Greyhound Regiment* (Cincinnati: Eighty-Third Ohio Volunteer Infantry Association, 1912), 30; H. F. Staples, ed., *Proceedings of the Forty-Fourth Annual Session of the Homeopathic Medical Society of the State of Ohio* (Cleveland: Publication Committee, 1908), 41; *85th Anniversary Membership Registry and Roster of All Members of the Kansas Society of the National Society, Sons of the American Revolution, from 1892 to 1977* (Topeka: Sons of the American Revolution, 1977), 32.

[20] The Memphis & Charleston Railroad ran from Memphis to Chattanooga, TN, and passed through Corinth, MS. Davis et al., *Official Military Atlas of the Civil War,* plate 149, 154.

[21] For USG's account on the decision to not dig in defensively at Shiloh, see Ulysses S. Grant, *The Personal Memoirs of Ulysses S. Grant: The Complete Annotated Edition,* ed. John F.

(Owl Creek) to our right front; and Lick Creek, with a similar confluent, on our left, thus narrowing the space over which we could be attacked to about a mile and a half or two miles.

At a later period of the war, we could have rendered this position impregnable in one night, but at this time we did not do it, and it may be it is well we did not. From about the 1st of April we were conscious that the rebel cavalry in our front was getting bolder and more saucy; and on Friday, the 4th of April, it dashed down and carried off one of our picket-guards, composed of an officer and seven men, posted a couple of miles out on the Corinth road. Colonel Buckland sent a company to its relief, then followed himself with a regiment, and, fearing lest he might be worsted, I called out his whole brigade and followed some four or five miles, when the cavalry in advance encountered artillery. I then, after dark, drew back to our lines, and reported the fact by letter to General Grant, at Savannah;[22] but thus far we had not positively detected the presence of infantry, for cavalry regiments generally had a couple of guns along, and I supposed the guns that opened on us on the evening of Friday, April 4th, belonged to the cavalry that was hovering along our whole front.

Saturday passed in our camps without any unusual event, the weather being wet and mild, and the roads back to the steamboat—landing being heavy with mud; but on Sunday morning, the 6th, early, there was a good deal of picket-firing, and I got breakfast, rode out along my lines, and, about four hundred yards to the front of Appler's regiment,[23] received from some bushes in a ravine to the left front a volley which killed my orderly, Holliday.[24] About the same time I saw the rebel lines of battle in front coming down on us as far as the eye could reach. All my troops were in line of battle, ready, and the ground was favorable to us. I gave the necessary orders to the battery (Waterhouse's)[25] attached to Hildebrand's brigade, and cautioned the men to reserve

---

Marszalek, David S. Nolen, and Louie P. Gallo (Cambridge, MA: Belknap Press of Harvard University Press, 2017), 244.

[22] For WTS's Apr. 5 letter to USG, see *OR*, I, 10(II), 93.

[23] Jesse J. Appler commanded the 53rd Ohio Inf. in Apr. 1861. Nelson W. Evans, *A History of Scioto County, Ohio, Together with a Pioneer Record of Southern Ohio* (self-pub., 1903), 221, 226.

[24] Thomas D. Holliday commanded Co. H in the 2nd Illinois Cav. *OR*, I, 10(I), 249.

[25] Allen C. Waterhouse (1832–1912) commanded Battery E of the 1st Illinois Light Art. "Col. Waterhouse Dies in Chicago," *Herald and Review* (Decatur, IL), May 12, 1912, 2; Winston Groom, *Shiloh, 1862* (Washington, DC: National Geographic, 2012), 422.

their fire till the rebels had crossed the ravine of Owl Creek, and had begun the ascent; also, sent staff-officers to notify Generals McClernand and Prentiss of the coming blow. Indeed, McClernand had already sent three regiments to the support of my left flank, and they were in position when the onset came.

In a few minutes the battle of "Shiloh" began with extreme fury, and lasted two days. Its history has been well given, and it has been made the subject of a great deal of controversy. Hildebrand's brigade was soon knocked to pieces, but Buckland's and McDowell's[26] kept their organization throughout. Stuart's was driven back to the river, and did not join me in person till the second day of the battle. I think my several reports of that battle are condensed and good, made on the spot, when all the names and facts were fresh in my memory, and are herewith given entire:

HEADQUARTERS FIRST DIVISION,
PITTSBURG LANDING, *March* 17, 1862.

Captain WM. MCMICHAEL, *Assistant Adjutant-General to General* C. F. SMITH, *Savannah, Tennessee.*

SIR: Last night I dispatched a party of cavalry, at 6 P. M., under the command of Lieutenant-Colonel Heath, Fifth Ohio Cavalry, for a strong reconnoissance, if possible, to be converted into an attack upon the Memphis road. The command got off punctually, followed at twelve o'clock at night by the First Brigade of my division, commanded by Colonel McDowell, the other brigades to follow in order.

About one at night the cavalry returned, reporting the road occupied in force by the enemy, with whose advance-guard they skirmished, driving them back about a mile, taking two prisoners, and having their chief guide, Thomas Maxwell, Esq., and three men of the Fourth Illinois wounded.

Inclosed please find the report of Lieutenant-Colonel Heath; also a copy of his instructions, and the order of march. As soon as the cavalry returned, I saw that an attempt on the road was frustrated, and accordingly have placed McDowell's brigade to our right front, guarding the pass of Snake Creek; Stuart's brigade to the left front, to

[26] John A. McDowell (1825–1887) commanded the 2nd Brig., 5th Div., Army of the Tennessee. Roger D. Hunt, *Colonels in Blue: Illinois, Iowa, Minnesota and Wisconsin* (Jefferson, NC: McFarland, 2017), s.v. "John Adair McDowell."

watch the pass of Lick Creek; and I shall this morning move directly out on the Corinth road, about eight miles to or toward Pea Ridge, which is a key-point to the southwest.

General Hurlbut's division will be landed to-day, and the artillery and infantry disposed so as to defend Pittsburg, leaving my division entire for any movement by land or water.

As near as I can learn, there are five regiments of rebel infantry at Purdy; at Corinth, and distributed along the railroad to Iuca, are probably thirty thousand men; but my information from prisoners is very indistinct. Every road and path is occupied by the enemy's cavalry, whose orders seem to be, to fire a volley, retire, again fire and retire. The force on the Purdy road attacked and driven by Major Bowman yesterday, was about sixty strong. That encountered last night on the Corinth road was about five companies of Tennessee cavalry, sent from Purdy about 2 P. M. yesterday.

I hear there is a force of two regiments on Pea Ridge, at the point where the Purdy and Corinth roads come together.

I am satisfied we cannot reach the Memphis & Charleston road without a considerable engagement, which is prohibited by General Halleck's instructions, so that I will be governed by your orders of yesterday, to occupy Pittsburg strongly, extend the pickets so as to include a semicircle of three miles, and push a strong reconnoissance as far out as Lick Creek and Pea Ridge.

I will send down a good many boats to-day, to be employed as you may direct; and would be obliged if you would send a couple of thousand sacks of corn, as much hay as you can possibly spare, and, if possible, a barge of coal.

I will send a steamboat under care of the gunboat, to collect corn from cribs on the river-bank.

I have the honor to be your obedient servant,

W. T. SHERMAN,
Brigadier-General, commanding First Division.

HEADQUARTERS, STEAMBOAT CONTINENTAL,
PITTSBURG, *March* 18, 1862.

Captain RAWLINS, *Assistant Adjutant-General to General* GRANT.

SIR: The division surgeon having placed some one hundred or more sick on board the Fanny Bullitt, I have permitted her to take them to

Savannah. There is neither house nor building of any kind that can be used for a hospital here.

I hope to receive an order to establish floating hospitals, but in the mean time, by the advice of the surgeon, allow these sick men to leave. Let me hope that it will meet your approbation.

The order for debarkation came while General Sherman was absent with three brigades, and no men are left to move the effects of these brigades.

The landing, too, is small, with scarcely any chance to increase it; therefore there is a great accumulation of boats. Colonel McArthur has arrived, and is now cutting a landing for himself.

General Sherman will return this evening. I am obliged to transgress, and write myself in the mean time,

Respectfully your obedient servant,

J. H. HAMMOND, *Assistant Adjutant-General.*

P. S—4 P. M.—Just back; have been half-way to Corinth and to Purdy. All right. Have just read this letter, and approve all but floating hospitals; regimental surgeons can take care of all sick, except chronic cases, which can always be sent down to Paducah.

Magnificent plain for camping and drilling, and a military point of great strength. The enemy has felt us twice, at great loss and demoralization; will report at length this evening; am now much worn out.

W. T. SHERMAN, *Brigadier-General.*

HEADQUARTERS FIRST DIVISION,
PITTSBURG LANDING, *March* 19, 1862.

Captain RAWLINS, *Assistant Adjutant-General to General* GRANT, *Savannah, Tennessee.*

SIR: I have just returned from an extensive reconnoissance toward Corinth and Purdy, and am strongly impressed with the importance of this position, both for its land advantages and its strategic position. The ground itself admits of easy defense by a small command, and yet affords admirable camping-ground for a hundred thousand men. I will as soon as possible make or cause to be made a topographical sketch of the position. The only drawback is that, at this stage of water, the space for landing is contracted too much for the immense fleet now here discharging.

I will push the loading and unloading of boats, but suggest that you send at once (Captain Dodd, if possible) the best quartermaster you can, that he may control and organize this whole matter. I have a good commissary, and will keep as few provisions afloat as possible.

Yours, etc.,

W. T. Sherman, *Brigadier-General commanding.*

Headquarters Sherman's Division,
Camp Shiloh, near Pittsburg Landing, Tennessee, *April* 2, 1862.

Captain J. A. Rawlins, *Assistant Adjutant-General to General* Grant.

Sir: In obedience to General Grant's instructions of March 31st, with one section of Captain Muench's Minnesota Battery, two twelve-pound howitzers, a detachment of Fifth Ohio Cavalry of one hundred and fifty men, under Major Ricker, and two battalions of infantry from the Fifty-seventh and Seventy-seventh Ohio, under the command of Colonels Hildebrand and Mungen, I marched to the river, and embarked on the steamers Empress and Tecumseh. The gunboat Cairo did not arrive at Pittsburg, until after midnight, and at 6 A. M. Captain Bryant, commanding the gunboat, notified me that he was ready to proceed up the river. I followed, keeping the transports within about three hundred yards of the gunboat. About 1 P. M., the Cairo commenced shelling the battery above the mouth of Indian Creek, but elicited no reply. She proceeded up the river steadily and cautiously, followed close by the Tyler and Lexington, all throwing shells at the points where, on former visits of the gunboats, enemy's batteries were found. In this order all followed, till it was demonstrated that all the enemy's batteries, including that at Chickasaw, were abandoned.

I ordered the battalion of infantry under Colonel Hildebrand to disembark at Eastport, and with the other battalion proceeded to Chickasaw and landed. The battery at this point had evidently been abandoned some time, and consisted of the remains of an old Indian mound, partly washed away by the river, which had been fashioned into a two-gun battery, with a small magazine. The ground to its rear had evidently been overflowed during the late freshet, and led to the removal of the guns to Eastport, where the batteries were on high, elevated ground, accessible at all seasons from the country to the rear.

Upon personal inspection, I attach little importance to Chickasaw as a military position. The people, who had fled during the approach of the gunboats, returned to the village, and said the place had been occupied by one Tennessee regiment and a battery of artillery from Pensacola. After remaining at Chickasaw some hours, all the boats dropped back to Eastport, not more than a mile below, and landed there. Eastport Landing during the late freshet must have been about twelve feet under water, but at the present stage the landing is the best I have seen on the Tennessee River.

The levee is clear of trees or snags, and a hundred boats could land there without confusion.

The soil is of sand and gravel, and very firm. The road back is hard, and at a distance of about four hundred yards from the water begin the gravel hills of the country. The infantry scouts sent out by Colonel Hildebrand found the enemy's cavalry mounted, and watching the Iuca road, about two miles back of Eastport. The distance to Iuca is only eight miles, and Iuca is the nearest point and has the best road by which the Charleston & Memphis Railroad can be reached. I could obtain no certain information as to the strength of the enemy there, but am satisfied that it would have been folly to have attempted it with my command. Our object being to dislodge the enemy from the batteries recently erected near Eastport, and this being attained, I have returned, and report the river to be clear to and beyond Chickasaw.

I have the honor to be, your obedient servant,

W. T. SHERMAN,
Brigadier-General commanding Division.

HEADQUARTERS FIFTH DIVISION,
CAMP SHILOH, *April* 5, 1862.

Captain J. A. RAWLINS, *Assistant Adjutant-General, District of Western Tennessee.*

SIR: I have the honor to report that yesterday, about 3 P. M., the lieutenant commanding and seven men of the advance pickets imprudently advanced from their posts and were captured. I ordered Major Ricker, of the Fifth Ohio Cavalry, to proceed rapidly to the picket-station, ascertain the truth, and act according to circumstances. He reached the station, found the pickets had been captured as reported, and that a company of infantry sent by the brigade commander had gone forward in pursuit of some cavalry. He rapidly advanced some two miles, and found them engaged, charged the enemy, and drove them along the Ridge road, till he met and received three discharges of artillery, when he very properly wheeled under cover, and returned till he met me.

As soon as I heard artillery, I advanced with two regiments of infantry, and took position, and remained until the scattered companies of infantry and cavalry had returned. This was after night.

I infer that the enemy is in some considerable force at Pea Ridge, that yesterday morning they crossed a brigade of two regiments of infantry, one regiment of cavalry, and one battery of field-artillery, to the ridge on which the Corinth road lies. They halted the infantry and artillery at a point about five miles in my front, sent a detachment to the lane of General Meaks, on the north of Owl Creek, and the cavalry down toward our camp. This cavalry captured a part of our advance pickets, and afterward engaged the two companies of Colonel Buckland's regiment, as described by him in his report herewith inclosed. Our cavalry drove them back upon their artillery and Infantry, killing many, and bringing off ten prisoners, all of the First Alabama Cavalry, whom I send to you.

We lost of the pickets one first-lieutenant and seven men of the Ohio Seventieth Infantry (list inclosed); one major, one lieutenant, and one private of the Seventy-second Ohio, taken prisoners; eight privates wounded (names in full, embraced in report of Colonel Buckland, inclosed herewith).

We took ten prisoners, and left two rebels wounded and many killed on the field.

I have the honor to be, your obedient servant,

W. T. SHERMAN,
Brigadier-General, commanding Division.

HEADQUARTERS FIFTH DIVISION,
CAMP SHILOH, *April* 10, 1862.

Captain J. A. RAWLINS, *Assistant Adjutant-General to General* GRANT.

SIR: I had the honor to report that, on Friday the 4th inst., the enemy's cavalry drove in our pickets, posted about a mile and a half in advance of my centre, on the main Corinth road, capturing one first-lieutenant and seven men; that I caused a pursuit by the cavalry of my division, driving them back about five miles, and killing many. On Saturday the enemy's cavalry was again very bold, coming well down to our front; yet I did not believe they designed any thing but a strong demonstration. On Sunday morning early, the 6th inst., the enemy drove our advance-guard back on the main body, when I ordered under arms all my division, and sent word to General McClernand, asking him to support my left; to General Prentiss, giving him notice that the enemy was in our front in force, and to General Hurlbut, asking him to support General Prentiss. At that time—7 A. M.—my division was arranged as follows:

First Brigade, composed of the Sixth Iowa, Colonel J. A. McDowell; Fortieth Illinois, Colonel Hicks; Forty-sixth Ohio, Colonel Worthington; and the Morton battery, Captain Behr, on the extreme right, guarding the bridge on the Purdy road over Owl Creek.

Second Brigade, composed of the Fifty-fifth Illinois, Colonel D. Stuart; the Fifty-fourth Ohio, Colonel T. Kilby Smith; and the Seventy-first Ohio, Colonel Mason, on the extreme left, guarding the ford over Lick Creek.

Third Brigade, composed of the Seventy-seventh Ohio, Colonel Hildebrand; the Fifty-third Ohio, Colonel Appler; and the Fifty-seventh Ohio, Colonel Mungen, on the left of the Corinth road, its right resting on Shiloh meeting-house.

Fourth Brigade, composed of the Seventy-second Ohio, Colonel Buckland; the Forty-eighth Ohio, Colonel Sullivan; and the Seventieth Ohio, Colonel Cockerill, on the right of the Corinth road, its left resting on Shiloh meeting-house.

Two batteries of artillery—Taylor's and Waterhouse's—were posted, the former at Shiloh, and the latter on a ridge to the left, with a front-fire over open ground between Mungen's and Appler's regiments. The cavalry, eight companies of the Fourth Illinois, under Colonel Dickey, were posted in a large open field to the left and rear of Shiloh meeting-house, which I regarded as the centre of my position.

Shortly after 7 A. M., with my entire staff, I rode along a portion of our front, and when in the open field before Appler's regiment, the enemy's pickets opened a brisk fire upon my party, killing my orderly, Thomas D. Holliday, of Company H, Second Illinois Cavalry. The fire came from the bushes which line a small stream that rises in the field in front of Appler's camp, and flows to the north along my whole front.

This valley afforded the enemy partial cover; but our men were so posted as to have a good fire at them as they crossed the valley and ascended the rising ground on our side.

About 8 A. M. I saw the glistening bayonets of heavy masses of infantry to our left front in the woods beyond the small stream alluded to, and became satisfied for the first time that the enemy designed a determined attack on our whole camp.

All the regiments of my division were then in line of battle at their proper posts. I rode to Colonel Appler, and ordered him to hold his ground at all hazards, as he held the left flank of our first line of battle, and I informed him that he had a good battery on his right, and strong support to his rear. General McClernand had promptly and energetically responded to my request, and had sent me three regiments which were posted to protect Waterhouse's battery and the left flank of my line.

The battle opened by the enemy's battery, in the woods to our front, throwing shells into our camp. Taylor's and Waterhouse's batteries promptly responded, and I then observed heavy battalions of infantry passing obliquely to the left, across the open field in Appler's front; also, other columns advancing directly upon my division. Our infantry and artillery opened along the whole line, and the battle became general. Other heavy masses of the enemy's forces kept passing across the field to our left, and directing their course on General Prentiss. I saw at once that the enemy designed to pass my left flank, and fall upon Generals McClernand and Prentiss, whose line of camps was almost parallel with the Tennessee River, and about two miles back from it. Very soon the sound of artillery and musketry announced that General Prentiss was engaged; and about 9 A. M. I judged that he was falling back. About this time Appler's regiment broke in disorder, followed by Mungen's regiment, and the enemy pressed forward on Waterhouse's battery thereby exposed.

The three Illinois regiments in immediate support of this battery stood for some time; but the enemy's advance was so vigorous, and the fire so severe, that when Colonel Raith, of the Forty-third Illinois, received a severe wound and fell from his horse, his regiment and the others manifested disorder, and the enemy got possession of three guns of this (Waterhouse's) battery. Although our left was thus turned, and the enemy was pressing our whole line, I deemed Shiloh so important, that I remained by it and renewed my orders to Colonels McDowell and Buckland to hold their ground; and we did hold these positions until about 10 A. M., when the enemy had got his artillery to the rear of our left flank and some change became absolutely necessary. Two regiments of Hildebrand's brigade—Appler's and Mungen's—had already disappeared to the rear, and Hildebrand's own regiment was in disorder. I therefore gave orders for Taylor's battery—still at Shiloh—to fall back as far as the Purdy and Hamburg road, and for McDowell and Buckland to adopt that road as their new line. I rode across the angle and met Behr's battery at the cross-roads, and ordered it immediately to come into battery, action right. Captain Behr gave the order, but he was almost immediately shot from his horse, when drivers and gunners fled in disorder, carrying off the caissons, and abandoning five out of six guns, without firing a shot. The enemy pressed on, gaining this battery, and we were again forced to choose a new line of defense. Hildebrand's brigade had substantially disappeared from the field, though he himself bravely remained. McDowell's and Buckland's brigades maintained their organizations, and were conducted by my aides, so as to join on General McClernand's right, thus abandoning my original camps and line. This was about 10 ½ A. M., at which time the enemy had made a furious attack on General McClernand's whole front. He struggled most determinedly, but, finding him pressed, I moved McDowell's brigade directly against the left flank of the enemy, forced him back some distance, and then directed the men to avail themselves of every cover-trees, fallen timber, and a wooded valley to our right. We held this position for four long hours, sometimes gaining and at others losing ground; General McClernand and myself acting in perfect concert, and struggling to maintain this line. While we were so hard pressed, two Iowa regiments approached from the rear, but could not be brought up to the severe fire that was raging in our front, and General Grant, who visited us on that ground, will remember our situation about 3 P. M.; but about 4 P. M. it was evident that Hurlbut's line had been driven back to the river; and knowing that General Lew Wallace was coming with reënforcements from Crump's Landing, General McClernand and I, on consultation, selected a new line of defense, with its right covering a bridge by which General Wallace had to approach. We fell back as well as we could, gathering in addition to our own such scattered forces as we could find, and formed the new line.

During this change the enemy's cavalry charged us, but were handsomely repulsed by the Twenty-ninth Illinois Regiment. The Fifth Ohio Battery, which had come up, rendered good service in holding the enemy in check for some time, and Major Taylor also came up with another battery and got into position, just in time to get a good flank-fire upon the enemy's column, as he pressed on General McClernand's right, checking his advance; when General McClernand's division made a fine charge on the enemy and drove him back into the ravines to our front and right. I had a clear field, about two hundred yards wide, in my immediate front, and contented myself with keeping the enemy's infantry at that distance during the rest of the day. In this position we rested for the night. My command had become decidedly of a mixed character. Buckland's brigade was the only one that retained its organization. Colonel Hildebrand was personally there, but his brigade was not. Colonel McDowell had been severely injured by a fall off his horse, and had gone to the river, and the three regiments of his brigade were not in line. The Thirteenth Missouri, Colonel Crafts J. Wright, had reported to me on the field, and fought well, retaining its regimental organization; and it formed a part of my line during Sunday night and all Monday. Other fragments of regiments and companies had also fallen into my division, and acted with it during the remainder of the battle. Generals Grant and Buell visited me in our bivouac that evening, and from them I learned the situation of affairs on other parts of the field. General Wallace arrived from Crump's Landing shortly after dark, and formed his line to my right rear. It rained hard during the night, but our men were in good spirits, lay on their arms, being satisfied with such bread and meat as could be gathered at the neighboring camps, and determined to redeem on Monday the losses of Sunday.

At daylight of Monday I received General Grant's orders to advance and recapture our original camps. I dispatched several members of my staff to bring up all the men they could find, especially the brigade of Colonel Stuart, which had been separated from the division all the day before; and at the appointed time the division, or rather what remained of it, with the Thirteenth Missouri and other fragments, moved forward and reoccupied the ground on the extreme right of General McClernand's camp, where we attracted the fire of a battery located near Colonel McDowell's former headquarters. Here I remained, patiently waiting for the sound of General Buell's advance upon the main Corinth road. About 10 A. M. the heavy firing in that direction, and its steady approach, satisfied me; and General Wallace being on our right flank with his well-conducted division, I led the head of my column to General McClernand's right, formed line of battle, facing south, with Buckland's brigade directly across the ridge, and Stuart's brigade on its right in the woods; and thus advanced, steadily and slowly, under a heavy fire of musketry and artillery. Taylor had just got to me from the rear, where he had gone for ammunition, and brought up three guns, which I ordered into position, to advance by hand firing. These guns belonged to Company A, Chicago Light Artillery, commanded by Lieutenant P. P. Wood, and did most excellent service. Under cover of their fire, we advanced till we reached the point where the Corinth road crosses the line of McClernand's camp, and here I saw for the first time the well-ordered and compact columns of General Buell's Kentucky forces, whose soldierly movements at once gave confidence to our newer and less disciplined men. Here I saw Willich's regiment advance upon a point of water-oaks and thicket, behind which I knew the enemy was in great strength, and enter it in beautiful style. Then arose the severest musketry-fire I ever heard, and lasted some twenty minutes, when this splendid regiment had to fall back. This green point of timber is about five hundred yards east of Shiloh meeting-house, and it was evident here was to be the struggle. The enemy could also be seen forming his lines to the south. General McClernand sending to me for artillery, I detached to him the three guns of Wood's battery, with which he speedily drove them back, and, seeing some others to the rear, I sent one of my staff to bring them forward, when, by almost providential decree, they proved to be two twenty-four-pound howitzers belonging to McAlister's battery, and served as well as guns ever could be.

This was about 2 P. M. The enemy had one battery close by Shiloh, and another near the Hamburg road, both pouring grape and canister upon any column of troops that advanced upon the green point of water-oaks. Willich's regiment had been repulsed, but a whole brigade of McCook's division advanced beautifully, deployed, and entered this dreaded wood. I ordered my second brigade (then commanded by Colonel T. Kilby Smith, Colonel Stuart being wounded) to form on its right, and my fourth brigade, Colonel Buckland, on its right; all to advance abreast with this Kentucky brigade before mentioned, which I afterward found to be Rousseau's brigade of McCook's division. I gave personal direction to the twenty-four-pounder guns, whose well-directed fire first silenced the enemy's guns to the left, and afterward at the Shiloh meeting-house.

Rousseau's brigade moved in splendid order steadily to the front, sweeping every thing before it, and at 4 P. M. we stood upon the ground of our original front line; and the enemy was in full retreat. I directed my several brigades to resume at once their original camps.

Several times during the battle, cartridges gave out; but General Grant had thoughtfully kept a supply coming from the rear. When I appealed to regiments to stand fast, although out of cartridges, I did so because, to retire a regiment for any cause, has a bad effect on others. I commend the Fortieth Illinois and Thirteenth Missouri for thus holding their ground under heavy fire, although their cartridge-boxes were empty.

I am ordered by General Grant to give personal credit where I think it is due, and censure where I think it merited. I concede that General McCook's splendid division from Kentucky drove back the enemy along the Corinth road, which was the great centre of this field of battle, where Beauregard commanded in person, supported by Bragg's, Polk's, and Breckenridge's divisions. I think Johnston was killed by exposing himself in front of his troops, at the time of their attack on Buckland's brigade on Sunday morning; although in this I may be mistaken.

My division was made up of regiments perfectly new, nearly all having received their muskets for the first time at Paducah. None of them had ever been under fire or beheld heavy columns of an enemy bearing down on them as they did on last Sunday.

To expect of them the coolness and steadiness of older troops would be wrong. They knew not the value of combination and organization. When individual fears seized them, the first impulse was to get away. My third brigade did break much too soon, and I am not yet advised where they were during Sunday afternoon and Monday morning. Colonel Hildebrand, its commander, was as cool as any man I ever saw, and no one could have made stronger efforts to hold his men to their places than he did. He kept his own regiment with individual exceptions in hand, an hour after Appler's and Mungen's regiments had left their proper field of action. Colonel Buckland managed his brigade well. I commend him to your notice as a cool, intelligent, and judicious gentleman, needing only confidence and experience to make a good commander. His subordinates, Colonels Sullivan and Cockerill, behaved with great gallantry; the former receiving a severe wound on Sunday, and yet commanding and holding his regiment well in hand all day, and on Monday, until his right arm was broken by a shot. Colonel Cockerill held a larger proportion of his men than any colonel in my division, and was with me from first to last.

Colonel J. A. McDowell, commanding the first brigade, held his ground on Sunday, till I ordered him to fall back, which he did in line of battle; and when ordered, he conducted the attack on the enemy's left in good style. In falling back to the next position, he was thrown from his horse and injured, and his brigade was not in position on Monday morning. His subordinates, Colonels Hicks and Worthington, displayed great personal courage. Colonel Hicks led his regiment in the attack on Sunday, and received a wound, which it is feared may prove mortal. He is a brave and gallant gentleman, and deserves well of his country. Lieutenant-Colonel Walcutt, of the Ohio Forty-sixth, was severely wounded on Sunday, and has been disabled ever since. My second brigade, Colonel Stuart, was detached nearly two miles from my headquarters. He had to fight his own battle on Sunday, against superior numbers, as the enemy interposed between him and General Prentiss early in the day. Colonel Stuart was wounded severely, and yet reported for duty on Monday morning, but was compelled to leave during the day, when the command devolved on Colonel T. Kilby Smith, who was always in the thickest of the fight, and led the brigade handsomely.

I have not yet received Colonel Stuart's report of the operations of his brigade during the time he was detached, and must therefore forbear to mention names. Lieutenant-Colonel Kyle, of the Seventy-first, was mortally wounded on Sunday, but the regiment itself I did not see, as only a small fragment of it was with the brigade when it joined the division on Monday morning. Great credit is due the fragments of men of the disordered regiments who kept in the advance. I observed and noticed them, but until the brigadiers and colonels make their reports, I cannot venture to name individuals, but will in due season notice all who kept in our front line, as well as those who preferred to keep back near the steamboat-landing. I will also send a full list of the killed, wounded, and missing, by name, rank, company, and regiment. At present I submit the result in figures:

The enemy captured seven of our guns on Sunday, but on Monday we recovered seven; not the identical guns we had lost, but enough in number to balance the account. At the time of recovering our camps our men were so fatigued that we could not follow the retreating masses of the enemy; but on the following day I followed up with Buckland's and Hildebrand's brigade for six miles, the result of which I have already reported.

REGIMENTS, ETC.	KILLED.		WOUNDED.		MISSING.	
	Officers.	Men.	Officers.	Men.	Officers.	Men.
Sixth Iowa	2	49	3	117	..	39
Fortieth Illinois	1	42	7	148	..	2
Forty-sixth Ohio	2	32	3	147	..	52
Fifty-fifth Illinois	1	45	8	183	..	41
Fifty-fourth Ohio	2	22	5	128	..	32
Seventy-first Ohio	1	12	..	52	1	45
Seventy-seventh Ohio	1	48	7	107	3	53
Fifty-seventh Ohio	2	7	..	82	..	33
Fifty-third Ohio	..	7	..	89	..	5
Seventy-second Ohio	2	13	5	85	..	49
Forty-eighth Ohio	1	13	3	70	1	45
Seventieth Ohio	..	9	1	53	1	39
Taylor's Battery, no report	..	..	..	..	..	..
Behr's	1	..	..	..	..	..
Barrett's	..	1	..	5	..	..
Waterhouse's	..	1	3	14	..	..
Orderly Holliday	..	1	..	..	..	..
Total	16	302	45	1,280	6	435

BATTLE OF SHILOH.
RECAPITULATION.

Officers killed	16
Officers wounded	45
Officers missing	6
Soldiers killed	302
Soldiers wounded	1,280
Soldiers missing	435
Aggregate loss in the division	2,084

Of my personal staff, I can only speak with praise and thanks. I think they smelled as much gunpowder and heard as many cannon-balls and bullets as must satisfy their ambition. Captain Hammond, my chief of staff, though in feeble health, was very active in rallying broken troops, encouraging the steadfast and aiding to form the lines of defense and attack. I recommend him to your notice. Major Sanger's intelligence, quick perception, and rapid execution, were of very great value to me, especially in bringing into line the batteries that coöperated so efficiently in our movements. Captains McCoy and Dayton, aides-de-camp, were with me all the time, carrying orders, and acting with coolness, spirit, and courage. To Surgeon Hartshorne and Dr. L'Hommedieu hundreds of wounded men are indebted for the kind and excellent treatment received on the field of battle and in the various temporary hospitals created along the line of our operations. They worked day and night, and did not rest till all the wounded of our own troops as well as of the enemy were in safe and comfortable shelter. To Major Taylor, chief of artillery, I feel under deep obligations, for his good sense and judgment in managing the batteries, on which so much depended. I inclose his report and indorse his recommendations. The cavalry of my command kept to the rear, and took little part in the action; but it would have been madness to have exposed horses to the musketry-fire under which we were compelled to remain from Sunday at 8 A. M. till Monday at 4 P. M.

Captain Kossack, of the engineers, was with me all the time, and was of great assistance. I inclose his sketch of the battle-field, which is the best I have seen, and which will enable you to see the various positions occupied by my division, as well as of the others that participated in the battle. I will also send in, during the day, the detailed reports of my brigadiers and colonels, and will indorse them with such remarks as I deem proper.

I am, with much respect, your obedient servant,

W. T. SHERMAN,
Brigadier-General commanding Fifth Division.

HEADQUARTERS FIFTH DIVISION,
Tuesday, April 8, 1862.

SIR: With the cavalry placed at my command and two brigades of my fatigued troops, I went this morning out on the Corinth road. One after another of the abandoned camps of the enemy lined the roads, with hospital-flags for their protection; at all we found more or less wounded and dead men. At the forks of the road I found the head of General T. J. Wood's division of Buell's Army. I ordered cavalry to examine both roads leading toward Corinth, and found the enemy on both. Colonel Dickey, of the Fourth Illinois Cavalry, asking for reënforcements, I ordered General Wood to advance the head of his column cautiously on the left-hand road, while I conducted the head of the third brigade of my division up the right-hand road. About half a mile from the forks was a clear field, through which the road passed, and, immediately beyond, a space of some two hundred yards of fallen timber, and beyond that an extensive rebel camp. The enemy's cavalry could be seen in this camp; after reconnoisance, I ordered the two advance companies of the Ohio Seventy-seventh, Colonel Hildebrand, to deploy forward as skirmishers, and the regiment itself forward into line, with an interval of one hundred yards. In this order we advanced cautiously until the skirmishers were engaged. Taking it for granted this disposition would clear the camp, I held Colonel Dickey's Fourth Illinois Cavalry ready for the charge. The enemy's cavalry came down boldly at a charge, led by General Forrest in person, breaking through our line of skirmishers; when the regiment of infantry, without cause, broke, threw away their muskets, and fled. The ground was admirably adapted for a defense of infantry against cavalry, being miry and covered with fallen timber.

As the regiment of infantry broke, Dickey's Cavalry began to discharge their carbines, and fell into disorder. I instantly sent orders to the rear for the brigade to form line of battle, which was promptly executed. The broken infantry and cavalry rallied on this line, and, as the enemy's cavalry came to it, our cavalry in turn charged and drove them from the field. I advanced the entire brigade over the same ground and sent Colonel Dickey's cavalry a mile farther on the road. On examining the ground which had been occupied by the Seventy-seventh Ohio, we found fifteen of our men dead and about twenty-five wounded. I sent for wagons and had all the wounded carried back to camp, and caused the dead to be buried, also the whole rebel camp to be destroyed.

Here we found much ammunition for field-pieces, which was destroyed; also two caissons, and a general hospital, with about two hundred and eighty Confederate wounded, and about fifty of our own wounded men. Not having the means of bringing them off, Colonel Dickey, by my orders, took a surrender, signed by the medical director (Lyle) and by all the attending surgeons, and a pledge to report themselves to you as prisoners of war; also a pledge that our wounded should be carefully attended to, and surrendered to us to-morrow as soon as ambulances could go out. I inclose this written document, and request that you cause wagons or ambulances for our wounded to be sent to-morrow, and that wagons be sent to bring in the many tents belonging to us which are pitched along the road for four miles out. I did not destroy them, because I knew the enemy could not move them. The roads are very bad, and are strewed with abandoned wagons, ambulances, and limber-boxes. The enemy has succeeded in carrying off the guns, but has crippled his batteries by abandoning the hind limber-boxes of at least twenty caissons. I am satisfied the enemy's infantry and artillery passed Lick Creek this morning, traveling all of last night, and that he left to his rear all his cavalry, which has protected his retreat; but signs of confusion and disorder mark the whole road. The check sustained by us at the fallen timber delayed our advance, so that night came upon us before the wounded were provided for and the dead buried, and our troops being fagged out by three days' hard fighting, exposure, and privation, I ordered them back to their camps, where they now are.

I have the honor to be, your obedient servant,

W. T. Sherman,
Brigadier-General commanding Division.

General Grant did not make an official report of the battle of Shiloh, but all its incidents and events were covered by the reports of division commanders and subordinates.[27] Probably no single battle of the war gave rise to such wild and damaging reports. It was publicly asserted at the North that our army was taken completely by surprise; that the rebels caught us in our tents; bayoneted the men in their beds; that General Grant was drunk; that Buell's opportune arrival saved the Army of the Tennessee from utter annihilation, etc. These reports were in a measure sustained by the published opinions of Generals Buell, Nelson, and others,[28] who had reached the steamboat-landing from the east, just before nightfall of the 6th, when there was a large crowd of frightened, stampeded men, who clamored and declared that our army was all destroyed and beaten. Personally I saw General Grant, who with his staff visited me about 10 A. M. of the 6th, when we were desperately engaged. But we had checked the headlong assault of our enemy, and then held our ground. This gave him great satisfaction, and he told me that things did not look as well over on the left. He also told me that on his way up from Savannah that morning he had stopped at Crump's Landing, and had ordered Lew Wallace's division to cross over Snake Creek,[29] so as to come up on my right, telling me to look out for him. He came again just before dark,[30] and described the last assault made by

[27] For USG's reasons for not submitting a post-battle report, see Grant, *The Personal Memoirs,* 252.

[28] For all the post-battle reports on the Battle of Shiloh, see *OR,* I, 10 (I), 98–627.

[29] In the first edition of the memoirs (1875), WTS identified the creek as "Lick Creek."

[30] In the first edition of the memoirs (1875), this portion of the text read, "He again came to me just before dark . . ."

the rebels at the ravine, near the steamboat-landing, which he had repelled by a heavy battery collected under Colonel J. D. Webster and other officers,[31] and he was convinced that the battle was over for that day. He ordered me to be ready to assume the offensive in the morning, saying that, as he had observed at Fort Donelson at the crisis of the battle, both sides seemed defeated, and whoever assumed the offensive was sure to win. General Grant also explained to me that General Buell had reached the bank of the Tennessee River opposite Pittsburg Landing, and was in the act of ferrying his troops across at the time he was speaking to me.

About half an hour afterward General Buell himself rode up to where I was, accompanied by Colonels Fry, Michler,[32] and others of his staff. I was dismounted at the time, and General Buell made of me a good many significant inquiries about matters and things generally. By the aid of a manuscript map made by myself, I pointed out to him our positions as they had been in the morning, and our then positions; I also explained that my right then covered the bridge over Snake Creek by which we had all day been expecting Lew Wallace; that McClernand was on my left, Hurlbut on his left, and so on.[33] But Buell said he had come up from the landing, and had not seen our men, of whose existence in fact he seemed to doubt. I insisted that I had five thousand good men still left in line, and thought that McClernand had as many more, and that with what was left of Hurlbut's, W. H. L. Wallace's, and Prentiss's divisions, we ought to have eighteen thousand men fit for battle. I reckoned that ten thousand of our men were dead, wounded, or prisoners, and that the enemy's loss could not be much less. Buell said that Nelson's, McCook's, and Crittenden's divisions of his army, containing eighteen thousand men, had arrived and could cross over in the night, and be ready for the next day's battle. I argued that with these reënforcements we could sweep the field. Buell seemed to mistrust us, and repeatedly said that he did not like the looks of things, especially about the boat-landing, and I really feared he would not cross over his army that night, lest he should become involved in our general disaster. He did not, of course, understand the shape

[31] Joseph D. Webster (1811–1876) was the chief of staff for the Army of the Tennessee during the battle. *CWHC*, 558.

[32] Nathaniel Michler (1827–1877) was a captain and topographical engineer in the Army of the Ohio during the battle. He was later brevetted colonel in Apr. 1865. *CWHC*, 389.

[33] In the first edition of the memoirs (1875), this portion of the text read, "I also explained to him that my right then covered the bridge over Lick Creek by which we had all day been expecting Lew Wallace; that McClernand was on my left, Hurlbut on his left, and so on."

of the ground, and asked me for the use of my map, which I lent him on the promise that he would return it. He handed it to Major Michler to have it copied, and the original returned to me, which Michler did two or three days after the battle. Buell did cross over that night, and the next day we assumed the offensive and swept the field, thus gaining the battle decisively. Nevertheless, the controversy was started and kept up, mostly to the personal prejudice of General Grant, who as usual maintained an imperturbable silence.

After the battle, a constant stream of civilian surgeons, and sanitary commission agents, men and women, came up the Tennessee to bring relief to the thousands of maimed and wounded soldiers for whom we had imperfect means of shelter and care. These people caught up the camp-stories, which on their return home they retailed through their local papers, usually elevating their own neighbors into heroes, but decrying all others. Among them was Lieutenant-Governor Stanton, of Ohio, who published in Belfontaine, Ohio, a most abusive article about General Grant and his subordinate generals.[34] As General Grant did not and would not take up the cudgels, I did so. My letter in reply to Stanton, dated June 10, 1862, was published in the *Cincinnati Commercial* soon after its date. To this Lieutenant-Governor Stanton replied, and I further rejoined in a letter dated July 12, 1862. These letters are too personal to be revived. By this time the good people of the North had begun to have their eyes opened, and to give us in the field more faith and support. Stanton was never again elected to any public office, and was commonly spoken of as "the late Mr. Stanton." He is now dead, and I doubt not in life he often regretted his mistake in attempting to gain popular fame by abusing the army-leaders, then as now an easy and favorite mode of gaining notoriety, if not popularity. Of course, subsequent events gave General Grant and most of the other actors in that battle their appropriate place in history, but the danger of sudden popular clamors is well illustrated by this case.

[34] Benjamin Stanton (1809–1873) was elected lieutenant governor of Ohio in 1861 and wrote a report on his visit to Shiloh after the battle in late Apr. 1862. He asserted, "That the disasters of Sunday, April 6th, were the result of a surprise, which is justly chargeable upon the commanding officers, and not upon the men on whom the responsibility is now sought to be thrown. Whenever the occasion shall demand, justify, or excuse a statement of the facts and circumstances upon which this opinion is based, and the names of the officers whose criminal negligence has occasioned the disasters of that day, I shall be prepared to give them." John C. Hover et al., *Memoirs of the Miami Valley* (Chicago: Robert O. Law, 1919), 1:201; "Report of Lieut. Gov. Stanton," *Daily Ohio Statesman* (Columbus, OH), May 1, 1862, 2.

The battle of Shiloh, or Pittsburg Landing, was one of the most fiercely contested of the war. On the morning of April 6, 1862, the five divisions of McClernand, Prentiss, Hurlbut, W. H. L. Wallace, and Sherman, aggregated about thirty-two thousand men. We had no intrenchments of any sort, on the theory that as soon as Buell arrived we would march to Corinth to attack the enemy. The rebel army, commanded by General Albert Sidney Johnston, was, according to their own reports and admissions, forty-five thousand strong,[35] had the momentum of attack, and beyond all question fought skillfully from early morning till about 2 P. M., when their commander-in-chief was killed by a Minié-ball in the calf of his leg, which penetrated the boot and severed the main artery. There was then a perceptible lull for a couple of hours, when the attack was renewed, but with much less vehemence, and continued up to dark. Early at night the division of Lew Wallace arrived from the other side of Snake Creek, not having fired a shot. A very small part of General Buell's army was on our side of the Tennessee River that evening, and their loss was trivial.

During that night, the three divisions of McCook, Nelson, and Crittenden, were ferried across the Tennessee, and fought with us the next day (7th). During that night, also, the two wooden gunboats, Tyler, commanded by Lieutenant Gwin, and Lexington, Lieutenant Shirk, both of the regular navy, caused shells to be thrown toward that part of the field of battle known to be occupied by the enemy. Beauregard afterward reported his entire loss as ten thousand six hundred and ninety-nine. Our aggregate loss, made up from official statements, shows seventeen hundred killed, seven thousand four hundred and ninety-five wounded, and three thousand and twenty-two prisoners; aggregate, twelve thousand two hundred and seventeen, of which twenty-one hundred and sixty-seven were in Buell's army, leaving for that of Grant ten thousand and fifty. This result is a fair measure of the amount of fighting done by each army.[36]

[35] According to official reports, the Confederate Army had 40,335 troops at the start of the battle. *OR,* I, 10(I), 396.

[36] WTS received subsequent criticism for his actions during the Battle of Shiloh. In 1875, former U.S. Army officer Henry Van Boynton claimed, "Ever since this battle, most who believed that the Union army was unexpectedly attacked on that occasion, have laid the chief load of responsibility upon General Grant, and he through all these years has made no effort to shift the burden. But now it will appear through the records which these Memoirs have called out, that General Sherman was mainly responsible, since he was encamped in advance." Henry Van Boynton, *Sherman's Historical Raid: The Memoirs in the Light of the Record—A Review Based upon Compilations from the Files of the War Office* (Cincinnati: Wilstach and Baldwin, 1875), 25–26.

11

Shiloh to Memphis.

APRIL TO JULY, 1862.

WHILE the "Army of the Tennessee," under Generals Grant and C. F. Smith, was operating up the Tennessee River, another force, styled the "Army of the Mississippi," commanded by Major-General John Pope, was moving directly down the Mississippi River, against that portion of the rebel line which, under Generals Polk and Pillow, had fallen back from Columbus, Kentucky, to Island Number Ten and New Madrid. This army had the full coöperation of the gunboat fleet, commanded by Admiral Foote, and was assisted by the high flood of that season, which enabled General Pope, by great skill and industry, to open a canal from a point above Island Number Ten to New Madrid below, by which he interposed between the rebel army and its available line of supply and retreat.[1] At the very time that we were fighting the bloody battle on the Tennessee River, General Pope and Admiral Foote were bombarding the batteries on Island Number Ten, and the Kentucky shore abreast of it; and General Pope having crossed over by steamers a part of his army to the east bank, captured a large part of this rebel army, at and near Tiptonville.[2]

General Halleck still remained at St. Louis, whence he gave general directions to the armies of General Curtis, Generals Grant, Buell, and Pope;[3] and instead of following up his most important and brilliant successes directly down the Mississippi, he concluded to bring General Pope's army around to the Tennessee, and to come in person to command there. The

[1] Construction of the canal began on Mar. 23, 1862, and took two weeks to complete. Thomas F. Army Jr., *Engineering Victory: How Technology Won the Civil War* (Baltimore: Johns Hopkins University Press, 2016), 107–109.

[2] Pope captured Tiptonville, TN, and Island Number Ten on the morning of Apr. 8, 1862. John Pope, *The Military Memoirs of General John Pope,* ed. Peter Cozzens and Robert I. Girardi (Chapel Hill: University of North Carolina Press, 1998), 55–58.

[3] In the first edition of the memoirs (1875), this portion of WTS's text read, "to the armies of General Curtis, General Grant, and General Pope."

gunboat fleet pushed on down the Mississippi, but was brought up again all standing by the heavy batteries at Fort Pillow, about fifty miles above Memphis. About this time Admiral Farragut, with another large sea-going fleet, and with the coöperating army of General Butler,[4] was entering the Mississippi River by the Passes, and preparing to reduce Forts Jackson and St. Philip in order to reach New Orleans; so that all minds were turned to the conquest of the Mississippi River, and surely adequate means were provided for the undertaking.

The battle of Shiloh had been fought, as described, on the 6th and 7th of April; and when the movement of the 8th had revealed that our enemy was gone, in full retreat, leaving killed, wounded, and much property by the way, we all experienced a feeling of relief. The struggle had been so long, so desperate and bloody, that the survivors seemed exhausted and nerveless; we appreciated the value of the victory, but realized also its great cost of life. The close of the battle had left the Army of the Tennessee on the right, and the Army of the Ohio on the left; but I believe neither General Grant nor Buell exercised command, the one over the other; each of them having his hands full in repairing damages. All the division, brigade, and regimental commanders were busy in collecting stragglers, regaining lost property, in burying dead men and horses, and in providing for their wounded. Some few new regiments came forward, and some changes of organization became necessary. Then, or very soon after, I consolidated my four brigades into three, which were commanded: First, Brigadier-General Morgan L. Smith;[5] Second, Colonel John A. McDowell; Third, Brigadier-General J. W. Denver.[6] About the same time I was promoted to major-general volunteers.[7]

The Seventy-first Ohio was detached to Clarksville, Tennessee, and the Sixth and Eighth Missouri were transferred to my division.

In a few days after the battle, General Halleck arrived by steamboat from St. Louis, pitched his camp near the steamboat-landing, and assumed

[4] Benjamin F. Butler (1818–1893) joined the U.S. Army as a major general in May 1861. He commanded the Army of the Gulf in Apr. 1862. *CWHC,* 156–157.

[5] Morgan L. Smith (1821–1874) was placed in command of the 1st Brig., 5th Div., Army of the Tennessee, on May 12, 1862. *CWHC,* 498.

[6] James W. Denver (1817–1892), namesake of Denver, CO, was a prominent politician who joined the U.S. Army as a brigadier general on Aug. 14, 1861. He took command of the 3rd Brig., 5th Div., Army of the Tennessee, on May 16, 1862. *CWHC,* 207.

[7] WTS was promoted to major general on May 1, 1862. *CWHC,* 485.

personal command of all the armies.[8] He was attended by his staff, composed of General G. W. Cullum, U. S. Engineers, as his chief of staff; Colonel George Thom, U. S. Engineers;[9] and Colonels Kelton[10] and Kemper,[11] adjutants-general. It soon became manifest that his mind had been prejudiced by the rumors which had gone forth to the detriment of General Grant; for in a few days he issued an order, reorganizing and rearranging the whole army.[12] General Buell's Army of the Ohio constituted the centre; General Pope's army, then arriving at Hamburg Landing, was the left; the right was made up of mine and Hurlbut's divisions, belonging to the old Army of the Tennessee, and two new ones, made up from the fragments of the divisions of Prentiss and C. F. Smith, and of troops transferred thereto, commanded by Generals T. W. Sherman and Davies.[13] General George H. Thomas was taken from Buell, to command the right. McClernand's and Lew Wallace's divisions were styled the reserve, to be commanded by McClernand. General Grant was substantially left out, and was named "second in command," according to some French notion, with no clear, well-defined command or authority. He still retained his old staff, composed of Rawlins, adjutant-general; Riggin, Lagow, and Hilyer, aides;[14] and he had a small company of the Fourth Illinois Cavalry as an escort. For more than a month he thus remained, without any apparent authority, frequently visiting me and others, and rarely com-

[8] Halleck arrived at Shiloh, TN, on Apr. 11, 1862. Timothy B. Smith, *The Untold Story of Shiloh: The Battle and the Battlefield* (Knoxville: University of Tennessee Press, 2006), 75.

[9] George Thom (1819–1891) graduated from the USMA in 1839 and became a captain in the topographical engineers. He served as an additional aide-de-camp from Nov. 1861 to May 1866. *USMA,* 1:741–743, 4:52.

[10] John C. Kelton (1828–1893) graduated from the USMA in 1851 and became an additional aide-de-camp as a colonel on Jan. 4, 1862. He was promoted to assistant adjutant general for Halleck on July 11, 1862. *USMA,* 2:459–460, 4:82.

[11] A. C. Kemper (1832–1905), a medical doctor from Dublin, Ireland, was a captain on Halleck's staff in Apr. 1862. "Obituary Notes," *Medical Record: A Weekly Journal of Medicine and Surgery,* no. 9 (Aug. 1905), 68:347; *OR,* I, 10(I), 114.

[12] For Halleck's order, see *OR,* I, 10(II), 144–145.

[13] Thomas A. Davies (1809–1900) graduated from the USMA in 1829 and was promoted to brigadier general on Mar. 7, 1862. In Apr., he commanded the 2nd Div., Army of the Tennessee. *USMA,* 1:438–439, 4:33, 5:34; *CWHC,* 200–201.

[14] John Riggin Jr. (1835–1886) was an aide-de-camp to USG from Dec. 1861 to Oct. 1863. Clark B. Lagow (1837–1915) was an aide-de-camp to USG from Aug. 1861 to Nov. 1863, and William S. Hillyer (1830–1874) was an aide-de-camp to USG from Sept. 1861 to May 1863. *CWHC,* 297, 337, 454.

plaining; but I could see that he felt deeply the indignity, if not insult, heaped upon him.

General Thomas at once assumed command of the right wing, and, until we reached Corinth, I served immediately under his command. We were classmates, intimately acquainted, had served together before in the old army, and in Kentucky, and it made to us little difference who commanded the other, provided the good cause prevailed.

Corinth was about thirty miles distant, and we all knew that we should find there the same army with which we had so fiercely grappled at Shiloh, reorganized, reënforced, and commanded in chief by General Beauregard in place of Johnston, who had fallen at Shiloh. But we were also reënforced by Buell's and Pope's armies; so that before the end of April our army extended from Snake Creek[15] on the right to the Tennessee River, at Hamburg, on the left, and must have numbered nearly one hundred thousand men.

Ample supplies of all kinds reached us by the Tennessee River, which had a good stage of water; but our wagon transportation was limited, and much confusion occurred in hauling supplies to the several camps. By the end of April, the several armies seemed to be ready, and the general forward movement on Corinth began.[16] My division was on the extreme right of the right wing, and marched out by the "White House,"[17] leaving Monterey or Pea Ridge to the south. Crossing Lick Creek, we came into the main road about a mile south of Monterey, where we turned square to the right, and came into the Purdy road, near "Elams." Thence we followed the Purdy road to Corinth, my skirmishers reaching at all times the Mobile & Ohio Railroad. Of course our marches were governed by the main centre, which followed the direct road from Pittsburg Landing to Corinth; and this movement was provokingly slow. We fortified almost every camp at night, though we had encountered no serious opposition, except from cavalry, which gave ground easily as we advanced. The opposition increased as we neared Corinth, and at a place called Russell's we had a sharp affair of one brigade, under the immediate direction of Brigadier-General Morgan L. Smith, assisted by the brigade of

[15] In the first edition of the memoirs (1875), this portion of WTS's text read, "Snake River."

[16] Halleck ordered his army to move on Corinth, MS, on Apr. 30, 1862. John F. Marszalek, *Commander of All Lincoln's Armies: A Life of General Henry W. Halleck* (Cambridge, MA: Belknap Press of Harvard University Press, 2004), 123.

[17] For a detailed map of U.S. Army troop movements leading up to the siege of Corinth, see George B. Davis et al., *Official Military Atlas of the Civil War* (New York: Fairfax Press, 1983), plate 13.

General Denver. This affair occurred on the 19th of May, and our line was then within about two miles of the northern intrenchments of Corinth.

On the 27th I received orders from General Halleck "to send a force the next day to drive the rebels from the house in our front, on the Corinth road, to drive in their pickets as far as possible, and to make a strong demonstration on Corinth itself;" authorizing me to call on any adjacent division for assistance.[18]

I reconnoitred the ground carefully, and found that the main road led forward along the fence of a large cotton-field to our right front, and ascended a wooded hill, occupied in some force by the enemy, on which was the farm-house referred to in General Halleck's orders. At the farther end of the field was a double log-house, whose chinking had been removed; so that it formed a good block-house from which the enemy could fire on any person approaching from our quarter.

General Hurlbut's division was on my immediate left, and General McClernand's reserve on our right rear. I asked of each the assistance of a brigade. The former sent General Veatch's,[19] and the latter General John A. Logan's[20] brigade. I asked the former to support our left flank, and the latter our right flank. The next morning early, Morgan L. Smith's brigade was deployed under cover on the left, and Denver's on the right, ready to move forward rapidly at a signal. I had a battery of four twenty-pound Parrott guns, commanded by Captain Silversparre.[21] Colonel Ezra Taylor, chief of artillery,[22] had two of these guns moved up silently by hand behind a small knoll, from

[18] For Halleck's order to WTS, see *OR,* I, 10(II), 216.

[19] James C. Veatch (1819–1895) was an Indiana legislator who took command of the 25th Indiana Inf. as a colonel in Aug. 1861. He was promoted to brigadier general on Apr. 28, 1862, and commanded the 2nd Brig., 4th Div., Army of the Tennessee, during the march on Corinth. *CWHC,* 544.

[20] John A. Logan (1826–1886) represented Illinois in the U.S. House of Representatives from 1859 to 1862 and was appointed brigadier general in the U.S. Army in Mar. 1862. He commanded the 1st Brig., 1st Div., Army of the Tennessee, during the march on Corinth. *CWHC,* 351.

[21] Axel Silversparre (1834–1906), of Sweden, was captain of Co. H, 1st Illinois Art., during the Civil War. Allan Kastrup, *The Swedish Heritage in America: The Swedish Element in America and American-Swedish Relations in Their Historical Perspective* (St. Paul: Swedish Council of America, 1975), 285; "Soldiers' Home," *Dayton Herald* (Dayton, OH), Nov. 23, 1896, 4.

[22] Ezra Taylor (1820–1885) served as WTS's chief of artillery throughout the Civil War. He was later appointed inspector of provisions on the Board of Trade in Chicago. "Obituary. Gen. Ezra Taylor," *Chicago Tribune,* Oct. 26, 1885, 2.

the crest of which the enemy's block-house and position could be distinctly seen; when all were ready, these guns were moved to the crest, and several quick rounds were fired at the house, followed after an interval by a single gun. This was the signal agreed on, and the troops responded beautifully, crossed the field in line of battle, preceded by their skirmishers who carried the position in good style, and pursued the enemy for half a mile beyond.

The main line halted on the crest of the ridge, from which we could look over the parapets of the rebel works at Corinth, and hear their drum and bugle calls. The rebel brigade had evidently been taken by surprise in our attack; it soon rallied and came back on us with the usual yell, driving in our skirmishers, but was quickly checked when it came within range of our guns and line of battle. Generals Grant and Thomas happened to be with me during this affair, and were well pleased at the handsome manner in which the troops behaved. That night we began the usual entrenchments, and the next day brought forward the artillery and the rest of the division, which then extended from the Mobile & Ohio Railroad, at Bowie Hill Cut, to the Corinth & Purdy road, there connecting with Hurlbut's division. That night, viz., May 29th, we heard unusual sounds in Corinth, the constant whistling of locomotives, and soon after daylight occurred a series of explosions followed by a dense smoke rising high over the town. There was a telegraph line connecting my headquarters with those of General Halleck, about four miles off, on the Hamburg road. I inquired if he knew the cause of the explosions and of the smoke, and he answered to "advance with my division and feel the enemy if still in my front."[23] I immediately dispatched two regiments from each of my three brigades to feel the immediate front, and in a very short time advanced with the whole division. Each brigade found the rebel parapets abandoned, and pushed straight for the town, which lies in the northeast angle of intersection of the Mobile & Ohio and Memphis & Charleston Railroads. Many buildings had been burned by the enemy on evacuation, which had begun the night before at 6 P. M., and continued through the night, the rear-guard burning their magazine at the time of withdrawing, about daybreak. Morgan L. Smith's brigade followed the retreating rear-guard some four miles to the Tuscumbia Bridge, which was found burned. I halted the other brigades at the college, about a mile to the southwest of the town, where I was overtaken by General Thomas in person.

The heads of all the columns had entered the rebel lines about the same time, and there was some rather foolish clamor for the first honors, but in

[23] For the relevant correspondence between WTS and Halleck, see *OR,* I, 10(II), 228.

fact there was no honor in the event. Beauregard had made a clean retreat to the south, and was only seriously pursued by cavalry from General Pope's flank. But he reached Tupelo, where he halted for reorganization; and there is no doubt that at the moment there was much disorganization in his ranks, for the woods were full of deserters whom we did not even take prisoners, but advised them to make their way home and stay there. We spent the day at and near the college, when General Thomas, who applied for orders at Halleck's headquarters, directed me to conduct my division back to the camp of the night before, where we had left our trains. The advance on Corinth had occupied all of the month of May, the most beautiful and valuable month of the year for campaigning in this latitude. There had been little fighting, save on General Pope's left flank about Farmington; and on our right. I esteemed it a magnificent drill, as it served for the instruction of our men in guard and picket duty, and in habituating them to out-door life; and by the time we had reached Corinth I believe that army was the best then on this continent, and could have gone where it pleased. The four subdivisions were well commanded, as were the divisions and brigades of the whole army. General Halleck was a man of great capacity, of large acquirements, and at the time possessed the confidence of the country, and of most of the army. I held him in high estimation, and gave him credit for the combinations which had resulted in placing this magnificent army of a hundred thousand men, well equipped and provided, with a good base, at Corinth, from which he could move in any direction.

Had he held his force as a unit, he could have gone to Mobile, or Vicksburg, or anywhere in that region, which would by one move have solved the whole Mississippi problem; and, from what he then told me, I believe he intended such a campaign, but was overruled from Washington. Be that as it may, the army had no sooner settled down at Corinth before it was scattered: General Pope was called to the East,[24] and his army distributed among the others; General Thomas was relieved from the command of the right wing, and reassigned to his division in the Army of the Ohio; and that whole army under General Buell was turned east along the Memphis & Charleston road, to march for Chattanooga. McClernand's "reserve" was turned west to Bolivar and Memphis. General Halleck took post himself at Corinth, assigned Lieutenant-Colonel McPherson to take charge of the railroads, with instructions to repair them as far as Columbus, Kentucky, and to collect cars and

[24] U.S. Secretary of War Stanton asked Pope to visit Washington, DC, in a letter dated June 19, 1862. *OR,* I, 17(II), 17–18.

locomotives to operate them to Corinth and Grand Junction. I was soon dispatched with my own and Hurlbut's divisions northwest fourteen miles to Chewalla, to save what could be of any value out of six trains of cars belonging to the rebels which had been wrecked and partially burned at the time of the evacuation of Corinth.

A short time before leaving Corinth I rode from my camp to General Halleck's headquarters, then in tents just outside of the town, where we sat and gossiped for some time, when he mentioned to me casually that General Grant was going away the next morning. I inquired the cause, and he said that he did not know, but that Grant had applied for a thirty days' leave, which had been given him. Of course we all knew that he was chafing under the slights of his anomalous position, and I determined to see him on my way back.[25] His camp was a short distance off the Monterey road, in the woods, and consisted of four or five tents, with a sapling railing around the front. As I rode up, Majors Rawlins, Lagow, and Hilyer, were in front of the camp, and piled up near them were the usual office and camp chests, all ready for a start in the morning. I inquired for the general, and was shown to his tent, where I found him seated on a camp-stool, with papers on a rude camp-table; he seemed to be employed in assorting letters, and tying them up with red tape into convenient bundles. After passing the usual compliments, I inquired if it were true that he was going away. He said, "Yes." I then inquired the reason, and he said "Sherman, you know. You know that I am in the way here. I have stood it as long as I can, and can endure it no longer." I inquired where he was going to, and he said, "St. Louis." I then asked if he had any business there, and he said, "Not a bit." I then begged him to stay, illustrating his case by my own.

Before the battle of Shiloh, I had been cast down by a mere newspaper assertion of "crazy;" but that single battle had given me new life, and now I was in high feather; and I argued with him that, if he went away, events would go right along, and he would be left out; whereas, if he remained, some happy accident might restore him to favor and his true place. He certainly appreciated my friendly advice, and promised to wait awhile; at all events, not to go without seeing me again, or communicating with me. Very soon after this, I was ordered to Chewalla, where, on the 6th of June, I received a note from

[25] For USG's description of his interaction with WTS, see Ulysses S. Grant, *The Personal Memoirs of Ulysses S. Grant: The Complete Annotated Edition,* ed. John F. Marszalek, David S. Nolen, and Louie P. Gallo (Cambridge, MA: Belknap Press of Harvard University Press, 2017), 262–263.

him, saying that he had reconsidered his intention, and would remain. I cannot find the note, but my answer I have kept.

CHEWALLA, *June* 6, 1862.

Major-General GRANT.

MY DEAR SIR: I have just received your note, and am rejoiced at your conclusion to remain; for you could not be quiet at home for a week when armies were moving, and rest could not relieve your mind of the gnawing sensation that injustice had been done you.

. . . .

My orders at Chewalla were to rescue the wrecked trains there, to reconnoitre westward and estimate the amount of damage to the railroad as far as Grand Junction, about fifty miles. We camped our troops on high, healthy ground to the south of Chewalla, and after I had personally reconnoitred the country, details of men were made and volunteer locomotive engineers obtained to superintend the repairs. I found six locomotives and about sixty cars, thrown from the track, parts of the machinery detached and hidden in the surrounding swamp, and all damaged as much by fire as possible. It seems that these trains were inside of Corinth during the night of evacuation, loading up with all sorts of commissary stores, etc., and about daylight were started west; but the cavalry-picket stationed at the Tuscumbia bridge had, by mistake or panic, burned the bridge before the trains got to them. The trains, therefore, were caught, and the engineers and guards hastily scattered the stores into the swamp, and disabled the trains as far as they could, before our cavalry had discovered their critical situation. The weather was hot, and the swamp fairly stunk with the putrid flour and fermenting sugar and molasses; I was so much exposed there in the hot sun, pushing forward the work, that I got a touch of malarial fever, which hung on me for a month, and forced me to ride two days in an ambulance, the only time I ever did such a thing during the whole war. By the 7th I reported to General Halleck that the amount of work necessary to reëstablish the railroad between Corinth and Grand Junction was so great, that he concluded not to attempt its repair, but to rely on the road back to Jackson (Tennessee), and forward to Grand Junction; and I was ordered to move to Grand Junction, to take up the repairs from there toward Memphis.

The evacuation of Corinth by Beauregard, and the movements of General McClernand's force toward Memphis, had necessitated the evacuation of

Fort Pillow, which occurred about June 1st;[26] soon followed by the further withdrawal of the Confederate army from Memphis, by reason of the destruction of the rebel gunboats in the bold and dashing attack by our gunboats under command of Admiral Davis, who had succeeded Foote.[27] This occurred June 7th.[28] Admiral Farragut had also captured New Orleans after the terrible passage of Forts Jackson and St. Philip on May 24th, and had ascended the river as high as Vicksburg;[29] so that it seemed as though, before the end of June, we should surely have full possession of the whole river. But it is now known that the progress of our Western armies had aroused the rebel government to the exercise of the most stupendous energy. Every man capable of bearing arms at the South was declared to be a soldier, and forced to act as such. All their armies were greatly reënforced, and the most despotic power was granted to enforce discipline and supplies. Beauregard was replaced by Bragg, a man of more ability—of greater powers of organization, of action, and discipline—but naturally exacting and severe, and not possessing the qualities to attract the love of his officers and men. He had a hard task to bring into order and discipline that mass of men to whose command he succeeded at Tupelo, with which he afterward fairly outmanœuvred General Buell, and forced him back from Chattanooga to Louisville. It was a fatal mistake, however, that halted General Halleck at Corinth, and led him to disperse and scatter the best materials for a fighting army that, up to that date, had been assembled in the West.

During the latter part of June and first half of July, I had my own and Hurlbut's divisions about Grand Junction, Lagrange, Moscow, and Lafayette,[30] building railroad-trestles and bridges, fighting off cavalry detachments coming

[26]The Confederate Army evacuated Fort Pillow on June 4, 1862. Myron J. Smith Jr., *The USS Carondelet: A Civil War Ironclad on Western Waters* (Jefferson, NC: McFarland, 2010), 118.

[27]Charles H. Davis (1807–1877) took command of the U.S. Navy's "Western Flotilla" on May 9, 1862. *CWHC,* 201.

[28]Contrary to WTS's assertion, Memphis was captured by the U.S. Navy on June 6. The U.S. Army suffered only one casualty, compared to 180 Confederate losses. Terry L. Jones, ed., *Historical Dictionary of the Civil War* (Lanham, MD: Scarecrow Press, 2011), 1:34.

[29]The U.S. Navy captured Forts Jackson and St. Phillip on Apr. 25, 1862, and New Orleans on May 2. Rufus Kinsley, *Diary of a Christian Soldier,* ed. David C. Rankin (Cambridge: Cambridge University Press, 2004), 92.

[30]Lafayette, TN, was a town situated approximately fifteen miles due west of La Grange, TN, and approximately thirty miles southeast of Memphis, along the Memphis and Charleston Railroad. Davis et al., *Official Military Atlas of the Civil War,* plate 154.

from the south, and waging an everlasting quarrel with planters about their negroes and fences—they trying, in the midst of moving armies, to raise a crop of corn. On the 17th of June I sent a detachment of two brigades, under General M. L. Smith, to Holly Springs, in the belief that I could better protect the railroad from some point in front than by scattering our men along it; and, on the 23d, I was at Lafayette Station, when General Grant, with his staff and a very insignificant escort, arrived from Corinth *en route* for Memphis, to take command of that place and of the District of West Tennessee. He came very near falling into the hands of the enemy, who infested the whole country with small but bold detachments of cavalry.[31] Up to that time I had received my orders direct from General Halleck at Corinth, but soon after I fell under the immediate command of General Grant and so continued to the end of the war;[32] but, on the 29th, General Halleck notified me that "a division of troops under General C.S. Hamilton of 'Rosecrans's army corps,'[33] had passed the Hatchie from Corinth," and was destined for Holly Springs, ordering me to "coöperate as far as advisable," but "not to neglect the protection of the road."[34] I ordered General Hurlbut to leave detachments at Grand Junction and Lagrange, and to march for Holly Springs. I left detachments at Moscow and Lafayette, and, with about four thousand men, marched for the same point. Hurlbut and I met at Hudsonville, and thence marched to the Coldwater, within four miles of Holly Springs. We encountered only small detachments of rebel cavalry under Colonels Jackson[35] and Pierson, and drove them into and through Holly Springs; but they hung about, and I kept an infantry brigade in Holly Springs to keep them out. I heard nothing from General Hamilton till

[31] For USG's description of the incident, see Ulysses S. Grant, *The Personal Memoirs,* 264–265.

[32] USG effectively took command of the Dept. of the Mississippi after Halleck was promoted to general-in-chief of the U.S. Army on July 23, 1862. Grant, *The Personal Memoirs,* 268; *CWHC,* 274.

[33] In the first edition of the memoirs (1875), WTS identified Charles S. Hamilton (1822–1891) as "John Hamilton." Charles graduated from the USMA in 1843 and commanded the 3rd Div., Army of the Mississippi, in June 1862. William S. Rosecrans (1819–1898) graduated from the USMA in 1838 and took command of the Army of the Mississippi on June 26, 1862. *CWHC,* 275, 461.

[34] For Halleck's full order to WTS, see *OR,* I, 17(II), 48–49.

[35] William H. Jackson (1835–1903) graduated from the USMA in 1856 and resigned from the U.S. Army in May 1861. He was a colonel in the Confederate Army's 1st Tennessee Cav. in June 1862. *CWHC,* 317.

the 5th of July, when I received a letter from him dated Rienzi, saying that he had been within nineteen miles of Holly Springs and had turned back for Corinth; and on the next day, July 6th, I got a telegraph order from General Halleck, of July 2d, sent me by courier from Moscow, "not to attempt to hold Holly Springs, but to fall back and protect the railroad."[36] We accordingly marched back twenty-five miles—Hurlbut to Lagrange, and I to Moscow. The enemy had no infantry nearer than the Tallahatchee bridge, but their cavalry was saucy and active, superior to ours, and I despaired of ever protecting a railroad, presenting a broad front of one hundred miles, from their dashes.

About this time, we were taunted by the Confederate soldiers and citizens with the assertion that Lee had defeated McClellan at Richmond; that he would soon be in Washington; and that our turn would come next. The extreme caution of General Halleck also indicated that something had gone wrong, and, on the 16th of July, at Moscow, I received a dispatch from him, announcing that he had been summoned to Washington, which he seemed to regret, and which at that moment I most deeply deplored.[37] He announced that his command would devolve on General Grant, who had been summoned around from Memphis to Corinth by way of Columbus, Kentucky, and that I was to go into Memphis to take command of the District of West Tennessee, vacated by General Grant. By this time, also, I was made aware that the great army that had assembled at Corinth at the end of May had been scattered and dissipated, and that terrible disasters had befallen our other armies in Virginia and the East.[38]

I soon received orders to move to Memphis, taking Hurlbut's division along. We reached Memphis on the 21st, and on the 22d I posted my three brigades mostly in and near Fort Pickering,[39] and Hurlbut's division next

[36] For WTS's response to Halleck, see *OR,* I, 17(II), 79.

[37] For Halleck's dispatch to WTS, see *OR,* I, 17(II), 100.

[38] The Seven Days' Battle was a series of battles where the U.S. Army, under the command of George B. McClellen, was repelled by the Confederate Army near Richmond, VA. In total, the U.S. Army suffered 15,299 casualties. Bud Hannings, *Every Day of the Civil War: A Chronological Encyclopedia* (Jefferson, NC: McFarland, 2010), 195–201.

[39] Fort Pickering, situated along the Mississippi River just south of Memphis, was constructed by the Confederate Army in 1861. Based on a dispatch to USG, WTS arrived in Memphis on the morning of July 20, 1862. John D. Bennett, *Placenames of the Civil War* (Jefferson, NC: McFarland, 2012), s.v. "Fort Pickering (Shelby) TN"; *OR,* I, 17(II), 109; I, 49(II), 899–901.

below on the river-bank by reason of the scarcity of water, except in the Mississippi River itself. The weather was intensely hot. The same order that took us to Memphis required me to send the division of General Lew Wallace (then commanded by Brigadier-General A. P. Hovey)[40] to Helena, Arkansas, to report to General Curtis, which was easily accomplished by steamboat. I made my own camp in a vacant lot, near Mr. Moon's house, and gave my chief attention to the construction of Fort Pickering, then in charge of Major Prime, United States Engineers; to perfecting the drill and discipline of the two divisions under my command; and to the administration of civil affairs.

At the time when General Halleck was summoned from Corinth to Washington, to succeed McClellan as commander-in-chief, I surely expected of him immediate and important results. The Army of the Ohio was at the time marching toward Chattanooga, and was strung from Eastport by Huntsville to Bridgeport, under the command of General Buell. In like manner, the Army of the Tennessee was strung along the same general line, from Memphis to Tuscumbia, and was commanded by General Grant, with no common commander for both these forces: so that the great army which General Halleck had so well assembled at Corinth, was put on the defensive, with a frontage of three hundred miles. Soon thereafter the rebels displayed peculiar energy and military skill. General Bragg had reorganized the army of Beauregard at Tupelo, carried it rapidly and skillfully toward Chattanooga, whence he boldly assumed the offensive, moving straight for Nashville and Louisville, and compelling General Buell to fall back to the Ohio River at Louisville.

The army of Van Dorn and Price had been brought from the trans-Mississippi Department to the east of the river, and was collected at and about Holly Springs, where, reënforced by Armstrong's and Forrest's cavalry,[41] it amounted to about forty thousand brave and hardy soldiers. These were General Grant's immediate antagonists, and so many and large detachments had been drawn from him, that for a time he was put on the defensive. In person he had his headquarters at Corinth, with the three divisions of Hamilton, Davies, and McKean,[42] under the immediate orders of General Rosecrans. General

[40] Alvin P. Hovey (1821–1891) was the founder of the Illinois State Normal School and was its president from 1857 to 1861. He commanded the 1st Brig., 3rd Div., Army of the Tennessee, in July 1862. *CWHC,* 305.

[41] Nathan B. Forrest (1821–1877), a trader of enslaved people, commanded a cavalry brigade in the Army of the Mississippi in July 1862. *CWHC,* 240.

[42] William W. McKean (1800–1865) graduated from the USMA in 1831 and commanded the 6th Div., Dist. of Corinth, Army of the Tennessee, in July 1862. *CWHC,* 379–380.

Ord had succeeded to the division of McClernand (who had also gone to Washington), and held Bolivar and Grand Junction.[43] I had in Memphis my own and Hurlbut's divisions, and other smaller detachments were strung along the Memphis & Charleston road. But the enemy's detachments could strike this road at so many points, that no use could be made of it, and General Grant had to employ the railroads, from Columbus, Kentucky, to Corinth and Grand Junction, by way of Jackson, Tennessee, a point common to both roads, and held in some force.

In the early part of September the enemy in our front manifested great activity, feeling with cavalry at all points, and on the 13th General Van Dorn threatened Corinth, while General Price seized the town of Iuka, which was promptly abandoned by a small garrison under Colonel Murphy.[44] Price's force was about eight thousand men, and the general impression was that he was *en route* for Eastport, with the purpose to cross the Tennessee River in the direction of Nashville, in aid of General Bragg, then in full career for Kentucky. General Grant determined to attack him in force, prepared to regain Corinth before Van Dorn could reach it. He had drawn Ord to Corinth, and moved him, by Burnsville, on Iuka, by the main road, twenty-six miles. General Grant accompanied this column as far as Burnsville. At the same time he had dispatched Rosecrans by roads to the south, *via* Jacinto, with orders to approach Iuka by the two main roads, coming into Iuka from the south, viz., the Jacinto and Fulton roads.[45]

On the 18th General Ord encountered the enemy about four miles out of Iuka. His orders contemplated that he should not make a serious attack, until Rosecrans had gained his position on the south; but, as usual, Rosecrans had encountered difficulties in the confusion of roads, his head of column did not reach the vicinity of Iuka till 4 P. M. of the 19th, and then his troops were long drawn out on the single Jacinto road, leaving the Fulton road clear for Price's use. Price perceived his advantage, and attacked with vehemence the head of Rosecrans's column, Hamilton's division, beating it back, capturing a battery,

[43] On Aug. 13, USG ordered Ord to examine the condition of the fortifications at Bolivar. McClernand took a leave of absence and visited Pres. Lincoln in Washington, DC, on Sept. 30. Richard L. Kiper, *Major General John Alexander McClernand: Politician in Uniform* (Kent, OH: Kent State University Press, 1999), 136; *OR,* I, 17(II), 167; *PUSG,* 5:299–302*n.*

[44] Robert C. Murphy (1827–1888) was a colonel in the 8th Wisconsin Inf. "Daily Death Roll," *Evening Star* (Washington, DC), Apr. 10, 1888, 6; Grant, *The Personal Memoirs,* 279*n.*

[45] For a detailed map of the Battle of Iuka, see Davis et al., *Official Military Atlas of the Civil War,* plate 25, map 2.

and killing and disabling seven hundred and thirty-six men, so that when night closed in Rosecrans was driven to the defensive, and Price, perceiving his danger, deliberately withdrew by the Fulton road, and the next morning was gone.[46] Although General Ord must have been within four or six miles of this battle, he did not hear a sound; and he or General Grant did not know of it till advised the next morning by a courier who had made a wide circuit to reach them.[47] General Grant was much offended with General Rosecrans because of this affair, but in my experience these concerted movements generally fail, unless with the very best kind of troops, and then in a country on whose roads some reliance can be placed, which is not the case in Northern Mississippi. If Price was aiming for Tennessee, he failed, and was therefore beaten. He made a wide circuit by the south, and again joined Van Dorn.

On the 6th of September, at Memphis, I received an order from General Grant dated the 2d, to send Hurlbut's division to Brownsville, in the direction of Bolivar, thence to report by letter to him at Jackson.[48] The division started the same day, and, as our men and officers had been together side by side from the first landing at Shiloh, we felt the parting like the breaking up of a family. But General Grant was forced to use every man, for he knew well that Van Dorn could attack him at pleasure, at any point of his long line. To be the better prepared, on the 23d of September he took post himself at Jackson, Tennessee, with a small reserve force, and gave Rosecrans command of Corinth, with his three divisions and some detachments, aggregating about twenty thousand men. He posted General Ord with his own and Hurlbut's divisions at Bolivar, with outposts toward Grand Junction and Lagrange. These amounted to nine or ten thousand men, and I held Memphis with my own division, amounting to about six thousand men. The whole of General Grant's men at that time may have aggregated fifty thousand, but he had to defend a frontage of a hundred and fifty miles, guard some two hundred miles of railway, and as much river. Van Dorn had forty thousand men, united, at perfect liberty to move in any direction, and to choose his own point of attack, under cover of woods, and a superior body of cavalry, familiar with every foot of the ground. Therefore General Grant had good

[46] The U.S. Army suffered 790 casualties during the Battle of Iuka. Gerald L. Earley, *Strategies of North and South: A Comparative Analysis of the Union and Confederate Campaigns* (Jefferson, NC: McFarland, 2021), 120.

[47] For an analysis of the phenomenon known as an "acoustic shadow," see Charles D. Ross, *Civil War Acoustic Shadows* (Shippensburg, PA: White Mane, 2001).

[48] See *PUSG,* 6:10.

reason for telegraphing to General Halleck, on the 1st of October, that his position was precarious, "but I hope to get out of it all right."[49] In Memphis my business was to hold fast that important flank, and by that date Fort Pickering had been made very strong, and capable of perfect defense by a single brigade. I therefore endeavored by excursions to threaten Van Dorn's detachments to the southeast and east. I repeatedly sent out strong detachments toward Holly Springs, which was his main depot of supply; and General Grierson, with his Sixth Illinois,[50] the only cavalry I had, made some bold and successful dashes at the Coldwater, compelling Van Dorn to cover it by Armstrong's whole division of cavalry. Still, by the 1st of October, General Grant was satisfied that the enemy was meditating an attack in force on Bolivar or Corinth; and on the 2d Van Dorn made his appearance near Corinth, with his entire army. On the 3d he moved down on that place from the north and northwest. General Rosecrans went out some four miles to meet him, but was worsted and compelled to fall back within the line of his forts. These had been begun under General Halleck, but were much strengthened by General Grant, and consisted of several detached redoubts, bearing on each other, and inclosing the town and the depots of stores at the intersection of the two railroads. Van Dorn closed down on the forts by the evening of the 3d, and on the morning of the 4th assaulted with great vehemence. Our men, covered by good parapets, fought gallantly, and defended their posts well, inflicting terrible losses on the enemy, so that by noon the rebels were repulsed at all points, and drew off, leaving their dead and wounded in our hands. Their losses, were variously estimated, but the whole truth will probably never be known, for in that army reports and returns were not the fashion. General Rosecrans admitted his own loss to be three hundred and fifteen killed, eighteen hundred and twelve wounded, and two hundred and thirty-two missing or prisoners, and claimed on the part of the rebels fourteen hundred and twenty-three dead, two thousand and twenty-five prisoners and wounded. Of course, most of the wounded must have gone off or been carried off, so that, beyond doubt, the rebel army lost at Corinth fully six thousand men.

Meantime, General Grant, at Jackson, had dispatched Brigadier-General McPherson, with a brigade, directly for Corinth, which reached General Rosecrans after the battle; and, in anticipation of his victory, had ordered him to pursue instantly, notifying him that he had ordered Ord's and Hurlbut's

[49] For USG's telegram to Halleck, see *OR*, I, 17(II), 250.

[50] Benjamin H. Grierson (1826–1911) commanded the 3rd Brig., Cav. D, 17th Corps, Army of the Tennessee. *CWHC*, 268.

divisions rapidly across to Pocahontas, so as to strike the rebels in flank. On the morning of the 5th, General Ord reached the Hatchie River, at Davis's bridge, with four thousand men; crossed over and encountered the retreating army, captured a battery and several hundred prisoners, dispersing the rebel advance, and forcing the main column to make a wide circuit by the south in order to cross the Hatchie River. Had General Rosecrans pursued promptly, and been on the heels of this mass of confused and routed men, Van Dorn's army would surely have been utterly ruined; as it was, Van Dorn regained Holly Springs somewhat demoralized.

General Rosecrans did not begin his pursuit till the next morning, the 5th, and it was then too late. General Grant was again displeased with him, and never became fully reconciled. General Rosecrans was soon after relieved, and transferred to the Army of the Cumberland, in Tennessee, of which he afterward obtained the command, in place of General Buell, who was removed.[51]

The effect of the battle of Corinth was very great. It was, indeed, a decisive blow to the Confederate cause in our quarter, and changed the whole aspect of affairs in West Tennessee. From the timid defensive we were at once enabled to assume the bold offensive. In Memphis I could see its effects upon the citizens, and they openly admitted that their cause had sustained a death-blow. But the rebel government was then at its maximum strength; Van Dorn was reënforced, and very soon Lieutenant-General J. C. Pemberton[52] arrived and assumed the command, adopting for his line the Tallahatchie River, with an advance-guard along the Coldwater, and smaller detachments forward at Grand Junction and Hernando. General Grant, in like manner, was reënforced by new regiments.

Out of those which were assigned to Memphis I organized two new brigades, and placed them under officers who had gained skill and experience during the previous campaign.

[51] Rosecrans provided his justification for delaying the pursuit of the retreating Confederate Army in his post-battle report. He stated, "Having ridden over it and satisfied myself of the fact I rode over all our lines, announcing the result of the fight in person, and notified our victorious troops that after two days of fighting, two almost sleepless nights of preparation, movement, and march, I wished them to replenish their cartridge-boxes, haversacks, and stomachs, take an early sleep, and start in pursuit by daylight." *OR,* I, 17(I), 170.

[52] John C. Pemberton (1814–1881) graduated from the USMA in 1837 and resigned from the U.S. Army in Apr. 1861. He joined the Confederate Army and was placed in command of the Dept. of Mississippi and East Louisiana on Oct. 10, 1863. *CWHC,* 424.

12

Memphis to Arkansas Post.

JULY, 1862 TO JANUARY, 1863.

When we first entered Memphis, July 21, 1862, I found the place dead; no business doing, the stores closed, churches, schools, and every thing shut up. The people were all more or less in sympathy with our enemies, and there was a strong prospect that the whole civil population would become a dead weight on our hands. Inasmuch as the Mississippi River was then in our possession northward, and steamboats were freely plying with passengers and freight, I caused all the stores to be opened, churches, schools, theatres, and places of amusement, to be reëstablished, and very soon Memphis resumed its appearance of an active, busy, prosperous place. I also restored the mayor (whose name was Parks)[1] and the city government to the performance of their public functions, and required them to maintain a good civil police.

Up to that date neither Congress nor the President had made any clear, well-defined rules touching the negro slaves, and the different generals had issued orders according to their own political sentiments. Both Generals Halleck and Grant regarded the slave as still a slave, only that the labor of the slave belonged to his owner, if faithful to the Union, or to the United States, if the master had taken up arms against the Government, or adhered to the fortunes of the rebellion. Therefore, in Memphis, we received all fugitives, put them to work on the fortifications, supplied them with food and clothing, and reserved the question of payment of wages for future decision. No force was allowed to be used to restore a fugitive slave to his master in any event; but if the master proved his loyalty, he was usually permitted to see his slave, and, if he could persuade him to return home, it was permitted. Cotton, also, was a fruitful subject of controversy. The Secretary of the Treasury, Mr. Chase, was extremely anxious at that particular time to promote the purchase of

[1] John Park (1812–1897) was born in Ireland and immigrated to the United States with his family in 1819. He served as the mayor of Memphis from 1861 to 1866. "John Park Peacefully Dies," *Commercial Appeal* (Memphis, TN), Aug. 8, 1897, 6.

cotton, because each bale was worth, in gold, about three hundred dollars, and answered the purpose of coin in our foreign exchanges. He therefore encouraged the trade, so that hundreds of greedy speculators flocked down the Mississippi, and resorted to all sorts of measures to obtain cotton from the interior, often purchasing it from negroes who did not own it, but who knew where it was concealed. This whole business was taken from the jurisdiction of the military, and committed to Treasury agents appointed by Mr. Chase.

Other questions absorbed the attention of military commanders; and by way of illustration I here insert a few letters from my "letter-book," which contains hundreds on similar subjects:

HEADQUARTERS FIFTH DIVISION,
MEMPHIS, TENNESSEE, *August* 11, 1862.

Hon. S. P. CHASE, *Secretary of the Treasury.*

SIR: Your letter of August 2d, just received, invites my discussion of the cotton question.

I will write plainly and slowly, because I know you have no time to listen to trifles. This is no trifle; when one nation is at war with another, all the people of the one are enemies of the other: then the rules are plain and easy of understanding. Most unfortunately, the war in which we are now engaged has been complicated with the belief on the one hand that all on the other are *not* enemies. It would have been better if, at the outset, this mistake had not been made, and it is wrong longer to be misled by it. The Government of the United States may now safely proceed on the proper rule that all in the South *are* enemies of all in the North; and not only are they unfriendly, but all who can procure arms now bear them as organized regiments, or as guerrillas. There is not a garrison in Tennessee where a man can go beyond the sight of the flag-staff without being shot or captured. It so happened that these people had cotton, and, whenever they apprehended our large armies would move, they destroyed the cotton in the belief that, of course, we would seize it, and convert it to our use. They did not and could not dream that we would pay money for it. It had been condemned to destruction by their own acknowledged government, and was therefore lost to their people; and could have been, without injustice, taken by us, and sent away, either as absolute prize of war, or for future compensation. But the commercial enterprise of the Jews soon discovered that ten cents would buy a pound of cotton behind our army; that four cents would take it to Boston, where they could receive thirty cents in gold. The bait was too tempting, and it spread like fire, when here they discovered that salt, bacon, powder, fire-arms, percussion-caps, etc., etc., were worth as much as gold; and, strange to say, this traffic was not only permitted, but encouraged. Before we in the interior could know it, hundreds, yea thousands of barrels of salt and millions of dollars had been disbursed; and I have no doubt that Bragg's army at Tupelo, and Van Dorn's at Vicksburg, received enough salt to make bacon, without which they could not have moved their armies in mass; and that from ten to twenty thousand fresh arms, and a due supply of cartridges, have also been got, I am equally satisfied. As soon as I got to Memphis, having seen the effect in the interior, I ordered (only as to my own command) that gold, silver, and Treasury notes, were contraband of war, and should not go into the interior, where all were hostile. It is idle to talk about Union men here: many want peace, and fear war and its results; but all prefer a Southern, independent government, and are fighting or working for it. Every gold dollar that was spent for cotton, was sent to the seaboard, to be exchanged for bank-notes and Confederate scrip, which will buy goods here, and are taken in ordinary transactions. I therefore required cotton to be paid for in such notes, by an obligation to pay at the end of the war, or by a deposit of the price in the hands of a trustee, viz., the United States Quartermaster. Under these rules cotton is being obtained about as fast as by any other process, and yet the enemy receives no "aid or comfort." Under the "gold" rule, the country people who had concealed their cotton from the burners, and who openly scorned our greenbacks, were willing enough to take Tennessee money, which will buy their groceries; but now that the trade is to be encouraged, and gold paid out, I admit that cotton will be sent in by our open enemies, who can make better use of gold than they can of their hidden bales of cotton.

I may not appreciate the foreign aspect of the question, but my views on this may be ventured. If England ever threatens war because we don't furnish her cotton, tell her plainly if she can't employ and feed her own people, to send them here, where they cannot only earn an honest living, but soon secure independence by moderate labor. We are not bound to furnish her cotton. She has more reason to fight the South for burning that cotton, than us for not shipping it. To aid the South on this ground would be hypocrisy which the world would detect at once. Let her make her ultimatum, and there are enough generous minds in Europe that will counteract her in the balance. Of course her motive is to cripple a power that rivals her in commerce and manufactures, that threatens even to usurp her history. In twenty more years of prosperity, it will require a close calculation to determine whether England, her laws and history, claim for a home the Continent of America or the Isle of Britain. Therefore, finding us in a death-struggle for existence, she seems to seek a quarrel to destroy both parts in detail.

Southern people know this full well, and will only accept the alliance of England in order to get arms and manufactures in exchange for their cotton. The Southern Confederacy will accept no other mediation, because she knows full well that in *Old* England her slaves and slavery will receive no more encouragement than in *New* England.

France certainly does not need our cotton enough to disturb her equilibrium, and her mediation would be entitled to a more respectful consideration than on the part of her present ally. But I feel assured the French will not encourage rebellion and secession anywhere as a political doctrine. Certainly all the German states must be our ardent friends; and, in case of European intervention, they could not be kept down.

With great respect, your obedient servant,

W. T. SHERMAN, *Major-General.*

HEADQUARTERS FIFTH DIVISION, ARMY OF THE TENNESSEE,
MEMPHIS, July 23, 1862.

Dr. E. S. PLUMMER *and others, Physicians in Memphis, Signers to a Petition.*

GENTLEMEN: I have this moment received your communication, and assure you that it grieves my heart thus to be the instrument of adding to the seeming cruelty and hardship of this unnatural war.

On my arrival here, I found my predecessor (General Hovey) had issued an order permitting the departure south of all persons subject to the conscript law of the Southern Confederacy. Many applications have been made to me to modify this order, but I regarded it as a condition precedent by which I was bound in honor, and therefore I have made no changes or modifications; nor shall I determine what action I shall adopt in relation to persons unfriendly to our cause who remain after the time limited by General Hovey's order has expired. It is now sunset, and all who have not availed themselves of General Hovey's authority, and who remain in Memphis, are supposed to be loyal and true men.

I will only say that I cannot allow the personal convenience of even a large class of ladies to influence me in my determination to make Memphis a safe place of operations for an army, and all people who are unfriendly should forthwith prepare to depart in such direction as I may hereafter indicate.

Surgeons are not liable to be made prisoners of war, but they should not reside within the lines of an army which they regard as hostile. The situation would be too delicate.

I am, with great respect, your obedient servant,

W. T. SHERMAN, *Major-General.*

HEADQUARTERS, MEMPHIS, *July* 24, 1862.

SAMUEL SAWYER, *Esq.*, *Editor Union Appeal, Memphis.*

DEAR SIR: It is well I should come to an understanding at once with the press as well as the people of Memphis, which I am ordered to command; which means, to control for the interest, welfare, and glory of the *whole* Government of the United States.

Personalities in a newspaper are wrong and criminal. Thus, though you meant to be complimentary in your sketch of my career, you make more than a dozen mistakes of fact, which I need not correct, as I don't desire my biography to be written till I am dead. It is enough for the world to know that I live and am a soldier, bound to obey the orders of my superiors, the laws of my country, and to venerate its Constitution; and that, when discretion is given me, I shall exercise it wisely and account to my superiors.

I regard your article headed "City Council—General Sherman and Colonel Slack," as highly indiscreet. Of course, no person who can jeopardize the safety of Memphis can remain here, much less exercise public authority; but I must take time, and be satisfied that injustice be not done.

If the parties named be the men you describe, the fact should not be published, to put them on their guard and thus to encourage their escape. The evidence should be carefully collected, authenticated, and then placed in my hands. But your statement of facts is entirely qualified, in my mind, and loses its force by your negligence of the very simple facts within your reach as to myself: I had been in the army six years in 1846; am not related by blood to any member of Lucas, Turner & Co.; was associated with them in business six years (instead of two); am not colonel of the Fifteenth Infantry, but of the Thirteenth. Your correction, this morning, of the acknowledged error as to General Denver and others, is still erroneous. General Morgan L. Smith did not belong to my command at the battle of Shiloh at all, but he was transferred to my division just before reaching Corinth. I mention these facts in kindness, to show you how wrong it is to speak of persons.

I will attend to the judge, mayor, Boards of Aldermen, and policemen, all in good time.

Use your influence to reëstablish system, order, government. You may rest easy that no military commander is going to neglect internal safety, or to guard against external danger; but to do right requires time, and more patience than I usually possess. If I find the press of Memphis actuated by high principle and a sole devotion to their country, I will be their best friend; but, if I find them personal, abusive, dealing in innuendoes and hints at a blind venture, and looking to their own selfish aggrandizement and fame, then they had better look out; for I regard such persons as greater enemies to their country and to mankind than the men who, from a mistaken sense of State pride, have taken up muskets, and fight us about as hard as we care about. In haste, but in kindness, yours, etc.,

W. T. SHERMAN, *Major-General.*

HEADQUARTERS FIFTH DIVISION,
MEMPHIS, TENNESSEE, *July* 27, 1862.

JOHN PARK, *Mayor of Memphis, present.*

SIR: Yours of July 24th is before me, and has received, as all similar papers ever will, my careful and most respectful consideration. I have the most unbounded respect for the civil law, courts, and authorities, and shall do all in my power to restore them to their proper use, viz., the protection of life, liberty, and property.

Unfortunately, at this time, civil war prevails in the land, and necessarily the military, for the time being, must be superior to the civil authority, but it does not therefore destroy it. Civil courts and executive officers should still exist and perform duties, without which civil or municipal bodies would soon pass into disrespect—an end to be avoided. I am glad to find in Memphis a mayor and municipal authorities not only in existence, but in the co-exercise of important functions, and I shall endeavor to restore one or more civil tribunals for the arbitration of contracts and punishment of crimes, which the military have neither time nor inclination to interfere with. Among these, first in importance is the maintenance of order, peace, and quiet, within the jurisdiction of Memphis. To insure this, I will keep a strong provost guard in the city, but will limit their duty to guarding public property held or claimed by the United States, and for the arrest and confinement of State prisoners and soldiers who are disorderly or improperly away from their regiments. This guard ought not to arrest citizens for disorder or minor crimes. This should be done by the city police. I understand that the city police is too weak in numbers to accomplish this perfectly, and I therefore recommend that the City Council at once take steps to increase this force to a number which, in their judgment, day and night can enforce your ordinances as to peace, quiet, and order; so that any change in our military dispositions will not have a tendency to leave your people unguarded. I am willing to instruct the provost guard to assist the police force when any combination is made too strong for them to overcome; but the city police should be strong enough for any probable contingency. The cost of maintaining this police force must necessarily fall upon all citizens equitably.

I am not willing, nor do I think it good policy, for the city authorities to collect the taxes belonging to the State and County, as you recommend; for these would have to be refunded. Better meet the expenses at once by a new tax on all interested. Therefore, if you, on consultation with the proper municipal body, will frame a good bill for the increase of your police force, and for raising the necessary means for their support and maintenance, I will approve it and aid you in the collection of the tax. Of course, I cannot suggest how this tax should be laid, but I think that it should be made uniform on all interests, real estate, and personal property, including money and merchandise.

All who are protected should share the expenses in proportion to the interests involved. I am, with respect, your obedient servant,

W. T. Sherman, *Major-General commanding.*

HEADQUARTERS FIFTH DIVISION,
MEMPHIS, *August* 7, 1862.

Captain FITCH, *Assistant Quartermaster, Memphis, Tennessee.*

SIR: The duties devolving on the quartermaster of this post, in addition to his legitimate functions, are very important and onerous, and I am fully aware that the task is more than should devolve on one man. I will endeavor to get you help in the person of some commissioned officer, and, if possible, one under bond, as he must handle large amounts of money in trust; but, for the present, we must execute the duties falling to our share as well as possible. On the subject of vacant houses, General Grant's orders are: "Take possession of all vacant stores and houses in the city, and have them rented at reasonable rates; rent to be paid monthly in advance. These buildings, with their tenants, can be turned over to proprietors on proof of loyalty; also take charge of such as have been leased out by disloyal owners."

I understand that General Grant takes the rents and profits of this class of real property under the rules and laws of war, and not under the confiscation act of Congress; therefore the question of title is not involved—simply the possession, and the rents and profits of houses belonging to our enemies, which are not vacant, we hold in trust for them or the Government, according to the future decisions of the proper tribunals.

Mr. McDonald, your chief agent in renting and managing this business, called on me last evening and left with me written questions, which it would take a volume to answer and a Webster to elucidate; but as we can only attempt plain, substantial justice, I will answer these questions as well as I can, briefly and to the point:

First. When ground is owned by parties who have gone south, and have leased the ground to parties now in the city who own the improvements on the ground?

Answer. The United States takes the rents due the owner of the land; does not disturb the owner of the improvements.

Second. When parties owning houses have gone south, and the tenant has given his notes for the rent in advance?

Answer. Notes are mere evidence of the debt due landlord. The tenant pays the rent to the quartermaster, who gives a bond of indemnity against the notes representing the debt for the particular rent.

Third. When the tenant has expended several months' rent in repairs on the house?

Answer. Of course, allow all such credits on reasonable proof and showing.

Fourth. When the owner has gone south, and parties here hold liens on the property and are collecting the rents to satisfy their liens?

Answer. The rent of a house can only be mortgaged to a person in possession. If a loyal tenant be in possession and claim the rent from himself as due to himself on some other debt, allow it; but, if not in actual possession of the property, rents are not good liens for a debt, but must be paid to the quartermaster.

Fifth. Of parties claiming foreign protection?

Answer. Many claim foreign protection who are not entitled to it. If they are foreign subjects residing for business in this country, they are entitled to consideration and protection so long as they obey the laws of the country. If they occupy houses belonging to absent rebels, they must pay rent to the quartermaster. If they own property, they must occupy it by themselves, tenants, or servants.

Eighth. When houses are occupied and the owner has gone south, leaving an agent to collect rent for his benefit?

Answer. Rent must be paid to the quartermaster. No agent can collect and remit money south without subjecting himself to arrest and trial for aiding and abetting the public enemy.

Ninth. When houses are owned by loyal citizens, but are unoccupied?

Answer. Such should not be disturbed, but it would be well to advise them to have some servant at the house to occupy it.

Tenth. When parties who occupy the house are creditors of the owner, who has gone south?

Answer. You only look to collection of rents. Any person who transmits money south is liable to arrest and trial for aiding and abetting the enemy; but I do not think it our business to collect debts other than rents.

Eleventh. When the parties who own the property have left the city under General Hovey's Order No. 1, but are in the immediate neighborhood, on their plantations?

Answer. It makes no difference where they are, so they are absent.

Twelfth. When movable property is found in stores that are closed?

Answer. The goods are security for the rent. If the owner of the goods prefers to remove the goods to paying rent, he can do so.

Thirteenth. When the owner lives in town, and refuses to take the oath of allegiance?

Answer. If the house be occupied, it does not fall under the order. If the house be vacant, it does. The owner can recover his property by taking the oath.

All persons in Memphis residing within our military lines are presumed to be loyal, good citizens, and may at any moment be called to serve on juries, *posses comitatus,* or other civil service required by the Constitution and laws of our country. Should they be called upon to do such duty, which would require them to acknowledge their allegiance and subordination to the Constitution of the United States, it would then be too late to refuse. So long as they remain quiet and conform to these laws, they are entitled to protection in their property and lives.

We have nothing to do with confiscation. We only deal with possession, and therefore the necessity of a strict accountability, because the United States assumes the place of trustee, and must account to the rightful owner for his property, rents, and profits. In due season courts will be established to execute the laws, the confiscation act included, when we will be relieved of this duty and trust. Until that time, every opportunity should be given to the wavering and disloyal to return to their allegiance to the Constitution of their birth or adoption. I am, etc.,

W. T. SHERMAN,
Major-General commanding.

HEADQUARTERS FIFTH DIVISION,
MEMPHIS, TENNESSEE, *August* 26, 1862.

Major-General GRANT, *Corinth, Mississippi.*

SIR: In pursuance of your request that I should keep you advised of matters of interest here, in addition to the purely official matters, I now write.

I dispatched promptly the thirteen companies of cavalry, nine of Fourth Illinois, and four of Eleventh Illinois, to their respective destinations, punctually on the 23d instant, although the order was only received on the 22d. I received at the same time, from Colonel Dickey, the notice that the bridge over Hatchie was burned, and therefore I prescribed their order of march *via* Bolivar. They started at 12 M. of the 23d, and I have no news of them since. None of the cavalry ordered to me is yet heard from.

The guerrillas have destroyed several bridges over Wolf Creek; one at Raleigh, on the road by which I had prescribed trade and travel to and from the city. I have a strong guard at the lower bridge over Wolf River, by which we can reach the country to the north of that stream; but, as the Confederates have burned their own bridges, I will hold them to my order, and allow no trade over any other road than the one prescribed, using the lower or Randolph road for our own convenience. I am still satisfied there is no large force of rebels anywhere in the neighborhood. All the navy gunboats are below except the St. Louis, which lies off the city. When Commodore Davis passes down from Cairo, I will try to see him, and get him to exchange the St. Louis for a fleeter boat not iron-clad; one that can move up and down the river, to break up ferry-boats and canoes, and to prevent all passing across the river. Of course, in spite of all our efforts, smuggling is carried on. We occasionally make hauls of clothing, gold-lace, buttons, etc., but I am satisfied that salt and arms are got to the interior somehow. I have addressed the Board of Trade a letter on this point, which will enable us to control it better.

You may have been troubled at hearing reports of drunkenness here. There was some after pay-day, but generally all is as quiet and orderly as possible. I traverse the city every day and night, and assert that Memphis is and has been as orderly a city as St. Louis, Cincinnati, or New York.

Before the city authorities undertook to license saloons, there was as much whiskey here as now, and it would take all my command as custom-house inspectors, to break open all the parcels and packages containing liquor. I can destroy all groggeries and shops where soldiers get liquor just as we would in St. Louis.

The newspapers are accusing me of cruelty to the sick; as base a charge as was ever made. I would not let the Sanitary Committee carry off a boat-load of sick, because I have no right to. We have good hospitals here, and plenty of them. Our regimental hospitals are in the camps of the men, and the sick do much better there than in the general hospitals; so say my division surgeon and the regimental surgeons. The civilian doctors would, if permitted, take away our entire command. General Curtis sends his sick up here, but usually no nurses; and it is not right that nurses should be taken from my command for his sick. I think that, when we are endeavoring to raise soldiers and to instruct them, it is bad policy to keep them at hospitals as attendants and nurses.

I send you Dr. Derby's acknowledgment that he gave the leave of absence of which he was charged. I have placed him in arrest, in obedience to General Halleck's orders, but he remains in charge of the Overton Hospital, which is not full of patients.

The State Hospital also is not full, and I cannot imagine what Dr. Derby wants with the Female Academy on Vance Street. I will see him again, and now that he is the chief at Overton Hospital, I think he will not want the academy. Still, if he does, under your orders I will cause it to be vacated by the children and Sisters of Mercy. They have just advertised for more scholars, and will be sadly disappointed. If, however, this building or any other be needed for a hospital, it must be taken; but really, in my heart, I do not see what possible chance there is, under present circumstances, of filling with patients the two large hospitals now in use, besides the one asked for. I may, however, be mistaken in the particular building asked for by Dr. Derby, and will go myself to see.

The fort is progressing well, Captain Jenney having arrived. Sixteen heavy guns are received, with a large amount of shot and shell, but the platforms are not yet ready; still, if occasion should arise for dispatch, I can put a larger force to work. Captain Prime, when here, advised that the work should proceed regularly under the proper engineer officers and laborers.

I am, etc.,
W. T. SHERMAN, *Major-General commanding.*

HEADQUARTERS FIFTH DIVISION,
MEMPHIS, TENNESSEE, *September* 4, 1862.

Colonel J. C. KELTON, *Assistant Adjutant-General, Headquarters of the Army, Washington, D. C.*

DEAR COLONEL: Please acknowledge to the major-general commanding the receipt by me of his letter, and convey to him my assurances that I have promptly modified my first instructions about cotton, so as to conform to his orders. Trade in cotton is now free, but in all else I endeavor so to control it that the enemy shall receive no contraband goods, or any aid or comfort; still I feel sure that the officers of steamboats are sadly tempted by high prices to land salt and other prohibited articles at waypoints along the river. This, too, in time will be checked.

All seems well here and hereabout; no large body of the enemy within striking distance. A force of about two thousand cavalry passed through Grand Junction north last Friday, and fell on a detachment of the Bolivar army at Middleburg, the result of which is doubtless reported to you. As soon as I heard of the movement, I dispatched a force to the southeast by way of diversion, and am satisfied that the enemy's infantry and artillery fell back in consequence behind the Tallahatchie.

The weather is very hot, country very dry, and dust as bad as possible. I hold my two divisions ready, with their original complement of transportation, for field service.

Of course all things most now depend on events in front of Washington and in Kentucky.

The gunboat Eastport and four transports loaded with prisoners of war destined for Vicksburg have been lying before Memphis for two days, but are now steaming up to resume their voyage.

Our fort progresses well, but our guns are not yet mounted. The engineers are now shaping the banquette to receive platforms. I expect Captain Prime from Corinth in two or three days.

I am, with great respect, yours,

W. T. Sherman, *Major-General commanding.*

Headquarters Fifth Division,
Memphis, Tennessee, *September* 21, 1862.

Editor Bulletin.

Sir: Your comments on the recent orders of Generals Halleck and McClellan afford the occasion appropriate for me to make public the fact that there is a law of Congress, as old as our Government itself, but reënacted on the 10th of April, 1806, and in force ever since. That law reads:

"All officers and soldiers are to behave themselves orderly in quarters and on the march; and whoever shall commit any waste or spoil, either in walks of trees, parks, warrens, fish-ponds, houses and gardens, cornfields, inclosures or meadows, or shall maliciously destroy any property whatever belonging to the inhabitants of the United States, unless by order of the commander-in-chief of the armies of said United

States, shall (besides such penalties as they are liable to by law) be punished according to the nature and degree of the offense, by the judgment of a general or regimental court-martial."

Such is the law of Congress; and the orders of the commander-in-chief are, that officers or soldiers convicted of straggling and pillaging shall be punished with death. These orders have not come to me officially, but I have seen them in newspapers, and am satisfied that they express the determination of the commander-in-chief. Straggling and pillaging have ever been great military crimes; and every officer and soldier in my command knows what stress I have laid upon them, and that, so far as in my power lies, I will punish them to the full extent of the law and orders.

The law is one thing, the execution of the law another. God himself has commanded: "Thou shalt not kill," "thou shalt not steal," "thou shalt not covet thy neighbor's goods," etc. Will any one say these things are not done now as well as before these laws were announced at Sinai? I admit the law to be that "no officer or soldier of the United States shall commit waste or destruction of cornfields, orchards, potato-patches, or any kind of pillage on the property of friend or foe near Memphis," and that I stand prepared to execute the law as far as possible.

No officer or soldier should enter the house or premises of any peaceable citizen, no matter what his politics, unless on business; and no such officer or soldier can force an entrance unless he have a written order from a commanding officer or provost-marshal, which written authority must be exhibited if demanded. When property such as forage, building or other materials are needed by the United States, a receipt will be given by the officer taking them, which receipt should be presented to the quartermaster, who will substitute therefor a regular voucher, to be paid according to the circumstances of the case. If the officer refuse to give such receipt, the citizen may fairly infer that the property is wrongfully taken, and he should, for his own protection, ascertain the name, rank, and regiment of the officer, and report him in writing. If any soldier commits waste or destruction, the person whose property is thus wasted must find out the name, company, and regiment of the actual transgressor. In order to punish there must be a trial, and there must be testimony. It is not sufficient that a general accusation be made, that soldiers are doing this or that. I cannot punish my whole command, or a whole battalion, because one or two bad soldiers do wrong. The punishment must reach the perpetrators, and no one can identify them as well as the party who is interested. The State of Tennessee does not hold itself responsible for acts of larceny committed by her citizens, nor does the United States or any other nation. These are individual acts of wrong, and punishment can only be inflicted on the wrong-doer. I know the difficulty of identifying particular soldiers, but difficulties do not alter the importance of principles of justice. They should stimulate the parties to increase their efforts to find out the actual perpetrators of the crime.

Colonels of regiments and commanders of corps are liable to severe punishment for permitting their men to leave their camps to commit waste or destruction; but I know full well that many of the acts attributed to soldiers are committed by citizens and negroes, and are charged to soldiers because of a desire to find fault with them; but this only reacts upon the community and increases the mischief. While every officer would willingly follow up an accusation against any one or more of his men whose names or description were given immediately after the discovery of the act, he would naturally resent any general charge against his *good* men, for the criminal conduct of a few bad ones.

I have examined into many of the cases of complaint made in this general way, and have felt mortified that our soldiers should do acts which are nothing more or less than stealing, but I was powerless without some clew whereby to reach the rightful party. I know that the great mass of our soldiers would scorn to steal or commit crime, and I will not therefore entertain vague and general complaints, but stand prepared always to follow up any reasonable complaint when the charge is definite and the names of witnesses furnished.

I know, moreover, in some instances when our soldiers are complained of, that they have been insulted by sneering remarks about "Yankees," "Northern barbarians," "Lincoln's hirelings," etc. People who use such language must seek redress through some one else, for I will not tolerate insults to our country or cause. When people forget their obligations to a Government that made them respected among the nations of the earth, and speak contemptuously of the flag which is the silent emblem of that country, I will not go out of my way to protect them or their property. I will punish the soldiers for trespass or waste if adjudged by a court-martial, because they disobey orders; but soldiers are men and citizens as well as soldiers, and should promptly resent any insult to their country, come from what quarter it may. I mention this phase because it is too common. Insult to a soldier does not justify pillage, but it takes from the officer the disposition he would otherwise feel to follow up the inquiry and punish the wrong-doers.

Again, armies in motion or stationary must commit some waste. Flankers must let down fences and cross fields; and, when an attack is contemplated or apprehended, a command will naturally clear the ground of houses, fences, and trees. This is waste, but is the natural consequence of war, chargeable on those who caused the war. So in fortifying a place, dwelling-houses must be taken, materials used, even wasted, and great damage done, which in the end may prove useless. This, too, is an expense not chargeable to us, but to those who made the war; and generally war is destruction and nothing else.

We must bear this in mind, that however peaceful things look, we are really *at war;* and much that looks like waste or destruction is only the removal of objects that obstruct our fire, or would afford cover to an enemy.

This class of waste must be distinguished from the wanton waste committed by army-stragglers, which is wrong, and can be punished by the death-penalty if proper testimony can be produced.

Yours, etc.,

W. T. SHERMAN, *Major-General commanding.*

Satisfied that, in the progress of the war, Memphis would become an important depot, I pushed forward the construction of Fort Pickering, kept most of the troops in camps back of the city, and my own headquarters remained in tents on the edge of the city, near Mr. Moon's house, until, on the approach of winter, Mrs. Sherman came down with the children[2] to visit me, when I took a house nearer the fort.

All this time battalion and brigade drills were enforced, so that, when the season approached for active operations farther south, I had my division in the best possible order, and about the 1st of November it was composed as follows:

[2] In July 1862, WTS and Ellen had six children—Maria Sherman, Mary Sherman, William T. Sherman Jr., Thomas E. Sherman (1856–1933), Eleanor M. Sherman (1859–1915), and Rachel Ewing Sherman (1861–1919). Thomas T. Sherman, *Sherman Genealogy Including Families of Essex, Suffolk and Norfolk, England* (Madison: University of Wisconsin, 1920), 397–399.

First Brigade, Brigadier-General M. L. SMITH.—Eighth Missouri, Colonel G. A. Smith; Sixth Missouri, Colonel Peter E. Bland; One Hundred and Thirteenth Illinois, Colonel George B. Hoge; Fifty-fourth Ohio, Colonel T. Kilby Smith; One Hundred and Twentieth Illinois, Colonel G. W. McKeaig.

Second Brigade, Colonel JOHN ADAIR MCDOWELL.—Sixth Iowa, Lieutenant-Colonel John M. Corse; Fortieth Illinois, Colonel J. W. Booth; Forty-sixth Ohio, Colonel C. C. Walcutt; Thirteenth United States Infantry, First Battalion, Major D. Chase.

Third Brigade, Brigadier-General J. W. DENVER.—Forty-eighth Ohio, Colonel P. J. Sullivan; Fifty-third Ohio, Colonel W. S. Jones; Seventieth Ohio, Colonel J. R. Cockerill.

Fourth Brigade, Colonel DAVID STUART.—Fifty-fifth Illinois, Colonel O. Malmburg; Fifty-seventh Ohio, Colonel W. Mungen; Eighty-third Indiana, Colonel B. Spooner; One Hundred and Sixteenth Illinois, Colonel Tupper; One Hundred and Twenty-seventh Illinois, Lieutenant-Colonel Eldridge.

Fifth Brigade, Colonel R. P. BUCKLAND.—Seventy-second Ohio, Lieutenant-Colonel D. W. C. Loudon; Thirty-second Wisconsin, Colonel J. W. Howe; Ninety-third Indiana, Colonel Thomas; Ninety-third Illinois, Major J. M. Fisher.

Subsequently, Brigadier-General J. G. Lauman[3] arrived at Memphis, and I made up a sixth brigade, and organized these six brigades into three divisions, under Brigadier-Generals M. L. Smith, J. W. Denver, and J. G. Lauman.

About the 17th of November I received an order from General Grant, dated—

LAGRANGE, *November* 15, 1862.

Meet me at Columbus, Kentucky, on Thursday next. If you have a good map of the country south of you, take it up with you.

U. S. GRANT, *Major-General.*

I started forthwith by boat, and met General Grant, who had reached Columbus by the railroad from Jackson, Tennessee. He explained to me that he proposed to move against Pemberton, then intrenched on a line behind the Tallahatchie River below Holly Springs; that he would move on

[3] Jacob G. Lauman (1813–1867) took command of the 3rd Div., Dist. of Memphis, 8th Corps, Army of the Tennessee, on Nov. 23, 1862. *CWHC,* 340.

Holly Springs and Abberville, from Grand Junction; that McPherson, with the troops at Corinth, would aim to make junction with him at Holly Springs; and that he wanted me to leave in Memphis a proper garrison, and to aim for the Tallahatchie, so as to come up on his right by a certain date. He further said that his ultimate object was to capture Vicksburg, to open the navigation of the Mississippi River, and that General Halleck had authorized him to call on the troops in the Department of Arkansas, then commanded by General S. R. Curtis, for coöperation. I suggested to him that if he would request General Curtis to send an expedition from some point on the Mississippi, near Helena, then held in force, toward Grenada, to the rear of Pemberton, it would alarm him for the safety of his communications, and would assist us materially in the proposed attack on his front. He authorized me to send to the commanding officer at Helena a request to that effect, and, as soon as I reached Memphis, I dispatched my aide, Major McCoy, to Helena, who returned, bringing me a letter from General Frederick Steele, who had just reached Helena with Osterhaus's division, and who was temporarily in command, General Curtis having gone to St. Louis. This letter contained the assurance that he "would send from Friar's Point a large force under Brigadier-General A. P. Hovey in the direction of Grenada, aiming to reach the Tallahatchie at Charleston, on the next Monday, Tuesday, or Wednesday (December 1st) at furthest." My command was appointed to start on Wednesday, November 24th, and meantime Major-General S. A. Hurlbut, having reported for duty, was assigned to the command of Memphis, with four regiments of infantry, one battery of artillery, two companies of Thielman's cavalry[4] and the certain prospect of soon receiving a number of new regiments, known to be *en route.*

I marched out of Memphis punctually with three small divisions, taking different roads till we approached the Tallahatchie, when we converged on Wyatt[5] to cross the river, there a bold, deep stream, with a newly-constructed fort behind. I had Grierson's Sixth Illinois Cavalry with me, and with it opened communication with General Grant when we were abreast of Holly

[4] Christian Thielemann (1809–1875) commanded an independent battalion of Illinois Cav. in late 1862. Roger D. Hunt, *Colonels in Blue: Illinois, Iowa, Minnesota, and Wisconsin* (Jefferson, NC: McFarland, 2017), s.v. "Christian Thielemann."

[5] Wyatt, MS, was located approximately twenty miles south of Holly Springs, MS. George B. Davis et al., *Official Military Atlas of the Civil War* (New York: Fairfax Press, 1983), plate 154.

Springs. We reached Wyatt on the 2d day of December without the least opposition, and there learned that Pemberton's whole army had fallen back to the Yalabusha, near Grenada, in a great measure by reason of the exaggerated reports concerning the Helena force, which had reached Charleston; and some of General Hovey's cavalry, under General Washburn,[6] having struck the railroad in the neighborhood of Coffeeville, naturally alarmed General Pemberton for the safety of his communications, and made him let go his Tallahatchie line with all the forts which he had built at great cost in labor. We had to build a bridge at Wyatt, which consumed a couple of days, and on the 5th of December my whole command was at College Hill, ten miles from Oxford,[7] whence I reported to General Grant in Oxford.

On the 8th I received the following letter:

OXFORD, MISSISSIPPI, *December* 8, 1862.—*Morning.*

General SHERMAN, *College Hill.*

DEAR GENERAL: The following is a copy of dispatch just received from Washington:

WASHINGTON, *December* 7, 1862.—12 M.

General GRANT:

The capture of Grenada may change our plans in regard to Vicksburg. You will move your troops as you may deem best to accomplish the great object in view. You will retain, till further orders, all troops of General Curtis now in your department. Telegraph to General Allen in St. Louis for all steamboats you may require. Ask Porter to coöperate. Telegraph what are your present plans.

H. W. HALLECK, *General-in-Chief.*

I wish you would come over this evening and stay to-night, or come in the morning. I would like to talk with you about this matter. My notion is to send two divisions back to Memphis, and fix upon a day when they should effect a landing, and press from here with this command at the proper time to coöperate. If I do not do this I will move our present force to Grenada, including Steele's, repairing road as

[6] Cadwallader C. Washburn (1818–1882) commanded the 3rd Cav. Div., Dist. of Arkansas, Dept. of the Missouri, in Dec. 1862. *CWHC,* 555.

[7] See Davis et al., *Official Military Atlas of the Civil War,* plate 154.

we proceed, and establish a depot of provisions there. When a good ready is had, to move immediately on Jackson, Mississippi, cutting loose from the road. Of the two plans I look most favorably on the former.

Come over and we will talk this matter over.

Yours truly,

U. S. Grant, *Major-General.*

I repaired at once to Oxford, and found General Grant in a large house with all his staff, and we discussed every possible chance.[8] He explained to me that large reënforcements had been promised, which would reach Memphis very soon, if not already there; that the entire gunboat fleet, then under the command of Admiral D. D. Porter,[9] would coöperate; that we could count on a full division from the troops at Helena; and he believed that, by a prompt movement, I could make a lodgment up the Yazoo and capture Vicksburg from the rear; that its garrison was small, and he, at Oxford, would so handle his troops as to hold Pemberton away from Vicksburg. I also understood that, if Pemberton should retreat south, he would follow him up, and would expect to find me at the Yazoo River, if not inside of Vicksburg. I confess, at that moment I did not dream that General McClernand, or anybody else, was scheming for the mere honor of capturing Vicksburg. We knew at the time that General Butler had been reënforced by General Banks at New Orleans, and the latter was supposed to be working his way up-stream from New Orleans, while we were working down. That day General Grant dispatched to General Halleck, in Washington, as follows:

Oxford, *December* 8, 1862.

Major-General H. W. Halleck, *Washington, D. C.:*

General Sherman will command the expedition down the Mississippi. He will have a force of about forty thousand men; will land above Vicksburg (up the Yazoo, if practicable), and cut the Mississippi

[8] USG established his headquarters in the home of James Brown, a member of the University of Mississippi's board of trustees. Timothy B. Smith, *The Decision Was Always My Own: Ulysses S. Grant and the Vicksburg Campaign* (Carbondale: Southern Illinois University Press, 2018), 17.

[9] David D. Porter (1813–1891) of the U.S. Navy took command of the Mississippi River Squadron on Oct. 9, 1862. *CWHC,* 434–435.

Central road and the road running east from Vicksburg, where they cross Black River. I will coöperate from here, my movements depending on those of the enemy. With the large cavalry force now at my command, I will be able to have them show themselves at different points on the Tallahatchie and Yalabusha; and, when an opportunity occurs, make a real attack. After cutting the two roads, General Sherman's movements to secure the end desired will necessarily be left to his judgment.I will occupy this road to Coffeeville.

U. S. Grant, *Major-General.*

I was shown this dispatch before it was sent, and afterward the general drew up for me the following letter of instructions in his own handwriting, which I now possess:

Headquarters Thirteenth Army Corps,
Department of the Tennessee, Oxford, Mississippi,
December 8, 1862.

Major-General W. T. Sherman, *commanding Right Wing Army in the Field, present.*

General: You will proceed with as little delay as practicable to Memphis, Tennessee, taking with you one division of your present command. On your arrival at Memphis you will assume command of all the troops there, and that portion of General Curtis's forces at present east of the Mississippi River, and organize them into brigades and divisions in your own way.

As soon as possible move with them down the river to the vicinity of Vicksburg, and, with the coöperation of the gunboat fleet under command of Flag-Officer Porter, proceed to the reduction of that place in such manner as circumstances and your own judgment may dictate.

The amount of rations, forage, land transportation, etc., necessary to take, will be left entirely to yourself.

The quartermaster in St. Louis will be instructed to send you transportation for thirty thousand men. Should you still find yourself deficient, your quartermaster will be authorized to make up the deficiency from such transports as may come into the port of Memphis.

On arriving in Memphis put yourself in communication with Admiral Porter, and arrange with him for his coöperation.

Inform me at the earliest practicable day of the time when you will embark, and such plans as may then be matured. I will hold the forces here in readiness to coöperate with you in such manner as the movements of the enemy may make necessary.

Leave the District of Memphis in the command of an efficient officer and with a garrison of four regiments of infantry, the siege-guns, and what ever cavalry force may be there.

One regiment of infantry and at least a section of artillery will also be left at Friar's Point or Delta, to protect the stores of the cavalry post that will be left there.

Yours truly,

U. S. Grant, *Major-General.*

I also insert here another letter, dated the 14th instant, sent afterward to me at Memphis, which completes all instructions received by me governing the first movement against Vicksburg:

Headquarters Department of the Tennessee,
Oxford, Mississippi, *December* 14, 1862.

Major-General Sherman, *commanding, etc., Memphis, Tennessee:*

I have not had one word from Grierson since he left, and am getting uneasy about him. I hope General Gorman will give you no difficulty about retaining the troops on this side the river, and Steele to command them. The twenty-one thousand men you have, with the twelve thousand from Helena, will make a good force. The enemy are as yet on the Yalabusha. I am pushing down on them slowly, but so as to keep up the impression of a continuous move. I feel particularly anxious to have the Helena cavalry on this side of the river; if not now, at least after you start. If Gorman will send them, instruct them where to go and how to communicate with me. My headquarters will probably be in Coffeeville one week hence. In the mean time I will order transportation, etc. . . . It would be well if you could have two or three small boats suitable for navigating the Yazoo. It may become necessary for me to look to that base for supplies before we get through. . . .

U. S. Grant, *Major-General.*

When we rode to Oxford from College Hill, there happened a little circumstance which seems worthy of record. While General Van Dorn had his headquarters in Holly Springs, viz., in October, 1862, he was very short of the comforts and luxuries of life, and resorted to every possible device to draw from the abundant supplies in Memphis. He had no difficulty whatever in getting spies into the town for information, but he had trouble in getting bulky supplies out through our guards, though sometimes I connived at his supplies of cigars, liquors, boots, gloves, etc., for his individual use; but medicines and large supplies of all kinds were confiscated, if attempted to be passed out. As we rode that morning toward Oxford, I observed in a farmer's barn-yard a wagon that looked like a city furniture-wagon with springs. We were always short of wagons, so I called the attention of the quartermaster, Colonel J. Condit Smith,[10] saying, "There is a good wagon; go for it." He dropped out of the retinue with an orderly, and after we had ridden a mile or so he overtook us, and I asked him, "What luck?" He answered, "All right; I have secured that wagon, and I also got another," and explained that he had gone to the farmer's house to inquire about the furniture-wagon, when the farmer said it did not belong to him, but to some party in Memphis, adding that in his barn was another belonging to the same party. They went to the barn, and there found a handsome city hearse, with pall and plumes. The farmer said they had had a big funeral out of Memphis, but when it reached his house, the coffin was found to contain a fine assortment of medicines for the use of Van Dorn's army. Thus under the pretense of a first-class funeral, they had carried through our guards the very things we had tried to prevent. It was a good trick, but diminished our respect for such pageants afterward.

As soon as I was in possession of General Grant's instructions of December 8th, with a further request that I should dispatch Colonel Grierson, with his cavalry, across by land to Helena, to notify General Steele of the general plan, I returned to College Hill, selected the division of Brigadier-General Morgan L. Smith to return with me to Memphis; started Grierson on his errand to Helena, and ordered Generals Denver and Lauman to report to General Grant for further orders. We started back by the most direct route, reached Memphis by noon of December 12th, and began immediately the preparations for the Vicksburg movement. There I found two irregular divisions which had arrived at Memphis in my absence, commanded respectively by Brigadier-General A. J. Smith and Brigadier-General George W. Morgan.[11] These were designated the

[10] John C. Smith (1830–1883) was the chief quartermaster under WTS's command in 1862. John W. Jordan, *Colonial and Revolutionary Families of Pennsylvania* (New York: Lewis, 1911), 2:793.

[11] George W. Morgan (1820–1893) served as the U.S. consul to France from 1856 to 1858 and U.S. minister to Portugal from 1858 to 1861. He joined the U.S. Army as a brigadier general in

First and Third Divisions, leaving the Second Division of Morgan L. Smith to retain its original name and number.

I also sent orders, in the name of General Grant, to General Gorman, who meantime had replaced General Steele in command of Helena, in lieu of the troops which had been east of the Mississippi and had returned, to make up a strong division to report to me on my way down. This division was accordingly organized, and was commanded by Brigadier-General Frederick Steele, constituting my Fourth Division.

Meantime a large fleet of steamboats was assembling from St. Louis and Cairo, and Admiral Porter dropped down to Memphis with his whole gunboat fleet, ready to coöperate in the movement. The preparations were necessarily hasty in the extreme, but this was the essence of the whole plan, viz., to reach Vicksburg as it were by surprise, while General Grant held in check Pemberton's army about Grenada, leaving me to contend only with the smaller garrison of Vicksburg and its well-known strong batteries and defenses. On the 19th the Memphis troops were embarked, and steamed down to Helena, where on the 21st General Steele's division was also embarked; and on the 22d we were all rendezvoused at Friar's Point, in the following order, viz.:

Steamer Forest Queen, general headquarters, and battalion Thirteenth United States Infantry.

First Division, Brigadier-General A. J. SMITH.—Steamers Des Arc, division headquarters and escort; Metropolitan, Sixth Indiana; J. H. Dickey, Twenty-third Wisconsin; J. C. Snow, Sixteenth Indiana; Hiawatha, Ninety-sixth Ohio; J. S. Pringle, Sixty-seventh Indiana; J. W. Cheeseman, Ninth Kentucky; R. Campbell, Ninety-seventh Indiana; Duke of Argyle, Seventy-seventh Illinois; City of Alton, One Hundred and Eighth and Forty-eighth Ohio; City of Louisiana, Mercantile Battery; Ohio Belle, Seventeenth Ohio Battery; Citizen, Eighty-third Ohio; Champion, commissary-boat; General Anderson, Ordnance.

Second Division, Brigadier-General M. L. SMITH.—Steamers Chancellor, headquarters, and Thielman's cavalry; Planet, One Hundred and Sixteenth Illinois; City of Memphis, Batteries A and B (Missouri Artillery), Eighth Missouri, and section of Parrott guns; Omaha, Fifty-seventh Ohio; Sioux City, Eighty-third Indiana; Spread

---

Nov. 1861 and took command of the 2nd Div., Right Wing, 8th Corps, Army of the Tennessee, on Dec. 13, 1862. *CWHC,* 397.

Eagle, One Hundred and Twenty-seventh Illinois; Ed. Walsh, One Hundred and Thirteenth Illinois; Westmoreland, Fifty-fifth Illinois, headquarters Fourth Brigade; Sunny South, Fifty-fourth Ohio; Universe, Sixth Missouri; Robert Allen, commissary-boat.

Third Division, Brigadier-General G. W. MORGAN.—Steamers Empress, division headquarters; Key West, One Hundred and Eighteenth Illinois;[12] Sam Gaty, Sixty-ninth Indiana; Northerner, One Hundred and Twentieth Ohio; Belle Peoria, headquarters Second Brigade, two companies Forty-ninth Ohio, and pontoons; Die Vernon, Third Kentucky; War Eagle, Forty-ninth Indiana (eight companies), and Foster's battery; Henry von Phul, headquarters Third Brigade, and eight companies Sixteenth Ohio; Fanny Bullitt, One Hundred and Fourteenth Ohio, and Lamphere's battery; Crescent City, Twenty-second Kentucky and Fifty-fourth Indiana; Des Moines, Forty-second Ohio; Pembina, Lamphere's and Stone's batteries; Lady Jackson, commissary-boat.

Fourth Division, Brigadier-General FREDERICK STEELE—Steamers Continental, headquarters, escort and battery; John J. Roe, Fourth and Ninth Iowa; Nebraska, Thirty-first Iowa; Key West, First Iowa Artillery; John Warner, Thirteenth Illinois; Tecumseh, Twenty-sixth Iowa; Decatur, Twenty-eighth Iowa; Quitman, Thirty-fourth Iowa; Kennett, Twenty-ninth Missouri; Gladiator, Thirtieth Missouri; Isabella, Thirty-first Missouri; D. G. Taylor, quartermaster's stores and horses; Sucker State, Thirty-second Missouri; Dakota, Third Missouri; Tutt, Twelfth Missouri; Emma, Seventeenth Missouri; Adriatic, First Missouri; Meteor, Seventy-sixth Ohio; Polar Star, Fifty-eighth Ohio.

At the same time were communicated the following instructions:

HEADQUARTERS RIGHT WING, THIRTEENTH ARMY CORPS,
FOREST QUEEN, *December* 23, 1862.

To Commanders of Divisions, Generals F. STEELE, GEORGE W. MORGAN, A. J. SMITH, *and* M. L. SMITH:

With this I hand to each of you a copy of a map, compiled from the best sources, and which in the main is correct. It is the same used by Admiral Porter and myself. Complete military success can only be

[12] In the first edition of the memoirs (1875), this portion of WTS's text read, "One Hundred and Eighteenth Indiana."

accomplished by united action on some *general plan,* embracing usually a large district of country. In the present instance, our object is to secure the navigation of the Mississippi River and its main branches, and to hold them as military channels of communication and for commercial purposes. The river, above Vicksburg, has been gained by conquering the country to its rear, rendering its possession by our enemy useless and unsafe to him, and of great value to us. But the enemy still holds the river from Vicksburg to Baton Rouge, navigating it with his boats, and the possession of it enables him to connect his communications and routes of supply, east and west. To deprive him of this will be a severe blow, and, if done effectually, will be of great advantage to us, and probably the most decisive act of the war. To accomplish this important result we are to act our part—an important one of the great *whole.* General Banks, with a large force, has reënforced General Butler in Louisiana, and from that quarter an expedition, by water and land, is coming northward. General Grant, with the Thirteenth Army Corps, of which we compose the right wing, is moving southward. The naval squadron (Admiral Porter) is operating with his gunboat fleet by water, each in perfect harmony with the other.

General Grant's left and centre were at last accounts approaching the Yalabusha, near Grenada, and the railroad to his rear, by which he drew his supplies, was reported to be seriously damaged. This may disconcert him somewhat, but only makes more important our line of operations. At the Yalabusha General Grant may encounter the army of General Pemberton, the same which refused him *battle* on the line of the Tallahatchie, which was strongly fortified; but, as he will not have time to fortify it, he will hardly stand there; and, in that event, General Grant will immediately advance down the high ridge between the Big Black and Yazoo, and will expect to meet us on the Yazoo and receive from us the supplies which he needs, and which he knows we carry along. Parts of this general plan are to coöperate with the naval squadron in the reduction of Vicksburg; to secure possession of the land lying between the Yazoo and Big Black; and to act in concert with General Grant against Pemberton's forces, supposed to have Jackson, Mississippi, as a point of concentration. Vicksburg is doubtless very strongly fortified, both against the river and land approaches. Already the gunboats have secured the Yazoo up for twenty-three miles, to a fort on the Yazoo at Haines's Bluff, giving us a choice for a landing-place at some point up the Yazoo below this fort, or on the island which lies between Vicksburg and the present mouth of the Yazoo. (*See* map [*b, c, d*], Johnson's plantation.)

But, before any actual collision with the enemy, I purpose, after our whole *land-force* is rendezvoused at Gaines's Landing, Arkansas, to proceed in order to Milliken's Bend (*a*), and there dispatch a brigade, without wagons or any incumbrances whatever, to the Vicksburg & Shreveport Railroad (at *h* and *k*), to destroy that effectually, and to cut off that fruitful avenue of supply; then to proceed to the mouth of the Yazoo, and, after possessing ourselves of the latest and most authentic information from naval officers now there, to land our whole force on the Mississippi side, and then to reach the point where the Vicksburg & Jackson Railroad crosses the Big Black (*f*); after which to attack Vicksburg *by land,* while the gunboats assail it by water. It may be necessary (looking to Grant's approach), before attacking Vicksburg, to reduce the battery at *Haine's Bluff* first, so as to enable some of the lighter gunboats and transports to ascend the Yazoo and communicate with General Grant. The detailed manner of accomplishing all these results will be communicated in due season, and these general points are only made known at this time, that commanders may study the maps, and also that in the event of non-receipt of orders all may act in perfect concert by following the general movement, unless specially detached.

You all now have the same map, so that no mistakes or confusion need result from different names of localities. All possible preparations as to wagons, provisions, axes, and intrenching-tools, should be made in advance, so that when we do land there will be no want of them. When we begin to act on shore, we must do the work quickly and effectually. The gunboats under Admiral Porter will do their full share, and I feel every assurance that the army will not fall short in its work.

Division commanders may read this to regimental commanders, and furnish brigade commanders a copy. They should also cause as many copies of the map to be made on the same scale as possible, being very careful in copying the names.

The points marked *e* and *g* (Allan's and Mount Albans) are evidently strategical points that will figure in our future operations, and these positions should be well studied.

I am, with great respect, your obedient servant,

W. T. Sherman, *Major-General.*

The Mississippi boats were admirably calculated for handling troops, horses, guns, stores, etc., easy of embarkation and disembarkation, and supplies of all kinds were abundant, except fuel. For this we had to rely on wood, but most of the wood-yards, so common on the river before the war, had been exhausted, so that we had to use fence-rails, old dead timber, the logs of houses, etc. Having abundance of men and plenty of axes, each boat could daily procure a supply.

In proceeding down the river, one or more of Admiral Porter's gunboats took the lead; others were distributed throughout the column, and some brought up the rear. We manœuvred by divisions and brigades when in motion, and it was a magnificent sight as we thus steamed down the river. What few inhabitants remained at the plantations on the river-bank were unfriendly, except the slaves; some few guerrilla-parties infested the banks, but did not dare to molest so strong a force as I then commanded.

We reached Milliken's Bend on Christmas-day, when I detached one brigade (Burbridge's),[13] of A. J. Smith's division, to the southwest, to break up the railroad leading from Vicksburg toward Shreveport, Louisiana. Leaving A. J. Smith's division there to await the return of Burbridge, the remaining three divisions proceeded, on the 26th, to the mouth of the Yazoo, and up that river to Johnson's plantation, thirteen miles, and there disembarked—Steele's division above the mouth of Chickasaw Bayou, Morgan's division near the house of Johnson (which had been burned by the gunboats on a former occasion), and M. L. Smith's just below. A. J. Smith's division arrived the next night, and disembarked below that of M. L. Smith. The place of our disembarkation was in fact an island, separated from the high bluff known as Walnut Hills, on which the town of Vicksburg stands, by a broad and shallow bayou—evidently an old channel of the Yazoo.[14] On our right was another wide bayou, known as Old River; and on the left still another, much narrower, but too deep to be forded, known as Chickasaw Bayou. All the island was densely wooded, except Johnson's plantation, immediately on the bank of the Yazoo, and a series of old cotton-fields along Chickasaw Bayou. There was a road from Johnson's plantation directly to Vicksburg, but it crossed numerous bayous and deep swamps by bridges, which had been destroyed;

[13] Stephen G. Burbridge (1831–1894) took command of the 1st Brig., 1st Div., Right Wing, 8th Corps, Army of the Tennessee, on Dec. 18, 1862. *CWHC,* 154.

[14] The Old River, or False River, extended approximately six miles south of the Yazoo River. For a detailed map of WTS's operations near Vicksburg, see Davis et al., *Official Military Atlas of the Civil War,* plates 36–37.

and this road debouched on level ground at the foot of the Vicksburg bluff, opposite strong forts, well prepared and defended by heavy artillery. On this road I directed General A. J. Smith's division, not so much by way of a direct attack as a diversion and threat.

Morgan was to move to his left, to reach Chickasaw Bayou, and to follow it toward the bluff, about four miles above A. J. Smith. Steele was on Morgan's left, across Chickasaw Bayou, and M. L. Smith on Morgan's right. We met light resistance at all points, but skirmished, on the 27th, up to the main bayou, that separated our position from the bluffs of Vicksburg, which were found to be strong by nature and by art, and seemingly well defended. On reconnoitring the front in person, during the 27th and 28th, I became satisfied that General A. J. Smith could not cross the intervening obstacles under the heavy fire of the forts immediately in his front, and that the main bayou was impassable, except at two points—one near the head of Chickasaw Bayou, in front of Morgan, and the other about a mile lower down, in front of M. L. Smith's division.

During the general reconnoissance of the 28th General Morgan L. Smith received a severe and dangerous wound in his hip, which completely disabled him and compelled him to go to his steamboat, leaving the command of his division to Brigadier-General D. Stuart;[15] but I drew a part of General A. J. Smith's division, and that general himself, to the point selected for passing the bayou, and committed that special task to his management.

General Steele reported that it was physically impossible to reach the bluffs from his position, so I ordered him to leave but a show of force there, and to return to the west side of Chickasaw Bayou in support of General Morgan's left. He had to countermarch and use the steamboats in the Yazoo to get on the firm ground on our side of the Chickasaw.

On the morning of December 29th all the troops were ready and in position. The first step was to make a lodgment on the foot-hills and bluffs abreast of our position, while diversions were made by the navy toward Haines's Bluff, and by the first division directly toward Vicksburg. I estimated the enemy's forces, then strung from Vicksburg to Haines's Bluff, at fifteen thousand men, commanded by the rebel Generals Martin Luther Smith[16] and Stephen D.

[15] Smith took an enemy bullet in the hip but ultimately survived. In his report of the incident, WTS asserted, "I cannot exaggerate the loss to me personally and officially of General Morgan L. Smith at that critical moment." *OR,* I, 17(I), 607.

[16] Martin L. Smith (1819–1866) graduated from the USMA in 1842. He resigned from the U.S. Army to join the Confederate Army in Apr. 1861. In Dec. 1862, he commanded the 2nd Div., Dept. of the Mississippi and East Louisiana. *CWHC,* 497.

Lee.[17] Aiming to reach firm ground beyond this bayou, and to leave as little time for our enemy to reënforce as possible, I determined to make a show of attack along the whole front, but to break across the bayou at the two points named, and gave general orders accordingly. I pointed out to General Morgan the place where he could pass the bayou, and he answered, "General, in ten minutes after you give the signal I'll be on those hills." He was to lead his division in person, and was to be supported by Steele's division. The front was very narrow, and immediately opposite, at the base of the hills about three hundred yards from the bayou, was a rebel battery, supported by an infantry force posted on the spurs of the hill behind. To draw attention from this, the real point of attack, I gave instructions to commence the attack at the flanks.

I went in person about a mile to the right rear of Morgan's position, at a place convenient to receive reports from all other parts of the line; and about noon of December 29th gave the orders and signal for the main attack. A heavy artillery-fire opened along our whole line, and was replied to by the rebel batteries, and soon the infantry-fire opened heavily, especially on A. J. Smith's front, and in front of General George W. Morgan. One brigade (De Courcey's)[18] of Morgan's troops crossed the bayou safely, but took to cover behind the bank, and could not be moved forward. Frank Blair's brigade, of Steele's division, in support, also crossed the bayou, passed over the space of level ground to the foot of the hills; but, being unsupported by Morgan, and meeting a very severe cross-fire of artillery, was staggered and gradually fell back, leaving about five hundred men behind, wounded and prisoners; among them Colonel Thomas Fletcher, afterward Governor of Missouri.[19] Part of Thayer's brigade took a wrong direction,[20] and did not cross the bayou at all; nor did General Morgan cross in person. This attack failed; and I have always felt that it was due to the failure of General G. W. Morgan to obey his orders, or to fulfill his promise made in person. Had he used with skill and

[17] Stephen D. Lee (1833–1908) graduated from the USMA in 1854 and resigned from the U.S. Army to join the Confederate Army in Feb. 1861. *CWHC*, 345.

[18] John Fitzroy De Courcy (1821–1890) was the 31st Baron Kingsale of Ireland. He fought with the Turkish Contingent during the Crimean War and later moved to the United States, where he joined the U.S. Army. "Death of an Irish Peer," *Leicester Mercury* (Leicester, England), Nov. 26, 1890, 2.

[19] Thomas C. Fletcher (1827–1899) commanded the 1st Brig., Dist. of St. Louis, Dept. of the Missouri. He later served as the governor of Missouri from 1865 to 1869. *CWHC*, 237.

[20] In the first edition of the memoirs (1875), this portion of WTS's text read, "Thayer's brigade, of Steele's division, took a wrong direction . . ."

boldness one of his brigades, in addition to that of Blair's, he could have made a lodgment on the bluff, which would have opened the door for our whole force to follow.[21] Meantime the Sixth Missouri Infantry, at heavy loss, had also crossed the bayou at the narrow passage lower down, but could not ascend the steep bank; right over their heads was a rebel battery, whose fire was in a measure kept down by our sharp-shooters (Thirteenth United States Infantry) posted behind logs, stumps, and trees, on our side of the bayou.

The men of the Sixth Missouri actually scooped out with their hands caves in the bank, which sheltered them against the fire of the enemy, who, right over their heads, held their muskets outside the parapet vertically, and fired down. So critical was the position, that we could not recall the men till after dark, and then one at a time. Our loss had been pretty heavy, and we had accomplished nothing, and had inflicted little loss on our enemy. At first I intended to renew the assault, but soon became satisfied that, the enemy's attention having been drawn to the only two practicable points, it would prove too costly, and accordingly resolved to look elsewhere for a point below Haines's Bluff, or Blake's plantation.[22] That night I conferred with Admiral Porter, who undertook to cover the landing; and the next day (December 30th) the boats were all selected, but so alarmed were the captains and pilots, that we had to place sentinels with loaded muskets to insure their remaining at their posts. Under cover of night, Steele's division, and one brigade of Stuart's, were drawn out of line, and quietly embarked on steamboats in the Yazoo River. The night of December 30th was appointed for this force, under the command of General Fred Steele, to proceed up the Yazoo just below Haines's Bluff, there to disembark about daylight, and make a dash for the hills. Meantime we had strengthened our positions near Chickasaw Bayou, had all our guns in good position with parapets, and had every thing ready to renew our attack as soon as we heard the sound of battle above.

At midnight I left Admiral Porter on his gunboat; he had his fleet ready and the night was propitious. I rode back to camp and gave orders for all to be ready by daybreak; but when daylight came I received a note from General

[21] For more on Morgan's actions during the Chickasaw Bayou campaign, and his subsequent report on the operations against Vicksburg in Dec. 1862, see the section "Chickasaw Bayou" in the Appendix to Volume I; also see *OR,* I, 17(I), 637–640.

[22] Blake's plantation was located approximately ten miles south of Haines's Bluff and two miles south of the Yazoo River. Davis et al., *Official Military Atlas of the Civil War,* plate 36, map 1.

Steele reporting that, before his boats had got up steam, the fog had settled down on the river so thick and impenetrable, that it was simply impossible to move; so the attempt had to be abandoned. The rain, too, began to fall, and the trees bore water-marks ten feet above our heads, so that I became convinced that the part of wisdom was to withdraw. I ordered the stores which had been landed to be reëmbarked on the boats, and preparations made for all the troops to regain their proper boats during the night of the 1st of January, 1863. From our camps at Chickasaw we could hear the whistles of the trains arriving in Vicksburg, could see battalions of men marching up toward Haines's Bluff, and taking post at all points in our front. I was more than convinced that heavy reënforcements were coming to Vicksburg; whether from Pemberton at Grenada, Bragg in Tennessee, or from other sources, I could not tell; but at no point did the enemy assume the offensive; and when we drew off our rear-guard, on the morning of the 2d, they simply followed up the movement, timidly. Up to that moment I had not heard a word from General Grant since leaving Memphis; and most assuredly I had listened for days for the sound of his guns in the direction of Yazoo City. On the morning of January 2d, all my command were again afloat in their proper steamboats, when Admiral Porter told me that General McClernand had arrived at the mouth of the Yazoo in the steamboat Tigress, and that it was rumored he had come down to supersede me. Leaving my whole force where it was, I ran down to the mouth of the Yazoo in a small tug-boat, and there found General McClernand, with orders from the War Department to command the expeditionary force on the Mississippi River.[23] I explained what had been done, and what was the actual state of facts; that the heavy reënforcements pouring into Vicksburg must be Pemberton's army, and that General Grant must be near at hand. He informed me that General Grant was not coming at all; that his depot at Holly Springs had been captured by Van Dorn, and that he had drawn back from Coffeeville and Oxford to Holly Springs and Lagrange; and, further, that Quinby's[24] division of Grant's army was actually at Memphis for stores when he passed down. This,

[23] On Dec. 18, 1862, Halleck telegraphed USG to inform him that Pres. Lincoln had ordered McClernand to take command of the expeditionary force on the Mississippi River. USG then ordered Gen. Thomas Davies to inform WTS of Lincoln's order. According to USG, the dispatch never reached WTS because his lines of communication were interrupted. *OR,* I, 17(II), 425, 461–462; Ulysses S. Grant, *The Personal Memoirs of Ulysses S. Grant: The Complete Annotated Edition,* ed. John F. Marszalek, David S. Nolen and Louie P. Gallo (Cambridge, MA: Belknap Press of Harvard University Press, 2017), 302.

[24] In the first edition of the memoirs (1875), WTS listed the name as "Quimby."

then, fully explained how Vicksburg was being reënforced. I saw that any attempt on the place from the Yazoo was hopeless; and, with General McClernand's full approval, we all came out of the Yazoo, and on the 3d of January rendezvoused at Milliken's Bend, about ten miles above. On the 4th General McClernand issued his General Order No. 1, assuming command of the Army of the Mississippi, divided into two corps; the first to be commanded by General Morgan, composed of his own and A. J. Smith's divisions; and the second, composed of Steele's and Stuart's divisions, to be commanded by me. Up to that time the army had been styled the right wing of (General Grant's) Thirteenth Army Corps, and numbered about thirty thousand men. The aggregate loss during the time of my command, mostly on the 29th of December, was one hundred and seventy-five killed, nine hundred and thirty wounded, and seven hundred and forty-three prisoners. According to Badeau,[25] the rebels lost sixty-three killed, one hundred and thirty-four wounded, and ten prisoners.

It afterward transpired that Van Dorn had captured Holly Springs on the 20th of December, and that General Grant fell back very soon after.[26] General Pemberton, who had telegraphic and railroad communication with Vicksburg, was therefore at perfect liberty to reënforce the place with a garrison equal, if not superior, to my command. The rebels held high, commanding ground, and could see every movement of our men and boats, so that the only possible hope of success consisted in celerity and surprise, and in General Grant's holding all of Pemberton's army hard pressed meantime. General Grant was perfectly aware of this, and had sent me word of the change, but it did not reach me in time; indeed, I was not aware of it until after my assault of December 29th, and until the news was brought me by General McClernand as related. General McClernand was appointed to this command by President Lincoln in person, who had no knowledge of what was then going on down the river. Still, my relief, on the heels of a failure, raised the usual cry, at the North, of "repulse, failure, and bungling."[27] There was no bungling on my part, for I

[25] Adam Badeau (1831–1895) was USG's military secretary during the Civil War. He authored *Military History of Ulysses S. Grant* (1868) and *Grant in Peace: From Appomattox to Mount McGregor* (1887). *CWHC,* 111–112.

[26] USG moved his headquarters to Memphis, TN, on Jan. 10, 1863. Grant, *The Personal Memoirs,* 303.

[27] On Jan. 16, 1863, the *New York Herald* published an article that stated, "The repulse of McClellan from the gates of Richmond, the disastrous retreat of Pope, the Fredericksburg and Vicksburg disasters, are the results of the bungling combinations of Stanton and Halleck. We have had enough of them." On Feb. 1, Thomas Knox, a correspondent for the newspaper,

never worked harder or with more intensity of purpose in my life; and General Grant, long after, in his report of the operations of the siege of Vicksburg, gave us all full credit for the skill of the movement, and described the almost impregnable nature of the ground;[28] and, although in all official reports I assumed the whole responsibility, I have ever felt that had General Morgan promptly and skillfully sustained the lead of Frank Blair's brigade on that day, we should have broken the rebel line, and effected a lodgment on the hills behind Vicksburg.[29] General Frank Blair was outspoken and indignant against Generals Morgan and De Courcey at the time, and always abused me for assuming the whole blame. But, had we succeeded, we might have found ourselves in a worse trap, when General Pemberton was at full liberty to turn his whole force against us.

While I was engaged at Chickasaw Bayou, Admiral Porter was equally busy in the Yazoo River, threatening the enemy's batteries at Haines's and Snyder's Bluffs above. In a sharp engagement he lost one of his best officers, in the person of Captain Gwin, United States Navy, who, though on board an ironclad, insisted on keeping his post on deck, where he was struck in the breast by a round shot, which carried away the muscle, and contused the lung within, from which he died a few days after. We of the army deplored his loss quite as much as his fellows of the navy, for he had been intimately associated with us in our previous operations on the Tennessee River, at Shiloh and above, and we had come to regard him as one of us.

On the 4th of January, 1863, our fleet of transports was collected at Milliken's Bend, about ten miles above the mouth of the Yazoo, Admiral Porter remaining with his gunboats at the Yazoo. General John A. McClernand was in chief command, General George W. Morgan commanded the First Corps and I the Second Corps of the Army of the Mississippi.

I had learned that a small steamboat, the Blue Wing, with a mail, towing coal-barges and loaded with ammunition, had left Memphis for the Yazoo, about the 20th of December, had been captured by a rebel boat which had come out of the Arkansas River,[30] and had been carried up that river to Fort

---

wrote to WTS to apologize for any misrepresentation related to the expedition. *OR,* I, 17(II), 580–586; "The Vicksburg Failure—The Country Disheartened—President Lincoln Must Reorganize the War Office," *New York Herald,* Jan. 16, 1863, 4.

[28] For USG's comments on WTS's actions during the expedition, see *OR,* I, 17(I), 479–480.

[29] For WTS's full report on the expedition, see *OR,* I, 17(I), 601–626.

[30] On Dec. 28, 1862, the *Blue Wing No. 2* was attacked, and ultimately captured, by Confederate horse artillery situated along the shore of the Mississippi River, approximately eight miles

Hindman.[31] We had reports from this fort, usually called the "Post of Arkansas," about forty miles above the mouth, that it was held by about five thousand rebels, was an inclosed work, commanding the passage of the river, but supposed to be easy of capture from the rear. At that time I don't think General McClernand had any definite views or plans of action. If so, he did not impart them to me. He spoke in general terms of opening the navigation of the Mississippi, "cutting his way to the sea," etc., etc., but the *modus operandi* was not so clear. Knowing full well that we could not carry on operations against Vicksburg as long as the rebels held the Post of Arkansas, whence to attack our boats coming and going without convoy, I visited him on his boat, the Tigress, took with me a boy who had been on the Blue Wing, and had escaped, and asked leave to go up the Arkansas, to clear out the Post. He made various objections, but consented to go with me to see Admiral Porter about it. We got up steam in the Forest Queen, during the night of January 4th, stopped at the Tigress, took General McClernand on board, and proceeded down the river by night to the admiral's boat, the Black Hawk, lying in the mouth of the Yazoo. It must have been near midnight, and Admiral Porter was in *déshabille.* We were seated in his cabin and I explained my views about Arkansas Post, and asked his coöperation. He said that he was short of coal, and could not use wood in his iron-clad boats. Of these I asked for two, to be commanded by Captain Shirk or Phelps, or some officer of my acquaintance. At that moment, poor Gwin lay on his bed, in a state-room close by, dying from the effect of the cannon shot received at Haines's Bluff, as before described. Porter's manner to McClernand was so curt that I invited him out into a forward-cabin where he had his charts, and asked him what he meant by it. He said that "he did not like him;" that in Washington, before coming West, he had been introduced to him by President Lincoln, and he had taken a strong prejudice against him. I begged him, for the sake of harmony, to waive that, which he promised to do. Returning to the cabin, the conversation was resumed, and, on our offering to tow his gunboats up the river to save coal, and on renewing the request for Shirk to command the detachment, Porter said, "Suppose I go along myself?" I answered, if he would do so, it would insure

---

below Napoleon, AR. Myron J. Smith Jr., *Tinclads in the Civil War: Union Light-Draught Gunboat Operations on Western Waters, 1862–1865* (Jefferson, NC: McFarland, 2010), 86.

[31] Fort Hindman was constructed by the Confederate Army in 1862 and was most likely named after Confederate Gen. Thomas C. Hindman. John D. Bennett, *Placenames of the Civil War: Cities, Towns, Villages, Railroad Stations, Forts, Camps, Islands, Rivers, Creeks, Fords and Ferries* (Jefferson, NC: McFarland, 2012), s.v. "Fort Hindman (Arkansas) AR."

the success of the enterprise. At that time I supposed General McClernand would send me on this business, but he concluded to go himself, and to take his whole force. Orders were at once issued for the troops not to disembark at Milliken's Bend, but to remain as they were on board the transports. My two divisions were commanded—the First, by Brigadier-General Frederick Steele, with three brigades, commanded by Brigadier-Generals F. P. Blair, C. E. Hovey,[32] and J. M. Thayer;[33] the Second, by Brigadier-General D. Stuart, with two brigades, commanded by Colonels G. A. Smith and T. Kilby Smith.[34]

The whole army, embarked on steamboats convoyed by the gunboats, of which three were iron-clads, proceeded up the Mississippi River to the mouth of White River, which we reached January 8th. On the next day we continued up White River to the "Cut-off;"[35] through this to the Arkansas, and up the Arkansas to Notrib's farm,[36] just below Fort Hindman. Early the next morning we disembarked. Stuart's division, moving up the river along the bank, soon encountered a force of the enemy intrenched behind a line of earthworks, extending from the river across to the swamp. I took Steele's division, marching by the flank by a road through the swamp to the firm ground behind, and was moving up to get to the rear of Fort Hindman, when General McClernand overtook me, with the report that the rebels had abandoned their first position, and had fallen back into the fort. By his orders, we countermarched, recrossed the swamp, and hurried forward to overtake Stuart, marching for Fort Hindman. The first line of the rebels was about four miles below Fort Hindman, and the intervening space was densely wooded and obscure, with the exception of some old fields back of and close to the fort.

[32] Charles E. Hovey (1827–1897) took command of the 2nd Brig., 1st Div., 2nd Corps, Army of the Mississippi. *CWHC,* 305.

[33] John M. Thayer (1820–1906) took command of the 3rd Brig., 1st Div., 2nd Corps, Army of the Mississippi, on Jan. 4, 1863. After the war, he served as the governor of Wyoming Territory from 1875 to 1878 and governor of Nebraska from 1887 to 1891. *CWHC,* 526.

[34] For more on the meeting between WTS, Porter, and McClernand, see the section "Arkansas Post (Extracts from Admiral Porter's Journal)" in the Appendix to Volume I.

[35] In early 1863, U.S. Naval commander Thomas O. Selfridge Sr. constructed a canal at the confluence of the Mississippi and Arkansas Rivers, near Napoleon, AR. The canal effectively prevented Confederate forces on the Arkansas River from attacking U.S. Naval boats traversing the Mississippi River. Thomas O. Selfridge Jr., *Memoirs of Thomas O. Selfridge, Jr., Rear Admiral, U.S.N.* (New York: G. P. Putnam's Sons, 1924), 76–79.

[36] Notrib's farm was located a few miles downriver from Arkansas Post. *OR,* I, 17(I), 711 (map).

During the night, which was a bright moonlight one, we reconnoitred close up, and found a large number of huts which had been abandoned, and the whole rebel force had fallen back into and about the fort. Personally I crept up to a stump so close that I could hear the enemy hard at work, pulling down houses, cutting with axes, and building intrenchments. I could almost hear their words, and I was thus listening when, about 4 A. M. the bugler in the rebel camp sounded as pretty a reveille as I ever listened to.

When daylight broke it revealed to us a new line of parapet straight across the peninsula, connecting Fort Hindman, on the Arkansas River bank, with the impassable swamp about a mile to its left or rear. This peninsula was divided into two nearly equal parts by a road. My command had the ground to the right of the road, and Morgan's corps that to the left. McClernand had his quarters still on the Tigress, back at Notrib's farm, but moved forward that morning (January 11th) to a place in the woods to our rear, where he had a man up a tree, to observe and report the movements.

There was a general understanding with Admiral Porter that he was to attack the fort with his three ironclad gunboats directly by its water-front, while we assaulted by land in the rear. About 10 A. M. I got a message from General McClernand, telling me where he could be found, and asking me what we were waiting for. I answered that we were then in close contact with the enemy, viz., about five or six hundred yards off; that the next movement must be a direct assault; that this should be simultaneous along the whole line; and that I was waiting to hear from the gunboats; asking him to notify Admiral Porter that we were all ready. In about half an hour I heard the clear ring of the navy-guns; the fire gradually increasing in rapidity and advancing toward the fort. I had distributed our field-guns, and, when I judged the time had come, I gave the orders to begin. The intervening ground between us and the enemy was a dead level, with the exception of one or two small gullies, and our men had no cover but the few standing trees and some logs on the ground. The troops advanced well under a heavy fire, once or twice falling to the ground for a sort of rest or pause. Every tree had its group of men, and behind each log was a crowd of sharp-shooters, who kept up so hot a fire that the rebel troops fired wild. The fire of the fort proper was kept busy by the gunboats and Morgan's corps, so that all my corps had to encounter was the direct fire from the newly-built parapet across the peninsula. This line had three sections of field-guns, that kept things pretty lively, and several round-shot came so near me that I realized that they were aimed at my staff; so I dismounted, and made them scatter.

As the gunboats got closer up I saw their flags actually over the parapet of Fort Hindman, and the rebel gunners scamper out of the embrasures and run down into the ditch behind. About the same time a man jumped up on the rebel parapet just where the road entered, waving a large white flag, and numerous smaller white rags appeared above the parapet along the whole line. I immediately ordered, "Cease firing!" and sent the same word down the line to General Steele, who had made similar progress on the right, following the border of the swamp. I ordered my aide, Colonel Dayton, to jump on his horse and ride straight up to the large white flag, and when his horse was on the parapet I followed with the rest of my staff. All firing had ceased, except an occasional shot away to the right, and one of the captains (Smith) of the Thirteenth Regulars was wounded after the display of the white flag. On entering the line, I saw that our muskets and guns had done good execution; for there was a horse-battery, and every horse lay dead in the traces. The fresh-made parapet had been knocked down in many places, and dead men lay around very thick. I inquired who commanded at that point, and a Colonel Garland[37] stepped up and said that he commanded that brigade. I ordered him to form his brigade, stack arms, hang the belts on the muskets, and stand waiting for orders. Stuart's division had been halted outside the parapet. I then sent Major Hammond down the rebel line to the right, with orders to stop Steele's division outside, and to have the other rebel brigade stack its arms in like manner, and to await further orders. I inquired of Colonel Garland who commanded in chief, and he said that General Churchill[38] did, and that he was inside the fort. I then rode into the fort, which was well built, with good parapets, drawbridge, and ditch, and was an in closed work of four bastions. I found it full of soldiers and sailors, its parapets toward the river well battered in, and Porter's gunboats in the river, close against the fort, with their bows on shore. I soon found General Churchill, in conversation with Admiral Porter and General A. J. Smith, and about this time my adjutant-general, Major J. H. Hammond, came and reported that General Deshler,[39] who commanded the rebel brigade facing and opposed to Steele, had refused to stack arms and surrender, on the ground that he had received no orders from his commanding

[37] Robert R. Garland (c. 1821–1870) was the state inspector of Texas and commanded the 6th Texas Inf. during the war. Jefferson Davis, *The Papers of Jefferson Davis,* ed. Lynda L. Crist, Mary S. Dix, and Kenneth H. Williams (Baton Rouge: LSU Press, 1995), 8:365*n.*

[38] Thomas J. Churchill (1824–1905) joined the Confederate Army as a colonel in June 1861. He was transferred to the Dist. of Arkansas in Dec. 1862. *CWHC,* 172–173.

[39] James Deshler (1833–1863) graduated from the USMA in 1854 and commanded the 2nd Brig., 2nd Div., 2nd Corps, Trans-Mississippi Dept., in Jan. 1863. He was shot and killed on Sept. 20, 1863, at the Battle of Chickamauga. *CWHC,* 594.

general; that nothing separated this brigade from Steele's men except the light parapet, and that there might be trouble there at any moment. I advised General Churchill to send orders at once, because a single shot might bring the whole of Steele's division on Deshler's brigade, and I would not be responsible for the consequences; soon afterward, we both concluded to go in person. General Churchill had the horses of himself and staff in the ditch; they were brought in, and we rode together to where Garland was standing, and Churchill spoke to him in an angry tone, "Why did you display the white flag!" Garland replied, "I received orders to do so from one of your staff." Churchill denied giving such an order, and angry words passed between them. I stopped them, saying that it made little difference then, as they were in our power. We continued to ride down the line to its extreme point, where we found Deshler in person, and his troops were still standing to the parapet with their muskets in hand. Steele's men were on the outside. I asked Deshler: "What does this mean? You are a regular officer, and ought to know better." He answered, snappishly, that "he had received no orders to surrender;" when General Churchill said: "You see, sir, that we are in their power, and you may surrender." Deshler turned to his staff-officers and ordered them to repeat the command to "stack arms," etc., to the colonels of his brigade. I was on my horse, and he was on foot. Wishing to soften the blow of defeat, I spoke to him kindly, saying that I knew a family of Deshlers in Columbus, Ohio, and inquired if they were relations of his. He disclaimed any relation with people living north of the Ohio, in an offensive tone, and I think I gave him a piece of my mind that he did not relish. He was a West Point graduate, small but very handsome, and was afterward killed in battle. I never met him again.[40]

Returning to the position where I had first entered the rebel line, I received orders from General McClernand, by one of his staff, to leave General A. J. Smith in charge of the fort and prisoners, and with my troops to remain outside. The officer explained that the general was then on the Tigress, which had moved up from below, to a point in the river just above the fort; and not understanding his orders, I concluded to go and see him in person. My troops were then in possession of two of the three brigades which composed the army opposed to us; and my troops were also in possession of all the ground of the peninsula outside the "fort proper" (Hindman). I found General McClernand on the Tigress, in high spirits. He said repeatedly: "Glorious! glorious! my star

[40] For more on the challenge of capturing Arkansas Post, and the Confederate Army's refusal to stack arms and surrender, see the section "Arkansas Post (Statement from J. H. Hammond)" in the Appendix to Volume I.

is ever in the ascendant!" He spoke complimentarily of the troops, but was extremely jealous of the navy. He said: "I'll make a splendid report;" "I had a man up a tree;"[41] etc. I was very hungry and tired, and fear I did not appreciate the honors in reserve for us, and asked for something to eat and drink. He very kindly ordered something to be brought, and explained to me that by his "orders" he did not wish to interfere with the actual state of facts; that General A. J. Smith would occupy "Fort Hindman," which his troops had first entered, and I could hold the lines outside, and go on securing the prisoners and stores as I had begun. I returned to the position of Garland's brigade and gave the necessary orders for marching all the prisoners, disarmed, to a pocket formed by the river and two deep gullies just above the fort, by which time it had become quite dark. After dark another rebel regiment arrived from Pine Bluff, marched right in, and was also made prisoners. There seemed to be a good deal of feeling among the rebel officers against Garland, who asked leave to stay with me that night, to which I of course consented. Just outside the rebel parapet was a house which had been used for a hospital. I had a room cleaned out, and occupied it that night. A cavalry-soldier lent me his battered coffee-pot with some coffee and scraps of hard bread out of his nose-bag; Garland and I made some coffee, ate our bread together, and talked politics by the fire till quite late at night, when we lay down on straw that was saturated with the blood of dead or wounded men. The next day the prisoners were all collected on their boats, lists were made out, and orders given for their transportation to St. Louis, in charge of my aide, Major Sanger. We then proceeded to dismantle and level the forts, destroy or remove the stores, and we found in the magazine the very ammunition which had been sent for us in the Blue Wing, which was secured and afterward used in our twenty-pound Parrott guns.

On the 13th we reëmbarked; the whole expedition returned out of the river by the direct route down the Arkansas during a heavy snow-storm, and rendezvoused in the Mississippi, at Napoleon, at the mouth of the Arkansas. Here General McClernand told me he had received a letter from General Grant at Memphis, who disapproved of our movement up the Arkansas; but that communication was made before he had learned of our complete success.[42] When informed of this, and of the promptness with which it had been

[41] McClernand was referring to a man he placed in a tree to observe the Confederate surrender at Arkansas Post from a distance. For more on the story of the "man up a tree," see the section "Arkansas Post (Letter from L. M. Dayton)" in the Appendix to Volume I; also see Harry Hansen, *The Civil War: A History* (New York: Signet Classics, 2010), 331.

[42] For USG's letter to McClernand, see *PUSG:* 7, 210–212.

executed, he could not but approve. We were then ordered back to Milliken's Bend, to await General Grant's arrival in person. We reached Milliken's Bend January 21st.

McClernand's report of the capture of Fort Hindman almost ignored the action of Porter's fleet altogether.[43] This was unfair, for I know that the admiral led his fleet in person in the river-attack, and that his guns silenced those of Fort Hindman, and drove the gunners into the ditch.

The aggregate loss in my corps at Arkansas Post was five hundred and nineteen, viz., four officers and seventy-five men killed, thirty-four officers and four hundred and six men wounded. I never knew the losses in the gunboat fleet, or in Morgan's corps; but they must have been less than in mine, which was more exposed.[44] The number of rebel dead must have been nearly one hundred and fifty;[45] of prisoners, by actual count, we secured four thousand seven hundred and ninety-one, and sent them north to St. Louis.

[43] For McClernand's report on the capture of Arkansas Post, see *OR,* I, 17(I), 699–710.

[44] According to McClernand's post-battle report, his forces suffered a total of 1,061 casualties. For a full report of the casualties, see *OR,* I, 17(I),716–719.

[45] Confederate Gen. Churchill claimed in his post-battle report that his losses did not "exceed sixty killed and seventy-five or eighty wounded." *OR,* I, 17(I),782.

13

Vicksburg.

JANUARY TO JULY, 1863.

THE CAMPAIGN OF 1863, resulting in the capture of Vicksburg, was so important, that its history has been well studied and well described in all the books treating of the civil war, more especially by Dr. Draper, in his "History of the Civil War in America,"[1] and in Badeau's "Military History of General Grant." In the latter it is more fully and accurately given than in any other, and is well illustrated by maps and original documents. I now need only attempt to further illustrate Badeau's account by some additional details. When our expedition came out of the Arkansas River, January 18, 1863, and rendezvoused at the river-bank, in front of the town of Napoleon, Arkansas, we were visited by General Grant in person, who had come down from Memphis in a steamboat. Although at this time Major-General J. A. McClernand was in command of the Army of the Mississippi, by virtue of a confidential order of the War Department, dated October 21, 1862, which order bore the indorsement of President Lincoln, General Grant still exercised a command over him, by reason of his general command of the Department of the Tennessee. By an order (No. 210) of December 18, 1862, from the War Department, received at Arkansas Post, the Western armies had been grouped into five *corps d'armée,* viz.: the Thirteenth, Major-General McClernand; the Fourteenth, Major-General George H. Thomas, in Middle Tennessee; the Fifteenth, Major-General W. T. Sherman; the Sixteenth, Major-General Hurlbut, then at or near Memphis; and the Seventeenth, Major-General McPherson, also at and back of Memphis.[2] General Grant when at Napoleon, on the 18th of January, ordered McClernand with his own and my corps to return to Vicksburg, to dis-

[1] John W. Draper (1811–1882) was born in England and in 1833 moved to the United States, where he studied medicine and chemistry at the University of Pennsylvania. He published *History of the American Civil War* in 1867. "Dr. John W. Draper," *Centre Democrat* (Bellefonte, PA), Jan. 12, 1882, 5.

[2] See *OR,* I, 17(II), 432–433.

embark on the west bank, and to resume work on a canal across the peninsula, which had been begun by General Thomas Williams[3] the summer before, the object being to turn the Mississippi River at that point, or at least to make a passage for our fleet of gunboats and transports across the peninsula, opposite Vicksburg.[4] General Grant then returned to Memphis, ordered to Lake Providence, about sixty miles above us, McPherson's corps, the Seventeenth, and then came down again to give his personal supervision to the whole movement.[5]

The Mississippi River was very high and rising, and we began that system of canals on which we expended so much hard work fruitlessly: first, the canal at Young's plantation, opposite Vicksburg;[6] second, that at Lake Providence; and third, at the Yazoo Pass, leading into the head-waters of the Yazoo River. Early in February the gunboats Indianola and Queen of the West ran the batteries of Vicksburg. The latter was afterward crippled in Red River, and was captured by the rebels; and the Indianola was butted and sunk about forty miles below Vicksburg. We heard the booming of the guns, but did not know of her loss till some days after.[7] During the months of January and February, we were digging the canal and fighting off the water of the Mississippi, which continued to rise and threatened to drown us. We had no sure place of refuge except the narrow levee, and such steamboats as remained abreast of our camps. My two divisions furnished alternately a detail of five hundred men a day, to work on the canal. So high was the water in the beginning of March, that McClernand's corps was moved to higher ground, at Milliken's Bend, but I remained at Young's plantation, laid off a due proportion of the levee for each subdivision of my command, and assigned other parts to such steamboats as lay at the levee. My own headquarters were in

[3]Thomas Williams (1815–1862) graduated from the USMA in 1837 and served in the Mexican-American War. He was shot and killed on Aug. 5, 1862, during the Battle of Baton Rouge. *CWHC,* 572; "Funeral of Gen. Williams," *Daily Delta* (New Orleans), Aug. 8, 1862, 2.

[4]Thomas and his infantry brigade started digging a canal opposite Vicksburg on June 27, 1862. For USG's order to McClernand, see *PUSG,* 7:231–233. William Wiley, *The Civil War Diary of a Common Soldier,* ed. Terrence J. Winschel (Baton Rouge: LSU Press, 2001), 38*n.*

[5]USG returned to Memphis on Jan. 19, 1862. *PUSG,* 7:xxii.

[6]Young's plantation was approximately ten miles upriver from Vicksburg. George B. Davis et al., *Official Military Atlas of the Civil War* (New York: Fairfax Press, 1983), plate 155.

[7]The *Indianola* and the *Queen of the West* failed to run the batteries of Vicksburg on Feb. 2, 1862. However, the *Indianola* successfully ran the batteries on Feb. 13. The following day, the *Queen of the West* ran aground in the Red River and was captured by the Confederate Army. *PUSG,* 7:xxiii.

Mrs. Grove's house,[8] which had the water all around it, and could only be reached by a plank-walk from the levee, built on posts.

General Frederick Steele commanded the first division, and General D. Stuart the second; this latter division had been reenforced by General Hugh Ewing's brigade, which had arrived from West Virginia.[9]

At the time of its date I received the following note from General Grant:

MILLIKEN'S BEND, *March* 16, 1863

General SHERMAN.

DEAR SIR: I have just returned from a reconnoissance up Steele's Bayou, with the admiral (Porter), and five of his gunboats. With some labor in cutting tree-tops out of the way, it will be navigable for any class of steamers.

I want you to have your pioneer corps, or one regiment of good men for such work, detailed, and at the landing as soon as possible.

The party will want to take with them their rations, arms, and sufficient camp and garrison equipage for a few days. I will have a boat at any place you may designate, as early as the men can be there. The Eighth Missouri (being many of them boatmen) would be excellent men for this purpose.

As soon as you give directions for these men to be in readiness, come up and see me, and I will explain fully. The tug that takes this is instructed to wait for you. A full supply of axes will be required.

Very respectfully,

U. S. GRANT, *Major-General.*

This letter was instantly (8 A. M.) sent to Colonel Giles A. Smith, commanding the Eighth Missouri, with orders to prepare immediately. He returned it at 9.15, with an answer that the regiment was all ready.[10] I went up to Milliken's Bend in the tug, and had a conference with the general, resulting in these orders:

[8] Mrs. Grove's house was located approximately five miles below Young's Point along the Tuscumbia Bend on the Mississippi River. Davis et al., *Official Military Atlas of the Civil War,* plate 36, map 1.

[9] Ewing took command of the 3rd Brig., 2nd Div., 15th Corps, Army of the Tennessee, on Jan. 12, 1863. *CWHC,* 230.

[10] See *PUSG,* 7:423–424.

Headquarters Department of the Tennessee,
Before Vicksburg, *March* 16, 1863.

Major-General W. T. Sherman, *commanding Fifteenth Army Corps.*

General: You will proceed as early as practicable up Steele's Bayou, and through Black Bayou to Deer Creek, and thence with the gun-boats now there by any route they may take to get into the Yazoo River, for the purpose of determining the feasibility of getting an army through that route to the east bank of that river, and at a point from which they can act advantageously against Vicksburg.

Make such details from your army corps as may be required to clear out the channel of the various bayous through which transports would have to run, and to hold such points as in your judgment should be occupied.

I place at your disposal to-day the steamers Diligent and Silver Wave, the only two suitable for the present navigation of this route. Others will be supplied you as fast as required, and they can be got.

I have given directions (and you may repeat them) that the party going on board the steamer Diligent push on until they reach Black Bayou, only stopping sufficiently long at any point before reaching there to remove such obstructions as prevent their own progress. Captain Kossak, of the Engineers, will go with this party. The other boat-load will commence their work in Steele's Bayou, and make the navigation as free as possible all the way through.

There is but little work to be done in Steele's Bayou, except for about five miles about midway of the bayou. In this portion many overhanging trees will have to be removed, and should be dragged out of the channel.

Very respectfully,
U. S. Grant, *Major-General.*

On returning to my camp at Young's Point, I started these two boats up the Yazoo and Steele's Bayou, with the Eighth Missouri and some pioneers, with axes, saws, and all the tools necessary. I gave orders for a part of Stuart's division to proceed in the large boats up the Mississippi River to a point at Gwin's plantation,[11] where a bend of Steele's Bayou neared the main river;

[11] Gwin's plantation, owned by California senator William M. Gwin, was located approximately thirty miles upriver from Young's Point. Myron J. Smith Jr., *The Fight for the Yazoo,*

and the next day, with one or two staff-officers and orderlies, got a navy-tug, and hurried up to overtake Admiral Porter. About sixty miles up Steele's Bayou we came to the gunboat Price, Lieutenant Woodworth,[12] United States Navy, commanding, and then turned into Black Bayou, a narrow, crooked channel, obstructed by overhanging oaks, and filled with cypress and cotton-wood trees. The gunboats had forced their way through, pushing aside trees a foot in diameter. In about four miles we overtook the gunboat fleet just as it was emerging into Deer Creek. Along Deer Creek the alluvium was higher, and there was a large cotton-plantation belonging to a Mr. Hill, who was absent, and the negroes were in charge of the place. Here I overtook Admiral Porter, and accompanied him a couple of miles up Deer Creek, which was much wider and more free of trees, with plantations on both sides at intervals. Admiral Porter thought he had passed the worst, and that he would be able to reach the Rolling Fork and Sunflower. He requested me to return and use all possible means to clear out Black Bayou. I returned to Hill's plantation, which was soon reached by Major Coleman, with a part of the Eighth Missouri;[13] the bulk of the regiment and the pioneers had been distributed along the bayous, and set to work under the general supervision of Captain Kossak. The Diligent and Silver Wave then returned to Gwin's plantation and brought up Brigadier-General Giles A. Smith, with the Sixth Missouri, and part of the One Hundred and Sixteenth Illinois. Admiral Porter was then working up Deer Creek with his iron-clads, but he had left me a tug, which enabled me to reconnoitre the country, which was all under water except the narrow strip along Deer Creek. During the 19th I heard the heavy navy-guns booming more frequently than seemed consistent with mere guerrilla operations; and that night I got a message from Porter, written on tissue-paper, brought me through the swamp by a negro, who had it concealed in a piece of tobacco.

The admiral stated that he had met a force of infantry and artillery which gave him great trouble by killing the men who had to expose themselves out-

---

August 1862–July 1864: Swamps, Forts and Fleets on Vicksburg's Northern Flank (Jefferson, NC: McFarland, 2012), 246.

[12] Selim Woodworth (1815–1871) joined the U.S. Navy as a midshipman in 1838 and was elected as a California state senator in 1849. *ORN,* I, 24, 485; Frank Soule, John H. Gihon, and James Nisbet, *The Annals of San Francisco* (New York: D. Appleton, 1854), 794–797.

[13] David C. Coleman (1825–1909) joined the 8th Missouri Inf. as a first lieutenant on July 4, 1861. *CHWC,* 180; "Gen. Coleman to Be Buried Wednesday," *St. Louis Globe-Democrat,* Aug. 17, 1909, 6.

side the iron armor to shove off the bows of the boats, which had so little headway that they would not steer. He begged me to come to his rescue as quickly as possible. Giles A. Smith had only about eight hundred men with him, but I ordered him to start up Deer Creek at once, crossing to the east side by an old bridge at Hill's plantation, which we had repaired for the purpose; to work his way up to the gunboat-fleet, and to report to the admiral that I would come up with every man I could raise as soon as possible. I was almost alone at Hill's, but took a canoe, paddled down Black Bayou to the gunboat Price, and there, luckily, found the Silver Wave with a load of men just arrived from Gwin's plantation. Taking some of the parties who were at work along the bayou into an empty coal-barge, we tugged it up by a navy-tug, followed by the Silver Wave, crashing through the trees, carrying away pilot-house, smoke-stacks, and every thing above-deck; but the captain (McMillan, of Pittsburg) was a brave fellow,[14] and realized the necessity. The night was absolutely black, and we could only make two and a half of the four miles. We then disembarked, and marched through the canebrake, carrying lighted candles in our hands, till we got into the open cotton-fields at Hill's plantation, where we lay down for a few hours' rest. These men were a part of Giles A. Smith's brigade, and part belonged to the brigade of T. Kilby Smith, the senior officer present being Lieutenant-Colonel Rice,[15] Fifty-fourth Ohio, an excellent young officer. We had no horses.

On Sunday morning, March 21st, as soon as daylight appeared, we started, following the same route which Giles A. Smith had taken the day before; the battalion of the Thirteenth United States Regulars, Major Chase, in the lead. We could hear Porter's guns, and knew that moments were precious. Being on foot myself, no man could complain, and we generally went at the double-quick, with occasional rests. The road lay along Deer Creek, passing several plantations; and occasionally, at the bends, it crossed the swamp, where the water came above my hips. The smaller drummer-boys had to carry their drums on their heads, and most of the men slang their cartridge-boxes around their necks. The soldiers generally were glad to have their general and field officers afoot, but we gave them a fair specimen of marching, accomplishing about

[14] John S. McMillin (1817–1893) purchased the *Silver Wave* in 1854. Boyd Crumrine, *Pittsburgh Reports: Containing Cases Decided by the Federal and State Courts of Pennsylvania* (Philadelphia: John Campbell and Son, 1873), 3:391–392; "A Noted Blockade-Runner Dead," *Ottawa Free Trader* (Ottawa, IL), Mar. 18, 1893, 12.

[15] Americus V. Rice (1835–1904) was promoted to lieutenant colonel on Feb. 8, 1862. *CWHC*, 451–452.

twenty-one miles by noon. Of course, our speed was accelerated by the sounds of the navy-guns, which became more and more distinct, though we could see nothing. At a plantation near some Indian mounds we met a detachment of the Eighth Missouri, that had been up to the fleet, and had been sent down as a picket to prevent any obstructions below. This picket reported that Admiral Porter had found Deer Creek badly obstructed, had turned back; that there was a rebel force beyond the fleet, with some six-pounders, and nothing between us and the fleet. So I sat down on the door-sill of a cabin to rest, but had not been seated ten minutes when, in the wood just ahead, not three hundred yards off, I heard quick and rapid firing of musketry. Jumping up, I ran up the road, and found Lieutenant-Colonel Rice, who said the head of his column had struck a small force of rebels with a working gang of negroes, provided with axes, who on the first fire had broken and run back into the swamp. I ordered Rice to deploy his brigade, his left on the road, and extending as far into the swamp as the ground would permit, and then to sweep forward until he uncovered the gunboats. The movement was rapid and well executed, and we soon came to some large cotton-fields and could see our gunboats in Deer Creek, occasionally firing a heavy eight-inch gun across the cotton-field into the swamp behind. About that time Major Kirby, of the Eighth Missouri,[16] galloped down the road on a horse he had picked up the night before, and met me. He explained the situation of affairs, and offered me his horse. I got on *bareback,* and rode up the levee, the sailors coming out of their iron-clads and cheering most vociferously as I rode by, and as our men swept forward across the cotton-field in full view. I soon found Admiral Porter, who was on the deck of one of his iron-clads, with a shield made of the section of a smoke-stack, and I doubt if he was ever more glad to meet a friend than he was to see me. He explained that he had almost reached the Rolling Fork, when the woods became full of sharp-shooters, who, taking advantage of trees, stumps, and the levee, would shoot down every man that poked his nose outside the protection of their armor; so that he could not handle his clumsy boats in the narrow channel. The rebels had evidently dispatched a force from Haines's Bluff up the Sunflower to the Rolling Fork, had anticipated the movement of Admiral Porter's fleet, and had completely obstructed the channel of the upper part of Deer Creek by felling trees into it, so that further progress in that direction was simply

[16] Dennis T. Kirby (1838–1922) joined the 8th Missouri Inf. as a captain on June 25, 1861. *CWHC,* 335.

impossible.[17] It also happened that, at the instant of my arrival, a party of about four hundred rebels, armed and supplied with axes, had passed around the fleet and had got below it, intending in like manner to block up the channel by the felling of trees, so as to cut off retreat. This was the force we had struck so opportunely at the time before described. I inquired of Admiral Porter what he proposed to do, and he said he wanted to get out of that scrape as quickly as possible. He was actually working back when I met him, and, as we then had a sufficient force to cover his movement completely, he continued to back down Deer Creek. He informed me at one time things looked so critical that he had made up his mind to blow up the gunboats, and to escape with his men through the swamp to the Mississippi River. There being no longer any sharp-shooters to bother the sailors, they made good progress; still, it took three full days for the fleet to back out of Deer Creek into Black Bayou, at Hill's plantation, whence Admiral Porter proceeded to his post at the mouth of the Yazoo, leaving Captain Owen[18] in command of the fleet. I reported the facts to General Grant, who was sadly disappointed at the failure of the fleet to get through to the Yazoo above Haines's Bluff, and ordered us all to resume our camps at Young's Point. We accordingly steamed down, and regained our camps on the 27th. As this expedition up Deer Creek was but one of many efforts to secure a footing from which to operate against Vicksburg, I add the report of Brigadier-General Giles A. Smith, who was the first to reach the fleet:

Headquarters First Brigade, Second Division,
Fifteenth Army Corps, Young's Point, Louisiana, *March* 28, 1863.

Captain L. M. Dayton, *Assistant Adjutant-General.*

Captain: I have the honor to report the movements of the First Brigade in the expedition up Steele's Bayou, Black Bayou, and Deer Creek.

The Sixth Missouri and One Hundred and Sixteenth Illinois regiments embarked at the mouth of Muddy Bayou on the evening of Thursday, the 18th of March, and proceeded up Steele's Bayou to the

[17] On Mar. 19, 1863, Confederate Gen. John C. Pemberton ordered Gen. W. W. Loring to prevent the U.S. Army from taking Deer Creek. *OR,* I, 24(III), 677–680.

[18] Elias K. Owen (1834–1877) joined the U.S. Navy as a midshipman in 1848. Myron J. Smith Jr., *Ironclad Captains of the Civil War* (Jefferson, NC: McFarland, 2018), s.v. "Owen, Elias Kane."

mouth of Black; thence up Black Bayou to Hill's plantation, at its junction with Deer Creek, where we arrived on Friday at four o'clock P. M., and joined the Eighth Missouri, Lieutenant-Colonel Coleman commanding, which had arrived at that point two days before. General Sherman had also established his headquarters there, having preceded the Eighth Missouri in a tug, with no other escort than two or three of his staff, reconnoitring all the different bayous and branches, thereby greatly facilitating the movements of the troops, but at the same time exposing himself beyond precedent in a commanding general. At three o'clock of Saturday morning, the 20th instant, General Sherman having received a communication from Admiral Porter at the mouth of Rolling Fork, asking for a speedy coöperation of the land forces with his fleet, I was ordered by General Sherman to be ready, with all the available force at that point, to accompany him to his relief; but before starting it was arranged that I should proceed with the force at hand (eight hundred men), while he remained, again entirely unprotected, to hurry up the troops expected to arrive that night, consisting of the Thirteenth Infantry and One Hundred and Thirteenth Illinois Volunteers, completing my brigade, and the Second Brigade, Colonel T. Kilby Smith commanding.

This, as the sequel showed, proved a very wise measure, and resulted in the safety of the whole fleet. At daybreak we were in motion, with a regular guide. We had proceeded but about six miles, when we found the enemy had been very busy felling trees to obstruct the creek.

All the negroes along the route had been notified to be ready at night fall to continue the work. To prevent this as much as possible, I ordered all able-bodied negroes to be taken along, and warned some of the principal inhabitants that they would be held responsible for any more obstructions being placed across the creek. We reached the admiral about four o'clock P. M., with no opposition save my advance-guard (Company A, Sixth Missouri) being fired into from the opposite side of the creek, killing one man, and slightly wounding another; having no way of crossing, we had to content ourselves with driving them beyond musket-range. Proceeding with as little loss of time as possible, I found the fleet obstructed in front by fallen trees, in rear by a sunken coal-barge, and surrounded by a large force of rebels with an abundant supply of artillery, but wisely keeping their main force out of range of the admiral's guns. Every tree and stump covered a sharpshooter, ready to pick off any luckless marine who showed his head above-decks, and entirely preventing the working-parties from removing obstructions.

In pursuance of orders from General Sherman, I reported to Admiral Porter for orders, who turned over to me all the land-forces in his fleet (about one hundred and fifty men), together with two howitzers, and I was instructed by him to retain a sufficient force to clear out the sharp-shooters, and to distribute the remainder along the creek for six or seven miles below, to prevent any more obstructions being placed in it during the night. This was speedily arranged, our skirmishers capturing three prisoners. Immediate steps were now taken to remove the coal-barge, which was accomplished about daylight on Sunday morning, when the fleet moved back toward Black Bayou. By three o'clock P. M. we had only made about six miles, owing to the large number of trees to be removed; at this point, where our progress was very slow, we discovered a long line of the enemy filing along the edge of the woods, and taking position on the creek below us, and about one mile ahead of our advance. Shortly after, they opened fire on the gunboats from batteries behind the cavalry and infantry. The boats not only replied to the batteries, which they soon silenced, but poured a destructive fire into their lines. Heavy skirmishing was also heard in our front, supposed to be by three companies from the Sixth and Eighth Missouri, whose position, taken the previous night to guard the creek, was beyond the point reached by the enemy, and consequently liable to be cut off or captured. Captain Owen, of the Louisville, the leading boat, made every effort to go through the obstructions and aid in the rescuing of the men. I ordered Major Kirby, with four companies of the Sixth Missouri, forward, with two companies deployed. He soon met General Sherman, with the Thirteenth Infantry and One Hundred and Thirteenth Illinois, driving the enemy before them, and opening communication along the creek with the gunboats. Instead of our three companies referred to as engaging the enemy, General Sherman had arrived at a very opportune moment with the two regiments mentioned above, and the Second Brigade. The enemy, not expecting an attack from that quarter, after some hot skirmishing, retreated. General Sherman immediately ordered the Thirteenth Infantry and One Hundred and Thirteenth Illinois to pursue; but, after following their trace for about two miles, they were recalled.

We continued our march for about two miles, when we bivouacked for the night. Early on Monday morning (March 22d) we continued our march, but owing to the slow progress of the gunboats did not reach Hill's plantation until Tuesday, the 23d instant, where we remained until the 25th; we then reëmbarked, and arrived at Young's Point on Friday, the 27th instant.

Below you will find a list of casualties. Very respectfully,

GILES A. SMITH,
Colonel Eighth Missouri, commanding First Brigade.

P. S.—I forgot to state above that the Thirteenth Infantry and One Hundred and Thirteenth Illinois being under the immediate command of General Sherman, he can mention them as their conduct deserves.

On the 3d of April, a division of troops, commanded by Brigadier-General J. M. Tuttle,[19] was assigned to my corps, and was designated the Third Division; and, on the 4th of April, Brigadier-General D. Stuart was relieved from the command of the Second Division, to which Major-General Frank P. Blair was appointed by an order from General Grant's headquarters. Stuart had been with me from the time we were at Benton Barracks, in command of the Fifty-fifth Illinois, then of a brigade, and finally of a division; but he had failed in securing a confirmation by the Senate to his nomination as brigadier-general, by reason of some old affair at Chicago, and, having resigned his commission as colonel, he was out of service.[20] I esteemed him very highly, and was actually mortified that the service should thus be deprived of so excellent and gallant an officer. He afterward settled in New Orleans as a lawyer, and died about 1867 or 1868.[21]

[19] James M. Tuttle (1823–1892) was wounded at the Battle of Fort Donelson and later promoted to brigadier general on June 9, 1862. *CWHC*, 538.

[20] In 1860, Stuart was falsely accused of having an extramarital affair with Mary Burch, the wife of Chicago banker Isaac H. Burch. Stuart was later nominated as brigadier general by Pres. Lincoln on Nov. 29, 1862, but three members of his regiment, including the chaplain, protested the appointment because of the adultery allegation. On Mar. 11, 1863, the U.S. Senate denied his confirmation. Stuart resigned from the Army on Apr. 3. *CWHC*, 611; *The Only Complete Report of the Burch Divorce Case* (New York: Robert M. DeWitt, 1860), 1–7; *The Story of the Fifty-Fifth Regiment Illinois Volunteer Infantry in the Civil War, 1861–1865* (Clinton, MA: W. J. Coulter, 1887), 184–185.

[21] Stuart died of paralysis in Detroit, MI, on Sept. 11, 1868. *CWHC*, 611.

On the 6th of April, my command, the Fifteenth Corps, was composed of three divisions:

The First Division, commanded by Major-General Fred Steele; and his three brigades by Colonel Manter,[22] Colonel Charles R. Wood,[23] and Brigadier-General John M. Thayer.

The Second Division, commanded by Major-General Frank P. Blair; and his three brigades by Colonel Giles A. Smith, Colonel Thomas Kilby Smith, and Brigadier-General Hugh Ewing.

The Third Division, commanded by Brigadier-General J. M. Tuttle; and his three brigades by Brigadier-General R. P. Buckland, Colonel J. A. Mower,[24] and Brigadier-General John E. Smith.[25]

My own staff then embraced: Dayton, McCoy, and Hill, aides; J. H. Hammond, assistant adjutant-general; Sanger, inspector-general; McFeeley, commissary;[26] J. Condit Smith, quartermaster; Charles McMillan, medical director;[27] Ezra Taylor, chief of artillery; Jno. C. Neely, ordnance-officer;[28] Jenney and Pitzman,[29] engineers.

[22] Frank H. Manter (1824–1864) died in Arkansas after accidentally falling off his horse. *History of Lorain County, Ohio* (Philadelphia: Williams Brothers, 1879), 134.

[23] Charles R. Woods (1827–1885) graduated from the USMA in 1852 and commanded the 2nd Brig., 1st Div., 15th Corps, Army of the Tennessee, in mid-1863. *CWHC,* 580–581.

[24] Joseph A. Mower (1827–1870) took command of the 2nd Brig., 3rd Div., 15th Corps, Army of the Tennessee, on Apr. 3. *CWHC,* 401.

[25] John E. Smith (1816–1897) was born in Berne, Switzerland, and he and his family moved to the United States in 1817. On Apr. 23, 1863, he took command of his own brigade in the 3rd Div., 15th Corps, Army of the Tennessee. *CWHC,* 497.

[26] Robert MacFeely (1824–1901) graduated from the USMA in 1850 and was promoted to lieutenant general, U.S. Army Commissary of Subsistence, on Jan. 1, 1863. *CWHC,* 358.

[27] Charles McMillan (c. 1825–1890) was the medical director for multiple generals, including WTS, USG, and Logan. "The Late Dr. McMillan," *Evening Star* (Washington, DC), Jan. 8, 1890, 8.

[28] John C. Neely (1840–1920) joined WTS's staff as an acting ordnance officer on May 2, 1862. In the first edition of the memoirs (1875), WTS did not list Neely's first name or middle initial. "John C. Neely Dead in Chicago," *Republican-Northwestern* (Belvidere, IL), Feb. 6, 1920, 5; Emily W. Leavitt, *The Blair Family of New England* (Boston: David Clapp and Son, 1900), 123–124.

[29] Julius Pitzman (1837–1923) was born in Germany and moved to St. Louis at an early age. He joined the U.S. Army as a first lieutenant in 1861. "Julius Pitzman, Worker for City Improvement and Pioneer, Is Dead," *St. Louis Globe-Democrat,* Sept. 1, 1923, 1, 3.

By this time it had become thoroughly demonstrated that we could not divert the main river Mississippi, or get practicable access to the east bank of the Yazoo, in the rear of Vicksburg, by any of the passes; and we were all in the habit of discussing the various chances of the future. General Grant's headquarters were at Milliken's Bend, in tents, and his army was strung along the river all the way from Young's Point up to Lake Providence, at least sixty miles. I had always contended that the best way to take Vicksburg was to resume the movement which had been so well begun the previous November, viz., for the main army to march by land down the country inland of the Mississippi River; while the gunboat-fleet and a minor land-force should threaten Vicksburg on its river-front.

I reasoned that, with the large force then subject to General Grant's orders—viz., four army corps—he could easily resume the movement from Memphis, by way of Oxford and Grenada, to Jackson, Mississippi, or down the ridge between the Yazoo and Big Black; but General Grant would not, for reasons other than military, take any course which looked like a step backward;[30] and he himself concluded on the river movement below Vicksburg, so as to appear like connecting with General Banks, who at the same time was besieging Port Hudson from the direction of New Orleans.

Preliminary orders had already been given, looking to the digging of a canal, to connect the river at Duckport with Willow Bayou, back of Milliken's Bend, so as to form a channel for the conveyance of supplies, by way of Richmond, to New Carthage;[31] and several steam dredge-boats had come from the upper rivers to assist in the work. One day early in April, I was up at General Grant's headquarters, and we talked over all these things with absolute freedom.[32] Charles A. Dana, Assistant Secretary of War,[33] was there, and

[30] In his personal memoirs, USG stated, "One of my superstitions had always been when I started to go any where, or to do anything, not to turn back, or stop until the thing intended was accomplished." Ulysses S. Grant, *The Personal Memoirs of Ulysses S. Grant: The Complete Annotated Edition,* ed. John F. Marszalek, David S. Nolen, and Louie P. Gallo (Cambridge, MA: Belknap Press of Harvard University Press, 2017), 30.

[31] See Davis et al., *Official Military Atlas of the Civil War,* plate 155.

[32] USG met with WTS and others on Apr. 1, 1863. *PUSG,* 8:xxi.

[33] Charles A. Dana (1819–1897) arrived at USG's headquarters on Apr. 6, 1863. Officially, he was sent by Secretary of War Edwin M. Stanton as a special commissioner to "investigate and report upon the condition of the pay service in the Western armies," but he also had been directed to observe Grant and inform Stanton and Lincoln about him. He later served as the assistant secretary of war from Jan. 1864 until his resignation in July 1865. *CWHC,* 198;

Wilson,[34] Rawlins, Frank Blair, McPherson, etc. We all knew, what was notorious, that General McClernand was still intriguing against General Grant, in hopes to regain the command of the whole expedition, and that others were raising a clamor against General Grant in the newspapers at the North.[35] Even Mr. Lincoln and General Halleck seemed to be shaken; but at no instant of time did we (his personal friends) slacken in our loyalty to him. One night, after such a discussion, and believing that General McClernand had no real plan of action shaped in his mind, I wrote my letter of April 8, 1863, to Colonel Rawlins, which letter is embraced in full at page 616 of Badeau's book, and which I now reproduce here:

HEADQUARTERS FIFTEENTH ARMY CORPS,
CAMP NEAR VICKSBURG, *April* 8, 1863.

Colonel J. A. RAWLINS, *Assistant Adjutant-General to General* GRANT.

SIR: I would most respectfully suggest (for reasons which I will not name) that General Grant call on his corps commanders for their opinions, concise and positive, on the best general plan of a campaign. Unless this be done, there are men who will, in any result falling below the popular standard, claim that *their* advice was unheeded, and that fatal consequence resulted therefrom. My own opinions are—

First. That the Army of the Tennessee is now far in advance of the other grand armies of the United States.

Second. That a corps from Missouri should forthwith be moved from St. Louis to the vicinity of Little Rock, Arkansas; supplies collected there while the river is full, and land communication with Memphis opened *via* Des Arc on the White, and Madison on the St. Francis River.

Charles A. Dana, *Recollections of the Civil War, with the Leaders at Washington and in the Field in the Sixties* (New York: D. Appleton, 1913), 20–21; William S. McFeely, *Grant: A Biography* (New York: W. W. Norton, 1981), 128.

[34] James H. Wilson (1837–1925) graduated from the USMA in 1860 and was an assistant inspector general of the Army of the Tennessee in 1863. *CWHC*, 574.

[35] The *Chicago Tribune* criticized USG for his treatment of McClernand in the lead-up to the Vicksburg Campaign. The reporter stated, "What Gen. McClernand has undertaken to do he has done well. We hope Gen. Grant will be more successful in conducting this great enterprise than he was in conducting the enterprise against Grenada." "Gen. McClernand," *Chicago Tribune,* Feb. 23, 1863, 2.

Third. That as much of the Yazoo Pass, Coldwater, and Tallahatchie Rivers, as can be gained and fortified, be held, and the main army be transported thither by land and water; that the road back to Memphis be secured and reopened, and, as soon as the waters subside, Grenada be attacked, and the swamp-road across to Helena be patrolled by cavalry.

Fourth. That the line of the Yalabusha be the base from which to operate against the points where the Mississippi Central crosses Big Black, above Canton; and, lastly, where the Vicksburg & Jackson Railroad crosses the same river (Big Black). The capture of Vicksburg would result.

Fifth. That a minor force be left in this vicinity, not to exceed ten thousand men, with only enough steamboats to float and transport them to any desired point; this force to be held always near enough to act with the gunboats when the main army is known to be near Vicksburg—Haines's Bluff or Yazoo City.

Sixth. I do doubt the capacity of Willow Bayou (which I estimate to be fifty miles long and very tortuous) as a military channel, to supply an army large enough to operate against Jackson, Mississippi, or the Black River Bridge; and such a channel will be very vulnerable to a force coming from the west, which we must expect. Yet this canal will be most useful as the way to convey coals and supplies to a fleet that should navigate the lower reach of the Mississippi between Vicksburg and the Red River.

Seventh. The chief reason for operating *solely* by water was the season of the year and high water in the Tallahatchie and Yalabusha Rivers. The spring is now here, and soon these streams will be no serious obstacle, save in the ambuscades of the forest, and whatever works the enemy may have erected at or near Grenada. North Mississippi is too valuable for us to allow the enemy to hold it and make crops this year.

I make these suggestions, with the request that General Grant will read them and give them, as I know he will, a share of his thoughts. I would prefer that he should not answer this letter, but merely give it as much or as little weight as it deserves. Whatever plan of action he may adopt will receive from me the same zealous coöperation and energetic support as though conceived by myself. I do not believe General Banks will make any serious attack on Port Hudson this spring. I am, etc.,

W. T. Sherman, *Major-General.*

This is the letter which some critics have styled a "protest." We never had a council of war at any time during the Vicksburg campaign. We often met casually, regardless of rank or power, and talked and gossiped of things in general, as officers do and should. But my letter speaks for itself. It shows my opinions clearly at that stage of the game, and was meant partially to induce General Grant to call on General McClernand for a similar expression of opinion, but, so far as I know, he did not.[36] He went on quietly to work out his own designs; and he has told me, since the war, that had we possessed in December, 1862, the experience of marching and maintaining armies without a regular base, which we afterward acquired, he would have gone on from Oxford as first contemplated, and would not have turned back because of the destruction of his depot at Holly Springs by Van Dorn.[37] The distance from Oxford to the rear of Vicksburg is little greater than by the circuitous route we afterward followed, from Bruinsburg[38] to Jackson and Vicksburg, during which we had neither depot nor train of supplies. I have never criticised General Grant's strategy on this or any other occasion, but I thought then that he had lost an opportunity, which cost him and us six months' extra-hard work, for we might have captured Vicksburg from the direction of Oxford in January, quite as easily as was afterward done in July, 1863.

General Grant's orders for the general movement past Vicksburg, by Richmond and Carthage, were dated April 20, 1863.[39] McClernand was to lead off with his corps, McPherson next, and my corps (the Fifteenth) to bring up the rear. Preliminary thereto, on the night of April 16th, seven iron-clads led by Admiral Porter in person, in the Benton, with three transports, and ten barges in tow, ran the Vicksburg batteries by night. Anticipating a scene, I had four yawl-boats hauled across the swamp, to the reach of the river below Vicksburg, and manned them with soldiers, ready to pick up any of the disabled wrecks as

[36] In his personal memoirs, USG stated, "Colonel Rawlins showed me the letter, but I did not see any reason for changing my plans. The letter was not answered and the subject was not subsequently mentioned between Sherman and myself to the end of the war, that I remember of." Grant, *The Personal Memoirs,* 375.

[37] On Dec. 20, 1862, Van Dorn captured Holly Springs, MS, and destroyed U.S. Army supplies. *PUSG,* 7:xxi.

[38] Bruinsburg, MS, was located on the Mississippi River near the mouth of Bayou Pierre, and approximately ten miles south of Grand Gulf, MS. Christopher R. Gabel, *The Vicksburg Campaign: November 1862–July 1863* (Washington, DC: Center of Military History, U.S. Army, 2013), 32 (map).

[39] For Special Orders No. 110, see *PUSG,* 8:98–99.

they floated by. I was out in the stream when the fleet passed Vicksburg, and the scene was truly sublime. As soon as the rebel gunners detected the Benton, which was in the lead, they opened on her, and on the others in succession, with shot and shell; houses on the Vicksburg side and on the opposite shore were set on fire, which lighted up the whole river; and the roar of cannon, the bursting of shells, and finally the burning of the Henry Clay, drifting with the current, made up a picture of the terrible not often seen. Each gunboat returned the fire as she passed the town, while the transports hugged the opposite shore. When the Benton had got abreast of us, I pulled off to her, boarded, had a few words with Admiral Porter, and as she was drifting rapidly toward the lower batteries at Warrenton, I left, and pulled back toward the shore, meeting the gunboat Tuscumbia towing the transport Forest Queen into the bank out of the range of fire. The Forest Queen, Captain Conway,[40] had been my flag-boat up the Arkansas, and for some time after, and I was very friendly with her officers. This was the only transport whose captain would not receive volunteers as a crew, but her own officers and *crew* stuck to their boat, and carried her safely below the Vicksburg batteries, and afterward rendered splendid service in ferrying troops across the river at Grand Gulf[41] and Bruinsburg. In passing Vicksburg, she was damaged in the hull and had a steam-pipe cut away, but this was soon repaired.[42] The Henry Clay was set on fire by bursting shells, and burned up; one of my yawls picked up her pilot floating on a piece of wreck, and the bulk of her crew escaped in their own yawl-boat to the shore above.[43] The Silver Wave, Captain McMillan, the same that was with us up Steele's Bayou, passed safely, and she also rendered good service afterward.

Subsequently, on the night of April 26th, six other transports with numerous barges loaded with hay, corn, freight, and provisions, were drifted

[40] C. Dan Conway, a steamboat captain from Indiana, was praised by WTS as a person to whom "the U.S. owes a debt of gratitude that can never be paid" for his actions during the Vicksburg Campaign. *PUSG,* 8:523*n;* "Widow of Civil War Hero Will Be Buried Today," *Indianapolis Star,* Oct. 18, 1905, 5.

[41] Grand Gulf, MS, was located approximately ten miles upriver of Bruinsburg. Gabel, *The Vicksburg Campaign,* 32 (map).

[42] According to a reporter aboard the *Forest Queen,* when the boat passed the Vicksburg batteries, Capt. Conway "carried a chair close up to the forward railing of the upper deck, seated himself, lighted a cigar, and remained in this position during the tremendous fire through which he passed . . . Captain Conway rode through the storm, never leaving his seat nor losing the light of his cigar." Franc B. Wilkie, *Pen and Powder* (Boston: Tickner, 1888), 313.

[43] The pilot was named "Taylor." *OR,* I, 24(III), 207–208.

past Vicksburg; of these the Tigress was hit, and sunk just as she reached the river-bank below, on our side. I was there with my yawls, and saw Colonel Lagow, of General Grant's staff, who had passed the batteries in the Tigress, and I think he was satisfied never to attempt such a thing again. Thus General Grant's army had below Vicksburg an abundance of stores, and boats with which to cross the river. The road by which the troops marched was very bad, and it was not until the 1st of May that it was clear for my corps. While waiting my turn to march, I received a letter from General Grant, written at Carthage, saying that he proposed to cross over and attack Grand Gulf, about the end of April, and he thought I could put in my time usefully by making a "feint" on Haines's Bluff, but he did not like to order me to do it, because it might be reported at the North that I had again been "repulsed, etc." Thus we had to fight a senseless clamor at the North, as well as a determined foe and the obstacles of Nature. Of course, I answered him that I would make the "feint," regardless of public clamor at a distance, and I did make it most effectually; using all the old boats I could get about Milliken's Bend and the mouth of the Yazoo, but taking only ten small regiments, selected out of Blair's division, to make a show of force.[44] We afterward learned that General Pemberton in Vicksburg had previously dispatched a large force to the assistance of General Bowen,[45] at Grand Gulf and Port Gibson, which force had proceeded as far as Hankinson's Ferry, when he discovered our ostentatious movement up the Yazoo, recalled his men, and sent them up to Haines's Bluff to meet us. This detachment of rebel troops must have marched nearly sixty miles without rest, for afterward, on reaching Vicksburg, I heard that the men were perfectly exhausted, and lay along the road in groups, completely fagged out. This diversion, made with so much pomp and display, therefore completely fulfilled its purpose, by leaving General Grant to contend with a minor force, on landing at Bruinsburg, and afterward at Port Gibson and Grand Gulf.

In May the waters of the Mississippi had so far subsided that all our canals were useless, and the roads had become practicable. After McPherson's corps had passed Richmond, I took up the route of march, with Steele's and Tuttle's divisions. Blair's division remained at Milliken's Bend to protect our depots

[44] For USG's Apr. 27, 1863, letter to WTS and WTS's response, see *OR,* I, 24(III), 240, 242–243.

[45] John S. Bowen (1830–1863) graduated from the USMA in 1853 and resigned from the U.S. Army in May 1856. He joined the Confederate Army and died of dysentery near Edwards, MS, on July 13, 1863. *CWHC,* 138.

there, till relieved by troops from Memphis, and then he was ordered to follow us. Our route lay by Richmond and Roundabout Bayou; then, following Bayou Vidal we struck the Mississippi at Perkins's plantation. Thence the route followed Lake St. Joseph to a plantation called Hard Times, about five miles above Grand Gulf.[46] The road was more or less occupied by wagons and detachments belonging to McPherson's corps; still we marched rapidly and reached Hard Times on the 6th of May. Along the Bayou or Lake St. Joseph were many very fine cotton-plantations, and I recall that of a Mr. Bowie,[47] brother-in-law of the Hon. Reverdy Johnson, of Baltimore.[48] The house was very handsome, with a fine, extensive grass-plot in front. We entered the yard, and, leaving our horses with the headquarters escort, walked to the house. On the front-porch I found a magnificent grand-piano, with several satin-covered arm-chairs, in one of which sat a Union soldier (one of McPherson's men), with his feet on the keys of the piano, and his musket and knapsack lying on the porch. I asked him what he was doing there, and he answered that he was "taking a rest;" this was manifest and I started him in a hurry, to overtake his command. The house was tenantless, and had been completely ransacked; articles of dress and books were strewed about, and a handsome boudoir with mirror front had been cast down, striking a French bedstead, shivering the glass. The library was extensive, with a fine collection of books; and hanging on the wall were two full-length portraits of Reverdy Johnson and his wife, one of the most beautiful ladies of our country,[49] with whom I had been acquainted in Washington at the time of General Taylor's administration. Behind the mansion was the usual double row of cabins called the "quarters." There I found an old negro (a family servant) with several women, whom I sent to the house to put things in order; telling the old

[46] Hard Times Plantation was situated along the Mississippi River in Louisiana. For a detailed map of the area, see Davis et al., *Official Military Atlas of the Civil War,* plate 36, map 1.

[47] Thomas F. Bowie (1808–1869) served in the Maryland House of Representatives from 1842 to 1846 and in the U.S. House of Representatives from 1855 to 1859. Andrew Johnson, *The Papers of Andrew Johnson,* ed. Paul H. Bergeron (Knoxville: University of Tennessee Press, 1995) 12:102*n;* "The Late Thomas F. Bowie," *Baltimore Sun,* Nov. 5, 1869, 2.

[48] Reverdy Johnson (1796–1876) served as a U.S. senator from 1845 to 1849 and U.S. attorney general for Zachary Taylor. Gilbert J. Clark, *Life Sketches of Eminent Lawyers, American, English and Canadian* (Kansas City: Lawyers' International, 1895), 2:51–54.

[49] Mary M. Johnson (1801–1873), the daughter of Maryland governor Robert Bowie, married Reverdy Johnson on Nov. 16, 1819. "Death of Mrs. Reverdy Johnson," *Pittsburgh Post* (Pittsburgh, PA), Mar. 25, 1873, 1.

man that other troops would follow, and he must stand on the porch to tell any officers who came along that the property belonged to Mr. Bowie, who was the brother-in-law of our friend Mr. Reverdy Johnson, of Baltimore, asking them to see that no further harm was done. Soon after we left the house I saw some negroes carrying away furniture which manifestly belonged to the house, and compelled them to carry it back; and after reaching camp that night, at Hard Times, I sent a wagon back to Bowie's plantation, to bring up to Dr. Hollingsworth's house[50] the two portraits for safe keeping; but before the wagon had reached Bowie's the house was burned, whether by some of our men or by negroes I have never learned.[51]

At the river there was a good deal of scrambling to get across, because the means of ferriage were inadequate; but by the aid of the Forest Queen and several gunboats I got my command across during the 7th of May, and marched out to Hankinson's Ferry (eighteen miles), relieving General Crocker's division of McPherson's corps.[52] McClernand's corps and McPherson's were still ahead, and had fought the battle of Port Gibson, on the 11th. I overtook General Grant in person at Auburn,[53] and he accompanied my corps all the way into Jackson, which we reached May 14th. McClernand's corps had been left in observation toward Edwards's Ferry. McPherson had fought at Raymond, and taken the left-hand road toward Jackson, *via* Clinton, while my troops were ordered by General Grant in person to take the right-hand road leading through Mississippi Springs. We reached Jackson at the same time; McPherson fighting on the Clinton road, and my troops

[50] Jeremiah Y. Hollingsworth (1813–1888) earned his doctor of medicine degree from the University of Pennsylvania in 1834. *Biographical Memoranda Respecting All Who Ever Were Members of the Class of 1832 in Yale College* (New Haven, CT: Tuttle, Morehouse and Taylor, 1880), 145–148; Jefferson Davis, *The Papers of Jefferson Davis,* ed. Lynda L. Crist and Suzanne S. Gibbs (Baton Rouge: LSU Press, 2012), 13:392*n.*

[51] U.S. Army soldier Alexander G. Downing visited the Bowie Plantation on May 12. He wrote, "The main Bowie residence was burned and household articles, among which is a grand piano, are strewn about the large lawn . . . The plantation borders the west bank of Lake St. Joseph, the public highway being just between it and the lake. This plantation, containing several thousand acres, is all planted to corn, which is now in tassel and silk." Alexander G. Downing, *Downing's Civil War Diary,* ed. Olynthus B. Clark (Des Moines: Historical Department of Iowa, 1916), 114–115.

[52] Marcellus M. Crocker (1830–1865) was relieved of command of the 7th Div., 17th Corps, Army of the Tennessee, on May 16, 1863. *CWHC,* 191.

[53] Auburn, MS, was located approximately twenty-five miles southwest of Jackson, MS. For a detailed map of the area, see Davis et al., *Official Military Atlas of the Civil War,* plate 36, map 1.

fighting just outside the town, on the Raymond road, where we captured three entire field-batteries, and about two hundred prisoners of war.[54] The rebels, under General Joe Johnston, had retreated through the town northward on the Canton road. Generals Grant, McPherson, and I, met in the large hotel facing the State-House, where the former explained to us that he had intercepted dispatches from Pemberton to Johnston, which made it important for us to work smart to prevent a junction of their respective forces.[55] McPherson was ordered to march back early the next day on the Clinton road to make junction with McClernand, and I was ordered to remain one day to break up railroads, to destroy the arsenal, a foundery, the cotton-factory of the Messrs. Green, etc., etc., and then to follow McPherson.[56]

McPherson left Jackson early on the 15th, and General Grant during the same day. I kept my troops busy in tearing up railroad-tracks, etc., but early on the morning of the 16th received notice from General Grant that a battle was imminent near Edwards's Depot; that he wanted me to dispatch one of my divisions immediately, and to follow with the other as soon as I had completed the work of destruction. Steele's division started immediately, and later in the day I followed with the other division (Tuttle's). Just as I was leaving Jackson, a very fat man came to see me, to inquire if his hotel, a large, frame-building near the depot, were doomed to be burned. I told him we had no intention to burn it, or any other house, except the machine-shops, and such buildings as could easily be converted to hostile uses. He professed to be a law-abiding Union man, and I remember to have said that this fact was manifest from the sign of his hotel, which was the "Confederate Hotel;" the sign "United States" being faintly painted out, and "Confederate" painted over it! I remembered that hotel, as it was the supper-station for the New Orleans trains when I used to travel the road before the war. I had not the least pur-

[54] For WTS's contemporary report of events, see *OR,* I, 24(I), 751–758.

[55] The Bowman House was built in 1857 and was a Confederate Army headquarters before being captured. Mary C. Miller, *Lost Landmarks of Mississippi* (Jackson: University Press of Mississippi, 2002), 47.

[56] In Apr. 1874, the U.S. Congress's "Committee on War-Claims" denied Joshua and Thomas Green's claim of $982,201.75 as reimbursement for the destruction of their property by the U.S. Army in 1863. The committee declared that "the seizure and destruction in whatever property was seized and destroyed were *flagrante bello* in a State in rebellion, as a military necessity, and that the property was such as might add to the strength of the enemy and enable him to carry on hostilities." *Reports of the Committees of the House of Representatives for the First Session of the Forty-Third Congress* (Washington, DC: GPO, 1874), vol. 2, Report 376.

pose, however, of burning it, but, just as we were leaving the town, it burst out in flames and was burned to the ground. I never found out exactly who set it on fire, but was told that in one of our batteries were some officers and men who had been made prisoners at Shiloh, with Prentiss's division, and had been carried past Jackson in a railroad-train; they had been permitted by the guard to go to this very hotel for supper, and had nothing to pay but greenbacks, which were refused, with insult, by this same law-abiding landlord. These men, it was said, had quietly and stealthily applied the fire underneath the hotel just as we were leaving the town.

About dark we met General Grant's staff-officer near Bolton Station,[57] who turned us to the right, with orders to push on to Vicksburg by what was known as the upper Jackson Road, which crossed the Big Black at Bridgeport. During that day (May 16th) the battle of Champion Hills had been fought and won by McClernand's and McPherson's corps, aided by one division of mine (Blair's), under the immediate command of General Grant; and McPherson was then following the mass of Pemberton's army, disordered and retreating toward Vicksburg by the Edwards's Ferry road. General Blair's division had come up from the rear, was temporarily attached to McClernand's corps, taking part with it in the battle of Champion Hills, but on the 17th it was ordered by General Grant across to Bridgeport, to join me there.

Just beyond Bolton there was a small hewn-log house, standing back in a yard, in which was a well; at this some of our soldiers were drawing water. I rode in to get a drink, and, seeing a book on the ground, asked some soldier to hand it to me. It was a volume of the Constitution of the United States, and on the title-page was written the name of Jefferson Davis. On inquiry of a negro, I learned that the place belonged to the then President of the Southern Confederation. His brother Joe Davis's plantation was not far off; one of my staff-officers went there, with a few soldiers, and took a pair of carriage-horses, without my knowledge at the time.[58] He found Joe Davis at home, an old man, attended by a young and affectionate niece; but they were overwhelmed with grief to see their country overrun and swarming with Federal troops.

We pushed on, and reached the Big Black early, Blair's troops having preceded us by an hour or so. I found General Blair in person, and he reported

[57] Bolton Depot was situated along the Vicksburg and Jackson Railroad, approximately twenty miles west of Jackson. Davis et al., *Official Military Atlas of the Civil War,* plate 36, map 1.

[58] Joe Davis's plantation was located approximately two miles northwest of Bolton Depot. Buck T. Foster, *Sherman's Mississippi Campaign* (Tuscaloosa: University of Alabama Press, 2006), 49.

that there was no bridge across the Big Black; that it was swimming-deep; and that there was a rebel force on the opposite side, intrenched. He had ordered a detachment of the Thirteenth United States Regulars, under Captain Charles Ewing, to strip some artillery-horses, mount the men, and swim the river above the ferry, to attack and drive away the party on the opposite bank. I did not approve of this risky attempt, but crept down close to the brink of the river bank, behind a corn-crib belonging to a plantation house near by, and saw the parapet on the opposite bank. Ordering a section of guns to be brought forward by hand behind this corn-crib, a few well-directed shells brought out of their holes the little party that was covering the crossing, viz., a lieutenant and ten men, who came down to the river-bank and surrendered. Blair's pontoon-train was brought up, consisting of India-rubber boats, one of which was inflated, used as a boat, and brought over the prisoners. A pontoon-bridge was at once begun, finished by night, and the troops began the passage. After dark, the whole scene was lit up with fires of pitch-pine. General Grant joined me there, and we sat on a log, looking at the passage of the troops by the light of those fires; the bridge swayed to and fro under the passing feet, and made a fine war-picture. At daybreak we moved on, ascending the ridge, and by 10 A. M. the head of my column, long drawn out, reached the Benton road, and gave us command of the peninsula between the Yazoo and Big Black. I dispatched Colonel Swan, of the Fourth Iowa Cavalry, to Haines's Bluff, to capture that battery from the rear, and he afterward reported that he found it abandoned, its garrison having hastily retreated into Vicksburg, leaving their guns partially disabled, a magazine full of ammunition, and a hospital full of wounded and sick men.[59] Colonel Swan saw one of our gunboats lying about two miles below in the Yazoo, to which he signaled. She steamed up, and to its commander the cavalry turned over the battery at Haines's Bluff, and rejoined me in front of Vicksburg.[60] Allowing a couple of hours for rest and to close up the column, I resumed the march straight on Vicksburg. About two miles before reaching the forts, the road forked; the left was the main Jackson road, and the right was the "graveyard" road, which entered Vicksburg near a large cemetery. General Grant in person directed me to take the right-hand road, but, as McPherson had not

[59] Simeon D. Swan (1832–1900) was promoted to lieutenant colonel on June 4, 1862. He discovered that Haines's Bluff was abandoned on May 19, 1863. *OR,* I, 24(I), 755; George A. Ide, *History of Union County, Iowa* (Chicago: S. J. Clarke, 1908), 509–511.

[60] The USS *Baron DeKalb,* commanded by John G. Walker (1835–1907), took control of the battery at Haines's Bluff. *ORN,* I, 25, 133; Smith, *The Fight for the Yazoo,* 325.

yet got up from the direction of the railroad-bridge at Big Black, I sent the Eighth Missouri on the main Jackson road, to push the rebel skirmishers into town, and to remain until relieved by McPherson's advance, which happened late that evening, May 18th. The battalion of the Thirteenth United States Regulars, commanded by Captain Washington, was at the head of the column on the right-hand road, and pushed the rebels close behind their parapets; one of my staff, Captain Pitzman, receiving a dangerous wound in the hip, which apparently disabled him for life. By night Blair's whole division had closed up against the defenses of Vicksburg, which were found to be strong and well manned; and, on General Steele's head of column arriving, I turned it still more to the right, with orders to work its way down the bluff, so as to make connection with our fleet in the Mississippi River. There was a good deal of desultory fighting that evening, and a man was killed by the side of General Grant and myself, as we sat by the road-side looking at Steele's division passing to the right. General Steele's men reached the road which led from Vicksburg up to Haines's Bluff, which road lay at the foot of the hills, and intercepted some prisoners and wagons which were coming down from Haines's Bluff.

All that night McPherson's troops were arriving by the main Jackson road, and McClernand's by another near the railroad, deploying forward as fast as they struck the rebel works. My corps (the Fifteenth) had the right of the line of investment; McPherson's (the Seventeenth) the centre; and McClernand's (the Thirteenth) the left, reaching from the river above to the railroad below. Our lines connected, and invested about three-quarters of the land-front of the fortifications of Vicksburg. On the supposition that the garrison of Vicksburg was demoralized by the defeats at Champion Hills and at the railroad crossing of the Big Black, General Grant ordered an assault at our respective fronts on the 19th. My troops reached the top of the parapet, but could not cross over. The rebel parapets were strongly manned, and the enemy fought hard and well. My loss was pretty heavy, falling chiefly on the Thirteenth Regulars, whose commanding officer, Captain Washington, was killed, and several other regiments were pretty badly cut up.[61] We, however, held the ground up to the ditch till night, and then drew back only a short distance, and began to counter-trench. On the graveyard road, our parapet was within less than fifty yards of the rebel ditch.

[61] Edward C. Washington (c. 1820–1863) was killed during the engagement at the Big Black River on May 19, 1863. WTS reported a total of seventy-seven casualties. OR, I, 24(I), 756; John C. White, "A Review of the Services of the Regular Army during the Civil War," *Journal of the Military Service Institution of the United States,* no. 172 (July–Aug. 1911): 49:98.

On the 20th of May, General Grant called the three corps commanders together, viz., McClernand, McPherson, and Sherman. We compared notes, and agreed that the assault of the day before had failed, by reason of the natural strength of the position, and because we were forced by the nature of the ground to limit our attacks to the strongest parts of the enemy's line, viz., where the three principal roads entered the city.

It was not a council of war, but a mere consultation, resulting in orders from General Grant for us to make all possible preparations for a renewed assault on the 22d, simultaneously, at 10 A. M. I reconnoitred my front thoroughly in person, from right to left, and concluded to make my real attack at the right flank of the bastion, where the graveyard road entered the enemy's intrenchments, and at another point in the curtain about a hundred yards to its right (our left); also to make a strong demonstration by Steele's division, about a mile to our right, toward the river. All our field-batteries were put in position, and were covered by good epaulements; the troops were brought forward, in easy support, concealed by the shape of the ground; and to the minute, viz., 10 A. M. of May 22d, the troops sprang to the assault. A small party, that might be called a forlorn hope, provided with plank to cross the ditch, advanced at a run, up to the very ditch; the lines of infantry sprang from cover, and advanced rapidly in line of battle. I took a position within two hundred yards of the rebel parapet, on the off slope of a spur of ground, where by advancing two or three steps I could see every thing. The rebel line, concealed by the parapet, showed no sign of unusual activity, but as our troops came in fair view, the enemy rose behind their parapet and poured a furious fire upon our lines; and, for about two hours, we had a severe and bloody battle, but at every point we were repulsed. In the very midst of this, when shell and shot fell furious and fast, occurred that little episode which has been celebrated in song and story, of the boy Orion P. Howe, badly wounded, bearing me a message for cartridges, calibre 54, described in my letter to the Hon. E. M. Stanton, Secretary of War. This boy was afterward appointed a cadet to the United States Naval Academy, at Annapolis, but he could not graduate, and I do not now know what has become of him.[62]

[62] On Aug. 8, 1863, WTS wrote to Stanton about Orion P. Howe's (1848–1930) actions during the events leading up to the Siege of Vicksburg. In 1864, poet George H. Boker wrote a poem based on Howe titled "Before Vicksburg." Howe was later appointed to the Naval Academy in Annapolis, MD, in July 1865. He dropped out two years later due to poor grades. He did, however, graduate from New York University with a degree in dentistry in 1892, and in 1896 Pres. Grover Cleveland awarded him the Medal of Honor for his actions during the

After our men had been fairly beaten back from off the parapet, and had got cover behind the spurs of ground close up to the rebel works, General Grant came to where I was, on foot, having left his horse some distance to the rear. I pointed out to him the rebel works, admitted that my assault had failed, and he said the result with McPherson and McClernand was about the same. While he was with me, an orderly or staff-officer came and handed him a piece of paper, which he read and handed to me. I think the writing was in pencil, on a loose piece of paper, and was in General McClernand's hand-writing, to the effect that "his troops had captured the rebel parapet in his front," that, "the flag of the Union waved over the stronghold of Vicksburg," and asking him (General Grant) to give renewed orders to McPherson and Sherman to press their attacks on their respective fronts, lest the enemy should concentrate on him (McClernand).[63] General Grant said, "I don't believe a word of it;" but I reasoned with him, that this note was official, and must be credited, and I offered to renew the assault at once with new troops. He said he would instantly ride down the line to McClernand's front, and if I did not receive orders to the contrary, by 3 o'clock P. M., I might try it again. Mower's fresh brigade was brought up under cover, and some changes were made in Giles Smith's brigade; and, punctually at 3 P. M., hearing heavy firing down along the line to my left, I ordered the second assault. It was a repetition of the first, equally unsuccessful and bloody. It also transpired that the same thing had occurred with General McPherson, who lost in this second assault some most valuable officers and men, without adequate result; and that General McClernand, instead of having taken any single point of the rebel main parapet, had only taken one or two small outlying lunettes open to the rear, where his men were at the mercy of the rebels behind their main parapet, and most of them were actually thus captured.[64] This affair caused great feeling with us, and severe criticisms on General McClernand, which led finally to

---

attack on the Stockade Redan outside of Vicksburg. Sculley Bradley, *George Henry Boker: Poet and Patriot* (Philadelphia: University of Pennsylvania Press, 1927), 209–210; William F. Vilas, *A View of the Vicksburg Campaign: A Paper Read before the Madison Literary Club, October 14, 1907* (Madison, WI: Democrat, 1908), 99–100; A. J. Schenkman, *Unexpected Bravery: Women and Children of the Civil War* (Lanham, MD: Globe Pequot, 2021), 45, 54–59.

[63] On May 22, 1863, McClernand wrote to USG, "We are hotly engaged with the enemy. We have part possession of two forts, and the Stars and Stripes are floating over there. A vigorous push ought to be made all along the line." *OR,* I, 24(I), 172.

[64] McClernand's losses at the Battle of Big Black River were 226 killed, 972 wounded, and 145 missing. *OR,* I, 24(I), 151.

his removal from the command of the Thirteenth Corps, to which General Ord succeeded. The immediate cause, however, of General McClernand's removal was the publication of a sort of congratulatory order addressed to his troops, first published in St. Louis, in which he claimed that he had actually succeeded in making a lodgment in Vicksburg, but had lost it, owing to the fact that McPherson and Sherman did not fulfill their parts of the general plan of attack.[65] This was simply untrue. The two several assaults made May 22d, on the lines of Vicksburg, had failed, by reason of the great strength of the position and the determined fighting of its garrison. I have since seen the position at Sevastopol, and without hesitation I declare that at Vicksburg to have been the more difficult of the two.[66]

Thereafter our proceedings were all in the nature of a siege. General Grant drew more troops from Memphis, to prolong our general line to the left, so as completely to invest the place on its land-side, while the navy held the river both above and below.[67] General Mower's brigade of Tuttle's division was also sent across the river to the peninsula, so that by May 31st Vicksburg was completely beleaguered. Good roads were constructed from our camps to the several landing-places on the Yazoo River, to which points our boats brought us ample supplies; so that we were in a splendid condition for a siege, while our enemy was shut up in a close fort, with a large civil population of men, women, and children to feed, in addition to his combatant force. If we could prevent sallies, or relief from the outside, the fate of the garrison of Vicksburg was merely a question of time.

I had my headquarters camp close up to the works, near the centre of my corps, and General Grant had his bivouac behind a ravine to my rear. We estimated Pemberton's whole force in Vicksburg at thirty thousand men, and it was well known that the rebel General Joseph E. Johnston was engaged in collecting another strong force near the Big Black, with the intention to attack our rear, and thus to afford Pemberton an opportunity to escape with his men. Even then the ability of General Johnston was recognized, and General Grant told me that he was about the only general on that side whom he feared. Each corps kept strong pickets well to the rear; but, as the rumors of

[65] For McClernand's congratulatory order to his troops, see *OR,* I, 24(I), 159.

[66] In his book *Sevastopol Sketches,* famed Russian author Leo Tolstoy wrote about his experience as a soldier in the Crimean War during the Siege of Sevastopol in 1854–1855. See Leo Tolstoy, *Sevastopol,* trans. Isabel F. Hapgood (New York: Thomas Y. Cromwell, 1888).

[67] Two brigades from Missouri, equaling approximately 8,000 troops, were sent south to reinforce USG. *OR,* I, 24(III), 402.

Johnston's accumulating force reached us, General Grant concluded to take stronger measures. He had received from the North General J. G. Parkes's corps (Ninth), which had been posted at Haines's Bluff; then, detailing one division from each of the three *corps d'armée* investing Vicksburg, he ordered me to go out, take a general command of all, and to counteract any movement on the part of General Johnston to relieve Vicksburg.[68] I reconnoitred the whole country, from Haines's Bluff to the railroad bridge, and posted the troops thus: Parkes's two divisions from Haines's Bluff out to the Benton or ridge road; Tuttle's division, of my corps, joining on and extending to a plantation called Young's, overlooking Bear Creek valley, which empties into the Big Black above Messinger's Ferry; then McArthur's division, of McPherson's corps, took up the line, and reached to Osterhaus's division of McClernand's corps, which held a strong fortified position at the railroad-crossing of the Big Black River. I was of opinion that, if Johnston should cross the Big Black, he could by the favorable nature of the country be held in check till a concentration could be effected by us at the point threatened. From the best information we could gather, General Johnston had about thirty or forty thousand men.[69] I took post near a plantation of one Trible, near Markham's, and frequently reconnoitred the whole line, and could see the enemy engaged in like manner, on the east side of Big Black; but he never attempted actually to cross over, except with some cavalry, just above Bear Creek, which was easily driven back. I was there from June 20th to the 4th of July. In a small log-house near Markham's was the family of Mr. Klein,[70] whose wife[71] was the daughter of Mrs. Day, of New Orleans, who in turn was the sister of Judge T. W. Bartley, my brother-in-law. I used frequently to drop in and take a meal with them, and Mrs. Klein

[68] For USG's June 11, 1863, order to WTS, see *OR,* I, 24(III), 402.

[69] Johnston had approximately 25,000 troops under his command in June 1863. Matthew F. Steele, *American Campaigns* (Washington, DC: Byron S. Adams, 1909), 1:356.

[70] John A. Klein (1812–1884) moved to Vicksburg in 1836 and built the Cedar Grove House in 1840. He served as the vice president of the Vicksburg and Meridian Railroad. Jim Fraiser, *The Majesty of the Mississippi Delta* (Gretna, LA: Pelican, 2005), 18; *In and About Vicksburg: An Illustrated Guide Book to the City of Vicksburg, Mississippi* (Vicksburg, MS: Gibraltar, 1890), 189.

[71] Elizabeth B. Day-Klein (1826–1909) was the daughter of Sylvanus and Susannah Day. She married John Klein in 1842 and was known for hosting guests at the family home. "Passing of a Venerable Lady," *Vicksburg American* (Vicksburg, MS), Jan. 16, 1909, 8; Margery F. D. Hanson and Richard E. Hanson, *Day unto Day: A Study of the Day Family in America* (Burlington, VT: Queen City, 1978), 19, 46, 114.

was generally known as the general's cousin, which doubtless saved her and her family from molestation, too common on the part of our men.

One day, as I was riding the line near a farm known as Parson Fox's,[72] I heard that the family of a Mr. Wilkinson, of New Orleans, was "refugeeing" at a house near by. I rode up, inquired, and found two young girls of that name, who said they were the children of General Wilkinson, of Louisiana, and that their brother had been at the Military School at Alexandria. Inquiring for their mother, I was told she was spending the day at Parson Fox's.[73] As this house was on my route, I rode there, went through a large gate into the yard, followed by my staff and escort, and found quite a number of ladies sitting on the porch. I rode up and inquired if that were Parson Fox's. The parson, a fine-looking, venerable old man, rose, and said that he was Parson Fox. I then inquired for Mrs. Wilkinson, when an elderly lady answered that she was the person. I asked her if she were from Plaquemine Parish, Louisiana, and she said she was. I then inquired if she had a son who had been a cadet at Alexandria when General Sherman was superintendent, and she answered yes. I then announced myself, inquired after the boy, and she said he was inside of Vicksburg, an artillery lieutenant. I then asked about her husband, whom I had known, when she burst into tears, and cried out in agony, "You killed him at Bull Run, where he was fighting for his country!" I disclaimed killing anybody at Bull Run; but all the women present (nearly a dozen) burst into loud lamentations, which made it most uncomfortable for me, and I rode away. On the 3d of July, as I sat at my bivouac by the road-side near Trible's, I saw a poor, miserable horse, carrying a lady, and led by a little negro boy, coming across a cotton-field toward me; as they approached I recognized poor Mrs. Wilkinson, and helped her to dismount. I inquired what had brought her to me in that style, and she answered that she *knew* Vicksburg was going to surrender, and she wanted to go right away to see her boy. I had a telegraph-wire to General Grant's headquarters, and had heard that there were symptoms of surrender, but as yet nothing definite. I tried to console and dissuade her, but she was resolved, and I could not help giving her a letter to General Grant, explaining to him who she was, and asking him to give her the earliest opportunity to see her son. The distance was

[72] Parson Fox's Farm was located approximately ten miles northeast of Vicksburg, on the west side of the Big Black River. William B. Feis, *Secret Service: The Intelligence War from Belmont to Appomattox* (Lincoln: University of Nebraska Press, 2002), 143 (map).

[73] Robert A. Wilkinson (1809–1862) was married to Mary F. Wilkinson. They had six children—Robert, Horatio, Katherine, Rose, Belle, and Mollie. Robert Jr. was one of the first cadets at the Louisiana State Seminary.

fully twenty miles, but off she started, and I afterward learned that my letter had enabled her to see her son, who had escaped unharmed. Later in the day I got by telegraph General Grant's notice of the negotiations for surrender; and, by his directions, gave general orders to my troops to be ready at a moment's notice to cross the Big Black, and go for Joe Johnston.[74]

The next day (July 4, 1863) Vicksburg surrendered, and orders were given for at once attacking General Johnston. The Thirteenth Corps (General Ord) was ordered to march rapidly, and cross the Big Black at the railroad-bridge; the Fifteenth by Messinger's, and the Ninth (General Parkes) by Birdsong's Ferry—all to converge on Bolton. My corps crossed the Big Black during the 5th and 6th of July, and marched for Bolton, where we came in with General Ord's troops; but the Ninth Corps was delayed in crossing at Birdsong's. Johnston had received timely notice of Pemberton's surrender, and was in full retreat for Jackson.[75] On the 8th all our troops reached the neighborhood of Clinton, the weather fearfully hot, and water scarce. Johnston had marched rapidly, and in retreating had caused cattle, hogs, and sheep, to be driven into the ponds of water, and there shot down; so that we had to haul their dead and stinking carcasses out to use the water. On the 10th of July we had driven the rebel army into Jackson, where it turned at bay behind the intrenchments, which had been enlarged and strengthened since our former visit in May. We closed our lines about Jackson; my corps (Fifteenth) held the centre, extending from the Clinton to the Raymond road; Ord's (Thirteenth) on the right, reaching Pearl River below the town; and Parkes's (Ninth) the left, above the town.

On the 11th we pressed close in, and shelled the town from every direction. One of Ords brigades (Lauman's) got too close, and was very roughly handled and driven back in disorder. General Ord accused the commander (General Lauman) of having disregarded his orders, and attributed to him personally the disaster and heavy loss of men. He requested his relief, which I granted, and General Lauman went to the rear, and never regained his division.[76] He died after the war, in Iowa, much respected, as before that time he had been universally esteemed a most gallant and excellent officer. The weather was fearfully hot, but we continued to press the siege day and night, using our artillery pretty freely; and on the morning of July 17th the place

[74] For the relevant correspondence between USG and WTS, see *PUSG,* 8:460.

[75] According to his post-battle report, Johnston learned of the fall of Vicksburg on July 5, 1863. *OR,* I, 24(I), 245.

[76] Lauman commanded the 4th Div., 8th Corps, Army of the Tennessee, on July 11. He took command of the 4th Div., 17th Corps, Army of the Tennessee, on Aug. 7. *CWHC,* 340.

was found evacuated. General Steele's division was sent in pursuit as far as Brandon (fourteen miles), but General Johnston had carried his army safely off, and pursuit in that hot weather would have been fatal to my command.

Reporting the fact to General Grant, he ordered me to return, to send General Parkes's corps to Haines's Bluff, General Ord's back to Vicksburg, and he consented that I should encamp my whole corps near the Big Black, pretty much on the same ground we had occupied before the movement, and with the prospect of a period of rest for the remainder of the summer. We reached our camps on the 27th of July.

Meantime, a division of troops, commanded by Brigadier-General W. Sooy Smith,[77] had been added to my corps. General Smith applied for and received a sick-leave on the 20th of July; Brigadier-General Hugh Ewing was assigned to its command; and from that time it constituted the Fourth Division of the Fifteenth Army Corps.[78]

Port Hudson had surrendered to General Banks on the 8th of July (a necessary consequence of the fall of Vicksburg), and thus terminated probably the most important enterprise of the civil war—the recovery of the complete control of the Mississippi River, from its source to its mouth—or, in the language of Mr. Lincoln, the Mississippi went "unvexed to the sea."[79]

I put my four divisions into handsome, clean camps, looking to health and comfort alone, and had my headquarters in a beautiful grove near the house of that same Parson Fox where I had found the crowd of weeping rebel women waiting for the fate of their friends in Vicksburg.

The loss sustained by the Fifteenth Corps in the assault of May 19th, at Vicksburg, was mostly confined to the battalion of the Thirteenth Regulars, whose commanding officer, Captain Washington, was mortally wounded, and afterward died in the hands of the enemy, which battalion lost seventy-seven men out of the two hundred and fifty engaged; the Eighty-third Indiana (Colonel Spooner), and the One Hundred and Twenty seventh Illinois (Lieutenant-Colonel Eldridge), the aggregate being about two hundred.

[77] William S. Smith (1830–1916) graduated from the USMA in 1853 and was promoted to brigadier general in Apr. 1862. *CWHC,* 500.

[78] Smith's 1st Div., 16th Corps, Army of the Tennessee, was reorganized and formed into the 4th Div., 15th Corps, Army of the Tennessee, on July 28. *CWHC,* 230.

[79] In an Aug. 26, 1863, letter to Illinois politician J. C. Conkling, Pres. Abraham Lincoln asserted, "The signs look better. The Father of Waters again goes unvexed to the sea." Abraham Lincoln, *The Collected Works of Abraham Lincoln,* ed. Roy P. Basler, Marion D. Pratt, and Lloyd A. Dunlap (New Brunswick. NJ: Rutgers University Press, 1953), 6:409.

In the assaults of the 22d, the loss in the Fifteenth Corps was about six hundred.

In the attack on Jackson, Mississippi, during the 11th–16th of July, General Ord reported the loss in the Thirteenth Army Corps seven hundred and sixty-two, of which five hundred and thirty-three were confined to Lauman's division; General Parkes reported, in the Ninth Corps, thirty-seven killed, two hundred and fifty-eight wounded, and thirty-three missing: total, three hundred and twenty-eight. In the Fifteenth Corps the loss was less; so that, in the aggregate, the loss as reported by me at the time was less than a thousand men, while we took that number alone of prisoners.

In General Grant's entire army before Vicksburg, composed of the Ninth, part of the Sixteenth, and the whole of the Thirteenth, Fifteenth, and Seventeenth Corps, the aggregate loss, as stated by Badeau, was—

Killed	1,243
Wounded	7,095
Missing	535
Total	8,873

Whereas the Confederate loss, as stated by the same author, was:

Surrendered at Vicksburg	32,000
Captured at Champion Hills	3,000
Captured at Big Black Bridge	2,000
Captured at Port Gibson	2,000
Captured with Loring	4,000
Killed and wounded	10,000
Stragglers	3,000
Total	56,000

Besides which, "a large amount of public property, consisting of railroads, locomotives, cars, steamers, cotton, guns, muskets, ammunition, etc., etc., was captured in Vicksburg."[80]

The value of the capture of Vicksburg, however, was not measured by the list of prisoners, guns, and small-arms, but by the fact that its possession

[80] See Adam Badeau, *Military History of Ulysses S. Grant: From April, 1861, to April, 1865* (New York: D. Appleton, 1881), 1:398–399.

secured the navigation of the great central river of the continent, bisected fatally the Southern Confederacy, and set the armies which had been used in its conquest free for other purposes; and it so happened that the event coincided as to time with another great victory which crowned our arms far away, at Gettysburg, Pennsylvania. That was a defensive battle, whereas ours was offensive in the highest acceptation of the term, and the two, occurring at the same moment of time, should have ended the war; but the rebel leaders were mad, and seemed determined that their people should drink of the very lowest dregs of the cup of war, which they themselves had prepared.

The campaign of Vicksburg, in its conception and execution, belonged exclusively to General Grant, not only in the great whole, but in the thousands of its details. I still retain many of his letters and notes, all in his own handwriting, prescribing the routes of march for divisions and detachments, specifying even the amount of food and tools to be carried along. Many persons gave his adjutant general, Rawlins, the credit for these things, but they were in error; for no commanding general of an army ever gave more of his personal attention to details, or wrote so many of his own orders, reports, and letters, as General Grant. His success at Vicksburg justly gave him great fame at home and abroad. The President conferred on him the rank of major-general in the regular army, the highest grade then existing by law; and General McPherson and I shared in his success by receiving similar commissions as brigadier-generals in the regular army.[81]

But our success at Vicksburg produced other results not so favorable to our cause—a general relaxation of effort, and desire to escape the hard drudgery of camp: officers sought leaves of absence to visit their homes, and soldiers obtained furloughs and discharges on the most slender pretexts; even the General Government seemed to relax in its efforts to replenish our ranks with new men, or to enforce the draft, and the politicians were pressing their schemes to reorganize or patch up some form of civil government, as fast as the armies gained partial possession of the States.

In order to illustrate this peculiar phase of our civil war, I give at this place copies of certain letters which have not heretofore been published:

[81] USG's and WTS's promotions were backdated to July 4. McPherson received his promotion to brigadier general on Aug. 1. *CWHC*, 264, 383–384, 485.

[PRIVATE.]

WASHINGTON, *August* 29, 1863.

Major-General W. T. SHERMAN, *Vicksburg, Mississippi.*

MY DEAR GENERAL: The question of reconstruction in Louisiana, Mississippi, and Arkansas, will soon come up for decision of the Government, and not only the length of the war, but our ultimate and complete success, will depend upon its decision. It is a difficult matter, but I believe it can be successfully solved, if the President will consult opinions of cool and discreet men, who are capable of looking at it in all its bearings and effects. I think he is disposed to receive the advice of our generals who have been in these States, and know much more of their condition than gassy politicians in Congress. General Banks has written pretty fully on the subject. I wrote to General Grant, immediately after the fall of Vicksburg, for his views in regard to Mississippi, but he has not yet answered.

I wish you would consult with Grant, McPherson, and others of cool, good judgment, and write me your views fully, as I may wish to use them with the President. You had better write me unofficially, and then your letter will not be put on file, and cannot hereafter be used against you. You have been in Washington enough to know how every thing a man writes or says is picked up by his enemies and misconstrued. With kind wishes for your further success,

I am yours truly,

H. W. HALLECK.

[PRIVATE AND CONFIDENTIAL.]

HEADQUARTERS, FIFTEENTH ARMY CORPS,
CAMP ON BIG BLACK, MISSISSIPPI, *September* 17, 1863.

H. W. HALLECK, *Commander-in-Chief, Washington, D. C.*

DEAR GENERAL: I have received your letter of August 29th, and with pleasure confide to you fully my thoughts on the important matters you suggest, with absolute confidence that you will use what is valuable, and reject the useless or superfluous.

That part of the continent of North America known as Louisiana, Mississippi, and Arkansas, is in my judgment the key to the whole interior. The valley of the Mississippi is America, and, although railroads have changed the economy of intercommunication, yet the water-channels still mark the lines of fertile land, and afford cheap carriage to the heavy products of it.

The inhabitants of the country on the Monongahela, the Illinois, the Minnesota, the Yellowstone, and Osage, are as directly concerned in the security of the Lower Mississippi as are those who dwell on its very banks in Louisiana; and now that the nation has recovered its possession, this generation of men will make a fearful mistake if they again commit its charge to a people liable to misuse their position, and assert, as was recently done, that, because they dwelt on the banks of this mighty stream, they had a right to control its navigation.

I would deem it very unwise at this time, or for years to come, to revive the State governments of Louisiana, etc., or to institute in this quarter any civil government in which the local people have much to say. They had a government so mild and paternal that they gradually forgot they had any at all, save what they themselves controlled; they asserted an absolute right to seize public moneys, forts, arms, and even to shut up the natural avenues of travel and commerce. They chose *war*—they ignored and denied all the obligations of the solemn contract of government and appealed to force.

We accepted the issue, and now they begin to realize that war is a two-edged sword, and it may be that many of the inhabitants cry for *peace.* I know them well, and the very impulses of their nature; and to deal with the inhabitants of that part of the South which borders on the great river, we must recognize the classes into which they have divided themselves:

First. The large planters, owning lands, slaves, and all kinds of personal property. These are, on the whole, the ruling class. They are educated, wealthy, and easily approached. In some districts they are bitter as gall, and have given up slaves, plantations, and all, serving in the armies of the Confederacy; whereas, in others, they are conservative. None dare admit a friendship for us, though they say freely that they were at the outset opposed to war and disunion. I *know* we can manage this class, but only by *action.* Argument is exhausted, and words have lost their usual meaning. Nothing but the logic of events touches their understanding; but, of late, this has worked a wonderful change. If our country were like Europe, crowded with people, I would say it would be easier to replace this class than to reconstruct it, subordinate to the policy of the nation; but, as this is not the case, it is better to allow the planters, with individual exceptions, gradually to recover their plantations, to hire any species of labor, and to adapt themselves to the new order of things. Still, their friendship and assistance to reconstruct order out of the present ruin cannot be depended on. They watch the operations of our armies, and hope still for a Southern Confederacy that will restore to them the slaves and privileges which they feel are otherwise lost forever. In my judgment, we have two more battles to win before we should even bother our minds with the idea of restoring civil order—viz., one near Meridian, in November, and one near Shreveport, in February and March next, when Red River is navigable by our gunboats. When these are done, then, and not until then, will the planters of Louisiana, Arkansas, and Mississippi, submit. Slavery is already gone, and, to cultivate the land, negro or other labor must be hired. This, of itself, is a vast revolution, and time must be afforded to allow men to adjust their minds and habits to this new order of things. A civil government of the representative type would suit this class far less than a pure military role, readily adapting itself to actual occurrences, and able to enforce its laws and orders promptly and emphatically.

Second. The smaller farmers, mechanics, merchants, and laborers. This class will probably number three-quarters of the whole; have, in fact, no real interest in the establishment of a Southern Confederacy, and have been led or driven into war on the false theory that they were to be benefited somehow—they knew not how. They are essentially tired of the war, and would slink back home if they could. These are the real *tiers état* of the South, and are hardly worthy a thought; for they swerve to and fro according to events which they do not comprehend or attempt to shape. When the time for reconstruction comes, they will want the old political system of caucuses, Legislatures, etc., to amuse them and make them believe they are real sovereigns; but in all things they will follow blindly the lead of the planters. The Southern politicians, who understand this class, use them as the French do their masses—seemingly consult their prejudices, while they make their orders and enforce them. We should do the same.

Third. The Union men of the South. I must confess I have little respect for this class. They allowed a clamorous set of demagogues to muzzle and drive them as a pack of curs. Afraid of shadows, they submit tamely to squads of dragoons, and permit them, without a murmur, to burn their cotton, take their horses, corn, and every thing; and, when we reach them, they are full of complaints if our men take a few fence-rails for fire, or corn to feed our horses. They give us no assistance or information, and are loudest in their complaints at the smallest excesses of our soldiers. Their sons, horses, arms, and every thing useful, are in the army against us, and they stay at home, claiming all the exemptions of peaceful citizens. I account them as nothing in this great game of war.

Fourth. The young bloods of the South: sons of planters, lawyers about towns, good billiard-players and sportsmen, men who never did work and never will. War suits them, and the rascals are brave, fine riders, bold to rashness, and dangerous subjects in every sense. They care not a sou for niggers, land, or anything. They hate Yankees *per se,* and don't bother their brains about the past, present, or future. As long as they have good horses, plenty of forage, and an open country, they are happy. This is a larger class than most men suppose, and they are the most dangerous set of men that this war has turned loose upon the world. They are splendid riders, first-rate shots, and utterly reckless. Stewart, John Morgan, Forrest, and Jackson, are the types and leaders of this class. These men must all be killed or employed by us before we can hope for peace. They have no property or future, and therefore cannot be influenced by anything, except personal considerations. I have two brigades of these fellows in my front, commanded by Cosby, of the old army, and Whitfield, of Texas. Stephen D. Lee is in command of the whole. I have frequent interviews with their officers, a good understanding with them, and am inclined to think, when the resources of their country are exhausted, we must employ them. They are the best cavalry in the world, but it will tax Mr. Chase's genius for finance to supply them with horses. At present horses cost them nothing; for they take where they find, and don't bother their brains as to who is to pay for them; the same may be said of the cornfields, which have, as they believe, been cultivated by a good-natured people for their special benefit. We propose to share with them the free use of these cornfields, planted by willing hands, that will never gather the crops.

Now that I have sketched the people who inhabit the district of country under consideration, I will proceed to discuss the future.

A civil government now, for any part of it, would be simply ridiculous. The people would not regard it, and even the military commanders of the antagonistic parties would treat it lightly. Governors would be simply petitioners for military assistance, to protect supposed friendly interests, and military commanders would refuse to disperse and weaken their armies for military reasons. Jealousies would arise between the two conflicting powers, and, instead of contributing to the end of the war, would actually defer it. Therefore, I contend that the interests of the United States, and of the real parties concerned, demand the continuance of the simple military rule, till after *all* the organized armies of the South are dispersed, conquered, and subjugated.

The people of all this region are represented in the Army of Virginia, at Charleston, Mobile, and Chattanooga. They have sons and relations in each of the rebel armies, and naturally are interested in their fate. Though we hold military possession of the key-points of their country, still they contend, and naturally, that should Lee succeed in Virginia, or Bragg at Chattanooga, a change will occur here also. We cannot for this reason attempt to reconstruct parts of the South as we conquer it, till all idea of the establishment of a Southern Confederacy is abandoned. We should avail ourselves of the present lull to secure the strategical points that will give us an advantage in the future military movements, and we should treat the idea of civil government as one in which we as a nation have a minor or subordinate interest. The opportunity is good to impress on the population the truth that they are more interested in civil government than we are; and that, to enjoy the protection of laws, they must not be passive observers of events, but must aid and sustain the constituted authorities in enforcing the laws; they must not only submit themselves, but should pay their share of taxes, and render personal services when called on.

It seems to me, in contemplating the history of the past two years, that all the people of our country, North, South, East, and West, have been undergoing a salutary political schooling, learning lessons which might have been acquired from the experience of other people; but we had all become so wise in our own conceit that we would only learn by actual experience of our own. The people even of small and unimportant localities, North as well as South, had reasoned themselves into the belief that their opinions were superior to the aggregated interest of the whole nation. Half our territorial nation rebelled, on a doctrine of secession that they themselves now scout; and a real numerical majority actually believed that a little State was endowed with such sovereignty that it could defeat the policy of the great whole. I think the present war has exploded that notion, and were this war to cease now, the experience gained, though dear, would be worth the expense.

Another great and important natural truth is still in contest, and can only be solved by war. Numerical majorities by vote have been our great arbiter. Heretofore all men have cheerfully submitted to it in questions left open, but numerical majorities are not necessarily physical majorities. The South, though numerically inferior, contend they can whip the Northern superiority of numbers, and therefore by natural law they contend that they are not bound to submit. This issue is the only real one, and in my judgment all else should be deferred to it. War alone can decide it, and it is the only question now left for us as a people to decide. Can we whip the South? If we can, our numerical majority has both the natural and constitutional right to govern them. If we cannot whip them, they contend for the natural right to select their own government, and they have the argument. Our armies must prevail over theirs; our officers, marshals, and courts, must penetrate into the innermost recesses of their land, before we have the natural right to demand their submission.

I would banish all minor questions, assert the broad doctrine that as a nation the United States has the right, and also the physical power, to penetrate to every part of our national domain, and that we will do it—that we will do it in our own time and in our own way; that it makes no difference whether it be in one year, or two, or ten, or twenty; that we will remove and destroy every obstacle, if need be, take every life, every acre of land, every particle of property, every thing that to us seems proper; that we will not cease till the end is attained; that all who do not aid us are enemies, and that we will not account to them for our acts. If the people of the South oppose, they do so at their peril; and if they stand by, mere lookers-on in this domestic tragedy, they have no right to immunity, protection, or share in the final results.

I even believe and contend further that, in the North, every member of the nation is bound by both natural and constitutional law to "maintain and defend the Government against all its enemies and opposers whomsoever." If they fail to do it they are derelict, and can be punished, or deprived of all advantages arising from the labors of those who do. If any man, North or South, withholds his share of taxes, or his physical assistance in this, the crisis of our history, he should be deprived of all voice in the future elections of this country, and might be banished, or reduced to the condition of a mere denizen of the land.

War is upon us, none can deny it. It is not the choice of the Government of the United States, but of a faction; the Government was forced to accept the issue, or to submit to a degradation fatal and disgraceful to all the inhabitants. In accepting war, *it* should be "pure and simple" as applied to the belligerents. I would keep it so, till all traces of the war are effaced; till those who appealed to it are sick and tired of it, and come to the emblem of our nation, and sue for peace. I would not coax them, or even meet them half-way, but make them so sick of war that generations would pass away before they would again appeal to it.

I know what I say when I repeat that the insurgents of the South sneer at all overtures looking to their interests. They scorn the alliance with the Copperheads; they tell me to my face that they respect Grant, McPherson, and our brave associates who fight manfully and well for a principle, but despise the Copperheads and sneaks at the North, who profess friendship for the South and opposition to the war, as mere covers for their knavery and poltroonery.

God knows that I deplore this fratricidal war as much as any man living, but it is upon us, a physical fact; and there is only one honorable issue from it. We must fight it out, army against army, and man against man; and I know, and you know, and civilians begin to realize the fact, that reconciliation and reconstruction will be easier through and by means of strong, well-equipped, and organized armies than through any species of conventions that can be framed. The issues are made, and all discussion is out of place and ridiculous. The section of thirty-pounder Parrott rifles now drilling before my tent is a more convincing argument than the largest Democratic meeting the State of New York can possibly assemble at Albany; and a simple order of the War Department to draft enough men to fill our skeleton regiments would be more convincing as to our national perpetuity than an humble pardon to Jeff. Davis and all his misled host.

The only government needed or deserved by the States of Louisiana, Arkansas, and Mississippi, now exists in Grant's army. This needs, simply, enough privates to fill its ranks; all else will follow in due season. This army has its well-defined code of laws and practice, and can adapt itself to the wants and necessities of a city, the country, the rivers, the sea, indeed to all parts of this land. It better subserves the interest and policy of the General Government, and the people here prefer it to any weak or servile combination that would at once, from force of habit, revive and perpetuate local prejudices and passions. The people of this country have forfeited all right to a voice in the councils of the nation. They know it and feel it, and in after-years they will be the better citizens from the dear-bought experience of the present crisis. Let them learn now, and learn it well, that good citizens must obey as well as command. Obedience to law, absolute—yea, even abject—is the lesson that this war, under Providence, will teach the free and enlightened American citizen. As a nation, we shall be the better for it.

I never have apprehended foreign interference in our family quarrel. Of course, governments founded on a different and it may be an antagonistic principle with ours naturally feel a pleasure at our complications, and, it may be, wish our downfall; but in the end England and France will join with us in jubilation at the triumph of constitutional government over faction. Even now the English manifest this. I do not profess to understand Napoleon's design in Mexico, and I do not see that his taking military possession of Mexico concerns us. We have as much territory now as we want. The Mexicans have failed in self-government, and it was a question as to what nation she should fall a prey. That is now solved, and I don't see that we are damaged. We have the finest part of the North American Continent, all we can people and can take care of; and, if we can suppress rebellion in our own land, and compose the strife generated by it, we shall have enough people, resources, and wealth, if well combined, to defy interference from any and every quarter.

I therefore hope the Government of the United States will continue, as heretofore, to collect, in well-organized armies, the physical strength of the nation; applying it, as heretofore, in asserting the national authority; and in persevering, without relaxation, to the end. This, whether near or far off, is not for us to say; but, fortunately, we have no choice. We must succeed—no other choice is left us except degradation. The South must be ruled by us, or she will rule us. We must conquer them, or ourselves be conquered. There is no middle course. They ask, and will have, nothing else, and talk of compromise is bosh; for we know they would even scorn the offer.

I wish the war could have been deferred for twenty years, till the superabundant population of the North could flow in and replace the losses sustained by war; but this could not be, and we are forced to take things as they are.

All therefore I can now venture to advise is to raise the draft to its maximum, fill the present regiments to as large a standard as possible, and push the war, pure and simple. Great attention should be paid to the discipline of our armies, for on them may be founded the future stability of the Government.

The cost of the war is, of course, to be considered, but finances will adjust themselves to the actual state of affairs; and, even if we would, we could not change the cost. Indeed, the larger the cost now, the less will it be in the end; for the end must be attained somehow, regardless of loss of life and treasure, and is merely a question of time.

Excuse so long a letter. With great respect, etc.,

W. T. SHERMAN, *Major-General.*

General Halleck, on receipt of this letter, telegraphed me that Mr. Lincoln had read it carefully, and had instructed him to obtain my consent to have it published. At the time, I preferred not to be drawn into any newspaper controversy, and so wrote to General Halleck; and the above letter has never been, to my knowledge, published; though Mr. Lincoln more than once referred to it with marks of approval.

HEADQUARTERS FIFTEENTH ARMY CORPS,
CAMP ON BIG BLACK, *September* 17, 1863.

Brigadier-General J. A. RAWLINS, *Acting Assistant Adjutant-General, Vicksburg.*

DEAR GENERAL: I inclose for your perusal, and for you to read to General Grant such parts as you deem interesting, letters received by me from Prof. Mahan and General Halleck, with my answers. After you have read my answer to General Halleck, I beg you to inclose it to its address, and return me the others.

I think Prof. Mahan's very marked encomium upon the campaign of Vicksburg is so flattering to General Grant, that you may offer to let him keep the letter, if he values such a testimonial. I have never written a word to General Halleck since my report of last December, after the affair at Chickasaw, except a short letter a few days ago, thanking him for the kind manner of his transmitting to me the appointment of brigadier-general. I know that in Washington I am incomprehensible, because at the outset of the war I would not go it blind and rush headlong into a war unprepared and with an utter ignorance of its extent and purpose. I was then construed *unsound;* and now that I insist on war pure and simple, with no admixture of civil compromises, I am supposed vindictive. You remember what *Polonius* said to his son *Laertes:* "Beware of entrance to a quarrel; but, being in, bear it, that the opposed may beware of thee." What is true of the single man, is equally true of a nation. Our leaders seemed at first to thirst for the quarrel, willing, even anxious, to array against us all possible elements of opposition; and now, being in, they would hasten to quit long before the "opposed" has received that lesson which he needs. I would make this war as severe as possible, and show no symptoms of tiring till the South begs for mercy; indeed, I know, and you know, that the end would be reached quicker by such a course than by any seeming yielding on our part. I don't want our Government to be bothered by patching up local governments, or by trying to reconcile any class of men. The South has done her worst, and now is the time for us to pile on our blows thick and fast.

Instead of postponing the draft till after the elections, we ought now to have our ranks full of drafted men; and, at best, if they come at all, they will reach us when we should be in motion.

I think General Halleck would like to have the honest, candid opinions of all of us, viz., Grant, McPherson, and Sherman. I have given mine, and would prefer, of course, that it should coincide with the others. Still, no matter what my opinion may be, I can easily adapt my conduct to the plans of others, and am only too happy when I find theirs better than mine.

If no trouble, please show Halleck's letter to McPherson, and ask him to write also. I know his regiments are like mine (mere squads), and need filling up. Yours truly,

W. T. Sherman, *Major-General.*

14

Chattanooga and Knoxville.

JULY TO DECEMBER, 1863.

AFTER the fall of Vicksburg, and its corollary, Port Hudson, the Mississippi River was wholly in the possession of the Union forces, and formed a perfect line of separation in the territories of our opponents. Thenceforth, they could not cross it save by stealth, and the military affairs on its west bank became unimportant. Grant's army had seemingly completed its share of the work of war, and lay, as it were, idle for a time. In person General Grant went to New Orleans to confer with General Banks, and his victorious army was somewhat dispersed.[1] Parke's corps (Ninth) returned to Kentucky, and afterward formed part of the Army of the Ohio, under General Burnside; Ord's corps (Thirteenth) was sent down to Natchez, and gradually drifted to New Orleans and Texas; McPherson's (Seventeenth) remained in and near Vicksburg; Hurlbut's (Sixteenth) was at Memphis; and mine (Fifteenth) was encamped along the Big Black, about twenty miles east of Vicksburg. This corps was composed of four divisions: Steele's (the First) was posted at and near the railroad-bridge; Blair's (the Second), next in order, near Parson Fox's; the Third Division (Tuttle's) was on the ridge about the head of Bear Creek; and the Fourth (Ewing's) was at Messinger's Ford. My own headquarters were in tents in a fine grove of old oaks near Parson Fox's house, and the battalion of the Thirteenth Regulars was the headquarters guard.[2]

All the camps were arranged for health, comfort, rest, and drill. It being midsummer, we did not expect any change till the autumn months, and accordingly made ourselves as comfortable as possible. There was a short railroad in operation from Vicksburg to the bridge across the Big Black, whence

[1] USG arrived in New Orleans on Sept. 2, 1863. *PUSG,* 9:xxii.

[2] See William T. Sherman, *Sherman's Civil War: Selected Correspondence of William T. Sherman, 1860–1865,* ed. Brooks D. Simpson and Jean V. Berlin (Chapel Hill: University of North Carolina Press, 2014), 511–512.

supplies in abundance were hauled to our respective camps.[3] With a knowledge of this fact Mrs. Sherman came down from Ohio with Minnie, Lizzie, Willie, and Tom, to pay us a visit in our camp at Parson Fox's. Willie was then nine years old, was well advanced for his years, and took the most intense interest in the affairs of the army. He was a great favorite with the soldiers, and used to ride with me on horseback in the numerous drills and reviews of the time. He then had the promise of as long a life as any of my children, and displayed more interest in the war than any of them. He was called a "sergeant" in the regular battalion, learned the manual of arms, and regularly attended the parade and guard-mounting of the Thirteenth, back of my camp. We made frequent visits to Vicksburg, and always stopped with General McPherson, who had a large house, and boarded with a family (Mrs. Edwards's) in which were several interesting young ladies. General Grant occupied another house (Mrs. Lum's)[4] in Vicksburg during that summer, and also had his family with him. The time passed very agreeably, diversified only by little events of not much significance, among which I will recount only one.

While we occupied the west bank of the Big Black, the east bank was watched by a rebel cavalry-division, commanded by General Armstrong.[5] He had four brigades, commanded by Generals Whitfield,[6] Stark,[7] Cosby,[8] and Wirt Adams.[9] Quite frequently they communicated with us by flags of truce on trivial matters, and we reciprocated, merely to observe them. One day a flag of truce, borne by a Captain B——, of Louisville, Kentucky, escorted by

[3] See George B. Davis et al., *Official Military Atlas of the Civil War* (New York: Fairfax Press, 1983), plate 36, map 1.

[4] In Sept. 1866, Ann O. Lum (d. 1870) requested government assistance from USG to help rebuild her Vicksburg property that was destroyed by the war. Her request was granted in Nov. *PUSG,* 9:78*n;* "Funeral Notice," *Vicksburg Herald,* Apr. 1, 1870, 2.

[5] Francis C. Armstrong (1835–1909) served in the U.S. Army as a captain at the First Battle of Bull Run in July 1861. He resigned in Aug. to join the Confederate Army. In the summer of 1863, he commanded the 1st Cav. Brig., 2nd Div., Army of Tennessee. *CWHC,* 107–108.

[6] John W. Whitfield (1818–1879) joined the Confederate Army as a captain in July 1861. In the summer of 1863 he commanded a cavalry brigade in W. H. Jackson's division in the Dept. of Mississippi and East Louisiana. *CWHC,* 566.

[7] William E. Starke (1815–1888) joined the Confederate Army in Feb. 1862 as a colonel in the 28th Mississippi Cav. *CWHC,* 506.

[8] George B. Cosby (1830–1909) graduated from the USMA in 1852 and resigned from the U.S. Army in May 1861 to join the Confederate Army as a captain. *CWHC,* 186.

[9] William W. Adams (1819–1888) joined the Confederate Army as a colonel in Oct. 1861. He was promoted to brigadier general in Sept. 1863. *CWHC,* 99.

about twenty-five men, was reported at Messinger's Ferry, and I sent orders to let them come right into my tent.[10] This brought them through the camps of the Fourth Division, and part of the Second; and as they drew up in front of my tent, I invited Captain B——and another officer with him (a major from Mobile) to dismount, to enter my tent, and to make themselves at home. Their escort was sent to join mine, with orders to furnish them forage and every thing they wanted. B——had brought a sealed letter for General Grant at Vicksburg, which was dispatched to him. In the evening we had a good supper, with wine and cigars, and, as we sat talking, B——spoke of his father and mother, in Louisville, got leave to write them a long letter without its being read by any one, and then we talked about the war. He said: "What is the use of your persevering? It is simply impossible to subdue eight millions of people;" asserting that "the feeling in the South had become so embittered that a reconciliation was impossible." I answered that, "sitting as we then were, we appeared very comfortable, and surely there was no trouble in our becoming friends." "Yes," said he, "that is very true of us, but we are gentlemen of education, and can easily adapt ourselves to any condition of things; but this would not apply equally well to the common people, or to the common soldiers." I took him out to the camp-fires behind the tent, and there were the men of his escort and mine mingled together, drinking their coffee, and happy as soldiers always seem. I asked B——what he thought of that, and he admitted that I had the best of the argument. Before I dismissed this flag of truce, his companion consulted me confidentially as to what disposition he ought to make of his family, then in Mobile, and I frankly gave him the best advice I could.

While we were thus lying idle in camp on the Big Black, the Army of the Cumberland, under General Rosecrans, was moving against Bragg at Chattanooga; and the Army of the Ohio, General Burnside, was marching toward East Tennessee. General Rosecrans was so confident of success that he somewhat scattered his command, seemingly to surround and capture Bragg in Chattanooga; but the latter, reënforced from Virginia, drew out of Chattanooga, concentrated his army at Lafayette, and at Chickamauga fell on Rosecrans, defeated him, and drove him into Chattanooga. The whole country

[10] On Sept. 9, 1863, in a letter to his brother John, WTS wrote, "I have frequent communications with the Confederate Army by flags of Truce, and with the citizens of the Interior. The former seem confident yet of their ultimate independence, but of course calculate on anarchy north and European complications." Sherman, *Selected Correspondence,* 540.

seemed paralyzed by this unhappy event; and the authorities in Washington were thoroughly stampeded. From the East the Eleventh Corps (Slocum),[11] and the Twelfth Corps (Howard),[12] were sent by rail to Nashville, and forward under command of General Hooker; orders were also sent to General Grant, by Halleck, to send what reënforcements he could spare immediately toward Chattanooga.[13]

Bragg had completely driven Rosecrans's army into Chattanooga; the latter was in actual danger of starvation, and the railroad to his rear seemed inadequate to his supply. The first intimation which I got of this disaster was on the 22d of September, by an order from General Grant to dispatch one of my divisions immediately into Vicksburg, to go toward Chattanooga,[14] and I designated the First, General Osterhaus[15]—Steele meantime having been appointed to the command of the Department of Arkansas, and had gone to Little Rock.[16] General Osterhaus marched the same day, and on the 23d I was summoned to Vicksburg in person, where General Grant showed me the alarming dispatches from General Halleck, which had been sent from Memphis by General Hurlbut, and said, on further thought, that he would send me and my whole corps.[17] But, inasmuch as one division of McPherson's corps (John E. Smith's) had already started, he instructed me to leave one of my divisions on the Big Black, and to get the other two ready to follow at once. I designated the Second, then commanded by Brigadier-General Giles A. Smith, and the Fourth, commanded by Brigadier-General Corse.

On the 25th I returned to my camp on Big Black, gave all the necessary orders for these divisions to move, and for the Third (Tuttle's) to remain, and went into Vicksburg with my family. The last of my corps designed for this

[11] Henry W. Slocum (1827–1894) graduated from the USMA in 1852 and was promoted to major general on July 4, 1862. In Sept. 1863 he commanded the 12th Corps, Army of the Cumberland. *CWHC,* 491.

[12] Oliver O. Howard (1830–1909) graduated from the USMA in 1854 and was promoted to major general in Nov. 1862. In Sept. 1863 he commanded the 11th Corps, Army of the Cumberland. *CWHC,* 305–306.

[13] For Halleck's order to USG, see *OR,* I, 30(III), 923.

[14] For USG's order to WTS, see *OR,* I, 30(I), 161–162.

[15] Peter J. Osterhaus (1823–1917) was born in Prussia and immigrated to Illinois in 1849. He commanded the 1st Div., 13th Corps, Army of the Tennessee, in the fall of 1863. *CWHC,* 411.

[16] Steele commanded the Army of Arkansas from July 27, 1863 to Dec. 22, 1864. *CWHC,* 508.

[17] USG requested a visit from WTS on Sept. 22. *OR,* I, 30(III), 772.

expedition started from camp on the 27th, reached Vicksburg the 28th, and were embarked on boats provided for them. General Halleck's dispatches dwelt upon the fact that General Rosecrans's routes of supply were overtaxed, and that we should move from Memphis eastward, repairing railroads as we progressed, as far as Athens, Alabama, whence I was to report to General Rosecrans, at Chattanooga, by letter.

I took passage for myself and family in the steamer Atlantic, Captain Henry McDougall.[18] When the boat was ready to start, Willie was missing. Mrs. Sherman supposed him to have been with me, whereas I supposed he was with her. An officer of the Thirteenth went up to General McPherson's house for him, and soon returned, with Captain Clift leading him, carrying in his hands a small double-barreled shot-gun; and I joked him about carrying away captured property. In a short time we got off. As we all stood on the guards to look at our old camps at Young's Point, I remarked that Willie was not well, and he admitted that he was sick. His mother put him to bed, and consulted Dr. Roler, of the Fifty-fifth Illinois,[19] who found symptoms of typhoid fever. The river was low; we made slow progress till above Helena; and, as we approached Memphis, Dr. Roler told me that Willie's life was in danger, and he was extremely anxious to reach Memphis for certain medicines and for consultation. We arrived at Memphis on the 2d of October, carried Willie up to the Gayoso Hotel,[20] and got the most experienced physician there, who acted with Dr. Roler, but he sank rapidly, and died the evening of the 3d of October. The blow was a terrible one to us all, so sudden and so unexpected, that I could not help reproaching myself for having consented to his visit in that sickly region in the summer-time. Of all my children, he seemed the most precious. Born in San Francisco, I had watched with intense interest his development, and he seemed more than any of the children to take an interest in my special profession. Mrs. Sherman, Minnie, Lizzie, and Tom, were with him at the time, and we all, helpless and overwhelmed, saw him die.

[18] Harry McDougal assisted the U.S. Army and Navy during the Vicksburg Campaign in 1863. See, *PUSG*, 9:120.

[19] Edward O. F. Roler (1833–1907) moved to Chicago in 1856 and joined the U.S. Army as the assistant surgeon of the 42nd Illinois Volunteers in 1861. He later joined WTS's staff. *History of Medicine and Surgery and Physicians and Surgeons of Chicago* (Chicago: Biographical, 1922), 93.

[20] The Gayoso Hotel, named after Spanish explorer Don Manuel Gayoso de Lemos, opened in 1844 and was located on Main Street. *Tennessee: A Guide to the State* (New York: Viking, 1939), 221.

Being in the very midst of an important military enterprise, I had hardly time to pause and think of my personal loss. We procured a metallic casket, and had a military funeral, the battalion of the Thirteenth United States Regulars acting as escort from the Gayoso Hotel to the steamboat Grey Eagle, which conveyed him and my family up to Cairo, whence they proceeded to our home at Lancaster, Ohio, where he was buried. I here give my letter to Captain C. C. Smith, who commanded the battalion at the time,[21] as exhibiting our intense feelings:

GAYOSO HOUSE, MEMPHIS, TENNESSEE,
October 4, 1863—*Midnight.*

Captain C. C. SMITH, *commanding Battalion Thirteenth United States Regulars.*

MY DEAR FRIEND: I cannot sleep to-night till I record an expression of the deep feelings of my heart to you, and to the officers and soldiers of the battalion, for their kind behavior to my poor child. I realize that you all feel for my family the attachment of kindred, and I assure you of full reciprocity.

Consistent with a sense of duty to my profession and office, I could not leave my post, and sent for the family to come to me in that fatal climate, and in that sickly period of the year, and behold the result! The child that bore my name, and in whose future I reposed with more confidence than I did in my own plan of life, now floats a mere corpse, seeking a grave in a distant land, with a weeping mother, brother, and sisters, clustered about him. For myself, I ask no sympathy. On, on I must go, to meet a soldier's fate, or live to see our country rise superior to all factions, till its flag is adored and respected by ourselves and by all the powers of the earth.

But Willie was, or thought he was, a sergeant in the Thirteenth. I have seen his eye brighten, his heart beat, as he beheld the battalion under arms, and asked me if they were not *real* soldiers. Child as he was, he had the enthusiasm, the pure love of truth, honor, and love of country, which should animate all soldiers.

[21] Charles C. Smith (1823–1891) was appointed captain of the 13th Regulars in May 1861. "Capt. Charles C. Smith Dead," *National Tribune* (Washington, DC), Aug. 27, 1891, 5.

God only knows why he should die thus young. He is dead, but will not be forgotten till those who knew him in life have followed him to that same mysterious end.

Please convey to the battalion my heart-felt thanks, and assure each and all that if in after-years they call on me or mine, and mention that they were of the Thirteenth Regulars when Willie was a sergeant, they will have a key to the affections of my family that will open all it has; that we will share with them our last blanket, our last crust!

Your friend,

W. T. SHERMAN, *Major-General.*

Long afterward, in the spring of 1867, we had his body disinterred and brought to St. Louis, where he is now buried in a beautiful spot, in Calvary Cemetery, by the side of another child, "Charles," who was born at Lancaster, in the summer of 1864, died early, and was buried at Notre Dame, Indiana.[22] His body was transferred at the same time to the same spot. Over Willie's grave is erected a beautiful marble monument, designed and executed by the officers and soldiers of that battalion which claimed him as a sergeant and comrade.

During the summer and fall of 1863 Major-General S. A. Hurlbut was in command at Memphis. He supplied me copies of all dispatches from Washington, and all the information he possessed of the events about Chattanooga. Two of these dispatches cover all essential points:

WASHINGTON CITY, *September* 15, 1863—5 P. M.

Major-General S. A. HURLBUT, *Memphis:*

All the troops that can possibly be spared in West Tennessee and on the Mississippi River should be sent without delay to assist General Rosecrans on the Tennessee River.

Urge Sherman to act with all possible promptness.

If you have boats, send them down to bring up his troops.

Information just received indicates that a part of Lee's army has been sent to reënforce Bragg.

H. W. HALLECK, *General-in-Chief.*

[22] Charles C. Sherman (1864–1864), the child born to Ellen and WTS, died of pneumonia at five months of age on Dec. 4, 1864. "Charles Celestine Sherman," *New York Times,* Dec. 25, 1864, 4.

WASHINGTON, *September* 19, 1863—4 P. M.

Major-General S. A. HURLBUT, *Memphis, Tennessee:*

Give me definite information of the number of troops sent toward Decatur, and where they are. Also, what other troops are to follow, and when.

Has any thing been heard from the troops ordered from Vicksburg?

No efforts must be spared to support Rosecrans's right, and to guard the crossings of the Tennessee River.

H. W. HALLECK, *General-in-Chief.*

My special orders were to repair the Memphis & Charleston Railroad eastward as I progressed, as far as Athens, Alabama, to draw supplies by that route, so that, on reaching Athens, we should not be dependent on the roads back to Nashville, already overtaxed by the demand of Rosecrans's army.

On reaching Memphis, October 2d, I found that Osterhaus's division had already gone by rail as far as Corinth, and that John E. Smith's division was in the act of starting by cars. The Second Division, then commanded by Brigadier-General Giles A. Smith, reached Memphis at the same time with me; and the Fourth Division, commanded by Brigadier-General John M. Corse, arrived a day or two after. The railroad was in fair condition as far as Corinth, ninety-six miles, but the road was badly stocked with locomotives and cars, so that it took until the 9th to get off the Second Division, when I gave orders for the Fourth Division and wagon-trains to march by the common road.

On Sunday morning, October 11th, with a special train loaded with our orderlies and clerks, the horses of our staff, the battalion of the Thirteenth United States Regulars, and a few officers going forward to join their commands, among them Brigadier-General Hugh Ewing, I started for Corinth.

At Germantown, eight miles, we passed Corse's division (Fourth) on the march, and about noon the train ran by the depot at Colliersville, twenty-six miles out. I was in the rear car with my staff, dozing, but observed the train slacking speed and stopping about half a mile beyond the depot. I noticed some soldiers running to and fro, got out at the end of the car, and soon Colonel Anthony (Sixty-sixth Indiana),[23] who commanded the post, rode up and said that his pickets had just been driven in, and there was an appearance of an attack by a large force of cavalry coming from the southeast. I ordered the men to get off the train, to form on the knoll near the railroad-cut, and

[23] Dewitt C. Anthony (1828–1891) was promoted to colonel of the 66th Indiana Inf. on Sept. 11, 1862. *CWHC*, 107.

soon observed a rebel officer riding toward us with a white flag. Colonel Anthony and Colonel Dayton (one of my aides) were sent to meet him, and to keep him in conversation as long as possible. They soon returned, saying it was the adjutant of the rebel general Chalmers,[24] who demanded the surrender of the place. I instructed them to return and give a negative answer, but to delay him as much as possible, so as to give us time for preparation. I saw Anthony, Dayton, and the rebel bearer of the flag, in conversation, and the latter turn his horse to ride back, when I ordered Colonel McCoy to run to the station, and get a message over the wires as quick as possible to Memphis and Germantown, to hurry forward Corse's division. I then ordered the train to back to the depot, and drew back the battalion of regulars to the small earth redoubt near it. The depot-building was of brick, and had been punctured with loop-holes. To its east, about two hundred yards, was a small square earthwork or fort, into which were put a part of the regulars along with the company of the Sixty-sixth Indiana already there. The rest of the men were distributed into the railroad-cut, and in some shallow rifle-trenches near the depot. We had hardly made these preparations when the enemy was seen forming in a long line on the ridge to the south, about four hundred yards off, and soon after two parties of cavalry passed the railroad on both sides of us, cutting the wires and tearing up some rails. Soon they opened on us with artillery (of which we had none), and their men were dismounting and preparing to assault. To the south of us was an extensive cornfield, with the corn still standing, and on the other side was the town of Colliersville. All the houses near, that could give shelter to the enemy, were ordered to be set on fire, and the men were instructed to keep well under cover and to reserve their fire for the assault, which seemed inevitable. A long line of rebel skirmishers came down through the cornfield, and two other parties approached us along the railroad on both sides.

In the fort was a small magazine containing some cartridges. Lieutenant James, a fine, gallant fellow, who was ordnance-officer on my staff, asked leave to arm the orderlies and clerks with some muskets which he had found in the depot, to which I consented; he marched them into the magazine, issued cartridges, and marched back to the depot to assist in its defense. Afterward he came to me, said a party of the enemy had got into the woods near the depot, and was annoying him, and he wanted to charge and drive it away.

[24] James R. Chalmers (1831–1898) joined the Confederate Army as a captain on Mar. 16, 1861. In Oct. 1863 he commanded a cavalry division in the Dept. of Mississippi and East Louisiana. *CWHC,* 168.

I advised him to be extremely cautious, as our enemy vastly outnumbered us, and had every advantage in position and artillery; but instructed him, if they got too near, he might make a sally. Soon after, I heard a rapid fire in that quarter, and Lieutenant James was brought in on a stretcher, with a ball through his breast, which I supposed to be fatal.[25]

The enemy closed down on us several times, and got possession of the rear of our train, from which they succeeded in getting five of our horses, among them my favorite mare Dolly; but our men were cool and practised shots (with great experience acquired at Vicksburg), and drove them back. With their artillery they knocked to pieces our locomotive and several of the cars, and set fire to the train; but we managed to get possession again, and extinguished the fire. Colonel Audenreid, aide-de-camp,[26] was provoked to find that his valise of nice shirts had been used to kindle the fire. The fighting continued all round us for three or four hours, when we observed signs of drawing off, which I attributed to the rightful cause, the rapid approach of Corse's division, which arrived about dark, having marched the whole distance from Memphis, twenty-six miles, on the double-quick. The next day we repaired damages to the railroad and locomotive, and went on to Corinth.

At Corinth, on the 16th, I received the following important dispatches:

MEMPHIS, *October* 14, 1863—11 A. M.

Arrived this morning. Will be off in a few hours. My orders are only to go to Cairo, and report from there by telegraph. McPherson will be in Canton to-day. He will remain there until Sunday or Monday next, and reconnoitre as far eastward as possible with cavalry, in the mean time.

U. S. GRANT, *Major-General.*

[25] In the 1875 first edition (and subsequent editions) of the memoirs, the following note appeared here: "After the fight we sent him back to Memphis, where his mother and father came from their home on the North River to nurse him. Young James was recovering from his wound, but was afterward killed by a fall from his horse, near his home, when riding with the daughters of Mr. Hamilton Fish, now Secretary of State."

[26] Joseph C. Audenried (1839–1880) graduated from the USMA in 1861 and served as WTS's aide-de-camp from Oct. 1, 1863, until his death on June 3, 1880. *USMA,* 2:824–825.

WASHINGTON, *October* 14, 1863—1 P. M.

Major-General W. T. SHERMAN, *Corinth:*

Yours of the 10th is received. The important matter to be attended to is that of supplies. When Eastport can be reached by boats, the use of the railroad can be dispensed with; but until that time it must be guarded as far as used. The Kentucky Railroad can barely supply General Rosecrans. All these matters must be left to your judgment as circumstances may arise. Should the enemy be so strong as to prevent your going to Athens, or connecting with General Rosecrans, you will nevertheless have assisted him greatly by drawing away a part of the enemy's forces.

H. W. HALLECK, *Major-General.*

On the 18th, with my staff and a small escort, I rode forward to Burnsville, and on the 19th to Iuka, where, on the next day, I was most agreeably surprised to hear of the arrival at Eastport (only ten miles off) of two gunboats, under the command of Captain Phelps, which had been sent up the Tennessee River by Admiral Porter, to help us.

Satisfied that, to reach Athens and to communicate with General Rosecrans, we should have to take the route north of the Tennessee River, on the 24th I ordered the Fourth Division to cross at Eastport with the aid of the gunboats, and to move to Florence. About the same time, I received the general orders assigning General Grant to command the Military Division of the Mississippi, authorizing him, on reaching Chattanooga, to supersede General Rosecrans by General George H. Thomas, with other and complete authority, as set forth in the following letters of General Halleck, which were sent to me by General Grant; and the same orders devolved on me the command of the Department and Army of the Tennessee.

HEADQUARTERS OF THE ARMY,
WASHINGTON, D. C., *October* 16, 1863.

Major-General U. S. GRANT, *Louisville.*

GENERAL: You will receive herewith the orders of the President of the United States, placing you in command of the Departments of the Ohio, Cumberland, and Tennessee. The organization of these departments will be changed as you may deem most practicable. You will immediately proceed to Chattanooga, and relieve General Rosecrans. You can communicate with Generals Burnside and

Sherman by telegraph. A summary of the orders sent to these officers will be sent to you immediately. It is left optional with you to supersede General Rosecrans by General G. H. Thomas or not. Any other changes will be made on your request by telegram.

One of the first objects requiring your attention is the supply of your armies. Another is the security of the passes in the Georgia mountains, to shut out the enemy from Tennessee and Kentucky. You will consult with General Meigs and Colonel Scott in regard to transportation and supplies.

Should circumstances permit, I will visit you personally in a few days for consultation.

H. W. Halleck, *General-in-Chief.*

Headquarters of the Army,
Washington, D. C., *October* 20, 1863.

Major-General Grant, *Louisville.*

General: In compliance with my promise, I now proceed to give you a brief statement of the objects aimed at by General Rosecrans and General Burnside's movement into East Tennessee, and of the measures directed to be taken to attain these objects.

It has been the constant desire of the government, from the beginning of the war, to rescue the loyal inhabitants of East Tennessee from the hands of the rebels, who fully appreciated the importance of continuing their hold upon that country. In addition to the large amount of agricultural products drawn from the upper valley of the Tennessee, they also obtained iron and other materials from the vicinity of Chattanooga. The possession of East Tennessee would cut off one of their most important railroad communications, and threaten their manufactories at Rome, Atlanta, etc.

When General Buell was ordered into East Tennessee in the summer of 1862, Chattanooga was comparatively unprotected; but Bragg reached there before Buell, and, by threatening his communications, forced him to retreat on Nashville and Louisville. Again, after the battle of Perryville, General Buell was urged to pursue Bragg's defeated army, and drive it from East Tennessee. The same was urged upon his successor, but the lateness of the season or other causes prevented further operations after the battle of Stone River.

Last spring, when your movements on the Mississippi River had drawn out of Tennessee a large force of the enemy, I again urged General

Rosecrans to take advantage of that opportunity to carry out his projected plan of campaign, General Burnside being ready to coöperate, with a diminished but still efficient force. But he could not be persuaded to act in time, preferring to lie still till your campaign should be terminated. I represented to him, but without avail, that by this delay Johnston might be able to reënforce Bragg with the troops then operating against you.

When General Rosecrans finally determined to advance, he was allowed to select his own lines and plans for carrying out the objects of the expedition. He was directed, however, to report his movements daily, till he crossed the Tennessee, and to connect his left, so far as possible, with General Burnside's right. General Burnside was directed to move simultaneously, connecting his right, as far as possible, with General Rosecrans's left, so that, if the enemy concentrated upon either army, the other could move to its assistance. When General Burnside reached Kingston and Knoxville, and found no considerable number of the enemy in East Tennessee, he was instructed to move down the river and coöperate with General Rosecrans.

These instructions were repeated some fifteen times, but were not carried out, General Burnside alleging as an excuse that he believed that Bragg was in retreat, and that General Rosecrans needed no reënforcements. When the latter had gained possession of Chattanooga he was directed not to move on Rome as he proposed, but simply to hold the mountain-passes, so as to prevent the ingress of the rebels into East Tennessee. That object accomplished, I considered the campaign as ended, at least for the present. Future operations would depend upon the ascertained strength and movements of the enemy. In other words, the main objects of the campaign were the restoration of East Tennessee to the Union, and by holding the two extremities of the valley to secure it from rebel invasion.

The moment I received reliable information of the departure of Longstreet's corps from the Army of the Potomac, I ordered forward to General Rosecrans every available man in the Department of the Ohio, and again urged General Burnside to move to his assistance. I also telegraphed to Generals Hurlbut, Sherman, and yourself, to send forward all available troops in your department. If these forces had been sent to General Rosecrans by Nashville, they could not have been supplied; I therefore directed them to move by Corinth and the Tennessee River. The necessity of this has been proved by the fact that the reënforcements sent to him from the Army of the Potomac have not been able, for the want of railroad transportation, to reach General Rosecrans's army in the field.

In regard to the relative strength of the opposing armies, it is believed that General Rosecrans when he first moved against Bragg had double, if not treble, his force. General Burnside, also, had more than double the force of Buckner; and, even when Bragg and Buckner united, Rosecrans's army was very greatly superior in number. Even the eighteen thousand men sent from Virginia, under Longstreet, would not have given the enemy the superiority. It is now ascertained that the greater part of the prisoners parolled by you at Vicksburg, and General Banks at Port Hudson, were illegally and improperly declared exchanged, and forced into the ranks to swell the rebel numbers at Chickamauga. This outrageous act, in violation of the laws of war, of the cartel entered into by the rebel authorities, and of all sense of honor, gives us a useful lesson in regard to the character of the enemy with whom we are contending. He neither regards the rules of civilized warfare, nor even his most solemn engagements. You may, therefore, expect to meet in arms thousands of unexchanged prisoners released by you and others on parole, not to serve again till duly exchanged.

Although the enemy by this disgraceful means has been able to concentrate in Georgia and Alabama a much larger force than we anticipated, your armies will be abundantly able to defeat him. Your difficulty will not be in the want of men, but in the means of supplying them at this season of the year. A single-track railroad can supply an army of sixty or seventy thousand men, with the usual number of cavalry and artillery; but beyond that number, or with a large mounted force, the difficulty of supply is very great.

I do not know the present condition of the road from Nashville to Decatur, but, if practicable to repair it, the use of that triangle will be of great assistance to you. I hope, also, that the recent rise of water in the Cumberland and Tennessee Rivers will enable you to employ water transportation to Nashville, Eastport, or Florence.

If you reoccupy the passes of Lookout Mountain, which should never have been given up, you will be able to use the railroad and river from Bridgeport to Chattanooga. This seems to me a matter of vital importance, and should receive your early attention.

I submit this summary in the hope that it will assist you in fully understanding the objects of the campaign, and the means of attaining these objects. Probably the Secretary of War, in his interviews with you at Louisville, has gone over the same ground.

Whatever measures you may deem proper to adopt under existing circumstances, you will receive all possible assistance from the authorities at Washington. You have never, heretofore, complained that such assistance has not been afforded you in your operations, and I think you will have no cause of complaint in your present campaign. Very respectfully, your obedient servant,

H. W. HALLECK, *General-in-Chief.*

General Frank P. Blair, who was then ahead with the two divisions of Osterhaus and John E. Smith, was temporarily assigned to the command of the Fifteenth Corps. General Hurlbut remained at Memphis in command of the Sixteenth Corps, and General McPherson at Vicksburg with the Seventeenth. These three corps made up the Army of the Tennessee.

I was still busy in pushing forward the repairs to the railroad-bridge at Bear Creek, and in patching up the many breaks between it and Tuscumbia, when on the 27th of October, as I sat on the porch of a house, I was approached by a dirty, black-haired individual with mixed dress and strange demeanor, who inquired for me, and, on being assured that I was in fact the man, he handed me a letter from General Blair at Tuscumbia, and another short one, which was a telegraph-message from General Grant at Chattanooga, addressed to me through General George Crook, commanding at Huntsville, Alabama,[27] to this effect:

Drop all work on Memphis & Charleston Railroad, cross the Tennessee, and hurry eastward with all possible dispatch toward Bridgeport, till you meet further orders from me.

U. S. GRANT.[28]

The bearer of this message was Corporal Pike, who described to me, in his peculiar way, that General Crook had sent him in a canoe; that he had paddled down the Tennessee River, over Muscle Shoals, was fired at all the

[27] George Crook (1828–1890) graduated from the USMA in 1852 and was in command of the 2nd Div., Cav. Corps, Army of the Cumberland, in Oct. 1863. *CWHC,* 191–192.

[28] For USG's full letter to WTS, dated Oct. 24, 1863, see *OR,* I, 31(I), 713.

way by guerrillas, but on reaching Tuscumbia he had providentially found it in possession of our troops. He had reported to General Blair, who sent him on to me at Iuka. This Pike proved to be a singular character; his manner attracted my notice at once, and I got him a horse, and had him travel with us eastward to about Elkton, whence I sent him back to General Crook at Huntsville; but told him, if I could ever do him a personal service, he might apply to me. The next spring when I was in Chattanooga, preparing for the Atlanta campaign, Corporal Pike made his appearance and asked a fulfillment of my promise. I inquired what he wanted, and he said he wanted to do something *bold*, something that would make him a hero. I explained to him, that we were getting ready to go for Joe Johnston at Dalton, that I expected to be in the neighborhood of Atlanta about the 4th of July, and wanted the bridge across the Savannah River at Augusta, Georgia, to be burnt about that time, to produce alarm and confusion behind the rebel army. I explained to Pike that the chances were three to one that he would be caught and hanged; but the greater the danger the greater seemed to be his desire to attempt it. I told him to select a companion, to disguise himself as an East Tennessee refugee, work his way over the mountains into North Carolina, and at the time appointed to float down the Savannah River and burn that bridge. In a few days he had made his preparations and took his departure. The bridge was not burnt, and I supposed that Pike had been caught and hanged.

When we reached Columbia, South Carolina, in February, 1865, just as we were leaving the town, in passing near the asylum, I heard my name called, and saw a very dirty fellow followed by a file of men running toward me, and as they got near I recognized Pike. He called to me to identify him as one of *my* men; he was then a prisoner under guard, and I instructed the guard to bring him that night to my camp some fifteen miles up the road, which was done. Pike gave me a graphic narrative of his adventures, which would have filled a volume; told me how he had made two attempts to burn the bridge, and failed; and said that at the time of our entering Columbia he was a prisoner in the hands of the rebels, under trial for his life, but in the confusion of their retreat he made his escape and got into our lines, where he was again made a prisoner by our troops because of his looks. Pike got some clothes, cleaned up, and I used him afterward to communicate with Wilmington, North Carolina. Some time after the war, he was appointed a lieutenant of the Regular Cavalry, and was killed in Oregon, by the accidental discharge of a pistol. Just before his death he wrote me, saying that he was tired of the monotony of garrison-life, and wanted to turn Indian, join the Cheyennes on the Plains, who were then giving us great trouble, and, after he had gained their confidence, he would betray them into our hands. Of course I wrote him that he must try and settle down and become a gentleman as well as an officer, apply himself to his duties, and forget the wild desires of his nature, which were well enough in time of war, but not suited to his new condition as an officer; but, poor fellow! he was killed by an accident, which probably saved him from a slower but harder fate.[29]

At Iuka I issued all the orders to McPherson and Hurlbut necessary for the Department of the Tennessee during my absence, and, further, ordered the collection of a force out of the Sixteenth Corps, of about eight thousand men, to be commanded by General G. M. Dodge,[30] with orders to follow as far east as Athens, Tennessee, there to await instructions. We instantly discontinued all attempts to repair the Charleston Railroad; and the remaining three divisions of the Fifteenth Corps marched to Eastport, crossed the Tennessee River by the aid of the gunboats, a ferry-boat, and a couple of transports which had come up, and hurried eastward.

In person I crossed on the 1st of November, and rode forward to Florence, where I overtook Ewing's division. The other divisions followed rapidly. On the road to Florence I was accompanied by my staff, some clerks, and mounted orderlies. Major Ezra Taylor was chief of artillery, and one of his sons was a clerk at headquarters.[31] The latter seems to have dropped out of the column, and gone to a farm-house near the road. There was no organized force of the rebel army north of the Tennessee River, but the country was full of guerrillas. A party of these pounced down on the farm, caught young Taylor and another of the clerks, and after reaching Florence, Major Taylor heard of the capture of his son, and learned that when last seen he was stripped of his hat and coat, was tied to the tail-board of a wagon, and driven

[29] James Pike (1834–1867) was accidentally shot and killed while pursuing Native Americans in Oregon. A year before his death, he wrote a memoir that provided context related to his attempt to burn the bridge across the Savanah River near Augusta, GA. See James Pike, *Scout and Ranger: Being the Personal Adventures of James Pike of the Texas Rangers in 1859–60,* ed. Carl L. Cannon (Princeton, NJ: Princeton University Press, 1932).

[30] Grenville M. Dodge (1831–1916) took command of the Left Wing, 16th Corps, Army of the Tennessee, on Oct. 15, 1863. *CWHC,* 211–212.

[31] Ezra Taylor had two sons, William and James, under his command in Nov. 1863. William was a sergeant major, and James was a recruit who was discharged on Nov. 18, 1863. Alfred T. Andreas, *History of Chicago* (self-pub., 1885), 2:520; "Major William N. Taylor," *Chicago Evening Post,* Aug. 6, 1869, 4; J. N. Reece, *Report of the Adjutant General of the State of Illinois* (Springfield, IL: Journal, 1901), 8:605–608.

rapidly to the north of the road we had traveled. The major appealed to me to do something for his rescue. I had no cavalry to send in pursuit, but knowing that there was always an understanding between these guerrillas and their friends who staid at home, I sent for three or four of the principal men of Florence (among them a Mr. Foster, who had once been a Senator in Congress), explained to them the capture of young Taylor and his comrade, and demanded their immediate restoration. They, of course, remonstrated, denied all knowledge of the acts of these guerrillas, and claimed to be peaceful citizens of Alabama, residing at home. I insisted that these guerrillas were their own sons and neighbors; that they knew their haunts, and could reach them if they wanted, and they could effect the restoration to us of these men; and I said, moreover, they must do it within twenty-four hours, or I would take them, strip them of their hats and coats, and tie them to the tail-boards of our wagons till they were produced. They sent off messengers at once, and young Taylor and his comrade were brought back the next day.

Resuming our march eastward by the large road, we soon reached Elk River, which was wide and deep, and could only be crossed by a ferry, a process entirely too slow for the occasion; so I changed the route more by the north, to Elkton, Winchester, and Deckerd. At this point we came in communication with the Army of the Cumberland, and by telegraph with General Grant, who was at Chattanooga. He reiterated his orders for me and my command to hurry forward with all possible dispatch, and in person I reached Bridgeport during the night of November 13th, my troops following behind by several roads. At Bridgeport I found a garrison guarding the railroad-bridge and pontoon-bridge there, and staid with the quartermaster, Colonel William G. Le Duc (who was my school-mate at How's School in 1836).[32] There I received a dispatch from General Grant, at Chattanooga, to come up in person, leaving my troops to follow as fast as possible. At that time there were two or three small steamboats on the river, engaged in carrying stores up as far as Kelly's Ferry.[33] In one of these I took passage, and on reaching Kelly's Ferry found orderlies, with one of General Grant's private horses, waiting for me, on which I rode into Chattanooga, November 14th. Of course, I was heartily welcomed by Generals Grant, Thomas, and all, who realized the extraordinary efforts we had made to come to their relief.

[32] William G. LeDuc (1823–1917) was the assistant quartermaster, 11th Corps, Army of the Cumberland, in Nov. 1863. *CWHC,* 342.

[33] Kelly's Ferry crossed the Tennessee River approximately ten miles west of Chattanooga, TN. Davis et al., *Official Military Atlas of the Civil War,* plate 149.

The next morning we walked out to Fort Wood,[34] a prominent salient of the defenses of the place, and from its parapet we had a magnificent view of the panorama. Lookout Mountain, with its rebel flags and batteries, stood out boldly, and an occasional shot fired toward Wauhatchee[35] or Moccasin Point gave life to the scene. These shots could barely reach Chattanooga, and I was told that one or more shot had struck a hospital inside the lines. All along Missionary Ridge were the tents of the rebel beleaguering force; the lines of trench from Lookout up toward the Chickamauga were plainly visible; and rebel sentinels, in a continuous chain, were walking their posts in plain view, not a thousand yards off. "Why," said I, "General Grant, you are besieged;" and he said, "It is too true." Up to that moment I had no idea that things were so bad. The rebel lines actually extended from the river, below the town, to the river above, and the Army of the Cumberland was closely held to the town and its immediate defenses. General Grant pointed out to me a house on Missionary Ridge, where General Bragg's headquarters were known to be.[36] He also explained the situation of affairs generally; that the mules and horses of Thomas's army were so starved that they could not haul his guns; that forage, corn, and provisions, were so scarce that the men in hunger stole the few grains of corn that were given to favorite horses; that the men of Thomas's army had been so demoralized by the battle of Chickamauga that he feared they could not be got out of their trenches to assume the offensive; that Bragg had detached Longstreet with a considerable force up into East Tennessee, to defeat and capture Burnside; that Burnside was in danger, etc.; and that he (Grant) was extremely anxious to attack Bragg in position, to defeat him, or at least to force him to recall Longstreet. The Army of the Cumberland had so long been in the trenches that he wanted my troops to hurry up, to take the offensive *first;* after which, he had no doubt the Cumberland army would fight well. Meantime the Eleventh and Twelfth Corps, under General Hooker, had been advanced from Bridgeport along the

[34] Fort Wood, originally named Fort Creighton, was constructed by the Confederate Army approximately one-half mile south of the Tennessee River and one mile east of Chattanooga. Davis et al., *Official Military Atlas of the Civil War,* plate 111, map 10; Zella Armstrong, *The History of Hamilton County* (Johnson City, TN: Overmountain, 1993), 2:48, 285.

[35] Wauhatchee, TN, was located approximately four miles southeast of Chattanooga. Davis et al., *Official Atlas of the Civil War,* plate 49, map 1.

[36] Bragg's headquarters were located approximately one mile southeast of Chattanooga. James R. Sullivan, *Chickamauga and Chattanooga Battlefields* (Washington, DC: National Park Service, 1956), 54 (map).

railroad to Wauhatchee, but could not as yet pass Lookout Mountain. A pontoon-bridge had been thrown across the Tennessee River at Brown's Ferry,[37] by which supplies were hauled into Chattanooga from Kelly's and Wauhatchee.

Another bridge was in course of construction at Chattanooga, under the immediate direction of Quartermaster-General Meigs, but at the time all wagons, etc., had to be ferried across by a flying-bridge. Men were busy and hard at work everywhere inside our lines, and boats for another pontoon-bridge were being rapidly constructed under Brigadier-General W. F. Smith, familiarly known as "Baldy Smith,"[38] and this bridge was destined to be used by my troops, at a point of the river about four miles above Chattanooga, just below the mouth of the Chickamauga River.[39] General Grant explained to me that he had reconnoitred the rebel line from Lookout Mountain up to Chickamauga, and he believed that the northern portion of Missionary Ridge was not fortified at all; and he wanted me, as soon as my troops got up, to lay the new pontoon-bridge by night, cross over, and attack Bragg's right flank on that part of the ridge abutting on Chickamauga Creek, near the tunnel; and he proposed that we should go at once to look at the ground. In company with Generals Thomas, W. F. Smith, Brannan,[40] and others, we crossed by the flying-bridge, rode back of the hills some four miles, left our horses, and got on a hill overlooking the whole ground about the mouth of the Chickamauga River, and across to the Missionary Hills near the tunnel. Smith and I crept down behind a fringe of trees that lined the river-bank, to the very point selected for the new bridge, where we sat for some time, seeing the rebel pickets on the opposite bank, and almost hearing their words.

Having seen enough, we returned to Chattanooga; and in order to hurry up my command, on which so much depended, I started back to Kelly's in hopes to catch the steamboat that same evening; but on my arrival the boat had gone. I applied to the commanding officer, got a rough boat manned by four soldiers, and started down the river by night. I occasionally took a turn

[37] Brown's Ferry crossed the Tennessee River approximately two miles west of Chattanooga. Davis et al., *Official Military Atlas of the Civil War,* plate 49, map 1.

[38] William F. Smith (1824–1903) graduated from the USMA in 1845 and was an engineer in the Military Div. of Mississippi in Nov. 1863. *CWHC,* 499–500.

[39] For the exact location of the bridge built by Smith's men, see Davis et al., *Official Military Atlas of the Civil War,* plate 49, map 1.

[40] John M. Brannan (1819–1892) graduated from the USMA in 1841 and was brevetted colonel in Nov. 1863. *CWHC,* 142.

at the oars to relieve some tired man, and about midnight we reached Shell Mound, where General Whittaker, of Kentucky, furnished us a new and good crew, with which we reached Bridgeport by daylight. I started Ewing's division in advance, with orders to turn aside toward Trenton, to make the enemy believe we were going to turn Bragg's left by pretty much the same road Rosecrans had followed; but with the other three divisions I followed the main road, *via* the Big Trestle at Whitesides, and reached General Hooker's headquarters, just above Wauhatchee, on the 20th; my troops strung all the way back to Bridgeport.[41] It was on this occasion that the Fifteenth Corps gained its peculiar badge: as the men were trudging along the deeply-cut, muddy road, of a cold, drizzly day, one of our Western soldiers left his ranks and joined a party of the Twelfth Corps at their camp-fire. They got into conversation, the Twelfth-Corps men asking what troops we were, etc., etc. In turn, our fellow (who had never seen a corps-badge, and noticed that every thing was marked with a star) asked if they were all brigadier-generals. Of course they were not, but the star was their corps-badge, and every wagon, tent, hat, etc., had its star. Then the Twelfth-Corps men inquired what corps he belonged to, and he answered, "The Fifteenth Corps." "What is your badge?" "Why," said he (and he was an Irishman), suiting the action to the word, "forty rounds in the cartridge-box, and twenty in the pocket!" At that time Blair commanded the corps; but Logan succeeded soon after, and, hearing the story, adopted the cartridge-box and forty rounds as the corps-badge.[42]

The condition of the roads was such, and the bridge at Brown's so frail, that it was not until the 23d that we got three of my divisions behind the hills near the point indicated above Chattanooga for crossing the river. It was determined to begin the battle with these three divisions, aided by a division of Thomas's army, commanded by General Jeff. C. Davis,[43] that was already near that point. All the details of the battle of Chattanooga, so far as I was a witness, are so fully given in my official report herewith, that I need add

[41] For a detailed map of the area surrounding Chattanooga, see Davis et al., *Official Military Atlas of the Civil War,* plate 149.

[42] On Feb. 14, 1865, Gen. John A. Logan issued General Orders Number 10, which established the "Forty Round" badge for the 15th U.S. Army Corps. Charles W. Wills, *Army Life of an Illinois Soldier: Including a Day-by-Day Record of Sherman's March to the Sea,* ed. Mary E. Kellog (Carbondale: Southern Illinois University Press, 1996), 347.

[43] Jefferson C. Davis (1828–1879), who had avoided prosecution for the murder of U.S. Army General William "Bull" Nelson on Sept. 29, 1862, was in command of the 2nd Div., 14th Corps, Army of the Cumberland, in Nov. 1863. *CWHC,* 202.

nothing to it. It was a magnificent battle in its conception, in its execution, and in its glorious results; hastened somewhat by the supposed danger of Burnside, at Knoxville, yet so completely successful, that nothing is left for cavil or fault-finding.[44] The first day was lowering and overcast, favoring us greatly, because we wanted to be concealed from Bragg, whose position on the mountain-tops completely overlooked us and our movements. The second day was beautifully clear, and many a time, in the midst of its carnage and noise, I could not help stopping to look across that vast field of battle, to admire its sublimity.

The object of General Hooker's and my attacks on the extreme flanks of Bragg's position was, to disturb him to such an extent, that he would naturally detach from his centre as against us, so that Thomas's army could break through his centre. The whole plan succeeded admirably; but it was not until after dark that I learned the complete success at the centre, and received General Grant's orders to pursue on the north side of Chickamauga Creek.

HEADQUARTERS MILITARY DIVISION OF THE MISSISSIPPI,
CHATTANOOGA, TENNESSEE, *November* 25, 1863.

Major-General SHERMAN.

GENERAL: No doubt you witnessed the handsome manner in which Thomas's troops carried Missionary Ridge this afternoon, and can feel a just pride, too, in the part taken by the forces under your command in taking first so much of the same range of hills, and then in attracting the attention of so many of the enemy as to make Thomas's part certain of success. The next thing now will be to relieve Burnside. I have heard from him to the evening of the 23d. At that time he had from ten to twelve days' supplies, and spoke hopefully of being able to hold out that length of time.

My plan is to move your forces out gradually until they reach the railroad between Cleveland and Dalton. Granger will move up the south side of the Tennessee with a column of twenty thousand men, taking no wagons, or but few, with him. His men will carry four days' rations, and the steamer Chattanooga, loaded with rations, will accompany the expedition.

[44] WTS failed to capture Tunnel Hill on the north end of Missionary Ridge during the battle on Nov. 24. Instead, he mistakenly captured Billy Goat Hill, about one mile away from Tunnel Hill. John F. Marszalek, *Sherman: A Soldier's Passion for Order* (New York: Free Press, 1993), 244–245.

I take it for granted that Bragg's entire force has left. If not, of course, the first thing is to dispose of him. If he has gone, the only thing necessary to do to-morrow will be to send out a reconnoissance to ascertain the whereabouts of the enemy. Yours truly,

U. S. GRANT, *Major-General.*

P. S.—On reflection, I think we will push Bragg with all our strength to-morrow, and try if we cannot cut off a good portion of his rear troops and trains. His men have manifested a strong disposition to desert for some time past, and we will now give them a chance. I will instruct Thomas accordingly. Move the advance force early, on the most easterly road taken by the enemy.

U. S. G.

This compelled me to reverse our column, so as to use the bridge across the Chickamauga at its mouth. The next day we struck the rebel rear at Chickamauga Station,[45] and again near Graysville. There we came in contact with Hooker's and Palmer's troops, who had reached Ringgold.[46] There I detached Howard to cross Taylor's Ridge, and strike the railroad which comes from the north by Cleveland to Dalton. Hooker's troops were roughly handled at Ringgold, and the pursuit was checked. Receiving a note from General Hooker, asking help, I rode forward to Ringgold to explain the movement of Howard; where I met General Grant, and learned that the rebels had again retreated toward Dalton. He gave orders to discontinue the pursuit, as he meant to turn his attention to General Burnside, supposed to be in great danger at Knoxville, about one hundred and thirty miles northeast. General Grant returned and spent part of the night with me, at Graysville. We talked over matters generally, and he explained that he had ordered General Gordon Granger, with the Fourth Corps, to move forward rapidly to Burnside's help, and that he must return to Chattanooga to push him. By reason of the scarcity of food, especially of forage, he consented that, instead of going back, I might keep out in the country; for in motion I could pick up some forage

[45] Chickamauga Station was situated on the Western and Atlantic Railroad approximately seven miles southeast of Chattanooga. Davis et al., *Official Military Atlas of the Civil War,* plate 48.

[46] John M. Palmer (1817–1900) commanded the 14th Corps, Army of the Cumberland, in Nov. 1863. *CWHC,* 415.

and food, especially on the Hiawassee River, whereas none remained in Chattanooga.

Accordingly, on the 29th of November, my several columns marched to Cleveland, and the next day we reached the Hiawassee at Charleston, where the Chattanooga & Knoxville Railroad crosses it. The railroad-bridge was partially damaged by the enemy in retreating, but we found some abandoned stores. There and thereabouts I expected some rest for my weary troops and horses; but, as I rode into town, I met Colonel J. H. Wilson and C. A. Dana (Assistant Secretary of War), who had ridden out from Chattanooga to find me, with the following letter from General Grant, and copies of several dispatches from General Burnside, the last which had been received from him by way of Cumberland Gap:

HEADQUARTERS MILITARY DIVISION OF THE MISSISSIPPI,
CHATTANOOGA, TENNESSEE, *November* 29, 1863.

Major-General W. T. SHERMAN:

News are received from Knoxville to the morning of the 27th. At that time the place was still invested, but the attack on it was not vigorous. Longstreet evidently determined to starve the garrison out. Granger is on the way to Burnside's relief, but I have lost all faith in his energy or capacity to manage an expedition of the importance of this one. I am inclined to think, therefore, I shall have to send you. Push as rapidly as you can to the Hiawassee, and determine for yourself what force to take with you from that point. Granger has his corps with him, from which you will select in conjunction with the force now with you. In plain words, you will assume command of all the forces now moving up the Tennessee, including the garrison at Kingston, and from that force organize what you deem proper to relieve Burnside. The balance send back to Chattanooga. Granger has a boat loaded with provisions, which you can issue, and return the boat. I will have another loaded, to follow you. Use, of course, as sparingly as possible from the rations taken with you, and subsist off the country all you can.

It is expected that Foster is moving, by this time, from Cumberland Gap on Knoxville. I do not know what force he will have with him, but presume it will range from three thousand five hundred to five thousand. I leave this matter to you, knowing that you will do better acting upon your discretion than you could trammeled with instructions. I will only add, that the last advices from Burnside himself indicated his ability to hold out with rations only to about the 3d of December.

Very respectfully,
U. S. GRANT, *Major-General commanding.*

This showed that, on the 27th of November, General Burnside was in Knoxville, closely besieged by the rebel General Longstreet; that his provisions were short, and that, unless relieved by December 3d, he might have to surrender. General Grant further wrote that General Granger, instead of moving with great rapidity as ordered, seemed to move "slowly, and with reluctance;" and, although he (General Grant) hated to call on me and on my tired troops, there was no alternative. He wanted me to take command of every thing within reach, and to hurry forward to Knoxville.

All the details of our march to Knoxville are also given in my official report. By extraordinary efforts Long's small brigade of cavalry[47] reached Knoxville during the night of the 3d, purposely to let Burnside know that I was rapidly approaching with an adequate force to raise the siege.

With the head of my infantry column I reached Marysville, about fifteen miles short of Knoxville, on the 5th of December, when I received official notice from Burnside that Longstreet had raised the siege, and had started in retreat up the valley toward Virginia. Halting all the army, except Granger's two divisions, on the morning of the 6th, with General Granger and some of my staff I rode into Knoxville. Approaching from the south and west, we crossed the Holston on a pontoon-bridge, and in a large pen on the Knoxville side I saw a fine lot of cattle, which did not look much like starvation. I found General Burnside and staff domiciled in a large, fine mansion, looking very comfortable, and in a few words he described to me the leading events of the previous few days, and said he had already given orders looking to the pursuit of Longstreet. I offered to join in the pursuit, though in fact my men were worn out, and suffering in that cold season and climate. Indeed, on our way up I personally was almost frozen, and had to beg leave to sleep in the house of a family at Athens.

Burnside explained to me that, reënforced by Granger's two divisions of ten thousand men, he would be able to push Longstreet out of East Tennessee, and he hoped to capture much of his artillery and trains. Granger was present at our conversation, and most unreasonably, I thought, remonstrated against being left; complaining bitterly of what he thought was hard treatment to his men and himself. I know that his language and manner at that

[47] Long commanded the 2nd Brig., 2nd Cav. Div., Dept. of the Cumberland, in Nov. 1863. *CWHC,* 352.

time produced on my mind a bad impression, and it was one of the causes which led me to relieve him as a corps commander in the campaign of the next spring. I asked General Burnside to reduce his wishes to writing, which he did in the letter of December 7th, embodied in my official report. General Burnside and I then walked along his lines and examined the salient, known as Fort Sanders, where, some days before, Longstreet had made his assault, and had sustained a bloody repulse.[48]

Returning to Burnside's quarters, we all sat down to a good dinner, embracing roast-turkey. There was a regular dining- table, with clean table-cloth, dishes, knives, forks, spoons, etc., etc. I had seen nothing of this kind in my field experience, and could not help exclaiming that I thought "they were starving," etc.; but Burnside explained that Longstreet had at no time completely invested the place, and that he had kept open communication with the country on the south side of the river Holston, more especially with the French Broad settlements, from whose Union inhabitants he had received a good supply of beef, bacon, and corn-meal. Had I known of this, I should not have hurried my men so fast; but until I reached Knoxville I thought his troops there[49] were actually in danger of starvation. Having supplied General Burnside all the help he wanted, we began our leisurely return to Chattanooga, which we reached on the 16th; when General Grant in person ordered me to restore to General Thomas the divisions of Howard and Davis, which belonged to his army, and to conduct my own corps (the Fifteenth) to North Alabama for winter-quarters.

HEADQUARTERS DEPARTMENT AND ARMY OF THE TENNESSEE,
BRIDGEPORT, ALABAMA, *December* 19, 1863.

Brigadier-General JOHN A. RAWLINS, *Chief of Staff to General* GRANT, *Chattanooga.*

GENERAL: For the first time, I am now at leisure to make an official record of events with which the troops under my command have been connected during the eventful campaign which has just closed.

During the month of September last, the Fifteenth Army Corps, which I had the honor to command, lay in camps along the Big Black,

[48] Fort Sanders was situated approximately one-half mile west of Knoxville, TN. Davis et al., *Official Military Atlas of the Civil War,* plate 48.

[49] In the first edition of the memoirs (1875), this section read "our troops there."

about twenty miles east of Vicksburg, Mississippi. It consisted of four divisions. The First, commanded by Brigadier-General P. J. Osterhaus, was composed of two brigades, led by Brigadier-General C. R. Woods and Colonel J. A. Williamson (of the Fourth Iowa).

The Second, commanded by Brigadier-General Morgan L. Smith, was composed of two brigades, led by Brigadier-Generals Giles A. Smith and J. A. J. Lightburn.

The Third, commanded by Brigadier-General J. M. Tuttle, was composed of three brigades, led by Brigadier-Generals J. A. Mower and R. P. Buckland, and Colonel J. J. Wood (of the Twelfth Iowa).

The Fourth, commanded by Brigadier-General Hugh Ewing, was composed of three brigades, led by Brigadier-General J. M. Corse, Colonel Loomis (Twenty-sixth Illinois), and Colonel J. R. Cockerill (of the Seventieth Ohio).

On the 22d day of September I received a telegraphic dispatch from General Grant, then at Vicksburg, commanding the Department of the Tennessee, requiring me to detach one of my divisions to march to Vicksburg, there to embark for Memphis, where it was to form a part of an army to be sent to Chattanooga, to reënforce General Rosecrans. I designated the First Division, and at 4 P. M. the same day it marched for Vicksburg, and embarked the next day.

On the 23d of September I was summoned to Vicksburg by the general commanding, who showed me several dispatches from the general-in-chief, which led him to suppose he would have to send me and my whole corps to Memphis and eastward, and I was instructed to prepare for such orders. It was explained to me that, in consequence of the low stage of water in the Mississippi, boats had arrived irregularly, and had brought dispatches that seemed to conflict in their meaning, and that General John E. Smith's division (of General McPherson's corps) had been ordered up to Memphis, and that I should take that division and leave one of my own in its stead, to hold the line of the Big Black. I detailed my third division (General Tuttle) to remain and report to Major-General McPherson, commanding the Seventeenth Corps, at Vicksburg; and that of General John E. Smith, already started for Memphis, was styled the Third Division, Fifteenth Corps, though it still belongs to the Seventeenth Army Corps. This division is also composed of three brigades, commanded by General Matthias,

Colonel J. B. Raum (of the Fifty-sixth Illinois), and Colonel J. I. Alexander (of the Fifty-ninth Indiana).

The Second and Fourth Divisions were started for Vicksburg the moment I was notified that boats were in readiness, and on the 27th of September I embarked in person in the steamer Atlantic, for Memphis, followed by a fleet of boats conveying these two divisions. Our progress was slow, on account of the unprecedentedly low water in the Mississippi, and the scarcity of coal and wood. We were compelled at places to gather fence-rails, and to land wagons and haul wood from the interior to the boats; but I reached Memphis during the night of the 2d of October, and the other boats came in on the 3d and 4th.

On arrival at Memphis I saw General Hurlbut, and read all the dispatches and letters of instruction of General Halleck, and therein derived my instructions, which I construed to be as follows:

To conduct the Fifteenth Army Corps, and all other troops which could be spared from the line of the Memphis & Charleston Railroad, to Athens, Alabama, and thence report by letter for orders to General Rosecrans, commanding the Army of the Cumberland, at Chattanooga; to follow substantially the railroad eastward, repairing it as I moved; to look to my own line for supplies; and in no event to depend on General Rosecrans for supplies, as the roads to his rear were already overtaxed to supply his present army.

I learned from General Hurlbut that General Osterhaus's division was already out in front of Corinth, and that General John E. Smith was still at Memphis, moving his troops and material by railroad as fast as its limited stock would carry them. General J. D. Webster was superintendent of the railroad, and was enjoined to work night and day, and to expedite the movement as rapidly as possible; but the capacity of the road was so small, that I soon saw that I could move horses, mules, and wagons faster by land, and therefore I dispatched the artillery and wagons by the road under escort, and finally moved the entire Fourth Division by land.

The enemy seems to have had early notice of this movement, and he endeavored to thwart us from the start. A considerable force assembled in a threatening attitude at Salem, south of Salisbury Station; and General Carr, who commanded at Corinth, felt compelled to turn back and use a part of my troops, that had already reached Corinth, to resist the threatened attack.

On Sunday, October 11th, having put in motion my whole force, I started myself for Corinth, in a special train, with the battalion of the Thirteenth United States Regulars as escort. We reached Collierville Station about noon, just in time to take part in the defense made of that station by Colonel D. C. Anthony, of the Sixty-sixth Indiana, against an attack made by General Chalmers with a force of about three thousand cavalry, with eight pieces of artillery. He was beaten off, the damage to the road repaired, and we resumed our journey the next day, reaching Corinth at night.

I immediately ordered General Blair forward to Iuka, with the First Division, and, as fast as I got troops up, pushed them forward of Bear Creek, the bridge of which was completely destroyed, and an engineer regiment, under command of Colonel Flad, was engaged in its repairs.

Quite a considerable force of the enemy was assembled in our front, near Tuscumbia, to resist our advance. It was commanded by General Stephen D. Lee, and composed of Roddy's and Ferguson's brigades, with irregular cavalry, amounting in the aggregate to about five thousand.

In person I moved from Corinth to Burnsville on the 18th, and to Iuka on the 19th of October.

Osterhaus's division was in the advance, constantly skirmishing with the enemy; he was supported by General Morgan L. Smith's, both divisions under the general command of Major-General Blair. General John E. Smith's division covered the working-party engaged in rebuilding the railroad.

Foreseeing difficulty in crossing the Tennessee River, I had written to Admiral Porter, at Cairo, asking him to watch the Tennessee and send up some gunboats the moment the stage of water admitted; and had also requested General Allen, quartermaster at St. Louis, to dispatch to Eastport a steam ferry-boat.

The admiral, ever prompt and ready to assist us, had two fine gunboats at Eastport, under Captain Phelps, the very day after my arrival at Iuka; and Captain Phelps had a coal-barge decked over, with which to cross our horses and wagons before the arrival of the ferry-boat.

Still following literally the instructions of General Halleck, I pushed forward the repairs of the railroad, and ordered General Blair, with the two leading divisions, to drive the enemy beyond Tuscumbia. This he did successfully, after a pretty severe fight at Cane Creek, occupying Tuscumbia on the 27th of October.

In the mean time many important changes in command had occurred, which I must note here, to a proper understanding of the case.

General Grant had been called from Vicksburg, and sent to Chattanooga to command the military division of the Mississippi, composed of the three Departments of the Ohio, Cumberland, and Tennessee; and the Department of the Tennessee had been devolved on me, with instructions, however, to retain command of the army in the field. At Iuka I made what appeared to me the best disposition of matters relating to the department, giving General McPherson full powers in Mississippi and General Hurlbut in West Tennessee, and assigned General Blair to the command of the Fifteenth Army Corps; and summoned General Hurlbut from Memphis, and General Dodge from Corinth, and selected out of the Sixteenth Corps a force of about eight thousand men, which I directed General Dodge to organize with all expedition, and with it to follow me eastward.

On the 27th of October, when General Blair, with two divisions, was at Tuscumbia, I ordered General Ewing, with the Fourth Division, to cross the Tennessee (by means of the gunboats and scow) as rapidly as possible at Eastport, and push forward to Florence, which he did; and the same day a messenger from General Grant floated down the Tennessee over Muscle Shoals, landed at Tuscumbia, and was sent to me at Iuka. He bore a short message from the general to this effect: "Drop all work on the railroad east of Bear Creek; push your command toward Bridgeport till you meet orders;" etc. Instantly the order was executed; the order of march was reversed, and all the columns were directed to Eastport, the only place where we could cross the Tennessee. At first we only had the gunboats and coal-barge; but the ferry-boat and two transports arrived on the 31st of October, and the work of crossing was pushed with all the vigor possible. In person I crossed, and passed to the head of the column at Florence on the 1st of November, leaving the rear divisions to be conducted by General Blair, and marched to Rogersville and Elk River. This was found impassable. To ferry would have consumed to much time, and to build a bridge still more; so there was no alternative but to turn up Elk River by way of Gilbertsboro, Elkton, etc., to the stone bridge at Fayetteville, where we crossed the Elk, and proceeded to Winchester and Deckerd.

At Fayetteville I received orders from General Grant to come to Bridgeport with the Fifteenth Army Corps, and to leave General

Dodge's command at Pulaski, and along the railroad from Columbia to Decatur. I instructed General Blair to follow with the Second and First Divisions by way of New Market, Larkinsville, and Bellefonte, while I conducted the other two divisions by way of Deckerd; the Fourth Division crossing the mountain to Stevenson, and the Third by University Place and Swedon's Cove.

In person I proceeded by Swedon's Cove and Battle Creek, reaching Bridgeport on the night of November 13th. I immediately telegraphed to the commanding general my arrival, and the positions of my several divisions, and was summoned to Chattanooga. I took the first steamboat during the night of the 14th for Kelly's Ferry, and rode into Chattanooga on the 15th. I then learned the part assigned me in the coming drama, was supplied with the necessary maps and information, and rode, during the 16th, in company with Generals Grant, Thomas, W. F. Smith, Brannan, and others, to the positions occupied on the west bank of the Tennessee, from which could be seen the camps of the enemy, compassing Chattanooga and the line of Missionary Hills, with its terminus on Chickamauga Creek, the point that I was expected to take, hold, and fortify. Pontoons, with a full supply of balks and chesses, had been prepared for the bridge over the Tennessee, and all things had been prearranged with a foresight that elicited my admiration. From the hills we looked down on the amphitheatre of Chattanooga as on a map, and nothing remained but for me to put my troops in the desired position. The plan contemplated that, in addition to crossing the Tennessee River and making a lodgment on the terminus of Missionary Ridge, I should demonstrate against Lookout Mountain, near Trenton, with a part of my command.

All in Chattanooga were impatient for action, rendered almost acute by the natural apprehensions felt for the safety of General Burnside in East Tennessee.

My command had marched from Memphis, three hundred and thirty miles, and I had pushed them as fast as the roads and distance would admit, but I saw enough of the condition of men and animals in Chattanooga to inspire me with renewed energy. I immediately ordered my leading division (General Ewing's) to march *via* Shellmound to Trenton, demonstrating against Lookout Ridge, but to be prepared to turn quickly and follow me to Chattanooga and in person I returned to Bridgeport, rowing a boat down the Tennessee from Kelly's Ferry, and immediately on arrival put in motion my divisions in the order in which they had arrived. The bridge of boats at Bridgeport was frail, and, though used day and night, our passage was slow; and the road thence to Chattanooga was dreadfully cut up and encumbered with the wagons of the other troops stationed along the road. I reached General Hooker's headquarters during a rain, in the afternoon of the 20th, and met General Grant's orders for the general attack on the next day. It was simply impossible for me to fulfill my part in time; only one division (General John E. Smith's) was in position. General Ewing was still at Trenton, and the other two were toiling along the terrible road from Shellmound to Chattanooga. No troops ever were or could be in better condition than mine, or who labored harder to fulfill their part. On a proper representation, General Grant postponed the attack. On the 21st I got the Second Division over Brown's-Ferry Bridge, and General Ewing got up; but the bridge broke repeatedly, and delays occurred which no human sagacity could prevent. All labored night and day, and General Ewing got over on the 23d; but my rear division was cut off by the broken bridge at Brown's Ferry, and could not join me. I offered to go into action with my three divisions, supported by General Jeff. C. Davis, leaving one of my best divisions (Osterhaus's) to act with General Hooker against Lookout Mountain. That division has not joined me yet, but I know and feel that it has served the country well, and that it has reflected honor on the Fifteenth Army Corps and the Army of the Tennessee. I leave the record of its history to General Hooker, or whomsoever has had its services during the late memorable events, confident that all will do it merited honor.

At last, on the 23d of November, my three divisions lay behind the hills opposite the mouth of the Chickamauga. I dispatched the brigade of the Second Division, commanded by General Giles A. Smith, under cover of the hills, to North Chickamauga Creek, to man the boats designed for the pontoon-bridge, with orders (at midnight) to drop down silently to a point above the mouth of the South Chickamauga, there land two regiments, who were to move along the river-bank quietly, and capture the enemy's river-pickets.

General Giles A. Smith then was to drop rapidly below the mouth of the Chickamauga, disembark the rest of his brigade, and dispatch the boats across for fresh loads. These orders were skillfully executed, and every rebel picket but one was captured. The balance of General Morgan L. Smith's division was then rapidly ferried across; that of General John E. Smith followed, and by daylight of November 24th two divisions of about eight thousand men were on the east bank of the Tennessee, and had thrown up a very respectable rifle-trench as a *téte du pont.* As soon as the day dawned, some of the boats were taken from the use of ferrying, and a pontoon-bridge was begun, under the immediate direction of Captain Dresser, the whole planned and supervised by General William F. Smith in person. A pontoon-bridge was also built at the same time over Chickamauga Creek, near its mouth, giving communication with the two regiments which had been left on the north side, and fulfilling a most important purpose at a later stage of the drama. I will here bear my willing testimony to the completeness of this whole business. All the officers charged with the work were present, and manifested a skill which I cannot praise too highly. I have never beheld any work done so quietly, so well; and I doubt if the history of war can show a bridge of that extent (viz., thirteen hundred and fifty feet) laid so noiselessly and well, in so short a time. I attribute it to the genius and intelligence of General William F. Smith. The steamer Dunbar arrived up in the course of the morning, and relieved Ewing's division of the labor of rowing across; but by noon the pontoon-bridge was done, and my three divisions were across, with men, horses, artillery, and every thing.

General Jeff. C. Davis's division was ready to take the bridge, and I ordered the columns to form in order to carry the Missionary Hills. The movement had been carefully explained to all division commanders, and at 1 P. M. we marched from the river in three columns in echelon: the left, General Morgan L. Smith, the column of direction, following substantially Chickamauga Creek; the centre, General John E. Smith, in columns, doubled on the centre, at one brigade interval to the right and rear; the right, General Ewing, in column at the same distance to the right rear, prepared to deploy to the right, on the supposition that we would meet an enemy in that direction. Each head of column was covered by a good line of skirmishers, with supports. A light drizzling rain prevailed, and the clouds hung low, cloaking our movement from the enemy's tower of observation on Lookout Mountain. We soon gained the foot-hills; our skirmishers crept up the face of the hills, followed by their supports, and at 3.30 P. M. we had gained, with no loss, the desired point. A brigade of each division was pushed rapidly to the top of the hill, and the enemy for the first time seemed to realize the movement, but too late, for we were in possession. He opened with artillery, but General Ewing soon got some of Captain Richardson's guns up that steep hill and gave back artillery, and the enemy's skirmishers made one or two ineffectual dashes at General Lightburn, who had swept round and got a farther hill, which was the real continuation of the ridge. From studying all the maps, I had inferred that Missionary Ridge was a continuous hill; but we found ourselves on two high points, with a deep depression between us and the one immediately over the tunnel, which was my chief objective point. The ground we had gained, however, was so important, that I could leave nothing to chance, and ordered it to be fortified during the night. One brigade of each division was left on the hill, one of General Morgan L. Smith's closed the gap to Chickamauga Creek, two of General John E. Smith's were drawn back to the base in reserve, and General Ewing's right was extended down into the plain, thus crossing the ridge in a general line, facing southeast.

The enemy felt our left flank about 4 P. M., and a pretty smart engagement with artillery and muskets ensued, when he drew off; but it cost us dear, for General Giles A. Smith was severely wounded, and had to go to the rear; and the command of the brigade devolved on Colonel Tupper (One Hundred and Sixteenth Illinois), who managed it with skill during the rest of the operations. At the moment of my crossing the bridge, General Howard appeared, having come with three regiments from Chattanooga, along the east bank of the Tennessee, connecting my new position with that of the main army in Chattanooga. He left the three regiments attached temporarily to General Ewing's right, and returned to his own corps at Chattanooga. As night closed in, I ordered General Jeff. C. Davis to keep one of his brigades at the bridge, one close up to my position, and one intermediate. Thus we passed the night, heavy details being kept busy at work on the intrenchments on the hill. During the night the sky cleared away bright, a cold frost filled the air, and our camp-fires revealed to the enemy and to our friends in Chattanooga our position on Missionary Ridge. About midnight I received, at the hands of Major Rowley (of General Grant's staff), orders to attack the enemy at "dawn of day," with notice that General Thomas would attack in force *early* in the day. Accordingly, before day I was in the saddle, attended by all my staff; rode to the extreme left of our position near Chickamauga Creek; thence up the hill, held by General Lightburn; and round to the extreme right of General Ewing. Catching as accurate an idea of the ground as possible by the dim light of morning, I saw that our line of attack was in the direction of Missionary Ridge, with wings supporting on either flank. Quite a valley lay between us and the next hill of the series, and this hill presented steep sides, the one to the west partially cleared, but the other covered with the native forest. The crest of the ridge was narrow and wooded. The farther point of this hill was held by the enemy with a breastwork of logs and fresh earth, filled with men and two guns. The enemy was also seen in great force on a still higher hill beyond the tunnel, from which he had a fine plunging fire on the hill in dispute. The gorge between, through which several roads and the railroad-tunnel pass, could not be seen from our position, but formed the natural *place d'armes,* where the enemy covered his masses to resist our contemplated movement of turning his right flank and endangering his communications with his depot at Chickamauga Station.

As soon as possible, the following dispositions were made: The brigades of Colonels Cockrell and Alexander, and General Lightburn, were to hold our hill as the key-point. General Corse, with as much of his brigade as could operate along the narrow ridge, was to attack from our right centre. General Lightburn was to dispatch a good regiment from his position to coöperate with General Corse; and General Morgan L. Smith was to move along the east base of Missionary Ridge, connecting with General Corse; and Colonel Loomis, in like manner, to move along the west base, supported by the two reserve brigades of General John E. Smith.

The sun had hardly risen before General Corse had completed his preparations and his bugle sounded the "forward!" The Fortieth Illinois, supported by the Forty-sixth Ohio, on our right centre, with the Thirtieth Ohio (Colonel Jones), moved down the face of our hill, and up that held by the enemy. The line advanced to within about eighty yards of the intrenched position, where General Corse found a secondary crest, which he gained and held. To this point he called his reserves, and asked for reënforcements, which were sent; but the space was narrow, and it was not well to crowd the men, as the enemy's artillery and musketry fire swept the approach to his position, giving him great advantage. As soon as General Corse had made his preparations, he assaulted, and a close, severe contest ensued, which lasted more than an hour, gaining and losing ground, but never the position first obtained, from which the enemy in vain attempted to drive him. General Morgan L. Smith kept gaining ground on the left spurs of

Missionary Ridge, and Colonel Loomis got abreast of the tunnel and railroad embankment on his side, drawing the enemy's fire, and to that extent relieving the assaulting party on the hill-crest. Captain Callender had four of his guns on General Ewing's hill, and Captain Woods his Napoleon battery on General Lightburn's; also, two guns of Dillon's battery were with Colonel Alexander's brigade. All directed their fire as carefully as possible, to clear the hill to our front, without endangering our own men. The fight raged furiously about 10 A. M., when General Corse received a severe wound, was brought off the field, and the command of the brigade and of the assault at that key-point devolved on that fine young, gallant officer, Colonel Walcutt, of the Forty-sixth Ohio, who fulfilled his part manfully. He continued the contest, pressing forward at all points. Colonel Loomis had made good progress to the right, and about 2 P. M. General John E. Smith, judging the battle to be most severe on the hill, and being required to support General Ewing, ordered up Colonel Raum's and General Matthias's brigades across the field to the summit that was being fought for. They moved up under a heavy fire of cannon and musketry, and joined Colonel Walcutt; but the crest was so narrow that they necessarily occupied the west face of the hill. The enemy, at the time being massed in great strength in the tunnel-gorge, moved a large force under cover of the ground and the thick bushes, and suddenly appeared on the right rear of this command. The suddenness of the attack disconcerted the men, exposed as they were in the open field; they fell back in some disorder to the lower edge of the field, and reformed. These two brigades were in the nature of supports, and did not constitute a part of the real attack. The movement, seen from Chattanooga (five miles off) with spy-glasses, gave rise to the report, which even General Meigs has repeated, that we were repulsed on the left. It was *not so.* The real attacking columns of General Corse, Colonel Loomis, and General Smith, were not repulsed. They engaged in a close struggle all day persistently, stubbornly, and well. When the two reserve brigades of General John E. Smith fell back as described, the enemy made a show of pursuit, but were in their turn caught in flank by the well-directed fire of our brigade on the wooded crest, and hastily sought cover behind the hill.

Thus matters stood about 3 P. M. The day was bright and clear, and the amphitheatre of Chattanooga lay in beauty at our feet. I had watched for the attack of General Thomas "*early in the day.*"

Column after column of the enemy was streaming toward me; gun after gun poured its concentric shot on us, from every hill and spur that gave a view of any part of the ground held by us. An occasional shot from Fort Wood and Orchard Knob, and some musketry-fire and artillery over about Lookout Mountain, was all that I could detect on our side; but about 3 P. M. I noticed the white line of musketry-fire in front of Orchard Knoll extending farther and farther right and left and on. We could only hear a faint echo of sound, but enough was seen to satisfy me that General Thomas was at last moving on the *centre.* I knew that our attack had drawn vast masses of the enemy to our flank, and felt sure of the result. Some guns which had been firing on us all day were silent, or were turned in a different direction.

The advancing line of musketry-fire from Orchard Knoll disappeared to us behind a spur of the hill, and could no longer be seen; and it was not until night closed in that I knew that the troops in Chattanooga had swept across Missionary Ridge and broken the enemy's centre. Of course, the victory was won, and pursuit was the next step.

I ordered General Morgan L. Smith to feel to the tunnel, and it was found vacant, save by the dead and wounded of our own and the enemy commingled. The reserve of General Jeff. C. Davis was ordered to march at once by the pontoon-bridge across Chickamauga Creek, at its mouth, and push forward for the depot.

General Howard had reported to me in the early part of the day, with the remainder of his army corps (the Eleventh), and had been posted to connect my left with Chickamauga Creek. He was ordered to repair an old broken bridge about two miles up the Chickamauga, and to follow General Davis at 4 A. M., and the Fifteenth Army Corps was ordered to follow at daylight. But General Howard found that to repair the bridge was more of a task than was at first supposed, and we were all compelled to cross the Chickamauga on the new pontoon-bridge at its mouth. By about 11 A. M. General Jeff. C. Davis's division reached the depot, just in time to see it in flames. He found the enemy occupying two hills, partially intrenched, just beyond the depot. These he soon drove away. The depot presented a scene of desolation that war alone exhibits—corn-meal and corn in huge burning piles, broken wagons, abandoned caissons, two thirty-two-pounder rifled-guns with carriages burned, pieces of pontoons, balks and chesses, etc., destined doubtless for the famous invasion of Kentucky, and all manner of things, burning and broken. Still, the enemy kindly left us a good supply of forage for our horses, and meal, beans, etc., for our men.

Pausing but a short while, we passed on, the road filled with broken wagons and abandoned caissons, till night. Just as the head of the column emerged from a dark, miry swamp, we encountered the rear-guard of the retreating enemy. The fight was sharp, but the night closed in so dark that we could not move. General Grant came up to us there. At daylight we resumed the march, and at Graysville, where a good bridge spanned the Chickamauga, we found the corps of General Palmer on the south bank, who informed us that General Hooker was on a road still farther south, and we could hear his guns near Ringgold.

As the roads were filled with all the troops they could possibly accommodate, I turned to the east, to fulfill another part of the general plan, viz., to break up all communication between Bragg and Longstreet.

We had all sorts of rumors as to the latter, but it was manifest that we should interpose a proper force between these two armies. I therefore directed General Howard to move to Parker's Gap, and thence send rapidly a competent force to Red Clay, or the Council-Ground, there to destroy a large section of the railroad which connects Dalton and Cleveland. This work was most successfully and fully accomplished that day. The division of General Jeff. C. Davis was moved close up to Ringgold, to assist General Hooker if needed, and the Fifteenth Corps was held at Graysville, for any thing that might turn up. About noon I had a message from General Hooker, saying he had had a pretty hard fight at the mountain-pass just beyond Ringgold, and he wanted me to come forward to turn the position. He was not aware at the time that Howard, by moving through Parker's Gap toward Red Clay, had already turned it. So I rode forward to Ringgold in person, and found the enemy had already fallen back to Tunnel Hill. He was already out of the valley of the Chickamauga, and on ground whence the waters flow to the Coosa. He was out of Tennessee.

I found General Grant at Ringgold, and, after some explanations as to breaking up the railroad from Ringgold back to the State line, as soon as some cars loaded with wounded men could be pushed back to Chickamauga depot, I was ordered to move slowly and leisurely back to Chattanooga.

On the following day the Fifteenth Corps destroyed absolutely and effectually the railroad from a point half-way between Ringgold and

Graysville, back to the State line; and General Grant, coming to Graysville, consented that, instead of returning direct to Chattanooga, I might send back all my artillery-wagons and impediments, and make a circuit by the north as far as the Hiawassee River.

Accordingly, on the morning of November 29th, General Howard moved from Parker's Gap to Cleveland, General Davis by way of McDaniel's Gap, and General Blair with two divisions of the Fifteenth Corps by way of Julien's Gap, all meeting at Cleveland that night. Here another good break was made in the Dalton & Cleveland road. On the 30th the army moved to Charleston, General Howard approaching so rapidly that the enemy evacuated with haste, leaving the bridge but partially damaged, and five car-loads of flour and provisions on the north bank of the Hiawassee.

This was to have been the limit of our operations. Officers and men had brought no baggage or provisions, and the weather was bitter cold. I had already reached the town of Charleston, when General Wilson arrived with a letter from General Grant, at Chattanooga, informing me that the latest authentic accounts from Knoxville were to the 27th, at which time General Burnside was completely invested, and had provisions only to include the 3d of December; that General Granger had left Chattanooga for Knoxville, by the river-road, with a steamboat following him in the river; but he feared that General Granger could not reach Knoxville in time, and ordered me to take command of all troops moving for the relief of Knoxville, and hasten to General Burnside. Seven days before, we had left our camps on the other side of the Tennessee with two days' rations, without a change of clothing—stripped for the fight, with but a single blanket or coat per man, from myself to the private included.

Of course, we then had no provisions save what we gathered by the road, and were ill supplied for such a march. But we learned that twelve thousand of our fellow-soldiers were beleaguered in the mountain town of Knoxville, eighty-four miles distant; that they needed relief, and must have it in three days. This was enough—and it had to be done. General Howard that night repaired and planked the railroad-bridge, and at daylight the army passed over the Hiawassee and marched to Athens, fifteen miles. I had supposed rightly that General Granger was about the mouth of the Hiawassee, and had sent him notice of my orders; that General Grant had sent me a copy of his written instructions, which were full and complete, and that he must push for Kingston, near which we would make a junction. But by the time I reached Athens I had better studied the geography, and sent him orders, which found him at Decatur, that Kingston was out of our way; that he should send his boat to Kingston, but with his command strike across to Philadelphia, and report to me there. I had but a small force of cavalry, which was, at the time of my receipt of General Grant's orders, scouting over about Benton and Columbus. I left my aide, Major McCoy, at Charleston, to communicate with this cavalry and hurry it forward. It overtook me in the night at Athens.

On the 2d of December the army moved rapidly north toward Loudon, twenty-six miles distant. About 11 A. M., the cavalry passed to the head of the column, was ordered to push to Loudon, and, if possible, to save a pontoon-bridge across the Tennessee, held by a brigade of the enemy commanded by General Vaughn. The cavalry moved with such rapidity as to capture every picket; but the brigade of Vaughn had artillery in position, covered by earthworks, and displayed a force too respectable to be carried by a cavalry dash, so that darkness closed in before General Howard's infantry got up. The enemy abandoned the place in the night, destroying the pontoons, running three locomotives and forty-eight cars into the Tennessee River, and abandoned much provision, four guns, and other material, which General Howard took at daylight. But the bridge was gone, and we were forced to turn east and trust to General Burnside's bridge at Knoxville. It was all-important that General Burnside should have notice of our coming, and but one day of the time remained.

Accordingly, at Philadelphia, during the night of the 2d of December, I sent my aide (Major Audenried) forward to Colonel Long, commanding the brigade of cavalry at Loudon, to explain to him how all-important it was that notice of our approach should reach General Burnside within twenty-four hours, ordering him to select the best materials of his command, to start at once, ford the Little Tennessee, and push into Knoxville at whatever cost of life and horse-flesh. Major Audenried was ordered to go along. The distance to be traveled was about forty miles, and the roads villainous. Before day they were off, and at daylight the Fifteenth Corps was turned from Philadelphia for the Little Tennessee at Morgantown, where my maps represented the river as being very shallow; but it was found too deep for fording, and the water was freezing cold—width two hundred and forty yards, depth from two to five feet; horses could ford, but artillery and men could not. A bridge was indispensable. General Wilson (who accompanied me) undertook to superintend the bridge, and I am under many obligations to him, as I was without an engineer, having sent Captain Jenny back from Graysville to survey our field of battle. We had our pioneers, but only such tools as axes, picks, and spades. General Wilson, working partly with cut wood and partly with square trestles (made of the houses of the late town of Morgantown), progressed apace, and by dark of December 4th troops and animals passed over the bridge, and by daybreak of the 5th the Fifteenth Corps (General Blair's) was over, and Generals Granger's and Davis's divisions were ready to pass; but the diagonal bracing was imperfect for want of spikes, and the bridge broke, causing delay. I had ordered General Blair to move out on the Marysville road five miles, there to await notice that General Granger was on a parallel road abreast of him, and in person I was at a house where the roads parted, when a messenger rode up, bringing me a few words from General Burnside, to the effect that Colonel Long had arrived at Knoxville with his cavalry, and that all was well with him there; Longstreet still lay before the place, but there were symptoms of his speedy departure.

I felt that I had accomplished the first great step in the problem for the relief of General Burnside's army, but still urged on the work. As soon as the bridge was mended, all the troops moved forward. General Howard had marched from Loudon, had found a pretty good ford for his horses and wagons at Davis's, seven miles below Morgantown, and had made an ingenious bridge of the wagons left by General Vaughn at Loudon, on which to pass his men. He marched by Unitia and Louisville. On the night of the 5th all the heads of columns communicated at Marysville, where I met Major Van Buren (of General Burnside's staff), who announced that Longstreet had the night before retreated on the Rutledge, Rogersville, and Bristol road, leading to Virginia; that General Burnside's cavalry was on his heels; and that the general desired to see me in person as soon as I could come to Knoxville. I ordered all the troops to halt and rest, except the two divisions of General Granger, which were ordered to move forward to Little River, and General Granger to report in person to General Burnside for orders. His was the force originally designed to reënforce General Burnside, and it was eminently proper that it should join in the stern-chase after Longstreet.

On the morning of December 6th I rode from Marysville into Knoxville, and met General Burnside. General Granger arrived later in the day. We examined his lines of fortifications, which were a wonderful production for the short time allowed in their selection of ground and construction of work. It seemed to me that they were nearly impregnable. We examined the redoubt named "Sanders," where, on the Sunday previous, three brigades of the enemy had assaulted and met a bloody repulse. Now, all was peaceful and quiet; but a few hours before, the deadly bullet sought its victim all round about that hilly barrier.

The general explained to me fully and frankly what he had done, and what he proposed to do. He asked of me nothing but General Granger's command; and suggested, in view of the large force I had brought from Chattanooga, that I should return with due expedition to the line of the Hiawassee, lest Bragg, reënforced, might take advantage of our absence to resume the offensive. I asked him to reduce this to writing, which he did, and I here introduce it as part of my report:

HEADQUARTERS ARMY OF THE OHIO,
KNOXVILLE, *December* 7, 1863.

Major-General W. T. SHERMAN, *commanding, etc.*

GENERAL: I desire to express to you and your command my most hearty thanks and gratitude for your promptness in coming to our relief during the siege of Knoxville, and I am satisfied your approach served to raise the siege. The emergency having passed, I do not deem, for the present, any other portion of your command but the corps of General Granger necessary for operations in this section; and, inasmuch as General Grant has weakened the forces immediately with him in order to relieve us (thereby rendering the position of General Thomas less secure), I deem it advisable that all the troops now here, save those commanded by General Granger, should return at once to within supporting distance of the forces in front of Bragg's army. In behalf of my command, I desire again to thank you and your command for the kindness you have done us.

I am, general, very respectfully, your obedient servant,
A. E. BURNSIDE, *Major-General commanding.*

Accordingly, having seen General Burnside's forces move out of Knoxville in pursuit of Longstreet, and General Granger's move in, I put in motion my own command to return. General Howard was ordered to move, *via* Davis's Ford and Sweetwater, to Athens, with a guard forward at Charleston, to hold and repair the bridge which the enemy had retaken after our passage up. General Jeff. C. Davis moved to Columbus, on the Hiawassee, *via* Madisonville, and the two divisions of the Fifteenth Corps moved to Tellico Plains, to cover movement of cavalry across the mountains into Georgia, to overtake a wagon-train which had dodged us on our way up, and had escaped by way of Murphy. Subsequently, on a report from General Howard that the enemy held Charleston, I diverted General Ewing's division to Athens, and went in person to Tellico with General Morgan L. Smith's division. By the 9th all our troops were in position, and we held the rich country between the Little Tennessee and the Hiawassee. The cavalry, under Colonel Long, passed the mountain at Tellico, and proceeded about seventeen miles beyond Murphy, when Colonel Long, deeming his farther pursuit of the wagon-train useless, returned on the 12th to Tellico. I then ordered him and the division of General Morgan L. Smith to move to Charleston, to which point I had previously ordered the corps of General Howard.

On the 14th of December all of my command in the field lay along the Hiawassee. Having communicated to General Grant the actual state of affairs, I received orders to leave, on the line of the Hiawassee, all the cavalry, and come to Chattanooga with the rest of my command. I left the brigade of cavalry commanded by Colonel Long, reënforced by the Fifth Ohio Cavalry (Lieutenant-Colonel Heath)—the only cavalry properly belonging to the Fifteenth Army Corps—at Charleston, and with the remainder moved by easy marches, by Cleveland and Tyner's Depot, into Chattanooga, where I received in person from General Grant orders to transfer back to their appropriate commands the corps of General Howard and the division commanded by General Jeff. C. Davis, and to conduct the Fifteenth Army Corps to its new field of operations.

It will thus appear that we have been constantly in motion since our departure from the Big Black, in Mississippi, until the present moment. I have been unable to receive from subordinate commanders the usual full, detailed reports of events, and have therefore been compelled to make up this report from my own personal memory; but, as soon as possible, subordinate reports will be received and duly forwarded.

In reviewing the facts, I must do justice to the men of my command for the patience, cheerfulness, and courage which officers and men have displayed throughout, in battle, on the march, and in camp. For long periods, without regular rations or supplies of any kind, they have marched through mud and over rocks, sometimes barefooted, without a murmur. Without a moment's rest after a march of over four hundred miles, without sleep for three successive nights, we crossed the Tennessee, fought our part of the battle of Chattanooga, pursued the enemy out of Tennessee, and then turned more than a hundred and twenty miles north and compelled Longstreet to raise the siege of Knoxville, which gave so much anxiety to the whole country. It is hard to realize the importance of these events without recalling the memory of the general feeling which pervaded all minds at Chattanooga prior to our arrival. I cannot speak of the Fifteenth Army Corps without a seeming vanity; but as I am no longer its commander, I assert that there is no better body of soldiers in America than it. I wish all to feel a just pride in its real honors.

To General Howard and his command, to General Jeff. C. Davis and his, I am more than usually indebted for the intelligence of commanders and fidelity of commands. The brigade of Colonel Bushbeck, belonging to the Eleventh Corps, which was the first to come out of Chattanooga to my flank, fought at the Tunnel Hill, in connection with General Ewing's division, and displayed a courage almost amounting to rashness. Following the enemy almost to the tunnel-gorge, it lost many valuable lives, prominent among them Lieutenant-Colonel Taft, spoken of as a most gallant soldier.

In General Howard throughout I found a polished and Christian gentleman, exhibiting the highest and most chivalric traits of the soldier. General Davis handled his division with artistic skill, more especially at the moment we encountered the enemy's rear-guard, near Graysville, at nightfall. I must award to this division the credit of the best order during our movement through East Tennessee, when long marches and the necessity of foraging to the right and left gave some reason for disordered ranks.

Inasmuch as exception may be taken to my explanation of the temporary confusion, during the battle of Chattanooga, of the two brigades of General Matthias and Colonel Raum, I will here state that I saw the whole, and attach no blame to any one. Accidents will happen in battle, as elsewhere; and at the point where they so manfully went to relieve the pressure on other parts of our assaulting line, they exposed themselves unconsciously to an enemy vastly superior in force, and favored by the shape of the ground. Had that enemy come out on equal terms, those brigades would have shown their mettle, which has been tried more than once before and *stood* the test of fire. They reformed their ranks, and were ready to support General Ewing's division in a very few minutes; and the circumstance would have hardly called for notice on my part, had not others reported what was seen from Chattanooga, a distance of nearly five miles, from where could only be seen the troops in the open field in which this affair occurred.

I now subjoin the best report of casualties I am able to compile from the records thus far received:

CORPS, DIVISIONS, ETC.	Killed.	Wounded.	Missing.	Total.
FIFTEENTH ARMY CORPS:				
First Division....................	67	364	66	497
Second Division..................	No report.	62 (in hosp.)	....	62
Third Division...................	89	288	122	499
Fourth Division..................	72	535	21	628
Total............................				1,686
ELEVENTH ARMY CORPS:				
Bushbeck's Brigade...............	37	145	81	263
Aggregate Loss...................				1,949

No report from General Davis's division, but loss is small.

Among the killed were some of our most valuable officers: Colonels Putnam, Ninety-third Illinois; O'Meara, Ninetieth Illinois; and Torrence, Thirtieth Iowa; Lieutenant-Colonel Taft, of the Eleventh Corps; and Major Bushnell, Thirteenth Illinois.

Among the wounded are Brigadier-Generals Giles A. Smith, Corse, and Matthias; Colonel Raum; Colonel Waugelin, Twelfth Missouri; Lieutenant-Colonel Partridge, Thirteenth Illinois; Major P. I. Welsh, Fifty-sixth Illinois; and Major Nathan McAlla, Tenth Iowa.

Among the missing is Lieutenant-Colonel Archer, Seventeenth Iowa.

My report is already so long, that I must forbear mentioning acts of individual merit. These will be recorded in the reports of division commanders, which I will cheerfully indorse; but I must say that it is but justice that colonels of regiments, who have so long and so well commanded brigades, as in the following cases, should be commissioned to the grade which they have filled with so much usefulness and credit to the public service, viz.: Colonel J. R. Cockerell, Seventieth

Ohio; Colonel J. M. Loomis, Twenty-sixth Illinois; Colonel C. C. Walcutt, Forty-sixth Ohio; Colonel J. A. Williamson, Fourth Iowa; Colonel G. B. Raum, Fifty-sixth Illinois; Colonel J. I. Alexander, Fifty-ninth Indiana.

My personal staff, as usual, have served their country with fidelity, and credit to themselves, throughout these events, and have received my personal thanks.

Inclosed you will please find a map of that part of the battle-field of Chattanooga fought over by the troops under my command, surveyed and drawn by Captain Jenney, engineer on my staff. I have the honor to be, your obedient servant, W. T. Sherman, *Major-General commanding.*

[General Order No. 68.]

War Department, Adjutant-General's Office,
Washington, *February* 21, 1864.

Public Resolution—No. 12.

Joint resolution tendering the thanks of Congress to Major-General W. T. Sherman and others.

Be it resolved by the Senate and House of Representatives of the United States of America in Congress assembled, That the thanks of Congress and of the people of the United States are due, and that the same are hereby tendered, to Major-General W. T. Sherman, commander of the Department and Army of the Tennessee, and the officers and soldiers who served under him, for their gallant and arduous services in marching to the relief of the Army of the Cumberland, and for their gallantry and heroism in the battle of Chattanooga, which contributed in a great degree to the success of our arms in that glorious victory.

Approved February 19, 1864.

By order of the Secretary of War:

E. D. Townsend, *Assistant Adjutant-General.*

On the 19th of December I was at Bridgeport, and gave all the orders necessary for the distribution of the four divisions of the Fifteenth Corps along the railroad from Stevenson to Decatur, and the part of the Sixteenth Corps, commanded by General Dodge, along the railroad from Decatur to Nashville, to make the needed repairs, and to be in readiness for the campaign of the succeeding year; and on the 21st I went up to Nashville, to confer with General Grant and conclude the arrangements for the winter. At that time

General Grant was under the impression that the next campaign would be up the valley of East Tennessee, in the direction of Virginia; and as it was likely to be the last and most important campaign of the war, it became necessary to set free as many of the old troops serving along the Mississippi River as possible. This was the real object and purpose of the Meridian campaign, and of Banks's expedition up Red River to Shreveport during that winter.

15

Meridian Campaign.

JANUARY AND FEBRUARY, 1864.

THE WINTER OF 1863–'64 opened very cold and severe; and it was manifest after the battle of Chattanooga, November 25, 1863, and the raising of the siege of Knoxville, December 5th, that military operations in that quarter must in a measure cease, or be limited to Burnside's force beyond Knoxville. On the 21st of December General Grant had removed his headquarters to Nashville, Tennessee, leaving General George H. Thomas at Chattanooga, in command of the Department of the Cumberland, and of the army round about that place; and I was at Bridgeport, with orders to distribute my troops along the railroad from Stevenson to Decatur, Alabama, and from Decatur up toward Nashville.[1]

General G. M. Dodge, who was in command of the detachment of the Sixteenth Corps, numbering about eight thousand men, had not participated with us in the battle of Chattanooga, but had remained at and near Pulaski, Tennessee, engaged in repairing that railroad, as auxiliary to the main line which led from Nashville to Stevenson, and Chattanooga. General John A. Logan had succeeded to the command of the Fifteenth Corps, by regular appointment of the President of the United States, and had relieved General Frank P. Blair, who had been temporarily in command of that corps during the Chattanooga and Knoxville movement.[2]

At that time I was in command of the Department of the Tennessee, which embraced substantially the territory on the east bank of the Mississippi River, from Natchez up to the Ohio River, and thence along the Tennessee River as high as Decatur and Bellefonte, Alabama. General McPherson was at Vicks-

[1] On Dec. 8, 1863, USG instructed WTS, "Keep your troops in the valley of Upper Tennessee until it seems clear that the enemy has entirely abandoned the States." *OR,* I, 31(III), 356.

[2] Logan officially took command of the 15th Corps, Army of the Tennessee, on Dec. 11. *CWHC,* 351.

burg and General Hurlbut at Memphis, and from them I had the regular reports of affairs in that quarter of my command. The rebels still maintained a considerable force of infantry and cavalry in the State of Mississippi, threatening the river, whose navigation had become to us so delicate and important a matter. Satisfied that I could check this by one or two quick moves inland, and thereby set free a considerable body of men held as local garrisons, I went up to Nashville and represented the case to General Grant, who consented that I might go down the Mississippi River, where the bulk of my command lay, and strike a blow on the east of the river, while General Banks from New Orleans should in like manner strike another to the west; thus preventing any further molestation of the boats navigating the main river, and thereby widening the gap in the Southern Confederacy.[3]

After having given all the necessary orders for the distribution, during the winter months, of that part of my command which was in Southern and Middle Tennessee, I went to Cincinnati and Lancaster, Ohio, to spend Christmas with my family; and on my return I took Minnie with me down to a convent at Reading, near Cincinnati,[4] where I left her, and took the cars for Cairo, Illinois, which I reached January 3d, a very cold and bitter day. The ice was forming fast, and there was great danger that the Mississippi River would become closed to navigation. Admiral Porter, who was at Cairo, gave me a small gunboat (the Juliet), with which I went up to Paducah, to inspect that place, garrisoned by a small force, commanded by Colonel S. G. Hicks, Fortieth Illinois, who had been with me and was severely wounded at Shiloh. Returning to Cairo, we started down the Mississippi River, which was full of floating ice. With the utmost difficulty we made our way through it, for hours floating in the midst of immense cakes, that chafed and ground our boat so that at times we were in danger of sinking. But about the 10th of January we reached Memphis,[5] where I found General Hurlbut, and explained to him my purpose to collect from his garrisons and those of McPherson about twenty thousand men, with which in February to march out from Vicksburg

[3] WTS arrived in Nashville, TN, on Dec. 20. and left for Louisville, KY, on Dec. 22. William T. Sherman, *Sherman's Civil War: Selected Correspondence of William T. Sherman, 1860–1865*, ed. Brooks D. Simpson and Jean V. Berlin (Chapel Hill: University of North Carolina Press, 1999), 574–576.

[4] WTS took his daughter Maria to the Mount Notre Dame Seminary. John F. Marszalek, *Sherman: A Soldier's Passion for Order* (New York: Free Press, 2003), 248; Sherman, *Sherman's Civil War*, 583–584.

[5] For WTS's contemporary account of the trip, see Sherman, *Sherman's Civil War*, 584–585.

as far as Meridian, break up the Mobile & Ohio Railroad, and also the one leading from Vicksburg to Selma, Alabama. I instructed him to select two good divisions, and to be ready with them to go along. At Memphis I found Brigadier-General W. Sooy Smith, with a force of about twenty-five hundred cavalry, which he had by General Grant's orders brought across from Middle Tennessee, to assist in our general purpose, as well as to punish the rebel General Forrest, who had been most active in harassing our garrisons in West Tennessee and Mississippi.

After staying a couple of days at Memphis, we continued on in the gunboat Silver Cloud to Vicksburg, where I found General McPherson, and, giving him similar orders, instructed him to send out spies to ascertain and bring back timely information of the strength and location of the enemy. The winter continued so severe that the river at Vicksburg was full of floating ice, but in the Silver Cloud we breasted it manfully, and got back to Memphis by the 20th. A chief part of the enterprise was to destroy the rebel cavalry commanded by General Forrest, who were a constant threat to our railway communications in Middle Tennessee, and I committed this task to Brigadier-General W. Sooy Smith. General Hurlbut had in his command about seven thousand five hundred cavalry, scattered from Columbus, Kentucky, to Corinth, Mississippi, and we proposed to make up an aggregate cavalry force of about seven thousand "effective," out of these and the twenty-five hundred which General Smith had brought with him from Middle Tennessee. With this force General Smith was ordered to move from Memphis straight for Meridian, Mississippi, and to start by February 1st. I explained to him personally the nature of Forrest as a man, and of his peculiar force; told him that in his route he was sure to encounter Forrest, who always attacked with a vehemence for which he must be prepared, and that, after he had repelled the first attack, he must in turn assume the most determined offensive, overwhelm him and utterly destroy his whole force. I knew that Forrest could not have more than four thousand cavalry, and my own movement would give employment to every other man of the rebel army not immediately present with him, so that he (General Smith) might safely act on the hypothesis I have stated.

Having completed all these preparations in Memphis, being satisfied that the cavalry force would be ready to start by the 1st of February, and having seen General Hurlbut with his two divisions embark in steamers for Vicksburg, I also reëmbarked for the same destination on the 27th of January.

On the 1st of February we rendezvoused in Vicksburg, where I found a spy who had been sent out two weeks before, had been to Meridian, and brought back correct information of the state of facts in the interior of Mississippi. Lieutenant-General (Bishop) Polk was in chief command, with headquarters at Meridian, and had two divisions of infantry, one of which (General Loring's) was posted at Canton, Mississippi, the other (General French's)[6] at Brandon. He had also two divisions of cavalry—Armstrong's, composed of the three brigades of Ross,[7] Stark, and Wirt Adams, which were scattered from the neighborhood of Yazoo City to Jackson and below; and Forrest's, which was united, toward Memphis, with headquarters at Como. General Polk seemed to have no suspicion of our intentions to disturb his serenity.

Accordingly, on the morning of February 3d, we started in two columns, each of two divisions, preceded by a light force of cavalry, commanded by Colonel E. F. Winslow.[8] General McPherson commanded the right column, and General Hurlbut the left. The former crossed the Big Black at the railroad-bridge, and the latter seven miles above, at Messinger's. We were lightly equipped as to wagons, and marched without deployment straight for Meridian, distant one hundred and fifty miles. We struck the rebel cavalry beyond the Big Black, and pushed them pell-mell into and beyond Jackson during the 6th. The next day we reached Brandon, and on the 9th Morton, where we perceived signs of an infantry concentration, but the enemy did not give us battle, and retreated before us. The rebel cavalry were all around us, so we kept our columns compact and offered few or no chances for their dashes. As far as Morton we had occupied two roads, but there we were forced into one. Toward evening of the 12th, Hurlbut's column passed through Decatur, with orders to go into camp four miles beyond at a creek. McPherson's head of column was some four miles behind, and I personally detached one of Hurlbut's regiments to guard the cross-roads at Decatur till the head of McPherson's column should come in sight.[9] Intending to spend the night in

[6] Samuel G. French (1818–1910) graduated from the USMA in 1843 and later joined the Confederate Army. In Feb. 1864 he commanded a division in the Dept. of Alabama, Mississippi, and East Louisiana. *CWHC,* 244.

[7] Lawrence S. Ross (1838–1898), an aide-de-camp to Sam Houston in TX, joined the Confederate Army as a private in the Texas Cav. in Apr. 1861. In Feb. 1864 he commanded a brigade in W. H. Jackson's Cav. Div., Southern District, Dept. of Alabama and East Mississippi. *CWHC,* 462.

[8] Edward F. Winslow (1837–1914) commanded a cavalry brigade in the 17th Corps, Army of the Tennessee, in Feb. 1864. *CWHC,* 575.

[9] WTS ordered Hurlbut to camp near the Little Chunky River. *OR,* I, 32 (II), 383; George B. Davis et al., *Official Military Atlas of the Civil War* (New York: Fairfax Press, 1983), plate 155.

Decatur, I went to a double log-house, and arranged with the lady for some supper. We unsaddled our horses, tied them to the fence inside the yard, and, being tired, I lay down on a bed and fell asleep. Presently I heard shouts and hallooing, and then heard pistol-shots close to the house. My aide, Major Audenried, called me and said we were attacked by rebel cavalry, who were all around us. I jumped up and inquired where was the regiment of infantry I had myself posted at the cross-roads. He said a few moments before it had marched past the house, following the road by which General Hurlbut had gone, and I told him to run, overtake it, and bring it back. Meantime, I went out into the back-yard, saw wagons passing at a run down the road, and horsemen dashing about in a cloud of dust, firing their pistols, their shots reaching the house in which we were. Gathering the few orderlies and clerks that were about, I was preparing to get into a corn-crib at the back side of the lot, wherein to defend ourselves, when I saw Audenried coming back with the regiment, on a run, deploying forward as they came. This regiment soon cleared the place and drove the rebel cavalry back toward the south, whence they had come.

It transpired that the colonel of this infantry regiment, whose name I do not recall, had seen some officers of McPherson's staff (among them Inspector-General Strong)[10] coming up the road at a gallop, raising a cloud of dust; supposing them to be the head of McPherson's column, and being anxious to get into camp before dark, he had called in his pickets and started down the road, leaving me perfectly exposed. Some straggling wagons, escorted by a New Jersey regiment, were passing at the time, and composed the rear of Hurlbut's train. The rebel cavalry, seeing the road clear of troops, and these wagons passing, struck them in flank, shot down the mules of three or four wagons, broke the column, and began a general skirmish. The escort defended their wagons as well as they could, and thus diverted their attention; otherwise I would surely have been captured. In a short time the head of McPherson's column came up, went into camp, and we spent the night in Decatur.

The next day we pushed on, and on the 14th entered Meridian, the enemy retreating before us toward Demopolis, Alabama. We at once set to work to destroy an arsenal, immense storehouses, and the railroad in every direction. We staid in Meridian five days, expecting every hour to hear of General Sooy Smith, but could get no tidings of him whatever. A large force

[10] William E. Strong (1840–1891) was promoted to assistant inspector general, Army of the Tennessee, in Jan. 1864. *CWHC,* 517.

of infantry was kept at work all the time in breaking up the Mobile & Ohio Railroad south and north; also the Jackson & Selma Railroad, east and west. I was determined to damage these roads so that they could not be used again for hostile purposes during the rest of the war. I never had the remotest idea of going to Mobile, but had purposely given out that idea to the people of the country, so as to deceive the enemy and to divert their attention. Many persons still insist that, because we did not go to Mobile on this occasion, I had failed; but in the following letter to General Banks, of January 31st, written from Vicksburg before starting for Meridian, it will be seen clearly that I indicated my intention to keep up the delusion of an attack on Mobile by land, whereas I promised him to be back to Vicksburg by the 1st of March, so as to coöperate with him in his contemplated attack on Shreveport:

HEADQUARTERS DEPARTMENT OF THE TENNESSEE,
VICKSBURG, *January* 31, 1864.

Major-General N. P. BANKS, *commanding Department of the Gulf, New Orleans.*

GENERAL: I received yesterday, at the hands of Captain Dunham, aide-de-camp, your letter of the 25th inst., and hasten to reply. Captain Dunham has gone to the mouth of White River, *en route* for Little Rock, and the other officers who accompanied him have gone up to Cairo, as I understand, to charter twenty-five steamboats for the Red River trip. The Mississippi River, though low for the season, is free of ice and in good boating order; but I understand that Red River is still low. I had a man in from Alexandria yesterday, who reported the falls or rapids at that place impassable save by the smallest boats. My inland expedition is now moving, and I will be off for Jackson and Meridian to-morrow. The only fear I have is in the weather. All the other combinations are good. I want to keep up the delusion of an attack on Mobile and the Alabama River, and therefore would be obliged if you would keep up an irritating foraging or other expedition in that direction.

My orders from General Grant will not, as yet, justify me in embarking for Red River, though I am very anxious to move in that direction. The moment I learned that you were preparing for it, I sent a communication to Admiral Porter, and dispatched to General Grant at Chattanooga, asking if he wanted me and Steele to coöperate with you against Shreveport; and I will have his answer in time, for you cannot do any thing till Red River has twelve feet of water on the rapids at Alexandria. That will be from March to June. I have lived on Red River, and know somewhat of the phases of that stream. The expedition on Shreveport should be made rapidly, with simultaneous movements from Little Rock on Shreveport, from Opelousas on Alexandria, and a combined force of gunboats and transports directly up Red River. Admiral Porter will be able to have a splendid fleet by March 1st. I think Steele could move with ten thousand infantry and five thousand cavalry. I could take about ten thousand, and you could, I suppose, have the same. Your movement from Opelousas, simultaneous with mine up the river, would compel Dick Taylor to leave Fort De Russy (near Marksville), and the whole combined force could appear at Shreveport about a day appointed beforehand.

I doubt if the enemy will risk a siege at Shreveport, although I am informed they are fortifying the place, and placing many heavy guns in position. It would be better for us that they should stand there, as we might make large and important captures. But I do not believe the enemy will fight a force of thirty thousand men, acting in concert with gunboats.

I will be most happy to take part in the proposed expedition, and hope, before you have made your final dispositions, that I will have the necessary permission. Half the Army of the Tennessee is near the Tennessee River, beyond Huntsville, Alabama, awaiting the completion of the railroad, and, by present orders, I will be compelled to hasten there to command it in person, unless meantime General Grant modifies the plan. I have now in this department only the force left to hold the river and the posts, and I am seriously embarrassed by the promises made the veteran volunteers for furlough. I think, by March 1st, I can put afloat for Shreveport ten thousand men, provided I succeed in my present movement in cleaning out the State of Mississippi, and in breaking up the railroads about Meridian.

I am, with great respect, your obedient servant,

W. T. SHERMAN, *Major-General commanding.*

The object of the Meridian expedition was to strike the roads inland, so to paralyze the rebel forces that we could take from the defense of the Mississippi River the equivalent of a corps of twenty thousand men, to be used in the next Georgia campaign; and this was actually done. At the same time, I wanted to destroy General Forrest, who, with an irregular force of cavalry, was constantly threatening Memphis and the river above, as well as our routes of supply in Middle Tennessee. In this we failed utterly, because General W. Sooy Smith did not fulfill his orders, which were clear and specific, as contained in my letter of instructions to him of January 27th, at Memphis, and my personal explanations to him at the same time.[11] Instead of starting at the date ordered, February 1st, he did not leave Memphis till the 11th, waiting for Waring's brigade[12] that was ice-bound near Columbus, Kentucky; and then, when he did start, he allowed General Forrest to head him off and to defeat him with an inferior force, near West Point, below Okalona, on the Mobile & Ohio Railroad.[13]

We waited at Meridian till the 20th to hear from General Smith, but hearing nothing whatever, and having utterly destroyed the railroads in and around that junction, I ordered General McPherson to move back slowly toward Canton. With Winslow's cavalry, and Hurlbut's infantry, I turned north to Marion, and thence to a place called "Union," whence I dispatched the cavalry farther north to Philadelphia and Louisville, to feel as it were for General Smith, and then turned all the infantry columns toward Canton, Mississippi. On the 26th we all reached Canton, but we had not heard a word of General Smith, nor was it until some time after (at Vicksburg) that I learned the whole truth of General Smith's movement and of his failure. Of course I did not and could not approve of his conduct, and I know that he yet chafes under the censure. I had set so much store on his part of the project that I was disappointed, and so reported officially to General Grant.[14] General Smith never regained my confidence as a soldier, though I still regard him as a most accomplished gentleman and a skillful engineer. Since the close of the war he has appealed to me to relieve him of that censure, but I could not do it, because it would falsify history.[15]

[11] For WTS's instructions to W. S. Smith, dated Jan. 27, 1864, see the section "Meridian Campaign" in the Appendix to Volume I.

[12] George E. Waring (1833–1898) commanded a cavalry regiment known as the Frémont Hussars. In the first edition of the memoirs (1875), this portion of WTS's text read "some regiment" instead of "Waring's brigade." See W. S. Smith to WTS, July 9, 1875, in the section "Meridian Campaign" in the Appendix to Volume I.

[13] For Smith's post-battle report, see *OR,* I, 32(I), 251–260.

[14] For WTS's complete report on the Meridian Campaign, including casualty figures, see *OR,* I, 32(I), 173–194.

[15] For the relevant correspondence between WTS and Smith, see the section "Meridian Campaign" in the Appendix to Volume I.

Having assembled all my troops in and about Canton, on the 27th of February I left them under the command of the senior major-general, Hurlbut, with orders to remain till about the 3d of March, and then to come into Vicksburg leisurely; and, escorted by Winslow's cavalry, I rode into Vicksburg on the last day of February. There I found letters from General Grant, at Nashville, and General Banks, at New Orleans, concerning his (General Banks's) projected movement up Red River. I was authorized by the former to contribute aid to General Banks for a limited time; but General Grant insisted on my returning in person to my own command about Huntsville, Alabama, as soon as possible, to prepare for the spring campaign.

About this time we were much embarrassed by a general order of the War Department, promising a thirty-days furlough to all soldiers who would "veteranize"—viz., reënlist for the rest of the war.[16] This was a judicious and wise measure, because it doubtless secured the services of a very large portion of the men who had almost completed a three-years enlistment, and were therefore veteran soldiers in feeling and in habit. But to furlough so many of our men at that instant of time was like disbanding an army in the very midst of battle.

In order to come to a perfect understanding with General Banks, I took the steamer Diana and ran down to New Orleans to see him.[17] Among the many letters which I found in Vicksburg on my return from Meridian was one from Captain D. F. Boyd, of Louisiana, written from the jail in Natchez, telling me that he was a prisoner of war in our hands; had been captured in Louisiana by some of our scouts; and he bespoke my friendly assistance. Boyd was Professor of Ancient Languages at the Louisiana Seminary of Learning during my administration in 1859–'60; was an accomplished scholar, of moderate views in politics, but, being a Virginian, was drawn, like all others of his kind, into the vortex of the rebellion by the events of 1861, which broke up colleges and every thing at the South. Natchez, at this time, was in my command, and was held by a strong division, commanded by Brigadier-General J. W. Davidson. In the Diana we stopped at Natchez, and I made a hasty inspection of the place. I sent for Boyd, who was in good health, but quite dirty, and begged me to take him out of prison, and to effect his ex-

[16] General Orders No. 376, which granted furloughs to reenlisted volunteers, were issued by Stanton on Nov. 21, 1863. *General Orders, Adjutant General's Office, for 1863* (Washington, DC: GPO, 1864), s.v. "General Orders No. 376."

[17] WTS stayed in New Orleans for two days in early Mar. 1864. Sherman, *Sherman's Civil War,* 604–608.

change. I receipted for him; took him along with me to New Orleans; offered him money, which he declined; allowed him to go free in the city; and obtained from General Banks a promise to effect his exchange, which was afterward done.[18] Boyd is now my legitimate successor in Louisiana, viz., President of the Louisiana University, which is the present title of what had been the Seminary of Learning. After the war was over, Boyd went back to Alexandria, reorganized the old institution, which I visited in 1866; but the building was burnt down by an accident or by an incendiary about 1868, and the institution was then removed to Baton Rouge, where it now is, under its new title of the University of Louisiana.[19]

We reached New Orleans on the 2d of March. I found General Banks, with his wife and daughter,[20] living in a good house, and he explained to me fully the position and strength of his troops, and his plans of action for the approaching campaign. I dined with him, and, rough as I was—just out of the woods—attended, that night, a very pleasant party at the house of a lady, whose name I cannot recall, but who is now the wife of Captain Arnold, Fifth United States Artillery.[21] At this party were also Mr. and Mrs. Frank Howe.[22] I found New Orleans much changed since I had been familiar with it in 1853 and in 1860–'61. It was full of officers and soldiers. Among the former were General T. W. Sherman, who had lost a leg at Port Hudson, and General Charles P. Stone, whom I knew so well in California, and who is now

[18] See Sherman, *Sherman's Civil War,* 606.

[19] On Oct. 25, 1869, WTS wrote to Boyd to express his concern about the status of the seminary, "I was shocked, beyond expression, to read, some days ago, the short statement that our Seminary had burned down, supposed to be the work of an incendiary." *Annual Report of the Board of Supervisors of the Louisiana State Seminary of Learning and Military Academy* (New Orleans: A. L. Lee, 1870), 26.

[20] Mary Palmer Banks (1819–1901) married Nathaniel Banks in 1847. They had four children, including two daughters, Mary and Maude. James G. Hollandsworth Jr., *Pretense of Glory: The Life of General Nathaniel P. Banks* (Baton Rouge: LSU Press, 1998); "Recent Deaths: Mrs. Mary P. Banks," *Boston Evening Transcript,* Feb. 1, 1901, 5.

[21] Abby P. Coffin (1835–1904) married Richard Arnold in 1866. "Impressive Services: Funeral of Mrs. Abby Parker Coffin Arnold at Trinity," *Boston Globe,* Oct. 4, 1904, 9; John D. Wright, *The Routledge Encyclopedia of Civil War Era Biographies* (New York: Routledge, 2013), s.v. "Arnold, Richard, 1828–82."

[22] Frank E. Howe (1829–1883) was acting as a special agent for the U.S. Treasury while visiting New Orleans in Mar. 1864. Salmon P. Chase, *The Salmon P. Chase Papers,* ed. John Niven et al. (Kent, OH: Kent State University Press, 1007), 4:361–365; "Col. Frank E. Howe Dead," *New York Times,* May 24, 1883, 1.

in the Egyptian service as chief of staff.[23] The bulk of General Banks's army was about Opelousas, under command of General Franklin, ready to move on Alexandria. General Banks seemed to be all ready, but intended to delay his departure a few days to assist in the inauguration of a civil government for Louisiana, under Governor Hahn.[24] In Lafayette Square I saw the arrangements of scaffolding for the fireworks and benches for the audience. General Banks urged me to remain over the 4th of March, to participate in the ceremonies, which he explained would include the performance of the "Anvil Chorus" by all the bands of his army, and during the performance the church-bells were to be rung, and cannons were to be fired by electricity. I regarded all such ceremonies as out of place at a time when it seemed to me every hour and every minute were due to the war. General Banks's movement, however, contemplated my sending a force of ten thousand men in boats up Red River from Vicksburg, and that a junction should occur at Alexandria by March 17th. I therefore had no time to wait for the grand pageant of the 4th of March, but took my departure from New Orleans in the Diana the evening of March 3d.

On the next day, March 4th, I wrote to General Banks a letter, which was extremely minute in conveying to him how far I felt authorized to go under my orders from General Grant.[25] At that time General Grant commanded the Military Division of the Mississippi, embracing my own Department of the Tennessee and that of General Steele in Arkansas, but not that of General Banks in Louisiana. General Banks was acting on his own powers, or under the instructions of General Halleck in Washington, and our assistance to him was designed as a loan of ten thousand men for a period of thirty days. The instructions of March 6th to General A. J. Smith, who commanded this detachment, were full and explicit on this point. The Diana reached Vicksburg on the 6th, where I found that the expeditionary army had come in from Canton. One division of five thousand men was made up out of Hurlbut's command, and placed under Brigadier-General T. Kilby Smith; and a similar division was made out of McPherson's and Hurlbut's troops, and placed under Brigadier-General Joseph A. Mower; the whole commanded by Brigadier-General A. J. Smith. General Hurlbut, with the rest of his command, returned to Memphis, and General McPherson remained at Vicksburg. General A. J. Smith's com-

[23] Charles P. Stone (1824–1887) graduated from the USMA in 1845 and was Banks's chief of staff in Mar. 1864. He joined the Egyptian Army as a brigadier general on Mar. 30, 1870. *USMA*, 2:214–219.

[24] Michael Hahn (1830–1886) was born in Bavaria and in 1840 moved to Louisiana, where he became a lawyer. He served as the governor of Louisiana in 1864–1865. *CWHC*, 272.

[25] For WTS's Mar. 4, 1864, letter to Banks, see *OR*, I, 34(II), 94.

mand was in due season embarked, and proceeded to Red River, which it ascended, convoyed by Admiral Porter's fleet. General Mower's division was landed near the outlet of the Atchafalaya, marched up by land and captured the fort below Alexandria known as Fort De Russy, and the whole fleet then proceeded up to Alexandria, reaching it on the day appointed, viz., March 17th, where it waited for the arrival of General Banks, who, however, did not come till some days after. These two divisions participated in the whole of General Banks's unfortunate Red River expedition, and were delayed so long up Red River, and subsequently on the Mississippi, that they did not share with their comrades the successes and glories of the Atlanta campaign, for which I had designed them; and, indeed, they did not join our army till just in time to assist General George H. Thomas to defeat General Hood[26] before Nashville, on the 15th and 16th of December, 1864.

General Grant's letter of instructions, which was brought me by General Butterfield,[27] who had followed me to New Orleans, enjoined on me, after concluding with General Banks the details for his Red River expedition, to make all necessary arrangements for furloughing the men entitled to that privilege, and to hurry back to the army at Huntsville, Alabama. I accordingly gave the necessary orders to General McPherson, at Vicksburg, and continued up the river toward Memphis. On our way we met Captain Badeau, of General Grant's staff, bearing the following letter, of March 4th, which I answered on the 10th, and sent the answer by General Butterfield, who had accompanied me up from New Orleans. Copies of both were also sent to General McPherson, at Vicksburg.

[PRIVATE.]

NASHVILLE, TENNESSEE, *March* 4, 1864.

DEAR SHERMAN: The bill reviving the grade of lieutenant-general in the army has become a law, and my name has been sent to the Senate for the place.

I now receive orders to report at Washington immediately, *in person,* which indicates either a confirmation or a likelihood of confirmation.

[26] John Bell Hood (1831–1879) graduated from the USMA in 1853 and resigned from the U.S. Army to join the Confederate Army in Apr. 1861. He was promoted to major general on Oct. 10, 1862. *CWHC,* 302–303.

[27] Daniel Butterfield (1831–1901) was the chief of staff for the 11th and 12th Corps, Army of the Cumberland, Military Div. of the Mississippi, in Mar. 1864. *CWHC,* 157–158.

I start in the morning to comply with the order, but I shall say very distinctly on my arrival there that I shall accept no appointment which will require me to make that city my headquarters. This, however, is not what I started out to write about.

While I have been eminently successful in this war, in at least gaining the confidence of the public, no one feels more than I how much of this success is due to the energy, skill, and the harmonious putting forth of that energy and skill, of those whom it has been my good fortune to have occupying subordinate positions under me.

There are many officers to whom these remarks are applicable to a greater or less degree, proportionate to their ability as soldiers; but what I want is to express my thanks to you and McPherson, as *the men* to whom, above all others, I feel indebted for whatever I have had of success. How far your advice and suggestions have been of assistance, you know. How far your execution of whatever has been given you to do entitles you to the reward I am receiving, you cannot know as well as I do. I feel all the gratitude this letter would express, giving it the most flattering construction.

The word *you* I use in the plural, intending it for McPherson also. I should write to him, and will some day, but, starting in the morning, I do not know that I will find time just now. Your friend,

U. S. Grant, *Major-General.*

[Private and Confidential]

Near Memphis, *March* 10, 1864.

General Grant.

Dear General: I have your more than kind and characteristic letter of the 4th, and will send a copy of it to General McPherson at once.

You do yourself injustice and us too much honor in assigning to us so large a share of the merits which have led to your high advancement. I know you approve the friendship I have ever professed to you, and will permit me to continue as heretofore to manifest it on all proper occasions.

You are now Washington's legitimate successor, and occupy a position of almost dangerous elevation; but if you can continue as heretofore to be yourself, simple, honest, and unpretending, you will enjoy through life the respect and love of friends, and the homage of millions of human beings who will award to you a large share for securing to them and their descendants a government of law and stability.

I repeat, you do General McPherson and myself too much honor. At Belmont you manifested your traits, neither of us being near; at Donelson also you illustrated your whole character. I was not near, and General McPherson in too subordinate a capacity to influence you.

Until you had won Donelson, I confess I was almost cowed by the terrible array of anarchical elements that presented themselves at every point; but that victory admitted the ray of light which I have followed ever since.

I believe you are as brave, patriotic, and just, as the great prototype Washington; as unselfish, kind-hearted, and honest, as a man should be; but the chief characteristic in your nature is the simple faith in success you have always manifested, which I can liken to nothing else than the faith a Christian has in his Saviour.

This faith gave you victory at Shiloh and Vicksburg. Also, when you have completed your best preparations, you go into battle without hesitation, as at Chattanooga—no doubts, no reserve; and I tell you that it was this that made us act with confidence. I knew wherever I was that you thought of me, and if I got in a tight place you would come—if alive.

My only points of doubt were as to your knowledge of grand strategy, and of books of science and history; but I confess your common-sense seems to have supplied all this.

Now as to the future. Do not stay in Washington. Halleck is better qualified than you are to stand the buffets of intrigue and policy. Come out West; take to yourself the whole Mississippi Valley; let us make it dead-sure, and I tell you the Atlantic slope and Pacific shores will follow its destiny as sure as the limbs of a tree live or die with the main trunk! We have done much; still much remains to be done. Time and time's influences are all with us; we could almost afford to sit still and let these influences work. Even in the seceded States your word *now* would go further than a President's proclamation, or an act of Congress.

For God's sake and for your country's sake, come out of Washington! I foretold to General Halleck, before he left Corinth, the inevitable result to him, and I now exhort you to come out West. Here lies the seat of the coming empire; and from the West, when our task is done, we will make short work of Charleston and Richmond, and the impoverished coast of the Atlantic. Your sincere friend,

W. T. SHERMAN.

We reached Memphis on the 13th, where I remained some days, but on the 14th of March received from General Grant a dispatch to hurry to Nashville in person by the 17th, if possible. Disposing of all matters then pending, I took a steamboat to Cairo, the cars thence to Louisville and Nashville, reaching that place on the 17th of March, 1864.

I found General Grant there. He had been to Washington and back, and was ordered to return East to command all the armies of the United States, and personally the Army of the Potomac. I was to succeed him in command of the Military Division of the Mississippi, embracing the Departments of the Ohio, Cumberland, Tennessee, and Arkansas.[28] General Grant was of course very busy in winding up all matters of business, in transferring his command to me, and in preparing for what was manifest would be the great and closing campaign of our civil war. Mrs. Grant[29] and some of their children were with him, and occupied a large house in Nashville, which was used as an office, dwelling, and every thing combined.[30]

On the 18th of March I had issued orders assuming command of the Military Division of the Mississippi, and was seated in the office, when the general came in and said they were about to present him a sword, inviting me to come and see the ceremony. I went back into what was the dining-room of the house; on the table lay a rose-wood box, containing a sword, sash, spurs, etc., and round about the table were grouped Mrs. Grant, Nelly, and one or two of the boys.[31] I was introduced to a large, corpulent gentleman, as the mayor, and another citizen, who had come down from Galena to make this presentation of a sword to their fellow-townsman.[32] I think that Rawlins,

[28] USG officially received his commission as lieutenant general on Mar. 9, 1864. Three days later, General Orders No. 98 placed WTS in command of the Military Div. of the Mississippi. Ulysses S. Grant, *The Personal Memoirs of Ulysses S. Grant: The Complete Annotated Edition,* ed. John F. Marszalek, David S. Nolen, and Louie P. Gallo (Cambridge, MA: Belknap Press of Harvard University Press, 2017), 469*n.*

[29] Julia D. Grant (1826–1902) married USG in Aug. 1848. "Mrs. Julia D. Grant Dies in Washington," *Hattiesburg Daily News,* Dec. 15, 1902, 1.

[30] USG's headquarters was in the home of Tennessee banker Daniel F. Carter. *PUSG,* 10:123*n.*

[31] USG and Julia had four children: Frederick (1850–1912), Ulysses Jr. (1852–1929), Jesse (1858–1934), and Ellen (1855–1922). Grant, *The Personal Memoirs,* 4, 146*n.*

[32] Stephenson T. Napper and Halstead S. Townsend, residents of Jo Daviess County, IL, brought the sword to Nashville. According to Julia D. Grant, the sword was presented to USG by "Mr. L. S. Felt of Galena and dear Mr. Charles Rogers of New York, formerly a resident of Galena." Julia D. Grant, *Personal Memoirs of Julia D. Grant,* ed. John Y. Simon (New York: G. P. Putnam's Sons, 1975), 128; *PUSG,* 10:215*n.*

Bowers,[33] Badeau, and one or more of General Grant's personal staff, were present. The mayor rose and in the most dignified way read a finished speech to General Grant, who stood, as usual, very awkwardly; and the mayor closed his speech by handing him the resolutions of the City Council engrossed on parchment, with a broad ribbon and large seal attached. After the mayor had fulfilled his office so well, General Grant said: "Mr. Mayor, as I knew that this ceremony was to occur, and as I am not used to speaking, I have written something in reply." He then began to fumble in his pockets, first his breast-coat pocket, then his pants, vest; etc., and after considerable delay he pulled out a crumpled piece of common yellow cartridge-paper, which he handed to the mayor. His whole manner was awkward in the extreme, yet perfectly characteristic, and in strong contrast with the elegant parchment and speech of the mayor. When read, however, the substance of his answer was most excellent, short, concise, and, if it had been delivered by word of mouth, would have been all that the occasion required.[34]

I could not help laughing at a scene so characteristic of the man who then stood prominent before the country; and to whom all had turned as the only one qualified to guide the nation in a war that had become painfully critical. With copies of the few letters referred to, and which seem necessary to illustrate the subject-matter, I close this chapter.

HEADQUARTERS DEPARTMENT OF THE TENNESSEE,
STEAMER DIANA (UNDER WEIGH), *March* 4, 1864.

Major-General N. P. BANKS, *commanding Department of the Gulf, New Orleans.*

GENERAL: I had the honor to receive your letter of the 2d instant yesterday at New Orleans, but was unable to answer, except verbally, and I now reduce it to writing.

I will arrive at Vicksburg the 6th instant, and I expect to meet there my command from Canton, out of which I will select two divisions of about ten thousand men, embark them under a good commander, and order him:

1st. To rendezvous at the mouth of Red River, and, in concert with Admiral Porter (if he agree), to strike Harrisonburg a *hard* blow.

[33] Theodore S. Bowers (1832–1866) was assistant adjutant general in the Military Div. of the Mississippi in mid-Mar. 1864. *CWHC,* 139.

[34] For a full transcript of USG's speech, see *PUSG,* 10:214–215.

2d. To return to Red River and ascend it, aiming to reach Alexandria on the 17th of March, to report to you.

3d. That, as this command is designed to operate by water, it will not be encumbered with much land transportation, say two wagons to a regiment, but with an ample supply of stores, including mortars and heavy rifled guns, to be used against fortified places.

4th. That I have calculated, and so reported to General Grant, that this detachment of his forces in no event is to go beyond Shreveport, and that you will spare them the moment you can, trying to get them back to the Mississippi River in thirty days from the time they actually enter Red River.

The year is wearing away fast, and I would like to carry to General Grant at Huntsville, Alabama, every man of his military division, as early in April as possible, for I am sure we ought to move from the base of the Tennessee River to the south before the season is too far advanced, say as early as April 15th next.

I feel certain of your complete success, provided you make the concentration in time, to assure which I will see in person to the embarkation and dispatch of my quota, and I will write to General Steele, conveying to him my personal and professional opinion that the present opportunity is the most perfect one that will ever offer itself to him to clean out his enemies in Arkansas.

Wishing you all honor and success, I am, with respect, your friend and servant,

W. T. Sherman, *Major-General.*

Headquarters Department of the Tennessee,
Vicksburg, *March* 6, 1864.

Brigadier-General A. J. Smith, *commanding Expedition up Red River, Vicksburg, Mississippi.*

General: By an order this day issued, you are to command a strong, well-appointed detachment of the Army of the Tennessee, sent to reënforce a movement up Red River, but more especially against the fortified position at Shreveport.

You will embark your command as soon as possible, little encumbered with wagons or wheeled vehicles, but well supplied with fuel, provisions, and ammunition. Take with you the twelve mortars, with their ammunition, and all the thirty-pound Parrotts the ordnance-officer will supply. Proceed to the mouth of Red River and confer with

Admiral Porter. Consult with him, and in all the expedition rely on him implicitly, as he is the approved friend of the Army of the Tennessee, and has been associated with us from the beginning. I have undertaken with General Banks that you will be at Alexandria, Louisiana, on or before the 17th day of March; and you will, if time allows, coöperate with the navy in destroying Harrisonburg, up Black River; but as I passed Red River yesterday I saw Admiral Porter, and he told me he had already sent an expedition to Harrisonburg, so that I suppose that part of the plan will be accomplished before you reach Red River; but, in any event, be careful to reach Alexandria about the 17th of March.

General Banks will start by land from Franklin, in the Têche country, either the 5th or 7th, and will march *via* Opelousas to Alexandria. You will meet him there, report to him, and act under his orders. My understanding with him is that his forces will move by land, *via* Natchitoches, to Shreveport, while the gunboat-fleet is to ascend the river with your transports in company. Red River is very low for the season, and I doubt if any of the boats can pass the falls or rapids at Alexandria. What General Banks proposes to do in that event I do not know; but my own judgment is that Shreveport ought not to be attacked until the gunboats can reach it. Not that a force marching by land cannot do it alone, but it would be bad economy in war to invest the place with an army so far from heavy guns, mortars, ammunition, and provisions, which can alone reach Shreveport by water. Still, I do not know about General Banks's plans in that event; and whatever they may be, your duty will be to conform, in the most hearty manner.

My understanding with General Banks is that he will not need the coöperation of your force beyond thirty days from the date you reach Red River. As soon as he has taken Shreveport, or as soon as he can spare you, return to Vicksburg with all dispatch, gather up your detachments, wagons, tents, transportation, and all property pertaining to so much of the command as belongs to the Sixteenth Army Corps, and conduct it to Memphis, where orders will await you. My present belief is your division, entire, will be needed with the Army of the Tennessee, about Huntsville or Bridgeport. Still, I will leave orders with General Hurlbut, at Memphis, for you on your return.

I believe if water will enable the gunboats to cross the rapids at Alexandria, you will be able to make a quick, strong, and effective blow at our enemy in the West, thus widening the belt of our territory, and making the breach between the Confederate Government and its outlying trans-Mississippi Department more perfect.

It is understood that General Steele makes a simultaneous move from Little Rock, on Shreveport or Natchitoches, with a force of about ten thousand men. Banks will have seventeen thousand, and you ten thousand. If these can act concentrically and simultaneously, you will make short work of it, and then General Banks will have enough force to hold as much of the Red River country as he deems wise, leaving you to bring to General Grant's main army the seven thousand five hundred men of the Sixteenth Corps now with you. Having faith in your sound judgment and experience, I confide this important and delicate command to you, with certainty that you will harmonize perfectly with Admiral Porter and General Banks, with whom you are to act, and thereby insure success.

I am, with respect, your obedient servant,

W. T. SHERMAN, *Major-General commanding.*

HEADQUARTERS DEPARTMENT OF THE TENNESSEE,
MEMPHIS, *March* 14, 1864.

Major-General MCPHERSON, *commanding, etc., Vicksburg, Mississippi.*

DEAR GENERAL: I wrote you at length on the 11th, by a special bearer of dispatches, and now make special orders to cover the movements therein indicated. It was my purpose to await your answer, but I am summoned by General Grant to be in Nashville on the 17th, and it will keep me moving night and day to get there by that date. I must rely on you, for you understand that we *must* reënforce the great army at the centre (Chattanooga) as much as possible, at the same time not risking the safety of any point on the Mississippi which is fortified and armed with heavy guns. I want you to push matters as rapidly as possible, and to do all you can to put two handsome divisions of your own corps at Cairo, ready to embark up the Tennessee River by the 20th or 30th of April at the *very furthest.* I wish it could be done quicker; but the promise of these thirty-days furloughs in the States of enlistment, though politic, is very unmilitary. It deprives us of our ability to calculate as to time; but do the best you can. Hurlbut can do nothing till A. J. Smith returns from Red River. I will then order him to occupy Grenada temporarily, and to try and get those locomotives that we need here. I may also order him with cavalry and infantry to march toward Tuscaloosa, at the same time that we move from the Tennessee River about Chattanooga.

I don't know as yet the grand strategy of the next campaign, but on arrival at Nashville I will soon catch the main points, and will advise you of them.

Steal a furlough and run to Baltimore *incog.;* but get back in time to take part in the next grand move.

Write me fully and frequently of your progress. I have ordered the quartermaster to send down as many boats as he can get, to facilitate your movements. Mules, wagons, etc., can come up afterward by transient boats. I am truly your friend,

W. T. Sherman, *Major-General commanding.*

[Special Field Order No. 28.]

Headquarters Department of the Tennessee,
Memphis, Tenn., *March* 14, 1864.

1. Major-General McPherson will organize two good divisions of his corps (Seventeenth) of about five thousand men, each embracing in part the reënlisted veterans of his corps whose furloughs will expire in April, which he will command in person, and will rendezvous at Cairo, Illinois, and report by telegraph and letter to the general commanding at department headquarters, wherever they may be. These divisions will be provided with new arms and accoutrements, and land transportation (wagons and mules) out of the supplies now at Vicksburg, which will be conveyed to Cairo by or before April 15th.

. . . .

4. During the absence of General McPherson from the district of Vicksburg, Major-General Hurlbut will exercise command over all the troops in the Department of the Tennessee from Cairo to Natchez, inclusive, and will receive special instructions from department headquarters.

By order of Major-General W. T. Sherman:

L. M. Dayton, *Aide-de-Camp.*[35]

[35] In the first edition of the memoirs (1875), the phrase "END OF VOL. I." was centered at the bottom of the page. In subsequent editions that included the Appendix to Volume I, this phrase has been removed.

Volume II

16

Atlanta Campaign—Nashville and Chattanooga to Kenesaw.

MARCH, APRIL, AND MAY, 1864.

ON THE 18TH DAY OF MARCH, 1864, at Nashville, Tennessee, I relieved Lieutenant-General Grant in command of the Military Division of the Mississippi, embracing the Departments of the Ohio, Cumberland, Tennessee, and Arkansas, commanded respectively by Major-Generals Schofield, Thomas, McPherson, and Steele. General Grant was in the act of starting East to assume command of all the armies of the United States, but more particularly to give direction in person to the Armies of the Potomac and James, operating against Richmond; and I accompanied him as far as Cincinnati on his way, to avail myself of the opportunity to discuss privately many little details incident to the contemplated changes, and of preparation for the great events then impending. Among these was the intended assignment to duty of many officers of note and influence, who had, by the force of events, drifted into inactivity and discontent. Among these stood prominent Generals McClellan, Burnside, and Fremont, in the East; and Generals Buell, McCook, Negley, and Crittenden, at the West. My understanding was that General Grant thought it wise and prudent to give all these officers appropriate commands, that would enable them to regain the influence they had lost; and, as a general reorganization of all the armies was then necessary, he directed me to keep in mind especially the claims of Generals Buell, McCook, and Crittenden, and endeavor to give them commands that would be as near their rank and dates of commission as possible; but I was to do nothing until I heard further from him on the subject, as he explained that he would have to consult the Secretary of War before making final orders. General Buell and his officers had been subjected to a long ordeal by a court of inquiry, touching their conduct of the campaign in Tennessee and Kentucky, that resulted in the battle of Perryville, or Chaplin's Hills, October 8,

1862, and they had been substantially acquitted;[1] and, as it was manifest that we were to have some hard fighting, we were anxious to bring into harmony every man and every officer of skill in the profession of arms. Of these, Generals Buell and McClellan were prominent in rank, and also by reason of their fame acquired in Mexico, as well as in the earlier part of the civil war.

After my return to Nashville I addressed myself to the task of organization and preparation, which involved the general security of the vast region of the South which had been already conquered, more especially the several routes of supply and communication with the active armies at the front, and to organize a large army to move into Georgia, coincident with the advance of the Eastern armies against Richmond. I soon received from Colonel J. B. Fry—now of the Adjutant-General's Department, but then at Washington in charge of the Provost-Marshal-General's office—a letter asking me to do something for General Buell. I answered him frankly, telling him of my understanding with General Grant, and that I was still awaiting the expected order of the War Department, assigning General Buell to my command. Colonel Fry, as General Buell's special friend, replied that he was very anxious that I should make specific application for the services of General Buell by name, and inquired what I proposed to offer him. To this I answered that, after the agreement with General Grant that he would notify me from Washington, I could not with propriety press the matter, but if General Buell should be assigned to me specifically I was prepared to assign him to command all the troops on the Mississippi River from Cairo to Natchez, comprising about three divisions, or the equivalent of a *corps d'armée.*[2] General Grant never afterward communicated to me on the subject at all; and I inferred that Mr. Stanton, who was notoriously vindictive in his prejudices, would not consent to the employment of these high officers. General Buell, toward the close of the war, published a bitter political letter, aimed at General Grant, reflecting on his general management of the war, and stated that both Generals Canby and Sherman had offered him a subordinate command, which he had declined because he had once outranked us. This was not true as to me, or Canby either, I think, for both General Canby and I ranked him at West Point and in the old army, and he (General Buell) was only superior

[1] In Oct. 1862, several governors from Northern states planned a convention in Washington, DC, to call for the removal of McClellan and Buell. Buell, however, was dismissed before the meeting was held. Stephen D. Engle, *Don Carlos Buell: Most Promising of All* (Chapel Hill: University of North Carolina Press, 1999), 319–320.

[2] For WTS's full response to Fry on Apr. 10, 1864, see *OR,* I, 32(III), 319–320.

to us in the date of his commission as major-general, for a short period in 1862. This newspaper communication, though aimed at General Grant, re-acted on himself, for it closed his military career.[3] General Crittenden afterward obtained authority for service, and I offered him a division, but he declined it for the reason, as I understood it, that he had at one time commanded a corps. He is now in the United States service, commanding the Seventeenth Infantry.[4] General McCook obtained a command under General Canby, in the Department of the Gulf, where he rendered good service, and he is also in the regular service, lieutenant-colonel Tenth Infantry.[5]

I returned to Nashville from Cincinnati about the 25th of March, and started at once, in a special car attached to the regular train, to inspect my command at the front, going to Pulaski, Tennessee, where I found General G. M. Dodge; thence to Huntsville, Alabama, where I had left a part of my personal staff and the records of the department during the time we had been absent at Meridian; and there I found General McPherson, who had arrived from Vicksburg, and had assumed command of the Army of the Tennessee. General McPherson accompanied me, and we proceeded by the cars to Stevenson, Bridgeport, etc., to Chattanooga, where we spent a day or two with General George H. Thomas, and then continued on to Knoxville, where was General Schofield. He returned with us to Chattanooga, stopping by the way a few hours at Loudon, where were the headquarters of the Fourth Corps (Major-General Gordon Granger). General Granger, as usual, was full of complaints at the treatment of his corps since I had left him with General Burnside, at Knoxville, the preceding November; and he stated to me personally that he had a leave of absence in his pocket, of which he intended to take advantage very soon. About the end of March, therefore, the three army commanders and myself were together at Chattanooga. We had nothing like a council of war, but conversed freely and frankly on all matters of interest then in progress or impending. We all knew that, as soon as the spring was fairly open, we should have to move directly against our antagonist, General Jos. E. Johnston, then securely intrenched at Dalton, thirty miles distant; and

[3] In Jan. 1865 the *United States Service Magazine* published a letter by WTS that refuted claims made by Buell about the Battle of Shiloh. On Feb. 18, 1865, Buell published a response to WTS's criticism in the *New York World.* Engle, *Don Carlos Buell,* 346–349.

[4] Crittenden resigned from the U.S. Army in Dec. 1864 and rejoined in July 1866. He was transferred to the 17th Inf. in Mar. 1869. *CWHC,* 191.

[5] Alexander M. McCook was transferred to the 10th Inf. in Mar. 1869 and later served as WTS's aide-de-camp from June 1875 to Dec. 1880. *CWHC,* 374.

the purpose of our conference at the time was to ascertain our own resources, and to distribute to each part of the army its appropriate share of work. We discussed every possible contingency likely to arise, and I simply instructed each army commander to make immediate preparations for a hard campaign, regulating the distribution of supplies that were coming up by rail from Nashville as equitably as possible. We also agreed on some subordinate changes in the organization of the three separate armies which were destined to take the field; among which was the consolidation of the Eleventh and Twelfth Corps (Howard and Slocum) into a single corps, to be commanded by General Jos. Hooker. General Howard was to be transferred to the Fourth Corps, *vice* Gordon Granger to avail himself of his leave of absence; and General Slocum was to be ordered down the Mississippi River, to command the District of Vicksburg. These changes required the consent of the President, and were all in due time approved.

The great question of the campaign was one of supplies. Nashville, our chief depot, was itself partially in a hostile country, and even the routes of supply from Louisville to Nashville by rail, and by way of the Cumberland River, had to be guarded. Chattanooga (our starting-point) was one hundred and thirty-six miles in front of Nashville, and every foot of the way, especially the many bridges, trestles, and culverts, had to be strongly guarded against the acts of a local hostile population and of the enemy's cavalry. Then, of course, as we advanced into Georgia, it was manifest that we should have to repair the railroad, use it, and guard it likewise. General Thomas's army was much the largest of the three, was best provided, and contained the best corps of engineers, railroad managers, and repair parties, as well as the best body of spies and provost-marshals. On him we were therefore compelled in a great measure to rely for these most useful branches of service. He had so long exercised absolute command and control over the railroads in his department, that the other armies were jealous, and these thought the Army of the Cumberland got the lion's share of the supplies and other advantages of the railroads. I found a good deal of feeling in the Army of the Tennessee on this score, and therefore took supreme control of the roads myself, placed all the army commanders on an equal footing, and gave to each the same control, so far as orders of transportation for men and stores were concerned. Thomas's spies brought him frequent and accurate reports of Jos. E. Johnston's[6] army at Dalton, giving its strength anywhere between forty and fifty thousand men, and these were being reënforced by troops from Mississippi, and by the

[6] In the first edition of the memoirs (1875), WTS rendered the name as just "Jos. Johnston."

Georgia militia, under General G. W. Smith.[7] General Johnston seemed to be acting purely on the defensive, so that we had time and leisure to take all our measures deliberately and fully. I fixed the date of May 1st, when all things should be in readiness for the grand forward movement, and then returned to Nashville; General Schofield going back to Knoxville, and McPherson to Huntsville, Thomas remaining at Chattanooga.

On the 2d of April, at Nashville, I wrote to General Grant, then at Washington, reporting to him the results of my visit to the several armies, and asked his consent to the several changes proposed, which was promptly given by telegraph.[8] I then addressed myself specially to the troublesome question of transportation and supplies. I found the capacity of the railroads from Nashville forward to Decatur, and to Chattanooga, so small, especially in the number of locomotives and cars, that it was clear that they were barely able to supply the daily wants of the armies then dependent on them, with no power of accumulating a surplus in advance. The cars were daily loaded down with men returning from furlough, with cattle, horses, etc.; and, by reason of the previous desolation of the country between Chattanooga and Knoxville, General Thomas had authorized the issue of provisions to the suffering inhabitants.

We could not attempt an advance into Georgia without food, ammunition, etc.; and ordinary prudence dictated that we should have an accumulation at the front, in case of interruption to the railway by the act of the enemy, or by common accident. Accordingly, on the 6th of April, I issued a general order, limiting the use of the railroad-cars to transporting only the essential articles of food, ammunition, and supplies for the army proper, forbidding any further issues to citizens, and cutting off all civil traffic; requiring the commanders of posts within thirty miles of Nashville to haul out their own stores in wagons; requiring all troops destined for the front to march, and all beef-cattle to be driven on their own legs.[9] This was a great help, but of course it naturally raised a howl. Some of the poor Union people of East Tennessee appealed to President Lincoln, whose kind heart responded promptly to their request. He telegraphed me to know if I could not modify

[7] Gustavus W. Smith (1821–1896) graduated from the USMA in 1842 and served in the Mexican-American War. He resigned from the U.S. Army in Dec. 1854 and joined the Confederate Army in Sept. 1861. He resigned from the Confederate Army in Feb. 1863 to join the Georgia Militia. *CWHC,* 495.

[8] For WTS's full letter to USG, see *OR,* I, 32(III), 221.

[9] For General Orders No. 6, dated Apr. 6, 1864, see *OR,* I, 32(III), 279–280.

or repeal my orders; but I answered him that a great campaign was impending, on which the fate of the nation hung; that our railroads had but a limited capacity, and could not provide for the necessities of the army and of the people too; that one or the other must quit, and we could not until the army of Jos. Johnston was conquered, etc., etc. Mr. Lincoln seemed to acquiesce, and I advised the people to obtain and drive out cattle from Kentucky, and to haul out their supplies by the wagon-road from the same quarter, by way of Cumberland Gap.[10] By these changes we[11] nearly or quite doubled our daily accumulation of stores at the front, and yet even this was not found enough.

I accordingly called together in Nashville the master of transportation, Colonel Anderson,[12] the chief quartermaster, General J. L. Donaldson,[13] and the chief commissary, General Amos Beckwith, for conference. I assumed the strength of the army to move from Chattanooga into Georgia at one hundred thousand men, and the number of animals to be fed, both for cavalry and draught, at thirty-five thousand; then, allowing for occasional wrecks of trains, which were very common, and for the interruption of the road itself by guerrillas and regular raids, we estimated it would require one hundred and thirty cars, of ten tons each, to reach Chattanooga daily, to be reasonably certain of an adequate supply. Even with this calculation, we could not afford to bring forward hay for the horses and mules, nor more than five pounds of oats or corn per day for each animal. I was willing to risk the question of forage in part, because I expected to find wheat and corn fields, and a good deal of grass, as we advanced into Georgia at that season of the year. The problem then was to deliver at Chattanooga and beyond one hundred and thirty car-loads daily, leaving the beef-cattle to be driven on the hoof, and all the troops in excess of the usual train-guards to march by the ordinary roads. Colonel Anderson promptly explained that he did not possess cars or locomotives enough to do this work. I then instructed and authorized him to hold on to all trains that arrived at Nashville from Louisville, and to allow

[10] For Pres. Lincoln's full response to WTS on May 5, see *OR,* I, 38(IV), 33–34.

[11] In the first edition of the memoirs (1875), this portion of the text read "I" instead of "we."

[12] Adna Anderson (1827–1889) was made chief engineer and superintendent of military railroads in the United States in 1864. "General Anderson, a Well-Known Railroad Man, Dies by His Own Hand," *South Bend Tribune* (South Bend, IN), May 16, 1889, 2.

[13] James L. Donaldson (1814–1885) graduated from the USMA in 1836 and served in the Mexican-American War. He was the chief quartermaster of the Dept. of the Cumberland from Aug. 1864 to June 1865. *USMA,* 1:637–641.

none to go back until he had secured enough to fill the requirements of our problem. At the time he only had about sixty serviceable locomotives, and about six hundred cars of all kinds, and he represented that to provide for all contingencies he must have at least one hundred locomotives and one thousand cars. As soon as Mr. Guthrie, the President of the Louisville & Nashville Railroad, detected that we were holding on to all his locomotives and cars, he wrote me, earnestly remonstrating against it, saying that he would not be able with diminished stock to bring forward the necessary stores from Louisville to Nashville. I wrote to him, frankly telling him exactly how we were placed, appealed to his patriotism to stand by us, and advised him in like manner to hold on to all trains coming into Jeffersonville, Indiana.[14] He and General Robert Allen, then quartermaster-general at Louisville, arranged a ferry-boat so as to transfer the trains over the Ohio River from Jeffersonville, and in a short time we had cars and locomotives from almost every road at the North; months afterward I was amused to see, away down in Georgia, cars marked "Pittsburg & Fort Wayne," "Delaware & Lackawanna," "Baltimore & Ohio," and indeed with the names of almost every railroad north of the Ohio River. How these railroad companies ever recovered their property, or settled their transportation accounts, I have never heard, but to this fact, as much as to any other single fact, I attribute the perfect success which afterward attended our campaigns; and I have always felt grateful to Mr. Guthrie, of Louisville, who had sense enough and patriotism enough to subordinate the interests of his railroad company to the cause of his country.

About this time, viz., the early part of April, I was much disturbed by a bold raid made by the rebel General Forrest up between the Mississippi and Tennessee Rivers. He reached the Ohio River at Paducah, but was handsomely repulsed by Colonel Hicks. He then swung down toward Memphis, assaulted and carried Fort Pillow, massacring a part of its garrison, composed wholly of negro troops. At first I discredited the story of the massacre, because, in preparing for the Meridian campaign, I had ordered Fort Pillow to be evacuated, but it transpired afterward that General Hurlbut had retained a small garrison at Fort Pillow to encourage the enlistment of the blacks as soldiers, which was a favorite political policy at that day. The massacre at Fort Pillow occurred April 12, 1864, and has been the subject of congressional inquiry. No doubt Forrest's men acted like a set of barbarians, shooting down the helpless negro garrison after the fort was in their possession; but I am told that Forrest personally disclaims any active participation

[14] For WTS's full response to James Guthrie on May 1, 1864, see *OR,* I, 38(IV), 4–5.

in the assault, and that he stopped the firing as soon as he could. I also take it for granted that Forrest did not lead the assault in person, and consequently that he was to the rear, out of sight if not of hearing at the time, and I was told by hundreds of our men, who were at various times prisoners in Forrest's possession, that he was usually very kind to them. He had a desperate set of fellows under him, and at that very time there is no doubt the feeling of the Southern people was fearfully savage on this very point of our making soldiers out of their late slaves, and Forrest may have shared the feeling.[15]

I also had another serious cause of disturbance about that time. I wanted badly the two divisions of troops which had been loaned to General Banks in the month of March previously, with the express understanding that their absence was to endure only one month, and that during April they were to come out of Red River, and be again within the sphere of my command. I accordingly instructed one of my inspector-generals, John M. Corse, to take a fleet steamboat at Nashville, proceed *via* Cairo, Memphis, and Vicksburg, to General Banks up the Red River, and to deliver the following letter of April 3d, as also others, of like tenor, to Generals A. J. Smith and Fred Steele, who were supposed to be with him:

HEADQUARTERS MILITARY DIVISION OF THE MISSISSIPPI,
NASHVILLE, TENNESSEE, *April* 3, 1864.

Major-General N. P. BANKS, *commanding Department of the Gulf, Red River.*

GENERAL: The thirty days for which I loaned you the command of General A. J. Smith will expire on the 10th instant. I send with this Brigadier-General J. M. Corse, to carry orders to General A. J. Smith, and to give directions for a new movement, which is preliminary to the general campaign. General Corse may see you and explain in full, but, lest he should not find you in person, I will simply state that Forrest, availing himself of the absence of our furloughed men and of the detachment with you, has pushed up between the Mississippi and Tennessee Rivers, even to the Ohio. He attacked Paducah, but got the worst of it, and he still lingers about the place. I hope that he will

[15] In his post-battle report on the Fort Pillow Massacre, Confederate Gen. Nathan B. Forrest asserted, "It is hoped that these facts will demonstrate to the Northern people that negro soldiers cannot cope with southerners." *OR,* I, 32(I), 610.

remain thereabouts till General A. J. Smith can reach his destined point, but this I can hardly expect; yet I want him to reach by the Yazoo a position near Grenada, thence to operate against Forrest, after which to march across to Decatur, Alabama. You will see that he has a big job, and therefore should start at once. From all that I can learn, my troops reached Alexandria, Louisiana, at the time agreed on, viz., March 17th, and I hear of them at Natchitoches, but cannot hear of your troops being above Opelousas.

Steele is also moving. I leave Steele's entire force to coöperate with you and the navy, but, as I before stated, I must have A. J. Smith's troops now as soon as possible.

I beg you will expedite their return to Vicksburg, if they have not already started, and I want them if possible to remain in the same boats they have used up Red River, as it will save the time otherwise consumed in transfer to other boats.

All is well in this quarter, and I hope by the time you turn against Mobile our forces will again act toward the same end, though from distant points. General Grant, now having lawful control, will doubtless see that all minor objects are disregarded, and that all the armies act on a common plan.

Hoping, when this reaches you, that you will be in possession of Shreveport, I am, with great respect, etc.,

W. T. SHERMAN, *Major-General commanding.*

Rumors were reaching us thick and fast of defeat and disaster in that quarter; and I feared then, what afterward actually happened, that neither General Banks nor Admiral Porter could or would spare those two divisions. On the 23d of April, General Corse returned, bringing full answers to my letters, and I saw that we must go on without them. This was a serious loss to the Army of the Tennessee, which was also short by two other divisions that were on their veteran furlough, and were under orders to rendezvous at Cairo, before embarking for Clifton, on the Tennessee River.

On the 10th of April, 1864, the headquarters of the three Armies of the Cumberland, Tennessee, and Ohio, were at Chattanooga., Huntsville, and Knoxville, and the tables on page 16, *et seq.*,[16] give their exact condition and strength.

[16] See tables beginning on p. 498 in this chapter.

The Department of the Arkansas was then subject to my command, but General Fred Steele, its commander, was at Little Rock, remote from me, acting in coöperation with General Banks, and had full employment for every soldier of his command; so that I never depended on him for any men, or for any participation in the Georgia campaign. Soon after, viz., May 8th, that department was transferred to the Military Division of "the Gulf," or "Southwest," Major-General E. R. S. Canby commanding, and General Steele served with him in the subsequent movement against Mobile.

In Generals Thomas, McPherson, and Schofield, I had three generals of education and experience, admirably qualified for the work before us. Each has made a history of his own, and I need not here dwell on their respective merits as men, or as commanders of armies, except that each possessed special qualities of mind and of character which fitted them in the highest degree for the work then in contemplation.[17]

By the returns of April 10, 1864, it will be seen that the Army of the Cumberland had on its muster-rolls—

	Men.
Present and absent	171,450
Present for duty	88,883

The Army of the Tennessee—

	Men.
Present and absent	134,763
Present for duty	64,957

The Army of the Ohio—

	Men.
Present and absent	46,052
Present for duty	26,242

The department and army commanders had to maintain strong garrisons in their respective departments, and also to guard their respective lines of

[17] U.S. Army Col. Charles H. Grosvenor wrote of WTS's assessment of Thomas, "Nothing that you have written of him and his campaigns do I criticize as untrue, unjust, or even injudicious and ill-timed." See C. H. Grosvenor to WTS, July 12, 1875, in Appendix to Volume II.

supply. I therefore, in my mind, aimed to prepare out of these three armies, by the 1st of May, 1864, a compact army for active operations in Georgia, of about the following numbers:

	Men.
Army of the Cumberland	50,000
Army of the Tennessee	35,000
Army of the Ohio	15,000
Total	100,000

and, to make these troops as mobile as possible, I made the strictest possible orders in relation to wagons and all species of incumbrances and impedimenta whatever. Each officer and soldier was required to carry on his horse or person food and clothing enough for five days. To each regiment was allowed but one wagon and one ambulance, and to the officers of each company one pack-horse or mule.

Each division and brigade was provided a fair proportion of wagons for a supply-train, and these were limited in their loads to carry food, ammunition, and clothing. Tents were forbidden to all save the sick and wounded, and one tent only was allowed to each headquarters for use as an office. These orders were not absolutely enforced, though in person I set the example, and did not have a tent, nor did any officer about me have one; but we had wall tent-flies, without poles, and no tent-furniture of any kind. We usually spread our flies over saplings, or on fence-rails or posts improvised on the spot. Most of the general officers, except Thomas, followed my example strictly; but he had a regular headquarters-camp. I frequently called his attention to the orders on this subject, rather jestingly than seriously. He would break out against his officers for having such luxuries, but, needing a tent himself, and being good-natured and slow to act, he never enforced my orders perfectly. In addition to his regular wagon-train, he had a big wagon which could be converted into an office, and this we used to call "Thomas's circus." Several times during the campaign I found quartermasters hid away in some comfortable nook to the rear, with tents and mess-fixtures which were the envy of the passing soldiers; and I frequently broke them up, and distributed the tents to the surgeons of brigades. Yet my orders actually reduced the transportation, so that I doubt if any army ever went forth to battle with fewer impedimenta, and where the regular and necessary supplies of food, ammunition, and clothing, were issued, as called for, so regularly and so well.

Transcript from the Tri-Monthly Return of the Department of the Cumberlan

COMMANDS.	Number of Regiments.	Number of Companies.	For Duty.					
			General Officers.	General Staff-Officers.	Field, Staff, and Company Officers.	Total commissioned.	Enlisted Men.	Aggregate.
Department Staff.	...	.....	3	19	.....	22	.....	2
Fourth Army Corps.	75	751	6	17	826	849	15,323	16,17
Fourteenth Army Corps.	60	600	7	13	686	706	18,931	19,63
Eleventh and Twelfth Ar'y C'rps*.	55	561	9	46	864	919	20,028	20,94
District of Nashville.	18	196	5	8	396	409	8,820	9,22
Cavalry Command.	26	293	1	12	542	555	10,472	11,02
Reserve Artillery.	...	12	...	...	31	31	1,073	1,10
Tenth Ohio Sharp-shooters.	1	14	...	...	30	30	596	62
Post of Chattanooga.	...	.....	1	3	123	127	3,153	3,28
Engineer Brigade.	4	40	...	...	30	30	1,020	1,05
Unassigned Infantry.	4	42	...	...	102	102	2,975	3,07
" Cavalry.	8	88	...	...	79	79	1,588	1,66
" Artillery.	....	9	...	...	20	20	871	89
Signal Corps.	..	.....	...	24	.....	24	130	154
Grand Total.	251	2,606	32	142	3,729	3,903	84,980	88,88

*Consolidated, and named Twentieth Army Corps.

My personal staff was then composed of Captain J. C. McCoy, aide-de-camp; Captain L. M. Dayton, aide-de-camp; Captain J. C. Audenried, aide-de-camp; Brigadier-General J. D. Webster, chief of staff; Major R. M. Sawyer, assistant adjutant-general;[18] Captain Montgomery Rochester, assistant adjutant-general.[19] These last three were left at Nashville in charge of the office, and were

[18] R. M. Sawyer (1835–1866) joined the 1st Wisconsin Volunteers at the start of the war and quickly rose through the ranks to become WTS's assistant adjutant general. "Death of an Army Officer," *Daily Missouri Republican* (St. Louis), Dec. 28, 1866, 2.

[19] Montgomery Rochester (1832–1909) joined the 13th New York Volunteers as a quartermaster in May 1861. He served on WTS's staff in 1864–1865. "Deaths," *Cincinnati Enquirer,*

ommanded by Major-General THOMAS, *for April 10, 1864.*

PRESENT.							ABSENT.					
							On Detachment Service.					
Special, Extra, or Daily Duty.		Sick.		In Arrest or Confineme't.			Within the Department.		Without the Department.		With Leave.	
Commissioned Officers.	Enlisted Men.	Commissioned Officers.	Enlisted Men.	Commissioned Officers.	Enlisted Men.	Aggregate.	Commissioned Officers.	Enlisted Men.	Commissioned Officers.	Enlisted Men.	Commissioned Officers.	Enlisted Men.
...	.....	...	.....	...	...	22	1	.....	1	.....	2	......
80	1,505	27	726	5	82	18,597	301	4,484	95	384	782	8,266
126	1,866	53	1,210	11	132	23,035	326	4,823	114	457	408	5,724
82	1,874	37	1,378	12	161	24,491	207	2,628	120	627	189	2,614
74	2,221	26	907	9	216	12,682	104	1,431	36	175	23	796
49	1,442	23	404	6	72	13,023	175	2,762	62	847	136	1,899
...	17	1	35	...	5	1,162	5	10	13	6	6	159
5	154	...	50	1	18	854	4	57	...	.....	2	12
18	296	5	155	...	49	3,803	33	574	17	76	21	342
13	345	...	53	...	8	1,469	17	162	10	36	40	520
16	282	...	324	...	24	3,723	25	152	...	11	36	559
3	204	9	168	4	26	2,081	9	184	4	5	4	108
1	16	2	38	1	4	953	5	4	6	3	4	145
...	.....	...	1	...	...	155	3	36	...	.....	.....	4
467	10,222	183	5,449	49	797	106,050	1,215	17,307	478	2,627	1,653	21,148

empowered to give orders in my name, communication being generally kept up by telegraph.

Subsequently were added to my staff, and accompanied me in the field, Brigadier-General W. F. Barry, chief of artillery; Colonel O. M. Poe, chief of engineers; Colonel L. C. Easton, chief quartermaster;[20] Colonel Amos Beck-

Feb. 4, 1909, 7; *The Union Army: A History of Military Affairs in the Loyal States, 1861–65* (Madison, WI: Federal, 1908), 8:389–390.

[20] Langdon C. Easton (1814–1884) graduated from the USMA in 1838 and became quartermaster in the Military Div. of the Mississippi in May 1864. *CWHC,* 221.

Transcript from the Tri-Monthly Return of the

COMMANDS.	ABSENT.				PRESENT AND ABSENT.			
	Sick.		Without Authority.					
	Commissioned Officers.	Enlisted Men.	Commissioned Officers.	Enlisted Men.	Commissioned Officers.	Enlisted Men.	Aggregate.	Aggregate Last Return.
Department Staff.	1	. . . . . .	. . .	. . . . .	27	. . . . .	27	27
Fourth Army Corps.	82	5,685	27	408	2,248	36,863	39,111	39,112
Fourteenth Army Corps.	50	4,004	26	369	1,820	37,516	39,336	38,941
Eleventh and Twelfth Army Corps.	41	3,728	11	371	1,618	33,409	35,027	34,858
District of Nashville	7	983	5	357	693	15,906	16,599	18,074
Cavalry Command.	44	2,800	17	237	1,067	20,935	22,002	22,002
Reserve Artillery.	1	116	2	49	59	1,470	1,529	3,074
Fourth Ohio Sharp-shooters. .	2	43	2	3	46	933	979	980
Post of Chattanooga.	3	518	31	35	255	5,198	5,453	3,981
Engineer Brigade.	3	270	2	15	115	2,429	2,544	2,572
Unassigned Infantry.	1	244	1	40	181	4,611	4,792	4,010
" Cavalry.	. . .	174	. . .	70	112	2,527	2,639	2,265
" Artillery.	. . .	83	. . .	8	39	1,172	1,211	775
Signal Corps.	1	1	. . .	1	28	173	201	192
Grand Total.	236	18,649	124	1,963	8,308	163,142	171,450	170,863

Official: E. D. Townsend, *Adjutant-General.* GEO. H. THOMAS, *Major-General commanding.*

with, chief commissary; Captain Thos. G. Baylor, chief of ordnance;[21] Surgeon E. D. Kittoe, medical director;[22] Brigadier-General J. M. Corse,

[21]Thomas Baylor (1837–1890) graduated from the USMA in 1857 and became the chief of ordnance for the Military Div. of the Mississippi in Aug. 1864. He served on WTS's staff from May 1864 to Apr. 1865. *USMA,* 2:679, 4:107.

[22]Edward D. Kittoe (1814–1887) joined the 45th Illinois Volunteers in Aug. 1861 and served as medical director for the Army of the Tennessee before joining WTS's staff. He remained on WTS's staff until the fall of Vicksburg. "Edward D. Kittoe: This Eminent Physician Dies of Heart Disease at Galena," *Nashville Banner,* Sept. 30, 1887, 1.

Department of the Cumberland—(Continued.)

Present for duty equipped.						Horses.		Guns.	
Infantry.		Cavalry.		Artillery.					
Commissioned Officers.	Enlisted Men.	Commissioned Officers.	Enlisted Men.	Commissioned Officers.	Enlisted Men.	Serviceable.	Unserviceable.	Number.	
.....	......	...	.....	...	.....	......	......	...	Brig.-Gen. W.D. Whipple.
785	14,115	...	.....	15	381	295	25	24	Maj.-Gen. O.O. Howard.
686	18,406	...	.....	28	782	664	52	42	Maj.-Gen. J.M. Palmer.
838	18,297	1	50	25	988	802	44	52	Maj.-Gen J. Hooker.
302	8,006	2	89	24	739	589	10	65	Maj.-Gen. L.H. Rousseau.
104	1,376	363	6,786	6	188	9,022	1,969	12	Brig.-Gen. K. Garrard.
.....	......	...	.....	27	940	481	4	38	Brig.-Gen. J.M. Brannan.
80	596	...	.....	...	.....	......	......	...	Capt. G.M. Barber.
66	1,189	...	.....	20	1,050	......	......	89	Maj.-Gen. J.B. Steedman.
30	1,020	...	.....	...	.....	218	7	...	Gen. O.M. Poe.
96	3,001	...	.....	...	.....	......	......	...	Maj.-Gen Carl Schurz.
.....	......	79	1,204	...	.....	658	545	...	In the field with other
.....	......	...	.....	20	871	54	11	28	Divisions of the cavalry.
.....	......	...	.....	...	.....	......	......	...	Col. J. Barnett, 1st Ohio L.A.
									Capt. P. Babcock, Jr.
2,987	66,006	445	8,129	165	5,939	12,783	2,667	350	

inspector-general; Lieutenant-Colonel C. Ewing, inspector-general; and Lieutenant-Colonel Willard Warner, inspector-general.[23]

These officers constituted my staff proper at the beginning of the campaign, which remained substantially the same till the close of the war, with very few exceptions; viz.: Surgeon John Moore, United States Army, relieved

[23] Willard Warner (1826–1906) commanded an Ohio regiment during the Civil War and later served as a U.S. senator from Alabama. "General Warner Dead," *Chattanooga News,* Nov. 23, 1906, 4; "Death Came at His Desk," *Chattanooga Daily Times,* Nov. 24, 1906, 5.

Transcript from the Tri-Monthly Return of the Department and Army of th

COMMANDS.	Number of Regiments.	Number of Companies.	PRESENT. For Duty. General Officers.	General Staff-Officers.	Field, Staff, and Company Officers.	Total commissioned.	Enlisted Men.	Aggregate.	Special, Extra, or Daily Duty. Commissioned Officers.	Enlisted Men.
Department Staff.	. . .	. . . . .	1	4	. . . . .	5	. . . . ..	5	. . .	. . . . .
Fifteenth Army Corps	56	571	9	13	728	750	14,919	15,669	94	1,925
Sixteenth Army Corps	71	811	10	35	1,355	1,400	31,345	32,745	169	4,402
Seventeenth Army Corps. . . .	58	627	6	30	598	634	15,890	16,524	76	2,134
Signal Detachment.	. . .	. . . . .	. . .	. . .	. . . . .	1	13	14	. . .	. . . . .
Total Force—Department and Army of the Tennessee	185	2,009	26	82	2,681	2,790	62,167	64,957	339	8,461

Transcript from the Tri-Monthly Retur

COMMANDS.	ABSENT. Without Authority. Commissioned Officers.	Enlisted Men.	PRESENT AND ABSENT. Commissioned Officers.	Enlisted Men.	Aggregate.	Aggregate Last Return.
Department Staff.	. . .	. . . . .	5	. . . .	5	5
Fifteenth Army Corps.	19	262	1,689	30,354	32,043	31,522
Sixteenth Army Corps.	23	966	2,768	57,055	59,823	58,245
Seventeenth Army Corps	14	395	2,069	40,790	42,859	42,859
Signal Detachment.	. . .	7	4	29	33	26
Total Force—Department and Army of the Tennessee.	56	1,630	6,535	128,228	134,763	132,657

Official: E. D. Townsend, *Adjutant-General.* J. B. McPherson, *Major-General commanding.*

nnessee, commanded by Major-General McPherson, *for April 10, 1864.*

					ABSENT.							
					On Detached Service.							
Sick.		In Arrest or Confineme't.			Within the Department.		Without the Department.		With Leave.		Sick.	
Commissioned Officers.	Enlisted Men.	Commissioned Officers.	Enlisted Men.	Aggregate.	Commissioned Officers.	Enlisted Men.	Commissioned Officers.	Enlisted Men.	Commissioned Officers.	Enlisted Men.	Commissioned Officers.	Enlisted Men.
...	.....	...	...	5	...	.....	...	......	......	....	...	.....
52	1,302	7	152	19,201	215	3,055	102	354	394	5,069	56	3,316
81	3,042	23	193	40,655	299	3,191	195	1,560	494	8,298	84	4,058
58	2,348	15	96	21,251	461	7,660	128	534	660	10,148	28	1,585
...	.....	...	...	14	1	7	1	2	1	....	...	.....
191	6,692	45	441	81,126	976	13,913	426	2,450	1,549	23,515	168	8,959

f the Department and Army of the Tennessee—(Continued.)

PRESENT FOR DUTY EQUIPPED.						HORSES.		GUNS.	
Infantry.		Cavalry.		Artillery.					
Commissioned Officers.	Enlisted Men.	Commissioned Officers.	Enlisted Men.	Commissioned Officers.	Enlisted Men.	Serviceable.	Unserviceable.	Number.	
.....	.....	...	.....	...	.....	.....	.....	...	Colonel W.T. Clark.
689	11,053	27	350	31	1,165	1,086	243	57	Major-General J.A. Logan.
554	11,107	152	3,681	80	2,840	5,779	1,064	173	Major-General G.M. Dodge.
400	8,545	91	2,137	59	2,005	2,911	1,016	58	Major-General Frank P. Blair
.....	.....	...	.....	...	.....	31	.....	...	Captain O.H. Howard.
1,643	30,705	270	6,168	170	6,010	9,807	2,323	288	

Transcript from the Tri-Monthly Return of the Department of the Ohi

COMMANDS.	Number of Regiments.	Number of Companies.	PRESENT. For Duty. General Officers.	General Staff-Officers.	Field Staff, and Company Officers.	Total commissioned.	Enlisted Men.	Aggregate.	Special, Extra, or Daily Duty. Commissioned Officers.	Enlisted Men.
Twenty-third Army Corps. . .	24	326	4	7	675	686	14,733	15,419	88	1,968
Cavalry Corps.	14	167	1	4	209	214	5,419	5,633	42	673
District of the Clinch.	4	37	1	3	79	83	1,406	1,489	9	118
Defenses of Knoxville.	2	42	. . .	. . .	123	123	3,507	3,630	19	354
Newport Barracks.	. . .	. . .	. . .	. . .	2	2	69	71	. . .	5
Total Force—Department of the Ohio.	44	572	6	14	1,088	1,108	25,134	26,242	158	3,118

Transcript from the Tri-Monthly Return o

COMMANDS.	ABSENT. Without Authority. Commissioned Officers.	Enlisted Men.	PRESENT AND ABSENT. Commissioned Officers.	Enlisted Men.	Aggregate.	Aggregate Last Return.
Twenty-third Army Corps	13	970	1,141	25,892	27,033	26,999
Cavalry Corps.	9	314	504	10,340	10,844	10,844
District of the Clinch.	1	373	119	2,353	2,472	2,478
Defenses of Knoxville.	3	99	198	5,415	5,613	5,613
Newport Barracks.	. . .	1	2	88	90	224
Total Force—Department of the Ohio.	26	1,757	1,964	44,088	46,052	46,158

Official: E. D. Townsend, *Adjutant-General.* J. M. Schofield, *Major-General commanding.*

mmanded by Major-General Schofield, *for April 10, 1864.*

Sick.		In Arrest or Confineme't.		Aggregate.	ABSENT. On Detached Service.. Within the Department.		Without the Department.		With Leave.		Sick.	
Commissioned Officers.	Enlisted Men.	Commissioned Officers.	Enlisted Men.		Commissioned Officers.	Enlisted Men.	Commissioned Officers.	Enlisted Men.	Commissioned Officers.	Enlisted Men.	Commissioned Officers.	Enlisted Men.
50	1,490	8	313	19,336	221	3,365	15	133	36	512	24	2,408
19	557	4	37	6,965	141	1,660	14	35	32	270	29	1,375
5	120	2	21	1,764	9	69	1	14	4	3	5	229
4	552	4	16	4,579	31	314	3	78	7	54	4	441
...	1	...	10	87	...	.....	...	...	...	1	...	1
78	2,720	18	397	32,731	402	5,408	33	260	79	840	62	4,454

e Department of the Ohio—(Continued.)

PRESENT FOR DUTY EQUIPPED. Infantry.		Cavalry.		Artillery.		HORSES.		GUNS.	
Commissioned Officers.	Enlisted Men.	Commissioned Officers.	Enlisted Men.	Commissioned Officers.	Enlisted Men.	Serviceable.	Unserviceable.	Number.	
545	11,500	76	1,180	49	1,614	427	67	...	Major-General J. D. Cox.
	1,184	125	2,917	...	.....	1,888	424	...	Major-General G. Stoneman.
57	897	16	245		291	5	...	...	Brig.-General T. T. Garrard.
54	455	...	.....	9	1,884	12	...	602	Brigadier-General D. Tillson.
21	......	...	.....	57	.....	.....	...	...	Colonel J. P. Sanderson.
677	14,036	217	4,342	115	3,789	2,332	491	602	

Surgeon Kittoe of the volunteers (about Atlanta) as medical director;[24] Major Henry Hitchcock joined as judge-advocate,[25] and Captain G. Ward Nichols reported as an extra aide-de-camp (after the fall of Atlanta)[26] at Gaylesville,[27] just before we started for Savannah.

During the whole month of April the preparations for active war were going on with extreme vigor, and my letter-book shows an active correspondence with Generals Grant, Halleck, Thomas, McPherson, and Schofield on thousands of matters of detail and arrangement, most of which are embraced in my testimony before the Committee on the Conduct of the War, vol. i., Appendix.

When the time for action approached, viz., May 1, 1864, the actual armies prepared to move into Georgia resulted as follows, present for battle:

Army of the Cumberland, Major-General Thomas

	Men.
Infantry	54,568
Artillery	2,377
Cavalry	3,828
Aggregate	60,773
Number of field-guns, 130.	

[24] John Moore (1826–1907) graduated from New York University with a medical degree in 1850. He was appointed colonel and medical director of volunteers in 1865 and later served as the surgeon general of the U.S. Army in 1886. Howard A. Kelly, *A Cyclopedia of American Medical Biography* (Philadelphia: W. B. Saunders, 1912), vol. 2, s.v. "Moore, John."

[25] Henry Hitchcock (1829–1902), a close friend of WTS, graduated from Yale University and practiced law in New York before the start of the Civil War. "Life Story of the Original of Stephen Brice of 'The Crisis,'" *St. Louis Dispatch,* Mar. 19, 1902, 4.

[26] George W. Nichols (1831–1885) was an American journalist. He published *The Story of the Great March from the Diary of a Staff Officer* (1865), which detailed his experience with WTS during the last year of the war. "George Ward Nichols: Death of the Author of 'Sherman's March to the Sea,'" *St. Joseph Herald* (St. Joseph, MO), Sept. 16, 1885, 1.

[27] Gaylesville, AL, was located approximately eighty miles northwest of Atlanta, GA. George B. Davis et al., *Official Military Atlas of the Civil War* (New York: Fairfax Press, 1983), plate 149.

Army of the Tennessee, Major-General McPherson.

	Men.
Infantry	22,437
Artillery	1,404
Cavalry	624
Aggregate	24,465
Guns, 96.	

Army of the Ohio, Major-General Schofield.

	Men.
Infantry	11,183
Artillery	679
Cavalry	1,697
Aggregate	13,559
Guns, 28.	
Grand aggregate, 98,797 men and 254 guns.	

These figures do not embrace the cavalry divisions which were still incomplete, viz., of General Stoneman, at Lexington, Kentucky, and of General Garrard,[28] at Columbia, Tennessee, who were then rapidly collecting horses, and joined us in the early stage of the campaign. General Stoneman, having a division of about four thousand men and horses, was attached to Schofield's Army of the Ohio. General Garrard's division, of about four thousand five hundred men and horses, was attached to General Thomas's command; and he had another irregular division of cavalry, commanded by Brigadier-General E. McCook. There was also a small brigade of cavalry, belonging to the Army of the Cumberland, attached temporarily to the Army of the Tennessee, which was commanded by Brigadier-General Judson Kilpatrick.[29] These cavalry commands changed constantly in strength and numbers, and

[28] Kenner Garrard (1827–1879) graduated from the USMA in 1851 and commanded the 2nd Cav. Div., Dept. of the Cumberland, at the start of the Atlanta Campaign. *CWHC,* 250.

[29] Judson Kilpatrick (1836–1881) graduated from the USMA in 1861 and commanded the 3rd Div., Cav. Corps, Dept. of the Cumberland, at the start of the Atlanta Campaign. *CWHC,* 332.

were generally used on the extreme flanks, or for some special detached service, as will be hereinafter related. The Army of the Tennessee was still short by the two divisions detached with General Banks, up Red River, and two other divisions on furlough in Illinois, Indiana, and Ohio, but which were rendezvousing at Cairo, under Generals Leggett[30] and Crocker, to form a part of the Seventeenth Corps, which corps was to be commanded by Major-General Frank P. Blair, then a member of Congress, in Washington. On the 2d of April I notified him by letter that I wanted him to join and to command these two divisions, which ought to be ready by the 1st of May. General Blair, with these two divisions, constituting the Seventeenth Army Corps, did not actually overtake us until we reached Acworth and Big Shanty,[31] in Georgia, about the 9th of June, 1864.

In my letter of April 4th to General John A. Rawlins, chief of staff to General Grant at Washington, I described at length all the preparations that were in progress for the active campaign thus contemplated, and therein estimated Schofield at twelve thousand, Thomas at forty-five thousand, and McPherson at thirty thousand.[32] At first I intended to open the campaign about May 1st, by moving Schofield on Dalton from Cleveland, Thomas on the same objective from Chattanooga, and McPherson on Rome and Kingston from Gunter's Landing.[33] My intention was merely to threaten Dalton in front, and to direct McPherson to act vigorously against the railroad below Resaca, far to the rear of the enemy. But by reason of his being short of his estimated strength by the four divisions before referred to, and thus being reduced to about twenty-four thousand men, I did not feel justified in placing him so far away from the support of the main body of the army, and therefore subsequently changed the plan of campaign, so far as to bring that army up to Chattanooga, and to direct it thence through Ship's Gap[34] against the rail-

[30] Mortimer D. Leggett (1821–1896) commanded the 3rd Div., 17th Corps, Army of the Tennessee in 1864. *CWHC,* 346.

[31] Big Shanty, modern-day Kennesaw, GA, began as a railroad town in 1830, and was the site of Camp McDonald, the training ground for the Georgia Militia. Joe Bozeman, Robert Jones, and Sallie Loy, *Images of America: Kennesaw* (Charleston, SC: Arcadia, 2006), 7–9.

[32] For WTS's full letter to Rawlins, see *OR,* I, 32(III), 247–249.

[33] Gunter's Landing was the original name of modern-day Guntersville, AL. Thomas M. Owen and Marie B. Owen, *History of Alabama and Dictionary of Alabama Biography* (Chicago: S. J. Clarke, 1921), vol. 1, s.v. "Guntersville."

[34] Ship's Gap was located near Lafayette, GA, approximately twenty miles northwest of Resaca, GA. Hiram S. Williams, *This War So Horrible: The Civil War Diary of Hiram Smith*

road to Johnston's rear, at or near Resaca, distant from Dalton only eighteen miles, and in full communication with the other armies by roads behind Rockyface Ridge, of about the same length.

On the 10th of April I received General Grant's letter of April 4th from Washington, which formed the basis of all the campaigns of the year 1864, and subsequently received another of April 19th, written from Culpepper, Virginia, both of which are now in my possession, in his own handwriting, and are here given entire. These letters embrace substantially all the orders he ever made on this particular subject, and these, it will be seen, devolved on me the details both as to the plan and execution of the campaign by the armies under my immediate command. These armies were to be directed against the rebel army commanded by General Joseph E. Johnston, then lying on the defensive, strongly intrenched at Dalton, Georgia; and I was required to follow it up closely and persistently, so that in no event could any part be detached to assist General Lee in Virginia; General Grant undertaking in like manner to keep Lee so busy that he could not respond to any calls of help by Johnston. Neither Atlanta, nor Augusta, nor Savannah, was the objective, but the "army of Jos. Johnston," go where it might.

[PRIVATE AND CONFIDENTIAL.]

HEADQUARTERS ARMIES OF THE UNITED STATES,
WASHINGTON, D. C., *April* 4, 1864.

Major-General W. T. SHERMAN, *commanding Military Division of the Mississippi.*

GENERAL: It is my design, if the enemy keep quiet and allow me to take the initiative in the spring campaign, to work all parts of the army together, and somewhat toward a common centre. For your information I now write you my programme, as at present determined upon.

I have sent orders to Banks, by private messenger, to finish up his present expedition against Shreveport with all dispatch; to turn over the defense of Red River to General Steele and the navy, and to return your troops to you, and his own to New Orleans; to abandon all of Texas, except the Rio Grande, and to hold that with not to exceed four thousand men; to reduce the number of troops on the Mississippi to

---

Williams, ed. Lewis N. Wynne and Robert A. Taylor (Tuscaloosa: University of Alabama Press, 1993), 22 (map).

the lowest number necessary to hold it, and to collect from his command not less than twenty-five thousand men. To this I will add five thousand from Missouri. With this force he is to commence operations against Mobile as soon as he can. It will be impossible for him to commence too early.

Gillmore joins Butler with ten thousand men, and the two operate against Richmond from the south side of James River. This will give Butler thirty-three thousand men to operate with, W. F. Smith commanding the right wing of his forces, and Gillmore the left wing. I will stay with the Army of the Potomac, increased by Burnside's corps of not less than twenty-five thousand effective men, and operate directly against Lee's army, wherever it may be found.

Sigel collects all his available force in two columns, one, under Ord and Averill, to start from Beverly, Virginia, and the other, under Crook, to start from Charleston, on the Kanawha, to move against the Virginia & Tennessee Railroad.

Crook will have all cavalry, and will endeavor to get in about Saltville, and move east from there to join Ord. His force will be all cavalry, while Ord will have from ten to twelve thousand men of all arms.

You I propose to move against Johnston's army, to break it up, and to get into the interior of the enemy's country as far as you can, inflicting all the damage you can against their war resources.

I do not propose to lay down for you a plan of campaign, but simply to lay down the work it is desirable to have done, and leave you free to execute it in your own way. Submit to me, however, as early as you can, your plan of operations.

As stated, Banks is ordered to commence operations as soon as he can. Gillmore is ordered to report at Fortress Monroe by the 18th inst., or as soon thereafter as practicable. Sigel is concentrating now. None will move from their places of rendezvous until I direct, except Banks. I want to be ready to move by the 25th inst., if possible; but all I can now direct is that you get ready as soon as possible. I know you will have difficulties to encounter in getting through the mountains to where supplies are abundant, but I believe you will accomplish it.

From the expedition from the Department of West Virginia I do not calculate on very great results; but it is the only way I can take troops from there. With the long line of railroad Sigel has to protect, he can spare no troops, except to move directly to his front. In this way he must get through to inflict great damage on the enemy, or the enemy must detach from one of his armies a large force to prevent it. In other words, if Sigel can't skin himself, he can hold a leg while some one else skins.

I am, general, very respectfully, your obedient servant,

U. S. Grant, *Lieutenant-General.*

Headquarters Military Division of the Mississippi,
Nashville, Tennessee, *April* 10, 1864.

Lieutenant-General U. S. Grant, *Commander-in-Chief, Washington, D. C.*

Dear General: Your two letters of April 4th are now before me, and afford me infinite satisfaction. That we are now all to act on a common plan, converging on a common centre, looks like enlightened war.

Like yourself, you take the biggest load, and from me you shall have thorough and hearty coöperation. I will not let side issues draw me off from your main plans in which I am to knock Jos. Johnston, and to do as much damage to the resources of the enemy as possible. I have heretofore written to General Rawlins and to Colonel Comstock (of your staff) somewhat of the method in which I propose to act. I have seen all my army, corps, and division commanders, and have signified only to the former, viz., Schofield, Thomas, and McPherson, our general plans, which I inferred from the purport of our conversation here and at Cincinnati.

First, I am pushing stores to the front with all possible dispatch, and am completing the army organization according to the orders from Washington, which are ample and perfectly satisfactory.

It will take us all of April to get in our furloughed veterans, to bring up A. J. Smith's command, and to collect provisions and cattle on the line of the Tennessee. Each of the armies will guard, by detachments of its own, its rear communications.

At the signal to be given by you, Schofield, leaving a select garrison at Knoxville and Loudon, with twelve thousand men will drop down to the Hiawassee, and march against Johnston's right by the old Federal road. Stoneman, now in Kentucky, organizing the cavalry forces of the Army of the Ohio, will operate with Schofield on his left front—it may be, pushing a select body of about two thousand cavalry by Ducktown or Elijah toward Athens, Georgia.

Thomas will aim to have forty-five thousand men of all arms, and move straight against Johnston, wherever he may be, fighting him cautiously, persistently, and to the best advantage. He will have two divisions of cavalry, to take advantage of any offering.

McPherson will have nine divisions of the Army of the Tennessee, if A. J. Smith gets here, in which case he will have full thirty thousand of the best men in America. He will cross the Tennessee at Decatur and Whitesburg, march toward Rome, and feel for Thomas. If Johnston falls behind the Coosa, then McPherson will push for Rome; and if Johnston falls behind the Chattahoochee, as I believe he will, then McPherson will cross over and join Thomas.

McPherson has no cavalry, but I have taken one of Thomas's divisions, viz., Garrard's, six thousand strong, which is now at Columbia, mounting, equipping, and preparing. I design this division to operate on McPherson's right, rear, or front, according as the enemy appears. But the moment I detect Johnston falling behind the Chattahoochee, I propose to cast off the effective part of this cavalry division, after crossing the Coosa, straight for Opelika, West Point, Columbus, or Wetumpka, to break up the road between Montgomery and Georgia. If Garrard can do this work well, he can return to the Union army; but should a superior force interpose, then he will seek safety at Pensacola and join Banks, or, after rest, will act against any force that he can find east of Mobile, till such time as he can reach me.

Should Johnston fall behind the Chattahoochee, I will feign to the right, but pass to the left and act against Atlanta or its eastern communications, according to developed facts.

This is about as far ahead as I feel disposed to look, but I will ever bear in mind that Johnston is at all times to be kept so busy that he cannot in any event send any part of his command against you or Banks.

If Banks can at the same time carry Mobile and open up the Alabama River, he will in a measure solve the most difficult part of my problem, viz., "provisions." But in that I must venture. Georgia has a million of inhabitants. If they can live, we should not starve. If the enemy interrupt our communications, I will be absolved from all obligations to subsist on our own resources, and will feel perfectly justified in taking whatever and wherever we can find.

I will inspire my command, if successful, with the feeling that beef and salt are all that is absolutely necessary to life, and that parched corn once fed General Jackson's army on that very ground.

As ever, your friend and servant,

W. T. SHERMAN, *Major-General.*

HEADQUARTERS ARMIES IN THE FIELD,
CULPEPPER COURT-HOUSE, VIRGINIA, *April* 19, 1864.

Major-General W. T. SHERMAN, *commanding Military Division of the Mississippi.*

GENERAL: Since my letter to you of April 4th I have seen no reason to change any portion of the general plan of campaign, if the enemy remain still and allow us to take the initiative. Rain has continued so uninterruptedly until the last day or two that it will be impossible to move, however, before the 27th, even if no more should fall in the mean time. I think Saturday, the 30th, will probably be the day for our general move.

Colonel Comstock, who will take this, can spend a day with you, and fill up many little gaps of information not given in any of my letters.

What I now want more particularly to say is, that if the two main attacks, yours and the one from here, should promise great success, the enemy may, in a fit of desperation, abandon one part of their line of defense, and throw their whole strength upon the other, believing a single defeat without any victory to sustain them better than a defeat all along their line, and hoping too, at the same time, that the army, meeting with no resistance, will rest perfectly satisfied with their laurels, having penetrated to a given point south, thereby enabling them to throw their force first upon one and then on the other.

With the majority of military commanders they might do this.

But you have had too much experience in traveling light, and subsisting upon the country, to be caught by any such *ruse.* I hope my experience has not been thrown away. My directions, then, would be, if the enemy in your front show signs of joining Lee, follow him up to the full extent of your ability. I will prevent the concentration of Lee upon your front, if it is in the power of this army to do it.

The Army of the Potomac looks well, and, so far as I can judge, officers and men feel well.

Yours truly,

U. S. Grant, *Lieutenant-General.*

Headquarters Military Division of the Mississippi,
Nashville, Tennessee, *April* 24, 1864.

Lieutenant-General Grant, *commanding Armies of the United States, Culpepper, Virginia.*

General: I now have, at the hands of Colonel Comstock, of your staff, the letter of April 19th, and am as far prepared to assume the offensive as possible. I only ask as much time as you think proper, to enable me to get up McPherson's two divisions from Cairo. Their furloughs will expire about this time, and some of them should now be in motion for Clifton, whence they will march to Decatur, to join General Dodge.

McPherson is ordered to assemble the Fifteenth Corps near Larkin's, and to get the Sixteenth and Seventeenth Corps (Dodge and Blair) at Decatur at the earliest possible moment. From these two points he will direct his forces on Lebanon, Summerville, and Lafayette, where he will act against Johnston, if he accept battle at Dalton; or move in the direction of Rome, if the enemy give up Dalton, and fall behind the Oostenaula or Etowah. I see that there is some risk in dividing our forces, but Thomas and Schofield will have strength enough to cover all the valleys as far as Dalton; and, should Johnston turn his whole force against McPherson, the latter will have his bridge at Larkin's, and the route to Chattanooga *via* Wills's Valley and the Chattanooga Creek, open for retreat; and if Johnston attempt to leave Dalton, Thomas will have force enough to push on through Dalton to Kingston, which will checkmate him. My own opinion is that Johnston will be compelled to hang to his railroad, the only possible avenue of supply to his army, estimated at from forty-five to sixty thousand men.

At Lafayette all our armies will be together, and if Johnston stands at Dalton we must attack him in position. Thomas feels certain that he has no material increase of force, and that he has not sent away Hardee, or any part of his army. Supplies are the great question. I have materially increased the number of cars daily. When I got here, the average was from sixty-five to eighty per day. Yesterday the report was one hundred and ninety-three; to-day, one hundred and thirty-four;

and my estimate is that one hundred and forty-five cars per day will give us a day's supply and a day's accumulation.

McPherson is ordered to carry in wagons twenty day's rations, and to rely on the depot at Ringgold for the renewal of his bread. Beeves are now being driven on the hoof to the front; and the commissary, Colonel Beckwith, seems fully alive to the importance of the whole matter.

Our weakest point will be from the direction of Decatur, and I will be forced to risk something from that quarter, depending on the fact that the enemy has no force available with which to threaten our communications from that direction.

Colonel Comstock will explain to you personally much that I cannot commit to paper. I am, with great respect,

W. T. SHERMAN, *Major-General.*

On the 28th of April I removed my headquarters to Chattanooga, and prepared for taking the field in person. General Grant had first indicated the 30th of April as the day for the simultaneous advance, but subsequently changed the day to May 5th. McPherson's troops were brought forward rapidly to Chattanooga, partly by rail and partly by marching. Thomas's troops were already in position (his advance being out as far as Ringgold—eighteen miles), and Schofield was marching down by Cleveland to Red Clay and Catoosa Springs. On the 4th of May, Thomas was in person at Ringgold, his left at Catoosa, and his right at Leet's Tan-yard. Schofield was at Red Clay, closing upon Thomas's left; and McPherson was moving rapidly into Chattanooga, and out toward Gordon's Mill.

On the 5th I rode out to Ringgold, and on the very day appointed by General Grant from his headquarters in Virginia the great campaign was begun. To give all the minute details will involve more than is contemplated, and I will endeavor only to trace the principal events, or rather to record such as weighed heaviest on my own mind at the time, and which now remain best fixed in my memory.

My general headquarters and official records remained back at Nashville, and I had near me only my personal staff and inspectors-general, with about half a dozen wagons, and a single company of Ohio sharp-shooters (commanded by Lieutenant McCrory)[35] as headquarters or camp guard. I also had a small com-

[35] William McCrory (1839–1893) enlisted in the 7th Independent Co. of Ohio Sharpshooters in Nov. 1862. His company served as WTS's headquarters guards during the Atlanta Campaign until the close of the war. "To Col. M'Crory," *Star Tribune* (Minneapolis), Feb. 23, 1893, 8.

pany of irregular Alabama cavalry (commanded by Lieutenant Snelling),[36] used mostly as orderlies and couriers. No wall-tents were allowed, only the flies. Our mess establishment was less in bulk than that of any of the brigade commanders; nor was this from an indifference to the ordinary comforts of life, but because I wanted to set the example, and gradually to convert all parts of that army into a mobile machine, willing and able to start at a minute's notice, and to subsist on the scantiest food. To reap absolute success might involve the necessity even of dropping all wagons, and to subsist on the chance food which the country was known to contain. I had obtained not only the United States census-tables of 1860, but a compilation made by the Controller of the State of Georgia for the purpose of taxation, containing in considerable detail the "population and statistics" of every county in Georgia. One of my aides (Captain Dayton) acted as assistant adjutant-general, with an order-book, letter-book, and writing-paper, that filled a small chest not much larger than an ordinary candle-box. The only reports and returns called for were the ordinary tri-monthly returns of "effective strength." As these accumulated they were sent back to Nashville, and afterward were embraced in the archives of the Military Division of the Mississippi, changed in 1865 to the Military Division of the Missouri, and I suppose they were burned in the Chicago fire of 1870. Still, duplicates remain of all essential papers in the archives of the War Department.

The 6th of May was given to Schofield and McPherson to get into position, and on the 7th General Thomas moved in force against Tunnel Hill, driving off a mere picket-guard of the enemy, and I was agreeably surprised to find that no damage had been done to the tunnel or the railroad. From Tunnel Hill I could look into the gorge by which the railroad passed through a straight and well-defined range of mountains, presenting sharp palisade faces, and known as "Rocky Face." The gorge itself was called the "Buzzard Roost." We could plainly see the enemy in this gorge and behind it, and Mill Creek which formed the gorge, flowing toward Dalton, had been dammed up, making a sort of irregular lake, filling the road, thereby obstructing it, and the enemy's batteries crowned the cliffs on either side. The position was very strong, and I knew that such a general as was my antagonist (Jos. Johnston), who had been there six months, had fortified it to the maximum. Therefore I had no intention to attack the position seriously in front, but depended on McPherson to capture and hold the railroad to its rear, which

[36] David R. Snelling (1836–1901) deserted from the Confederate Army to join the U.S. Army in early 1863. James C. Bonner, "David R. Snelling: A Story of Desertion and Defection in the Civil War," *North Carolina Historical Review* 41, no. 2 (Apr. 1964):275; *OR,* I, 23(I), 63.

would force Johnston to detach largely against him, or rather, as I expected, to evacuate his position at Dalton altogether. My orders to Generals Thomas and Schofield were merely to press strongly at all points in front, ready to rush in on the first appearance of "let go," and, if possible, to catch our enemy in the confusion of retreat.

All the movements of the 7th and 8th were made exactly as ordered, and the enemy seemed quiescent, acting purely on the defensive.

I had constant communication with all parts of the army, and on the 9th McPherson's head of column entered and passed through Snake Creek, perfectly undefended, and accomplished a complete surprise to the enemy. At its farther *débouché* he met a cavalry brigade, easily driven, which retreated hastily north toward Dalton, and doubtless carried to Johnston the first serious intimation that a heavy force of infantry and artillery was to his rear and within a few miles of his railroad. I got a short note from McPherson that day (written at 2 P. M., when he was within a mile and a half of the railroad, above and near Resaca), and we all felt jubilant. I renewed orders to Thomas and Schofield to be ready for the instant pursuit of what I expected to be a broken and disordered army, forced to retreat by roads to the east of Resaca, which were known to be very rough and impracticable.

That night I received further notice from McPherson that he had found Resaca too strong for a surprise; that in consequence he had fallen back three miles to the mouth of Snake-Creek Gap, and was there fortified. I wrote him the next day the following letters, copies of which are in my letter-book; but his to me were mere notes in pencil, not retained:[37]

HEADQUARTERS MILITARY DIVISION OF THE MISSISSIPPI,
IN THE FIELD, TUNNEL HILL, GEORGIA, *May* 11, 1864—*Morning.*

Major-General MCPHERSON, *commanding army of the Tennessee, Sugar Valley, Georgia.*

GENERAL: I received by courier (in the night) yours of 5 and 6.30 P. M. of yesterday.

You now have your twenty-three thousand men, and General Hooker is in close support, so that you can hold all of Jos. Johnston's army in check should he abandon Dalton. He cannot afford to abandon Dalton, for he has fixed it up on purpose to receive us, and he observes that we are close at hand, waiting for him to quit. He

[37] For McPherson's letter to WTS on the morning of May 11, 1864, see *OR,* I, 38(IV), 138–139.

cannot afford a detachment strong enough to fight you, as his army will not admit of it.

Strengthen your position; fight any thing that comes; and threaten the safety of the railroad all the time. But, to tell the truth, I would rather the enemy would stay in Dalton two more days, when he may find in his rear a larger party than he expects in an open field. At all events, we can then choose our own ground, and he will be forced to move out of his works. I do not intend to put a column into Buzzard-Roost Gap at present.

See that you are in easy communication with me and with all headquarters. After to-day the supplies will be at Ringgold. Yours,

W. T. SHERMAN, *Major-General commanding.*

HEADQUARTERS MILITARY DIVISION OF THE MISSISSIPPI,
IN THE FIELD, TUNNEL HILL, GEORGIA, *May* 11, 1864—*Evening.*

General MCPHERSON, *Sugar Valley.*

GENERAL: The indications are that Johnston is evacuating Dalton. In that event, Howard's corps and the cavalry will pursue; all the rest will follow your route. I will be down early in the morning.

Try to strike him if possible about the forks of the road.

Hooker must be with you now, and you may send General Garrard by Summerville to threaten Rome and that flank. I will cause all the lines to be felt at once.

W. T. SHERMAN, *Major-General commanding.*

McPherson had startled Johnston in his fancied security, but had not done the full measure of his work. He had in hand twenty-three thousand of the best men of the army, and could have walked into Resaca (then held only by a small brigade), or he could have placed his whole force astride the railroad above Resaca, and there have easily withstood the attack of all of Johnston's army, with the knowledge that Thomas and Schofield were on his heels. Had he done so, I am certain that Johnston would not have ventured to attack him in position, but would have retreated eastward by Spring Place, and we should have captured half his army and all his artillery and wagons at the very beginning of the campaign.

Such an opportunity does not occur twice in a single life, but at the critical moment McPherson seems to have been a little cautious.[38] Still, he was perfectly justified by his orders, and fell back and assumed an unassailable defen-

[38] In the first edition of his memoirs (1875), WTS used the word "timid" instead of "cautious."

sive position in Sugar Valley, on the Resaca side of Snake-Creek Gap. As soon as informed of this, I determined to pass the whole army through Snake-Creek Gap, and to move on Resaca with the main army.

But during the 10th, the enemy showed no signs of evacuating Dalton, and I was waiting for the arrival of Garrard's and Stoneman's cavalry, known to be near at hand, so as to secure the full advantages of victory, of which I felt certain. Hooker's Twentieth Corps was at once moved down to within easy supporting distance of McPherson; and on the 11th, perceiving signs of evacuation of Dalton, I gave all the orders for the general movement, leaving the Fourth Corps (Howard) and Stoneman's cavalry in observation in front of Buzzard-Roost Gap, and directing all the rest of the army to march through Snake-Creek Gap, straight on Resaca. The roads were only such as the country afforded, mere rough wagon-ways, and these converged to the single narrow track through Snake-Creek Gap; but during the 12th and 13th the bulk of Thomas's and Schofield's armies were got through, and deployed against Resaca, McPherson on the right, Thomas in the centre, and Schofield on the left. Johnston, as I anticipated, had abandoned all his well-prepared defenses at Dalton, and was found inside of Resaca with the bulk of his army, holding his divisions well in hand, acting purely on the defensive, and fighting well at all points of conflict. A complete line of intrenchments was found covering the place, and this was strongly manned at all points. On the 14th we closed in, enveloping the town on its north and west, and during the 15th we had a day of continual battle and skirmish. At the same time I caused two pontoon-bridges to be laid across the Oostenaula River at Lay's Ferry, about three miles below the town, by which we could threaten Calhoun, a station on the railroad seven miles below Resaca. At the same time, May 14th, I dispatched General Garrard, with his cavalry division, down the Oostenaula by the Rome road, with orders to cross over, if possible, and to attack or threaten the railroad at any point below Calhoun and above Kingston.

During the 15th, without attempting to assault the fortified works, we pressed at all points, and the sound of cannon and musketry rose all day to the dignity of a battle. Toward evening McPherson moved his whole line of battle forward, till he had gained a ridge overlooking the town, from which his field-artillery could reach the railroad-bridge across the Oostenaula. The enemy made several attempts to drive him away, repeating the sallies several times, and extending them into the night; but in every instance he was repulsed with bloody loss.

Hooker's corps had also some heavy and handsome fighting that afternoon and night on the left, where the Dalton road entered the intrenchments, capturing a four-gun intrenched battery, with its men and guns; and generally all our men showed the finest fighting qualities.

Howard's corps had followed Johnston down from Dalton, and was in line; Stoneman's division of cavalry had also got up, and was on the extreme left, beyond the Oostenaula.

On the night of May 15th Johnston got his army across the bridges, set them on fire, and we entered Resaca at daylight. Our loss up to that time was about six hundred dead and thirty-three hundred and seventy-five wounded—mostly light wounds that did not necessitate sending the men to the rear for treatment.[39] That Johnston had deliberately designed in advance to give up such strong positions as Dalton and Resaca, for the purpose of drawing us farther south, is simply absurd. Had he remained in Dalton another hour, it would have been his total defeat, and he only evacuated Resaca because his safety demanded it.[40] The movement by us through Snake-Creek Gap was a total surprise to him. My army about doubled his in size, but he had all the advantages of natural positions, of artificial forts and roads, and of concentrated action. We were compelled to grope our way through forests, across mountains, with a large army, necessarily more or less dispersed. Of course, I was disappointed not to have crippled his army more at that particular stage of the game; but, as it resulted, these rapid successes gave us the initiative, and the usual impulse of a conquering army.

Johnston having retreated in the night of May 15th, immediate pursuit was begun. A division of infantry (Jeff. C. Davis's) was at once dispatched down the valley toward Rome, to support Garrard's cavalry, and the whole army was ordered to pursue, McPherson by Lay's Ferry, on the right, Thomas directly by

[39] In a letter to his wife, dated May 20, 1864, WTS stated, "We have a thousand prisoners, have killed and wounded 5,000 and have ourselves lost less than 4,000. We have had no time to count noses." William T. Sherman, *Sherman's Civil War: Selected Correspondence of William T. Sherman, 1860–1865*, ed. Brooks D. Simpson and Jean V. Berlin (Chapel Hill: University of North Carolina Press, 2014), 636.

[40] In his post-battle report, Johnston provided his reasoning for abandoning Dalton and Resaca: "The fact that a part of Polk's troops were still in the rear, and the great numerical superiority of the Federal army, made it expedient to risk battle only when position or some blunder on the part of the enemy might give us counterbalancing advantages. I, therefore, determined to fall back slowly until circumstances should put the chances of battle in our favor, keeping so near the U.S. army as to prevent its sending re-enforcements to Grant, and hoping, by taking advantage of positions and opportunities, to reduce the odds against us by partial engagements." *OR*, I, 38(III), 615.

the railroad, and Schofield by the left, by the old road that crossed the Oostenaula above Echota or Newtown. We hastily repaired the railroad-bridge at Resaca, which had been partially burned, and built a temporary floating-bridge out of timber and materials found on the spot; so that Thomas got his advance corps over during the 16th, and marched as far as Calhoun, where he came into communication with McPherson's troops, which had crossed the Oostenaula at Lay's Ferry by our pontoon-bridges, previously laid. Inasmuch as the bridge at Resaca was overtaxed, Hooker's Twentieth Corps was also diverted to cross by the fords and ferries above Resaca, in the neighborhood of Echota.[41]

On the 17th, toward evening, the head of Thomas's column, Newton's division,[42] encountered the rear-guard of Johnston's army near Adairsville. I was near the head of column at the time, trying to get a view of the position of the enemy from an elevation in an open field. My party attracted the fire of a battery; a shell passed through the group of staff-officers and burst just beyond, which scattered us promptly. The next morning the enemy had disappeared, and our pursuit was continued to Kingston, which we reached during Sunday forenoon, the 19th.

From Resaca the railroad runs nearly due south, but at Kingston it makes junction with another railroad from Rome, and changes direction due east. At that time McPherson's head of column was about four miles to the west of Kingston, at a country place called "Woodlawn;" Schofield and Hooker were on the direct roads leading from Newtown to Cassville, diagonal to the route followed by Thomas. Thomas's head of column, which had followed the country roads alongside of the railroad, was about four miles east of Kingston, toward Cassville, when about noon I got a message from him that he had found the enemy, drawn up in line of battle, on some extensive, open ground, about half-way between Kingston and Cassville, and that appearances indicated a willingness and preparation for battle.

Hurriedly sending orders to McPherson to resume the march, to hasten forward by roads leading to the south of Kingston, so as to leave for Thomas's troops and trains the use of the main road, and to come up on his right, I rode forward rapidly, over some rough gravel hills, and about six miles from Kingston found General Thomas, with his troops deployed; but he reported that the enemy had fallen back in echelon of divisions, steadily and in superb

[41] For Gen. Grenville Dodge's account of the Battle of Resaca, see the section "General G. M. Dodge's account of the part taken by the Sixteenth Army Corps in the movement on Resaca. Attack of the 4th of July, and battle of Atlanta, July 22, 1864" in Appendix to Volume II.

[42] John Newton (1822–1895) graduated from the USMA in 1842 and commanded the 2nd Div., 4th Corps, Army of the Cumberland, in May 1864. *CWHC,* 405–406.

order, into Cassville. I knew that the roads by which Generals Hooker and Schofield were approaching would lead them to a seminary near Cassville,[43] and that it was all-important to secure the point of junction of these roads with the main road along which we were marching. Therefore I ordered General Thomas to push forward his deployed lines as rapidly as possible; and, as night was approaching, I ordered two field-batteries to close up at a gallop on some woods which lay between us and the town of Cassville. We could not see the town by reason of these woods, but a high range of hills just back of the town was visible over the tree-tops. On these hills could be seen fresh-made parapets, and the movements of men, against whom I directed the artillery to fire at long range. The stout resistance made by the enemy along our whole front of a couple of miles indicated a purpose to fight at Cassville; and, as the night was closing in, General Thomas and I were together, along with our skirmish-lines near the seminary, on the edge of the town, where musket-bullets from the enemy were cutting the leaves of the trees pretty thickly about us. Either Thomas or I remarked that that was not the place for the two senior officers of a great army, and we personally went back to the battery, where we passed the night on the ground. During the night I had reports from McPherson, Hooker, and Schofield. The former was about five miles to my right rear, near the "nitre-caves;" Schofield was about six miles north, and Hooker between us, within two miles. All were ordered to close down on Cassville at daylight, and to attack the enemy wherever found. Skirmishing was kept up all night, but when day broke the next morning, May 20th, the enemy was gone, and our cavalry was sent in pursuit. These reported him beyond the Etowah River. We were then well in advance of our railroad-trains, on which we depended for supplies; so I determined to pause a few days to repair the railroad, which had been damaged but little, except at the bridge at Resaca, and then to go on.

Nearly all the people of the country seemed to have fled with Johnston's army; yet some few families remained, and from one of them I procured the copy of an order which Johnston had made at Adairsville, in which he recited that he had retreated as far as strategy required, and that his army must be prepared for battle at Cassville.[44] The newspapers of the South, many of

[43] WTS was most likely referring to Cherokee Baptist College. Charles E. Jones, *Education in Georgia* (Washington, DC: GPO, 1889), 71*n*.

[44] On May 19, 1864, Johnston issued a General Order from Cassville: "By your courage and skill you have repulsed every assault of the enemy. By marches by day and by marches by night you have defeated every attempt upon your communications. Your communications are secured. You will now turn and march to meet his advancing columns." *OR,* I, 38(IV), 728.

which we found, were also loud in denunciation of Johnston's falling back before us without a serious battle, simply resisting by his skirmish-lines and by his rear-guard. But his friends proclaimed that it was all *strategic;* that he was deliberately drawing us farther and farther into the meshes, farther and farther away from our base of supplies, and that in due season he would not only halt for battle, but assume the bold offensive. Of course it was to my interest to bring him to battle as soon as possible, when our numerical superiority was at the greatest; for he was picking up his detachments as he fell back, whereas I was compelled to make similar and stronger detachments to repair the railroads as we advanced, and to guard them. I found at Cassville many evidences of preparation for a grand battle, among them a long line of fresh intrenchments on the hill beyond the town, extending nearly three miles to the south, embracing the railroad-crossing. I was also convinced that the whole of Polk's corps had joined Johnston from Mississippi, and that he had in hand three full corps, viz., Hood's, Polk's, and Hardee's, numbering about sixty thousand men, and could not then imagine why he had declined battle, and did not learn the real reason till after the war was over, and then from General Johnston himself.

In the autumn of 1865, when in command of the Military Division of the Missouri, I went from St. Louis to Little Rock, Arkansas, and afterward to Memphis. Taking a steamer for Cairo, I found as fellow-passengers Generals Johnston and Frank Blair. We were, of course, on the most friendly terms, and on our way up we talked over our battles again, played cards, and questioned each other as to particular parts of our mutual conduct in the game of war. I told Johnston that I had seen his order of preparation, in the nature of an address to his army, announcing his purpose to retreat no more, but to accept battle at Cassville. He answered that such was his purpose; that he had left Hardee's corps in the open fields to check Thomas, and gain time for his formation on the ridge, just behind Cassville; and it was this corps which General Thomas had seen deployed, and whose handsome movement in retreat he had reported in such complimentary terms. Johnston described how he had placed Hood's corps on the right, Polk's in the centre, and Hardee's on the left. He said he had ridden over the ground, given to each corps commander his position, and orders to throw up parapets during the night; that he was with Hardee on his extreme left as the night closed in, and as Hardee's troops fell back to the position assigned them for the intended battle of the next day; and that, after giving Hardee some general instructions, he and his staff rode back to Cassville. As he entered the town, or village, he met Generals Hood and Polk. Hood inquired of him if he had had any thing to eat, and he said no, that he was both hungry and tired, when Hood invited him to go and share a supper which had been prepared for him at a house close by. At the supper they discussed the chances of the impending battle, when Hood spoke of the ground assigned him as being enfiladed by our (Union) artillery, which Johnston disputed, when General Polk chimed in with the remark that General Hood was right; that the cannon-shots fired by us at nightfall had enfiladed their general line of battle, and that for this reason he feared they could not hold their men. General Johnston was surprised at this, for he understood General Hood to be one of those who professed to criticise his strategy, contending that, instead of retreating, he should have risked a battle. General Johnston said he was provoked, accused them of having been in conference, with being beaten before battle, and added that he was unwilling to engage in a critical battle with an army so superior to his own in numbers, with two of his three corps commanders dissatisfied with the ground and positions assigned them. He then and there made up his mind to retreat still farther south, to put the Etowah River and the Allatoona range between us; and he at once gave orders to resume the retrograde movement.

This was my recollection of the substance of the conversation, of which I made no note at the time; but, at a meeting of the Society of the Army of the Cumberland some years after, at Cleveland, Ohio, about 1868, in a short after-dinner speech, I related this conversation, and it got into print.[45] Subsequently, in the spring of 1870, when I was at New Orleans, *en route* for Texas, General Hood called to see me at the St. Charles Hotel, explained that he had seen my speech reprinted in the newspapers and gave me his version of the same event, describing the halt at Cassville, the general orders for battle on that ground, and the meeting at supper with Generals Johnston and Polk, when the chances of the battle to be fought the next day were freely and fully discussed; and he stated that he had argued against fighting the battle purely on the defensive, but had asked General Johnston to permit him with his own corps and part of Polk's to quit their lines, and to march rapidly to attack and overwhelm Schofield, who was known to be separated from Thomas by an interval of nearly five miles, claiming that he could have defeated Schofield, and got back to his position in time to meet General Thomas's attack in front. He also stated that he had then contended with Johnston for the "offensive-defensive" game, instead of the "pure defensive," as proposed by General John-

[45] WTS delivered his speech at the fourth reunion of the Society of the Army of the Cumberland in late Nov. 1870. For a full copy of the speech, see "General Sherman: His Speech at the Gathering of the Army of the Cumberland, What He Intended to Do with Johnston's Army," *Carlisle Weekly Herald* (Carlisle, PA), Dec. 1, 1870, 2.

ston; and he said that it was at this time that General Johnston had taken offense, and that it was for this reason he had ordered the retreat that night. As subsequent events estranged these two officers, it is very natural they should now differ on this point;[46] but it was sufficient for us that the rebel army did retreat that night, leaving us masters of all the country above the Etowah River.

For the purposes of rest, to give time for the repair of the railroads, and to replenish supplies, we lay by some few days in that quarter—Schofield with Stoneman's cavalry holding the ground at Cassville Depot, Cartersville, and the Etowah Bridge; Thomas holding his ground near Cassville, and McPherson that near Kingston. The officer intrusted with the repair of the railroads was Colonel W. W. Wright, a railroad-engineer,[47] who, with about two thousand men, was so industrious and skillful that the bridge at Resaca was rebuilt in three days, and cars loaded with stores came forward to Kingston on the 24th. The telegraph also brought us the news of the bloody and desperate battles of the Wilderness, in Virginia, and that General Grant was pushing his operations against Lee with terrific energy. I was therefore resolved to give my enemy no rest.

In early days (1844), when a lieutenant of the Third Artillery, I had been sent from Charleston, South Carolina, to Marietta, Georgia, to assist Inspector-General Churchill to take testimony concerning certain losses of horses and accoutrements by the Georgia Volunteers during the Florida War; and after completing the work at Marietta we transferred our party over to Bellefonte, Alabama. I had ridden the distance on horseback, and had noted well the topography of the country, especially that about Kenesaw, Allatoona, and the Etowah River. On that occasion I had stopped some days with a Colonel Tumlin, to see some remarkable Indian mounds on the Etowah River, usually called the "Hightower." I therefore knew that the Allatoona Pass was very strong, would be hard to force, and resolved not even to attempt it, but to turn the position, by moving from Kingston to Marietta *via* Dallas; accordingly I made orders on the 20th to get ready for the march to begin on the 23d. The Army of the Cumberland was ordered to march for Dallas, by Euharlee and Stilesboro'; Davis's division, then in Rome, by Van Wert; the Army of the Ohio to keep on the left of Thomas, by a place called

[46] After the war, Johnston and Hood publicly blamed each other for the failures of the Confederate Army during the Atlanta Campaign. John B. Hood, *The Lost Papers of Confederate General John Bell Hood,* ed. Stephen M. Hood (El Dorado Hills, CA: Savas Beatie, 2015), 126–127.

[47] William W. Wright (1824–1882) became the principal assistant engineer of the Pennsylvania Railroad's Western Div. in 1854, and he served in the U.S. Army's engineer corps during the Civil War. "A Debauch Ended by Death," *St. Joseph Herald* (St. Joseph, MO), Mar. 15, 1882, 2.

Burnt Hickory;[48] and the Army of the Tennessee to march for a position a little to the south, so as to be on the right of the general army, when grouped about Dallas.

The movement contemplated leaving our railroad, and to depend for twenty days on the contents of our wagons; and as the country was very obscure, mostly in a state of nature, densely wooded, and with few roads, our movements were necessarily slow. We crossed the Etowah by several bridges and fords, and took as many roads as possible, keeping up communication by cross-roads, or by couriers through the woods. I personally joined General Thomas, who had the centre, and was consequently the main column, or "column of direction." The several columns followed generally the valley of the Euharlee, a tributary coming into the Etowah from the south, and gradually crossed over a ridge of mountains, parts of which had once been worked over for gold, and were consequently full of paths and unused wagon-roads or tracks. A cavalry picket of the enemy at Burnt Hickory was captured, and had on his person an order from General Johnston, dated at Allatoona, which showed that he had detected my purpose of turning his position,[49] and it accordingly became necessary to use great caution, lest some of the minor columns should fall into ambush, but, luckily the enemy was not much more familiar with that part of the country than we were. On the other side of the Allatoona range, the Pumpkin-Vine Creek, also a tributary of the Etowah, flowed north and west; Dallas, the point aimed at, was a small town on the other or east side of this creek, and was the point of concentration of a great many roads that led in every direction. Its possession would be a threat to Marietta and Atlanta, but I could not then venture to attempt either, till I had regained the use of the railroad, at least as far down as its *débouché* from the Allatoona range of mountains. Therefore, the movement was chiefly designed to compel Johnston to give up Allatoona.

On the 25th all the columns were moving steadily on Dallas—McPherson and Davis away off to the right, near Van Wert; Thomas on the main road in the centre, with Hooker's Twentieth Corps ahead, toward Dallas; and Schofield to the left rear. For the convenience of march, Hooker had his three divisions on separate roads, all leading toward Dallas, when, in the afternoon, as he approached a bridge across Pumpkin-Vine Creek, he found it held by a

[48] Burnt Hickory, GA, was located approximately twenty miles northwest of Marietta. "The Great Battle-Field of North Georgia in 1864: On the Line of Western and Atlantic Railway," *Confederate Veteran* 5 (Jan. 1897): 286.

[49] For the relevant correspondence between Johnston and his generals on May 20–24, 1864, see *OR,* I, 38(IV), 731–742.

cavalry force, which was driven off, but the bridge was on fire. This fire was extinguished, and Hooker's leading division (Geary's)[50] followed the retreating cavalry on a road leading due east toward Marietta, instead of Dallas. This leading division, about four miles out from the bridge, struck a heavy infantry force, which was moving down from Allatoona toward Dallas, and a sharp battle ensued. I came up in person soon after, and as my map showed that we were near an important cross-road called "New Hope," from a Methodist meeting-house there of that name, I ordered General Hooker to secure it if possible that night. He asked for a short delay, till he could bring up his other two divisions, viz., of Butterfield and Williams,[51] but before these divisions had got up and were deployed, the enemy had also gained corresponding strength. The woods were so dense, and the resistance so spirited, that Hooker could not carry the position, though the battle was noisy, and prolonged far into the night. This point, "New Hope," was the accidental intersection of the road leading from Allatoona to Dallas with that from Van Wert to Marietta, was four miles northeast of Dallas, and from the bloody fighting there for the next week was called by the soldiers "Hell-Hole."

The night was pitch-dark, it rained hard, and the convergence of our columns toward Dallas produced much confusion. I am sure similar confusion existed in the army opposed to us, for we were all mixed up. I slept on the ground, without cover, alongside of a log, got little sleep, resolved at daylight to renew the battle, and to make a lodgment on the Dallas and Allatoona road if possible, but the morning revealed a strong line of intrenchments facing us, with a heavy force of infantry and guns. The battle was renewed, and without success. McPherson reached Dallas that morning, viz., the 26th, and deployed his troops to the southeast and east of the town, placing Davis's division of the Fourteenth Corps, which had joined him on the road from Rome, on his left; but this still left a gap of at least three miles between Davis and Hooker. Meantime, also, General Schofield was closing up on Thomas's left.

Satisfied that Johnston in person was at New Hope with all his army, and that it was so much nearer my "objective," the railroad, than Dallas, I concluded to draw McPherson from Dallas to Hooker's right, and gave orders

[50] In May 1864, Geary commanded the 2nd Div., 20th Corps, Army of the Cumberland. *CWHC*, 251–252.

[51] Alpheus S. Williams (1810–1878) commanded the 1st Div., 20th Corps, Army of the Cumberland, in May 1864. He later served as a U.S. congressman from Michigan from 1875 to 1878. *CWHC*, 571.

accordingly;[52] but McPherson also was confronted with a heavy force, and, as he began to withdraw according to his orders, on the morning of the 28th he was fiercely assailed on his right; a bloody battle ensued, in which he repulsed the attack, inflicting heavy loss on his assailants, and it was not until the 1st of June that he was enabled to withdraw from Dallas, and to effect a close junction with Hooker in front of New Hope. Meantime Thomas and Schofield were completing their deployments, gradually overlapping Johnston on his right, and thus extending our left nearer and nearer to the railroad, the nearest point of which was Acworth, about eight miles distant. All this time a continual battle was in progress by strong skirmish-lines, taking advantage of every species of cover, and both parties fortifying each night by rifle-trenches, with head-logs, many of which grew to be as formidable as first-class works of defense. Occasionally one party or the other would make a dash in the nature of a sally, but usually it sustained a repulse with great loss of life. I visited personally all parts of our lines nearly every day, was constantly within musket-range, and though the fire of musketry and cannon resounded day and night along the whole line, varying from six to ten miles, I rarely saw a dozen of the enemy at any one time; and these were always skirmishers dodging from tree to tree, or behind logs on the ground, or who occasionally showed their heads above the hastily-constructed but remarkably strong rifle-trenches. On the occasion of my visit to McPherson on the 30th of May, while standing with a group of officers, among whom were Generals McPherson, Logan, Barry, and Colonel Taylor, my former chief of artillery, a Minié-ball passed through Logan's coat-sleeve, scratching the skin, and struck Colonel Taylor square in the breast; luckily he had in his pocket a famous memorandum-book, in which he kept a sort of diary, about which we used to joke him a good deal; its thickness and size saved his life, breaking the force of the ball, so that after traversing the book it only penetrated the breast to the ribs, but it knocked him down and disabled him for the rest of the campaign. He was a most competent and worthy officer, and now lives in poverty in Chicago, sustained in part by his own labor, and in part by a pitiful pension recently granted.

On the 1st of June General McPherson closed in upon the right, and, without attempting further to carry the enemy's strong position at New Hope Church,[53] I held our general right in close contact with it, gradually, carefully, and steadily working by the left, until our strong infantry-lines had

[52] WTS sent his order to McPherson on May 26, 1864. See *OR,* I, 38(IV), 322.

[53] New Hope Church was located a few miles west of Marietta. Sherman, *Sherman's Civil War,* 637 (map).

reached and secured possession of all the wagon-roads between New Hope, Allatoona, and Acworth, when I dispatched Generals Garrard's and Stoneman's divisions of cavalry into Allatoona, the first around by the west end of the pass, and the latter by the direct road. Both reached their destination without opposition, and orders were at once given to repair the railroad forward from Kingston to Allatoona, embracing the bridge across the Etowah River. Thus the real object of my move on Dallas was accomplished, and on the 4th of June I was preparing to draw off from New Hope Church, and to take position on the railroad in front of Allatoona, when, General Johnston himself having evacuated his position, we effected the change without further battle, and moved to the railroad, occupying it from Allatoona and Acworth forward to Big Shanty, in sight of the famous Kenesaw Mountain.

Thus, substantially in the month of May, we had steadily driven our antagonist from the strong positions of Dalton, Resaca, Cassville, Allatoona, and Dallas; had advanced our lines in strong, compact order from Chattanooga to Big Shanty, nearly a hundred miles of as difficult country as was ever fought over by civilized armies; and thus stood prepared to go on, anxious to fight, and confident of success as soon as the railroad communications were complete to bring forward the necessary supplies. It is now impossible to state accurately our loss of life and men in any one separate battle; for the fighting was continuous, almost daily, among trees and bushes, on ground where one could rarely see a hundred yards ahead.

The aggregate loss in the several corps for the month of May is reported as follows in the usual monthly returns sent to the Adjutant-General's office, which are, therefore, official:

Casualties during the Month of May, 1864 (Major-General SHERMAN, *commanding.)*

ARMY OF THE CUMBERLAND (MAJOR-GENERAL THOMAS).

CORPS.	Killed and Missing.	Wounded.	Total.
Fourth (Howard)	576	1,910	2,486
Fourteenth (Palmer)	147	655	802
Twentieth (Hooker)	571	2,997	3,568
Total	1,294	5,562	6,856

ARMY OF THE TENNESSEE (MAJOR-GENERAL McPHERSON).

CORPS.	Killed and Missing.	Wounded.	Total.
Fifteenth (Logan)	122	624	746
Sixteenth (Dodge)	94	430	524
Seventeenth (Blair)	(Not yet up.)	1	1
Total	216	1,055	1,271

ARMY OF THE OHIO (MAJOR-GENERAL SCHOFIELD).

CORPS.	Killed and Missing.	Wounded.	Total.
Twenty-third (Schofield).	226	757	983
Cavalry.	127	62	189
Total.	353	819	1,172
Grand aggregate.	1,868	7,436	9,299

General Joseph E. Johnston, in his "Narrative of his Military Operations," just published (March 27, 1874), gives the effective strength of his army at and about Dalton on the 1st of May, 1864 (page 302),[54] as follows:

Infantry	37,652
Artillery	2,812
Cavalry	2,392
Total	42,856

During May, and prior to reaching Cassville, he was further reënforced (page 352):

Polk's corps of three divisions	12,000
Martin's[55] division of cavalry	3,500
Jackson's[56] division of cavalry	3,900

And at New Hope Church, May 26th:

Brigade of Quarles[57]	2,200
Grand-total	64,456

[54] See Joseph E. Johnston, *Narrative of Military Operations, Directed, during the Late War between the States* (New York: D. Appleton, 1874), 302.

[55] William T. Martin (1823–1910) joined the Confederate Army in July 1861 and commanded the 1st Div., Cav. Corps, Army of Tennessee, in May 1864. *CHWC,* 366.

[56] William H. Jackson (1835–1903) graduated from the USMA in 1856 and joined the Confederate Army in Mar. 1861. He commanded a cavalry division in the 3rd Corps, Army of Tennessee, in May 1864. *CWHC,* 316–317.

[57] William A. Quarles (1825–1893) joined the Confederate Army in Oct. 1861 and commanded a brigade in Walthall's Div., 3rd Corps, Army of Tennessee, in late May 1864. *CWHC,* 442.

His losses during the month of May are stated by him, as taken from the report of Surgeon Foard[58] (page 325):

FROM DALTON TO CASSVILLE.

CORPS.	Killed.	Wounded.	Total.
Hardee's.	116	850	966
Hood's.	283	1,564	1,847
Polk's.	46	529	575
Total.	445	2,943	3,388

AT NEW HOPE CHURCH (PAGE 335.)

CORPS.	Killed.	Wounded.	Total.
Hardee's.	156	879	1,035
Hood's.	103	756	859
Polk's.	17	94	111
Total.	276	1,729	2,005
Total killed and wounded during May..	721	4,672	5,393

These figures include only the killed and wounded, whereas my statement of losses embraces the "missing," which are usually "prisoners," and of these we captured, during the whole campaign of four and a half months, exactly 12,983, whose names, rank, and regiments, were officially reported to the Commissary-General of Prisoners; and assuming a due proportion for the month of May, viz., one-fourth, makes 3,245 to be added to the killed and wounded given above, making an aggregate loss in Johnston's army, from Dalton to New Hope, inclusive, of 8,638, against ours of 9,299.

Therefore General Johnston is greatly in error, in his estimates on page 357, in stating our loss, as compared with his, at six or ten to one.

I always estimated my force at about double his, and could afford to lose two to one without disturbing our relative proportion; but I also reckoned that, in the natural strength of the country, in the abundance of mountains, streams, and forests, he had a fair offset to our numerical superiority, and

[58] Andrew J. Foard (1829–1868) earned his medical degree and served as an assistant surgeon in the U.S. Army from 1853 to 1861. He joined the Confederate Army at the start of the war and became Johnston's medical director after the Battle of Murfreesboro in Jan. 1863. "The Late Dr. A. J. Foard," *The Tennessean* (Nashville, TN), May 16, 1868, 2.

therefore endeavored to act with reasonable caution while moving on the vigorous "offensive."

With the drawn battle of New Hope Church, and our occupation of the natural fortress of Allatoona, terminated the month of May, and the first stage of the campaign.

17

Atlanta Campaign—Battles about Kenesaw Mountain.

JUNE, 1864.

ON THE 1ST OF JUNE our three armies were well in hand, in the broken and densely-wooded country fronting the enemy intrenched at New Hope Church, about five miles north of Dallas. General Stoneman's division of cavalry had occupied Allatoona, on the railroad, and General Garrard's division was at the western end of the pass, about Stilesboro'. Colonel W. W. Wright, of the Engineers, was busily employed in repairing the railroad and rebuilding the bridge across the Etowah (or High tower) River, which had been destroyed by the enemy on his retreat; and the armies were engaged in a general and constant skirmish along a front of about six miles—McPherson the right, Thomas the centre, and Schofield on the left. By gradually covering our front with parapet, and extending to the left, we approached the railroad toward Acworth and overlapped the enemy's right. By the 4th of June we had made such progress that Johnston evacuated his lines in the night, leaving us masters of the situation, when I deliberately shifted McPherson's army to the extreme left, at and in front of Acworth, with Thomas's about two miles on his right, and Schofield's on his right—all facing east. Heavy rains set in about the 1st of June, making the roads infamous; but our marches were short, as we needed time for the repair of the railroad, so as to bring supplies forward to Allatoona Station. On the 6th I rode back to Allatoona, seven miles, found it all that was expected, and gave orders for its fortification and preparation as a "secondary base." General Blair arrived at Acworth on the 8th with his two divisions of the Seventeenth Corps—the same which had been on veteran furlough—had come up from Cairo by way of Clifton, on the Tennessee River, and had followed our general route to Allatoona, where he had left a garrison of about fifteen hundred men. His effective strength, as reported, was nine thousand.[1] These, with new

[1] Blair took command of the 17th Corps, Army of the Tennessee, on May 4, 1864. *CWHC,* 133.

regiments and furloughed men who had joined early in the month of May, equaled our losses from battle, sickness, and by detachments; so that the three armies still aggregated about one hundred thousand effective men.[2]

On the 10th of June the whole combined army moved forward six miles, to "Big Shanty," a station on the railroad, whence we had a good view of the enemy's position, which embraced three prominent hills, known as Kenesaw, Pine Mountain, and Lost Mountain. On each of these hills the enemy had signal-stations and fresh lines of parapets. Heavy masses of infantry could be distinctly seen with the naked eye, and it was manifest that Johnston had chosen his ground well, and with deliberation had prepared for battle; but his line was at least ten miles in extent—too long, in my judgment, to be held successfully by his force, then estimated at sixty thousand.[3] As his position, however, gave him a perfect view over our field, we had to proceed with due caution. McPherson had the left, following the railroad, which curved around the north base of Kenesaw; Thomas the centre, obliqued to the right, deploying below Kenesaw and facing Pine Hill; and Schofield, somewhat refused, was on the general right, looking south, toward Lost Mountain.

On the 11th the Etowah bridge was done; the railroad was repaired up to our very skirmish line, close to the base of Kenesaw, and a loaded train of cars came to Big Shanty. The locomotive, detached, was run forward to a water-tank within the range of the enemy's guns on Kenesaw, whence the enemy opened fire on the locomotive; but the engineer was not afraid, went on to the tank, got water, and returned safely to his train, answering the guns with the screams of his engine, heightened by the cheers and shouts of our men.

The rains continued to pour, and made our developments slow and dilatory, for there were no roads, and these had to be improvised by each division for its own supply-train from the depot in Big Shanty to the camps. Meantime each army was deploying carefully before the enemy, intrenching every camp, ready as against a sally. The enemy's cavalry was also busy in our rear, compelling us to detach cavalry all the way back as far as Resaca, and to strengthen all the infantry posts as far as Nashville. Besides, there was great danger, always in my mind, that Forrest would collect a heavy cavalry command in Mississippi, cross the Tennessee River, and break up our railroad below Nashville. In anticipation of this very danger, I had sent General

[2] By June 1, 1864, WTS's command of about 100,000 men had suffered approximately 9,300 casualties. John F. Marszalek, *Sherman: A Soldier's Passion for Order* (New York: Free Press, 1993), 269.

[3] Johnston had approximately 65,000 troops under his command. Marszalek, *Sherman*, 269.

Sturgis to Memphis to take command of all the cavalry in that quarter, to go out toward Pontotoc, engage Forrest and defeat him; but on the 14th of June I learned that General Sturgis had himself been defeated on the 10th of June, and had been driven by Forrest back into Memphis in considerable confusion.[4] I expected that this would soon be followed by a general raid on all our roads in Tennessee. General A. J. Smith, with the two divisions of the Sixteenth and Seventeenth Corps which had been with General Banks up Red River, had returned from that ill-fated expedition, and had been ordered to General Canby at New Orleans, who was making a diversion about Mobile; but, on hearing of General Sturgis's defeat, I ordered General Smith to go out from Memphis and renew the offensive, so as to keep Forrest off our roads. This he did finally, defeating Forrest at Tupelo, on the 13th, 14th, and 15th days of July; and he so stirred up matters in North Mississippi that Forrest could not leave for Tennessee.[5] This, for a time, left me only the task of covering the roads against such minor detachments of cavalry as Johnston could spare from his immediate army, and I proposed to keep these too busy in their own defense to spare detachments.

By the 14th the rain slackened, and we occupied a continuous line of ten miles, intrenched, conforming to the irregular position of the enemy, when I reconnoitred, with a view to make a break in their line between Kenesaw and Pine Mountain. When abreast of Pine Mountain I noticed a rebel battery on its crest, with a continuous line of fresh rifle-trench about half-way down the hill. Our skirmishers were at the time engaged in the woods about the base of this hill between the lines, and I estimated the distance to the battery on the crest at about eight hundred yards. Near it, in plain view, stood a group of the enemy, evidently observing us with glasses. General Howard, commanding the Fourth Corps, was near by, and I called his attention to this group, and ordered him to compel it to keep behind its cover. He replied that his orders from General Thomas were to spare artillery-ammunition. This was right, according to the general policy, but I explained to him that we must keep up the *morale* of a bold offensive, that he must use his artillery, force the enemy to remain on the timid defensive, and ordered him to cause a battery close by

[4] Sturgis left Memphis with approximately 8,000 troops and twenty-two pieces of artillery on June 1, 1864. He encountered Forrest's troops at Brice's Cross Roads, four miles west of Baldwyn, MS. The Confederates pushed Sturgis's forces back to Memphis by June 15. Robert M. Browning, *Forrest: The Confederacy's Relentless Warrior* (Washington, DC: Potomac Books, 2004), 60–66; *OR*, I, 39(I), 220–231.

[5] For Smith's and Forrest's reports on the Battle of Tupelo, see *OR*, I, 39(I), 250–256, 320–324.

to fire three volleys. I continued to ride down our line, and soon heard, in quick succession, the three volleys. The next division in order was Geary's, and I gave him similar orders. General Polk, in my opinion, was killed by the second volley fired from the first battery referred to.

In a conversation with General Johnston, after the war, he explained that on that day he had ridden in person from Marietta to Pine Mountain, held by Bates's division,[6] and was accompanied by Generals Hardee and Polk. When on Pine Mountain, reconnoitring, quite a group of soldiers, belonging to the battery close by, clustered about him. He noticed the preparations of our battery to fire, and cautioned these men to scatter. They did so, and he likewise hurried behind the parapet, from which he had an equally good view of our position; but General Polk, who was dignified and corpulent, walked back slowly, not wishing to appear too hurried or cautious in the presence of the men, and was struck across the breast by an unexploded shell, which killed him instantly. This is my memory of the conversation, and it is confirmed by Johnston himself in his "Narrative," page 337, except that he calculated the distance of our battery at six hundred yards, and says that Polk was killed by the third shot; I know that our guns fired by volley, and believe that he was hit by a shot of the second volley.[7] It has been asserted that I fired the gun which killed General Polk, and that I knew it was directed against that general.[8] The fact is, at that distance we could not even tell that the group were officers at all; I was on horseback, a couple of hundred yards off, before my orders to fire were executed, had no idea that our shot had taken effect, and continued my ride down along the line to Schofield's extreme

[6] William B. Bate (1826–1905), a Tennessee legislator who joined the Confederate Army, was wounded at the Battle of Shiloh. In mid-1864 he commanded a division in the 1st Corps, Army of Tennessee. Later he served as the governor of Tennessee from 1883 to 1887. *CWHC,* 121.

[7] Johnston wrote, "Polk, unconsciously exposed by his characteristic insensibility to danger, fell by the third shot, which passed from left to right through the middle of his chest. The death of this eminent Christian and soldier, who had been distinguished in every battle in which the Army of Tennessee had been engaged, produced deep sorrow in our troops. Major-General Loring, the officer next in rank in the corps, succeeded temporarily to its command." Joseph E. Johnston, *Narrative of Military Operations, Directed, during the Late War between the States* (New York: D. Appleton, 1874), 337.

[8] Alexander Davidson and Bernard Stuvé claimed, "While thus making observations, Gen. Polk, the Episcopal bishop of Louisiana, was struck by a 3-inch ball from our guns, and instantly killed. In company with Johnston and Hardee, the group was discovered on its lofty lookout, and, at the instance of Sherman, a gun was turned upon it and fired." Alexander Davidson and Bernard Stuvé, *A Complete History of Illinois from 1673 to 1873* (Springfield: Illinois Journal, 1874), 840*n*.

flank, returning late in the evening to my headquarters at Big Shanty, where I occupied an abandoned house.[9] In a cotton-field back of that house was our signal-station, on the roof of an old gin-house. The signal-officer reported that by studying the enemy's signals he had learned the "key," and that he could read their signals. He explained to me that he had translated a signal about noon, from Pine Mountain to Marietta, "Send an ambulance for General Polk's body;" and later in the day another, "Why don't you send an ambulance for General Polk?" From this we inferred that General Polk had been killed, but how or where we knew not; and this inference was confirmed later in the same day by the report of some prisoners who had been captured.[10]

On the 15th we advanced our general lines, intending to attack at any weak point discovered between Kenesaw and Pine Mountain; but Pine Mountain was found to be abandoned, and Johnston had contracted his front somewhat, on a direct line, connecting Kenesaw with Lost Mountain. Thomas and Schofield thereby gained about two miles of most difficult country, and McPherson's left lapped well around the north end of Kenesaw. We captured a good many prisoners, among them a whole infantry regiment, the Fourteenth Alabama, three hundred and twenty strong.

On the 16th the general movement was continued, when Lost Mountain was abandoned by the enemy. Our right naturally swung round, so as to threaten the railroad below Marietta, but Johnston had still further contracted and strengthened his lines, covering Marietta and all the roads below.

On the 17th and 18th the rain again fell in torrents, making army movements impossible, but we devoted the time to strengthening our positions, more especially the left and centre, with a view gradually to draw from the

[9] On June 12, 1864, WTS described his headquarters at Big Shanty in a letter to his wife Ellen: "I am in an old house with a fire burning which is not uncomfortable. Johnston has 60,000 Infantry, 15,000 Cavalry and a good deal of militia. We must have a terrific Battle, and he wants to choose and fortify his ground." William T. Sherman, *Sherman's Civil War: Selected Correspondence of William T. Sherman, 1860–1865*, ed. Brooks D. Simpson and Jean V. Berlin (Chapel Hill: University of North Carolina Press, 1999), 646–647.

[10] O. H. Howard, of the signal corps, recorded the incident in his journal: "During the day we discovered that the enemy's signal officers were working with a new code which was, of course, unintelligible to us . . . Directing three officers to write and record the numbers, a considerable record was made, and at night, with the assistance of Lieut. Sampson, I succeeded in deciphering the letters of the new code . . . On the next day our knowledge of the new code was made perfect by letters and abbreviations discovered and added by Lieutenants Edge, Worley, Allen, and myself." J. Willard Brown, *The Signal Corps, U.S.A. in the War of the Rebellion* (Boston: U.S. Veteran Signal Corps Association, 1896), 527.

left to add to the right; and we had to hold our lines on the left extremely strong, to guard against a sally from Kenesaw against our depot at Big Shanty. Garrard's division of cavalry was kept busy on our left, McPherson had gradually extended to his right, enabling Thomas to do the same still farther; but the enemy's position was so very strong, and everywhere it was covered by intrenchments, that we found it as dangerous to assault as a permanent fort. We in like manner covered our lines of battle by similar works, and even our skirmishers learned to cover their bodies by the simplest and best forms of defensive works, such as rails or logs, piled in the form of a simple lunette, covered on the outside with earth thrown up at night.

The enemy and ourselves used the same form of rifle-trench, varied according to the nature of the ground, viz.: the trees and bushes were cut away for a hundred yards or more in front, serving as an abatis or entanglement; the parapets varied from four to six feet high, the dirt taken from a ditch outside and from a covered way inside, and this parapet was surmounted by a "head-log," composed of the trunk of a tree from twelve to twenty inches at the butt, lying along the interior crest of the parapet and resting in notches cut in other trunks which extended back, forming an inclined plane, in case the head-log should be knocked inward by a cannon-shot. The men of both armies became extremely skillful in the construction of these works, because each man realized their value and importance to himself, so that it required no orders for their construction. As soon as a regiment or brigade gained a position within easy distance for a sally, it would set to work with a will, and would construct such a parapet in a single night; but I endeavored to spare the soldiers this hard labor by authorizing each division commander to organize out of the freedmen who escaped to us a pioneer corps of two hundred men, who were fed out of the regular army supplies, and I promised them ten dollars a month, under an existing act of Congress. These pioneer detachments became very useful to us during the rest of the war, for they could work at night while our men slept; they in turn were not expected to fight, and could therefore sleep by day. Our enemies used their slaves for a similar purpose, but usually kept them out of the range of fire by employing them to fortify and strengthen the position to their rear *next* to be occupied in their general retrograde. During this campaign hundreds if not thousands of miles of similar intrenchments were built by both armies, and, as a rule, whichever party attacked got the worst of it.

On the 19th of June the rebel army again fell back on its flanks, to such an extent that for a time I supposed it had retreated to the Chattahoochee River, fifteen miles distant; but as we pressed forward we were soon undeceived, for we found it still more concentrated, covering Marietta and the railroad.

These successive contractions of the enemy's line encouraged us and discouraged him, but were doubtless justified by sound reasons. On the 20th Johnston's position was unusually strong. Kenesaw Mountain was his salient; his two flanks were refused and covered by parapets and by Noonday and Nose's Creeks. His left flank was his weak point, so long as he acted on the "defensive," whereas, had he designed to contract the extent of his line for the purpose of getting in reserve a force with which to strike "offensively" from his right, he would have done a wise act, and I was compelled to presume that such was his object. We were also so far from Nashville and Chattanooga that we were naturally sensitive for the safety of our railroad and depots, so that the left (McPherson) was held *very strong.*

About this time came reports that a large cavalry force of the enemy had passed around our left flank, evidently to strike this very railroad somewhere below Chattanooga. I therefore reënforced the cavalry stationed from Resaca to Cassville, and ordered forward from Huntsville, Alabama, the infantry division of General John E. Smith, to hold Kingston securely.[11]

While we were thus engaged about Kenesaw, General Grant had his hands full with Lee, in Virginia. General Halleck was the chief of staff at Washington, and to him I communicated almost daily. I find from my letter-book that on the 21st of June I reported to him tersely and truly the condition of facts on that day: "This is the nineteenth day of rain, and the prospect of fair weather is as far off as ever. The roads are impassable; the fields and woods become quagmires after a few wagons have crossed over. Yet we are at work all the time. The left flank is across Noonday Creek, and the right is across Nose's Creek. The enemy still holds Kenesaw, a conical mountain, with Marietta behind it, and has his flanks retired, to cover that town and the railroad behind. I am all ready to attack the moment the weather and roads will permit troops and artillery to move with any thing like life."[12]

The weather has a wonderful effect on troops: in action and on the march, rain is favorable; but in the woods, where all is blind and uncertain, it seems almost impossible for an army covering ten miles of front to act in concert during wet and stormy weather. Still I pressed operations with the utmost earnestness, aiming always to keep our fortified lines in absolute contact with the enemy, while with the surplus force we felt forward, from one flank or the other, for his line of communication and retreat. On the 22d of June I rode

[11] In June 1864, Smith commanded the 3rd Div., 15th Corps, Army of the Tennessee. *CWHC,* 497.

[12] WTS wrote to Halleck from Big Shanty on June 21, 1864. See *OR,* I, 38(IV), 544.

the whole line, and ordered General Thomas in person to advance his extreme right corps (Hooker's); and instructed General Schofield, by letter, to keep his entire army, viz., the Twenty-third Corps, as a strong right flank in close support of Hooker's deployed line.[13] During this day the sun came out, with some promise of clear weather, and I had got back to my bivouac about dark, when a signal message was received, dated—

KULP HOUSE, 5.30 P. M.

General SHERMAN:

We have repulsed two heavy attacks, and feel confident, our only apprehension being from our extreme right flank. Three entire corps are in front of us.

Major-General HOOKER.

Hooker's corps (the Twentieth) belonged to Thomas's army; Thomas's headquarters were two miles nearer to Hooker than mine; and Hooker, being an old army officer, knew that he should have reported this fact to Thomas and not to me; I was, moreover, specially disturbed by the assertion in his report that he was uneasy about his *right flank,* when Schofield had been specially ordered to protect that. I first inquired of my adjutant, Dayton, if he were certain that General Schofield had received his orders, and he answered that the envelope in which he had sent them was receipted by General Schofield himself. I knew, therefore, that General Schofield must be near by, in close support of Hooker's right flank. General Thomas had before this occasion complained to me of General Hooker's disposition to "switch off," leaving wide gaps in his line, so as to be independent, and to make *glory* on his own account. I therefore resolved not to overlook this breach of discipline and propriety. The rebel army was only composed of three corps; I had that very day ridden six miles of their lines, found them everywhere strongly occupied, and therefore Hooker could not have encountered "three entire corps." Both McPherson and Schofield had also complained to me of this same tendency of Hooker to widen the gap between his own corps and his proper army (Thomas's), so as to come into closer contact with one or other of the wings, asserting that he was the senior by commission to both McPherson and Schofield, and that in the event of battle he should assume command over them, by virtue of his older commission.

[13] For WTS's order to Schofield on June 21, 1864, see *OR,* I, 38(IV), 551.

They appealed to me to protect them. I had heard during that day some cannonading and heavy firing down toward the "Kulp House," which was about five miles southeast of where I was, but this was nothing unusual, for at the same moment there was firing along our lines full ten miles in extent. Early the next day (23d) I rode down to the "Kulp House," which was on a road leading from Powder Springs to Marietta, about three miles distant from the latter. On the way I passed through General Butterfield's division of Hooker's corps, which I learned had not been engaged at all in the battle of the day before; then I rode along Geary's and Williams's divisions,[14] which occupied the field of battle, and the men were engaged in burying the dead. I found General Schofield's corps on the Powder Springs road, its head of column abreast of Hooker's right, therefore constituting "a strong right flank," and I met Generals Schofield and Hooker together. As rain was falling at the moment, we passed into a little church standing by the road-side, and I there showed General Schofield Hooker's signal-message of the day before. He was very angry, and pretty sharp words passed between them, Schofield saying that his head of column (Hascall's division) had been, at the time of the battle, actually in advance of Hooker's line; that the attack or sally of the enemy struck his troops before it did Hooker's; that General Hooker knew of it at the time; and he offered to go out and show me that the dead men of his advance division (Hascall's) were lying farther out than any of Hooker's. General Hooker pretended not to have known this fact. I then asked him why he had called on me for help, until he had used all of his own troops; asserting that I had just seen Butterfield's division, and had learned from him that he had not been engaged the day before at all; and I asserted that the enemy's sally must have been made by one corps (Hood's), in place of three, and that it had fallen on Geary's and Williams's divisions, which had repulsed the attack handsomely. As we rode away from that church General Hooker was by my side, and I told him that such a thing must not occur again; in other words, I reproved him more gently than the occasion demanded, and from that time he began to sulk. General Hooker had come from the East with great fame as a "fighter," and at Chattanooga he was glorified by his "battle above the clouds," which I fear turned his head. He seemed jealous of all the army commanders, because in years, former rank, and experience, he thought he was our superior.

[14] In the first edition of the memoirs (1875), this portion of WTS's text read "Ward's division" instead of "Williams's division."

On the 23d of June I telegraphed to General Halleck this summary, which I cannot again better state:

> We continue to press forward on the principle of an advance against fortified positions. The whole country is one vast fort, and Johnston must have at least fifty miles of connected trenches, with abatis and finished batteries. We gain ground daily, fighting all the time. On the 21st General Stanley gained a position near the south end of Kenesaw, from which the enemy attempted in vain to drive him; and the same day General T. J. Wood's division took a hill, which the enemy assaulted three times at night without success, leaving more than a hundred dead on the ground. Yesterday the extreme right (Hooker and Schofield) advanced on the Powder Springs road to within three miles of Marietta. The enemy made a strong effort to drive them away, but failed signally, leaving more than two hundred dead on the field. Our lines are now in close contact, and the fighting is incessant, with a good deal of artillery-fire. As fast as we gain one position the enemy has another all ready, but I think he will soon have to let go Kenesaw, which is the key to the whole country. The weather is now better, and the roads are drying up fast. Our losses are light, and, notwithstanding the repeated breaks of the road to our rear, supplies are ample.

During the 24th and 25th of June General Schofield extended his right as far as prudent, so as to compel the enemy to thin out his lines correspondingly, with the intention to make two strong assaults at points where success would give us the greatest advantage. I had consulted Generals Thomas, McPherson, and Schofield, and we all agreed that we could not with prudence stretch out any more, and therefore there was no alternative but to attack "fortified lines," a thing carefully avoided up to that time. I reasoned, if we could make a breach anywhere near the rebel centre, and thrust in a strong head of column, that with the one moiety of our army we could hold in check the corresponding wing of the enemy, and with the other sweep in flank and overwhelm the other half. The 27th of June was fixed as the day for the attempt, and in order to oversee the whole, and to be in close communication with all parts of the army, I had a place cleared on the top of a hill to the rear of Thomas's centre, and had the telegraph-wires laid to it. The points of attack were chosen, and the troops were all prepared with as little demonstration as possible. About 9 A. M. of the day appointed, the troops moved to the assault, and all along our lines for ten miles a furious fire of artillery and musketry was kept up. At all points the enemy met us with determined courage and in great force. McPherson's attacking column fought up the face of the lesser Kenesaw, but could not reach the summit. About a mile to the right (just below the Dallas road) Thomas's assaulting column reached the parapet, where Brigadier-General Harker[15] was shot down mortally wounded, and Brigadier-General Daniel McCook (my old law-partner) was desperately wounded, from the effects of which he afterward died.[16] By 11.30 the assault was in fact over, and had failed. We had not broken the rebel line at either point, but our assaulting columns held their ground within a few yards of the rebel trenches, and there covered themselves with parapet. McPherson lost about five hundred men and several valuable officers, and Thomas lost nearly two thousand men. This was the hardest fight of the campaign up to that date, and it is well described by Johnston in his "Narrative" (pages 342, 343), where he admits his loss in killed and wounded as—

	Men.
Hood's corps (not reported)	
Hardee's corps	286
Loring's (Polk's)	522
Total	808

This, no doubt, is a true and fair statement; but, as usual, Johnston overestimates our loss, putting it at six thousand, whereas our entire loss was about twenty-five hundred, killed and wounded.[17]

While the battle was in progress at the centre, Schofield crossed Olley's Creek on the right, and gained a position threatening Johnston's line of retreat; and, to increase the effect, I ordered Stoneman's cavalry to proceed rapidly still farther to the right, to Sweetwater. Satisfied of the bloody cost of attacking intrenched lines, I at once thought of moving the whole army to

[15] Charles G. Harker (1835–1864) graduated from the USMA in 1858 and was in command of the 3rd Brig., 2nd Div., 4th Corps, Army of the Cumberland, when he was shot through the right arm and spine at Resaca on May 14, 1864. He died on June 27. *CWHC,* 280.

[16] McCook was shot in the right lung at Kennesaw Mountain, GA, on June 27, 1864, and died on July 17. *CWHC,* 374.

[17] For a summary of U.S. Army casualties at the Battle of Kennesaw Mountain, see Albert Castel, *Decision in the West: The Atlanta Campaign of 1864* (Lawrence: University Press of Kansas, 1992), 319.

the railroad at a point (Fulton)[18] about ten miles below Marietta, or to the Chattahoochee River itself, a movement similar to the one afterward so successfully practised at Atlanta. All the orders were issued to bring forward supplies enough to fill our wagons, intending to strip the railroad back to Allatoona, and leave that place as our depot, to be covered as well as possible by Garrard's cavalry. General Thomas, as usual, shook his head, deeming it risky to leave the railroad; but something had to be done, and I had resolved on this move, as reported in my dispatch to General Halleck on July 1st:

> General Schofield is now south of Olley's Creek, and on the head of Nickajack. I have been hurrying down provisions and forage, and to-morrow night propose to move McPherson from the left to the extreme right, back of General Thomas. This will bring my right within three miles of the Chattahoochee River, and about five miles from the railroad. By this movement I think I can force Johnston to move his whole army down from Kenesaw to defend his railroad and the Chattahoochee, when I will (by the left flank) reach the railroad below Marietta; but in this I must cut loose from the railroad with ten days' supplies in wagons. Johnston may come out of his intrenchments to attack Thomas, which is exactly what I want, for General Thomas is well intrenched on a line parallel with the enemy south of Kenesaw. I think that Allatoona and the line of the Etowah are strong enough for me to venture on this move. The movement is substantially down the Sandtown road straight for Atlanta.

McPherson drew out of his lines during the night of July 2d, leaving Garrard's cavalry, dismounted, occupying his trenches, and moved to the rear of the Army of the Cumberland, stretching down the Nickajack; but Johnston detected the movement, and promptly abandoned Marietta and Kenesaw. I expected as much, for, by the earliest dawn of the 3d of July, I was up at a large spy-glass mounted on a tripod, which Colonel Poe, United States Engineers, had at his bivouac close by our camp. I directed the glass on Kenesaw, and saw some of our pickets crawling up the hill cautiously; soon they stood upon the very top, and I could plainly see their movements as they ran along the crest just abandoned by the enemy. In a minute I roused my staff, and

[18] See George B. Davis et al., *Official Military Atlas of the Civil War* (New York: Fairfax Press, 1983), plate 149.

started them off with orders in every direction for a pursuit by every possible road, hoping to catch Johnston in the confusion of retreat, especially at the crossing of the Chattahoochee River.[19]

I must close this chapter here, so as to give the actual losses during June, which are compiled from the official returns by months. These losses, from June 1st to July 3d, were all substantially sustained about Kenesaw and Marietta, and it was really a continuous battle, lasting from the 10th day of June till the 3d of July, when the rebel army fell back from Marietta toward the Chattahoochee River. Our losses were:

ARMY OF THE CUMBERLAND.

CORPS.	Killed and Missing.	Wounded.	Total.
Fourth (Howard)	602	1,542	2,144
Fourteenth (Palmer)	353	1,466	1,819
Twentieth (Hooker)	322	1,246	1,568
Total, Army of the Cumberland	1,277	4,254	5,531

ARMY OF THE TENNESSEE.

CORPS.	Killed and Missing.	Wounded.	Total.
Fifteenth (Logan)	179	687	866
Sixteenth (Dodge)	52	157	209
Seventeenth (Blair)	47	212	259
Total, Army of the Tennessee	278	1,056	1,334

ARMY OF THE OHIO.

CORPS.	Killed and Missing.	Wounded.	Total.
Twenty-third (Schofield)	105	362	467
Cavalry	130	68	198
Total, Army of the Ohio	235	430	665
Loss in June, aggregate	1,790	5,740	7,530

[19] David S. Stanley, who commanded the 1st Div., 4th Corps, Army of the Cumberland, referred to WTS's decision to attack Johnston at Kennesaw Mountain as "murderous, cruel and wholly unjustifiable." He wrote, "Indeed he coolly says in his memoirs, that he was bound to show Joe Johnston that he would attack him everywhere. A fine answer to the four thousand dead and mangled left in front of Kenesaw." Marszalek, *Sherman,* 274; David S. Stanley, *Personal Memoirs of D. S. Stanley, U.S.A.* (Cambridge, MA: Harvard University Press, 1917), 173.

Johnston makes his statement of losses from the report of his surgeon Foard, for pretty much the same period, viz., from June 4th to July 4th (page 576):

CORPS.	Killed and Missing.	Wounded.	Total.
Hardee's.	200	1,433	1,633
Hood's.	140	1,121	1,261
Polk's.	128	926	1,054
Total.	468	3,480	3,948

In the tabular statement the "missing" embraces the prisoners; and, giving two thousand as a fair proportion of prisoners captured by us for the month of June (twelve thousand nine hundred and eighty-three in all the campaign), makes an aggregate loss in the rebel army of fifty-nine hundred and forty-eight, to ours of seventy-five hundred and thirty—a less proportion than in the relative strength of our two armies, viz., as six to ten, thus maintaining our relative superiority, which the desperate game of war justified.

18

Atlanta Campaign—Battles about Atlanta.

JULY, 1864.

As BEFORE EXPLAINED, on the 3d of July, by moving McPherson's entire army from the extreme left, at the base of Kenesaw to the right, below Olley's Creek, and stretching it down the Nickajack toward Turner's Ferry of the Chattahoochee,[1] we forced Johnston to choose between a direct assault on Thomas's intrenched position, or to permit us to make a lodgment on his railroad below Marietta, or even to cross the Chattahoochee. Of course, he chose to let go Kenesaw and Marietta, and fall back on an intrenched camp prepared by his orders in advance on the north and west bank of the Chattahoochee, covering the railroad-crossing and his several pontoon-bridges. I confess I had not learned beforehand of the existence of this strong place, in the nature of a *tête-du-pont,* and had counted on striking him an effectual blow in the expected confusion of his crossing the Chattahoochee, a broad and deep river then to his rear. Ordering every part of the army to pursue vigorously on the morning of the 3d of July, I rode into Marietta, just quitted by the rebel rear-guard, and was terribly angry at the cautious pursuit by Garrard's cavalry, and even by the head of our infantry columns. But Johnston had in advance cleared and multiplied his roads, whereas ours had to cross at right angles from the direction of Powder Springs toward Marrietta, producing delay and confusion. By night Thomas's head of column ran up against a strong rear-guard intrenched at Smyrna camp-ground, six miles below Marietta, and there on the next day we celebrated our Fourth of July, by a noisy but not a desperate battle, designed chiefly to hold the enemy there till Generals McPherson and Schofield could get well into position below him, near the Chattahoochee crossings.

[1] For WTS's July 3, 1864, order to McPherson, and for a detailed map of McPherson's movements, see *OR,* I, 38(V), 36–37, 57.

It was here that General Noyes, late Governor of Ohio, lost his leg.[2] I came very near being shot myself while reconnoitring in the second story of a house on our picket-line, which was struck several times by cannon-shot, and perfectly riddled with musket-balls.

During the night Johnston drew back all his army and trains inside the *tête-du-pont* at the Chattahoochee, which proved one of the strongest pieces of field-fortification I ever saw. We closed up against it, and were promptly met by a heavy and severe fire. Thomas was on the main road in immediate pursuit; next on his right was Schofield; and McPherson on the extreme right, reaching the Chattahoochee River below Turner's Ferry. Stoneman's cavalry was still farther to the right, along down the Chattahoochee River as far as opposite Sandtown; and on that day I ordered Garrard's division of cavalry up the river eighteen miles, to secure possession of the factories at Roswell, as well as to hold an important bridge and ford at that place.

About three miles out from the Chattahoochee the main road forked, the right branch following substantially the railroad, and the left one leading straight for Atlanta, *via* Paice's Ferry[3] and Buckhead. We found the latter unoccupied and unguarded, and the Fourth Corps (Howard's) reached the river at Paice's Ferry. The right-hand road was perfectly covered by the *tête-du-pont* before described, where the resistance was very severe, and for some time deceived me, for I was pushing Thomas with orders to fiercely assault his enemy, supposing that he was merely opposing us to gain time to get his trains and troops across the Chattahoochee; but, on personally reconnoitring, I saw the abatis and the strong redoubts, which satisfied me of the preparations that had been made by Johnston in anticipation of this very event. While I was with General Jeff. C. Davis, a poor negro came out of the abatis, blanched with fright, said he had been hidden under a log all day, with a perfect storm of shot, shells, and musket-balls, passing over him, till a short lull had enabled him to creep out and make himself known to our skirmishers, who in turn had sent him back to where we were. This negro explained that he with about a thousand slaves had been at work a month or more on these very lines, which, as he

[2] Edward F. Noyes (1832–1890) joined the 39th Ohio Inf. as a major in July 1861 and was promoted to colonel in Nov. 1862. He lost his left foot in battle at Ruff Mill, GA, and was discharged on Apr. 22, 1865. He later served as governor of Ohio from 1872 to 1874. *CWHC,* 407.

[3] Pace's Ferry was situated on the Chattahoochee River approximately six miles north of Atlanta. Richard M McMurray, *Atlanta 1864: Last Chance for the Confederacy* (Lincoln: University of Nebraska Press, 2000), 148 (map).

explained, extended from the river about a mile above the railroad-bridge to Turner's Ferry below, being in extent from five to six miles.

Therefore, on the 5th of July we had driven our enemy to cover in the valley of the Chattahoochee, and we held possession of the river above for eighteen miles, as far as Roswell, and below ten miles to the mouth of the Sweetwater. Moreover, we held the high ground and could overlook his movements, instead of his looking down on us, as was the case at Kenesaw.

From a hill just back of Vining's Station I could see the houses in Atlanta, nine miles distant, and the whole intervening valley of the Chattahoochee; could observe the preparations for our reception on the other side, the camps of men and large trains of covered wagons; and supposed, as a matter of course, that Johnston had passed the river with the bulk of his army, and that he had only left on our side a corps to cover his bridges; but in fact he had only sent across his cavalry and trains. Between Howard's corps at Paice's Ferry and the rest of Thomas's army pressing up against this *tête-du-pont,* was a space concealed by dense woods, in crossing which I came near riding into a detachment of the enemy's cavalry; and later in the same day Colonel Frank Sherman, of Chicago, then on General Howard's staff, did actually ride straight into the enemy's camp, supposing that our lines were continuous. He was carried to Atlanta, and for some time the enemy supposed they were in possession of the commander-in-chief of the opposing army.[4]

I knew that Johnston would not remain long on the west bank of the Chattahoochee, for I could easily practise on that ground to better advantage our former tactics of intrenching a moiety in his front, and with the rest of our army cross the river and threaten either his rear or the city of Atlanta itself, which city was of vital importance to the existence not only of his own army, but of the Confederacy itself. In my dispatch of July 6th to General Halleck, at Washington, I state that—

> Johnston (in his retreat from Kenesaw) has left two breaks in the railroad—one above Marietta and one near Vining's Station. The former is already repaired, and Johnston's army has heard the sound of our locomotives. The telegraph is finished to Vining's Station, and the field-wire has just reached my bivouac, and will be ready to convey this message as soon as it is written and translated into cipher.

[4] Francis T. Sherman (1825–1905) was chief of staff in the 4th Corps, Army of the Cumberland, when he was captured by Confederate forces on July 7, 1864. He was exchanged on Oct. 4. *CWHC,* 484.

> I propose to study the crossings of the Chattahoochee, and, when all is ready, to move quickly. As a beginning, I will keep the troops and wagons well back from the river, and only display to the enemy our picket-line, with a few field-batteries along at random. I have already shifted Schofield to a point in our left rear, whence he can in a single move reach the Chattahoochee at a point above the railroad-bridge, where there is a ford. At present the waters are turbid and swollen from recent rains; but if the present hot weather lasts, the water will run down very fast. We have pontoons enough for four bridges, but, as our crossing will be resisted, we must manœuvre some. All the regular crossing-places are covered by forts, apparently of long construction; but we shall cross in due time, and, instead of attacking Atlanta direct, or any of its forts, I propose to make a circuit, destroying all its railroads. This is a delicate movement, and must be done with caution. Our army is in good condition and full of confidence; but the weather is intensely hot, and a good many men have fallen with sunstroke. The country is high and healthy, and the sanitary condition of the army is good.[5]

At this time Stoneman was very active on our extreme right, pretending to be searching the river below Turner's Ferry for a crossing, and was watched closely by the enemy's cavalry on the other side. McPherson, on the right, was equally demonstrative at and near Turner's Ferry. Thomas faced substantially the intrenched *tête-du-pont,* and had his left on the Chattahoochee River, at Paice's Ferry. Garrard's cavalry was up at Roswell, and McCook's[6] small division of cavalry was intermediate, above Soap's Creek. Meantime, also, the railroad-construction party was hard at work, repairing the railroad up to our camp at Vining's Station.

Of course, I expected every possible resistance in crossing the Chattahoochee River, and had made up my mind to feign on the right, but actually

[5] WTS omitted the first part of his July 6, 1864, dispatch to Halleck. The missing section read, "I have just received Secretary Stanton's dispatch, and do not understand how Semmes and crew were allowed to leave the sinking Alabama in an English yacht. I would have preferred the President had not proclaimed martial law in Kentucky, but simply allowed the military commanders to arrest and banish all malcontents, while the honest and industrious stay-at-homes were encouraged by the increase of security." *OR,* I, 38(V), 65–66.

[6] Edward M. McCook (1833–1909), a lawyer, joined the U.S. 1st Cav. as a second lieutenant in May 1861 and was promoted to brigadier general in Apr. 1864. *CWHC,* 374.

to cross over by the left. We had already secured a crossing-place at Roswell, but one nearer was advisable; General Schofield had examined the river well, found a place just below the mouth of Soap's Creek which he deemed advantageous, and was instructed to effect an early crossing there, and to intrench a good position on the other side, viz., the east bank. But, preliminary thereto, I had ordered General Rousseau, at Nashville, to collect, out of the scattered detachments of cavalry in Tennessee, a force of a couple of thousand men, to rendezvous at Decatur, Alabama, thence to make a rapid march for Opelika, to break up the railroad-links between Georgia and Alabama, and then to make junction with me about Atlanta; or, if forced, to go on to Pensacola, or even to swing across to some of our posts in Mississippi. General Rousseau asked leave to command this expedition himself, to which I consented, and on the 6th of July he reported that he was all ready at Decatur, and I gave him orders to start. He moved promptly on the 9th, crossed the Coosa below the "Ten Islands" and the Tallapoosa below "Horseshoe Bend," having passed through Talladega. He struck the railroad west of Opelika, tore it up for twenty miles, then turned north and came to Marietta on the 22d of July, whence he reported to me. This expedition was in the nature of a raid, and must have disturbed the enemy somewhat; but, as usual, the cavalry did not work hard, and their destruction of the railroad was soon repaired. Rousseau, when he reported to me in person before Atlanta, on the 23d of July, stated his entire loss to have been only twelve killed and thirty wounded.[7] He brought in four hundred captured mules and three hundred horses, and also told me a good story. He said he was far down in Alabama, below Talladega, one hot, dusty day, when the blue clothing of his men was gray with dust; he had halted his column along a road, and he in person, with his staff, had gone to the house of a planter, who met him kindly on the front-porch. He asked for water, which was brought, and as the party sat on the porch in conversation he saw, in a stable-yard across the road, quite a number of good mules. He remarked to the planter, "My good sir, I fear I must take some of your mules." The planter remonstrated, saying he had already contributed liberally to the *good cause;* that it was only last week he had given to General Roddy[8] ten mules. Rousseau replied, "Well, in this war you should be at least neutral—that is, you should be as liberal to us as to Roddy" (a rebel cavalry general). "Well, ain't you on our side?" "No," said Rousseau; "I am General

[7] For Lovell H. Rousseau's report on his raid through Alabama, and his relevant correspondence with WTS, see *OR,* I, 38(II), 904–911.

[8] Philip D. Roddey (1826–1897) commanded a Confederate cavalry division in the Dept. of Alabama, Mississippi, and East Louisiana, in July 1864. *CWHC,* 458.

Rousseau, and all these men you see are Yanks." "Great God! is it possible? Are these Yanks? Who ever supposed they would come away down here in Alabama?" Of course, Rousseau took his ten mules.

Schofield effected his crossing at Soap's Creek very handsomely on the 9th, capturing the small guard that was watching the crossing. By night he was on the high ground beyond, strongly intrenched, with two good pontoon-bridges finished, and was prepared, if necessary, for an assault by the whole Confederate army. The same day Garrard's cavalry also crossed over at Roswell, drove away the cavalry-pickets, and held its ground till relieved by Newton's division of Howard's corps, which was sent up temporarily, till it in turn was relieved by Dodge's corps (Sixteenth) of the Army of the Tennessee, which was the advance of the whole of that army.

That night Johnston evacuated his trenches, crossed over the Chattahoochee, burned the railroad-bridge and his pontoon and trestle bridges, and left us in full possession of the north or west bank—besides which, we had already secured possession of the two good crossings at Roswell and Soap's Creek. I have always thought Johnston neglected his opportunity there, for he had lain comparatively idle while we got control of both banks of the river above him.

On the 13th I ordered McPherson, with the Fifteenth Corps, to move up to Roswell, to cross over, prepare good bridges, and to make a strong *tête-du-pont* on the farther side. Stoneman had been sent down to Campbellton,[9] with orders to cross over and to threaten the railroad below Atlanta, if he could do so without too much risk; and General Blair, with the Seventeenth Corps, was to remain at Turner's Ferry, demonstrating as much as possible, thus keeping up the feint below while we were actually crossing above. Thomas was also ordered to prepare his bridges at Powers's[10] and Paice's Ferries. By crossing the Chattahoochee above the railroad-bridge, we were better placed to cover our railroad and depots than below, though a movement across the river below the railroad, to the south of Atlanta, might have been more decisive. But we were already so far from home, and would be compelled to accept battle whenever offered, with the Chattahoochee to *our* rear, that it became imperative for me to take all prudential measures the

[9] Campbellton, GA, was located approximately fifteen miles southwest of Atlanta along the Chattahoochee River. George B. Davis et al., *Official Military Atlas of the Civil War* (New York: Fairfax Press, 1983), plate 149.

[10] On July 12, 1864, a bridge made up of twenty-two pontoons was constructed across the Chattahoochee River at Power's Ferry, approximately fifteen miles north of Atlanta. The bridge was dismantled on July 21. McMurray, *Atlanta 1864*, 148 (map); *OR*, I, 38(III), 68.

case admitted of, and I therefore determined to pass the river above the railroad-bridge—McPherson on the left, Schofield in the centre, and Thomas on the right.

On the 13th I reported to General Halleck as follows:

> All is well. I have now accumulated stores at Allatoona and Marietta, both fortified and garrisoned points. Have also three places at which to cross the Chattahoochee in our possession, and only await General Stoneman's return from a trip down the river, to cross the army in force and move on Atlanta.
>
> Stoneman is now out two days, and had orders to be back on the fourth or fifth day at furthest.

From the 10th to the 15th we were all busy in strengthening the several points for the proposed passage of the Chattahoochee, in increasing the number and capacity of the bridges, rearranging the garrisons to our rear, and in bringing forward supplies. On the 15th General Stoneman got back to Powder Springs, and was ordered to replace General Blair at Turner's Ferry, and Blair, with the Seventeenth Corps, was ordered up to Roswell to join McPherson.

On the 17th we began the general movement against Atlanta, Thomas crossing the Chattahoochee at Powers's and Paice's, by pontoon-bridges; Schofield moving out toward Cross Keys,[11] and McPherson toward Stone Mountain. We encountered but little opposition except by cavalry. On the 18th all the armies moved on a general right wheel, Thomas to Buckhead, forming line of battle facing Peach-Tree Creek; Schofield was on his left, and McPherson well over toward the railroad between Stone Mountain and Decatur, which he reached at 2 P. M. of that day, about four miles from Stone Mountain, and seven miles east of Decatur, and there he turned toward Atlanta, breaking up the railroad as he progressed, his advance-guard reaching Decatur about night, where he came into communication with Schofield's troops, which had also reached Decatur. About 10 A. M. of that day (July 18th), when the armies were all in motion, one of General Thomas's staff-officers brought me a citizen, one of our spies, who had just come out of Atlanta, and had brought a newspaper of the same day, or of the day before, containing Johnston's order relinquishing the command of the Confederate forces in Atlanta, and Hood's

[11] Cross Keys, GA, was located approximately ten miles north of Atlanta. Davis et al., *Official Military Atlas of the Civil War,* plate 149.

order assuming the command.[12] I immediately inquired of General Schofield, who was his classmate at West Point, about Hood, as to his general character, etc., and learned that he was bold even to rashness, and courageous in the extreme; I inferred that the change of commanders meant "fight." Notice of this important change was at once sent to all parts of the army, and every division commander was cautioned to be always prepared for battle in any shape. This was just what we wanted, viz., to fight in open ground, on any thing like equal terms, instead of being forced to run up against prepared intrenchments; but, at the same time, the enemy having Atlanta behind him, could choose the time and place of attack, and could at pleasure mass a superior force on our weakest points. Therefore, we had to be constantly ready for sallies.

On the 19th the three armies were converging toward Atlanta, meeting such feeble resistance that I really thought the enemy intended to evacuate the place. McPherson was moving astride of the railroad, near Decatur; Schofield along a road leading toward Atlanta, by Colonel Howard's house and the distillery;[13] and Thomas was crossing "Peach-Tree" in line of battle, building bridges for nearly every division as deployed. There was quite a gap between Thomas and Schofield, which I endeavored to close by drawing two of Howard's divisions nearer Schofield. On the 20th I was with General Schofield near the centre, and soon after noon heard heavy firing in front of Thomas's right, which lasted an hour or so, and then ceased. I soon learned that the enemy had made a furious sally, the blow falling on Hooker's corps (the Twentieth), and partially on Johnson's division of the Fourteenth, and Newton's of the Fourth. The troops had crossed Peach-Tree Creek, were deployed, but at the time were resting for noon, when, without notice, the enemy came pouring out of their trenches down upon them, they became commingled, and fought in many places hand to hand. General Thomas happened to be near the rear of Newton's division, and got some field-batteries in a good position, on the north side of Peach-Tree Creek, from which he directed a furious fire on a mass of the enemy, which was passing around Newton's left and exposed flank. After a couple of

[12] Johnston issued General Orders No. 4, relinquishing command of the Army and Department of Tennessee to Hood, on July 17, 1864. Hood acknowledged receipt of his appointment the following day but requested that Confederate president Jefferson Davis revoke the order. Hood argued, "I deem it dangerous to change the commanders of this army at this particular time, and to be to the interest of the service that no change should be made until the fate of Atlanta is decided." Davis denied Hood's request. *OR,* I, 38(V), 887–889.

[13] For a detailed map of the Atlanta area during the campaign, see Davis et al., *Official Military Atlas of the Civil War,* plate 60.

hours of hard and close conflict, the enemy retired slowly within his trenches, leaving his dead and many wounded on the field. Johnson's and Newton's losses were light, for they had partially covered their fronts with light parapet; but Hooker's whole corps fought in open ground, and lost about fifteen hundred men. He reported four hundred rebel dead left on the ground, and that the rebel wounded would number four thousand; but this was conjectural, for most of them got back within their own lines. We had, however, met successfully a bold sally, had repelled it handsomely, and were also put on our guard; and the event illustrated the future tactics of our enemy. This sally came from the Peach-Tree line, which General Johnston had carefully prepared in advance, from which to fight us *outside* of Atlanta. We then advanced our lines in compact order, close up to these finished intrenchments, overlapping them on our left. From various parts of our lines the houses inside of Atlanta were plainly visible, though between us were the strong parapets, with ditch, *fraise, chevaux-de-frise,* and abatis, prepared long in advance by Colonel Jeremy F. Gilmer, formerly of the United States Engineers.[14] McPherson had the Fifteenth Corps astride the Augusta Railroad, and the Seventeenth deployed on its left. Schofield was next on his right, then came Howard's, Hooker's, and Palmer's corps, on the extreme right. Each corps was deployed with strong reserves, and their trains were parked to their rear. McPherson's trains were in Decatur, guarded by a brigade commanded by Colonel Sprague of the Sixty-third Ohio.[15] The Sixteenth Corps (Dodge's) was crowded out of position on the right of McPherson's line, by the contraction of the circle of investment; and, during the previous afternoon, the Seventeenth Corps (Blair's) had pushed its operations on the farther side of the Augusta Railroad, so as to secure possession of a hill, known as Leggett's Hill, which Leggett's and Force's divisions[16] had carried by assault.[17] Giles A. Smith's division was on Leggett's left, deployed with a weak left flank "in air," in military phraseology.

[14] Jeremy F. Gilmer (1818–1883) graduated from the USMA in 1839 and was an engineer in the Dept. of the Pacific before the start of the Civil War. He resigned from the U.S. Army to join the Confederate Army in Mar. 1861. *CWHC,* 598.

[15] John W. Sprague (1817–1893) joined the 63rd Ohio as a colonel in Jan. 1862. During the Atlanta Campaign, he commanded the 2nd Brig., 4th Div., Dist. of Corinth, 16th Corps, Army of the Tennessee. *CWHC,* 503.

[16] Manning F. Force (1824–1899) commanded the 1st Brig., 3rd Div., 17th Corps, Army of the Tennessee, in July 1864. He was wounded in the face during the Battle of Atlanta and later received the Medal of Honor for his actions during the battle. *CWHC,* 239.

[17] In the first edition of the memoirs (1875), this portion of WTS's text read, "known as Leggett's Hill, because General Leggett's division had carried it by assault. Giles A. Smith's division was on

The evening before General Gresham, a great favorite, was badly wounded;[18] and there also Colonel Tom Reynolds, now of Madison, Wisconsin, was shot through the leg. When the surgeons were debating the propriety of amputating it in his hearing, he begged them to spare the leg, as it was very valuable, being an "imported leg." He was of Irish birth, and this well-timed piece of wit saved his leg, for the surgeons thought, if he could perpetrate a joke at such a time, they would trust to his vitality to save his limb.[19]

During the night, I had full reports from all parts of our line, most of which was partially intrenched as against a sally, and finding that McPherson was stretching out too much on his left flank, I wrote him a note early in the morning not to extend so much by his left; for we had not troops enough to completely invest the place, and I intended to destroy utterly all parts of the Augusta Railroad to the east of Atlanta, then to withdraw from the left flank and add to the right. In that letter I ordered McPherson not to extend any farther to the left, but to employ General Dodge's corps (Sixteenth), then forced out of position, to destroy every rail and tie of the railroad, from Decatur up to his skirmish-line, and I wanted him (McPherson) to be ready, as soon as General Garrard returned from Covington (whither I had sent him), to move to the extreme right of Thomas, so as to reach if possible the railroad below Atlanta, viz., the Macon road.[20] In the morning we found the strong line of parapet, "Peach-Tree line," to the front of Schofield and Thomas, abandoned, and our lines were advanced rapidly close up to Atlanta. For some moments I supposed the enemy intended to evacuate, and in person

---

Leggett's left, deployed with a weak left flank 'in air,' in military phraseology. It was in carrying this hill that General Gresham, a great favorite, was badly wounded . . ."

[18] Walter Q. Gresham (1832–1895) commanded the 4th Div., 17th Corps, Army of the Tennessee, during the Battle of Atlanta. He was wounded in the left knee at Bald Hill, GA, on July 20, 1864. He later served as the U.S. postmaster general from 1883 to 1884, U.S. secretary of the treasury for Sept.–Oct. 1884, and U.S. secretary of state from 1893 to 1895. *CWHC,* 268.

[19] Thomas Reynolds (1814–1893), a close friend of WTS, was born in County Longford, Ireland, and moved to the United States when he was twenty-two years old. "General Thomas Reynolds," *Inter Ocean* (Chicago), Mar. 5, 1893, 11; "Death of Gen. Thomas Reynolds," *Chicago Tribune,* Mar. 5, 1893, 5.

[20] McPherson received WTS's order, written in pencil, at approximately 7 A.M. on July 22, 1864. The letter was preserved by one of McPherson's staff members. *Report of the Proceedings of the Society of the Army of the Tennessee, at the Eleventh Annual Meeting Held at St. Paul, Minnesota, September 5th and 6th, 1877* (Cincinnati: Society of the Army of the Tennessee, 1885), 240.

was on horseback at the head of Schofield's troops, who had advanced in front of the Howard House[21] to some open ground, from which we could plainly see the whole rebel line of parapets, and I saw their men dragging up from the intervening valley, by the distillery, trees and saplings for abatis. Our skirmishers found the enemy down in this valley, and we could see the rebel main line strongly manned, with guns in position at intervals. Schofield was dressing forward his lines, and I could hear Thomas farther to the right engaged, when General McPherson and his staff rode up. We went back to the Howard House, a double frame-building with a porch, and sat on the steps, discussing the chances of battle, and of Hood's general character. McPherson had also been of the same class at West Point with Hood, Schofield, and Sheridan. We agreed that we ought to be unusually cautious and prepared at all times for sallies and for hard fighting, because Hood, though not deemed much of a scholar, or of great mental capacity, was undoubtedly a brave, determined, and rash man; and the change of commanders at that particular crisis argued the displeasure of the Confederate Government with the cautious but prudent conduct of General Jos. Johnston.

McPherson was in excellent spirits, well pleased at the progress of events so far, and had come over purposely to see me about the order I had given him to use Dodge's corps to break up the railroad, saying that the night before he had gained a position on Leggett's Hill from which he could look over the rebel parapet, and see the high smoke-stack of a large foundery in Atlanta; that before receiving my order he had diverted Dodge's two divisions (then in motion) from the main road, along a diagonal one that led to his extreme left flank, then held by Giles A. Smith's division (Seventeenth Corps), for the purpose of strengthening that flank; and that he had sent some intrenching-tools there, to erect some batteries from which he intended to knock down that foundery, and otherwise to damage the buildings inside of Atlanta. He said he could put all his pioneers to work, and do with them in the time indicated all I had proposed to do with General Dodge's two divisions. Of course I assented at once, and we walked down the road a short distance, sat down by the foot of a tree where I had my map, and on it pointed out to him Thomas's position and his own. I then explained minutely that, after we had sufficiently broken up the Augusta road, I wanted to shift his whole army around by the rear to Thomas's extreme right, and hoped thus to reach the

[21] The Howard House was situated approximately three miles east of Atlanta. Davis et al., *Official Military Atlas of the Civil War,* plate 88, map 1.

other railroad at East Point.[22] While we sat there we could hear lively skirmishing going on near us (down about the distillery), and occasionally round-shot from twelve or twenty-four pound guns came through the trees in reply to those of Schofield, and we could hear similar sounds all along down the lines of Thomas to our right, and his own to the left; but presently the firing appeared a little more brisk (especially over about Giles A. Smith's division), and then we heard an occasional gun back toward Decatur. I asked him what it meant. We took my pocket-compass (which I always carried), and by noting the direction of the sound, we became satisfied that the firing was too far to our left rear to be explained by known facts, and he hastily called for his horse, his staff, and his orderlies.

McPherson was then in his prime (about thirty-four years old),[23] over six feet high, and a very handsome man in every way, was universally liked, and had many noble qualities. He had on his boots outside his pantaloons, gauntlets on his hands, had on his major-general's uniform, and wore a sword-belt, but no sword. He hastily gathered his papers (save one, which I now possess) into a pocket-book, put it in his breast-pocket, and jumped on his horse, saying he would hurry down his line and send me back word what these sounds meant. His adjutant-general, Clark,[24] Inspector-General Strong, and his aides, Captains Steele[25] and Gile,[26] were with him. Although the sound of musketry on our left grew in volume, I was not so much disturbed by it as by the sound of artillery back toward Decatur. I ordered Schofield at once to send a brigade back to Decatur (some five miles) and was walking up and down the porch of the Howard House, listening, when one of McPherson's staff, with his horse

[22] East Point, GA, was situated approximately two miles south of Atlanta near the intersection of the Atlanta & West Point and Macon & Western Railroads. Davis et al., *Official Military Atlas of the Civil War,* plate 57, map 1.

[23] McPherson was thirty-five years old in July 1864. *CWHC,* 383–384.

[24] William T. Clark (1831–1905) was brevetted brigadier general for his actions during the Atlanta Campaign on July 22, 1864. In 1870 he was elected to represent Texas in the U.S. House of Representatives, where he served until he was expelled in 1872. *CWHC,* 175.

[25] George R. Steele (1836–1897) was promoted to captain and became McPherson's aide-de-camp after the Battle of Corinth in 1862. After McPherson's death, Steele was assigned to the staff of Gen. Francis P. Blair until the end of the war. "Major Steele Dead," *Decatur Daily Republican* (Decatur, IL), May 19, 1897, 8.

[26] David H. Gile (1836–1898) joined McPherson's staff as an aide-de-camp on Mar. 1, 1863, and resigned from the U.S. Army on Nov. 4, 1864. *Report of the Proceedings of the Society of the Army of the Tennessee at the Thirtieth Meeting, Held at Toledo, Ohio, October 26–27, 1898* (Cincinnati: F.W. Freeman, 1899), 136.

covered with sweat, dashed up to the porch, and reported that General McPherson was either "killed or a prisoner."[27] He explained that when they had left me a few minutes before, they had ridden rapidly across to the railroad, the sounds of battle increasing as they neared the position occupied by General Giles A. Smith's division, and that McPherson had sent first one, then another of his staff to bring some of the reserve brigades of the Fifteenth Corps over to the exposed left flank; that he had reached the head of Dodge's corps (marching by the flank on the diagonal road as described), and had ordered it to hurry forward to the same point; that then, almost if not entirely alone, he had followed this road leading across the wooded valley behind the Seventeenth Corps, and had disappeared in these woods, doubtless with a sense of absolute security. The sound of musketry was there heard, and McPherson's horse came back, bleeding, wounded, and riderless. I ordered the staff-officer who brought this message to return at once, to find General Logan (the senior officer present with the Army of the Tennessee), to report the same facts to him, and to instruct him to drive back this supposed small force, which had evidently got around the Seventeenth Corps through the blind woods in rear of our left flank. I soon dispatched one of my own staff (McCoy, I think) to General Logan with similar orders, telling him to refuse his left flank, and to fight the battle (holding fast to Leggett's Hill) with the Army of the Tennessee; that I would personally look to Decatur and to the safety of his rear, and would reënforce him if he needed it. I dispatched orders to General Thomas on our right, telling him of this strong sally, and my inference that the lines in his front had evidently been weakened by reason thereof, and that he ought to take advantage of the opportunity to make a lodgment in Atlanta, if possible.

Meantime the sounds of the battle rose on our extreme left more and more furious, extending to the place where I stood, at the Howard House. Within an hour an ambulance came in (attended by Colonels Clark and Strong, and Captains Steele and Gile), bearing McPherson's body. I had it carried inside of the Howard House, and laid on a door wrenched from its hinges. Dr. Hewitt, of the army,[28] was there, and I asked him to examine the wound. He opened the coat and shirt, saw where the ball had entered and where it came out, or rather lodged under the skin, and he reported that McPherson must have died in a

[27] In his post-battle report, WTS stated that Gen. William T. Clark was the staff member who informed him of McPherson's fate. *OR,* I, 38(I), 73.

[28] Henry S. Hewit (c. 1829–1873) served as the medical director for USG until he was transferred to Gen. Schofield's staff after the Battle of Shiloh. *PUSG,* 23:17–18; "Was Grant Drunk at Pittsburg Landing?," *Nashville Union and American* (Nashville, TN), Oct. 21, 1873, 2.

few seconds after being hit; that the ball had ranged upward across his body, and passed near the heart. He was dressed just as he left me, with gauntlets and boots on, but his pocket-book was gone. On further inquiry I learned that his body must have been in possession of the enemy some minutes, during which time it was rifled of the pocket-book, and I was much concerned lest the letter I had written him that morning should have fallen into the hands of some one who could read and understand its meaning. Fortunately the spot in the woods where McPherson was shot was regained by our troops in a few minutes, and the pocket-book found in the haversack of a prisoner of war captured at the time, and it and its contents were secured by one of McPherson's staff.[29]

While we were examining the body inside the house, the battle was progressing outside, and many shots struck the building, which I feared would take fire; so I ordered Captains Steele and Gile to carry the body to Marietta. They reached that place the same night, and, on application, I ordered his personal staff to go on and escort the body to his home, in Clyde, Ohio, where it was received with great honor, and it is now buried in a small cemetery, close by his mother's house, which cemetery is composed in part of the family orchard, in which he used to play when a boy. The foundation is ready laid for the equestrian monument now in progress, under the auspices of the Society of the Army of the Tennessee.[30]

The reports that came to me from all parts of the field revealed clearly what was the game of my antagonist, and the ground somewhat favored him. The railroad and wagon-road from Decatur to Atlanta lie along the summit, from which the waters flow, by short, steep valleys, into the "Peach-Tree" and

[29] McPherson's belongings were recovered by troops from the division led by Gen. John W. Fuller (1827–1891). In a letter to Gen. Dodge, Fuller wrote, "I send this that General Sherman may know that they did not remain in the hands of the enemy long enough to be read. They were taken from a rebel who had just been stripping General McPherson's body; another who had the General's glass was also taken. They were sent to the rear. If nobody objects, I should be obliged if General Dodge will return these papers to me." *CWHC,* 246; *Report of the Proceedings of the Society of the Army of the Tennessee at the Eleventh Annual Meeting Held at St. Paul, Minnesota, September 5th and 6th, 1877,* 248.

[30] On July 22, 1881, a bronze statue of McPherson standing was unveiled at the family cemetery. WTS gave a eulogy that read, in part, "You knew his genial, hearty nature, his attachment to his family and neighbors, but you could not see the man as I have seen him, in danger, in battle, when every muscle and every tissue was in full action, when the heroic qualities shown out as a star in the darkest night." Nevin O. Winter, *A History of Northwest Ohio* (Chicago: Lewis, 1917), 267.

Chattahoochee, to the west, and by other valleys, of gentler declivity, toward the east (Ocmulgee). The ridges and level ground were mostly cleared, and had been cultivated as corn or cotton fields; but where the valleys were broken, they were left in a state of nature—wooded, and full of undergrowth. McPherson's line of battle was across this railroad, along a general ridge, with a gentle but cleared valley to his front, between him and the defenses of Atlanta; and another valley, behind him, was clear of timber in part, but to his left rear the country was heavily wooded. Hood, during the night of July 21st, had withdrawn from his Peach-Tree line, had occupied the fortified line of Atlanta, facing north and east, with Stewart's[31]—formerly Polk's—corps and part of Hardee's, and with G. W. Smith's division of militia. His own corps, and part of Hardee's, had marched out to the road leading from McDonough to Decatur, and had turned so as to strike the left and rear of McPherson's line "in air." At the same time he had sent Wheeler's division of cavalry[32] against the trains parked in Decatur. Unluckily for us, I had sent away the whole of Garrard's division of cavalry during the night of the 20th, with orders to proceed to Covington, thirty miles east, to burn two important bridges across the Ulcofauhatchee[33] and Yellow Rivers, to tear up the railroad, to damage it as much as possible from Stone Mountain eastward, and to be gone four days; so that McPherson had no cavalry in hand to guard that flank.[34]

The enemy was therefore enabled, under cover or the forest, to approach quite near before he was discovered; indeed, his skirmish-line had worked through the timber and got into the field to the rear of Giles A. Smith's division of the Seventeenth Corps unseen, had captured Murray's battery of regular artillery,[35] moving through these woods entirely unguarded, and had

[31] Alexander P. Stewart (1821–1908) graduated from the USMA in 1842 and resigned from the U.S. Army in 1845. He joined the Confederate Army at the start of the war and commanded the 3rd Corps, Army of Tennessee, in July 1864. *CWHC,* 511.

[32] Joseph Wheeler II (1836–1906) graduated from the USMA in 1854 and resigned from the U.S. Army to join the Confederate Army at the start of the war. In July 1864 he commanded the Cav. Corps in the Army of Tennessee. *CWHC,* 563.

[33] The Ulcofauhatchee River was the name of the modern-day Alcovey River. Lary M. Dilsaver and Craig E. Colten, eds., *The American Environment: Interpretations of Past Geographies* (Lanham, MD: Rowman and Littlefield, 1992), 24–25.

[34] For WTS's full order to Garrard, see *OR,* I, 38(V), 209.

[35] Eli H. Murray (1843–1896) was a colonel in the 3rd Brig., 3rd Div., Cav. Corps, Military Div. of the Mississippi, in July 1864. According to Giles A. Smith's post-battle report, two pieces of artillery were taken from Co. F of the 2nd Illinois Art. *CWHC,* 402; *OR,* I, 38(III), 582.

got possession of several of the hospital camps. The right of this rebel line struck Dodge's troops in motion; but, fortunately, this corps (Sixteenth) had only to halt, face to the left, and was in line of battle; and this corps not only held in check the enemy, but drove him back through the woods.[36] About the same time this same force had struck General Giles A. Smith's left flank, doubled it back, captured four guns in position and the party engaged in building the very battery which was the special object of McPherson's visit to me, and almost enveloped the entire left flank. The men, however, were skillful and brave, and fought for a time with their backs to Atlanta. They gradually fell back, compressing their own line, and gaining strength by making junction with Leggett's division of the Seventeenth Corps, well and strongly posted on the hill. One or two brigades of the Fifteenth Corps, ordered by McPherson, came rapidly across the open field to the rear, from the direction of the railroad, filled up the gap from Blair's new left to the head of Dodge's column—now facing to the general left—thus forming a strong left flank, at right angles to the original line of battle. The enemy attacked, boldly and repeatedly, the whole of this flank, but met an equally fierce resistance; and on that ground a bloody battle raged from little after noon till into the night. A part of Hood's plan of action was to sally from Atlanta at the same moment; but this sally was not, for some reason, simultaneous, for the first attack on our extreme left flank had been checked and repulsed before the sally came from the direction of Atlanta. Meantime, Colonel Sprague, in Decatur, had got his teams harnessed up, and safely conducted his train to the rear of Schofield's position, holding in check Wheeler's cavalry till he had got off all his trains, with the exception of three or four wagons. I remained near the Howard House, receiving reports and sending orders, urging Generals Thomas and Schofield to take advantage of the absence from their front of so considerable a body as was evidently engaged on our left, and, if possible, to make a lodgment in Atlanta itself; but they reported that the lines to their front, at all accessible points, were strong, by nature and by art, and were fully manned. About 4 P. M. the expected sally came from Atlanta, directed mainly against Leggett's Hill and along the Decatur road. At Leggett's Hill they were met and bloodily repulsed. Along the railroad they were more successful. Sweeping over a small force with two guns, they reached our main line, broke through it, and got possession of De

[36] For Dodge's account of the Battle of Atlanta, see the section "General G. M. Dodge's account of the part taken by the Sixteenth Army Corps in the movement on Resaca. Attack of the 4th of July, and battle of Atlanta, July 22, 1864" in Appendix to Volume II.

Gress's battery[37] of four twenty-pound Parrotts, killing every horse, and turning the guns against us. General Charles R. Wood's division of the Fifteenth Corps was on the extreme right of the Army of the Tennessee, between the railroad and the Howard House, where he connected with Schofield's troops. He reported to me in person that the line on his left had been swept back, and that his connection with General Logan, on Leggett's Hill, was broken. I ordered him to wheel his brigades to the left, to advance in echelon, and to catch the enemy in flank. General Schofield brought forward all his available batteries, to the number of twenty guns, to a position to the left front of the Howard House, whence we could overlook the field of action, and directed a heavy fire over the heads of General Wood's men against the enemy; and we saw Wood's troops advance and encounter the enemy, who had secured possession of the old line of parapet which had been held by our men. His right crossed this parapet, which he swept back, taking it in flank; and, at the same time, the division which had been driven back along the railroad was rallied by General Logan in person, and fought for their former ground. These combined forces drove the enemy into Atlanta, recovering the twenty pound Parrott guns—but one of them was found "bursted" while in the possession of the enemy. The two six-pounders farther in advance were, however, lost, and had been hauled back by the enemy into Atlanta. Poor Captain de Gress came to me in tears, lamenting the loss of his favorite guns; when they were regained he had only a few men left, and not a single horse. He asked an order for a reëquipment, but I told him he must beg and borrow of others till he could restore his battery, now reduced to three guns. How he did so I do not know, but in a short time he did get horses, men, and finally another gun, of the same special pattern, and served them with splendid effect till the very close of the war.[38] This battery had also been with me from Shiloh till that time.

[37] Francis DeGress (1840–1883) was born in Prussia and moved to the United States at a young age. He joined the 1st Illinois Light Art. at the start of the war and served as the chief of artillery under Gen. John Logan during the Atlanta Campaign. "Major Francis DeGress," *New York Tribune,* Jan. 5, 1883, 3.

[38] DeGress described the incident in his post-battle report: "The enemy charged our works about 4 P.M.; was repulsed in my front, but broke through our center, and changing front charged my battery, which I was obliged to leave after spiking the guns, and after all my support had left me. As soon as my battery was recaptured I had the guns unspiked and fired again

The battle of July 22d is usually called the battle of Atlanta. It extended from the Howard House to General Giles A. Smith's position, about a mile beyond the Augusta Railroad, and then back toward Decatur, the whole extent of ground being fully seven miles. In part the ground was clear and in part densely wooded. I rode over the whole of it the next day, and it bore the marks of a bloody conflict. The enemy had retired during the night inside of Atlanta, and we remained masters of the situation outside. I purposely allowed the Army of the Tennessee to fight this battle almost unaided, save by demonstrations on the part of General Schofield and Thomas against the fortified lines to their immediate fronts, and by detaching, as described, one of Schofield's brigades to Decatur, because I knew that the attacking force could only be a part of Hood's army, and that, if any assistance were rendered by either of the other armies, the Army of the Tennessee would be jealous. Nobly did they do their work that day, and terrible was the slaughter done to our enemy, though at sad cost to ourselves, as shown by the following reports:

HEADQUARTERS MILITARY DIVISION OF THE MISSISSIPPI,
IN THE FIELD, NEAR ATLANTA, *July* 23, 1864.

General HALLECK, *Washington, D. C.*

Yesterday morning the enemy fell back to the intrenchments proper of the city of Atlanta, which are in a general circle, with a radius of one and a half miles, and we closed in. While we were forming our lines, and selecting positions for our batteries, the enemy appeared suddenly out of the dense woods in heavy masses on our extreme left, and struck the Seventeenth Corps (General Blair) in flank, and was forcing it back, when the Sixteenth Corps (General Dodge) came up and checked the movement, but the enemy's cavalry got well to our rear, and into Decatur, and for some hours our left flank was completely enveloped. The fight that resulted was continuous until night, with heavy loss on both sides. The enemy took one of our batteries (Murray's, of the Regular Army) that was marching in its place in column in the road, unconscious of danger. About 4 P. M. the enemy sallied against the division of General Morgan L. Smith, of the Fifteenth Corps, which occupied an abandoned line of rifle-trench near the

at the retreating enemy. One of my guns, injured since the 25th of June, burst at the third round." *OR*, I, 38(III), 265.

railroad east of the city, and forced it back some four hundred yards, leaving in his hands for the time two batteries, but the ground and batteries were immediately after recovered by the same troops reën-forced. I cannot well approximate our loss, which fell heavily on the Fifteenth and Seventeenth Corps, but count it as three thousand; I know that, being on the defensive, we have inflicted equally heavy loss on the enemy.

General McPherson, when arranging his troops about 11.00 A. M., and passing from one column to another, incautiously rode upon an ambuscade without apprehension, at some distance ahead of his staff and orderlies, and was shot dead.

W. T. SHERMAN, *Major-General commanding.*

HEADQUARTERS MILITARY DIVISION OF THE MISSISSIPPI,
IN THE FIELD, NEAR ATLANTA, GEORGIA, *July* 25, 1864—8 A. M.

Major-General HALLECK, *Washington, D. C.*

GENERAL: I find it difficult to make prompt report of results, coupled with some data or information, without occasionally making mistakes. McPherson's sudden death, and Logan succeeding to the command as it were in the midst of battle, made some confusion on our extreme left; but it soon recovered and made sad havoc with the enemy, who had practised one of his favorite games of attacking our left when in motion, and before it had time to cover its weak flank. After riding over the ground and hearing the varying statements of the actors, I directed General Logan to make an official report of the actual result, and I herewith inclose it.

Though the number of dead rebels seems excessive, I am disposed to give full credit to the report that our loss, though only thirty-five hundred and twenty-one killed, wounded, and missing, the enemy's dead alone on the field nearly equaled that number, viz., thirty-two hundred and twenty. Happening at that point of the line when a flag of truce was sent in to ask permission for each party to bury its dead, I gave General Logan authority to permit a temporary truce on that flank *alone,* while our labors and fighting proceeded at all others.

I also send you a copy of General Garrard's report of the breaking of the railroad toward Augusta. I am now grouping my command to attack the Macon road, and with that view will intrench a strong line of circumvallation with flanks, so as to have as large an infantry column as possible, with all the cavalry to swing round to the south and east, to strike that road at or below East Point.

I have the honor to be, your obedient servant,

W. T. Sherman, *Major-General commanding.*

Headquarters Department and Army of the Tennessee,
before Atlanta, Georgia, *July* 24, 1864.

Major-General W. T. Sherman, *commanding Military Division of the Mississippi.*

General: I have the honor to report the following general summary of the result of the attack of the enemy on this army on the 22d inst.

Total loss, killed, wounded, and missing, thirty-five hundred and twenty-one, and ten pieces of artillery.

We have buried and delivered to the enemy, under a flag of truce sent in by them, in front of the Third Division, Seventeenth Corps, one thousand of their killed.

The number of their dead in front of the Fourth Division of the same corps, including those on the ground not now occupied by our troops, General Blair reports, will swell the number of their dead on his front to two thousand.

The number of their dead buried in front of the Fifteenth Corps, up to this hour, is three hundred and sixty, and the commanding officer reports that at least as many more are yet unburied, burying-parties being still at work.

The number of dead buried in front of the Sixteenth Corps is four hundred and twenty-two. We have over one thousand of their wounded in our hands, the larger number of the wounded being carried off during the night, after the engagement, by them.

We captured eighteen stands of colors, and have them now. We also captured five thousand stands of arms.

The attack was made on our lines seven times, and was seven times repulsed. Hood's and Hardee's corps and Wheeler's cavalry engaged us.

We have sent to the rear one thousand prisoners, including thirty-three commissioned officers of high rank.

We still occupy the field, and the troops are in fine spirits. A detailed and full report will be furnished as soon as completed.

Recapitulation.

Our total loss	3,521
Enemy's dead, thus far reported, buried, and delivered to them	3,220
Total prisoners sent North	1,017
Total prisoners, wounded, in our hands	1,000
Estimated loss of the enemy, at least	10,000

Very respectfully, your obedient servant,
JOHN A. LOGAN, *Major-General.*

On the 22d of July General Rousseau reached Marietta, having returned from his raid on the Alabama road at Opelika, and on the next day General Garrard also returned from Covington, both having been measurably successful. The former was about twenty-five hundred strong, the latter about four thousand, and both reported that their horses were jaded and tired, needing shoes and rest. But, about this time, I was advised by General Grant (then investing Richmond) that the rebel Government had become aroused to the critical condition of things about Atlanta, and that I must look out for Hood being greatly reënforced.[39] I therefore was resolved to push matters, and at once set about the original purpose of transferring the whole of the Army of the Tennessee to our right flank, leaving Schofield to stretch out so as to rest his left on the Augusta road, then torn up for thirty miles eastward; and, as auxiliary thereto, I ordered all the cavalry to be ready to pass around Atlanta on both flanks, to break up the Macon road at some point below, so as to cut off all supplies to the rebel army inside, and thus to force it to evacuate, or come out and fight us on equal terms.

But it first became necessary to settle the important question of who should succeed General McPherson? General Logan had taken command of the Army of the Tennessee by virtue of his seniority, and had done well; but I did not consider him equal to the command of three corps. Between him and General Blair there existed a natural rivalry. Both were men of great courage and talent, but were politicians by nature and experience, and it may be that for this reason they were mistrusted by regular officers like Generals Schofield, Thomas, and myself. It was all-important that there should exist a perfect understanding among the army commanders, and at a conference with General George H. Thomas at the headquarters of General Thomas J. Woods, commanding a

[39] WTS did not receive USG's July 21, 1864, dispatch until July 25. *OR,* I, 38(V), 210–211, 247.

division in the Fourth Corps, he (Thomas) remonstrated warmly against my recommending that General Logan should be regularly assigned to the command of the Army of the Tennessee by reason of his accidental seniority. We discussed fully the merits and qualities of every officer of high rank in the army, and finally settled on Major-General O. O. Howard as the best officer who was present and available for the purpose; on the 24th of July I telegraphed to General Halleck this preference, and it was promptly ratified by the President. General Howard's place in command of the Fourth Corps was filled by General Stanley, one of his division commanders, on the recommendation of General Thomas. All these promotions happened to fall upon West-Pointers, and doubtless Logan and Blair had some reason to believe that we intended to monopolize the higher honors of the war for the regular officers. I remember well my own thoughts and feelings at the time, and feel sure that I was not intentionally partial to any class. I wanted to succeed in taking Atlanta, and needed commanders who were purely and technically soldiers, men who would obey orders and execute them promptly and on time; for I knew that we would have to execute some most delicate manœuvres, requiring the utmost skill, nicety, and precision. I believed that General Howard would do all these faithfully and well, and I think the result has justified my choice. I regarded both Generals Logan and Blair as "volunteers," that looked to personal fame and glory as auxiliary and secondary to their political ambition, and not as professional soldiers.[40]

As soon as it was known that General Howard had been chosen to command the Army of the Tennessee, General Hooker applied to General Thomas to be relieved of the command of the Twentieth Corps, and General Thomas forwarded his application to me approved and *heartily* recommended. I at once telegraphed to General Halleck, recommending General Slocum (then at Vicksburg) to be his successor, because Slocum had been displaced from the command of his corps at the time when the Eleventh and Twelfth were united and made the Twentieth.[41]

[40] U.S. Army Gen. John W. Sprague defended WTS's comments on Blair and Logan. "Your views of these gentlemen as soldiers are precisely the same as those expressed by hundreds of volunteer officers during the war, and who felt for both those gentlemen only the highest respect and most kindly feelings." See John W. Sprague to WTS, July 13, 1875, in Appendix to Volume II.

[41] Special Field Orders, No. 205, issued on July 27, relieved Hooker of command of the 20th Corps, Army of the Cumberland. *OR,* I, 38(V), 272–274.

General Hooker was offended because he was not chosen to succeed McPherson; but his chances were not even considered; indeed, I had never been satisfied with him since his affair at the Kulp House, and had been more than once disposed to relieve him of his corps, because of his repeated attempts to interfere with Generals McPherson and Schofield. I had known Hooker since 1836, and was intimately associated with him in California, where we served together on the staff of General Persifer F. Smith. He had come to us from the East with a high reputation as a "fighter," which he had fully justified at Chattanooga and Peach-Tree Creek; at which latter battle I complimented him on the field for special gallantry, and afterward in official reports.[42] Still, I did feel a sense of relief when he left us.[43] We were then two hundred and fifty miles in advance of our base, dependent on a single line of railroad for our daily food. We had a bold, determined foe in our immediate front, strongly intrenched, with communication open to his rear for supplies and reënforcements, and every soldier realized that we had plenty of hard fighting ahead, and that all honors had to be fairly earned.[44]

Until General Slocum joined (in the latter part of August), the Twentieth Corps was commanded by General A. S. Williams, the senior division commander present. On the 25th of July the army, therefore, stood thus: the Army of the Tennessee (General O. O. Howard commanding) was on the left, pretty much on the same ground it had occupied during the battle of the 22d, all ready to move rapidly by the rear to the extreme right beyond Proctor's Creek; the Army of the Ohio (General Schofield) was next in order, with its left flank reaching the Augusta Railroad; next in order, conforming closely with the rebel intrenchments of Atlanta, was General Thomas's Army of the Cumberland, in the order of—the Fourth Corps (Stanley's), the Twentieth Corps (Williams's), and the Fourteenth Corps (Palmer's). Palmer's right division (Jefferson C. Davis's) was strongly refused along Proctor's Creek. This

[42] For WTS's full report on the Atlanta Campaign, see *OR,* I, 38(I), 59–117.

[43] In the first edition of the memoirs (1875), this portion of WTS's text, starting with "I had known Hooker . . . ," read, "I am told that he says that Thomas and I were jealous of him; but this is hardly probable, for we on the spot did not rate his fighting qualities as high as he did, and I am, moreover, convinced that both he and General Butterfield went to the rear for personal reasons."

[44] In the first edition of the memoirs (1875), the end of the paragraph read, "General Hooker, moreover, when he got back to Cincinnati, reported (I was told) that we had run up against a rock at Atlanta, and that the country ought to be prepared to hear of disaster from that quarter."

line was about five miles long, and was intrenched as against a sally about as strong as was our enemy. The cavalry was assembled in two strong divisions; that of McCook (including the brigade of Harrison[45] which had been brought in from Opelika by General Rousseau) numbered about thirty-five hundred effective cavalry, and was posted to our right rear, at Turner's Ferry, where we had a good pontoon-bridge; and to our left rear, at and about Decatur, were the two cavalry divisions of Stoneman, twenty-five hundred, and Garrard, four thousand, united for the time and occasion under the command of Major-General George Stoneman, a cavalry-officer of high repute. My plan of action was to move the Army of the Tennessee to the right rapidly and boldly against the railroad below Atlanta, and at the same time to send all the cavalry around by the right and left to make a lodgment on the Macon road about Jonesboro'.

All the orders were given, and the morning of the 27th was fixed for commencing the movement. On the 26th I received from General Stoneman a note asking permission (after having accomplished his orders to break up the railroad at Jonesboro') to go on to Macon to rescue our prisoners of war known to be held there, and then to push on to Andersonville, where was the great depot of Union prisoners, in which were penned at one time as many as twenty-three thousand of our men, badly fed and harshly treated.[46] I wrote him an answer consenting substantially to his proposition, only modifying it by requiring him to send back General Garrard's division to its position on our left flank after he had broken up the railroad at Jonesboro'.[47] Promptly, and on time, all got off, and General Dodge's corps (the Sixteenth, of the Army of the Tennessee) reached its position across Proctor's Creek the same evening, and early the next morning (the 28th) Blair's corps (the Seventeenth) deployed on his right, both corps covering their front with the usual parapet; the Fifteenth Corps (General Logan's) came up that morning on the right of Blair, strongly refused, and began to prepare the usual cover. As General Jeff. C. Davis's division was, as it were, left out of line, I ordered it on the evening before to march down toward Turner's Ferry, and then to take a road laid down on our maps which led from there toward

[45] Benjamin Harrison (1833–1901) commanded the 1st Brig., 3rd Div., 20th Corps, Army of the Cumberland, in July 1864. He later served one term as a U.S. senator from Indiana from 1881 to 1887 and one term as president of the United States from 1889 to 1893. *CWHC*, 283.

[46] In Feb. 1864 the Confederate Army established Andersonville Prison in Macon County, GA, to house U.S. Army prisoners of war. By July, Andersonville, known for its extremely poor sanitary and health conditions, was the largest prison in the country. John C. Inscoe, *The Civil War in Georgia: A New Georgia Encyclopedia Companion* (Athens: University of Georgia Press, 2011), s.v. "Andersonville Prison."

[47] For the July 26 correspondence between WTS and Stoneman, see *OR*, I, 38(V), 264–265.

East Point, ready to engage any enemy that might attack our general right flank, after the same manner as had been done to the left flank on the 22d.

Personally on the morning of the 28th I followed the movement, and rode to the extreme right, where we could hear some skirmishing and an occasional cannon-shot. As we approached the ground held by the Fifteenth Corps, a cannon-ball passed over my shoulder and killed the horse of an orderly behind; and seeing that this gun enfiladed the road by which we were riding, we turned out of it and rode down into a valley, where we left our horses and walked up to the hill held by Morgan L. Smith's division of the Fifteenth Corps. Near a house I met Generals Howard and Logan, who explained that there was an intrenched battery to their front, with the appearance of a strong infantry support. I then walked up to the ridge, where I found General Morgan L. Smith. His men were deployed and engaged in rolling logs and fence-rails, preparing a hasty cover. From this ridge we could overlook the open fields near a meeting-house known as "Ezra Church," close by the Poor-House.[48] We could see the fresh earth of a parapet covering some guns (that fired an occasional shot), and there was also an appearance of activity beyond. General Smith was in the act of sending forward a regiment from his right flank to feel the position of the enemy, when I explained to him and to Generals Logan and Howard that they must look out for General Jeff. C. Davis's division, which was coming up from the direction of Turner's Ferry.

As the skirmish-fire warmed up along the front of Blair's corps, as well as along the Fifteenth Corps (Logan's), I became convinced that Hood designed to attack this right flank, to prevent, if possible, the extension of our line in that direction. I regained my horse, and rode rapidly back to see that Davis's division had been dispatched as ordered. I found General Davis in person, who was unwell, and had sent his division that morning early, under the command of his senior brigadier, Morgan;[49] but, as I attached great importance to the movement, he mounted his horse, and rode away to overtake and to hurry forward the movement, so as to come up on the left rear of the enemy, during the expected battle.

By this time the sound of cannon and musketry denoted a severe battle as in progress, which began seriously at 11 ½ A. M., and ended substantially by 4

[48] Ezra Church was situated approximately two miles northwest of Atlanta. Davis et al., *Official Military Atlas of the Civil War,* plate 60, map 1.

[49] In his post-battle report, Davis wrote, "At this time my health, which had not been good for some days, required me to turn over the active and immediate command of the troops to General Morgan." James D. Morgan (1810–1896) commanded the 1st Brig., 2nd Div., 14th Corps, Army of the Cumberland, on July 28, 1864. *CWHC,* 397; *OR,* I, 38(I), 635.

P. M. It was a fierce attack by the enemy on our extreme right flank, well posted and partially covered. The most authentic account of the battle is given by General Logan, who commanded the Fifteenth Corps, in his official report to the Adjutant-General of the Army of the Tennessee, thus:

HEADQUARTERS FIFTEENTH ARMY CORPS,
BEFORE ATLANTA, GEORGIA, *July* 29, 1864.

Lieutenant-Colonel WILLIAM T. CLARK, *Assistant Adjutant-General, Army of the Tennessee, present.*

COLONEL: I have the honor to report that, in pursuance of orders, I moved my command into position on the right of the Seventeenth Corps, which was the extreme right of the army in the field, during the night of the 27th and morning of the 28th; and, while advancing in line of battle to a more favorable position, we were met by the rebel infantry of Hardee's and Lee's corps, who made a determined and desperate attack on us at 11 ½ A. M. of the 28th (yesterday).

My lines were only protected by logs and rails, hastily thrown up in front of them.

The first onset was received and checked, and the battle commenced and lasted until about three o'clock in the evening. During that time six successive charges were made, which were six times gallantly repulsed, each time with fearful loss to the enemy.

Later in the evening my lines were several times assaulted vigorously, but each time with like result.

The worst of the fighting occurred on General Harrow's and Morgan L. Smith's fronts, which formed the centre and right of the corps.

The troops could not have displayed greater courage, nor greater determination not to give ground; had they shown less, they would have been driven from their position.

Brigadier-Generals C. R. Woods, Harrow, and Morgan L. Smith, division commanders, are entitled to equal credit for gallant conduct and skill in repelling the assault.

My thanks are due to Major-Generals Blair and Dodge for sending me reënforcements at a time when they were much needed.

My losses were fifty killed, four hundred and forty-nine wounded, and seventy-three missing: aggregate, five hundred and seventy-two.

The division of General Harrow captured five battle-flags. There were about fifteen hundred or two thousand muskets left on the ground. One hundred and six prisoners were captured, exclusive of seventy-three wounded, who were sent to our hospital, and are being cared for by our surgeons.

Five hundred and sixty-five rebels have up to this time been buried, and about two hundred are supposed to be yet unburied.

A large number of their wounded were undoubtedly carried away in the night, as the enemy did not withdraw till near daylight. The enemy's loss could not have been less than six or seven thousand men.

A more detailed report will hereafter be made.

I am, very respectfully,
Your obedient servant,

JOHN A. LOGAN,
Major-General, commanding Fifteenth Army Corps.

General Howard, in transmitting this report, added:

I wish to express my high gratification with the conduct of the troops engaged. I never saw better conduct in battle. General Logan, though ill and much worn out, was indefatigable, and the success of the day is as much attributable to him as to any one man.

This was, of course, the first fight in which General Howard had commanded the Army of the Tennessee, and he evidently aimed to reconcile General Logan in his disappointment, and to gain the heart of his army, to which he was a stranger. He very properly left General Logan to fight his own corps, but exposed himself freely; and, after the firing had ceased, in the afternoon he walked the lines; the men, as reported to me, gathered about him in the most affectionate way, and he at once gained their respect and confidence. To this fact I at the time attached much importance, for it put me at ease as to the future conduct of that most important army.

At no instant of time did I feel the least uneasiness about the result on the 28th, but wanted to reap fuller results, hoping that Davis's division would come up at the instant of defeat, and catch the enemy in flank; but the woods were dense, the roads obscure, and as usual this division got on the wrong road, and did not come into position until about dark. In like manner, I thought that Hood had greatly weakened his main lines inside of Atlanta, and accordingly sent repeated orders to Schofield and Thomas to make an attempt to break in; but both reported that they found the parapets very strong and full manned.

Our men were unusually encouraged by this day's work, for they realized that we could compel Hood to come out from behind his fortified lines to attack us at a disadvantage. In conversation with me, the soldiers of the Fifteenth Corps, with whom I was on the most familiar terms, spoke of the affair of the 28th as the easiest thing in the world; that, in fact, it was a common slaughter of the enemy; they pointed out where the rebel lines had been, and how they themselves had fired deliberately, had shot down their antagonists, whose bodies still lay unburied, and marked plainly their lines of battle, which must have halted within easy musket-range of our men, who were partially protected by their improvised line of logs and fence-rails. All bore willing testimony to the courage and spirit of the foe, who, though repeatedly repulsed, came back with increased determination some six or more times.

The next morning the Fifteenth Corps wheeled forward to the left over the battle-field of the day before, and Davis's division still farther prolonged the line, which reached nearly to the ever-to-be-remembered "Sandtown road."[50]

Then, by further thinning out Thomas's line, which was well entrenched, I drew another division of Palmer's corps (Baird's)[51] around to the right, to further strengthen that flank. I was impatient to hear from the cavalry raid, then four days out, and was watching for its effect, ready to make a bold push for the possession of East Point. General Garrard's division returned to Decatur on the 31st, and reported that General Stoneman had posted him at Flat Rock,[52] while he (Stoneman) went on. The month of July therefore closed with our infantry line strongly entrenched, but drawn out from the Augusta road on the left to the Sandtown road on the right, a distance of full ten measured miles.

The enemy, though evidently somewhat intimidated by the results of their defeats on the 22d and 28th, still presented a bold front at all points, with fortified lines that defied a direct assault. Our railroad was done to the rear of our camps, Colonel W. W. Wright having reconstructed the bridge across the Chattahoochee in six days; and our garrisons and detachments to the rear had so effectually guarded the railroad that the trains from Nashville arrived daily, and our substantial wants were well supplied.

The month, though hot in the extreme, had been one of constant conflict, without intermission, and on four several occasions—viz., July 4th, 20th,

[50] Sandtown Road was used by Gen. Schofield to advance his troops south during the Battle of Kennesaw Mountain. The road was located west of Marietta, GA. Davis et al., *Official Military Atlas of the Civil War,* plate 57, map 1; Richard M. McMurry, *The Road Past Kennesaw: The Atlanta Campaign of 1864* (Washington, DC: National Park Service, 1972), 25.

[51] In the first edition of the memoirs (1875), WTS identified the division as "Ward's" instead of "Baird's."

[52] Flat Rock, GA, was located approximately ten miles southeast of Atlanta. Davis et al., *Official Military Atlas of the Civil War,* plate 149.

22d, and 28th—these affairs had amounted to real battles, with casualty lists by the thousands. Assuming the correctness of the rebel surgeon Foard's report, on page 577 of Johnston's "Narrative," commencing with July 4th and terminating with July 31st, we have:

CORPS.	Killed.	Wounded.	Total.
Hardee's.	523	2,774	3,297
Lee's.	351	2,408	2,759
Stewart's.	436	2,141	2,577
Wheeler's Cavalry.	29	156	185
Engineers.	2	21	23
Total.	1,341	7,500	8,841
To these I add us as prisoners, at least.			2,000
Aggregate loss of the enemy in July, 1864.			10,841

Our losses, as compiled from the official returns for July, 1864, are:

ARMY OF THE CUMBERLAND.

CORPS.	Killed and Missing.	Wounded.	Total.
Fourth.	116	432	548
Fourteenth.	317	1,084	1,401
Twentieth.	541	1,480	2,021
Total, Army of the Cumberland.	974	2,996	3,970

ARMY OF THE TENNESSEE.

CORPS.	Killed and Missing.	Wounded.	Total.
Fifteenth.	590	797	1,387
Sixteenth.	289	721	1,010
Seventeenth.	1,361	1,203	2,564
Total, Army of the Tennessee.	2,240	2,721	4,961

ARMY OF THE OHIO.

CORPS.	Killed and Missing.	Wounded.	Total.
Twenty-third.	95	167	262
Cavalry.	495	31	526
Total, Army of the Ohio.	590	198	788
Aggregate loss for July.	3,804	5,915	9,719

In this table the column of "killed and missing" embraces the prisoners that fell into the hands of the enemy, mostly lost in the Seventeenth Corps, on the 22d of July, and does not embrace the losses in the cavalry divisions of Garrard and McCook, which, however, were small for July. In all other respects the statement is absolutely correct. I am satisfied, however, that Surgeon Foard could not have been in possession of data sufficiently accurate to enable him to report the losses in actual battle of men who never saw the hospital. During the whole campaign I had rendered to me tri-monthly statements of "effective strength," from which I carefully eliminated the figures not essential for my conduct, so that at all times I knew the exact fighting-strength of each corps, division, and brigade, of the whole army, and also endeavored to bear in mind our losses both on the several fields of battle and by sickness, and well remember that I always estimated that during the month of July we had inflicted heavier loss on the enemy than we had sustained ourselves, and the above figures prove it conclusively. Before closing this chapter, I must record one or two minor events that occurred about this time, that may prove of interest.

On the 24th of July I received a dispatch from Inspector-General James A. Hardie, then on duty at the War Department in Washington, to the effect that Generals Osterhaus and Alvan P. Hovey had been appointed major-generals. Both of these had begun the campaign with us in command of divisions, but had gone to the rear—the former by reason of sickness, and the latter dissatisfied with General Schofield and myself about the composition of his division of the Twenty-third Corps. Both were esteemed as first-class officers, who had gained special distinction in the Vicksburg campaign. But up to that time, when the newspapers announced daily promotions elsewhere, no prominent officers serving with me had been advanced a peg, and I felt hurt. I answered Hardie on the 25th, in a dispatch which has been made public, closing with this language: "If the rear be the post of honor, then we had better all change front on Washington."[53] To my amazement, in a few days I received from President Lincoln himself an answer, in which he caught me fairly. I have not preserved a copy of that dispatch, and suppose it was burned up in the Chicago fire; but it was characteristic of Mr. Lincoln, and was dated the 26th or 27th day of July, contained unequivocal expressions of respect for those who were fighting hard and unselfishly, offering us a full share of the honors and rewards of the war, and saying that, in the cases of Hovey and Osterhaus, he was influenced mainly by the recommendations of Generals Grant and Sherman. On the 27th I replied direct, apologizing

[53] For WTS's full response to Hardie, see *OR*, I, 38(V), 247.

somewhat for my message to General Hardie, saying that I did not suppose such messages ever reached him personally, explaining that General Grant's and Sherman's recommendations for Hovey and Osterhaus had been made when the events of the Vicksburg campaign were fresh with us, and that my dispatch of the 25th to General Hardie had reflected chiefly the feelings of the officers then present with me before Atlanta.[54] The result of all this, however, was good, for another dispatch from General Hardie, of the 28th, called on me to nominate eight colonels for promotion as brigadier-generals. I at once sent a circular note to the army-commanders to nominate two colonels from the Army of the Ohio and three from each of the others; and the result was, that on the 29th of July I telegraphed the names of—Colonel William Gross, Thirty-sixth Indiana; Colonel Charles C. Walcutt, Forty-sixth Ohio; Colonel James W. Riley, One Hundred and Fourth Ohio; Colonel L. P. Bradley, Fifty-first Illinois; Colonel J. W. Sprague, Sixty-third Ohio; Colonel Joseph A. Cooper, Sixth East Tennessee; Colonel John T. Croxton, Fourth Kentucky; Colonel William W. Belknap, Fifteenth Iowa.[55] These were promptly appointed brigadier-generals, were already in command of brigades or divisions; and I doubt if eight promotions were ever made fairer, or were more honestly earned, during the whole war.[56]

[54] After the war, WTS sent a large collection of Civil War–era letters to Chicago for storage, but most were destroyed in the Great Chicago Fire of 1871. Lincoln's July 26 letter to WTS survived. It read, in part, "I beg you to believe we do not act in a spirit of disregarding merit. We expect to await your programme for further changes and promotions in your army. My profoundest thanks to you and your whole army for the present campaign so far." Marszalek, *Sherman,* 473; *OR,* I, 38(V), 259–260, and see 271 for WTS's July 27th reply to Lincoln.

[55] During the Atlanta Campaign, William Gross (1812–1900) commanded the 3rd Brig., 1st Div., 4th Corps, Army of the Cumberland; Charles C. Walcutt (1838–1898) commanded the 2nd Brig., 4th Div., 15th Corps, Army of the Tennessee; James W. Reilly (1828–1905) commanded the 1st Brig., 3rd Div., 23rd Corps, Army of the Ohio; Luther P. Bradley (1822–1910) commanded the 3rd Brig., 2nd Div., 4th Corps, Army of the Cumberland; John W. Sprague commanded the 2nd Brig., 4th Div., Dist. of Corinth, 16th Corps, Army of the Tennessee; Joseph A. Cooper (1823–1910) commanded the 1st Brig., 2nd Div., 23rd Corps, Army of the Ohio; John T. Croxton (1836–1874) commanded the 1st Brig., 1st Cav. Div., Dept. of the Cumberland; William W. Belknap (1829–1890) commanded the 3rd Brig., 4th Div., 17th Corps, Army of the Tennessee. Each man was promoted to brigadier general on July 30, 1864. *CWHC,* 126, 140, 184, 193, 270, 449, 503, 548.

[56] For the relevant correspondence between WTS and Hardie regarding military promotions, see *OR,* I, 38(V), 247, 278, 289, 300.

19

Capture of Atlanta.

AUGUST AND SEPTEMBER, 1864.

THE MONTH OF AUGUST opened hot and sultry, but our position before Atlanta was healthy, with ample supply of wood, water, and provisions. The troops had become habituated to the slow and steady progress of the siege; the skirmish-lines were held close up to the enemy, were covered by rifle-trenches or logs, and kept up a continuous clatter of musketry. The mainlines were held farther back, adapted to the shape of the ground, with muskets loaded and stacked for instant use. The field-batteries were in select positions, covered by handsome parapets, and occasional shots from them gave life and animation to the scene. The men loitered about the trenches carelessly, or busied themselves in constructing ingenious huts out of the abundant timber, and seemed as snug, comfortable, and happy, as though they were at home. General Schofield was still on the extreme left, Thomas in the centre, and Howard on the right. Two divisions of the Fourteenth Corps (Baird's and Jeff. C. Davis's) were detached to the right rear, and held in reserve.

I thus awaited the effect of the cavalry movement against the railroad about Jonesboro', and had heard from General Garrard that Stoneman had gone on to Macon; during that day (August 1st) Colonel Brownlow, of a Tennessee cavalry regiment,[1] came in to Marietta from General McCook, and reported that McCook's whole division had been overwhelmed, defeated, and captured at Newnan. Of course, I was disturbed by this wild report, though I discredited it, but made all possible preparations to strengthen our guards along the railroad to the rear, on the theory that the force of cavalry which had defeated McCook would at once be on the railroad about Marietta. At the same time Garrard was ordered to occupy the trenches on our left, while Schofield's whole army moved to the extreme right, and extended the line toward East Point. Thomas was also ordered still further to thin out

[1] James P. Brownlow (1842–1879) commanded the 1st Brig., 1st Cav. Div., Dept. of the Cumberland, in Aug. 1864. *CWHC,* 149.

his lines, so as to set free the other division (Johnson's) of the Fourteenth Corps (Palmer's), which was moved to the extreme right rear, and held in reserve ready to make a bold push from that flank to secure a footing on the Macon Railroad at or below East Point.

These changes were effected during the 2d and 3d days of August, when General McCook came in and reported the actual results of his cavalry expedition. He had crossed the Chattahoochee River below Campbellton, by his pontoon-bridge; had then marched rapidly across to the Macon Railroad at Lovejoy's Station, where he had reason to expect General Stoneman; but, not hearing of him, he set to work, tore up two miles of track, burned two trains of cars, and cut away five miles of telegraph-wire. He also found the wagon-train belonging to the rebel army in Atlanta, burned five hundred wagons, killed eight hundred mules; and captured seventy-two officers and three hundred and fifty men. Finding his progress eastward, toward McDonough, barred by a superior force, he turned back to Newnan, where he found himself completely surrounded by infantry and cavalry. He had to drop his prisoners and fight his way out, losing about six hundred men in killed and captured, and then returned with the remainder to his position at Turner's Ferry.[2] This was bad enough, but not so bad as had been reported by Colonel Brownlow. Meantime, rumors came that General Stoneman was down about Macon, on the east bank of the Ocmulgee. On the 4th of August Colonel Adams[3] got to Marietta with his small brigade of nine hundred men belonging to Stoneman's cavalry, reporting, as usual, all the rest lost, and this was partially confirmed by a report which came to me all the way round by General Grant's headquarters before Richmond.[4] A few days afterward Colonel Capron also got in, with another small brigade perfectly demoralized,[5] and confirmed the report that General Stoneman had covered the escape of these two small brigades, himself standing with a reserve of seven hundred men, with which he surrendered to a Colonel

[2] For Gen. Edward M. McCook's report on his expedition, including reports from his brigade and regimental commanders, see *OR,* I, 38(II), 750–803.

[3] Silas Adams (1839–1906) commanded the 1st Kentucky Volunteer Cav. regiment in Aug. 1864. He later served in the U.S. House of Representatives from 1892 to 1894. "Silas Adams: Dead at His Home in Casey County—The Cause of His Death Was Pneumonia," *Owensboro Daily Tribune* (Owensboro, KY), May 7, 1896, 1.

[4] For USG's dispatch to WTS, see *OR,* I, 38(V), 349–350.

[5] Horace Capron (1804–1885) commanded the 3rd Brig., Cav. Div., District of Kentucky, Army of the Ohio, in early Aug. 1864. *CWHC,* 162–163. For his report on the Atlanta Campaign, see *OR,* I, 38(II), 925–930.

Iverson.[6] Thus another of my cavalry divisions was badly damaged, and out of the fragments we hastily reorganized three small divisions under Brigadier-Generals Garrard, McCook, and Kilpatrick.

Stoneman had not obeyed his orders to attack the railroad *first* before going to Macon and Andersonville, but had crossed the Ocmulgee River high up near Covington, and had gone down that river on the east bank. He reached Clinton,[7] and sent out detachments which struck the railroad leading from Macon to Savannah at Griswold Station,[8] where they found and destroyed seventeen locomotives and over a hundred cars; then went on and burned the bridge across the Oconee, and reunited the division before Macon. Stoneman shelled the town across the river, but could not cross over by the bridge, and returned to Clinton, where he found his retreat obstructed, as he supposed, by a superior force. There he became bewildered, and sacrificed himself for the safety of his command. He occupied the attention of his enemy by a small force of seven hundred men, giving Colonels Adams and Capron leave, with their brigades, to cut their way back to me at Atlanta. The former reached us entire, but the latter was struck and scattered at some place farther north, and came in by detachments. Stoneman surrendered, and remained a prisoner until he was exchanged some time after, late in September, at Rough and Ready.[9]

I now became satisfied that cavalry could not, or would not, make a sufficient lodgment on the railroad below Atlanta, and that nothing would suffice but for us to reach it with the main army. Therefore the most urgent efforts to that end were made, and to Schofield, on the right, was committed the charge of this special object. He had his own corps (the Twenty-third), composed of eleven thousand and seventy-five infantry and eight hundred and eighty-five artillery, with McCook's broken division of cavalry, seventeen hundred and fifty-four men and horses. For this purpose I also placed the Fourteenth Corps (Palmer) under his orders. This corps numbered at the time seventeen thousand two hundred and eighty-eight infantry and eight

[6] Alfred Iverson Jr. (1829–1911) resigned from the U.S. Army to join the Confederate Army in Mar. 1861. In Aug. 1864 he commanded his own brigade in Gen. Wheeler's Cav. Corps, Army of Tennessee. *CWHC,* 314.

[7] Clinton, GA, was located approximately sixty miles southeast of Atlanta. George B. Davis et al., *Official Military Atlas of the Civil War* (New York: Fairfax Press, 1983), plate 101, map 21.

[8] Griswold Station was located approximately ten miles northeast of Macon. Davis et al., *Official Military Atlas of the Civil War,* plate 101, map 21.

[9] Rough and Ready, GA, was located approximately five miles south of Atlanta. Davis et al., *Official Military Atlas of the Civil War,* plate 101, map 21.

hundred and twenty-six artillery; but General Palmer claimed to rank General Schofield in the date of his commission as major-general, and denied the latter's right to exercise command over him. General Palmer was a man of ability, but was not enterprising. His three divisions were compact and strong, well commanded, admirable on the defensive, but slow to move or to act on the offensive. His corps (the Fourteenth) had sustained, up to that time, fewer hard knocks than any other corps in the whole army, and I was anxious to give it a chance. I always expected to have a desperate fight to get possession of the Macon road, which was then the vital objective of the campaign. Its possession by us would, in my judgment, result in the capture of Atlanta, and give us the fruits of victory, although the destruction of Hood's army was the real object to be desired. Yet Atlanta was known as the "Gate-City of the South,"[10] was full of founderies, arsenals, and machine-shops, and I knew that its capture would be the death-knell of the Southern Confederacy.

On the 4th of August I ordered General Schofield to make a bold attack on the railroad, anywhere about East Point, and ordered General Palmer to report to him for duty.[11] He at once denied General Schofield's right to command him; but, after examining the dates of their respective commissions, and hearing their arguments, I wrote to General Palmer.

August 4th—10.45 P. M.

From the statements made by yourself and General Schofield to-day, my decision is, that he ranks you as a major-general, being of the same date of present commission, by reason of his previous superior rank as *brigadier-general.* The movements of to-morrow are so important that the orders of the superior on that flank must be regarded as military orders, and not in the nature of coöperation. I did hope that there would be no necessity for my making this decision; but it is better for all parties interested that no question of rank should occur in actual battle. The Sandtown road, and the railroad, if possible, must be

[10] The nickname "Gate City" was given to Atlanta during a banquet in Charleston, SC, that celebrated the completion of the Charleston and Memphis railroad in 1857. A toast for Atlanta was read aloud: "The Gate City, the only tribute which she requires of those who pass through her boundaries is that they stop long enough to partake of the hospitality of her citizens." Franklin M. Garrett, *Atlanta and Environs: A Chronicle of Its People and Events, 1820s–1870s* (Athens: University of Georgia Press, 1969), 1:432.

[11] For WTS's Aug. 4 orders to Schofield, see *OR,* I, 38(V), 358–359.

> gained to-morrow, if it costs half your command. I regard the loss of time this afternoon as equal to the loss of two thousand men.

I also communicated the substance of this to General Thomas, to whose army Palmer's corps belonged, who replied on the 5th:

> I regret to hear that Palmer has taken the course he has, and I know that he intends to offer his resignation as soon as he can properly do so. I recommend that his application be granted.[12]

And on the 5th I again wrote to General Palmer, arguing the point with him, advising him, as a friend, not to resign at that crisis lest his motives might be misconstrued, and because it might damage his future career in civil life; but, at the same time, I felt it my duty to say to him that the operations on that flank, during the 4th and 5th, had not been satisfactory—not imputing to him, however, any want of energy or skill, but insisting that "the events did not keep pace with my desires."[13] General Schofield had reported to me that night:

> I am compelled to acknowledge that I have totally failed to make any aggressive movement with the Fourteenth Corps. I have ordered General Johnson's division to replace General Hascall's this evening, and I propose to-morrow to take my own troops (Twenty-third Corps)

[12] WTS did not include the full transcript of Thomas's Aug. 5 letter. The full letter read: "Your dispatch received. I regret to hear that Palmer has taken the course he has, and as I know he intends to offer his resignation as soon as he feels he can do so without injury to himself I recommend that his application to be relieved from the command of the Fourteenth Army Corps be granted. I earnestly recommend Brig. Gen. J. C. Davis for major-general U.S. Volunteers for past services and uniform gallantry in battle, and apply to have him assigned to the command of the Fourteenth Army Corps. I have everybody on the lookout for any movement of the enemy." *OR,* I, 38(V), 369–370.

[13] In his autobiography, Palmer wrote, "After General Sherman wrote to me that I could not 'disregard the friendly advice of two such men as General Thomas and myself,' I wrote to General Sherman that, 'pending active operations, I request that my application to be relieved be regarded as withdrawn,' but when I received General Sherman's note suggesting excuses for my resignation, I wrote the letter of 10:45, August 5, 1864, which ended my connection with the Army of the Cumberland." John M. Palmer, *Personal Recollections of John M. Palmer: The Story of an Earnest Life* (Cincinnati: Robert Clarke, 1901), 221.

> to the right, and try to recover what has been lost by two days' delay. The force may likely be too small.[14]

I sanctioned the movement, and ordered two of Palmer's divisions—Davis's and Baird's—to follow *en échelon* in support of Schofield, and summoned General Palmer to meet me in person. He came on the 6th to my headquarters, and insisted on his resignation being accepted, for which formal act I referred him to General Thomas. He then rode to General Thomas's camp, where he made a written resignation of his office as commander of the Fourteenth Corps, and was granted the usual leave of absence to go to his home in Illinois, there to await further orders. General Thomas recommended that the resignation be accepted; that Johnson, the senior division commander of the corps, should be ordered back to Nashville as chief of cavalry, and that Brigadier-General Jefferson C. Davis, the next in order, should be promoted major-general, and assigned to command the corps. These changes had to be referred to the President, in Washington, and were, in due time, approved and executed; and thenceforward I had no reason to complain of the slowness or inactivity of that splendid corps.[15] It had been originally formed by General George H. Thomas, had been commanded by him in person, and had imbibed somewhat his personal character, viz., steadiness, good order, and deliberation—nothing hasty or rash, but always safe, "slow, and sure."

On August 7th I telegraphed to General Halleck:

> Have received to-day the dispatches of the Secretary of War and of General Grant, which are very satisfactory. We keep hammering away all the time, and there is no peace, inside or outside of Atlanta. To-day General Schofield got round the line which was assaulted yesterday by General Reilly's brigade, turned it and gained the ground where the assault had been made, and got possession of all our dead and wounded. He continued to press on that flank, and brought on a noisy but not a bloody battle. He drove the enemy behind his main breastworks, which cover the railroad from Atlanta to East Point, and captured a good many of the skirmishers, who are of his best

[14] In the letter, Schofield also stated, "The efforts of yesterday and to-day on this flank have been much worse than mere failures." Palmer, *Personal Recollections,* 380.

[15] Palmer was relieved of command of the 14th Corps, Army of the Cumberland, on Aug. 6. He later served as governor of Illinois from 1869 to 1873 and U.S. senator from Illinois from 1891 to 1897. *CWHC,* 415.

> troops—for the militia hug the breastworks close. I do not deem it prudent to extend any more to the right, but will push forward daily by parallels, and make the inside of Atlanta too hot to be endured. I have sent back to Chattanooga for two thirty-pound Parrotts, with which we can pick out almost any house in town. I am too impatient for a siege, and don't know but this is as good a place to fight it out on, as farther inland. One thing is certain, whether we get inside of Atlanta or not, it will be a used-up community when we are done with it.

In Schofield's extension on the 5th, General Reilly's brigade had struck an outwork, which he promptly attacked, but, as usual, got entangled in the trees and bushes which had been felled, and lost about five hundred men, in killed and wounded; but, as above reported, this outwork was found abandoned the next day, and we could see from it that the rebels were extending their lines, parallel with the railroad, about as fast as we could add to our line of investment. On the 10th of August the Parrott thirty-pounders were received and placed in position; for a couple of days we kept up a sharp fire from all our batteries converging on Atlanta, and at every available point we advanced our infantry-lines, thereby shortening and strengthening the investment; but I was not willing to order a direct assault, unless some accident or positive neglect on the part of our antagonist should reveal an opening. However, it was manifest that no such opening was intended by Hood, who felt secure behind his strong defenses. He had repelled our cavalry attacks on his railroad, and had damaged us seriously thereby, so I expected that he would attempt the same game against our rear. Therefore I made extraordinary exertions to recompose our cavalry divisions, which were so essential, both for defense and offense. Kilpatrick was given that on our right rear, in support of Schofield's exposed flank; Garrard retained that on our general left; and McCook's division was held somewhat in reserve, about Marietta and the railroad. On the 10th, having occasion to telegraph to General Grant, then in Washington, I used this language:

> Since July 28th Hood has not attempted to meet us outside his parapets. In order to possess and destroy effectually his communications, I may have to leave a corps at the railroad-bridge, well intrenched, and cut loose with the balance to make a circle of desolation around Atlanta. I do not propose to assault the works, which are too strong, nor to proceed by regular approaches. I have lost a good many

> regiments, and will lose more, by the expiration of service; and this is the only reason why I want reënforcements. We have killed, crippled, and captured more of the enemy than we have lost by his acts.[16]

On the 12th of August I heard of the success of Admiral Farragut in entering Mobile Bay, which was regarded as a most valuable auxiliary to our operations at Atlanta; and learned that I had been commissioned a major-general in the regular army, which was unexpected, and not desired until successful in the capture of Atlanta.[17] These did not change the fact that we were held in check by the stubborn defense of the place, and a conviction was forced on my mind that our enemy would hold fast, even though every house in the town should be battered down by our artillery. It was evident that we must decoy him out to fight us on something like equal terms, or else, with the whole army, raise the siege and attack his communications. Accordingly, on the 13th of August, I gave general orders for the Twentieth Corps to draw back to the railroad-bridge at the Chattahoochee, to protect our trains, hospitals, spare artillery, and the railroad-depot, while the rest of the army should move bodily to some point on the Macon Railroad below East Point.

Luckily, I learned just then that the enemy's cavalry, under General Wheeler, had made a wide circuit around our left flank, and had actually reached our railroad at Tilton Station, above Resaca, captured a drove of one thousand of our beef-cattle, and was strong enough to appear before Dalton, and demand of its commander, Colonel Raum, the surrender of the place. General John E. Smith, who was at Kingston, collected together a couple of thousand men, and proceeded in cars to the relief of Dalton, when Wheeler retreated northward toward Cleveland. On the 16th another detachment of the enemy's cavalry appeared in force about Allatoona and the Etowah bridge, when I became fully convinced that Hood had sent *all* of his cavalry to raid upon our railroads. For some days our communication with Nashville was interrupted by the destruction of the telegraph-lines, as well as railroad. I at once ordered strong reconnoissances forward from our flanks on the left by Garrard, and on the right by Kilpatrick. The former moved with so much caution that I was displeased; but Kilpatrick, on the contrary, displayed so much zeal and activity that I was attracted to him at once. He reached Fairburn Station, on the West Point road,

[16] For a full transcription of WTS's dispatch to USG on Aug. 10, see *OR,* I, 38(V), 447.

[17] WTS was promoted to major general in the U.S. Army on Aug. 12. *CWHC,* 485.

and tore it up, returning safely to his position on our right flank.[18] I summoned him to me, and was so pleased with his spirit and confidence, that I concluded to suspend the general movement of the main army, and to send him with his small division of cavalry to break up the Macon road about Jonesboro', in the hopes that it would force Hood to evacuate Atlanta, and that I should thereby not only secure possession of the city itself, but probably could catch Hood in the confusion of retreat; and, further to increase the chances of success, I ordered General Thomas to detach two brigades of Garrard's division of cavalry from the left to the right rear, to act as a reserve in support of General Kilpatrick. Meantime, also, the utmost activity was ordered along our whole front by the infantry and artillery. Kilpatrick got off during the night of the 18th, and returned to us on the 22d, having made the complete circuit of Atlanta. He reported that he had destroyed three miles of the railroad about Jonesboro', which he reckoned would take ten days to repair; that he had encountered a division of infantry and a brigade of cavalry (Ross's); that he had captured a battery and destroyed three of its guns, bringing one in as a trophy, and he also brought in three battle-flags and seventy prisoners.[19] On the 23d, however, we saw trains coming into Atlanta from the south, when I became more than ever convinced that cavalry could not or would not work hard enough to disable a railroad properly, and therefore resolved at once to proceed to the execution of my original plan. Meantime, the damage done to our own railroad and telegraph by Wheeler, about Resaca and Dalton, had been repaired, and Wheeler himself was too far away to be of any service to his own army, and where he could not do us much harm, viz., up about the Hiawassee. On the 24th I rode down to the Chattahoochee bridge, to see in person that it could be properly defended by the single corps proposed to be left there for that purpose, and found that the rebel works, which had been built by Johnston to resist us, could be easily utilized against themselves; and on returning to my camp, at 7.15 P. M. that same evening, I telegraphed to General Halleck as follows:

> Heavy fires in Atlanta all day, caused by our artillery. I will be all ready, and will commence the movement around Atlanta by the south, tomorrow night, and for some time you will hear little of us. I will

[18] On Aug. 15, Kilpatrick destroyed a depot at Fairburn Station, situated on the Atlanta and West Point Railroad approximately twenty miles southwest of Atlanta. For a detailed map of the area, see Davis et al., *Official Military Atlas of the Civil War,* plate 60; *OR,* I, 38(II), 858.

[19] For Kilpatrick's full report on his movements during the Atlanta Campaign, see *OR,* I, 38(II), 855–862.

> keep open a courier line back to the Chattahoochee bridge, by way of Sandtown. The Twentieth Corps will hold the railroad-bridge, and I will move with the balance of the army, provisioned for twenty days.

Meantime General Dodge (commanding the Sixteenth Corps) had been wounded in the forehead, had gone to the rear, and his two divisions were distributed to the Fifteenth and Seventeenth Corps. The real movement commenced on the 25th, at night. The Twentieth Corps drew back and took post at the railroad-bridge, and the Fourth Corps (Stanley) moved to his right rear, closing up with the Fourteenth Corps (Jeff. C. Davis) near Utoy Creek; at the same time Garrard's cavalry, leaving their horses out of sight, occupied the vacant trenches, so that the enemy did not detect the change at all. The next night (26th) the Fifteenth and Seventeenth Corps, composing the Army of the Tennessee (Howard), drew out of their trenches, made a wide circuit, and came up on the extreme right of the Fourth and Fourteenth Corps of the Army of the Cumberland (Thomas) along Utoy Creek, facing south. The enemy seemed to suspect something that night, using his artillery pretty freely; but I think he supposed we were going to retreat altogether. An artillery-shot, fired at random, killed one man and wounded another, and the next morning some of his infantry came out of Atlanta and found our camps abandoned. It was afterward related that there was great rejoicing in Atlanta "that the Yankees were gone;" the fact was telegraphed all over the South, and several trains of cars (with ladies) came up from Macon to assist in the celebration of their grand victory.[20]

On the 28th (making a general left-wheel, pivoting on Schofield) both Thomas and Howard reached the West Point Railroad, extending from East Point to Red-Oak Station and Fairburn, where we spent the next day (29th) in breaking it up thoroughly. The track was heaved up in sections the length of a regiment, then separated rail by rail; bonfires were made of the ties and of fence-rails on which the rails were heated, carried to trees or telegraph-poles, wrapped around and left to cool. Such rails could not be used again; and, to be still more certain, we filled up many deep cuts with trees, brush, and earth, and commingled with them loaded shells, so arranged that they would explode on

[20] On Sept. 1, 1864, the *Daily Progress* (Raleigh, NC) issued a statement about WTS's army in Atlanta. It read, "Some of the Georgia papers are jubilant over Sherman's late change of base, and are even predicting an early and disastrous retreat for him . . . We would gladly accept these sanguine speculations, but after an examination of our maps and Railroad Guides, we are sorry to say that we cannot." "The Situation at Atlanta," *Daily Progress* (Raleigh, NC), Sept. 1, 1864, 2.

an attempt to haul out the bushes. The explosion of one such shell would have demoralized a gang of negroes, and thus would have prevented even the attempt to clear the road.

Meantime Schofield, with the Twenty-third Corps, presented a bold front toward East Point, daring and inviting the enemy to sally out to attack him in position. His first movement was on the 30th, to Mount Gilead Church, then to Morrow's Mills, facing Rough and Ready. Thomas was on his right, within easy support, moving by cross-roads from Red Oak to the Fayetteville road, extending from Couch's to Renfrew's; and Howard was aiming for Jonesboro'.

I was with General Thomas that day, which was hot but otherwise very pleasant. We stopped for a short noon-rest near a little church (marked on our maps as Shoal-Creek Church), which stood back about a hundred yards from the road, in a grove of native oaks. The infantry column had halted in the road, stacked their arms, and the men were scattered about—some lying in the shade of the trees, and others were bringing corn-stalks from a large corn-field across the road to feed our horses, while still others had arms full of the roasting-ears, then in their prime. Hundreds of fires were soon started with the fence-rails, and the men were busy roasting the ears. Thomas and I were walking up and down the road which led to the church, discussing the chances of the movement, which he thought were extra-hazardous, and our path carried us by a fire at which a soldier was roasting his corn. The fire was built artistically; the man was stripping the ears of their husks, standing them in front of his fire, watching them carefully, and turning each ear little by little, so as to roast it nicely. He was down on his knees intent on his business, paying little heed to the stately and serious deliberations of his leaders. Thomas's mind was running on the fact that we had cut loose from our base of supplies, and that seventy thousand men were then dependent for their food on the chance supplies of the country (already impoverished by the requisitions of the enemy), and on the contents of our wagons. Between Thomas and his men there existed a most kindly relation, and he frequently talked with them in the most familiar way. Pausing awhile, and watching the operations of this man roasting his corn, he said, "What are you doing?" The man looked up smilingly: "Why, general, I am laying in a supply of provisions." "That is right, my man, but don't waste your provisions." As we resumed our walk, the man remarked, in a sort of musing way, but loud enough for me to hear: "There he goes, there goes the old man, economizing as usual." "Economizing" with corn, which cost only the labor of gathering and roasting!

As we walked, we could hear General Howard's guns at intervals, away off to our right front, but an ominous silence continued toward our left, where I was expecting at each moment to hear the sound of battle. That night we reached Renfrew's, and had reports from left to right (from General Schofield, about Morrow's Mills, to General Howard, within a couple of miles of Jonesboro'). The next morning (August 31st) all moved straight for the railroad. Schofield reached it near Rough and Ready, and Thomas at two points between there and Jonesboro'. Howard found an intrenched foe (Hardee's corps) covering Jonesboro', and his men began at once to dig their accustomed rifle-pits. Orders were sent to Generals Thomas and Schofield to turn straight for Jonesboro', tearing up the railroad-track as they advanced. About 3 P. M. the enemy sallied from Jonesboro' against the Fifteenth corps, but was easily repulsed, and driven back within his lines. All hands were kept busy tearing up the railroad, and it was not until toward evening of the 1st day of September that the Fourteenth Corps (Davis) closed down on the north front of Jonesboro', connecting on his right with Howard, and his left reaching the railroad, along which General Stanley was moving, followed by Schofield. General Davis formed his divisions in line about 4 P. M., swept forward over some old cotton-fields in full view, and went over the rebel parapet handsomely, capturing the whole of Govan's[21] brigade, with two field-batteries of ten guns. Being on the spot, I checked Davis's movement, and ordered General Howard to send the two divisions of the Seventeenth Corps (Blair) round by his right rear, to get below Jonesboro', and to reach the railroad, so as to cut off retreat in that direction. I also dispatched orders after orders to hurry forward Stanley, so as to lap around Jonesboro' on the east, hoping thus to capture the whole of Hardee's corps. I sent first Captain Audenried (aide-de-camp), then Colonel Poe, of the Engineers, and lastly General Thomas himself (and that is the only time during the campaign I can recall seeing General Thomas urge his horse into a gallop). Night was approaching, and the country on the farther side of the railroad was densely wooded. General Stanley had come up on the left of Davis, and was deploying, though there could not have been on his front more than a skirmish-line. Had he moved straight on by the flank, or by a slight circuit to his left, he would have inclosed the whole ground occupied by Hardee's corps, and that corps could not have escaped us; but night came on, and Hardee did escape.[22]

[21] Daniel C. Govan (c. 1829–1911) commanded a brigade in Patrick Cleburne's Div., 1st Corps, Army of Tennessee, when he was captured by the U.S. Army in Sept. 1864. He was exchanged for Gen. George Stoneman on Oct. 2. *CWHC*, 260–261.

[22] For Stanley's response to WTS's critique of his movements, see "D.S. Stanley to WTS, Sept. 24, 1875" in the Appendix to Volume II.

Meantime General Slocum had reached his corps (the Twentieth), stationed at the Chattahoochee bridge, had relieved General A. S. Williams in command, and orders had been sent back to him to feel forward occasionally toward Atlanta, to observe the effect when we had reached the railroad. That night I was so restless and impatient that I could not sleep, and about midnight there arose toward Atlanta sounds of shells exploding, and other sound like that of musketry. I walked to the house of a farmer close by my bivouac, called him out to listen to the reverberations which came from the direction of Atlanta (twenty miles to the north of us), and inquired of him if he had resided there long. He said he had, and that these sounds were just like those of a battle. An interval of quiet then ensued, when again, about 4 A. M., arose other similar explosions, but I still remained in doubt whether the enemy was engaged in blowing up his own magazines, or whether General Slocum had not felt forward, and become engaged in a real battle.

The next morning General Hardee was gone, and we all pushed forward along the railroad south, in close pursuit, till we ran up against his lines at a point just above Lovejoy's Station. While bringing forward troops and feeling the new position of our adversary, rumors came from the rear that the enemy had evacuated Atlanta, and that General Slocum was in the city. Later in the day I received a note in Slocum's own handwriting, stating that he had heard during the night the very sounds that I have referred to; that he had moved rapidly up from the bridge about daylight, and had entered Atlanta unopposed. His letter was dated inside the city, so there was no doubt of the fact.[23] General Thomas's bivouac was but a short distance from mine, and, before giving notice to the army in general orders, I sent one of my staff-officers to show him the note. In a few minutes the officer returned, soon followed by Thomas himself, who again examined the note, so as to be perfectly certain that it was genuine. The news seemed to him too good to be true. He snapped his fingers, whistled, and almost danced, and, as the news spread to the army, the shouts that arose from our men, the wild hallooing and glorious laughter, were to us a full recompense for the labor and toils and hardships through which we had passed in the previous three months.

A courier-line was at once organized, messages were sent back and forth from our camp at Lovejoy's to Atlanta, and to our telegraph-station at the Chattahoochee bridge. Of course, the glad tidings flew on the wings of electricity to all parts of the North, where the people had patiently awaited news of their husbands, sons, and brothers, away down in "Dixie Land;" and congratulations came pouring back full of good-will and patriotism. This vic-

[23] For Slocum's Sept. 3 letter, see *OR,* I, 38(II), 20.

tory was most opportune; Mr. Lincoln himself told me afterward that even he had previously felt in doubt, for the summer was fast passing away; that General Grant seemed to be checkmated about Richmond and Petersburg, and my army seemed to have run up against an impassable barrier, when, suddenly and unexpectedly, came the news that "Atlanta was ours, and fairly won."[24] On this text many a fine speech was made, but none more eloquent than that by Edward Everett, in Boston. A presidential election then agitated the North. Mr. Lincoln represented the national cause, and General McClellan had accepted the nomination of the Democratic party, whose platform was that the war was a failure, and that it was better to allow the South to go free to establish a separate government, whose corner-stone should be slavery. Success to our arms at that instant was therefore a political necessity; and it was all-important that something startling in our interest should occur before the election in November. The brilliant success at Atlanta filled that requirement, and made the election of Mr. Lincoln certain. Among the many letters of congratulation received, those of Mr. Lincoln and General Grant seem most important:

EXECUTIVE MANSION,
WASHINGTON, D. C., *September* 3, 1864.

The national thanks are rendered by the President to Major-General W. T. Sherman and the gallant officers and soldiers of his command before Atlanta, for the distinguished ability and perseverance displayed in the campaign in Georgia, which, under Divine favor, has resulted in the capture of Atlanta. The marches, battles, sieges, and other military operations, that have signalized the campaign, must render it famous in the annals of war, and have entitled those who have participated therein to the applause and thanks of the nation.

ABRAHAM LINCOLN,
President of the United States

CITY POINT, VIRGINIA, *September* 4, 1864—9 P. M.

Major-General SHERMAN:

I have just received your dispatch announcing the capture of Atlanta. In honor of your great victory, I have ordered a salute to be

[24] In a Sept. 3 telegram to Halleck, WTS wrote, "So Atlanta is ours, and fairly won. I shall not push much farther on this raid, but in a day or so will move to Atlanta and give my men some rest." *OR,* I, 38(V), 777.

fired with *shotted* guns from every battery bearing upon the enemy. The salute will be fired within an hour, amid great rejoicing.

U. S. Grant, *Lieutenant-General.*

These dispatches were communicated to the army in general orders,[25] and we all felt duly encouraged and elated by the praise of those competent to bestow it.

The army still remained where the news of success had first found us, viz., Lovejoy's; but, after due refection, I resolved not to attempt at that time a further pursuit of Hood's army, but slowly and deliberately to move back, occupy Atlanta, enjoy a short period of rest, and to think well over the next step required in the progress of events. Orders for this movement were made on the 5th September, and three days were given for each army to reach the place assigned it, viz.: the Army of the Cumberland in and about Atlanta; the Army of the Tennessee at East Point; and the Army of the Ohio at Decatur.[26]

Personally I rode back to Jonesboro' on the 6th, and there inspected the rebel hospital, full of wounded officers and men left by Hardee in his retreat. The next night we stopped at Rough and Ready, and on the 8th of September we rode into Atlanta, then occupied by the Twentieth Corps (General Slocum). In the Court-House Square was encamped a brigade, embracing the Massachusetts Second and Thirty-third Regiments, which had two of the finest bands of the army, and their music was to us all a source of infinite pleasure during our sojourn in that city. I took up my headquarters in the house of Judge Lyons,[27] which stood opposite one corner of the Court-House Square, and at once set about a measure already ordered, of which I had thought much and long, viz., to remove the entire civil population, and to deny to all civilians from the rear the expected profits of civil trade. Hundreds of sutlers and traders were waiting at Nashville and Chattanooga, greedy to reach Atlanta with their wares and goods, with which to drive a profitable trade with the inhabitants. I gave positive orders that none of these traders, except three (one for each separate army), should be permitted to

[25] For Special Field Orders No. 66, issued on Sept. 6, see *OR,* I, 38(I), 87.

[26] For Special Field Orders No. 245, issued on Sept. 5, see *OR,* I, 38(V), 805.

[27] Richard F. Lyon (1817–1893) served on the Georgia Supreme Court from 1859 to 1866. His Atlanta home was located at the corner of Washington and Mitchell Streets. Frank M. Garrett, *Atlanta and Environs: A Chronicle of Its People and Events, 1880s–1930s* (Athens: University of Georgia Press, 1969), 2:850; "Judge Richard F. Lyon Dead," *Weekly Telegraph* (Macon, GA), May 29, 1893, 6.

come nearer than Chattanooga; and, moreover, I peremptorily required that all the citizens and families resident in Atlanta should go away, giving to each the option to go south or north, as their interests or feelings dictated. I was resolved to make Atlanta a pure military garrison or depot, with no civil population to influence military measures. I had seen Memphis, Vicksburg, Natchez, and New Orleans, all captured from the enemy, and each at once was garrisoned by a full division of troops, if not more; so that success was actually crippling our armies in the field by detachments to guard and protect the interests of a hostile population.[28]

I gave notice of this purpose, as early as the 4th of September, to General Halleck, in a letter concluding with these words:

> If the people raise a howl against my barbarity and cruelty, I will answer that war is war, and not popularity-seeking. If they want peace, they and their relatives must stop the war.[29]

I knew, of course, that such a measure would be strongly criticised, but made up my mind to do it with the absolute certainty of its justness, and that time would sanction its wisdom. I knew that the people of the South would read in this measure two important conclusions: one, that we were in earnest; and the other, if they were sincere in their common and popular clamor "to die in the last ditch," that the opportunity would soon come.[30]

Soon after our reaching Atlanta, General Hood had sent in by a flag of truce a proposition, offering a general exchange of prisoners, saying that he was authorized to make such an exchange by the Richmond authorities, out of the vast number of our men then held captive at Andersonville, the same whom General Stoneman had hoped to rescue at the time of his raid. Some of these prisoners had already escaped and got in, had described the pitiable condition of the remainder, and, although I felt a sympathy for their hardships and sufferings as deeply as any man could, yet as nearly all the prisoners

[28] For a list of citizens affected by Special Field Order No. 67, see the section "Official account of the people sent south, their numbers and luggage, under Special Field Order No. 67, issued by Major-General W. T. Sherman, Atlanta, Georgia, September 4, 1864," in Appendix to Volume II.

[29] For WTS's full Sept. 4 letter to Halleck, see *OR*, I, 38(V), 794.

[30] The motto "Die in the last ditch" was used throughout the Confederacy. In Apr. 1863, John B. Jones, a clerk in the Confederate war department, wrote in his diary, "Our people will die in the last ditch rather than be subjugated and see the confiscation of their property." John B. Jones, *A Rebel War Clerk's Diary at the Confederate States Capitol* (Philadelphia: J. B. Lippincott, 1866), 1:302; "The Last Ditch," *The Indiana Progress* (Indiana, PA), Apr. 5, 1865, 2.

who had been captured by us during the campaign had been sent, as fast as taken, to the usual depots North, they were then beyond my control. There were still about two thousand, mostly captured at Jonesboro', who had been sent back by cars, but had not passed Chattanooga. These I ordered back, and offered General Hood to exchange them for Stoneman, Buell, and such of my own army as would make up the equivalent; but I would not exchange for his prisoners *generally*, because I knew these would have to be sent to their own regiments, away from my army, whereas all we could give him could at once be put to duty in his immediate army. Quite an angry correspondence grew up between us, which was published at the time in the newspapers, but it is not to be found in any book of which I have present knowledge, and therefore is given here, as illustrative of the events referred to, and of the feelings of the actors in the game of war at that particular crisis, together with certain other original letters of Generals Grant and Halleck, never hitherto published.[31]

HEADQUARTERS ARMIES OF THE UNITED STATES,
CITY POINT, VIRGINIA, *September* 12, 1864.

Major-General W. T. SHERMAN, *commanding Military Division of the Mississippi.*

GENERAL: I send Lieutenant-Colonel Horace Porter, of my staff, with this. Colonel Porter will explain to you the exact condition of affairs here, better than I can do in the limits of a letter. Although I feel myself strong enough now for offensive operations, I am holding on quietly, to get advantage of recruits and convalescents, who are coming forward very rapidly. My lines are necessarily very long, extending from Deep Bottom, north of the James, across the peninsula formed by the Appomattox and the James, and south of the Appomattox to the Weldon road. This line is very strongly fortified, and can be held with comparatively few men; but, from its great length, necessarily takes many in the aggregate. I propose, when I do move, to extend my left so as to control what is known as the Southside, or Lynchburg & Petersburg road; then, if possible, to keep the Danville road cut. At the same time this move is made, I want to send a force of from six to ten

[31] On Sept. 17, 1864, the *Macon Telegraph* published part of the correspondence between WTS and Hood. The correspondence was later published in the *OR.* "The Atlanta Exiles," *Macon Telegraph* (Macon, GA), Sept. 17, 1864, 2; *OR,* I, 39(II), 414–430.

thousand men against Wilmington. The way I propose to do this is to land the men north of Fort Fisher, and hold that point. At the same time a large naval fleet will be assembled there, and the iron-clads will run the batteries as they did at Mobile. This will give us the same control of the harbor of Wilmington that we now have of the harbor of Mobile. What you are to do with the forces at your command, I do not exactly see. The difficulties of supplying your army, except when they are constantly moving beyond where you are, I plainly see. If it had not been for Price's movement, Canby could have sent twelve thousand more men to Mobile. From your command on the Mississippi, an equal number could have been taken. With these forces, my idea would have been to divide them, sending one-half to Mobile, and the other half to Savannah. You could then move as proposed in your telegram, so as to threaten Macon and Augusta equally. Whichever one should be abandoned by the enemy, you could take and open up a new base of supplies. My object now in sending a staff-officer to you is not so much to suggest operations for you as to get your views, and to have plans matured by the time every thing can be got ready. It would probably be the 5th of October before any of the plans here indicated will be executed. If you have any promotions to recommend, send the names forward, and I will approve them.

In conclusion, it is hardly necessary for me to say that I feel you have accomplished the most gigantic undertaking given to any general in this war, and with a skill and ability that will be acknowledged in history as unsurpassed, if not unequaled. It gives me as much pleasure to record this in your favor as it world in favor of any living man, myself included.

Truly yours,

U. S. Grant, *Lieutenant-General.*

Headquarters Military Division of the Mississippi,
in the Field, Atlanta, Georgia, *September* 20, 1864.

Lieutenant-General U. S. Grant, *Commander-in-Chief, City Point, Virginia.*

General: I have the honor to acknowledge, at the hands of Lieutenant-Colonel Porter, of your staff, your letter of September 12th, and accept with thanks the honorable and kindly mention of the services of this army in the great cause in which we are all engaged.

I send by Colonel Porter all official reports which are completed, and will in a few days submit a list of names which are deemed worthy of promotion.

I think we owe it to the President to save him the invidious task of selection among the vast number of worthy applicants, and have ordered my army commanders to prepare their lists with great care, and to express their preferences, based upon claims of actual capacity and services rendered.

These I will consolidate, and submit in such a form that, if mistakes are made, they will at least be sanctioned by the best contemporaneous evidence of merit, for I know that vacancies do not exist equal in number to that of the officers who really deserve promotion.

As to the future, I am pleased to know that your army is being steadily reënforced by a good class of men, and I hope it will go on until you have a force that is numerically double that of your antagonist, so that with one part you can watch him, and with the other push out boldly from your left flank, occupy the Southside Railroad, compel him to attack you in position, or accept battle on your own terms.

We ought to ask our country for the largest possible armies that can be raised, as so important a thing as the self-existence of a great nation should not be left to the fickle chances of war.

Now that Mobile is shut out to the commerce of our enemy, it calls for no further effort on our part, unless the capture of the city can be followed by the occupation of the Alabama River and the railroad to Columbus, Georgia, when that place would be a magnificent auxiliary to my further progress into Georgia; but, until General Canby is much reënforced, and until he can more thoroughly subdue the scattered armies west of the Mississippi, I suppose that much cannot be attempted by him against the Alabama River and Columbus, Georgia.

The utter destruction of Wilmington, North Carolina, is of importance only in connection with the necessity of cutting off all foreign trade to our enemy, and if Admiral Farragut can get across the bar, and move quickly, I suppose he will succeed. From my knowledge of the mouth of Cape Fear River, I anticipate more difficulty in getting the heavy ships across the bar than in reaching the town of Wilmington; but, of course, the soundings of the channel are well known at Washington, as well as the draught of his iron-clads, so that it must be demonstrated to be feasible, or else it would not be attempted. If successful, I suppose that Fort Caswell will be occupied, and the fleet at once sent to the Savannah River. Then the reduction of that city is the next question. It once in our possession, and the river open to us, I would not hesitate to cross the State of Georgia with sixty thousand men, hauling some stores, and depending on the country for the balance. Where a million of people find subsistence, my army won't starve; but, as you know, in a country like Georgia, with few roads and innumerable streams, an inferior force can so delay an army and harass it, that it would not be a formidable object; but if the enemy knew that we had our boats in the Savannah River I could rapidly move to Milledgeville, where there is abundance of corn and meat, and could so threaten Macon and Augusta that the enemy would doubtless give up Macon for Augusta; then I would move so as to interpose between Augusta and Savannah, and force him to give us Augusta, with the only powder-mills and factories remaining in the South, or let us have the use of the Savannah River. Either horn of the dilemma will be worth a battle. I would prefer his holding Augusta (as the probabilities are); for then, with the Savannah River in our possession, the taking of Augusta would be a mere matter of time. This campaign can be made in the winter.

But the more I study the game, the more am I convinced that it would be wrong for us to penetrate farther into Georgia without an objective beyond. It would not be productive of much good. I can start east and make a circuit south and back, doing vast damage to the State, but resulting in no permanent good; and by mere threatening to do so, I hold a rod over the Georgians, who are not over-loyal to the South. I will therefore give it as my opinion that your army and Canby's should be reënforced to the maximum; that, after you get Wilmington, you should strike for Savannah and its river; that General Canby should hold the Mississippi River, and send a force to take Columbus, Georgia, either by way of the Alabama or Appalachicola River; that I should keep Hood employed and put my army in fine order for a march on Augusta, Columbia, and Charleston; and start as soon as Wilmington is sealed to commerce, and the city of Savannah is in our possession.

I think it will be found that the movements of Price and Shelby, west of the Mississippi, are mere diversions. They cannot hope to enter Missouri except as raiders; and the truth is, that General Rosecrans should be ashamed to take my troops for such a purpose. If you will secure Wilmington and the city of Savannah from your centre, and let

General Canby have command over the Mississippi River and country west of it, I will send a force to the Alabama and Appalachicola, provided you give me one hundred thousand of the drafted men to fill up my old regiments; and if you will fix a day to be in Savannah, I will insure our possession of Macon and a point on the river below Augusta. The possession of the Savannah River is more than fatal to the possibility of Southern independence. They may stand the fall of Richmond, but not of all Georgia.

I will have a long talk with Colonel Porter, and tell him every thing that may occur to me of interest to you.

In the mean time, know that I admire your dogged perseverance and pluck more than ever. If you can whip Lee and I can march to the Atlantic, I think Uncle Abe will give us a twenty days' leave of absence to see the young folks. Yours as ever,

W. T. Sherman, *Major-General.*

Headquarters of the Army,
Washington, *September* 16, 1864.

General W. T. Sherman, *Atlanta, Georgia.*

My dear General: Your very interesting letter of the 4th is just received. Its perusal has given me the greatest pleasure. I have not written before to congratulate you on the capture of Atlanta, the objective point of your brilliant campaign, for the reason that I have been suffering from my annual attack of "coryza," or hay-cold. It affects my eyes so much that I can scarcely see to write. As you suppose, I have watched your movements most attentively and critically, and I do not hesitate to say that your campaign has been the most brilliant of the war. Its results are less striking and less complete than those of General Grant at Vicksburg, but then you have had greater difficulties to encounter, a longer line of communications to keep up, and a longer and more continuous strain upon yourself and upon your army.

You must have been very considerably annoyed by the State negro recruiting-agents. Your letter was a capital one, and did much good. The law was a ridiculous one; it was opposed by the War Department, but passed through the influence of Eastern manufacturers, who hoped to escape the draft in that way. They were making immense fortunes out of the war, and could well afford to *purchase* negro recruits, and thus save their employés at home.

I fully agree with you in regard to the policy of a stringent draft; but, unfortunately, political influences are against us, and I fear it will not amount to much. Mr. Seward's speech at Auburn, again prophesying, for the twentieth time, that the rebellion would be crushed in a few months, and saying that there would be no draft, as we now had enough soldiers to end the war, etc., has done much harm, in a military point of view. I have seen enough of politics here to last me for life. You are right in avoiding them. McClellan may possibly reach the White House, but he will lose the respect of all honest, high-minded patriots, by his affiliation with such traitors and Copperheads as B—, V—, W—, S—, & Co. He would not stand upon the traitorous Chicago platform, but he had not the manliness to oppose it. A major-general in the United States Army, and yet not one word to utter against rebels or the rebellion! I had much respect for McClellan before he became a politician, but very little after reading his letter accepting the nomination.

Hooker certainly made a mistake in leaving before the capture of Atlanta. I understand that, when here, he said that you would fail; your army was discouraged and dissatisfied, etc., etc. He is most unmeasured in his abuse of me. I inclose you a specimen of what he publishes in Northern papers, wherever he goes. They are dictated by himself and written by W. B. and such worthies. The funny part of the business is, that I had nothing whatever to do with his being relieved on either occasion. Moreover, I have never said any thing to the President or Secretary of War to injure him in the slightest degree, and he knows that perfectly well. His animosity arises from another source. He is aware that I know some things about his character and conduct in California, and, fearing that I may use that information against him, he seeks to ward off its effect by making it appear that I am his personal enemy, am jealous of him, etc. I know of no other reason for his hostility to me. He is welcome to abuse me as much as he pleases; I don't think it will do him much good, or me much harm. I know very little of General Howard, but believe him to be a true, honorable man. Thomas is also a noble old war-horse. It is true, as you say, that he is slow, but he is always sure.

I have not seen General Grant since the fall of Atlanta, and do not know what instructions he has sent you. I fear that Canby has not the means to do much by way of Mobile. The military effects of Banks's disaster are now showing themselves by the threatened operations of Price & Co. toward Missouri, thus keeping in check our armies west of the Mississippi.

With many thanks for your kind letter, and wishes for your future success, yours truly,

H. W. HALLECK.

HEADQUARTERS MILITARY DIVISION OF THE MISSISSIPPI,
ATLANTA, GEORGIA, *September* 20, 1864.

Major-General HALLECK, *Chief of Staff, Washington, D. C.*

GENERAL: I have the honor herewith to submit copies of a correspondence between General Hood, of the Confederate Army, the Mayor of Atlanta, and myself, touching the removal of the inhabitants of Atlanta.

In explanation of the tone which marks some of these letters, I will only call your attention to the fact that, after I had announced my determination, General Hood took upon himself to question my motives. I could not tamely submit to such impertinence; and I have also seen that, in violation of all official usage, he has published in the Macon newspapers such parts of the correspondence as suited his purpose. This could have had no other object than to create a feeling on the part of the people; but if he expects to resort to such artifices, I think I can meet him there too.

It is sufficient for my Government to know that the removal of the inhabitants has been made with liberality and fairness, that it has been attended with no force, and that no women or children have suffered, unless for want of provisions by their natural protectors and friends.

My real reasons for this step were:

We want all the houses of Atlanta for military storage and occupation.

We want to contract the lines of defense, so as to diminish the garrison to the limit necessary to defend its narrow and vital parts, instead of embracing, as the lines now do, the vast suburbs. This contraction of the lines, with the necessary citadels and redoubts, will make it necessary to destroy the very houses used by families as residences.

Atlanta is a fortified town, was stubbornly defended, and fairly captured. As captors, we have a right to it.

The residence here of a poor population would compel us, sooner or later, to feed them or to see them starve under our eyes.

The residence here of the families of our enemies would be a temptation and a means to keep up a correspondence dangerous and hurtful to our cause; a civil population calls for provost-guards, and absorbs the attention of officers in listening to everlasting complaints and special grievances that are not military.

These are my reasons; and, if satisfactory to the Government of the United States, it makes no difference whether it pleases General Hood and *his* people or not. I am, with respect, your obedient servant,

W. T. SHERMAN, *Major-General commanding.*

HEADQUARTERS MILITARY DIVISION OF THE MISSISSIPPI,
IN THE FIELD, ATLANTA, GEORGIA, *September* 7, 1864.

General HOOD, *commanding Confederate Army.*

GENERAL: I have deemed it to the interest of the United States that the citizens now residing in Atlanta should remove, those who prefer it to go south, and the rest north. For the latter I can provide food and transportation to points of their election in Tennessee, Kentucky, or farther north. For the former I can provide transportation by cars as far as Rough and Ready, and also wagons; but, that their removal may be made with as little discomfort as possible, it will be necessary for you to help the families from Rough and Ready to the cars at Lovejoy's. If you consent, I will undertake to remove all the families in Atlanta who prefer to go south to Rough and Ready, with all their movable effects, viz., clothing, trunks, reasonable furniture, bedding, etc., with their servants, white and black, with the proviso that no force shall be used toward the blacks, one way or the other. If they want to go with their masters or mistresses, they may do so; otherwise they will be sent away, unless they be men, when they may be employed by our quartermaster. Atlanta is no place for families or non-combatants, and I have no desire to send them north if you will assist in conveying them south. If this proposition meets your views, I will consent to a truce in the neighborhood of Rough and Ready, stipulating that any wagons, horses, animals, or persons sent there for the purposes herein stated, shall in no manner be harmed or molested; you in your turn agreeing that any cars, wagons, or carriages, persons or animals sent to the same point, shall not be interfered with. Each of us might send a guard of, say, one hundred men, to maintain order, and limit the truce to, say, two days after a certain time appointed.

I have authorized the mayor to choose two citizens to convey to you this letter, with such documents as the mayor may forward in explanation, and shall await your reply. I have the honor to be your obedient servant.

W. T. Sherman, *Major-General commanding.*

Headquarters Army of Tennessee,
Office Chief of Staff, *September* 9, 1864.

Major-General W. T. Sherman, *commanding United States Forces in Georgia.*

General: Your letter of yesterday's date, borne by James M. Ball and James R. Crew, citizens of Atlanta, is received. You say therein, "I deem it to be to the interest of the United States that the citizens now residing in Atlanta should remove," etc. I do not consider that I have any alternative in this matter. I therefore accept your proposition to declare a truce of two days, or such time as may be necessary to accomplish the purpose mentioned, and shall render all assistance in my power to expedite the transportation of citizens in this direction. I suggest that a staff-officer be appointed by you to superintend the removal from the city to Rough and Ready, while I appoint a like officer to control their removal farther south; that a guard of one hundred men be sent by either party as you propose, to maintain order at that place, and that the removal begin on Monday next.

And now, sir, permit me to say that the unprecedented measure you propose transcends, in studied and ingenious cruelty, all acts ever before brought to my attention in the dark history of war.

In the name of God and humanity, I protest, believing that you will find that you are expelling from their homes and firesides the wives and children of a brave people. I am, general, very respectfully, your obedient servant,

J. B. Hood, *General.*

Headquarters Military Division of the Mississippi,
in the field, Atlanta, Georgia, *September* 10, 1864.

General J. B. Hood, *commanding Army of Tennessee, Confederate Army.*

General: I have the honor to acknowledge the receipt of your letter of this date, at the hands of Messrs. Ball and Crew, consenting to the arrangements I had proposed to facilitate the removal south of the people of Atlanta, who prefer to go in that direction. I inclose you a copy of my orders, which will, I am satisfied, accomplish my purpose perfectly.

You style the measures proposed "unprecedented," and appeal to the dark history of war for a parallel, as an act of "studied and ingenious cruelty." It is not unprecedented; for General Johnston himself very wisely and properly removed the families all the way from Dalton down, and I see no reason why Atlanta should be excepted. Nor is it necessary to appeal to the dark history of war, when recent and modern examples are so handy. You yourself burned dwelling-houses along your parapet, and I have seen to-day fifty houses that you have rendered uninhabitable because they stood in the way of your forts and men. You defended Atlanta on a line so close to town that every cannon-shot and many musket-shots from our line of investment, that overshot their mark, went into the habitations of women and children. General Hardee did the same at Jonesboro', and General Johnston did the same, last summer, at Jackson, Mississippi. I have not accused you of heartless cruelty, but merely instance these cases of very recent occurrence, and could go on and enumerate hundreds of others, and challenge any fair man to judge which of us has the heart of pity for the families of a "brave people."

I say that it is kindness to these families of Atlanta to remove them now, at once, from scenes that women and children should not be exposed to, and the "brave people" should scorn to commit their wives and children to the rude barbarians who thus, as you say, violate the laws of war, as illustrated in the pages of its dark history.

In the name of common-sense, I ask you not to appeal to a just God in such a sacrilegious manner. You who, in the midst of peace and prosperity, have plunged a nation into war—dark and cruel war—who dared and badgered us to battle, insulted our flag, seized our arsenals and forts that were left in the honorable custody of peaceful ordnance-sergeants, seized and made "prisoners of war" the very garrisons sent to protect your people against negroes and Indians, long before any overt act was committed by the (to you) hated Lincoln Government; tried to force Kentucky and Missouri into rebellion, spite of themselves; falsified the vote of Louisiana; turned loose your privateers to plunder unarmed ships; expelled Union families by the thousands, burned their houses, and declared, by an act of your Congress, the confiscation of all debts due Northern men for goods had and received! Talk thus to the marines, but not to me, who have seen these things, and who will this day make as much sacrifice for the peace and honor of the South as the best-born Southerner among you! If we must be enemies, let us be men, and fight it out as we propose to do, and not deal in such hypocritical appeals to God and humanity. God will judge us in due time, and he will pronounce whether it be more humane to fight with a town full of women and the families of a brave people at our back, or to remove them in time to places of safety among their own friends and people. I am, very respectfully, your obedient servant,

W. T. Sherman, *Major-General commanding.*

Headquarters Army of Tennessee,
September 12, 1864.

Major-General W. T. Sherman, *commanding Military Division of the Mississippi.*

General: I have the honor to acknowledge the receipt of your letter of the 9th inst., with its inclosure in reference to the women, children, and others, whom you have thought proper to expel from their homes in the city of Atlanta. Had you seen proper to let the matter rest there, I would gladly have allowed your letter to close this correspondence, and, without your expressing it in words, would have been willing to believe that, while "the interests of the United States," in your opinion, compelled you to an act of barbarous cruelty, you regretted the necessity, and we would have dropped the subject; but you have chosen to indulge in statements which I feel compelled to notice, at least so far as to signify my dissent, and not allow silence in regard to them to be construed as acquiescence.

I see nothing in your communication which induces me to modify the language of condemnation with which I characterized your order. It but strengthens me in the opinion that it stands "preëminent in the dark history of war for studied and ingenious cruelty." Your original order was stripped of all pretenses; you announced the edict for the sole reason that it was "to the interest of the United States." This alone you offered to us and the civilized world as an all-sufficient reason for disregarding the laws of God and man. You say that "General Johnston himself very wisely and properly removed the families all the way from Dalton down." It is due to that gallant soldier and gentleman to say that no act of his distinguished career gives the least color to your unfounded aspersions upon his conduct. He depopulated no villages, nor towns, nor cities, either friendly or hostile. He offered and extended friendly aid to his unfortunate fellow-citizens who desired to flee from your fraternal embraces. You are equally unfortunate in your attempt to find a justification for this act of cruelty, either in the defense of Jonesboro', by General Hardee, or of Atlanta, by myself. General Hardee defended his position in front of Jonesboro' at the expense of injury to the houses; an ordinary, proper, and justifiable act of war. I defended Atlanta at the same risk and cost. If there was any fault in either case, it was your own, in not giving notice, especially in the case of Atlanta, of your purpose to shell the town, which is usual in war among civilized nations. No inhabitant was expelled from his home and fireside by the orders of General Hardee or myself, and therefore your recent order can find no support from the conduct of either of us. I feel no other emotion other than pain in reading that portion of your letter which attempts to justify your shelling Atlanta without notice under pretense that I defended Atlanta upon a line so close to town that every cannon-shot and many musket-balls from your line of investment, that overshot their mark, went into the habitations of women and children. I made no complaint of your firing into Atlanta in any way you thought proper. I make none now, but there are a hundred thousand witnesses that you fired into the habitations of women and children for weeks, firing far above and miles beyond my line of defense. I have too good an opinion, founded both upon observation and experience, of the skill of your artillerists, to credit the insinuation that they for several weeks unintentionally fired too high for my modest field-works, and slaughtered women and children by accident and want of skill.

The residue of your letter is rather discussion. It opens a wide field for the discussion of questions which I do not feel are committed to me. I am only a general of one of the armies of the Confederate States, charged with military operations in the field, under the direction of my superior officers, and I am not called upon to discuss with you the causes of the present war, or the political questions which led to or resulted from it. These grave and important questions have been committed to far abler hands than mine, and I shall only refer to them so far as to repel any unjust conclusion which might be drawn from my silence. You charge my country with "daring and badgering you to battle." The truth is, we sent commissioners to you, respectfully offering a peaceful separation, before the first gun was fired on either side. You say we insulted your flag. The truth is, we fired upon it, and those who fought under it, when you came to our doors upon the mission of subjugation. You say we seized upon your forts and arsenals, and made prisoners of the garrisons sent to protect us against negroes and Indians. The truth is, we, by force of arms, drove out insolent intruders and took possession of our own forts and arsenals, to resist your claims to dominion over masters, slaves, and Indians, all of whom are to this day, with a unanimity unexampled in the history of the world, warring against your attempts to become their masters. You say that we tried to force Missouri and Kentucky into rebellion in spite of themselves. The truth is, my Government, from the beginning of this struggle to this hour, has again and again offered, before the whole world, to leave it to the unbiased will of these States, and all others, to determine for themselves whether they will cast their destiny with your Government or ours; and your Government has resisted this fundamental principle of free institutions with the bayonet, and labors daily, by force and fraud, to fasten its hateful tyranny upon the unfortunate freemen of these States. You say we falsified the vote of Louisiana. The truth is, Louisiana not only separated herself from your Government by nearly a unanimous vote of her people, but has vindicated the act upon every battle-field from Gettysburg to the Sabine, and has exhibited an heroic devotion to her decision which challenges the admiration and respect of every man capable of feeling sympathy for the oppressed or admiration for heroic valor. You say that we turned loose pirates to plunder your unarmed ships. The truth is, when you robbed us of our part of the navy, we built and bought a few vessels, hoisted the flag of our country, and swept the seas, in defiance of your navy, around the whole circumference of the globe. You say we have expelled Union families by thousands. The truth is, not a single family has been expelled from the Confederate States, that I am aware of; but, on the contrary, the moderation of our Government toward traitors has been a fruitful theme of denunciation by its enemies and well-meaning friends of our cause. You say my Government, by acts of Congress, has confiscated "all debts due Northern men for goods sold and delivered." The truth is, our Congress gave due and ample time to your merchants and traders to depart from our shores with their ships, goods, and effects, and only sequestrated the property of our enemies in retaliation for their acts—declaring us traitors, and confiscating our property wherever their power extended, either in their country or our own. Such are your accusations, and such are the facts known of all men to be true.

You order into exile the whole population of a city; drive men, women, and children from their homes at the point of the bayonet, under the plea that it is to the interest of your Government, and on the claim that it is an act of "kindness to these families of Atlanta." Butler only banished from New Orleans the registered enemies of his Government, and acknowledged that he did it as a punishment. You issue a sweeping edict, covering all the inhabitants of a city, and add insult to the injury heaped upon the defenseless by assuming that you have done them a kindness. This you follow by the assertion that you will "make as much sacrifice for the peace and honor of the South as the best-born Southerner." And, because I characterize what you call a kindness as being real cruelty, you presume to sit in judgment between me and my God; and you decide that my earnest prayer to the Almighty Father to save our women and children from what you call kindness, is a "sacrilegious, hypocritical appeal."

You came into our country with your army, avowedly for the purpose of subjugating free white men, women, and children, and not only intend to rule over them, but you make negroes your allies, and desire to place over us an inferior race, which we have raised from barbarism to its present position, which is the highest ever attained by that race, in any country, in all time. I must, therefore, decline to accept your statements in reference to your kindness toward the people of Atlanta, and your willingness to sacrifice every thing for the peace and honor of the South, and refuse to be governed by your decision in regard to matters between myself, my country, and my God.

You say, "Let us fight it out like men." To this my reply is—for myself, and I believe for all the true men, ay, and women and children, in my country—we will fight you to the death! Better die a thousand deaths than submit to live under you or your Government and your negro allies!

Having answered the points forced upon me by your letter of the 9th of September, I close this correspondence with you; and, notwithstanding your comments upon my appeal to God in the cause of humanity, I again humbly and reverently invoke his almighty aid in defense of justice and right. Respectfully, your obedient servant,

J. B. Hood, *General.*

Atlanta, Georgia, *September* 11, 1864.

Major-General W. T. Sherman.

Sir: We the undersigned, Mayor and two of the Council for the city of Atlanta, for the time being the only legal organ of the people of the said city, to express their wants and wishes, ask leave most earnestly but respectfully to petition you to reconsider the order requiring them to leave Atlanta.

At first view, it struck us that the measure would involve extraordinary hardship and loss, but since we have seen the practical execution of it so far as it has progressed, and the individual condition of the people, and heard their statements as to the inconveniences, loss, and suffering attending it, we are satisfied that the amount of it will involve in the aggregate consequences appalling and heart-rending.

Many poor women are in advanced state of pregnancy, others now having young children, and whose husbands for the greater part are either in the army, prisoners, or dead. Some say: "I have such a one sick at my house; who will wait on them when I am gone?" Others say: "What are we to do? We have no house to go to, and no means to buy, build, or rent any; no parents, relatives, or friends, to go to." Another says: "I will try and take this or that article of property, but such and such things I must leave behind, though I need them much." We reply to them: "General Sherman will carry your property to Rough and Ready, and General Hood will take it thence on." And they will reply to that: "But I want to leave the railroad at such a place, and cannot get conveyance from there on."

We only refer to a few facts, to try to illustrate in part how this measure will operate in practice. As you advanced, the people north of this fell back; and before your arrival here, a large portion of the people had retired south, so that the country south of this is already crowded, and without houses enough to accommodate the people, and we are informed that many are now staying in churches and other out-buildings.

This being so, how is it possible for the people still here (mostly women and children) to find any shelter? And how can they live through the winter in the woods—no shelter or subsistence, in the midst of strangers who know them not, and without the power to assist them much, if they were willing to do so?

This is but a feeble picture of the consequences of this measure. You know the woe, the horrors, and the suffering, cannot be described by words; imagination can only conceive of it, and we ask you to take these things into consideration.

We know your mind and time are constantly occupied with the duties of your command, which almost deters us from asking your attention to this matter, but thought it might be that you had not considered this subject in all of its awful consequences, and that on more reflection you, we hope, would not make this people an exception to all mankind, for we know of no such instance ever having occurred—surely never in the United States—and what has this *helpless* people done, that they should be driven from their homes, to wander strangers and outcasts, and exiles, and to subsist on charity?

We do not know as yet the number of people still here; of those who are here, we are satisfied a respectable number, if allowed to remain at home, could subsist for several months without assistance, and a respectable number for a much longer time, and who might not need assistance at any time.

In conclusion, we most earnestly and solemnly petition you to reconsider this order, or modify it, and suffer this unfortunate people to remain at home, and enjoy what little means they have.

Respectfully submitted:

James M. Calhoun, *Mayor.*
E. E. Rawson, *Councilman.*
S. C. Wells, *Councilman.*

Headquarters Military Division of the Mississippi,
in the Field, Atlanta, Georgia, *September* 12, 1864.

James M. Calhoun, *Mayor,* E. E. Rawson *and* S. C. Wells, *representing City Council of Atlanta.*

Gentlemen: I have your letter of the 11th, in the nature of a petition to revoke my orders removing all the inhabitants from Atlanta. I have read it carefully, and give full credit to your statements of the distress that will be occasioned, and yet shall not revoke my orders, because they were not designed to meet the humanities of the case, but to prepare for the future struggles in which millions of good people outside of Atlanta have a deep interest. We must have peace, not only at Atlanta, but in all America. To secure this, we must stop the war that now desolates our once happy and favored country. To stop war, we must defeat the rebel armies which are arrayed against the laws and Constitution that all must respect and obey. To defeat those armies, we must prepare the way to reach them in their recesses, provided with the arms and instruments which enable us to accomplish our purpose. Now, I know the vindictive nature of our enemy, that we may have many years of military operations from this quarter; and, therefore, deem it wise and prudent to prepare in time. The use of Atlanta for warlike purposes is inconsistent with its character as a home for families. There will be no manufactures, commerce, or agriculture here, for the maintenance of families, and sooner or later want will compel the inhabitants to go. Why not go now, when all the arrangements are completed for the transfer, instead of waiting till the plunging shot of contending armies will renew the scenes of the past month? Of course, I do not apprehend any such thing at this moment, but you do not suppose this army will be here until the war is over. I cannot discuss this subject with you fairly, because I cannot impart to you what we propose to do, but I assert that our military plans make it necessary for the inhabitants to go away, and I can only renew my offer of services to make their exodus in any direction as easy and comfortable as possible.

You cannot qualify war in harsher terms than I will. War is cruelty, and you cannot refine it; and those who brought war into our country deserve all the curses and maledictions a people can pour out. I know I had no hand in making this war, and I know I will make more sacrifices to-day than any of you to secure peace. But you cannot have peace and a division of our country. If the United States submits to a division now, it will not stop, but will go on until we reap the fate of Mexico, which is eternal war. The United States does and must assert its authority, wherever it once had power; for, if it relaxes one bit to pressure, it is gone, and I believe that such is the national feeling. This feeling assumes various shapes, but always comes back to that of Union. Once admit the Union, once more acknowledge the authority of the national Government, and, instead of devoting your houses and streets and roads to the dread uses of war, I and this army become at once your protectors and supporters, shielding you from danger, let it come from what quarter it may. I know that a few individuals cannot resist a torrent of error and passion, such as swept the South into rebellion, but you can point out, so that we may know those who desire a government, and those who insist on war and its desolation.

You might as well appeal against the thunder-storm as against these terrible hardships of war. They are inevitable, and the only way the people of Atlanta can hope once more to live in peace and quiet at home, is to stop the war, which can only be done by admitting that it began in error and is perpetuated in pride.

We don't want your negroes, or your horses, or your houses, or your lands, or any thing you have, but we do want and will have a just obedience to the laws of the United States. That we will have, and, if it involves the destruction of your improvements, we cannot help it.

You have heretofore read public sentiment in your newspapers, that live by falsehood and excitement; and the quicker you seek for truth in other quarters, the better. I repeat then that, by the original compact of Government, the United States had certain rights in Georgia, which have never been relinquished and never will be; that the South began war by seizing forts, arsenals, mints, custom-houses, etc., etc., long before Mr. Lincoln was installed, and before the South had one jot or tittle of provocation. I myself have seen in Missouri, Kentucky, Tennessee, and Mississippi, hundreds and thousands of women and children fleeing from your armies and desperadoes, hungry and with bleeding feet. In Memphis, Vicksburg, and Mississippi, we fed thousands upon thousands of the families of rebel soldiers left on our hands, and whom we could not see starve. Now that war comes home to you, you feel very different. You deprecate its horrors, but did not feel them when you sent car-loads of soldiers and ammunition, and moulded shells and shot, to carry war into Kentucky and Tennessee, to desolate the homes of hundreds and thousands of good people who only asked to live in peace at their old homes, and under the Government of their inheritance. But these comparisons are idle. I want peace, and believe it can only be reached through union and war, and I will ever conduct war with a view to perfect and early success.

But, my dear sirs, when peace does come, you may call on me for any thing. Then will I share with you the last cracker, and watch with you to shield your homes and families against danger from every quarter.

Now you must go, and take with you the old and feeble, feed and nurse them, and build for them, in more quiet places, proper habitations to shield them against the weather until the mad passions of men cool down, and allow the Union and peace once more to settle over your old homes at Atlanta. Yours in haste,

W. T. Sherman, *Major-General commanding.*

HEADQUARTERS MILITARY DIVISION OF THE MISSISSIPPI,
IN THE FIELD, ATLANTA, GEORGIA, *September* 14, 1864.

General J. B. HOOD, *commanding Army of the Tennessee, Confederate Army.*

GENERAL: Yours of September 12th is received, and has been carefully perused. I agree with you that this discussion by two soldiers is out of place, and profitless; but you must admit that you began the controversy by characterizing an official act of mine in unfair and improper terms. I reiterate my former answer, and to the only new matter contained in your rejoinder add: We have no "negro allies" in this army; not a single negro soldier left Chattanooga with this army, or is with it now. There are a few guarding Chattanooga, which General Steedman sent at one time to drive Wheeler out of Dalton.

I was not bound by the laws of war to give notice of the shelling of Atlanta, a "fortified town, with magazines, arsenals, founderies, and public stores;" you were bound to take notice. See the books.

This is the conclusion of our correspondence, which I did not begin, and terminate with satisfaction. I am, with respect, your obedient servant,

W. T. SHERMAN, *Major-General commanding.*

HEADQUARTERS OF THE ARMY,
WASHINGTON, *September* 28, 1864,

Major-General SHERMAN, *Atlanta, Georgia.*

GENERAL: Your communications of the 20th in regard to the removal of families from Atlanta, and the exchange of prisoners, and also the official report of your campaign, are just received. I have not had time as yet to examine your report. The course which you have pursued in removing rebel families from Atlanta, and in the exchange of prisoners, is fully approved by the War Department. Not only are you justified by the laws and usages of war in removing these people, but I think it was your duty to your own army to do so. Moreover, I am fully of opinion that the nature of your position, the character of the war, the conduct of the enemy (and especially of non-combatants and women of the territory which we have heretofore conquered and occupied), will justify you in gathering up all the forage and provisions which your army may require, both for a siege of Atlanta and for your supply in your march farther into the enemy's country. Let the disloyal families of the country, thus stripped, go to their husbands, fathers, and natural protectors, in the rebel ranks; we have tried three years of conciliation and kindness without any reciprocation; on the contrary, those thus treated have acted as spies and guerrillas in our rear and within our lines. The safety of our armies, and a proper regard for the lives of our soldiers, require that we apply to our inexorable foes the severe rules of war. We certainly are not required to treat the so-called non-combatant rebels better than they themselves treat each other. Even here in Virginia, within fifty miles of Washington, they strip their own families of provisions, leaving them, as our army advances, to be fed by us, or to starve within our lines. We have fed this class of people long enough. Let them go with their husbands and fathers in the rebel ranks; and if they won't go, we must send them to their friends and natural protectors. I would destroy every mill and factory within reach which I did not want for my own use. This the rebels have done, not only in Maryland and Pennsylvania, but also in Virginia and other rebel States, when compelled to fall back before our armies. In many sections of the country they have not left a mill to grind grain for their own suffering families, lest we might use them to supply our armies. We must do the same.

I have endeavored to impress these views upon our commanders for the last two years. You are almost the only one who has properly applied them. I do not approve of General Hunter's course in burning private houses or uselessly destroying private property. That is barbarous. But I approve of taking or destroying whatever may serve as supplies to us or to the enemy's army.

Very respectfully, your obedient servant,

H. W. Halleck, *Major-General, Chief of Staff.*

In order to effect the exchange of prisoners, to facilitate the exodus of the people of Atlanta, and to keep open communication with the South, we established a neutral camp, at and about the railroad-station next south of Atlanta, known as "Rough and Ready," to which point I dispatched Lieutenant-Colonel Willard Warner, of my staff, with a guard of one hundred men, and General Hood sent Colonel Clare,[32] of his staff, with a similar guard; these officers and men harmonized perfectly, and parted good friends when their work was done. In the mean time I also had reconnoitred the entire rebel

[32] William Clare (1839–1870), who was wounded at the Battle of Shiloh, was on the staff of multiple Confederate generals, including Bragg, Beauregard, Johnson, and Hood. For Warner's assessment of his own conduct during the Atlanta Campaign, see Williard Warner to Ellen Ewing Sherman, Feb. 22, 1876, in the Appendix to Volume II; "Tribute of Respect to the Memory of Major William Clare, Deceased," *Nashville Union and American,* Nov. 23, 1870, 1.

lines about Atlanta, which were well built, but were entirely too extensive to be held by a single corps or division of troops, so I instructed Colonel Poe, United States Engineers, on my staff, to lay off an inner and shorter line, susceptible of defense by a smaller garrison.

By the middle of September all these matters were in progress, the reports of the past campaign were written up and dispatched to Washington,[33] and our thoughts began to turn toward the future. Admiral Farragut had boldly and successfully run the forts at the entrance to Mobile Bay, which resulted in the capture of Fort Morgan, so that General Canby was enabled to begin his regular operations against Mobile City, with a view to open the Alabama River to navigation.[34] My first thoughts were to concert operations with him, either by way of Montgomery, Alabama, or by the Appalachicola; but so long a line, to be used as a base for further operations eastward, was not advisable, and I concluded to await the initiative of the enemy, supposing that he would be forced to resort to some desperate campaign by the clamor raised at the South on account of the great loss to them of the city of Atlanta.[35]

General Thomas occupied a house on Marietta Street which had a veranda with high pillars. We were sitting there one evening, talking about things generally, when General Thomas asked leave to send his trains back to Chattanooga, for the convenience and economy of forage. I inquired of him if he supposed we would be allowed much rest at Atlanta, and he said he thought we would, or that at all events it would not be prudent for us to go much farther into Georgia because of our already long line of communication, viz., three hundred miles from Nashville. This was true; but there we were, and we could not afford to remain on the defensive, simply holding Atlanta and fighting for the safety of its railroad. I insisted on his retaining all trains, and on keeping all his divisions ready to move at a moment's warning. All the army, officers and men, seemed to relax more or less, and sink into a condition of idleness. General Schofield was permitted to go to Knoxville, to look after matters in his Department of the Ohio; and Generals Blair and Logan went home to look after politics. Many of the regiments were entitled to, and

[33] For the U.S. Army's reports on the Atlanta Campaign, see *OR,* I, 38(I, II).

[34] On Aug. 5, 1864, Farragut attacked Mobile Bay with eighteen ships. Canby had approximately 2,000 troops when he captured Fort Morgan on Aug. 23. Spencer C. Tucker, ed., *American Civil War: A State-by-State Encyclopedia* (Santa Barbara: ABC-CLIO, 2017), vol. 1, s.v. "Mobile Bay, Battle of (August 5, 1864)."

[35] U.S. Army general Thomas W. Sweeny was displeased that WTS omitted any mention of his operations with the 2nd Div., 16th Corps, Army of the Tennessee, during the Atlanta Campaign. See T. W. Sweeny to WTS, Oct. 30, 1876, in the Appendix to Volume II.

claimed, their discharge, by reason of the expiration of their term of service; so that with victory and success came also many causes of disintegration.

The rebel General Wheeler was still in Middle Tennessee, threatening our railroads, and rumors came that Forrest was on his way from Mississippi to the same theatre, for the avowed purpose of breaking up our railroads and compelling us to fall back from our conquest. To prepare for this, or any other emergency, I ordered Newton's division of the Fourth Corps back to Chattanooga, and Corse's division of the Seventeenth Corps to Rome, and instructed General Rousseau at Nashville, Granger at Decatur, and Steadman at Chattanooga, to adopt the most active measures to protect and insure the safety of our roads.

Hood still remained about Lovejoy's Station, and, up to the 15th of September, had given no signs of his future plans; so that with this date I close the campaign of Atlanta, with the following review of our relative losses during the months of August and September, with a summary of those for the whole campaign, beginning May 6 and ending September 15, 1864. The losses for August and September are added together, so as to include those about Jonesboro':

ARMY OF THE CUMBERLAND—(MAJOR-GENERAL THOMAS.)

CORPS.	Killed and Missing.	Wounded.	Total.
Fourth (Stanley)	166	416	582
Fourteenth (Davis, Palmer)	444	1,809	2,253
Twentieth (Williams, Slocum)	71	189	260
Total	681	2,414	3,095

ARMY OF THE TENNESSEE—(MAJOR-GENERAL O. O. HOWARD.)

CORPS.	Killed and Missing.	Wounded.	Total.
Fifteenth (Logan)	143	430	573
Sixteenth (Dodge)	40	217	257
Seventeenth (Blair)	102	258	360
Total	285	905	1,190

ARMY OF THE OHIO—(MAJOR-GENERAL SCHOFIELD.)

CORPS.	Killed and Missing.	Wounded.	Total.
Twenty-third (Cox)	146	279	425
Cavalry (Garrard, McCook, Kilpatrick)	296	133	429
Total	442	412	854
Grand Aggregate	1,408	3,731	5,139

Hood's losses, as reported for the same period, page 577, Johnston's "Narrative:"[36]

CORPS.	Killed.	Wounded.	Total.
Hardee's.	141	1,018	1,159
Lee's.	248	1,631	1,879
Stewart's.	93	574	667
Total.	482	3,223	3,705

To which should be added:

Prisoner's captured by us	3,738
Giving his total loss	7,443

On recapitulating the entire losses of each army during the entire campaign, from May to September, inclusive, we have, in the Union army, as per table appended:

Killed	4,423
Wounded	22,822
Missing	4,442
Aggregate loss	31,687

In the Southern army, according to the reports of Surgeon Foard (pp. 576, 577, Johnston's "Narrative"):

Killed (Johnston)	1,221
" (Hood)	1,823
Total killed	3,044

[36] See Joseph E. Johnston, *Narrative of Military Operations, Directed, during the Late War between the States* (New York: D. Appleton, 1874),

Wounded (Johnston)	8,229
" (Hood)	10,723
Total killed and wounded	21,996
Add prisoners captured by us, and officially reported at the time (*see* table)	12,983
Aggregate loss to Southern army	34,979

The foregoing figures are official, and are very nearly correct. I see no room for error save in the cavalry, which was very much scattered, and whose reports are much less reliable than of the infantry and artillery; but as Surgeon Foard's tables do not embrace Wheeler's, Jackson's, and Martin's divisions of cavalry, I infer that the comparison, as to cavalry losses, is a "stand-off."

I have no doubt that the Southern officers flattered themselves that they had killed and crippled of us two and even six to one, as stated by Johnston; but they were simply mistaken, and I herewith submit official tabular statements made up from the archives of the War Department, in proof thereof:

I have also had a careful tabular statement compiled from official records in the adjutant-general's office, giving the "effective strength" of the army under my command for each of the months of May, June, July, August, and September, 1864, which enumerate every man (infantry, artillery, and cavalry) for duty. The recapitulation clearly exhibits the actual truth. We opened the campaign with 98,797 (ninety-eight thousand seven hundred and ninety-seven) men. Blair's two divisions joined us early in June, giving 112,819 (one hundred and twelve thousand eight hundred and nineteen), which number gradually became reduced to 106,070 (one hundred and six thousand and seventy men), 91,675 (ninety-one thousand six hundred and seventy-five), and 81,758 (eighty-one thousand seven hundred and fifty-eight) at the end of the campaign. This gradual reduction was not altogether owing to death and wounds, but to the expiration of service, or by detachments sent to points at the rear.

Statement showing the Losses sustained in Battle by the Army under Command of General W. T. SHERMAN, *from May to September, 1864, inclusive.*

COMMANDS.	May.		June.		July.		August.		September.		Total Killed or Missing.	Total Wounded.	Aggregate.	REMARKS.
	Killed or Missing.	Wounded.	Killed or Missing.	Wounded.	Killed or Missing.	Wounded.	Killed or Missing.	Wounded.	Killed or Missing.	Wounded.				
Fourth Corps.	576	1,910	602	1,542	116	432	106	152	60	264	1,460	4,300	5,760	
Fourteenth Corps.	147	655	353	1,466	317	1,084	180	801	264	1,008	1,261	5,014	6,275	
Twentieth Corps.	571	2,997	322	1,246	541	1,480	70	189	1	.....	1,505	5,912	7,417	
Total—Army of the Cumberland.	1,294	5,562	1,277	4,254	974	2,996	356	1,142	325	1,272	4,226	15,226	19,452	
Fifteenth Corps.	122	624	179	687	590	797	108	367	35	63	1,034	2,538	3,572	
Sixteenth Corps.	*a* 94 *b* 40	*a* 430 *b* 209	*a* 52 *c* 20	*a* 157 *c* 102	*a* 289 *d* 26	*a* 721 *d* 146	*a* 40	*a* 217 *e* 3	....	....	475 *86	1,525 *460	2,000 *546	Left wing broken up September, 1864, and troops transferred to Fifteenth and Seventeenth Corps.
Seventeenth Corps.		1	47	212	1,361	1,203	74	212	28	46	1,510	1,674	3,184	
Total—Army of the Tennessee.	256	1,264	298	1,158	2,266	2,867	222	799	63	109	3,105	6,197	9,302	
Twenty-third Corps.	226	757	105	362	95	167	142	270	4	9	572	1,565	2,137	
Cavalry.	127	62	130	68	495	31	199	110	97	23	1,048	294	1,342	
Grand Total.	1,903	7,645	1,810	5,842	3,830	6,061	919	2,321	489	1,413	*8,951	*23,282	*32,233	

a Left wing in Atlanta campaign.
b Right wing on Red River expedition.
c Right wing at Lake Chicot, La.
d Right wing at Tupelo, Miss.
e Right wing skirmishes in Mississippi.

*These figures have been obtained principally from the monthly returns of the several army corps, and are believed to be approximately correct. The killed and missing, being reported in the same column on the returns, cannot be shown separately in this table, but from another source of information (Regimental Rolls and Returns) the aggregate number of missing during the period in question is found to have been 4,442. Deducting this number from the 8,951 of both classes would give 4,508 as the number killed. Then subtracting the casualties (86 killed and 460 wounded) of the right wing, Sixteenth Army Corps, not engaged in the Atlanta campaign, would give the losses of General Sherman's immediate command from Chattanooga to Atlanta as follows: Killed, 4,423; wounded, 22,822; missing, 4,442—total 31,687.

E. D. TOWNSEND, ADJUTANT-GENERAL.

HEADQUARTERS MILITARY DIVISION OF THE MISSISSIPPI, IN THE FIELD, ATLANTA, GEORGIA, *SEPTEMBER* 15, 1864.

Prisoners and Deserters taken by "Army in the Field," Military Division of the Mississippi, during May, June, July, and August, 1864.

COMMANDS.	PRISONERS.		DESERTERS.		
	Commissioned Officers.	Enlisted Men.	Commissioned Officers.	Enlisted Men.	Aggregate.
Army of the Cumberland.	121	3,838	21	1,543	5,523
Army of the Tennessee.	133	2,591	5	576	3,305
Army of the Ohio.	16	781	1	292	1,090
Total.	270	7,210	27	2,411	9,918

To which add the prisoners and deserters taken by the Army of the Cumberland,
September 1st to 20th. 3,065
Making aggregate. 12,983
Reports from armies of the Tennessee and Ohio include the whole campaign, to September 15, 1864. . . . .

W.T. Sherman,
Major-General United States Army commanding.

Statement showing the Effective Strength of the Army under Gener

Commands.	June 1.						July			
	Infantry.		Cavalry.		Artillery.		Infantry.		Cavalry.	
	Commissioned Officers.	Enlisted Men.	Commissioned Officers.	Enlisted Men.	Commissioned Officers.	Enlisted Men.	Commissioned Officers.	Enlisted Men.	Commissioned Officers.	Enlisted Men.
Fourth Army Corps.	999	15,453	. . .	. . . . . .	21	754	878	13,338	. . . . . .	. . . . .
Fourteenth Army Corps.	1,007	21,618	. . .	. . . . . .	21	802	906	17,900	. . . . . .	. . . . .
Twentieth Army Corps.	808	15,071	3	68	25	826	734	13,057	3	6
Total—A'y of the C'mb'rl'd.	2,814	52,142	3	68	67	2,382	2,518	44,295	3	6
Fifteenth Army Corps.	636	11,044	. . .	. . . . . .	25	792	612	10,396	. . . . . .	. . . . .
Sixteenth A.C. (left wing).	408	9,053	26	322	12	540	441	9,625	4	3
Seventeenth Army Corps.	387	8,380	4	83	17	904	380	7,812	9	9
Total—Army of the Tenn.	1,431	28,477	30	405	54	2,236	1,433	27,833	13	12
Twenty-third Army Corps.	406	9,040	. . . . . .	. . . . . .	20	505	498	11,509	. . . . . .	. . . . .
Garrard's Cavalry.	. . . . . .	. . . . . .	200	4,822	3	130	. . . . . .	. . . . . .	180	4,04
Stoneman's Cavalry.	. . . . . .	. . . . . .	138	2,753	. . .	. . . . . .	. . . . . .	. . . . . .	128	2,53
McCook's Cavalry.	. . . . . .	. . . . . .	152	2,570	3	79	. . . . . .	. . . . . .	161	2,16
Kilpatrick's Cavalry.	. . . . . .	. . . . . .	89	1,678	5	117	. . . . . .	. . . . . .	128	2,48
Grand Aggregate.	4,651	89,659	612	12,296	152	5,449	4,449	88,637	613	11,42

T. SHERMAN, *during the Campaign against Atlanta, Georgia, 1864.*

		August 1.						September 1.					
Artillery.		Infantry.		Cavalry.		Artillery.		Infantry.		Cavalry.		Artillery.	
Commissioned Officers.	Enlisted Men.	Commissioned Officers.	Enlisted Men.	Commissioned Officers.	Enlisted Men.	Commissioned Officers.	Enlisted Men.	Commissioned Officers.	Enlisted Men.	Commissioned Officers.	Enlisted Men.	Commissioned Officers.	Enlisted Men.
16	724	827	11,837	......	......	20	835	736	10,678	......	......	22	682
21	780	847	16,441	......	......	19	707	720	13,733	......	......	22	774
24	786	645	11,112	3	40	27	751	649	10,955	3	35	31	740
61	2,290	2,319	39,390	3	40	66	2,293	2,105	35,366	3	35	75	2,196
23	757	508	8,033	......	......	14	578	523	7,691	......	......	9	447
16	620	402	8,111	29	370	11	422	322	7,054	3	27	11	401
23	947	280	5,541	5	29	22	923	225	4,962	4	23	16	705
62	2,324	1,190	21,685	34	399	47	1,923	1,070	19,707	7	50	36	1,553
24	875	490	10,585	......	......	25	860	407	9,019	......	......	15	540
3	122	......	......	179	3,699	3	111	......	......	166	2,911	3	104
.....	......	......	......	96	1,803	......	......	......	......	101	1,835	......	......
3	75	......	......	120	1,634	3	60	......	......	132	1,720	3	73
4	102	......	......	144	2,366	4	104	......	......	166	2,268	4	88
157	5,788	3,999	71,660	579	9,941	148	5,351	3,582	64,092	575	8,819	136	4,554

RECAPITULATION—ATLANTA CAMPAIGN.

ARM.	June 1.	July 1.	August 1.	September 1.
Infantry.	94,310	88,086	75,659	67,674
Cavalry.	12,908	12,039	10,517	9,394
Artillery.	5,601	5,945	5,499	4,690
Aggregate.	112,819	106,070	91,675	81,758

20

Atlanta and After—Pursuit of Hood.

SEPTEMBER AND OCTOBER, 1864.

BY THE MIDDLE OF SEPTEMBER, matters and things had settled down in Atlanta, so that we felt perfectly at home. The telegraph and railroads were repaired, and we had uninterrupted communication to the rear. The trains arrived with regularity and dispatch, and brought us ample supplies. General Wheeler had been driven out of Middle Tennessee, escaping south across the Tennessee River at Bainbridge; and things looked as though we were to have a period of repose.[1]

One day, two citizens, Messrs. Hill[2] and Foster,[3] came into our lines at Decatur, and were sent to my headquarters. They represented themselves as former members of Congress, and particular friends of my brother John Sherman; that Mr. Hill had a son killed in the rebel army as it fell back before us somewhere near Cassville, and they wanted to obtain the body, having learned from a comrade where it was buried. I gave them permission to go by rail to the rear, with a note to the commanding officer, General John E.

[1]On Aug. 31, 1864, Hood ordered Confederate cavalry general Joseph Wheeler to retreat into Bainbridge, AL, located on the south bank of the Tennessee River and approximately ten miles east of Florence, AL. George B. Davis et al., *Official Military Atlas of the Civil War* (New York: Fairfax Press, 1983), plate 149.

[2]Joshua Hill (1812–1891) resigned from the U.S. House of Representatives in 1861 but was ultimately opposed to secession. Soon after the war, he served one partial term as a U.S. senator from Georgia from 1871 to 1873. "Hon. Joshua Hill: Death of the Ex-Senator at His Home in Madison," *Atlanta Constitution,* Mar. 7, 1891, 1.

[3]In the first edition of the memoirs (1875), WTS identified the person as "Nelson." Thomas A. R. Nelson (1812–1873) represented Tennessee in the U.S. Congress at the start of the Civil War. After the war, he briefly served on the Tennessee Supreme Court. Nathaniel G. Foster (1809–1869) was a lawyer and a preacher from Madison, GA. *History of the Baptist Denomination in Georgia* (Atlanta: James P. Harrison, 1881), s.v. "Nathaniel Greene Foster"; "Tribute of Respect: The Late Thomas A. R. Nelson," *Morristown Gazette* (Morristown, TN), 1.

Smith, at Cartersville, requiring him to furnish them an escort and an ambulance for the purpose.[4] I invited them to take dinner with our mess, and we naturally ran into a general conversation about politics and the devastation and ruin caused by the war. They had seen a part of the country over which the army had passed, and could easily apply its measure of desolation to the remainder of the State, if necessity should compel us to go ahead.

Mr. Hill resided at Madison, on the main road to Augusta, and seemed to realize fully the danger; said that further resistance on the part of the South was madness, that he hoped Governor Brown, of Georgia,[5] would so proclaim it, and withdraw his people from the rebellion, in pursuance of what was known as the policy of "separate State action."[6] I told him, if he saw Governor Brown, to describe to him fully what he had seen, and to say that if he remained inert, I would be compelled to go ahead, devastating the State in its whole length and breadth; that there was no adequate force to stop us, etc.; but if he would issue his proclamation withdrawing his State troops from the armies of the Confederacy, I would spare the State, and in our passage across it confine the troops to the main roads, and would, moreover, pay for all the corn and food we needed. I also told Mr. Hill that he might, in my name, invite Governor Brown to visit Atlanta; that I would give him a safeguard, and that if he wanted to make a speech, I would guarantee him as full and respectable an audience as any he had ever spoken to. I believe that

[4] Joshua Hill wrote a letter to the superintendent of the West Point Railroad, saying, "You have doubtless heard of the cruel affliction this abominable war has brought to my hearthstone. I can't help thinking this was more than I merited. My poor boy met his death on Thursday morning on the 19th of May, as I am informed, about 2 ½ miles above Cass Station beyond Ben Johnson's House on the road leading from Cassville to Kingston, about a ½ mile from the R. road. He is said to have been brought by some comrades nearer the R.R. and left by the side of the public road, somewhere about or near a deserted cabin or perhaps nearer still to a small frame house near the R.R." Hill's son, Hugh Legare Hill (1846–1864), was the only person killed in the skirmish. A. A. Hoehling, *Last Train from Atlanta* (Lanham, MD: Stackpole, 1992), 59–60.

[5] Joseph E. Brown (1821–1894) served as the governor of Georgia from 1857 to 1865. After the war, he joined the Republican Party and advocated for civil rights. Richard Zuczek, ed., *Reconstruction: A Historical Encyclopedia of the American Mosaic* (Santa Barbara: ABC-CLIO, 2016), s.v. "Brown, Joseph Emerson."

[6] In a letter to WTS after the capture of Atlanta, Gov. Brown wrote that Georgia "will never make separate terms with the enemy which may free her territory from invasion and leave her confederates in the lurch." Thomas R. Hay, "Joseph Emerson Brown: Governor of Georgia, 1857–1865," *Georgia Historical Quarterly* 13, no. 2 (June 1929):103*n*.

Mr. Hill, after reaching his home at Madison, went to Milledgeville, the capital of the State,[7] and delivered the message to Governor Brown. I had also sent similar messages by Judge Wright of Rome, Georgia,[8] and by Mr. King, of Marietta.[9] On the 15th of September I telegraphed to General Halleck as follows:

> My report is done, and will be forwarded as soon as I get in a few more of the subordinate reports. I am awaiting a courier from General Grant. All well; the troops are in good, healthy camps, and supplies are coming forward finely. Governor Brown has disbanded his militia, to gather the corn and sorghum of the State. I have reason to believe that he and Stephens want to visit me, and have sent them a hearty invitation. I will exchange two thousand prisoners with Hood, but no more.

Governor Brown's action at that time is fully explained by the following letter, since made public, which was then only known to us in part by hearsay:

> EXECUTIVE DEPARTMENT,
> MILLEDGEVILLE, GEORGIA, *September* 10, 1864.
>
> *General* J. B. HOOD, *commanding Army of Tennessee.*
>
> GENERAL: As the militia of the State were called out for the defense of Atlanta during the campaign against it, which has terminated by the fall of the city into the hands of the enemy, and as many of these left their homes without preparation (expecting to be gone but a few weeks), who have remained in service over three months (most of the time in the trenches), justice requires that they be permitted, while the enemy are preparing for the winter campaign, to return to their homes, and look for a time after important interests, and prepare themselves

[7] The capital was officially moved from Milledgeville to Atlanta in 1868. Spencer C. Tucker, ed., *American Civil War: A State-by-State Encyclopedia* (Santa Barbara: ABC-CLIO, 2015), vol. 1, s.v. "Milledgeville, Georgia."

[8] Augustus R. Wright (1813–1891) worked as a lawyer and a judge before the start of the Civil War. He later served as a member of the 1877 Georgia constitutional convention. Thomas A. Scott, ed., *Cornerstones of Georgia History: Documents That Formed the State* (Athens: University of Georgia Press, 1995), 115; "Judge Wright Dead," *Atlanta Journal,* Apr. 1, 1891, 5.

[9] William King (1804–1884) was a cotton trader and prominent citizen of Marietta, GA. "Obituary: King," *Atlanta Constitution,* Jan. 20, 1884, 7.

for such service as may be required when another campaign commences against other important points in the State. I therefore hereby withdraw said organization from your command. . . .

JOSEPH C. BROWN

This militia had composed a division under command of Major-General Gustavus W. Smith, and were thus dispersed to their homes, to gather the corn and sorghum, then ripe and ready for the harvesters.

On the 17th I received by telegraph from President Lincoln this dispatch:

WASHINGTON, D. C., *September* 17, 1864—10 A. M.

Major-General SHERMAN:

I feel great interest in the subjects of your dispatch, mentioning corn and sorghum, and the contemplated visit to you.

A. LINCOLN, *President of the United States.*

I replied at once:

HEADQUARTERS MILITARY DIVISION OF THE MISSISSIPPI, IN THE FIELD, ATLANTA, GEORGIA, *September* 17, 1864.

President LINCOLN, *Washington, D. C.:*

I will keep the department fully advised of all developments connected with the subject in which you feel interested.

Mr. Wright, former member of Congress from Rome, Georgia, and Mr. King, of Marietta, are now going between Governor Brown and myself. I have said to them that some of the people of Georgia are engaged in rebellion, begun in error and perpetuated in pride, but that Georgia can now save herself from the devastations of war preparing for her, only by withdrawing her quota out of the Confederate Army, and aiding me to expel Hood from the borders of the State; in which event, instead of desolating the land as we progress, I will keep our men to the high-roads and commons, and pay for the corn and meat we need and take.

I am fully conscious of the delicate nature of such assertions, but it would be a magnificent stroke of policy if we could, without surrendering principle or a foot of ground, arouse the latent enmity of Georgia against Davis.

The people do not hesitate to say that Mr. Stephens was and is a Union man at heart; and they say that Davis will not trust him or let him have a share in his Government.

W. T. Sherman, *Major-General.*

I have not the least doubt that Governor Brown, at that time, seriously entertained the proposition; but he hardly felt ready to act, and simply gave a furlough to the militia, and called a special session of the Legislature, to meet at Milledgeville, to take into consideration the critical condition of affairs in the State.[10]

On the 20th of September Colonel Horace Porter arrived from General Grant, at City Point, bringing me the letter of September 12th, asking my general views as to what should next be done. He staid several days at Atlanta, and on his return carried back to Washington my full reports of the past campaign, and my letter of September 20th to General Grant in answer to his of the 12th.[11]

About this time we detected signs of activity on the part of the enemy. On the 21st Hood shifted his army across from the Macon road, at Lovejoy's, to the West Point road, at Palmetto Station,[12] and his cavalry appeared on the west side of the Chattahoochee, toward Powder Springs; thus, as it were, stepping aside, and opening wide the door for us to enter Central Georgia. I inferred, however, that his real purpose was to assume the offensive against our railroads, and on the 24th a heavy force of cavalry from Mississippi, under General Forrest, made its appearance at Athens, Alabama, and captured its garrison.

General Newton's division (of the Fourth Corps), and Corse's (of the Seventeenth), were sent back by rail, the former to Chattanooga, and the latter to Rome. On the 25th I telegraphed to General Halleck:

Hood seems to be moving, as it were, to the Alabama line, leaving open the road to Macon, as also to Augusta; but his cavalry is busy on all our roads. A force, number estimated as high as eight thousand, are

[10] On Sept 28, 1864, WTS wrote to Pres. Lincoln, "Brown is at Milledgeville trying to get a Legislature to meet next month, but he is afraid to act unless in concert with other Governors." *OR,* I, 39(II), 501.

[11] For WTS's full report on the Atlanta Campaign, and his relevant correspondence with USG, see *OR,* I, 38(I), 59–117, 38(II), 364–365, 411–413.

[12] Palmetto Station was situated along the Atlanta and West Point Railroad approximately twenty miles southwest of Atlanta. Davis et al., *Official Military Atlas of the Civil War,* plate 148.

reported to have captured Athens, Alabama; and a regiment of three hundred and fifty men sent to its relief. I have sent Newton's division up to Chattanooga in cars, and will send another division to Rome. If I were sure that Savannah would soon be in our possession, I should be tempted to march for Milledgeville and Augusta; but I must first secure what I have. Jeff. Davis is at Macon.

W. T. SHERMAN, *Major-General.*

On the next day I telegraphed further that Jeff. Davis was with Hood at Palmetto Station. One of our spies was there at the time, who came in the next night, and reported to me the substance of his speech to the soldiers. It was a repetition of those he had made at Columbia, South Carolina, and Macon, Georgia, on his way out, which I had seen in the newspapers. Davis seemed to be perfectly upset by the fall of Atlanta, and to have lost all sense and reason. He denounced General Jos. Johnston and Governor Brown as little better than traitors; attributed to them personally the many misfortunes which had befallen their cause, and informed the soldiers that now the tables were to be turned; that General Forrest was already on our roads in Middle Tennessee; and that Hood's army would soon be there. He asserted that the Yankee army would have to retreat or starve, and that the retreat would prove more disastrous than was that of Napoleon from Moscow.[13] He promised his Tennessee and Kentucky soldiers that their feet should soon tread their "native soil," etc., etc. He made no concealment of these vainglorious boasts, and thus gave us the full key to his future designs. To be forewarned was to be forearmed, and I think we took full advantage of the occasion.

On the 26th I received this dispatch:

CITY POINT, VIRGINIA, *September* 26, 1864—10 A. M.

Major-General SHERMAN, *Atlanta:*

It will be better to drive Forrest out of Middle Tennessee as a first step, and do any thing else you may feel your force sufficient for. When

[13] In a speech delivered at Macon, GA, Confederate president Davis asserted, "Sherman cannot keep up his long line of communication and retreat. Sooner or later he must; and when that day comes the fate that befell the army of the French Empire in its retreat from Moscow will be reacted. Our cavalry and our people will harass and destroy his army as did the Cossacks that of Napoleon; and the Yankee General, like him, will escape with only a body guard." "Desperate Speech by Jeff. Davis at Macon," *New York Times,* Oct. 7, 1864, 1.

a movement is made on any part of the sea-coast, I will advise you. If Hood goes to the Alabama line, will it not be impossible for him to subsist his army?

U. S. GRANT, *Lieutenant-General.*

Answer:

HEADQUARTERS MILITARY DIVISION OF THE MISSISSIPPI,
IN THE FIELD, ATLANTA, GEORGIA, *September* 26, 1864.

GENERAL: I have your dispatch of to-day. I have already sent one division (Newton's) to Chattanooga, and another (Corse's) to Rome.

Our armies are much reduced, and if I send back any more, I will not be able to threaten Georgia much. There are men enough to the rear to whip Forrest, but they are necessarily scattered to defend the roads.

Can you expedite the sending to Nashville of the recruits that are in Indiana and Ohio? They could occupy the forts.

Hood is now on the West Point road, twenty-four miles south of this, and draws his supplies by that road. Jefferson Davis is there to-day, and superhuman efforts will be made to break my road.

Forrest is now lieutenant-general, and commands all the enemy's cavalry.

W. T. SHERMAN, *Major-General.*

General Grant first thought I was in error in supposing that Jeff. Davis was at Macon and Palmetto, but on the 27th I received a printed copy of his speech made at Macon on the 22d,[14] which was so significant that I ordered it to be telegraphed entire as far as Louisville, to be sent thence by mail to Washington, and on the same day received this dispatch:

WASHINGTON, D. C., *September* 27, 1864—9 A. M.

Major-General SHERMAN, *Atlanta:*

You say Jeff. Davis is on a visit to General Hood. I judge that Brown and Stephens are the objects of his visit.

A. LINCOLN, *President of the United States.*

[14] Davis delivered the speech at Macon, GA, on Sept. 23. *New York Times,* Oct. 7, 1864, 1; *OR,* I, 39(II), 488–489.

To which I replied:

HEADQUARTERS MILITARY DIVISION OF THE MISSISSIPPI,
IN THE FIELD, ATLANTA, GEORGIA, *September* 28, 1864.

President LINCOLN, *Washington, D. C.:*

I have positive knowledge that Mr. Davis made a speech at Macon, on the 22d, which I mailed to General Halleck yesterday. It was bitter against General Jos. Johnston and Governor Brown. The militia are on furlough. Brown is at Milledgeville, trying to get a Legislature to meet next month, but he is afraid to act unless in concert with other Governors. Judge Wright, of Rome, has been here, and Messrs. Hill and Nelson, former members of Congress, are here now, and will go to meet Wright at Rome, and then go back to Madison and Milledgeville.

Great efforts are being made to reënforce Hood's army, and to break up my railroads, and I should have at once a good reserve force at Nashville. It would have a bad effect, if I were forced to send back any considerable part of my army to guard roads, so as to weaken me to an extent that I could not act offensively if the occasion calls for it.

W. T. SHERMAN, *Major-General.*

All this time Hood and I were carrying on the foregoing correspondence relating to the exchange of prisoners, the removal of the people from Atlanta, and the relief of our prisoners of war at Andersonville. Notwithstanding the severity of their imprisonment, some of these men escaped from Andersonville, and got to me at Atlanta. They described their sad condition: more than twenty-five thousand prisoners confined in a stockade designed for only ten thousand; debarred the privilege of gathering wood out of which to make huts; deprived of sufficient healthy food, and the little stream that ran through their prison-pen poisoned and polluted by the offal from their cooking and butchering houses above. On the 22d of September I wrote to General Hood, describing the condition of our men at Andersonville, purposely refraining from casting odium on him or his associates for the treatment of these men, but asking his consent for me to procure from our generous friends at the North the articles of clothing and comfort which they wanted, viz., under-clothing, soap, combs, scissors, etc.—all needed to keep them in health—and to send these stores with a train, and an officer to issue them. General Hood, on the 24th, promptly consented, and I telegraphed to my friend Mr. James E. Yeatman, Vice-President of the Sanitary Commission at St. Louis,[15] to send us all the under-clothing and soap he could spare, specifying twelve hundred fine-tooth combs, and four hundred pairs of shears to cut hair. These articles indicate the plague that most afflicted our prisoners at Andersonville.

Mr. Yeatman promptly responded to my request, expressed the articles, but they did not reach Andersonville in time, for the prisoners were soon after removed; these supplies did, however, finally overtake them at Jacksonville, Florida, just before the war closed.[16]

On the 28th I received from General Grant two dispatches:

CITY POINT, VIRGINIA, *September* 27, 1864—8.30 A. M.

Major-General SHERMAN:

It is evident, from the tone of the Richmond press and from other sources of information, that the enemy intend making a desperate effort to drive you from where you are. I have directed all new troops from the West, and from the East too, if necessary, in case none are ready in the West, to be sent to you. If General Burbridge is not too far on his way to Abingdon, I think he had better be recalled and his surplus troops sent into Tennessee.

U. S. GRANT, *Lieutenant-General.*

CITY POINT, VIRGINIA, *September* 27, 1864—10.30 A. M.

Major-General SHERMAN:

I have directed all recruits and new troops from all the Western States to be sent to Nashville, to receive their further orders from you. I was mistaken about Jeff. Davis being in Richmond on Thursday last. He was then on his way to Macon.

U. S. GRANT, *Lieutenant-General.*

Forrest having already made his appearance in Middle Tennessee, and Hood evidently edging off in that direction, satisfied me that the general movement against our roads had begun. I therefore determined to send Gen-

[15] James E. Yeatman (1818–1901) was also a St. Louis merchant, banker, and philanthropist. "James E. Yeatman Dead: St. Louis Philanthropist Breathes His Last," *Elm Creek Beacon* (Elm Creek, NE), July 12, 1901, 6.

[16] WTS wrote to Yeatman about supplies for prisoners of war on Sept. 22 and 27, 1864. *OR,* II, 7, 857–858, 885.

eral Thomas back to Chattanooga, with another division (Morgan's, of the Fourteenth Corps), to meet the danger in Tennessee. General Thomas went up on the 29th, and Morgan's division followed the same day, also by rail. And I telegraphed to General Halleck:

> I take it for granted that Forrest will cut our road, but think we can prevent him from making a serious lodgment. His cavalry will travel a hundred miles where ours will ten. I have sent two divisions up to Chattanooga and one to Rome, and General Thomas started to-day to drive Forrest out of Tennessee. Our roads should be watched from the rear, and I am glad that General Grant has ordered reserves to Nashville. I prefer for the future to make the movement on Milledgeville, Millen, and Savannah. Hood now rests twenty-four miles south, on the Chattahoochee, with his right on the West Point road. He is removing the iron of the Macon road. I can whip his infantry, but his cavalry is to be feared.

There was great difficulty in obtaining correct information about Hood's movements from Palmetto Station. I could not get spies to penetrate his camps, but on the 1st of October I was satisfied that the bulk of his infantry was at and across the Chattahoochee River, near Campbellton, and that his cavalry was on the west side, at Powder Springs. On that day I telegraphed to General Grant:

> Hood is evidently across the Chattahoochee, below Sweetwater. If he tries to get on our road, this side of the Etowah, I shall attack him; but if he goes to the Selma & Talladega road, why will it not do to leave Tennessee to the forces which Thomas has, and the reserves soon to come to Nashville, and for me to destroy Atlanta and march across Georgia to Savannah or Charleston, breaking roads and doing irreparable damage? We cannot remain on the defensive.

The Selma & Talladega road herein referred to was an unfinished railroad from Selma, Alabama, through Talladega, to Blue Mountain, a terminus sixty-five miles southwest of Rome and about fifteen miles southeast of Gadsden, where the rebel army could be supplied from the direction of Montgomery and Mobile, and from which point Hood could easily threaten Middle Tennessee. My first impression was, that Hood would make for that point; but by the 3d of October the indications were that he would strike our railroad nearer us, viz., about Kingston or Marietta.

Orders were at once made for the Twentieth Corps (Slocum's) to hold Atlanta and the bridges of the Chattahoochee, and the other corps were put in motion for Marietta.

The army had undergone many changes since the capture of Atlanta. General Schofield had gone to the rear, leaving General J. D. Cox in command of the Army of the Ohio (Twenty-third Corps).[17] General Thomas, also, had been dispatched to Chattanooga, with Newton's division of the Fourth Corps and Morgan's of the Fourteenth Corps, leaving General D. S. Stanley, the senior major-general of the two corps of his Army of the Cumberland, remaining and available for this movement, viz., the Fourth and Fourteenth, commanded by himself and Major-General Jeff. C. Davis; and after General Dodge was wounded, his corps (the Sixteenth) had been broken up, and its two divisions were added to the Fifteenth and Seventeenth Corps, constituting the Army of the Tennessee, commanded by Major-General O. O. Howard.[18] Generals Logan and Blair had gone home to assist in the political canvass, leaving their corps, viz., the Fifteenth and Seventeenth, under the command of Major-Generals Osterhaus and T. E. G. Ransom.[19]

These five corps were very much reduced in strength, by detachments and by discharges, so that for the purpose of fighting Hood I had only about sixty thousand infantry and artillery, with two small divisions of cavalry (Kilpatrick's and Garrard's). General Elliott[20] was the chief of cavalry to the Army of the Cumberland, and was the senior officer of that arm of service present for duty with me.

We had strong railroad guards at Marietta and Kenesaw, Allatoona, Etowah Bridge, Kingston, Rome, Resaca, Dalton, Ringgold, and Chattanooga. All the important bridges were likewise protected by good block-houses, admirably constructed, and capable of a strong defense against cavalry or infantry; and at nearly all the regular railroad-stations we had smaller detachments intrenched. I had little fear of the enemy's cavalry damaging our roads seriously, for they rarely made a break which could not be repaired in a few days; but it

[17] Jacob D. Cox Jr. (1828–1900) was placed in command of the Army of the Ohio for Oct. 5–22. *OR,* I, 39(III), 88, 401–402.

[18] On Aug. 19, 1864, during the battle for Atlanta, Dodge was wounded in the head. *CWHC,* 212.

[19] Thomas E. G. Ransom (1834–1864) took command of the 17th Corps, Army of the Tennessee, on Sept. 22, 1864. *CWHC,* 446.

[20] Washington L. Elliot (1825–1888) took command of the Cav. Corps, Army of the Cumberland, on Nov. 20, 1863. *CWHC,* 225.

was absolutely necessary to keep General Hood's infantry off our main route of communication and supply. Forrest had with him in Middle Tennessee about eight thousand cavalry, and Hood's army was estimated at from thirty-five to forty thousand men, infantry and artillery, including Wheeler's cavalry, then about three thousand strong.

We crossed the Chattahoochee River during the 3d and 4th of October, rendezvoused at the old battle-field of Smyrna Camp, and the next day reached Marietta and Kenesaw. The telegraph-wires had been cut above Marietta, and learning that heavy masses of infantry, artillery, and cavalry, had been seen from Kenesaw (marching north), I inferred that Allatoona was their objective point; and on the 4th of October I signaled from Vining's Station to Kenesaw, and from Kenesaw to Allatoona, over the heads of the enemy, a message for General Corse, at Rome, to hurry back to the assistance of the garrison at Allatoona. Allatoona was held by a small brigade, commanded by Lieutenant-Colonel Tourtellotte, my present aide-de-camp.[21] He had two small redoubts on either side of the railroad, overlooking the village of Allatoona, and the warehouses, in which were stored over a million rations of bread.

Reaching Kenesaw Mountain about 8 A. M. of October 5th (a beautiful day), I had a superb view of the vast panorama to the north and west. To the southwest, about Dallas, could be seen the smoke of camp-fires, indicating the presence of a large force of the enemy, and the whole line of railroad from Big Shanty up to Allatoona (full fifteen miles) was marked by the fires of the burning railroad. We could plainly see the smoke of battle about Allatoona, and hear the faint reverberation of the cannon.

From Kenesaw I ordered the Twenty-third Corps (General Cox) to march due west on the Burnt Hickory road, and to burn houses or piles of brush as it progressed, to indicate the head of column, hoping to interpose this corps between Hood's main army at Dallas and the detachment then assailing Allatoona.[22] The rest of the army was directed straight for Allatoona, northwest, distant eighteen miles. The signal-officer on Kenesaw[23] reported that since daylight he had failed to obtain any answer to his call for Allatoona; but, while I

[21] John E. Tourtellotte (1833–1891) commanded the 4th Minnesota Inf. in early Oct. 1864. *CWHC,* 534.

[22] WTS to Cox, Oct. 6, 1864, *OR,* I, 39(III), 114–115.

[23] Samuel Bachtell (1833–1907) was appointed chief signal officer of the Army of the Cumberland in Sept. 1864 and was soon transferred to WTS's staff. "Bachtell," *National Tribune* (Washington, DC), May 16, 1907, 7; *The History of Wyandot County, Ohio* (Chicago: Leggett and Conaway, 1884), 693.

was with him, he caught a faint glimpse of the tell-tale flag through an embrasure, and after much time he made out these letters—"C.," "R.," "S.," "E.," "H.," "E.," "R.," and translated the message—"Corse is here." It was a source of great relief, for it gave me the first assurance that General Corse had received his orders, and that the place was adequately garrisoned.

I watched with painful suspense the indications of the battle raging there, and was dreadfully impatient at the slow progress of the relieving column, whose advance was marked by the smokes which were made according to orders, but about 2 P. M. I noticed with satisfaction that the smoke of battle about Allatoona grew less and less, and ceased altogether about 4 P. M. For a time I attributed this result to the effect of General Cox's march, but later in the afternoon the signal-flag announced the welcome tidings that the attack had been fairly repulsed, but that General Corse was wounded. The next day my aide, Colonel Dayton, received this characteristic dispatch:

ALLATOONA, GEORGIA, *October* 6, 1864—2 P. M.

Captain L. M. DAYTON, *Aide-de-Camp:*

I am short a cheek-bone and an ear, but am able to whip all h—l yet! My losses are very heavy. A force moving from Stilesboro' to Kingston gives me some anxiety. Tell me where Sherman is.

JOHN M. CORSE, Brigadier-General.

Inasmuch as the enemy had retreated southwest, and would probably next appear at Rome, I answered General Corse with orders to get back to Rome with his troops as quickly as possible.

General Corse's report of this fight at Allatoona is very full and graphic. It is dated Rome, October 27, 1864; recites the fact that he received his orders by signal to go to the assistance of Allatoona on the 4th, when he telegraphed to Kingston for cars, and a train of thirty empty cars was started for him, but about ten of them got off the track and caused delay. By 7 P. M. he had at Rome a train of twenty cars, which he loaded up with Colonel Rowett's brigade,[24] and part of the Twelfth Illinois Infantry; started at 8 P. M., reached Allatoona (distant thirty-five miles) at 1 A M. of the 5th, and sent the train back for more men; but the road was in bad order, and no more men came in time. He found Colonel Tourtellotte's garrison composed of eight hundred

[24] Richard Rowett (1830–1887) commanded the 3rd Brig., 2nd Div., 15th Corps, Army of the Tennessee, in Oct. 1864. *CWHC,* 463.

and ninety men; his reënforcement was one thousand and fifty-four: total for the defense, nineteen hundred and forty-four. The outposts were already engaged, and as soon as daylight came he drew back the men from the village to the ridge on which the redoubts were built.

The enemy was composed of French's division of three brigades, variously reported from four to five thousand strong. This force gradually surrounded the place by 8 A. M., when General French sent in by flag of truce this note:

AROUND ALLATOONA, *October* 5, 1864.

Commanding Officer, United States Forces, Allatoona:

I have placed the forces under my command in such positions that you are surrounded, and to avoid a needless effusion of blood I call on you to surrender your forces at once, and unconditionally.

Five minutes will be allowed you to decide. Should you accede to this, you will be treated in the most honorable manner as prisoners of war.

I have the honor to be, very respectfully yours,

S. G. FRENCH,
Major-General commanding forces Confederate States.

General Corse answered immediately:

HEADQUARTERS FOURTH DIVISION, FIFTEENTH CORPS,
ALLATOONA, GEORGIA, 8.30 A. M., *October* 5, 1864.

Major-General S. G. FRENCH, *Confederate States, etc.:*

Your communication demanding surrender of my command I acknowledge receipt of, and respectfully reply that we are prepared for the "needless effusion of blood" whenever it is agreeable to you.

I am, very respectfully, your obedient servant,

JOHN M. CORSE,
Brigadier-General commanding forces United States.

Of course the attack began at once, coming from front, flank, and rear. There were two small redoubts, with slight parapets and ditches, one on each side of the deep railroad-cut. These redoubts had been located by Colonel Poe, United States Engineers, at the time of our advance on Kenesaw, the previous June. Each redoubt overlooked the storehouses close by the railroad, and each could aid the other defensively by catching in flank the attacking force of the other. Our troops at first endeavored to hold some ground outside the redoubts, but were soon driven inside, when the enemy made repeated assaults, but were always driven back. About 11 A. M., Colonel Redfield, of the Thirty-ninth Iowa, was killed,[25] and Colonel Rowett was wounded, but never ceased to fight and encourage his men. Colonel Tourtellotte was shot through the hips, but continued to command. General Corse was, at 1 P. M., shot across the face, the ball cutting his ear, which stunned him, but he continued to encourage his men and to give orders. The enemy (about 1.30 P. M.) made a last and desperate effort to carry one of the redoubts, but was badly cut to pieces by the artillery and infantry fire from the other, when he began to draw off, leaving his dead and wounded on the ground.

Before finally withdrawing, General French converged a heavy fire of his cannon on the block-house at Allatoona Creek, about two miles from the depot, set it on fire, and captured its garrison, consisting of four officers and eighty-five men. By 4 P. M. he was in full retreat south, on the Dallas road, and got by before the head of General Cox's column had reached it; still several ambulances and stragglers were picked up by this command on that road. General Corse reported two hundred and thirty-one rebel dead, four hundred and eleven prisoners, three regimental colors, and eight hundred muskets captured.

Among the prisoners was a Brigadier-General Young,[26] who thought that French's aggregate loss would reach two thousand. Colonel Tourtellotte says that, for days after General Corse had returned to Rome, his men found and buried at least a hundred more dead rebels, who had doubtless been wounded, and died in the woods near Allatoona. I know that when I reached Allatoona, on the 9th, I saw a good many dead men, which had been collected for burial.

Corse's entire loss, officially reported, was:

GARRISON.	Killed.	Wounded.	Missing.	Total.
Officers.	6	23	6	35
Men.	136	330	206	672
Total.	142	353	212	707

[25] James Redfield (1824–1864) was killed while leading his men into battle at Rome, GA, on Oct. 6, 1864. *Obituary Record of Graduates of Yale College, Deceased from July, 1859, to July 1870* (New Haven, CT: Tuttle, Morehouse, and Taylor, 1870), s.v. "James Redfield."

[26] Pierce M. B. Young (1836–1896) joined the Confederate Army at the start of the war and was detached from the Army of Northern Virginia when he was wounded and captured at Allatoona on Oct. 5. *CWHC,* 585.

I esteemed this defense of Allatoona so handsome and important, that I made it the subject of a general order, viz., No. 86, of October 7, 1864:

> The general commanding avails himself of the opportunity, in the handsome defense made of Allatoona, to illustrate the most important principle in war, that fortified posts should be defended to the last, regardless of the relative numbers of the party attacking and attacked. . . . The thanks of this army are due and are hereby accorded to General Corse, Colonel Tourtellotte, Colonel Rowett, officers, and men, for their determined and gallant defense of Allatoona, and it is made an example to illustrate the importance of preparing in time, and meeting the danger, when present, boldly, manfully, and well.
>
> Commanders and garrisons of the posts along our railroad are hereby instructed that they must hold their posts to the last minute, sure that the time gained is valuable and necessary to their comrades at the front.
>
> By order of Major-General W. T. Sherman,
>
> L. M. Dayton, *Aide-de-Camp.*

The rebels had struck our railroad a heavy blow, burning every tie, bending the rails for eight miles, from Big Shanty to above Acworth, so that the estimate for repairs called for thirty-five thousand new ties, and six miles of iron. Ten thousand men were distributed along the break to replace the ties, and to prepare the road-bed, while the regular repair-party, under Colonel W. W. Wright, came down from Chattanooga with iron, spikes, etc., and in about seven days the road was all right again.[27] It was by such acts of extraordinary energy that we discouraged our adversaries, for the rebel soldiers felt that it was a waste of labor for them to march hurriedly, on wide circuits, day and night, to burn a bridge and tear up a mile or so of track, when they knew that we could lay it back so quickly. They supposed that we had men and money without limit, and that we always kept on hand, distributed along the road, duplicates of every bridge and culvert of any importance.

A good story is told of one who was on Kenesaw Mountain during our advance in the previous June or July. A group of rebels lay in the shade of a tree, one hot day, overlooking our camps about Big Shanty. One soldier remarked to his fellows:

[27] In a dispatch dated Oct. 7, Gen. Thomas informed WTS that Col. Wright promised "to have the road in running order as far as Allatoona in one week." *OR,* I, 39(III), 139.

"Well, the Yanks will have to git up and git now, for I heard General Johnston himself say that General Wheeler had blown up *the tunnel* near Dalton, and that the Yanks would have to retreat, because they could get no more rations."

"Oh, hell!" said a listener, "don't you know that old Sherman carries a *duplicate* tunnel along?"[28]

After the war was over, General Johnston inquired of me who was our chief railroad-engineer. When I told him that it was Colonel W. W. Wright, a civilian, he was much surprised, said that our feats of bridge-building and repairs of roads had excited his admiration; and he instanced the occasion at Kenesaw in June, when an officer from Wheeler's cavalry had reported to him in person that he had come from General Wheeler, who had made a bad break in our road about Tilton Station, which he said would take at least a fortnight to repair; and, while they were talking, a train was seen coming down the road, which had passed that very break, and had reached me at Big Shanty as soon as the fleet horseman had reached him (General Johnston) at Marietta!

I doubt whether the history of war can furnish more examples of skill and bravery than attended the defense of the railroad from Nashville to Atlanta during the year 1864.

In person I reached Allatoona on the 9th of October, still in doubt as to Hood's immediate intentions. Our cavalry could do little against his infantry in the rough and wooded country about Dallas, which masked the enemy's movements; but General Corse, at Rome, with Spencer's First Alabama Cavalry and a mounted regiment of Illinois Infantry,[29] could feel the country south of Rome about Cedartown and Villa Rica; and reported the enemy to be in force at both places. On the 9th I telegraphed to General Thomas, at Nashville, as follows:

I came up here to relieve our road. The Twentieth Corps remains at Atlanta. Hood reached the road and broke it up between Big Shanty and Acworth. He attacked Allatoona, but was repulsed. We have plenty of bread and meat, but forage is scarce. I want to destroy all the road below Chattanooga,

[28] On Oct. 12, 1864, the *Edgefield Advertiser* (Edgefield, SC) published an article stating that "Forrest has destroyed every railway bridge from Decatur, Alabama, to Pulaski, Tennessee, together with miles of trestlework and all water tanks on the road. The damage done cannot be repaired in two months even if Sherman has 'duplicates of cuts, tunnels, and embankments.'" "Gen. Forrest," *Edgefield Advertiser* (Edgefield, SC), Oct. 12, 1864, 2.

[29] George E. Spencer (1836–1893) joined the 1st Alabama Cav. as a colonel on Sept. 11, 1863. After the war, he served as a U.S. senator from Alabama from 1868 to 1879. *CWHC*, 502.

including Atlanta, and to make for the sea-coast. We cannot defend this long line of road.[30]

And on the same day I telegraphed to General Grant, at City Point:

> It will be a physical impossibility to protect the roads, now that Hood, Forrest, Wheeler, and the whole batch of devils, are turned loose without home or habitation. I think Hood's movements indicate a diversion to the end of the Selma & Talladega road, at Blue Mountain, about sixty miles southwest of Rome, from which he will threaten Kingston, Bridgeport, and Decatur, Alabama. I propose that we break up the railroad from Chattanooga forward, and that we strike out with our wagons for Milledgeville, Millen, and Savannah. Until we can repopulate Georgia, it is useless for us to occupy it; but the utter destruction of its roads, houses, and people, will cripple their military resources. By attempting to hold the roads, we will lose a thousand men each month, and will gain no result. I can make this march, and make Georgia howl! We have on hand over eight thousand head of cattle and three million rations of bread, but no corn. We can find plenty of forage in the interior of the State.

Meantime the rebel General Forrest had made a bold circuit in Middle Tennessee, avoiding all fortified points, and breaking up the railroad at several places; but, as usual, he did his work so hastily and carelessly that our engineers soon repaired the damage—then, retreating before General Rousseau, he left the State of Tennessee, crossing the river near Florence, Alabama, and got off unharmed.

On the 10th of October the enemy appeared south of the Etowah River at Rome, when I ordered all the armies to march to Kingston, rode myself to Cartersville with the Twenty-third Corps (General Cox), and telegraphed from there to General Thomas at Nashville:

> It looks to me as though Hood was bound for Tuscumbia. He is now crossing the Coosa River below Rome, looking west. Let me know if you can hold him with your forces now in Tennessee and the expected reënforcements, as, in that event, you know what I propose to do.
>
> I will be at Kingston to-morrow. I think Rome is strong enough to resist any attack, and the rivers are all high. If he turns up by Summerville, I will get in behind him.

[30] For WTS's full telegram to Gen. Thomas, see *OR,* I, 39(III), 169–170.

And on the same day to General Grant, at City Point:

> Hood is now crossing the Coosa, twelve miles below Rome, bound west. If he passes over to the Mobile & Ohio Railroad, had I not better execute the plan of my letter sent you by Colonel Porter, and leave General Thomas, with the troops now in Tennessee, to defend the State? He will have an ample force when the reënforcements ordered reach Nashville.[31]

I found General John E. Smith at Cartersville, and on the 11th rode on to Kingston, where I had telegraphic communications in all directions.

From General Corse, at Rome, I learned that Hood's army had disappeared, but in what direction he was still in doubt; and I was so strongly convinced of the wisdom of my proposition to change the whole tactics of the campaign, to leave Hood to General Thomas, and to march across Georgia for Savannah or Charleston, that I again telegraphed to General Grant:

> We cannot now remain on the defensive. With twenty-five thousand infantry and the bold cavalry he has, Hood can constantly break my road. I would infinitely prefer to make a wreck of the road and of the country from Chattanooga to Atlanta, including the latter city; send back all my wounded and unserviceable men, and with my effective army move through Georgia, smashing things to the sea. Hood may turn into Tennessee and Kentucky, but I believe he will be forced to follow me. Instead of being on the defensive, I will be on the offensive. Instead of my guessing at what he means to do, he will have to guess at my plans. The difference in war would be fully twenty-five per cent. I can make Savannah, Charleston, or the mouth of the Chattahoochee (Appalachicola). Answer quick, as I know we will not have the telegraph long.[32]

I received no answer to this at the time, and the next day went on to Rome, where the news came that Hood had made his appearance at Resaca, and had demanded the surrender of the place, which was commanded by Colonel Weaver,[33] reënforced by Brevet Brigadier-General Raum. General Hood had

[31] WTS wrote his dispatch to USG from Cartersville, GA, on Oct. 10. *OR*, I, 39(III), 174.

[32] WTS wrote his telegram to USG from Kingston, GA, on Oct. 11. *OR*, I, 39(III), 202.

[33] In a dispatch to Clark R. Wever (1835–1874), WTS wrote, "In case you are threatened you should concentrate your force at the forts at the bridge. Have abatis made at once on the land

evidently marched with rapidity up the Chattooga Valley, by Summerville, Lafayette, Ship's Gap, and Snake-Creek Gap, and had with him his whole army, except a small force left behind to watch Rome. I ordered Resaca to be further reënforced by rail from Kingston, and ordered General Cox[34] to make a bold reconnoissance down the Coosa Valley, which captured and brought into Rome some cavalrymen and a couple of field-guns, with their horses and men. At first I thought of interposing my whole army in the Chattooga Valley, so as to prevent Hood's escape south; but I saw at a glance that he did not mean to fight, and in that event, after damaging the road all he could, he would be likely to retreat eastward by Spring Place, which I did not want him to do; and, hearing from General Raum that he still held Resaca safe, and that General Edward McCook had also got there with some cavalry reënforcements, I turned all the heads of columns for Resaca, viz., General Cox's, from Rome; General Stanley's, from McGuire's;[35] and General Howard's, from Kingston. We all reached Resaca during that night, and the next morning (13th) learned that Hood's whole army had passed up the valley toward Dalton, burning the railroad and doing all the damage possible.

On the 12th he had demanded the surrender of Resaca in the following letter:

HEADQUARTERS ARMY OF TENNESSEE,
IN THE FIELD, *October* 12, 1864. }

To the Officer commanding the United States Forces at Resaca, Georgia.

SIR: I demand the immediate and unconditional surrender of the post and garrison under your command, and, should this be acceded to, all white officers and soldiers will be parolled in a few days. If the place is carried by assault, no prisoners will be taken. Most respectfully, your obedient servant,

J. B. HOOD, *General.*

---

side. Keep a strong cavalry picket at Snake Creek Gap. As long as the Oostenaula is high the troops at Adairsville and Calhoun should go to Resaca." *CWHC*, 562; *OR*, I, 39(III), 208.

[34] In the first edition of the memoirs (1875), this portion of WTS's text read "General Corse" instead of "General Cox." See J. D. Cox to WTS, Oct. 19, 1875, in the Appendix to Volume II.

[35] McGuire, GA, was located approximately sixty miles northwest of Atlanta. Davis et al., *Official Military Atlas of the Civil War*, plate 149.

To this Colonel Weaver, then in command, replied:

HEADQUARTERS SECOND BRIGADE, THIRD DIVISION, FIFTEENTH CORPS,
RESACA, GEORGIA, *October* 12, 1864.

To General J. B. HOOD:

Your communication of this date just received. In reply, I have to state that I am somewhat surprised at the concluding paragraph, to the effect that, if the place is carried by assault, no prisoners will be taken. In my opinion I can hold this post. If you want it, come and take it.

I am, general, very respectfully, your most obedient servant,

CLARK R. WEAVER, *Commanding Officer.*

This brigade was very small, and as Hood's investment extended only from the Oostenaula, below the town, to the Connesauga above, he left open the approach from the south, which enabled General Raum and the cavalry of Generals McCook and Watkins to reënforce from Kingston.[36] In fact, Hood, admonished by his losses at Allatoona, did not attempt an assault at all, but limited his attack to the above threat, and to some skirmishing, giving his attention chiefly to the destruction of the railroad, which he accomplished all the way up to Tunnel Hill, nearly twenty miles, capturing *en route* the regiment of black troops at Dalton (Johnson's Forty-fourth United States colored).[37] On the 14th, I turned General Howard through Snake-Creek Gap, and sent General Stanley around by Tilton, with orders to cross the mountain to the west, so as to capture, if possible, the force left by the enemy in Snake-Creek Gap. We found this gap very badly obstructed by fallen timber, but got through that night, and the next day the main army was at Villanow. On the morning of the 16th, the leading division of General Howard's column, commanded by General Charles R. Woods, carried Ship's Gap, taking prisoners part of the Twenty-fourth South Carolina Regiment, which had been left there to hold us in check.

The best information there obtained located Hood's army at Lafayette, near which place I hoped to catch him and force him to battle; but, by the time we had got enough troops across the mountain at Ship's Gap, Hood had escaped down the valley of the Chattooga, and all we could do was to follow him as closely as possible. From Ship's Gap I dispatched couriers to Chattanooga, and

[36] In the first edition of the memoirs (1875), WTS omitted "Watkins" from the sentence.

[37] Lewis Johnson (1841–1900) took command of the 44th U.S. Colored Inf. as a colonel on Sept. 16, 1864. *CWHC*, 321.

received word back that General Schofield was there, endeavoring to coöperate with me, but Hood had broken up the telegraph, and thus had prevented quick communication. General Schofield did not reach me till the army had got down to Gaylesville, about the 21st of October.[38]

It was at Ship's Gap that a courier brought me the cipher message from General Halleck which intimated that the authorities in Washington were willing I should undertake the march across Georgia to the sea. The translated dispatch named "Horse-i-bar Sound" as the point where the fleet would await my arrival. After much time I construed it to mean, "Ossabaw Sound," below Savannah, which was correct.[39]

On the 16th I telegraphed to General Thomas, at Nashville:

> Send me Morgan's and Newton's old divisions. Reëstablish the road, and I will follow Hood wherever he may go. I think he will move to Blue Mountain. We can maintain our men and animals on the country.

General Thomas's reply was:

> NASHVILLE, *October* 17, 1864—10.30 A. M.
>
> *Major-General* SHERMAN:
>
> Your dispatch from Ship's Gap, 5 P. M. of the 16th, just received. Schofield, whom I placed in command of the two divisions (Wagner's and Morgan's), was to move up Lookout Valley this A. M., to intercept Hood, should he be marching for Bridgeport. I will order him to join you with the two divisions, and will reconstruct the road as soon as possible. Will also reorganize the guards for posts and block-houses. . . . Mower and Wilson have arrived, and are on their way to join you. I hope you will adopt Grant's idea of turning Wilson loose, rather than undertake the plan of a march with the whole force through Georgia to the sea, inasmuch as General Grant cannot coöperate with you as at first arranged.
>
> GEORGE H. THOMAS, *Major-General.*

[38] Schofield did not arrive at Gaylesville, AL, until Oct. 22. *OR,* I, 39(III), 391, 401–402.

[39] On Oct. 16, WTS wrote to USG, "I got the dispatch in cipher about providing me a place to come out on salt water, but the cipher is imperfect and I cannot make out whether Savannah or Mobile be the point preferred." *OR,* I, 39(III), 304–305.

So it is clear that at that date neither General Grant nor General Thomas heartily favored my proposed plan of campaign. On the same day, I wrote to General Schofield at Chattanooga:

> Hood is not at Dear Head Cove. We occupy Ship's Gap and Lafayette. Hood is moving south *via* Summerville, Alpine, and Gadsden. If he enters Tennessee, it will be to the west of Huntsville, but I think he has given up all such idea. I want the road repaired to Atlanta; the sick and wounded men sent north of the Tennessee; my army recomposed; and I will then make the interior of Georgia feel the weight of war. It is folly for us to be moving our armies on the reports of scouts and citizens. We must maintain the offensive. Your first move on Trenton and Valley Head was right—the move to defend Caperton's Ferry is wrong. Notify General Thomas of these my views. We must follow Hood till he is beyond the reach of mischief, and then resume the offensive.

The correspondence between me and the authorities at Washington, as well as with the several army commanders, given at length in the report of the Committee on the Conduct of the War, is full on all these points.[40]

After striking our road at Dalton, Hood was compelled to go on to Chattanooga and Bridgeport, or to pass around by Decatur and abandon altogether his attempt to make us let go our hold of Atlanta by attacking our communications. It was clear to me that he had no intention to meet us in open battle, and the lightness and celerity of his army convinced me that I could not possibly catch him on a stern-chase. We therefore quietly followed him down the Chattooga Valley to the neighborhood of Gadsden, but halted the main armies near the Coosa River, at the mouth of the Chattooga, drawing our supplies of corn and meat from the farms of that comparatively rich valley and of the neighborhood.

General Slocum, in Atlanta, had likewise sent out, under strong escort, large trains of wagons to the east, and brought back corn, bacon, and all kinds of provisions, so that Hood's efforts to cut off our supplies only reacted on his own people. So long as the railroads were in good order, our supplies came full and regular from the North; but when the enemy broke our railroads we were perfectly justified in stripping the inhabitants of all they had. I remember well the appeal of a very respectable farmer against our men driving away his fine flock of sheep. I explained to him that General Hood had broken our railroad;

[40] See *Supplemental Report of the Joint Committee on the Conduct of the War* (Washington, DC: GPO, 1866), 1:1–391.

that we were a strong, hungry crowd, and needed plenty of food; that Uncle Sam was deeply interested in our continued health and would soon repair these roads, but meantime we must eat; we preferred Illinois beef, but mutton would have to answer. Poor fellow! I don't believe he was convinced of the wisdom or wit of my explanation. Very soon after reaching Lafayette we organized a line of supply from Chattanooga to Ringgold by rail, and thence by wagons to our camps about Gaylesville. Meantime, also, Hood had reached the neighborhood of Gadsden, and drew his supplies from the railroad at Blue Mountain.

On the 19th of October I telegraphed to General Halleck, at Washington:

> Hood has retreated rapidly by all the roads leading south. Our advance columns are now at Alpine and Melville Post-Office. I shall pursue him as far as Gaylesville. The enemy will not venture toward Tennessee except around by Decatur. I propose to send the Fourth Corps back to General Thomas, and leave him, with that corps, the garrisons, and new troops, to defend the line of the Tennessee River; and with the rest I will push into the heart of Georgia and come out at Savannah, destroying all the railroads of the State. The break in our railroad at Big Shanty is almost repaired, and that about Dalton should be done in ten days. We find abundance of forage in the country.

On the same day I telegraphed to General L. C. Easton, chief-quartermaster, who had been absent on a visit to Missouri, but had got back to Chattanooga:

> Go in person to superintend the repairs of the railroad, and make all orders in my name that will expedite its completion. I want it finished, to bring back from Atlanta to Chattanooga the sick and wounded men and surplus stores. On the 1st of November I want nothing in front of Chattanooga except what we can use as food and clothing and haul in our wagons. There is plenty of corn in the country, and we only want forage for the posts. I allow ten days for all this to be done, by which time I expect to be at or near Atlanta.

I telegraphed also to General Amos Beckwith, chief-commissary in Atlanta, who was acting as chief-quartermaster during the absence of General Easton:

> Hood will escape me. I want to prepare for my big raid. On the 1st of November I want nothing in Atlanta but what is necessary for war. Send all trash to the rear at once, and have on hand thirty days'

> food and but little forage. I propose to abandon Atlanta, and the railroad back to Chattanooga, to sally forth to ruin Georgia and bring up on the sea-shore. Make all dispositions accordingly. I will go down the Coosa until I am sure that Hood has gone to Blue Mountain.

On the 21st of October I reached Gaylesville, had my bivouac in an open field back of the village, and remained there till the 28th. During that time General Schofield arrived, with the two divisions of Generals Wagner (formerly Newton's) and Morgan, which were returned to their respective corps (the Fourth and Fourteenth), and General Schofield resumed his own command of the Army of the Ohio, then on the Coosa River, near Cedar Bluff.[41] General Joseph A. Mower also arrived, and was assigned to command a division in the Seventeenth Corps; and General J. H. Wilson came, having been sent from Virginia by General Grant, for the purpose of commanding all my cavalry. I first intended to organize this cavalry into a corps of three small divisions, to be commanded by General Wilson; but the horses were well run down, and, at Wilson's instance, I concluded to retain only one division of four thousand five hundred men, with selected horses, under General Kilpatrick, and to send General Wilson back with all the rest to Nashville, to be reorganized and to act under General Thomas in the defense of Tennessee. Orders to this effect were made on the 24th of October.[42]

General Grant, in designating General Wilson to command my cavalry, predicted that he would, by his personal activity, increase the effect of that arm "fifty per cent.," and he advised that he should be sent south, to accomplish all that I had proposed to do with the main army; but I had not so much faith in cavalry as he had, and preferred to adhere to my original intention of going myself with a competent force.[43]

About this time I learned that General Beauregard had reached Hood's army at Gadsden; that, without assuming direct command of that army, he had authority from the Confederate Government to direct all its movements, and to call to his assistance the whole strength of the South. His orders, on assuming command, were full of alarm and desperation, dated—

[41] Schofield resumed command of the 23rd Corps, Army of the Ohio, on Oct. 22. *CWHC,* 473.

[42] See *OR,* I, 39(III), 414–415.

[43] On Oct. 4, USG wrote to WTS, "General Wilson has been ordered to report to you, and that he may have rank to command your cavalry I have asked that he be brevetted a major-general, and assigned with that rank. I believe Wilson will add 50 per cent. to the effectiveness of your cavalry." *OR,* I, 39(III), 64.

Headquarters Military Division of the West,
October 17, 1864.

In assuming command, at this critical juncture, of the Military Division of the West, I appeal to my countrymen, of all classes and sections, for their generous support. In assigning me to this responsible position, the President of the Confederate States has extended to me the assurance of his earnest support. The Executives of your States meet me with similar expressions of their devotion to our cause. The noble army in the field, composed of brave men and gallant officers, are strangers to me, but I know they will do all that patriots can achieve. . . .

The army of Sherman still defiantly holds Atlanta. He can and must be driven from it. It is only for the good people of Georgia and surrounding States to speak the word, and the work is done. We have abundant provisions. There are men enough in the country, liable to and able for service, to accomplish the result. . . .

My countrymen, respond to this call as you have done in days that are past, and, with the blessing of a kind and overruling Providence, the enemy shall be driven from your soil. The security of your wives and daughters from the insults and outrages of a brutal foe shall be established soon, and be followed by a permanent and honorable peace. The claims of home and country, wife and children, uniting with the demands of honor and patriotism, summon us to the field. We cannot, dare not, will not fail to respond. Full of hope and confidence, I come to join you in your struggles, sharing your privations, and, with your brave and true men, to strike the blow that shall bring success to our arms, triumph to our cause, and peace to our country!

. . . .

G. T. Beauregard, *General.*[44]

Notwithstanding this somewhat boastful order or appeal, General Beauregard did not actually accompany General Hood on his disastrous march to Nashville, but took post at Corinth, Mississippi, to control the movement of his supplies and to watch me.[45]

[44] See *OR,* I, 39(III), 825–826.

[45] In his post-battle report, Confederate Gen. Beauregard stated, "To add to the chances of success I remained two days at Gadsden after the departure of the army, to issue the necessary

At Gaylesville the pursuit of Hood by the army under my immediate command may be said to have ceased. During this pursuit, the Fifteenth Corps was commanded by its senior major-general present, P. J. Osterhaus, in the absence of General John A. Logan; and the Seventeenth Corps was commanded by Brigadier-General T. E. G. Ransom, the senior officer present, in the absence of General Frank P. Blair.

General Ransom was a young, most gallant, and promising officer, son of the Colonel Ransom who was killed at Chapultepec, in the Mexican War. He had served with the Army of the Tennessee in 1862 and 1863, at Vicksburg, where he was severely wounded. He was not well at the time we started from Atlanta, but he insisted on going along with his command. His symptoms became more aggravated on the march, and when we were encamped near Gaylesville, I visited him in company with Surgeon John Moore, United States Army, who said that the case was one of typhoid fever, which would likely prove fatal. A few days after, viz., the 28th, he was being carried on a litter toward Rome; and as I rode from Gaylesville to Rome, I passed him by the way, stopped, and spoke with him, but did not then suppose he was so near his end. The next day, however, his escort reached Rome, bearing his dead body. The officer in charge reported that, shortly after I had passed, his symptoms became so much worse that they stopped at a farm-house by the road-side, where he died that evening. His body was at once sent to Chicago for burial, and a monument has been ordered by the Society of the Army of the Tennessee to be erected in his memory.[46]

On the 26th of October I learned that Hood's whole army had made its appearance about Decatur, Alabama, and at once caused a strong reconnoissance to be made down the Coosa to near Gadsden, which revealed the truth that the enemy was gone, except a small force of cavalry, commanded by General Wheeler, which had been left to watch us. I then finally resolved on my future course, which was to leave Hood to be encountered by General Thomas, while I should carry into full effect the long-contemplated project of marching for the sea-coast, and thence to operate toward Richmond. But it was all-important to

---

orders to secure railroad communications in Mississippi and Middle Alabama for the transportation of supplies, and to direct Major-General Forrest, who was then operating in West Tennessee, to report to General Hood with his command." Beauregard arrived in Corinth, MS, on Nov. 18. *OR,* I, 45(I), 647–648, 1223.

[46] Ransom was interred at Rosehill Cemetery in Chicago. *CWHC,* 446.

me and to our cause that General Thomas should have an ample force, equal to any and every emergency.

He then had at Nashville about eight or ten thousand new troops, and as many more civil employés of the Quartermaster's Department, which were not suited for the field, but would be most useful in manning the excellent forts that already covered Nashville. At Chattanooga, he had General Steedman's division, about five thousand men, besides garrisons for Chattanooga, Bridgeport, and Stevenson; at Murfreesboro' he also had General Rousseau's division, which was full five thousand strong, independent of the necessary garrisons for the railroad. At Decatur and Huntsville, Alabama, was the infantry division of General R. S. Granger, estimated at four thousand;[47] and near Florence, Alabama, watching the crossings of the Tennessee, were General Edward Hatch's division of cavalry, four thousand;[48] General Croxton's brigade, twenty-five hundred; and Colonel Capron's brigade, twelve hundred; besides which, General J. H. Wilson had collected in Nashville about ten thousand dismounted cavalry, for which he was rapidly collecting the necessary horses for a remount. All these aggregated about forty-five thousand men. General A. J. Smith at that time was in Missouri, with the two divisions of the Sixteenth Corps which had been diverted to that quarter to assist General Rosecrans in driving the rebel General Price out of Missouri. This object had been accomplished, and these troops, numbering from eight to ten thousand, had been ordered to Nashville. To these I proposed at first to add only the Fourth Corps (General Stanley), fifteen thousand; and that corps was ordered from Gaylesville to march to Chattanooga, and thence report for orders to General Thomas; but subsequently, on the 30th of October, at Rome, Georgia, learning from General Thomas that the new troops promised by General Grant were coming forward very slowly, I concluded to further reënforce him by General Schofield's corps (Twenty-third), twelve thousand, which corps accordingly marched for Resaca, and there took the cars for Chattanooga. I then knew that General Thomas would have an ample force with which to encounter General Hood anywhere in the open field, besides garrisons to secure the railroad to his rear and as far forward as Chattanooga. And, moreover, I was more than convinced that he would have ample time for

[47] Robert S. Granger (1816–1894) graduated from the USMA in 1838 and was in command of the Dist. of Northern Alabama, Dept. of the Cumberland, in Oct. 1864. *CWHC,* 263.

[48] Edward Hatch (1832–1889) was in command of the 1st Div., Cav. Corps, Dist. of West Tennessee, Military Div. of West Mississippi, in Oct. 1864. *CWHC,* 286–287.

preparation; for, on that very day, General R. S. Granger had telegraphed me from Decatur, Alabama:

> I omitted to mention another reason why Hood will go to Tuscumbia before crossing the Tennessee River. He was evidently out of supplies. His men were all grumbling; the first thing the prisoners asked for was something to eat. Hood could not get any thing if he should cross this side of Rogersville.

I knew that the country about Decatur and Tuscumbia, Alabama, was bare of provisions, and inferred that General Hood would have to draw his supplies, not only of food, but of stores, clothing, and ammunition, from Mobile, Montgomery, and Selma, Alabama, by the railroad around by Meridian and Corinth, Mississippi, which we had most effectually disabled the previous winter.

General Hood did not make a serious attack on Decatur, but hung around it from October 26th to the 30th, when he drew off and marched for a point on the south side of the Tennessee River, opposite Florence, where he was compelled to remain nearly a month, to collect the necessary supplies for his contemplated invasion of Tennessee and Kentucky.

The Fourth Corps (Stanley) had already reached Chattanooga, and had been transported by rail to Pulaski, Tennessee; and General Thomas ordered General Schofield, with the Twenty-third Corps, to Columbia, Tennessee, a place intermediate between Hood (then on the Tennessee River, opposite Florence) and Forrest, opposite Johnsonville.

On the 31st of October General Croxton, of the cavalry, reported that the enemy had crossed the Tennessee River four miles above Florence, and that he had endeavored to stop him, but without success. Still, I was convinced that Hood's army was in no condition to march for Nashville, and that a good deal of further delay might reasonably be counted on. I also rested with much confidence on the fact that the Tennessee River below Muscle Shoals was strongly patrolled by gunboats, and that the reach of the river above Muscle Shoals, from Decatur as high up as our railroad at Bridgeport, was also guarded by gunboats, so that Hood, to cross over, would be compelled to select a point inaccessible to these gunboats. He actually did choose such a place, at the old railroad-piers, four miles above Florence, Alabama, which is below Muscle Shoals and above Colbert Shoals.

On the 31st of October Forrest made his appearance on the Tennessee River opposite Johnsonville (whence a new railroad led to Nashville), and with his cavalry and field-pieces actually crippled and captured two gunboats with five of our transports, a feat of arms which, I confess, excited my admiration.

There is no doubt that the month of October closed to us looking decidedly squally; but, somehow, I was sustained in the belief that in a very few days the tide would turn.

On the 1st of November I telegraphed very fully to General Grant, at City Point, who must have been disturbed by the wild rumors that filled the country,[49] and on the 2d of November received (at Rome) this dispatch:

CITY POINT, *November* 1, 1864—6 P. M.

Major-General SHERMAN:

Do you not think it advisable, now that Hood has gone so far north, to entirely ruin him before starting on your proposed campaign? With Hood's army destroyed, you can go where you please with impunity. I believed and still believe, if you had started south while Hood was in the neighborhood of you, he would have been forced to go after you. Now that he is far away he might look upon the chase as useless, and he will go in one direction while you are pushing in the other. If you can see a chance of destroying Hood's army, attend to that first, and make your other move secondary.

U. S. GRANT, *Lieutenant-General.*

My answer is dated—

ROME, GEORGIA, *November* 2, 1864.

Lieutenant-General U. S. GRANT, *City Point, Virginia:*

Your dispatch is received. If I could hope to overhaul Hood, I would turn against him with my whole force; then he would retreat to the southwest, drawing me as a decoy away from Georgia, which is his chief object. If he ventures north of the Tennessee River, I may turn in that direction, and endeavor to get below him on his line of retreat;

[49] In the telegram, WTS wrote, "As you foresaw, and as Jeff. Davis threatened, the enemy is now in the full tide of execution of his grand plan to destroy my communications and defeat this army . . . Hood's cavalry may do a good deal of damage, and I have sent Wilson back with all dismounted cavalry retaining only about 4,500. This is the best I can do, and shall, therefore, when I can get to Atlanta the necessary stores, move as soon as possible." *OR,* I, 39(III), 576–577.

but thus far he has not gone above the Tennessee River. General Thomas will have a force strong enough to prevent his reaching any country in which we have an interest; and he has orders, if Hood turns to follow me, to push for Selma, Alabama. No single army can catch Hood, and I am convinced the best results will follow from our defeating Jeff. Davis's cherished plan of making me leave Georgia by manœuvring. Thus far I have confined my efforts to thwart this plan, and have reduced baggage so that I can pick up and start in any direction; but I regard the pursuit of Hood as useless. Still, if he attempts to invade Middle Tennessee, I will hold Decatur, and be prepared to move in that direction; but, unless I let go of Atlanta, my force will not be equal to his.

W. T. Sherman, *Major-General.*

By this date, under the intelligent and energetic action of Colonel W. W. Wright, and with the labor of fifteen hundred men, the railroad break of fifteen miles about Dalton was repaired so far as to admit of the passage of cars, and I transferred my headquarters to Kingston as more central; and from that place, on the same day (November 2d), again telegraphed to General Grant.

Kingston, Georgia, *November* 2, 1864.

Lieutenant-General U. S. Grant, *City Point, Virginia:*

If I turn back, the whole effect of my campaign will be lost. By my movements I have thrown Beauregard (Hood) well to the west, and Thomas will have ample time and sufficient troops to hold him until the reënforcements from Missouri reach him. We have now ample supplies at Chattanooga and Atlanta, and can stand a month's interruption to our communications. I do not believe the Confederate army can reach our railroad-lines except by cavalry-raids, and Wilson will have cavalry enough to checkmate them. I am clearly of opinion that the best results will follow my contemplated movement through Georgia.

W. T. Sherman, *Major-General.*

That same day I received, in answer to the Rome dispatch, the following:

City Point, Virginia, *November* 2, 1864—11.30 a. m.

Major-General Sherman:

Your dispatch of 9 A. M. yesterday is just received. I dispatched you the same date, advising that Hood's army, now that it had worked so far north, ought to be looked upon now as the "object." With the force, however, that you have left with General Thomas, he must be able to take care of Hood and destroy him.

I do not see that you can withdraw from where you are to follow Hood, without giving up all we have gained in territory. I say, then, go on as you propose.

U. S. GRANT, *Lieutenant-General.*

This was the first time that General Grant ordered[50] the "march to the sea," and, although many of his warm friends and admirers insist that he was the author and projector of that march, and that I simply executed his plans, General Grant has never, in my opinion, thought so or said so.[51] The truth is fully given in an original letter of President Lincoln, which I received at Savannah, Georgia, and have at this instant before me, every word of which is in his own familiar handwriting. It is dated—

WASHINGTON, *December* 26, 1864.

. . . .

When you were about leaving Atlanta for the Atlantic coast, I was anxious, if not fearful; but, feeling that you were the better judge, and remembering "nothing risked, nothing gained," I did not interfere. Now, the undertaking being a success, the honor is all yours; for I believe none of us went further than to acquiesce; and, taking the work of General

[50] In the first edition of the memoirs (1875), WTS used the word "assented" instead of "ordered." See J. W. Draper to WTS, May 24, 1875, in the Appendix to Volume II, for a possible motivation for the amendment.

[51] On Apr. 4, 1864, USG wrote a confidential letter to WTS, which read, "You, I propose, to move against Johnston's army, to break it up and to get into the interior of the enemy's country as far as you can, inflicting all the damage you can against their war resources. I do not propose to lay down for you a plan of campaign, but simply lay down the work it is desirable to have done and leave you free to execute it in your own way. Submit to me, however, as early as you can, your plan of operations." For more on the planning of the "March to the Sea," see J. W. Draper to WTS, May 25, 1875, in the Appendix to Volume II; Ulysses S. Grant, *The Personal Memoirs of Ulysses S. Grant: The Complete Annotated Edition,* ed. John F. Marszalek, David S. Nolen, and Louie P. Gallo (Cambridge. MA: Belknap Press of Harvard University Press, 2017), 480.

> Thomas into account, as it should be taken, it is indeed a great success. Not only does it afford the obvious and immediate military advantages, but, in showing to the world that your army could be divided, putting the stronger part to an important new service, and yet leaving enough to vanquish the old opposing force of the whole, Hood's army, it brings those who sat in darkness to see a great light. But what next? I suppose it will be safer if I leave General Grant and yourself to decide.
>
> A. LINCOLN.[52]

Of course, this judgment, made after the event, was extremely flattering and was all I ever expected, a recognition of the truth and of its importance. I have often been asked, by well-meaning friends, when the thought of that march first entered my mind. I knew that an army which had penetrated Georgia as far as Atlanta could not turn back. It must go ahead, but when, how, and where, depended on many considerations. As soon as Hood had shifted across from Lovejoy's to Palmetto, I saw the move in my "mind's eye;" and, after Jeff. Davis's speech at Palmetto, of September 26th, I was more positive in my conviction, but was in doubt as to the time and manner. When General Hood first struck our railroad above Marietta, we were not ready, and I was forced to watch his movements further, till he had "carromed" off to the west of Decatur. Then I was perfectly convinced, and had no longer a shadow of doubt. The only possible question was as to Thomas's strength and ability to meet Hood in the open field. I did not suppose that General Hood, though rash, would venture to attack fortified places like Allatoona, Resaca, Decatur, and Nashville; but he did so, and in so doing he played into our hands perfectly.

On the 2d of November I was at Kingston, Georgia, and my four corps—the Fifteenth, Seventeenth, Fourteenth, and Twentieth—with one division of cavalry, were strung from Rome to Atlanta. Our railroads and telegraph had been repaired, and I deliberately prepared for the march to Savannah, distant three hundred miles from Atlanta. All the sick and wounded men had been sent back by rail to Chattanooga; all our wagon-trains had been carefully overhauled and loaded, so as to be ready to start on an hour's notice, and there was no serious enemy in our front.

[52] WTS omitted the first and last lines of the letter from Pres. Lincoln, which read, "Many, many thanks for your Christmas gift, the capture of Savannah . . . Please make my grateful acknowledgements to your whole army, officers and men." *OR,* I, 44, 783, 809.

General Hood remained still at Florence, Alabama, occupying both banks of the Tennessee River, busy in collecting shoes and clothing for his men, and the necessary ammunition and stores with which to invade Tennessee, most of which had to come from Mobile, Selma, and Montgomery, Alabama, over railroads that were still broken. Beauregard was at Corinth, hastening forward these necessary preparations.

General Thomas was at Nashville, with Wilson's dismounted cavalry and a mass of new troops and quartermaster's employés amply sufficient to defend the place. The Fourth and Twenty-third Corps, under Generals Stanley and Schofield, were posted at Pulaski, Tennessee, and the cavalry of Hatch, Croxton, and Capron, were about Florence, watching Hood. Smith's (A. J.) two divisions of the Sixteenth Corps were still in Missouri, but were reported as ready to embark at Lexington for the Cumberland River and Nashville. Of course, General Thomas saw that on him would likely fall the real blow, and was naturally anxious. He still kept Granger's division at Decatur, Rousseau's at Murfreesboro', and Steedman's at Chattanooga, with strong railroad guards at all the essential points intermediate, confident that by means of this very railroad he could make his concentration sooner than Hood could possibly march up from Florence.

Meantime, General F. P. Blair had rejoined his corps (Seventeenth), and we were receiving at Kingston recruits and returned furlough-men, distributing them to their proper companies.[53] Paymasters had come down to pay off our men before their departure to a new sphere of action, and commissioners were also on hand from the several States to take the vote of our men in the presidential election then agitating the country.

On the 6th of November, at Kingston, I wrote and telegraphed to General Grant, reviewing the whole situation, gave him my full plan of action, stated that I was ready to march as soon as the election was over, and appointed November 10th as the day for starting.[54] On the 8th I received this dispatch.

City Point, Virginia, *November* 7, 1864—10.30 p. m.

Major-General Sherman:

Your dispatch of this evening received. I see no present reason for changing your plan. Should any arise, you will see it, or if I do I will

[53] Gen. Francis Blair returned to command of the 17th Corps, Army of the Tennessee, on Oct. 31. *CWHC,* 133.

[54] See *OR,* I, 39(III), 658–661.

inform you. I think every thing here is favorable now. Great good fortune attend you! I believe you will be eminently successful, and, at worst, can only make a march less fruitful of results than hoped for.

U. S. GRANT, *Lieutenant-General.*

Meantime trains of cars were whirling by, carrying to the rear an immense amount of stores which had accumulated at Atlanta, and at the other stations along the railroad; and General Steedman had come down to Kingston, to take charge of the final evacuation and withdrawal of the several garrisons below Chattanooga.

On the 10th of November the movement may be said to have fairly begun. All the troops designed for the campaign were ordered to march for Atlanta, and General Corse, before evacuating his post at Rome, was ordered to burn all the mills, factories, etc., etc., that could be useful to the enemy, should he undertake to pursue us, or resume military possession of the country. This was done on the night of the 10th, and next day Corse reached Kingston. On the 11th General Thomas and I interchanged full dispatches. He had heard of the arrival of General A. J. Smith's two divisions at Paducah, which would surely reach Nashville much sooner than General Hood could possibly do from Florence, so that he was perfectly satisfied with his share of the army.[55]

On the 12th, with a full staff, I started from Kingston for Atlanta; and about noon of that day we reached Cartersville, and sat on the edge of a porch to rest, when the telegraph operator, Mr. Van Valkenburg, or Eddy,[56] got the wire down from the poles to his lap, in which he held a small pocket instrument. Calling "Chattanooga," he received this message from General Thomas, dated—

NASHVILLE, *November* 12, 1864—8.30. A. M.

Major-General SHERMAN:

Your dispatch of twelve o'clock last night is received. I have no fears that Beauregard can do us any harm now, and, if he attempts to follow

[55] See *OR,* I, 39(III), 746–747.

[56] Charles G. Eddy (1841–1893) joined the U.S. Army in July 1862 and was a telegrapher and cypher clerk on WTS's staff. After the war, he served as vice president of the Norfolk and Western Railroad. F. S. Van Valkenburg enlisted in the U.S. Army in 1861 and was transferred to the telegraph corps, where he was tasked with tapping Confederate telegraph lines. Soon after, he was made chief operator for Nashville, TN, and then joined WTS's staff as a cipher operator. "Suicide of Charles G. Eddy," *Roanoke Times,* Aug. 12, 1893, 1; "F. S Van Valkenburgh in Mexico," *Telegraph and Telephone Age,* June 1, 1914, 317.

you, I will follow him as far as possible. If he does not follow you, I will then thoroughly organize my troops, and believe I shall have men enough to ruin him unless he gets out of the way very rapidly.

The country of Middle Alabama, I learn, is teeming with supplies this year, which will be greatly to our advantage. I have no additional news to report from the direction of Florence.

I am now convinced that the greater part of Beauregard's army is near Florence and Tuscumbia, and that you will have at least a clear road before you for several days, and that your success will fully equal your expectations.

George H. Thomas, *Major-General.*

I answered simply: "Dispatch received—all right." About that instant of time, some of our men burnt a bridge, which severed the telegraph-wire, and all communication with the rear ceased thenceforth.

As we rode on toward Atlanta that night, I remember the railroad-trains going to the rear with a furious speed; the engineers and the few men about the trains waving us an affectionate adieu. It surely was a strange event—two hostile armies marching in opposite directions, each in the full belief that it was achieving a final and conclusive result in a great war; and I was strongly inspired with the feeling that the movement on our part was a direct attack upon the rebel army and the rebel capital at Richmond, though a full thousand miles of hostile country intervened, and that, for better or worse, it would end the war.

21

The March to the Sea—from Atlanta to Savannah.

NOVEMBER AND DECEMBER, 1864.

On the 12th of November the railroad and telegraph communications with the rear were broken, and the army stood detached from all friends, dependent on its own resources and supplies. No time was to be lost; all the detachments were ordered to march rapidly for Atlanta, breaking up the railroad *en route,* and generally to so damage the country as to make it untenable to the enemy. By the 14th all the troops had arrived at or near Atlanta, and were, according to orders, grouped into two wings, the right and left, commanded respectively by Major-Generals O. O. Howard and H. W. Slocum, both comparatively young men, but educated and experienced officers, fully competent to their command.

The right wing was composed of the Fifteenth Corps, Major-General P. J. Osterhaus commanding, and the Seventeenth Corps, Major-General Frank P. Blair commanding.

The left wing was composed of the Fourteenth Corps, Major-General Jefferson C. Davis commanding, and the Twentieth Corps, Brigadier-General A. S. Williams commanding.

The Fifteenth Corps had four divisions, commanded by Brigadier-Generals Charles R. Woods, W. B. Hazen,[1] John E. Smith, and John M. Corse.

The Seventeenth Corps had three divisions, commanded by Major-General J. A. Mower, and Brigadier-Generals M. D. Leggett and Giles A. Smith.

The Fourteenth Corps had three divisions, commanded by Brigadier-Generals W. P. Carlin, James D. Morgan, and A. Baird.[2]

[1] William B. Hazen (1830–1887) graduated from the USMA in 1855 and was in command of the 2nd Div., 15th Corps, Army of the Tennessee, in Nov. 1864. *CWHC,* 291.

[2] William P. Carlin (1829–1903) graduated from the USMA in 1850 and commanded the 1st Div., 15th Corps, Army of the Tennessee. James D. Morgan (1810–1896) commanded the 2nd Div., 14th Corps, Army of the Cumberland. *CWHC,* 163, 397.

The Twentieth Corps had also three divisions, commanded by Brigadier-Generals N. J. Jackson, John W. Geary, and W. T. Ward.[3]

The cavalry division was held separate, subject to my own orders. It was commanded by Brigadier-General Judson Kilpatrick, and was composed of two brigades, commanded by Colonels Eli H. Murray, of Kentucky, and Smith D. Atkins, of Illinois.[4]

The strength of the army, as officially reported, is given in the following tables, and shows an aggregate of fifty-five thousand three hundred and twenty-nine infantry, five thousand and sixty-three cavalry, and eighteen hundred and twelve artillery—in all, sixty-two thousand two hundred and four officers and men. (*See* table for December 1st.)

RECAPITULATION—ATLANTA TO SAVANNAH.

Arm.	November 10.	December 1.	December 20.
Infantry.	52,796	55,329	54,255
Cavalry.	4,961	5,063	4,584
Artillery.	1,788	1,812	1,759
Aggregate.	59,545	62,204	60,598

The most extraordinary efforts had been made to purge this army of non-combatants and of sick men, for we knew well that there was to be no place of safety save with the army itself; our wagons were loaded with ammunition, provisions, and forage, and we could ill afford to haul even sick men in the ambulances, so that all on this exhibit may be assumed to have been able-bodied, experienced soldiers, well armed, well equipped and provided, as far as human foresight could, with all the essentials of life, strength, and vigorous action.

[3]Nathaniel J. Jackson (1818–1892) commanded the 1st Div., 20th Corps, Army of Georgia. William T. Ward (1808–1878) commanded the 3rd Div., 20th Corps, Army of Georgia. *CWHC*, 316, 553.

[4]Eli H. Murray (1843–1896) commanded the 1st Brig., 3rd Div., Cav. Corps, Military Div. of the Mississippi. Smith D. Atkins (1836–1913) commanded the 2nd Brig., 3rd Div., Cav. Corps, Military Div. of the Mississippi. *CWHC*, 109, 402.

Effective Strength of the Army commanded by General W.T. SHERMA

COMMANDS.	November 10.					
	Infantry.		Cavalry.		Artillery.	
	Commissioned Officers.	Enlisted Men.	Commissioned Officers.	Enlisted Men.	Commissioned Officers.	Enlisted Men.
Fifteenth Army Corps.	724	14,568	. . . . . .	. . . . . .	11	376
Seventeenth Army Corps.	420	10,667	2	43	5	266
Total—Right Wing.	1,144	25,235	2	43	16	642
Fourteenth Army Corps.	556	12,397	. . . . . .	. . . . . .	11	388
Twentieth Army Corps.	602	12,862	. . . . . .	. . . . . .	25	607
Total—Left Wing.	1,158	25,259	. . . . . .	. . . . . .	36	995
Kilpatrick's Cavalry.	. . . . . .	. . . . . .	244	4,672	4	95
Grand Aggregate.	2,302	50,494	246	4,715	56	1,732

The two general orders made for this march appear to me, even at this late day, so clear, emphatic, and well-digested, that no account of that historic event is perfect without them, and I give them entire, even at the seeming appearance of repetition; and, though they called for great sacrifice and labor on the part of the officers and men, I insist that these orders were obeyed as well as any similar orders ever were, by an army operating wholly in an enemy's country, and dispersed, as we necessarily were, during the subsequent period of nearly six months.

[Special Field Orders, No. 119.]

HEADQUARTERS MILITARY DIVISION OF THE MISSISSIPPI,
IN THE FIELD, KINGSTON, GEORGIA, *November* 8, 1864.

The general commanding deems it proper at this time to inform the officers and men of the Fourteenth, Fifteenth, Seventeenth, and Twentieth Corps, that he has organized them into an army for a special purpose, well known to the War Department and to General Grant. It is sufficient for you to know that it involves a departure from our present *ring the March from Atlanta to Savannah, Georgia,* 1864.

December 1.						December 20.					
Infantry.		Cavalry.		Artillery.		Infantry.		Cavalry.		Artillery.	
Commissioned Officers.	Enlisted Men.	Commissioned Officers.	Enlisted Men.	Commissioned Officers.	Enlisted Men.	Commissioned Officers.	Enlisted Men.	Commissioned Officers.	Enlisted Men.	Commissioned Officers.	Enlisted Men.
750	15,144	......	......	17	362	753	14,441	......	......	12	367
418	11,314	2	30	10	318	436	11,293	2	30	7	278
1,168	26,458	2	30	27	680	1,189	25,734	2	30	19	645
623	13,339	......	......	11	443	621	13,170	......	......	11	434
638	13,103	......	......	22	529	631	12,910	......	......	24	526
1,261	26,442	......	......	33	972	1,252	26,080	......	......	35	960
......	......	251	4,780	4	96	......	......	201	4,351	4	96
2,429	52,900	253	4,810	64	1,748	2,441	51,814	203	4,381	58	1,701

base, and a long and difficult march to a new one. All the chances of war have been considered and provided for, as far as human sagacity can. All he asks of you is to maintain that discipline, patience, and courage, which have characterized you in the past; and he hopes, through you, to strike a blow at our enemy that will have a material effect in producing what we all so much desire, his complete overthrow. Of all things, the most important is, that the men, during marches and in camp, keep their places and do not scatter about as stragglers or foragers, to be picked up by a hostile people in detail. It is also of the utmost importance that our wagons should not be loaded with any thing but provisions and ammunition. All surplus servants, non-combatants, and refugees, should now go to the rear, and none should be encouraged to encumber us on the march. At some future time we will be able to provide for the poor whites and blacks who seek to escape the bondage under which they are now suffering. With these few simple cautions, he hopes to lead you to achievements equal in importance to those of the past.

By order of Major-General W. T. Sherman,

L. M. Dayton, *Aide-de-Camp.*

[Special Field Orders, No. 120.]

HEADQUARTERS MILITARY DIVISION OF THE MISSISSIPPI, IN THE FIELD, KINGSTON, GEORGIA, *November* 9, 1864.

1. For the purpose of military operations, this army is divided into two wings viz.:

The right wing, Major-General O. O. Howard commanding, composed of the Fifteenth and Seventeenth Corps; the left wing, Major-General H. W. Slocum commanding, composed of the Fourteenth and Twentieth Corps.

2. The habitual order of march will be, wherever practicable, by four roads, as nearly parallel as possible, and converging at points hereafter to be indicated in orders. The cavalry, Brigadier-General Kilpatrick commanding, will receive special orders from the commander-in-chief.

3. There will be no general train of supplies, but each corps will have its ammunition-train and provision-train, distributed habitually as follows: Behind each regiment should follow one wagon and one ambulance; behind each brigade should follow a due proportion of ammunition-wagons, provision-wagons, and ambulances. In case of danger, each corps commander should change this order of march, by having his advance and rear brigades unencumbered by wheels. The separate columns will start habitually at 7 A. M., and make about fifteen miles per day, unless otherwise fixed in orders.

4. The army will forage liberally on the country during the march. To this end, each brigade commander will organize a good and sufficient foraging party, under the command of one or more discreet officers, who will gather, near the route traveled, corn or forage of any kind, meat of any kind, vegetables, corn-meal, or whatever is needed by the command, aiming at all times to keep in the wagons at least ten days' provisions for his command, and three days' forage. Soldiers must not enter the dwellings of the inhabitants, or commit any trespass; but, during a halt or camp, they may be permitted to gather turnips, potatoes, and other vegetables, and to drive in stock in sight of their camp. To regular foraging-parties must be intrusted the gathering of provisions and forage, at any distance from the road traveled.

5. To corps commanders alone is intrusted the power to destroy mills, houses, cotton-gins, etc.; and for them this general principle is laid down: In districts and neighborhoods where the army is unmo-

lested, no destruction of such property should be permitted; but should guerrillas or bushwhackers molest our march, or should the inhabitants burn bridges, obstruct roads, or otherwise manifest local hostility, then army commanders should order and enforce a devastation more or less relentless, according to the measure of such hostility.

6. As for horses, mules, wagons, etc., belonging to the inhabitants, the cavalry and artillery may appropriate freely and without limit; discriminating, however, between the rich, who are usually hostile, and the poor and industrious, usually neutral or friendly. Foraging-parties may also take mules or horses, to replace the jaded animals of their trains, or to serve as pack-mules for the regiments or brigades. In all foraging, of whatever kind, the parties engaged will refrain from abusive or threatening language, and may, where the officer in command thinks proper, give written certificates of the facts, but no receipts; and they will endeavor to leave with each family a reasonable portion for their maintenance,

7. Negroes who are able-bodied and can be of service to the several columns may be taken along; but each army commander will bear in mind that the question of supplies is a very important one, and that his first duty is to see to those who bear arms.

8. The organization, at once, of a good pioneer battalion for each army corps, composed if possible of negroes, should be attended to. This battalion should follow the advance-guard, repair roads and double them if possible, so that the columns will not be delayed after reaching bad places. Also, army commanders should practise the habit of giving the artillery and wagons the road, marching their troops on one side, and instruct their troops to assist wagons at steep hills or bad crossings of streams.

9. Captain O. M. Poe, chief-engineer, will assign to each wing of the army a pontoon-train, fully equipped and organized; and the commanders thereof will see to their being properly protected at all times.

By order of Major-General W. T. Sherman,

L. M. Dayton, *Aide-de-Camp.*

The greatest possible attention had been given to the artillery and wagon trains. The number of guns had been reduced to sixty-five, or about one gun to each thousand men, and these were generally in batteries of four guns each.

Each gun, caisson, and forge, was drawn by four teams of horses. We had in all about twenty-five hundred wagons, with teams of six mules to each, and six hundred ambulances, with two horses to each. The loads were made comparatively light, about twenty-five hundred pounds net; each wagon carrying in addition the forage needed by its own team. Each soldier carried on his person forty rounds of ammunition, and in the wagons were enough cartridges to make up about two hundred rounds per man, and in like manner two hundred rounds of assorted ammunition were carried for each gun.

The wagon-trains were divided equally between the four corps, so that each had about eight hundred wagons, and these usually on the march occupied five miles or more of road. Each corps commander managed his own train; and habitually the artillery and wagons had the road, while the men, with the exception of the advance and rear guards, pursued paths improvised by the side of the wagons, unless they were forced to use a bridge or causeway in common.

I reached Atlanta during the afternoon of the 14th, and found that all preparations had been made—Colonel Beckwith, chief commissary, reporting one million two hundred thousand rations in possession of the troops, which was about twenty days' supply, and he had on hand a good supply of beef-cattle to be driven along on the hoof. Of forage, the supply was limited, being of oats and corn enough for five days, but I knew that within that time we would reach a country well stocked with corn, which had been gathered and stored in cribs, seemingly for our use, by Governor Brown's militia.

Colonel Poe, United States Engineers, of my staff, had been busy in his special task of destruction. He had a large force at work, had leveled the great depot, round-house, and the machine-shops of the Georgia Railroad, and had applied fire to the wreck. One of these machine-shops had been used by the rebels as an arsenal, and in it were stored piles of shot and shell, some of which proved to be loaded, and that night was made hideous by the bursting of shells, whose fragments came uncomfortably near Judge Lyon's house, in which I was quartered. The fire also reached the block of stores near the depot, and the heart of the city was in flames all night, but the fire did not reach the parts of Atlanta where the court-house was, or the great mass of dwelling-houses.[5]

The march from Atlanta began on the morning of November 15th, the right wing and cavalry following the railroad southeast toward Jonesboro', and General Slocum with the Twentieth Corps leading off to the east by De-

[5] On Nov. 16, 1864, Henry M. Hitchcock, one of WTS's staff officers, wrote in his diary, "saw no dwelling destroyed, and outside of the central business part of town [there was] comparatively little damage . . . ¼ of area of town destroyed, but this the largest and best built business part." John F. Marszalek, *Sherman: A Soldier's Passion for Order* (New York: Free Press, 1993), 299.

catur and Stone Mountain, toward Madison. These were divergent lines, designed to threaten both Macon and Augusta at the same time, so as to prevent a concentration at our intended destination, or "objective," Milledgeville, the capital of Georgia, distant southeast about one hundred miles. The time allowed each column for reaching Milledgeville was seven days. I remained in Atlanta during the 15th with the Fourteenth Corps, and the rear-guard of the right wing, to complete the loading of the trains, and the destruction of the buildings of Atlanta which could be converted to hostile uses, and on the morning of the 16th started with my personal staff, a company of Alabama cavalry, commanded by Lieutenant Snelling, and an infantry company, commanded by Lieutenant McCrory, which guarded our small train of wagons.[6]

My staff was then composed of Major L. M. Dayton, aide-de-camp and acting adjutant-general, Major J. C. McCoy, and Major J. C. Audenried, aides. Major Ward Nichols had joined some weeks before at Gaylesville, Alabama, and was attached as an acting aide-de-camp. Also Major Henry Hitchcock had joined at the same time as judge-advocate. Colonel Charles Ewing was inspector-general, and Surgeon John Moore medical director. These constituted our mess. We had no tents, only the flies, with which we nightly made bivouacs with the assistance of the abundant pine-boughs, which made excellent shelter, as well as beds.

Colonel L. C. Easton was chief-quartermaster; Colonel Amos Beckwith, chief-commissary; Colonel O. M. Poe, chief-engineer; and Colonel T. G. Baylor, chief of ordnance. These invariably rode with us during the day, but they had a separate camp and mess at night.

General William F. Barry had been chief of artillery in the previous campaign, but at Kingston his face was so swollen with erysipelas that he was reluctantly compelled to leave us for the rear; and he could not, on recovering, rejoin us till we had reached Savannah.

About 7 A. M. of November 16th we rode out of Atlanta by the Decatur road, filled by the marching troops and wagons of the Fourteenth Corps; and reaching the hill, just outside of the old rebel works, we naturally paused to look back upon the scenes of our past battles. We stood upon the very ground whereon was fought the bloody battle of July 22d, and could see the copse of wood where McPherson fell. Behind us lay Atlanta, smouldering and in ruins, the black smoke rising high in air, and hanging like a pall over the ruined city. Away off in the distance, on the McDonough road, was the rear of

[6] For a detailed map of WTS's movements during the March to the Sea, see George B. Davis et al., *Official Military Atlas of the Civil War* (New York: Fairfax Press, 1983), plate 101, map 21.

Howard's column, the gun-barrels glistening in the sun, the white-topped wagons stretching away to the south; and right before us the Fourteenth Corps, marching steadily and rapidly, with a cheery look and swinging pace, that made light of the thousand miles that lay between us and Richmond. Some band, by accident, struck up the anthem of "John Brown's soul goes marching on;" the men caught up the strain, and never before or since have I heard the chorus of "Glory, glory, hallelujah!" done with more spirit, or in better harmony of time and place.

Then we turned our horses' heads to the east; Atlanta was soon lost behind the screen of trees, and became a thing of the past. Around it clings many a thought of desperate battle, of hope and fear, that now seem like the memory of a dream; and I have never seen the place since. The day was extremely beautiful, clear sunlight, with bracing air, and an unusual feeling of exhilaration seemed to pervade all minds—a feeling of something to come, vague and undefined, still full of venture and intense interest. Even the common soldiers caught the inspiration, and many a group called out to me as I worked my way past them, "Uncle Billy, I guess Grant is waiting for us at Richmond!" Indeed, the general sentiment was that we were marching for Richmond, and that there we should end the war, but how and when they seemed to care not; nor did they measure the distance, or count the cost in life, or bother their brains about the great rivers to be crossed, and the food required for man and beast, that had to be gathered by the way. There was a "devil-may-care" feeling pervading officers and men, that made me feel the full load of responsibility, for success would be accepted as a matter of course, whereas, should we fail, this "march" would be adjudged the wild adventure of a crazy fool. I had no purpose to march direct for Richmond by way of Augusta and Charlotte, but always designed to reach the sea-coast first at Savannah or Port Royal, South Carolina, and even kept in mind the alternative of Pensacola.

The first night out we camped by the road-side near Lithonia. Stone Mountain, a mass of granite, was in plain view, cut out in clear outline against the blue sky; the whole horizon was lurid with the bonfires of rail-ties, and groups of men all night were carrying the heated rails to the nearest trees, and bending them around the trunks. Colonel Poe had provided tools for ripping up the rails and twisting them when hot; but the best and easiest way is the one I have described, of heating the middle of the iron-rails on bonfires made of the cross-ties, and then winding them around a telegraph-pole or the trunk of some convenient sapling. I attached much importance to this destruction of the railroad, gave it my own personal attention, and made reiterated orders to others on the subject.

The next day we passed through the handsome town of Covington, the soldiers closing up their ranks, the color-bearers unfurling their flags, and the bands striking up patriotic airs. The white people came out of their houses to behold the sight, spite of their deep hatred of the invaders, and the negroes were simply frantic with joy. Whenever they heard my name, they clustered about my horse, shouted and prayed in their peculiar style, which had a natural eloquence that would have moved a stone. I have witnessed hundreds, if not thousands, of such scenes; and can now see a poor girl, in the very ecstasy of the Methodist "shout," hugging the banner of one of the regiments, and jumping up to the "feet of Jesus."[7]

I remember, when riding around by a by-street in Covington, to avoid the crowd that followed the marching column, that some one brought me an invitation to dine with a sister of Sam. Anderson, who was a cadet at West Point with me;[8] but the messenger reached me after we had passed the main part of the town. I asked to be excused, and rode on to a place designated for camp, at the crossing of the Ulcofauhachee River, about four miles to the east of the town. Here we made our bivouac, and I walked up to a plantation-house close by, where were assembled many negroes, among them an old, gray-haired man, of as fine a head as I ever saw.[9] I asked him if he understood about the war and its progress. He said he did; that he had been looking for the "angel of the Lord"[10] ever since he was knee-high, and, though we professed to be fighting for the Union, he supposed that slavery was the cause, and that our success

[7] WTS referred to the exuberant shouting and physical activity that accompanied worship practices in some Methodist communities in the nineteenth century. Ruth Alden Doan, "Worship, Experience, and the Creation of Methodist Place," in *By the Vision of Another World: Worship in American History*, ed. James D. Bratt (Grand Rapids. MI: Eerdmans, 2012), 48–49.

[8] Samuel S. Anderson (1819–1901) graduated from the USMA in 1841 and resigned from the U.S. Army to join the Confederate Army. *USMA*, 2:83, 5:53.

[9] On Nov. 18, an enslaved Black man named Stephen had a long conversation with WTS. Stephen was enslaved by Judge John Harris (1802–1878) of Covington, GA. Sarah J. Harris-Keifer, *Genealogical and Biographical Sketches of the New Jersey Branch of the Harris Family, in the United States* (Madison. WI: Democrat, 1888), 157; Henry M. Hitchcock, *Marching with Sherman: Passages from the Letters and Campaign Diaries of Henry Hitchcock, Major and Assistant Adjutant General of Volunteers, November 1864–May 1865*, ed. M. A. DeWolfe Howe (New Haven, CT: Yale University Press, 1927), 67–72.

[10] The "Angel of the Lord" is mentioned numerous times throughout the Bible. Theologians debate the angel's identity. Some New Testament theologians claim the Angel of the Lord was Jesus Christ manifest. Rosemary Guiley, *The Encyclopedia of Angels*, 2nd ed. (New York: Facts on File, 2004), s.v. "Angel of the Lord (Angel of Yahweh)."

was to be his freedom. I asked him if all the negro slaves comprehended this fact, and he said they surely did. I then explained to him that we wanted the slaves to remain where they were, and not to load us down with useless mouths, which would eat up the food needed for our fighting-men; that our success was their assured freedom; that we could receive a few of their young, hearty men as pioneers; but that, if they followed us in swarms of old and young, feeble and helpless, it would simply load us down and cripple us in our great task. I think Major Henry Hitchcock was with me on that occasion, and made a note of the conversation, and I believe that old man spread this message to the slaves, which was carried from mouth to mouth, to the very end of our journey, and that it in part saved us from the great danger we incurred of swelling our numbers so that famine would have attended our progress.[11] It was at this very plantation that a soldier passed me with a ham on his musket, a jug of sorghum-molasses under his arm, and a big piece of honey in his hand, from which he was eating, and, catching my eye, he remarked *sotto voce* and carelessly to a comrade, "Forage liberally on the country," quoting from my general orders. On this occasion, as on many others that fell under my personal observation, I reproved the man, explained that foraging must be limited to the regular parties properly detailed, and that all provisions thus obtained must be delivered to the regular commissaries, to be fairly distributed to the men who kept their ranks.

From Covington the Fourteenth Corps (Davis's), with which I was traveling, turned to the right for Milledgeville, *via* Shady Dale. General Slocum was ahead at Madison, with the Twentieth Corps, having torn up the railroad as far as that place, and thence had sent Geary's division on to the Oconee, to burn the bridges across that stream, when this corps turned south by Eatonton, for Milledgeville, the common "objective" for the first stage of the "march." We found abundance of corn, molasses, meal, bacon, and sweet-potatoes. We also took a good many cows and oxen, and a large number of mules. In all these the country was quite rich, never before having been visited by a hostile army; the recent crop had been excellent, had been just gathered and laid by for the winter. As a rule, we destroyed none, but kept our wagons full, and fed our teams bountifully.

The skill and success of the men in collecting forage was one of the features of this march. Each brigade commander had authority to detail a company of foragers, usually about fifty men, with one or two commissioned officers selected for their boldness and enterprise. This party would be dispatched before

[11] For Hitchcock's full version of events, see Hitchcock, *Marching with Sherman,* 71–72.

daylight with a knowledge of the intended day's march and camp; would proceed on foot five or six miles from the route traveled by their brigade, and then visit every plantation and farm within range. They would usually procure a wagon or family carriage, load it with bacon, corn-meal, turkeys, chickens, ducks, and every thing that could be used as food or forage, and would then regain the main road, usually in advance of their train. When this came up, they would deliver to the brigade commissary the supplies thus gathered by the way. Often would I pass these foraging-parties at the road-side, waiting for their wagons to come up, and was amused at their strange collections—mules, horses, even cattle, packed with old saddles and loaded with hams, bacon, bags of corn-meal, and poultry of every character and description. Although this foraging was attended with great danger and hard work, there seemed to be a charm about it that attracted the soldiers, and it was a privilege to be detailed on such a party. Daily they returned mounted on all sorts of beasts, which were at once taken from them and appropriated to the general use; but the next day they would start out again on foot, only to repeat the experience of the day before. No doubt, many acts of pillage, robbery, and violence, were committed by these parties of foragers, usually called "bummers;" for I have since heard of jewelry taken from women, and the plunder of articles that never reached the commissary; but these acts were exceptional and incidental. I never heard of any cases of murder or rape; and no army could have carried along sufficient food and forage for a march of three hundred miles; so that foraging in some shape was necessary. The country was sparsely settled, with no magistrates or civil authorities who could respond to requisitions, as is done in all the wars of Europe; so that this system of foraging was simply indispensable to our success. By it our men were well supplied with all the essentials of life and health, while the wagons retained enough in case of unexpected delay, and our animals were well fed. Indeed, when we reached Savannah, the trains were pronounced by experts to be the finest in flesh and appearance ever seen with any army.

Habitually each corps followed some main road, and the foragers, being kept out on the exposed flank, served all the military uses of flankers. The main columns gathered, by the roads traveled, much forage and food, chiefly meat, corn, and sweet-potatoes, and it was the duty of each division and brigade quartermaster to fill his wagons as fast as the contents were issued to the troops. The wagon-trains had the right to the road *always,* but each wagon was required to keep closed up, so as to leave no gaps in the column. If for any purpose any wagon or group of wagons dropped out of place, they had to wait for the rear. And this was always dreaded, for each brigade commander wanted his train up at camp as soon after reaching it with his men as possible.

I have seen much skill and industry displayed by these quartermasters on the march, in trying to load their wagons with corn and fodder by the way without losing their place in column. They would, while marching, shift the loads of wagons, so as to have six or ten of them empty. Then, riding well ahead, they would secure possession of certain stacks of fodder near the road, or cribs of corn, leave some men in charge, then open fences and a road back for a couple of miles, return to their trains, divert the empty wagons out of column, and conduct them rapidly to their forage, load up and regain their place in column without losing distance. On one occasion I remember to have seen ten or a dozen wagons thus loaded with corn from two or three full cribs, almost without halting. These cribs were built of logs, and roofed. The train-guard, by a lever, had raised the whole side of the crib a foot or two; the wagons drove close alongside, and the men in the cribs, lying on their backs, kicked out a wagon-load of corn in the time I have taken to describe it.

In a well-ordered and well-disciplined army, these things might be deemed irregular, but I am convinced that the ingenuity of these younger officers accomplished many things far better than I could have ordered, and the marches were thus made, and the distances were accomplished, in the most admirable way. Habitually we started from camp at the earliest break of dawn, and usually reached camp soon after noon. The marches varied from ten to fifteen miles a day, though sometimes on extreme flanks it was necessary to make as much as twenty, but the rate of travel was regulated by the wagons; and, considering the nature of the roads, fifteen miles per day was deemed the limit.

The pontoon-trains were in like manner distributed in about equal proportions to the four corps, giving each a section of about nine hundred feet. The pontoons were of the skeleton pattern, with cotton-canvas covers, each boat, with its proportion of balks and chesses,[12] constituting a load for one wagon. By uniting two such sections together, we could make a bridge of eighteen hundred feet, enough for any river we had to traverse; but habitually the leading brigade would, out of the abundant timber, improvise a bridge before the pontoon-train could come up, unless in the cases of rivers of considerable magnitude, such as the Ocmulgee, Oconee, Ogeechee, Savannah, etc.

On the 20th of November I was still with the Fourteenth Corps, near Eatonton Factory, waiting to hear of the Twentieth Corps; and on the 21st we camped near the house of a man named Mann; the next day, about 4 P. M.,

[12] For a detailed account related to the assembly, and disassembly, of pontoon bridges during the war, see Herman Haupt, *Military Bridges: With Suggestions of New Expedients and Constructions for Crossing Streams and Chasms* (New York: D. Van Nostrand, 1864), 150–191.

General Davis had halted his head of column on a wooded ridge, overlooking an extensive slope of cultivated country, about ten miles short of Milledgeville, and was deploying his troops for camp when I got up. There was a high, raw wind blowing, and I asked him why he had chosen so cold and bleak a position. He explained that he had accomplished his full distance for the day, and had there an abundance of wood and water. He explained further that his advance-guard was a mile or so ahead; so I rode on, asking him to let his rear division, as it came up, move some distance ahead into the depression or valley beyond. Riding on some distance to the border of a plantation, I turned out of the main road into a cluster of wild-plum bushes, that broke the force of the cold November wind, dismounted, and instructed the staff to pick out the place for our camp.

The afternoon was unusually raw and cold. My orderly was at hand with his invariable saddle-bags, which contained a change of under-clothing, my maps, a flask of whiskey, and bunch of cigars. Taking a drink and lighting a cigar, I walked to a row of negro-huts close by, entered one and found a soldier or two warming themselves by a wood-fire. I took their place by the fire, intending to wait there till our wagons had got up, and a camp made for the night. I was talking to the old negro woman, when some one came and explained to me that, if I would come farther down the road, I could find a better place. So I started on foot, and found on the main road a good double-hewed-log house, in one room of which Colonel Poe, Dr. Moore, and others, had started a fire. I sent back orders to the "plum-bushes" to bring our horses and saddles up to this house, and an orderly to conduct our headquarter wagons to the same place. In looking around the room, I saw a small box, like a candle-box, marked "Howell Cobb," and, on inquiring of a negro, found that we were at the plantation of General Howell Cobb, of Georgia, one of the leading rebels of the South, then a general in the Southern army, and who had been Secretary of the United States Treasury in Mr. Buchanan's time.[13] Of course, we confiscated his property, and found it rich in corn, beans, pea-nuts, and sorghum-molasses. Extensive fields were all round the house; I sent word back to General Davis to explain whose plantation it was, and instructed him to spare nothing. That night huge bonfires consumed the fence-rails, kept our soldiers warm, and the teamsters and men, as well as the slaves, carried off an immense quantity of corn and provisions of all sorts.

In due season the headquarter wagons came up, and we got supper. After supper I sat on a chair astride, with my back to a good fire, musing, and became conscious that an old negro, with a tallow-candle in his hand, was scanning

[13] Howell Cobb (1815–1868) was a major general in the Confederate Army, Georgia Reserve Forces, in Nov. 1864. *CWHC*, 178.

my face closely. I inquired, "What do you want, old man?" He answered, "Dey say you is Massa Sherman." I answered that such was the case, and inquired what he wanted. He only wanted to look at me, and kept muttering, "Dis nigger can't sleep dis night." I asked him why he trembled so, and he said that he wanted to be sure that we were in fact "Yankees," for on a former occasion some rebel cavalry had put on light-blue overcoats, personating Yankee troops, and many of the negroes were deceived thereby, himself among the number—had shown them sympathy, and had in consequence been unmercifully beaten therefor. This time he wanted to be certain before committing himself; so I told him to go out on the porch, from which he could see the whole horizon lit up with camp-fires, and he could then judge whether he had ever seen any thing like it before. The old man became convinced that the "Yankees" had come at last, about whom he had been dreaming all his life; and some of the staff-officers gave him a strong drink of whiskey, which set his tongue going. Lieutenant Snelling, who commanded my escort, was a Georgian, and recognized in this old negro a favorite slave of his uncle,[14] who resided about six miles off; but the old slave did not at first recognize his young master in our uniform. One of my staff-officers asked him what had become of his young master, George. He did not know, only that he had gone off to the war, and he supposed him killed, as a matter of course. His attention was then drawn to Snelling's face, when he fell on his knees and thanked God that he had found his young master alive and along with the Yankees. Snelling inquired all about his uncle and the family, asked my permission to go and pay his uncle a visit, which I granted, of course, and the next morning he described to me his visit. The uncle was not cordial, by any means, to find his nephew in the ranks of the host that was desolating the land, and Snelling came back, having exchanged his tired horse for a fresher one out of his uncle's stables, explaining that surely some of the "bummers" would have got the horse had he not.

The next morning, November 23d, we rode into Milledgeville, the capital of the State, whither the Twentieth Corps had preceded us; and during that day the left wing was all united, in and around Milledgeville. From the inhabitants we learned that some of Kilpatrick's cavalry had preceded us by a couple of days, and that all of the right wing was at and near Gordon, twelve miles off, viz., the place where the branch railroad came to Milledgeville from the Macon & Savannah road. The first stage of the journey was, therefore, complete, and absolutely successful.

[14] David Lester, the uncle of David R. Snelling, owned a plantation approximately twelve miles outside of Milledgeville, GA. "David R. Snelling: A Story of Desertion and Defection in the Civil War," *North Carolina Historical Review* 41, no. 2 (Apr. 1964): 276–279.

General Howard soon reported by letter the operations of his right wing, which, on leaving Atlanta, had substantially followed the two roads toward Macon, by Jonesboro' and McDonough, and reached the Ocmulgee at Planters' Factory,[15] which they crossed, by the aid of the pontoon-train, during the 18th and 19th of November. Thence, with the Seventeenth Corps (General Blair's) he (General Howard) had marched *via* Monticello toward Gordon, having dispatched Kilpatrick's cavalry, supported by the Fifteenth Corps (Osterhaus's), to feign on Macon. Kilpatrick met the enemy's cavalry about four miles out of Macon, and drove them rapidly back into the bridge-defenses held by infantry. Kilpatrick charged these, got inside the parapet, but could not hold it, and retired to his infantry supports, near Griswold Station.[16] The Fifteenth Corps tore up the railroad-track eastward from Griswold, leaving Charles R. Wood's division behind as a rear-guard—one brigade of which was intrenched across the road, with some of Kilpatrick's cavalry on the flanks. On the 22d of November General G. W. Smith, with a division of troops, came out of Macon, attacked this brigade (Walcutt's) in position, and was handsomely repulsed and driven back into Macon. This brigade was in part armed with Spencer repeating-rifles, and its fire was so rapid that General Smith insists to this day that he encountered a whole division; but he is mistaken; he was beaten by one brigade (Walcutt's), and made no further effort to molest our operations from that direction. General Walcutt was wounded in the leg, and had to ride the rest of the distance to Savannah in a carriage.

Therefore, by the 23d, I was in Milledgeville with the left wing, and was in full communication with the right wing at Gordon. The people of Milledgeville remained at home, except the Governor (Brown), the State officers, and Legislature, who had ignominiously fled, in the utmost disorder and confusion; standing not on the order of their going, but going at once—some by rail, some by carriages, and many on foot. Some of the citizens who remained behind described this flight of the "brave and patriotic" Governor Brown. He had occupied a public building known as the "Governor's Mansion,"[17] and had hastily stripped it of carpets, curtains, and furniture of all sorts, which were removed to a train of

[15] Planters' Factory was located approximately twenty-five miles northwest of Macon, GA. Davis et al., *Official Military Atlas of the Civil War,* plate 101, map 21.

[16] Griswold Station was located approximately ten miles northeast of Macon. Davis et al., *Official Military Atlas of the Civil War,* plate 101, map 21.

[17] The Old Governor's Mansion operated as the official residence of the state's governor from 1839 to 1868. John C. Inscoe, ed., *The Civil War in Georgia: A New Georgia Encyclopedia Companion* (Athens: University of Georgia Press, 2011), s.v. "Milledgeville."

freight-cars, which carried away these things—even the cabbages and vegetables from his kitchen and cellar—leaving behind muskets, ammunition, and the public archives. On arrival at Milledgeville I occupied the same public mansion, and was soon overwhelmed with appeals for protection. General Slocum had previously arrived with the Twentieth Corps, had taken up his quarters at the Milledgeville Hotel,[18] established a good provost-guard, and excellent order was maintained. The most frantic appeals had been made by the Governor and Legislature for help from every quarter, and the people of the State had been called out *en masse* to resist and destroy the invaders of their homes and firesides. Even the prisoners and convicts of the penitentiary were released on condition of serving as soldiers, and the cadets were taken from their military college for the same purpose.[19] These constituted a small battalion, under General Harry Wayne, a former officer of the United States Army, and son of the then Justice Wayne of the Supreme Court.[20] But these hastily retreated east across the Oconee River, leaving us a good bridge, which we promptly secured.

At Milledgeville we found newspapers from all the South, and learned the consternation which had filled the Southern mind at our temerity; many charging that we were actually fleeing for our lives and seeking safety at the hands of our fleet on the sea-coast. All demanded that we should be assailed, "front, flank, and rear;" that provisions should be destroyed in advance, so that we would starve; that bridges should be burned, roads obstructed, and no mercy shown us. Judging from the tone of the Southern press of that day, the outside world must have supposed us ruined and lost. I give a few of these appeals as samples, which to-day must sound strange to the parties who made them:

[18] The Milledgeville Hotel, built in 1855, was located on the corner of Wayne and Greene Streets. Amy E. Clark-Davis, *Images of America: Milledgeville* (Charleston, SC: Arcadia, 2011), 22.

[19] The Georgia Military Institute, founded in 1851, was in Marietta, GA. The college was destroyed by WTS's forces. Joseph D. Clemens et al., *History and Catalogue of the Sigma Alpha Epsilon Fraternity* (Harrisburg, PA: Meyers, 1893), 113.

[20] Henry C. Wayne (1815–1883), son of U.S. Supreme Court justice James M. Wayne (1790–1867), graduated from the USMA in 1838 and joined the Confederate Army at the start of the Civil War. His battalion from the Georgia Military Institute went into active service in May 1864. For Wayne's response to WTS's claims regarding his actions during the March to the Sea, see Henry C. Wayne to WTS, Oct. 23, 1875, in the Appendix to Volume II. Also see *CWHC*, 557; *Webster's Guide to American History: A Chronological, Geographical, and Biographical Survey and Compendium* (Springfield, MA: G. & C. Merriam, 1971), 777.

Corinth, Mississippi, *November* 18, 1864.

To the People of Georgia:

Arise for the defense of your native soil! Rally around your patriotic Governor and gallant soldiers! Obstruct and destroy all the roads in Sherman's front, flank, and rear, and his army will soon starve in your midst. Be confident. Be resolute. Trust in an overruling Providence, and success will soon crown your efforts. I hasten to join you in the defense of your homes and firesides.

G. T. Beauregard.

Richmond, *November* 18, 1864.

To the People of Georgia:

You have now the best opportunity ever yet presented to destroy the enemy. Put every thing at the disposal of our generals; remove all provisions from the path of the invader, and put all obstructions in his path.

Every citizen with his gun, and every negro with his spade and axe, can do the work of a soldier. You can destroy the enemy by retarding his march.

Georgians, be firm! Act promptly, and fear not!

B. H. Hill, *Senator.*

I most cordially approve the above.

James A. Seddon, *Secretary of War.*

Richmond, *November* 19, 1864.

To the People of Georgia:

We have had a special conference with President Davis and the Secretary of War, and are able to assure you that they have done and are still doing all that can be done to meet the emergency that presses upon you. Let every man fly to arms! Remove your negroes, horses, cattle, and provisions from Sherman's army, and burn what you cannot carry. Burn all bridges, and block up the roads in his route. Assail the invader in front, flank, and rear, by night and by day. Let him have no rest.

Julian Hartridge, Mark Blandford,
J. H. Echols, Geo. N. Lester,
John T. Shuemake, Jas. M. Smith,
Members of Congress.

Of course, we were rather amused than alarmed at these threats, and made light of the feeble opposition offered to our progress. Some of the officers (in the spirit of mischief) gathered together in the vacant hall of Representatives, elected a Speaker, and constituted themselves the Legislature of the State of Georgia! A proposition was made to repeal the ordinance of secession, which was well debated, and resulted in its repeal by a fair vote! I was not present at these frolics, but heard of them at the time, and enjoyed the joke.[21]

Meantime orders were made for the total destruction of the arsenal and its contents, and of such public buildings as could be easily converted to hostile uses. But little or no damage was done to private property, and General Slocum, with my approval, spared several mills, and many thousands of bales of cotton, taking what he knew to be worthless bonds, that the cotton should not be used for the Confederacy. Meantime the right wing continued its movement along the railroad toward Savannah, tearing up the track and destroying its iron. At the Oconee was met a feeble resistance from Harry Wayne's troops, but soon the pontoon-bridge was laid, and that wing crossed over. Kilpatrick's cavalry was brought into Milledgeville, and crossed the Oconee by the bridge near the town; and on the 23d I made the general orders for the next stage of the march as far as Millen. These were, substantially, for the right wing to follow the Savannah Railroad, by roads on its south; the left wing was to move to Sandersville, by Davisboro' and Louisville, while the cavalry was ordered by a circuit to the north, and to march rapidly for Millen, to rescue our prisoners of war confined there. The distance was about a hundred miles.

General Wheeler, with his division of rebel cavalry, had succeeded in getting ahead of us between Milledgeville and Augusta; and General W. J. Hardee had been dispatched by General Beauregard from Hood's army to oppose our progress directly in front.[22] He had, however, brought with him no troops, but relied on his influence with the Georgians (of whose State he was a native) to arouse the people, and with them to annihilate Sherman's army!

[21] Soldiers from the 3rd Wisconsin and the 107th New York regiments held a mock session in the statehouse at Milledgeville on Nov. 23. According to the *Augusta Chronicle,* "The Yankees kicked up quite a fuss in the Statehouse. They had a mock Legislature, elected Speaker, Clerk, &c., and were introducing bills, resolutions, &c., at a furious rate, when a courier burst into their midst, almost breathless with the announcement—'The Yankees are coming'—when the whole concern absquatulated with the most precipitate haste and alarm." "Incidents of Sherman's March," *New York Times,* Dec. 18, 1864, 1; James C. Bonner, "Sherman at Milledgeville in 1864," *Journal of Southern History* 22, no. 3 (Aug. 1956): 284.

[22] See *OR,* I, 45(I), 1213.

On the 24th we renewed the march, and I accompanied the Twentieth Corps, which took the direct road to Sandersville, which we reached simultaneously with the Fourteenth Corps, on the 26th. A brigade of rebel cavalry was deployed before the town, and was driven in and through it by our skirmish-line. I myself saw the rebel cavalry apply fire to stacks of fodder standing in the fields at Sandersville, and gave orders to burn some unoccupied dwellings close by. On entering the town, I told certain citizens (who would be sure to spread the report) that, if the enemy attempted to carry out their threat to burn their food, corn, and fodder, in our route, I would most undoubtedly execute to the letter the general orders of devastation made at the outset of the campaign. With this exception, and one or two minor cases near Savannah, the people did not destroy food, for they saw clearly that it would be ruin to themselves.

At Sandersville I halted the left wing until I heard that the right wing was abreast of us on the railroad. During the evening a negro was brought to me, who had that day been to the station (Tenille), about six miles south of the town. I inquired of him if there were any Yankees there, and he answered, "Yes." He described in his own way what he had seen. "First, there come along some cavalry-men, and they burned the depot; then come along some infantry-men, and they tore up the track, and burned it;" and just before he left they had "sot fire to the well!"

The next morning, viz., the 27th, I rode down to the station, and found General Corse's division (of the Fifteenth Corps) engaged in destroying the railroad, and saw the well which my negro informant had seen "burnt." It was a square pit about twenty-five feet deep, boarded up, with wooden steps leading to the bottom, wherein was a fine copper pump, to lift the water to a tank above. The soldiers had broken up the pump, heaved in the steps and lining, and set fire to the mass of lumber in the bottom of the well, which corroborated the negro's description.

From this point Blair's corps, the Seventeenth, took up the work of destroying the railroad, the Fifteenth Corps following another road leading eastward, farther to the south of the railroad. While the left wing was marching toward Louisville, north of the railroad, General Kilpatrick had, with his cavalry division, moved rapidly toward Waynesboro', on the branch railroad leading from Millen to Augusta. He found Wheeler's division of rebel cavalry there, and had considerable skirmishing with it; but, learning that our prisoners had been removed two days before from Millen, he returned to Louisville on the 29th, where he found the left wing. Here he remained a couple of days to rest his horses, and, receiving orders from me to engage Wheeler and give him all the fighting he wanted, he procured from General Slocum the assistance of the infantry division of General Baird, and moved back for Waynesboro' on the 2d of December, the remainder of the left wing continuing its march on toward Millen. Near Waynesboro' Wheeler was again encountered, and driven through the town and beyond Brier Creek, toward Augusta, thus keeping up the delusion that the main army was moving toward Augusta. General Kilpatrick's fighting and movements about Waynesboro' and Brier Creek were spirited, and produced a good effect by relieving the infantry column and the wagon-trains of all molestation during their march on Millen. Having thus covered that flank, he turned south and followed the movement of the Fourteenth Corps to Buckhead Church, north of Millen and near it.

On the 3d of December I entered Millen with the Seventeenth Corps (General Frank P. Blair), and there paused one day, to communicate with all parts of the army. General Howard was south of the Ogeechee River, with the Fifteenth Corps, opposite Scarboro'. General Slocum was at Buckhead Church, four miles north of Millen, with the Twentieth Corps. The Fourteenth (General Davis) was at Lumpkin's Station, on the Augusta road, about ten miles north of Millen, and the cavalry division was within easy support of this wing. Thus the whole army was in good position and in good condition. We had largely subsisted on the country; our wagons were full of forage and provisions; but, as we approached the sea-coast, the country became more sandy and barren, and food became more scarce; still, with little or no loss, we had traveled two-thirds of our distance, and I concluded to push on for Savannah. At Millen I learned that General Bragg was in Augusta, and that General Wade Hampton[23] had been ordered there from Richmond, to organize a large cavalry force with which to resist our progress.

General Hardee was ahead, between us and Savannah, with McLaw's division,[24] and other irregular troops, that could not, I felt assured, exceed ten thousand men. I caused the fine depot at Millen to be destroyed, and other damage done, and then resumed the march directly on Savannah, by the four main roads. The Seventeenth Corps (General Blair) followed substantially the railroad, and, along with it, on the 5th of December, I reached Ogeechee Church, about fifty miles from Savannah, and found there fresh earthworks,

[23] Wade Hampton III (1818–1902) joined the Confederate Army at the start of the war and took command of the Cav. Corps, Army of Northern Virgina, in Aug. 1864. After the war, he served as the governor of South Carolina. *CWHC,* 277.

[24] Lafayette McLaws (1821–1897) was in command of Subdist. 5, Dist. of South Carolina, Dept. of South Carolina, Georgia, and Florida, in Dec. 1864. *CWHC,* 381.

which had been thrown up by McLaw's division; but he must have seen that both his flanks were being turned, and prudently retreated to Savannah without a fight. All the columns then pursued leisurely their march toward Savannah, corn and forage becoming more and more scarce, but rice-fields beginning to occur along the Savannah and Ogeechee Rivers, which proved a good substitute, both as food and forage. The weather was fine, the roads good, and every thing seemed to favor us. Never do I recall a more agreeable sensation than the sight of our camps by night, lit up by the fires of fragrant pine-knots. The trains were all in good order, and the men seemed to march their fifteen miles a day as though it were nothing. No enemy opposed us, and we could only occasionally hear the faint reverberation of a gun to our left rear, where we knew that General Kilpatrick was skirmishing with Wheeler's cavalry, which persistently followed him. But the infantry columns had met with no opposition whatsoever. McLaw's division was falling back before us, and we occasionally picked up a few of his men as prisoners, who insisted that we would meet with strong opposition at Savannah.

On the 8th, as I rode along, I found the column turned out of the main road, marching through the fields. Close by, in the corner of a fence, was a group of men standing around a handsome young officer, whose foot had been blown to pieces by a torpedo planted in the road. He was waiting for a surgeon to amputate his leg, and told me that he was riding along with the rest of his brigade-staff of the Seventeenth Corps, when a torpedo trodden on by his horse had exploded, killing the horse and literally blowing off all the flesh from one of his legs. I saw the terrible wound, and made full inquiry into the facts. There had been no resistance at that point, nothing to give warning of danger, and the rebels had planted eight-inch shells in the road, with friction-matches to explode them by being trodden on. This was not war, but murder, and it made me very angry. I immediately ordered a lot of rebel prisoners to be brought from the provost-guard, armed with picks and spades, and made them march in close order along the road, so as to explode their own torpedoes, or to discover and dig them up.[25] They begged hard, but I reiterated the order, and could hardly help laughing at their stepping so gingerly along the road, where it was supposed sunken torpedoes might explode at each step, but they found no other torpedoes till near Fort

[25] For more information on the use of land mines during the Civil War, see Earl J. Hess, *Civil War Torpedoes and the Global Development of Landmine Warfare* (Lanham, MD: Rowman and Littlefield, 2023).

McAllister.[26] That night we reached Pooler's Station, eight miles from Savannah, and during the next two days, December 9th and 10th, the several corps reached the defenses of Savannah—the Fourteenth Corps on the left, touching the river; the Twentieth Corps next; then the Seventeenth; and the Fifteenth on the extreme right; thus completely investing the city. Wishing to reconnoitre the place in person, I rode forward by the Louisville road, into a dense wood of oak, pine, and cypress, left the horses, and walked down to the railroad-track, at a place where there was a side-track, and a cut about four feet deep. From that point the railroad was straight, leading into Savannah, and about eight hundred yards off were a rebel parapet and battery. I could see the cannoneers preparing to fire, and cautioned the officers near me to scatter, as we would likely attract a shot. Very soon I saw the white puff of smoke, and, watching close, caught sight of the ball as it rose in its flight, and, finding it coming pretty straight, I stepped a short distance to one side, but noticed a negro very near me in the act of crossing the track at right angles. Some one called to him to look out; but, before the poor fellow understood his danger, the ball (a thirty-two-pound round shot) struck the ground, and rose in its first ricochet, caught the negro under the right jaw, and literally carried away his head, scattering blood and brains about. A soldier close by spread an overcoat over the body, and we all concluded to get out of that railroad-cut. Meantime, General Mower's division of the Seventeenth Corps had crossed the canal to the right of the Louisville road, and had found the line of parapet continuous; so at Savannah we had again run up against the old familiar parapet, with its deep ditches, canals, and bayous, full of water; and it looked as though another siege was inevitable. I accordingly made a camp or bivouac near the Louisville road, about five miles from Savannah, and proceeded to invest the place closely, pushing forward reconnoissances at every available point.

As soon as it was demonstrated that Savannah was well fortified, with a good garrison, commanded by General William J. Hardee, a competent soldier, I saw that the first step was to open communication with our fleet, supposed to be waiting for us with supplies and clothing in Ossabaw Sound.

General Howard had, some nights previously, sent one of his best scouts, Captain Duncan,[27] with two men, in a canoe, to drift past Fort McAllister,

[26] In July 1861 the Confederate Army used enslaved people to construct Fort McAllister at the mouth of the Ogeechee River. Roger S. Durham, *Images of America: Fort McAllister* (Charleston, SC: Arcadia, 2004), 11–13.

[27] In his autobiography, O. O. Howard stated, "I selected Captain William Duncan, who had escaped from capture and had returned to my escort, and told him to take with him Sergeant

and to convey to the fleet a knowledge of our approach. General Kilpatrick's cavalry had also been transferred to the south bank of the Ogeechee, with orders to open communication with the fleet. Leaving orders with General Slocum to press the siege, I instructed General Howard to send a division with all his engineers to King's Bridge, fourteen and a half miles southwest from Savannah, to rebuild it. On the evening of the 12th I rode over myself, and spent the night at Mr. King's house, where I found General Howard, with General Hazen's division of the Fifteenth Corps. His engineers were hard at work on the bridge, which they finished that night, and at sunrise Hazen's division passed over. I gave General Hazen, in person, his orders to march rapidly down the right bank of the Ogeechee, and without hesitation to assault and carry Fort McAllister by storm. I knew it to be strong in heavy artillery, as against an approach from the sea, but believed it open and weak to the rear. I explained to General Hazen, fully, that on his action depended the safety of the whole army, and the success of the campaign. Kilpatrick had already felt the fort, and had gone farther down the coast to Kilkenny Bluff, or St. Catharine's Sound, where, on the same day, he had communication with a vessel belonging to the blockading fleet; but, at the time, I was not aware of this fact, and trusted entirely to General Hazen and his division of infantry, the Second of the Fifteenth Corps, the same old division which I had commanded at Shiloh and Vicksburg, in which I felt a special pride and confidence.[28]

Having seen General Hazen fairly off, accompanied by General Howard, I rode with my staff down the left bank of the Ogeechee, ten miles to the rice-plantation of a Mr. Cheeves,[29] where General Howard had established a signal-station to overlook the lower river, and to watch for any vessel of the blockading squadron, which the negroes reported to be expecting us, because they nightly sent up rockets, and daily dispatched a steamboat up the Ogeechee as near to Fort McAllister as it was safe.

Myron J. Amick and Private George W. Quimby and proceed down the Ogeechee, passing Confederate stations, the King's Bridge, Fort McAllister, and all obstructions, and go out to sea and communicate with the fleet." O. O. Howard, *Autobiography of Oliver Otis Howard* (New York: Baker and Taylor, 1908), 2:83–85.

[28] Kilpatrick reached St. Catharine's Sound on Dec. 13. *OR,* I, 44, 366.

[29] Dr. John R. Cheves owned a 2,000-acre rice plantation along the Ogeechee River. Karen B. Bell, "'The Ogeechee Troubles': Federal Land Restoration and the 'Lived Realities' of Temporary Proprietors, 1865–1868," *Georgia Historical Quarterly* 85, no. 3 (Fall 2001): 380; Davis et al., *Official Military Atlas of the Civil War,* plate 69, map 4.

On reaching the rice-mill at Cheeves's, I found a guard and a couple of twenty-pound Parrott guns, of De Gres's battery, which fired an occasional shot toward Fort McAllister, plainly seen over the salt-marsh, about three miles distant. Fort McAllister had the rebel flag flying, and occasionally sent a heavy shot back across the marsh to where we were, but otherwise every thing about the place looked as peaceable and quiet as on the Sabbath.

The signal-officer had built a platform on the ridge-pole of the rice-mill. Leaving our horses behind the stacks of rice-straw, we all got on the roof of a shed attached to the mill, wherefrom I could communicate with the signal-officer above, and at the same time look out toward Ossabaw Sound, and across the Ogeechee River at Fort McAllister. About 2 P. M. we observed signs of commotion in the fort, and noticed one or two guns fired inland, and some musket-skirmishing in the woods close by.

This betokened the approach of Hazen's division, which had been anxiously expected, and soon thereafter the signal-officer discovered about three miles above the fort a signal-flag, with which he conversed, and found it to belong to General Hazen, who was preparing to assault the fort, and wanted to know if I were there. On being assured of this fact, and that I expected the fort to be carried before night, I received by signal the assurance of General Hazen that he was making his preparations, and would soon attempt the assault. The sun was rapidly declining, and I was dreadfully impatient. At that very moment some one discovered a faint cloud of smoke, and an object gliding, as it were, along the horizon above the tops of the sedge toward the sea, which little by little grew till it was pronounced to be the smoke-stack of a steamer coming up the river. "It must be one of our squadron!" Soon the flag of the United States was plainly visible, and our attention was divided between this approaching steamer and the expected assault. When the sun was about an hour high, another signal-message came from General Hazen that he was all ready, and I replied to go ahead, as a friendly steamer was approaching from below. Soon we made out a group of officers on the deck of this vessel, signaling with a flag, "Who are you?" The answer went back promptly, "General Sherman." Then followed the question, "Is Fort McAllister taken?" "Not yet, but it will be in a minute!" Almost at that instant of time, we saw Hazen's troops come out of the dark fringe of woods that encompassed the fort, the lines dressed as on parade, with colors flying, and moving forward with a quick, steady pace. Fort McAllister was then all alive, its big guns belching forth dense clouds of smoke, which soon enveloped our assaulting lines. One color went down, but was up in a moment. On the lines advanced, faintly seen in the white, sulphurous smoke; there was a pause, a cessation of fire; the smoke cleared away, and the parapets were blue with our men, who fired their muskets in the air, and shouted so that we actually heard them, or felt that we did. Fort McAllister was taken, and the good news was instantly sent by the signal-officer to our navy friends on the approaching gunboat, for a point of timber had shut out Fort McAllister from their view, and they had not seen the action at all, but must have heard the cannonading.

During the progress of the assault, our little group on Cheeves's mill hardly breathed; but no sooner did we see our flags on the parapet than I exclaimed, in the language of the poor negro at Cobb's plantation, "This nigger will have no sleep this night!"

I was resolved to communicate with our fleet that night, which happened to be a beautiful moonlight one. At the wharf belonging to Cheeves's mill was a small skiff, that had been used by our men in fishing or in gathering oysters. I was there in a minute, called for a volunteer crew, when several young officers, Nichols and Merritt among the number; said they were good oarsmen, and volunteered to pull the boat down to Fort McAllister.[30] General Howard asked to accompany me; so we took seats in the stern of the boat, and our crew of officers pulled out with a will. The tide was setting in strong, and they had a hard pull, for, though the distance was but three miles in an air-line, the river was so crooked that the actual distance was fully six miles. On the way down we passed the wreck of a steamer which had been sunk some years before, during a naval attack on Fort McAllister.[31]

Night had fairly set in when we discovered a soldier on the beach. I hailed him, and inquired if he knew where General Hazen was. He answered that the general was at the house of the overseer of the plantation (McAllister's),[32]

[30] Nehemiah Merritt and George W. Nichols (1831–1885) were with WTS during the assault on Fort McAllister. Nichols described WTS's demeanor in his diary: "General Sherman walked nervously to and fro, turning quickly now and then from viewing the scene of conflict to observe the sun sinking slowly behind the tree-tops." After the war, Nichols published an article on James "Wild Bill" Hickok in *Harper's Weekly Magazine* which cemented Hickok as an American folk legend. George W. Nichols, *The Story of the Great March from the Diary of a Staff Officer* (New York: Harper, 1865), 89; George Nichols, "Wild Bill," *Harper's New Monthly Magazine,* Feb. 1867, 273–285; *OR,* I, 44, 719.

[31] The USS *Montauk* sank the CSS *Rattlesnake* near Fort McAllister on Feb. 28, 1863. Spencer C. Tucker, ed., *The Civil War Naval Encyclopedia* (Santa Barbara: ABC-CLIO, 2010), s.v. "February 1863."

[32] Joseph L. McAllister (1820–1864) was killed in battle while fighting for the Confederate Army at Trevellian Station, VA, on June 11, 1864. Durham, *Images of America: Fort* McAllister,

and that he could guide me to it. We accordingly landed, tied our boat to a drift-log, and followed our guide through bushes to a frame-house, standing in a grove of live-oaks, near a row of negro quarters. General Hazen was there with his staff, in the act of getting supper; he invited us to join them, which we accepted promptly, for we were really very hungry. Of course, I congratulated Hazen most heartily on his brilliant success, and praised its execution very highly, as it deserved, and he explained to me more in detail the exact results. The fort was an inclosed work, and its land-front was in the nature of a bastion and curtains, with good parapet, ditch, *fraise,* and *chevaux-de-frise,* made out of the large branches of live-oaks. Luckily, the rebels had left the larger and unwieldy trunks on the ground, which served as a good cover for the skirmish-line, which crept behind these logs, and from them kept the artillerists from loading and firing their guns accurately.

The assault had been made by three parties in line, one from below, one from above the fort, and the third directly in rear, along the capital. All were simultaneous, and had to pass a good abatis and line of torpedoes, which actually killed more of the assailants than the heavy guns of the fort, which generally overshot the mark. Hazen's entire loss was reported, killed and wounded, ninety-two. Each party reached the parapet about the same time, and the garrison inside, of about two hundred and fifty men (about fifty of them killed or wounded), were in his power. The commanding officer, Major Anderson,[33] was at that moment a prisoner, and General Hazen invited him in to take supper with us, which he did.[34]

Up to this time General Hazen did not know that a gunboat was in the river below the fort; for it was shut off from sight by a point of timber, and I was determined to board her that night, at whatever risk or cost, as I wanted some news of what was going on in the outer world. Accordingly, after supper, we all walked down to the fort, nearly a mile from the house where we had been, entered Fort McAllister, held by a regiment of Hazen's troops, and the sentinel cautioned us to be very careful, as the ground outside the fort was full of torpe-

---

10–11; Carolyn C. Swiggart, *Shades of Gray: The Clay and McAllister Families of Bryan, Georgia* (Darien, CT: Two Bytes, 1999), 56–57.

[33] George W. Anderson (1839–1906) took command of Fort McAllister in Feb. 1863. Joseph G. B. Bulloch, *A History and Genealogy of the Habersham Family* (Columbia, SC: R. L. Bryan, 1901), 214; Durham, *Images of America: Fort McAllister,* 20.

[34] The U.S. Army suffered 134 casualties during the assault on Fort McAllister on Dec. 13. James B. Swan, *Chicago's Irish Legion: The 90th Illinois Volunteers in the Civil War* (Carbondale: Southern Illinois University Press, 2009), 184.

does. Indeed, while we were there, a torpedo exploded, tearing to pieces a poor fellow who was hunting for a dead comrade. Inside the fort lay the dead as they had fallen, and they could hardly be distinguished from their living comrades, sleeping soundly side by side in the pale moonlight. In the river, close by the fort, was a good yawl tied to a stake, but the tide was high, and it required some time to get it in to the bank; the commanding officer,[35] whose name I cannot recall, manned the boat with a good crew of his men, and, with General Howard, I entered, and pulled down-stream, regardless of the warnings all about the torpedoes.

The night was unusually bright, and we expected to find the gunboat within a mile or so; but, after pulling down the river fully three miles, and not seeing the gunboat, I began to think she had turned and gone back to the sound; but we kept on, following the bends of the river, and about six miles below McAllister we saw her light, and soon were hailed by the vessel at anchor. Pulling alongside, we announced ourselves, and were received with great warmth and enthusiasm on deck by half a dozen naval officers, among them Captain Williamson,[36] United States Navy. She proved to be the Dandelion, a tender of the regular gunboat Flag, posted at the mouth of the Ogeechee. All sorts of questions were made and answered, and we learned that Captain Duncan had safely reached the squadron, had communicated the good news of our approach, and they had been expecting us for some days. They explained that Admiral Dahlgren commanded the South-Atlantic Squadron, which was then engaged in blockading the coast from Charleston south, and was on his flagship, the Harvest Moon, lying in Wassaw Sound;[37] that General J. G. Foster was in command of the Department of the South, with his headquarters at Hilton Head;[38] and that several ships loaded with stores for the army were lying in Tybee Roads and in Port Royal Sound. From these officers I also learned that

[35] Gen. O. O. Howard described the incident in his autobiography. "The instant that we received the sure word that the fort was ours we ran for a small rowboat that was close at hand and proceeded as fast as the oarsman could speed us down the Ogeechee to the vicinity of Fort McAllister." Howard, *Autobiography of Oliver Otis Howard,* 2:91.

[36] James C. Williamson (1813–1871) joined the U.S. Navy in 1832 and was commissioned as captain in 1866. "Obituary: Captain James C. Williamson," *Philadelphia Inquirer,* July 27, 1871, 4.

[37] John A. B. Dahlgren (1809–1870) took command of the *Harvest Moon* in Feb. 1864. *CWHC,* 197–198.

[38] John G. Foster (1823–1874) graduated from the USMA in 1846 and took command of the Dept. of the South on May 26, 1864. *CWHC,* 241.

General Grant was still besieging Petersburg and Richmond, and that matters and things generally remained pretty much the same as when we had left Atlanta. All thoughts seemed to have been turned to us in Georgia, cut off from all communication with our friends; and the rebel papers had reported us to be harassed, defeated, starving, and fleeing for safety to the coast. I then asked for pen and paper, and wrote several hasty notes to General Foster, Admiral Dahlgren, General Grant, and the Secretary of War, giving in general terms the actual state of affairs, the fact of the capture of Fort McAllister, and of my desire that means should be taken to establish a line of supply from the vessels in port up the Ogeechee to the rear of the army.[39] As a sample, I give one of these notes, addressed to the Secretary of War, intended for publication to relieve the anxiety of our friends at the North generally:

ON BOARD DANDELION, OSSABAW SOUND,
December 13, 1864—11.50 P. M.

To Hon. E. M. STANTON, *Secretary of War, Washington, D. C.:*

To-day, at 5 P. M., General Hazen's division of the Fifteenth Corps carried Fort McAllister by assault, capturing its entire garrison and stores. This opened to us Ossabaw Sound, and I pushed down to this gunboat to communicate with the fleet. Before opening communication we had completely destroyed all the railroads leading into Savannah, and invested the city. The left of the army is on the Savannah River three miles above the city, and the right on the Ogeechee, at King's Bridge. The army is in splendid order, and equal to any thing. The weather has been fine, and supplies were abundant. Our march was most agreeable, and we were not at all molested by guerrillas.

We reached Savannah three days ago, but, owing to Fort McAllister, could not communicate; but, now that we have McAllister, we can go ahead.

We have already captured two boats on the Savannah River and prevented their gunboats from coming down.

I estimate the population of Savannah at twenty-five thousand, and the garrison at fifteen thousand. General Hardee commands.

We have not lost a wagon on the trip; but have gathered a large supply of negroes, mules, horses, etc., and our teams are in far better condition than when we started.

[39] See *OR*, I, 44, 700–701, 726.

My first duty will be to clear the army of surplus negroes, mules, and horses. We have utterly destroyed over two hundred miles of rails, and consumed stores and provisions that were essential to Lee's and Hood's armies.

The quick work made with McAllister, the opening of communication with our fleet, and our consequent independence as to supplies, dissipate all their boasted threats to head us off and starve the army.

I regard Savannah as already *gained.*

Yours truly,

W. T. Sherman, *Major-General.*

By this time the night was well advanced, and the tide was running ebb-strong; so I asked Captain Williamson to tow us up as near Fort McAllister as he would venture for the torpedoes, of which the navy-officers had a wholesome dread. The Dandelion steamed up some three or four miles, till the lights of Fort McAllister could be seen, when she anchored, and we pulled to the fort in our own boat. General Howard and I then walked up to the McAllister House, where we found General Hazen and his officers asleep on the floor of one of the rooms. Lying down on the floor, I was soon fast asleep, but shortly became conscious that some one in the room was inquiring for me among the sleepers. Calling out, I was told that an officer of General Foster's staff[40] had just arrived from a steamboat anchored below McAllister; that the general was extremely anxious to see me on important business, but that he was lame from an old Mexican-War wound, and could not possibly come to me. I was extremely weary from the incessant labor of the day and night before, but got up, and again walked down the sandy road to McAllister, where I found a boat awaiting us, which carried us some three miles down the river, to the steamer W. W. Coit (I think),[41] on board of which we found General Foster. He had just come from Port Royal, expecting to find Admiral Dahlgren in Ossabaw Sound, and, hearing of the capture of Fort McAllister, he had come up to see me. He described fully the condition of affairs with his own command in South Carolina. He had made several serious efforts to effect

[40] In his post-battle report, WTS wrote, "After making communications to those officers, and a short communication to the War Department, I returned to Fort McAllister that night, and before daylight was overtaken by Major (Edward N.) Strong, of General Foster's staff, advising me that General Foster had arrived in the Ogeechee, near Fort McAllister, and was very anxious to meet me onboard his boat." *OR,* I, 44, 11.

[41] WTS identified Foster's boat as the *Nemaha* in his post-battle report. *OR,* I, 44, 11.

a lodgment on the railroad which connects Savannah with Charleston near Pocotaligo, but had not succeeded in reaching the railroad itself, though he had a full division of troops, strongly intrenched, near Broad River, within cannon-range of the railroad. He explained, moreover, that there were at Port Royal abundant supplies of bread and provisions, as well as of clothing, designed for our use. We still had in our wagons and in camp abundance of meat, but we needed bread, sugar, and coffee, and it was all-important that a route of supply should at once be opened, for which purpose the aid and assistance of the navy were indispensable. We accordingly steamed down the Ogeechee River to Ossabaw Sound, in hopes to meet Admiral Dahlgren, but he was not there, and we continued on by the inland channel to Wassaw Sound, where we found the Harvest Moon, and Admiral Dahlgren. I was not personally acquainted with him at the time, but he was so extremely kind and courteous that I was at once attracted to him. There was nothing in his power, he said, which he would not do to assist us, to make our campaign absolutely successful. He undertook at once to find vessels of light draught to carry our supplies from Port Royal to Cheeves's Mill, or to King's Bridge above, whence they could be hauled by wagons to our several camps; he offered to return with me to Fort McAllister, to superintend the removal of the torpedoes, and to relieve me of all the details of this most difficult work. General Foster then concluded to go on to Port Royal, to send back to us six hundred thousand rations, and all the rifled guns of heavy calibre, and ammunition on hand, with which I thought we could reach the city of Savannah, from the positions already secured. Admiral Dahlgren then returned with me in the Harvest Moon to Fort McAllister. This consumed all of the 14th of December; and by the 15th I had again reached Cheeves's Mill, where my horse awaited me, and rode on to General Howard's headquarters at Anderson's plantation, on the plank-road, about eight miles back of Savannah. I reached this place about noon, and immediately sent orders to my own headquarters, on the Louisville road, to have them brought over to the plank-road, as a place more central and convenient; gave written notice to Generals Slocum and Howard of all the steps taken, and ordered them to get ready to receive the siege-guns, to put them in position to bombard Savannah, and to prepare for the general assault.[42] The country back of Savannah is very low, and intersected with innumerable saltwater creeks, swamps, and rice-fields. Fortunately the weather was good and the roads were passable, but, should the winter rains set in, I knew that we would be much embarrassed. There-

[42] See *OR,* I, 44, 718–719.

fore, heavy details of men were at once put to work to prepare a wharf and depot at King's Bridge, and the roads leading thereto were corduroyed in advance. The Ogeechee Canal was also cleared out for use; and boats, such as were common on the river plantations, were collected, in which to float stores from our proposed base on the Ogeechee to the points most convenient to the several camps.

Slocum's wing extended from the Savannah River to the canal, and Howard's wing from the canal to the extreme right, along down the Little Ogeechee. The enemy occupied not only the city itself, with its long line of outer works, but the many forts which had been built to guard the approaches from the sea—such as at Beaulieu, Rosedew, White Bluff, Bonaventura, Thunderbolt, Cansten's Bluff, Forts Tatnall, Boggs, etc., etc.[43] I knew that General Hardee could not have a garrison strong enough for all these purposes, and I was therefore anxious to break his lines before he could receive reënforcements from Virginia or Augusta. General Slocum had already captured a couple of steamboats trying to pass down the Savannah River from Augusta, and had established some of his men on Argyle and Hutchinson Islands above the city, and wanted to transfer a whole corps to the South Carolina bank; but, as the enemy had iron-clad gunboats in the river, I did not deem it prudent, because the same result could be better accomplished from General Foster's position at Broad River.

Fort McAllister was captured as described, late in the evening of December 13th, and by the 16th many steamboats had passed up as high as King's Bridge; among them one which General Grant had dispatched with the mails for the army, which had accumulated since our departure from Atlanta, under charge of Colonel A. H. Markland.[44] These mails were most welcome to all the officers and soldiers of the army, which had been cut off from friends and the world for two months, and this prompt receipt of letters from home had an excellent effect, making us feel that home was near. By this vessel also came Lieutenant Dunn, aide-de-camp,[45] with the following letter of December 3d, from General Grant, and on the next day Colonel Babcock, United States

[43] For a detailed map of the works around Savannah, see Davis et al., *Official Military Atlas of the Civil War*, plate 70, map 2.

[44] Absalom H. Markland (1825–1888) was superintendent of U.S. Army mail while USG was in command of the army during the war. "Death of Col. Ab. Markland," *Lexington Herald-Leader* (Lexington, KY), May 25, 1888, 1.

[45] William M. Dunn (1814–1887) served as Gen. George B. McClellan's aide-de-camp in the summer of 1861. *CWHC*, 218.

Engineers,[46] arrived with the letter of December 6th, both of which are in General Grant's own handwriting, and are given entire:

HEADQUARTERS ARMIES OF THE UNITED STATES,
CITY POINT, VIRGINIA, *December* 3, 1864.

Major-General W. T. SHERMAN, *commanding Armies near Savannah, Georgia.*

GENERAL: The little information gleaned from the Southern press indicating no great obstacle to your progress, I have directed your mails (which had been previously collected in Baltimore by Colonel Markland, special agent of the Post-Office Department) to be sent as far as the blockading squadron off Savannah, to be forwarded to you as soon as heard from on the coast.

Not liking to rejoice before the victory is assured, I abstain from congratulating you and those under your command, until bottom has been struck. I have never had a fear, however, for the result.

Since you left Atlanta no very great progress has been made here. The enemy has been closely watched, though, and prevented from detaching against you. I think not one man has gone from here, except some twelve or fifteen hundred dismounted cavalry. Bragg has gone from Wilmington. I am trying to take advantage of his absence to get possession of that place. Owing to some preparations Admiral Porter and General Butler are making to blow up Fort Fisher (which, while hoping for the best, I do not believe a particle in), there is a delay in getting this expedition off. I hope they will be ready to start by the 7th, and that Bragg will not have started back by that time.

In this letter I do not intend to give you any thing like directions for future action, but will state a general idea I have, and will get your views after you have established yourself on the sea-coast. With your veteran army I hope to get control of the only two through routes from east to west possessed by the enemy before the fall of Atlanta. The condition will be filled by holding Savannah and Augusta, or by

[46] Orville E. Babcock (1835–1884) graduated from the USMA in 1861 and served as USG's aide-de-camp from Mar. 1864 to July 1866. Babcock served as Pres. Grant's secretary and was later implicated in the Whiskey Ring scandal. *CWHC,* 111; Ulysses S. Grant, *The Personal Memoirs of Ulysses S. Grant: The Complete Annotated Edition,* ed. John F. Marszalek, David S. Nolen, and Louie P. Gallo (Cambridge, MA: Belknap Press of Harvard University Press, 2017), 547*n.*

holding any other port to the east of Savannah and Branchville. If Wilmington falls, a force from there can coöperate with you.

Thomas has got back into the defenses of Nashville, with Hood close upon him. Decatur has been abandoned, and so have all the roads, except the main one leading to Chattanooga. Part of this falling back was undoubtedly necessary, and all of it may have been. It did not look so, however, to me. In my opinion, Thomas far outnumbers Hood in infantry. In cavalry Hood has the advantage in *morale* and numbers. I hope yet that Hood will be badly crippled, if not destroyed. The general news you will learn from the papers better than I can give it.

After all becomes quiet, and roads become so bad up here that there is likely to be a week or two when nothing can be done, I will run down the coast to see you. If you desire it, I will ask Mrs. Sherman to go with me.

Yours truly,
U. S. GRANT, *Lieutenant-General.*

HEADQUARTERS ARMIES OF THE UNITED STATES,
CITY POINT, VIRGINIA, *December* 6, 1864.

Major-General W. T. SHERMAN, *commanding Military Division of the Mississippi.*

GENERAL: On reflection since sending my letter by the hands of Lieutenant Dunn, I have concluded that the most important operation toward closing out the rebellion will be to close out Lee and his army.

You have now destroyed the roads of the South so that it will probably take them three months without interruption to reëstablish a through line from east to west. In that time I think the job here will be effectually completed.

My idea now is that you establish a base on the sea-coast, fortify and leave in it all your artillery and cavalry, and enough infantry to protect them, and at the same time so threaten the interior that the militia of the South will have to be kept at home. With the balance of your command come here by water with all dispatch. Select yourself the officer to leave in command, but you I want in person. Unless you see objections to this plan which I cannot see, use every vessel going to you for purposes of transportation.

Hood has Thomas close in Nashville. I have said all I can to force him to attack, without giving the positive order until to-day. To-day, however, I could stand it no longer, and gave the order without any reserve. I think the battle will take place to-morrow. The result will probably be known in New York before Colonel Babcock (the bearer of this) will leave it. Colonel Babcock will give you full information of all operations now in progress. Very respectfully your obedient servant,

U. S. GRANT, *Lieutenant-General.*

The contents of these letters gave me great uneasiness, for I had set my heart on the capture of Savannah, which I believed to be practicable, and to be near; for me to embark for Virginia by sea was so complete a change from what I had supposed would be the course of events that I was very much concerned. I supposed, as a matter of course, that a fleet of vessels would soon pour in, ready to convey the army to Virginia, and as General Grant's orders contemplated my leaving the cavalry, trains, and artillery, behind, I judged Fort McAllister to be the best place for the purpose, and sent my chief-engineer, Colonel Poe, to that fort, to reconnoitre the ground, and to prepare it so as to make a fortified camp large enough to accommodate the vast herd of mules and horses that would thus be left behind. And as some time might be required to collect the necessary shipping, which I estimated at little less than a hundred steamers and sailing-vessels, I determined to push operations, in hopes to secure the city of Savannah before the necessary fleet could be available. All these ideas are given in my answer to General Grant's letters (dated December 16, 1864) herewith, which is a little more full than the one printed in the report of the Committee on the Conduct of the War, because in that copy I omitted the matter concerning General Thomas, which now need no longer be withheld:

HEADQUARTERS MILITARY DIVISION OF THE MISSISSIPPI,
IN THE FIELD, NEAR SAVANNAH, *December* 16, 1864.

Lieutenant-General U. S. GRANT, *Commander-in-Chief, City Point, Virginia.*

GENERAL: I received, day before yesterday, at the hands of Lieutenant Dunn, your letter of December 3d, and last night, at the hands of Colonel Babcock, that of December 6th. I had previously made you a hasty scrawl from the tugboat Dandelion, in Ogeechee River, advising you that the army had reached the sea-coast, destroying all the railroads across the State of Georgia, investing closely the city of Savannah, and had made connection with the fleet.

Since writing that note, I have in person met and conferred with General Foster and Admiral Dahlgren, and made all the arrangements which were deemed essential for reducing the city of Savannah to our possession. But, since the receipt of yours of the 6th, I have initiated measures looking principally to coming to you with fifty or sixty thousand infantry, and incidentally to capture Savannah, if time will allow.

At the time we carried Fort McAllister by assault so handsomely, with its twenty-two guns and entire garrison, I was hardly aware of its importance; but, since passing down the river with General Foster and up with Admiral Dahlgren, I realize how admirably adapted are Ossabaw Sound and Ogeechee River to supply an army operating against Savannah. Seagoing vessels can easily come to King's Bridge, a point on Ogeechee River, fourteen and a half miles due west of Savannah, from which point we have roads leading to all our camps. The country is low and sandy, and cut up with marshes, which in wet weather will be very bad, but we have been so favored with weather that they are all now comparatively good, and heavy details are constantly employed in double-corduroying the marshes, so that I have no fears even of bad weather. Fortunately, also, by liberal and judicious foraging, we reached the sea-coast abundantly supplied with forage and provisions, needing nothing on arrival except bread. Of this we started from Atlanta, with from eight to twenty days' supply per corps, and some of the troops only had one day's issue of bread during the trip of thirty days; yet they did not want, for sweet-potatoes were very abundant, as well as corn-meal, and our soldiers took to them naturally. We started with about five thousand head of cattle, and arrived with over ten thousand, of course consuming mostly turkeys, chickens, sheep, hogs, and the cattle of the country. As to our mules and horses, we left Atlanta with about twenty-five hundred wagons, many of which were drawn by mules which had not recovered from the Chattanooga starvation, all of which were replaced, the poor mules shot, and our transportation is now in superb condition. I have no doubt the State of Georgia has lost, by our operations, fifteen thousand first-rate mules. As to horses, Kilpatrick collected all his remounts, and it looks to me, in riding along our columns, as though every officer had three or four led horses, and each regiment seems to be followed by at least fifty negroes and foot-sore soldiers, riding on horses and mules. The custom was for each brigade to send out daily a foraging-party of about fifty men, on foot, who invariably returned mounted, with several wagons loaded with poultry, potatoes, etc., and as the army is composed of about forty brigades, you can estimate approximately the number of horses collected. Great numbers of these were shot by my order, because of the disorganizing effect on our infantry of having too many idlers mounted. General Easton is now engaged in collecting statistics on this subject, but I know the Government will never receive full accounts of our captures, although the result aimed at was fully attained, viz., to deprive our enemy of them. All these animals I will have sent to Port Royal, or collected behind Fort McAllister, to be used by General Saxton in his farming operations, or by the Quartermaster's Department, after they are systematically accounted for. While General Easton is collecting transportation for my troops to James River, I will throw to Port Royal Island all our means of transportation I can, and collect the rest near Fort McAllister, covered by the Ogeechee River and intrenchments to be erected, and for which Captain Poe, my chief-engineer, is now reconnoitring the ground, but in the mean time will act as I have begun, as though the city of Savannah were my objective: namely, the troops will continue to invest Savannah closely, making attacks and feints wherever we have fair ground to stand upon, and I will place some thirty-pound Parrotts, which I have got from General Foster, in position, near enough to reach the centre of the city, and then will demand its surrender. If General Hardee is alarmed, or fears starvation, he may surrender; otherwise I will bombard the city, but not risk the lives of our men by assaults across the narrow causeways, by which alone I can now reach it.

If I had time, Savannah, with all its dependent fortifications, would surely fall into our possession, for we hold all its avenues of supply.

The enemy has made two desperate efforts to get boats from above to the city, in both of which he has been foiled—General Slocum (whose left flank rests on the river) capturing and burning the first boat, and in the second instance driving back two gunboats and capturing the steamer Resolute, with seven naval officers and a crew of twenty-five seamen. General Slocum occupies Argyle Island and the upper end of Hutchinson Inland, and has a brigade on the South Carolina shore opposite, and is very urgent to pass one of his corps over to that shore. But, in view of the change of plan made necessary by your order of the 6th, I will maintain things *in statu quo* till I have got all my transportation to the rear and out of the way, and until I have sea-transportation for the troops you require at James River, which I will accompany and command in person. Of course, I will leave Kilpatrick, with his cavalry (say five thousand three hundred), and, it may be, a division of the Fifteenth Corps; but, before determining on this, I must see General Foster, and may arrange to shift his force (now over above the Charleston Railroad, at the head of Broad River) to the Ogeechee, where, in coöperation with Kilpatrick's cavalry, he can better threaten the State of Georgia than from the direction of Port Royal. Besides, I would much prefer not to detach from my regular corps any of its veteran divisions, and would even prefer that other less valuable troops should be sent to reënforce Foster from some other quarter. My four corps, full of experience and full of ardor, coming to you *en masse,* equal to sixty thousand fighting-men, will be a reënforcement that Lee cannot disregard. Indeed, with my present command, I had expected, after reducing Savannah, instantly to march to Columbia, South Carolina; thence to Raleigh, and thence to report to you. But this would consume, it may be, six weeks' time after the fall of Savannah; whereas, by sea, I can probably reach you with my men and arms before the middle of January.

I myself am somewhat astonished at the attitude of things in Tennessee. I purposely delayed at Kingston until General Thomas assured me that he was all ready, and my last dispatch from him of the 12th of November was full of confidence, in which he promised me that he would ruin Hood if he dared to advance from Florence, urging me to go ahead, and give myself no concern about Hood's army in Tennessee.

Why he did not turn on him at Franklin, after checking and discomfiting him, surpasses my understanding. Indeed, I do not approve of his evacuating Decatur, but think he should have assumed the offensive against Hood from Pulaski, in the direction of Waynesburg. I know full well that General Thomas is slow in mind and in action; but he is judicious and brave, and the troops feel great confidence in him. I still hope he will out-manœuvre and destroy Hood.

As to matters in the Southeast, I think Hardee, in Savannah, has good artillerists, some five or six thousand good infantry, and, it may be, a mongrel mass of eight to ten thousand militia. In all our marching through Georgia, he has not forced us to use any thing but a skirmish-line, though at several points he had erected fortifications and tried to alarm us by bombastic threats. In Savannah he has taken refuge in a line constructed behind swamps and overflowed rice-fields, extending from a point on the Savannah River about three miles above the city, around by a branch of the Little Ogeechee, which stream is impassable from its salt-marshes and boggy swamps, crossed only by narrow causeways or common corduroy-roads.

There must be twenty-five thousand citizens, men, women, and children, in Savannah, that must also be fed, and how he is to feed them beyond a few days I cannot imagine. I know that his requisitions for corn on the interior counties were not filled, and we are in possession of the rice-fields and mills, which could alone be of service to him in this neighborhood. He can draw nothing from South Carolina, save from a small corner down in the southeast, and that by a disused wagon-road. I could easily get possession of this, but hardly deem it worth the risk of making a detachment, which would be in danger by its isolation from the main army. Our whole army is in fine condition as to health, and the weather is splendid. For that reason alone I feel a personal dislike to turning northward. I will keep Lieutenant Dunn here until I know the result of my demand for the surrender of Savannah, but, whether successful or not, shall not delay my execution of your order of the 6th, which will depend alone upon the time it will require to obtain transportation by sea.

I am, with respect, etc., your obedient servant,
W. T. Sherman, *Major-General United States Army.*

Having concluded all needful preparations, I rode from my headquarters, on the plank-road, over to General Slocum's headquarters, on the Macon road, and thence dispatched (by flag of truce) into Savannah, by the hands of Colonel Ewing, inspector-general, a demand for the surrender of the place. The following letters give the result. General Hardee refused to surrender, and I then resolved to make the attempt to break his line of defense at several places, trusting that some one would succeed.

Headquarters Military Division of the Mississippi,
in the Field, Savannah, Georgia, *December* 17, 1864.

General William J. Hardee, *commanding Confederate Forces in Savannah.*

General: You have doubtless observed, from your station at Rosedew that sea-going vessels now come through Ossabaw Sound and up the Ogeechee to the rear of my army, giving me abundant supplies of all kinds, and more especially heavy ordnance necessary for the reduction of Savannah. I have already received guns that can cast heavy and destructive shot as far as the heart of your city; also, I have for some days held and controlled every avenue by which the people and garrison of Savannah can be supplied, and I am therefore justified in demanding the surrender of the city of Savannah, and its dependent forts, and shall wait a reasonable time for your answer, before opening with heavy ordnance. Should you entertain the proposition, I am prepared to grant liberal terms to the inhabitants and garrison; but should I be forced to resort to assault, or the slower and surer process of starvation, I shall then feel justified in resorting to the harshest measures, and shall make little effort to restrain my army—burning to avenge the national wrong which they attach to Savannah and other large cities which have been so prominent in dragging our country into civil war. I inclose you a copy of General Hood's demand for the surrender of the town of Resaca, to be used by you for what it is worth.

I have the honor to be your obedient servant,

W. T. Sherman, *Major-General.*

Headquarters Department South Carolina, Georgia, and Florida,
Savannah, Georgia, *December* 17, 1864.

Major-General W. T. Sherman, *commanding Federal Forces near Savannah, Georgia.*

General: I have to acknowledge the receipt of a communication from you of this date, in which you demand "the surrender of Savannah and its dependent forts," on the ground that you "have received guns that can cast heavy and destructive shot into the heart of the city," and for the further reason that you "have, for some days, held and controlled every avenue by which the people and garrison can be supplied." You add that, should you be "forced to resort to assault, or to the slower and surer process of starvation, you will then feel justified in resorting to the harshest measures, and will make little effort to restrain your army," etc., etc. The position of your forces (a half-mile beyond the outer line for the land-defense of Savannah) is, at the nearest point, at least four miles from the heart of the city. That and the interior line are both intact.

Your statement that you have, for some days, held and controlled every avenue by which the people and garrison can be supplied, is incorrect. I am in free and constant communication with my department.

Your demand for the surrender of Savannah and its dependent forts is refused.

With respect to the threats conveyed in the closing paragraphs of your letter (of what may be expected in case your demand is not complied with), I have to say that I have hitherto conducted the military operations intrusted to my direction in strict accordance with the rules of civilized warfare, and I should deeply regret the adoption of any course by you that may force me to deviate from them in future. I have the honor to be, very respectfully, your obedient servant,

W. J. Hardee, *Lieutenant-General.*

Headquarters Military Division of the Mississippi, in the Field, near Savannah, Georgia, *December* 18, 1864—8 p. m.

Lieutenant-General U. S. Grant, *City Point, Virginia.*

General: I wrote you at length (by Colonel Babcock) on the 16th instant. As I therein explained my purpose, yesterday I made a demand on General Hardee for the surrender of the city of Savannah, and to-day received his answer—refusing; copies of both letters are herewith inclosed. You will notice that I claim that my lines are within easy cannon-range of the heart of Savannah; but General Hardee asserts that we are four and a half miles distant. But I myself have been to the intersection of the Charleston and Georgia Central Railroads, and the three-mile post is but a few yards beyond, within the line of our pickets. The enemy has no pickets outside of his fortified line (which is a full quarter of a mile within the three-mile post), and I have the evidence of Mr. R. R. Cuyler, President of the Georgia Central Railroad (who was a prisoner in our hands), that the mile-posts are measured from the Exchange, which is but two squares back from the river. By to-morrow morning I will have six thirty-pound Parrotts in position, and General Hardee will learn whether I am right or not. From the left of our line, which is on the Savannah River, the spires can be plainly seen; but the country is so densely wooded with pine and live-oak, and lies so flat, that we can see nothing from any other portion of our lines. General Slocum feels confident that he can make a successful assault at one or two points in front of General Davis's (Fourteenth) corps. All of General Howard's troops (the right wing) lie behind the Little Ogeechee, and I doubt if it can be passed by troops in the face of an enemy. Still, we can make strong feints, and if I can get a sufficient number of boats, I shall make a coöperative demonstration up Vernon River or Wassaw Sound. I should like very much indeed to take Savannah before coming to you; but, as I wrote to you before, I will do nothing rash or hasty, and will embark for the James River as soon as General Easton (who is gone to Port Royal for that purpose) reports to me that he has an approximate number of vessels for the transportation of the contemplated force. I fear even this will cost more delay than you anticipate, for already the movement of our transports and the gunboats has required more time than I had expected. We have had dense fogs; there are more mud-banks in the Ogeechee than were reported, and there are no pilots whatever. Admiral Dahlgren promised to have the channel buoyed and staked, but it is not done yet. We find only six feet of water up to King's Bridge at low tide, about ten feet up to the rice-mill, and sixteen to Fort McAllister. All these points may be used by us, and we have a good, strong bridge across Ogeechee at King's, by which our wagons can go to Fort McAllister, to which point I am sending all wagons not absolutely necessary for daily use, the negroes, prisoners of war, sick, etc., *en route* for Port Royal. In relation to Savannah, you will remark that General Hardee refers to his still being in communication with his department. This language he thought would deceive me; but I am confirmed in the belief that the route to which he refers (the Union Plank-road on the South Carolina shore) is inadequate to feed his army and the people of Savannah, and General Foster assures me that he has his force on that very road, near the head of Broad River, so that cars no longer run between Charleston and Savannah. We hold this end of the Charleston Railroad, and have destroyed it from the three-mile post back to the bridge (about twelve miles). In anticipation of leaving this country, I am continuing the destruction of their railroads, and at this moment have two divisions and the cavalry at work breaking up the Gulf Railroad from the Ogeechee to the Altamaha; so that, even if I do not take Savannah, I will leave it in a bad way. But I still hope that events will give me time to take Savannah, even if I have to assault with some loss. I am satisfied that, unless we take it, the gunboats never will, for they can make no impression upon the batteries which guard every approach from the sea. I have a faint belief that, when Colonel Babcock reaches you, you will delay operations long enough to enable me to succeed here. With Savannah in our possession, at some future time if not now, we can punish South Carolina as she deserves, and as thousands of the people in Georgia hoped we would do. I do sincerely believe that the whole United States, North and South, would rejoice to have this army turned loose on South Carolina, to devastate that State in the manner we have done in Georgia, and it would have a direct and immediate bearing on your campaign in Virginia.

I have the honor to be your obedient servant,

W. T. Sherman, *Major-General United States Army.*

As soon as the army had reached Savannah, and had opened communication with the fleet, I endeavored to ascertain what had transpired in Tennessee since our departure. We received our letters and files of newspapers, which contained full accounts of all the events there up to about the 1st of December. As before described, General Hood had three full corps of infantry—S. D. Lee's, A. P. Stewart's, and Cheatham's,[47] at Florence, Alabama—with Forrest's corps of cavalry, numbering in the aggregate about forty-five thousand men. General Thomas was in Nashville, Tennessee, quietly engaged in reorganizing his army out of the somewhat broken forces at his disposal. He had posted his only two regular corps, the Fourth and Twenty-third, under the general command of Major-General J. M. Schofield, at Pulaski, directly in front of Florence, with the three brigades of cavalry (Hatch, Croxton, and Capron), commanded by Major-General Wilson, watching closely for Hood's initiative.

This force aggregated about thirty thousand men, was therefore inferior to the enemy; and General Schofield was instructed, in case the enemy made a general advance, to fall back slowly toward Nashville, fighting, till he should be reënforced by General Thomas in person. Hood's movement was probably hurried by reason of my advance into Georgia; for on the 17th his infantry columns marched from Florence in the direction of Waynesboro', turning Schofield's position at Pulaski. The latter at once sent his trains to the rear, and on the 21st fell back to Columbia, Tennessee. General Hood followed up this movement, skirmished lightly with Schofield at Columbia, began the passage of Duck River, below the town, and Cheatham's corps reached the vicinity of Spring Hill, whither General Schofield had sent General Stanley, with two of his divisions, to cover the movement of his trains. During the night of November 29th General Schofield passed Spring Hill with his trains and army,

[47] Benjamin F. Cheatham (1820–1886) joined the Confederate Army as a brigadier general at the start of the war and commanded the 1st Corps, Army of Tennessee, in Dec. 1864. *CWHC,* 170–171.

and took post at Franklin, on the south side of Harpeth River. General Hood now attaches serious blame to General Cheatham for not attacking General Schofield in flank while in motion at Spring Hill, for he was bivouacked within eight hundred yards of the road at the time of the passage of our army.[48] General Schofield reached Franklin on the morning of November 30th, and posted his army in front of the town, where some rifle-intrenchments had been constructed in advance. He had the two corps of Stanley and Cox (Fourth and Twenty-third), with Wilson's cavalry on his flanks, and sent his trains behind the Harpeth.

General Hood closed upon him the same day, and assaulted his position with vehemence, at one time breaking the line and wounding General Stanley seriously; but our men were veterans, cool and determined, and fought magnificently.[49] The rebel officers led their men in person to the several persistent assaults, continuing the battle far into the night, when they drew off, beaten and discomfited.

Their loss was very severe, especially in general officers; among them Generals Cleburn and Adams, division commanders.[50] Hood's loss on that day was afterward ascertained to be (Thomas's report): Buried on the field, seventeen hundred and fifty; left in hospital at Franklin, thirty-eight hundred; and seven hundred and two prisoners captured and held: aggregate, six thousand two hundred and fifty-two. General Schofield's loss, reported officially, was one hundred and eighty-nine killed, one thousand and thirty-three wounded, and eleven hundred and four prisoners or missing: aggregate,

[48] In his autobiography, Confederate general John B. Hood provided his perspective on the failure to attack Schofield at Spring Hill. "I at once directed Stewart to halt, and turning to Cheatham, I exclaimed with deep emotion, as I felt the golden opportunity fast slipping from me, 'General, why in the name of God have you not attacked the enemy, and taken possession of that pike?' He replied that the line looked a little too long for him, and that Stewart should form on his right. I could hardly believe it possible that this brave old soldier, who had given proof of such courage and ability upon so many hard-fought fields, would even make such a report." John B. Hood, *Advance and Retreat: Personal Experiences in the United States and Confederate States Armies* (New Orleans: G. T. Beauregard, 1880), 286.

[49] Gen. David S. Stanley was wounded in the neck during the assault on Nov. 30. He survived the injury and soon returned to service. *CWHC*, 504–505.

[50] Patrick R. Cleburne (1828–1864) was born in Ireland and immigrated to the United States in 1849. He was shot in the abdomen and died from his wounds. John Adams (1825–1864) graduated from the USMA in 1846 and was shot and killed while trying to attack the U.S. Army's defenses. *CWHC*, 99.

twenty-three hundred and twenty-six. The next day General Schofield crossed the Harpeth without trouble, and fell back to the defenses of Nashville.

Meantime General Thomas had organized the employés of the Quartermaster's Department into a corps, commanded by the chief-quartermaster, General J. L. Donaldson, and placed them in the fortifications of Nashville, under the general direction of Major-General Z. B. Tower, now of the United States Engineers. He had also received the two veteran divisions of the Sixteenth Corps, under General A. J. Smith, long absent and long expected; and he had drawn from Chattanooga and Decatur (Alabama) the divisions of Steedman and of R. S. Granger. These, with General Schofield's army and about ten thousand good cavalry, under General J. H. Wilson, constituted a strong army, capable not only of defending Nashville, but of beating Hood in the open field. Yet Thomas remained inside of Nashville, seemingly passive, until General Hood had closed upon him and had intrenched his position.

General Thomas had furthermore held fast to the railroad leading from Nashville to Chattanooga, leaving strong guards at its principal points, as at Murfreesboro', Deckerd, Stevenson, Bridgeport, Whitesides, and Chattanooga. At Murfreesboro' the division of Rousseau was reënforced and strengthened up to about eight thousand men.

At that time the weather was cold and sleety, the ground was covered with ice and snow, and both parties for a time rested on the defensive. Thus matters stood at Nashville, while we were closing down on Savannah, in the early part of December, 1864; and the country, as well as General Grant, was alarmed at the seeming passive conduct of General Thomas; and General Grant at one time considered the situation so dangerous that he thought of going to Nashville in person, but General John A. Logan, happening to be at City Point, was sent out to supersede General Thomas; luckily for the latter, he acted in time, gained a magnificent victory, and thus escaped so terrible a fate.[51]

On the 18th of December, at my camp by the side of the plank-road, eight miles back of Savannah, I received General Hardee's letter declining to surrender, when nothing remained but to assault. The ground was difficult, and, as all former assaults had proved so bloody, I concluded to make one more effort to completely surround Savannah on all sides, so as further to excite Hardee's fears, and, in case of success, to capture the whole of his army. We had already completely invested the place on the north, west, and south, but

[51] Logan started for Nashville, TN, on Dec. 13. Thomas, however, attacked the Confederate forces on Dec. 15. As a result, Logan, who had reached Louisville, KY, was ordered to return to Washington, DC. *PUSG,* 12:127–128*n.*

there remained to the enemy, on the east, the use of the old dike or plank-road leading into South Carolina, and I knew that Hardee would have a pontoon-bridge across the river. On examining my maps, I thought that the division of John P. Hatch,[52] belonging to General Foster's command, might be moved from its then position at Broad River, by water, down to Bluffton, from which it could reach this plank-road, fortify and hold it—at some risk, of course, because Hardee could avail himself of his central position to fall on this detachment with his whole army. I did not want to make a mistake like "Ball's Bluff"[53] at that period of the war; so, taking one or two of my personal staff, I rode back to King's Bridge, leaving with Generals Howard and Slocum orders to make all possible preparations, but not to attack, during my two or three days' absence; and there I took a boat for Wassaw Sound, whence Admiral Dahlgren conveyed me in his own boat (the Harvest Moon) to Hilton Head, where I represented the matter to General Foster, and he promptly agreed to give his personal attention to it. During the night of the 20th we started back, the wind blowing strong, Admiral Dahlgren ordered the pilot[54] of the Harvest Moon to run into Tybee, and to work his way through to Wassaw Sound and the Ogeechee River by the Romney Marshes. We were caught by a low tide and stuck in the mud. After laboring some time, the admiral ordered out his barge; in it we pulled through this intricate and shallow channel, and toward evening of December 21st we discovered, coming toward us, a tug, called the Red Legs, belonging to the Quartermaster's Department, with a staff-officer on board, bearing letters from Colonel Dayton to myself and the admiral, reporting that the city of Savannah had been found evacuated on the morning of December 21st, and was then in our possession. General Hardee had crossed the Savannah River by a pontoon-bridge, carrying off his men and light artillery, blowing up his iron-clads and navy-yard, but leaving for us all the heavy guns, stores, cotton, railway-cars, steamboats, and an immense amount of public and private property. Admiral Dahlgren

[52] John P. Hatch (1822–1901) graduated from the USMA in 1845 and received a Medal of Honor for his actions at South Mountain, MD, in Sept. 1862. *CWHC,* 287.

[53] On Oct 21, 1861, U.S. Army forces were severely defeated by Confederate forces at the Battle of Ball's Bluff near Leesburg, VA. The defeat led to the establishment of the Joint Committee on the Conduct of the War. Spencer C. Tucker, *Almanac of American Military History* (Santa Barbara: ABC-CLIO, 2012), s.v. "October 21, 1861."

[54] John K. Crosby (1831–1904) took command of the *Harvest Moon* on Oct. 7, 1864. "Dared Many Perils: Capt. John K. Crosby, Old-Time Shipmaster, Passes Away," *Little River Monitor* (Little River, KS), Oct. 20, 1904, 2.

concluded to go toward a vessel (the Sonoma) of his blockading fleet, which lay at anchor near Beaulieu, and I transferred to the Red Legs, and hastened up the Ogeechee River to King's Bridge, whence I rode to my camp that same night. I there learned that, early on the morning of December 21st, the skirmishers had detected the absence of the enemy, and had occupied his lines simultaneously along their whole extent; but the left flank (Slocum), especially Geary's division of the Twentieth Corps, claimed to have been the first to reach the heart of the city.

Generals Slocum and Howard moved their headquarters at once into the city, leaving the bulk of their troops in camps outside. On the morning of December 22d I followed with my own headquarters, and rode down Bull Street to the custom-house, from the roof of which we had an extensive view over the city, the river, and the vast extent of marsh and rice-fields on the South Carolina side. The navy-yard, and the wreck of the iron-clad ram Savannah, were still smouldering, but all else looked quiet enough. Turning back, we rode to the Pulaski Hotel, which I had known in years long gone, and found it kept by a Vermont man with a lame leg, who used to be a clerk in the St. Louis Hotel, New Orleans, and I inquired about the capacity of his hotel for headquarters.[55] He was very anxious to have us for boarders, but I soon explained to him that we had a full mess equipment along, and that we were not in the habit of paying board; that one wing of the building would suffice for our use, while I would allow him to keep an hotel for the accommodation of officers and gentlemen in the remainder. I then dispatched an officer to look around for a livery-stable that could accommodate our horses, and, while waiting there, an English gentleman, Mr. Charles Green,[56] came and said that he had a fine house completely furnished, for which he had no use, and offered it as headquarters. He explained, moreover, that General Howard had informed him, the day before, that I would want his house for headquarters. At first I felt strongly disinclined to make use of any private dwelling, lest complaints should arise of damage and loss of furniture, and so expressed myself to Mr. Green; but, after riding about the city, and finding

[55] The Pulaski Hotel, built around 1839, was located at the corner of Bull and West Bryan Streets in Savannah. WTS visited the hotel while he was stationed at Fort Moultrie, SC, in the mid-1840s. Hitchcock, *Marching with Sherman,* 198–199; Whip M. Triplett, *Postcard History Series: Savannah* (Charleston, SC: Arcadia, 2006), 25.

[56] Charles Green (1807–1881) was born in England and in 1826 moved to the United States, where he became a prominent lawyer in Savannah. "Death of Charles Green," *Savannah Morning News,* Aug. 17, 1881, 4.

his house so spacious, so convenient, with large yard and stabling, I accepted his offer, and occupied that house during our stay in Savannah. He only reserved for himself the use of a couple of rooms above the dining-room, and we had all else, and a most excellent house it was in all respects.[57]

I was disappointed that Hardee had escaped with his army, but on the whole we had reason to be content with the substantial fruits of victory. The Savannah River was found to be badly obstructed by torpedoes, and by log piers stretched across the channel below the city, which piers were filled with the cobble stones that formerly paved the streets. Admiral Dahlgren was extremely active, visited me repeatedly in the city, while his fleet still watched Charleston, and all the avenues, for the blockade-runners that infested the coast, which were notoriously owned and managed by Englishmen, who used the island of New Providence (Nassau) as a sort of entrepot. One of these small blockade-runners came into Savannah after we were in full possession, and the master did not discover his mistake till he came ashore to visit the custom-house.[58] Of course his vessel fell a prize to the navy. A heavy force was at once set to work to remove the torpedoes and obstructions in the main channel of the river, and, from that time forth, Savannah became the great depot of supply for the troops operating in that quarter.

Meantime, on the 15th and 16th of December, were fought, in front of Nashville, the great battles in which General Thomas so nobly fulfilled his promise to ruin Hood, the details of which are fully given in his own official reports, long since published.[59] Rumors of these great victories reached us at Savannah by piecemeal, but his official report came on the 24th of December, with a letter from General Grant, giving in general terms the events up to the 18th, and I wrote at once through my chief of staff, General Webster, to General Thomas, complimenting him in the highest terms. His brilliant victory at Nashville was necessary to mine at Savannah to make a complete whole, and this fact was perfectly comprehended by Mr. Lincoln, who recognized it fully in his personal letter of December 26th, hereinbefore quoted at length, and which is also claimed at the time, in my Special Field Order No. 6, of January 8, 1865, here given:

[57] In 1853 Green paid approximately $93,000 to construct the house located on Macon Street. Peter Beney, *The Majesty of Savannah* (Gretna, LA: Pelican, 1992), 32.

[58] The *Acacia,* commanded by William Barrymore, captured the English-built blockade runner *Julia* near Port Royal, SC, on Dec. 23. Davis et al., *Official Military Atlas of the Civil War,* plate 144; *ORN,* I, 143–145.

[59] See *OR,* I, 45(I), 32–59.

[Special Field Order No. 6.]

HEADQUARTERS MILITARY DIVISION OF THE MISSISSIPPI,
IN THE FIELD, SAVANNAH, GEORGIA, *January* 8, 1865.

The general commanding announces to the troops composing the Military Division of the Mississippi that he has received from the President of the United States, and from Lieutenant-General Grant, letters conveying their high sense and appreciation of the campaign just closed, resulting in the capture of Savannah and the defeat of Hood's army in Tennessee.

In order that all may understand the importance of events, it is proper to revert to the situation of affairs in September last. We held Atlanta, a city of little value to us, but so important to the enemy that Mr. Davis, the head of the rebellious faction in the South, visited his army near Palmetto, and commanded it to regain the place and also to ruin and destroy us, by a series of measures which he thought would be effectual. That army, by a rapid march, gained our railroad near Big Shanty, and afterward about Dalton. We pursued it, but it moved so rapidly that we could not overtake it, and General Hood led his army successfully far over toward Mississippi, in hope to decoy us out of Georgia. But we were not thus to be led away by him, and preferred to lead and control events ourselves. Generals Thomas and Schofield, commanding the departments to our rear, returned to their posts and prepared to decoy General Hood into their meshes, while we came on to complete the original journey. We quietly and deliberately destroyed Atlanta, and all the railroads which the enemy had used to carry on war against us, occupied his State capital, and then captured his commercial capital, which had been so strongly fortified from the sea as to defy approach from that quarter. Almost at the moment of our victorious entry into Savannah came the welcome and expected news that our comrades in Tennessee had also fulfilled nobly and well their part, had decoyed General Hood to Nashville and then turned on him, defeating his army thoroughly, capturing all his artillery, great numbers of prisoners, and were still pursuing the fragments down in Alabama. So complete a success in military operations, extending over half a continent, is an achievement that entitles it to a place in the military history of the world. The armies

> serving in Georgia and Tennessee, as well as the local garrisons of Decatur, Bridgeport, Chattanooga, and Murfreesboro', are alike entitled to the common honors, and each regiment may inscribe on its colors, at pleasure, the word "Savannah" or "Nashville." The general commanding embraces, in the same general success, the operations of the cavalry under Generals Stoneman, Burbridge, and Gillem, that penetrated into Southwest Virginia, and paralyzed the efforts of the enemy to disturb the peace and safety of East Tennessee. Instead of being put on the defensive, we have at all points assumed the bold offensive, and have completely thwarted the designs of the enemies of our country.
>
> By order of Major-General W. T. Sherman,
>
> L. M. Dayton, *Aide-de-Camp.*

Here terminated the "March to the Sea," and I only add a few letters, selected out of many, to illustrate the general feeling of rejoicing throughout the country at the time. I only regarded the march from Atlanta to Savannah as a "shift of base," as the transfer of a strong army, which had no opponent, and had finished its then work, from the interior to a point on the sea-coast, from which it could achieve other important results. I considered this march as a means to an end, and not as an essential act of war. Still, then, as now, the march to the sea was generally regarded as something extraordinary, something anomalous, something out of the usual order of events; whereas, in fact, I simply moved from Atlanta to Savannah, as one step in the direction of Richmond, a movement that had to be met and defeated, or the war was necessarily at an end.

Were I to express my measure of the relative importance of the march to the sea, and of that from Savannah northward, I would place the former at one, and the latter at ten, or the maximum.

I now close this long chapter by giving a tabular statement of the losses during the march, and the number of prisoners captured. The property captured consisted of horses and mules by the thousand, and of quantities of subsistence stores that aggregate very large, but may be measured with sufficient accuracy by assuming that sixty-five thousand men obtained abundant food for about forty days, and thirty-five thousand animals were fed for a like period, so as to reach Savannah in splendid flesh and condition. I also add a few of the more important letters that passed between Generals Grant, Halleck, and myself, which illustrate our opinions at that stage of the war:

STATEMENT OF CASUALITIES AND PRISONERS CAPTURED BY THE ARMY IN THE FIELD, CAMPAIGN OF GEORGIA.

	KILLED.		W'UND'D.		MISSING.			CAPTURED.		
COMMANDS.	Commissioned Officers.	Enlisted Men.	Commissioned Officers.	Enlisted Men.	Commissioned Officers.	Enlisted Men.	Aggregate.	Commissioned Officers.	Enlisted Men.	Aggregate.
Right Wing, Army of the Tennessee, Major-General O.O. Howard commanding........	5	35	11	172	....	19	242	34	632	666
Left Wing, Fourteenth and Twentieth Corps, Major-General H.W. Slocum commanding...	2	23	6	112	1	258	402	30	409	439
Cavalry Division, Brigadier-General J. Kilpatrick commanding..........................	3	35	7	120	....	....	120	13	220	233
Total.............................	10	93	24	404	1	277	764	77	1,261	1,338

L. M. Dayton, *Assistant Adjutant-General.*

Headquarters of the Army,
Washington, *December* 16, 1864.

Major-General Sherman *(via Hilton Head).*

General: Lieutenant-General Grant informs me that, in his last dispatch sent to you, he suggested the transfer of your infantry to Richmond. He now wishes me to say that you will retain your entire force, at least for the present, and, with such assistance as may be given you by General Foster and Admiral Dahlgren, operate from such base as you may establish on the coast. General Foster will obey such instructions as may be given by you.

Should you have captured Savannah, it is thought that by transferring the water-batteries to the land side that place may be made a good depot and base of operations on Augusta, Branchville, or Charleston. If Savannah should not be captured, or if captured and not deemed suitable for this purpose, perhaps Beaufort would serve as a depot. As the rebels have probably removed their most valuable property from Augusta, perhaps Branchville would be the most important point at which to strike in order to sever all connection between Virginia and the Southwestern Railroad.

General Grant's wishes, however, are, that this whole matter of your future actions should be entirely left to your discretion.

We can send you from here a number of complete batteries of field-artillery, with or without horses, as you may desire; also, as soon as General Thomas can spare them, all the fragments, convalescents, and furloughed men of your army. It is reported that Thomas defeated Hood yesterday, near Nashville, but we have no particulars nor official reports, telegraphic communication being interrupted by a heavy storm.

Our last advices from you was General Howard's note, announcing his approach to Savannah. Yours truly,

H. W. Halleck, *Major-General, Chief-of-Staff.*

Headquarters of the Army,
Washington, *December* 18, 1864.

Major-General W. T. Sherman, *Savannah (via Hilton Head).*

My dear General: Yours of the 13th, by Major Anderson, is just received. I congratulate you on your splendid success, and shall very soon expect to hear of the crowning work of your campaign—the capture of Savannah. Your march will stand out prominently as the great one of this great war. When Savannah falls, then for another wide swath through the centre of the Confederacy. But I will not anticipate. General Grant is expected here this morning, and will probably write you his own views.

I do not learn from your letter, or from Major Anderson, that you are in want of any thing which we have not provided at Hilton Head. Thinking it probable that you might want more field-artillery, I had prepared several batteries, but the great difficulty of foraging horses on the sea-coast will prevent our sending any unless you actually need them. The hay-crop this year is short, and the Quartermaster's Department has great difficulty in procuring a supply for our animals.

General Thomas has defeated Hood, near Nashville, and it is hoped that he will completely crush his army. Breckenridge, at last accounts, was trying to form a junction near Murfreesboro', but, as Thomas is between them, Breckenridge must either retreat or be defeated.

General Rosecrans made very bad work of it in Missouri, allowing Price with a small force to overrun the State and destroy millions of property.

Orders have been issued for all officers and detachments having three months or more to serve, to rejoin your army *via* Savannah. Those having less than three months to serve, will be retained by General Thomas.

Should you capture Charleston, I hope that by *some accident* the place may be destroyed, and, if a little salt should be sown upon its site, it may prevent the growth of future crops of nullification and secession.

Yours truly,
H. W. HALLECK, *Major-General, Chief-of-Staff.*

[CONFIDENTIAL]

HEADQUARTERS ARMIES OF THE UNITED STATES,
WASHINGTON, D. C., *December* 18, 1864.

To Major-General W. T. SHERMAN, *commanding Military Division of the Mississippi.*

MY DEAR GENERAL: I have just received and read, I need not tell you with how much gratification, your letter to General Halleck. I congratulate you and the brave officers and men under your command on the successful termination of your most brilliant campaign. I never had a doubt of the result. When apprehensions for your safety were expressed by the President, I assured him with the army you had, and you in command of it, there was no danger but you would *strike* bottom on salt-water some place; that I would not feel the same security—in fact, would not have intrusted the expedition to any other living commander.

It has been very hard work to get Thomas to attack Hood. I gave him the most peremptory order, and had started to go there myself, before he got off. He has done magnificently, however, since he started. Up to last night, five thousand prisoners and forty-nine pieces of captured artillery, besides many wagons and innumerable small-arms, had been received in Nashville. This is exclusive of the enemy's loss at Franklin, which amounted to thirteen general officers killed, wounded, and captured. The enemy probably lost five thousand men at Franklin, and ten thousand in the last three days' operations. Breckenridge is said to be making for Murfreesboro'.

I think he is in a most excellent place. Stoneman has nearly wiped out John Morgan's old command, and five days ago entered Bristol. I did think the best thing to do was to bring the greater part of your army here, and wipe out Lee. The turn affairs now seem to be taking has shaken me in that opinion. I doubt whether you may not accomplish more toward that result where you are than if brought here, especially as I am informed, since my arrival in the city, that it would take about two months to get you here with all the other calls there are for ocean transportation.

I want to get your views about what ought to be done, and what can be done. If you capture the garrison of Savannah, it certainly will compel Lee to detach from Richmond, or give us nearly the whole South. My own opinion is that Lee is averse to going out of Virginia, and if the cause of the South is lost he wants Richmond to be the last place surrendered. If he has such views, it may be well to indulge him until we get every thing else in our hands.

Congratulating you and the army again upon the splendid results of your campaign, the like of which is not read of in past history, I subscribe myself, more than ever, if possible, your friend,

U. S. Grant, *Lieutenant-General.*

Headquarters Armies of the United States,
City Point, Virginia, *December* 26, 1864.

Major-General W. T. Sherman, *Savannah, Georgia.*

General: Your very interesting letter of the 22d inst., brought by Major Gray, of General Foster's staff, is just at hand. As the major starts back at once, I can do no more at present than simply acknowledge its receipt. The capture of Savannah, with all its immense stores, must tell upon the people of the South. All well here.

Yours truly,

U. S. Grant, *Lieutenant-General.*

Headquarters Military Division of the Mississippi,
Savannah, Georgia, *December* 24, 1864.

Lieutenant-General U. S. Grant, *City Point, Virginia.*

General: Your letter of December 18th is just received. I feel very much gratified at receiving the handsome commendation you pay my army. I will, in general orders, convey to the officers and men the substance of your note.

I am also pleased that you have modified your former orders, for I feared that the transportation by sea would very much disturb the unity and *morale* of my army, now so perfect.

The occupation of Savannah, which I have heretofore reported, completes the first part of our game, and fulfills a great part of your instructions; and we are now engaged in dismantling the rebel forts which bear upon the sea-channels, and transferring the heavy ordnance and ammunition to Fort Pulaski and Hilton Head, where they can be more easily guarded than if left in the city.

The rebel inner lines are well adapted to our purpose, and with slight modifications can be held by a comparatively small force; and in about ten days I expect to be ready to sally forth again. I feel no doubt whatever as to our future plans. I have thought them over so long and well that they appear as clear as daylight. I left Augusta untouched on purpose, because the enemy will be in doubt as to my objective point, after we cross the Savannah River, whether it be Augusta or Charleston, and will naturally divide his forces. I will then move either on Branchville or Columbia, by any curved line that gives us the best supplies, breaking up in our course as much railroad as possible; then, ignoring Charleston and Augusta both, I would occupy Columbia and Camden, pausing there long enough to observe the effect. I would then strike for the Charleston & Wilmington Railroad, somewhere between the Santee and Cape Fear Rivers, and, if possible, communicate with the fleet under Admiral Dahlgren (whom I find a most agreeable gentleman, accommodating himself to our wishes and plans). Then I would favor an attack on Wilmington, in the belief that Porter and Butler will fail in their present undertaking. Charleston is now a mere desolated wreck, and is hardly worth the time it would take to starve it out. Still, I am aware that, historically and politically, much importance is attached to the place, and it may be that, apart from its military importance, both you and the Administration may prefer I should give it more attention; and it would be well for you to give me some general idea on that subject, for otherwise I would treat it as I have expressed, as a point of little importance, after all its railroads leading into the interior have been destroyed or occupied by us. But, on the hypothesis of ignoring Charleston and taking Wilmington, I would then favor a movement direct on Raleigh. The game is then up with Lee, unless he comes out of Richmond, avoids you and fights me; in which case I should reckon on your being on his heels. Now that Hood is used up by Thomas, I feel disposed to bring the matter to an issue as quick as possible. I feel confident that I can break up the whole railroad system of South Carolina and North Carolina, and be on the Roanoke, either at Raleigh or Weldon, by the time spring fairly opens; and, if you feel confident that you can whip Lee outside of his intrenchments, I feel equally confident that I can handle him in the open country.

One reason why I would ignore Charleston is this: that I believe Hardee will reduce the garrison to a small force, with plenty of provisions; I know that the neck back of Charleston can be made impregnable to assault, and we will hardly have time for siege operations.

I will have to leave in Savannah a garrison, and, if Thomas can spare them, I would like to have all detachments, convalescents, etc., belonging to these four corps, sent forward at once. I do not want to cripple Thomas, because I regard his operations as all-important, and I have ordered him to pursue Hood down into Alabama, trusting to the country for supplies.

I reviewed one of my corps to-day, and shall continue to review the whole army. I do not like to boast, but believe this army has a confidence in itself that makes it almost invincible. I wish you could run down and see us; it would have a good effect, and show to both armies that they are acting on a common plan. The weather is now cool and pleasant, and the general health very good. Your true friend,

W. T. SHERMAN, *Major-General.*

HEADQUARTERS MILITARY DIVISION OF THE MISSISSIPPI,
IN THE FIELD, SAVANNAH, *December* 24, 1864.

Major-General H. W. HALLECK, *Chief-of-Staff, Washington, D. C.*

GENERAL: I had the pleasure of receiving your two letters of the 16th and 18th instant to-day, and feel more than usually flattered by the high encomiums you have passed on our recent campaign, which is now complete by the occupation of Savannah.

I am also very glad that General Grant has changed his mind about embarking my troops for James River, leaving me free to make the broad swath you describe through South and North Carolina, and still more gratified at the news from Thomas, in Tennessee, because it fulfills my plans, which contemplated his being able to dispose of Hood, in case he ventured north of the Tennessee River. So, I think, on the whole, I can chuckle over Jeff. Davis's disappointment in not turning my Atlanta campaign into a "Moscow disaster."

I have just finished a long letter to General Grant, and have explained to him that we are engaged in shifting our base from the Ogeechee to the Savannah River, dismantling all the forts made by the enemy to bear upon the salt-water channels, transferring the heavy ordnance, etc., to Fort Pulaski and Hilton Head, and in remodeling the enemy's interior lines to suit our future plans and purposes. I have also laid down the programme for a campaign which I can make this winter, and which will put me in the spring on the Roanoke, in direct communication with General Grant on James River. In general terms, my plan is to turn over to General Foster the city of Savannah, to sally forth with my army resupplied, cross the Savannah, feign on Charleston and Augusta, but strike between, breaking *en route* the Charleston & Augusta Railroad, also a large part of that from Branchville and Camden toward North Carolina, and then rapidly to move for some point of the railroad from Charleston to Wilmington, between the Santee and Cape Fear Rivers; then, communicating with the fleet in the neighborhood of Georgetown, I would turn upon Wilmington or Charleston, according to the importance of either. I rather prefer Wilmington, as a live place, over Charleston, which is dead and unimportant when its railroad communications are broken. I take it for granted that the present movement on Wilmington will fail. If I should determine to take Charleston, I would turn across the country (which I have hunted over many a time) from Santee to Mount Pleasant, throwing one wing on the peninsula between the Ashley and Cooper. After accomplishing one or other of these ends, I would make a bee-line for Raleigh or Weldon, when Lee would be forced to come out of Richmond, or acknowledge himself beaten. He would, I think, by the use of the Danville Railroad, throw himself rapidly between me and Grant, leaving Richmond in the hands of the latter. This would not alarm me, for I have an army which I think can manœuvre, and I would force him to attack me at a disadvantage, always under the supposition that Grant would be on his heels; and, if the worst come to the worst, I can fight my way down to Albermarle Sound, or Newbern.

I think the time has come now when we should attempt the boldest moves, and my experience is, that they are easier of execution than more timid ones, because the enemy is disconcerted by them—as, for instance, my recent campaign.

I also doubt the wisdom of concentration beyond a certain extent, for the roads of this country limit the amount of men that can be brought to bear in any one battle, and I do not believe that any one general can handle more than sixty thousand men in battle.

I think our campaign of the last month, as well as every step I take from this point northward, is as much a direct attack upon Lee's army as though we were operating within the sound of his artillery.

I am very anxious that Thomas should follow up his success to the very utmost point. My orders to him before I left Kingston were, after beating Hood, to follow him as far as Columbus, Mississippi, or Selma, Alabama, both of which lie in districts of country which are rich in corn and meat.

I attach more importance to these deep incisions into the enemy's country, because this war differs from European wars in this particular: we are not only fighting hostile armies, but a hostile people, and must make old and young, rich and poor, feel the hard hand of war, as well as their organized armies. I know that this recent movement of mine through Georgia has had a wonderful effect in this respect. Thousands who had been deceived by their lying newspapers to believe that we were being whipped all the time now realize the truth, and have no appetite for a repetition of the same experience. To be sure, Jeff. Davis has his people under pretty good discipline, but I think faith in him is much shaken in Georgia, and before we have done with her South Carolina will not be quite so tempestuous.

I will bear in mind your hint as to Charleston, and do not think "salt" will be necessary. When I move, the Fifteenth Corps will be on the right of the right wing, and their position will naturally bring them into Charleston first; and, if you have watched the history of that corps, you will have remarked that they generally do their work pretty well. The truth is, the whole army is burning with an insatiable desire to wreak vengeance upon South Carolina. I almost tremble at her fate, but feel that she deserves all that seems in store for her.

Many and many a person in Georgia asked me why we did not go to South Carolina; and, when I answered that we were *en route* for that State, the invariable reply was, "Well, if you will make those people feel the utmost severities of war, we will pardon you for your desolation of Georgia."

I look upon Columbia as quite as bad as Charleston, and I doubt if we shall spare the public buildings there as we did at Milledgeville.

I have been so busy lately that I have not yet made my official report, and I think I had better wait until I get my subordinate reports before attempting it, as I am anxious to explain clearly not only the reasons for every step, but the amount of execution done, and this I cannot do until I get the subordinate reports; for we marched the whole distance in four or more columns, and, of course, I could only be present with one, and generally that one engaged in destroying railroads. This work of destruction was performed better than usual, because I had an engineer-regiment, provided with claws to twist the bars after being heated. Such bars can never be used again, and the only way in which a railroad line can be reconstructed across Georgia is, to make a new road from Fairburn Station (twenty-four miles southwest of Atlanta) to Madison, a distance of one hundred miles; and, before that can be done, I propose to be on the road from Augusta to Charleston, which is a continuation of the same. I felt somewhat disappointed at Hardee's escape, but really am not to blame. I moved as quickly as possible to close up the "Union Causeway," but intervening obstacles were such that, before I could get troops on the road, Hardee had slipped out. Still, I know that the men that were in Savannah will be lost in a measure to Jeff. Davis, for the Georgia troops, under G. W. Smith, declared they would not fight in South Carolina, and they have gone north, *en route* for Augusta, and I have reason to believe the North Carolina troops have gone to Wilmington; in other words, they are scattered. I have reason to believe that Beauregard was present in Savannah at the time of its evacuation, and think that he and Hardee are now in Charleston, making preparations for what they suppose will be my next step.

Please say to the President that I have received his kind message (through Colonel Markland), and feel thankful for his high favor. If I disappoint him in the future, it shall not be from want of zeal or love to the cause.

From you I expect a full and frank criticism of my plans for the future, which may enable me to correct errors before it is too late. I do not wish to be rash, but want to give my rebel friends no chance to accuse us of want of enterprise or courage.

Assuring you of my high personal respect, I remain, as ever,

your friend,

W. T. Sherman, *Major-General.*

[General Order No. 3.]

War Department, Adjutant-General's Office,
Washington, *January* 14, 1865.

The following resolution of the Senate and House of Representatives is published to the army:

[Public Resolution—No. 4.]

Joint resolution tendering the thanks of the people and of Congress to Major-General William T. Sherman, and the officers and soldiers of his command, for their gallant conduct in their late brilliant movement through Georgia.

Be it resolved by the Senate and House of Representatives of the United States of America in Congress assembled, That the thanks of the people and of the Congress of the United States are due and are hereby tendered to Major-General William T. Sherman, and through him to the officers and men under his command, for their gallantry and good conduct in their late campaign from Chattanooga to Atlanta, and the triumphal march thence through Georgia to Savannah, terminating in the capture and occupation of that city; and that the President cause a copy of this joint resolution to be engrossed and forwarded to Major-General Sherman. Approved, January 10, 1865.

By order of the Secretary of War,
W. A. Nichols, *Assistant Adjutant-General.*

22

Savannah and Pocotaligo.

DECEMBER, 1864, AND JANUARY, 1865.

THE CITY OF SAVANNAH was an old place, and usually accounted a handsome one. Its houses were of brick or frame, with large yards, ornamented with shrubbery and flowers; its streets perfectly regular, crossing each other at right angles; and at many of the intersections were small inclosures in the nature of parks. These streets and parks were lined with the handsomest shade-trees of which I have knowledge, viz., the willow-leaf live-oak, evergreens of exquisite beauty; and these certainly entitled Savannah to its reputation as a handsome town more than the houses, which, though comfortable, would hardly make a display on Fifth Avenue or the Boulevard Haussmann of Paris. The city was built on a plateau of sand about forty feet above the level of the sea, abutting against the river, leaving room along its margin for a street of stores and warehouses. The custom-house, court-house, post-office, etc., were on the plateau above. In rear of Savannah was a large park, with a fountain, and between it and the court-house was a handsome monument, erected to the memory of Count Pulaski, who fell in 1779 in the assault made on the city at the time it was held by the English during the Revolutionary War.[1] Outside of Savannah there was very little to interest a stranger, except the cemetery of Bonaventura, and the ride along the Wilmington Channel by way of Thunderbolt, where might be seen some groves of the majestic live-oak trees, covered with gray and funereal

[1] Casimir Pulaski (c. 1745–1779) was born in Poland and moved to America in 1777. He was killed during the siege of Savannah on Oct. 11, 1779. The citizens of Savannah erected a statue of him on Jan. 6, 1855. *The National Cyclopedia of American Biography Being the History of the United States* (New York: James T. White, 1898), vol. 1, s.v. "Pulaski, Casimir."

moss, which were truly sublime in grandeur, but gloomy after a few days' camping under them.[2]

Within an hour of taking up my quarters in Mr. Green's house, Mr. A. G. Browne, of Salem, Massachusetts, United States Treasury agent for the Department of the South,[3] made his appearance to claim possession, in the name of the Treasury Department, of all captured cotton, rice, buildings, etc. Having use for these articles ourselves, and having fairly earned them, I did not feel inclined to surrender possession, and explained to him that the quartermaster and commissary could manage them more to my liking than he; but I agreed, after the proper inventories had been prepared, if there remained any thing for which we had no special use, I would turn it over to him. It was then known that in the warehouses were stored at least twenty-five thousand bales of cotton, and in the forts one hundred and fifty large, heavy sea-coast guns; although afterward, on a more careful count, there proved to be more than two hundred and fifty sea-coast or siege guns, and thirty-one thousand bales of cotton. At that interview Mr. Browne, who was a shrewd, clever Yankee, told me that a vessel was on the point of starting for Old Point Comfort, and, if she had good weather off Cape Hatteras, would reach Fortress Monroe by Christmas-day, and he suggested that I might make it the occasion of sending a welcome Christmas gift to the President, Mr. Lincoln, who peculiarly enjoyed such pleasantry. I accordingly sat down and wrote on a slip of paper, to be left at the telegraph-office at Fortress Monroe for transmission, the following:

SAVANNAH, GEORGIA, *December* 22, 1864.

To His Excellency President LINCOLN, *Washington, D. C.:*

I beg to present you as a Christmas-gift the city of Savannah, with one hundred and fifty heavy guns and plenty of ammunition, also about twenty-five thousand bales of cotton.

W. T. SHERMAN, *Major-General.*

[2] See George B. Davis et al., *Official Military Atlas of the Civil War* (New York: Fairfax Press, 1983), plate 70, map 2.

[3] Albert G. Browne (1805–1885) worked for the Boston Hemp Company before being appointed as an agent for the U.S. Treasury. *Annals of the Massachusetts Charitable Mechanic Association, 1795–1892* (Boston: Press of Rockwell and Churchill, 1892), s.v. "Albert G. Browne"; "News from All Around," *Sun-Journal* (Lewiston, ME), Oct. 12, 1885, 3.

This message actually reached him on Christmas-eve, was extensively published in the newspapers, and made many a household unusually happy on that festive day; and it was in the answer to this dispatch that Mr. Lincoln wrote me the letter of December 28th, already given, beginning with the words, "many, many thanks," etc., which he sent at the hands of General John A. Logan, who happened to be in Washington, and was coming to Savannah, to rejoin his command.

On the 23d of December were made the following general orders for the disposition of the troops in and about Savannah:

[Special Field Order No. 139.]

HEADQUARTERS MILITARY DIVISION OF THE MISSISSIPPI, IN THE FIELD, SAVANNAH, GEORGIA, *December* 23, 1864.

Savannah, being now in our possession, the river partially cleared out, and measures having been taken to remove all obstructions, will at once be made a grand depot for future operations:

1. The chief-quartermaster, General Easton, will, after giving the necessary orders touching the transports in Ogeechee River and Ossabaw Sound, come in person to Savannah, and take possession of all public buildings, vacant storerooms, warehouses, etc., that may be now or hereafter needed for any department of the army. No rents will be paid by the Government of the United States during the war, and all buildings must be distributed according to the accustomed rules of the Quartermaster's Department, as though they were public property.

2. The chief commissary of subsistence, Colonel A. Beckwith, will transfer the grand depot of the army to the city of Savannah, secure possession of the needful buildings and offices, and give the necessary orders, to the end that the army may be supplied abundantly and well.

3. The chief-engineer, Captain Poe, will at once direct which of the enemy's forts are to be retained for our use, and which dismantled and destroyed. The chief ordnance-officer, Captain Baylor, will in like manner take possession of all property pertaining to his department captured from the enemy, and cause the same to be collected and conveyed to points of security; all the heavy coast-guns will be dismounted and carried to Fort Pulaski.

4. The troops, for the present, will be grouped about the city of Savannah, looking to convenience of camps; General Slocum taking

from the Savannah River around to the seven-mile post on the Canal, and General Howard thence to the sea; General Kilpatrick will hold King's Bridge until Fort McAllister is dismantled, and the troops withdrawn from the south side of the Ogeechee, when he will take post about Anderson's plantation, on the plank-road, and picket all the roads leading from the north and west.

5. General Howard will keep a small guard at Forts Rosedale, Beaulieu, Wimberley, Thunderbolt, and Bonaventura, and he will cause that shore and Skidaway Island to be examined very closely, with a view to finding many and convenient points for the embarkation of troops and wagons on sea-going vessels.

By order of Major-General W. T. Sherman,

L. M. Dayton, *Aide-de-Camp.*

[Special Field Order No. 143.]

Headquarters Military Division of the Mississippi,
in the Field, Savannah, Georgia, *December* 26, 1864.

The city of Savannah and surrounding country will be held as a military post, and adapted to future military uses, but, as it contains a population of some twenty thousand people, who must be provided for, and as other citizens may come, it is proper to lay down certain general principles, that all within its military jurisdiction may understand their relative duties and obligations.

1. During war, the military is superior to civil authority, and, where interests clash, the civil must give way; yet, where there is no conflict, every encouragement should be given to well-disposed and peaceful inhabitants to resume their usual pursuits. Families should be disturbed as little as possible in their residences, and tradesmen allowed the free use of their shops, tools, etc.; churches, schools, and all places of amusement and recreation, should be encouraged, and streets and roads made perfectly safe to persons in their pursuits. Passes should not be exacted within the line of outer pickets, but if any person shall abuse these privileges by communicating with the enemy, or doing any act of hostility to the Government of the United States, he or she will be punished with the utmost rigor of the law. Commerce with the outer world will be resumed to an extent commensurate with the wants of the citizens, governed by the restrictions and rules of the Treasury Department.

2. The chief quartermaster and commissary of the army may give suitable employment to the people, white and black, or transport them to such points as they may choose where employment can be had; and may extend temporary relief in the way of provisions and vacant houses to the worthy and needy, until such time as they can help themselves. They will select first the buildings for the necessary uses of the army; next, a sufficient number of stores, to be turned over to the Treasury agent for trade-stores. All vacant storehouses or dwellings, and all buildings belonging to absent rebels, will be construed and used as belonging to the United States, until such time as their titles can be settled by the courts of the United States.

3. The Mayor and City Council of Savannah will continue to exercise their functions, and will, in concert with the commanding officer of the post and the chief-quartermaster, see that the fire-companies are kept in organization, the streets cleaned and lighted, and keep up a good understanding between the citizens and soldiers. They will ascertain and report to the chief commissary of subsistence, as soon as possible, the names and number of worthy families that need assistance and support. The mayor will forth with give public notice that the time has come when all must choose their course, viz., remain within our lines, and conduct themselves as good citizens, or depart in peace. He will ascertain the names of all who choose to leave Savannah, and report their names and residence to the chief-quartermaster, that measures may be taken to transport them beyond our lines.

4. Not more than two newspapers will be published in Savannah; their editors and proprietors will be held to the strictest accountability, and will be punished severely, in person and property, for any libelous publication, mischievous matter, premature news, exaggerated statements, or any comments whatever upon the acts of the constituted authorities; they will be held accountable for such articles, even though copied from other papers.

By order of Major-General W. T. Sherman,

L. M. Dayton, *Aide-de-Camp.*

It was estimated that there were about twenty thousand inhabitants in Savannah, all of whom had participated more or less in the war, and had no special claims to our favor, but I regarded the war as rapidly drawing to a close, and it was becoming a political question as to what was to be done with the people of the South, both white and black, when the war was actually over. I concluded to give them the option to remain or to join their friends in Charleston or Augusta, and so announced in general orders.[4] The mayor, Dr. Arnold, was completely "subjugated," and, after consulting with him, I authorized him to assemble his City Council to take charge generally of the interests of the people; but warned all who remained that they must be strictly subordinate to the military law, and to the interests of the General Government. About two hundred persons, mostly the families of men in the Confederate army, prepared to follow the fortunes of their husbands and fathers, and these were sent in a steamboat under a flag of truce, in charge of my aide Captain Audenried, to Charleston harbor, and there delivered to an officer of the Confederate army. But the great bulk of the inhabitants chose to remain in Savannah, generally behaved with propriety, and good social relations at once arose between them and the army. Shortly after our occupation of Savannah, a lady was announced at my headquarters by the orderly or sentinel at the front-door, who was ushered into the parlor, and proved to be the wife of General G. W. Smith, whom I had known about 1850, when Smith was on duty at West Point. She was a native of New London, Connecticut, and very handsome.[5] She began her interview by presenting me a letter from her husband, who then commanded a division of the Georgia militia in the rebel army, which had just quitted Savannah, which letter began, "Dear Sherman: The fortunes of war, etc., compel me to leave my wife in Savannah, and I beg for her your courteous protection," etc., etc. I inquired where she lived, and if anybody was troubling her. She said she was boarding with a lady whose husband had, in like manner with her own, gone off with Hardee's army; that a part of the house had been taken for the use of Major-General Ward, of Kentucky; that her landlady was approaching her confinement, and was nervous at the noise which the younger staff-officers made at night, etc. I explained to her that I could give but little personal attention to such matters, and referred her to General Slocum, whose troops occupied the city. I afterward visited her house, and saw, personally, that she had no reason to complain. Shortly afterward Mr. Hardee, a merchant of Savannah, came to me and presented a letter from his brother, the general, to the same effect, alleging that his brother was a civilian, had never taken up arms, and asked of

[4] See *OR,* I, 47(II), 60–62.

[5] Lucretia S. Bassett (1822–1881) married Gustavus W. Smith on Oct. 3, 1844. Thomas H. Carter, *A Gunner in Lee's Army: The Civil War Letters of Thomas Henry Carter,* ed. Graham T. Dozier (Chapel Hill: University of North Carolina Press, 2014), 89*n.*

me protection for his family, his cotton, etc. To him I gave the general assurance that no harm was designed to any of the people of Savannah who would remain quiet and peaceable, but that I could give him no guarantee as to his cotton, for over it I had no absolute control; and yet still later I received a note from the wife of General A. P. Stewart (who commanded a corps in Hood's army), asking me to come to see her. This I did, and found her to be a native of Cincinnati, Ohio, wanting protection, and who was naturally anxious about the fate of her husband, known to be with General Hood, in Tennessee, retreating before General Thomas.[6] I remember that I was able to assure her that he had not been killed or captured, up to that date, and think that I advised her, instead of attempting to go in pursuit of her husband, to go to Cincinnati, to her uncle, Judge Storer,[7] there await the issue of events.

Before I had reached Savannah, and during our stay there, the rebel officers and newspapers represented the conduct of the men of our army as simply infamous; that we respected neither age nor sex; that we burned every thing we came across—barns, stables, cotton-gins, and even dwelling-houses; that we ravished the women and killed the men, and perpetrated all manner of outrages on the inhabitants. Therefore it struck me as strange that Generals Hardee and Smith should commit their families to our custody, and even bespeak our personal care and attention. These officers knew well that these reports were exaggerated in the extreme, and yet tacitly assented to these false publications, to arouse the drooping energies of the people of the South.

As the division of Major-General John W. Geary, of the Twentieth Corps, was the first to enter Savannah, that officer was appointed to command the place, or to act as a sort of governor. He very soon established a good police, maintained admirable order, and I doubt if Savannah, either before or since, has had a better government than during our stay. The guard-mountings and parades, as well as the greater reviews, became the daily resorts of the ladies, to hear the music of our excellent bands; schools were opened, and the churches every Sunday were well filled with most devout and respectful congregations; stores were reopened, and markets for provisions, meat, wood, etc., were established, so that each family, regardless of race, color, or

[6] Harriet Chase (1823–1898) married A. P. Stewart on Aug. 7, 1845. "Mrs. Harriet C. Stewart: Sudden Death of the Wife of Gen. A. P. Stewart Occasioned by an Apoplectic Stroke," *Chattanooga Daily Times*, Jan. 5, 1898, 2.

[7] Bellamy Storer (1796–1875) served as the judge of the Cincinnati superior court from 1854 to 1872. *Biographical Directory of the United States Congress, 1774–2005* (Washington, DC: GPO, 2005), s.v. "Storer, Bellamy."

opinion, could procure all the necessaries and even luxuries of life, provided they had money. Of course, many families were actually destitute of this, and to these were issued stores from our own stock of supplies. I remember to have given to Dr. Arnold, the mayor, an order for the contents of a large warehouse of rice, which he confided to a committee of gentlemen, who went North (to Boston), and soon returned with one or more cargoes of flour, hams, sugar, coffee, etc., for gratuitous distribution, which relieved the most pressing wants until the revival of trade and business enabled the people to provide for themselves.

A lady, whom I had known in former years as Miss Josephine Goodwin,[8] told me that, with a barrel of flour and some sugar which she had received gratuitously from the commissary, she had baked cakes and pies, in the sale of which she realized a profit of fifty-six dollars.

Meantime Colonel Poe had reconnoitred and laid off new lines of parapet, which would enable a comparatively small garrison to hold the place, and a heavy detail of soldiers was put to work thereon; Generals Easton and Beckwith had organized a complete depot of supplies; and, though vessels arrived almost daily with mails and provisions, we were hardly ready to initiate a new and hazardous campaign. I had not yet received from General Grant or General Halleck any modification of the orders of December 6, 1864, to embark my command for Virginia by sea; but on the 2d of January, 1865, General J. G. Barnard, United States Engineers, arrived direct from General Grant's headquarters, bearing the following letter, in the general's own handwriting, which, with my answer, is here given:

HEADQUARTERS ARMIES OF THE UNITED STATES,
CITY POINT, VIRGINIA, *December* 27, 1864.

Major-General W. T. SHERMAN, *commanding Military Division of the Mississippi.*

GENERAL: Before writing you definite instructions for the next campaign, I wanted to receive your answer to my letter written from Washington. Your confidence in being able to march up and join this army pleases me, and I believe it can be done. The effect of such a campaign will be to disorganize the South, and prevent the organization of new armies from their broken fragments. Hood is now

[8] Abby Josephine Goodwin (1824–1870) married William F. Law in Savannah on Aug. 27, 1846. Lyon G. Tyler, ed., *William and Mary College Quarterly Historical Magazine* (Richmond: Whittet and Shepperson, 1900), s.v. "The Goodwins of Baltimore, Maryland."

retreating, with his army broken and demoralized. His loss in men has probably not been far from twenty thousand, besides deserters. If time is given, the fragments may be collected together and many of the deserters reassembled. If we can, we should act to prevent this. Your spare army, as it were, moving as proposed, will do it.

In addition to holding Savannah, it looks to me that an intrenched camp ought to be held on the railroad between Savannah and Charleston. Your movement toward Branchville will probably enable Foster to reach this with his own force. This will give us a position in the South from which we can threaten the interior without marching over long, narrow causeways, easily defended, as we have heretofore been compelled to do. Could not such a camp be established about Pocotaligo or Coosawhatchie?

I have thought that, Hood being so completely wiped out for present harm, I might bring A. J. Smith here, with fourteen to fifteen thousand men. With this increase I could hold my lines, and move out with a greater force than Lee has. It would compel Lee to retain all his present force in the defenses of Richmond or abandon them entirely. This latter contingency is probably the only danger to the easy success of your expedition. In the event you should meet Lee's army, you would be compelled to beat it or find the sea-coast. Of course, I shall not let Lee's army escape if I can help it, and will not let it go without following to the best of my ability.

Without waiting further directions, then, you may make your preparations to start on your northern expedition without delay. Break up the railroads in South and North Carolina, and join the armies operating against Richmond as soon as you can. I will leave out all suggestions about the route you should take, knowing that your information, gained daily in the course of events, will be better than any that can be obtained now.

It may not be possible for you to march to the rear of Petersburg; but, failing in this, you could strike either of the sea-coast ports in North Carolina held by us. From there you could take shipping. It would be decidedly preferable, however, if you could march the whole distance.

From the best information I have, you will find no difficulty in supplying your army until you cross the Roanoke. From there here is but a few days' march, and supplies could be collected south of the river to bring you through. I shall establish communication with you there, by steamboat and gunboat. By this means your wants can be partially supplied. I shall hope to hear from you soon, and to hear your plan, and about the time of starting.

Please instruct Foster to hold on to all the property in Savannah, and especially the cotton. Do not turn it over to citizens or Treasury agents, without orders of the War Department.

Very respectfully, your obedient servant,

U. S. Grant, *Lieutenant-General.*

Headquarters Military Division of the Mississippi,
in the Field, Savannah, Georgia, *January* 2, 1865.

Lieutenant-General U. S. Grant, *City Point.*

General: I have received, by the hands of General Barnard, your note of 26th and letter of 27th December.

I herewith inclose to you a copy of a *projet* which I have this morning, in strict confidence, discussed with my immediate commanders.

I shall need, however, larger supplies of stores, especially grain. I will inclose to you, with this, letters from General Easton, quartermaster, and Colonel Beckwith, commissary of subsistence, setting forth what will be required, and trust you will forward them to Washington with your sanction, so that the necessary steps may be taken at once to enable me to carry out this plan on time.

I wrote you very fully on the 24th, and have nothing to add. Every thing here is quiet, and if I can get the necessary supplies in our wagons, shall be ready to start at the time indicated in my *projet* (January 15th). But, until those supplies are in hand, I can do nothing; after they are, I shall be ready to move with great rapidity.

I have heard of the affair at Cape Fear. It has turned out as you will remember I expected.

I have furnished General Easton a copy of the dispatch from the Secretary of War. He will retain possession of all cotton here, and ship it as fast as vessels can be had to New York.

I shall immediately send the Seventeenth Corps over to Port Royal, by boats, to be furnished by Admiral Dahlgren and General Foster (without interfering with General Easton's vessels), to make a lodgment on the railroad at Pocotaligo.

General Barnard will remain with me a few days, and I send this by a staff-officer, who can return on one of the vessels of the supply-fleet. I suppose that, now that General Butler has got through with them, you can spare them to us.

My report of recent operations is nearly ready, and will be sent you in a day or two, as soon as some further subordinate reports come in.

I am, with great respect, very truly, your friend,

W. T. Sherman, *Major-General.*

[Entirely Confidential.]

PROJET FOR JANUARY.

1. Right wing to move men and artillery by transports to head of Broad River and Beaufort; reëstablish Port Royal Ferry, and mass the wing at or in the neighborhood of Pocotaligo.

Left wing and cavalry to work slowly across the causeway toward Hardeeville, to open a road by which wagons can reach their corps about Broad River; also, by a rapid movement of the left, to secure Sister's Ferry, and Augusta road out to Robertsville.

In the mean time, all guns, shot, shell, cotton, etc., to be moved to a safe place, easy to guard, and provisions and wagons got ready for another *swath,* aiming to have our army in hand about the head of Broad River, say Pocotaligo, Robertsville, and Coosawhatchie, by the 15th January.

2. The whole army to move with loaded wagons by the roads leading in the direction of Columbia, which afford the best chance of forage and provisions. Howard to be at Pocotaligo by the 15th January, and Slocum to be at Robertsville, and Kilpatrick at or near Coosawhatchie about the same date. General Foster's troops to occupy Savannah, and gunboats to protect the rivers as soon as Howard gets Pocotaligo.

W. T. Sherman, *Major-General.*

Therefore, on the 2d of January, I was authorized to march with my entire army north by land, and concluded at once to secure a foothold or starting-point on the South Carolina side, selecting Pocotaligo and Hardeeville as the points of rendezvous for the two wings; but I still remained in doubt as to the wishes of the Administration, whether I should take Charleston *en route,* or confine my whole attention to the incidental advantages of breaking up the railways of South and North Carolina, and the greater object of uniting my army with that of General Grant before Richmond.

General Barnard remained with me several days, and was regarded then, as now, one of the first engineers of the age, perfectly competent to advise me on the strategy and objects of the new campaign. He expressed himself delighted with the high spirit of the army, the steps already taken, by which we had captured Savannah, and he personally inspected some of the forts, such as Thunderbolt and Causten's Bluff,[9] by which the enemy had so long held at bay the whole of our navy, and had defeated the previous attempts made in April, 1862, by the army of General Gillmore, which had bombarded and captured Fort Pulaski, but had failed to reach the city of Savannah. I think General Barnard expected me to invite him to accompany us northward in his official capacity; but Colonel Poe, of my staff, had done so well, and was so perfectly competent, that I thought it unjust to supersede him by a senior in his own corps. I therefore said nothing of this to General Barnard, and soon after he returned to his post with General Grant, at City Point, bearing letters and full personal messages of our situation and wants.

We were very much in want of light-draught steamers for navigating the shallow waters of the coast, so that it took the Seventeenth Corps more than a week to transfer from Thunderbolt to Beaufort, South Carolina. Admiral Dahlgren had supplied the Harvest Moon and the Pontiac, and General Foster gave us a couple of hired steamers; I was really amused at the effect this short sea-voyage had on our men, most of whom had never before looked upon the ocean. Of course, they were fit subjects for sea-sickness, and afterward they begged me never again to send them to sea, saying they would rather march a thousand miles on the worst roads of the South than to spend a single night on the ocean. By the 10th General Howard had collected the bulk of the Seventeenth Corps (General Blair) on Beaufort Island, and began his march for Pocotaligo, twenty-five miles inland. They crossed the channel between the island and main-land during Saturday, the 14th of January, by a pontoon-bridge, and marched out to Garden's Corners, where there was some light skirmishing; the next day, Sunday, they continued on to Pocotaligo, finding the strong fort there abandoned, and accordingly made a lodgment on the railroad, having lost only two officers and eight men.

About the same time General Slocum crossed two divisions of the Twentieth Corps over the Savannah River, above the city, occupied Hardeeville by

[9] Causten's Bluff was located on the east side of the city approximately one mile south of the Savannah River. Davis et al., *Official Military Atlas of the Civil War,* plate 70, map 2.

one division and Purysburg by another.[10] Thus, by the middle of January, we had effected a lodgment in South Carolina, and were ready to resume the march northward; but we had not yet accumulated enough provisions and forage to fill the wagons, and other causes of delay occurred, of which I will make mention in due order.

On the last day of December, 1864, Captain Breese, United States Navy, flag-officer to Admiral Porter,[11] reached Savannah, bringing the first news of General Butler's failure at Fort Fisher, and that the general had returned to James River with his land-forces, leaving Admiral Porter's fleet anchored off Cape Fear, in that tempestuous season. Captain Breese brought me a letter from the admiral, dated December 29th, asking me to send him from Savannah one of my old divisions, with which he said he would make short work of Fort Fisher; that he had already bombarded and silenced its guns, and that General Butler had failed because he was afraid to attack, or even give the order to attack, after (as Porter insisted) the guns of Fort Fisher had been actually silenced by the navy.

I answered him promptly on the 31st of December, that I proposed to march north *inland*, and that I would prefer to leave the rebel garrisons on the coast, instead of dislodging and piling them up in my front as we progressed.[12] From the chances, as I then understood them, I supposed that Fort Fisher was garrisoned by a comparatively small force, while the whole division of General Hoke[13] remained about the city of Wilmington; and that, if Fort Fisher were captured, it would leave General Hoke free to join the larger force that would naturally be collected to oppose my progress northward. I accordingly answered Admiral Porter to this effect, declining to loan him the use of one of my divisions. It subsequently transpired, however, that, as soon as General Butler reached City Point, General Grant was unwilling to rest under a sense of failure, and accordingly dispatched back the same troops, reënforced and commanded by General A. H. Terry,[14] who, on the 15th day of January, successfully assaulted and

[10] For a detailed map of the area, see Davis et al., *Official Military Atlas of the Civil War*, plate 70, map 2.

[11] Kidder R. Breese (1831–1881) was appointed fleet captain after U.S. Navy Admiral David D. Porter took command of the North Atlantic Squadron in Sept. 1864. "Captain Kidder R. Breese," *Philadelphia Inquirer*, Sept. 14, 1881, 8.

[12] See *ORN*, I, 11, 388–389, 397–398.

[13] Robert F. Hoke (1837–1912), a major general in the Confederate Army, commanded a division in the Dept. of North Carolina and South Virginia in Jan. 1865. *CWHC*, 300–301.

[14] Alfred H. Terry (1827–1890) commanded the 10th Provisional Corps, Dept. of North Carolina, during the second assault on Fort Fisher on Jan. 15. *CWHC*, 524.

captured Fort Fisher, with its entire garrison.[15] After the war was over, about the 20th of May, when I was giving my testimony before the Congressional Committee on the Conduct of the War, the chairman of the committee, Senator B. F. Wade, of Ohio,[16] told me that General Butler had been summoned before that committee during the previous January, and had just finished his demonstration to their entire satisfaction that Fort Fisher could not be carried by assault, when they heard the newsboy in the hall crying out an "extra." Calling him in, they inquired the news, and he answered, "Fort Fisher done took!" Of course, they all laughed, and none more heartily than General Butler himself.[17]

On the 11th of January there arrived at Savannah a revenue-cutter, having on board Simeon Draper, Esq., of New York City,[18] the Hon. E. M. Stanton, Secretary of War, Quartermaster-General Meigs, Adjutant-General Townsend, and a retinue of civilians, who had come down from the North to regulate the civil affairs of Savannah.

I was instructed by Mr. Stanton to transfer to Mr. Draper the custom-house, post-office, and such other public buildings as these civilians needed in the execution of their office, and to cause to be delivered into their custody the captured cotton. This was accomplished by—

[Special Field Orders, No. 10.]

HEADQUARTERS MILITARY DIVISION OF THE MISSISSIPPI,
IN THE FIELD, SAVANNAH, GEORGIA, *January* 12, 1865.

1. Brevet Brigadier-General Easton, chief-quartermaster, will turn over to Simeon Draper, Esq., agent of the United States Treasury Department, all cotton now in the city of Savannah, prize of war,

[15] The U.S. Army captured ninety-six officers and 1,164 enlisted men during the Second Battle of Fort Fisher. For Gen. Terry's post-battle report, see *OR,* I, 46(I), 394–401.

[16] Benjamin F. Wade (1800–1878), a prominent abolitionist, served three terms as a U.S. senator starting in 1851. "Hon. B. F. Wade," *Somerset Press* (Somerset, OH), Mar. 14, 1878, 1.

[17] For Butler's full testimony to Congress related to the First Battle of Fort Fisher, see *Report of the Joint Committee on the Conduct of the War, at the Second Session, Thirty-Eighth Congress: Fort Fisher Expedition* (Washington, DC: GPO, 1865), 3–51.

[18] Simeon Draper (1806–1866), a merchant, was appointed collector of the Port of New York by Pres. Lincoln in 1864. Richard F. Miller, ed., *States at War* (Hanover, NH: University Press of New England, 2012), 1:433*n;* "Funeral of Simeon Draper," *National Republican* (Washington, DC), Nov. 12, 1866, 1.

taking his receipt for the same in gross, and returning for it to the quartermaster-general. He will also afford Mr. Draper all the facilities in his power in the way of transportation, labor, etc., to enable him to handle the cotton with expedition.

2. General Easton will also turn over to Mr. Draper the custom-house, and such other buildings in the city of Savannah as he may need in the execution of his office.

By order of General W. T. Sherman,

L. M. Dayton, *Aide-de-Camp.*

Up to this time all the cotton had been carefully guarded, with orders to General Easton to ship it by the return-vessels to New York, for the adjudication of the nearest prize-court, accompanied with invoices and all evidence of title to ownership. Marks, numbers, and other figures, were carefully preserved on the bales, so that the court might know the history of each bale. But Mr. Stanton, who surely was an able lawyer, changed all this, and ordered the obliteration of all the marks; so that no man, friend or foe, could trace his identical cotton. I thought it strange at the time, and think it more so now; for I am assured that claims, real and fictitious, have been *proved up* against this identical cotton of three times the quantity actually captured, and that reclamations on the Treasury have been *allowed* for more than the actual quantity captured, viz., thirty-one thousand bales.[19]

Mr. Stanton staid in Savannah several days, and seemed very curious about matters and things in general. I walked with him through the city, especially the bivouacs of the several regiments that occupied the vacant squares, and he seemed particularly pleased at the ingenuity of the men in constructing their temporary huts. Four of the "dog-tents," or *tentes d'abri,* buttoned together, served for a roof, and the sides were made of clapboards, or rough boards brought from demolished houses or fences. I remember his marked admiration for the hut of a soldier who had made his door out of a handsome parlor mirror, the glass gone and its gilt frame serving for his door.

[19] In his autobiography, Gen. Edward D. Townsend, who accompanied Stanton to Savannah, wrote, "After personally examining the stores containing the cotton, hearing private claims to certain lots, indicating the marks to be put on the bales, and what disposition should be made of them, the Secretary, on consultation with General Sherman, appointed Mr. Draper to have the charge of the cotton, and General John W. Geary, who belonged to Sherman's army, to be left in military command of Savannah when the army marched northward." Edward D. Townsend, *Anecdotes of the Civil War in the United States* (New York: D. Appleton, 1884), 116–117.

He talked to me a great deal about the negroes, the former slaves, and I told him of many interesting incidents, illustrating their simple character and faith in our arms and progress. He inquired particularly about General Jeff. C. Davis, who, he said, was a Democrat, and hostile to the negro. I assured him that General Davis was an excellent soldier, and I did not believe he had any hostility to the negro; that in our army we had no negro soldiers, and, as a rule, we preferred white soldiers, but that we employed a large force of them as servants, teamsters, and pioneers, who had rendered admirable service.[20] He then showed me a newspaper account of General Davis taking up his pontoon-bridge across Ebenezer Creek, leaving sleeping negro men, women, and children, on the other side, to be slaughtered by Wheeler's cavalry. I had heard such a rumor, and advised Mr. Stanton, before becoming prejudiced, to allow me to send for General Davis, which he did, and General Davis explained the matter to his entire satisfaction. The truth was, that, as we approached the seaboard, the freedmen in droves, old and young, followed the several columns to reach a place of safety. It so happened that General Davis's route into Savannah followed what was known as the "River-road," and he had to make constant use of his pontoon-train—the head of his column reaching some deep, impassable creek before the rear was fairly over another. He had occasionally to use the pontoons both day and night. On the occasion referred to, the bridge was taken up from Ebenezer Creek while some of the camp-followers remained asleep on the farther side, and these were picked up by Wheeler's cavalry. Some of them, in their fright, were drowned in trying to swim over, and others may have been cruelly killed by Wheeler's men, but this was a mere supposition.[21] At all events, the same thing might have resulted to General Howard, or to any other of the many most humane commanders who filled the army. General Jeff. C. Davis was strictly a soldier, and doubtless hated to have his wagons

[20] See Edmund L. Drago, "How Sherman's March through Georgia Affected the Slaves," *Georgia Historical Quarterly* 57, no. 3 (Fall 1973): 361–375.

[21] U.S. Army general Jefferson C. Davis ordered the removal of the pontoon bridge on Ebenezer Creek, just outside of Savannah, on Dec. 9. James A. Connolly, one of Davis's lieutenant colonels, was critical of his decision: "The idea of five or six hundred black women, children, and old men being thus returned to slavery by such an infernal copperhead as Jeff C. Davis was entirely too much for my Democracy . . . I told his staff officers what I thought of such inhuman, barbarous proceeding in language which may possibly result in a reprimand from his serene Highness . . . but I don't care a fig." James P. Jones, "General Jeff C. Davis, U.S.A. and Sherman's Georgia Campaign," *Georgia Historical Quarterly* 47, no. 3 (Sept. 1963): 242–244; John F. Marszalek, *Sherman: A Soldier's Passion for Order* (New York: Free Press, 1993), 312–313.

and columns encumbered by these poor negroes, for whom we all felt sympathy, but a sympathy of a different sort from that of Mr. Stanton, which was not of pure humanity, but of *politics.* The negro question was beginning to loom up among the political eventualities of the day, and many foresaw that not only would the slaves secure their freedom, but that they would also have votes. I did not dream of such a result then, but knew that slavery, as such, was dead forever, and did not suppose that the former slaves would be suddenly, without preparation, manufactured into voters, equal to all others, politically and socially.[22] Mr. Stanton seemed desirous of coming into contact with the negroes to confer with them, and he asked me to arrange an interview for him. I accordingly sent out and invited the most intelligent of the negroes, mostly Baptist and Methodist preachers, to come to my rooms to meet the Secretary of War. Twenty responded, and were received in my room up-stairs in Mr. Green's house, where Mr. Stanton and Adjutant-General Townsend took down the conversation in the form of questions and answers. Each of the twenty gave his name and partial history, and then selected Garrison Frazier[23] as their spokesman:

> *First Question.* State what your understanding is in regard to the acts of Congress and President Lincoln's proclamation touching the colored people in the rebel States?
>
> *Answer.* So far as I understand President Lincoln's proclamation to the rebel States, it is, that if they will lay down their arms and submit to the laws of the United States, before the 1st of January, 1863, all should be well; but if they did not, then all the slaves in the Southern States should be free, henceforth and forever. That is what I understood.
>
> *Second Question.* State what you understand by slavery, and the freedom that was to be given by the President's proclamation?
>
> *Answer.* Slavery is receiving by irresistible power the work of another man, and not by his consent. The freedom, as I understand it, prom-

[22] For more on WTS's treatment of formerly enslaved people in his lines, and their civil rights, see A. Baird to Gerrit Smith, Jan. 1865, and WTS to A. Baird, Apr. 3, 1865, in the Appendix to Volume II.

[23] Garrison Frazer (b. 1798) purchased freedom for himself and his wife in 1857 for $1,000. He was described as "endowed with fair natural gifts, a commanding presence, and a good voice." Josef C. James, "Sherman at Savannah," *Journal of Negro History* 39, no. 2 (Apr. 1954): 128; James M. Simms, *The First Colored Baptist Church in North America: Constituted at Savannah, Georgia, January 20, A.D. 1788* (Philadelphia: J. B. Lippincott, 1888), 261–262.

ised by the proclamation, is taking us from under the yoke of bondage and placing us where we can reap the fruit of our own labor, and take care of ourselves and assist the Government in maintaining our freedom.

. . . .

Fourth Question. State in what manner you would rather live—whether scattered among the whites, or in colonies by yourselves?

Answer. I would prefer to live by ourselves, for there is a prejudice against us in the South that will take years to get over; but I do not know that I can answer for my brethren.

(All but Mr. Lynch, a missionary from the North, agreed with Frazier, but he thought they ought to live together, along with the whites.)

. . . .

Eighth Question. If the rebel leaders were to arm the slaves, what would be its effect?

Answer. I think they would fight as long as they were before the "bayonet," and just as soon as they could get away they would desert, in my opinion.

. . . .

Tenth Question. Do you understand the mode of enlistment of colored persons in the rebel States by State agents, under the act of Congress; if yes, what is your understanding?

Answer. My understanding is, that colored persons enlisted by State agents are enlisted as substitutes, and give credit to the State and do not swell the army, because every black man enlisted by a State agent leaves a white man at home; and also that larger bounties are given, or promised, by the State agents than are given by the United States. The great object should be to push through this rebellion the shortest way; and there seems to be something wanting in the enlistment by State agents, for it don't strengthen the army, but takes one away for every colored man enlisted.

Eleventh Question. State what, in your opinion, is the best way to enlist colored men as soldiers?

Answer. I think, sir, that all compulsory operations should be put a stop to. The ministers would talk to them, and the young men would enlist. It is my opinion that it would be far better for the State agents to stay at home and the enlistments be made for the United States under the direction of General Sherman.

Up to this time I was present, and, on Mr. Stanton's intimating that he wanted to ask some questions affecting me, I withdrew, and then he put the twelfth and last question:

> *Twelfth Question.* State what is the feeling of the colored people toward General Sherman, and how far do they regard his sentiments and actions as friendly to their rights and interests, or otherwise?
>
> *Answer.* We looked upon General Sherman, prior to his arrival, as a man, in the providence of God, specially set apart to accomplish this work, and we unanimously felt inexpressible gratitude to him, looking upon him as a man who should be honored for the faithful performance of his duty. Some of us called upon him immediately upon his arrival, and it is probable he did not meet the secretary with more courtesy than he did us. His conduct and deportment toward us characterized him as a friend and gentleman. We have confidence in General Sherman, and think what concerns us could not be in better hands. This is our opinion now, from the short acquaintance and intercourse we have had.[24]

It certainly was a strange fact that the great War Secretary should have catechized negroes concerning the character of a general who had commanded a hundred thousand men in battle, had captured cities, conducted sixty-five thousand men successfully across four hundred miles of hostile territory, and had just brought tens of thousands of freedmen to a place of security; but because I had not loaded down my army by other hundreds of thousands of poor negroes, I was construed by others as hostile to the black race. I had received from General Halleck, at Washington, a letter warning me that there were certain influential parties near the President who were torturing him with suspicions of my fidelity to him and his negro policy; but I shall always believe that Mr. Lincoln, though a civilian, knew better, and appreciated my motives and character. Though this letter of General Halleck has always been treated by me as confidential, I now insert it here at length:

> HEADQUARTERS OF THE ARMY,
> WASHINGTON, D. C., *December* 30, 1864.
>
> *Major-General* W. T. SHERMAN, *Savannah.*
>
> MY DEAR GENERAL: I take the liberty of calling your attention, in this private and friendly way, to a matter which may possibly

[24] For a full list of the Black men in attendance, see James, "Sherman at Savannah," 128–129.

hereafter be of more importance to you than either of us may now anticipate.

While almost every one is praising your great march through Georgia, and the capture of Savannah, there is a certain class having now great influence with the President, and very probably anticipating still more on a change of cabinet, who are decidedly disposed to make a point against you. I mean in regard to "inevitable Sambo." They say that you have manifested an almost *criminal* dislike to the negro, and that you are not willing to carry out the wishes of the Government in regard to him, but repulse him with contempt! They say you might have brought with you to Savannah more than fifty thousand, thus stripping Georgia of that number of laborers, and opening a road by which as many more could have escaped from their masters; but that, instead of this, you drove them from your ranks, prevented their following you by cutting the bridges in your rear, and thus caused the massacre of large numbers by Wheeler's cavalry.

To those who know you as I do, such accusation will pass as the idle winds, for we presume that you discouraged the negroes from following you because you had not the means of supporting them, and feared they might seriously embarrass your march. But there are others, and among them some in high authority, who think or pretend to think otherwise, and they are decidedly disposed to make a point against you.

I do not write this to induce you to conciliate this class of men by doing any thing which you do not deem right and proper, and for the interest of the Government and the country; but simply to call your attention to certain things which are viewed here somewhat differently than from your stand-point. I will explain as briefly as possible:

Some here think that, in view of the scarcity of labor in the South, and the probability that a part, at least, of the able-bodied slaves will be called into the military service of the rebels, it is of the greatest importance to open outlets by which these slaves can escape into our lines, and they say that the route you have passed over should be made the route of escape, and Savannah the great place of refuge. These, I know, are the views of some of the leading men in the Administration, and they now express dissatisfaction that you did not carry them out in your great raid.

Now that you are in possession of Savannah, and there can be no further fears about supplies, would it not be possible for you to reopen these avenues of escape for the negroes, without interfering with your

> military operations? Could not such escaped slaves find at least a partial supply of food in the rice-fields about Savannah, and cotton plantations on the coast?
>
> I merely throw out these suggestions. I know that such a course would be approved by the Government, and I believe that a manifestation on your part of a desire to bring the slaves within our lines will do much to silence your opponents. You will appreciate my motives in writing this private letter.
>
> Yours truly,
>
> H. W. Halleck.

There is no doubt that Mr. Stanton, when he reached Savannah, shared these thoughts, but luckily the negroes themselves convinced him that he was in error, and that they understood their own interests far better than did the men in Washington, who tried to make political capital out of this negro question. The idea that such men should have been permitted to hang around Mr. Lincoln, to torture his life by suspicions of the officers who were toiling with the single purpose to bring the war to a successful end, and thereby to liberate *all* slaves, is a fair illustration of the influences that poison a political capital.

My aim then was, to whip the rebels, to humble their pride, to follow them to their inmost recesses, and make them fear and dread us. "Fear of the Lord is the beginning of wisdom."[25] I did not want them to cast in our teeth what General Hood had once done in Atlanta, that we had to call on *their* slaves to help us to subdue them. But, as regards kindness to the race, encouraging them to patience and forbearance, procuring them food and clothing, and providing them with land whereon to labor, I assert that no army ever did more for that race than the one I commanded in Savannah. When we reached Savannah, we were beset by ravenous State agents from Hilton Head, who enticed and carried away our servants, and the corps of pioneers which we had organized, and which had done such excellent service. On one occasion, my own aide-de-camp, Colonel Audenried, found at least a hundred poor negroes shut up in a house and pen, waiting for the night, to be conveyed stealthily to Hilton Head. They appealed to him for protection, alleging that they had been told that they *must be* soldiers, that "Massa Lincoln" wanted them, etc. I never denied the slaves a full opportunity for voluntary enlistment, but I did prohibit force to be used, for I knew that the State agents were more influenced by the profit they derived from the large

[25] WTS quoted Proverbs 9:10: "The fear of the Lord is the beginning of wisdom: and the knowledge of the holy is understanding" (King James Version).

bounties then being paid than by any love of country or of the colored race. In the language of Mr. Frazier, the enlistment of every black man "did not strengthen the army, but took away one white man from the ranks."

During Mr. Stanton's stay in Savannah we discussed this negro question very fully; he asked me to draft an order on the subject, in accordance with my own views, that would meet the pressing necessities of the case, and I did so. We went over this order, No. 15, of January 16, 1865, very carefully. The secretary made some verbal modifications, when it was approved by him in all its details, I published it, and it went into operation at once. It provided fully for the enlistment of colored troops, and gave the freedmen certain possessory rights to land, which afterward became matters of judicial inquiry and decision. Of course, the military authorities at that day, when war prevailed, had a perfect right to grant the possession of any vacant land to which they could extend military protection, but we did not undertake to give a fee-simple title; and all that was designed by these special field orders was to make temporary provisions for the freedmen and their families during the rest of the war, or until Congress should take action in the premises. All that I now propose to assert is, that Mr. Stanton, Secretary of War, saw these orders in the rough, and approved every paragraph thereof, before they were made public:

[Special Field Orders, No. 15.]

Headquarters Military Division of the Mississippi,
in the Field, Savannah, Georgia, *January* 16, 1865.

1. The islands from Charleston south, the abandoned rice-fields along the rivers for thirty miles back from the sea, and the country bordering the St. John's River, Florida, are reserved and set apart for the settlement of the negroes now made free by the acts of war and the proclamation of the President of the United States.

2. At Beaufort, Hilton Head, Savannah, Fernandina, St. Augustine, and Jacksonville, the blacks may remain in their chosen or accustomed vocations; but on the islands, and in the settlements hereafter to be established, no white person whatever, unless military officers and soldiers detailed for duty, will be permitted to reside; and the sole and exclusive management of affairs will be left to the freed people themselves, subject only to the United States military authority, and the acts of Congress. By the laws of war, and orders of the President of the United States, the negro is free, and must be dealt with as such. He

cannot be subjected to conscription, or forced military service, save by the written orders of the highest military authority of the department, under such regulations as the President or Congress may prescribe. Domestic servants, blacksmiths, carpenters, and other mechanics, will be free to select their own work and residence, but the young and able-bodied negroes must be encouraged to enlist as soldiers in the service of the United States, to contribute their share toward maintaining their own freedom, and securing their rights as citizens of the United States.

Negroes so enlisted will be organized into companies, battalions, and regiments, under the orders of the United States military authorities, and will be paid, fed, and clothed, according to law. The bounties paid on enlistment may, with the consent of the recruit, go to assist his family and settlement in procuring agricultural implements, seed, tools, boots, clothing, and other articles necessary for their livelihood.

3. Whenever three respectable negroes, heads of families, shall desire to settle on land, and shall have selected for that purpose an island or a locality clearly defined within the limits above designated, the Inspector of Settlements and Plantations will himself, or by such subordinate officer as he may appoint, give them a license to settle such island or district, and afford them such assistance as he can to enable them to establish a peaceable agricultural settlement. The three parties named will subdivide the land, under the supervision of the inspector, among themselves, and such others as may choose to settle near them, so that each family shall have a plot of not more than forty acres of tillable ground, and, when it borders on some water-channel, with not more than eight hundred feet water-front, in the possession of which land the military authorities will afford them protection until such time as they can protect themselves, or until Congress shall regulate their title. The quartermaster may, on the requisition of the Inspector of Settlements and Plantations, place at the disposal of the inspector one or more of the captured steamers to ply between the settlements and one or more of the commercial points heretofore named, in order to afford the settlers the opportunity to supply their necessary wants, and to sell the products of their land and labor.

4. Whenever a negro has enlisted in the military service of the United States, he may locate his family in any one of the settlements at pleasure, and acquire a homestead, and all other rights and privileges of a settler, as though present in person. In like manner, negroes may settle their families and engage on board the gunboats, or in fishing, or

in the navigation of the inland waters, without losing any claim to land or other advantages derived from this system. But no one, unless an actual settler as above defined, or unless absent on Government service, will be entitled to claim any right to land or property in any settlement by virtue of these orders.

5. In order to carry out this system of settlement, a general officer will be detailed as Inspector of Settlements and Plantations, whose duty it shall be to visit the settlements, to regulate their police and general arrangement, and who will furnish personally to each head of a family, subject to the approval of the President of the United States, a possessory title in writing, giving as near as possible the description of boundaries; and who shall adjust all claims or conflicts that may arise under the same, subject to the like approval, treating such titles altogether as possessory. The same general officer will also be charged with the enlistment and organization of the negro recruits, and protecting their interests while absent from their settlements; and will be governed by the rules and regulations prescribed by the War Department for such purposes.

6. Brigadier-General R. Saxton is hereby appointed Inspector of Settlements and Plantations, and will at once enter on the performance of his duties. No change is intended or desired in the settlement now on Beaufort Island, nor will any rights to property heretofore acquired be affected thereby.

By order of Major-General W. T. Sherman,

L. M. Dayton, *Assistant Adjutant-General.*

I saw a good deal of the secretary socially, during the time of his visit to Savannah. He kept his quarters on the revenue-cutter with Simeon Draper, Esq., which cutter lay at a wharf in the river, but he came very often to my quarters at Mr. Green's house. Though appearing robust and strong, he complained a good deal of internal pains, which he said threatened his life, and would compel him soon to quit public office. He professed to have come from Washington purposely for rest and recreation, and he spoke unreservedly of the bickerings and jealousies at the national capital; of the interminable quarrels of the State Governors about their quotas, and more particularly of the financial troubles that threatened the very existence of the Government itself. He said that the price of every thing had so risen in comparison with the depreciated money, that there was danger of national bankruptcy, and he appealed to me, as a soldier and patriot, to hurry up matters so as to bring the war to a close.

He left for Port Royal about the 15th of January, and promised to go North without delay, so as to hurry back to me the supplies I had called for, as indispensable for the prosecution of the next stage of the campaign. I was quite impatient to get off myself, for a city-life had become dull and tame, and we were all anxious to get into the pine-woods again, free from the importunities of rebel women asking for protection, and of the civilians from the North who were coming to Savannah for cotton and all sorts of profit.

On the 18th of January General Slocum was ordered to turn over the city of Savannah to General J. G. Foster, commanding the Department of the South, who proposed to retain his own headquarters at Hilton Head, and to occupy Savannah by General Grover's division of the Nineteenth Corps, just arrived from James River;[26] and on the next day, viz., January 19th, I made the first general orders for the move.

These were substantially to group the right wing of the army at Pocotaligo, already held by the Seventeenth Corps, and the left wing and cavalry at or near Robertsville, in South Carolina. The army remained substantially the same as during the march from Atlanta, with the exception of a few changes in the commanders of brigades and divisions, the addition of some men who had joined from furlough, and the loss of others from the expiration of their term of service. My own personal staff remained the same, with the exception that General W. F. Barry had rejoined us at Savannah, perfectly recovered from his attack of erysipelas, and continued with us to the end of the war. Generals Easton and Beckwith remained at Savannah, in charge of their respective depots, with orders to follow and meet us by sea with supplies when we should reach the coast at Wilmington or Newbern, North Carolina.

Of course, I gave out with some ostentation, especially among the rebels, that we were going to Charleston or Augusta; but I had long before made up my mind to waste no time on either, further than to play off on their fears, thus to retain for their protection a force of the enemy which would otherwise concentrate in our front, and make the passage of some of the great rivers that crossed our route more difficult and bloody.

Having accomplished all that seemed necessary, on the 21st of January, with my entire headquarters, officers, clerks, orderlies, etc., with wagons and horses, I embarked in a steamer for Beaufort, South Carolina, touching at Hilton Head, to see General Foster. The weather was rainy and bad, but we reached Beaufort safely on the 23d, and found some of General Blair's troops

[26] Cuvier Grover (1828–1885) graduated from the USMA in 1850 and took command of the Dist. of Savannah, Dept. of the South, on Jan 18, 1865. *CWHC,* 270.

there. The bulk of his corps (Seventeenth) was, however, up on the railroad about Pocotaligo, near the head of Broad River, to which their supplies were carried from Hilton Head by steamboats. General Hatch's division (of General Foster's command) was still at Coosawhatchie or Tullafinny,[27] where the Charleston & Savannah Railroad crosses the river of that name. All the country between Beaufort and Pocotaligo was low alluvial land, cut up by an infinite number of salt-water sloughs and fresh-water creeks, easily susceptible of defense by a small force; and why the enemy had allowed us to make a lodgment at Pocotaligo so easily I did not understand, unless it resulted from fear or ignorance. It seemed to me then that the terrible energy they had displayed in the earlier stages of the war was beginning to yield to the slower but more certain industry and discipline of our Northern men. It was to me manifest that the soldiers and people of the South entertained an undue fear of our Western men, and, like children, they had invented such ghostlike stories of our prowess in Georgia, that they were scared by their own inventions. Still, this was a power, and I intended to utilize it. Somehow, our men had got the idea that South Carolina was the cause of all our troubles; her people were the first to fire on Fort Sumter, had been in a great hurry to precipitate the country into civil war; and therefore on them should fall the scourge of war in its worst form. Taunting messages had also come to us, when in Georgia, to the effect that, when we should reach South Carolina, we would find a people less passive, who would fight us to the bitter end, daring us to come over, etc.; so that I saw and felt that we would not be able longer to restrain our men as we had done in Georgia.

Personally I had many friends in Charleston, to whom I would gladly have extended protection and mercy, but they were beyond my personal reach, and I would not restrain the army lest its vigor and energy should be impaired; and I had every reason to expect bold and strong resistance at the many broad and deep rivers that lay across our path.

General Foster's Department of the South had been enlarged to embrace the coast of North Carolina, so that the few troops serving there, under the command of General Innis N. Palmer,[28] at Newbern, became subject to my command. General A. H. Terry held Fort Fisher, and a rumor came that he had taken the city of Wilmington; but this was premature. He had about

[27] The Charleston and Savannah Railroad crossed the Tullifinny River approximately thirty miles northwest of Beaufort Island. Davis et al., *Official Military Atlas of the Civil War,* plate 144.

[28] Innis N. Palmer (1824–1900) graduated from the USMA in 1846 and was placed in command of the Dist. of North Carolina, Dept. of the South, on Jan. 31. *CWHC,* 414.

eight thousand men. General Schofield was also known to be *en route* from Nashville for North Carolina, with the entire Twenty-third Corps, so that I had every reason to be satisfied that I would receive additional strength as we progressed northward, and before I should need it.

General W. J. Hardee commanded the Confederate forces in Charleston, with the Salkiehatchie River as his line of defense. It was also known that General Beauregard had come from the direction of Tennessee, and had assumed the general command of all the troops designed to resist our progress.

The heavy winter rains had begun early in January, rendered the roads execrable, and the Savannah River became so swollen that it filled its many channels, overflowing the vast extent of rice-fields that lay on the east bank. This flood delayed our departure two weeks; for it swept away our pontoon-bridge at Savannah, and came near drowning John E. Smith's division of the Fifteenth Corps, with several heavy trains of wagons that were *en route* from Savannah to Pocotaligo by the old causeway.[29]

General Slocum had already ferried two of his divisions across the river, when Sister's Ferry, about forty miles above Savannah, was selected for the passage of the rest of his wing and of Kilpatrick's cavalry. The troops were in motion for that point before I quitted Savannah, and Captain S. B. Luce, United States Navy,[30] had reported to me with a gunboat (the Pontiac) and a couple of transports, which I requested him to use in protecting Sister's Ferry during the passage of Slocum's wing, and to facilitate the passage of the troops all he could. The utmost activity prevailed at all points, but it was manifest we could not get off much before the 1st day of February; so I determined to go in person to Pocotaligo, and there act as though we were bound for Charleston. On the 24th of January I started from Beaufort with a part of my staff, leaving the rest to follow at leisure, rode across the island to a pontoon-bridge that spanned the channel between it and the main-land, and thence rode by Garden's Corners to a plantation not far from Pocotaligo, occupied by General Blair. There we found a house, with a majestic avenue of live-oaks, whose limbs had been cut away by the troops for firewood, and desolation marked one of those splendid

[29] On Jan. 19, 1865, Smith's troops were caught in a torrential downpour while crossing a causeway on Cheves's rice plantation. No one drowned, but nine wagons were lost to the flood. *OR,* I, 47(I), 314–315.

[30] Stephen B. Luce (1827–1917), founder of the Naval War College in Newport, RI, was known for attacking blockade runners along the South Carolina coast during the war. "Founder of Naval War College Dies," *Fresno Morning Republican* (Fresno, CA), July 29, 1917, 10; *ORN,* I, 16, 207–208.

South Carolina estates where the proprietors formerly had dispensed a hospitality that distinguished the old *régime* of that proud State. I slept on the floor of the house, but the night was so bitter cold that I got up by the fire several times, and when it burned low I rekindled it with an old mantel-clock and the wreck of a bedstead which stood in a corner of the room—the only act of vandalism that I recall done by myself personally during the war.

The next morning I rode to Pocotaligo, and thence reconnoitred our entire line down to Coosawhatchie. Pocotaligo Fort was on low, alluvial ground, and near it began the sandy pine-land which connected with the firm ground extending inland, constituting the chief reason for its capture at the very first stage of the campaign. Hatch's division was ordered to that point from Coosawhatchie, and the whole of Howard's right wing was brought near by, ready to start by the 1st of February. I also reconnoitred the point of the Salkiehatchie River, where the Charleston Railroad crossed it, found the bridge protected by a rebel battery on the farther side, and could see a few men about it; but the stream itself was absolutely impassable, for the whole bottom was overflowed by its swollen waters to the breadth of a full mile. Nevertheless, Force's and Mower's divisions of the Seventeenth Corps were kept active, seemingly with the intention to cross over in the direction of Charleston, and thus to keep up the delusion that that city was our immediate "objective."[31] Meantime, I had reports from General Slocum of the terrible difficulties he had encountered about Sister's Ferry, where the Savannah River was reported nearly three miles wide, and it seemed for a time almost impossible for him to span it at all with his frail pontoons. About this time (January 25th), the weather cleared away bright and cold, and I inferred that the river would soon run down, and enable Slocum to pass the river before February 1st. One of the divisions of the Fifteenth Corps (Corse's) had also been cut off by the loss of the pontoon-bridge at Savannah, so that General Slocum had with him, not only his own two corps, but Corse's division and Kilpatrick's cavalry, without which it was not prudent for me to inaugurate the campaign. We therefore rested quietly about Pocotaligo, collecting stores and making final preparations, until the 1st of February, when I learned that the cavalry and two divisions of the Twentieth Corps

[31] In the first edition of the memoirs (1875), this portion of WTS's text read, "Nevertheless, a division (Mower's) of the Seventeenth Corps was kept active, seemingly with the intention to cross over in the direction of Charleston, and thus to keep up the delusion that that city was our immediate 'objective.'" For more on WTS's motivation for amending this section of the memoirs, see M. F. Force to WTS, Aug. 31, 1875, in the Appendix to Volume II.

were fairly across the river, and then gave the necessary orders for the march northward.

Before closing this chapter, I will add a few original letters that bear directly on the subject, and tend to illustrate it:

HEADQUARTERS ARMIES OF THE UNITED STATES,
WASHINGTON, D. C., *January* 21, 1865.

Major-General W. T. SHERMAN, *commanding Military Division of the Mississippi.*

GENERAL: Your letters brought by General Barnard were received at City Point, and read with interest. Not having them with me, however, I cannot say that in this I will be able to satisfy you on all points of recommendation. As I arrived here at 1 P. M., and must leave at 6 P. M., having in the mean time spent over three hours with the secretary and General Halleck, I must be brief. Before your last request to have Thomas make a campaign into the heart of Alabama, I had ordered Schofield to Annapolis, Maryland, with his corps. The advance (six thousand) will reach the seaboard by the 23d, the remainder following as rapidly as railroad transportation can be procured from Cincinnati. The corps numbers over twenty-one thousand men.

. . . .

Thomas is still left with a sufficient force, surplus to go to Selma under an energetic leader. He has been telegraphed to, to know whether he could go, and, if so, by which of several routes he would select. No reply is yet received. Canby has been ordered to act offensively from the sea-coast to the interior, toward Montgomery and Selma. Thomas's forces will move from the north at an early day, or some of his troops will be sent to Canby. Without further reënforcement Canby will have a moving column of twenty thousand men.

Fort Fisher, you are aware, has been captured. We have a force there of eight thousand effective. At Newbern about half the number. It is rumored, through deserters, that Wilmington also has fallen. I am inclined to believe the rumor, because on the 17th we knew the enemy were blowing up their works about Fort Caswell, and that on the 18th Terry moved on Wilmington.

If Wilmington is captured, Schofield will go there. If not, he will be sent to Newbern. In either event, all the surplus forces at the two points will move to the interior, toward Goldsboro', in coöperation with your movements. From either point, railroad communications can be run out, there being here abundance of rolling-stock suited to the gauge of those roads.

There have been about sixteen thousand men sent from Lee's army south. Of these, you will have fourteen thousand against you, if Wilmington is not held by the enemy, casualties at Fort Fisher having overtaken about two thousand.

All other troops are subject to your orders as you come in communication with them. They will be so instructed. From about Richmond I will watch Lee closely, and if he detaches many men, or attempts to evacuate, will pitch in. In the meantime, should you be brought to a halt anywhere, I can send two corps of thirty thousand effective men to your support, from the troops about Richmond.

To resume: Canby is ordered to operate to the interior from the Gulf. A. J. Smith may go from the north, but I think it doubtful. A force of twenty-eight or thirty thousand will coöperate with you from Newbern or Wilmington, or both. You can call for reënforcements.

This will be handed you by Captain Hudson, of my staff, who will return with any message you may have for me. If there is any thing I can do for you in the way of having supplies on shipboard, at any point on the sea-coast, ready for you, let me know it.

Yours truly,

U. S. Grant, *Lieutenant-General.*

Headquarters Military Division of the Mississippi,
in the Field, Pocotaligo, South Carolina, *January* 29, 1865.

Lieutenant-General U. S. Grant, *City Point, Virginia.*

Dear General: Captain Hudson has this moment arrived with your letter of January 21st, which I have read with interest.

The capture of Fort Fisher has a most important bearing on my campaign, and I rejoice in it for many reasons, because of its intrinsic importance, and because it gives me another point of security on the seaboard. I hope General Terry will follow it up by the capture of Wilmington, although I do not look for it, from Admiral Porter's dispatch to me. I rejoice that Terry was not a West-Pointer, that he belonged to your army, and that he had the same troops with which Butler feared to make the attempt.

Admiral Dahlgren, whose fleet is reënforced by some more iron-clads, wants to make an assault *à la* Fisher on Fort Moultrie, but I withhold my consent, for the reason that the capture of all Sullivan's Island is not conclusive as to Charleston; the capture of James Island would be, but all pronounce that impossible at this time. Therefore, I am moving (as hitherto designed) for the railroad west of Branchville, then will swing across to Orangeburg, which will interpose my army between Charleston and the interior. Contemporaneous with this, Foster will demonstrate up the Edisto, and afterward make a lodgment at Bull's Bay, and occupy the common road which leads from Mount Pleasant toward Georgetown. When I get to Columbia, I think I shall move straight for Goldsboro', *via* Fayetteville. By this circuit I cut all roads, and devastate the land; and the forces along the coast, commanded by Foster, will follow my movement, taking any thing the enemy lets go, or so occupy his attention that he cannot detach all his forces against me. I feel sure of getting Wilmington, and may be Charleston, and being at Goldsboro', with its railroads finished back to Morehead City and Wilmington, I can easily take Raleigh, when it seems that Lee must come out. If Schofield comes to Beaufort, he should be pushed out to Kinston, on the Neuse, and may be Goldsboro' (or, rather, a point on the Wilmington road, south of Goldsboro'). It is not necessary to storm Goldsboro', because it is in a distant region, of no importance in itself, and, if its garrison is forced to draw supplies from its north, it, will be eating up the same stores on which Lee depends for his command.

I have no doubt Hood will bring his army to Augusta. Canby and Thomas should penetrate Alabama as far as possible, to keep employed at least a part of Hood's army; or, what would accomplish the same thing, Thomas might reoccupy the railroad from Chattanooga forward to the Etowah, viz., Rome, Kingston, and Allatoona, thereby threatening Georgia. I know that the Georgia troops are disaffected. At Savannah I met delegates from several counties of the southwest, who manifested a decidedly hostile spirit to the Confederate cause. I nursed the feeling as far as possible, and instructed Grover to keep it up.

My left wing must now be at Sister's Ferry, crossing the Savannah River to the east bank. Slocum has orders to be at Robertsville to-morrow, prepared to move on Barnwell. Howard is here, all ready to start for the Augusta Railroad at Midway.

We find the enemy on the east side of the Salkiehatchie, and cavalry in our front; but all give ground on our approach, and seem to be merely watching us. If we start on Tuesday, in one week we shall be near Orangeburg, having broken up the Augusta road from the Edisto westward twenty or twenty-five miles. I will be sure that every rail is twisted. Should we encounter too much opposition near Orangeburg, then I will for a time neglect that branch, and rapidly move on Columbia, and fill up the triangle formed by the Congaree and Wateree (tributaries of the Santee), breaking up that great centre of the Carolina roads. Up to that point I feel full confidence, but from there may have to manœuvre some, and will be guided by the questions of weather and supplies.

You remember we had fine weather last February for our Meridian trip, and my memory of the weather at Charleston is, that February is usually a fine month. Before the March storms come we should be within striking distance of the coast. The months of April and May will be the best for operations from Goldsboro' to Raleigh and the Roanoke. You may rest assured that I will keep my troops well in hand, and, if I get worsted, will aim to make the enemy pay so dearly that you will have less to do. I know that this trip is necessary; it must be made sooner or later; I am on time, and in the right position for it. My army is large enough for the purpose, and I ask no reënforcement, but simply wish the utmost activity to be kept up at all other points, so that concentration against me may not be universal.

I expect that Jeff. Davis will move heaven and earth to catch me, for success to this column is fatal to his dream of empire. Richmond is not more vital to his cause than Columbia and the heart of South Carolina.

If Thomas will not move on Selma, order him to occupy Rome, Kingston, and Allatoona, and again threaten Georgia in the direction of Athens.

I think the "poor white trash" of the South are falling out of their ranks by sickness, desertion, and every available means; but there is a large class of vindictive Southerners who will fight to the last. The squabbles in Richmond, the howls in Charleston, and the disintegration elsewhere, are all good omens for us; we must not relax one iota, but, on the contrary, pile up our efforts. I would, ere this, have been off, but we had terrific rains, which caught us in motion, and nearly drowned some of the troops in the rice-fields of the Savannah, swept away our causeway (which had been carefully corduroyed), and made the swamps hereabout mere lakes of slimy mud. The weather is now good, and I have the army on *terra firma.* Supplies, too, came for a long time by daily driblets instead of in bulk; this is now all remedied, and I hope to start on Tuesday.

I will issue instructions to General Foster, based on the reënforcements of North Carolina; but if Schofield come, you had better relieve Foster, who cannot take the field, and needs an operation on his leg. Let Schofield take command, with his headquarters at Beaufort, North Carolina, and with orders to secure Goldsboro' (with its railroad communication back to Beaufort and Wilmington). If Lee lets us get that position, he is gone up.

I will start with my Atlanta army (sixty thousand), supplied as before, depending on the country for all food in excess of thirty days. I will have less cattle on the hoof, but I hear of hogs, cows, and calves, in Barnwell and the Columbia districts. Even here we have found some forage. Of course, the enemy will carry off and destroy some forage, but I will burn the houses where the people burn their forage, and they will get tired of it.

I must risk Hood, and trust to you to hold Lee or be on his heels if he comes south. I observe that the enemy has some respect for my name, for they gave up Pocotaligo without a fight when they heard that the attacking force belonged to my army. I will try and keep up that feeling, which is a real power. With respect, your friend,

W. T. SHERMAN, *Major-General commanding.*

P. S.—I leave my chief-quartermaster and commissary behind to follow coastwise.

W. T. S.

[Dispatch No. 6.]

FLAG-STEAMER PHILADELPHIA,
SAVANNAH RIVER, *January* 4, 1865.

Hon. GIDEON WELLES, *Secretary of the Navy.*

SIR: I have already apprised the Department that the army of General Sherman occupied the city of Savannah on the 21st of December.

The rebel army, hardly respectable in numbers or condition, escaped by crossing the river and taking the Union Causeway toward the railroad.

I have walked about the city several times, and can affirm that its tranquillity is undisturbed. The Union soldiers who are stationed within its limits are as orderly as if they were in New York or Boston. . . . One effect of the march of General Sherman through Georgia has been to satisfy the people that their credulity has been imposed upon by the lying assertions of the rebel Government, affirming the inability of the United States Government to withstand the armies of rebeldom. They have seen the old flag of the United States carried by its victorious legions through their State, almost unopposed, and placed in their principal city without a blow.

Since the occupation of the city General Sherman has been occupied in making arrangements for its security after he leaves it for the march that he meditates. My attention has been directed to such measures of coöperation as the number and quality of my force permit.

On the 2d I arrived here from Charleston, whither, as I stated in my dispatch of the 29th of December, I had gone in consequence of information from the senior officer there that the rebels contemplated issuing from the harbor, and his request for my presence. Having placed a force there of seven monitors, sufficient to meet such an emergency, and not perceiving any sign of the expected raid, I returned to Savannah, to keep in communication with General Sherman and be ready to render any assistance that might be desired. General Sherman has fully informed me of his plans, and, so far as my means permit, they shall not lack assistance by water.

On the 3d the transfer of the right wing to Beaufort was began, and the only suitable vessel I had at hand (the Harvest Moon) was sent to Thunderbolt to receive the first embarkation. This took place about 3 P. M., and was witnessed by General Sherman and General Barnard (United States Engineers) and myself. The Pontiac is ordered around to assist, and the army transports also followed the first move by the Harvest Moon.

I could not help remarking the unbroken silence that prevailed in the large array of troops; not a voice was to be heard, as they gathered in masses on the bluff to look at the vessels. The notes of a solitary bugle alone came from their midst.

General Barnard made a brief visit to one of the rebel works (Causten's Bluff) that dominated this water-course—the best approach of the kind to Savannah.

I am collecting data that will fully exhibit to the Department the powerful character of the defenses of the city and its approaches.

General Sherman will not retain the extended limits they embrace, but will contract the line very much.

General Foster still holds the position near the Tullifinny. With his concurrence I have detached the fleet brigade, and the men belonging to it have returned to their vessels. The excellent service performed by this detachment has fully realized my wishes, and exemplified the efficiency of the organization—infantry and light artillery handled as skirmishers. The howitzers were always landed as quickly as the men, and were brought into action before the light pieces of the land-service could be got ashore.

I regret very much that the reduced complements of the vessels prevent me from maintaining the force in constant organization. With three hundred more marines and five hundred seamen I could frequently operate to great advantage, at the present time, when the attention of the rebels is so engrossed by General Sherman.

It is said that they have a force at Hardeeville, the pickets of which were retained on the Union Causeway until a few days since, when some of our troops crossed the river and pushed them back. Concurrently with this, I caused the Sonoma to anchor so as to sweep the ground in the direction of the causeway.

The transfer of the right-wing (thirty thousand men) to Beaufort will so imperil the rebel force at Hardeeville that it will be cut off or dispersed, if not moved in season.

Meanwhile I will send the Dai-Ching to St. Helena, to meet any want that may arise in that quarter, while the Mingo and Pontiac will be ready to act from Broad River.

The general route of the army will be northward; but the exact direction must be decided more or less by circumstances which it may not be possible to foresee.

My coöperation will be confined to assistance in attacking Charleston, or in establishing communication at Georgetown, in case the army pushes on without attacking Charleston, and time alone will show which of these will eventuate.

The weather of the winter first, and the condition of the ground in spring, would permit little advantage to be derived from the presence of the army at Richmond until the middle of May. So that General Sherman has no reason to move in haste, but can choose such objects as he prefers, and take as much time as their attainment may demand. The Department will learn the objects in view of General Sherman more precisely from a letter addressed by him to General Halleck, which he read to me a few days since.

I have the honor to be, very respectfully, your obedient servant,

J. A. Dahlgren,

Rear-Admiral, commanding South-Atlantic Blockading-Squadron.

Headquarters Military Division of the Mississippi,
in the Field, Pocotaligo, South Carolina, *January* 29, 1865.

Major-General J. G. Foster, *commanding Department of the South.*

General: I have just received dispatches from General Grant, stating that Schofield's corps (the Twenty-third), twenty-one thousand strong, is ordered east from Tennessee, and will be sent to Beaufort, North Carolina. That is well; I want that force to secure a point on the railroad about Goldsboro', and then to build the railroad out to that point. If Goldsboro' be too strong to carry by a rapid movement, then a point near the Neuse, south of Goldsboro', will answer, but the bridge and position about Kinston, should be held and fortified strong. The movement should be masked by the troops already at Newbern. Please notify General Palmer that these troops are coming, and to be prepared to receive them. Major-General Schofield will command in person, and is admirably adapted for the work. If it is possible, I want him to secure Goldsboro', with the railroad back to Morehead City and Wilmington. As soon as General Schofield reaches Fort Macon, have him to meet some one of your staff, to explain in full the details of the situation of affairs with me; and you can give him the chief command of all troops at Cape Fear and in North Carolina. If he finds the enemy has all turned south against me, he need not follow, but turn his attention against Raleigh; if he can secure Goldsboro' and Wilmington, it will be as much as I expect before I have passed the Santee. Send him all detachments of men that have come to join my army. They can be so organized and officered as to be efficient, for they are nearly all old soldiers who have been detached or on furlough. Until I pass the Santee, you can better use these detachments at Bull's Bay, Georgetown, etc.

I will instruct General McCallum, of the Railroad Department, to take his men up to Beaufort, North Carolina, and employ them on the road out. I do not know that he can use them on any road here. I did instruct him, while awaiting information from North Carolina, to have them build a good trestle-bridge across Port Royal ferry; but I now suppose the pontoon-bridge will do. If you move the pontoons, be sure to make a good road out to Garden's Corners, and mark it with sign-boards—obstructing the old road, so that, should I send back any detachments, they would not be misled.

I prefer that Hatch's force should not be materially weakened until I am near Columbia, when you may be governed by the situation of affairs about Charleston. If you can break the railroad between this and Charleston, then this force could be reduced.

I am, with respect, etc.,
W. T. SHERMAN, *Major-General commanding.*

HEADQUARTERS MILITARY DIVISION OF THE MISSISSIPPI,
IN THE FIELD, SAVANNAH, *January* 19, 1865.

Hon. EDWIN M. STANTON, *Secretary of War, Washington, D. C.*

SIR: When you left Savannah a few days ago, you forgot the map which General Geary had prepared for you, showing the route by which his division entered the city of Savannah, being the first troops to occupy that city. I now send it to you.

I avail myself of the opportunity also to inclose you copies of all my official orders touching trade and intercourse with the people of Georgia, as well as for the establishment of the negro settlements.

Delegations of the people of Georgia continue to come in, and I am satisfied that, by judicious handling and by a little respect shown to their prejudices, we can create a schism in Jeff. Davis's dominions. All that I have conversed with realize the truth that slavery as an institution is defunct, and the only questions that remain are what disposition shall be made of the negroes themselves. I confess myself unable to offer a complete solution for these questions, and prefer to leave it to the slower operations of time. We have given the initiative, and can afford to await the working of the experiment.

As to trade-matters, I also think it is to our interest to keep the Southern people somewhat dependent on the articles of commerce to which they have hitherto been accustomed. General Grover is now here, and will, I think, be able to handle this matter judiciously, and may gradually relax, and invite cotton to come in in large quantities. But at first we should manifest no undue anxiety on that score; for the rebels would at once make use of it as a power against us. We should assume a tone of perfect contempt for cotton and every thing else in comparison with the great object of the war—*the restoration of the Union, with all its rights and power.* If the rebels burn cotton as a war measure, they simply play into our hands by taking away the only product of value they have to exchange in foreign ports for war-ships and munitions. By such a course, also, they alienate the feelings of a large class of small farmers who look to their little parcels of cotton to exchange for food and clothing for their families. I hope the Government will not manifest too much anxiety to obtain cotton in large quantities, and especially that the President will not indorse the contracts for the purchase of large quantities of cotton. Several contracts, involving from six to ten thousand bales, indorsed by Mr. Lincoln, have been shown me, but were not in such a form as to amount to an order to compel me to facilitate their execution.

As to Treasury agents, and agents to take charge of confiscated and abandoned property, whose salaries depend on their fees, I can only say that, as a general rule, they are mischievous and disturbing elements to a military government, and it is almost impossible for us to study the law and regulations so as to understand fully their powers and duties. I rather think the Quartermaster's Department of the army could better fulfill all their duties and accomplish all that is aimed at by the law. Yet on this subject I will leave Generals Foster and Grover to do the best they can.

I am, with great respect, your obedient servant,
W. T. Sherman, *Major-General commanding.*

Headquarters Military Division of the Mississippi,
in the Field, Savannah, Georgia, *January* 2, 1865.

Hon. Edwin M. Stanton, *Secretary of War, Washington, D. C.*

Sir: I have just received from Lieutenant-General Grant a copy of that part of your telegram to him of December 26th relating to cotton, a copy of which has been immediately furnished to General Easton, chief-quartermaster, who will be strictly governed by it.

I had already been approached by all the consuls and half the people of Savannah on this cotton question, and my invariable answer was that all the cotton in Savannah was prize of war, belonged to the United States, and nobody should recover a bale of it with my consent; that, as cotton had been one of the chief causes of this war, it should help to pay its expenses; that all cotton became tainted with treason from the hour the first act of hostility was committed against the United States some time in December, 1860; and that no bill of sale subsequent to that date could convey title.

My orders were that an officer of the Quartermaster's Department, United States Army, might furnish the holder, agent, or attorney, a mere certificate of the fact of seizure, with description of the bales' marks, etc., the cotton then to be turned over to the agent of the Treasury Department, to be shipped to New York for sale. But, since the receipt of your dispatch, I have ordered General Easton to make the shipment himself to the quartermaster at New York, where you can dispose of it at pleasure. I do not think the Treasury Department ought to bother itself with the prizes or captures of war.

Mr. Barclay, former consul at New York, representing Mr. Molyneux, former consul here, but absent a long time, called on me with reference to cotton claimed by English subjects. He seemed amazed when I told him I should pay no respect to consular certificates, that in no event would I treat an English subject with more favor than one of our own deluded citizens, and that for my part I was unwilling to fight for cotton for the benefit of Englishmen openly engaged in smuggling arms and instruments of war to kill us; that, on the contrary, it would afford me great satisfaction to conduct my army to Nassau, and wipe out that nest of pirates. I explained to him, however, that I was not a diplomatic agent of the General Government of the United States, but that my opinion, so frankly expressed, was that of a soldier, which it would be well for him to heed. It appeared, also, that he owned a plantation on the line of investment of Savannah, which, of course, was pillaged, and for which he expected me to give some certificate entitling him to indemnification, which I declined emphatically.

I have adopted in Savannah rules concerning property—severe but just—founded upon the laws of nations and the practice of civilized governments, and am clearly of opinion that we should claim all the belligerent rights over conquered countries, that the people may realize the truth that war is no child's play.

I embrace in this a copy of a letter, dated December 31, 1864, in answer to one from Solomon Cohen (a rich lawyer) to General Blair, his personal friend, as follows:

Major-General F. P. Blair, *commanding Seventeenth Army Corps.*

General: Your note, inclosing Mr. Cohen's of this date, is received, and I answer frankly through you his inquiries.

1. No one can practise law as an attorney in the United States without acknowledging the supremacy of our Government. If I am not in error, an attorney is as much an officer of the court as the clerk, and it would be a novel thing in a government to have a court to administer law which denied the supremacy of the government itself.

2. No one will be allowed the privileges of a merchant, or, rather, to trade is a privilege which no one should seek of the Government without in like manner acknowledging its supremacy.

3. If Mr. Cohen remains in Savannah as a denizen, his property, real and personal, will not be disturbed unless its temporary use be necessary for the military authorities of the city. The title to property will not be disturbed in any event, until adjudicated by the courts of the United States.

4. If Mr. Cohen leaves Savannah under my Special Order No. 143, it is a public acknowledgment that he "adheres to the enemies of the United States," and all his property becomes forfeited to the United States. But, as a matter of favor, he will be allowed to carry with him clothing and furniture for the use of himself, his family, and servants, and will be transported within the enemy's lines, but not by way of Port Royal.

These rules will apply to all parties, and from them no exception will be made.

I have the honor to be, general, your obedient servant,

W. T. Sherman, *Major-General.*

This letter was in answer to specific inquiries; it is clear, and covers all the points, and, should I leave before my orders are executed, I will endeavor to impress upon my successor, General Foster, their wisdom and propriety.

I hope the course I have taken in these matters will meet your approbation, and that the President will not refund to parties claiming cotton or other property, without the strongest evidence of loyalty and friendship on the part of the claimant, or unless some other positive end is to be gained.

I am, with great respect, your obedient servant,

W. T. Sherman, *Major-General commanding.*

23

Campaign of the Carolinas.

FEBRUARY AND MARCH, 1865.

ON THE 1ST DAY of February, as before explained, the army designed for the active campaign from Savannah northward was composed of two wings, commanded respectively by Major-Generals Howard and Slocum, and was substantially the same that had marched from Atlanta to Savannah. The same general orders were in force, and this campaign may properly be classed as a continuance of the former.

The right wing, less Corse's division, Fifteenth Corps, was grouped at or near Pocotaligo, South Carolina, with its wagons filled with food, ammunition, and forage, all ready to start, and only waiting for the left wing, which was detained by the flood in the Savannah River. It was composed as follows:

Fifteenth Corps, Major-General JOHN A. LOGAN.

First Division, Brigadier-General Charles R. Woods; Second Division, Major-General W. B. Hazen; Third Division, Brigadier-General John E. Smith; Fourth Division, Brigadier-General John M. Corse. Artillery brigade, eighteen guns, Lieutenant-Colonel W. H. Ross, First Michigan Artillery.

Seventeenth Corps, Major-General FRANK P. BLAIR, JR.

First Division, Major-General Joseph A. Mower; Second Division, Brigadier-General M. F. Force; Fourth Division, Brigadier-General Giles A. Smith. Artillery brigade, fourteen guns, Major A. C. Waterhouse, First Illinois Artillery.

The left wing, with Corse's division and Kilpatrick's cavalry, was at and near Sister's Ferry, forty miles above the city of Savannah, engaged in crossing the river, then much swollen. It was composed as follows:

Fourteenth Corps, Major-General JEFF. C. DAVIS.

First Division, Brigadier-General W. P. Carlin; Second Division, Brigadier-General John D. Morgan; Third Division, Brigadier-

General A. Baird. Artillery brigade, sixteen guns, Major Charles Houghtaling, First Illinois Artillery.

Twentieth Corps, Brigadier-General A. S. WILLIAMS.

First Division, Brigadier-General N. J. Jackson; Second Division, Brigadier-General J. W. Geary; Third Division, Brigadier-General W. T. Ward. Artillery brigade, sixteen guns, Major J. A. Reynolds, First New York Artillery.

Cavalry Division, Brigadier-General JUDSON KILPATRICK.

First Brigade, Colonel T. J. Jordan, Ninth Pennsylvania Cavalry; Second Brigade, Colonel S. D. Atkins, Ninety-second Illinois Volunteers; Third Brigade, Colonel George E. Spencer, First Alabama Cavalry. One battery of four guns.[1]

The actual strength of the army, as given in the following official tabular statements, was at the time sixty thousand and seventy-nine men, and sixty-eight guns. The trains were made up of about twenty-five hundred wagons, with six mules to each wagon, and about six hundred ambulances, with two horses each. The contents of the wagons embraced an ample supply of ammunition for a great battle; forage for about seven days, and provisions for twenty days, mostly of bread, sugar, coffee, and salt, depending largely for fresh meat on beeves driven on the hoof and such cattle, hogs, and poultry, as we expected to gather along our line of march.

RECAPITULATION—CAMPAIGN OF THE CAROLINAS.

ARM.	February 1.	March 1.	April 1.	April 10.
Infantry.	53,923	51,598	74,105	80,968
Cavalry.	4,438	4,401	4,781	5,537
Artillery.	1,718	1,677	2,264	2,443
Aggregate.	60,079	57,676	81,150	88,948

The enemy occupied the cities of Charleston and Augusta, with garrisons capable of making a respectable if not successful defense, but utterly unable to meet our veteran columns in the open field. To resist or delay our progress north, General Wheeler had his division of cavalry (reduced to the size of a brigade by his hard and persistent fighting ever since the beginning of the Atlanta campaign), and General Wade Hampton had been dispatched from the Army of Virginia to his native State of South Carolina, with a great

[1] For the order of battle of WTS's army on Feb. 1, 1865, see *OR,* I, 47(I), 46–60.

Effective Strength of the Army under General W. T. SHERM

COMMANDS.	February 1.						March			
	Infantry.		Cavalry.		Artillery.		Infantry.		Cavalry.	
	Commissioned Officers.	Enlisted Men.	Commissioned Officers.	Enlisted Men.	Commissioned Officers.	Enlisted Men.	Commissioned Officers.	Enlisted Men.	Commissioned Officers.	Enlisted Men.
Fifteenth A'ry C'rps. . . .	720	14,638	2	14	10	371	733	14,076	2	
Seventeenth A. C's. . . .	466	11,220	4	43	6	258	441	10,675	4	
Total, Right Wing.	1,186	25,858	6	57	16	629	1,174	24,751	6	
Fourteenth A. C'ps. . . .	596	13,372	. . .	. . . . . .	8	444	571	12,192	. . .	. . . .
Twentieth A. Corps. . . .	579	12,332	. . .	. . . . . .	22	501	610	12,300	. . .	. . . .
Total, Left Wing.	1,175	25,704	. . .	. . . . . .	30	945	1,181	24,492	. . .	. . . .
Tenth Army Corps. . . .	. . . . . .	. . . . . .	.	. . . . . .	. . .	. . . . . .	. . . . . .	. . . . . .	. . .	. . . .
Twenty-third A.C.	. . . . . .	. . . . . .	. . . . .	. . . . . .	. . .	. . . . . .	. . . . . .	. . . . . .	. . .	. . . .
Kilpatrick's Cav'ry.	. . . . . .	. . . . . .	. 180	4,195	4	94	. . . . . .	. . . . . .	173	4,1
Grand Aggregate.	2,361	51,562	186	4,252	50	1,668	2,355	49,243	179	4,2

flourish of trumpets, and extraordinary powers to raise men, money, and horses, with which "to stay the progress of the invader," and "to punish us for our insolent attempt to invade the glorious State of South Carolina!"[2] He was supposed at the time to have, at and near Columbia, two small divisions of cavalry commanded by himself and General Butler.[3]

Of course, I had a species of contempt for these scattered and inconsiderable forces, knew that they could hardly delay us an hour; and the only serious question that occurred to me was, would General Lee sit down in Richmond (besieged by General Grant), and permit us, almost unopposed, to

[2] In early Jan. 1865, Hampton asked to be transferred to South Carolina. He claimed, "In Virginia, we have fought like men; but in South Carolina, we will fight like lions." *Yorkville Enquirer* (York, SC), Jan. 18, 1865, 1.

[3] Matthew C. Butler (1836–1909), nephew of famed U.S. Navy commander Oliver H. Perry, joined the Confederate Army in June 1861 and joined Hampton's cavalry corps in July 1864. *CWHC*, 157.

ing the Campaign of the Carolinas, 1865.

		April 1.						April 10.					
Artillery.		Infantry.		Cavalry.		Artillery.		Infantry.		Cavalry		Artillery.	
	Enlisted Men.	Commissioned Officers.	Enlisted Men.	Commissioned Officers.	Enlisted Men.	Commissioned Officers.	Enlisted Men.	Commissioned Officers.	Enlisted Men.	Commissioned Officers.	Enlisted Men.	Commissioned Officers.	Enlisted Men.
4	348	747	14,668	2	11	15	366	708	14,536	2	21	13	390
5	266	475	11,614	4	42	7	252	478	12,395	2	28	8	253
9	614	1,222	26,282	6	53	22	618	1,186	26,931	4	49	21	643
7	438	516	12,193	. . .	. . . . . .	6	408	561	14,092	. . .	. . . . . .	8	437
3	481	614	11,375	. . .	. . . . . .	23	486	639	11,832	. . .	. . . . . .	18	476
0	919	1,130	23,568	. . .	. . . . . .	29	894	1,200	25,924	. . .	. . . . . .	26	913
.	. . . . . .	372	9,841	15	559	3	124	392	11,335	. . .	. . . . . .	6	366
.	. . . . . .	547	11,143	. . .	. . . . . .	13	480	641	13,359	. . .	. . . . . .	11	282
4	91	. . . . . .		155	3,993	4	77	. . . . . .	. . . . . .	178	5,306	5	170
3	1,624	3,271	70,834	176	4,605	71	2,193	3,419	77,549	182	5,355	69	2,374

pass through the States of South and North Carolina, cutting off and consuming the very supplies on which he depended to feed his army in Virginia, or would he make an effort to escape from General Grant, and endeavor to catch us inland somewhere between Columbia and Raleigh? I knew full well at the time that the broken fragments of Hood's army (which had escaped from Tennessee) were being hurried rapidly across Georgia, by Augusta, to make junction in my front; estimating them at the maximum twenty-five thousand men, and Hardee's, Wheeler's, and Hampton's forces at fifteen thousand, made forty thousand; which, if handled with spirit and energy, would constitute a formidable force, and might make the passage of such rivers as the Santee and Cape Fear a difficult undertaking. Therefore, I took all possible precautions, and arranged with Admiral Dahlgren and General Foster to watch our progress inland by all the means possible, and to provide for us points of security along the coast; as, at Bull's Bay, Georgetown, and the mouth of Cape Fear River. Still, it was extremely desirable in *one* march to reach Goldsboro' in the State of North Carolina (distant four hundred and twenty-five miles), a point of great convenience for ulterior operations, by reason of the two railroads which meet there, coming from the sea-coast at Wilmington and Newbern. Before leaving Savannah I had sent to Newbern Colonel W. W. Wright, of the Engineers, with orders to look to these railroads, to collect rolling-stock, and to have the roads repaired out as far as possible in six weeks—the time estimated as necessary for us to march that distance.[4]

The question of supplies remained still the one of vital importance, and I reasoned that we might safely rely on the country for a considerable quantity of forage and provisions, and that, if the worst came to the worst, we could live several months on the mules and horses of our trains. Nevertheless, time was equally material, and the moment I heard that General Slocum had finished his pontoon-bridge at Sister's Ferry, and that Kilpatrick's cavalry was over the river, I gave the general orders to march, and instructed all the columns to aim for the South Carolina Railroad to the west of Branchville, about Blackville and Midway.[5]

The right wing moved up the Salkiehatchie, the Seventeenth Corps on the right, with orders on reaching Rivers's Bridge to cross over, and the Fifteenth Corps by Hickory Hill to Beaufort's Bridge.[6] Kilpatrick was instructed to march by way of Barnwell; Corse's division and the Twentieth Corps to take such roads as would bring them into communication with the Fifteenth Corps about Beaufort's Bridge. All these columns started promptly on the 1st of February. We encountered Wheeler's cavalry, which had obstructed the road by felling trees, but our men picked these up and threw them aside, so that this obstruction hardly delayed us an hour. In person I accompanied the Fifteenth Corps (General Logan) by McPhersonville and Hickory Hill, and kept couriers going to and fro to General Slocum with instructions to hurry as much as possible, so as to make a junction of the whole army on the South Carolina Railroad about Blackville.[7]

I spent the night of February 1st at Hickory Hill Post-Office, and that of the 2d at Duck Branch Post-Office, thirty-one miles out from Pocotaligo. On the 3d the Seventeenth Corps was opposite Rivers's Bridge, and the Fifteenth approached Beaufort's Bridge. The Salkiehatchie was still over its banks, and

[4] See *OR*, I, 47(II), 157.

[5] Slocum's men constructed a pontoon bridge at Sister's Ferry on Jan. 29, 1865. *OR*, I, 47(I), 419–420.

[6] For a detailed map of the South Carolina coast during this period, see George B. Davis et al., *Official Military Atlas of the Civil War* (New York: Fairfax Press, 1983), plate 144.

[7] WTS ordered Slocum to move on Blackville, SC, on Feb. 7. See *OR*, I, 47(II), 335.

presented a most formidable obstacle. The enemy appeared in some force on the opposite bank, had cut away all the bridges which spanned the many deep channels of the swollen river, and the only available passage seemed to be along the narrow causeways which constituted the common roads. At Rivers's Bridge Generals Mower and Giles A. Smith led their heads of column through this swamp, the water up to their shoulders, crossed over to the pine-land, turned upon the rebel brigade which defended the passage, and routed it in utter disorder. It was in this attack that General Wager Swayne lost his leg, and he had to be conveyed back to Pocotaligo. Still, the loss of life was very small, in proportion to the advantages gained, for the enemy at once abandoned the whole line of the Salkiehatchie, and the Fifteenth Corps passed over at Beaufort's Bridge, without opposition.[8]

On the 5th of February I was at Beaufort's Bridge, by which time General A. S. Williams had got up with five brigades of the Twentieth Corps; I also heard of General Kilpatrick's being abreast of us, at Barnwell, and then gave orders for the march straight for the railroad at Midway. I still remained with the Fifteenth Corps, which, on the 6th of February, was five miles from Bamberg. As a matter of course, I expected severe resistance at this railroad, for its loss would sever all the communications of the enemy in Charleston with those in Augusta.

Early on the 7th, in the midst of a rain-storm, we reached the railroad, almost unopposed, striking it at several points. General Howard told me a good story concerning this, which will bear repeating: He was with the Seventeenth Corps, marching straight for Midway, and when about five miles distant he began to deploy the leading division, so as to be ready for battle. Sitting on his horse by the road-side, while the deployment was making, he saw a man coming down the road, riding as hard as he could, and as he approached he recognized him as one of his own "foragers," mounted on a white horse, with a rope bridle and a blanket for saddle. As he came near he called out, "Hurry up, general; we have got the railroad!" So, while we, the generals, were proceeding deliberately to prepare for a serious battle, a parcel of our foragers, in search of plunder, had got ahead and actually captured the South Carolina Railroad, a line of vital importance to the rebel Government.

As soon as we struck the railroad, details of men were set to work to tear up the rails, to burn the ties and twist the bars. This was a most important railroad, and I proposed to destroy it completely for fifty miles, partly to

[8] Wager Swayne (1834–1902), son of U.S. Supreme Court justice Noah H. Swayne, lost his right leg during the battle at River's Bridge on Feb. 2. *CWHC,* 519.

prevent a possibility of its restoration and partly to utilize the time necessary for General Slocum to get up.[9]

The country thereabouts was very poor, but the inhabitants mostly remained at home. Indeed, they knew not where to go. The enemy's cavalry had retreated before us, but his infantry was reported in some strength at Branchville, on the farther side of the Edisto; yet on the appearance of a mere squad of our men they burned their own bridges—the very thing I wanted, for we had no use for them, and they had.

We all remained strung along this railroad till the 9th of February—the Seventeenth Corps on the right, then the Fifteenth, Twentieth, and cavalry, at Blackville. General Slocum reached Blackville that day, with Geary's division of the Twentieth Corps, and reported the Fourteenth Corps (General Jeff. C. Davis's) to be following by way of Barnwell. On the 10th I rode up to Blackville, where I conferred with Generals Slocum and Kilpatrick, became satisfied that the whole army would be ready within a day, and accordingly made orders for the next movement north to Columbia, the right wing to strike Orangeburg *en route.* Kilpatrick was ordered to demonstrate strongly toward Aiken, to keep up the delusion that we might turn to Augusta; but he was notified that Columbia was the next objective, and that he should cover the left flank against Wheeler, who hung around it. I wanted to reach Columbia before any part of Hood's army could possibly get there. Some of them were reported as having reached Augusta, under the command of General Dick Taylor.

Having sufficiently damaged the railroad, and effected the junction of the entire army, the general march was resumed on the 11th, each corps crossing the South Edisto by separate bridges, with orders to pause on the road leading from Orangeburg to Augusta, till it was certain that the Seventeenth Corps had got possession of Orangeburg. This place was simply important as its occupation would sever the communications between Charleston and Columbia. All the heads of column reached this road, known as the Edgefield road, during the 12th, and the Seventeenth Corps turned to the right, against Orangeburg. When I reached the head of column opposite Orangeburg, I found Giles A. Smith's division halted, with a battery unlimbered, exchanging shots with a party on the opposite side of the Edisto. He reported

[9] In his post-battle report, General O. O. Howard wrote, "During the 7th both corps reached the Augusta and Charleston Railroad, the Fifteenth at Bamberg and the Seventeenth about four miles to the east of Midway . . . On arrival at the railroad reconnaissance were made to the several bridges across the Edisto." *OR,* I, 47(I), 195.

that the bridge was gone, and that the river was deep and impassable. I then directed General Blair to send a strong division below the town, some four or five miles, to effect a crossing there.[10] He laid his pontoon-bridge, but the bottom on the other side was overflowed, and the men had to wade through it, in places as deep as their waists. I was with this division at the time, on foot, trying to pick my way across the overflowed bottom; but, as soon as the head of column reached the sand-hills, I knew that the enemy would not long remain in Orangeburg, and accordingly returned to my horse, on the west bank, and rode rapidly up to where I had left Giles A. Smith. I found him in possession of the broken bridge, abreast of the town, which he was repairing, and I was among the first to cross over and enter the town. By and before the time either Force's[11] or Giles A. Smith's skirmishers entered the place, several stores were on fire, and I am sure that some of the towns-people told me that a Jew merchant had set fire to his own cotton and store, and from this the fire had spread. This, however, was soon put out, and the Seventeenth Corps (General Blair) occupied the place during that night. I remember to have visited a large hospital, on the hill near the railroad depot, which was occupied by the orphan children who had been removed from the asylum in Charleston. We gave them protection, and, I think, some provisions.[12] The railroad and depot were destroyed by order, and no doubt a good deal of cotton was burned, for we all regarded cotton as hostile property, a thing to be destroyed. General Blair was ordered to break up this railroad, forward to the point where it crossed the Santee, and then to turn for Columbia. On the morning of the 13th I again joined the Fifteenth Corps, which crossed the North Edisto by Snilling's Bridge, and moved straight for Columbia, around the head of Caw-Caw Swamp. Orders were sent to all the columns to turn for Columbia, where it was supposed the enemy had concentrated all the men they could from Charleston, Augusta, and even from Virginia. That night I was with the Fifteenth Corps, twenty-one miles from Columbia, where my aide, Colonel Audenried, picked up a rebel officer on the road, who, supposing him to be of the same service with himself, answered all his questions frankly, and revealed the truth that there was nothing in Columbia except Hampton's cavalry. The

[10] In the first edition of the memoirs (1875), WTS identified the division as "Mower's."

[11] In the first edition of the memoirs (1875), WTS suggested the skirmishers belonged to Mower, not Force.

[12] The orphaned children were initially moved from Charleston, SC, in Aug. 1863, to a seminary for young ladies in Orangeburg, SC. Newton B. Jones, "The Charleston Orphan House, 1860–1876," *South Carolina Historical Magazine* 62, no. 2 (Oct. 1961): 209–210.

fact was, that General Hardee, in Charleston, took it for granted that we were after Charleston; the rebel troops in Augusta supposed they were "our objective;" so they abandoned poor Columbia to the care of Hampton's cavalry, which was confused by the rumors that poured in on it, so that both Beauregard and Wade Hampton, who were in Columbia, seem to have lost their heads.

On the 14th the head of the Fifteenth Corps, Charles R. Woods's division, approached the Little Congaree, a broad, deep stream, tributary to the Main Congaree, six or eight miles below Columbia. On the opposite side of this stream was a newly-constructed fort, and on our side a wide extent of old cotton-fields, which had been overflowed, and was covered with a deep slime. General Woods had deployed his leading brigade, which was skirmishing forward, but he reported that the bridge was gone, and that a considerable force of the enemy was on the other side. I directed General Howard or Logan to send a brigade by a circuit to the left, to see if this stream could not be crossed higher up, but at the same time knew that General Slocum's route would bring him to Columbia behind this stream, and that his approach would uncover it. Therefore, there was no need of exposing much life. The brigade, however, found means to cross the Little Congaree, and thus uncovered the passage by the main road, so that General Woods's skirmishers at once passed over, and a party was set to work to repair the bridge, which occupied less than an hour, when I passed over with my whole staff. I found the new fort unfinished and unoccupied, but from its parapet could see over some old fields bounded to the north and west by hills skirted with timber. There was a plantation to our left, about half a mile, and on the edge of the timber was drawn up a force of rebel cavalry of about a regiment, which advanced, and charged upon some of our foragers, who were plundering the plantation; my aide, Colonel Audenried, who had ridden forward, came back somewhat hurt and bruised, for, observing this charge of cavalry, he had turned for us, and his horse fell with him in attempting to leap a ditch. General Woods's skirmish-line met this charge of cavalry, and drove it back into the woods and beyond. We remained on that ground during the night of the 15th, and I camped on the nearest dry ground behind the Little Congaree, where on the next morning were made the written orders for the government of the troops while occupying Columbia. These are dated February 16, 1865, in these words:

General Howard will cross the Saluda and Broad Rivers as near their mouths as possible, occupy Columbia, destroy the public buildings, railroad property, manufacturing and machine shops; but will spare libraries, asylums, and private dwellings. He will then move to Winns-

> boro', destroying *en route* utterly that section of the railroad. He will also cause all bridges, trestles, water-tanks, and depots on the railroad back to the Wateree to be burned, switches broken, and such other destruction as he can find time to accomplish consistent with proper celerity.

These instructions were embraced in General Order No. 26, which prescribed the routes of march for the several columns as far as Fayetteville, North Carolina, and is conclusive that I then regarded Columbia as simply one point on our general route of march, and not as an important conquest.[13]

During the 16th of February the Fifteenth Corps reached the point opposite Columbia, and pushed on for the Saluda Factory three miles above, crossed that stream, and the head of column reached Broad River just in time to find its bridge in flames, Butler's cavalry having just passed over into Columbia. The head of Slocum's column also reached the point opposite Columbia the same morning, but the bulk of his army was back at Lexington. I reached this place early in the morning of the 16th, met General Slocum there, and explained to him the purport of General Order No. 26, which contemplated the passage of his army across Broad River at Alston, fifteen miles above Columbia. Riding down to the river-bank, I saw the wreck of the large bridge which had been burned by the enemy, with its many stone piers still standing, but the superstructure gone. Across the Congaree River lay the city of Columbia, in plain, easy view. I could see the unfinished State-House, a handsome granite structure, and the ruins of the railroad depot, which were still smouldering. Occasionally a few citizens or cavalry could be seen running across the streets, and quite a number of negroes were seemingly busy in carrying off bags of grain or meal, which were piled up near the burned depot.

Captain De Gres had a section of his twenty-pound Parrott guns unlimbered, firing into the town. I asked him what he was firing for; he said he could see some rebel cavalry occasionally at the intersections of the streets, and he had an idea that there was a large force of infantry concealed on the opposite bank, lying low, in case we should attempt to cross over directly into the town. I instructed him not to fire any more into the town, but consented to his bursting a few shells near the depot, to scare away the negroes who were appropriating the bags of corn and meal which we wanted, also to fire three shots at the unoccupied State-House. I stood by and saw these fired, and then all firing ceased. Although this matter of firing into Columbia has

[13] See *OR*, I, 47 (II), 444–445.

been the subject of much abuse and investigation, I have yet to hear of any single person having been killed in Columbia by our cannon.[14] On the other hand, the night before, when Woods's division was in camp in the open fields at Little Congaree, it was shelled all night by a rebel battery from the other side of the river. This provoked me much at the time, for it was wanton mischief, as Generals Beauregard and Hampton must have been convinced that they could not prevent our entrance into Columbia. I have always contended that I would have been justified in retaliating for this unnecessary act of war, but did not, though I always characterized it as it deserved.

The night of the 16th I camped near an old prison bivouac opposite Columbia, known to our prisoners of war as "Camp Sorghum,"[15] where remained the mud-hovels and holes in the ground which our prisoners had made to shelter themselves from the winter's cold and the summer's heat. The Fifteenth Corps was then ahead, reaching to Broad River, about four miles above Columbia; the Seventeenth Corps was behind, on the river-bank opposite Columbia; and the left wing and cavalry had turned north toward Alston.

The next morning, viz., February 17th, I rode to the head of General Howard's column, and found that during the night he had ferried Stone's brigade of Woods's division of the Fifteenth Corps across by rafts made of the pontoons, and that brigade was then deployed on the opposite bank to cover the construction of a pontoon-bridge nearly finished.

I sat with General Howard on a log, watching the men lay this bridge; and about 9 or 10 A. M. a messenger came from Colonel Stone on the other side, saying that the Mayor of Columbia had come out of the city to surrender the place, and asking for orders.[16] I simply remarked to General Howard that he

[14] On Feb. 27, 1865, Confederate general Wade Hampton wrote to WTS, "You have permitted, if you have not ordered, the commission of these offenses against humanity and the rules of war; you fired into the city of Columbia without a word of warning; after its surrender by the mayor, who demanded protection to private property, you laid the whole city in ashes, leaving amidst its ruins thousands of old men and helpless women and children, who are likely to perish of starvation and exposure." *OR,* I, 47(II), 596–597.

[15] According to Willard W. Glazier, a prisoner of war who escaped from Sorghum in 1864, the camp was named after the principal ration issued to prisoners. Willard W. Glazier, *The Capture, the Prison Pen and the Escape, Giving an Account of Prison Life in the South* (Albany, NY: J. Munsell, 1866), 162, 193–230.

[16] Thomas J. Goodwyn (1800–1877), a physician who served as mayor of Columbia during the war, wrote to WTS, "The Confederate forces having evacuated Columbia, I deem it my duty, as Mayor and representative of the city, to ask for its citizens the treatment accorded by

had his orders, to let Colonel Stone go on into the city, and that we would follow as soon as the bridge was ready. By this same messenger I received a note in pencil from the Lady Superioress of a convent or school in Columbia, in which she claimed to have been a teacher in a convent in Brown County, Ohio, at the time my daughter Minnie was a pupil there, and therefore asking special protection.[17] My recollection is, that I gave the note to my brother-in-law, Colonel Ewing, then inspector-general on my staff, with instructions to see this lady, and assure her that we contemplated no destruction of any private property in Columbia at all.[18]

As soon as the bridge was done, I led my horse over it, followed by my whole staff. General Howard accompanied me with his, and General Logan was next in order, followed by General C. R. Woods, and the whole of the Fifteenth Corps. Ascending the hill, we soon emerged into a broad road leading into Columbia, between old fields of corn and cotton, and, entering the city, we found seemingly all its population, white and black, in the streets. A high and boisterous wind was prevailing from the north, and flakes of cotton were flying about in the air and lodging in the limbs of the trees, reminding us of a Northern snow-storm. Near the market-square we found Stone's brigade halted, with arms stacked, and a large detail of his men, along with some citizens, engaged with an old fire-engine, trying to put out the fire in a long pile of burning cotton-bales, which I was told had been fired by the rebel cavalry on withdrawing from the city that morning. I know that, to avoid this row of burning cotton-bales, I had to ride my horse on the side-

the usages of civilized warfare." John S. Goodwin, "The Goodwyn Families in America," *William and Mary College Quarterly Historical Magazine* 8, no. 2 (Oct. 1899): 35; *Report of the Committee Appointed to Collect Testimony in Relation to the Destruction of Columbia, S.C.* (Columbia, SC: Bryan, 1893), 3.

[17] Ellen Lynch (c. 1825–1887), also known as Mother Mary Baptista Aloysius, was the mother superior of the Ursuline Convent and Academy when WTS captured Columbia. The convent was established in 1858 by a colony of Catholics from Brown County, OH. Marjorie J. Spruill, Valinda W. Littlefield, and Joan M. Johnson, ed., *South Carolina Women: Their Lives and Times* (Athens: University of Georgia Press, 2009), 1:214.

[18] According to Sarah A. Richardson, a pupil at the convent, a "Major FitzGibbons" delivered WTS's letter to Mother Mary Baptista Aloysius. It read, "Commanding officer near: Protect the Convent. Colonel Palmer, 25th Iowa, furnish ninety-six men for this duty. J. W. Jenkins, P. M. Sergt., J. C. Motte, Co. 25, 26." Sarah A. Richardson, "The Burning of the Ursuline Convent by Sherman," in *South Carolina Women in the Confederacy,* ed. Thomas Taylor et al. (Columbia: State, 1903), 299–300.

walk. In the market-square had collected a large crowd[19] of whites and blacks, among whom was the mayor of the city, Dr. Goodwin, quite a respectable old gentleman, who was extremely anxious to protect the interests of the citizens. He was on foot, and I on horseback, and it is probable I told him then not to be uneasy, that we did not intend to stay long, and had no purpose to injure the private citizens or private property. About this time I noticed several men trying to get through the crowd to speak with me, and called to some black people to make room for them; when they reached me, they explained that they were officers of our army, who had been prisoners, had escaped from the rebel prison and guard, and were of course overjoyed to find themselves safe with us. I told them that, as soon as things settled down, they should report to General Howard, who would provide for their safety, and enable them to travel with us. One of them handed me a paper, asking me to read it at my leisure; I put it in my breast-pocket and rode on. General Howard was still with me, and, riding down the street which led by the right to the Charleston depot, we found it and a large storehouse burned to the ground, but there were, on the platform and ground near by, piles of cotton bags filled with corn and corn-meal, partially burned.[20]

A detachment of Stone's brigade was guarding this, and separating the good from the bad. We rode along the railroad-track, some three or four hundred yards, to a large foundery, when some man rode up and said the rebel cavalry were close by, and he warned us that we might get shot. We accordingly turned back to the market-square, and *en route* noticed that several of the men were evidently in liquor, when I called General Howard's attention to it. He left me and rode toward General Woods's head of column, which was defiling through the town. On reaching the market-square, I again met Dr. Goodwin, and inquired where he proposed to quarter me, and he said that he had selected the house of Blanton Duncan, Esq., a citizen of Louisville, Kentucky, then a resident there, who had the contract for manufacturing the Confederate money, and had fled with Hampton's cavalry.[21] We all rode some six or eight squares back from the new State-House, and found

[19] In the first edition of the memoirs (1875), WTS described the crowd as "immense" instead of "large."

[20] For more on the Burning of Columbia, see "Extracts of my Military Record, submitted to the Retiring Board by which I was retired in May, 1870," in Appendix to Volume II.

[21] Blanton Duncan (1827–1902) joined the Confederate Army as a lieutenant colonel in Oct. 1861. *CWHC*, 595.

a very good modern house, completely furnished, with stabling and a large yard, took it as our headquarters, and occupied it during our stay. I considered General Howard as in command of the place, and referred the many applicants for guards and protection to him. Before our headquarter-wagons had got up, I strolled through the streets of Columbia, found sentinels posted at the principal intersections, and generally good order prevailing, but did not again return to the main street, because it was filled with a crowd of citizens watching the soldiers marching by.

During the afternoon of that day, February 17th, the whole of the Fifteenth Corps passed through the town and out on the Camden and Winnsboro' roads. The Seventeenth Corps did not enter the city at all, but crossed directly over to the Winnsboro' road from the pontoon-bridge at Broad River, which was about four miles above the city.

After we had got, as it were, settled in Blanton Duncan's house, say about 2 P. M., I overhauled my pocket according to custom, to read more carefully the various notes and memoranda received during the day, and found the paper which had been given me, as described, by one of our escaped prisoners. It proved to be the song of "Sherman's March to the Sea," which had been composed by Adjutant S. H. M. Byers, of the Fifth Iowa Infantry, when a prisoner in the asylum at Columbia, which had been beautifully written off by a fellow-prisoner, and handed to me in person. This appeared to me so good that I at once sent for Byers, attached him to my staff, provided him with horse and equipment, and took him as far as Fayetteville, North Carolina, whence he was sent to Washington as bearer of dispatches. He is now United States consul at Zurich, Switzerland, where I have since been his guest.[22] I insert the song here for convenient reference and preservation. Byers said that there was an excellent glee-club among the prisoners in Columbia, who used to sing it well, with an audience often of rebel ladies:

[22] Samuel H. M. Byers (1838–1933) wrote "Sherman's March to the Sea" in Jan. 1865. He claimed that "a comrade composed music for it, and in a day almost I was the most famous man in prison. It was sung, copied, recited, by everybody there, and soon a comrade carried it through the rebel lines, and the song was taken up by the whole of Sherman's army. It was sung in nearly every theatre in the land, and would have been sung in Ford's Theatre the night of Lincoln's assassination had it not been for that dire event." After the war, in 1869, Byers was appointed consul to Switzerland and served in that capacity for fifteen years before being named consul general for Italy. "S. H. M. Byers and His Famous Song," *Current Literature,* Jan.–June 1897, 404.

SHERMAN'S MARCH TO THE SEA.

Composed by Adjutant Byers, *Fifth Iowa Infantry.*
Arranged and sung by the Prisoners in Columbia Prison.

I.

Our camp-fires shone bright on the mountain
   That frowned on the river below,
As we stood by our guns in the morning,
   And eagerly watched for the foe;
When a rider came out of the darkness
   That hung over mountain and tree,
And shouted, "Boys, up and be ready!
   For Sherman will march to the sea!"

Chorus.

Then sang we a song of our chieftain,
   That echoed over river and lea;
And the stars of our banner shone brighter
   When Sherman marched down to the sea!

II.

Then cheer upon cheer for bold Sherman
   Went up from each valley and glen,
And the bugles reëchoed the music
   That came from the lips of the men;
For we knew that the stars in our banner
   More bright in their splendor would be,
And that blessings from Northland world greet us,
   When Sherman marched down to the sea!
Then sang we a song, etc.

III.

Then forward, boys! forward to battle!
   We marched on our wearisome way,
We stormed the wild hills of Resaca—
   God bless those who fell on that day!

Then Kenesaw frowned in its glory,
  Frowned down on the flag of the free;
But the East and the West bore our standard,
  And Sherman marched on to the sea!
Then sang we a song, etc.

IV.

Still onward we pressed, till our banners
  Swept out from Atlanta's grim walls,
And the blood of the patriot dampened
  The soil where the traitor-flag falls;
But we paused not to weep for the fallen,
  Who slept by each river and tree,
Yet we twined them a wreath of the laurel,
  As Sherman marched down to the sea!
Then sang we a song, etc.

V.

Oh, proud was our army that morning,
  That stood where the pine darkly towers,
When Sherman said, "Boys, you are weary,
  But to-day fair Savannah is ours!"
Then sang we the song of our chieftain,
  That echoed over river and lea,
And the stars in our banner shone brighter
  When Sherman camped down by the sea!

Toward evening of February 17th, the mayor, Dr. Goodwin, came to my quarters at Duncan's house, and remarked that there was a lady in Columbia who professed to be a special friend of mine. On his giving her name, I could not recall it, but inquired as to her maiden or family name. He answered Poyas. It so happened that, when I was a lieutenant at Fort Moultrie, in 1842—'46, I used very often to visit a family of that name on the east branch of Cooper River, about forty miles from Fort Moultrie, and to hunt with the son, Mr. James Poyas, an elegant young fellow and a fine sportsman. His father, mother, and several sisters, composed the family, and were extremely hospitable. One of the ladies was very fond of painting in water-colors, which was one of my weaknesses, and on one occasion I had presented her with a volume treating of water-colors.

Of course, I was glad to renew the acquaintance, and proposed to Dr. Goodwin that we should walk to her house and visit this lady, which we did.[23] The house stood beyond the Charlotte depot, in a large lot, was of frame, with a high porch, which was reached by a set of steps outside. Entering this yard, I noticed ducks and chickens, and a general air of peace and comfort that was really pleasant to behold at that time of universal desolation; the lady in question met us at the head of the steps and invited us into a parlor which was perfectly neat and well furnished. After inquiring about her father, mother, sisters, and especially her brother James, my special friend, I could not help saying that I was pleased to notice that our men had not handled her house and premises as roughly as was their wont. "I owe it to you, general," she answered. "Not at all. I did not know you were here till a few minutes ago." She reiterated that she was indebted to me for the perfect safety of her house and property, and added, "You remember, when you were at our house on Cooper River in 1845, you gave me a book;" and she handed me the book in question, on the fly leaf of which was written: "To Miss ______ Poyas, with the compliments of W. T. Sherman, First-lieutenant Third Artillery." She then explained that, as our army approached Columbia, there was a doubt in her mind whether the terrible Sherman who was devastating the land were W. T. Sherman or T. W. Sherman, both known to be generals in the Northern army; but, on the supposition that he was her old acquaintance, when Wade Hampton's cavalry drew out of the city, calling out that the Yankees were coming, she armed herself with this book, and awaited the crisis. Soon the shouts about the market-house announced that the Yankees had come; very soon men were seen running up and down the streets; a parcel of them poured over the fence, began to chase the chickens and ducks, and to enter her house. She observed one large man, with full beard, who exercised some authority, and to him she appealed in the name of "his general." "What do you know of Uncle Billy?" "Why," she said, "when he was a young man he used to be our friend in Charleston, and here is a book he gave me." The officer or soldier took the book, looked at the inscription, and, turning to his fellows, said: "Boys, that's so; that's Uncle Billy's writing, for I have seen it often before." He at once commanded the party to stop pillaging, and left a man in charge of the house, to protect her until the regular provost-guard should be established. I then asked her if the regular guard or sentinel had been as good to her. She assured me that he was a very nice young man; that he had been telling

[23] Mary C. Poyas (1826–1882) married William H. Walker and gave birth to their son, Robert, in June 1864. *The National Cyclopedia of American Biography* (New York: James T. White, 1922), vol. 18, s.v. "Walker, Robert Murdoch."

her all about his family in Iowa; and that at that very instant of time he was in another room minding her baby. Now, this lady had good sense and tact, and had thus turned aside a party who, in five minutes more, would have rifled her premises of all that was good to eat or wear. I made her a long social visit, and, before leaving Columbia, gave her a half-tierce of rice and about one hundred pounds of ham from our own mess-stores.

In like manner, that same evening I found in Mrs. Simons another acquaintance—the wife of the brother of Hon. James Simons, of Charleston, who had been Miss Wragg.[24] When Columbia was on fire that night, and her house in danger, I had her family and effects carried to my own headquarters, gave them my own room and bed, and, on leaving Columbia the next day, supplied her with a half-barrel of hams and a half-tierce of rice. I mention these specific facts to show that, personally, I had no malice or desire to destroy that city or its inhabitants, as is generally believed at the South.

Having walked over much of the suburbs of Columbia in the afternoon, and being tired, I lay down on a bed in Blanton Duncan's house to rest. Soon after dark I became conscious that a bright light was shining on the walls; and, calling some one of my staff (Major Nichols, I think) to inquire the cause, he said there seemed to be a house on fire down about the market-house. The same high wind still prevailed, and, fearing the consequences, I bade him go in person to see if the provost-guard were doing its duty. He soon returned, and reported that the block of buildings directly opposite the burning cotton of that morning was on fire, and that it was spreading; but he had found General Woods on the ground, with plenty of men trying to put the fire out, or, at least, to prevent its extension. The fire continued to increase, and the whole heavens became lurid. I dispatched messenger after messenger to Generals Howard, Logan, and Woods, and received from them repeated assurances that all was being done that could be done, but that the high wind was spreading the flames beyond all control. These general officers were on the ground all night, and Hazen's division had been brought into the city to assist Woods's division, already there. About eleven o'clock at night I went down-town myself, Colonel Dayton with me; we walked to Mr. Simons's house, from which I could see the flames rising high in the air, and could hear the roaring of the fire. I advised the ladies to move to my headquarters, had our own headquarter-wagons hitched up, and their effects carried there, as a place of greater safety. The whole air was full of sparks and of flying masses of cotton,

[24] Sarah Wragg (1814–1901) married James Simons. Her family was instrumental in the founding of Charleston, SC. Robert B. Simons, *Thomas Grange Simons III, His Forebears and Relations* (self-pub., 1954), 66.

shingles, etc., some of which were carried four or five blocks, and started new fires. The men seemed generally under good control, and certainly labored hard to girdle the fire, to prevent its spreading; but, so long as the high wind prevailed, it was simply beyond human possibility. Fortunately, about 3 or 4 A. M., the wind moderated, and gradually the fire was got under control; but it had burned out the very heart of the city, embracing several churches, the old State-House, and the school or asylum of that very Sister of Charity who had appealed for my personal protection. Nickerson's Hotel, in which several of my staff were quartered, was burned down, but the houses occupied by myself, Generals Howard and Logan, were not burned at all.[25] Many of the people thought that this fire was deliberately planned and executed. This is not true. It was accidental, and in my judgment began with the cotton which General Hampton's men had set fire to on leaving the city (whether by his orders or not is not material), which fire was partially subdued early in the day by our men; but, when night came, the high wind fanned it again into full blaze, carried it against the frame-houses, which caught like tinder, and soon spread beyond our control.

This whole subject has since been thoroughly and judicially investigated, in some cotton cases, by the mixed commission on American and British claims, under the Treaty of Washington, which commission failed to award a verdict in favor of the English claimants, and thereby settled the fact that the destruction of property in Columbia, during that night, did not result from the acts of the General Government of the United States—that is to say, from my army. In my official report of this conflagration, I distinctly charged it to General Wade Hampton, and confess I did so pointedly, to shake the faith of his people in him, for he was in my opinion boastful,[26] and professed to be the special champion of South Carolina.[27]

[25] According to George W. Nichols, "General Sherman and his officers worked with their own hands until long after midnight, trying to save life and property . . . Whatever may have been the cause of the disaster, the direful result is deprecated by General Sherman most emphatically; for however heinous the crimes of this people against our common country, we do not war against women and children and helpless persons." George W. Nichols, *The Story of the Great March: From the Diary of a Staff Officer* (New York: Harper, 1865), 165–166.

[26] In the first edition of the memoirs (1875), WTS described Hampton as a "braggart" instead of "boastful." For more insight into the motivation for the omission, see D. F. Boyd to WTS, July 17, 1875, in the Appendix to Volume II.

[27] WTS gave his testimony on the burning of Columbia to George H. Butler, the U.S. consul general of Egypt, while visiting Cairo, Egypt, on Mar. 30, 1872. *British and American Claims, Appendix, Testimony* 3, no. 37 (1873): 2–12.

The morning sun of February 18th rose bright and clear over a ruined city. About half of it was in ashes and in smouldering heaps. Many of the people were houseless, and gathered in groups in the suburbs, or in the open parks and spaces, around their scanty piles of furniture. General Howard, in concert with the mayor, did all that was possible to provide other houses for them; and by my authority he turned over to the Sisters of Charity the Methodist College,[28] and to the mayor five hundred beef-cattle, to help feed the people; I also gave the mayor (Dr. Goodwin) one hundred muskets, with which to arm a guard to maintain order after we should leave the neighborhood. During the 18th and 19th we remained in Columbia, General Howard's troops engaged in tearing up and destroying the railroad, back toward the Wateree, while a strong detail, under the immediate supervision of Colonel O. M. Poe, United States Engineers, destroyed the State Arsenal, which was found to be well supplied with shot, shell, and ammunition. These were hauled in wagons to the Saluda River, under the supervision of Colonel Baylor, chief of ordnance, and emptied into deep water, causing a very serious accident by the bursting of a percussion-shell, as it struck another on the margin of the water. The flame followed back a train of powder which had sifted out, reached the wagons, still partially loaded, and exploded them, killing sixteen men and destroying several wagons and teams of mules. We also destroyed several valuable founderies and the factory of Confederate money. The dies had been carried away, but about sixty handpresses remained. There was also found an immense quantity of money, in various stages of manufacture, which our men spent and gambled with in the most lavish manner.

Having utterly ruined Columbia, the right wing began its march northward, toward Winnsboro', on the 20th, which we reached on the 21st, and found General Slocum, with the left wing, who had come by the way of Alston. Thence the right wing was turned eastward, toward Cheraw, and Fayetteville, North Carolina, to cross the Catawba River at Peay's Ferry. The cavalry was ordered to follow the railroad north as far as Chester, and then to turn east to Rocky Mount, the point indicated for the passage of the left wing.[29] In person I reached Rocky Mount on the 22d, with the Twentieth Corps, which laid its pontoon-bridge and crossed over during the 23d. Kilpatrick arrived the next

[28] The Columbia Female College, known today as Columbia College, was founded in 1854 and remained open until the consequences of the Civil War forced its closure in 1865. The school later reopened in 1873. Charles Israel and Elizabeth DuRant, *Columbia College* (Charleston, SC: Arcadia, 2001), 7.

[29] For a detailed map of the region, see Davis et al., *Official Military Atlas of the Civil War*, plates 138–139.

day, in the midst of heavy rain, and was instructed to cross the Catawba at once, by night, and to move up to Lancaster, to make believe we were bound for Charlotte, to which point I heard that Beauregard had directed all his detachments, including a corps of Hood's old army, which had been marching parallel with us, but had failed to make junction with the forces immediately opposing us. Of course, I had no purpose of going to Charlotte, for the right wing was already moving rapidly toward Fayetteville, North Carolina. The rain was so heavy and persistent that the Catawba River rose fast, and soon after I had crossed the pontoon-bridge at Rocky Mount it was carried away, leaving General Davis, with the Fourteenth Corps, on the west bank. The roads were infamous, so I halted the Twentieth Corps at Hanging Rock for some days, to allow time for the Fourteenth to get over.

General Davis had infinite difficulty in reconstructing his bridge, and was compelled to use the fifth chains of his wagons for anchor-chains, so that we were delayed nearly a week in that neighborhood. While in camp at Hanging Rock two prisoners were brought to me—one a chaplain, the other a boy, son of Richard Bacot, of Charleston, whom I had known as a cadet at West Point.[30] They were just from Charleston, and had been sent away by General Hardee in advance, because he was, they said, evacuating Charleston. Rumors to the same effect had reached me through the negroes, and it was, moreover, reported that Wilmington, North Carolina, was in possession of the Yankee troops; so that I had every reason to be satisfied that our march was fully reaping all the fruits we could possibly ask for. Charleston was, in fact, evacuated by General Hardee on the 18th of February, and was taken possession of by a brigade of General Foster's troops, commanded by General Schimmelpfennig,[31] the same day. Hardee had availed himself of his only remaining railroad, by Florence to Cheraw; had sent there much of his ammunition and stores, and reached it with the effective part of the garrison in time to

[30] Richard H. Bacot (1820–1862) graduated from the USMA in 1841 and resigned from the U.S. Army in 1843. Before the start of the Civil War, he was a clerk in the U.S. Custom House in Charleston, SC. His son, Richard D. Bacot (1848–1927), joined the Confederate Army at age sixteen and later purchased a patent medicine show. He then changed his name to "Dr. Richard Coleman." *USMA,* 2:94; "'Dr. Coleman' of Georgia Is Bacot of South Carolina," *The State* (Columbia, SC), June 1, 1927, 1.

[31] Alexander Schimmelfennig (1824–1865) was born in Prussia and moved to the United States in 1853. He joined the U.S. Army in Sept. 1861 and was wounded in the arm and head during the Battle of Gettysburg on July 1, 1863. In Feb. 1865 he commanded the Northern Dist., Dept. of the South. *CWHC,* 472.

escape across the Pedee River before our arrival. Wilmington was captured by General Terry on the 22d of February; but of this important event we only knew by the vague rumors which reached us through rebel sources.

General Jeff. C. Davis got across the Catawba during the 27th, and the general march was resumed on Cheraw. Kilpatrick remained near Lancaster, skirmishing with Wheeler's and Hampton's cavalry, keeping up the delusion that we proposed to move on Charlotte and Salisbury, but with orders to watch the progress of the Fourteenth Corps, and to act in concert with it, on its left rear. On the 1st of March I was at Finlay's Bridge across Lynch's Creek, the roads so bad that we had to corduroy nearly every foot of the way; but I was in communication with all parts of the army, which had met no serious opposition from the enemy. On the 2d of March we entered the village of Chesterfield, skirmishing with Butler's cavalry, which gave ground rapidly. There I received a message from General Howard, who reported that he was already in Cheraw with the Seventeenth Corps, and that the Fifteenth was near at hand.[32]

General Hardee had retreated eastward across the Pedee, burning the bridge. I therefore directed the left wing to march for Sneedsboro', about ten miles above Cheraw, to cross the Pedee there, while I in person proposed to cross over and join the right wing in Cheraw. Early in the morning of the 3d of March I rode out of Chesterfield along with the Twentieth Corps, which filled the road, forded Thompson's Creek, and, at the top of the hill beyond, found a road branching off to the right, which corresponded with the one on my map leading to Cheraw. Seeing a negro standing by the road-side, looking at the troops passing, I inquired of him what road that was. "Him lead to Cheraw, master!" "Is it a good road, and how far?" "A very good road, and eight or ten miles." "Any guerrillas?" "Oh! no, master, dey is gone two days ago; you could have played cards on der coat-tails, dey was in sich a hurry!" I was on my Lexington horse, who was very handsome and restive, so I made signal to my staff to follow, as I proposed to go without escort. I turned my horse down the road, and the rest of the staff followed. General Barry took up the questions about the road, and asked the same negro what he was doing there. He answered, "Dey say Massa Sherman will be along soon!" "Why," said General Barry, "that was General Sherman you were talking to." The poor negro, almost in the attitude of prayer, exclaimed: "De great God! just look at his horse!" He ran up and trotted by my side for a mile or so, and gave me all the information he possessed, but he seemed to admire the horse more than the rider.

[32] See *OR*, I, 47(II), 644, 661–662.

We reached Cheraw in a couple of hours in a drizzling rain, and, while waiting for our wagons to come up, I staid with General Blair in a large house, the property of a blockade-runner, whose family remained. General Howard occupied another house farther down-town. He had already ordered his pontoon-bridge to be laid across the Pedee, there a large, deep, navigable stream, and Mower's division was already across, skirmishing with the enemy about two miles out. Cheraw was found to be full of stores which had been sent up from Charleston prior to its evacuation, and which could not be removed. I was satisfied, from inquiries, that General Hardee had with him only the Charleston garrison, that the enemy had not divined our movements, and that consequently they were still scattered from Charlotte around to Florence, then behind us. Having thus secured the passage of the Pedee, I felt no uneasiness about the future, because there remained no further great impediment between us and Cape Fear River, which I felt assured was by that time in possession of our friends. The day was so wet that we all kept in-doors; and about noon General Blair invited us to take lunch with him. We passed down into the basement dining-room, where the regular family table was spread with an excellent meal; and during its progress I was asked to take some wine, which stood upon the table in venerable bottles. It was so very good that I inquired where it came from. General Blair simply asked, "Do you like it?" but I insisted upon knowing where he had got it; he only replied by asking if I liked it, and wanted some. He afterward sent to my bivouac a case containing a dozen bottles of the finest madeira I ever tasted; and I learned that he had captured, in Cheraw, the wine of some of the old aristocratic families of Charleston, who had sent it up to Cheraw for safety, and heard afterward that Blair had found about eight wagon-loads of this wine, which he distributed to the army generally, in very fair proportions.

After finishing our lunch, as we passed out of the dining- room, General Blair asked me if I did not want some saddle-blankets, or a rug for my tent, and, leading me into the hall to a space under the stairway, he pointed out a pile of carpets which had also been sent up from Charleston for safety. After our headquarter-wagons got up, and our bivouac was established in a field near by, I sent my orderly (Walter) over to General Blair, and he came back staggering under a load of carpets, out of which the officers and escort made excellent tent-rugs, saddle-cloths, and blankets. There was an immense amount of stores in Cheraw, which were used or destroyed; among them twenty-four guns, two thousand muskets, and thirty-six hundred barrels of gunpowder. By the carelessness of a soldier, an immense pile of this powder was exploded, which shook the town badly, and killed and maimed several of our men.[33]

We remained in or near Cheraw till the 6th of March, by which time the army was mostly across the Pedee River, and was prepared to resume the march on Fayetteville. In a house where General Hardee had been, I found a late *New York Tribune,* of fully a month later date than any I had seen. It contained a mass of news of great interest to us, and one short paragraph which I thought extremely mischievous. I think it was an editorial, to the effect that at last the editor had the satisfaction to inform his readers that General Sherman would next be heard from about Goldsboro', because his supply-vessels from Savannah were known to be rendezvousing at Morehead City. Now, I knew that General Hardee had read that same paper, and that he would be perfectly able to draw his own inferences. Up to that moment I had endeavored so to feign to our left that we had completely misled our antagonists; but this was no longer possible, and I concluded that we must be ready for the concentration in our front of all the force subject to General Jos. Johnston's orders, for I was there also informed that he had been restored to the full command of the Confederate forces in South and North Carolina.[34]

On the 6th of March I crossed the Pedee, and all the army marched for Fayetteville: the Seventeenth Corps kept well to the right, to make room; the Fifteenth Corps marched by a direct road; the Fourteenth Corps also followed a direct road from Sneedsboro', where it had crossed the Pedee; and the Twentieth Corps, which had come into Cheraw for the convenience of the pontoon-bridge, diverged to the left, so as to enter Fayetteville next after the Fourteenth Corps, which was appointed to lead into Fayetteville. Kilpatrick held his cavalry still farther to the left rear on the roads from Lancaster, by way of Wadesboro' and New Gilead, so as to cover our trains from Hampton's and Wheeler's cavalry, who had first retreated toward the north. I traveled with the Fifteenth Corps, and on the 8th of March reached Laurel Hill, North Carolina. Satisfied

[33] According to General O. O. Howard, "The sudden thunderous explosion for the time appeared to paralyze men and animals. The mules and horses near by ran off wildly in a stampede. One officer and three enlisted men were killed outright, and at least a dozen or more of the soldiers were disabled. Thus disaster followed acts of inexcusable carelessness!" O. O. Howard, *Autobiography of Oliver Otis Howard: Major General of the United States Army* (New York: Baker and Taylor, 1908), 2:135–136.

[34] Confederate general Joseph E. Johnston took command of the Dept. of South Carolina and Southern Virgina on Mar. 6. *CWHC,* 323.

that our troops must be at Wilmington, I determined to send a message there; I called for my man, Corporal Pike, whom I had rescued as before described, at Columbia, who was then traveling with our escort, and instructed him in disguise to work his way to the Cape Fear River, secure a boat, and float down to Wilmington to convey a letter, and to report our approach. I also called on General Howard for another volunteer, and he brought me a very clever young sergeant, who is now a commissioned officer in the regular army. Each of these got off during the night by separate routes, bearing the following message, reduced to the same cipher we used in telegraphic messages:

HEADQUARTERS MILITARY DIVISION OF THE MISSISSIPPI, IN THE FIELD, LAUREL HILL, *Wednesday, March* 8, 1865.

Commanding Officer, Wilmington, North Carolina:

We are marching for Fayetteville, will be there Saturday, Sunday, and Monday, and will then march for Goldsboro'.

If possible, send a boat up Cape Fear River, and have word conveyed to General Schofield that I expect to meet him about Goldsboro'. We are all well and have done finely. The rains make our roads difficult, and may delay us about Fayetteville, in which case I would like to have some bread, sugar, and coffee. We have abundance of all else. I expect to reach Goldsboro' by the 20th instant.

W. T. SHERMAN, *Major-General.*

On the 9th I was with the Fifteenth Corps, and toward evening reached a little church called Bethel, in the woods, in which we took refuge in a terrible storm of rain, which poured all night, making the roads awful. All the men were at work corduroying the roads, using fence-rails and split saplings, and every foot of the way had thus to be corduroyed to enable the artillery and wagons to pass. On the 10th we made some little progress; on the 11th I reached Fayetteville, and found that General Hardee, followed by Wade Hampton's cavalry, had barely escaped across Cape Fear River, burning the bridge which I had hoped to save. On reaching Fayetteville I found General Slocum already in possession with the Fourteenth Corps, and all the rest of the army was near at hand. A day or two before, General Kilpatrick, to our left rear, had divided his force into two parts, occupying roads behind the Twentieth Corps, interposing between our infantry columns and Wade Hampton's cavalry. The latter, doubtless to make junction with General Hardee, in Fayetteville, broke across this line, captured the house in which General Kilpatrick and the brigade-commander, General Spencer, were, and for a time held possession of the camp and artillery of the brigade. However, General Kilpatrick and most of his men escaped into a swamp with their arms, reorganized and returned, catching Hampton's men in turn, scattered and drove them away, recovering most of his camp and artillery; but Hampton got off with Kilpatrick's private horses and a couple hundred prisoners, of which he boasted much in passing through Fayetteville.

It was also reported that, in the morning after Hardee's army was all across the bridge at Cape Fear River, Hampton, with a small bodyguard, had remained in town, ready to retreat and burn the bridge as soon as our forces made their appearance. He was getting breakfast at the hotel when the alarm was given, when he and his escort took saddle, but soon realized that the alarm came from a set of our foragers, who, as usual, were extremely bold and rash. On these he turned, scattered them, killing some and making others prisoners; among them General Howard's favorite scout, Captain Duncan. Hampton then crossed the bridge and burned it.

I took up my quarters at the old United States Arsenal,[35] which was in fine order, and had been much enlarged by the Confederate authorities, who never dreamed that an invading army would reach it from the west; and I also found in Fayetteville the widow and daughter of my first captain (General Childs), of the Third Artillery, learned that her son Fred had been the ordnance-officer in charge of the arsenal, and had of course fled with Hardee's army.[36]

During the 11th the whole army closed down upon Fayetteville, and immediate preparations were made to lay two pontoon bridges, one near the burned bridge, and another about four miles lower down.

[35] Eliza B. Stinson, a resident of North Carolina at the time, described the arsenal as "the handsomest collection of buildings the town could boast of, included three fine residences for the officials. The buildings were all painted cream-color, with brown trimming, and were arranged in a hollow rectangle with the citadel in the center." Eliza Stinson, "How the Arsenal Was Taken," in *Our Women in the War: The Lives They Lived; The Deaths They Died* (Charleston, SC: News and Courier Book Presses, 1885), 22.

[36] Anne Coryton Childs (1800–1875) married Thomas Childs in 1819. In 1865 she had two surviving daughters, Catharine R. Childs (1819–1896) and Mary V. Childs (1833–1912). Her son, Frederick L. Childs (1831–1894), graduated from the USMA in 1855 and resigned from the U.S. Army on Mar. 4, 1861, to join the Confederate Army. Elias Child, *Genealogy of the Child, Childs, and Childe Families* (Utica, NY: Curtiss and Childs, 1881), 677–679; *USMA*, 2:613.

Sunday, March 12th, was a day of Sabbath stillness in Fayetteville. The people generally attended their churches, for they were a very pious people, descended in a large measure from the old Scotch Covenanters, and our men too were resting from the toils and labors of six weeks of as hard marching as ever fell to the lot of soldiers. Shortly after noon was heard in the distance the shrill whistle of a steamboat, which came nearer and nearer, and soon a shout, long and continuous, was raised down by the river, which spread farther and farther, and we all felt that it meant a messenger from home. The effect was electric, and no one can realize the feeling unless, like us, he has been for months cut off from all communication with friends, and compelled to listen to the croakings and prognostications of open enemies. But in a very few minutes came up through the town to the arsenal on the plateau behind a group of officers, among whom was a large, florid seafaring man, named Ainsworth,[37] bearing a small mail-bag from General Terry, at Wilmington, having left at 2 P. M. the day before. Our couriers had got through safe from Laurel Hill, and this was the prompt reply.

As in the case of our former march from Atlanta, intense anxiety had been felt for our safety, and General Terry had been prompt to open communication. After a few minutes' conference with Captain Ainsworth about the capacity of his boat, and the state of facts along the river, I instructed him to be ready to start back at 6 P. M., and ordered Captain Byers to get ready to carry dispatches to Washington. I also authorized General Howard to send back by this opportunity some of the fugitives who had traveled with his army all the way from Columbia, among whom were Mrs. Feaster and her two beautiful daughters.[38]

I immediately prepared letters for Secretary Stanton, Generals Halleck and Grant, and Generals Schofield, Foster, Easton, and Beckwith, all of which have been published, but I include here only those to the Secretary of War, and Generals Grant and Terry, as samples of the whole.[39]

[37] Charles Ainsworth, acting ensign of the *Davidson,* was honorably discharged from the U.S. Navy in 1866. Edward W. Callahan, ed., *List of Officers of the Navy of the United States and of the Marine Corps from 1775 to 1900* (New York: L. R. Hamersly, 1901), 19.

[38] Amelia Feaster (1819–1870) and her daughter, Marie Boozer (1846–1908), were prominent socialites in South Carolina. Peter Cozzens, ed., *Battles and Leaders of the Civil War* (Urbana: University of Illinois Press, 2004), 6:525; *Lineage Book: National Society of the Daughters of the American Revolution* (Washington, DC: Daughters of the American Revolution, 1838), 163:180.

[39] See *OR,* I, 47(II), 794–795, 799–800, 804.

HEADQUARTERS MILITARY DIVISION OF THE MISSISSIPPI,
IN THE FIELD, FAYETTEVILLE, NORTH CAROLINA,
Sunday, March 12, 1865.

Hon. E. M. STANTON, *Secretary of War.*

DEAR SIR: I know you will be pleased to hear that my army has reached this point, and has opened communication with Wilmington. A tug-boat came up this morning, and will start back at 6 P. M.

I have written a letter to General Grant, the substance of which he will doubtless communicate, and it must suffice for me to tell you what I know will give you pleasure—that I have done all that I proposed, and the fruits seem to me ample for the time employed. Charleston, Georgetown, and Wilmington, are incidents, while the utter demolition of the railroad system of South Carolina, and the utter destruction of the enemy's arsenals of Columbia, Cheraw, and Fayetteville, are the principals of the movement. These points were regarded as inaccessible to us, and now no place in the Confederacy is safe against the army of the West. Let Lee hold on to Richmond, and we will destroy his country; and then of what use is Richmond? He must come out and fight us on open ground, and for that we must ever be ready. Let him stick behind his parapets, and he will perish.

I remember well what you asked me, and think I am on the right road, though a long one. My army is as united and cheerful as ever, and as full of confidence in itself and its leaders. It is utterly impossible for me to enumerate what we have done, but I inclose a slip just handed me, which is but partial. At Columbia and Cheraw we destroyed nearly all the gunpowder and cartridges which the Confederacy had in this part of the country. This arsenal is in fine order, and has been much enlarged. I cannot leave a detachment to hold it, therefore shall burn it, blow it up with gunpowder, and then with rams knock down its walls. I take it for granted the United States will never again trust North Carolina with an arsenal to appropriate at her pleasure.

Hoping that good fortune may still attend my army.

I remain your servant,

W. T. SHERMAN, *Major-General.*

HEADQUARTERS MILITARY DIVISION OF THE MISSISSIPPI,
IN THE FIELD, FAYETTEVILLE, NORTH CAROLINA, *March* 12, 1865.

Lieutenant-General U. S. GRANT, *commanding United States Army, City Point, Virginia.*

DEAR GENERAL: We reached this place yesterday at noon; Hardee, as usual, retreating across the Cape Fear, burning his bridges; but our pontoons will be up to-day, and, with as little delay as possible, I will be after him toward Goldsboro'.

A tug has just come up from Wilmington, and before I get off from here, I hope to get from Wilmington some shoes and stockings, sugar, coffee, and flour. We are abundantly supplied with all else, having in a measure lived off the country.

The army is in splendid health, condition, and spirits, though we have had foul weather, and roads that would have stopped travel to almost any other body of men I ever heard of.

Our march, was substantially what I designed—straight on Columbia, feigning on Branchville and Augusta. We destroyed, in passing, the railroad from the Edisto nearly up to Aiken; again, from Orangeburg to the Congaree; again, from Columbia down to Kingsville on the Wateree, and up toward Charlotte as far as the Chester line; thence we turned east on Cheraw and Fayetteville. At Columbia we destroyed immense arsenals and railroad establishments, among which were forty-three cannon. At Cheraw we found also machinery and material of war sent from Charleston, among which were twenty-five guns and thirty-six hundred barrels of powder; and here we find about twenty guns and a magnificent United States' arsenal.

We cannot afford to leave detachments, and I shall therefore destroy this valuable arsenal, so the enemy shall not have its use; and the United States should never again confide such valuable property to a people who have betrayed a trust.

I could leave here to-morrow, but want to clear my columns of the vast crowd of refugees and negroes that encumber us. Some I will send down the river in boats, and the rest to Wilmington by land, under small escort, as soon as we are across Cape Fear River.

I hope you have not been uneasy about us, and that the fruits of this march will be appreciated. It had to be made not only to destroy the valuable depots by the way, but for its incidents in the necessary fall of Charleston, Georgetown, and Wilmington. If I can now add Goldsboro' without too much cost, I will be in a position to aid you materially in the spring campaign.

Jos. Johnston may try to interpose between me here and Schofield about Newbern; but I think he will not try that, but concentrate his scattered armies at Raleigh, and I will go straight at him as soon as I get our men reclothed and our wagons reloaded.

Keep everybody busy, and let Stoneman push toward Greensboro' or Charlotte from Knoxville; even a feint in that quarter will be most important.

The railroad from Charlotte to Danville is all that is left to the enemy, and it will not do for me to go there, on account of the red-clay hills which are impassable to wheels in wet weather.

I expect to make a junction with General Schofield in ten days.

Yours truly,

W. T. Sherman, *Major-General.*

Headquarters Military Division of the Mississippi,
in the Field, Fayetteville, North Carolina, *March* 12, 1865.

Major-General Terry, *commanding United States Forces. Wilmington, North Carolina.*

General: I have just received your message by the tug which left Wilmington at 2 p. m. yesterday, which arrived here without trouble. The scout who brought me your cipher-message started back last night with my answers, which are superseded by the fact of your opening the river.

General Howard just reports that he has secured one of the enemy's steamboats below the city, General Slocum will try to secure two others known to be above, and we will load them with refugees (white and black) who have clung to our skirts, impeded our movements, and consumed our food.

We have swept the country well from Savannah to here, and the men and animals are in fine condition. Had it not been for the foul weather, I would have caught Hardee at Cheraw or here; but at Columbia, Cheraw, and here, we have captured immense stores, and destroyed machinery, guns, ammunition, and property, of inestimable value to our enemy. At all points he has fled from us, "standing not on the order of his going."

The people of South Carolina, instead of feeding Lee's army, will now call on Lee to feed them.

I want you to send me all the shoes, stockings, drawers, sugar, coffee, and flour, you can spare; finish the loads with oats or corn. Have the boats escorted, and let them run at night at any risk. We must not give time for Jos. Johnston to concentrate at Goldsboro'. We cannot prevent his concentrating at Raleigh, but he shall have no rest. I want General Schofield to go on with his railroad from Newbern as far as he can, and you should do the same from Wilmington. If we can get the roads to and secure Goldsboro' by April 10th, it will be soon enough; but every day now is worth a million of dollars. I can whip Jos. Johnston provided he does not catch one of my corps in flank, and I will see that the army marches hence to Goldsboro' in compact form.

I must rid our army of from twenty to thirty thousand useless mouths; as many to go down Cape Fear as possible, and the rest to go in vehicles or on captured horses *via* Clinton to Wilmington.

I thank you for the energetic action that has marked your course, and shall be most happy to meet you. I am, truly your friend,

W. T. Sherman, *Major-General.*

In quick succession I received other messages from General Terry, of older date, and therefore superseded by that brought by the tug Davidson, viz., by two naval officers, who had come up partly by canoes and partly by land; General Terry had also sent the Thirteenth Pennsylvania Cavalry to search for us, under Colonel Kerwin,[40] who had dispatched Major Berks with fifty men,[41] who reached us at Fayetteville; so that, by March 12th, I was in full communication with General Terry and the outside world. Still, I was anxious to reach Goldsboro', there to make junction with General Schofield, so as to be ready for the next and last stage of the war. I then knew that my special antagonist, General Jos. E. Johnston,[42] was back, with part of his old army; that he would not be misled by feints and false reports, and would somehow compel me to

[40] Michael Kerwin (1837–1912) joined the U.S. Army as a private in 1861 and reached the rank of brigadier general by the end of the war. Edward H. Daly, ed., *The Journal of the American Irish Historical Society* (New York: American Irish Historical Society, 1913), 12:276–277.

[41] In the first edition of the memoirs (1875), WTS did not specify which cavalry was sent or name Major Berks. Instead the text read, "General Terry had also sent a cavalry regiment to search for us, under Colonel Kerwin, who had dispatched two officers and fifty men . . ."

[42] In the first edition of the memoirs (1875), WTS did not include Johnston's middle initial.

exercise more caution than I had hitherto done. I then over-estimated his force at thirty-seven thousand infantry, supposed to be made up of S. D. Lee's corps, four thousand; Cheatham's, five thousand; Hoke's, eight thousand; Hardee's, ten thousand; and other detachments, ten thousand; with Hampton's, Wheeler's, and Butler's cavalry, about eight thousand. Of these, only Hardee and the cavalry were immediately in our front, while the bulk of Johnston's army was supposed to be collecting at or near Raleigh. I was determined, however, to give him as little time for organization as possible, and accordingly crossed Cape Fear River, with all the army, during the 13th and 14th, leaving one division as a rear-guard, until the arsenal could be completely destroyed. This was deliberately and completely leveled on the 14th, when fire was applied to the wreck. Little other damage was done at Fayetteville.

On the 14th the tug Davidson again arrived from Wilmington, with General Dodge, quartermaster, on board, reporting that there was no clothing to be had at Wilmington; but he brought up some sugar and coffee, which were most welcome, and some oats. He was followed by a couple of gunboats, under command of Captain Young, United States Navy,[43] who reached Fayetteville after I had left, and undertook to patrol the river as long as the stage of water would permit; and General Dodge also promised to use the captured steamboats for a like purpose. Meantime, also, I had sent orders to General Schofield, at Newbern, and to General Terry, at Wilmington, to move with their effective forces straight for Goldsboro', where I expected to meet them by the 20th of March.

On the 15th of March the whole army was across Cape Fear River, and at once began its march for Goldsboro'; the Seventeenth Corps still on the right, the Fifteenth next in order, then the Fourteenth and Twentieth on the extreme left; the cavalry acting in close concert with the left flank. With almost a certainty of being attacked on this flank, I had instructed General Slocum to send his corps-trains under strong escort by an interior road, holding four divisions ready for immediate battle. General Howard was in like manner ordered to keep his trains well to his right, and to have four divisions unencumbered, about six miles ahead of General Slocum, within easy support.

In the mean time, I had dispatched by land to Wilmington a train of refugees who had followed the army all the way from Columbia, South Carolina, under an escort of two hundred men, commanded by Major John A. Winson

[43] George W. Young commanded the *Eolus*. *OR*, I, 47(I), 23–24.

(One Hundred and Sixteenth Illinois Infantry),[44] so that we were disencumbered, and prepared for instant battle on our left and exposed flank.

In person I accompanied General Slocum, and during the night of March 15th was thirteen miles out on the Raleigh road. This flank followed substantially a road along Cape Fear River north, encountered pretty stubborn resistance by Hardee's infantry, artillery, and cavalry, and the ground favored our enemy; for the deep river, Cape Fear, was on his right, and North River on his left, forcing us to attack him square in front. I proposed to drive Hardee well beyond Averysboro', and then to turn to the right by Bentonsville for Goldsboro'. During the day it rained very hard, and I had taken refuge in an old cooper-shop, where a prisoner of war was brought to me (sent back from the skirmish-line by General Kilpatrick), who proved to be Colonel Albert Rhett, former commander of Fort Sumter.[45] He was a tall, slender, and handsome young man, dressed in the most approved rebel uniform, with high jackboots beautifully stitched, and was dreadfully mortified to find himself a prisoner in our hands. General Frank Blair happened to be with me at the moment, and we were much amused at Rhett's outspoken disgust at having been captured without a fight. He said he was a brigade commander, and that his brigade that day was Hardee's rear-guard; that his command was composed mostly of the recent garrisons of the batteries of Charleston Harbor, and had little experience in woodcraft; that he was giving ground to us as fast as Hardee's army to his rear moved back, and during this operation he was with a single aide in the woods, and was captured by two men of Kilpatrick's skirmish-line that was following up his retrograde movement. These men called on him to surrender, and ordered him, in language more forcible than polite, to turn and ride back. He first supposed these men to be of Hampton's cavalry, and threatened to report them to General Hampton for disrespectful language; but he was soon undeceived, and was conducted to Kilpatrick, who sent him back to General Slocum's guard.

The rain was falling heavily, and, our wagons coming up, we went into camp there, and had Rhett and General Blair to take supper with us, and our conversation was full and quite interesting. In due time, however, Rhett was

[44] WTS was most likely referring to John S. Windsor of the 116th Illinois. Mark A. Smith and Wade Sokolosky, *"No Such Army since the Days of Julius Caesar": Sherman's Carolinas Campaign from Fayetteville to Averasboro, March 1865* (El Dorado Hills, CA: Savas Beatie, 2017), 59.

[45] Alfred M. Rhett (1829–1889) graduated from Harvard in 1860 and took command of the Confederate forces at Fort Sumter after it was captured in Apr. 1861. "Biography of Col. Rhett," *Fairfield News and Herald* (Winnsboro, SC), Nov. 20, 1889, 1.

passed over by General Slocum to his provost-guard, with orders to be treated with due respect, and was furnished with a horse to ride.

The next day (the 16th) the opposition continued stubborn, and near Averysboro' Hardee had taken up a strong position, before which General Slocum deployed Jackson's division (of the Twentieth Corps), with part of Ward's. Kilpatrick was on his right front. Coming up, I advised that a brigade should make a wide circuit by the left, and, if possible, catch this line in flank. The movement was completely successful, the first line of the enemy was swept away, and we captured the larger part of Rhett's brigade, two hundred and seventeen men, including Captain Macbeth's battery of three guns, and buried one hundred and eight dead.

The deployed lines (Ward's and Jackson's) pressed on, and found Hardee again intrenched; but the next morning he was gone, in full retreat toward Smithfield. In this action, called the battle of Averysboro', we lost twelve officers and sixty-five men killed, and four hundred and seventy-seven men wounded; a serious loss, because every wounded man had to be carried in an ambulance. The rebel wounded (sixty-eight) were carried to a house near by, all surgical operations necessary were performed by our surgeons, and then these wounded men were left in care of an officer and four men of the rebel prisoners, with a scanty supply of food, which was the best we could do for them. In person I visited this house while the surgeons were at work, with arms and legs lying around loose, in the yard and on the porch; and in a room on a bed lay a pale, handsome young fellow, whose left arm had just been cut off near the shoulder. Some one used my name, when he asked, in a feeble voice, if I were General Sherman. He then announced himself as Captain Macbeth, whose battery had just been captured; and said that he remembered me when I used to visit his father's house, in Charleston. I inquired about his family, and enabled him to write a note to his mother, which was sent her afterward from Goldsboro'. I have seen that same young gentleman since in St. Louis, where he was a clerk in an insurance-office.

While the battle of Averysboro' was in progress, and I was sitting on my horse, I was approached by a man on foot, without shoes or coat, and his head bandaged by a handkerchief. He announced himself as the Captain Duncan who had been captured by Wade Hampton in Fayetteville, but had escaped; and, on my inquiring how he happened to be in that plight, he explained that when he was a prisoner Wade Hampton's men had made him "get out of his coat, hat, and shoes," which they appropriated to themselves. He said Wade Hampton had seen them do it, and he had appealed to him personally for protection, as an officer, but Hampton answered him with a curse. I sent Duncan to General Kilpatrick, and heard afterward that Kilpatrick had applied to General Slocum for his prisoner, Colonel Rhett, whom he made march on foot the rest of the way to Goldsboro', in retaliation. There was a story afloat that Kilpatrick made him "get out" of those fine boots, but restored them because none of his own officers had feet delicate enough to wear them. Of course, I know nothing of this personally, and have never seen Rhett since that night by the cooper-shop; and suppose that he is the editor who recently fought a duel in New Orleans.[46]

From Averysboro' the left wing turned east, toward Goldsboro', the Fourteenth Corps leading. I remained with this wing until the night of the 18th, when we were within twenty-seven miles of Goldsboro' and five from Bentonsville; and, supposing that all danger was over, I crossed over to join Howard's column, to the right, so as to be nearer to Generals Schofield and Terry, known to be approaching Goldsboro'. I overtook General Howard at Falling-Creek Church, and found his column well drawn out, by reason of the bad roads. I had heard some cannonading over about Slocum's head of column, and supposed it to indicate about the same measure of opposition by Hardee's troops and Hampton's cavalry before experienced; but during the day a messenger overtook me, and notified me that near Bentonsville General Slocum had run up against *Johnston's whole army.* I sent back orders for him to fight defensively to save time, and that I would come up with reënforcements from the direction of Cog's Bridge, by the road which we had reached near Falling-Creek Church. The country was very obscure, and the maps extremely defective.

By this movement I hoped General Slocum would hold Johnston's army facing west, while I would come on his rear from the east. The Fifteenth Corps, less one division (Hazen's), still well to the rear, was turned at once toward Bentonsville; Hazen's division was ordered to Slocum's flank, and orders were also sent for General Blair, with the Seventeenth Corps, to come to the same destination. Meantime the sound of cannon came from the direction of Bentonsville.

The night of the 19th caught us near Falling-Creek Church; but early the next morning the Fifteenth Corps, General C. R. Woods's division leading, closed down on Bentonsville, near which it was brought up by encountering a line of fresh parapet, crossing the road and extending north, toward Mill Creek.

After deploying, I ordered General Howard to proceed with due caution, using skirmishers alone, till he had made junction with General Slocum, on

[46] Alfred M. Rhett killed Ransom Calhoun in a duel in 1863. "Biography of Col. Rhett," *Fairfield News and Herald* (Winnsboro, SC), Nov. 20, 1889, 1.

his left. These deployments occupied all day, during which two divisions of the Seventeenth Corps also got up. At that time General Johnston's army occupied the form of a V, the angle reaching the road leading from Averysboro' to Goldsboro', and the flanks resting on Mill Creek, his lines embracing the village of Bentonsville.

General Slocum's wing faced one of these lines and General Howard's the other; and, in the uncertainty of General Johnston's strength, I did not feel disposed to invite a general battle, for we had been out from Savannah since the latter part of January, and our wagon-trains contained but little food. I had also received messages during the day from General Schofield, at Kinston, and General Terry, at Faison's Depot, approaching Goldsboro', both expecting to reach it by March 21st. During the 20th we simply held our ground and started our trains back to Kinston for provisions, which would be needed in the event of being forced to fight a general battle at Bentonsville. The next day (21st) it began to rain again, and we remained quiet till about noon, when General Mower, ever rash, broke through the rebel line on his extreme left flank, and was pushing straight for Bentonsville and the bridge across Mill Creek. I ordered him back to connect with his own corps; and, lest the enemy should concentrate on him, ordered the whole rebel line to be engaged with a strong skirmish-fire.

I think I made a mistake there, and should rapidly have followed Mower's lead with the whole of the right wing, which would have brought on a general battle, and it could not have resulted otherwise than successfully to us, by reason of our vastly superior numbers; but at the moment, for the reasons given, I preferred to make junction with Generals Terry and Schofield, before engaging Johnston's army, the strength of which was utterly unknown. The next day he was gone, and had retreated on Smithfield; and, the roads all being clear, our army moved to Goldsboro'. The heaviest fighting at Bentonsville was on the first day, viz., the 19th, when Johnston's army struck the head of Slocum's columns, knocking back Carlin's division; but, as soon as General Slocum had brought up the rest of the Fourteenth Corps into line, and afterward the Twentieth on its left, he received and repulsed all attacks, and held his ground as ordered, to await the coming back of the right wing. His loss, as reported, was nine officers and one hundred and forty-five men killed, eight hundred and sixteen wounded, and two hundred and twenty-six missing. He reported having buried of the rebel dead one hundred and sixty-seven, and captured three hundred and thirty-eight prisoners.

The loss of the right wing was two officers and thirty-five men killed, twelve officers and two hundred and eighty-nine men wounded, and seventy missing. General Howard reported that he had buried one hundred of the rebel dead, and had captured twelve hundred and eighty-seven prisoners.

Our total loss, therefore, at Bentonsville was:

	Officers.	Men.
Killed	11	180
Wounded	12	1,105
Missing	..	296
Total	23	1,581
Aggregate Loss		1,604

General Johnston, in his "Narrative" (p. 392),[47] asserts that his entire force at Bentonsville, omitting Wheeler's and Butler's cavalry, only amounted to fourteen thousand one hundred infantry and artillery; and (p. 393) states his losses as follows:

DATE.	Killed.	Wounded.	Missing.
On the 19th	180	1,220	515
On the 20th	6	90	31
On the 21st	37	157	107
Total	223	1,467	653
Aggregate Loss			2,343

Wide discrepancies exist in these figures: for instance, General Slocum accounts for three hundred and thirty-eight prisoners captured, and General Howard for twelve hundred and eighty-seven, making sixteen hundred and twenty-five in all, to Johnston's six hundred and fifty-three—a difference of eight hundred and seventy-two. I have always accorded to General Johnston due credit for boldness in his attack on our exposed flank at Bentonville, but I think he understates his strength, and doubt whether at the time he had accurate returns from his miscellaneous army, collected from Hoke, Bragg, Hardee, Lee, etc. After the first attack on Carlin's division, I doubt if the fighting was as desperate as described by him, p. 385, *et seq.* I was close up with the Fifteenth Corps, on the 20th and 21st, considered the fighting as

[47] See Joseph E. Johnston, *Narrative of Military Operations, Directed, during the Late War between the States* (New York: D. Appleton, 1874).

mere skirmishing, and know that my orders were to avoid a general battle, till we could be sure of Goldsboro', and of opening up a new base of supply. With the knowledge now possessed of his small force, of course I committed an error in not overwhelming Johnston's army on the 21st of March, 1865. But I was content then to let him go, and on the 22d of March rode to Cog's Bridge, where I met General Terry, with his two divisions of the Tenth Corps; and the next day we rode into Goldsboro', where I found General Schofield with the Twenty-third Corps, thus effecting a perfect junction of all the army at that point, as originally contemplated. During the 23d and 24th the whole army was assembled at Goldsboro'; General Terry's two divisions encamped at Faison's Depot to the south, and General Kilpatrick's cavalry at Mount Olive Station, near him, and there we all rested, while I directed my special attention to replenishing the army for the next and last stage of the campaign. Colonel W. W. Wright had been so indefatigable, that the Newbern Railroad was done, and a locomotive arrived in Goldsboro' on the 25th of March.

Thus was concluded one of the longest and most important marches ever made by an organized army in a civilized country. The distance from Savannah to Goldsboro' is four hundred and twenty-five miles, and the route traversed embraced five large navigable rivers, viz., the Edisto, Broad, Catawba, Pedee, and Cape Fear, at either of which a comparatively small force, well handled, should have made the passage most difficult, if not impossible. The country generally was in a state of nature, with innumerable swamps, with simply mud roads, nearly every mile of which had to be corduroyed. In our route we had captured Columbia, Cheraw, and Fayetteville, important cities and depots of supplies, had compelled the evacuation of Charleston City and Harbor, had utterly broken up all the railroads of South Carolina, and had consumed a vast amount of food and forage, essential to the enemy for the support of his own armies. We had in mid-winter accomplished the whole journey of four hundred and twenty-five miles in fifty days, averaging ten miles per day, allowing ten lay-days, and had reached Goldsboro' with the army in superb order, and the trains almost as fresh as when we had started from Atlanta.

It was manifest to me that we could resume our march, and come within the theatre of General Grant's field of operations in all April, and that there was no force in existence that could delay our progress, unless General Lee should succeed in eluding General Grant at Petersburg, make junction with General Johnston, and thus united meet me alone; and now that we had effected a junction with Generals Terry and Schofield, I had no fear even of that event. On reaching Goldsboro', I learned from General Schofield all the details of his operations about Wilmington and Newbern; also of the fight of the Twenty-third Corps about Kinston, with General Bragg. I also found Lieutenant Dunn, of General Grant's staff, awaiting me, with the general's letter of February 7th, covering instructions to Generals Schofield and Thomas; and his letter of March 16th, in answer to mine of the 12th, from Fayetteville.

These are all given here to explain the full reasons for the events of the war then in progress, with two or three letters from myself, to fill out the picture.

HEADQUARTERS ARMIES OF THE UNITED STATES,
CITY POINT, VIRGINIA, *February* 7, 1865.

Major-General W. T. SHERMAN, *commanding Military Division of the Mississippi.*

GENERAL: Without much expectation of it reaching you in time to be of any service, I have mailed to you copies of instructions to Schofield and Thomas. I had informed Schofield by telegraph of the departure of Mahone's division, south from the Petersburg front. These troops marched down the Weldon road, and, as they apparently went without baggage, it is doubtful whether they have not returned. I was absent from here when they left. Just returned yesterday morning from Cape Fear River. I went there to determine where Schofield's corps had better go to operate against Wilmington and Goldsboro'. The instructions with this will inform you of the conclusion arrived at.

Schofield was with me, and the plan of the movement against Wilmington fully determined before we started back; hence the absence of more detailed instructions to him. He will land one division at Smithville, and move rapidly up the south side of the river, and secure the Wilmington & Charlotte Railroad, and with his pontoon train cross over to the island south of the city, if he can. With the aid of the gunboats, there is no doubt but this move will drive the enemy from their position eight miles east of the city, either back to their line or away altogether. There will be a large force on the north bank of Cape Fear River, ready to follow up and invest the garrison, if they should go inside.

The railroads of North Carolina are four feet eight and one-half inches gauge. I have sent large parties of railroad-men there to build them up, and have ordered stock to run them. We have abundance of it idle from the non-use of the Virginia roads. I have taken every precaution to have supplies ready for you wherever you may turn up. I did this before when you left Atlanta, and regret that they did not reach you promptly when you reached salt-water. . . .

Alexander Stephens, R. M. T. Hunter, and Judge Campbell, are now at my headquarters, very desirous of going to Washington to see Mr. Lincoln, informally, on the subject of peace. The peace feeling within the rebel lines is gaining ground rapidly. This, however, should not relax our energies in the least, but should stimulate us to greater activity.

I have received your very kind letters, in which you say you would decline, or are opposed to, promotion. No one would be more pleased at your advancement than I, and if you should be placed in my position, and I put subordinate, it would not change our personal relations in the least. I would make the same exertions to support you that you have ever done to support me, and would do all in my power to make our cause win.

Yours truly,
U. S. GRANT, *Lieutenant-General.*

HEADQUARTERS ARMIES OF THE UNITED STATES,
CITY POINT, VIRGINIA, *January* 31, 1865.

Major-General G. H. THOMAS, *commanding Army of the Cumberland.*

GENERAL: With this I send you a letter from General Sherman. At the time of writing it, General Sherman was not informed of the depletion of your command by my orders. It will be impossible at present for you to move south as he contemplated, with the force of infantry indicated.

General Slocum is advised before this of the changes made, and that for the winter you will be on the defensive. I think, however, an expedition from East Tennessee, under General Stoneman might penetrate South Carolina, well down toward Columbia, destroying the railroad and military resources of the country, thus visiting a portion of the State which will not be reached by Sherman's forces. He might also be able to return to East Tennessee by way of Salisbury, North Carolina, thus releasing home our prisoners of war in rebel hands.

Of the practicability of doing this, General Stoneman will have to be the judge, making up his mind from information obtained while executing the first part of his instructions. Sherman's movements will attract the attention of all the force the enemy can collect, thus facilitating the execution of this.

Three thousand cavalry would be a sufficient force to take. This probably can be raised in the old Department of the Ohio, without taking any now under General Wilson. It would require, though, the reorganization of the two regiments of Kentucky Cavalry, which Stoneman had in his very successful raid into Southwestern Virginia.

It will be necessary, probably, for you to send, in addition to the force now in East Tennessee, a small division of infantry, to enable General Gillem to hold the upper end of Holston Valley, and the mountain-passes in rear of Stevenson.

You may order such an expedition. To save time, I will send a copy of this to General Stoneman, so that he can begin his preparations without loss of time, and can commence his correspondence with you as to these preparations.

As this expedition goes to destroy and not to fight battles, but to avoid them when practicable, particularly against any thing like equal forces, or where a great object is to be gained, it should go as light as possible. Stoneman's experience, in raiding will teach him in this matter better than he can be directed.

Let there be no delay in the preparations for this expedition, and keep me advised of its progress. Very respectfully, your obedient servant,

U. S. Grant, *Lieutenant-General.*

Headquarters Armies of the United States,
City Point, Virginia, *January* 31, 1865.

Major-General J. M. Schofield, *commanding Army of the Ohio.*

General: I have requested by telegraph that, for present purposes, North Carolina be erected into a department, and that you be placed in command of it, subject to Major-General Sherman's orders. Of course, you will receive orders from me direct until such time as General Sherman gets within communicating distance of you. This obviates the necessity of my publishing the order which I informed you would meet you at Fortress Monroe. If the order referred to should not be published from the Adjutant-General's office, you will read these instructions as your authority to assume command of all the troops in North Carolina, dating all official communications, "Headquarters Army of the Ohio." Your headquarters will be in the field, and with the portion of the army where you feel yourself most needed. In the first move you will go to Cape Fear River.

Your movements are intended as coöperative with Sherman's movement through the States of South and North Carolina. The first point to be obtained is to secure Wilmington. Goldsboro' will then be your objective point, moving either from Wilmington or Newbern, or both, as you may deem best. Should you not be able to reach Goldsboro', you will advance on the line or lines of railway connecting that place with the sea-coast, as near to it as you can, building the road behind you. The enterprise under you has two objects: the first is, to give General Sherman material aid, if needed, in his march north; the second, to open a base of supplies for him on the line of his march. As soon, therefore, as you can determine which of the two points, Wilmington or Newbern, you can best use for throwing supplies from to the interior, you will commence the accumulation of twenty days' rations and forage for sixty thousand men and twenty thousand animals. You will get of these as many as you can house and protect, to such point in the interior as you may be able to occupy.

I believe General Innis N. Palmer has received some instructions directly from General Sherman, on the subject of securing supplies for his army. You can learn what steps he has taken, and be governed in your requisitions accordingly. A supply of ordnance-stores will also be necessary.

Make all your requisitions upon the chiefs of their respective departments, in the field, with me at City Point. Communicate with me by every opportunity, and, should you deem it necessary at any time, send a special boat to Fortress Monroe, from which point you can communicate by telegraph.

The supplies referred to in these instructions are exclusive of those required by your own command.

The movements of the enemy may justify you, or even make it your imperative duty, to cut loose from your base and strike for the interior, to aid Sherman. In such case you will act on your own judgment, without waiting for instructions. You will report, however, what you propose doing. The details for carrying out these instructions are necessarily left to you. I would urge, however, if I did not know that you are already fully alive to the importance of it, prompt action. Sherman may be looked for in the neighborhood of Goldsboro' any time from the 22d to the 28th of February. This limits your time very materially.

If rolling-stock is not secured in the capture of Wilmington, it can be supplied from Washington. A large force of railroad-men has already been sent to Beaufort, and other mechanics will go to Fort Fisher in a day or two. On this point I have informed you by telegraph.

Very respectfully, your obedient servant,

U. S. Grant, *Lieutenant-General.*

Headquarters Armies of the United States,
City Point, Virginia, *March* 16, 1865.

Major-General W. T. Sherman, *commanding Military Division of the Mississippi.*

General: Your interesting letter of the 12th inst. is just received. I have never felt any uneasiness for your safety, but I have felt great anxiety to know just how you were progressing. I knew, or thought I did, that, with the magnificent army with you, you would come out safely somewhere.

To secure certain success, I deemed the capture of Wilmington of the greatest importance. Butler came near losing that prize to us. But Terry and Schofield have since retrieved his blunders, and I do not know but the first failure has been as valuable a success for the country as the capture of Fort Fisher. Butler may not see it in that light.

Ever since you started on the last campaign, and before, I have been attempting to get something done in the West, both to coöperate with you and to take advantage of the enemy's weakness there—to accomplish results favorable to us. Knowing Thomas to be slow beyond excuse, I depleted his army to reënforce Canby, so that he might act from Mobile Bay on the interior. With all I have said, he has not moved at last advices. Canby was sending a cavalry force, of about seven thousand, from Vicksburg toward Selma. I ordered Thomas to send Wilson from Eastport toward the same point, and to get him off as soon after the 20th of February as possible. He telegraphed me that he would be off by that date. He has not yet started, or had not at last advices. I ordered him to send Stoneman from East Tennessee into Northwest South Carolina, to be there about the time you would reach Columbia. He would either have drawn off the enemy's cavalry from you, or would have succeeded in destroying railroads, supplies, and other material, which you could not reach. At that time the Richmond papers were full of the accounts of your movements, and gave daily accounts of movements in West North Carolina. I supposed all the time it was Stoneman. You may judge my surprise when I afterward learned that Stoneman was still in Louisville, Kentucky, and that the troops in North Carolina were Kirk's forces! In order that Stoneman might get off without delay, I told Thomas that three thousand men would be sufficient for him to take. In the mean time I had directed Sheridan to get his cavalry ready, and, as soon as the snow in the mountains melted sufficiently, to start for Staunton, and go on and destroy the Virginia Central Railroad and canal. Time advanced, until he set the 28th of February for starting. I informed Thomas, and directed him to change the course of Stoneman toward Lynchburg, to destroy the road in Virginia up as near to that place as possible. Not hearing from Thomas, I telegraphed to him about the 12th, to know if Stoneman was yet off. He replied not, but that he (Thomas) would start that day for Knoxville, to get him off as soon as possible.

Sheridan has made his raid, and with splendid success, so far as heard. I am looking for him at "White House" to-day. Since about the 20th of last month the Richmond papers have been prohibited from publishing accounts of army movements. We are left to our own resources, therefore, for information. You will see from the papers what Sheridan has done; if you do not, the officer who bears this will tell you all.

Lee has depleted his army but very little recently, and I learn of none going south. Some regiments may have been detached, but I think no division or brigade. The determination seems to be to hold Richmond as long as possible. I have a force sufficient to leave enough to hold our lines (all that is necessary of them), and move out with plenty to whip his whole army. But the roads are entirely impassable. Until they improve, I shall content myself with watching Lee, and be prepared to pitch into him if he attempts to evacuate the place. I may bring Sheridan over—think I will—and break up the Danville and Southside Railroads. These are the last avenues left to the enemy.

Recruits have come in so rapidly at the West that Thomas has now about as much force as he had when he attacked Hood. I have stopped all who, under previous orders, would go to him, except those from Illinois.

Fearing the possibility of the enemy falling back to Lynchburg, and afterward attempting to go into East Tennessee or Kentucky, I have ordered Thomas to move the Fourth Corps to Bull's Gap, and to fortify there, and to hold out to the Virginia line, if he can. He has accumulated a large amount of supplies in Knoxville, and has been ordered not to destroy any of the railroad west of the Virginia line. I told him to get ready for a campaign toward Lynchburg, if it became necessary. He never can make one there or elsewhere; but the steps taken will prepare for any one else to take his troops and come east or go toward Rome, whichever may be necessary. I do not believe either will.

When I hear that you and Schofield are together, with your back upon the coast, I shall feel that you are entirely safe against any thing the enemy can do. Lee may evacuate Richmond, but he cannot get there with force enough to touch you. His army is now demoralized and deserting very fast, both to us and to their homes. A retrograde movement would cost him thousands of men, even if we did not follow.

Five thousand men, belonging to the corps with you, are now on their way to join you. If more reënforcements are necessary, I will send them. My notion is, that you should get Raleigh as soon as possible, and hold the railroad from there back. This may take more force than you now have.

From that point all North Carolina roads can be made useless to the enemy, without keeping up communications with the rear.

Hoping to hear soon of your junction with the forces from Wilmington and Newbern, I remain, very respectfully, your obedient servant,

U. S. Grant, *Lieutenant-General.*

Headquarters Military Division of the Mississippi, in the Field,
Cox's Bridge, Neuse River, North Carolina, *March* 22, 1865.

Lieutenant-General U. S. Grant, *Commander-in-Chief, City Point, Virginia.*

General: I wrote you from Fayetteville, North Carolina, on Tuesday, the 14th instant, that I was all ready to start for Goldsboro', to which point I had also ordered General Schofield, from Newbern, and General Terry, from Wilmington. I knew that General Jos. Johnston was supreme in command against me, and that he would have time to concentrate a respectable army to oppose the last stage of this march. Accordingly, General Slocum was ordered to send his main supply-train, under escort of two divisions, straight for Bentonsville, while he, with his other four divisions, disencumbered of all unnecessary wagons, should march toward Raleigh, by way of threat, as far as Averysboro'. General Howard, in like manner, sent his trains with the Seventeenth Corps, well to the right, and, with the four divisions of the Fifteenth Corps, took roads which would enable him to come promptly to the exposed left flank. We started on the 15th, but again the rains set in, and the roads, already bad enough, became horrible.

On Tuesday, the 15th, General Slocum found Hardee's army, from Charleston, which had retreated before us from Cheraw, in position across the narrow, swampy neck between Cape Fear and North Rivers, where the road branches off to Goldsboro'. There a pretty severe fight occurred, in which General Slocum's troops carried handsomely the advanced line, held by a South Carolina brigade, commanded by a Colonel Butler. Its Commander, Colonel Rhett, of Fort Sumter notoriety, with one of his staff, had the night before been captured, by Kilpatrick's scouts, from his very skirmish-line. The next morning Hardee was found gone, and was pursued through and beyond Averysboro'. General Slocum buried one hundred and eight dead rebels, and captured and destroyed three guns. Some eighty wounded rebels were left in our hands, and, after dressing their wounds, we left them in a house, attended by a Confederate officer and four privates, detailed out of our prisoners and paroled for the purpose.

We resumed the march toward Goldsboro'. I was with the left wing until I supposed all danger had passed; but, when General Slocum's head of column was within four miles of Bentonsville, after skirmishing as usual with cavalry, he became aware that there was infantry in his front. He deployed a couple of brigades, which, on advancing, sustained a partial repulse, but soon rallied, when he formed a line of the two leading divisions (Morgan's and Carlin's) of Jeff. C. Davis's corps. The enemy attacked these with violence, but was repulsed. This was in the forenoon of Sunday, the 19th. General Slocum brought forward the two divisions of the Twentieth Corps, hastily disposed of them for defense, and General Kilpatrick massed his cavalry on the left.

General Jos. Johnston had, the night before, marched his whole army (Bragg, Cheatham, S. D. Lee, Hardee, and all the troops he had drawn from every quarter), determined, as he told his men, to crash one of our corps, and then defeat us in detail. He attacked General Slocum in position from 3 P. M. on the 19th till dark; but was everywhere repulsed, and lost heavily. At the time, I was with the Fifteenth Corps, marching on a road more to the right; but, on hearing of General Slocum's danger, directed that corps toward Cox's Bridge, in the night brought Blair's corps over, and on the 20th marched rapidly on Johnston's flank and rear. We struck him about noon, forced him to assume the defensive, and to fortify. Yesterday we pushed him hard, and came very near crushing him, the right division of the Seventeenth Corps (Mower's) having broken in to within a hundred yards of where Johnston himself was, at the bridge across Mill Creek. Last night he retreated, leaving us in possession of the field, dead, and wounded. We have over two thousand prisoners from this affair and the one at Averysboro', and I am satisfied that Johnston's army was so roughly handled yesterday that we could march right on to Raleigh; but we have now been out six weeks, living precariously upon the collections of our foragers, our men "dirty, ragged, and saucy," and we must rest and fix up a little. Our entire losses thus far (killed, wounded, and prisoners) will be covered by twenty-five hundred, a great part of which are, as usual, slight wounds. The enemy has lost more than double as many, and we have in prisoners alone full two thousand.

I limited the pursuit, this morning, to Mill Creek, and will forthwith march the army to Goldsboro', there to rest, reclothe, and get some rations.

Our combinations were such that General Schofield entered Goldsboro' from Newbern; General Terry got Cox's Bridge, with pontoons laid, and a brigade across Neuse River intrenched; and we whipped Jos. Johnston—all on the same day.

After riding over the field of battle to-day, near Bentonsville, and making the necessary orders, I have ridden down to this place (Cox's Bridge) to see General Terry, and to-morrow shall ride into Goldsboro'.

I propose to collect there my army proper; shall post General Terry about Faison's Depot, and General Schofield about Kinston, partly to protect the road, but more to collect such food and forage as the country affords, until the railroads are repaired leading into Goldsboro'.

I fear these have not been pushed with the vigor I had expected; but I will soon have them both going. I shall proceed at once to organize three armies of twenty-five thousand men each, and will try and be all ready to march to Raleigh or Weldon, as we may determine, by or before April 10th.

I inclose you a copy of my orders of to-day. I would like to be more specific, but have not the data. We have lost no general officers nor any organization. General Slocum took three guns at Averysboro', and lost three others at the first dash on him at Bentonsville. We have all our wagons and trains in good order.

Yours truly,

W. T. SHERMAN, *Major-General.*

HEADQUARTERS MILITARY DIVISION OF THE MISSISSIPPI,
IN THE FIELD, GOLDSBORO', NORTH CAROLINA, *March* 23, 1865.

Lieutenant-General U. S. GRANT, *commanding the Armies of the United States, City Point, Virginia.*

GENERAL: On reaching Goldsboro' this morning, I found Lieutenant Dunn awaiting me with your letter of March 16th and dispatch of the 17th. I wrote you fully from Cox's Bridge yesterday, and since reaching Goldsboro' have learned that my letter was sent punctually to Newbern, whence it will be dispatched to you.

I am very glad to hear that General Sheridan did such good service between Richmond and Lynchburg, and hope he will keep the ball moving. I know that these raids and dashes disconcert our enemy and discourage him much.

General Slocum's two corps (Fourteenth and Twentieth) are now coming in. I will dispose of them north of Goldsboro', between the Weldon road and Little River. General Howard to-day is marching south of the Neuse, and to-morrow will come in and occupy ground north of Goldsboro', extending from the Weldon Railroad to that leading to Kinston.

I have ordered all the provisional divisions, made up of troops belonging to the regular corps, to be broken up, and the men to join their proper regiments and organizations; and have ordered General Schofield to guard the railroads back to Newbern and Wilmington, and to make up a movable column equal to twenty-five thousand men, with which to take the field. His army will be the centre, as on the Atlanta campaign. I do not think I want any more troops (other than absentees and recruits) to fill up the present regiments, and I can make up an army of eighty thousand men by April 10th. I will post General

Kilpatrick at Mount Olive Station on the Wilmington road, and then allow the army some rest.

We have sent all our empty wagons, under escort, with the proper staff-officers, to bring up from Kinston clothing and provisions. As long as we move we can gather food and forage; but, the moment we stop, trouble begins.

I feel sadly disappointed that our railroads are not done. I do not like to say there has been any neglect until I make inquiries; but it does seem to me the repairs should have been made ere this, and the road properly stocked. I can only hear of one locomotive (besides the four old ones) on the Newbern road, and two damaged locomotives (found by General Terry) on the Wilmington road. I left Generals Easton and Beckwith purposely to make arrangements in anticipation of my arrival, and have heard from neither, though I suppose them both to be at Morehead City.

At all events, we have now made a junction of all the armies, and if we can maintain them, will, in a short time, be in a position to march against Raleigh, Gaston, Weldon, or even Richmond, as you may determine.

If I get the troops all well placed, and the supplies working well, I may run up to see you for a day or two before diving again into the bowels of the country.

I will make, in a very short time, accurate reports of our operations for the past two months. Yours truly,

W. T. Sherman, *Major-General commanding.*

Headquarters Military Division of the Mississippi,
in the Field, Goldsboro', North Carolina, *March* 24, 1865.

Lieutenant-General U. S. Grant, *City Point, Virginia.*

General: I have kept Lieutenant Dunn over to-day that I might report further. All the army is now in, save the cavalry (which I have posted at Mount Olive Station, south of the Neuse) and General Terry's command (which to-morrow will move from Cox's Ferry to Faison's Depot, also on the Wilmington road). I send you a copy of my orders of this morning, the operation of which will, I think, soon complete our roads. The telegraph is now done to Morehead City, and by it I learn that stores have been sent to Kinston in boats, and that our wagons are loading with rations and clothing. By using the Neuse as high up as Kinston, hauling from there twenty-six miles, and by equipping the two roads to Morehead City and Wilmington, I feel certain we can not only feed and equip the army, but in a short time fill our wagons for another start. I feel certain, from the character of the fighting, that we have got Johnston's army afraid of us. He himself acts with timidity and caution. His cavalry alone manifests spirit, but limits its operations to our stragglers and foraging-parties. My marching columns of infantry do not pay the cavalry any attention, but walk right through it.

I think I see pretty clearly how, in one more move, we can checkmate Lee, forcing him to unite Johnston with him in the defense of Richmond, or to abandon the *cause.* I feel certain, if he leaves Richmond, Virginia leaves the Confederacy. I will study my maps a little more before giving my positive views. I want all possible information of the Roanoke as to navigability, how far up, and with what draught.

We find the country sandy, dry, with good roads, and more corn and forage than I had expected. The families remain, but I will gradually push them all out to Raleigh or Wilmington. We will need every house in the town. Lieutenant Dunn can tell you of many things of which I need not write.

Yours truly,
W. T. SHERMAN, *Major-General.*

HEADQUARTERS MILITARY DIVISION OF THE MISSISSIPPI,
IN THE FIELD, GOLDSBORO', NORTH CAROLINA, *April* 5, 1865.

Major-General GEORGE H. THOMAS, *commanding Department of the Cumberland.*

DEAR GENERAL: I can hardly help smiling when I contemplate my command—it is decidedly mixed. I believe, but am not certain, that you are in my jurisdiction, but I certainly cannot help you in the way of orders or men; nor do I think you need either. General Cruft has just arrived with his provisional division, which will at once be broken up and the men sent to their proper regiments, as that of Meagher was on my arrival here.

You may have some feeling about my asking that General Slocum should have command of the two corps that properly belong to you, viz., the Fourteenth and Twentieth, but you can recall that he was but a corps commander, and could not legally make orders of discharge, transfer, etc., which was imperatively necessary. I therefore asked that General Slocum should be assigned to command "an army in the field," called the Army of Georgia, composed of the Fourteenth and Twentieth Corps. The order is not yet made by the President, though I have recognized it because both General Grant and the President have sanctioned it, and promised to have the order made.

My army is now here, pretty well clad and provided, divided into three parts, of two corps each—much as our old Atlanta army was.

I expect to move on in a few days, and propose (if Lee remains in Richmond) to pass the Roanoke, and open communication with the Chowan and Norfolk. This will bring me in direct communication with General Grant.

This is an admirable point—country open, and the two railroads in good order back to Wilmington and Beaufort. We have already brought up stores enough to fill our wagons, and only await some few articles, and the arrival of some men who are marching up from the coast, to be off.

General Grant explained to me his orders to you, which, of course, are all right. You can make reports direct to Washington or to General Grant, but keep me advised occasionally of the general state of affairs, that I may know what is happening. I must give my undivided attention to matters here. You will hear from a thousand sources pretty fair accounts of our next march.

Yours truly,

W. T. SHERMAN, *Major-General.*

[LETTER FROM ADMIRAL DAHLGREN.]

SOUTH-ATLANTIC SQUADRON,
FLAG-SHIP PHILADELPHIA, CHARLESTON, *April* 20, 1865.

Major-General W. T. SHERMAN, *commanding Armies of the Tennessee, Georgia, and Mississippi.*

MY DEAR GENERAL: I was much gratified by a sight of your handwriting, which has just reached me from Goldsboro'; it was very suggestive of a past to me, when these regions were the scene of your operations.

As you progressed through South Carolina, there was no manifestation of weakness or of an intention to abandon Charleston, until within a few hours of the fact. On the 11th of February I was at Stono, and a spirited demonstration was made by General Schimmelpfennig and the vessels. He drove the rebels from their rifle-pits in front of the lines, extending from Fort Pringle, and pushed them vigorously. The next day I was at Bull's Bay, with a dozen steamers, among them the finest of the squadron. General Potter had twelve to fifteen hundred men, the object being to carry out your views. We made as much fuss as possible, and with better success than I anticipated, for it seems that the rebs conceived Stono to be a feint, and the real object at Bull's Bay, supposing, from the number of steamers and boats, that we had several thousand men. Now came an aide from General Gillmore, at Port Royal, with your cipher-dispatch from Midway, so I steamed down to Port Royal to see him. Next day was spent in vain efforts to decipher—finally it was accomplished. You thought that the state of the roads *might* force you to turn upon Charleston; so I went there on the 15th, but there was no sign yet of flinching. Then I went to Bull's Bay next day (16th), and found that the troops were not yet ashore, owing to the difficulties of shoal water. One of the gunboats had contrived to get up to within shelling range, and both soldiers and sailors were working hard. On the evening of the 16th I steamed down to Stono to see how matters were going there. Passing Charleston, I noticed two large fires, well inside—probably preparing to leave. On the 17th, in Stono, rumors were flying about loose of evacuation. In course of the morning, General Schimmelpfennig telegraphed me, from Morris Island, that there were symptoms of leaving; that he would again make a push at Stono, and asked for monitors. General Schimmelpfennig came down in the afternoon, and we met in the Folly Branch, near Secessionville. He was sure that the rebs would be off that night, so he was to assault them in front, while a monitor and gunboats stung their flanks both sides. I also sent an aide to order my battery of five eleven-inch guns, at Cumming's Point, to fire steadily all night on Sullivan's Island, and two monitors to close up to the island for the same object. Next morning (18th) the rascals were found to be off, and we broke in from all directions, by land and water. The main bodies had left at eight or nine in the evening, leaving detachments to keep up a fire from the batteries. I steamed round quickly, and soon got into the city, threading the streets with a large group of naval captains who had joined me. All was silent as the grave. No one to be seen but a few firemen.

No one can question the excellence of your judgment in taking the track you did, and I never had any misgivings, but it was natural to desire to go into the place with a strong hand, for, if any one spot in the land was foremost in the trouble, it was Charleston.

Your campaign was the final blow, grand in conception, complete in execution; and now it is yours to secure the last army which rebeldom possesses. I hear of your being in motion by the 9th, and hope that the result may be all that you wish.

Tidings of the murder of the President have just come, and shocked every mind. Can it be that such a resort finds root in any stratum of American opinion? Evidently it has not been the act of one man, nor of a madman. Who have prompted him?

I am grateful for your remembrance of my boy; the thought of him is ever nearest to my heart. Generous, brave, and noble, as I ever knew him to be, that he should close his young life so early, even under the accepted conditions of a soldier's life, as a son of the Union, would have been grief sufficient for me to bear; but that his precious remains should have been so treated by the brutes into whose hands they fell, adds even to the bitterness of death. I am now awaiting the hour when I can pay my last duties to his memory.

With my best and sincere wishes, my dear general, for your success and happiness, I am, most truly, your friend,

J. A. DAHLGREN.

[GENERAL ORDER NO. 50.]

WAR DEPARTMENT, ADJUTANT-GENERAL'S OFFICE,
WASHINGTON, *March* 27, 1865.

Ordered—1. That at the hour of noon, on the 14th day of April, 1865, Brevet Major-General Anderson will raise and plant upon the ruins of Fort Sumter, in Charleston Harbor, the same United States flag which floated over the battlements of that fort during the rebel assault, and which was lowered and saluted by him and the small force of his command when the works were evacuated on the 14th day of April, 1861.

2. That the flag, when raised, be saluted by one hundred guns from Fort Sumter, and by a national salute from every fort and rebel battery that fired upon Fort Sumter.

3. That suitable ceremonies be had upon the occasion, under the direction of Major-General William T. Sherman, whose military operations compelled the rebels to evacuate Charleston, or, in his absence, under the charge of Major-General Q. A. Gillmore, commanding the department. Among the ceremonies will be the delivery of a public address by the Rev. Henry Ward Beecher.

4. That the naval forces at Charleston, and their commander on that station, be invited to participate in the ceremonies of the occasion.

By order of the President of the United States,
EDWIN M. STANTON, *Secretary of War.*

[GENERAL ORDER NO. 41.]

HEADQUARTERS DEPARTMENT OF THE SOUTH,
HILTON HEAD, SOUTH CAROLINA, *April* 10, 1865.

Friday next, the 14th inst., will be the fourth anniversary of the capture of Fort Sumter by the rebels. A befitting celebration on that day, in honor of its reoccupation by the national forces, has been ordered by the President, in pursuance of which Brevet Major-General Robert Anderson, United States Army, will restore to its original place on the fort the identical flag which, after an honorable and gallant defense, he was compelled to lower to the insurgents in South Carolina, in April, 1861.

The ceremonies for the occasion will commence with prayer, at thirty minutes past eleven o'clock A. M.

At noon precisely, the flag will be raised and saluted with one hundred guns from Fort Sumter, and with a national salute from Fort Moultrie and Battery Bee on Sullivan's Island, Fort Putnam on Morris Island, and Fort Johnson on James's Island; it being eminently appropriate that the places which were so conspicuous in the inauguration of the rebellion should take a part not less prominent in this national rejoicing over the restoration of the national authority.

After the salutes, the Rev. Henry Ward Beecher will deliver an address.

The ceremonies will close with prayer and a benediction.

Colonel Stewart L. Woodford, chief of staff, under such verbal instructions as he may receive, is hereby charged with the details of the celebration, comprising all the arrangements that it may be necessary to make for the accommodation of the orator of the day, and the comfort and safety of the invited guests from the army and navy, and from civil life.

By command of Major-General Q. A. Gillmore,
W. L. M. BURGER, *Assistant Adjutant-General.*

Copy of Major ANDERSON's *Dispatch, announcing the Surrender of Fort Sumter, April* 14, 1861.

STEAMSHIP BALTIC, OFF SANDY HOOK,
April 18, 1861, 10.30 A. M.—*Via* NEW YORK.

Honorable S. CAMERON, *Secretary of War, Washington:*

Having defended Fort Sumter for thirty-four hours, until the quarters were entirely burned, the main gates destroyed by fire, the gorge-walls seriously injured, the magazine surrounded by flames, and its door closed from the effect of heat, four barrels and three cartridges of powder only being available, and no provisions remaining but pork, I accepted terms of evacuation offered by General Beauregard, being the same offered by him on the 11th inst., prior to the commencement of hostilities, and marched out of the fort, Sunday afternoon, the 14th inst., with colors flying and drums beating, bringing away company and private property, and saluting my flag with fifty guns.

ROBERT ANDERSON, *Major First Artillery, commanding.*

24

End of the War.—from Goldsboro' to Raleigh and Washington.

APRIL AND MAY, 1865.

As BEFORE DESCRIBED, the armies commanded respectively by Generals J. M. Schofield, A. H. Terry, and myself, effected a junction in and about Goldsboro', North Carolina, during the 22d and 23d of March, 1865, but it required a few days for all the troops and trains of wagons to reach their respective camps. In person I reached Goldsboro' on the 23d, and met General Schofield, who described fully his operations in North Carolina up to that date; and I also found Lieutenant Dunn, aide-de-camp to General Grant, with a letter from him of March 16th, giving a general description of the state of facts about City Point.[1] The next day I received another letter, more full, dated the 22d, which I give herewith.

Nevertheless, I deemed it of great importance that I should have a personal interview with the general, and determined to go in person to City Point as soon as the repairs of the railroad, then in progress under the personal direction of Colonel W. W. Wright, would permit:

HEADQUARTERS ARMIES OF THE UNITED STATES,
CITY POINT, VIRGINIA, *March* 22, 1865.

Major-General W. T. SHERMAN, *commanding Military Division of the Mississippi.*

GENERAL: Although the Richmond papers do not communicate the fact, yet I saw enough in them to satisfy me that you occupied Goldsboro' on the 19th inst. I congratulate you and the army on what may be regarded as the successful termination of the third campaign since leaving the Tennessee River, less than one year ago.

[1] See, *PUSG*, 14:172–176.

Since Sheridan's very successful raid north of the James, the enemy are left dependent on the Southside and Danville roads for all their supplies. These I hope to cut next week. Sheridan is at "White House," shoeing up and resting his cavalry. I expect him to finish by Friday night and to start the following morning, *via* Long Bridge, Newmarket, Bermuda Hundred, and the extreme left of the army around Petersburg. He will make no halt with the armies operating here, but will be joined by a division of cavalry, five thousand five hundred strong, from the Army of the Potomac, and will proceed directly to the Southside and Danville roads. His instructions will be to strike the Southside road as near Petersburg as he can, and destroy it so that it cannot be repaired for three or four days, and push on to the Danville road, as near to the Appomattox as he can get. Then I want him to destroy the road toward Burkesville as far as he can; then push on to the Southside road, west of Burkesville, and destroy it effectually. From that point I shall probably leave it to his discretion either to return to this army, crossing the Danville road south of Burkesville, or go and join you, passing between Danville and Greensboro'. When this movement commences I shall move out by my left, with all the force I can, holding present intrenched lines. I shall start with no distinct view, further than holding Lee's forces from following Sheridan. But I shall be along myself, and will take advantage of any thing that turns up. If Lee detaches, I will attack; or if he comes out of his lines I will endeavor to repulse him, and follow it up to the best advantage.

It is most difficult to understand what the rebels intend to do; so far but few troops have been detached from Lee's army. Much machinery has been removed, and material has been sent to Lynchburg, showing a disposition to go there. Points, too, have been fortified on the Danville road.

Lee's army is much demoralized, and great numbers are deserting. Probably, from returned prisoners, and such conscripts as can be picked up, his numbers may be kept up. I estimate his force now at about sixty-five thousand men.

Wilson started on Monday, with twelve thousand cavalry, from Eastport. Stoneman started on the same day, from East Tennessee, toward Lynchburg. Thomas is moving the Fourth Corps to Bull's Gap. Canby is moving with a formidable force on Mobile and the interior of Alabama.

I ordered Gillmore, as soon as the fall of Charleston was known, to hold all important posts on the sea-coast, and to send to Wilmington all surplus forces. Thomas was also directed to forward to Newbern all troops belonging to the corps with you. I understand this will give you about five thousand men, besides those brought east by Meagher.

I have been telegraphing General Meigs to hasten up locomotives and cars for you. General McCallum, he informs me, is attending to it. I fear they are not going forward as fast as I would like.

Let me know if you want more troops, or any thing else.

Very respectfully, your obedient servant,

U. S. GRANT, *Lieutenant-General.*

The railroad was repaired to Goldsboro' by the evening of March 25th, when, leaving General Schofield in chief command, with a couple of staff-officers I started for City Point, Virginia, on a locomotive, in company with Colonel Wright, the constructing engineer. We reached Newbern that evening, which was passed in the company of General Palmer and his accomplished lady,[2] and early the next morning we continued on to Morehead City, where General Easton had provided for us the small captured steamer Russia, Captain Smith. We put to sea at once and steamed up the coast, reaching Fortress Monroe on the morning of the 27th, where I landed and telegraphed to my brother, Senator Sherman, at Washington, inviting him to come down and return with me to Goldsboro'. We proceeded on up James River to City Point, which we reached the same afternoon. I found General Grant, with his family and staff, occupying a pretty group of huts on the bank of James River, overlooking the harbor, which was full of vessels of all classes, both war and merchant, with wharves and warehouses on an extensive scale. The general received me most heartily, and we talked over matters very fully. After I had been with him an hour or so, he remarked that the President, Mr. Lincoln, was then on board the steamer River Queen, lying at the wharf, and he proposed that we should call and see him. We walked down to the wharf, went on board, and found Mr. Lincoln alone, in the after-cabin. He remembered me perfectly, and at once engaged in a most interesting conversation. He was full of curiosity about the many incidents of our great march, which had reached him officially and through the newspapers, and seemed to enjoy very much the more ludicrous parts—about the "bummers," and their devices to collect food and forage when the outside world supposed us to be starving; but at the

[2] "Queen" Mary Mellon (1850–1894) had three daughters with William J. Palmer. Sarah Wagner, *4 U R Ranch at Wagon Wheel Gap Hot Springs Resort: A History* (Charleston, SC: History Press, 2020), 131.

same time he expressed a good deal of anxiety lest some accident might happen to the army in North Carolina during my absence. I explained to him that that army was snug and comfortable, in good camps, at Goldsboro'; that it would require some days to collect forage and food for another march; and that General Schofield was fully competent to command it in my absence. Having made a good, long, social visit, we took our leave and returned to General Grant's quarters, where Mrs. Grant had provided tea. While at the table, Mrs. Grant inquired if we had seen *Mrs.* Lincoln.[3] "No," said the general, "I did not ask for her;" and I added that I did not even know that she was on board. Mrs. Grant then exclaimed, "Well, you are a pretty pair!" and added that our neglect was unpardonable; when the general said we would call again the next day, and make amends for the unintended slight.[4]

Early the next day, March 28th, all the principal officers of the army and navy called to see me, Generals Meade,[5] Ord, Ingalls,[6] etc., and Admiral Porter. At this time the River Queen was at anchor out in the river, abreast of the wharf, and we again started to visit Mr. and *Mrs.* Lincoln. Admiral Porter accompanied us. We took a small tug at the wharf, which conveyed us on board, where we were again received most courteously by the President, who conducted us to the after-cabin. After the general compliments, General Grant inquired after *Mrs.* Lincoln, when the President went to her state-room, returned, and begged us to excuse her, as she was not well. We then again entered upon a general conversation, during which General Grant explained to the President that at that very instant of time General Sheridan was crossing James River from the north, by a pontoon-bridge below City Point; that he

[3] Mary Lincoln (1818–1882) attended Shelby Female Academy in Lexington, KY, before she married future U.S. president Abraham Lincoln. Spencer C. Tucker, ed., *American Civil War: A State-by-State Encyclopedia* (Santa Barbara: ABC-CLIO, 2017), vol. 1, s.v. "Lincoln, Mary Ann Todd (1818–1882)."

[4] According to Julia D. Grant, after she greeted Mary Lincoln aboard the *River Queen,* the president remarked, "Now, I am going to leave you two ladies together while the General and I go for a few moments to my room where we can have a little talk without being interrupted. Eh, General?" Julia D. Grant, *The Personal Memoirs of Julia Dent Grant (Mrs. Ulysses S. Grant),* ed. John Y. Simon (New York: G. P. Putnam's Sons, 1975), 142.

[5] George G. Meade (1815–1872) graduated from the USMA in 1835 and fought in the Mexican-American War and commanded the Army of the Potomac in Mar. 1865. *CWHC,* 384–385.

[6] Rufus Ingalls (1818–1893) graduated from the USMA in 1843 and served as a quartermaster in the general headquarters for armies in Virginia. *CWHC,* 313.

had a large, well-appointed force of cavalry, with which he proposed to strike the Southside and Danville Railroads, by which alone General Lee, in Richmond, supplied his army; and that, in his judgment, matters were drawing to a crisis, his only apprehension being that General Lee would not wait long enough. I also explained that my army at Goldsboro' was strong enough to fight Lee's army and Johnston's combined, provided that General Grant could come up within a day or so; that if Lee would only remain in Richmond another fortnight, I could march up to Burkesville, when Lee would have to starve inside of his lines, or come out from his intrenchments and fight us on equal terms.

Both General Grant and myself supposed that one or the other of us would have to fight one more bloody battle, and that it would be the *last.* Mr. Lincoln exclaimed, more than once, that there had been blood enough shed, and asked us if another battle could not be avoided. I remember well to have said that we could not control that event; that this necessarily rested with our enemy; and I inferred that both Jeff. Davis and General Lee would be forced to fight one more desperate and bloody battle. I rather supposed it would fall on me, somewhere near Raleigh; and General Grant added that, if Lee would only wait a few more days, he would have his army so disposed that if the enemy should abandon Richmond, and attempt to make junction with General Jos. Johnston in North Carolina, he (General Grant) would be on his heels. Mr. Lincoln more than once expressed uneasiness that I was not with my army at Goldsboro', when I again assured him that General Schofield was fully competent to command in my absence; that I was going to start back that very day, and that Admiral Porter had kindly provided for me the steamer Bat, which he said was much swifter than my own vessel, the Russia. During this interview I inquired of the President if he was all ready for the end of the war. What was to be done with the rebel armies when defeated? And what should be done with the political leaders, such as Jeff. Davis, etc.? Should we allow them to escape, etc.? He said he was all ready; all he wanted of us was to defeat the opposing armies, and to get the men composing the Confederate armies back to their homes, at work on their farms and in their shops. As to Jeff. Davis, he was hardly at liberty to speak his mind fully, but intimated that he ought to clear out, "escape the country," only it would not do for him to say so openly. As usual, he illustrated his meaning by a story: "A man once had taken the total-abstinence pledge. When visiting a friend, he was invited to take a drink, but declined, on the score of his pledge; when his friend suggested lemonade, which was accepted. In preparing the lemonade, the friend pointed to the brandy-bottle, and said the lemonade would be more palatable if he were to pour in a little brandy; when his guest said, if he could do so 'unbeknown' to him, he would not object." From which illustration I inferred that Mr. Lincoln wanted Davis to escape, "unbeknown" to him.[7]

I made no notes of this conversation at the time, but Admiral Porter, who was present, did, and in 1866 he furnished me an account thereof, which I insert below, but the admiral describes the first visit, of the 27th, whereas my memory puts Admiral Porter's presence on the following day. Still he may be right, and he may have been with us the day before, as I write this chiefly from memory. There were two distinct interviews; the first was late in the afternoon of March 27th, and the other about noon of the 28th, both in the after-cabin of the steamer River Queen; on both occasions Mr. Lincoln was full and frank in his conversation, assuring me that in his mind he was all ready for the civil reorganization of affairs at the South as soon as the war was over; and he distinctly authorized me to assure Governor Vance[8] and the people of North Carolina that, as soon as the rebel armies laid down their arms, and resumed their civil pursuits, they would at once be guaranteed all their rights as citizens of a common country; and that to avoid anarchy the State governments then in existence, with their civil functionaries, would be recognized by him as the government *de facto* till Congress could provide others.

I know, when I left him, that I was more than ever impressed by his kindly nature, his deep and earnest sympathy with the afflictions of the whole people, resulting from the war, and by the march of hostile armies through the South; and that his earnest desire seemed to be to end the war speedily, without more bloodshed or devastation, and to restore all the men of both sections to their homes. In the language of his second inaugural address, he seemed to have "charity for all, malice toward none," and, above all, an absolute faith in the courage, manliness, and integrity of the armies in the field.[9] When at rest or listening, his legs and arms seemed to hang almost lifeless, and his face was care-worn and haggard; but, the moment he began to talk, his face lightened up, his tall form, as it were, unfolded, and he was the very

[7] USG referred to the same story in his personal memoirs, which were posthumously released ten years after the first publication of WTS's memoirs in 1875. Ulysses S. Grant, *Personal Memoirs of U.S. Grant* (New York: Charles L. Webster, 1885), 532–533.

[8] Zebulon B. Vance (1830–1894) served as the Confederate governor of North Carolina from 1862 to 1865. *CWHC,* 541.

[9] See Ronald C. White Jr., *Lincoln's Greatest Speech: The Second Inaugural* (New York: Simon and Schuster, 2006), 17–18.

impersonation of good-humor and fellowship. The last words I recall as addressed to me were that he would feel better when I was back at Goldsboro'. We parted at the gangway of the River Queen, about noon of March 28th, and I never saw him again. Of all the men I ever met, he seemed to possess more of the elements of greatness, combined with goodness, than any other.

ADMIRAL PORTER'S ACCOUNT OF THE INTERVIEW WITH MR. LINCOLN.

THE day of General Sherman's arrival at City Point (I think the 27th of March, 1865), I accompanied him and General Grant on board the President's flag-ship, the Queen, where the President received us in the upper saloon, no one but ourselves being present.

The President was in an exceedingly pleasant mood, and delighted to meet General Sherman, whom he cordially greeted.

It seems that this was the first time he had met Sherman, to remember him, since the beginning of the war, and did not remember when he had seen him before, until the general reminded him of the circumstances of their first meeting.

This was rather singular on the part of Mr. Lincoln, who was, I think, remarkable for remembering people, having that kingly quality in an eminent degree. Indeed, such was the power of his memory, that he seemed never to forget the most minute circumstance.

The conversation soon turned on the events of Sherman's campaign through the South, with every movement of which the President seemed familiar.

He laughed over some of the stories Sherman told of his "bummers," and told others in return, which illustrated in a striking manner the ideas he wanted to convey. For example, he would often express his wishes by telling an apt story, which was quite a habit with him, and one that I think he adopted to prevent his committing himself seriously.

The interview between the two generals and the President lasted about an hour and a half, and, as it was a remarkable one, I jotted down what I remembered of the conversation, as I have made a practice of doing during the rebellion, when any thing interesting occurred.

I don't regret having done so, as circumstances afterward occurred (Stanton's ill-conduct toward Sherman) which tended to cast odium on General Sherman for allowing such liberal terms to Jos. Johnston.

Could the conversation that occurred on board the Queen, between the President and General Sherman, have been known, Sherman would not, and could not, have been censured. Mr. Lincoln, had he lived, would have acquitted the general of any blame, for he was only carrying out the President's wishes.

My opinion is, that Mr. Lincoln came down to City Point with the most liberal views toward the rebels. He felt confident that we would be successful, and was willing that the enemy should capitulate on the most favorable terms.

I don't know what the President would have done had he been left to himself, and had our army been unsuccessful, but he was then wrought up to a high state of excitement. He wanted peace on almost any terms, and there is no knowing what proposals he might have been willing to listen to. His heart was tenderness throughout, and, as long as the rebels laid down their arms, he did not care how it was done. I do not know how far he was influenced by General Grant, but I presume, from their long conferences, that they must have understood each other perfectly, and that the terms given to Lee after his surrender were authorized by Mr. Lincoln. I know that the latter was delighted when he heard that they had been given, and exclaimed, a dozen times, "Good!" "All right!" "Exactly the thing!" and other similar expressions. Indeed, the President more than once told me what he supposed the terms would be: if Lee and Johnston surrendered, he considered the war ended, and that all the other rebel forces would lay down their arms at once.

In this he proved to be right. Grant and Sherman were both of the same opinion, and so was every one else who knew any thing about the matter.

What signified *the terms* to them, so long as we obtained the actual surrender of people who only wanted a good opportunity to give up gracefully? The rebels had fought "to the last ditch," and all that they had left them was the hope of being handed down in history as having received honorable terms.

After hearing General Sherman's account of his own position, and that of Johnston, at that time, the President expressed fears that the rebel general would escape south again by the railroads, and that General Sherman would have to chase him anew, over the same ground; but the general pronounced this to be impracticable. He remarked: "I have him where he cannot move without breaking up his army, which, once disbanded, can never again be got together; and I have destroyed the Southern railroads, so that they cannot be used again for a long time." General Grant remarked, "What is to prevent their laying the rails again?" "Why," said General Sherman, "my 'bummers' don't do things by halves. Every rail, after having been placed over a hot fire, has been twisted as crooked as a ram's-horn, and they never can be used again."

This was the only remark made by General Grant during the interview, as he sat smoking a short distance from the President, intent, no doubt, on his own plans, which were being brought to a successful termination.

The conversation between the President and General Sherman, about the terms of surrender to be allowed Jos. Johnston, continued. Sherman energetically insisted that he could command his own terms, and that Johnston would have to yield to his demands; but the President was very decided about the matter, and insisted that the surrender of Johnston's army must be obtained on any terms.

General Grant was evidently of the same way of thinking, for, although he did not join in the conversation to any extent, yet he made no objections, and I presume had made up his mind to allow the best terms himself.

He was also anxious that Johnston should not be driven into Richmond, to reënforce the rebels there, who, from behind their strong intrenchments, would have given us incalculable trouble.

Sherman, as a subordinate officer, yielded his views to those of the President, and the terms of capitulation between himself and Johnston were exactly in accordance with Mr. Lincoln's wishes. He could not have done any thing which would have pleased the President better.

Mr. Lincoln did, in fact, arrange the (so considered) liberal terms offered General Jos. Johnston, and, whatever may have been General Sherman's private views, I feel sure that he yielded to the wishes of the President in every respect. It was Mr. Lincoln's policy that was carried out, and, had he lived long enough, he would have been but too glad to have acknowledged it. Had Mr. Lincoln lived, Secretary Stanton would have issued no false telegraphic dispatches, in the hope of killing off another general in the regular army, one who by his success had placed himself in the way of his own succession.

The disbanding of Jos. Johnston's army was so complete, that the pens and ink used in the discussion of the matter were all wasted.

It was asserted, by the rabid ones, that General Sherman had given up all that we had been fighting for, had conceded every thing to Jos. Johnston, and had, as the boys say, "knocked the fat into the fire;" but sober reflection soon overruled these harsh expressions, and, with those who knew General Sherman, and appreciated him, he was still the great soldier, patriot, and gentleman. In future times this matter will be looked at more calmly and dispassionately. The bitter animosities that have been engendered during the rebellion will have died out for want of food on which to live, and the very course Grant, Sherman, and others pursued, in granting liberal terms to the defeated rebels, will be applauded. The fact is, they met an old beggar in the road, whose crutches had broken from under him: they let him have only the broken crutches to get home with!

I sent General Sherman back to Newbern, North Carolina, in the steamer Bat.

While he was absent from his command he was losing no time, for he was getting his army fully equipped with stores and clothing; and, when he returned, he had a rested and regenerated army, ready to swallow up Jos. Johnston and all his ragamuffins.

Johnston was cornered, could not move without leaving every thing behind him, and could not go to Richmond without bringing on a famine in that destitute city.

I was with Mr. Lincoln all the time he was at City Point, and until he left for Washington. He was more than delighted with the surrender of Lee, and with the terms Grant gave the rebel general; and would have given Jos. Johnston twice as much, had the latter asked for it, and could he have been certain that the rebel would have surrendered without a fight. I again repeat that, had Mr. Lincoln lived, he would have shouldered *all* the responsibility.

One thing is certain: had Jos. Johnston escaped and got into Richmond, and caused a larger list of killed and wounded than we had, General Sherman would have been blamed. Then why not give him the full credit of capturing on the best terms the enemy's last important army and its best general, and putting an end to the rebellion?

It was a *finale* worthy of Sherman's great march through the swamps and deserts of the South, a march not excelled by any thing we read of in modern military history.

D. D. Porter, *Vice-Admiral.*

(Written by the admiral in 1866, at the United States Naval Academy at Annapolis, Md., and mailed to General Sherman at St. Louis, Mo.)

As soon as possible, I arranged with General Grant for certain changes in the organization of my army; and the general also undertook to send to North Carolina some tug-boats and barges to carry stores from Newbern up as far as Kinston, whence they could be hauled in wagons to our camps, thus relieving our railroads to that extent. I undertook to be ready to march north by April 10th, and then embarked on the steamer Bat, Captain Barnes,[10] for North Carolina. We steamed down James River, and at Old Point Comfort took on board my brother, Senator Sherman, and Mr. Edwin Stanton, son of the Secretary of War,[11] and proceeded at once to our destination. On our way down the river, Captain Barnes expressed himself extremely obliged to me for taking his vessel, as it had relieved him of a most painful dilemma. He explained that he had been detailed by Admiral Porter to escort the President's unarmed boat, the River Queen, in which capacity it became his special duty to look after Mrs. Lincoln. The day before my arrival at City Point, there had been a grand review of a part of the Army of the James, then commanded by General Ord. The President rode out from City Point with General Grant on horseback, accompanied by a numerous staff, including Captain Barnes and Mrs. Ord;[12] but Mrs. Lincoln and Mrs. Grant had followed in a carriage.

The cavalcade reached the review-ground some five or six miles out from City Point, found the troops all ready, drawn up in line, and after the usual presentation of arms, the President and party, followed by Mrs. Ord and Captain Barnes on horseback, rode the lines, and returned to the reviewing stand, which meantime had been reached by Mrs. Lincoln and Mrs. Grant in their carriage, which had been delayed by the driver taking a wrong road. Mrs. Lincoln, seeing Mrs. Ord and Captain Barnes riding with the retinue, and supposing that Mrs. Ord had

[10] John S. Barnes (1836–1911) graduated from the U.S. Naval Academy in 1854 and was a lieutenant commander when he commanded the *Bat.* "John S. Barnes Dead," *Boston Globe,* Nov. 24, 1911, 10; *PUSG,* 21:304*n.*

[11] Edwin L. Stanton (1842–1877) served as his father's private secretary during the war. Joseph Henry, *The Papers of Joseph Henry: January 1866–May 1878, the Smithsonian Years,* ed. Nathan Reingold and Marc Rothenberg (New York: Smithsonian Institution Press, 1972), 11:465*n.*

[12] Mary M. Thompson (1831–1894) married Edward O. C. Ord in San Francisco in 1854. According to Julia D. Grant, E. O. C. Ord made regular visits to USG in early 1865 to "report upon the condition of the Army of the James." Julia D. Grant, *The Personal Memoirs,* 136; John D. Wright, *The Routledge Encyclopedia of Civil War Era Biographies* (New York: Routledge, 2013), s.v. "Ord, Edward Otho Cresap, 1818–1883."

personated her, turned on Captain Barnes and gave him a fearful scolding; and even indulged in some pretty sharp upbraidings to Mrs. Ord.

This made Barnes's position very unpleasant, so that he felt much relieved when he was sent with me to North Carolina. The Bat was very fast, and on the morning of the 29th we were near Cape Hatteras; Captain Barnes, noticing a propeller coming out of Hatteras Inlet, made her turn back and pilot us in. We entered safely, steamed up Pamlico Sound into Neuse River, and the next morning, by reason of some derangement of machinery, we anchored about seven miles below Newbern, whence we went up in Captain Barnes's barge. As soon as we arrived at Newbern, I telegraphed up to General Schofield at Goldsboro' the fact of my return, and that I had arranged with General Grant for the changes made necessary in the reorganization of the army, and for the boats necessary to carry up the provisions and stores we needed, prior to the renewal of our march northward.

These changes amounted to constituting the left wing a distinct army, under the title of "the Army of Georgia," under command of General Slocum, with his two corps commanded by General Jeff. C. Davis and General Joseph A. Mower; the Tenth and Twenty-third Corps already constituted another army, "of the Ohio," under the command of Major-General Schofield, and his two corps were commanded by Generals J. D. Cox and A. H. Terry. These changes were necessary, because army commanders only could order courts-martial, grant discharges, and perform many other matters of discipline and administration which were indispensable; but my chief purpose was to prepare the whole army for what seemed among the probabilities of the time—to fight both Lee's and Johnston's armies combined, in case their junction could be formed before General Grant could possibly follow Lee to North Carolina.

General George H. Thomas, who still remained at Nashville, was not pleased with these changes, for the two corps with General Slocum, viz., the Fourteenth and Twentieth, up to that time, had remained technically a part of his "Army of the Cumberland;" but he was so far away, that I had to act to the best advantage with the troops and general officers actually present. I had specially asked for General Mower to command the Twentieth Corps, because I regarded him as one of the boldest and best fighting generals in the whole army. His predecessor, General A. S. Williams, the senior division commander present, had commanded the corps well from Atlanta to Goldsboro', and it may have seemed unjust to replace him at that precise moment; but I was resolved to be prepared for a most desperate and, as then expected, a final battle, should it fall on me.

I returned to Goldsboro' from Newbern by rail the evening of March 30th, and at once addressed myself to the task of reorganization and replenishment of stores, so as to be ready to march by April 10th, the day agreed on with General Grant.

The army was divided into the usual three parts, right and left wings, and centre. The tabular statements herewith will give the exact composition of these separate armies, which by the 10th of April gave the following effective strength:

RIGHT WING—ARMY OF THE TENNESSEE—GENERAL O. O. HOWARD.

COMMANDS.	Infantry.	Cavalry.	Artillery.	Total.
Fifteenth Corps.	15,244	23	403	15,670
Seventeenth Corps.	12,873	30	261	13,164
Aggregate.	28,117	53	664	28,834

LEFT WING—ARMY OF GEORGIA—GENERAL H. W. SLOCUM.

COMMANDS.	Infantry.	Cavalry.	Artillery.	Total.
Fourteenth Corps.	14,653	......	445	15,098
Twentieth Corps.	12,471	......	494	12,965
Aggregate.	27,124	......	939	28,063

CENTRE—ARMY OF THE OHIO—GENERAL J. M. SCHOFIELD.

COMMANDS.	Infantry.	Cavalry.	Artillery.	Total.
Tenth Corps.	11,727	......	372	12,099
Twenty-third Corps.	14,000	......	293	14,293
Aggregate.	25,727	......	665	26,392

CAVALRY DIVISION—BRIGADIER-GENERAL J. KILPATRICK

COMMANDS.	Infantry.	Cavalry.	Artillery.	Total.
Aggregate.	......	5,484	175	5,659

Totals.

Infantry.	80,968
Artillery.	2,443
Cavalry.	5,537
Aggregate.	88,948

Totals number of guns 91

ARMY OF THE TENNESSEE.
MAJOR-GENERAL O. O. HOWARD COMMANDING.
Fifteenth Army Corps—Major-General JOHN A. LOGAN *commanding.*

FIRST DIVISION.
Brevet-Major-General C. R. WOODS.

First Brigade.
Brevet Brig.–Gen. W. B. Woods.

27th Missouri Infantry.
12th Indiana Infantry.
76th Ohio Infantry.
26th Iowa Infantry.
31st Missouri Infantry.
32d Missouri Infantry.

Second Brigade.
Colonel R. F. Catterson

40th Illinois Infantry.
46th Ohio Infantry.
103d Illinois Infantry.
6th Iowa Infantry.
97th Indiana Infantry.
26th Illinois Infantry.
100th Indiana Infantry.

Third Brigade.
Colonel G. A. Stone.

4th Iowa Infantry.
9th Iowa Infantry.
25th Iowa Infantry.
30th Iowa Infantry.
31st Iowa Infantry.

SECOND DIVISION.
Major-General WILLIAM B. HAZEN.

First Brigade.
Colonel T. Jones

6th Missouri Infantry.
55th Illinois Infantry.
116th Illinois Infantry.
127th Illinois Infantry.
30th Ohio Infantry.
57th Ohio Infantry.

Second Brigade.
Colonel W. S. Jones

37th Ohio Infantry.
47th Ohio Infantry.
53d Ohio Infantry.
54th Ohio Infantry.
83d Indiana Infantry.
111th Illinois Infantry.

Third Brigade.
Brigadier-General J. M. Oliver

15th Michigan Infantry.
70th Ohio Infantry.
48th Illinois Infantry.
90th Illinois Infantry.
99th Indiana Infantry.

THIRD DIVISION.
Brevet Major-General J. E. SMITH

First Brigade.
Brigadier-General W. T. Clark.

18th Wisconsin Infantry.
59th Indiana Infantry.
63d Illinois Infantry.
48th Indiana Infantry.
93d Illinois Infantry.

Second Brigade.
Colonel J. E. Tourtellotte

56th Illinois Infantry.
10th Iowa Infantry.
80th Ohio Infantry.
17th Iowa Infantry.
Battalion 26th Missouri Infantry.
Battalion 10th Missouri Infantry.
4th Minnesota Infantry.

FOURTH DIVISION.
Brevet Major-General John M. Corse

First Brigade Brig-Gen. E. W. Rice.	Second Brigade Colonel R. N. Adams.	Third Brigade Colonel F. J. Hurlbut.
2d Iowa Infantry.	12th Illinois Infantry.	7th Illinois Infantry.
7th Iowa Infantry.	66th Illinois Infantry.	39th Iowa Infantry.
66th Indiana Infantry.	81st Ohio Infantry.	50th Illinois Infantry.
52nd Illinois Infantry.		57th Illinois Infantry.
		110th U.S. Col'd Inf.

DETACHMENTS.
Artillery Brigade.
Lieutenant-Colonel William H. Ross.

H, 1st Illinois Artillery.
12th Wisconsin Battery.
29th Missouri Infantry.
Signal Detachment.

H, 1st Missouri Artillery.
B, 1st Michigan Artillery

Seventeenth Army Corps—Major General F. P. Blair *commanding.*

FIRST DIVISION.
Brigadier-General M. F. Force.

First Brigade. Brig.-General J. W. Fuller	Second Brigade. Brig.-General J. W. Sprague	Third Brigade. Lieut.-Colonel J. S. Wright
18th Missouri Infantry.	25th Wisconsin Infantry.	10th Illinois Infantry.
27th Ohio Infantry.	35th New Jersey Infantry.	25th Indiana Infantry.
39th Ohio Infantry.	43d Ohio Infantry.	32d Wisconsin Infantry.
64th Illinois Infantry.	63d Ohio Infantry.	

THIRD DIVISION.
Brevet Major-General M. D. Leggett.

First Brigade. Brigadier-General Charles Ewing.	Second Brigade. Brigadier-General R. K. Scott.
16th Wisconsin Infantry.	20th Ohio Infantry.
45th Illinois Infantry.	68th Ohio Infantry.
31st Illinois Infantry.	78th Ohio Infantry.
20th Illinois Infantry.	19th Wisconsin Infantry.
30th Illinois Infantry.	
12th Wisconsin Infantry.	

FOURTH DIVISION.
Brevet Major-General G. A. Smith.

First Brigade.
Brigadier-General B. F. Potts

23d Indiana Infantry.
32d Ohio Infantry.
53d Indiana Infantry.
14th Illinois Infantry.
53d Illinois Infantry.
15th Illinois Infantry.

Third Brigade.
Brigadier-General W. W. Belknap.

11th Iowa Infantry.
13th Iowa Infantry.
15th Iowa Infantry.
16th Iowa Infantry.
32d Illinois Infantry.

DETACHMENTS.
Artillery Brigade.
Major Frederick Welker.

C Battalion, 1st Michigan Artillery.
1st Minnesota Battery.

15th Ohio Battery.

9th Illinois Mounted Infantry.
G Company, 11th Illinois
Cavalry.
Signal Detachment.

ARMY OF GEORGIA.
MAJOR-GENERAL H. W. SLOCUM COMMANDING.

Fourteenth Army Corps—
Brevet Major-General J. C. Davis *commanding*

FIRST DIVISION.
Brigadier-General C. C. Walcott.

First Brigade.
Brevet Brig.-General Hobart.

21st Wisconsin volunteers.
33d Ohio Volunteers.
94th Ohio Volunteers.
42d Indiana Volunteers.
88th Indiana Volunteers.
104th Illinois Volunteers.

Second Brigade.
Brevet Brig.-General Buell.

21st Michigan Volunteers.
13th Michigan Volunteers.
69th Ohio Volunteers.

Third Brigade.
Colonel Hambright.

21st Ohio Volunteers.
74th Ohio Volunteers.
78th Pennsylvania Volun.
79th Pennsylvania Volun.

SECOND DIVISION.
Brigadier-General J. D. Morgan.

First Brigade. Brigadier-General Vandever.	Second Brigade. Brigadier-General Mitchell.	Third Brigade. Lieutenant-Colonel Langley.
10th Michigan Volunteers.	121st Ohio Volunteers.	85th Illinois Volunteers.
14th Michigan Volunteers.	113th Ohio Volunteers.	86th Illinois Volunteers.
16th Illinois Volunteers.	108th Ohio Volunteers.	110th Illinois Volunteers.
60th Illinois Volunteers.	98th Ohio Volunteers.	125th Illinois Volunteers.
17th New York Volunteers.	78th Illinois Volunteers.	52d Ohio Volunteers.
	34th Illinois Volunteers.	22d Indiana Volunteers.
		37th Indiana (Det.) Volun.

THIRD DIVISION.
Brevet Major-General A. Baird.

First Brigade. Colonel M. C. Hunter.	Second Brigade. Lieutenant-Colonel Doan.	Third Brigade. Brig-General George S. Greene.
17th Ohio Volunteers.	2d Minnesota Volunteers.	14th Ohio Volunteers.
31st Ohio Volunteers.	105th Ohio Volunteers.	38th Ohio Volunteers.
89th Ohio Volunteers.	75th Indiana Volunteers.	10th Kentucky Volunteers
92d Ohio Volunteers.	87th Indiana Volunteers.	18th Kentucky Volunteers.
82d Ohio Volunteers.	101st Indiana Volunteers.	74th Indiana Volunteers.
23d Missouri (Det.) Volun.		
11th Ohio Volunteers.		

DETACHMENTS.
Artillery Brigade.
Major Charles Houghtaling.

Battery I, 2d Illinois.	5th Wisconsin Battery.
Battery C, 1st Illinois.	19th Indiana Battery.

Twentieth Army Corps—Major General J. A. MOWER *commanding.*

FIRST DIVISION.
Brevet Major-General A. S. Williams.

First Brigade. Colonel J. L. Selfridge.	Second Brigade. Colonel William Hawley.	Third Brigade. Brig.-General J. S. Robinson.
4th Pennsylvania Volunt'rs.	2d Massachusetts Volun.	31st Wisconsin Volunteers.
5th Connecticut Volunteers.	3d Wisconsin Volunteers.	61st Ohio Volunteers.
123d New York Volunteers.	13th New Jersey Volunt'rs.	82d Ohio Volunteers.
141st New York Volunteers.	107th New York Volunt'rs.	82d Illinois Volunteers.
	150th New York Volunt'rs.	101st Illinois Volunteers.
		143d New York Volun.

SECOND DIVISION.
Brevet Major-General John W. Geary.

First Brigade. Brevet Brig.-Gen. N. Pardee, Jr.	Second Brigade. Colonel P. H. Jones.	Third Brigade. Brevet Brig.-General Barnum.
5th Ohio Volunteers.	33d New Jersey Volunteers.	29th Pennsylvania Volun.
29th Ohio Volunteers.	73d Pennsylvania Volun.	111th Pennsylvania Volun.
66th Ohio Volunteers.	109th Pennsylvania Volun.	60th New York Volunteers.
28th Pennsylvania Volun.	119th New York Volun.	102d New York Volunt'rs.
147th Pennsylvania Volun.	134th New York Volun.	137th New York Volunt'rs.
Detachment K.P.B.	154th New York Volun.	149th New York Volunt'rs.

THIRD DIVISION.
Brevet Major-General W. T. Ward.

First Brigade. Colonel H. Case.	Second Brigade. Colonel Daniel Dustin.	Third Brigade. Brevet Brig-General Coggswell.
70th Indiana Volunteers.	19th Michigan Volunteers.	20th Connecticut Volun.
79th Ohio Volunteers.	22d Wisconsin Volunteers.	26th Wisconsin Volunt'rs.
102d Illinois Volunteers.	33d Indiana Volunteers.	33d Massachusetts Volun.
105th Illinois Volunteers.	85th Indiana Volunteers.	55th Ohio Volunteers.
129th Illinois Volunteers.		73d Ohio Volunteers.
		136th New York Volunt'rs.

Detachments.
Artillery Brigade.
Captain Winnegar.

Battery I, 1st New York.	Battery C, 1st Ohio.
Battery M, 1st New York.	Battery E, Independent Pennsylvania.

Pontoniers, 58th Indiana Veteran Volunteers.
Mechanics and Engineers, 1st Michigan.

ARMY OF THE OHIO.
MAJOR-GENERAL JOHN M. SCHOFIELD COMMANDING.

Tenth Army Corps-Major General A. H. TERRY *commanding.*

FIRST DIVISION.

Brevet Major-General H. W. BIRGE.

First Brigade. Colonel H. D. Washburn.	Second Brigade. Colonel Harvey Graham.	Third Brigade. Colonel N. W. Day.
8th Indiana Volunteers.	159th New York Volunteers.	38th Massachusetts Vol.
18th Indiana Volunteers.	13th Connecticut Volunt'rs.	156th New York Volun.
9th Connecticut Volunteers.	22d Iowa Volunteers.	128th New York Volun.
14th New Hampshire Volun.	131st New York Volunteers.	175th New York Volun.
12th Maine Volunteers.	28th Iowa Volunteers.	176th New York Volun.
14th Maine Volunteers.		24th Iowa Volunteers.
75th New York Volunteers.		

SECOND DIVISION.

Brevet Major-General A. AMES.

First Brigade. Colonel R. Daggett.	Second Brigade. Colonel J. S. Littell.	Third Brigade. Colonel G. F. Granger.
3d New York Volunteers.	47th New York Volunteers.	4th New Hampshire Vol.
112th New York Volunteers.	48th New York Volunteers.	9th Maine Volunteers.
117th New York Volunteers.	203d Pennsylvania Volun.	13th Indiana Volunteers.
142d New York Volunteers.	97th Pennsylvania Volun.	115th New York Volun.
	76th Pennsylvania Volun.	169th New York Volun.

THIRD DIVISION.

Brigadier-General C. J. PAINE.

First Brigade. Brevet Brig.-General D. Bates.	Second Brigade. Brevet Brig.-Gen. S. Duncan.	Third Brigade. Colonel J. H. Holman.
1st U.S.C.T.	4th U.S.C.T.	5th U.S.C.T.
30th U.S.C.T.	6th U.S.C.T.	27th U.S.C.T.
107th U.S.C.T.	39th U.S.C.T.	37th U.S.C.T.

DETACHMENTS.
Brigade (not numbered).
Brevet Brigadier-General J. C. ABBOTT.

3d New Hampshire Volunteers.
7th New Hampshire Volunteers.
16th New York Heavy Artillery (six companies).
16th New York Independent Battery.
22d Indiana Battery.
6th Connecticut Volunteers.
7th Connecticut Volunteers.

Light Company E, 3d United States Artillery.
Company A, 2d Pennsylvania Heavy Artillery.
Companies E and K, 12th New York Cavalry.
Detachment Signal Corps.

Twenty-third Army Corps—Major-General J.D. COX *commanding.*

FIRST DIVISION.
Brigadier-General THOMAS H. RUGER.

First Brigade.
Brevet Brig.-General J. N. Stiles.

120th Indiana Vol. Infantry.
124th Indiana Vol. Infantry.
128th Indiana Vol. Infantry.
180th Ohio Volun. Infantry.

Second Brigade.
Colonel J. C. McQuiston.

123d Indiana Vol. Infantry.
129th Indiana Vol. Infan'y.
130th Indiana Vol. Infan'y.
28th Michigan Vol. Infan'y.

Third Brigade.
Colonel M. T. Thomas.

8th Minnesota Vol. Infan.
174th Ohio Vol. Infantry.
178th Ohio Vol. Infantry.

Battery Elgin, Illinois Volunteers.

SECOND DIVISION.
Major-General D. N. COUCH.

First Brigade.
Colonel O. H. Moore.

25th Michigan Vol. Infantry.
26th Kentucky Vol. Infantry.

Second Brigade.
Colonel J. Mehringer.

23d Michigan Vol. Infantry.
80th Indiana Vol. Infantry.
118th Ohio Vol. Infantry.
107th Illinois Vol. Infantry.
111th Ohio Vol. Infantry.
19th Ohio Battery.

Third Brigade.
Colonel S. A. Strickland.

91st Indiana Vol. Infantry.
183d Ohio Vol. Infantry.
181st Ohio Vol. Infantry
50th Ohio Vol. Infantry.

THIRD DIVISION.
Brigadier-General S. P. Carter.

First Brigade. Colonel O. W. Steel.	Second Brigade. Colonel J. S. Casement.	Third Brigade. Colonel T. J. Henderson.
8th Tennessee Vol. Infantry.	177th Ohio Vol. Infantry.	112th Illinois Vol. Infan'y
12th Kentucky Vol. Infantry.	65th Indiana Vol. Infantry.	63d Indiana Vol. Infantry
16th Kentucky Vol. Infantry.	65th Illinois Vol. Infantry.	140th Indiana Vol. Infan'y
100th Ohio Volun. Infantry.	103d Ohio Volun. Infantry.	
104th Ohio Volun. Infantry.		

Battery D, 1st Ohio Light Artillery.

Cavalry Division—Major-General Judson Kilpatrick *commanding.*

First Brigade. Brev. Brig.-Gen. Thos. J. Jordan.	Second Brigade. Brevet Brig.-Gen. S. D. Atkins	Third Brigade. Colonel George E. Spencer.
9th Pennsylvania Cavalry.	92d Illinois Mounted Infan.	5th Kentucky Cavalry.
3d Kentucky Cavalry.	10th Ohio Cavalry.	5th Ohio Cavalry.
2d Kentucky Cavalry.	9th Ohio Cavalry.	1st Alabama Cavalry.
8th Indiana Cavalry.	1st Ohio Squadron.	13th Pennsylvania Cav.
3d Indiana Cavalry.	9th Michigan Cavalry.	

ARTILLERY.
Captain Y. V. Beebe.
10th Wisconsin Battery.

The railroads to our rear had also been repaired, so that stores were arriving very fast, both from Morehead City and Wilmington. The country was so level that a single locomotive could haul twenty-five and thirty cars to a train, instead of only ten, as was the case in Tennessee and Upper Georgia.

By the 5th of April such progress had been made, that I issued the following Special Field Orders, No. 48, prescribing the time and manner of the next march:

[Special Field Orders, No. 48.]

Headquarters Military Division of the Mississippi,
in the Field, Goldsboro', North Carolina, *April* 5, 1865.

Confidential to Army Commanders, Corps Commanders, and Chiefs of Staff Departments:

The next grand objective is to place this army (with its full equipment) north of Roanoke River, facing west, with a base for supplies at

Norfolk, and at Winton or Murfreesboro' on the Chowan, and in full communication with the Army of the Potomac, about Petersburg; and also to do the enemy as much harm as possible *en route:*

1. To accomplish this result the following general plan will be followed, or modified only by written orders from these headquarters, should events require a change:

(1.) On Monday, the 10th of April, all preparations are presumed to be complete, and the outlying detachments will be called in, or given directions to meet on the next march. All preparations will also be complete to place the railroad-stock back of Kinston on the one road, and below the Northeast Branch on the other.

(2.) On Tuesday, the 11th, the columns will draw out on their lines of march, say, about seven miles, and close up.

(3.) On Wednesday the march will begin in earnest, and will be kept up at the rate, say, of about twelve miles a day, or according to the amount of resistance. All the columns will dress to the left (which is the exposed flank), and commanders will study always to find roads by which they can, if necessary, perform a general left wheel, the wagons to be escorted to some place of security on the direct route of march. Foraging and other details may continue as heretofore, only more caution and prudence should be observed; and foragers should not go in advance of the *advance-guard,* but look more to our right rear for corn, bacon, and meal.

2. The left wing (Major-General Slocum commanding) will aim straight for the railroad-bridge near Smithfield; thence along up the Neuse River to the railroad-bridge over Neuse River, northeast of Raleigh (Powell's); thence to Warrenton, the general point of concentration.

The centre (Major-General Schofield commanding) will move to Whitley's Mill, ready to support the left until it is past Smithfield, when it will follow up (substantially) Little River to about Rolesville, ready at all times to move to the support of the left; after passing Tar River, to move to Warrenton.

The right wing (Major-General Howard commanding), preceded by the cavalry, will move rapidly on Pikeville and Nahunta, then swing across to Bulah to Folk's Bridge, ready to make junction with the other armies in case the enemy offers battle this side of Neuse River, about Smithfield; thence, in case of no serious opposition on the left, will work up toward Earpsboro', Andrews, B——, and Warrenton.

The cavalry (General Kilpatrick commanding), leaving its encumbrances with the right wing, will push as though straight for Weldon, until the enemy is across Tar River, and that bridge burned; then it will deflect toward Nashville and Warrenton, keeping up communication with general headquarters.

3. As soon as the army starts, the chief-quartermaster and commissary will prepare a resupply of stores at some point on Pamlico or Albemarle Sounds, ready to be conveyed to Kinston or Winton and Murfreesboro', according to developments. As soon as they have satisfactory information that the army is north of the Roanoke, they will forthwith establish a depot at Winton, with a sub-depot at Murfreesboro'. Major-General Schofield will hold, as heretofore, Wilmington (with the bridge across Northern Branch as an outpost), Newbern (and Kinston as its outpost), and will be prepared to hold Winton and Murfreesboro' as soon as the time arrives for that move. The navy has instructions from Admiral Porter to coöperate, and any commanding officer is authorized to call on the navy for assistance and coöperation, always in writing, setting forth the reasons, of which necessarily the naval commander must be the judge.

4. The general-in-chief will be with the centre habitually, but may in person shift to either flank where his presence may be needed, leaving a staff-officer to receive reports. He requires, absolutely, a report of each army or grand detachment each night, whether any thing material has occurred or not, for often the absence of an enemy is a very important fact in military prognostication.

By order of Major-General W. T. Sherman,
L. M. Dayton, *Assistant Adjutant-General.*

But the whole problem became suddenly changed by the news of the fall of Richmond and Petersburg, which reached us at Goldsboro', on the 6th of April. The Confederate Government, with Lee's army, had hastily abandoned Richmond, fled in great disorder toward Danville, and General Grant's whole army was in close pursuit. Of course, I inferred that General Lee would succeed in making junction with General Johnston, with at least a fraction of his army, somewhere to my front. I at once altered the foregoing orders, and prepared on the day appointed, viz., April 10th, to move straight on Raleigh, against the army of General Johnston, known to be at Smithfield, and supposed to have about thirty-five thousand men. Wade Hampton's cavalry was on his left front and Wheeler's on his right front, simply watching us and awaiting our initiative. Meantime the details of the great victories in Virginia came thick and fast, and on the 8th I received from General Grant this communication, in the form of a cipher-dispatch:

HEADQUARTERS ARMIES OF THE UNITED STATES,
WILSON'S STATION, *April* 5, 1865.

Major-General SHERMAN, *Goldsboro', North Carolina:*

All indications now are that Lee will attempt to reach Danville with the remnant of his force. Sheridan, who was up with him last night, reports all that is left with him—horse, foot, and dragoons—at twenty thousand, much demoralized. We hope to reduce this number one-half. I will push on to Burkesville, and, if a stand is made at Danville, will, in a very few days, go there. If you can possibly do so, push on from where you are, and let us see if we cannot finish the job with Lee's and Johnston's armies. Whether it will be better for you to strike for Greensboro' or nearer to Danville, you will be better able to judge when you receive this. Rebel armies now are the only strategic points to strike at.

U. S. GRANT, *Lieutenant-General.*

I answered immediately that we would move on the 10th, prepared to follow Johnston wherever he might go.[13] Promptly on Monday morning, April 10th, the army moved straight on Smithfield; the right wing making a circuit by the right, and the left wing, supported by the centre, moving on the two direct roads toward Raleigh, distant fifty miles. General Terry's and General Kilpatrick's troops moved from their positions on the south or west bank of the Neuse River in the same general direction, by Cox's Bridge. On the 11th we reached Smithfield, and found it abandoned by Johnston's army, which had retreated hastily on Raleigh, burning the bridges. To restore these consumed the remainder of the day, and during that night I received a message from General Grant, at Appomattox, that General Lee had surrendered to him his whole army, which I at once announced to the troops in orders:[14]

[13] See *OR,* I, 47(III), 99–100, 128–129.

[14] See *OR,* I, 47(III), 140.

[Special Field Orders, No. 54]

HEADQUARTERS MILITARY DIVISION OF THE MISSISSIPPI,
IN THE FIELD, SMITHFIELD, NORTH CAROLINA, *April* 12, 1865.

The general commanding announces to the army that he has official notice from General Grant that General Lee surrendered to him his entire army, on the 9th inst., at Appomattox Court-House, Virginia.

Glory to God and our country, and all honor to our comrades in arms, toward whom we are marching!

A little more labor, a little more toil on our part, the great race is won, and our Government stands regenerated, after four long years of war.

W. T. SHERMAN, *Major-General commanding.*

Of course, this created a perfect *furore,* of rejoicing, and we all regarded the war as over, for I knew well that General Johnston had no army with which to oppose mine. So that the only questions that remained were, would he surrender at Raleigh? or would he allow his army to disperse into guerrilla bands, to "die in the last ditch," and entail on his country an indefinite and prolonged military occupation, and of consequent desolation? I knew well that Johnston's army could not be caught; the country was too open; and, without wagons, the men could escape us, disperse, and assemble again at some place agreed on, and thus the war might be prolonged indefinitely.

I then remembered Mr. Lincoln's repeated expression that he wanted the rebel soldiers not only defeated, but "back at their homes, engaged in their civil pursuits." On the evening of the 12th I was with the head of Slocum's column, at Gulley's, and General Kilpatrick's cavalry was still ahead, fighting Wade Hampton's rear-guard, with orders to push it through Raleigh, while I would give a more southerly course to the infantry columns, so as, if possible, to prevent a retreat southward. On the 13th, early, I entered Raleigh, and ordered the several heads of column toward Ashville in the direction of Salisbury or Charlotte.[15] Before reaching Raleigh, a locomotive came down the road to meet me, passing through both Wade Hampton's and Kilpatrick's cavalry, bringing four gentlemen, with a letter from Governor Vance to me, asking protection for the

[15] For a contemporary map of North Carolina, see George B. Davis et al., *Official Military Atlas of the Civil War* (New York: Fairfax Press, 1983), plate 138.

citizens of Raleigh.[16] These gentlemen were, of course, dreadfully excited at the dangers through which they had passed. Among them were ex-Senator Graham,[17] Mr. Swain, president of Chapel Hill University,[18] and a Surgeon Warren, of the Confederate army.[19] They had come with a flag of truce, to which they were not entitled; still, in the interest of peace, I respected it, and permitted them to return to Raleigh with their locomotive, to assure the Governor and the people that the war was substantially over, and that I wanted the civil authorities to remain in the execution of their office till the pleasure of the President could be ascertained. On reaching Raleigh I found these same gentlemen, with Messrs. Badger,[20] Bragg,[21] Holden,[22] and others, but Governor Vance had fled, and could not be prevailed on to return, because he feared an arrest and imprisonment. From the Raleigh newspapers of the 10th I learned that General Stoneman, with his division of cavalry, had come across the mountains from East Tennessee, had destroyed the railroad at Salisbury, and was then supposed to be approaching Greensboro'. I also learned that General Wilson's cavalry corps was "smashing things" down about Selma and Montgomery, Alabama, and was pushing for Columbus and Macon, Georgia; and I also had reason to expect that General Sheridan would come down from Ap-

[16] For the correspondence between WTS and Vance on Apr. 12, see *OR,* I, 47(III), 178.

[17] William A. Graham (1804–1875) served as a U.S. senator from North Carolina from 1841 to 1843 and as a Confederate senator during the Civil War. "Death of Hon. Wm. A. Graham," *Wilmington Morning Star* (Wilmington, NC), Aug. 12, 1875, 1.

[18] David L. Swain (1801–1868) was elected governor of North Carolina in 1832 and served in that capacity until he was made president of the University of North Carolina in 1835. Marcus J. Wright et al., *Analytical Historical Reference* (Philadelphia: National Historical Association, 1906), vol. 3, s.v. "Swain, David L."

[19] Edward Warren (1828–1893) was surgeon general of North Carolina, among other medical roles in the Confederacy. In 1885 he published a memoir about his experience in the war titled *A Doctor's Experiences in Three Continents.* "Death of Dr. Edward Warren, Bey," *Henderson Gold Leaf* (Henderson, NC), Sept. 21, 1893.

[20] George E. Badger (1795–1866) was secretary of the U.S. Navy during William H. Harrison's brief presidency in 1841 and served as a U.S. senator from North Carolina from 1846 to 1855. He ultimately opposed secession. Benson J. Lossing, ed., *Harper's Encyclopedia of United States History* (New York: Harper and Brothers, 1906), vol. 1, s.v. "Badger, George Edmund."

[21] Thomas Bragg Jr. (1810–1872), brother of Confederate general Braxton Bragg, was the governor of North Carolina from 1855 to 1859 and later served as the attorney general of the Confederacy. *CWHC,* 141.

[22] William W. Holden (1818–1892) was the provisional governor of North Carolina after the war. *CWHC,* 301.

pomattox to join us at Raleigh with his superb cavalry corps. I needed more cavalry to check Johnston's retreat, so that I could come up to him with my infantry, and therefore had good reason to delay. I ordered the railroad to be finished up to Raleigh, so that I could operate from it as a base, and then made—

[Special Field Orders, No. 55.]

HEADQUARTERS MILITARY DIVISION OF THE MISSISSIPPI,
IN THE FIELD, RALEIGH, NORTH CAROLINA, *APRIL* 14, 1865.

The next movement will be on Ashboro', to turn the position of the enemy at the "Company's Shops" in rear of Haw River Bridge, and at Greensboro', and to cut off his only available line of retreat by Salisbury and Charlotte:

1. General Kilpatrick will keep up a show of pursuit in the direction of Hillsboro' and Graham, but be ready to cross Haw River on General Howard's bridge, near Pittsboro', and thence will operate toward Greensboro', on the right front of the right wing.

2. The right wing, Major-General Howard commanding, will move out on the Chapel Hill road, and send a light division up in the direction of Chapel Hill University to act in connection with the cavalry; but the main columns and trains will move *via* Hackney's Cross-Roads, and Trader's Hill, Pittsboro', St. Lawrence, etc., to be followed by the cavalry and light division, as soon as the bridge is laid over Haw River.

3. The centre, Major-General Schofield commanding, will move *via* Holly Springs, New Hill, Haywood, and Moffitt's Mills.

4. The left wing, Major-General Slocum commanding, will move rapidly by the Aven's Ferry road, Carthage, Caledonia, and Cox's Mills.

5. All the troops will draw well out on the roads designated during to-day and to-morrow, and on the following day will move with all possible rapidity for Ashboro'. No further destruction of railroads, mills, cotton, and produce, will be made without the specific orders of an army commander, and the inhabitants will be dealt with kindly, looking to an early reconciliation. The troops will be permitted, however, to gather forage and provisions as heretofore; only more care should be taken not to strip the poorer classes too closely.

By order of General W. T. Sherman,

L. M. DAYTON, *Assistant Adjutant-General.*

Thus matters stood, when on the morning of the 14th General Kilpatrick reported from Durham's Station, twenty-six miles up the railroad toward Hillsboro', that a flag of truce had come in from the enemy with a package from General Johnston addressed to me. Taking it for granted that this was preliminary to a surrender, I ordered the message to be sent me at Raleigh, and on the 14th received from General Johnston a letter dated April 13, 1865, in these words:

The results of the recent campaign in Virginia have changed the relative military condition of the belligerents. I am, therefore, induced to address you in this form the inquiry whether, to stop the further effusion of blood and devastation of property, you are willing to make a temporary suspension of active operations, and to communicate to Lieutenant-General Grant, commanding the armies of the United States, the request that he will take like action in regard to other armies, the object being to permit the civil authorities to enter into the needful arrangements to terminate the existing war.

To which I replied as follows:

HEADQUARTERS MILITARY DIVISION OF THE MISSISSIPPI,
IN THE FIELD, RALEIGH, NORTH CAROLINA,
April 14, 1865.

General J. E. JOHNSTON, *commanding Confederate Army.*

GENERAL: I have this moment received your communication of this date. I am fully empowered to arrange with you any terms for the suspension of further hostilities between the armies commanded by you and those commanded by myself, and will be willing to confer with you to that end. I will limit the advance of my main column, to-morrow, to Morrisville, and the cavalry to the university, and expect that you will also maintain the present position of your forces until each has notice of a failure to agree.

That a basis of action may be had, I undertake to abide by the same terms and conditions as were made by Generals Grant and Lee at Appomattox Court-House, on the 9th instant, relative to our two armies; and, furthermore, to obtain from General Grant an order to suspend the movements of any troops from the direction of Virginia. General Stoneman is under my command, and my order will suspend any devastation or destruction contemplated by him. I will add that I really desire to save the people of North Carolina the damage they would sustain by the march of this army through the central or western parts of the State.

I am, with respect, your obedient servant,

W. T. SHERMAN, *Major-General.*

I sent my aide-de-camp, Colonel McCoy, up to Durham's Station with this letter, with instructions to receive the answer, to telegraph its contents back to me at Raleigh, and to arrange for an interview. On the 16th I received a reply from General Johnston, agreeing to meet me the next day at a point midway between our advance at Durham and his rear at Hillsboro'. I ordered a car and locomotive to be prepared to convey me up to Durham's at eight o'clock of the morning of April 17th. Just as we were entering the car, the telegraph-operator, whose office was up-stairs in the depot-building, ran down to me and said that he was at that instant of time receiving a most important dispatch in cipher from Morehead City, which I ought to see. I held the train for nearly half an hour, when he returned with the message translated and written out. It was from Mr. Stanton, announcing the assassination of Mr. Lincoln, the attempt on the life of Mr. Seward and son,[23] and a suspicion that a like fate was designed for General Grant and all the principal officers of the Government.[24] Dreading the effect of such a message at that critical instant of time, I asked the operator if any one besides himself had seen it; he answered no. I then bade him not to reveal the contents by word or look till I came back, which I proposed to do the same afternoon. The train then started, and, as we passed Morris's Station, General Logan, commanding the Fifteenth Corps, came into my car, and I told him I wanted to see him on my return, as I had something very important to communicate. He knew I was going to meet General Johnston, and volunteered to say that he hoped I would succeed in obtaining his surrender, as the whole army dreaded the long march to Charlotte (one hundred and seventy-five

[23] Two of U.S. secretary of state William Seward's sons, Augustus H. Seward (1826–1876) and Frederick W. Seward (1830–1915), were injured when Lewis Powell (1844–1865) attempted to assassinate the secretary of state on Apr. 14, 1865. *USMA,* 2:340–341; "Death Takes Man Long in Service," *Princeton Daily Clarion* (Princeton, IN), Apr. 27, 1915, 3; Scott P. Johnson, *Political Assassins, Terrorists and Related Conspiracies in American History* (Jefferson, NC: McFarland, 2021), s.v. "Lewis Powell (Lewis Paint or Lewis Payne)."

[24] In the dispatch, Stanton told WTS, "I find evidence that an assassin is also on your track, and I beseech you to be more heedful than Mr. Lincoln was of such knowledge." *OR,* I, 47(III), 220–221.

miles), already begun, but which had been interrupted by the receipt of General Johnston's letter of the 13th. We reached Durham's, twenty-six miles, about 10 A. M., where General Kilpatrick had a squadron of cavalry drawn up to receive me. We passed into the house in which he had his headquarters, and soon after mounted some led horses, which he had prepared for myself and staff. General Kilpatrick sent a man ahead with a white flag, followed by a small platoon, behind which we rode, and were followed by the rest of the escort. We rode up the Hillsboro' road for about five miles, when our flag-bearer discovered another coming to meet him. They met, and word was passed back to us that General Johnston was near at hand, when we rode forward and met General Johnston on horseback, riding side by side with General Wade Hampton. We shook hands, and introduced our respective attendants.[25] I asked if there was a place convenient where we could be private, and General Johnston said he had passed a small farm-house a short distance back, when we rode back to it together side by side, our staff-officers and escorts following. We had never met before, though we had been in the regular army together for thirteen years; but it so happened that we had never before come together. He was some twelve or more years my senior; but we knew enough of each other to be well acquainted at once. We soon reached the house of a Mr. Bennett, dismounted, and left our horses with orderlies in the road. Our officers, on foot, passed into the yard, and General Johnston and I entered the small frame-house. We asked the farmer if we could have the use of his house for a few minutes, and he and his wife withdrew into a smaller log-house, which stood close by.[26]

As soon as we were alone together I showed him the dispatch announcing Mr. Lincoln's assassination, and watched him closely. The perspiration came out in large drops on his forehead, and he did not attempt to conceal his distress. He denounced the act as a disgrace to the age, and hoped I did not charge it to the Confederate Government. I told him I could not believe that he or General Lee, or the officers of the Confederate army, could possibly be privy to acts of assassination; but I would not say as much for Jeff. Davis,

[25] Johnston and Hampton were accompanied by sixty men, and WTS's escort consisted of approximately 200 soldiers and a group of reporters. Mark L. Bradley, *This Astounding Close: The Road to Bennett Place* (Chapel Hill: University of North Carolina Press, 2000), 157–158.

[26] James and Nancy Bennett lived on a farm near Durham, NC. The family lived there until 1890; the original buildings were destroyed by a fire in 1921. *The Big Book of Civil War Sites: From Fort Sumter to Appomattox, a Visitor's guide to the History, Personalities, and Places of America's Battlefields* (Lanham, MD: Rowman and Littlefield, 2023), s.v. "Bennett Place."

George Sanders,[27] and men of that stripe. We talked about the effect of this act on the country at large and on the armies, and he realized that it made my situation extremely delicate. I explained to him that I had not yet revealed the news to my own personal staff or to the army, and that I dreaded the effect when made known in Raleigh. Mr. Lincoln was peculiarly endeared to the soldiers, and I feared that some foolish woman or man in Raleigh might say something or do something that would madden our men, and that a fate worse than that of Columbia would befall the place.

I then told Johnston that he must be convinced that he could not oppose my army, and that, since Lee had surrendered, he could do the same with honor and propriety. He plainly and repeatedly admitted this, and added that any further fighting would be "*murder;*" but he thought that, instead of surrendering piecemeal, we might arrange terms that would embrace *all* the Confederate armies. I asked him if he could control other armies than his own; he said, not then, but intimated that he could procure authority from Mr. Davis. I then told him that I had recently had an interview with General Grant and President Lincoln, and that I was possessed of their views; that with them and the people North there seemed to be no vindictive feeling against the Confederate armies, but there was against Davis and his political adherents; and that the terms that General Grant had given to General Lee's army were certainly most generous and liberal. All this he admitted, but always recurred to the idea of a universal surrender, embracing his own army, that of Dick Taylor in Louisiana and Texas, and of Maury,[28] Forrest, and others, in Alabama and Georgia. General Johnston's account of our interview in his "Narrative" (page 402, *et seq.*) is quite accurate and correct, only I do not recall his naming the capitulation of Loeben, to which he refers.[29] Our

[27] George Sanders (1812–1873) was a businessman, arms dealer, and agent of the Hudson Bay Company before the war. Frederick Hatch, *Protecting President Lincoln: The Security Effort, the Thwarted Plots and the Disaster at Ford's Theater* (Jefferson, NC: McFarland, 2011), 62.

[28] Dabney H. Maury (1822–1900) graduated from the USMA in 1846 and was later dismissed from the U.S. Army in June 1861. He joined the Confederate Army and reached the rank of major general. *CWHC*, 368.

[29] In his autobiography, Johnston claimed to have suggested to WTS they might "as other generals had done, arrange the terms of a permanent peace, and among other precedents reminded him of the preliminaries of Leoben, and the terms in which Napoleon, then victorious, proposed negotiation to the Archduke Charles; and the sentiment he expressed, that the civic crown earned by preserving the life of one citizen confers truer glory than the highest achievement merely military. General Sherman replied, with heightened color, that he appreciated

conversation was very general and extremely cordial, satisfying me that it could have but one result, and that which we all desired, viz., to end the war as quickly as possible; and, being anxious to return to Raleigh before the news of Mr. Lincoln's assassination could be divulged, on General Johnston's saying that he thought that, during the night, he could procure authority to act in the name of all the Confederate armies in existence, we agreed to meet again the next day at noon at the same place, and parted, he for Hillsboro' and I for Raleigh.

We rode back to Durham's Station in the order we had come, and then I showed the dispatch announcing Mr. Lincoln's death. I cautioned the officers to watch the soldiers closely, to prevent any violent retaliation by them, leaving that to the Government at Washington; and on our way back to Raleigh in the cars I showed the same dispatch to General Logan and to several of the officers of the Fifteenth Corps that were posted at Morrisville and Jones's Station, all of whom were deeply impressed by it; but all gave their opinion that this sad news should not change our general course of action.

As soon as I reached Raleigh I published the following orders to the army, announcing the assassination of the President, and I doubt if, in the whole land, there were more sincere mourners over his sad fate than were then in and about Raleigh. I watched the effect closely, and was gratified that there was no single act of retaliation; though I saw and felt that one single word by me would have laid the city in ashes, and turned its whole population houseless upon the country, if not worse:

[Special Field Orders, No. 56.]

HEADQUARTERS MILITARY DIVISION OF THE MISSISSIPPI,
IN THE FIELD, RALEIGH, NORTH CAROLINA, *April* 17, 1865.

The general commanding announces, with pain and sorrow, that on the evening of the 14th instant, at the theatre in Washington city, his Excellency the President of the United States, Mr. Lincoln, was assassinated by one who uttered the State motto of Virginia. At the same time, the Secretary of State, Mr. Seward, while suffering from a

---

such a sentiment, and that to put an end to further devastation and bloodshed, and restore the Union, and with it the prosperity of the country, were to him objects of ambition." Joseph E. Johnston, *Narrative of Military Operations, Directed, during the Late War between the States* (New York: D. Appleton, 1874), 403.

broken arm, was also stabbed by another murderer in his own house, but still survives, and his son was wounded, supposed fatally. It is believed, by persons capable of judging, that other high officers were designed to share the same fate. Thus it seems that our enemy, despairing of meeting us in open, manly warfare, begins to resort to the assassin's tools.

Your general does not wish you to infer that this is universal, for he knows that the great mass of the Confederate army would scorn to sanction such acts, but he believes it the legitimate consequence of rebellion against rightful authority.

We have met every phase which this war has assumed, and must now be prepared for it in its last and worst shape, that of assassins and guerrillas; but woe unto the people who seek to expend their wild passions in such a manner, for there is but one dread result!

By order of Major-General W. T. Sherman,

L. M. Dayton, *Assistant Adjutant-General.*

During the evening of the 17th and morning of the 18th I saw nearly all the general officers of the army (Schofield, Slocum, Howard, Logan, Blair), and we talked over the matter of the conference at Bennett's house of the day before, and, without exception, all advised me to agree to some terms, for they all dreaded the long and harassing march in pursuit of a dissolving and fleeing army—a march that might carry us back again over the thousand miles that we had just accomplished. We all knew that if we could bring Johnston's army to bay, we could destroy it in an hour, but that was simply impossible in the country in which we found ourselves. We discussed all the probabilities, among which was, whether, if Johnston made a point of it, I should assent to the escape from the country of Jeff. Davis and his fugitive cabinet; and some one of my general officers, either Logan or Blair, insisted that, if asked for, we should even provide a vessel to carry them to Nassau from Charleston.

The next morning I again started in the cars to Durham's Station, accompanied by most of my personal staff, and by Generals Blair, Barry, Howard, etc., and, reaching General Kilpatrick's headquarters at Durham's, we again mounted, and rode, with the same escort of the day before, to Bennett's house, reaching there punctually at noon. General Johnston had not yet arrived, but a courier shortly came, and reported him as on the way. It must have been nearly 2 P. M. when he arrived, as before, with General Wade Hampton. He had halted his escort out of sight, and we again entered Bennett's house, and I closed the door. General Johnston then assured me that he had authority over all the Confederate armies, so that they would obey his orders to surrender on the same terms with his own, but he argued that, to obtain so cheaply this desirable result, I ought to give his men and officers some assurance of their political rights after their surrender. I explained to him that Mr. Lincoln's proclamation of amnesty, of December 8, 1863, still in force, enabled every Confederate soldier and officer, below the rank of colonel, to obtain an absolute pardon, by simply laying down his arms, and taking the common oath of allegiance, and that General Grant, in accepting the surrender of General Lee's army, had extended the same principle to *all* the officers, General Lee included; such a pardon, I understood, would restore to them all their rights of citizenship.[30] But he insisted that the officers and men of the Confederate army were unnecessarily alarmed about this matter, as a sort of bugbear. He then said that Mr. Breckenridge was near at hand, and he thought that it would be well for him to be present. I objected, on the score that he was then in Davis's cabinet, and our negotiations should be confined strictly to belligerents. He then said Breckenridge was a major-general in the Confederate army, and might sink his character of Secretary of War. I consented, and he sent one of his staff-officers back, who soon returned with Breckenridge, and he entered the room.[31] General Johnston and I then again went over the whole ground, and Breckenridge confirmed what he had said as to the uneasiness of the Southern officers and soldiers about their political rights in case of surrender. While we were in consultation, a messenger came with a parcel of papers, which General Johnston said were from Mr. Reagan, Postmaster-General.[32] He and Breckenridge looked over them, and, after some side conversation, he handed one of the papers to me. It was in Reagan's handwriting, and began with a long preamble and terms, so general and verbose, that I said they were inadmissible. Then recalling the conversation of Mr. Lincoln, at City Point, I sat down at the table, and wrote off the terms, which I thought concisely expressed his views and wishes, and explained that I was willing to submit these terms to the new Presi-

[30] See Abraham Lincoln, *The Writings of Abraham Lincoln,* ed. Arthur B. Lapsley (New York: Lamb, 1906), 7:28–32.

[31] Johnston wrote, "Thinking it probable that the confidential relations of the Secretary of War (Breckenridge) with Mr. Davis might enable him to remove the only obstacle to an adjustment, I requested him by telegraph to join me as soon as possible." Johnston, *Narrative of Military Operations,* 404.

[32] John H. Reagan (1818–1905) was the Confederacy's postmaster general. *CWHC,* 447–448.

dent, Mr. Johnson,[33] provided that both armies should remain *in statu quo* until the truce therein declared should expire. I had full faith that General Johnston would religiously respect the truce, which he did; and that I would be the gainer, for in the few days it would take to send the papers to Washington, and receive an answer, I could finish the railroad up to Raleigh, and be the better prepared for a long chase.

Neither Mr. Breckenridge nor General Johnston wrote one word of that paper. I wrote it myself, and announced it as the best I could do, and they readily assented.

While copies of this paper were being made for signature, the officers of our staffs commingled in the yard at Bennett's house, and were all presented to Generals Johnston and Breckenridge. All without exception were rejoiced that the war was over, and that in a very few days we could turn our faces toward home. I remember telling Breckenridge that he had better get away, as the feeling of our people was utterly hostile to the political element of the South, and to him especially, because he was the Vice-President of the United States, who had as such announced Mr. Lincoln, of Illinois, duly and properly elected the President of the United States, and yet that he had afterward openly rebelled and taken up arms against the Government. He answered me that he surely would give us no more trouble, and intimated that he would speedily leave the country forever. I may have also advised him that Mr. Davis too should get abroad as soon as possible.

The papers were duly signed; we parted about dark, and my party returned to Raleigh. Early the next morning, April 19th, I dispatched by telegraph to Morehead City to prepare a fleet-steamer to carry a messenger to Washington, and sent Major Henry Hitchcock down by rail, bearing the following letters, and agreement with General Johnston, with instructions to be very careful to let nothing escape him to the greedy newspaper correspondents, but to submit his papers to General Halleck, General Grant, or the Secretary of War, and to bring me back with all expedition their orders and instructions.

On their face they recited that I had no authority to make final terms involving civil or political questions, but that I submitted them to the proper quarter in Washington for their action; and the letters fully explained that the military situation was such that the delay was an advantage to us. I cared little

[33] Andrew Johnson (1808–1875) was sworn in as president of the United States on Apr. 15, 1865, and was impeached on Feb. 24, 1868. He was ultimately acquitted on May 26, 1868. *CWHC*, 319.

whether they were approved, modified, or disapproved *in toto;* only I wanted instructions. Many of my general officers, among whom, I am almost positive, were Generals Logan and Blair, urged me to accept the "terms," without reference at all to Washington, but I preferred the latter course:

HEADQUARTERS MILITARY DIVISION OF THE MISSISSIPPI,
IN THE FIELD, RALEIGH, NORTH CAROLINA, *April* 18, 1865.

General H. W. HALLECK, *Chief of Staff, Washington, D. C.*

GENERAL: I received your dispatch describing the man Clark, detailed to assassinate me. He had better be in a hurry, or he will be too late.

The news of Mr. Lincoln's death produced a most intense effect on our troops. At first I feared it would lead to excesses; but now it has softened down, and can easily be guided. None evinced more feeling than General Johnston, who admitted that the act was calculated to stain his cause with a dark hue; and he contended that the loss was most serious to the South, who had begun to realize that Mr. Lincoln was the best friend they had.

I cannot believe that even Mr. Davis was privy to the diabolical plot, but think it the emanation of a set of young men of the South, who are very devils. I want to throw upon the South the care of this class of men, who will soon be as obnoxious to their industrial classes as to us.

Had I pushed Johnston's army to an extremity, it would have dispersed, and done infinite mischief. Johnston informed me that General Stoneman had been at Salisbury, and was now at Statesville. I have sent him orders to come to me.

General Johnston also informed me that General Wilson was at Columbus, Georgia, and he wanted me to arrest his progress. I leave that to you.

Indeed, if the President sanctions my agreement with Johnston, our interest is to cease all destruction.

Please give all orders necessary according to the views the Executive may take, and influence him, if possible, not to vary the terms at all, for I have considered every thing, and believe that, the Confederate armies once dispersed, we can adjust all else fairly and well.

I am, yours, etc.,
W. T. SHERMAN, *Major-General commanding.*

HEADQUARTERS MILITARY DIVISION OF THE MISSISSIPPI,
IN THE FIELD, RALEIGH, NORTH CAROLINA, *April* 18, 1865.

Lieutenant-General U. S. GRANT, *or Major-General* HALLECK, *Washington, D. C.*

GENERAL: I inclose herewith a copy of an agreement made this day between General Joseph E. Johnston and myself, which, if approved by the President of the United States, will produce peace from the Potomac to the Rio Grande. Mr. Breckenridge was present at our conference, in the capacity of major-general, and satisfied me of the ability of General Johnston to carry out to their full extent the terms of this agreement; and if you will get the President to simply indorse the copy, and commission me to carry out the terms, I will follow them to the conclusion.

You will observe that it is an absolute submission of the enemy to the lawful authority of the United States, and disperses his armies absolutely; and the point to which I attach most importance is, that the dispersion and disbandment of these armies is done in such a manner as to prevent their breaking up into guerrilla bands. On the other hand, we can retain just as much of an army as we please. I agreed to the mode and manner of the surrender of arms set forth, as it gives the States the means of repressing guerrillas, which we could not expect them to do if we stripped them of all arms.

Both Generals Johnston and Breckenridge admitted that slavery was dead, and I could not insist on embracing it in such a paper, because it can be made with the States in detail. I know that all the men of substance South sincerely want peace, and I do not believe they will resort to war again during this century. I have no doubt that they will in the future be perfectly subordinate to the laws of the United States. The moment my action in this matter is approved, I can spare five corps, and will ask for orders to leave General Schofield here with the Tenth Corps, and to march myself with the Fourteenth, Fifteenth, Seventeenth, Twentieth, and Twenty-third Corps *via* Burkesville and Gordonsville to Frederick or Hagerstown, Maryland, there to be paid and mustered out.

The question of finance is now the chief one, and every soldier and officer not needed should be got home at work. I would like to be able to begin the march north by May 1st.

I urge, on the part of the President, speedy action, as it is important to get the Confederate armies to their homes as well as our own.

I am, with great respect, your obedient servant,

W. T. SHERMAN, *Major-General commanding.*

Memorandum, or Basis of Agreement, made this 18*th day of April,* A. D. 1865, *near Durham's Station, in the State of North Carolina, by and between General* JOSEPH E. JOHNSTON, *commanding the Confederate Army, and Major-General* WILLIAM T. SHERMAN, *commanding the Army of the United States in North Carolina, both present:*

1. The contending armies now in the field to maintain the *statu quo* until notice is given by the commanding general of any one to its opponent, and reasonable time—say, forty-eight hours—allowed.

2. The Confederate armies now in existence to be disbanded and conducted to their several State capitals, there to deposit their arms and public property in the State Arsenal; and each officer and man to execute and file an agreement to cease from acts of war, and to abide the action of the State and Federal authority. The number of arms and munitions of war to be reported to the Chief of Ordnance at Washington City, subject to the future action of the Congress of the United States, and, in the mean time, to be used solely to maintain peace and order within the borders of the States respectively.

3. The recognition, by the Executive of the United States, of the several State governments, on their officers and Legislatures taking the oaths prescribed by the Constitution of the United States, and, where conflicting State governments have resulted from the war, the legitimacy of all shall be submitted to the Supreme Court of the United States.

4. The reëstablishment of all the Federal Courts in the several States, with powers as defined by the Constitution of the United States and of the States respectively.

5. The people and inhabitants of all the States to be guaranteed, so far as the Executive can, their political rights and franchises, as well as their rights of person and property, as defined by the Constitution of the United States and of the States respectively.

6. The Executive authority of the Government of the United States not to disturb any of the people by reason of the late war, so long as they live in peace and quiet, abstain from acts of armed hostility, and obey the laws in existence at the place of their residence.

7. In general terms—the war to cease; a general amnesty, so far as the Executive of the United States can command, on condition of the disbandment of the Confederate armies, the distribution of the arms, and the resumption of peaceful pursuits by the officers and men hitherto composing said armies.

Not being fully empowered by our respective principals to fulfill these terms, we individually and officially pledge ourselves to promptly obtain the necessary authority, and to carry out the above programme.

W. T. SHERMAN, *Major-General,*
Commanding Army of the United States in North Carolina.
J. E. JOHNSTON, *General,*
Commanding Confederate States Army in North Carolina.

Major Hitchcock got off on the morning of the 20th, and I reckoned that it would take him four or five days to go to Washington and back. During that time the repairs on all the railroads and telegraph-lines were pushed with energy, and we also got possession of the railroad and telegraph from Raleigh to Weldon, in the direction of Norfolk. Meantime the troops remained *statu quo,* our cavalry occupying Durham's Station and Chapel Hill. General Slocum's head of column was at Aven's Ferry on Cape Fear River, and General Howard's was strung along the railroad toward Hillsboro'; the rest of the army was in and about Raleigh.

On the 20th I reviewed the Tenth Corps, and was much pleased at the appearance of General Paines's division of black troops,[34] the first I had ever seen as a part of an organized army; and on the 21st I reviewed the Twenty-third Corps, which had been with me to Atlanta, but had returned to Nashville, had formed an essential part of the army which fought at Franklin, and with which General Thomas had defeated General Hood in Tennessee. It had then been transferred rapidly by rail to Baltimore and Washington by General Grant's orders, and thence by sea to North Carolina. Nothing of interest happened at Raleigh till the evening of April 23d, when Major Hitchcock reported by telegraph his return to Morehead City, and that he would come up by rail during the night. He arrived at 6 A. M., April 24th, accompanied by General Grant and one or two officers of his staff, who had not telegraphed the fact of their being on the train, for pru-

[34] Charles J. Paine (1833–1916) commanded the 3rd Div., 10th Corps, Dept. of North Carolina, in Apr. 1865. A portion of his command contained nine regiments of U.S. Colored Troops. *CWHC,* 412–413; Bradley, *This Astounding Close,* 26.

dential reasons. Of course, I was both surprised and pleased to see the general, soon learned that my terms with Johnston had been disapproved, was instructed by him to give the forty-eight hours' notice required by the terms of the truce, and afterward to proceed to attack or follow him. I immediately telegraphed to General Kilpatrick, at Durham's, to have a mounted courier ready to carry the following message, then on its way up by rail, to the rebel lines:

HEADQUARTERS MILITARY DIVISION OF THE MISSISSIPPI,
IN THE FIELD, RALEIGH, NORTH CAROLINA, *April* 24, 1865—6 A. M.

General JOHNSTON, *commanding Confederate Army, Greensboro':*

You will take notice that the truce or suspension of hostilities agreed to between us will cease in forty-eight hours after this is received at your lines, under the first of the articles of agreement.

W. T. SHERMAN, *Major-General.*

At the same time I wrote another short note to General Johnston, of the same date:

I have replies from Washington to my communications of April 18th. I am instructed to limit my operations to your immediate command, and not to attempt civil negotiations. I therefore demand the surrender of your army on the same terms as were given to General Lee at Appomattox, April 9th instant, purely and simply.

Of course, both these papers were shown to General Grant at the time, before they were sent, and he approved of them.

At the same time orders were sent to all parts of the army to be ready to resume the pursuit of the enemy on the expiration of the forty-eight hours' truce, and messages were sent to General Gillmore (at Hilton Head) to the same effect, with instructions to get a similar message through to General Wilson, at Macon, by some means.

General Grant had brought with him, from Washington, written answers from the Secretary of War, and of himself, to my communications of the 18th, which I still possess, and here give the originals. They embrace the copy of a dispatch made by Mr. Stanton to General Grant, when he was pressing Lee at Appomattox, which dispatch, if sent me at the same time (as should have been done), would have saved a world of trouble. I did not understand that General Grant had come down to supersede me in command, nor did he intimate it, nor did I receive these communications as a serious reproof, but promptly acted on them, as is already shown; and in this connection I give my answer made to General Grant, at Raleigh, before I had received any answer from General Johnston to the demand for the surrender of his own army, as well as my answer to Mr. Stanton's letter, of the same date, both written on the supposition that I might have to start suddenly in pursuit of Johnston, and have no other chance to explain.

War Department, Washington City, *April* 21, 1865.

Lieutenant-General Grant.

General: The memorandum or basis agreed upon between General Sherman and General Johnston having been submitted to the President, they are disapproved. You will give notice of the disapproval to General Sherman, and direct him to resume hostilities at the earliest moment.

The instructions given to you by the late President, Abraham Lincoln, on the 3d of March, by my telegraph of that date, addressed to you, express substantially the views of President Andrew Johnson, and will be observed by General Sherman. A copy is herewith appended.

The President desires that you proceed immediately to the headquarters of Major-General Sherman, and direct operations against the enemy.

Yours truly,

Edwin M. Stanton, *Secretary of War.*

The following telegram was received 2 p. m., City Point, March 4, 1865 (from Washington, 12 m., March 3, 1865):

[Cipher.]

Office United States Military Telegraph,
Headquarters Armies of the United States.

Lieutenant-General Grant:

The President directs me to say to you that he wishes you to have no conference with General Lee, unless it be for the capitulation of Lee's army or on solely minor and purely military matters.

He instructs me to say that you are not to decide, discuss, or confer upon any political question; such questions the President holds in his own hands, and will submit them to no military conferences or conventions.

Meantime you are to press to the utmost your military advantages.

EDWIN M. STANTON, *Secretary of War.*

HEADQUARTERS ARMIES OF THE UNITED STATES,
WASHINGTON, D.C., *April* 21, 1865.

Major-General W. T. SHERMAN, *commanding Military Division of the Mississippi.*

GENERAL: The basis of agreement entered into between yourself and General J. E. Johnston, for the disbandment of the Southern army, and the extension of the authority of the General Government over all the territory belonging to it, sent for the approval of the President, is received.

I read it carefully myself before submitting it to the President and Secretary of War, and felt satisfied that it could not possibly be approved. My reason for these views I will give you at another time, in a more extended letter.

Your agreement touches upon questions of such vital importance that, as soon as read, I addressed a note to the Secretary of War, notifying him of their receipt, and the importance of immediate action by the President; and suggested, in view of their importance, that the entire Cabinet be called together, that all might give an expression of their opinions upon the matter. The result was a disapproval by the President of the basis laid down; a disapproval of the negotiations altogether—except for the surrender of the army commanded by General Johnston, and directions to me to notify you of this decision. I cannot do so better than by sending you the inclosed copy of a dispatch (penned by the late President, though signed by the Secretary of War) in answer to me, on sending a letter received from General Lee, proposing to meet me for the purpose of submitting the question of peace to a convention of officers.

Please notify General Johnston, immediately on receipt of this, of the termination of the truce, and resume hostilities against his army at the earliest moment you can, acting in good faith.

Very respectfully your obedient servant,

U. S. GRANT, *Lieutenant-General.*

HEADQUARTERS MILITARY DIVISION OF THE MISSISSIPPI,
IN THE FIELD, RALEIGH, NORTH CAROLINA, *April* 25, 1865.

Lieutenant-General U. S. GRANT, *present.*

GENERAL: I had the honor to receive your letter of April 21st, with inclosures, yesterday, and was well pleased that you came along, as you must have observed that I held the military control so as to adapt it to any phase the case might assume.

It is but just I should record the fact that I made my terms with General Johnston under the influence of the liberal terms you extended to the army of General Lee at Appomattox Court-House on the 9th, and the seeming policy of our Government, as evinced by the call of the Virginia Legislature and Governor back to Richmond, under yours and President Lincoln's very eyes.

It now appears this last act was done without any consultation with you or any knowledge of Mr. Lincoln, but rather in opposition to a previous policy well considered.

I have not the least desire to interfere in the civil policy of our Government, but would shun it as something not to my liking; but occasions do arise when a prompt seizure of results is forced on military commanders not in immediate communication with the proper authority. It is probable that the terms signed by General Johnston and myself were not clear enough on the point, well understood between us, that our negotiations did not apply to any parties outside the officers and men of the Confederate armies, which could easily have been remedied.

No surrender of any army not actually at the mercy of an antagonist was ever made without "terms," and these always define the military status of the surrendered. Thus you stipulated that the officers and men of Lee's army should not be molested at their homes so long as they obeyed the laws at the place of their residence.

I do not wish to discuss these points involved in our recognition of the State governments in actual existence, but will merely state my conclusions, to await the solution of the future.

Such action on our part in no manner recognizes for a moment the so-called Confederate Government, or makes us liable for its debts or acts.

The laws and acts done by the several States during the period of rebellion are void, because done without the oath prescribed by our Constitution of the United States, which is a "condition precedent."

We have a right to use any sort of machinery to produce military results; and it is the commonest thing for military commanders to use the civil governments *in actual existence* as a means to an end. I do believe we could and can use the present State governments lawfully, constitutionally, and as the very best possible means to produce the object desired, viz., entire and complete submission to the lawful authority of the United States.

As to punishment for past crimes, that is for the judiciary, and can in no manner of way be disturbed by our acts; and, so far as I can, I will use my influence that rebels shall suffer all the personal punishment prescribed by law, as also the civil liabilities arising from their past acts.

What we now want is the new form of law by which common men may regain the positions of industry, so long disturbed by the war.

I now apprehend that the rebel armies will disperse; and, instead of dealing with six or seven States, we will have to deal with numberless bands of desperadoes, headed by such men as Mosby, Forrest, Red Jackson, and others, who know not and care not for danger and its consequences.

I am, with great respect, your obedient servant,
W. T. Sherman, *Major-General commanding.*

Headquarters Military Division of the Mississippi,
in the Field, Raleigh, North Carolina, *April* 25, 1865.

Hon. E. M. Stanton, *Secretary of War, Washington.*

Dear Sir: I have been furnished a copy of your letter of April 21st to General Grant, signifying your disapproval of the terms on which General Johnston proposed to disarm and disperse the insurgents, on condition of amnesty, etc. I admit my folly in embracing in a military convention any civil matters; but, unfortunately, such is the nature of our situation that they seem inextricably united, and I understood from you at Savannah that the financial state of the country demanded military success, and would warrant a little bending to policy.

When I had my conference with General Johnston I had the public examples before me of General Grant's terms to Lee's army, and

General Weitzel's invitation to the Virginia Legislature to assemble at Richmond.

I still believe the General Government of the United States has made a mistake; but that is none of my business—mine is a different task; and I had flattered myself that, by four years of patient, unremitting, and successful labor, I deserved no reminder such as is contained in the last paragraph of your letter to General Grant. You may assure the President that I heed his suggestion. I am truly, etc.,

W. T. SHERMAN, *Major-General commanding.*

On the same day, but later, I received an answer from General Johnston, agreeing to meet me again at Bennett's house the next day, April 26th, at noon. He did not even know that General Grant was in Raleigh.

General Grant advised me to meet him, and to accept his surrender on the same terms as his with General Lee; and on the 26th I again went up to Durham's Station by rail, and rode out to Bennett's house, where we again met, and General Johnston, without hesitation, agreed to, and we executed, the following final terms:

Terms of a Military Convention, entered into this 26th day of April, 1865, at Bennett's House, near Durham's Station, North Carolina, between General JOSEPH E. JOHNSTON, *commanding the Confederate Army, and Major-General* W. T. SHERMAN, *commanding the United States Army in North Carolina:*

1. All acts of war on the part of the troops under General Johnston's command to cease from this date.

2. All arms and public property to be deposited at Greensboro', and delivered to an ordnance-officer of the United States Army.

3. Rolls of all the officers and men to be made in duplicate; one copy to be retained by the commander of the troops, and the other to be given to an officer to be designated by General Sherman. Each officer and man to give his individual obligation in writing not to take up arms against the Government of the United States, until properly released from this obligation.

4. The side-arms of officers, and their private horses and baggage, to be retained by them.

5. This being done, all the officers and men will be permitted to return to their homes, not to be disturbed by the United States

authorities, so long as they observe their obligation and the laws in force where they may reside.

W. T. Sherman, *Major-General,*
Commanding United States Forces in North Carolina.
J. E. Johnston, *General,*
Commanding Confederate States Forces in North Carolina.
Approved: U. S. Grant, *Lieutenant-General.*

I returned to Raleigh the same evening, and, at my request, General Grant wrote on these terms his approval, and then I thought the matter was surely at an end. He took the original copy, on the 27th returned to Newbern, and thence went back to Washington.

I immediately made all the orders necessary to carry into effect the terms of this convention, devolving on General Schofield the details of granting the parols and making the muster-rolls of prisoners, inventories of property, etc., of General Johnston's army at and about Greensboro', North Carolina, and on General Wilson the same duties in Georgia; but, thus far, I had been compelled to communicate with the latter through rebel sources, and General Wilson was necessarily confused by the conflict of orders and information. I deemed it of the utmost importance to establish for him a more reliable base of information and supply, and accordingly resolved to go in person to Savannah for that purpose. But, before starting, I received a *New York Times,* of April 24th, containing the following extraordinary communications:

[First Bulletin.]

War Department, Washington, *April* 22, 1865.

Yesterday evening a bearer of dispatches arrived from General Sherman. An agreement for a suspension of hostilities, and a memorandum of what is called a basis for peace, had been entered into on the 18th inst. by General Sherman, with the rebel General Johnston. Brigadier-General Breckenridge was present at the conference.

A cabinet meeting was held at eight o'clock in the evening, at which the action of General Sherman was disapproved by the President, by the Secretary of War, by General Grant, and by every member of the cabinet. General Sherman was ordered to resume hostilities immediately, and was directed that the instructions given by the late President, in the following telegram, which was penned by Mr. Lincoln himself, at the Capitol, on the night of the 3d of March, were approved by President Andrew Johnson, and were reiterated to govern the action of military commanders.

On the night of the 3d of March, while President Lincoln and his cabinet were at the Capitol, a telegram from General Grant was brought to the Secretary of War, informing him that General Lee had requested an interview or conference, to make an arrangement for terms of peace. The letter of General Lee was published in a letter to Davis and to the rebel Congress. General Grant's telegram was submitted to Mr. Lincoln, who, after pondering a few minutes, took up his pen and wrote with his own hand the following reply, which he submitted to the Secretary of State and Secretary of War. It was then dated, addressed, and signed, by the Secretary of War, and telegraphed to General Grant:

WASHINGTON, *March* 3, 1865—12 P. M.

Lieutenant-General GRANT:

The President directs me to say to you that he wishes you to have no conference with General Lee, unless it be for the capitulation of General Lee's army, or on some minor or purely military matter. He instructs me to say that you are not to decide, discuss, or confer upon any political questions. Such questions the President holds in his own hands, and will submit them to no military conferences or conventions.

Meantime you are to press to the utmost your military advantages.

EDWIN M. STANTON, *Secretary of War.*

The orders of General Sherman to General Stoneman to withdraw from Salisbury and join him will probably open the way for Davis to escape to Mexico or Europe with his plunder, which is reported to be very large, including not only the plunder of the Richmond banks, but previous accumulations.

A dispatch received by this department from Richmond says: "It is stated here, by respectable parties, that the amount of specie taken south by Jeff. Davis and his partisans is very large, including not only the plunder of the Richmond banks, but previous accumulations. They hope, it is said, to make terms with General Sherman, or some other commander, by which they will be permitted, with their effects, including this gold plunder, to go to Mexico or Europe. Johnston's negotiations look to this end."

After the cabinet meeting last night, General Grant started for North Carolina, to direct operations against Johnston's army.

EDWIN M. STANTON, *Secretary of War.*

Here followed the terms, and Mr. Stanton's ten reasons for rejecting them.

The publication of this bulletin by authority was an outrage on me, for Mr. Stanton had failed to communicate to me in advance, as was his duty, the purpose of the Administration to limit our negotiations to purely military matters; but, on the contrary, at Savannah he had authorized me to control all matters, *civil* and military.

By this bulletin, he implied that I had previously been furnished with a copy of his dispatch of March 3d to General Grant, which was not so; and he gave warrant to the impression, which was sown broadcast, that I might be bribed by banker's gold to permit Davis to escape. Under the influence of this, I wrote General Grant the following letter of April 28th, which has been published in the Proceedings of the Committee on the Conduct of the War.

I regarded this bulletin of Mr. Stanton as a personal and official insult, which I afterward publicly resented.

HEADQUARTERS MILITARY DIVISION OF THE MISSISSIPPI,
IN THE FIELD, RALEIGH, NORTH CAROLINA, *April* 28, 1865.

Lieutenant-General U. S. GRANT, *General-in-Chief, Washington, D. C.*

GENERAL: Since you left me yesterday, I have seen the *New York Times* of the 24th, containing a budget of military news, authenticated by the signature of the Secretary of War, Hon. E. M. Stanton, which is grouped in such a way as to give the public very erroneous impressions. It embraces a copy of the basis of agreement between myself and General Johnston, of April 18th, with comments, which it will be time enough to discuss two or three years hence, after the Government has experimented a little more in the machinery by which power reaches the scattered people of the vast country known as the "South."

In the mean time, however, I did think that my rank (if not past services) entitled me at least to trust that the Secretary of War would keep secret what was communicated for the use of none but the cabinet, until further inquiry could be made, instead of giving publicity to it along with documents which I never saw, and drawing therefrom inferences wide of the truth. I never saw or had furnished me a copy of President Lincoln's dispatch to you of the 3d of March, nor did Mr. Stanton or any human being ever convey to me its substance, or any thing like it. On the contrary, I had seen General Weitzel's invitation to the Virginia Legislature, made in Mr. Lincoln's very presence, and failed to discover any other official hint of a plan of reconstruction, or any ideas calculated to allay the fears of the people of the South, after the destruction of their armies and civil authorities would leave them without any government whatever.

We should not drive a people into anarchy, and it is simply impossible for our military power to reach all the masses of their unhappy country.

I confess I did not desire to drive General Johnston's army into bands of armed men, going about without purpose, and capable only of infinite mischief. But you saw, on your arrival here, that I had my army so disposed that his escape was only possible in a disorganized shape; and as you did not choose to "direct military operations in this quarter," I inferred that you were satisfied with the military situation; at all events, the instant I learned what was proper enough, the disapproval of the President, I acted in such a manner as to compel the surrender of General Johnston's whole army on the same terms which you had prescribed to General Lee's army, when you had it surrounded and in your absolute power.

Mr. Stanton, in stating that my orders to General Stoneman were likely to result in the escape of "Mr. Davis to Mexico or Europe," is in deep error. General Stoneman was not at "Salisbury," but had gone back to "Statesville." Davis was between us, and therefore Stoneman was beyond him. By turning toward me he was approaching Davis, and, had he joined me as ordered, I would have had a mounted force greatly needed for Davis's capture, and for other purposes. Even now I don't know that Mr. Stanton wants Davis caught, and as my official papers, deemed sacred, are hastily published to the world, it will be imprudent for me to state what has been done in that regard.

As the editor of the *Times* has (it may be) logically and fairly drawn from this singular document the conclusion that I am insubordinate, I can only deny the intention.

I have never in my life questioned or disobeyed an order, though many and many a time have I risked my life, health, and reputation, in obeying orders, or even hints to execute plans and purposes, not to my liking. It is not fair to withhold from me the plans and policy of Government (if any there be), and expect me to guess at them; for facts and events appear quite different from different stand-points. For four years I have been in camp dealing with soldiers, and I can assure you that the conclusion at which the cabinet arrived with such singular unanimity differs from mine. I conferred freely with the best officers in this army as to the points involved in this controversy, and, strange to say, they were singularly unanimous in the other conclusion. They will learn with pain and amazement that I am deemed insubordinate, and wanting in common-sense; that I, who for four years have labored day and night, winter and summer, who have brought an army of seventy thousand men in magnificent condition across a country hitherto deemed impassable, and placed it just where it was wanted, on the day appointed, have brought discredit on our Government! I do not wish to boast of this, but I do say that it entitled me to the courtesy of being consulted, before publishing to the world a proposition rightfully submitted to higher authority for adjudication, and then accompanied by statements which invited the dogs of the press to be let loose upon me. It is true that non-combatants, men who sleep in comfort and security while we watch on the distant lines, are better able to judge than we poor soldiers, who rarely see a newspaper, hardly hear from our families, or stop long enough to draw our pay. I envy not the task of "reconstruction," and am delighted that the Secretary of War has relieved me of it.

As you did not undertake to assume the management of the affairs of this army, I infer that, on personal inspection, your mind arrived at a different conclusion from that of the Secretary of War. I will therefore go on to execute your orders to the conclusion, and, when done, will with intense satisfaction leave to the civil authorities the execution of the task of which they seem so jealous. But, as an honest man and soldier, I invite them to go back to Nashville and follow my path, for they will see some things and hear some things that may disturb their philosophy.

With sincere respect,

W. T. SHERMAN, *Major-General commanding.*

P. S.—As Mr. Stanton's most singular paper has been published, I demand that this also be made public, though I am in no manner responsible to the press, but to the law, and my proper superiors.

W. T. S., *Major-General.*

On the 28th I summoned all the army and corps commanders together at my quarters in the Governor's mansion at Raleigh, where every thing was explained to them, and all orders for the future were completed. Generals Schofield, Terry, and Kilpatrick, were to remain on duty in the Department of North Carolina, already commanded by General Schofield, and the right and left wings were ordered to march under their respective commanding generals North by easy stages to Richmond, Virginia, there to await my return from the South.

On the 29th of April, with a part of my personal staff, I proceeded by rail to Wilmington, North Carolina, where I found Generals Hawley[35] and Potter, and the little steamer Russia, Captain Smith, awaiting me. After a short pause in Wilmington, we embarked, and proceeded down the coast to Port Royal and the Savannah River, which we reached on the 1st of May. There Captain Hosea,[36] who had just come from General Wilson at Macon, met us, bearing letters for me and General Grant, in which General Wilson gave a brief summary of his operations up to date. He had marched from Eastport, Mississippi, "five hundred miles in thirty days, took six thousand three hundred prisoners, twenty-three colors, and one hundred and fifty-six guns, defeating Forrest, scattering the militia, and destroying every railroad, iron establishment, and factory, in North Alabama and Georgia."[37]

He spoke in the highest terms of his cavalry, as "cavalry," claiming that it could not be *excelled,* and he regarded his corps as a model for modern cavalry in organization, armament, and discipline. Its strength was given at thirteen thousand five hundred men and horses on reaching Macon. Of course I was extremely gratified at his just confidence, and saw that all he wanted for efficient action was a sure base of supply, so that he need no longer depend for clothing, ammunition, food, and forage, on the country, which, now that war had ceased, it was our solemn duty to protect, instead of plunder. I accordingly ordered the captured steamer Jeff. Davis to be loaded with stores, to proceed at once up the Savannah River to Augusta, with a small detachment of troops to occupy the arsenal, and to open communication with General Wilson at Macon; and on the next day, May 2d, this steamer was followed by another with a full cargo of clothing, sugar, coffee, and bread, sent from Hilton Head

[35] Joseph R. Hawley (1826–1905) commanded the Dist. of Wilmington, Dept. of North Carolina, in Apr. 1865. *CWHC,* 288–289.

[36] Lewis M. Hosea (1842–1924) joined James H. Wilson's staff near the end of the war. "An Army Officer, Practitioner at the Bar, Legislator and Judge," *Ohio Law Reporter: A Weekly Journal* 22 (1925): 272–273.

[37] For Wilson's full dispatch to WTS, dated Apr. 21, 1865, see *OR,* I, 49(II), 424–25, 444.

by the department commander, General Gillmore, with a stronger guard commanded by General Molineux.[38] Leaving to General Gillmore, who was present, and in whose department General Wilson was, to keep up the supplies at Augusta, and to facilitate as far as possible General Wilson's operations inland, I began my return on the 2d of May. We went into Charleston Harbor, passing the ruins of old Forts Moultrie and Sumter without landing. We reached the city of Charleston, which was held by part of the division of General John P. Hatch, the same that we had left at Pocotaligo. We walked the old familiar streets—Broad, King, Meeting, etc.—but desolation and ruin were everywhere. The heart of the city had been burned during the bombardment, and the rebel garrison at the time of its final evacuation had fired the railroad-depots, which fire had spread, and was only subdued by our troops after they had reached the city.

I inquired for many of my old friends, but they were dead or gone, and of them all I only saw a part of the family of Mrs. Pettigru.[39] I doubt whether any city was ever more terribly punished than Charleston, but, as her people had for years been agitating for war and discord, and had finally inaugurated the civil war by an attack on the small and devoted garrison of Major Anderson, sent there by the General Government to defend them, the judgment of the world will be, that Charleston deserved the fate that befell her. Resuming our voyage, we passed into Cape Fear River by its mouth at Fort Caswell and Smithville, and out by the new channel at Fort Fisher, and reached Morehead City on the 4th of May. We found there the revenue-cutter Wayanda, on board of which were the Chief-Justice, Mr. Chase, and his daughter Nettie, now Mrs. Hoyt.[40] The Chief-Justice at that moment was absent on a visit to Newbern, but came back the next day. Meantime, by means of the telegraph, I was again in correspondence with General Schofield at Raleigh. He had made great progress in paroling the officers and men of Johnston's army at Greensboro', but was embarrassed by the utter confu-

[38] Edward L. Molineux (1833–1915) took command of the Dist. of North Georgia, Dept. of the South, on June 5, 1865. *CWHC,* 393.

[39] Jane C. Petigru (1820–1892), a notable painter from South Carolina, married William A. Carson in 1841. Caroline Petigru, *The Roman Years of a South Carolina Artist: Caroline Carson's Letters Home, 1872–1892,* ed. William H. Pease and Jane H. Pease (Columbia: University of South Carolina Press, 2003), xiii, xxii.

[40] Janet "Nettie" Chase (1847–1925), an artist and illustrator, married William S. Hoyt in 1871. Salmon P. Chase, *The Salmon P. Chase Papers,* ed. John Niven et al. (Kent, OH: Kent State University Press, 1993), 1:223*n*.

sion and anarchy that had resulted from a want of understanding on many minor points, and on the political questions that had to be met at the instant. In order to facilitate the return to their homes of the Confederate officers and men, he had been forced to make with General Johnston the following supplemental terms, which were of course ratified and approved:

MILITARY CONVENTION OF APRIL 26, 1865.
SUPPLEMENTAL TERMS.

1. The field transportation to be loaned to the troops for their march to their homes, and for subsequent use in their industrial pursuits. Artillery-horses may be used in field-transportation, if necessary.

2. Each brigade or separate body to retain a number of arms equal to *one-seventh* of its effective strength, which, when the troops reach the capitals of their States, will be disposed of as the general commanding the department may direct.

3. Private horses, and other private property of both officers and men, to be retained by them.

4. The commanding general of the Military Division of West Mississippi, Major-General Canby, will be requested to give transportation by water, from Mobile or New Orleans, to the troops from Arkansas and Texas.

5. The obligations of officers and soldiers to be signed by their immediate commanders.

6. Naval forces within the limits of General Johnston's command to be included in the terms of this convention.

J. M. SCHOFIELD, *Major-General,*
Commanding United States Forces in North Carolina.
J. E. JOHNSTON, *General,*
Commanding Confederate States Forces in North Carolina.

The total number of prisoners of war parolled by General Schofield, at Greensboro', North Carolina, as afterward officially reported, amounted to 36,817
And the total number who surrendered in Georgia and Florida, as reported by General J. H. Wilson, was 52,453
Aggregate surrendered under the capitulation of General J. E. Johnston .89,270

On the morning of the 5th I also received from General Schofield this dispatch:

RALEIGH, NORTH CAROLINA, *May* 5, 1865.
To Major-General W. T. SHERMAN, *Morehead City:*

When General Grant was here, as you doubtless recollect, he said the lines (for trade and intercourse) had been extended to embrace this and other States south. The order, it seems, has been modified so as to include only Virginia and Tennessee. I think it would be an act of wisdom to open this State to trade at once.

I hope the Government will make known its policy as to the organs of State government without delay. Affairs must necessarily be in a very unsettled state until that is done. The people are now in a mood to accept almost any thing which promises a definite settlement. "What is to be done with the freedmen?" is the question of all, and it is the all-important question. It requires prompt and wise action to prevent the negroes from becoming a huge elephant on our hands. If I am to govern this State, it is important for me to know it at once. If another is to be sent here, it cannot be done too soon, for he probably will undo the most that I shall have done. I shall be glad to hear from you fully, when you have time to write. I will send your message to General Wilson at once.

J. M. SCHOFIELD, *Major-General.*

I was utterly without instructions from any source on the points of General Schofield's inquiry, and under the existing state of facts could not even advise him, for by this time I was in possession of the second bulletin of Mr. Stanton, published in all the Northern papers, with comments that assumed that I was a common traitor and a public enemy; and high officials had even instructed my own subordinates to disobey my lawful orders. General Halleck, who had so long been in Washington as the chief of staff, had been sent on the 21st of April to Richmond, to command the armies of the Potomac and James, in place of General Grant, who had transferred his headquarters to the national capital, and he (General Halleck) was therefore in supreme command in Virginia, while my command over North Carolina had never been revoked or modified.

[Second Bulletin.]
WAR DEPARTMENT, WASHINGTON, *April* 27—9.30 A. M.

To Major-General DIX:

The department has received the following dispatch from Major-General Halleck, commanding the Military Division of the James. Generals Canby and Thomas were instructed some days ago that Sherman's arrangements with Johnston were disapproved by the President, and they were ordered to disregard it and push the enemy in every direction.

E. M. STANTON, *Secretary of War.*

RICHMOND, VIRGINIA, *April* 26—9.30 P. M.

HON. E. M. STANTON, *Secretary of War:*

Generals Meade, Sheridan, and Wright, are acting under orders to pay no regard to any truce or orders of General Sherman respecting hostilities, on the ground that Sherman's agreement could bind his command only, and no other.

They are directed to push forward, regardless of orders from any one except from General Grant, and cut off Johnston's retreat.

Beauregard has telegraphed to Danville that a new arrangement has been made with Sherman, and that the advance of the Sixth Corps was to be suspended until further orders.

I have telegraphed back to obey no orders of Sherman, but to push forward as rapidly as possible.

The bankers here have information to-day that Jeff. Davis's specie is moving south from Goldsboro', in wagons, as fast as possible.

I suggest that orders be telegraphed, through General Thomas, that Wilson obey no orders from Sherman, and notifying him and Canby, and all commanders on the Mississippi, to take measures to intercept the rebel chiefs and their plunder.

The specie taken with them is estimated here at from six to thirteen million dollars.

H. W. HALLECK, *Major-General commanding.*

Subsequently, before the Committee on the Conduct of the War, in Washington, on the 22d of May, I testified fully on this whole matter, and will abide the judgment of the country on the patriotism and wisdom of my public conduct in this connection. General Halleck's measures to capture General Johnston's army, actually surrendered to me at the time, at Greensboro', on the 26th of April, simply excited my contempt for a judgment such as he was supposed to possess. The assertion that Jeff. Davis's specie-train, of six to thirteen million dollars, was reported to be moving south from Goldsboro' in wagons as fast as possible, found plenty of willing ears, though my army of eighty thousand men had been at Goldsboro' from March 22d to the date of his dispatch, April 26th; and such a train would have been composed of from fifteen to thirty-two six-mule teams to have hauled this specie, even if it all were in gold. I suppose the exact amount of treasure which Davis had with him is now known to a cent; some of it was paid to his escort, when it disbanded at and near Washington, Georgia, and at the time of his capture he had a small parcel of gold and silver coin, not to exceed ten thousand dollars, which is now retained in the United States Treasury-vault at Washington, and shown to the curious.

The thirteen millions of treasure, with which Jeff. Davis was to corrupt our armies and buy his escape, dwindled down to the contents of a hand-valise!

To say that I was merely angry at the tone and substance of these published bulletins of the War Department, would hardly express the state of my feelings. I was outraged beyond measure, and was resolved to resent the insult, cost what it might. I went to the Wayanda and showed them to Mr. Chase, with whom I had a long and frank conversation, during which he explained to me the confusion caused in Washington by the assassination of Mr. Lincoln, the sudden accession to power of Mr. Johnson, who was then supposed to be bitter and vindictive in his feelings toward the South, and the wild pressure of every class of politicians to enforce on the new President their pet schemes. He showed me a letter of his own, which was in print, dated Baltimore, April 11th, and another of April 12th, addressed to the President, urging him to recognize the freedmen as equal in all respects to the whites. He was the first man, of any authority or station, who ever informed me that the Government of the United States would insist on extending to the former slaves of the South the elective franchise, and he gave as a reason the fact that the slaves, grateful for their freedom, for which they were indebted to the armies and Government of the North, would, by their votes, offset the disaffected and rebel element of the white population of the South. At that time quite a storm was prevailing at sea, outside, and our two vessels lay snug at the wharf at Morehead City. I saw a good deal of Mr. Chase, and several notes passed between us, of which I have the originals yet.[41] Always claiming that the South had herself freed all her slaves by rebellion, and that Mr. Lincoln's proclamation of freedom (of September 22, 1862) was binding on all officers of the General Government, I doubted the wisdom of at once clothing them with the elective franchise, without some previous preparation and qualification; and then realized the national loss in the death at that critical moment of Mr. Lincoln, who had long pondered over the difficult questions involved, who, at all events, would have been honest and frank, and would not have withheld from his army commanders at least a hint that would have been to them a guide. It was plain to me, therefore, that the manner of his assassination had stampeded the civil authorities in Washington, had unnerved them, and that they were then undecided as to the measures indispensably necessary to prevent anarchy at the South.

On the 7th of May the storm subsided, and we put to sea, Mr. Chase to the south, on his proposed tour as far as New Orleans, and I for James River. I reached Fortress Monroe on the 8th, and thence telegraphed my arrival to General Grant, asking for orders. I found at Fortress Monroe a dispatch from General Halleck, professing great friendship, and inviting me to accept his hospitality at Richmond. I answered by a cipher-dispatch that I had seen his dispatch to Mr. Stanton, of April 26th, embraced in the second bulletin, which I regarded as insulting, declined his hospitality, and added that I preferred we should not meet as I passed through Richmond.[42] I thence proceeded to City Point in the Russia, and on to Manchester, opposite Richmond, *via* Petersburg, by rail. I found that both wings of the army had arrived from Raleigh, and were in camp in and around Manchester, whence I again telegraphed General Grant, on the 9th of May, for orders, and also reported my arrival to General Halleck by letter. I found that General Halleck had ordered General Davis's corps (the Fourteenth) for review by himself. This I forbade. All the army knew of the insult that had been made me by the Secretary of War and General Halleck, and watched me closely to see if I would tamely submit. During the 9th I made a full and complete report of all these events, from the last report made at Goldsboro' up to date, and

[41] For the relevant correspondence between WTS and Salmon P. Chase, chief justice of the U.S. Supreme Court, see William T. Sherman, *Sherman's Civil War: Selected Correspondence of William T. Sherman, 1860–1865*, ed. Brooks D. Simpson and Jean V. Berlin (Chapel Hill: University of North Carolina Press, 1999), 888–891.

[42] See *OR*, I, 47(III), 435.

the next day received orders to continue the march to Alexandria, near Washington.[43]

On the morning of the 11th we crossed the pontoon-bridge at Richmond, marched through that city, and out on the Hanover Court-House road, General Slocum's left wing leading. The right wing (General Logan) followed the next day, viz., the 12th. Meantime, General O. O. Howard had been summoned to Washington to take charge of the new Bureau of Refugees, Freedmen, and Abandoned Lands, and, from that time till the army was finally disbanded, General John A. Logan was in command of the right wing, and of the Army of the Tennessee.[44] The left wing marched through Hanover Court-House, and thence took roads well to the left by Chilesburg; the Fourteenth Corps by New Market and Culpepper, Manassas, etc.; the Twentieth Corps by Spotsylvania Court-House and Chancellorsville. The right wing followed the more direct road by Fredericksburg. On my way north I endeavored to see as much of the battle-fields of the Army of the Potomac as I could, and therefore shifted from one column to the other, visiting *en route* Hanover Court-House, Spotsylvania, Fredericksburg, Dumfries, etc., reaching Alexandria during the afternoon of May 19th, and pitched my camp by the road-side, about half-way between Alexandria and the Long Bridge. During the same and next day the whole army reached Alexandria, and camped round about it; General Meade's Army of the Potomac had possession of the camps above, opposite Washington and Georgetown.

The next day (by invitation) I went over to Washington and met many friends—among them General Grant and President Johnson.[45] The latter occupied rooms in the house on the corner of Fifteenth and H Streets, belonging to Mr. Hooper.[46] He was extremely cordial to me, and knowing that

[43] See *OR,* I, 47(I), 29–40.

[44] Howard was the commissioner of the Bureau of Refugees, Freedman and Abandoned Lands from 1865 to 1869. *CWHC,* 306.

[45] USG invited WTS to Washington, DC, on May 19. He wrote, "I will be glad to see you as soon as you can come to the city. Can you not come in the evening or in the morning? I want to talk to you upon matters about which you feel sore—I think justly so, but which bear some more explanation on behalf of those who, you feel, have inflicted the injury." *OR,* I, 47(III), 531.

[46] Samuel Hooper (1808–1875) served in the U.S. Congress as a representative from Massachusetts from 1861 to 1874. Before moving into the White House, Pres. Johnson lived in Hooper's house after Lincoln's assassination. Frank R. Batchelder, "Washington Homes of New England Statesmen," *New England Magazine,* Sept. 1900–Feb. 1901, 395–396.

I was chafing under the censures of the War Department, especially of the two war bulletins of Mr. Stanton, he volunteered to say that he knew of neither of them till seen in the newspapers, and that Mr. Stanton had shown neither to him nor to any of his associates in the cabinet till they were published. Nearly all the members of the cabinet made similar assurances to me afterward, and, as Mr. Stanton made no friendly advances, and offered no word of explanation or apology, I declined General Grant's friendly offices for a reconciliation, but, on the contrary, resolved to resent what I considered an insult, as publicly as it was made. My brother, Senator Sherman, who was Mr. Stanton's neighbor, always insisted that Mr. Stanton had been frightened by the intended assassination of himself, and had become embittered thereby. At all events, I found strong military guards around his house, as well as all the houses occupied by the cabinet and by the principal officers of Government; and a sense of insecurity pervaded Washington, for which no reason existed.

On the 19th I received a copy of War Department Special Order No. 239, Adjutant-General's office, of May 18th, ordering a grand review, by the President and cabinet, of all the armies then near Washington; General Meade's to occur on Tuesday, May 23d, mine on Wednesday, the 24th; and on the 20th I made the necessary orders for my part. Meantime I had also arranged (with General Grant's approval) to remove, after the review, my armies from the south side of the Potomac to the north; both for convenience and because our men had found that the grounds assigned them had been used so long for camps that they were foul and unfit.

By invitation I was on the reviewing-stand, and witnessed the review of the Army of the Potomac (on the 23d), commanded by General Meade in person. The day was beautiful, and the pageant was superb. Washington was full of strangers, who filled the streets in holiday-dress, and every house was decorated with flags. The army marched by divisions in close column around the Capitol, down Pennsylvania Avenue, past the President and cabinet, who occupied a large stand prepared for the occasion, directly in front of the White House.

I had telegraphed to Lancaster for Mrs. Sherman, who arrived that day, accompanied by her father, the Hon. Thomas Ewing, and my son Tom, then eight years old.

During the afternoon and night of the 23d, the Fifteenth, Seventeenth, and Twentieth Corps, crossed Long Bridge, bivouacked in the streets about the Capitol, and the Fourteenth Corps closed up to the bridge. The morning of the 24th was extremely beautiful, and the ground was in splendid order for our review. The streets were filled with people to see the pageant, armed with bouquets of flowers for their favorite regiments or heroes, and every thing was propitious. Punctually at 9 A. M. the signal-gun was fired, when in person, attended by General Howard and all my staff, I rode slowly down Pennsylvania Avenue, the crowds of men, women, and children, densely lining the sidewalks, and almost obstructing the way. We were followed close by General Logan and the head of the Fifteenth Corps. When I reached the Treasury-building, and looked back, the sight was simply magnificent. The column was compact, and the glittering muskets looked like a solid mass of steel, moving with the regularity of a pendulum. We passed the Treasury-building, in front of which and of the White House was an immense throng of people, for whom extensive stands had been prepared on both sides of the avenue. As I neared the brick-house opposite the lower corner of Lafayette Square, some one asked me to notice Mr. Seward, who, still feeble and bandaged for his wounds, had been removed there that he might behold the troops. I moved in that direction and took off my hat to Mr. Seward, who sat at an upper window. He recognized the salute, returned it, and then we rode on steadily past the President, saluting with our swords. All on his stand arose and acknowledged the salute. Then, turning into the gate of the presidential grounds, we left our horses with orderlies, and went upon the stand, where I found Mrs. Sherman, with her father and son. Passing them, I shook hands with the President, General Grant, and each member of the cabinet. As I approached Mr. Stanton, he offered me his hand, but I declined it publicly, and the fact was universally noticed.[47] I then took my post on the left of the President, and for six hours and a half stood, while the army passed in the order of the Fifteenth, Seventeenth, Twentieth, and Fourteenth Corps. It was, in my judgment, the most magnificent army in existence—sixty-five thousand men, in splendid *physique,* who had just completed a march of nearly two thousand miles in a hostile country, in good drill, and who realized that they were being closely scrutinized by thousands of their fellow-countrymen and by foreigners. Division after division passed, each commander of an army corps or division coming on the stand during the passage of his command, to be presented to the President, cabinet, and spectators. The steadiness and firmness of the tread, the careful dress on the guides, the uniform intervals between the companies, all eyes directly to the front, and the tattered and bullet-riven flags, festooned with flowers, all attracted universal notice. Many

[47] Julia D. Grant wrote, "How well do I remember when Sherman's men came tramp, tramp, tramping by, and Sherman arose to go to the front to review his glorious men. What a defiant and angry glance he shot at Stanton, who actually arose and offered his hand to Sherman, he having reprimanded that distinguished officer for giving too liberal terms of surrender to General Joe Johnston." Julia D. Grant, *The Personal Memoirs,* 159.

good people, up to that time, had looked upon our Western army as a sort of mob; but the world then saw, and recognized the fact, that it was an army in the proper sense, well organized, well commanded and disciplined; and there was no wonder that it had swept through the South like a tornado. For six hours and a half that strong tread of the Army of the West resounded along Pennsylvania Avenue; not a soul of that vast crowd of spectators left his place; and, when the rear of the column had passed by, thousands of the spectators still lingered to express their sense of confidence in the strength of a Government which could claim such an army.

Some little scenes enlivened the day, and called for the laughter and cheers of the crowd. Each division was followed by six ambulances, as a representative of its baggage-train. Some of the division commanders had added, by way of variety, goats, milch-cows, and pack-mules, whose loads consisted of game-cocks, poultry, hams, etc., and some of them had the families of freed slaves along, with the women leading their children. Each division was preceded by its corps of black pioneers, armed with picks and spades. These marched abreast in double ranks, keeping perfect dress and step, and added much to the interest of the occasion. On the whole, the grand review was a splendid success, and was a fitting conclusion to the campaign and the war.

I will now conclude by a copy of my general orders taking leave of the army, which ended my connection with the war, though I afterward visited and took a more formal leave of the officers and men on July 4, 1865, at Louisville, Kentucky:

[Special Field Orders, No. 76.]

HEADQUARTERS MILITARY DIVISION OF THE MISSISSIPPI,
IN THE FIELD, WASHINGTON, D. C., *May* 30, 1865.

The general commanding announces to the Armies of the Tennessee and Georgia that the time has come for us to part. Our work is done, and armed enemies no longer defy us. Some of you will go to your homes, and others will be retained in military service till further orders.

And now that we are all about to separate, to mingle with the civil world, it becomes a pleasing duty to recall to mind the situation of national affairs when, but little more than a year ago, we were gathered about the cliffs of Lookout Mountain, and all the future was wrapped in doubt and uncertainty.

Three armies had come together from distant fields, with separate histories, yet bound by one common cause—the union of our country, and the perpetuation of the Government of our inheritance. There is no need to recall to your memories Tunnel Hill, with Rocky-Face Mountain and Buzzard-Roost Gap, and the ugly forts of Dalton behind.

We were in earnest, and paused not for danger and difficulty, but dashed through Snake-Creek Gap and fell on Resaca; then on to the Etowah, to Dallas, Kenesaw; and the heats of summer found us on the banks of the Chattahoochee, far from home, and dependent on a single road for supplies. Again we were not to be held back by any obstacle, and crossed over and fought four hard battles for the possession of the citadel of Atlanta. That was the crisis of our history. A doubt still clouded our future, but we solved the problem, destroyed Atlanta, struck boldly across the State of Georgia, severed all the main arteries of life to our enemy, and Christmas found us at Savannah.

Waiting there only long enough to fill our wagons, we again began a march which, for peril, labor, and results, will compare with any ever made by an organized army. The floods of the Savannah, the swamps of the Combahee and Edisto, the "high hills" and rocks of the Santee, the flat quagmires of the Pedee and Cape Fear Rivers, were all passed in mid-winter, with its floods and rains, in the face of an accumulating enemy; and, after the battles of Averysboro' and Bentonsville, we once more came out of the wilderness, to meet our friends at Goldsboro'. Even then we paused only long enough to get new clothing, to reload our wagons, again pushed on to Raleigh and beyond, until we met our enemy suing for peace, instead of war, and offering to submit to the injured laws of his and our country. As long as that enemy was defiant, nor mountains nor rivers, nor swamps, nor hunger, nor cold, had checked us; but when he, who had fought us hard and persistently, offered submission, your general thought it wrong to pursue him farther, and negotiations followed, which resulted, as you all know, in his surrender.

How far the operations of this army contributed to the final overthrow of the Confederacy and the peace which now dawns upon us, must be judged by others, not by us; but that you have done all that men could do has been admitted by those in authority, and we have a right to join in the universal joy that fills our land because the war is *over,* and our Government stands vindicated before the world by the joint action of the volunteer armies and navy of the United States.

To such as remain in the service, your general need only remind you that success in the past was due to hard work and discipline, and that the same work and discipline are equally important in the future. To such as

List of the Average Number of Miles marched by the Different Army Corps of the United States Forces under Command of Major-General W.T. SHERMAN, *United States Army, during his Campaigns in 1863–'64–'65*

ROUTE.	NUMBER OF MILES.						
	Fourth Corps.	Fourteenth Corps.	Fifteenth Corps.	Sixteenth Corps.	Sixteenth Corps. (Left Wing)	Seventeenth Corps.	Twentieth Corps.
From Vicksburg to Meridian, and back	. . . .	. . . .	. . . .	330	. . . .	335	. . . .
From Memphis to Chattanooga.	. . . .	. . . .	330	. . . .	. . . .	. . . .	. . . .
From Chattanooga to Knoxville, and back	110	. . . .	230	. . . .	. . . .	. . . .	. . . .
From Chattanooga to Huntsville (Paint Rock), Langston, etc., and back.	. . . .	. . . .	240	. . . .	. . . .	. . . .	. . . .
From Clifton to Rome.	. . . .	. . . .	. . . .	. . . .	. . . .	261	. . . .
From Chattanooga to Atlanta (average distance traversed in manœuvring)	. . . .	178	178	. . . .	178	89	178
Pursuit of Hood, and back to Atlanta	. . . .	270	270	. . . .	. . . .	270	270
From Atlanta to Savannah.	. . . .	283	285	. . . .	. . . .	290	287
From Savannah to Goldsboro'.	. . . .	425	423	. . . .	. . . .	478	420
From Goldsboro' to Washington, D.C.	. . . .	430	333	. . . .	. . . .	353	370
Total distance in miles.	110	1,586	2,289	330	178	2,076	1,525

Compiled from campaign maps at headquarters Military Division of the Mississippi, St. Louis, Missouri.

WILLIAM KOSSACK, *Captain,*
Additional Aide-de-Camp on Engineer Duty.

go home, he will only say that our favored country is so grand, so extensive, so diversified in climate, soil, and productions, that every man may find a home and occupation suited to his taste; none should yield to the natural impatience sure to result from our past life of excitement and adventure. You will be invited to seek new adventures abroad; do not yield to the temptation, for it will lead only to death and disappointment.

Your general now bids you farewell, with the full belief that, as in war you have been good soldiers, so in peace you will make good citizens; and if, unfortunately, new war should arise in our country, "Sherman's army" will be the first to buckle on its old armor, and come forth to defend and maintain the Government of our inheritance.

By order of Major-General W. T. Sherman,
L. M. DAYTON, *Assistant Adjutant-General.*

25

Conclusion—Military Lessons of the War.

HAVING THUS RECORDED a summary of events, mostly under my own personal supervision, during the years from 1846 to 1865, it seems proper that I should add an opinion of some of the useful military lessons to be derived therefrom.

That civil war, by reason of the existence of slavery, was apprehended by most of the leading statesmen of the half-century preceding its outbreak, is a matter of notoriety. General Scott told me on my arrival at New York, as early as 1850, that the country was on the eve of civil war; and the Southern politicians openly asserted that it was their purpose to accept as a *casus belli* the election of General Fremont in 1856; but, fortunately or unfortunately, he was beaten by Mr. Buchanan, which simply postponed its occurrence for four years. Mr. Seward had also publicly declared that no government could possibly exist half slave and half free;[1] yet the Government made no military preparation, and the Northern people generally paid no attention, took no warning of its coming, and would not realize its existence till Fort Sumter was fired on by batteries of artillery, handled by declared enemies, from the surrounding islands and from the city of Charleston.

General Bragg, who certainly was a man of intelligence, and who, in early life, ridiculed a thousand times, in my hearing, the threats of the people of South Carolina to secede from the Federal Union, said to me in New Orleans, in February, 1861, that he was convinced that the feeling between the slave and free States had become so embittered that it was better to part in peace; better to part anyhow; and, as a separation was inevitable, that the South should begin at once, because the possibility of a successful effort was

[1] In Oct. 1858, future U.S. secretary of state William Seward stated, "It is an irrepressible conflict between opposing and enduring forces, and either entirely a slaveholding nation, or entirely a free-labor nation." James W. Parins, *John Rollin Ridge* (Lincoln: University of Nebraska Press, 2004), 164.

yearly lessened by the rapid and increasing inequality between the two sections, from the fact that all the European immigrants were coming to the Northern States and Territories, and none to the Southern.

The slave population in 1860 was near four millions, and the money value thereof not far from twenty-five hundred million dollars.[2] Now, ignoring the moral side of the question, a cause that endangered so vast a moneyed interest was an adequate cause of anxiety and preparation, and the Northern leaders surely ought to have foreseen the danger and prepared for it. After the election of Mr. Lincoln in 1860, there was no concealment of the declaration and preparation for war in the South. In Louisiana, as I have related, men were openly enlisted, officers were appointed, and war was actually begun, in January, 1861. The forts at the mouth of the Mississippi were seized, and occupied by garrisons that hauled down the United States flag and hoisted that of the State. The United States Arsenal at Baton Rouge was captured by New Orleans militia, its garrison ignominiously sent off, and the contents of the arsenal distributed. These were as much acts of war as was the subsequent firing on Fort Sumter, yet no public notice was taken thereof; and when, months afterward, I came North, I found not one single sign of preparation. It was for this reason, somewhat, that the people of the South became convinced that those of the North were pusillanimous and cowardly, and the Southern leaders were thereby enabled to commit their people to the war, nominally in defense of their slave property. Up to the hour of the firing on Fort Sumter, in April, 1861, it does seem to me that our public men, our politicians, were blamable for not sounding the note of alarm.

Then, when war was actually begun, it was by a call for seventy-five thousand "ninety-day" men, I suppose to fulfill Mr. Seward's prophecy that the war would last but ninety days.[3]

The earlier steps by our political Government were extremely wavering and weak, for which an excuse can be found in the fact that many of the

[2]The institution of slavery in the United States was valued at approximately $3 billion in 1860, which accounted for 19 percent of the country's total wealth. Calvin Schermerhorn, *Unrequited Toil: A History of United States Slavery* (Cambridge: Cambridge University Press, 2018), 1–2.

[3]On Mar. 4, 1861, Seward stated, "I have not expected that in the ninety days, which are the allotted term of Congress—this great controversy would certainly be adjusted, peace restored, and the Union firmly reestablished." William H. Seward, *Seward at Washington as Senator and Secretary of State: A Memoir of His Life, with Selections from His Letters, 1846–1861,* ed. Frederick W. Seward (New York: Derby and Miller, 1891), 499.

Southern representatives remained in Congress, sharing in the public councils, and influencing legislation. But as soon as Mr. Lincoln was installed, there was no longer any reason why Congress and the cabinet should have hesitated. They should have measured the cause, provided the means, and left the Executive to apply the remedy.

At the time of Mr. Lincoln's inauguration, viz., March 4, 1861, the Regular Army, by law, consisted of two regiments of dragoons, two regiments of cavalry, one regiment of mounted rifles, four regiments of artillery, and ten regiments of infantry, admitting of an aggregate strength of thirteen thousand and twenty-four officers and men. On the subsequent 4th of May the President, by his own orders (afterward sanctioned by Congress), added a regiment of cavalry, a regiment of artillery, and eight regiments of infantry, which, with the former army, admitted of a strength of thirty-nine thousand nine hundred and seventy-three; but at no time during the war did the Regular Army attain a strength of twenty-five thousand men.[4]

To the new regiments of infantry was given an organization differing from any that had heretofore prevailed in this country—of three battalions of eight companies each; but at no time did more than one of these regiments attain its full standard; nor in the vast army of volunteers that was raised during the war were any of the regiments of infantry formed on the three-battalion system, but these were universally single battalions of ten companies; so that, on the reorganization of the Regular Army at the close of the war, Congress adopted the form of twelve companies for the regiments of cavalry and artillery, and that of ten companies for the infantry, which is the present standard.

Inasmuch as the Regular Army will naturally form the standard of organization for any increase or for new regiments of volunteers, it becomes important to study this subject in the light of past experience, and to select that form which is best for peace as well as war.

A cavalry regiment is now composed of twelve companies, usually divided into six squadrons, of two companies each, or better subdivided into three battalions of four companies each. This is an excellent form, easily admitting of subdivision as well as union into larger masses.

A single battalion of four companies, with a field-officer, will compose a good body for a garrison, for a separate expedition, or for a detachment; and, in war, three regiments would compose a good brigade, three brigades a divi-

[4] On Mar. 31, 1865, the U.S. Regular Army reported 13,880 troops present for duty, with 7,789 absent for a total of 21,669 troops on the rolls. *CWHC,* 46.

sion, and three divisions a strong cavalry corps, such as was formed and fought by Generals Sheridan and Wilson during the war.

In the artillery arm, the officers differ widely in their opinion of the true organization. A single company forms a battery, and habitually each battery acts separately, though sometimes several are united or "massed;" but these always act in concert with cavalry or infantry.

Nevertheless, the regimental organization for artillery has always been maintained in this country for classification and promotion. Twelve companies compose a regiment, and, though probably no colonel ever commanded his full regiment in the form of twelve batteries, yet in peace they occupy our heavy sea-coast forts or act as infantry; then the regimental organization is both necessary and convenient.

But the infantry composes the great mass of all armies, and the true form of the regiment or unit has been the subject of infinite discussion; and, as I have stated, during the civil war the regiment was a single battalion of ten companies. In olden times the regiment was composed of eight battalion companies and two flank companies. The first and tenth companies were armed with rifles, and were styled and used as "skirmishers;" but during the war they were never used exclusively for that special purpose, and in fact no distinction existed between them and the other eight companies.

The ten-company organization is awkward in practice, and I am satisfied that the infantry regiment should have the same identical organization as exists for the cavalry and artillery, viz., twelve companies, so as to be susceptible of division into three battalions of four companies each.

These companies should habitually be about one hundred men strong, giving twelve hundred to a regiment, which in practice would settle down to about one thousand men.

Three such regiments would compose a brigade, three brigades a division, and three divisions a corps. Then, by allowing to an infantry corps a brigade of cavalry and six batteries of field-artillery, we would have an efficient *corps d'armée* of thirty thousand men, whose organization would be simple and most efficient, and whose strength should never be allowed to fall below twenty-five thousand men.

The corps is the true unit for grand campaigns and battle, should have a full and perfect staff, and every thing requisite for separate action, ready at all times to be detached and sent off for any nature of service. The general in command should have the rank of lieutenant-general, and should be, by experience and education, equal to any thing in war. Habitually with us he was a major-general, specially selected and assigned to the command by an order of the President, constituting, in fact, a separate grade.

The division is the unit of administration, and is the legitimate command of a major-general.

The brigade is the next subdivision, and is commanded by a brigadier-general.

The regiment is the family. The colonel, as the father, should have a personal acquaintance with every officer and man, and should instill a feeling of pride and affection for himself, so that his officers and men would naturally look to him for personal advice and instruction. In war the regiment should never be subdivided, but should always be maintained entire. In peace this is impossible.

The company is the true unit of discipline, and the captain is the company. A good captain makes a good company, and he should have the power to reward as well as punish. The fact that soldiers would naturally like to have a good fellow for their captain is the best reason why he should be appointed by the colonel, or by some superior authority, instead of being elected by the men.

In the United States the people are the "sovereign," all power originally proceeds from them, and therefore the election of officers by the men is the common rule. This is wrong, because an army is not a popular organization, but an animated machine, an instrument in the hands of the Executive for enforcing the law, and maintaining the honor and dignity of the nation; and the President, as the constitutional commander-in-chief of the army and navy, should exercise the power of appointment (subject to the confirmation of the Senate) of the officers of "volunteers," as well as of "regulars."

No army can be efficient unless it be a unit for action; and the power must come from above, not from below: the President usually delegates his power to the commander-in-chief, and he to the next, and so on down to the lowest actual commander of troops, however small the detachment. No matter how troops come together, when once united, the highest officer in rank is held responsible, and should be consequently armed with the fullest power of the Executive, subject only to law and existing orders. The more simple the principle, the greater the likelihood of determined action; and the less a commanding officer is circumscribed by bounds or by precedent, the greater is the probability that he will make the best use of his command and achieve the best results.

The Regular Army and the Military Academy at West Point have in the past provided, and doubtless will in the future provide an ample supply of good officers for future wars; but, should their numbers be insufficient, we can always safely rely on the great number of young men of education and force of character throughout the country, to supplement them. At the close of our civil war, lasting four years, some of our best corps and division generals, as well as staff-officers, were from civil life; but I cannot recall any of the most successful who did not express a regret that he had not received in early life instruction in the elementary principles of the art of war, instead of being forced to acquire this knowledge in the dangerous and expensive school of actual war.

But the real difficulty was, and will be again, to obtain an adequate number of good soldiers. We tried almost every system known to modern nations, all with more or less success—voluntary enlistments, the draft, and bought substitutes—and I think that all officers of experience will confirm my assertion that the men who voluntarily enlisted at the outbreak of the war were the best, better than the conscript, and far better than the bought substitute. When a regiment is once organized in a State, and mustered into the service of the United States, the officers and men become subject to the same laws of discipline and government as the regular troops. They are in no sense "militia," but compose a part of the Army of the United States, only retain their State title for convenience, and yet may be principally recruited from the neighborhood of their original organization. Once organized, the regiment should be kept full by recruits, and when it becomes difficult to obtain more recruits the pay should be raised by Congress, instead of tempting new men by exaggerated bounties. I believe it would have been more economical to have raised the pay of the soldier to thirty or even fifty dollars a month than to have held out the promise of three hundred and even six hundred dollars in the form of bounty. Toward the close of the war, I have often heard the soldiers complain that the "stay-at-home" men got better pay, bounties, and food, than they who were exposed to all the dangers and vicissitudes of the battles and marches at the front. The feeling of the soldier should be that, in every event, the sympathy and preference of his government is for him who fights, rather than for him who is on provost or guard duty to the rear, and, like most men, he measures this by the amount of pay. Of course, the soldier must be trained to obedience, and should be "content with his wages;"[5] but whoever has commanded an army in the field knows the difference between a willing, contented mass of men, and one that feels a cause of grievance. There is a soul to an army

[5] WTS referred to Luke 3:14: "And the soldiers likewise demanded of him, saying, And what shall we do? And he said unto them, Do violence to no man, neither accuse any falsely; and be content with your wages" (King James Version).

as well as to the individual man, and no general can accomplish the full work of his army unless he commands the soul of his men, as well as their bodies and legs.

The greatest mistake made in our civil war was in the mode of recruitment and promotion. When a regiment became reduced by the necessary wear and tear of service, instead of being filled up at the bottom, and the vacancies among the officers filled from the best non-commissioned officers and men, the habit was to raise new regiments, with new colonels, captains, and men, leaving the old and experienced battalions to dwindle away into mere skeleton organizations. I believe with the volunteers this matter was left to the States exclusively, and I remember that Wisconsin kept her regiments filled with recruits, whereas other States generally filled their quotas by new regiments, and the result was that we estimated a Wisconsin regiment equal to an ordinary brigade. I believe that five hundred new men added to an old and experienced regiment were more valuable than a thousand men in the form of a new regiment, for the former by association with good, experienced captains, lieutenants, and non-commissioned officers, soon became veterans, whereas the latter were generally unavailable for a year. The German method of recruitment is simply perfect, and there is no good reason why we should not follow it substantially.

On a road, marching by the flank, it would be considered "good order" to have five thousand men to a mile, so that a full corps of thirty thousand men would extend six miles, but with the average trains and batteries of artillery the probabilities are that it would draw out to ten miles. On a long and regular march the divisions and brigades should alternate in the lead, the leading division should be on the road by the earliest dawn, and march at the rate of about two miles, or, at most, two and a half miles an hour, so as to reach camp by noon. Even then the rear divisions and trains will hardly reach camp much before night. Theoretically, a marching column should preserve such order that by simply halting and facing to the right or left, it would be in line of battle; but this is rarely the case, and generally deployments are made "forward," by conducting each brigade by the flank obliquely to the right or left to its approximate position in line of battle, and there deployed. In such a line of battle, a brigade of three thousand infantry would occupy a mile of "front;" but for a strong line of battle five thousand men with two batteries should be allowed to each mile, or a division would habitually constitute a double line with skirmishers and a reserve on a mile of "front."

The "feeding" of an army is a matter of the most vital importance, and demands the earliest attention of the general intrusted with a campaign. To be strong, healthy, and capable of the largest measure of physical effort, the soldier needs about three pounds gross of food per day, and the horse or mule about twenty pounds. When a general first estimates the quantity of food and forage needed for an army of fifty or one hundred thousand men, he is apt to be dismayed, and here a good staff is indispensable, though the general cannot throw off on them the responsibility. He must give the subject his personal attention, for the army reposes in him alone, and should never doubt the fact that their existence overrides in importance all other considerations. Once satisfied of this, and that all has been done that can be, the soldiers are always willing to bear the largest measure of privation. Probably no army ever had a more varied experience in this regard than the one I commanded in 1864—'65.

Our base of supply was at Nashville, supplied by railways and the Cumberland River, thence by rail to Chattanooga, a "secondary base," and thence forward a single-track railroad. The stores came forward daily, but I endeavored to have on hand a full supply for twenty days in advance. These stores were habitually in the wagon-trains, distributed to corps, divisions, and regiments, in charge of experienced quartermasters and commissaries, and became subject to the orders of the generals commanding these bodies. They were generally issued on provision returns, but these had to be closely scrutinized, for too often the colonels would make requisitions for provisions for more men than they reported for battle. Of course, there are always a good many non-combatants with an army, but, after careful study, I limited their amount to twenty-five per cent. of the "effective strength," and that was found to be liberal. An ordinary army-wagon drawn by six mules may be counted on to carry three thousand pounds net, equal to the food of a full regiment for one day, but, by driving along beef-cattle, a commissary may safely count the contents of one wagon as sufficient for two days' food for a regiment of a thousand men; and as a corps should have food on hand for twenty days ready for detachment, it should have three hundred such wagons, as a provision-train; and for forage, ammunition, clothing, and other necessary stores, it was found necessary to have three hundred more wagons, or six hundred wagons in all, for a *corps d'armée.*

These should be absolutely under the immediate control of the corps commander, who will, however, find it economical to distribute them in due proportion to his divisions, brigades, and even regiments. Each regiment ought usually to have at least one wagon for convenience to distribute stores, and each company two pack-mules, so that the regiment may always be certain of a meal on reaching camp without waiting for the larger trains.

On long marches the artillery and wagon-trains should always have the right of way, and the troops should improvise roads to one side, unless forced to use a bridge in common, and all trains should have escorts to protect them, and to assist them in bad places. To this end there is nothing like actual experience, only, unless the officers in command give the subject their personal attention, they will find their wagon-trains loaded down with tents, personal baggage, and even the arms and knapsacks of the escort. Each soldier should, if not actually "sick or wounded," carry his musket and equipments containing from forty to sixty rounds of ammunition, his shelter-tent, a blanket or overcoat, and an extra pair of pants, socks, and drawers, in the form of a scarf, worn from the left shoulder to the right side in lieu of knapsack, and in his haversack he should carry some bread, cooked meat, salt, and coffee. I do not believe a soldier should be loaded down too much, but, including his clothing, arms, and equipment, he can carry about fifty pounds without impairing his health or activity. A simple calculation will show that by such a distribution a corps will thus carry the equivalent of five hundred wagon-loads—an immense relief to the trains.

Where an army is near one of our many large navigable rivers, or has the safe use of a railway, it can usually be supplied with the full army ration, which is by far the best furnished to any army in America or Europe; but when it is compelled to operate away from such a base, and is dependent on its own train of wagons, the commanding officer must exercise a wise discretion in the selection of his stores. In my opinion there is no better food for man than beef-cattle driven on the hoof, issued liberally, with salt, bacon, and bread. Coffee has also become almost indispensable, though many substitutes were found for it, such as Indian-corn, roasted, ground, and boiled as coffee; the sweet-potato, and the seed of the okra plant prepared in the same way. All these were used by the people of the South, who for years could procure no coffee, but I noticed that the women always begged of us some *real* coffee, which seems to satisfy a natural yearning or craving more powerful than can be accounted for on the theory of habit. Therefore I would always advise that the coffee and sugar ration be carried along, even at the expense of bread, for which there are many substitutes. Of these, Indian-corn is the best and most abundant. Parched in a frying-pan, it is excellent food, or if ground, or pounded and boiled with meat of any sort, it makes a most nutritious meal. The potato, both Irish and sweet, forms an excellent substitute for bread, and at Savannah we found the rice also suitable, both for men and animals. For the former it should be cleaned of its husk in a hominy block, easily prepared out of a log, and sifted with a coarse corn-bag; but for horses it should be fed in the straw. During the Atlanta campaign we were supplied by our regular commissaries with all sorts of patent compounds, such as desiccated vegetables, and concentrated milk, meat-biscuit, and sausages, but somehow the men preferred the simpler and more familiar forms of food, and usually styled these "desecrated vegetables and consecrated milk." We were also supplied liberally with lime-juice, sauerkraut, and pickles, as an antidote to scurvy, and I now recall the extreme anxiety of my medical director, Dr. Kittoe, about the scurvy, which he reported at one time as spreading and imperiling the army.[6] This occurred at a crisis about Kenesaw, when the railroad was taxed to its utmost capacity to provide the necessary ammunition, food, and forage, and could not possibly bring us an adequate supply of potatoes and cabbage, the usual antiscorbutics, when providentially the blackberries ripened and proved an admirable antidote, and I have known the skirmish-line, without orders, to fight a respectable battle for the possession of some old fields that were full of blackberries. Soon, thereafter, the green corn or roasting-ear came into season, and I heard no more of the scurvy. Our country abounds with plants which can be utilized for a prevention to the scurvy; besides the above are the persimmon, the sassafras root and bud, the wild-mustard, the "agave," turnip-tops, the dandelion cooked as greens, and a decoction of the ordinary pine-leaf.[7]

For the more delicate and costly articles of food for the sick we relied mostly on the agents of the Sanitary Commission. I do not wish to doubt the value of these organizations, which gained so much applause during our civil war, for no one can question the motives of these charitable and generous people; but to be honest I must record an opinion that the Sanitary Commission should limit its operations to the hospitals at the rear, and should never appear at the front. They were generally local in feeling, aimed to furnish their personal friends and neighbors with a better class of food than the Government supplied, and the consequence was, that one regiment of a brigade would receive potatoes and fruit which would be denied another regiment close by. Jealousy would be the inevitable result, and in an army all parts should be equal; there should be no "partiality, favor, or affection." The Government should supply all essential wants, and in the hospitals to the rear will

[6] In his post-battle report on the Atlanta Campaign, Kittoe wrote, "For more than four months on short rations, but poorly housed and badly clothed, with no appreciable variation in diet, scurvy naturally prevailed to some extent in most regiments; in all a marked tendency to this disease was observable, and at one time apprehensions were felt that very serious loss would occur from this cause." *OR,* I, 38(I), 117.

[7] British general Edward B. Hamley complimented WTS on his philosophy concerning troop and supply movements. See, E.B. Hamley to WTS, July 28, 1875, and F. E. Spinner to WTS, June 22, 1875, in Appendix to Volume II.

be found abundant opportunities for the exercise of all possible charity and generosity. During the war I several times gained the ill-will of the agents of the Sanitary Commission because I forbade their coming to the front unless they would consent to distribute their stores equally among all, regardless of the parties who had contributed them.

The sick, wounded, and dead of an army are the subjects of the greatest possible anxiety, and add an immense amount of labor to the well men. Each regiment in an active campaign should have a surgeon and two assistants always close at hand, and each brigade and division should have an experienced surgeon as a medical director. The great majority of wounds and of sickness should be treated by the regimental surgeon, on the ground, under the eye of the colonel. As few should be sent to the brigade or division hospital as possible, for the men always receive better care with their own regiment than with strangers, and as a rule the cure is more certain; but when men receive disabling wounds, or have sickness likely to become permanent, the sooner they go far to the rear the better for all. The tent or the shelter of a tree is a better hospital than a house, whose walls absorb fetid and poisonous emanations, and then give them back to the atmosphere. To men accustomed to the open air, who live on the plainest food, wounds seem to give less pain, and are attended with less danger to life than to ordinary soldiers in barracks.

Wounds which, in 1861, would have sent a man to the hospital for months, in 1865 were regarded as mere scratches, rather the subject of a joke than of sorrow. To new soldiers the sight of blood and death always has a sickening effect, but soon men become accustomed to it, and I have heard them exclaim on seeing a dead comrade borne to the rear, "Well, Bill has turned up *his* toes to the daisies." Of course, during a skirmish or battle, armed men should *never* leave their ranks to attend a dead or wounded comrade—this should be seen to in advance by the colonel, who should designate his musicians or company cooks as hospital attendants, with a white rag on their arm to indicate their office. A wounded man should go himself (if able) to the surgeon near at hand, or, if he need help, he should receive it from one of the attendants and not a comrade. It is wonderful how soon the men accustom themselves to these simple rules. In great battles these matters call for a more enlarged attention, and then it becomes the duty of the division general to see that proper stretchers and field-hospitals are ready for the wounded, and trenches are dug for the dead. There should be no real neglect of the dead, because it has a bad effect on the living; for each soldier values himself and comrade as highly as though he were living in a good house at home.

The regimental chaplain, if any, usually attends the burials from the hospital, should make notes and communicate details to the captain of the company, and to the family at home. Of course it is usually impossible to mark the grave with names, dates, etc., and consequently the names of the "unknown" in our national cemeteries equal about one-half of all the dead.

Very few of the battles in which I have participated were fought as described in European text-books, viz., in great masses, in perfect order, manœuvring by corps, divisions, and brigades. We were generally in a wooded country, and, though our lines were deployed according to tactics, the men generally fought in strong skirmish-lines, taking advantage of the shape of ground, and of every cover. We were generally the assailants, and in wooded and broken countries the "defensive" had a positive advantage over us, for they were always ready, had cover, and always knew the ground to their immediate front; whereas we, their assailants, had to grope our way over unknown ground, and generally found a cleared field or prepared entanglements that held us for a time under a close and withering fire. Rarely did the opposing lines in compact order come into actual contact, but when, as at Peach-Tree Creek and Atlanta, the lines did become commingled, the men fought individually in every possible style, more frequently with the musket clubbed than with the bayonet, and in some instances the men clinched like wrestlers, and went to the ground together. Europeans frequently criticised our war, because we did not always take full advantage of a victory; the true reason was, that habitually the woods served as a screen, and we often did not realize the fact that our enemy had retreated till he was already miles away and was again intrenched, having left a mere skirmish-line to cover the movement, in turn to fall back to the new position.

Our war was fought with the muzzle-loading rifle. Toward the close I had one brigade (Walcutt's) armed with breech-loading "Spencer's;" the cavalry generally had breach-loading carbines, "Spencer's" and "Sharp's," both of which were good arms.[8]

[8] In the winter of 1862, Charles C. Walcutt (1838–1898) requested Colt revolving rifles. "A quick answer came to me from General (George B.) Wright, which said he was unable to get the Colt revolving rifle, but suggested that he could get me a new gun called the Spencer repeating rifle musket, which he thought a better gun than the Colt, and would get them for me if I would send him a requisition. General William Sooy Smith and General McPherson joined me in the requisition. General Sherman signed it, but under protest, saying some fool contractor was trying to take advantage of the Government. But the guns were shipped al-

The only change that breech-loading arms will probably make in the art and practice of war will be to increase the amount of ammunition to be expended, and necessarily to be carried along; to still further "thin out" the lines of attack, and to reduce battles to short, quick, decisive conflicts. It does not in the least affect the grand strategy, or the necessity for perfect organization, drill, and discipline. The companies and battalions will be more dispersed, and the men will be less under the immediate eye of their officers, and therefore a higher order of intelligence and courage on the part of the individual soldier will be an element of strength.

When a regiment is deployed as skirmishers, and crosses an open field or woods, under heavy fire, if each man runs forward from tree to tree, or stump to stump, and yet preserves a good general alignment, it gives great confidence to the men themselves, for they always keep their eyes well to the right and left, and watch their comrades; but when some few hold back, stick too close or too long to a comfortable log, it often stops the line and defeats the whole object. Therefore, the more we improve the fire-arm the more will be the necessity for good organization, good discipline and intelligence on the part of the individual soldier and officer. There is, of course, such a thing as individual courage, which has a value in war, but familiarity with danger, experience in war and its common attendants, and personal habit, are equally valuable traits, and these are the qualities with which we usually have to deal in war. All men naturally shrink from pain and danger, and only incur their risk from some higher motive, or from habit; so that I would define true courage to be a perfect sensibility of the measure of danger, and a mental willingness to incur it, rather than that insensibility to danger of which I have heard far more than I have seen. The most courageous men are generally unconscious of possessing the quality; therefore, when one professes it too openly, by words or bearing, there is reason to mistrust it. I would further illustrate my meaning by describing a man of true courage to be one who possesses all his faculties and senses perfectly when serious danger is actually present.

Modern wars have not materially changed the relative values or proportions of the several arms of service: infantry, artillery, cavalry, and engineers. If any thing, the infantry has been increased in value. The danger of cavalry attempting to charge infantry armed with breech-loading rifles was fully il-

---

though by this time we were dismounted . . . the guns followed us but did not reach us until we arrived at Chattanooga on return from Knoxville, where we had gone to the relief of General Burnside." Alfred E. Lee, *History of the City of Columbus: Capital of Ohio* (New York: Munsell, 1892), 182.

lustrated at Sedan, and with us very frequently.[9] So improbable has such a thing become that we have omitted the infantry-square from our recent tactics. Still, cavalry against cavalry, and as auxiliary to infantry, will always be valuable, while all great wars will, as heretofore, depend chiefly on the infantry. Artillery is more valuable with new and inexperienced troops than with veterans. In the early stages of the war the field-guns often bore the proportion of six to a thousand men; but toward the close of the war one gun, or at most two, to a thousand men, was deemed enough. Sieges, such as characterized the wars of the last century, are too slow for this period of the world, and the Prussians recently almost ignored them altogether, penetrated France between the forts, and left a superior force "in observation," to watch the garrison and accept its surrender when the greater events of the war ahead made further resistance useless; but earth-forts, and especially field-works, will hereafter play an important part in wars, because they enable a minor force to hold a superior one in check for a *time,* and time is a most valuable element in all wars. It was one of Prof. Mahan's maxims that the spade was as useful in war as the musket,[10] and to this I will add the axe. The habit of intrenching certainly does have the effect of making new troops timid. When a line of battle is once covered by a good parapet, made by the engineers or by the labor of the men themselves, it does require an effort to make them leave it in the face of danger; but when the enemy is intrenched, it becomes absolutely necessary to permit each brigade and division of the troops immediately opposed to throw up a corresponding trench for their own protection in case of a sudden sally. We invariably did this in all our recent campaigns, and it had no ill effect, though sometimes our troops were a little too slow in leaving their well-covered lines to assail the enemy in position or on retreat. Even our skirmishers were in the habit of rolling logs together, or of making a lunette of rails, with dirt in front, to cover their bodies; and, though it revealed their position, I cannot say that it worked a bad effect; so that, as a rule, it may safely be left to the men themselves. On the "defensive," there is no doubt of the propriety of fortifying; but in the assailing army the general must watch

[9] The Battle of Sedan occurred in northeastern France during the Franco-Prussian War in 1870. *The Encyclopedia Britannica: A Dictionary of Arts, Sciences, Literature and General Information,* 11th ed. (New York: Encyclopedia Britannica, 1911), vol. 2, s.v. "Sedan."

[10] Dennis Mahan, a professor of engineering at the USMA from 1830 to 1871, was quoted as saying that the "spade, implementing the terrain, went hand in hand with rifle and bayonet." Thomas L. Connelly and Archer Jones, *The Politics of Command: Factions and Ideas in Confederate Strategy* (Baton Rouge: LSU Press, 1973), 25.

closely to see that his men do not neglect an opportunity to drop his precautionary defenses, and act promptly on the "offensive" at every chance.

I have many a time crept forward to the skirmish-line to avail myself of the cover of the pickets' "little fort," to observe more closely some expected result; and always talked familiarly with the men, and was astonished to see how well they comprehended the general object, and how accurately they were informed of the state of facts existing miles away from their particular corps. Soldiers are very quick to catch the general drift and purpose of a campaign, and are always sensible when they are well commanded or well cared for. Once impressed with this fact, and that they are making progress, they bear cheerfully any amount of labor and privation.

In camp, and especially in the presence of an active enemy, it is much easier to maintain discipline than in barracks in time of peace. Crime and breaches of discipline are much less frequent, and the necessity for courts-martial far less. The captain can usually inflict all the punishment necessary, and the colonel *should* always. The field-officers' court is the best form for war, viz., one of the field-officers—the lieutenant-colonel or major—can examine the case and report his verdict, and the colonel should execute it. Of course, there are statutory offenses which demand a general court-martial, and these must be ordered by the division or corps commander; but the presence of one of our regular civilian judge-advocates in an army in the field would be a first-class nuisance, for technical courts always work mischief. Too many courts-martial in any command are evidence of poor discipline and inefficient officers.

For the rapid transmission of orders in an army covering a large space of ground, the magnetic telegraph is by far the best, though habitually the paper and pencil, with good mounted orderlies, answer every purpose. I have little faith in the signal-service by flags and torches, though we always used them; because, almost invariably when they were most needed, the view was cut off by intervening trees, or by mists and fogs. There was one notable instance in my experience, when the signal-flags carried a message of vital importance over the heads of Hood's army, which had interposed between me and Allatoona, and had broken the telegraph-wires—as recorded in Chapter XIX.; but the value of the magnetic telegraph in war cannot be exaggerated, as was illustrated by the perfect concert of action between the armies in Virginia and Georgia during 1864. Hardly a day intervened when General Grant did not know the exact state of facts with me, more than fifteen hundred miles away as the wires ran. So on the field a thin insulated wire may be run on improvised stakes or from tree to tree for six or more miles in a couple of hours, and I have seen operators so skillful, that by cutting the wire they would receive a message with their tongues from a distant station. As a matter of course, the ordinary commercial wires along the railways form the usual telegraph-lines for an army, and these are easily repaired and extended as the army advances, but each army and wing should have a small party of skilled men to put up the field-wire, and take it down when done. This is far better than the signal-flags and torches. Our commercial telegraph-lines will always supply for war enough skillful operators.

The value of railways is also fully recognized in war quite as much as, if not more so than, in peace. The Atlanta campaign would simply have been impossible without the use of the railroads from Louisville to Nashville—one hundred and eighty-five miles—from Nashville to Chattanooga—one hundred and fifty-one miles—and from Chattanooga to Atlanta—one hundred and thirty-seven miles. Every mile of this "single track" was so delicate, that one man could in a minute have broken or moved a rail, but our trains usually carried along the tools and means to repair such a break. We had, however, to maintain strong guards and garrisons at each important bridge or trestle—the destruction of which would have necessitated time for rebuilding. For the protection of a bridge, one or two log block-houses, two stories high, with a piece of ordnance and a small infantry guard, usually sufficed. The block-house had a small parapet and ditch about it, and the roof was made shot-proof by earth piled on. These points could usually be reached only by a dash of the enemy's cavalry, and many of these block-houses successfully resisted serious attacks by both cavalry and artillery. The only block-house that was actually captured on the main was the one described near Allatoona.[11]

Our trains from Nashville forward were operated under military rules, and ran about ten miles an hour in gangs of four trains of ten cars each. Four such groups of trains daily made one hundred and sixty cars, of ten tons each, carrying sixteen hundred tons, which exceeded the absolute necessity of the army, and allowed for the accidents that were common and inevitable. But, as I have recorded, that single stem of railroad, four hundred and seventy-three miles long, supplied an army of one hundred thousand men and thirty-five thousand animals for the period of one hundred and ninety-six days, viz., from May 1 to November 12, 1864. To have delivered regularly that amount of food and forage by ordinary wagons would have required thirty-six thousand eight hundred wagons of six mules each, allowing each wagon to have hauled two tons twenty miles each day, a simple impossibility in roads such as then existed in that region of country. Therefore, I reiterate that the Atlanta campaign

[11] See Chapter 20.

was an impossibility without these railroads; and only then, because we had the men and means to maintain and defend them, in addition to what were necessary to overcome the enemy. Habitually, a passenger-car will carry fifty men with their necessary baggage. Box-cars, and even platform-cars, answer the purpose well enough, but they should always have rough board-seats. For sick and wounded men, box-cars filled with straw or bushes were usually employed. Personally, I saw but little of the practical working of the railroads, for I only turned back once as far as Resaca; but I had daily reports from the engineer in charge, and officers who came from the rear often explained to me the whole thing, with a description of the wrecked trains all the way from Nashville to Atlanta. I am convinced that the risk to life to the engineers and men on that railroad fully equaled that on the skirmish-line, called for as high an order of courage, and fully equaled it in importance. Still, I doubt if there be any necessity in time of peace to organize a corps specially to work the military railroads in time of war, because in peace these same men gain all the necessary experience, possess all the daring and courage of soldiers, and only need the occasional protection and assistance of the necessary train-guard, which may be composed of the furloughed men coming and going, or of details made from the local garrisons to the rear.

For the transfer of large armies by rail, from one theatre of action to another by the rear—the cases of the transfer of the Eleventh and Twelfth Corps—General Hooker, twenty-three thousand men—from the East to Chattanooga, eleven hundred and ninety-two miles in seven days, in the fall of 1863; and that of the Army of the Ohio—General Schofield, fifteen thousand men—from the valley of the Tennessee to Washington, fourteen hundred miles in eleven days, *en route* to North Carolina in January, 1865, are the best examples of which I have any knowledge, and reference to these is made in the report of the Secretary of War, Mr. Stanton, dated November 22, 1865.[12]

Engineer troops attached to an army are habitually employed in supervising the construction of forts or field works of a nature more permanent than the lines used by the troops in motion, and in repairing roads and making bridges. I had several regiments of this kind that were most useful, but as a rule we used the infantry, or employed parties of freedmen, who worked on the trenches at night while the soldiers slept, and these in turn rested by day. Habitually the repair of the railroad and its bridges was committed to hired laborers, like the English navvies, under the supervision of

[12] See Edwin M. Stanton, *Annual Report of the Secretary of War* (Washington, DC: GPO, 1866), 1:87, 214.

Colonel W. W. Wright, a railroad-engineer, who was in the military service at the time, and his successful labors were frequently referred to in the official reports of the campaign.[13]

For the passage of rivers, each army corps had a pontoon-train with a detachment of engineers, and, on reaching a river, the leading infantry division was charged with the labor of putting it down. Generally the single pontoon-train could provide for nine hundred feet of bridge, which sufficed; but when the rivers were very wide two such trains would be brought together, or the single train was supplemented by a trestle-bridge, or bridges made on crib-work, out of timber found near the place. The pontoons in general use were skeleton frames, made with a hinge, so as to fold back and constitute a wagon-body. In this same wagon were carried the cotton canvas cover, the anchor and chains, and a due proportion of the balks, chesses, and lashings. All the troops became very familiar with their mechanism and use, and we were rarely delayed by reason of a river, however broad. I saw, recently, in Aldershot, England, a very complete pontoon-train; the boats were sheathed with wood and felt, made very light; but I think these were more liable to chafing and damage in rough handling than were our less expensive and rougher boats.[14] On the whole, I would prefer the skeleton frame and canvas cover to any style of pontoon that I have ever seen.

In relation to guards, pickets, and vedettes, I doubt if any discoveries or improvements were made during our war, or in any of the modern wars in Europe. These precautions vary with the nature of the country and the situation of each army. When advancing or retreating in line of battle, the usual skirmish-line constitutes the picket-line, and may have "reserves," but usually the main line of battle constitutes the reserve; and in this connection I will state that the recent innovation introduced into the new infantry tactics by General Upton is

[13] In his report on the Carolinas campaign, WTS wrote that "such industry displayed in the railroad management by Generals Easton and Beckwith and Colonel Wright and Mr. Van Dyne, that by the 11th of April our men were all reclad, the wagons reloaded, and a fair amount of forage accumulated ahead." *OR,* I, 47(I), 29.

[14] WTS visited a military camp in Aldershot, England, in 1871. According to one witness, Sir Hope Grant, WTS was "as vivacious and active as a young man of twenty-five, and in the most business-like way peered into every corner of the camp . . . At the conclusion of his visit he was entertained at luncheon by the Queen's Bays, and conducted to the railway station in their splendidly turned out drag and team. He wrote a letter warmly thanking them for driving him about in their fine 'truck.'" Hope Grant, *Life of General Sir Hope Grant with Selections from his Correspondence,* ed. Henry Knollys (Edinburgh: William Blackwood, 1894), 2:295–296.

admirable, for by it each regiment, brigade, and division deployed, sends forward as "skirmishers" the one man of each set of fours, to cover its own front, and these can be recalled or reënforced at pleasure by the bugle-signal.[15]

For flank-guards and rear-guards, one or more companies should be detached under their own officers, instead of making up the guard by detailing men from the several companies.

For regimental or camp guards, the details should be made according to existing army regulations; and all the guards should be posted early in the evening, so as to afford each sentinel or vedette a chance to study his ground before it becomes too dark.

In like manner as to the staff. The more intimately it comes into contact with the troops, the more useful and valuable it becomes. The almost entire separation of the staff from the line, as now practised by us, and hitherto by the French, has proved mischievous, and the great retinues of staff-officers with which some of our earlier generals began the war were simply ridiculous. I don't believe in a chief of staff at all, and any general commanding an army, corps, or division, that has a staff-officer who professes to know more than his chief, is to be pitied. Each regiment should have a competent adjutant, quartermaster, and commissary, with two or three medical officers. Each brigade commander should have the same staff, with the addition of a couple of young aides-de-camp, habitually selected from the subalterns of the brigade, who should be good riders, and intelligent enough to give and explain the orders of their general.

The same staff will answer for a division. The general in command of a separate army, and of a *corps d'armée,* should have the same professional assistance, with two or more good engineers, and his adjutant-general should exercise all the functions usually ascribed to a chief of staff, viz., he should possess the ability to comprehend the scope of operations, and to make verbally and in writing all the orders and details necessary to carry into effect the views of his general, as well as to keep the returns and records of events for the information of the next higher authority, and for history. A bulky staff implies a division of responsibility, slowness of action, and indecision, whereas a small staff implies activity and concentration of purpose. The smallness of General Grant's staff throughout the civil war forms the best model for future imita-

[15] Emory Upton (1839–1881) graduated from the USMA in 1861 and was promoted to major general in the U.S. Army in Mar. 1865. In 1867 he published *A New System of Infantry Tactics, Double and Single Rank, Adapted to American Topography and Improved Fire-Arms.* For Upton's response to WTS's comments regarding his military innovations, see E. Upton to WTS, May 29, 1875, in Appendix to Volume II; *CWHC,* 540.

tion. So of tents, officers' furniture, etc., etc. In real war these should all be discarded, and an army is efficient for action and motion exactly in the inverse ratio of its *impedimenta.* Tents should be omitted altogether, save one to a regiment for an office, and a few for the division hospital. Officers should be content with a tent fly, improvising poles and shelter out of bushes. The *tente d'abri,* or shelter-tent, carried by the soldier himself, is all-sufficient. Officers should never seek for houses, but share the condition of their men.

A recent message (July 18, 1874) made to the French Assembly by Marshal MacMahon, President of the French Republic,[16] submits a *projet de loi,* with a report prepared by a board of French generals on "army administration," which is full of information, and is as applicable to us as to the French. I quote from its very beginning: "The misfortunes of the campaign of 1870 have demonstrated the inferiority of our system. . . . Two separate organizations existed with parallel functions—the 'general' more occupied in giving direction to his troops than in providing for their material wants, which he regarded as the special province of the staff, and the 'intendant' (staff) often working at random, taking on his shoulders a crushing burden of functions and duties, exhausting himself with useless efforts, and aiming to accomplish an insufficient service, to the disappointment of everybody. This separation of the administration and command, this coexistence of two wills, each independent of the other, which paralyzed both and annulled the dualism," was condemned. It was decided by the board that this error should be "proscribed" in the new military system. The report then goes on at great length discussing the provisions of the "new law," which is described to be a radical change from the old one on the same subject. While conceding to the Minister of War in Paris the general control and supervision of the entire military establishment primarily, especially of the annual estimates or budget, and the great depots of supply, it distributes to the commanders of the *corps d'armée* in time of peace, and to all army commanders generally in time of war, the absolute command of the money, provisions, and stores, with the necessary staff-officers to receive, issue, and account for them. I quote further: "The object of this law is to confer on the commander of troops whatever liberty of action the case demands. He has the power even to go beyond the regulations, in circumstances of urgency and pressing necessity. The extraordinary measures he may take on these occasions may require their execution without delay. The staff-officer has but one duty

[16] Patrice de MacMahon (1808–1893) was president of the French Republic from 1873 to 1879. Charles Johnston and Carita Spencer, *Ireland's Story* (Boston: Houghton Mifflin, 1923), 342–343.

before obeying, and that is to submit his observations to the general, and to ask his orders in writing. With this formality his responsibility ceases, and the responsibility for the extraordinary act falls solely on the general who gives the order. The officers and agents charged with supplies are placed under the orders of the general in command of the troops, that is, they are obliged both in war and peace to obey, with the single qualification above named, of first making their observations and securing the written order of the general."

With us, to-day, the law and regulations are that, no matter what may be the emergency, the commanding general in Texas, New Mexico, and the remote frontiers, cannot draw from the arsenals a pistol-cartridge, or any sort of ordnance-stores, without first procuring an order of the Secretary of War in Washington. The commanding general—though intrusted with the lives of his soldiers and with the safety of a frontier in a condition of chronic war—cannot touch or be trusted with ordnance-stores or property, and that is declared to be the law! Every officer of the old army remembers how, in 1861, we were hampered with the old blue army-regulations, which tied our hands, and that to do any thing positive and necessary we had to tear it all to pieces—cut the red-tape, as it was called—a dangerous thing for an army to do, for it was calculated to bring the law and authority into contempt; but war was upon us, and overwhelming necessity overrides all law.

This French report is well worth the study of our army-officers, of all grades and classes, and I will only refer again, casually, to another part, wherein it discusses the subject of military correspondence: whether the staff-officer should correspond directly with his chief in Paris, submitting to his general copies, or whether he should be required to carry on his correspondence through his general, so that the latter could promptly forward the communication, indorsed with his own remarks and opinions. The latter is declared by the board to be the only safe role, because "the general should never be ignorant of any thing that is transpiring that concerns his command."

In this country, as in France, Congress controls the great questions of war and peace, makes all laws for the creation and government of armies, and votes the necessary supplies, leaving to the President to execute and apply these laws, especially the harder task of limiting the expenditure of public money to the amount of the annual appropriations. The executive power is further subdivided into the seven great departments, and to the Secretary of War is confided the general care of the military establishment, and his powers are further subdivided into ten distinct and separate bureaus.

The chiefs of these bureaus are under the immediate orders of the Secretary of War, who, through them, in fact commands the army from "his office," but cannot do so "in the field"—an absurdity in military if not civil law.

The subordinates of these staff-corps and departments are selected and chosen from the army itself, or fresh from West Point, and too commonly construe themselves into the *élite,* as made of better clay than the common soldier. Thus they separate themselves more and more from their comrades of the line, and in process of time realize the condition of that old officer of artillery who thought the army would be a delightful place for a gentleman if it were not for the d——d soldier; or, better still, the conclusion of the young lord in "Henry IV.," who told Harry Percy (Hotspur) that "but for these vile guns he would himself have been a soldier."[17] This is all wrong; utterly at variance with our democratic form of government and of universal experience; and now that the French, from whom we had copied the system, have utterly "proscribed" it, I hope that our Congress will follow suit. I admit, in its fullest force, the strength of the maxim that the civil law should be superior to the military in time of peace; that the army should be at all times subject to the direct control of Congress; and I assert that, from the formation of our Government to the present day, the Regular Army has set the highest example of obedience to law and authority; but, for the very reason that our army is comparatively so very small, I hold that it should be the best possible, organized and governed on true military principles, and that in time of peace we should preserve the "habits and usages of war," so that, when war does come, we may not again be compelled to suffer the disgrace, confusion, and disorder of 1861.

The commanding officers of divisions, departments, and posts, should have the amplest powers, not only to command their troops, but all the stores designed for their use, and the officers of the staff necessary to administer them, within the area of their command; and then with fairness they could be held to the most perfect responsibility. The President and Secretary of War can command the army quite as well through these generals as through the subordinate staff-officers. Of course, the Secretary would, as now, distribute the funds according to the appropriation bills, and reserve to himself the absolute control and supervision of the larger arsenals and depots of supply. The error lies in the law, or in the judicial interpretation thereof, and no code of army regulations can be made that meets the case, until Congress, like the French *Corps Législatif,* utterly annihilates and "proscribes" the old law and the system which has grown up under it.[18]

[17] This is an allusion to Shakespeare's play *Henry IV, Part 1.* The young lord mentioned by WTS was a privileged courtier. For the full context of the quote, see Shakespeare, *Henry IV, Part 1,* act 1, scene 3.

[18] British colonel Charles C. Chesney complimented WTS on his remarks concerning Europeans and warfare. See C. C. Chesney to WTS, Dec. 25, 1875, in Appendix to Volume II.

It is related of Napoleon that his last words were, "Tête d'armée!"[19] Doubtless, as the shadow of death obscured his memory, the last thought that remained for speech was of some event when he was directing an important "head of column." I believe that every general who has handled armies in battle must recall from his own experience the intensity of thought on some similar occasion, when by a single command he had given the finishing stroke to some complicated action; but to me recurs another thought that is worthy of record, and may encourage others who are to follow us in our profession. I never saw the rear of an army engaged in battle but I feared that some calamity had happened at the front—the apparent confusion, broken wagons, crippled horses, men lying about dead and maimed, parties hastening to and fro in seeming disorder, and a general apprehension of something dreadful about to ensue; all these signs, however, lessened as I neared the front, and there the contrast was complete—perfect order, men and horses full of confidence, and it was not unusual for general hilarity, laughing, and cheering. Although cannon might be firing, the musketry clattering, and the enemy's shot hitting close, there reigned a general feeling of strength and security that bore a marked contrast to the bloody signs that had drifted rapidly to the rear; therefore, for comfort and safety, I surely would rather be at the front than the rear line of battle. So also on the march, the head of a column moves on steadily, while the rear is alternately halting and then rushing forward to close up the gap; and all sorts of rumors, especially the worst, float back to the rear. Old troops invariably deem it a special privilege to be in the front—to be at the "head of column"—because experience has taught them that it is the easiest and most comfortable place, and danger only adds zest and stimulus to this fact.

The hardest task in war is to lie in support of some position or battery, under fire without the privilege of returning it; or to guard some train left in the rear, within hearing but out of danger; or to provide for the wounded and dead of some corps which is too busy ahead to care for its own.

To be at the head of a strong column of troops, in the execution of some task that requires brain, is the highest pleasure of war—a grim one and terrible, but which leaves on the mind and memory the strongest mark; to detect the weak point of an enemy's line; to break through with vehemence and thus lead to victory; or to discover some key-point and hold it with tenacity;

[19] Napoleon Bonaparte (1769–1821) was the emperor of France 1804–1815. His alleged last words were memorialized in the poem *The Death-Bed of Napoleon.* William J. Hillis, *A Metrical History of the Life and Times of Napoleon Bonaparte* (New York: G. P. Putnam's Sons, 1896), 3, 164, 487–490.

or to do some other distinct act which is afterward recognized as the real cause of success. These all become matters that are never forgotten. Other great difficulties, experienced by every general, are to measure truly the thousand-and-one reports that come to him in the midst of conflict; to preserve a clear and well-defined purpose at every instant of time, and to cause all efforts to converge to that end.

To do these things he must know perfectly the strength and quality of each part of his own army, as well as that of his opponent, and must be where he can personally see and observe with his own eyes, and judge with his own mind. No man can properly command an army from the rear, he must be "at its front;" and when a detachment is made, the commander thereof should be informed of the object to be accomplished, and left as free as possible to execute it in his own way; and when an army is divided up into several parts, the superior should always attend that one which he regards as most important. Some men think that modern armies may be so regulated that a general can sit in an office and play on his several columns as on the keys of a piano; this is a fearful mistake. The directing mind must be at the very head of the army—must be seen there, and the effect of his mind and personal energy must be felt by every officer and man present with it, to secure the best results. Every attempt to make war easy and safe will result in humiliation and disaster.

Lastly, mail facilities should be kept up with an army if possible, that officers and men may receive and send letters to their friends, thus maintaining the home influence of infinite assistance to discipline. Newspaper correspondents with an army, as a rule, are mischievous. They are the world's gossips, pick up and retail the camp scandal, and gradually drift to the headquarters of some general, who finds it easier to make reputation at home than with his own corps or division. They are also tempted to prophesy events and state facts which, to an enemy, reveal a purpose in time to guard against it. Moreover, they are always bound to see facts colored by the partisan or political character of their own patrons, and thus bring army officers into the political controversies of the day, which are always mischievous and wrong. Yet, so greedy are the people at large for war news, that it is doubtful whether any army commander can exclude all reporters, without bringing down on himself a clamor that may imperil his own safety. Time and moderation must bring a just solution to this modern difficulty.[20]

[20] U.S. Army general Albert M. Winn complimented WTS on his opinions of newspaper correspondents. See A. M. Winn to WTS, Dec. 15, 1880, in Appendix to Volume II.

26

After the War.

In the foregoing pages I have endeavored to describe the public events in which I was an actor or spectator before and during the civil war of 1861–'65, and it now only remains for me to treat of similar matters of general interest subsequent to the civil war. Within a few days of the grand review of May 24, 1865, I took leave of the army at Washington, and with my family went to Chicago to attend a fair held in the interest of the families of soldiers impoverished by the war.[1] I remained there about two weeks; on the 22d of June was at South Bend, Indiana, where two of my children were at school, and reached my native place, Lancaster, Ohio, on the 24th. On the 4th of July I visited at Louisville, Kentucky, the Fourteenth, Fifteenth, Sixteenth, and Seventeenth Army Corps, which had come from Washington, under the command of General John A. Logan, for "muster out," or "further orders." I then made a short visit to General George H. Thomas at Nashville, and returned to Lancaster, where I remained with the family till the receipt of General Orders No. 118 of June 27, 1865, which divided the whole territory of the United States into nineteen departments and five military divisions, the second of which was the military division of the "Mississippi," afterward changed to "Missouri," Major-General W. T. Sherman to command, with headquarters at St. Louis, to embrace the Departments of the Ohio, Missouri, and Arkansas.[2]

This chapter was not included in the first edition of WTS's *Memoirs* (1875). It was added to the second edition (1886) as the new closing chapter.

[1] WTS attended the Northwestern Sanitary Fair in June 1865. According to an eyewitness, "A great crowd gathered in the streets and called the General out and insisted on him making a speech. He came out on the balcony and said, 'No, if you want to hear me speak, contribute to the Fair, pay your entrance fee and come inside.' An army of people could not take General Sherman by surprise, even at a fair." Myra Bradwell, "General William Tecumseh Sherman," *Chicago Legal News: A Journal of Legal Intelligence* 23 (Feb. 21, 1891): 209.

[2] See *OR,* I, 46(III), 1298–1299.

This territorial command included the States north of the Ohio River, and the States and Territories north of Texas, as far west as the Rocky Mountains, including Montana, Utah, and New Mexico, but the part east of the Mississippi was soon transferred to another division. The department commanders were General E. O. C. Ord, at Detroit; General John Pope, at Fort Leavenworth; and General J. J. Reynolds,[3] at Little Rock, but these also were soon changed. I at once assumed command, and ordered my staff and headquarters from Washington to St. Louis, Missouri, going there in person on the 16th of July.

My thoughts and feelings at once reverted to the construction of the great Pacific Railway, which had been chartered by Congress in the midst of war, and was then in progress.[4] I put myself in communication with the parties engaged in the work, visiting them in person, and assured them that I would afford them all possible assistance and encouragement. Dr. Durant, the leading man of the Union Pacific,[5] seemed to me a person of ardent nature, of great ability and energy, enthusiastic in his undertaking, and determined to build the road from Omaha to San Francisco. He had an able corps of assistants, collecting materials, letting out contracts for ties, grading, etc., and I attended the celebration of the first completed division of sixteen and a half miles, from Omaha to Papillon. When the orators spoke so confidently of the determination to build two thousand miles of railway across the plains, mountains, and desert, devoid of timber, with no population, but on the contrary raided by the bold and bloody Sioux and Cheyennes, who had almost successfully defied our power for half a century, I was disposed to treat it jocularly, because I could not help recall our California experience of 1855–'56, when we celebrated the completion of twenty-two and a half miles of the same road eastward of Sacramento; on which occasion Edward Baker had electrified us by his unequalled oratory, painting the glorious things which would result from uniting the Western coast with the East by bands of iron. Baker then, with a poet's imagination, saw the vision of the mighty future, but not the gulf which meantime was destined to swallow up half a million of

[3] Joseph J. Reynolds (1822–1900) graduated from the USMA in 1843 and was in command of the Dept. of Arkansas from Dec. 1864 to Aug. 1865. *CWHC,* 451.

[4] Pres. Lincoln signed the Pacific Railway Act on July 1, 1862, authorizing the construction of a transcontinental railroad. Lawrence Ostresh and Jerry Hansen, *Images of Rail: Laramie Railroads* (Charleston, SC: Arcadia, 2014), 9.

[5] Thomas C. Durant (1820–1885), a graduate of Albany Medical College, was vice president of Union Pacific Railroad when the first transcontinental railroad was completed in 1869. Peter C. Holloran, *Historical Dictionary of New England,* 2nd ed. (Lanham, MD: Rowman and Littlefield, 2017), s.v. "Durant, Thomas C."

the brightest and best youth of our land, and that he himself would be one of the first victims far away on the banks of the Potomac (he was killed in battle at Balls Bluff, October 21, 1861).

The Kansas Pacific was designed to unite with the main branch about the 100° meridian, near Fort Kearney.[6] Mr. Shoemaker was its general superintendent and building contractor,[7] and this branch in 1865 was finished about forty miles to a point near Lawrence, Kansas. I may not be able to refer to these roads again except incidentally, and will, therefore, record here that the location of this branch afterward was changed from the Republican to the Smoky Hill Fork of the Kansas River, and is now the main line to Denver. The Union and Central Railroads from the beginning were pushed with a skill, vigor, and courage which always commanded my admiration, the two meeting at Promontory Point, Utah, July 15, 1869, and in my judgment constitute one of the greatest and most beneficent achievements of man on earth.

The construction of the Union Pacific Railroad was deemed so important that the President, at my suggestion, constituted on the 5th of March, 1866, the new Department of the Platte, General P. St. George Cooke commanding, succeeded by General C. C. Augur, headquarters at Omaha,[8] with orders to give ample protection to the working-parties, and to afford every possible assistance in the construction of the road; and subsequently in like manner the Department of Dakota was constituted, General A. H. Terry commanding, with headquarters at St. Paul, to give similar protection and encouragement to the Northern Pacific Railroad. These departments, with changed commanders, have continued up to the present day, and have fulfilled perfectly the uses for which they were designed.

During the years 1865 and 1866 the great plains remained almost in a state of nature, being the pasture-fields of about ten million buffalo, deer, elk, and

[6] Fort Kearny was constructed in 1848 approximately forty miles southwest of Grand Island, NE. The fort was named after Col. Stephen W. Kearny. It remained in operation until 1877. David Dary, *The Oregon Trail: An American Saga* (New York: Random House, 2004), 340.

[7] Robert M. Shoemaker (1815–1885) was superintendent and chief engineer of Union Pacific Railroad's eastern division. *Message of the President of the United States, and Accompanying Documents to the Two Houses of Congress at the Commencement of the First Session of the Thirty-Ninth Congress* (Washington, DC: GPO, 1865), 965; "The Condenser," *Lima News* (Lima, OH), Feb. 11, 1885, 1.

[8] Christopher C. Augur (1821–1898) graduated from the USMA in 1843 and reached the rank of major general during the Civil War. He commanded the Dept. of the Platte from 1865 to 1867. *CWHC*, 109.

antelope, and were in full possession of the Sioux, Cheyennes, Arapahoes, and Kiowas, a race of bold Indians, who saw plainly that the construction of two parallel railroads right through their country would prove destructive to the game on which they subsisted, and consequently fatal to themselves.[9]

The troops were posted to the best advantage to protect the parties engaged in building these roads, and in person I reconnoitred well to the front, traversing the buffalo regions from south to north, and from east to west, often with a very small escort, mingling with the Indians whenever safe, and thereby gained personal knowledge of matters which enabled me to use the troops to the best advantage. I am sure that without the courage and activity of the department commanders with the small bodies of regular troops on the plains during the years 1866–'69, the Pacific Railroads could not have been built; but once built and in full operation the fate of the buffalo and Indian was settled for all time to come.

At the close of the civil war there were one million five hundred and sixteen names on the muster-rolls, of which seven hundred and ninety-seven thousand eight hundred and seven were present, and two hundred and two thousand seven hundred and nine absent, of which twenty-two thousand nine hundred and twenty-nine were regulars, the others were volunteers, colored troops, and veteran reserves. The regulars consisted of six regiments of cavalry, five of artillery, and nineteen of infantry. By the act of July 28, 1866, the peace establishment was fixed at one general (Grant), one lieutenant-general (Sherman), five major-generals (Halleck, Meade, Sheridan, Thomas, and Hancock), ten brigadiers (McDowell, Cooke, Pope, Hooker, Schofield, Howard, Terry, Ord, Canby, and Rousseau), ten regiments of cavalry, five of artillery, and forty-five of infantry, admitting of an aggregate force of fifty-four thousand six hundred and forty-one men.[10]

All others were mustered out, and thus were remanded to their homes nearly a million of strong, vigorous men who had imbibed the somewhat erratic habits of the soldier; these were of every profession and trade in life,

[9] In a letter to his brother dated June 17, 1868, WTS wrote that "it will not be long before all the buffaloes are extinct near and between the railroads." By 1883 the bison population of the Great Plains had been effectively eradicated by white hunters and travelers. Andrew C. Isenberg, *The Destruction of the Bison: An Environmental History, 1750–1920* (Cambridge: Cambridge University Press, 2000), 128.

[10] The Army Reorganization Act of 1866 established the first Black regiments in the regular army. *The Oxford Essential Dictionary of the U.S. Military* (Oxford: Oxford University Press, 2001), s.v. "Army Reorganization Act."

who, on regaining their homes, found their places occupied by others, that their friends and neighbors were different, and that they themselves had changed. They naturally looked for new homes to the great West, to the new Territories and States as far as the Pacific coast, and we realize to-day that the vigorous men who control Kansas, Nebraska, Dakota, Montana, Colorado, etc., etc., were soldiers of the civil war. These men flocked to the plains, and were rather stimulated than retarded by the danger of an Indian war. This was another potent agency in producing the result we enjoy to-day, in having in so short a time replaced the wild buffaloes by more numerous herds of tame cattle, and by substituting for the useless Indians the intelligent owners of productive farms and cattle-ranches.[11]

While these great changes were being wrought at the West, in the East politics had resumed full sway, and all the methods of anti-war times had been renewed. President Johnson had differed with his party as to the best method of reconstructing the State governments of the South, which had been destroyed and impoverished by the war, and the press began to agitate the question of the *next* President. Of course, all Union men naturally turned to General Grant, and the result was jealousy of him by the personal friends of President Johnson and some of his cabinet. Mr. Johnson always seemed very patriotic and friendly, and I believed him honest and sincere in his declared purpose to follow strictly the Constitution of the United States in restoring the Southern States to their normal place in the Union; but the same cordial friendship subsisted between General Grant and myself, which was the outgrowth of personal relations dating back to 1839.[12] So I resolved to keep out of this conflict. In September, 1866, I was in the mountains of New Mexico, when a message reached me that I was wanted at Washington.[13] I had with me a couple of offi-

[11] WTS was echoing the derogatory, and completely unfounded, stereotype that Native Americans did not contribute to the development of the United States. Studies have shown that Native American people, and their culture, had an enormous impact on the growth of the United States. Devon A. Mihesuah, *American Indians: Stereotypes and Realities* (Atlanta: Clarity Press, 1996), 58–93.

[12] WTS was in his final year at the USMA when USG arrived as a cadet in 1839. *USMA:* 2:27.

[13] On Sept. 21, 1866, WTS wrote to John Rawlins from Fort Garland, CO, "New Mexico has been and now is a difficult problem to solve. It is very large and thinly settled." At the time, the New Mexico Territory stretched into modern-day Colorado. *Executive Documents Printed by Order of the House of Representatives during the Second Session of the Thirty-Ninth Congress, 1866–1867,* document 23 (Washington, DC: GPO, 1867), 6:14–16; William Thorndale and

cers and half a dozen soldiers as escort, and traveled down the Arkansas, through the Kiowas, Comanches, Cheyennes, and Arapahoes, all more or less disaffected, but reached St. Louis in safety, and proceeded to Washington, where I reported to General Grant.[14]

He explained to me that President Johnson wanted to see me. He did not know the why or wherefore, but supposed it had some connection with an order he (General Grant) had received to escort the newly appointed Minister, Hon. Lew Campbell, of Ohio,[15] to the court of Juarez, the President-elect of Mexico,[16] which country was still in possession of the Emperor Maximilian,[17] supported by a corps of French troops commanded by General Bazaine.[18] General Grant denied the right of the President to order him on a diplomatic mission unattended by troops; said that he had thought the matter over, would disobey the order, and stand the consequences. He manifested much feeling, and said it was a plot to get rid of him. I then went to President Johnson, who treated me with great cordiality, and said that he was very glad I had come; that General Grant was about to go to Mexico on business of importance, and he wanted me at Washington to command the army in General Grant's absence.[19] I then informed him that General Grant *would not go,* and he seemed amazed; said that it was generally understood that General Grant construed

---

William Dollarhide, *Map Guide to the U.S. Federal Censuses, 1790–1920* (Baltimore: Genealogical, 1987), 51 (map).

[14] USG wrote to WTS on Oct. 20, "Come to Washington without delay. Leave St. Louis by Tuesday if you can." WTS left for Washington, DC, on Oct. 23, and arrived on Oct. 25. Andrew Johnson, *The Papers of Andrew Johnson, August 1866–January 1867,* ed. Paul H. Bergeron et al. (Knoxville: University of Tennessee Press, 1994), 444*n; PUSG,* 16:338–339*n.*

[15] Lewis D. Campbell (1811–1882) was elected to the U.S. House of Representatives in 1849 and served in that capacity until 1858. He also served as the U.S. minister to Mexico in 1866–1867. "Death of Lewis D. Campbell," *Stark County Democrat* (Canton, OH), Dec. 6, 1882, 1.

[16] Benito Juárez (1806–1872) was president of Mexico from 1858 to 1872. "Benito Juárez," *Ventura Signal* (Ventura, CA), Sept. 28, 1872, 1.

[17] Ferdinand Maximilian Joseph (1832–1867), archduke of Austria, became the emperor of Mexico in May 1864. *The Encyclopedia Britannica: A Dictionary of Arts, Sciences, and General Literature,* 9th ed. (New York: Henry G. Allen, 1890), vol. 15, s.v. "Maximilian."

[18] François Achille Bazaine (1811–1888) was a French general who served in Mexico from 1862 to 1867. He was later sentenced to death by the French government for "treachery to his country," but he escaped from prison and moved to Spain. "Bazaine's Death," *Brooklyn Citizen,* Sept. 25, 1888, 4; David F. Marley, *Mexico at War: From the Struggle for Independence to the 21st Century Drug Wars* (Santa Barbara: ABC-CLIO, 2014), 39–43.

[19] WTS met with Pres. Andrew Johnson on the morning of Oct. 26. *PUSG,* 16:339*n.*

the occupation of the territories of our neighbor, Mexico, by French troops, and the establishment of an empire therein, with an Austrian prince at its head, as hostile to republican America, and that the Administration had arranged with the French Government for the withdrawal of Bazaine's troops, which would leave the country free for the President-elect Juarez to reoccupy the city of Mexico, etc., etc.; that Mr. Campbell had been accredited to Juarez, and the fact that he was accompanied by so distinguished a soldier as General Grant would emphasize the act of the United States. I simply reiterated that General Grant *would not go,* and that he, Mr. Johnson, could not afford to quarrel with him at that time. I further argued that General Grant was at the moment engaged on the most delicate and difficult task of reorganizing the army under the act of July 28, 1866; that if the real object was to put Mr. Campbell in official communication with President Juarez, supposed to be at El Paso or Monterey, either General Hancock, whose command embraced New Mexico, or General Sheridan, whose command included Texas, could fulfill the object perfectly; or, in the event of neither of these alternates proving satisfactory to the Secretary of State, that I could be easier spared than General Grant. "Certainly," answered the President, "if you will go, that will answer perfectly."[20]

The instructions of the Secretary of State, W. H. Seward, to Hon. Lewis D. Campbell, Minister to Mexico, dated October 25, 1866; a letter from President Johnson to Secretary of War Stanton, dated October 26, 1866; and the letter of Edwin M. Stanton, Secretary of War, to General Grant, dated October 27th, had been already prepared and printed, and the originals or copies were furnished me; but on the 30th of October, 1866, the following letter passed:

EXECUTIVE MANSION,
WASHINGTON, D. C., *October* 30, 1866.

SIR: General Ulysses S. Grant having found it inconvenient to assume the duties specified in my letter to you of the 26th inst., you will please relieve him, and assign them in all respects to William T. Sherman, Lieutenant-General of the Army of the United States. By way of guiding General Sherman in the performance of his duties, you

[20] WTS wrote about his interaction with Pres. Johnson in a letter to his wife, "Our conversation was very general . . . I do not believe the President will do more than consult with me on the General status of affairs out West, and then let me off— . . . I have no doubt there is some plan to get Grant out of the way, and to get me here, but I will be a party to no such move—There may be trouble ahead—but I shall steer clear of the breakers if I can, and in my own way." *PUSG,* 16:340*n.*

will furnish him with a copy of your special orders to General Grant made in compliance with my letter of the 26th inst., together with a copy of the instructions of the Secretary of State to Lewis D. Campbell, Esq., therein mentioned.

The lieutenant-general will proceed to the execution of his duties without delay.

Very respectfully yours,

ANDREW JOHNSON.

To the HON. EDWIN M. STANTON, *Secretary of War.*

At the Navy Department I learned that the United States ship Susquehanna, Captain Alden,[21] was fitting out in New York for the use of this mission, and that there would be time for me to return to St. Louis to make arrangements for a prolonged absence, as also to communicate with Mr. Campbell, who was still at his home in Hamilton, Ohio. By correspondence we agreed to meet in New York, November 8th, he accompanied by Mr. Plumb,[22] secretary of legation, and I by my aide, Colonel Audenried.

We embarked November 10th, and went to sea next day, making for Havana and Vera Cruz, and, as soon as we were outside of Sandy Hook, I explained to Captain Alden that my mission was ended, because I believed by substituting myself for General Grant I had prevented a serious quarrel between him and the Administration, which was unnecessary. We reached Havana on the 18th, with nothing to vary the monotony of an ordinary sea-voyage, except off Hatteras we picked up one woman and twenty men from open boats, who had just abandoned a propeller bound from Baltimore to Charleston which foundered. The sea was very rough, but by the personal skill and supervision of Captain Alden every soul reached our deck safely, and was carried to our consul at Havana. At Havana we were very handsomely entertained, especially by Señor Aldama, who took us by rail to his sugar-estates at Santa Rosa, and back by Matanzas.[23]

[21] James Alden Jr. (1809–1877) entered the U.S. Navy in 1828 and was promoted to commodore in 1866 for his actions during the Civil War. "Rear Admiral Alden," *Oakland Tribune* (Oakland, CA), Feb. 15, 1877, 4.

[22] Edward L. Plumb (1827–1912) served as U.S. charge d'affaires in Mexico and as the consul general in Havana, Cuba. "Plumb," *Washington Herald* (Washington, DC), Apr. 17, 1912, 2.

[23] Miguel Aldama (1821–1888), a wealthy planter, supported the Guerra Grande, a group of rebels who opposed the Spanish Empire's presence in Cuba. After Aldama moved to the

We took our departure thence on the 25th, and anchored under Isla Verde, off Vera Cruz, on the 29th.

Everything about Vera Cruz indicated the purpose of the French to withdraw, and also that the Emperor Maximilian would precede them, for the Austrian frigate Dandolo was in port, and an Austrian bark, on which were received, according to the report of our consul, Mr. Lane,[24] as many as eleven hundred packages of private furniture to be transferred to Miramar, Maximilian's home; and Lieutenant Clarin, of the French navy, who visited the Susquehanna from the French commodore, Clouet, told me, without reserve, that, if we had delayed eight days more, we would have found Maximilian gone. General Bazaine was reported to be in the city of Mexico with about twenty-eight thousand French troops; but instead of leaving Mexico in three detachments, viz., November, 1866, March, 1867, and November, 1867, as described in Mr. Seward's letter to Mr. Campbell, of October 25, 1866, it looked to me that, as a soldier, he would evacuate at some time before November, 1867, *all at once,* and not by detachments. Lieutenant Clarin telegraphed Bazaine at the city of Mexico the fact of our arrival, and he sent me a most courteous and pressing invitation to come up to the city; but, as we were accredited to the government of Juarez, it was considered *un*diplomatic to establish friendly relations with the existing authorities. Meantime we could not hear a word of Juarez, and concluded to search for him along the coast northward. (When I was in Versailles, France, July, 1872, learning that General Bazaine was in arrest for the surrender of his army and post at Metz, in 1870, I wanted to call on him to thank him for his courteous invitation to me at Vera Cruz in 1866. I inquired of President Thiers[25] if I could with propriety call on the marshal. He answered that it would be very acceptable, no doubt, but suggested for form's sake that I should consult the Minister of War, General de Cissey,[26] which I did, and he promptly assented. Accordingly, I called with my aide, Colonel Audenried, on

---

United States around 1868, pro-Spanish authorities took over his family's property in Havana. He returned to Cuba in 1878. Antoni Kapcia, *Historical Dictionary of Cuba,* 3rd ed. (London: Rowman and Littlefield, 2022), s.v. "Aldama, Miguel."

[24] Marquis D. L. Lane (1825–1872) served as consul to Vera Cruz from 1862 to 1867. Johnson, *The Papers of Andew Johnson,* 11:477*n.*

[25] Louis A. Thiers (1797–1877) was president of France from 1871 to 1873. *The Annual Statistician and Economist 1890* (San Francisco: L. P. McCarty, 1890), 332.

[26] Ernest Courtot de Cissey (1810–1882) was France's minister of war from 1871 to 1874. *Supplement to Encyclopedia Britannica: A Dictionary of Arts, Sciences, and General Literature,* 9th ed. (New York: J. M. Stoddart, 1885), vol. 2, s.v. "Cissey, Ernest Louis Octave Courtot de."

Marshal Bazaine, who occupied a small, two-story stone house at Versailles, in an inclosure with a high garden wall, at the front gate or door of which was a lodge, in which was a military guard. We were shown to a good room on the second floor, where was seated the marshal in military half-dress, with large head, full face, short neck, and evidently a man of strong physique. He did not speak English, but spoke Spanish perfectly. We managed to carry on a conversation in which I endeavored to convey my sense of his politeness in inviting me so cordially up to the city of Mexico, and my regret that the peculiar duty on which I was engaged did not admit of a compliance, or even of an intelligent explanation, at the time. He spoke of the whole Mexican business as a "sad affair," that the empire necessarily fell with the result of our civil war, and that poor Maximilian was sacrificed to his own high sense of honor.)

While on board the Susquehanna, on the 1st day of December, 1866, we received the proclamation made by the Emperor Maximilian at Orizaba, in which, notwithstanding the near withdrawal of the French troops, he declared his purpose to remain and "shed the last drop of his blood in defense of his dear country."[27] Undoubtedly many of the most substantial people of Mexico, having lost all faith in the stability of the native government, had committed themselves to what they considered the more stable government of Maximilian, and Maximilian, a man of honor, concluded at the last moment he could not abandon them; the consequence was his death.

Failing to hear of Juarez, we steamed up the coast to the Island of Lobos, and on to Tampico, off which we found the United States steamer Paul Jones, which, drawing less water than the Susquehanna, carried us over the bar to the city, then in possession of the Liberal party, which recognized Juarez as their constitutional President, but of Juarez and his whereabout we could hear not a word; so we continued up the coast and anchored off Brazos Santiago, December 7th. Going ashore in small boats, we found a railroad, under the management of General J. R. West, now one of the commissioners of the city of Washington,[28] who sent us up to Brownsville, Texas. We met on the way General Sheridan, returning from a tour of inspection of the Rio Grande frontier. On Sunday, December 9th, we were all

[27] For an English translation of Maximilian's proclamation, see *Papers Relating to Foreign Affairs, Accompanying the Annual Message of the President to the Second Session, Thirty-Ninth Congress* (Washington, DC: GPO, 1867), 3:14.

[28] Joseph R. West (1822–1898) was a U.S. senator from Louisiana from 1871 to 1877 and was on the Board of Commissioners of Washington, DC, from 1882 to 1885. "Death of Joseph R. West," *Evening Star* (Washington, DC), Nov. 1, 1898, 10.

at Matamoras, Mexico, where we met General Escobedo, one of Juarez's trusty lieutenants, who developed to us the general plan agreed on for the overthrow of the empire, and the reëstablishment of the republican government of Mexico.[29] He asked of us no assistance, except the loan of some arms, ammunition, clothing, and camp-equipage. It was agreed that Mr. Campbell should, as soon as he could get his baggage off the Susquehanna, return to Matamoras, and thence proceed to Monterey, to be received by Juarez in person as the accredited Minister of the United States to the Republic of Mexico. Meantime the weather off the coast was stormy, and the Susquehanna parted a cable, so that we were delayed some days at Brazos; but in due time Mr. Campbell got his baggage, and we regained the deck of the Susquehanna, which got up steam and started for New Orleans. We reached New Orleans December 20th, whence I reported fully everything to General Grant,[30] and on the 21st received the following dispatch:

WASHINGTON, *December* 21, 1866.

Lieutenant-General SHERMAN, *New Orleans.*

Your telegram of yesterday has been submitted to the President. You are authorized to proceed to St. Louis at your convenience. Your proceedings in the special and delicate duties assigned you are cordially approved by the President and Cabinet and this department.

EDWIN M. STANTON.

And on the same day I received this dispatch:

GALVESTON, *December* 21, 1866.

To General SHERMAN, *or General* SHERIDAN.

Will be in New Orleans to-morrow. Wish to see you both on arrival, on matters of importance.

LEWIS D. CAMPBELL, *Minister to Mexico.*

Mr. Campbell arrived on the 22d, but had nothing to tell of the least importance, save that he was generally disgusted with the whole thing, and had not found Juarez at all.

[29] Mariano Escobedo (1826–1902) served in the Mexican Army during the Mexican-American War. Marley, *Mexico at War,* s.v. "Escobedo Peña, Mariano Antonio Guadalupe."

[30] See *PUSG,* 16:373*n*–374*n*.

I am sure this whole movement was got up for the purpose of getting General Grant away from Washington, on the pretext of his known antagonism to the French occupation of Mexico, because he was looming up as a candidate for President, and nobody understood the *animus* and purpose better than did Mr. Stanton. He himself was not then on good terms with President Johnson, and with several of his associates in the Cabinet. By Christmas I was back in St. Louis.

By this time the conflict between President Johnson and Congress had become open and unconcealed. Congress passed the bill known as the "Tenure of Civil Office" on the 2d of March, 1867 (over the President's veto), the first clause of which, now section 1767 of the Revised Statutes, reads thus: "Every person who holds any civil office to which he has been or hereafter may be appointed, by and with the advice and consent of the Senate, and who shall have become duly qualified to act therein, shall be entitled to hold such office during the term for which he was appointed, unless sooner removed by and with the advice and consent of the Senate, or by the appointment with the like advice and consent of a successor in his place, except as herein otherwise provided."[31]

General E. D. Townsend, in his "Anecdotes of the Civil War," states tersely and correctly the preliminary circumstances of which I must treat. He says: "On Monday morning, August 5, 1867, President Johnson invited Mr. Stanton to resign as Secretary of War. Under the tenure-of-civil-office law, Mr. Stanton declined. The President a week after suspended him, and appointed General Grant, General-in-Chief of the Army, to exercise the functions. This continued until January 13, 1868, when according to the law the Senate passed a resolution *not* sustaining the President's action. The next morning General Grant came to my office and handed me the key of the Secretary's room, saying: 'I am to be found over at my office at army headquarters. I was served with a copy of the Senate resolution last evening.' I then went up-stairs and delivered the key of his room to Mr. Stanton."

The mode and manner of Mr. Stanton's regaining his office, and of General Grant's surrendering it, were at the time subjects of bitter controversy. Unhappily I was involved, and must bear testimony. In all January, 1868, I was a member of a board ordered to compile a code of articles of war and army

[31] For a full transcription of the Tenure of Office Act, see Edward McPherson, ed., *A Political Manual for 1869, Including a Classified Summary of the Important Executive, Legislative, Judicial, Politico-Military and General Facts* (Washington, DC: Philp and Solomon's, 1869), 413–414.

regulations, of which Major-General Sheridan and Brigadier-General C. C. Augur were associate members. Our place of meeting was in the room of the old War Department, second floor, next to the corner room occupied by the Secretary of War, with a door of communication. While we were at work it was common for General Grant and, afterward, for Mr. Stanton to drop in and chat with us on the social gossip of the time.

On Saturday, January 11th, General Grant said that he had more carefully read the law (tenure of civil office), and it was different from what he had supposed; that in case the Senate did not consent to the removal of Secretary of War Stanton, and he (Grant) should hold on, he should incur a liability of ten thousand dollars and five years' imprisonment. We all expected the resolution of Senator Howard, of Michigan,[32] virtually restoring Mr. Stanton to his office, would pass the Senate, and knowing that the President expected General Grant to *hold on,* I inquired if he had given notice of his change of purpose; he answered that there was no hurry, because he supposed Mr. Stanton would pursue toward him (Grant) the same course which he (Stanton) had required of him the preceding August, viz., would address him a letter claiming the office, and allow him a couple of days for the change. Still, he said he would go to the White House the same day and notify the President of his intended action.

That afternoon I went over to the White House to present General Pope, who was on a visit to Washington, and we found the President and General Grant together. We made our visit and withdrew, leaving them still together, and I always supposed the subject of this conference was the expected decision of the Senate, which would in effect restore Mr. Stanton to his civil office of Secretary of War. That evening I dined with the Hon. Reverdy Johnson, Senator from Maryland, and suggested to him that the best way to escape a conflict was for the President to nominate some good man as Secretary of War whose confirmation by the Senate would fall within the provisions of the law, and named General J. D. Cox, then Governor of Ohio, whose term of office was drawing to a close, who would, I knew, be acceptable to General Grant and the army generally. Mr. Johnson was most favorably impressed with this suggestion, and promised to call on the President the next day (Sunday), which he did, but President Johnson had made up his mind to meet the conflict boldly. I saw General Grant that afternoon at his house on I Street, and told him what I had done, and so anxious was he about it that he came to our room at the War

[32] Jacob M. Howard (1805–1871) served as a U.S. senator from Michigan from 1862 to 1871. "Hon. Jacob M. Howard," *Evening Telegraph* (Philadelphia), Apr. 3, 1871, 4.

Department the next morning (Monday), the 13th, and asked me to go in person to the White House to urge the President to send in the name of General Cox. I did so, saw the President, and inquired if he had seen Mr. Reverdy Johnson the day before about General Cox. He answered that he had, and thought well of General Cox, but would say no further.

Tuesday, January 14, 1868, came, and with it Mr. Stanton. He resumed possession of his former office; came into that where General Sheridan, General Augur, and I were at work, and greeted us very cordially. He said he wanted to see me when at leisure, and at half-past 10 A. M. I went into his office and found him and General Grant together. Supposing they had some special matters of business, I withdrew, with the remark that I was close at hand, and could come in at any moment. In the afternoon I went again into Mr. Stanton's office, and we had a long and most friendly conversation, but not one word was spoken about the "tenure-of-office" matter. I then crossed over Seventeenth Street to the headquarters of the army, where I found General Grant, who expressed himself as by no means pleased with the manner in which Mr. Stanton had regained his office, saying that he had sent a messenger for him that morning as of old, with word that "he wanted to see him." We then arranged to meet at his office the next morning at half-past nine, and go together to see the President.

That morning the *National Intelligencer* published an article accusing General Grant of acting in bad faith to the President, and of having prevaricated in making his personal explanation to the Cabinet, so that General Grant at first felt unwilling to go, but we went. The President received us promptly and kindly. Being seated, General Grant said, "Mr. President, whoever gave the facts for the article of the *Intelligencer* of this morning has made some serious mistakes." The President: "General Grant, let me interrupt you just there. I have not seen the *Intelligencer* of this morning, and have no knowledge of the contents of any article therein." General Grant then went on: "Well, the idea is given there that I have not kept faith with you. Now, Mr. President, I remember, when you spoke to me on this subject last summer, I did say that, like the case of the Baltimore police commissioners,[33] I did suppose Mr. Stanton could not regain his office except by a process through the courts." To this the President assented, saying he "remembered the reference to the case of the Baltimore commissioners," when General Grant resumed: "I said if I changed my

[33] On Apr. 17, 1860, the Baltimore Court of Appeals upheld *Baltimore v. State,* which gave states the legal authority to control their municipalities and police. See H. H. Walker Lewis, "The Baltimore Police Case of 1860," *Maryland Law Review* 26, no. 3 (Summer 1966): 215–228.

opinion I would give you notice, and put things as they were before my appointment as Secretary of War *ad interim.*"

We then entered into a general friendly conversation, both parties professing to be satisfied, the President claiming that he had always been most friendly to General Grant, and the latter insisting that he had taken the office, not for honor or profit, but in the general interests of the army.

As we withdrew, at the very door, General Grant said, "Mr. President, you should make some order that we of the army are not bound to obey the orders of Mr. Stanton as Secretary of War," which the President intimated he would do.

No such "orders" were ever made; many conferences were held, and the following letters are selected out of a great mass to show the general feeling at the time:

1321 K Street, Washington, *January* 28, 1868, *Saturday.*

To the President:

I neglected this morning to say that I had agreed to go down to Annapolis to spend Sunday with Admiral Porter. General Grant also has to leave for Richmond on Monday morning at 6 A. M.

At a conversation with the General after our interview, wherein I offered to go with him on Monday morning to Mr. Stanton, and to say that it was our joint opinion he should resign, it was found impossible by reason of his (General Grant) going to Richmond and my going to Annapolis. The General proposed this course: He will call on you to-morrow, and offer to go to Mr. Stanton to say, for the good of the Army and of the country, he ought to resign. This on Sunday. On Monday I will again call on you, and, if you think it necessary, I will do the same, viz., go to Mr. Stanton and tell him he should resign.

If he will not, then it will be time to contrive ulterior measures. In the mean time it so happens that no necessity exists for precipitating matters.

Yours truly,

W. T. Sherman, *Lieutenant-General.*

Dear General: On the point of starting, I have written the above, and will send a fair copy of it to the President. Please retain this, that in case of necessity I may have a copy. The President clearly stated to me that he relied on us in this category.

Think of the propriety of your putting in writing what you have to say tomorrow, even if you have to put it in the form of a letter to hand him in person, retaining a copy. I'm afraid that acting as a go-between for three persons, I may share the usual fate of meddlers, at last get kicks from all. We ought not to be involved in politics, but for the sake of the Army we are justified in trying at least to cut this Gordian knot, which they do not appear to have any practicable plan to do. In haste as usual,

W. T. SHERMAN.

HEADQUARTERS ARMIES OF THE UNITED STATES,
January 29, 1868.

DEAR SHERMAN: I called on the President and Mr. Stanton to-day, but without any effect.

I soon found that to recommend resignation to Mr. Stanton would have no effect, unless it was to incur further his displeasure; and, therefore, did not directly suggest it to him. I explained to him, however, the course I supposed he would pursue, and what I expected to do in that case, namely, to notify the President of his intentions, and thus leave him to violate the "Tenure-of-Office Bill" if he chose, instead of having me do it.

I would advise that you say nothing to Mr. Stanton on the subject unless he asks your advice. It will do no good, and may embarrass you. I did not mention your name to him, at least not in connection with his position, or what you thought upon it.

All that Mr. Johnson said was pacific and compromising. While I think he wanted the constitutionality of the "Tenure Bill" tested, I think now he would be glad either to get the vacancy of Secretary of War, or have the office just where it was during suspension.
Yours truly,

U. S. GRANT.

WASHINGTON, D. C., *January* 27, 1868.

To the President.

DEAR SIR: As I promised, I saw Mr. Ewing yesterday, and after a long conversation asked him to put down his opinion in writing, which he has done and which I now inclose.

I am now at work on these Army Regulations, and in the course of preparation have laid down the Constitution and laws now in force, clearer than I find them elsewhere; and beg leave herewith to inclose you three pages of printed matter for your perusal. My opinion is, if you will adopt these rules and make them an executive order to General Grant, they will so clearly define the duties of all concerned that no conflict can arise. I hope to get through this task in the course of this week, and want very much to go to St. Louis. For eleven years I have been tossed about so much that I really do want to rest, study, and make the acquaintance of my family. I do not think, since 1857, I have averaged thirty days out of three hundred and sixty-five at home.

Next summer also, in fulfillment of our promise to the Sioux, I must go to Fort Phil Kearney early in the spring, so that, unless I can spend the next two months at home, I might as well break up my house at St. Louis, and give up all prospect of taking care of my family.

For these reasons especially I shall soon ask leave to go to St. Louis, to resume my proper and legitimate command. With great respect,

W. T. SHERMAN, *Lieutenant-General.*

[INCLOSURE.]

WASHINGTON, D. C., *January* 25, 1868.

MY DEAR GENERAL: I am quite clear in the opinion that it is not expedient for the President to take any action now in the case of Stanton. So far as he and his interests are concerned, things are in the best possible condition. Stanton is in the Department, *not* his secretary, but the secretary of the Senate, who have taken upon themselves his sins, and who place him there under a large salary to annoy and obstruct the operations of the Executive. This the people well enough understand, and he is a stench in the nostrils of their own party.

I thought the nomination of Cox at the proper juncture would have been wise as a peace-offering, but perhaps it would have let off the Senate too easily from the effect of their arbitrary act. Now the dislodging of Stanton and filling the office even temporarily without the consent of the Senate would raise a question as to the legality of the President's acts, and he would belong to the attacked instead of the attacking party. If the war between Congress and the President is to go on, as I suppose it is, Stanton should be ignored by the President, left to perform his clerical duties which the law requires him to perform, and let the party bear the odium which is already upon them for placing him where he is. So much for the President.

As to yourself, I wish you as far as possible to keep clear of political complications. I do not think the President will require you to do an act of doubtful legality. Certainly he will not without sanction of the opinion of his Attorney-General; and you should have time, in a questionable case, to consult with me before called upon to act. The office of Secretary of War is a civil office, as completely so as that of Secretary of State; and you as a military officer cannot, I think, be required to assume or exercise it. This may, if necessary, be a subject for further consideration. Such, however, will not, I think, be the case. The appeal is to the people, and it is better for the President to persist in the course he has for some time pursued—let the aggressions all come from the other side; and I think there is no doubt he will do so.

Affectionately,

T. EWING.

To Lieutenant-General SHERMAN.

LIBRARY ROOM, WAR DEPARTMENT,
WASHINGTON, D. C., *January* 31, 1868.

To the President:

Since our interview of yesterday I have given the subject of our conversation all my thoughts, and I beg you will pardon my reducing the same to writing.

My personal preferences, as expressed, were to be allowed to return to St. Louis to resume my present command, because my command was important, large, suited to my rank and inclination, and because my family was well provided for there in house, facilities, schools, living, and agreeable society; while, on the other hand, Washington was for many (to me) good reasons highly objectionable, especially because it is the political capital of the country; and focus of intrigue, gossip, and slander. Your personal preferences were, as expressed, to make a new department East adequate to my rank, with headquarters at Washington, and assign me to its command, to remove my family here, and to avail myself of its schools, etc.; to remove Mr. Stanton from his office as Secretary of War, and have me to discharge the duties.

To effect this removal two modes were indicated: to simply cause him to quit the War-Office Building, and notify the Treasury Department and the Army Staff Departments no longer to respect him as Secretary of War; or to remove him and submit my name to the Senate for confirmation.

Permit me to discuss these points a little, and I will premise by saying that I have spoken to no one on the subject, and have not even seen Mr. Ewing, Mr. Stanbery, or General Grant, since I was with you.

It has been the rule and custom of our army, since the organization of the government, that the second officer of the army should be at the second (in importance) command, and remote from general headquarters. To bring me to Washington would put three heads to an army, yourself, General Grant, and myself, and we would be more than human if we were not to differ. In my judgment it would ruin the army, and would be fatal to one or two of us.

Generals Scott and Taylor proved themselves soldiers and patriots in the field, but Washington was fatal to both. This city, and the influences that centre here, defeated every army that had its headquarters here from 1861 to 1864, and would have overwhelmed General Grant at Spottsylvania and Petersburg, had he not been fortified by a strong reputation, already hard-earned, and because no one then living coveted the place; whereas, in the West, we made progress from the start, because there was no political capital near enough to poison our minds, and kindle into life that craving, itching for fame which has killed more good men than bullets. I have been with General Grant in the midst of death and slaughter—when the howls of people reached him after Shiloh; when messengers were speeding to and from his army to Washington, bearing slanders, to induce his removal before he took Vicksburg; in Chattanooga, when the soldiers were stealing the corn of the starving mules to satisfy their own hunger; at Nashville, when he was ordered to the "forlorn hope" to command the Army of the Potomac, so often defeated—and yet I never saw him more troubled than since he has been in Washington, and been compelled to read himself a "sneak and deceiver," based on reports of four of the Cabinet, and apparently with your knowledge. If this political atmosphere can disturb the equanimity of one so guarded and so prudent as he is, what will be the result with me, so careless, so outspoken as I am? Therefore, with my consent, Washington never.

> As to the Secretary of War, his office is twofold. As a Cabinet officer he should not be there without your hearty, cheerful assent, and I believe that is the judgment and opinion of every fair-minded man. As the holder of a civil office, having the supervision of moneys appropriated by Congress and of contracts for army supplies, I do think Congress, or the Senate by delegation from Congress, has a lawful right to be consulted. At all events, I would not risk a suit or contest on that phase of the question. The law of Congress, of March 2, 1867, prescribing the manner in which orders and instructions relating to "military movements" shall reach the army, gives you as constitutional Commander-in-Chief the very power you want to exercise, and enables you to prevent the Secretary from making any such orders and instructions; and consequently he cannot control the army, but is limited and restricted to a duty that an Auditor of the Treasury could perform. You certainly can afford to await the result. The Executive power is not weakened, but rather strengthened. Surely he is not such an obstruction as would warrant violence, or even a show of force, which would produce the very reaction and clamor that he hopes for to save him from the absurdity of holding an empty office "for the safety of the country."
>
> This is as much as I ought to say, and more too, but if it produces the result I will be more than satisfied, viz., that I be simply allowed to resume my proper post and duties in St. Louis. With great respect, yours truly,
>
> W. T. SHERMAN, *Lieutenant-General.*

On the 1st of February, the board of which I was the president submitted to the adjutant-general our draft of the "Articles of War and Army Regulations," condensed to a small compass, the result of our war experience. But they did not suit the powers that were, and have ever since slept the sleep that knows no waking, to make room for the ponderous document now in vogue, which will not stand the strain of a week's campaign in real war.

I hurried back to St. Louis to escape the political storm I saw brewing. The President repeatedly said to me that he wanted me in Washington, and I as often answered that nothing could tempt me to live in that center of intrigue and excitement; but soon came the following:

HEADQUARTERS ARMY OF THE UNITED STATES,
WASHINGTON, *February* 10, 1868.

DEAR GENERAL: I have received at last the President's reply to my last letter. He attempts to substantiate his statements by his Cabinet. In this view it is important that I should have a letter from you, if you are willing to give it, of what I said to you about the effect of the "Tenure-of-Office Bill," and my object in going to see the President on Saturday before the installment of Mr. Stanton. What occurred after the meeting of the Cabinet on the Tuesday following is not a subject under controversy now; therefore, if you choose to write down your recollection (and I would like to have it) on Wednesday, when you and I called on the President, and your conversation with him the last time you saw him, make that a separate communication.

Your order to come East was received several days ago, but the President withdrew it, I supposed to make some alteration, but it has not been returned.

Yours truly,

U. S. GRANT.

[TELEGRAM.]

WASHINGTON, D. C., *February* 13, 1868.

Lieutenant-General W. T. SHERMAN, *St. Louis.*

The order is issued ordering you to Atlantic Division.

U. S. GRANT, *General.*

[TELEGRAM.]

HEADQUARTERS MILITARY DIVISION OF THE MISSOURI,
ST. LOUIS, *February* 14, 1868.

General U. S. GRANT, *Washington, D. C.*

Your dispatch is received informing me that the order for the Atlantic Division has been issued, and that I am assigned to its command. I was in hopes I had escaped the danger, and now were I prepared I should resign on the spot, as it requires no foresight to predict such must be the inevitable result in the end. I will make one more desperate effort by mail, which please await.

W. T. SHERMAN, *Lieutenant-General.*

[TELEGRAM.]

WASHINGTON, *February* 14, 1868.

Lieutenant-General W. T. SHERMAN, *St. Louis.*

I think it due to you that your letter of January 31st to the President of the United States should be published, to correct misapprehension in the public mind about your willingness to come to Washington. It will not be published against your will.

U. S. GRANT, *General.*

(Sent in cipher.)

[TELEGRAM.]

HEADQUARTERS MILITARY DIVISION OF THE MISSOURI,
ST. LOUIS, MISSOURI, *February* 14, 1868.

General U. S. GRANT, *Washington, D. C.*

Dispatch of to-day received. Please await a letter I address this day through you to the President, which will in due time reach the public, covering the very point you make.

I don't want to come to Washington at all.

W. T. SHERMAN, *Lieutenant-General.*

[TELEGRAM.]

HEADQUARTERS MILITARY DIVISION OF THE MISSOURI,
ST. LOUIS, MISSOURI, *February* 14, 1868.

Hon. JOHN SHERMAN, *United States Senate, Washington, D. C.*

Oppose confirmation of myself as brevet general, on ground that it is unprecedented, and that it is better not to extend the system of brevets above major-general. If I can't avoid coming to Washington, I may have to resign.

W. T. SHERMAN, *Lieutenant-General.*

HEADQUARTERS OF THE ARMY,
WASHINGTON, D. C., *February* 12, 1868.

The following orders are published for the information and guidance of all concerned:

EXECUTIVE MANSION,
WASHINGTON, D. C., *February* 12, 1868.

GENERAL: You will please issue an order creating a military division to be styled the Military Division of the Atlantic, to be composed of the Department of the Lakes, the Department of the East, and the Department of Washington, to be commanded by Lieutenant-General W. T. Sherman, with his headquarters at Washington. Until further orders from the President, you will assign no officer to the permanent command of the Military Division of the Missouri.

Respectfully yours,
ANDREW JOHNSON.

GENERAL U. S. GRANT,
Commanding Armies of the United States, Washington, D. C.

Major-General P. H. Sheridan, the senior officer in the Military Division of the Missouri, will temporarily perform the duties of commander of the Military Division of the Missouri in addition to his duties of department commander. By command of General Grant:

E. D. TOWNSEND, *Assistant Adjutant-General.*

This order, if carried into effect, would have grouped in Washington:

1. The President, constitutional Commander-in-Chief.
2. The Secretary of War, congressional Commander-in-Chief.
3. The General of the Armies of the United States.
4. The Lieutenant-General of the Army.
5. The Commanding General of the Department of Washington.
6. The commander of the post of Washington.

At that date the garrison of Washington was a brigade of infantry and a battery of artillery. I never doubted Mr. Johnson's sincerity in wishing to befriend me, but this was the broadest kind of a farce, or meant mischief. I therefore appealed to him by letter to allow me to remain where I was, and where I could do service, *real service,* and received his most satisfactory answer.

HEADQUARTERS MILITARY DIVISION OF THE MISSOURI,
ST. LOUIS, MISSOURI, *February* 14, 1868.

General U. S. GRANT, *Washington, D. C.*

Dear General: Last evening, just before leaving my office, I received your note of the 10th, and had intended answering it according to your request; but, after I got home, I got your dispatch of yesterday, announcing that the order I dreaded so much was issued. I never felt so troubled in my life. Were it an order to go to Sitka, to the devil, to battle with rebels or Indians, I think you would not hear a whimper from me, but it comes in such a questionable form that, like Hamlet's ghost, it curdles my blood and mars my judgment. My first thoughts were of resignation, and I had almost made up my mind to ask Dodge for some place on the Pacific road, or on one of the Iowa roads, and then again various colleges ran through my memory, but hard times and an expensive family have brought me back to staring the proposition square in the face, and I have just written a letter to the President, which I herewith transmit through you, on which I will hang a hope of respite till you telegraph me its effect. The uncertainties ahead are too great to warrant my incurring the expense of breaking up my house and family here, and therefore in no event will I do this till I can be assured of some permanence elsewhere. If it were at all certain that you would accept the nomination of President in May, I would try and kill the intervening time, and then judge of the chances, but I do not want you to reveal your plans to me till you choose to do so.

I have telegraphed to John Sherman to oppose the nomination which the papers announce has been made of me for brevet general.

I have this minute received your cipher dispatch of to-day, which I have just answered and sent down to the telegraph-office, and the clerk is just engaged in copying my letter to the President to go with this. If the President or his friends pretend that I seek to go to Washington, it will be fully rebutted by letters I have written to the President, to you, to John Sherman, to Mr. Ewing, and to Mr. Stanbery. You remember that in our last talk you suggested I should write again to the President. I thought of it, and concluded my letter of January 31st, already delivered, was full and emphatic. Still, I did write again to Mr. Stanbery, asking him as a friend to interpose in my behalf. There are plenty of people who know my wishes, and I would avoid, if possible, the publication of a letter so confidential as that of January 31st, in which I notice I allude to the President's purpose of removing Mr. Stanton by force, a fact that ought not to be drawn out through me if it be possible to avoid it. In the letter herewith I confine myself to purely private matters, and will not object if it reaches the public in any proper way. My opinion is, the President thinks Mrs. Sherman would like to come to Washington by reason of her father and brothers being there. This is true, for Mrs. Sherman has an idea that St. Louis is unhealthy for our children, and because most of the Catholics here are tainted with the old secesh feeling. But I know better what is to our common interest, and prefer to judge of the proprieties myself. What I do object to is the false position I would occupy as between you and the President. Were there an actual army at or near Washington, I could be withdrawn from the most unpleasant attitude of a "go-between," but there is no army there, nor any military duties which you with a host of subordinates can not perform. Therefore I would be there with naked, informal, and sinecure duties, and utterly out of place. This you understand well enough, and the army too, but the President and the politicians, who flatter themselves they are saving the country, cannot and will not understand. My opinion is, the country is doctored to death, and if President and Congress would go to sleep like Rip Van Winkle, the country would go on under natural influences, and recover far faster than under their joint and several treatment. This doctrine would be accounted by Congress, and by the President too, as high treason, and therefore I don't care about saying so to either of them, but I know you can hear anything, and give it just what thought or action it merits.

Excuse this long letter, and telegraph me the result of my letter to the President as early as you can. If he holds my letter so long as to make it improper for me to await his answer, also telegraph me.

The order, when received, will, I suppose, direct me as to whom and how I am to turn over this command, which should, in my judgment, not be broken up, as the three departments composing the division should be under one head.

I expect my staff-officers to be making for me within the hour to learn their fate, so advise me all you can as quick as possible.

With great respect, yours truly,

W. T. Sherman, *Lieutenant-General.*

Headquarters Military Division of the Missouri,
St. Louis, Missouri, *February* 14, 1868.

To the President.

Dear Sir: It is hard for me to conceive you would purposely do me an unkindness unless under the pressure of a sense of public duty, or because you do not believe me sincere. I was in hopes, since my letter to you of the 31st of January, that you had concluded to pass over that purpose of yours expressed more than once in conversation—to organize a new command for me in the East, with headquarters in Washington; but a telegram from General Grant of yesterday says that "the order was issued ordering you" (me) "to Atlantic Division"; and the newspapers of this morning contain the same information, with the addition that I have been nominated as brevet general. I have telegraphed my own brother in the Senate to oppose my confirmation, on the ground that the two higher grades in the army ought not to be complicated with brevets, and I trust you will conceive my motives aright. If I could see my way clear to maintain my family, I should not hesitate a moment to resign my present commission, and seek some business wherein I would be free from these unhappy complications that seem to be closing about me, spite of my earnest efforts to avoid them; but necessity ties my hands, and I must submit with the best grace I can till I make other arrangements.

In Washington are already the headquarters of a department, and of the army itself, and it is hard for me to see wherein I can render military service there. Any staff-officer with the rank of major could surely fill any gap left between these two military officers; and, by being placed in Washington, I will be universally construed as a rival to the General-in-Chief, a position damaging to me in the highest degree. Our relations have always been most confidential and friendly, and if, unhappily, any cloud of differences should arise between us, my sense of personal dignity and duty would leave me no alternative but resignation. For this I am not yet prepared, but I shall proceed to arrange for it as rapidly as possible, so that when the time does come (as it surely will if this plan is carried into effect) I may act promptly.

Inasmuch as the order is now issued, I cannot expect a full revocation of it, but I beg the privilege of taking post at New York, or any point you may name within the new military division other than Washington. This privilege is generally granted to all military commanders, and I see no good reason why I too may not ask for it, and this simple concession, involving no public interest, will much soften the blow, which, right or wrong, I construe as one of the hardest I have sustained in a life somewhat checkered with adversity. With great respect, yours truly,

W. T. Sherman, *Lieutenant-General.*

WASHINGTON, D. C., 2 P. M., *February* 19, 1868.

Lieutenant-General W. T. SHERMAN, *St. Louis, Missouri:*

I have just received, with General Grant's indorsement of reference, your letter to me of the fourteenth (14th) inst.

The order to which you refer was made in good faith, and with a view to the best interests of the country and the service; as, however, your assignment to a new military division seems so objectionable, you will retain your present command.

ANDREW JOHNSON.

On that same 19th of February he appointed Adjutant-General Lorenzo Thomas to be Secretary of War *ad interim,* which finally resulted in the articles of impeachment and trial of President Johnson before the Senate. I was a witness on that trial, but of course the lawyers would not allow me to express any opinion of the President's motives or intentions, and restricted me to the facts set forth in the articles of impeachment, of which I was glad to know nothing. The final test vote revealed less than two thirds, and the President was consequently acquitted. Mr. Stanton resigned. General Schofield, previously nominated, was confirmed as Secretary of War, thus putting an end to what ought never to have happened at all.[34]

Indian Peace Commission.

On the 20th of July, 1867, President Johnson approved an act to establish peace with certain hostile Indian tribes, the first section of which reads as follows: "Be it enacted, etc., that the President of the United States be and is hereby authorized to appoint a commission to consist of three (3) officers of the army not below the rank of brigadier-general, who, together with N. G. Taylor, Commissioner of Indian Affairs, John B. Henderson, chairman of the Committee of Indian Affairs of the Senate, S. F. Tappan, and John B. Sanborn,[35]

[34] Schofield served as U.S. secretary of war from May 28, 1868, to Mar. 11, 1869. *CWHC,* 473.

[35] Nathaniel G. Taylor (1819–1887) was an orator and served as commissioner of Indian Affairs under Pres. Johnson. John B. Henderson (1826–1913) was a U.S. senator from Missouri from 1862 to 1869. Samuel F. Tappan (1831–1913) served in the U.S. Army during the Civil War and was a member of the peace commission. John B. Sanborn (1826–1904) was a member of the peace commission and later served in the Minnesota House and Senate. "General John B. Sanborn Dead," *Kansas City Times* (Kansas City, MO), May 17, 1904, 1; "J. B. Anderson Answers Call," *Evening Star* (Washington, DC), Apr. 13, 1913, 2; "Life of Adventure: Death of Col.

shall have power and authority to call together the chiefs and head men of such bands or tribes of Indians as are now waging war against the United States, or committing depredations on the people thereof, to ascertain the alleged reasons for their acts of hostility, and in their discretion, under the direction of the President, to make and conclude with said bands or tribes such treaty stipulations, subject to the action of the Senate, as may remove all just causes of complaint on their part, and at the same time establish security for person and property along the lines of railroad now being constructed to the Pacific and other thoroughfares of travel to the Western Territories, and such as will most likely insure civilization for the Indians, and peace and safety for the whites."[36]

The President named as the military members Lieutenant-General Sherman, Brigadier-Generals A. H. Terry and W. S. Harney. Subsequently, to insure a full attendance, Brigadier-General C. C. Augur was added to the commission, and his name will be found on most of the treaties. The commissioners met at St. Louis and elected N. G. Taylor, the Commissioner of Indian Affairs, president; J. B. Sanborn, treasurer; and A. S. H. White, Esq., of Washington, D. C.,[37] secretary. The year 1867 was too far advanced to complete the task assigned during that season, and it was agreed that a steamboat (St. John's) should be chartered to convey the commission up the Missouri River, and we adjourned to meet at Omaha. In the St. John's the commission proceeded up the Missouri River, holding informal "talks" with the Santees at their agency near the Niobrara, the Yanktonnais at Fort Thompson, and the Ogallallas, Minneconjous, Sans Arcs, etc., at Fort Sully. From this point runners were sent out to the Sioux occupying the country west of the Missouri River, to meet us in council at the Forks of the Platte that fall, and to Sitting Bull's band of outlaw

---

Samuel F. Tappan Ends Remarkable Career," *Evening Star* (Washington, DC), Jan. 12, 1913, 12; "Obituary Notes," *New York Times,* Apr. 2, 1887, 5.

[36] For a full transcript of Pres. Johnson's proclamation, see *The United States Army and Navy Journal, and Gazette of the Regular and Volunteer Forces* (New York: Army and Navy Journal, 1867), 4:816.

[37] Ashton S. H. White (1819–1902) was a clerk in the Dept. of the Interior from 1849 to 1876. He was also one of the aides who helped lay the cornerstone for the Washington Monument. *American Ancestry* (Albany, NY: Joel Munsell's Sons, 1893), 130; "Personal Notes about Washington People," *Washington Times* (Washington, DC), Mar. 28, 1902, 6; "The Surviving Marshals," *Evening Star* (Washington, DC), Feb. 21, 1885, 8.

Sioux,[38] and the Crows on the upper Yellowstone, to meet us in May, 1868, at Fort Laramie. We proceeded up the river to the mouth of the Cheyenne and turned back to Omaha, having ample time on this steamboat to discuss and deliberate on the problems submitted to our charge.

We all agreed that the nomad Indians should be removed from the vicinity of the two great railroads then in rapid construction, and be localized on one or other of the two great reservations south of Kansas and north of Nebraska; that agreements, not treaties, should be made for their liberal maintenance as to food, clothing, schools, and farming implements for ten years, during which time we believed that these Indians should become self-supporting. To the north we proposed to remove the various bands of Sioux, with such others as could be induced to locate near them; and to the south, on the Indian Territory already established, we proposed to remove the Cheyennes, Arapahoes, Kiowas, Comanches, and such others as we could prevail on to move thither.

At that date the Union Pacific construction had reached the Rocky Mountains at Cheyenne, and the Kansas Pacific to about Fort Wallace. We held council with the Ogallallas at the Forks of the Platte, and arranged to meet them all the next spring, 1868. In the spring of 1868 we met the Crows in council at Fort Laramie, the Sioux at the North Platte, the Shoshones or Snakes at Fort Hall, the Navajos at Fort Sumner, on the Pecos, and the Cheyennes and Arapahoes at Medicine Lodge. To accomplish these results the commission divided up into committees, General Augur going to the Shoshones, Mr. Tappan and I to the Navajos, and the remainder to Medicine Lodge. In that year we made treaties or arrangements with all the tribes which before had followed the buffalo in their annual migrations, and which brought them into constant conflict with the whites.

Mr. Tappan and I found it impossible to prevail on the Navajos to remove to the Indian Territory, and had to consent to their return to their former home, restricted to a limited reservation west of Santa Fé, about old Fort Defiance, and there they continue unto this day, rich in the possession of herds of sheep and goats, with some cattle and horses; and they have remained at peace ever since.

[38] Sitting Bull (c. 1837–1890) was a chief of the Sioux tribe; he attacked U.S. settlements in Iowa and Minnesota during the Civil War. He was known for his victory at the Battle of Little Bighorn, also known as the Battle of Greasy Grass, in 1876. *The Encyclopedia Britannica,* 11th ed. (New York: Encyclopedia Britannica, 1911), vol. 25, s.v. "Sitting Bull."

A part of our general plan was to organize the two great reservations into regular Territorial governments, with Governor, Council, courts, and civil officers. General Harney was temporarily assigned to that of the Sioux at the north, and General Hazen to that of the Kiowas, Comanches, Cheyennes, Arapahoes, etc., etc., at the south, but the patronage of the Indian Bureau was too strong for us, and that part of our labor failed. Still, the Indian Peace Commission of 1867–'68 did prepare the way for the great Pacific Railroads, which, for better or worse, have settled the fate of the buffalo and Indian forever. There have been wars and conflicts since with these Indians up to a recent period too numerous and complicated in their detail for me to unravel and record, but they have been the dying struggles of a singular race of brave men fighting against destiny, each less and less violent, till now the wild game is gone, the whites too numerous and powerful; so that the Indian question has become one of sentiment and charity, but not of war.

The peace, or "Quaker" policy, of which so much has been said, originated about thus: By the act of Congress, approved March 3, 1869, the forty-five regiments of infantry were reduced to twenty-five, and provision was made for the "muster out" of many of the surplus officers, and for retaining others to be absorbed by the usual promotions and casualties. On the 7th of May of that year, by authority of an act of Congress approved *June 30, 1834,* nine field-officers and fifty-nine captains and subalterns were detached and ordered to report to the Commissioner of Indian Affairs,[39] to serve as Indian superintendents and agents. Thus by an old law surplus army officers were made to displace the usual civil appointees, undoubtedly a change for the better, but most distasteful to members of Congress, who looked to these appointments as part of their proper patronage. The consequence was the law of July 15, 1870, which vacated the military commission of any officer who accepted or exercised the functions of a civil officer. I was then told that certain politicians called on President Grant, informing him that this law was chiefly designed to prevent his using army officers for Indian agents, "civil offices," which he believed to be both judicious and wise; army officers, as a rule, being better qualified to deal with Indians than the average political appointees. The President then quietly replied: "Gentlemen, you have defeated my plan of Indian management; but you shall not succeed in *your* purpose,

[39] Nathaniel G. Taylor was the commissioner of Indian Affairs in Mar. 1869. In Apr. he was replaced by Ely S. Parker (1828–1895). Parker, a chief of the Tonawanda Senecas and military secretary of USG, was the first Native American to hold that position. *CWHC,* 416.

for I will divide these appointments up among the religious churches, with which you dare not contend." The army officers were consequently relieved of their "civil offices," and the Indian agencies were apportioned to the several religious churches in about the proportion of their supposed strength—some to the Quakers, some to the Methodists, to the Catholics, Episcopalians, Presbyterians, etc., etc.—and thus it remains to the present time, these religious communities selecting the agents to be appointed by the Secretary of the Interior. The Quakers, being first named, gave name to the policy, and it is called the "Quaker" policy to-day. Meantime railroads and settlements by hardy, bold pioneers have made the character of Indian agents of small concern, and it matters little who are the beneficiaries.

As was clearly foreseen, General U. S. Grant was duly nominated, and on the 7th of November, 1868, was elected President of the United States for the four years beginning with March 4, 1869.

On the 15th and 16th of December, 1868, the four societies of the Armies of the Cumberland, Tennessee, Ohio, and Georgia, held a joint reunion at Chicago, at which were present over two thousand of the surviving officers and soldiers of the war. The ceremonies consisted of the joint meeting in Crosby's magnificent opera-house,[40] at which General George H. Thomas presided. General W. W. Belknap was the orator for the Army of the Tennessee, General Charles Cruft for the Army of the Cumberland, General J. D. Cox for the Army of the Ohio, and General William Cogswell for the Army of Georgia.[41] The banquet was held in the vast Chamber of Commerce, at which I presided. General Grant, President-elect, General J. M. Schofield, Secretary of War, General H. W. Slocum, and nearly every general officer of note was present except General Sheridan, who at the moment was fighting the Cheyennes in Southern Kansas and the Indian country.

At that time we discussed the army changes which would necessarily occur in the following March, and it was generally understood that I was to succeed General Grant as general-in-chief, but as to my successor, Meade, Thomas, and Sheridan were candidates. And here I will remark that General Grant, afterward famous as the "silent man," used to be very gossipy, and no one was

[40] The Crosby Opera House opened in 1865 and operated until it was destroyed in the Great Chicago Fire of 1871. Eugene H. Cropsey, *Crosby's Opera House: Symbol of Chicago's Cultural Awakening* (Madison, NJ: Fairleigh Dickinson University Press, 1999), 11.

[41] William Cogswell (1838–1895) graduated from Harvard Law School and was brevetted brigadier general during the Civil War. He represented Massachusetts in the U.S. House of Representatives from 1887 to 1895. *CWHC,* 179.

ever more fond than he of telling anecdotes of our West Point and early army life. At the Chicago reunion he told me that I would have to come to Washington, that he wanted me to effect a change as to the general staff, which he had long contemplated, and which was outlined in his letter to Mr. Stanton of January 29, 1866, given hereafter, which had been repeatedly published, and was well known to the military world; that on being inaugurated President on the 4th of March he would retain General Schofield as his Secretary of War until the change had become habitual; that the modern custom of the Secretary of War giving military orders to the adjutant-general and other staff officers was positively wrong and should be stopped. Speaking of General Grant's personal characteristics at that period of his life, I recall a conversation in his carriage, when, riding down Pennsylvania Avenue, he inquired of me in a humorous way, "Sherman, what special hobby do you intend to adopt?" I inquired what he meant, and he explained that all men had their special weakness or vanity, and that it was wiser to choose one's own than to leave the newspapers to affix one less acceptable, and that for his part he had chosen the "horse," so that when any one tried to pump him he would turn the conversation to his "horse." I answered that I would stick to the "theatre and balls," for I was always fond of seeing young people happy, and did actually acquire a reputation for "dancing," though I had not attempted the waltz, or anything more than the ordinary cotillon, since the war.

On the 24th of February, 1869, I was summoned to Washington, arriving on the 26th, taking along my aides, Lieutenant-Colonels Dayton and Audenried.

On the 4th of March General Grant was duly inaugurated President of the United States, and I was nominated and confirmed as General of the Army.

Major-General P. H. Sheridan was at the same time nominated and confirmed as lieutenant-general, with orders to command the Military Division of the Missouri, which he did, moving the headquarters from St. Louis to Chicago; and General Meade was assigned to command the Military Division of the Atlantic, with headquarters at Philadelphia.

At that moment General Meade was in Atlanta, Georgia, commanding the Third Military District under the "Reconstruction Act;" and General Thomas, whose post was in Nashville, was in Washington on a court of inquiry investigating certain allegations against General A. B. Dyer, Chief of Ordnance.[42] He occupied the room of the second floor in the building on the corner of H and Fifteenth Streets, since become Wormley's Hotel. I at the

[42] Alex B. Dyer (1815–1874) graduated from the USMA in 1837 and was chief of ordnance for the U.S. Army from 1864 to 1874. He invented the Dyer projectile. *CWHC,* 220.

time was staying with my brother, Senator Sherman, at his residence, 1321 K Street, and it was my habit each morning to stop at Thomas's room on my way to the office in the War Department to tell him the military news, and to talk over matters of common interest. We had been intimately associated as "man and boy" for thirty-odd years, and I profess to have had better opportunities to know him than any man then living. His fame as the "Rock of Chickamauga" was perfect, and by the world at large he was considered as the embodiment of strength, calmness, and imperturbability. Yet of all my acquaintances Thomas worried and fretted over what he construed neglects or acts of favoritism more than any other. At that time he was much worried by what he supposed was injustice in the promotion of General Sheridan, and still more that General Meade should have an Eastern station, which compelled him to remain at Nashville or go to the Pacific. General Thomas claimed that all his life he had been stationed in the South or remote West, and had not had a fair share of Eastern posts, whereas that General Meade had always been there. I tried to get him to go with me to see President Grant and talk the matter over frankly, but he would not, and I had to act as a friendly mediator. General Grant assured me at the time that he not only admired and respected General Thomas, but actually loved him as a man, and he authorized me in making up commands for the general officers to do any-thing and everything to favor him, only he could not recede from his former action in respect to Generals Sheridan and Meade.

Prior to General Grant's inauguration the army register showed as major-generals Halleck, Meade, Sheridan, Thomas, and Hancock. Therefore, the promotion of General Sheridan to be lieutenant-general did not "overslaugh" Thomas, but it did Meade and Halleck. The latter did not expect promotion; General Meade did, but was partially, not wholly, reconciled by being stationed at Philadelphia, the home of his family; and President Grant assured me that he knew of his own knowledge that General Sheridan had been nominated major-general before General Meade, but had waived dates out of respect for his age and longer service, and that he had nominated him as lieutenant-general by reason of his special fitness to command the Military Division of the Missouri, embracing all the wild Indians, at that very moment in a state of hostility. I gave General Thomas the choice of every other command in the army, and of his own choice he went to San Francisco, California, where he died, March 28, 1870. The truth is, Congress should have provided by law for three lieutenant-generals for these three pre-eminent soldiers, and should have dated their commissions with "Gettysburg,"

"Winchester," and "Nashville." It would have been a graceful act, and might have prolonged the lives of two most popular officers, who died soon after, feeling that they had experienced ingratitude and neglect.[43]

Soon after General Grant's inauguration as President, and, as I supposed, in fulfilment of his plan divulged in Chicago the previous December, were made the following:

HEADQUARTERS OF THE ARMY,
WASHINGTON, *March* 8, 1869.

General Orders No. 11:

The following orders of the President of the United States are published for the information and government of all concerned:

WAR DEPARTMENT,
WASHINGTON CITY, *March* 5, 1869.

By direction of the President, General William T. Sherman will assume command of the Army of the United States.

The chiefs of staff corps, departments, and bureaus will report to and act under the immediate orders of the general commanding the army.

Any official business which by law or regulation requires the action of the President or Secretary of War will be submitted by the General of the Army to the Secretary of War, and in general all orders from the President or Secretary of War to any portion of the army, line or staff, will be transmitted through the General of the Army.

J. M. SCHOFIELD, *Secretary of War.*

By command of the General of the Army.

E. D. TOWNSEND, *Assistant Adjutant-General.*

On the same day I issued my General Orders No. 12, assuming command and naming all the heads of staff departments and bureaus as members of my staff, adding to my then three aides, Colonels McCoy, Dayton, and

[43] Halleck died in Jan. 1872 and Meade died in Nov. 1872. *CWHC,* 274, 385.

Audenried, the names of Colonels Comstock, Horace Porter, and Dent,[44] agreeing with President Grant that the two latter could remain with him till I should need their personal services or ask their resignations.

I was soon made aware that the heads of several of the staff corps were restive under this new order of things, for by long usage they had grown to believe themselves not officers of the army in a technical sense, but a part of the War Department, the civil branch of the Government which connects the army with the President and Congress.

In a short time General John A. Rawlins, General Grant's former chief of staff, was nominated and confirmed as Secretary of War; and soon appeared this order:

HEADQUARTERS OF THE ARMY,
ADJUTANT-GENERAL'S OFFICE,
WASHINGTON, *March* 27, 1869.

General Orders No. 28:

The following orders received for the War Department are published for the government of all concerned:

WAR DEPARTMENT,
WASHINGTON CITY, *March* 26, 1869.

By direction of the President, the order of the Secretary of War, dated War Department, March 5, 1869, and published in General Orders No. 11, headquarters of the army, Adjutant-General's Office, dated March 8, 1869, except so much as directs General W. T. Sherman to assume command of the Army of the United States, is hereby rescinded.

All official business which by law or regulations requires the action of the President or Secretary of War will be submitted by the chiefs of staff corps, departments, and bureaus to the Secretary of War.

All orders and instructions relating to military operations issued by the President or Secretary of War will be issued through the General of the Army.

JOHN A. RAWLINS, *Secretary of War.*

[44] Frederick T. Dent (1820–1892), brother-in-law of USG, graduated from the USMA in 1843. He served as an aide-de-camp to WTS in 1869–1870. *CWHC,* 206–207.

By command of General SHERMAN:
E. D. TOWNSEND, *Assistant Adjutant-General.*

Thus we were thrown back on the old method in having a double-if not a treble-headed machine. Each head of a bureau in daily consultation with the Secretary of War, and the general to command without an adjutant, quartermaster, commissary, or any staff except his own aides, often reading in the newspapers of military events and orders before he could be consulted or informed. This was the very reverse of what General Grant, after four years' experience in Washington as general-in-chief, seemed to want, different from what he had explained to me in Chicago, and totally different from the demand he had made on Secretary of War Stanton in his complete letter of January 29, 1866. I went to him to know the cause. He said he had been informed by members of Congress that his action, as defined by his order of March 5th, was regarded as a violation of laws making provision for the bureaus of the War Department; that he had repealed his own orders, but not mine, and that he had no doubt that General Rawlins and I could draw the line of separation satisfactorily to us both. General Rawlins was very conscientious, but a very sick man when appointed Secretary of War. Several times he made orders through the adjutant-general to individuals of the army without notifying me, but always when his attention was called to it he apologized, and repeatedly said to me that he understood from his experience on General Grant's staff how almost insulting it was for orders to go to individuals of a regiment, brigade, division, or an army of any kind without the commanding officer being consulted or even advised. This habit is more common at Washington than any place on earth, unless it be in London, where nearly the same condition of facts exists. Members of Congress daily appeal to the Secretary of War for the discharge of some soldier on the application of a mother, or some young officer has to be dry-nursed, withdrawn from his company on the plains to be stationed near home. The Secretary of War, sometimes moved by private reasons, or more likely to oblige the member of Congress, grants the order, of which the commanding general knows nothing till he reads it in the newspapers. Also, an Indian tribe, goaded by the pressure of white neighbors, breaks out in revolt. The general-in-chief must reënforce the local garrisons not only with men, but horses, wagons, ammunition, and food. All the necessary information is in the staff bureaus in Washington, but the general has no *right* to call for it, and generally finds it more practicable to ask by telegraph of the distant division or department commanders for the information before making the formal orders. The general in actual command of the army should have a full staff, subject to his own command. If not, he cannot be held responsible for results.

General Rawlins sank away visibly, rapidly, and died in Washington, September 6, 1869, and I was appointed to perform the duties of his office till a successor could be selected.[45] I realized how much easier and better it was to have both offices conjoined. The army then had one constitutional commander-in-chief of both army and navy, and one actual commanding general, bringing all parts into real harmony. An army to be useful must be a unit, and out of this has grown the saying, attributed to Napoleon, but doubtless spoken before the days of Alexander,[46] that an army with an inefficient commander was better than one with two able heads. Our political system and methods, however, demanded a separate Secretary of War, and in October President Grant asked me to scan the list of the volunteer generals of good record who had served in the civil war, preferably from the "West." I did so, and submitted to him in writing the names of W. W. Belknap, of Iowa; G. M. Dodge, the Chief Engineer of the Union Pacific Railroad; and Lucius Fairchild, of Madison, Wisconsin.[47] I also named General John W. Sprague, then employed by the Northern Pacific Railroad in Washington Territory. General Grant knew them all personally, and said if General Dodge were not connected with the Union Pacific Railroad, with which the Secretary of War must necessarily have large transactions, he would choose him, but as the case stood, and remembering the very excellent speech made by General Belknap at the Chicago reunion of December, 1868, he authorized me to communicate with him to ascertain if he were willing to come to Washington as Secretary of War. General Belknap was then the collector of internal revenue at Keokuk, Iowa. I telegraphed him and received a prompt and favorable answer. His name was sent to the Senate, promptly confirmed, and he entered on his duties October 25, 1869. General Belknap surely had at that date as fair a fame as any officer of volunteers of my personal acquaintance. He took up the business where it was left off, and gradually fell into the current which led to the command of the army itself as of the legal and financial matters which properly pertain to the War Department. Orders granting leaves of absence to officers, transfers, discharges of

[45] John A. Rawlins died of tuberculosis. *CWHC,* 447.

[46] Alexander the Great (c. 356BC–323BC) was the king of Macedon. Richard Stoneman, *Alexander the Great: A Life in Legend* (New Haven, CT: Yale University Press, 2008), xvi–xvii.

[47] Lucius Fairchild (1831–1896) lost his left arm and was captured at the Battle of Gettysburg. He later served as the governor of Wisconsin from 1866 to 1872. *CWHC,* 231.

soldiers for favor, and all the old abuses, which had embittered the life of General Scott in the days of Secretaries of War Marcy and Davis, were renewed. I called his attention to these facts, but without sensible effect. My office was under his in the old War Department, and one day I sent my aide-de-camp, Colonel Audenried, up to him with some message, and when he returned red as a beet, very much agitated, he asked me as a personal favor never again to send him to General Belknap. I inquired his reason, and he explained that he had been treated with a rudeness and discourtesy he had never seen displayed by any officer to a soldier. Colonel Audenried was one of the most polished gentlemen in the army, noted for his personal bearing and deportment, and I had some trouble to impress on him the patience necessary for the occasion, but I promised on future occasions to send some other or go myself. Things went on from bad to worse, till in 1870 I received from Mr. Hugh Campbell, of St. Louis, a personal friend and an honorable gentleman,[48] a telegraphic message complaining that I had removed from his position Mr. Ward, post-trader at Fort Laramie,[49] with only a month in which to dispose of his large stock of goods, to make room for his successor.

It so happened that we of the Indian Peace Commission had been much indebted to this same trader, Ward, for advances of flour, sugar, and coffee, to provide for the Crow Indians, who had come down from their reservation on the Yellowstone to meet us in 1868, before our own supplies had been received. For a time I could not comprehend the nature of Mr. Campbell's complaint, so I telegraphed to the department commander, General C. C. Augur, at Omaha, to know if any such occurrence had happened, and the reasons therefor. I received a prompt answer that it was substantially true, and had been ordered by the Secretary of War. It so happened that during General Grant's command of the army Congress had given to the general of the army the appointment of "post-traders." He had naturally devolved it on the subordinate division and department commanders, but the legal power remained with the general of the army. I went up to the Secretary of War, showed him the telegraphic correspondence, and pointed out the existing law in the Revised Statutes. General Belknap was visibly taken aback, and explained that he had supposed the right of appointment rested with him, that Ward was an old

[48] Hugh Campbell was appointed by Pres. Lincoln to the Commission on War Claims on Oct. 25, 1861. *PUSG,* 10:355*n*.

[49] Seth E. Ward (1820–1903) was appointed sutler at Fort Laramie, WY, in 1856 and remained in that position until 1871. "Death of Seth E. Ward," *Missouri Telegraph* (Fulton, MO), Dec. 22, 1903, 2.

rebel Democrat, etc.; whereas Ward had been in fact the sutler of Fort Laramie, a United States military post, throughout the civil war. I told him that I should revoke his orders, and leave the matter where it belonged, to the local council of administration and commanding officers. Ward was unanimously reëlected and reinstated. He remained the trader of the post until Congress repealed the law, and gave back the power of appointment to the Secretary of War, when of course he had to go. But meantime he was able to make the necessary business arrangements which saved him and his partners the sacrifice which would have been necessary in the first instance. I never had any knowledge whatever of General Belknap's transactions with the traders at Fort Sill and Fort Lincoln which resulted in his downfall. I have never sought to ascertain his motives for breaking with me, because he knew I had always befriended him while under my military command, and in securing him his office of Secretary of War. I spoke frequently to President Grant of the growing tendency of his Secretary of War to usurp all the powers of the commanding general, which would surely result in driving me away. He as frequently promised to bring us together to agree upon a just line of separation of our respective offices, but never did.

Determined to bring the matter to an issue, I wrote the following letter:

HEADQUARTERS ARMY OF THE UNITED STATES,
WASHINGTON, D. C., *August* 17, 1870.

General W. W. BELKNAP, *Secretary of War.*

GENERAL: I must urgently and respectfully invite your attention when at leisure to a matter of deep interest to future commanding generals of the army more than to myself, of the imperative necessity of fixing and clearly defining the limits of the powers and duties of the general of the army or of whomsoever may succeed to the place of commander-in-chief.

The case is well stated by General Grant in his letter of January 29, 1866, to the Secretary of War, Mr. Stanton, hereto appended, and though I find no official answer recorded, I remember that General Grant told me that the Secretary of War had promptly assured him in conversation that he fully approved of his views as expressed in this letter.

At that time the subject was much discussed, and soon after Congress enacted the bill reviving the grade of general, which bill was approved July 25, 1866, and provided that the general, when commissioned, may be authorized under the direction and during the pleasure of the President to command the armies of the United States; and a few days after, viz., July 28, 1866, was enacted the law which defined the military peace establishment. The enacting clause reads: "That the military peace establishment of the United States shall hereafter consist of five regiments of artillery, ten regiments of cavalry, forty-five regiments of infantry, the professors and Corps of Cadets of the United States Military Academy, and such other forces as shall be provided for by this act, to be known as the army of the United States."

The act then recites in great detail all the parts of the army, making no distinction between the line and staff, but clearly makes each and every part an element of the whole.

Section 37 provides for a board to revise the army regulations and report; and declares that the regulations then in force, viz., those of 1863, should remain until Congress "shall act on said report;" and section 38 and last enacts that all laws and parts of laws inconsistent with the provisions of this act be and the same are hereby repealed.

Under the provisions of this law my predecessor, General Grant, did not hesitate to command and make orders to all parts of the army, the Military Academy, and staff, and it was under his advice that the new regulations were compiled in 1868 that drew the line more clearly between the high and responsible duties of the Secretary of War and the general of the army. He assured me many a time before I was called here to succeed him that he wanted me to perfect the distinction, and it was by his express orders that on assuming the command of the army I specifically placed the heads of the staff corps here in Washington in the exact relation to the army which they would bear to an army in the field.

I am aware that subsequently, in his orders of March 26th, he modified his former orders of March 5th, but only as to the heads of bureaus in Washington, who have, he told me, certain functions of office imposed on them by special laws of Congress, which laws, of course, override all orders and regulations, but I did not either understand from him in person, or from General Rawlins, at whose instance this order was made, that it was designed in any way to modify, alter, or change his purposes that division and department commanders, as well as the general of the army, should exercise the same command of the staff as they did of the line of the army.

I need not remind the Secretary that orders and reports are made to and from the Military Academy which the general does not even see, though the Military Academy is specifically named as a part of that army which he is required to command. Leaves of absence are granted, the stations of officers are changed, and other orders are now made directly to the army, not through the general, but direct through other officials and the adjutant-general. So long as this is the case I surely do not command the army of the United States, and am not responsible for it.

I am aware that the confusion results from the fact that the thirty-seventh section of the act of July 28, 1866, clothes the army regulations of 1863 with the sanction of law, but the next section repeals all laws and parts of laws inconsistent with the provisions of this act. The regulations of 1863 are but a compilation of orders made prior to the war, when such men as Davis and Floyd took pleasure in stripping General Scott of even the semblance of power, and purposely reduced him to a cipher in the command of the army.

Not one word can be found in those regulations speaking of the duties of the lieutenant-general commanding the army, or defining a single act of authority rightfully devolving on him. Not a single mention is made of the rights and duties of a commander-in-chief of the army. He is ignored, and purposely, too, as a part of the programme resulting in the rebellion, that the army without a legitimate head should pass into the anarchy which these men were shaping for the whole country.

I invite your attention to the army regulations of 1847, when our best soldiers lived, among whom was your own father, and see paragraphs 48 and 49, page 8, and they are so important that I quote them entire:

"48. The military establishment is placed under the orders of the major-general commanding in chief in all that regards its discipline and military control. Its fiscal arrangements properly belong to the administrative departments of the staff and to the Treasury Department under the direction of the Secretary of War.

"49. The general of the army will watch over the economy of the service in all that relates to the expenditure of money, supply of arms, ordnance and ordnance stores, clothing, equipments, camp-equipage, medical and hospital stores, barracks, quarters, transportation, Military Academy, pay, and subsistence: in short, everything which enters into the expenses of the military establishment, whether personal or material. He will also see that the estimates for the military service are based on proper data, and made for the objects contemplated by law, and necessary to the due support and useful employment of the army. In carrying into effect these important duties, he will call to his counsel and assistance the staff, and those officers proper, in his opinion, to be employed in verifying and inspecting all the objects which may require attention. The rules and regulations established for the government of the army, and the laws relating to the military establishment, are the guides to the commanding general in the performance of his duties."

Why was this, or why was all mention of any field of duty for the head of the army left out of the army regulations? Simply because Jefferson Davis had a purpose, and absorbed to himself, as Secretary of War, as General Grant well says, all the powers of commander-in-chief. Floyd succeeded him, and the last regulations of 1863 were but a new compilation of *their* orders, hastily collected and published to supply a vast army with a new edition.

I contend that all parts of these regulations inconsistent with the law of July 28, 1866, are repealed.

I surely do not ask for any power myself, but I hope and trust, now when we have a military President and a military Secretary of War, that in the new regulations to be laid before Congress next session the functions and duties of the commander-in-chief will be so clearly marked out and defined that they may be understood by himself and the army at large.

I am, with great respect, your obedient servant,

W. T. SHERMAN, *General.*

[INCLOSURE.]

WASHINGTON, *January* 29, 1866.

Hon. E. M. STANTON, *Secretary of War:*

From the period of the difficulties between Major-General (now Lieutenant-General) Scott with Secretary Marcy, during the administration of President Polk, the command of the army virtually passed into the hands of the Secretary of War.

From that day to the breaking out of the rebellion the general-in-chief never kept his headquarters in Washington, and could not, consequently, with propriety resume his proper functions. To administer the affairs of the army properly, headquarters and the adjutant-general's office must be in the same place.

During the war, while in the field, my functions as commander of all the armies was never impaired, but were facilitated in all essential matters by the Administration and by the War Department. Now, however, that the war is over, and I have brought my headquarters to the city, I find my present position embarrassing and, I think, out of place. I have been intending, or did intend, to make the beginning of the New Year the time to bring this matter before you, with the view of asking to have the old condition of affairs restored, but from diffidence about mentioning the matter have delayed. In a few words I will state what I conceive to be my duties and my place, and ask respectfully to be restored to them and it.

The entire adjutant-general's office should be under the entire control of the general-in-chief of the army. No orders should go to the army, or the adjutant-general, except through the general-in-chief. Such as require the action of the President would be laid before the Secretary of War, whose actions would be regarded as those of the President. In short, in my opinion, the general-in-chief stands between the President and the army in all official matters, and the Secretary of War is between the army (through the general-in-chief) and the President.

I can very well conceive that a rule so long disregarded could not, or would not, be restored without the subject being presented, and I now do so respectfully for your consideration.

U. S. Grant, *Lieutenant-General.*

General Belknap never answered that letter.

In August, 1870, was held at Des Moines, Iowa, an encampment of old soldiers which I attended, *en route* to the Pacific, and at Omaha received this letter:

Long Branch, New Jersey, *August* 18, 1870.

General W. T. Sherman.

Dear General: Your letter of the 7th inst. did not reach Long Branch until after I had left for St. Louis, and consequently is just before me for the first time. I do not know what changes recent laws, particularly the last army bill passed, make in the relations between the general of the army and the Secretary of War.

Not having this law or other statutes here, I cannot examine the subject now, nor would I want to without consultation with the Secretary of War. On our return to Washington I have no doubt but that the relations between the Secretary and yourself can be made pleasant, and the duties of each be so clearly defined as to leave no doubt where the authority of one leaves off and the other commences.

My own views, when commanding the army, were that orders to the army should go through the general. No changes should be made, however, either of the location of troops or officers, without the knowledge of the Secretary of War.

In peace, the general commanded them without reporting to the Secretary further than he chose the specific orders he gave from time to time, but subjected himself to orders from the Secretary, the latter deriving his authority to give orders from the President. As Congress has the right, however, to make rules and regulations for the government of the army, rules made by them whether they are as they should be or not, will have to govern. As before stated, I have not examined the recent law.

Yours truly,

U. S. GRANT.

To which I replied:

OMAHA, NEBRASKA, *September* 2, 1870.

General U. S. GRANT, *Washington, D. C.*

DEAR GENERAL: I have received your most acceptable letter of August 18th, and assure you that I am perfectly willing to abide by any decision you may make. We had a most enthusiastic meeting at Des Moines, and General Belknap gave us a fine, finished address. I have concluded to go over to San Francisco to attend the annual celebration of the Pioneers, to be held on the 9th instant; from there I will make a short tour, aiming to get back to St. Louis by the 1st of October, and so on to Washington without unnecessary delay.

Conscious of the heavy burdens already on you, I should refrain from adding one ounce to your load of care, but it seems to me now is the time to fix clearly and plainly the field of duty for the Secretary of War and the commanding general of the army, so that we may escape the unpleasant controversy that gave so much scandal in General Scott's time, and leave to our successors a clear field.

No matter what the result, I promise to submit to whatever decision you may make. I also feel certain that General Belknap thinks he is simply executing the law as it now stands, but I am equally certain that he does not interpret the law reviving the grade of general, and that fixing the "peace establishment" of 1868, as I construe them.

For instance, I am supposed to control the discipline of the Military Academy as a part of the army, whereas General Belknap ordered a court of inquiry in the case of the colored cadet, made the detail, reviewed the proceedings, and made his order, without my knowing a word of it, except through the newspapers; and more recently, when I went to Chicago to attend to some division business, I found the inspector-general (Hardie) under orders from the Secretary of War to go to Montana on some claim business.

All I ask is that such orders should go through me. If all the staff-officers are subject to receive orders direct from the Secretary of War it will surely clash with the orders they may be in the act of executing from me, or from their immediate commanders.

I ask that General Belknap draw up some clear, well-defined rules for my action, that he show them to me before publication, that I make on them my remarks, and then that you make a final decision. I promise faithfully to abide by it, or give up my commission.

Please show this to General Belknap, and I will be back early in October. With great respect, your friend,

W. T. SHERMAN.

I did return about October 15th, saw President Grant, who said nothing had been done in the premises, but that he would bring General Belknap and me together and settle this matter. Matters went along pretty much as usual till the month of August, 1871, when I dined at the Arlington with Admiral Alden and General Belknap. The former said he had been promoted to rear-admiral and appointed to command the European squadron, then at Villa Franca, near Nice, and that he was going out in the frigate Wabash, inviting me to go along. I had never been to Europe, and the opportunity was too tempting to refuse. After some preliminaries I agreed to go along, taking with me as aides-de-camp Colonel Audenried and Lieutenant Fred Grant.[50] The Wabash was being overhauled at the Navy-Yard at Boston, and was not ready to sail till November, when she came to New York, where we all embarked Saturday, November 11th.

I have very full notes of the whole trip, and here need only state that we went out to the Island of Madeira, and thence to Cadiz and Gibraltar. Here my party landed, and the Wabash went on to Villa Franca. From Gibraltar we made the general tour of Spain to Bordeaux, through the south of France to Marseilles, Toulon, etc., to Nice, from which place we rejoined the Wabash and brought ashore our baggage.

From Nice we went to Genoa, Turin, the Mont Cenis Tunnel, Milan, Venice, etc., to Rome. Thence to Naples, Messina, and Syracuse, where we took a steamer to Malta. From Malta to Egypt and Constantinople, to Sebastopol, Poti, and Tiflis. At Constantinople and Sebastopol my party was increased by Governor Curtin,[51] his son, and Mr. McGahan.

It was my purpose to have reached the Caspian, and taken boats to the Volga, and up that river as far as navigation would permit, but we were dissuaded by the Grand-Duke Michael, Governor-General of the Caucasas,[52] and took carriages six hundred miles to Taganrog, on the Sea of Azof, to which point the railroad system of Russia was completed. From Taganrog we took cars to Moscow and St. Petersburg. Here Mr. Curtin and party remained, he being our Minister at that court; also Fred Grant left us to visit his aunt at Copenhagen.[53] Colonel Audenried and I then completed the tour

[50] Frederick D. Grant (1850–1912), eldest son of USG, graduated from the USMA in 1871. He took a leave of absence from the army in June 1871 to join WTS on his trip to Europe. *USMA,* 3:182.

[51] Andrew G. Curtin (1815–1894) was the governor of Pennsylvania during the Civil War and was appointed minister to Russia by USG in 1869. "Death's Shining Marks, Two Great and Good Men Gone Hence," *Los Angeles Herald,* Oct. 8, 1894, 1.

[52] Michael Nikolaevich (1832–1909) became the viceroy of the Caucasus and commander in chief of the Caucasian army in 1863. "Grand Duke Michael's Life," *Grand Island Independent* (Grand Island, NE), Dec. 27, 1909, 4.

[53] Frederick D. Grant left for Copenhagen on June 1, 1872, to visit his father's sister, Mary Cramer (1839–1905), wife of Michael Cramer, the ambassador to Denmark. On June 13, WTS wrote to his wife about Frederick, "the papers make the most of Prince Fred—He is a good natured fellow, but cares for little. He went to see his Aunt at Copenhagen—& joined me at Berlin; but asked to stay a few days more, and at the time he was to join me, he wrote that he would go to Paris to see Nellie, and would rejoin me at Geneva, or Paris. Of course I go on my

of interior Europe, taking in Warsaw, Berlin, Vienna, Switzerland, France, England, Scotland, and Ireland, embarking for home in the good steamer Baltic, Saturday, September 7, 1872, reaching Washington, D. C., September 22d. I refrain from dwelling on this trip, because it would swell this chapter beyond my purpose.[54]

When I regained my office I found matters unchanged since my departure, the Secretary of War exercising all the functions of commander-in-chief, and I determined to allow things to run to their necessary conclusion. In 1873 my daughter Minnie also made a trip to Europe, and I resolved as soon as she returned that I would simply move back to St. Louis to execute my office there as best I could. But I was embarrassed by being the possessor of a large piece of property in Washington on I Street, near the corner of Third, which I could at the time neither sell nor give away. It came into my possession as a gift from friends in New York and Boston, who had purchased it of General Grant and transferred to me at the price of $65,000.

The house was very large, costly to light, heat, and maintain, and Congress had reduced my pay four or five thousand dollars a year, so that I was gradually being impoverished. Taxes, too, grew annually, from about four hundred dollars a year to fifteen hundred, besides all sorts of special taxes.

Finding myself caught in a dilemma, I added a new hall, and made out of it two houses, one of which I occupied, and the other I rented, and thus matters stood in 1873–'74. By the agency of Mr. Hall, a neighbor and broker, I effected a sale of the property to the present owner, Mr. Emory, at a fair price, accepting about half payment in notes, and the other half in a piece of property on E Street, which I afterward exchanged for a place in Côte Brilliante, a suburb of St. Louis, which I still own. Being thus footloose, and having repeatedly notified President Grant of my purpose, I wrote the Secretary of War on the 8th day of May, 1874, asking the authority of the President and the War Department to remove my headquarters to St. Louis.

---

course utterly regardless of him, and don't want any one to find fault with General Grant for sending him with me, as I know Mrs. Grant did it, and of course she did it as a mother, thinking herself very smart to catch the chance." Julia D. Grant, *The Personal Memoirs of Julia Dent Grant (Mrs. Ulysses S. Grant)*, ed. John Y. Simon (New York: G. P. Putnam's sons, 1975), 29; *PUSG*, 23:83*n*, 172.

[54] WTS detailed his trip abroad in letters to S. H. M. Byers, the U.S. consul general to Switzerland and Italy. S. H. M. Byers, *Twenty Years in Europe: A Consul-General's Memories of Noted People, with Letters from General W. T. Sherman* (Chicago: Rand McNally, 1900), 53–71.

On the 11th day of May General Belknap replied that I had the assent of the President and himself, inclosing the rough draft of an order to accomplish this result, which I answered on the 15th, expressing my entire satisfaction, only requesting delay in the publication of the orders till August or September, as I preferred to make the changes in the month of October.[55]

On the 3d of September these orders were made:

WAR DEPARTMENT, ADJUTANT-GENERAL'S OFFICE,
WASHINGTON, *September* 3, 1874.

General Orders No. 108.

With the assent of the President, and at the request of the General, the headquarters of the armies of the United States will be established at St. Louis, Missouri, in the month of October next.

The regulations and orders now governing the functions of the General of the Army, and those in relation to transactions of business with the War Department and its bureaus, will continue in force.

By order of the Secretary of War:

E. D. TOWNSEND, *Adjutant-General.*

Our daughter Minnie was married October 1, 1874, to Thomas W. Fitch, United States Navy,[56] and we all forthwith packed up and regained our own house at St. Louis, taking an office on the corner of Tenth and Locust Streets. The only staff I brought with me were the aides allowed by law, and, though we went through the forms of "command," I realized that it was a farce, and it did not need a prophet to foretell it would end in a tragedy. We made ourselves very comfortable, made many pleasant excursions into the interior, had a large correspondence, and escaped the mortification of being slighted by men in Washington who were using their temporary power for selfish ends.

Early in March, 1876, appeared in all the newspapers of the day the sensational report from Washington that Secretary of War Belknap had been detected in selling sutlerships in the army; that he had confessed it to Repre-

[55] In his letter to Secretary of War William Belknap, WTS wrote, "Strong reasons official and personal impel me to this step." Robert G. Athearn, *William Tecumseh Sherman and the Settlement of the West* (Norman: University of Oklahoma Press, 1995), 263.

[56] Thomas W. Fitch (1843–1915) was an assistant engineer in the U.S. Navy during the Civil War. He later owned steel plants in St. Louis and Pittsburgh. "Obituary: Lieutenant Thomas W. Fitch," *Brooklyn Daily Eagle,* Apr. 10, 1915, 2.

sentative Blackburn, of Kentucky;[57] that he had tendered his resignation, which had been accepted by the President; and that he was still subject to impeachment, would be impeached and tried by the Senate.[58] I was surprised to learn that General Belknap was dishonest in money matters, for I believed him a brave soldier, and I surely thought him honest; but the truth was soon revealed from Washington, and very soon after I received from Judge Alphonso Taft, of Cincinnati, a letter informing me that he had been appointed Secretary of War, and should insist on my immediate return to Washington.[59] I answered that I was ready to go to Washington, or anywhere, if assured of decent treatment.

I proceeded to Washington, when, on the 6th of April, were published these orders:

WAR DEPARTMENT, ADJUTANT-GENERAL'S OFFICE,
WASHINGTON, *April* 6, 1876.

General Orders No. 28.

The following orders of the President of the United States are hereby promulgated for the information and guidance of all concerned:

The headquarters of the army are hereby reëstablished at Washington City, and all orders and instructions relative to military operations or affecting the military control and discipline of the army issued by the President through the Secretary of War, shall be promulgated through the General of the Army, and the departments of the Adjutant-General and the Inspector-General shall report to him, and be under his control in all matters relating thereto.

By order of the Secretary of War:

E. D. TOWNSEND, *Adjutant-General.*

[57] Joseph C. S. Blackburn (1838–1918) was an aide-de-camp to Confederate general William Preston during the Civil War. He was elected to the U.S. House of Representatives in 1874 and to the U.S. Senate in 1898. L. F. Johnson, *History of the Frankfort Cemetery* (Frankfort, KY: Roberts, 1921), s.v. "Hon. Joseph C. S. Blackburn."

[58] On Mar. 2, 1876, news broke that Belknap had resigned as secretary of war. Pres. Grant gave temporary command of the office to the secretary of the U.S. Navy, George Robeson. "Belknap's Resignation Accepted," *Evening Star* (Washington, DC), Mar. 2, 1876, 1.

[59] Alphonso Taft (1810–1891), a founding member of the Republican Party, served as the secretary of war during Mar. 8–May 22, 1876. Walter H. Crockett, *Vermont: The Green Mountain State* (New York: Century, 1923), vol. 5, s.v. "Alphonso Taft."

This was all I had ever asked; accordingly my personal staff were brought back to Washington, where we resumed our old places; only I did not, for some time, bring back the family, and then only to a rented house on Fifteenth Street, which we occupied till we left Washington for good. During the period from 1876 to 1884 we had as Secretaries of War in succession, the Hons. Alphonso Taft, J. D. Cameron, George W. McCrary, Alexander Ramsey, and R. T. Lincoln,[60] with each and all of whom I was on terms of the most intimate and friendly relations.

And here I will record of Washington that I saw it, under the magic hand of Alexander R. Shepherd,[61] grow from a straggling, ill-paved city, to one of the cleanest, most beautiful, and attractive cities of the whole world. Its climate is salubrious, with as much sunshine as any city of America. The country immediately about it is naturally beautiful and romantic, especially up the Potomac, in the region of the Great Falls; and, though the soil be poor as compared with that of my present home, it is susceptible of easy improvement and embellishment. The social advantages cannot be surpassed even in London, Paris, or Vienna; and among the resident population, the members of the Supreme Court, Senate, House of Representatives, army, navy, and the several executive departments, may be found an intellectual class one cannot encounter in our commercial and manufacturing cities. The student may, without tax and without price, have access, in the libraries of Congress and of the several departments, to books of every nature and kind; and the museums of natural history are rapidly approaching a standard of comparison with the best of the world. Yet it is the usual and proper center of political intrigue, from which the army especially should keep aloof, because the army must be true and faithful to the powers that be, and not be subjected to a temptation to favor one or other of the great parties into which our people have divided, and will continue to divide, it may be, with advantage to the whole.

It would be a labor of love for me, in this connection, to pay a tribute of respect, by name, to the many able and most patriotic officers with whom I was so

[60] Secretaries of war from 1876 to 1885: James D. Cameron (1833–1918) served from 1876 to 1877, George W. McCrary (1835–1890) served from 1877 to 1879, Alexander Ramsey (1815–1903) served from 1879 to 1881, and Robert T. Lincoln (1843–1926), the son of Abraham Lincoln, served from 1881 to 1885. "Alexander Ramsey Dies at Age of 88," *Saint Paul Globe* (Saint Paul, MN), Apr. 23, 1903, 6; Kenneth J. Blume, *The A to Z of U.S. Diplomacy from the Civil War to World War I* (Lanham, MD: Scarecrow Press, 2010), 68, 202, 219, 377.

[61] Alexander R. Shepherd (1835–1902) led the Citizens' Reform Association in 1870 to push for municipal reform in Washington, DC. As a result, Shepherd was elected alderman and later served as the governor of the district. "Death of 'Boss' Shepherd," *Boston Evening Transcript,* Sept. 13, 1902, 24.

long associated as the commanding generals of military divisions and departments, as well as staff-officers; but I must forego the temptation, because of the magnitude of the subject, certain that each and all of them will find biographers better posted and more capable than myself; and I would also like to make recognition of the hundreds of acts of most graceful hospitality on the part of the officers and families at our remote military posts in the days, of the "adobe," the "jacal," and "dug-out," when a board floor and a shingle roof were luxuries expected by none except the commanding officer. I can see, in memory, a beautiful young city-bred lady, who had married a poor second-lieutenant, and followed him to his post on the plains, whose quarters were in a "dug-out" ten feet by about fifteen, seven feet high, with a dirt roof; four feet of the walls were the natural earth, the other three of sod, with holes for windows and corn-sacks for curtains. This little lady had her Saratoga trunk, which was the chief article of furniture; yet, by means of a rug on the ground-floor, a few candle-boxes covered with red cotton calico for seats, a table improvised out of a barrel-head, and a fireplace and chimney excavated in the back wall or bank, she had transformed her "hole in the ground" into a most attractive home for her young warrior husband; and she entertained me with a supper consisting of the best of coffee, fried ham, cakes, and jellies from the commissary, which made on my mind an impression more lasting than have any one of the hundreds of magnificent banquets I have since attended in the palaces and mansions of our own and foreign lands.

Still more would I like to go over again the many magnificent trips made across the interior plains, mountains, and deserts before the days of the completed Pacific Railroad, with regular "Doughertys" drawn by four smart mules, one soldier with carbine or loaded musket in hand seated alongside the driver; two in the back seat with loaded rifles swung in the loops made for them; the lightest kind of baggage, and generally a bag of oats to supplement the grass, and to attach the mules to their camp. With an outfit of two, three, or four of such, I have made journeys of as much as eighteen hundred miles in a single season, usually from post to post, averaging in distance about two hundred miles a week, with as much regularity as is done to-day by the steam-car its five hundred miles a day; but those days are gone, and, though I recognize the great national advantages of the more rapid locomotion, I cannot help occasionally regretting the change. One instance in 1866 rises in my memory, which I must record: Returning eastward from Fort Garland, we ascended the Rocky Mountains to the Sangre-de-Cristo Pass.[62] The road descending the

[62] WTS was at Fort Garland in late Sept. 1866. Richard I. Dodge, *The Sherman Tour Journals of Colonel Richard Irving Dodge,* ed. Wayne R. Kime (Norman: University of Oklahoma Press, 2002), 13.

mountain was very rough and sidling. I got out with my rifle, and walked ahead about four miles, where I awaited my "Dougherty."[63] After an hour or so I saw, coming down the road, a wagon; and did not recognize it as my own till quite near. It had been upset, the top all mashed in, and no means at hand for repairs. I consequently turned aside from the main road to a camp of cavalry near the Spanish Peaks, where we were most hospitably received by Major A—and his accomplished wife.[64] They occupied a large hospital-tent, which about a dozen beautiful greyhounds were free to enter at will. The ambulance was repaired, and the next morning we renewed our journey, escorted by the major and his wife on their fine saddle-horses. They accompanied us about ten miles of the way; and, though age has since begun to tell on them, I shall ever remember them in their pride and strength as they galloped alongside our wagons down the long slopes of the Spanish Peaks in a driving snow-storm.

And yet again would it be a pleasant task to recall the many banquets and feasts of the various associations of officers and soldiers, who had fought the good battles of the civil war, in which I shared as a guest or host, when we could indulge in a reasonable amount of glorification at deeds done and recorded, with wit, humor, and song; these when memory was fresh, and when the old soldiers were made welcome to the best of cheer and applause in every city and town of the land. But no! I must hurry to my conclusion, for this journey has already been sufficiently prolonged.

I had always intended to divide time with my natural successor, General P. H. Sheridan, and early notified him that I should about the year 1884 retire from the command of the army, leaving him about an equal period of time for the highest office in the army. It so happened that Congress had meantime by successive "enactments" cut down the army to twenty-five thousand men, the usual strength of a *corps d'armée*, the legitimate command of a lieutenant-general. Up to 1882 officers not disabled by wounds or sickness could only avail themselves

[63] Dougherty wagons were developed in St. Louis in the 1840s by a man named Dougherty. On Oct. 22, 1884, WTS wrote to G. W. W. Houghton, "I feel like Rip Van Winkle, when a carriage man inquires 'Who was Dougherty?' How soon we are forgotten when dead! Poor Dougherty, like Grimsby with his saddle, must turn in his coffin to feel that he is so soon forgotten of his fellows!" "The Story of the Convention: Being a Detailed Report of the Twelfth Annual Convention of the Carriage Builders' National Association," *Hub Magazine*, Mar. 1, 1885, 519.

[64] On Sept. 21, 1866, WTS wrote to John Rawlins from Fort Garland, CO, "I travelled on the eastside of the mountains. When abreast of it I sent a courier over with an order to the commanding officer to send to me a staff officer to report. The commanding officer, Colonel A. J. Alexander, of the third United States cavalry, came in person." *Executive Documents*, document 23, 6:14.

of the privileges of retirement on application, after thirty years of service, at sixty-two years of age; but on the 30th of June, 1882, a bill was passed which, by operation of the law itself, compulsorily retired all army-officers, regardless of rank, at the age of sixty-four years. At the time this law was debated in Congress, I was consulted by Senators and others in the most friendly manner, representing that, if I wanted it, an exception could justly and easily be made in favor of the general and lieutenant-general, whose commissions expired with their lives; but I invariably replied that I did not ask or expect an exception in my case, because no man could know or realize when his own mental and physical powers began to decline. I remembered well the experience of Gil Blas with the Bishop of Granada,[65] and favored the passage of the law fixing a positive period for retirement, to obviate in the future special cases of injustice such as I had seen in the recent past. The law was passed, and every officer then knew the very day on which he *must* retire, and could make his preparations accordingly. In my own case the law was liberal in the extreme, being "without reduction in his current pay and allowances."

I would be sixty-four years old on the 8th of February, 1884, a date inconvenient to move, and not suited to other incidents; so I resolved to retire on the 1st day of November, 1883, to resume my former home at St. Louis, and give my successor ample time to meet the incoming Congress. But, preliminary thereto, I concluded to make one more tour of the continent, going out to the Pacific by the Northern route, and returning by that of the thirty-fifth parallel. This we accomplished, beginning at Buffalo, June 21st, and ending at St. Louis, Missouri, September 30, 1883, a full and most excellent account of which can be found in Colonel Tidball's "Diary," which forms part of the report of the General of the Army for the year 1883.[66]

[65] *The Adventures of Gil Blas of Santillane,* a French novel published in four volumes between 1715 and 1735, was by Alain-René Lesage. It was translated into English by Tobias Smollett in 1750. In the book, an archbishop of Granada, whose mental faculties were compromised by apoplexy, dismissed Gil Blas after he questioned the archbishop's ability to perform his duties. Alain René Le Sage, *The Adventures of Gil Blas of Santillane,* trans. Tobias Smollett, ed. O. M. Brack Jr. and Leslie A. Chilton (Athens: University of Georgia Press, 2011), xiii, 292–293.

[66] John C. Tidball (1825–1906) graduated from the USMA in 1848 and was a member of the force that responded to John Brown's Raid at Harper's Ferry, VA, in 1859. He was brevetted major general on Apr. 2, 1865, for his actions during the Civil War. He later served as WTS's aide-de-camp from 1881 to 1884. *USMA,* 2:350–351, 5:67.

Before retiring also, as was my duty, I desired that my aides-de-camp who had been so faithful and true to me should not suffer by my act. All were to retain the rank of colonels of cavalry till the last day, February 8, 1884; but meantime each secured places, as follows:

Colonel O. M. Poe was lieutenant-colonel of the Engineer Corps United States Army, and was by his own choice assigned to Detroit in charge of the engineering works on the Upper Lakes, which duty was most congenial to him.

Colonel J. C. Tidball was assigned to command the Artillery School at Fort Monroe, by virtue of his commission as lieutenant-colonel, Third Artillery, a station for which he was specially qualified.

Colonel John E. Tourtelotte was then entitled to promotion to major of the Seventh Cavalry, a rank in which he could be certain of an honorable command.

The only remaining aide-de-camp was Colonel John M. Bacon, who utterly ignored self in his personal attachment to me. He was then a captain of the Ninth Cavalry, but with almost a certainty of promotion to be major of the Seventh before the date of my official retirement, which actually resulted.[67] The last two accompanied me to St. Louis, and remained with me to the end.[68]

[67] John M. Bacon (1844–1913) was a U.S. volunteer solider from Kentucky during the Civil War. In 1866 he was commissioned as a captain of cavalry in the U.S. Army. He joined WTS's staff in 1870. "Taps Sound for Honored Veteran," *Oregon Daily Journal* (Portland, OR), Mar. 20, 1913, 2.

[68] In the second edition of the memoirs (1886), WTS included the following footnote:

"It is but just that I should account for the other most zealous and friendly officers who had served as aides-de-camp near me during my command of the army.

Colonel James C. McCoy was a first lieutenant in the Forty-sixth Ohio Volunteers, and adjutant of his regiment at the time I made up my brigade at Paducah, Kentucky, March, 1862. I selected him as one of my two aides. He was a brave, patient officer, always ready for work of any kind, was with me throughout the war and afterward, until failing health compelled him to seek relief in Florida. At the close of the war, on the disbandment of the volunteer army, he was appointed second lieutenant of the Fourth Artillery, to enable him legally to continue as a staff-officer, and in fact he remained with me, sharing my fortunes, rising from first lieutenant to colonel, until his death in New York City, May 29, 1875.

Colonel L. M. Dayton was also an officer of volunteers, joined me as aide-de-camp before the battle of Shiloh, and continued with me throughout the war, much of the time acting as adjutant-general. Nearly all my records of that period are in his handwriting. Soon after the close of the war he married a most accomplished and wealthy lady of Cincinnati, and resigned December 31, 1870. He is now a well-known citizen and manufacturer of Cincinnati, Ohio.

Colonel J. C. Audenried was a graduate of West Point, class of 1861, served with the Army of the Potomac, and on the staff of General Sumner until his death, March 31, 1863; soon after

Having previously accomplished the removal of my family to St. Louis, and having completed my last journey to the Pacific, I wrote the following letter:

HEADQUARTERS ARMY UNITED STATES,
WASHINGTON, D. C., *October* 8, 1883.

---

which he was sent with dispatches to General Grant at Vicksburg. In July, 1863, General Grant sent him with dispatches to me at Jackson, Mississippi. Impressed by his handsome appearance and soldierly demeanor, I soon after offered him a place on my staff, which he accepted, and he remained with me until his death, in Washington, June 3, 1880. A more honorable, chivalrous, and courteous gentleman never lived than Colonel J.C. Audenried.

The vacancy created by the death of Colonel McCoy was filled, at my invitation, by Lieutenant-Colonel Alexander McDowell McCook, of the Tenth Infantry, one of the most loyal and enthusiastic of the army officers who had promptly, in 1861, joined the volunteers. This officer had been in continuous service from 1852, had filled every commission from second lieutenant up to a corps commander, which by the military usage of the world is recognized by the rank of lieutenant-general; yet, on the "reduction" of 1866, he was thrown back to the grade of lieutenant-colonel, and continued with the same cheerfulness and hearty zeal which had characterized his whole life. He remained with me until his promotion to the colonelcy of the Sixth Infantry, December 15, 1880. He is now in command of that regiment at Fort Douglas, Salt Lake City.

In like manner the vacancy made by Colonel McCook was filled by Lieutenant-Colonel Richard Irving Dodge, Twenty-third Infantry, then serving at a cantonment on the Upper Canadian—an officer who had performed cheerfully and well a full measure of frontier service, was a capital sportsman, and of a perfect war record. He also remained with me until his promotion as colonel of the Eleventh Infantry, January 26, 1882. He is now commanding his regiment and post at Fort Sully, Dakota. Anticipating my retirement, I never filled his vacancy.

As I have heretofore recorded, at the time I succeeded General Grant in the command of the army, March 5, 1869, I offered to provide for three of his then six aides-de-camp, viz., Colonels Horace Porter, Fred T. Dent, and Cyrus B. Comstock. The two former never officiated a day near me as aides-de-camp, but remained at the White House with President Grant until their resignation, January 1, 1873. Colonel Comstock did serve in my office until his resignation, May 3, 1870, to resume his appropriate functions in the Engineer Corps. He is an officer of great ability, of perfect integrity, and is still in the service.

Colonel W. D. Whipple, of the Adjutant-General's Department, also served on my staff as an aide-de-camp from January 1, 1873, until January 1, 1881, when his services were called for in his own corps, in which he is now serving, with a fair prospect to become its chief.

I beg, at this late date, to express my great respect for all these officers, who were faithful, intelligent, and patriotic—not only an official respect, but a personal affection for their qualities as men, in the full belief that they were model soldiers and gentlemen, such as should ever characterize the headquarters of the Army of the United States."

Hon. R. T. Lincoln, *Secretary of War.*

Sir: By the act of Congress, approved June 30, 1882, all army-officers are retired on reaching the age of sixty-four years. If living, I will attain that age on the 8th day of February, 1884; but as that period of the year is not suited for the changes necessary on my retirement, I have contemplated anticipating the event by several months, to enable the President to meet these changes at a more convenient season of the year, and also to enable my successor to be in office before the assembling of the next Congress.

I therefore request authority to turn over the command of the army to Lieutenant-General Sheridan on the 1st day of November, 1883, and that I be ordered to my home at St. Louis, Missouri, there to await the date of my legal retirement; and inasmuch as for a long time I must have much correspondence about war and official matters, I also ask the favor to have with me for a time my two present aides-de-camp, Colonels J. E. Tourtelotte and J. M. Bacon.

The others of my personal staff, viz., Colonels O. M. Poe and J. C. Tidball, have already been assigned to appropriate duties in their own branches of the military service, the engineers and artillery. All should retain the rank and pay as aides-de-camp until February 8, 1884. By or before the 1st day of November I can complete all official reports, and believe I can surrender the army to my successor in good shape and condition, well provided in all respects, and distributed for the best interests of the country.

I am grateful that my physical and mental strength remain unimpaired by years, and am thankful for the liberal provision made by Congress for my remaining years, which will enable me to respond promptly to any call the President may make for my military service or judgment as long as I live.

I have the honor to be your obedient servant,

W. T. Sherman, *General.*

The answer was:

War Department,

Washington City, *October* 10, 1883.

General W. T. Sherman, *Washington, D. C.*

General: I have submitted to the President your letter of the 8th instant, requesting that you be relieved of the command of the army on the 1st of November next, as a more convenient time for making the changes in military commands which must follow your retirement from active service, than would be the date of your retirement under the law.

In signifying his approval of your request, the President directs me to express to you his earnest hope that there may be given you many years of health and happiness in which to enjoy the gratitude of your fellow-citizens, well earned by your most distinguished public services.

It will give me pleasure to comply with your wishes respecting your aides-de-camp, and the necessary orders will be duly issued.

I have the honor to be, General, your obedient servant,

ROBERT T. LINCOLN, *Secretary of War.*

On the 27th day of October I submitted to the Secretary of War, the Hon. R. T. Lincoln, my last annual report, embracing among other valuable matters the most interesting and condensed report of Colonel O. M. Poe, A. D. C., of the "original conception, progress, and completion" of the four great transcontinental railways, which have in my judgment done more for the subjugation and civilization of the Indians than all other causes combined, and have made possible the utilization of the vast area of pasture-lands and mineral regions which before were almost inaccessible, for my agency in which I feel as much pride as for my share in any of the battles in which I took part.[69]

Promptly on the 1st of November were made the following general orders, and the command of the Army of the United States passed from me to Lieutenant-General P. H. Sheridan, with as little ceremony as would attend the succession of the lieutenant-colonel of a regiment to his colonel about to take a leave of absence:

HEADQUARTERS OF THE ARMY,
WASHINGTON, *November* 1, 1883.

General Orders No. 77:

By and with the consent of the President, as contained in General Orders No. 71, of October 13, 1883, the undersigned relinquishes command of the Army of the United States.

In thus severing relations which have hitherto existed between us, he thanks all officers and men for their fidelity to the high trust imposed

[69] For WTS's full report, see *Annual Report of the Secretary of War for the Year 1883* (Washington, DC: GPO, 1883), 1:41–317.

on them during his official life, and will, in his retirement, watch with parental solicitude their progress upward in the noble profession to which they have devoted their lives.

W. T. SHERMAN, *General.*

Official: R. C. DRUM, *Adjutant-General.*

HEADQUARTERS OF THE ARMY,
WASHINGTON, *November* 1, 1883.

General Orders No. 78:

In obedience to orders of the President, promulgated in General Orders No. 71, October 13, 1883, from these headquarters, the undersigned hereby assumes command of the Army of the United States.

The following-named officers compose the personal staff of the Lieutenant-General: Major Michael V. Sheridan, Assistant Adjutant-General and Military Secretary; Captain William J. Volkmar, of the Fifth Cavalry, Aide-de-Camp; Captain James F. Gregory, of the Corps of Engineers, Aide-de-Camp.

P. H. SHERIDAN, *Lieutenant-General.*

Official: R. C. DRUM, *Adjutant-General.*

After a few days in which to complete my social visits, and after a short visit to my daughter, Mrs. A. M. Thackara, at Philadelphia, I quietly departed for St. Louis; and, as I hope, for "good and all," the family was again reunited in the same place from which we were driven by a cruel, unnecessary civil war initiated in Charleston Harbor in April, 1861.

On the 8th day of February, 1884, I was sixty-four years of age, and therefore *retired* by the operation of the act of Congress, approved June 30, 1882; but the fact was gracefully noticed by President Arthur in the following general orders:

WAR DEPARTMENT, ADJUTANT-GENERAL'S OFFICE,
WASHINGTON, *February* 8, 1884.

The following order of the President is published to the army:

EXECUTIVE MANSION, *February* 8, 1884.

General William T. Sherman, General of the Army, having this day reached the age of sixty-four years, is, in accordance with the law, placed upon the retired list of the army, without reduction in his current pay and allowances.

The announcement of the severance from the command of the army of one who has been for so many years its distinguished chief, can but awaken in the minds, not only of the army, but of the people of the United States, mingled emotions of regret and gratitude—regret at the withdrawal from active military service of an officer whose lofty sense of duty has been a model for all soldiers since he first entered the army in July, 1840; and gratitude, freshly awakened, for the services of incalculable value rendered by him in the war for the Union, which his great military genius and daring did so much to end.

The President deems this a fitting occasion to give expression, in this manner, to the gratitude felt toward General Sherman by his fellow-citizens, and to the hope that Providence may grant him many years of health and happiness in the relief from the active duties of his profession.

CHESTER A. ARTHUR.

By order of the Secretary of War:

R. C. DRUM, *Adjutant-General.*

To which I replied:

ST. LOUIS, *February* 9, 1884.

His Excellency CHESTER A. ARTHUR, *President of the United States.*

DEAR SIR: Permit me with a soldier's frankness to thank you personally for the handsome compliment bestowed in general orders of yesterday, which are reported in the journals of the day. To me it was a surprise and a most agreeable one. I had supposed the actual date of my retirement would form a short paragraph in the common series of special orders of the War Department; but as the honored Executive of our country has made it the occasion for his own hand to pen a tribute of respect and affection to an officer passing from the active stage of life to one of ease and rest, I can only say I feel highly honored, and congratulate myself in thus rounding out my record of service in a manner most gratifying to my family and friends. Not only this, but I feel sure, when the orders of yesterday are read on parade to the regiments and garrisons of the United States, many a young hero will tighten his belt, and resolve anew to be brave and true to the starry flag, which we of our day have carried safely through one epoch of danger, but which may yet be subjected to other trials, which may demand similar sacrifices, equal fidelity and courage, and a larger measure of intelligence. Again thanking you for so marked a compliment, and reciprocating the kind wishes for the future,

I am, with profound respect, your friend and servant,

W. T. SHERMAN, *General.*

This I construe as the end of my military career. In looking back upon the past I can only say, with millions of others, that I have done many things I should not have done, and have left undone still more which ought to have been done; that I can see where hundreds of opportunities have been neglected, but on the whole am content; and feel sure that I can travel this broad country of ours, and be each night the welcome guest in palace or cabin; and, as

"all the world's a stage,
And all the men and women merely players,"[70]

I claim the privilege to ring down the curtain.

W. T. SHERMAN, *General.*

[70]The quote is from Shakespeare's play *As You Like It.* WTS, an avid theater patron, made one of his last public appearances at the Casino Theatre in New York on Feb. 4, 1891, to watch a performance of the play *Poor Jonathan.* He died of pneumonia ten days later. Edward Chase, *The Memorial Life of General William Tecumseh Sherman* (Chicago: R. S. Peale, 1891), 538; John F. Marszalek, *Sherman: A Soldier's Passion for Order* (New York: Free Press, 1993), 491–492; Shakespeare, *As You Like It,* act 2, scene 7, lines 139–140.

Appendix to Volume I.

CHICKASAW BAYOU.

Report of Brigadier-General G. W. Morgan.

HEADQUARTERS THIRD DIVISION, RIGHT WING,
THIRTEENTH ARMY CORPS,
STEAMER EMPRESS, *January* 3, 1863.

Major J. H. HAMMOND, *Chief of Staff.*

SIR: On the 1st instant, while pressed by many arduous duties, I was requested to report to the commanding general the operations of my division during the affair of the 27th, the action of the 28th, and the battle of the 29th ult.

I had not received the report of subordinate commanders, nor had I time to review the report I have the honor to submit.

Herewith I have the honor to forward these reports, connected with which I will submit a few remarks.

Brigadier-General Blair speaks of having discovered, while on his retreat from the enemy's works, a broad and easy road running from the left of my position to the enemy's lines. The road is neither broad nor easy, and was advanced over by De Courcey when leading his brigade to the charge. The road General Blair speaks of is the one running from Lake's Landing and intersecting with the Vicksburg road on the Chickasaw Bluffs. Its existence was known to me on the 28th ult., but it was left open intentionally by the enemy, and was commanded by a direct and cross fire from batteries and rifle-pits. The withdrawal of his brigade from the assault by Colonel De Courcey was justified by the failure of the corps of A. J. Smith, and the command of Colonel Lindsey, to advance simultaneously to the assault. Both had the same difficulties to encounter—impassable bayous. The enemy's line of battle was concave, and De Courcey advanced against his centre—hence he sustained a concentric fire, and the withdrawal of Steele from the front of the enemy's right on the 28th ult. enabled the enemy on the following day to concentrate his right upon his centre.

I regret to find, from the report of Brigadier-General Thayer, some one regiment skulked; this I did not observe, nor is it mentioned by General Blair, though his were the troops which occupied that portion of the field. As far as my observation extended, the troops bore themselves nobly; but the Sixteenth Ohio Infantry was peerless on the field, as it had ever been in camp or on the march. Lieutenant-Colonel Kershner, commanding, was wounded and taken prisoner. He is an officer of rare merit, and deserves to command a brigade. Lieutenant-Colonel Dister, commanding the Fifty-eighth Ohio, was killed within the enemy's works; and Lieutenant-Colonel Monroe, Twenty-second Kentucky, was struck down at the head of his regiment.

I again express my profound acknowledgments to Brigadier-Generals Blair and Thayer, and Colonels De Courcey, Lindsey, and Sheldon, brigade commanders. Also to Major M. C. Garber, assistant quartermaster; Captain S. S. Lyon, acting topographical engineer; Lieutenant Burdick, acting ordnance officer; Lieutenant Hutchins, acting chief of staff; Lieutenants H. G. Fisher and Smith, of Signal Corps; Lieutenant E. D. Saunders, my acting assistant adjutant-general; and Lieutenants English and Montgomery, acting aides-de-camp, for the efficient services rendered me.

Nor can I close this report without speaking in terms of high praise of the meritorious and gallant services of Captains Foster and Lamphier. Their batteries silenced several of the enemy's works, and throughout the operations rendered good service. My sincere acknowledgments are also due to Captain Griffith, commanding First Iowa Battery, and Captain Hoffman, commanding Fourth Ohio Battery.

I am, sir, very respectfully, your obedient servant,

George W. Morgan, *Brigadier-General Volunteers.*

Cincinnati, *February* 3, 1876.

My dear General: Regarding the attack at Chickasaw Bayou, my record shows the position of Steele on the left; Morgan to his right; Morgan L. Smith to his right, and A. J. Smith on the extreme right; the latter not expected to accomplish much more than a diversion, the result to come from the three other divisions, Morgan having the best opportunity. Saturday night they were in position; you were at Lake's plantation, right and rear of Morgan.

The attack for lodgment on the hills was ordered for Sunday morning, December 28th. I was sent to A. J. Smith before daylight, and returned to you soon after. You were with Morgan. You had fully explained to him the importance of *his* success, and that he should be *present* with the attacking column, which was to be a part of his division, supported by the remainder, and by Blair's brigade of Steele's division coöperating. The attack was to be simultaneous, by the four divisions, on a signal.

Morgan's answer to you was that, when the signal was given, he would *lead* his attack, and with his life he would be on the bluffs in fifteen minutes. He seemed of positive knowledge, and as sure of success. You then retired to a central point, to be in easy communication with Steele and Morgan L. Smith. The attack was made, and developed, in the case of Steele, M. L. Smith, and A. J. Smith, that to cross the bayou was impossible, if opposed by any force, and in each they were by a strong one. Morgan's attacking force succeeded in getting across the causeway and marsh, but he did *not* go with it, nor *support* it with more men, and a large number were captured from Blair's brigade *after* gaining the enemy's last line of works covering the bayou. At the time everybody blamed and criticised Morgan with the failure. You felt from the advance of his attack it must be successful, and, as it pushed forward, you sent me to urge on M. L. Smith, as Morgan was over, and he, Smith, must aid by persistent attack, and give Morgan as good a chance as could be to make his lodgment. . . .

I am, etc., L. M. DAYTON,

Late Colonel of the Staff, now of Cincinnati, Ohio.

General W. T. SHERMAN, *St. Louis, Missouri.*

[COPY.]

". . . . The expedition was wonderfully well provided with provisions, transportation, and munitions, and even axes, picks, and shovels, so much in use later in the war, evidenced the forethought that governed this force. The boats, from their open lower deck construction, proved admirable for transports, but their tinder-box construction made fire-traps of them, requiring unremitting vigilance. These points were well understood, and the readiness with which the troops adapted themselves to circumstances was a constant source of wonder and congratulations.

"The fleet collected at Friar's Point for final orders, and there the order of sailing was laid down with great minuteness, and private instructions issued to commanders of divisions, all of whom had personal interviews with the commanding general, and received personal explanations on pretty much every point involved. Our headquarters boat, the Forest Queen, was not very comfortable, nor well provided, but General Sherman submitted cheerfully, on the grounds of duty, and thought Conway a fine fellow. I was only able to concede that he was a good steamboat captain. . . .

"Our camp appointments were Spartan in the extreme, and in their simplicity would have met the demands of any demagogue in the land. The nights were cold and damp, and General Sherman uncomfortably active in his preparations, so that the assistant adjutant-general had no very luxurious post just then. We were surrounded with sloughs. The ground was wet, and the water, although in winter, was very unwholesome. Many of our men, to this day, have reminders of the Yazoo in ague, fevers, and diseases of the bowels. Cavalry was useless. One battalion of Illinois cavalry was strongly suspected of camping in the timber, until time passed enough to justify the suspicion of having been somewhere. Really the strength of Vicksburg was in being out of reach of attack. . . .

"My orders were to learn and report what was going on on the right, particularly to try and form an idea of the enemy's force in front of M. L. Smith's division, and at the sand-bar. Leaving my horse close in the rear of the Sixth Missouri, when the fire became too heavy for riding, I succeeded, by taking frequent cover, in reaching unhurt the verge of the bayou among the drift-logs. There, by concert of action with Lieutenant-Colonel Blood, of the Sixth Missouri, his regiment, and the Thirteenth Regular Infantry, kept up a heavy fire on everything that showed along the levee and earthworks in front. The enemy were behind the embankment, not over one hundred and fifty yards across the bayou. Several officers, including Colonel Blood, Colonel Kilby Smith, and myself, managed, by getting on the piles of drift, to see over the levee through the cleared fields beyond, even to the foot of the bluff. The chips and twigs flew around lively enough, but we staid up long enough to make sure that the enemy had as many men behind the levee as could get cover. We saw, also, a line of rifle-pits in the rear, commanding the rear of the levee, and still beyond, winding along the foot of the bluff, a road worn by long use deep into the side-hill, and with the side next us strengthened with a good earthwork, affording a covered line of communication in the rear. The fire of our men was so well maintained that we were able to see all these things, say a minute or more. Some of those who ventured were wounded, but those mentioned and myself escaped unhurt. I advised that men enough to hold the position, once across—say three hundred—should make a rush (protected as our lookout had been by a heavy fire) across the sand-bar, and get a footing under the other bank of the bayou, as the nucleus of an attacking force, if General Sherman decided to attack there, or to make a strong diversion if the attack was made at the head of Chickasaw Bayou, in front of Morgan. General A. J. Smith, commanding First and Second Divisions, approved of this. While returning to General Sherman, I passed along the Second and part of the Third Division. On the left of the Second I found a new Illinois regiment, high up in numbers, working its way into position. The colonel, a brave but inexperienced officer, was trying to lead his men according to the popular pictorial idea, viz., riding in advance waving his sword. I was leading my horse, and taking advantage of such cover as I could find on my course, but this man acted so bravely that I tried to save him. He did not accept my expostulations with very good grace, but was not rough about it. While I was begging him to dismount, he waved his sword and advanced. In a second he was shot through the chest, and dropped from his horse, plucky to the last. He died, I was told, within the hour.[1] Many of the regiments were new and inexperienced, but as a rule behaved well. The fire along the bayou was severe, but not very fatal, on account of the cover. I was constantly asked what news from Grant, for from the moment of our arrival in the Yazoo we were in expectation of either hearing his guns in the rear, or of having communication with him. This encouraged the men greatly, but the long waiting was disappointing, as the enemy was evidently in large force in the plenty of works, and a very strong position. Careful estimates and available information placed their force at fifteen to twenty thousand men. I returned to headquarters about the middle of the afternoon, and made my report to the general. We

[1] A footnote marked by an asterisk in the second edition reads: *Colonel Wyman, Thirteenth Illinois Infantry.

were busy till after midnight, and again early in the morning of the 29th, in preparing orders for the attack. These were unusually minute in detail. It seemed as though no contingency was left unprovided for. Urgent orders and cautions as to rations and ammunition were given. Drawings of the line of attack, orders for supports, all and everything was foreseen and given in writing, with personal explanations to commanders of divisions, brigades, and even commanders of regiments. Indeed, the commanding general, always careful as to detail, left nothing to chance, and with experienced and ordinate officers we would have succeeded, for the troops were good. The general plan involved a feint on our left toward Haines's Bluff, by the navy, under Admiral Porter, with whom we were in constant communication, while between him and General Sherman perfect harmony existed. On the right a demonstration by A. J. Smith was to be made. The Second Division (Stuart's) was to cross the sand-bar, and the Third (General Morgan's) was to cross on a small bridge over the slough at the head of Chickasaw Bayou, and, supported by Steele, was to push straight for the Bluff at the nearest spur where there was a battery in position, and to effect a lodgment there and in the earthworks. General Sherman gave his orders in person to Morgan and Steele. I understood Morgan to promise that he would lead his division in person, and he seemed to expect an easy victory, and expressed himself freely to that effect. The aides were sent out, until I was left alone with the general and a couple of orderlies. He located himself in a position easy of access, and the most convenient afforded to the point of attack. He directed me to see what I could, and report if I met anything that he should know. I galloped as fast as possible to the right, and found part of the Sixth Missouri pushing over the sand-bar covered by the Thirteenth Regulars with a heavy fire. We supposed, if once across, they could get up the bank and turn the levee against the enemy, and left with that impression. Being in heavy timber, I was not quite sure of my way back to the general, his location being new, and therefore pushed full gallop for Morgan's front, catching a good many stray shots from the sharpshooters behind the levee, as I was compelled to keep in sight of the bayou to hold direction. Something over half-way along Morgan's division front, the commander of a Kentucky regiment hailed me and said he must have support, as he was threatened by a masked battery, and the enemy was in force in his front, and might cross any moment. I answered, rather shortly: 'How the devil do you know there is a masked battery? If you can't get over, how can the rebels get at you?' He insisted on the battery, and danger. I finally told him the bayou was utterly impassable there, but, if he insisted the enemy could cross, I would insist on an advance on our side at that point. Hurrying on to make up lost time, I soon reached Morgan. He was making encouraging speeches in a general way, but stopped to ask me questions as to Steele's rank, date of commission, etc. I was very much disturbed at this, fearing want of harmony, and rode on to Steele, whom I found cursing Morgan so fiercely that I could not exactly make out the source of the trouble, or reason why; but saw want of concert clearly enough. I hastened back to General Sherman, and endeavored to impress my ideas on him and my fears; but, while he admitted the facts, he could not be made to believe that any jealousy or personal quarrel could lead to a failure to support each other, and a neglect of duty. The signal for attack had already been given, and the artillery had opened, when I left him again for Morgan's front. I found Morgan where I left him, and the troops advancing. I had understood that he was to lead his division, and asked about it, but, getting no satisfaction, pushed for the front, crossing the slough at the little bridge at the head of the bayou. I found the willows cut off eighteen inches or two feet long, with sharp points above the mud, making it slow and difficult to pass, save at the bridge. I overtook the rear of the advance about two or three hundred feet up the gentle slope, and was astonished to find how small a force was making the attack. I was also surprised to find that they were Steele's men instead of Morgan's. I also saw several regiments across the bayou, but not advancing; they were near the levee. A heavy artillery and infantry fire was going on all this time. While making my way along the column, from which there were very few falling back, a shell burst near me, and the concussion confused me at the time and left me with a headache for several months. When I got my wits about me again I found a good many coming back, but the main part of the force was compact and keeping up the fight. I did not get closer to the woods than about five hundred feet, and found that a large number had penetrated into the enemy's works. When our men fell back, very few ran, but came slowly and sullenly, far more angry than frightened. I found General Frank Blair on foot, and with him Colonel Sea, of Southwest Missouri, and learned that Colonel Thomas Fletcher, afterward Governor of Missouri, was captured with many of his men. They both insisted there on the spot, with those around us, that if all the men ordered up had gone up, or even all that crossed the bayou had moved forward, we could have readily established ourselves in the enemy's works. I was firmly of the same opinion at the time on the ground; and, an entrance effected, we could have brought the whole force on dry ground, and had a base of operations against Vicksburg—though probably, in view of later events, we would have had to stand a siege from Pemberton's army. After explanations with Blair, I rode to where the men were, who had crossed the bayou, but had not advanced with the others. I found them to be De Courcey's brigade, of Morgan's division, which General Sherman supposed to be in advance. In fact, it was the intended support that made the attack. A correspondence and controversy followed between General Blair and Colonel De Courcey, most of which I have, but nothing came of it. On reaching the bayou, I found that Thayer's brigade, of Steele's division, had in some way lost its direction and filed off to the right. Remembering the 'masked battery,' I suspected that had something to do with the matter, and, on following it up, I learned that the Kentucky colonel before mentioned had appealed for aid against the masked battery and invisible force of rebels, and that a regiment had been ordered to him. This regiment, filing off into the timber, had been followed by Thayer's brigade, supposing it to be advancing to the front, and thus left a single brigade to attack a superior force of the enemy in an intrenched and naturally strong position. By the time the mistake could be rectified, it was too late. Our loss was from one hundred and fifty to two hundred killed, and about seven hundred prisoners and wounded. During the afternoon I went with a flag of truce, with reference to burying the dead. I saw between eighty and one hundred of our men dead, all *stripped.* There were others closer into the enemy's works than I was allowed to go. On going later to where the Sixth Missouri crossed, I found that they were under the bank, and had dug in with their hands and bayonets, or anything in reach, to protect themselves from a vertical fire from the enemy overhead, who had a heavy force there. With great difficulty they were withdrawn at night. Next day arrangements were made to attempt a lodgment below Haines's Bluff. This was to be done by Steele's command, while the rest of the force attacked again where we had already tried. During the day locomotives whistled, and a great noise and fuss went on in our front, and we supposed that Grant was driving in Pemberton, and expected firing any moment up the Yazoo or in the rear of Vicksburg. Not hearing this, we concluded that Pemberton was throwing his forces into Vicksburg. A heavy fog prevented Steele from making his movement. Rain began to fall, and our location was not good to be in after a heavy rain, or with the river rising. During the night (I think) of January 1, 1863, our troops were embarked, material and provisions having been loaded during the day. A short time before daylight of the 2d, I went, by order of the general commanding, to our picket lines and carefully examined the enemy's lines, wherever a camp-fire indicated their presence. They were not very vigilant, and I once got close enough to hear them talk, but could understand nothing. Early in the morning I came in with the rear-guard, the enemy advancing his pickets and main guards only, and making no effort at all to press us. Once I couldn't resist the temptation to fire into a squad that came bolder than the rest, and the two shots were good ones. We received a volley in return that did come very close among us, but hurt none of my party. Very soon after our rear-guard was aboard, General Sherman learned from Admiral Porter that McClernand had arrived at the mouth of the Yazoo. He went, taking me and one other staff-officer, to see McClernand, and found that, under an order from the President, he had taken command of the Army of the Mississippi. He and his staff, of whom I only remember two—Colonels Scates and Braham, assistant adjutant-general and aide-de-camp—seemed to think they had a big thing, and, so far as I could judge, they had just that. All hands thought the country expected them to cut their way to the Gulf; and to us, who had just come out of the swamp, the cutting didn't seem such an easy job as to the new-comers. Making due allowance for the elevation they seemed to feel in view of their job, everything passed off pleasantly, and we learned that General Grant's communications had been cut at Holly Springs by the capture of Murphy and his force (at Holly Springs), and that he was either in Memphis by that time or would soon be. So that, everything considered, it was about as well that we did not get our forces on the bluffs of Walnut Hill."

The above statement was sent to General Sherman in a letter dated "Chicago, February 5, 1876," and signed "John H. Hammond." Hammond[2] was General Sherman's assistant adjutant-general at the Chickasaw Bayou.

[2] A footnote marked by an asterisk in the second edition reads: *Still living.

J. E. Tourtelotte, *Colonel and Aide-de-Camp.*

On 29th December, 1862, at Chickasaw Bayou, I was in command of the Thirty-first Missouri Volunteer Infantry, First Brigade, First Division, Fifteenth Army Corps (Blair's brigade). Colonel Wyman, of the Thirteenth Illinois Volunteer Infantry, having been killed, I was the senior colonel of the brigade. General Blair rode up to where my regiment lay, and said to me:

"We are to make a charge here; we will charge in two lines; your regiment will be in the first line, and the Twenty-ninth (Cavender's) will support you. Form here in the timber, and move out across the bayou on a double-quick, and go right on to the top of the heights in your front." He then told me to await a signal. I then attempted to make a reconnaissance of the ground over which we would have to charge, and rode out to the open ground in my front, and saw that there was water and soft mud in the bayou, and was fired upon by the sharp-shooters of the enemy, and turned and went back into the woods where my command lay. Soon after that General Blair came near me, and I told him there was water and mud in the bayou, and I doubted if we could get across. He answered me that General Morgan told him there was no water nor mud to hinder us. I remarked that I had seen it myself, and General Morgan, or any one else, could see it if he would risk being shot at pretty lively. I then told General Blair that it was certain destruction to us if we passed over the abatis upon the open ground where there had once been a corn-field; that we could never reach the base of the hill. He turned to me and said, "Can't you take your regiment up there?" I told him, "Yes, I can take my regiment anywhere, because the men do not know any better than to go," but remarked that old soldiers could not be got to go up there. General Blair then said: "Tom, if we succeed, this will be a grand thing; you will have the glory of leading the assault." He then went on to say that General Morgan's division would support us, and they were heroes of many battles, and pointed to the Fifty-eighth Ohio, then forming in the rear of the Thirteenth Illinois on my right, and said: "See these men? They are a part of Morgan's division, and are heroes of many battles." I laughingly said that they might be heroes, but the regiment did not number as many as one of my companies. He again assured me we would be supported by Morgan's division, and all I had to do was to keep right on and "keep going till you get into Vicksburg." I took my position in advance of my regiment and awaited the signal. When we heard it, we raised a shout, and started at a double-quick, the Thirteenth Illinois on my right. I saw no troops on my left. When we emerged from the woods, the enemy opened upon us; crossing the bayou under fire, and many of the men sinking in the mud and water, our line was very much disordered, but we pretty well restored it before reaching the abatis. Here we were greatly disordered, but somewhat restored the line on reaching the plateau or corn-field. The Twenty-ninth Missouri came on, gallantly supporting us. The Thirteenth Illinois came out upon the corn-field, and the Fifty-eighth Ohio followed close upon it. There was firing to my left, and as I afterward learned was from the Fourth Iowa of Thayer's brigade (and I believe of Steele's division). I was struck and fell, and my regiment went back in great disorder. The fire was terrific. I saw beyond the Thirteenth Illinois, to my right, a disordered line, and learned afterward it was the Sixteenth Ohio. When I was taken from the field by the enemy and taken into Vicksburg, I found among the wounded and prisoners men and officers of the Sixteenth and Fifty-eighth Ohio, and of the Twenty-ninth and Thirty-first Missouri, and Thirteenth Illinois. After I was exchanged and joined my command, General Blair laughingly remarked to me that I had literally obeyed his order and gone "straight on to Vicksburg." He lamented the cutting to pieces of our force on that day. We talked the whole matter over at his headquarters during the siege of Vicksburg. He said that if the charge had been made along our whole line with the same vigor of attack made by his brigade, and if we had been supported as Morgan promised to do, we might have succeeded. I dissented from the opinion that we could even then have succeeded. I asked him what excuse Morgan gave for failing to support us, and he said that Colonel or General De Courcey was in some manner to blame for that, but he said Morgan was mistaken as to the nature of the ground and generally as to the feasibility of the whole thing, and was responsible for the failure to afford us the support he had promised; that he and General Sherman and all of them were misled by the statements and opinions of Morgan as to the situation in our front, and Morgan was, on his part, deceived by the reports of his scouts about other matters as well as the matter of the water in the bayou.

THOMAS C. FLETCHER.

ARKANSAS POST.

Extracts from Admiral Porter's Journal.

SHERMAN and I had made arrangements to capture Arkansas Post.

On the 31st of December, while preparing to go out of the Yazoo, an army officer called to see me, and said that he belonged to General McClernand's staff, and that the general was at the mouth of the Yazoo River, and desired to see me at once. I sent word to the general that if he wished to see me he could have an opportunity by calling on board my flag-ship.

A few moments after I had heard the news of McClernand's arrival, I saw Sherman pulling about in a boat, and hailed him, informing him that McClernand was at the mouth of the Yazoo. Sherman then came on board, and, in consequence of this unexpected news, determined to postpone the movement out of the Yazoo River, and let McClernand take that upon himself.

General McClernand took my hint and came on board the flag-ship, but I soon discovered that any admiral, Grant, Sherman, or all the generals in the army, were nobody in his estimation. Sherman had been at McClernand's headquarters to see him and state the condition of affairs, and *he then suggested to the latter the plan of going to Arkansas Post.*

I had a number of fine maps hanging up in my cabin, and when McClernand came on board he examined them all with the eye of a connoisseur. He then stated to me as a new thing the plan *he proposed* (*!*) of going to Arkansas Post and stirring up our troops, which had been "demoralized by the *late defeat*" (Sherman was present, looking daggers at him). I answered, "Yes, General Sherman and myself have already arranged for going to Arkansas Post." Sherman then made some remark about the disposition of the troops in the coming expedition, when McClernand gave him rather a curt answer. McClernand then remarked, "If you will let me have three gunboats, I will go and take the place." Now General McClernand had about as much idea of what a gunboat was, or could do, as the man in the moon. He did not know, the difference between an ironclad and a "tin-clad." He had heard that gunboats had taken Fort Henry, and that was all he knew about them. I said to him: "I'll tell you what I will do, General

McClernand. If General Sherman goes in command of the troops, I will go myself in command of a proper force, and will insure the capture of the post." McClernand winced under this, and Sherman quietly walked off into the after-cabin. He beckoned me to come there, while McClernand was apparently deeply engaged in studying out a chart, making believe he was interested, in order to conceal his temper. Sherman said to me: "Admiral, how could you make such a remark to McClernand? He hates me already, and you have made him an enemy for life."

"I don't care," said I; "he shall not treat you rudely in my cabin, and I was glad of the opportunity of letting him know my sentiments." By this time, General McClernand having bottled up his wrath, or cooled down, I went in to him and we discussed the matter. He consented that Sherman should go in command of the troops, and the interview ended pleasantly enough.

The above extracts from Admiral Porter's journal were sent by the admiral to General Sherman, inclosed in a letter dated "Washington, May 29, 1875," and signed "David D. Porter."

J. E. TOURTELOTTE.

After leaving the Yazoo, the Army of the Mississippi rendezvous was at Milliken's Bend. During the night of January 4th or 5th, General McClernand came on board the Forest Queen, and with General Sherman went to the Black Hawk flag-boat. There an interview took place, during which the expedition to Arkansas Post took shape. General Sherman having asked leave to take the post, and Admiral Porter having decided to go along, McClernand thought best to go with his entire army, although the enemy were supposed to have only about four or five thousand men, and the fort was little more than a large earthwork commanding the river.

General Sherman's command was then entitled the Second Corps, Army of the Mississippi, and was comprised of the First Division, Blair's, Hovey's, and Thayer's brigades, commanded by Steele; and the Second Division, commanded by David Stuart, with Colonels Giles A. and Kilby Smith commanding brigades.

Our fleet was convoyed by three ironclads and several other gun-boats. The weather was bitterly cold for that latitude; we were four days getting into the Arkansas River, which we entered by the White River cut-off; and my recollection is, that our passing the mouth of the main river deceived the enemy as to our destination. The entrance through the cut-off was feasible by reason of high water, and I think made our appearance a surprise to the force at the post. We disembarked on the morning of the 10th of January. Stuart's division first encountered the enemy behind an earthwork about four miles from the fort, running across the solid ground from the river to a swamp. General Sherman in person took Steele's division, and followed a road leading to the rear of the earthwork just mentioned. We had got fairly under way when the rebels fell back to the fort, and McClernand, coming up, ordered us to fall back, and march up the river. It seemed to me then, and afterward, that it would have been better to have marched straight to the rear of the fort, as we started to do. We soon overtook Stuart and closed in, General Sherman on the right, Morgan's force on the left, reaching to the river, where the gunboats were, while Sherman reached from the road which connected the post with the back country, toward where the earthworks reached the river above the fort, and threatened their communications with Little Rock. The night was cold and cloudy, with some snow. There were a good many abandoned huts to our rear, but our forces in position lay on the frozen ground, sheltered as best they could, among the bushes and timber. We were so close that they could have reached us any time during the night with light artillery. The gunboats threw heavy shells into the fort and behind the earthworks all night, keeping the enemy awake and anxious. The heavy boom of the artillery was followed by the squeak, squeak of Admiral Porter's little tug, as he moved around making his arrangements for the morrow. The sounds were ridiculous by comparison. General Sherman and staff lay on the roots of an old oak-tree, that kept them partly clear of mud. The cold was sharp, my right boot being frozen solid in a puddle in the morning. About half-past two or three o'clock, General Sherman, with another and myself, crept in as close as possible and reconnoitred the position. The general managed to creep in much closer than the rest of us—in fact, so close as to cause us anxiety. The enemy worked hard all night on their abatis and intrenchments, and in the morning we found a ditch and parapet running clear across the point on which the post was situated. This point was cut by a road from the back country, across which was a heavy earthwork and a battery. This road was at the extremity of our left. General McClernand kept his head-quarters on his boat, the Tigress. He came up in the morning to a place in the woods in our rear. One of his staff, a cavalry-officer, climbed a tree to report movements; but from that point there was very little to be seen. Between ten and eleven o'clock the fire opened from the fleet, and we opened along the whole line from infantry and field-guns. Our men soon worked in close enough to keep down the fire of the enemy to a very marked degree.

. . . .

After reporting to General Sherman, and while explaining the position of the fleet, the smoke-stacks and flags appeared above the fort. What firing was going on in our immediate front ceased. A good many rebels were in plain sight, running away from the fort and scattering. While we were still surprised, the cry was raised that a white flag was hung out. I did not see it, but in a few minutes saw others along the line, and just as the general started for the fort I saw the flag not far from the white house, near the parapet. Orders were given to cease firing. Captain Dayton was sent to the fort where the first flag was raised. Some shots were fired and some men hurt after this. The first rebel officer we encountered was Colonel or General Garland, commanding brigade, who was ordered to put his men in line and stack arms, which was done. I was directed to pass along the line to the right, and cause the prisoners to stack arms and form our men in line, just outside the work. This I did till I reached Deshler's brigade, on our extreme right, or nearly so, and who was opposed to the right of Steele's force. Steele's men had rushed up to the very foot of the parapet, and some were on it, though they did not fire. The commander of the enemy (Deshler) refused to obey my orders to stack arms, and asked a good many questions as to "how it happened;" said he was not whipped, but held us in check, etc. I told him there were eight or nine thousand men right there, that a shot from me, or a call, would bring down on him, and that we had entire possession of the place. After sending two officers from the nearest troops to explain the condition to Steele, and to warn every officer they met to pass the word for everybody to be on the sharp lookout, I arranged with Deshler to keep quiet until I could bring his own commander, or orders from him. Returning to General Sherman, I found a party of young rebel officers, including Robert Johnston's son (rebel Senate) and Captain Wolf, quartermaster, of New Orleans, who declined to surrender except to gentlemen. Some German Missouri soldiers didn't relish the distinction, and were about clubbing them over the head, when I interfered and received their surrender. Hurrying back to the general, I reported the dangerous condition of things. He and General Churchill, commanding officer of the enemy, started for Deshler's brigade; meeting Garland, a quarrel and some recrimination followed between him and Churchill, as to where the fault of the surrender belonged, which was rather promptly silenced by General Sherman, who hurried to the scene of trouble. There, after some ill-natured talk, Deshler ordered his men to lay down their arms. I rode into the fort, and found the parapet badly torn up by the fire from the fleet. On going to the embrasure where I had seen the gun while on the river-bank talking to Captain Shirk, the piece was found split back about eighteen inches, and the lower half of the muzzle dropped out. A battered but unexploded shell lying with the piece explained that it must have struck the gun in the muzzle, almost squarely. On passing along the inside I saw from the torn condition of the earthworks how tremendous our fire was, and how the fire of the enemy was kept down. The fire of the navy had partly torn down the side of the fort next the river. A good many sailors were in the fort. General A. J. Smith, Admiral Porter, and General Burbridge were there—all in high spirits, but in some contention as to who got in first. Toward dark, or nearly so, an Arkansas regiment came in as reënforcements, but surrendered without any trouble. About the same time General Sherman received orders to put General A. J. Smith in charge of the fort, and stay outside with his men. As his troops were nearly all inside, and had four-fifths of the prisoners in charge, these orders were not very clear, and the general left for headquarters to find out what was meant. I went on collecting arms, and as our men were scattering a good deal and were greatly excited, I took the precaution to pass along the line and march the prisoners far enough from the stacked arms to be out of temptation. I was especially urged to this by hearing several rebel officers speak of their guns being still loaded. It was dark before all the prisoners were collected and under guard, including the regiment that arrived after the fight. I am confident that all the prisoners were under guard by General Sherman's troops.

Everything being secure, the staff-officers, all of whom had been busily engaged, scattered to compare notes and enjoy the victory. I found my way onboard the Tigress, where every one was greatly excited, and in high feather regarding our victory, the biggest thing since Donelson. I also obtained some food and small comforts for a few rebel officers, including young Johnston, Wolfe, and the Colonel Deshler already mentioned. Then hunted up General Sherman, whom I found sitting on a cracker-box in the white house already mentioned, near where the white flag first appeared. Garland was with him, and slept with him that night, while the rest of us laid around wherever we could. It was a gloomy, bloody house, and suggestive of war. Garland was blamed by the other Confederate officers for the white flag, and remained with us for safety. Next day was very cold. We worked hard at the lists of prisoners—nearly five thousand in number—all of whom were sent to St. Louis, in charge of our inspector-general, Major Sanger. Our loss was less than one hundred. The enemy, although behind intrenchments, lost more than double what we did. Their wounded were much worse hurt than ours, who were mostly hit around the head and arms.

The losses were nearly all in General Sherman's wing of the army. The loss in the fleet amounted to little, but their service was very valuable, and deserved great credit, though they received little. There was a good deal of sympathy between our part of the forces and the fleet people, and I then thought, and still think, if we had been on the left next the river, that in connection with the tremendous fire from the navy, we could have carried the work in an hour after we opened on it. Their missiles traversed the whole fortification, clear through to the hospitals at the upper end, and I stood five minutes in rifle-range of the fort next the river—not hit, and but seldom shot at, and no one hit near me.

On the 13th we embarked, in a snow-storm; collected at Napoleon, which seemed to be washing away; and steamed to Milliken's Bend, where we arrived on January 21st, and soon after went to Young's plantation, near Vicksburg.

The above statement from General Hammond was received by General Sherman, inclosed in a letter dated "Chicago, February 5, 1876" and signed "John H. Hammond," who was adjutant-general to General Sherman during the winter of 1862–'63.

J. E. TOURTELOTTE.

CINCINNATI, *February* 3, 1876.

MY DEAR GENERAL: At Arkansas Post the troops debarked from steamer January 9th, from one o'clock to dark, in the vicinity of Notrib's farm, and on the 10th moved out to get position; Steele to the right, crossing the low ground to the north, to get a higher ground, avoid crowding the moving columns, and gain the left (our right) and rear of the "post," and the river-bank above the post. Stuart took the river-road the movement commencing at 11 o'clock A. M. After crossing the low ground covered with water, you were called back with Steele, as Stuart had driven out the enemy's rifle-trench pickets, this giving more and feasible room for moving. Stuart was pushed forward, and by dark he and Steele were well up to their expected positions. Before daylight on the 11th you directed me to accompany you for a personal inspection of the ground to your front, which we made on foot, going so far forward that we could easily hear the enemy at work and moving about. Discovering the open fields, you at once directed Steele to move to the right and front, and pushed Stuart out so as to fully command them and the field-work of the enemy extending from the fort, to prevent further strengthening, as it was evident these works were the product of a recent thought. Stuart and Steele were prompt in taking position, but Morgan's command (not under your control) did not seem to work up, or keep in junction with you. At ten o'clock you sent me to McClernand to ascertain why the delay of attack. He attributed it to Admiral Porter, which was really unjust. The attack began at 1 P. M., by Admiral Porter, and the sound of his first gun had not died till your men were engaged—Wood's, Barrett's, and the Parrott batteries and infantry. It was lively for a time, and Stuart pushed clear up to the enemy's rifle-trenches, and forced them to keep sheltered. Hammond was mostly with Steele; Sanger sent to McClernand, and McCoy, myself, and John Taylor were with you and Stuart. At about half-past three I got your permission to go to Giles Smith's skirmish-line, and, thinking I saw evidence of the enemy weakening, I hurried back to you and reported my observations. I was so confident that a demand for it would bring a surrender, that I *asked permission* to make it, and, as you granted me, but refused to let another member of your staff, at his request, go with me, I rode directly down the road with only an orderly. Colonel Garland, commanding a brigade, was the first officer I saw, to whom, for you, I made the demand. All firing ceased at once, or in a few moments. I sent the orderly back to you, and you rode forward. It was then four o'clock.

During the attack, nobody seemed to think McClernand had any clear idea of what or how it was to be done. During the day he gave you no directions, nor came where you were; he was well to the rear, with his "man up a tree," who in the capacity of a lookout gave McClernand information, *from which* he based such instructions as he made to his subordinates. He was free to express himself as being a man of "destiny," and his "star" was in the ascendance. I am, etc.,

L. M. DAYTON, *late Colonel of the Staff, now of Cincinnati, Ohio.*

General W. T. SHERMAN.

MERIDIAN CAMPAIGN.

[Special Field Orders, No. 11.]

HEADQUARTERS DEPARTMENT OF THE TENNESSEE,
MEMPHIS, *January* 27, 1864

. . . .

V. The expedition is one of celerity, and all things must tend to that. Corps commanders and staff-officers will see that our movements are not encumbered by wheeled vehicles improperly loaded. Not a tent, from the commander-in-chief down, will be carried. The sick will be left behind, and the surgeons can find houses and sheds for all hospital purposes.

VI. All the cavalry in this department is placed under the orders and command of Brigadier-General W. S. Smith, who will receive special instructions.

. . . .

By order of Major-General W. T. SHERMAN:

L. M. DAYTON, *Aide-de-Camp.*

NOTE.—That same evening I started in a steamboat for Vicksburg.

W. T. S.

ST. LOUIS, 1885.

HEADQUARTERS DEPARTMENT OF THE TENNESSEE,
MEMPHIS, *January* 27, 1864.

Brigadier-General W. S. SMITH, *commanding Cavalry, etc., present.*

DEAR GENERAL: By an order issued this day I have placed all the cavalry of this department subject to your command. I estimate you can make a force of full seven thousand men, which I believe to be superior and better in all respects than the combined cavalry which the enemy has in all the State of Mississippi. I will in person start for Vicksburg to-day, and with four divisions of infantry, artillery, and cavalry move out for Jackson, Brandon, and Meridian, aiming to reach the latter place by February 10th. General Banks will feign on Pascagoula and General Logan on Rome. I want you with your cavalry to move from Colliersville on Pontotoc and Okolona; thence sweeping down near the Mobile & Ohio Railroad, disable that road as much as possible, consume or destroy the resources of the enemy along that road, break up the connection with Columbus, Mississippi, and finally reach me at or near Meridian as near the date I have mentioned as possible. This will call for great energy of action on your part, but I believe you are equal to it, and you have the best and most experienced troops in the service, and they will do anything that is possible. General Grierson is with you, and is familiar with the whole country. I will send up from Haines's Bluff an expedition of gunboats and transports combined, to feel up the Yazoo as far as the present water will permit. This will disconcert the enemy. My movement on Jackson will also divide the enemy, so that by no combination can he reach you with but a part of his force. I wish you to attack any force of cavalry you meet and follow them southward, but in no event be drawn into the forks of the streams that make up the Yazoo nor over into Alabama. Do not let the enemy draw you into minor affairs, but look solely to the greater object to destroy his communication from Okolona to Meridian, and thence eastward to Selma. From Okolona south you will find abundance of forage collected along the railroad, and the farmers have corn standing in the fields. Take liberally of all these, as well as horses, mules, cattle, etc. As a rule, respect dwellings and families as something too sacred to be disturbed by soldiers, but mills, barns, sheds, stables, and such like things use for the benefit or convenience of your command. If convenient, send into Columbus, Mississippi, and destroy all machinery there, and the bridge across the Tombigbee, which enables the enemy to draw the resources of the east side of the valley, but this is not of sufficient importance to delay your movement. Try and communicate with me by scouts and spies from the time you reach Pontotoc. Avoid any large force of infantry, leaving them to me. We have talked over this matter so much that the above covers all points not provided for in my published orders of to-day. I am, etc.,

W. T. Sherman, *Major-General, commanding.*

MEMPHIS, TENNESSEE, *January* 27, 1864.

Brigadier-General J. P. HATCH, *in charge of Cavalry Bureau, St. Louis, Missouri.*

SIR: Your favor of the 21st inst. is just received. Up to the present time eight hundred and eighteen horses have arrived here since Captain Hudson's visit to St. Louis. I wrote you upon his return several days ago that it would not be necessary to divert shipments to this point which could not reach us before February 1st. We shall certainly get off on our contemplated expedition before that time. The number of horses estimated for in this department by its chief quartermaster was two thousand, and this number, including those already sent, will, I think, completely mount all the dismounted cavalry of this department. Recruits for cavalry regiments are arriving freely, and this will swell our requisitions for a couple of months to come. I will as far as possible procure horses from the regions of country traversed by our cavalry.

. . . .

Yours truly, W. SOOY SMITH, *Brigadier-General,*
Chief of Cavalry, Military Division of the Mississippi.

MEMPHIS, TENNESSEE, *January* 28, 1864.

Brigadier-General GEORGE CROOK, *commanding Second Cavalry Division, Huntsville, Alabama.*

I start in about three days with seven thousand men to Meridian *via* Pontotoc. Demonstrate on Decatur, to hold Roddy.

W. SOOY SMITH, *Brigadier-General,*
Chief of Cavalry, Military Division of the Mississippi.

MAYWOOD, ILLINOIS, *July* 9, 1875.

General W. T. SHERMAN, *Commander-in-Chief, United States Army.*

SIR: Your letter of July 7th is just received.

Your entire statement in the "Memoirs" concerning my part in the Meridian campaign is incorrect.

You overstate my strength, placing it at seven thousand effective, when it was but six. The nominal strength of my command was seven thousand.

You understate the strength of my enemy, putting Forrest's force at four thousand. On our return to Nashville, you stated it, in General Grant's presence, to have been but twenty-five hundred. Before and during my movement I positively knew Forrest's strength to be full six thousand, and he has since told me so himself.

Instead of delaying from the 1st to the 11th of February for "some regiment that was ice-bound near Columbus, Kentucky," it was an entire brigade, Colonel Waring's, without which your orders to me were peremptory not to move. I asked you if I should wait its arrival, and you answered: "Certainly; if you go without it, you will be too weak, and I want you strong enough to go where you please."

The time set for our arrival at Meridian, the 10th of February, had arrived before it was possible for me, under your orders, to move from Memphis, and I would have been entirely justifiable if I had not started at all. But I was at that time, and at all times during the war, as earnest and anxious to carry out my orders, and do my full duty, as you or any other officer could be, and I set out to make a march of two hundred and fifty miles into the Confederacy, having to drive back a rebel force equal to my own. After the time had arrived for the full completion of my movement, I drove this force before me, and penetrated one hundred and sixty miles into the Confederacy—did more hard fighting, and killed, wounded, and captured more of the enemy than you did during the campaign—did my work most thoroughly, as far as I could go without encountering the rebel cavalry set loose by your return from Meridian, and brought off my command, with all the captured property and rescued negroes, with very small loss, considering that inflicted on the enemy, and the long-continued and very severe fighting. If I had disobeyed your orders, and started without Waring's brigade, I would have been "too weak," would probably have been defeated, and would have been subjected to just censure. Having awaited its arrival, as I was positively and distinctly ordered to do, it only remained for me to start upon its arrival, and accomplish all that I could of the work allotted to me. To have attempted to penetrate farther into the enemy's country, with the cavalry of Polk's army coming up to reënforce Forrest, would have insured the destruction of my entire command, situated as it was. I cannot now go into all the particulars, though I assure you that they make the proof of the correctness of my conduct as conclusive as I could desire it to be. I was not headed off and defeated by an inferior force near West Point. We had the fighting all our own way near West Point, and at all other points except at Okalona, on our return, when we had the worst of it for a little while, but finally checked the enemy handsomely, and continued our return march, fighting at the rear and on both flanks, repulsing all attacks and moving in perfect order. And so my movement was not a failure, except that I did not reach Meridian as intended, for the reason stated, and for many more which it is not necessary for me to detail here. On the other hand, it was a very decided success, inflicting a terrible destruction of supplies of every kind, and a heavy loss of men upon the enemy. You should have so reported it in the beginning. You should so amend your report and "Memoirs" now. This, and no less than this, is due from one soldier to another. It is due to the exalted position which you occupy, and, above all, it is due to that truthfulness in history which you claim to revere. If you desire it, I will endeavor to visit you, and in a friendly manner "fight our battles o'er again," and endeavor to convince you that you have always been mistaken as to the manner in which my part in the "Meridian campaign" was performed. But I will never rest until the wrong statements regarding it are fully and fairly corrected. Yours truly,

WILLIAM SOOY SMITH.

HEADQUARTERS ARMY OF THE UNITED STATES,
ST. LOUIS, MISSOURI, *July* 11, 1875.

General J. D. WEBSTER, *Chicago, Illinois.*

DEAR GENERAL: General W. Sooy Smith feels aggrieved and wronged by my account of his part in the Meridian campaign, in my "Memoirs," pages 394, 395, and properly appeals to me for correction.[3] I have offered to modify any words or form of expression that he may point out, but he asks me to completely change the whole that concerns him. This, of course, I will not do, as his part was material to the whole, and cannot be omitted or materially altered without changing the remainder, for his failure to reach Meridian by February 10th was the reason for other movements distant from him. I now offer him, what seems to me fair and liberal, that we submit the points at issue to you as arbitrator. You are familiar with the ground, the coincident history, and most, if not all, the parties.

I propose to supply you with—

1. Copy of my orders placing all the cavalry under General Smith's orders (with returns).

[3] See the relevant section in Chapter 15 "Meridian Campaign. January and February, 1864."

2. My letter of instructions to him of January 27th.

3. My official report of the campaign, dated Vicksburg, March 7, 1864.

4. General W. Sooy Smith's report of his operations, dated Nashville, Tennessee, March 4, 1864.

After reading these, I further propose that you address us questions which we will answer in writing, when you are to make us a concise, written decision, which I will have published in close connection with the subject in controversy. If General Smith will show you my letter to him of this date, and also deliver this with his written assent, I will promptly furnish you the above documents, and also procure from the official files a return of the cavalry force available at and near Memphis on the date of my orders, viz., January 27, 1864.

With great respect, your friend and servant,

W. T. SHERMAN, *General.*

NOTE.—General Smith never submitted his case to the arbitration offered. The whole will be made clear by the publication of the official records, which are already in print, though not yet issued. His orders were in writing, and I have no recollection of the "peremptory" verbal orders to which he refers, and quotes as from me.

ST. LOUIS, MISSOURI, 1885. W. T. S.

MAYWOOD, ILLINOIS, *July* 14, 1875.

General W. T. SHERMAN, *Commander-in-Chief, etc.*

DEAR GENERAL: Your letter of the 11th of July reaches me just as I am starting to spend the first vacation I have ever allowed myself—in the Territories, with my wife and son.

It indicates a spirit of fairness from which we have better things than an arbitration to hope for. Though, if we should reach such a necessity, there is no one living to whom our differences might more properly be referred than to General Webster. I make no objection to your writing *your* "Memoirs," and, as long as they refer to your own conduct, you are at liberty to write them as you like; but, when they refer to mine, and deal unjustly with my reputation, I, of right, object.

Neither do I wish to write *my* "Memoirs," unless compelled to do so to vindicate my good name. There were certain commands which were to make up mine. These, Waring's brigade included, were spoken of by us in the long conversation to which you refer. This brigade we knew was having a hard time of it in its movement from Columbus to Memphis. I asked you if I should move without it if it did not arrive, and you answered me as stated in my last letter to you. Those who immediately surrounded me during the painful delay that occurred will inform you how sorely I chafed under the restraint of that peremptory order.

In the conversation that occurred between us at Nashville, while all the orders, written and verbal, were still fresh in your memory, you did not censure me for waiting for Waring, but for allowing myself to be encumbered with fugitive negroes to such an extent that my command was measurably unfit for active movement or easy handling, and for turning back from West Point, instead of pressing on toward Meridian. Invitations had been industriously circulated, by printed circulars and otherwise, to the negroes to come into our lines, and to seek our protection wherever they could find it, and I considered ourselves pledged to receive and protect them. Your censure for so doing, and your remarks on that subject to me in Nashville, are still fresh in my memory, and of a character which you would now doubtless gladly disavow.

But we must meet and talk the whole matter over, and I will be at any trouble to see you when I return.

Meantime I will not let go the hope that I will convince you absolutely of your error, for the facts are entirely on my side. Yours truly,

WILLIAM SOOY SMITH.[4]

[4] In the 1886 second edition of the memoirs, the phrase "END OF VOL. I." was centered at the bottom of the page.

Appendix to Volume II.

UNIVERSITY, WASHINGTON SQUARE,
NEW YORK, *May* 24, 1875.

MY DEAR GENERAL: Now, I suppose, there can be no doubt that your decision to publish your war memoirs was correct. One would have supposed that, whatever else might be denied, your origination of the "march to the sea" would never have been called in question. Yet you see it is! If there is to be a battle upon that or any other point, it is better that it should be fought now, while you who know all the facts of the case are here to take care of your own reputation. If claims that every one has for the last ten years admitted to be just can be called in question now, what would not be possible hereafter?

I do not see with what face the persons who are engaged in this disreputable attempt can proceed. How are they going to get over your letter of October 10th to Grant, or those of the same day to Howard and to Thomas? Surely you would not have presumed, in writing to Grant on October 10th, to say, "Had I better not execute *the plan of my* letter," if the operation contemplated had been advised by him. Nor would you the next day have sent him the cipher dispatch that you did. To the same effect is your letter to Halleck of October 19th, and that of November 2d to Grant. Grant in his letter to you of that same date does not say, "Go on as *I* proposed," but "Go on as *you* propose."

So I repeat, as there is to be a controversy, let it come now. Of course, it is a disagreeable thing to have such an affair on one's hands—an affair which one would very gladly avoid if possible, but I think you are fortunate in discovering what envious rivals are ready to do.

I received from Appletons this morning a copy of the "Memoirs" as presented by yourself, and heartily thank you for bearing me in mind. They have got the book up in very good style, and in that respect have left nothing to be desired. In the course of this and the next week I shall read it through, but I did not care to delay writing to congratulate you on the event.

General Grant could by half a dozen words stifle all these shameful claims, and do you justice. He ought to do so.

With kindest regards to your family, believe me, my dear general,

Very truly yours,

J. W. Draper.

General Sherman.

West Point, *May* 29, 1875.

Dear General: The presentation to me of a copy of your "Memoirs" was no less pleasing than unexpected.

I have refrained from writing until I could finish the book, which I have read with absorbing interest. I feel personally indebted to you for this contribution to history, which will not only enhance your reputation, but, what will be more gratifying to you, will attract the attention of Europe to the achievements of our army and open up a fertile field of illustration to the future students of strategy and grand tactics. I see there are some criticisms in the press, but all lovers of the truth will be glad that you have been faithful in your narration. I can safely say, from my knowledge of the character of some of the delinquent officers, that you have treated them with tender consideration. I am glad to have read your book before going abroad, as it has made clear and well defined my knowledge of operations in the West and South, which before was but vague and shadowy, and will thus enable me to talk intelligently with all officers who may seek information. I wrote a few days since to the Secretary of War about my tour, and mentioned Audenried as a desirable officer to accompany me. The Secretary replied that Audenried had been abroad once, and that he thought it ought to be given to some officer serving with troops. I owe this tour entirely to you, and would be glad to have you suggest some one to accompany me—Alexander might like to go, but I doubt if he would like to leave his family so long. With many thanks for the "Memoirs," ever

Very respectfully yours,

E. Upton.

Note.—Lieutenant-Colonel George A. Forsyth, of Lieutenant-General Sheridan's staff, and Captain Joseph P. Sanger, of the First

Artillery, accompanied General Upton on his tour around the world, and have since contributed largely of military knowledge to the profession.

W. T. S.

St. Louis, 1885.

New York, *December* 12, 1875.

My dear General: It has often been a subject of discussion between not only officers of the volunteer and regular army, but military critics, as to how far General Lee's plans and movements during the campaign immediately preceding his surrender were influenced by your "march to the sea." Thinking the following extract of a letter written by General Lee, three years after the close of the war, might not have come under your notice, and regarding it as having a most important bearing upon the discussion referred to, being the unprejudiced testimony of the only person who could give the facts and reasons which controlled the movements of the Confederate forces operating for the defense of the Confederate capital, I have made a transcript of the following:

"Warm Springs, Virginia, *July* 27, 1868.

"*General* W. S. Smith.

. . . .

"As regards the movements of General Sherman, it was easy to see that, unless they were interrupted, I should be compelled to abandon the defense of Richmond, and with a view of arresting his progress I so weakened my force by sending reënforcements to South and North Carolina that I had not sufficient men to man my lines.

"Had they not been broken, I should have abandoned them as soon as General Sherman reached the Roanoke.

(Signed) "R. E. Lee."

Yours truly, G. A. Custer,

Brevet Major-General, United States Army.

General W. T. Sherman, *United States Army.*

11 Grosvenor Mansion,
Victoria Street, S. W., London, *December* 25, 1875.

General W. T. Sherman.

My dear Sir: There could be no more desirable gift than that which has just reached me of your (red) second volume from the publishers. I thank you again heartily, and add special thanks for your valuable remarks touching European war. I have nothing at present to offer you in return if it was at all possible to balance such a work, which it assuredly is not. I have been writing a little again on the Prussians, but mainly in the "Edinburgh," which I know is regularly republished with you. The newest foreign thing, however, is Ducrot's little book on "Tirailleurs," interesting mainly as showing how close the best French officers are copying the Germans. I am taking the liberty of sending you a copy, one of the first got over here.

Mrs. Chesney desires me to thank you heartily for the promise of the photograph, for which she will look anxiously. She unites with me in best wishes, and I am always

Yours very sincerely,
C. C. CHESNEY.

P. S.—I ought not to close this without adding that, deep as is my interest in your book, I never thought of *your* campaign as "all confusion." Indeed, may I not hope you remember my lecturing on your Atlanta advance very soon after it had taken place? One part only I had been very doubtful about—your Meridian campaign. I, of course, am the more pleased to now have it fully cleared. C. C. C.
(*Colonel of Engineers, English Army*).

Staff College, Farnbro Station,
(Near Aldershot, England), *July* 28, 1875.

Dear General Sherman: I have just had the greatest satisfaction to receive a copy of your "Memoirs," most valuable in any case; but my pleasure is greatly increased by the book being your own gift. I shall look with pride at its place on my shelves after my careful and profitable study of it. I was on the point of ordering it from a publisher's when it arrived. The world is greatly indebted to you for furnishing such important and authentic material toward the record of the second great historical epoch of your country, and students of military art owe you much for the clear narrative of matters essential to be known, but generally omitted from the histories of wars. Coming from whatever hand, the details of transport movement and supply would be of great value; but from you, who devised the plans and gave the orders, they are inestimable.

Last September, I and the officers under my charge went through a little sham campaign as training for staff duties, and I afterward published the record of it. I can scarcely expect that a leader who has conducted such famous operations will care to look at it; but I venture to send it for your kind acceptance, as well as a pamphlet I lately published on what may be called the philosophy of outposts, and I should consider it a great honor if you think them worthy of a glance. With renewed thanks for the kind favor, believe me, dear general,

Yours sincerely,

E. B. HAMLEY.

SONOMA, CALIFORNIA, *December* 15, 1880.

FRIEND SHERMAN: From time to time I have observed some unfavorable criticism of your "Memoirs," which is accounted for by your just estimate of newspaper correspondents in the closing of your "Military Lessons of the War." Those writers, having found employment on newspapers in every part of the country, never forget or forgive. However, as falsehood and ridicule are ephemeral, and truth eternal, you have the best of it.

I have just finished reading the volumes of your "Memoirs," and find them the most interesting pages I have ever perused. All the facts and circumstances, given as they occurred, are so faithfully and plainly related that they fairly photograph themselves upon the understanding.

It was a wise conclusion of yours to write that book, for I am now well convinced that justice never would have been meted out to you by future historians; the envy of others would have warped their judgment. The fact is, no one else could have given such details, for they could not be concentrated in the brains of any other individual.

If the history of the war was to be written for the schools, yours could not be condensed to advantage; and if for a standard library work, yours could not be improved as far as it goes.

Your triumphs never have been and never will be equaled, your glory will never be dim, and generations yet unborn will do honor to your name. Like every true American, I am proud of you, and take this occasion to say so.

Being now seventy, I am living on borrowed time. I see you will be sixty-two next April. I shall, on the 27th of that month, be seventy-one. Please reply. I want your signature. Remember me kindly to your wife and children.

Your friend,

A. M. WINN.

General W. T. SHERMAN, *Washington, D. C.*

COLUMBIA, SOUTH CAROLINA, *June* 22, 1872.

General W. T. SHERMAN, *Washington, D. C.*

GENERAL: I have just finished reading your "Memoirs," written by yourself, and have been so much pleased with them that I cannot resist the temptation to write you a line. I never before in my life became so much interested in a book. I could not put it down after commencing it, especially the second volume. It carries with it the stamp of truth in every line, and no one reading it can fail to see it. When your army moved in the spring of 1864, I was a captain in the Seventh Connecticut (General A. H. Terry's old regiment); was captured June 2d, and taken to Macon, Georgia; was there, and never shall I forget the day, when McPherson was killed. Not a prisoner but seemed to feel it as though he had been a brother. The feeling was, I assure you, not confined to Western soldiers. I remember well Stoneman's coming into stockade. When you took Atlanta I was in Charleston. The papers there tried to convince the people that Atlanta did not amount to much anyhow, and it was better on the whole that you should have it. On October 4th I was sent to this place, and with the rest of the officers, about eighteen hundred, sent into stockade on the Lexington side of the Congaree River. I made an unsuccessful attempt at escape on the 4th of November; was recaptured and brought back. Got out again on the night of 28th November, reached gunboat off Georgetown on morning of December 8th, and was at Hilton Head when you took Fort McAllister. On our passage down the river we laid up our boat in the day and traveled nights, and were furnished with provisions by the negroes, and never knew one to fail to respond with the best he or she could obtain when asked. We had been unable for some time to hear from you, or to know what was going on. I felt sure, however, you would go to Savannah. One morning I came across an old negro with more than ordinary intelligence, and I said to him, "Do you hear anything from General Sherman?" "Oh, yes, we hear young massa talk about Mr. Sherman" (it was and is now to a great extent the custom to call you Mr. Sherman by both whites and blacks, instead of General). "What does he say?" "He says Mr. Sherman cross de river, and dey don't know whar he's gwine, but dat dey got a army behind that can't catch up with him, and de army in front of him can't get out de way." I am much pleased with your plain talk about some of the rebel generals. The feeling of the people in this State toward the United States Government has not changed one *iota,* or toward those who fought in the Union cause, no matter how much they try, and do gloss it over at the centennials, where they are fêted and treated. I have lived here nine years among them, and know. I think every lover of the Union should have in his house your book, and that his children should read it as soon as they can read anything, to see and to know what it cost in life, hardship, and treasure to preserve for them this Government.

Very respectfully, your obedient servant,

JOHN B. DENNIS,
Late Brevet Brigadier-General U. S. Volunteers.

TREASURY OF THE UNITED STATES,
WASHINGTON, *June* 22, 1875.

MY DEAR GENERAL: I have just finished your "Memoirs." It is the only book, save one, that I have read in twenty years. You cannot imagine how I enjoyed it from beginning to end, for which please accept my thanks.

I was residing in the city of New York in 1846 when the "armed emigration" under Colonel Stevenson was organized, and saw the regiment leave for the Pacific coast. So I was able to follow you all the way through for twenty years to the close of the war of the rebellion, in which you acted so very conspicuous a part, and added so much to the glorious history of our country.

Entertained, instructed, and pleased as I was all the way through your narrative, I was particularly struck with the justice of your ideas and the force with which you expressed them, at the conclusion, in regard to your staff.

But comparatively, the evils flowing from this branch of the public service are to a degree limited, and show themselves in a mild form in the army, while in the civil departments they are intolerable.

The lowest clerk, and even a messenger, in the office proper of the head of a department is considered competent, and authorized to direct the official actions of the chiefs of the various bureaus.

This is utterly subversive of efficiency in the offices, and an absolute obstruction and hinderance to the correct and proper transaction of the public business.

Again thanking you for the enjoyment the reading of your book has afforded me, I am, most sincerely,

Your friend, F. E. SPINNER.

General William T. Sherman, *St. Louis, Missouri.*

Washington, D. C., *July* 5, 1875.

My dear General: Since I parted with you at Columbus, I have read your two volumes of "Memoirs" very carefully, and I cannot let the occasion pass without telling you how much pleasure they have given me. Though the general history of the war was very familiar to me, I read these volumes with a keenness of interest which I have rarely experienced. The fresh and vivid style, the graphic description of persons and events would make your book attractive even were the subject-matter less interesting than it is. While you have very frankly given your opinion of your associates in the war, I do not believe that a just criticism will charge you with doing any intentional injustice to any one. It was not possible that such great events could have transpired without bringing into sharp collision individual interests and opinions; and I believe it is far better that all controverted opinions should be debated while the actors are living. Judging from the effect of your book upon myself, I cannot doubt that it will greatly strengthen the affection with which you are cherished by the American people. With kindest regards, I am very truly yours,

J. A. Garfield.

General W. T. Sherman, *St. Louis, Missouri.*

Athens, Ohio, *July* 12, 1875.

General W. T. Sherman.

Dear Sir: I have from time to time read the ingenious and rather bitter reviews of certain portions of your "Memoirs" by General Boynton, in the *Cincinnati Gazette.*

So much as relates to your published comments and historical statements of the campaigns of General George H. Thomas, and more especially his last great campaign of 1864, I have read with great interest. Neither to General Boynton nor any one else do I yield the palm for devotion to the memory and history of General Thomas. I served under him, often under his observation, from October, 1862, until the end of the war, and until November 22, 1865. I commanded a brigade at Nashville, and served all through his campaigns of that year.

It may be in some degree gratifying to you that, jealous as I am of the fame of Thomas, gratified as I am for his unsought indorsement of my own character as a soldier, and confident as I am that his record is without a blemish, or "spot, or wrinkle, or any such thing," yet nothing that you have written of him and his campaigns do I criticise as untrue, unjust, or even injudicious and ill-timed.

The misgivings you had in your tent away off from us pressed heavily upon us around our camp-fires at Nashville. We who were in inferior positions of command felt, or at least feared, that the long delays were likely to be fatal in the end; and often, between November 30th and December 15th, as I rode along the familiar lines of our army, and saw the solid works of Hood going up, I felt the moments of delay were golden, and perhaps fatal ones to us.

That my impatience and misgiving was without reasonable cause now appears affirmatively; and yet it existed, and was reasonable at the time. Our apprehensions did not take the shape of doubts of the zeal or competency of Thomas, so much as a dread of some obstacles to our progress, of the existence and magnitude of which we did not know and comprehend.

I am, general, your obedient servant,
C. H. Grosvenor.

Kalama, Washington Territory, *July* 13, 1875.

Dear General: I have just finished reading your "Memoirs," and want to thank you for that valuable addition to the literature of our country. Many of the critics seem surprised that you should publish *facts* instead of fiction, and I don't wonder, as the latter has become so fashionable. The *facts* of your book will be invaluable in the future to the conscientious historian. I could but wonder at the ill-natured criticisms of some, without regard to your comments on Generals Blair and Logan. Your views of these gentlemen as soldiers are precisely the same as those expressed by hundreds of volunteer officers during the war, and who felt for both those gentlemen only the highest respect and most kindly feelings.

I am sure every soldier who had the good fortune to serve with you in the late war will, if possible, feel an increased affection for you, and wonder that you were able to draw so true a picture of the scenes of which you were the central figure.

Please accept, general, my grateful thanks, and believe me,

Respectfully, your sincere friend,
John W. Sprague.

General W. T. Sherman, *United States Army, St. Louis, Missouri.*

LOUISIANA STATE UNIVERSITY,
BATON ROUGE, LOUISIANA, *July* 17, 1875.

General W. T. SHERMAN, *St. Louis, Missouri.*

DEAR GENERAL: I have read your book pretty carefully, especially the chapter on Louisiana.

The book will no doubt prove what you design it to be, a valuable contribution to the future historian who may wish to write of the origin and conduct of our great civil war.

The chapter on California I could almost anticipate page after page. I had heard you talk it all in 1860–'61, and the California story is, I think, the best part of the work. I am sorry you left out Florida and West Point; and it would have been all the better had you gone back to Ohio, and "Nosey Josey," and other old Western characters that you used to have us laugh at.

As to the Louisiana portion of the "Memoirs," it is true in its aim and purpose, and almost faultless even in its details, and you know I had a good opportunity of testing its accuracy. From January 1, 1860, until you left the seminary, in February, 1861, I knew you very intimately, officially and personally. Our isolation in the pine-woods, and messing together, enabled our little party of professors to see and know more of each other than would otherwise have been the case. And, with the exception of a few minor and unimportant details, your account of our school, yourself, and your relations to it and to the State, and of Louisiana affairs generally, as given in your book, is true—given with remarkable fidelity. You may recollect that I staid at the seminary for you during the vacation of 1860, while you visited your family in Ohio. You necessarily wrote me on business frequently, and as the country (North and South) was then in considerable agitation, pending the presidential election, you wrote a good deal also of politics. All those letters I have preserved, as well as those you did me the honor to write me after you had left us in 1861, from New Orleans and St. Louis, as late as May 13th, and they bear you out in what you say in your book on Louisiana. Regarding what I knew of your opinions and intentions, gathered from daily talk and discussions, you were a Clay Whig (if you were of any party at all), and I a Calhoun Democrat; you denying the right of secession, and I maintaining it. I need only say that, for six months *before* Louisiana seceded, you even then, and at all times, denounced secession as *treason;* said if Louisiana did secede, you would resign your superintendency of our school, and go away, and you did so. All the while, however, you expressed the hope that there would be no *secession* of any of the Southern States; and I shall never forget how you received the news of the secession of South Carolina. I happened to be in your room with you when the mail was brought in, and when you read of the actual passage of the formal and solemn withdrawal by that State from the Union, *you cried like a little child,* exclaiming: "My God, you Southern people don't know what you are doing! Peaceable secession! There can be no *peaceable secession.* Secession means war. The North will fight you, and fight you hard, and God only knows how or where it will end!" Yet, even after that, you seemed to have a vague hope that something would take place to bring back the seceding States, and to prevent actual war, and your letters to me show that to have been your hope, as late as April 4, 1861. But all the while, before you left Louisiana and afterward, you said that, if war did come, every *true* man must take sides one way or the other; and, as for you, you would go with the North, or the Union, as it was then understood. Nevertheless, your letters from St. Louis, of April and May, show clearly that you were then checked, or restrained, from actively taking sides with the North, by what you believed to be the *partisan* nature of Mr. Lincoln's Administration, and from feelings of friendship for us in the South. I remember well how it grieved you to leave us, and how sorry were we to see you go, and how great an influence was brought to bear on you to keep you at your post at the head of our school.

Moore and Bragg and Beauregard and Dick Taylor all wrote you most urgently to stay. Some of these letters, left by you among the *official* letters, I recollect seeing as late as 1863. One of a very friendly nature from Beauregard, particularly, I remember seeing there. And General Taylor told me, during the war, that he had thought you would *not* leave the seminary after you had received a certain letter from him. All these gentlemen, so distinguished afterward, seemed attached to you personally, and were very anxious that you should remain as president of our school; and my impression then was, and now is, that they thought you could do so without compromising yourself in politics, or taking actively any part for the South, should war take place. I recollect a little incident at Manassas that tends to confirm me in this view. A few days after the battle, some of us from Louisiana spoke of the false rumor that you had been captured, when

Dr. S. A. Smith, our Vice-President of the Board of Supervisors, said: "By *Gemminy,* I wish it had been so; I would like to have a good long talk with him, and then make him go back home to the seminary!" The letters of Beauregard, Bragg, and others alluded to, you might possibly find. Major Gillespie, of Macon, Missouri, says that he removed all the books, papers, apparatus, etc., from the old seminary in 1864, by order of General T. Kilby Smith, of the Federal army, and that General Smith took charge of some of the articles himself. Who knows but he may have preserved those letters? [He did.—W. T. S.]

Any account of the war, however accurate and liberal, must be, to even Confederates, full of sadness. We made a struggle such as history may never tell of again. We lost so much of our best blood, only to *fail!*

There are some few things in your book that I regret. You have mistaken the character of some of the Confederate leaders. If you had known Mr. Davis and General Hampton personally and well, I know you well enough to say that you would not have done them the injustice you have in your book.

The burning of Columbia accounts for itself—one army retreating, stragglers falling behind; the other advancing, bummers in front, Confederate storehouses fired, and *cotton* (which the Confederates were afraid to burn, lest they would burn the town) *unbaled and scattered through the streets,* with *liquor* everywhere! Nothing but a miracle could have saved Columbia from burning. Such is the account given me in 1866, by one who was present, a Southern lad, a son of a prominent New Orleans gentleman; and I have always felt that neither you nor Hampton were to blame, and that there ought never to have been a word between you about it.

Mr. Jefferson Davis, whatever else may be said of him, is a humane, Christian gentleman. He was really opposed to the war, thought secession premature, but, as a States-rights man, went along with Mississippi into the Confederacy, and became, without his seeking, its president. He entered into the great struggle with his whole soul, and *failed* simply because God seems not to have meant us (of the South) to break up the Union! How else can you account for the death of Albert Sidney Johnston, from a mere *scratch,* just in the height of his victory at Shiloh; and the calling back of Jackson, by Lee, when in the act of making his final rush on McClellan at Harrison's Bar, when McClellan says (under oath) he expected to surrender his whole army?

And the killing of Jackson, by *his own men,* when Hooker's condition was so desperate at Chancellorsville? And Ewell standing still in the streets of Gettysburg and quietly looking on at Meade slowly and timidly crowning the heights with men and guns? And a *commissioned officer five days slow* in carrying to Dick Taylor and Kirby Smith the terrible straits of General Banks's army and Admiral Porter's fleet at Grand Ecore, after the defeat at Mansfield? And, that army captured and that fleet destroyed, would not the blockade of the Mississippi River have been raised, and Nashville fallen to Hood, and Jubal Early have taken Washington? The issues of war turn often upon trifles too small for man to see or consider; but God observes them all, integrates all such differentials, and uses them for His own wise purposes. He never meant us of the Confederacy to succeed, and it is the duty of every true Confederate soldier to acquiesce in *His* decision; to thank Him for the abolition of slavery, and the preservation of the American Union.

But I have wandered off from Mr. Davis. He had no more to do with the assassination of Mr. Lincoln than you had; and the sensible, far-seeing man he is must, for the sake of his own dear South, have regretted his death even more than you could have done. For then Mr. Lincoln's good sense and firmness had saved the Union; and we needed his kindness of heart and liberal views to save the South. It was a sad day for the South (and for the Union) when Mr. Lincoln was killed (by a crazy actor), and the national government fell into the hands of partisans and demagogues, and cowards and thieves, and nobody knew that better than Jefferson Davis; no one so soon *felt it in his own person,* and ever since, the *outrageous and ignominious treatment* which he received at Fortress Monroe, from men who would have done you likewise, if they had dared—an indignity imposed upon him merely because he was the able and conscientious bearer of a gallant and earnest (though unfortunate) people. I loved Jefferson Davis dearly, and I shall teach my children to love him and to revere his memory.

Please pardon the liberty I have taken as a friend to speak to you frankly, not too fully, about your book. In the last letter I had from you at St. Louis (May 13, 1861), before you had entered actively into the war, you say, "No matter what happens, I will ever consider you my personal friend." I am proud to know that this promise shown to me has been verified, and in all this great country, outside of your own immediate family, there is not one who rejoices more in your personal success and great fame than

Your humble but devoted friend,
D. F. Boyd.

Fort Wayne, Michigan, *September* 24, 1875.

General W. T. Sherman.

Dear General: I have carefully read your "Memoirs," and desire to express my admiration of the work as a vivid picture of the great part of the war your experience was made in. It is not to be supposed, indeed it is not possible, that all the actors in their varied scenes should be satisfied with the parts assigned them, neither is it possible that you could have a perfect and personal acquaintance of the circumstances of every portion of your widely extended theatres of movements and battles.

On page 108, second volume of the "Memoirs," it is stated: "General Stanley had come up on the left of General Davis, and was deploying, though there could not have been on his front more than a skirmish-line. Had he moved straight by the flank, or by a slight circuit to his left, he would have inclosed the whole ground occupied by Hardee's corps, and that corps could not have escaped us."[1] I have no copy of my official report with me, but have a copy of the daily journal of my chief of staff, Colonel J. S. Fullerton, written the night of September 1, 1864. I also ask you to read the inclosed extracts from letters to me from General Nathan Kimball, John Newton, and William Grose, to each of whom I addressed a note in order to get their recollections of the day's movements, and the state of the case. I give only extracts, as each of these letters contains private matter only interesting to myself.

In regard to the day's result at Jonesboro', I assure you I felt at the time, and have since felt, as discontented as yourself. I urged the movement in person, and at the time thought Newton unnecessarily slow (I think since he did all he could under the circumstances). The only criticism I have to make is the one made by General Grose, that "too much time was spent tearing up railroads." About 2, or half-past 2, p. m., Colonel Willard Warner came to me and said that you directed that a thorough destruction of the railroad be made. If we had marched on the enemy during the hours we spent burning ties, and

[1] See the relevant section in Chapter 19 "Capture of Atlanta. August and September, 1864."

making bows and loops of iron rails, we would have ruined Hardee's corps, sure enough. General Thomas never came near me, nor did I meet any one that afternoon who could give me the least information with regard to the situation of affairs. I accompanied Newton's division in its deployment, and urged them on. Just at dark I received a contused wound from a musket-ball in the groin that disabled me for the remainder of that day. I submit these papers to you, with the utmost good nature, to show you that your supposition in regard to the force of the enemy upon my front is a mistaken one. The great difficulty was the dense tangle of underbrush we had to traverse under artillery-fire, and the impossibility in consequence of the ranking generals being able to push the advance rapidly by any personal influence.

I am aware that there was much severe criticism made upon the Fourth Corps at the time, but I have always felt we had a record that could stand a little hammering, and this communication is intended only for yourself.

I am, very respectfully, your obedient servant,

D. S. Stanley, *Colonel Twenty-second Infantry,*
Brevet Major-General, U. S. Army.

[Inclosures.]

Extract from Diary of Brevet Brigadier-General J. S. Fullerton, Chief of Staff, Fourth Army Corps, U. S. Army, for the 1st day of September, 1864.

Atlanta & Macon Railroad, below
Rough and Ready, Georgia.

4 A. M.—Our working parties commenced to destroy the railroads.

4.30 A. M.—Received a note from department headquarters, of which the following is a copy:

"Renfrews, Georgia, *August* 31, 1864.

"*Major-General* D. S. Stanley,
"*Commanding Fourth Army Corps.*

"General: The major-general commanding directs that to-morrow morning early you commence the destruction of the Macon & Western Railroad in connection with General Schofield, who will receive orders from General Sherman.

"You will destroy, as far as you can, in the direction of Jonesboro', or until you meet with General Baird's division of the Fourteenth Corps, which you will probably find engaged in the same kind of work. Should you meet or overtake General Baird, you will report for further orders. Brigadier-General Garrard has been ordered to cover the flank of your column during your march down the road.

"Very respectfully,

"William D. Whipple, *A. A. G.*

"P. S.—General Baird struck the railroad at 5 p. m. to-day, and went to work immediately breaking the road. W. D. W."

5.30 a. m.—Directed division commanders to make immediate preparations to march. General Kimball's division to move down the railroad toward Jonesboro', followed by General Newton, these two divisions to destroy the railroad. General Wood's division to march carefully down the Griffin road (which runs parallel with the railroad) toward Jonesboro', and to take the artillery with him, all save two guns, which are to move with the column down the railroad.

8 a. m.—Kimball commenced to move down the railroad, followed by Newton, destroying the road as they marched.

10 a. m.—Arrived at the point on the railroad where Baird had destroyed it; he only destroyed about three hundred yards of it, and that partially. Went over to report our arrival at this point to General Thomas; this is at Morris Station.

11 a. m.—Found General Thomas; he said he had sent General Wood from the Macon (or Griffin) road to join the rest of the corps at Morris Station, and that, as soon as he arrived there, for General Stanley to put his troops in column, and to send a man on and report his readiness to move to him (General Thomas) as soon as he can. Gave the message to General Stanley at 12.15 p. m.

12.45 p. m.—General Wood has joined the command and started to General Thomas to inform him of the fact; found him near Jonesboro' with General Howard at 2.30 p. m. He sent word to General Stanley to push forward down the railroad for Jonesboro' at once. This message was delivered to General Stanley at 3.30 p. m., and the column commenced to move at 3.40 p. m., General Kimball leading, followed by Newton, then Wood.

4.45 p. m.—Head of the column arrived at a point near Jonesboro', where the enemy was fortified. General Davis's corps (Fourteenth) was then going into position (his formations are made) on the right of the railroad to assault the enemy's works. (Kimball and Newton only.)

4.50 P. M.—Orders were given division commanders to deploy on the left of the railroad, and to advance immediately after their formations were made upon the enemy's position, for the purpose of assaulting the same and assisting General Davis. These orders were obeyed, and the troops commenced to form for advance immediately—Kimball's division on the right and Newton's on the left, while Wood's division was massed close in the rear of our line for support to any part of the same. The troops of the First and Second Divisions made their formations and moved forward as rapidly as possible. In front of the First Division the underbrush was so thick that it was almost impossible to move through it, and Newton could not go before this division. It was necessary to keep up connection with it.

5.30 P. M.—We drove in the enemy's skirmishers after a brisk fight, and Kimball's division came up to the enemy's works at about 5.40 P. M. They were in a strong place, and just beyond a deep ravine, and he thought it not practicable to assault them; he made a feeble attempt to do so, and found he could not succeed. Newton moved up as fast as possible through such thick wood between, it was dark before he reached the enemy. He had completely turned his right flank, but it was too late in the day to accomplish anything.

7 P. M.—We commenced to barricade along our front.

7.30 P. M.—Received instructions to move upon the enemy's works to-morrow morning at daylight. At once directed division commanders to prepare for an assault at daylight, to get up plenty of ammunition, etc. We lost in killed and wounded about one hundred and fifteen to-day. Day clear and very hot. Thoroughly destroyed about five miles of the Macon railroad-track to-day. Took seventy enlisted men and five commissioned officers prisoners to-day.

A true copy:

D. S. STANLEY, *Colonel Twenty-second Infantry.*

Letter from Major-General Nathan Kimball.

SALT LAKE CITY, UTAH, *July* 3, 1875.

General D. S. STANLEY, *Fort Wayne, Michigan.*

DEAR GENERAL: Yours of June 14th ult. was duly received, but, being necessarily absent, I could not answer earlier. I note your reference to General Sherman's "Memoirs," which I have read, and regret that he has made such a great mistake.

Your recollection of the disposition of the enemy's force, and especially as to his position and strength at Jonesboro', to which you call my attention, is correct, as I remember it, and, though I have not my notes, journal, or any of my papers here to refresh my memory, I am certain that General Sherman is mistaken. My division, the First of the Fourth Corps, was deployed, my right resting on the railroad, and joined to Jeff. C. Davis's left. I found the enemy well posted on a ridge, or hill, being the bluff bank of a ravine, and in great force—whether Hardee's corps alone or more, I do not know. Their works or positions extended beyond my left, so that General Newton's division, which deployed and formed on my left, found them in his front, or at least in front of his right. Newton's left came round, when the enemy were yet resisting us, and captured their hospital just after dark. I know that my entire line was resisted by both infantry and artillery. You remember what difficulty I had in getting my battery in position under the fire from theirs. You were slightly wounded at that point just at dark. The line of works, barricade of logs and earth made and occupied by the enemy, continued from the railroad, at a point immediately opposite, to the line of works carried by Morgan's brigade of Jeff. C. Davis's command diagonally to the left along the ridge or bluff mentioned. The only way we could have passed around them by a flank movement would have been to march miles away to make the circuit, and left Jeff. C. Davis's left entirely exposed, and this would have enabled Hardee to turn Davis's flank and attack our line (Davis) in rear. After deploying we met a heavy skirmish-line, which retired to their main line, and fought us with as much determination as they ever did in any engagement. My own impression was, at the time, that the enemy was preparing to move around Davis's left, and believe that he would if we had not come up at the time we did. Their line of works encountered by us were freshly made, seemingly designed to retire to in case of failure to flank Davis, or on meeting a resisting column. Sherman is much mistaken in his ideas of that fight, so far as my division was concerned, and of your movement.

I am, as ever, truly your friend,

A true copy: NATHAN KIMBALL.

D. S. STANLEY, *Colonel Twenty-second Infantry.*

Extract from Letter of Brevet Major-General John Newton.

NEW YORK, *June* 22, 1875.

General D. S. STANLEY.

DEAR GENERAL: Yours of the 14th came to hand, and I have been trying to refresh my memory of the events spoken of.

Most of the details have escaped my mind. My impression is, that the order to you, having to come through several hands, was delayed in delivery. I remember this, because that, while the facts were fresh in my mind, I defended you against Sherman himself, who thought you were slow in coming up that day.

I remember the difficult ground through which my division forced its way, and how it was urged on both by you and myself, and that no time was lost, but we came in too late, i. e., at dark. I have only a slight remembrance about Kimball's action that day. For him to have advanced by a flank would have been absurd.

Yours truly,
JOHN NEWTON.

A true copy:
D. S. STANLEY, *Colonel Twenty-second Infantry.*

Extract from Letter of Brigadier-General WILLIAM GROSE.

NEWCASTLE, *July* 2, 1875.

General D. S. STANLEY.

MY DEAR GENERAL: Your kind note of 30th ult. came last evening. Truly glad and surprised to hear from you. It would do me so much good to see you and talk over old times.

General Sherman's "Memoirs" are creating quite a buzz. I inclose you an extract from my official report of the campaign covering the Jonesboro' day. I always thought the fault of that day's work lay in spending too much time in destroying railroads. From the time I had orders to leave the railroad and prolong line of First Brigade, it would have been impossible, even with a *slight circuit to the left,* to have gained Hardee's rear in daylight of that day by one unacquainted with the situation of the grounds.

Believe me, your humble friend and obedient servant,
WILLIAM GROSE.

A true copy:
D. S. Stanley, *Colonel Twenty-second Infantry.*

Extract from Report of General William Grose, commanding Third Brigade, First Division, Fourth Army Corps.

Atlanta, Georgia, *September* 5, 1864.

. . . .

September 1st.—Our division marched at 6 A. M., First Brigade in advance, moving on the railroad toward Jonesboro', and under orders spent most of the day in destruction of railroad as we advanced. At about four o'clock, P. M., the advance brigade of our division made junction with the left of the Fourteenth Corps on the railroad at a point about two miles north of Jonesboro', the First Brigade forward in line, its right near or upon the railroad. I was ordered by General Kimball to prolong the left of the First Brigade, which I did without halting until my advance was checked by getting into a thick bramble of underbrush and a swamp in a dense woodland, through which it was impossible to ride, and the enemy, with a heavy skirmish-line in our front, and his artillery in reach playing upon us, contributed to impede our progress. The course or direction when I entered the woods seemed to be about south, and upon emerging from it, at a distance from one-half to three-fourths of a mile, the brigade to my right had shifted to the right such an extent that I had to move right oblique to fill the space, and my left swinging around, so that when my lines came upon the lines of the enemy behind barricades, my front was about southwest, and by the time we got the lines straightened up, and the enemy's driven back, and the position of the enemy discovered, night came on. Yet my lines, Seventy-seventh Pennsylvania, Eighty-fourth and Eightieth Illinois, and Ninth Indiana in front line, pressed forward under a heavy canister-fire from the enemy's guns to within three hundred yards of their barricaded lines, when the fighting ceased at dark. One of General Newton's brigades had moved up toward my left, and his skirmish-line connected with the left of my front battle-line. The barricade of the enemy ceased opposite the left of my lines. During the night the enemy withdrew.

. . . .

A true copy:
D. S. Stanley, *Colonel Twenty-second Infantry.*

TOLEDO, *October* 19, 1875.

MY DEAR GENERAL: I have seen it stated in the newspapers that you are preparing a second edition of your "Memoirs," and that you have intimated you would add, as an appendix, the letters of any officers explaining acts or events in which they deemed you had not done them justice. I hope I am not too late to be heard when I advise you to do no such thing. There can be no good reason for making your book the vehicle of unlimited controversy. You are under no obligations to square your account of affairs by other men's memory, or to gauge your judgment of their conduct by their own estimate of it. Your book is your testimony, based on your memory, aided by orders and other memoranda, of what occurred under your own eye and command. As such it has very great historical value, though you would yourself be probably the last man to claim that it is infallible, or that other witnesses will not be examined by future historians. The time will come when not only public documents will be minutely scrutinized, but even for centuries new evidence will be discovered in private diaries, soldiers' correspondence, both Union and Confederate, and in the thousand-and-one unsuspected and unthought-of sources of circumstantial evidence, which will throw strong direct or side lights upon the events of the war. You cannot, if you would, embody all these in your book, and the controversy, if opened in the form hinted at in the beginning of this letter, would weigh your book down with bulky matter, which should be published, if at all, in some other form.

It is to be hoped that every officer who would be likely to contribute to the "Appendix" will give his own narrative of events in which he took part. He need not write a history. A pamphlet in the form of a *"mémoire pour servir"* would find a welcome place on the shelves of every public library, where it will be safe against the day when the case will be authoritatively and judicially made up by an historian worthy of the theme. Meanwhile, however, your book is your contribution to this material, and, in my opinion, it ought to be kept in its integrity as such.

I assume that in the cases in which you have expressed opinions of men's capacity, character, or efficiency, you would not be likely to change your mind by anything they could write. In nearly every instance in which your book expresses your judgment of men, I know from my personal intercourse with you that you held the same opinion in 1864–'65, and at all times since. Such rooted opinions must therefore be accepted as a fixed judgment from which the appeal should be taken, if any one feels wronged, by means of separate publications, and not through an appendix to your book. While on this subject permit me to say further that in my opinion it is too late to consider the question whether on the whole you would prefer not to have anything to say which could wound personal pride or feeling. If you were convinced that you had erred, I am confident you would take pleasure in admitting it frankly; but, if you are not, you owe it to yourself, in all good temper, to stand firmly by what you have said. No omissions from a new edition could take the facts away from the possession of the public. You used your best judgment in giving what you thought it would be useful and interesting to the world to know. We, who know you intimately, know that you have done it without rancor or desire to harm any one, and that you felt that the lesson of the war would not be properly taught if you did not have the courage of your opinions enough to say when a subordinate failed as well as when he succeeded. Instead of omitting anything which you still believe to be true, you should rather, as it seems to me, support your former statement by such circumstantial matters as will more perfectly put others in a position to understand the grounds of your conclusions. There are several instances in the book in which, judging from the impression left on my own mind, I think this should be done.

I have read the book with some care, and I can honestly say I have noticed but a single and that an unimportant instance, in which my memory of your opinion at the time differs from that you now express, and only one in which you seem to have made a slight mistake as to a fact within my personal knowledge. The latter I will mention, as it involves the credit due to another person. On page 154 of the second volume you speak of the reconnaissance made from Rome in October, 1864, to determine the course taken by Hood's army, and say that it was made by General Corse, and resulted in the capture of two guns and some prisoners, besides obtaining the information desired. The guns and prisoners were in fact taken by Kenner Garrard's cavalry, acting under my command, on the northwest side of the Coosa, Corse being on the southeast side. On first reading the passage, I thought it was a mere typographical error; but, on looking back at your special field order No. 90, I find (what I had forgotten) that Corse was ordered to make the reconnaissance on the southeast side of the river, and *Elliot* (paragraph II) to send cavalry on the other side, which he did by detaching Garrard's division. But from news you had you changed the order after it was written, and directed me orally and in person to follow Garrard out with the Twenty-third Corps, and take command of the whole reconnaissance on that side. We found the enemy's cavalry in position behind a fence-barricade, and at Garrard's request I let his dismounted cavalry charge them, simply keeping my own infantry in supporting distance. Garrard's work was very handsomely done, and I think you will recollect on reflection how pleased Elliot was when I reported the gallantry of the cavalry and their capture of the guns, for you were at the time feeling a little dissatisfied with what the mounted troops had accomplished for a little while before that. We brought you the definite news that Hood was on our side of the Coosa, making toward Resaca. It would be a miracle if in some small matters of this kind there should be absolutely no error of remembrance, especially as the written order seemed to accord best with the statement you have given. It is one of the exceptions which prove the rule.

I need not say what by this time so many have told you, that the country is your debtor for the writing of the book, and that, despite some irritations and heart-burnings, you will in the end find abundant reason to be glad of having written it.

Sincerely yours,

J. D. Cox.

General W. T. Sherman.

314 East 120th Street,
New York City, *October* 30, 1876.

General W. T. Sherman, *Washington, D. C.*

General: Having read your "Memoirs," I confess to being disappointed at the entire absence of any notice of the operations of my command (Second Division, Sixteenth Army Corps, Army of the Tennessee) during the Atlanta campaign of 1864. Knowing your high sense of justice, and that it is your intention to correct any mistakes or errors you may have unintentionally made in your first edition, I have the honor to inclose herewith extracts from my military history submitted to the Retiring Board, by which I was retired in May, 1870.

Hoping you will give this matter a favorable consideration, I have the honor to subscribe myself, general,

Your most obedient servant,

T. W. Sweeny, *Brigadier-General, U. S. Army.*

Note.—The "Atlanta army" consisted of three separate armies, embracing six corps, made up of nineteen divisions of infantry and four of cavalry. To have embraced these latter in the "Memoirs" would have swelled them to an unwieldy size, and I aimed to limit my narrative to the main armies, with occasional reference to the corps and detachments, leaving to history to collect the details. W. T. S.
St. Louis, 1885.

Extracts of my Military Record, submitted to the Retiring Board, by which I was retired in May, 1870.

Left Pulaski, Tennessee, with my division (Second Division, Sixteenth Army Corps) April 29, 1864; passed through Huntsville, Alabama, on the 2d of May, and encamped on Chickamauga Creek on the 7th; took possession of Snake-Creek Gap on the afternoon of the 8th, skirmishing heavily with the enemy. At daylight on the morning of the 9th the rebels attacked me with vigor and drove back my advance guard some distance, wounding the commanding officer, Lieutenant-Colonel Phillips, Ninth Illinois Mounted Infantry; but I finally succeeded in clearing the "Gap" and driving them before me into the works of Resaca. I held the heights commanding them the greater part of the day, and was prevented from making an assault by the orders of General G. M. Dodge. Prisoners captured that morning informed me that Resaca was garrisoned by one brigade of infantry and ten guns. Soon after my arrival, however, column after column of rebels came down on the run, and late in the afternoon we received orders to fall back to the mouth of the "Gap" and fortify. My division were the first troops of our army that entered the "Gap."

. . . .

On the 14th of May my division was detached and ordered to force a passage across the Oostenaula River at "Lay's Ferry." I made feints at two points, one above and the other below the real point of attack, and, while the enemy's attention was distracted, succeeded in throwing a few companies across in pontoon-boats. At this stage of affairs I received information from our cavalry that the enemy were laying a pontoon-bridge at Calhoun Ferry, about three miles above, evidently with the intention of crossing a large force to attack me. At the same time I received a message from our signal corps that heavy columns of the enemy's infantry were moving down on the opposite side of the river in the direction of Lay's Ferry, and cautioned me to be on my guard. I hastily recalled the companies I had thrown across the river, and sent a brigade to watch the enemy at Calhoun Ferry and report positively whether they intended to cross there or not. After a careful reconnaissance I discovered that the enemy were fortifying the other side, but showing no disposition to cross. I saw at once they concluded that that was the real point of attack, and I made my preparations accordingly. The withdrawal of the troops I had thrown across the river helped to strengthen this idea in their minds. At daylight on the morning of the 15th I commenced crossing in a flat-boat I had brought from the other side the evening before, and, when I had two regiments over, commenced laying my pontoon-bridges and fortifying on both sides. The bridges were soon laid, and two brigades crossed, when my artillery was put in position on the north bank so as to sweep the ground in front of the troops on the opposite side, the trees that obstructed the river having been cut down for the purpose. The enemy did not allow me to carry out my plans, however, unmolested. General Walker's division of Hardee's corps made a fierce charge just as I had got my two brigades across, with the intention of driving me into the river, but was handsomely repulsed, not without considerable loss to us, however. I then crossed the Third Brigade of my division, strengthened my position, my artillery remaining on the right bank of the river, and received orders from General Sherman through General Corse, who was with me, to hold the position at all hazards. I knew General Johnson had to do one of two things, as my position threatened his main line of retreat—either to mass heavily in my front during the night and drive me across the river, or abandon his position at Resaca. I therefore threw out a thin line of skirmishers selected for the purpose, with instructions to advance cautiously and feel the enemy and find out what he was doing. The movement commenced about midnight, and at two o'clock on the morning of the 16th I received the report that General Johnson's army was in full retreat south. When General Sherman heard it, he sent me orders to move out at daylight as far as the Rome and Calhoun cross-roads (about two and a half miles) and strike the enemy's flank. I did, and had Hardee's corps hurled at me in order to protect the railroad by which they were retreating. A sharp fight took place here, in which I lost several valuable officers, among them General Burke (Sixty-sixth Illinois and captain in the Fourteenth Regulars) and one of my brigade commanders. I held my position, however, until the rest of the Army of the Tennessee came to my assistance.

. . . .

Engaged in the battle of the 22d of July, 1864, in front of Atlanta, when General McPherson was killed. On the 21st Garrard's cavalry was sent about forty miles south to destroy part of the Augusta Railroad, leaving our left flank entirely exposed. The enemy was not slow in taking advantage of it. Blair's and Logan's corps were intrenched, and my division was moving from the right of the Fifteenth to the left of the Seventeenth Corps, when I learned from a scout of General Thomas that the enemy's columns were then forming in the woods with the intention of making a flank attack on the Army of the Tennessee while they attacked in front at the same time. I immediately moved forward, threw my division into position so as to receive the attack, and, after a severe fight which lasted between five and six hours, repulsed the enemy at every point, capturing nine hundred prisoners, four battle-flags, and killed the rebel General Walker. After the repulse, the Second Brigade of my division, Colonel Mersey, Ninth Illinois, commanding, was ordered by General Logan to recapture the works lost by the Second Division, Fifteenth Army Corps, and still held by the rebels, which they did in a very handsome manner, and recovered Captain De Gress's battery of twenty-pound Parrott guns.

T. W. Sweeny, *Brigadier-General, U. S. Army.*

BURNING OF COLUMBIA.

BEFORE THE MIXED COMMISSION ON AMERICAN AND BRITISH CLAIMS.

(Composed of Count Corti, of Italy; Hon. Russell Gurney, M. P., of London; and Hon. James S. Fraser, of Indiana.)

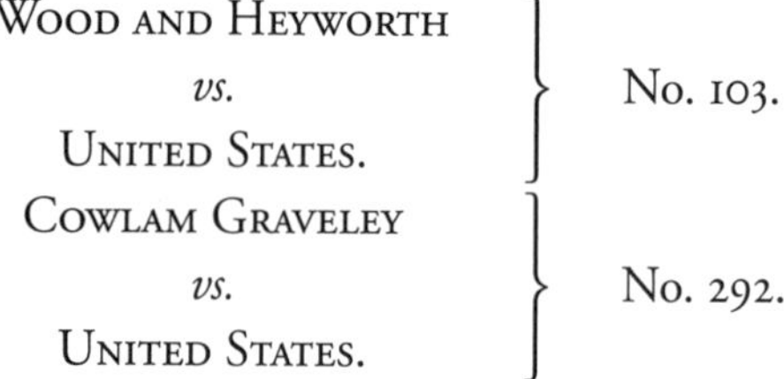

Wood and Heyworth
vs.
United States. } No. 103.

Cowlam Graveley
vs.
United States. } No. 292.

Depositions for Defence.

WASHINGTON, *December* 10, 1872.

Commission met pursuant to notice.

. . . .

Deposition of O. O. Howard.

The deposition of O. O. Howard, a witness produced, sworn, and examined on the part and behalf of the United States in the cause above entitled, now depending before the above-named Commission, taken before me, a United States Commissioner, in and for the District of Columbia, at Washington, in said District, on the 10th day of December, 1872, pursuant to a notice to that effect duly given by the agent and counsel for the United States.

Mr. A. S. Worthington appeared on behalf of the United States; Messrs. George R. Walker, Bartley, Denver, Mackay, and Wells, on behalf of claimants.

The said O. O. Howard, having been first by me duly sworn to tell the truth, the whole truth, and nothing but the truth, deposes and says:

My name is O. O. Howard; my age is forty-two years; my residence is District of Columbia; I am a native of Maine; my position is that of a brigadier-general in the United States Army.

Preliminary questions propounded by the officer taking this deposition:

Have you any interest, direct or indirect, in the claim which is the subject-matter of the above-entitled cause, or of this examination? If so, state the nature and extent of such interest.

Answer. I have no interest.

Being examined by Mr. Worthington, of counsel for the United States, the witness further deposes and says:

Question. State what your rank in the United States Army was in February, 1865.

A. I was major-general of volunteers at that time; I think I was not a brigadier-general in the regular army until March following.

Q. What was your command in February, 1865?

A. I commanded the Army of the Tennessee, constituting the right wing of General Sherman's army.

Q. Operating in the State of South Carolina?

A. Yes, sir.

Q. Please state the principal points through which your command passed in the march from Savannah to Goldsboro.

A. The principal portion of my command was transported to Beaufort, South Carolina; thence (marched) northward through Pocotaligo, Orangeburg, Columbia, Cheraw, Fayetteville; subordinate columns swept into different towns; General Slocum had the left wing; he was at the north of me; mine was the right line of march.

Q. During that march, under what orders from General Sherman were you acting in respect to private property?

A. They were to take such provisions as were necessary for the subsistence of the army, but generally to spare private property, with some few exceptions; cotton was excepted; I was directly instructed again and again to destroy the cotton. (Objected to by Mr. Walker, as the orders will show for themselves, they being the best testimony.)

A. (Continued.) I will put in evidence the orders I received from General Sherman, and the orders I issued on the subject, if it be desired.

Q. On what day did you enter the town of Columbia yourself?

A. The 17th of February, 1865.

Q. Please state, in your own way, your recollection of the circumstances attending the occupation of that city, and the destruction of a portion of it.

A. On the 15th of February, in the vicinity of Columbia, opposite thereto, across the Congaree, we met with much resistance at Little Congaree Creek, and had to push our way very slowly, the enemy retiring before us; when we arrived opposite Columbia, we found the bridge across the Congaree destroyed by fire; we moved up to where the two rivers, the Saluda and the Broad, conjoined to form the Congaree; the bridge across the Saluda was destroyed by fire by the enemy; we bridged that and crossed our troops; the other bridge, when we reached the land intervening between the two rivers, was still standing, but as we attempted to cross it, it was set on fire by the enemy, and having been covered with rosin, was in flames in a moment, so that even the Confederate cavalry rushed northward to save themselves, some of them without crossing; our troops spent the whole night getting across the Broad, which was a very difficult river; we ferried over a brigade at the beginning by means of ropes and boats; that brigade was the brigade of Colonel Stone, and pushed its way up the hill slowly against the enemy, retiring; the enemy passed through Columbia, and the mayor came to the outside of the city and surrendered the city, I think between ten and eleven o'clock, say ten o'clock; in the mean time a regular bridge was laid across the Broad River, and General Sherman and myself crossed over, riding side by side, before any other troops than this leading brigade had passed; it was about half-past ten that General Sherman and I rode over ahead of all the remaining portion of the troops that had not been ferried over, and rode directly on to the city, a distance of about three miles, entering it in what we called the main street; I believe the name, as it appears on the map, is Richardson Street; it was the one that leads directly to the Capitol; at every corner of the street we met crowds of people, principally negroes; not very far from the market-house we met the mayor of the city, who had a short conversation with General Sherman; as my troops alone were to have charge of the city, I observed very carefully the disposition of the guards of the leading brigade, Colonel Stone's; sentinels were located in front of buildings of any considerable importance, and on the main street the principal portion of the brigade was in rest, waiting for orders; there was only that one brigade; we were ahead of all the rest; near the brigade was an immense pile of cotton; bales were broken open in the middle of the streets, and were on fire; an engine was playing upon the fire, and soldiers and citizens were engaged apparently in extinguishing it; General Sherman was met with much enthusiasm by a company of soldiers; observing them closely, I saw that some of them were under the influence of drink.

Mr. Walker:

Q. How do you know that?

A. Only from the testimony of a great many who saw it. [The statement of the witness as to the rebel soldiers having set the depot on fire, was objected to by Mr. Walker, on the ground that the witness does not know it of his own personal knowledge.]

A. (Continued.) We rode to a foundry where guns had been cast, and observed that, and went afterward through several streets together, when I separated from General Sherman, selected my headquarters, and gave the necessary orders for the thorough care of the troops and of the city for the night. General Sherman took his headquarters at the house of Blanton Duncan, and I mine at a house near the university, belonging to one of the professors; after this disposition I lay down to take a little rest, and was awaked first about dark by one of my aides, who said the city was on fire. I sent the aide, Captain Gilbreth, immediately to ascertain where the fire was, and to call upon General Charles R. Wood, the division commander, who had the immediate command of the city, to prevent the extension of the fire; I then at once dressed myself and went to the scene; there I met General John A. Logan, who was my next in rank, and who commanded the corps; we consulted together, and took every precautionary measure we could think of to prevent the extension of the flames, sometimes ordering the tearing down of sheds and small buildings, protecting citizens, assisting them in the care of their property, and guarding it; much of the property was thrown into the streets; personally I set a great many soldiers during the night to extinguish the flames from the houses, and they went to the tops of the houses where water was passed up to them; nearly everything in my immediate vicinity was saved; a perfect gale from the northwest had commenced about the time we crossed the bridge, or before that, and continued all night or until, I should say, between two and three o'clock in the morning; it seemed at first utterly useless to attempt to stop the flames; they were so hot that many of our own soldiers were burnt up that night; when the wind changed, however, it was easy to prevent any further extension of the fire; it was done; some of our men behaved badly on account of being under the influence of drink, but they were replaced by fresh men as soon as their conduct came to the knowledge of the officer in charge; the first brigade—Stone's—was relieved by another brigade of General Wood's division, and finally the entire division of General Hazen was brought into the city to assist; all the men who misbehaved that we could seize upon were kept under guard until the next day and punished; there were quite a number of our men who had been taken prisoners and were held by the Confederates; they appeared in the streets of Columbia soon after our arrival; I do not know myself where they were confined; the penitentiary was also opened, and all its prisoners loosed; I found, during the night, a reckless mob very often, sometimes insulting ladies, and sometimes rushing into houses and pillaging; I did not see anybody setting fires; General Sherman himself staid up with us for the most of the night; General Logan and General Wood were on the ground all the time until the fire abated, and I believe did everything they could to prevent it. General Sherman's order to me to destroy certain classes of property is a part of our record, and I remember the tenor of it.

[Objected to, on the ground that the record testimony should be produced.]

A. (Continued.) I would like to make it a part of my testimony.

Mr. Worthington:

Q. State your recollection of it, General Howard.

A. It was that certain buildings of a certain nature should be destroyed, such as arsenals, armories, powder-mills, depots; but that private property and asylums so called should be protected. I saw that the wind was so high that it would be impossible to destroy that class of buildings by fire on the evening of the 17th of February, and therefore refrained at that time from putting the order into practical execution; on the 18th and 19th those buildings of that class that were left from the flames were destroyed. I have in my report an accurate list of them; the flames of this burning of the night of the 17th had destroyed a part of these other buildings included in the order. We destroyed also the railroad-track. Though the order was to destroy cotton in South Carolina, yet no cotton remained that I know of after this fire to be destroyed; none was destroyed, according to my recollection.

Q. State what actual hostilities occurred near Columbia immediately before its occupation, if any.

A. We had very heavy resistance on the other side in the vicinity of Congaree Creek, and all the way along; we had also very heavy resistance in crossing the Broad—the last river—the enemy's troops being posted in a very covered position; we hardly could reach them; they annoyed our troops and killed many; then we had our sleeping—camp shelled during the preceding night—the night of the 15th, if I remember correctly—from the Columbia side, from a battery in the vicinity of Columbia; it excited the hostile feeling of the officers and soldiers very much indeed; they thought it was contrary to the rules of war. After we crossed the river there was scarcely any resistance; I think there was none in the immediate vicinity of Columbia after the mayor met us.

Q. Do you know where those drunken soldiers obtained their liquor?

A. I know they obtained it in Columbia.

Mr. Walker: I would like the witness to state how he knew this; whether it is hearsay, or what.

The witness. It was not hearsay; I know the troops obtained it in Columbia; I know they had not any until they went into the city; I have testimony—for I investigated very thoroughly—that citizens carried pails of whiskey along the ranks, and that the men of the leading brigade of Colonel Stone drank with dippers out of pails.

Mr. Worthington:

Q. You have said that you made every disposition for the security of the private property immediately after your entry into the city. I wish you would state more particularly what measures you took for the security of private property.

A. The orders were general as to the manner of locating a brigade or division in a city, and this brigade or division conformed to the general order; I saw them, by my own observation, taking up a central place for the main portion of the brigade, and distributing different detachments to different parts of the city; locating sentinels very much as policemen are located in a city for its care: then I gave verbal instructions to General Charles R. Wood, General Logan not happening to be near me; they should have been given to General Logan, but I gave them directly to General Wood, and he, doubtless, reported my orders to General Logan; he, at any rate, obeyed the order. Seeing some of these men in the First Brigade under the influence of drink, my first order to him was to send in another brigade that had not had any drink, which he did; my next order went through General Logan, to send a division into the city, which was General Hazen's division; General Logan himself took the immediate disposition of those two divisions; they were under his command and formed a part of it; he had four divisions, and these were two of them; the sentinels I tested myself as to the orders that had been given them, and those in front of houses told me that they had orders to watch against all fires, or against any pillaging parties, and to see that no wrong should be done to private property where they were located; one or two executed the orders so thoroughly that after fire had caught roofs they hindered people from going in, but those sentinels were at once replaced, as it was the effect of the whiskey which did that; I took pains myself, as did my staff, to go about and to see as far as possible that everything was done rightly as ordered, for it was a fearful condition of things with such a fire, and with so many women and children in the city.

I would further say, to show our disposition toward the inhabitants, that, though we were in war, we left five hundred cattle for the people who had been burned out, and who were without food, and also provisions, and had them carted to the State-House, and we also assisted the mayor in a method by which he could get provisions from those outside the city.

Q. Were any applications made to you by the citizens before or during the war for guards to protect their property?

A. Constantly.

Q. What was your reply to them?

A. I always sent them; where we had not soldiers immediately at hand, my aides themselves went; Lieutenant McQueen, one of my staff-officers, stood sentinel the whole night, and protected the property of the Rev. A. T. Porter, of the Episcopal Church, and received his gratitude for it.

Q. Do I understand you to say that no cotton was burned in Columbia by your order?

A. None whatever.

Q. If the fire had not occurred, what would you have done with the cotton in Columbia?

Mr. Walker: I object to all answers to that question, and to all testimony elicited by it.

A. I had no specific orders to burn the cotton in Columbia, and I should not have burned it without consulting with the general-in-chief; if he had ordered it to be burned, I should have burned it; and if he had ordered it to be spared, I should have spared it.

By Mr. Worthington:

Q. Do you know anything about some rockets having been sent up in the vicinity of the State-House on the night of the 17th of February?

A. I do.

Q. State what you know about that.

A. The rockets were sent up by the signal corps; the left wing was quite a distance from us. General Blair's corps was located outside of the city, and one-half of General Logan's, and it was customary for the signal officers attached to each division or corps to communicate with their neighbors as to where they were, or to give any events of the day; they did it in the daytime by flags, and at night by rockets, and this was done at night; the signals meant nothing else, that I know of.

Q. Do you know of any understanding before the occupation of Columbia, or after it was occupied, that it was to be destroyed?

A. On the part of whom?

Q. On the part of anybody?

A. By the officers there was a distinct understanding that it should not be destroyed, and those were the orders; that is, the private property, asylums, etc.; on the part of the men I don't know anything about it; I have no knowledge whatever; they always had to obey orders.

. . . .

I, James O. Clephane, United States Commissioner for the District of Columbia, do hereby certify that, at the request of counsel for the United States, I caused the above-mentioned O. O. Howard, deponent in the foregoing deposition, to come before me at the time and place in the caption mentioned; that said deponent was by me sworn to tell the truth, the whole truth, and nothing but the truth; that said deposition was reduced to writing by me, and was carefully read to or by deponent before being signed by him, and deponent then and there, in my presence, subscribed the same; and I further certify that I have no interest, direct or indirect, in the claim to which the above deposition relates, and am not the agent or attorney of any person having any interest therein.

Witness my hand, at the city of Washington, D. C., this 10th day of December, 1872. JAMES O. CLEPHANE.

. . . .

NOTE.—Judgment in these cases was for the United States. W. T. S.

ALBANY, NEW YORK, *May* 15, 1876.

MY DEAR GENERAL: If you revise your "Memoirs," and wish to strengthen your position regarding the burning of Columbia, you are welcome to my testimony, etc. I was a prisoner of war at Columbia, and escaped at the time, and in the same manner and with Adjutant Byers, author of "The March to the Sea." From time of escape till the occupation, I was concealed in a barn on the outskirts of Columbia, and was an eye-witness to the going out of town of Hampton's troops, and their firing the depot, or surrounding warehouses, previous to departure. I was in the streets of the city before your coming in personally, and saw the cotton burning then. I am, general, very truly yours,

IRA B. SAMPSON,

Formerly Captain Company G, Second Massachusetts Artillery, at time of capture, March, 1864, Chief of Artillery sub-district of the Albemarle, North Carolina, under General H. W. Wessels.

To General W. T. SHERMAN, *St. Louis.*

POMEROY, OHIO, *August* 31, 1875.

General W. T. SHERMAN, *General of the Army.*

GENERAL: In your "Memoirs," giving the grand movements of the war, it is, of course, not to be expected that you could take time to verify all small details. And yet most of the officers as well as men were engaged only in details. It is a matter of little moment to history whether the commander is called Smith or Brown; but to the commander the difference is, whether he really was present in the war or not.

I confess when I first read your book I was vexed, because it looked as if you intentionally blotted me out of the war; not by mere omission to mention, for that might easily happen, but by describing some things I did, and giving credit for them to others.

I certainly was present in your command. From Acworth to the 21st July my brigade was the very whip-lash of the army: it always constituted the very extreme of one of the flanks, sometimes the right, sometimes the left. Though I then commanded only a brigade, General McPherson used to send orders directing me by name to command little expeditions. I had only four staff-officers besides a quartermaster. Yet, from Kenesaw to Pocotaligo, three of my staff were killed outright; one was mortally wounded; one was taken prisoner; and two were sent to hospital, broken down with exhaustion. I was myself wounded on the 22d July; at the time it was supposed to be a mortal wound. The Seventeenth Corps forced a crossing at Orangeburg; you say it was done by the divisions of Mower and Giles Smith. My division is not named or in any way referred to.

On the 10th February, the Seventeenth Corps lay in camp on the south fork of the Edisto, below Binnaker's Bridge. In the afternoon my division was moved across the river, and two miles beyond. At seven o'clock A. M. next day, I set out under orders to push to the crossing of the north fork at Orangeburg, and save the bridge, but not attempt to cross. I moved so rapidly that General Howard coming up found a gap of four miles between the rear of my train and the head of the next following division. On reaching the swamp bordering the river, I detached the Twentieth Ohio, which double-quicked over the causeway, charging and driving the hostile cavalry so that they could not pause to injure the causeway or the bridges over the small streams of the Edisto. Near the main stream the road bends, and a battery on the farther side of the river commanded the bridge and the road to the bend. I drew the men off the road at this point, and posted the Twentieth Ohio in the water under the trees that skirted the main stream, so as to cover the bridge with their rifles. Four of the enemy, dead, were picked up, and seven unhurt were captured in the swamp. I sent a party under Colonel Wiles, of the Second Brigade, up-stream, and a party from the First Brigade (Colonel Fairchild) down-stream, to find a place for crossing. Colonel Wiles found a place where, by clambering over fallen trees, men could scramble over singly. The other party found a place little more than a mile below the bridge, which, on their report, I went to examine, and found solid ground on our side extended to the river, while the farther side was a stretch of swamp. After supper I reported to General Blair. You and General Howard were both present. The instant I finished my verbal report to General Blair, you said to him: "Yes, the lower place is the place to cross; make your movement there—your feint at the bridge, your diversion above." My division was withdrawn from the bridge in the night, relieved by Giles Smith; and a road constructed for the pontoon train to the proposed crossing. In the morning I marched to the crossing-place. The pontoon-bridge was laid; I crossed over; General Mower's division was brought down to be in readiness in case of need, but did not cross. Emerging from the swamp on the farther side, I formed the division in lines in a long, open field, which extended all the way to the town. The enemy's battery was meanwhile playing across the river, over the bridge on to Giles Smith. I sent the Second Brigade, by a by-road across the woods, to the railroad below the town, and marched with the other brigade on to the enemy's battery at the bridge-head. It then turned its fire on to me, and withdrew as I approached. My skirmishers, dashing on through the town, fired on the train that left with the last of the enemy's infantry. I took possession of the town, and detailed the Twelfth Wisconsin, Colonel Proudfit, as provost guard. When my skirmish-line was passing through the town, and the first brigade was ascending the slope between the bridge and the town, an officer and three men from Giles Smith's division scrambled over the scantling of the bridge (for the enemy in the night had succeeded in burning some of the planking of the bridge without injuring the timbers) and joined me at the edge of the town. The bridge was repaired, and Giles Smith and Mower, later in the afternoon, marched their divisions over it.

General Mower stood ready to support me, just as, on the night of the 9th, I stood ready to support him at Binnaker's Bridge, but my division alone made the crossing at Orangeburg; and, moreover, I there saved the bridge, the only instance in your campaign where a contested bridge was saved and used by the army in crossing. I happened to be in advance the day we reached Orangeburg, and so made the crossing there; just as Mower and Giles Smith made the crossing of the rivers when they happened to be in advance.

You say that General Blair, while lying at Pocotaligo, kept General Mower busy making demonstrations upon the river to amuse and deceive the enemy. The fact is, one day General Mower took his division out to make a demonstration, but the country was so overflowed by water that he could not approach the river. Another day I made a demonstration on the high ground near the railroad-bridge. On the 30th January, the day we moved, I was sent to the river to make another. Next day, the Army of the Tennessee lying in camp, I was sent back to where the enemy had a work on the farther side of the river and silenced its fire. The work was reënforced, and kept up such a racket with artillery, that General Howard sent a staff-officer to inquire if there was a gunboat in the river. This was the only one of the four "demonstrations" that amounted to anything. Of the four, I made three, General Mower one, and you name General Mower as the only officer employed.

You give quite a detailed account of the battle of Atlanta of the 22d of July and the preliminary movements. On the 20th the Seventeenth Corps moved out from Decatur, General Gresham in front, my brigade (of General Leggett's division) supporting *en échelon* on his left; the rest of General Leggett's division in reserve. In the skirmishing during this advance General Gresham was wounded in the ankle and sent to the rear. At sunset his division halted at the base of a ridge, and I went into line and bivouacked on its left. The enemy, slightly intrenched on the summit of the hill, kept up a dropping fire through the night, so that I had to change my sleeping-place on the ground, my blankets being cut by their balls. Early next morning, the 21st, General Leggett came to the front and said to me, "I think I shall have to ask you to carry this hill." I made my own dispositions, formed the brigade into two lines with fixed bayonets, sent a skirmish-line dashing up the smooth surface of the hill to distract the fire of General Cleburne's men, who held it. I went up myself with the first line; Captain Walker, my adjutant, with the second. The men fell in groups under the fire, but closed continually on their colors, and swept over the works with a line as precise as on parade. The Twelfth and Sixteenth Wisconsin formed the first; Twentieth, Thirtieth, and Thirty-first Illinois the second line. The enemy fell back along the line some distance, but, as my brigade had no support, and I occupied only the extreme right of their line, they soon returned to the rest of their line, and I was subjected to a severe enfilading fire. I asked General Leggett to send up some twenty-four-pound howitzers attached to the division, and with them cleared out the woods until my men could throw up a line of work facing Atlanta, with a refused line from my right running down-hill toward my rear, so as to protect my right flank. General Leggett then brought up the rest of his division on to my left, extending the line that way, as it was threatened by bodies of troops in front. The night of the 21st I threw up heavy traverses, five to each regiment, and strengthened the works. In the night the enemy abandoned their line; and next morning, the 22d, the Fifteenth Corps moved up to my right, and Giles Smith, having succeeded General Gresham, moved out to General Leggett's left. In the battle of the 22d the enemy rolled up our line till they came to my brigade, intrenched in the traverses, and advanced no farther. In the two days forty per cent. of my brigade was lost. The Twentieth Illinois marched up the hill on the 21st over one hundred and fifty strong. At sunset of the 22d it numbered one officer and seventeen men, but held its place. Captain Walker, my assistant adjutant-general, was wounded. After ten years of suffering, he died of his wounds last winter. While making a tourniquet for him on the field, I was shot through the face. I was brevetted major-general "for especial gallantry before Atlanta on the 22d July"—the only brevet entitled "for especial gallantry" in that campaign. You mention General Gresham as the general officer who was wounded; and go so far into detail as to mention that Colonel Reynolds (lieutenant-colonel of one of my regiments) was wounded, yet my name is nowhere referred to in any way.

I might mention other similar instances. Taken together they all have an air of an intentional exclusion of my name as a participant in the war. Of course, there is nothing of the sort. You simply have not bothered yourself with details. But, if another edition of your book should be published, I hope this memorandum may secure a revision of these matters, of little moment to the world, or, indeed, to history, but of some moment to

Very respectfully and truly yours,

M. F. FORCE.

NOTE.—This may be another instance in which, by attempting to avoid details, which would swell the bulk of my intended volume into too large proportions, I may seem to have done individual injustice. There was not in the whole army a more intelligent, conscientious, zealous, or brave officer than General Force, for whom I always entertained the most profound respect and personal affection. I indorse all he says, have made the corrections, and publish his letter entire in this the final edition of my "Memoirs."

ST. LOUIS, 1885. W. T. S.

General G. M. Dodge's account of the part taken by the Sixteenth Army Corps in the movement on Resaca. Attack of the 4th of July, and battle of Atlanta, July 22, 1864.

General W. T. SHERMAN, *St. Louis, Missouri.*

DEAR GENERAL: Your suggestion to send you a brief *résumé* of the part taken by my corps (the Sixteenth) of the Army of the Tennessee, in the Atlanta campaign, was received some time ago. I reply as early as possible, in view of absence and other engagements.

I wish to refer to only such parts of the Atlanta campaign as have been to some extent the subject of public comment, through your "Memoirs," and to which my personal testimony may contribute light.

I shall therefore confine myself to the attempted surprise of Resaca, May 9, 1864, and some following events, and to the repulse of General Hood's rear movement at Atlanta, July 22d.

The Sixteenth Corps, as the vanguard of General McPherson's army, penetrated, first, through the Chattanooga Mountains, and made the attack of Resaca. The same corps, while moving to a new position around Atlanta, fell across the way of Hood's army, and met him on such opportunely good ground that the battle was accepted on the spot. I have never published my official report of the operations of the corps. I state these general facts to save you the trouble of explaining them again if you should ever make use of this letter. Your rapid and general summary of a maze of events, in which the part of a corps is more or less lost in the movement of several armies, has attracted my admiration for its clearness, and I can well see how the limitations of your book have compelled a severe distribution of prominence to the many detachments.

The left wing of the Sixteenth Corps (Dodge's), the other wing not being in this campaign, arrived at Chattanooga May 5th, in the evening, in the cars, the batteries and transportation following by road from Pulaski, Tennessee, and Athens, Alabama.

The same evening General McPherson's orders arrived to take the initiative for his army, and to move to Gordon's Mills. While marching there the next day, verbal orders came to push a portion of my command forward toward Villanow, and seize Ship's Gap. Sprague's brigade, of the Fourth Division, did this at midnight of the same day, and the next day we had passed through and occupied Villanow.

The third day (May 8th) my command, with the Second Division in advance, moved rapidly to Snake-Creek Gap, one day before my orders had contemplated, they advising me to march when the Fifteenth Army Corps had closed upon me. I had heard from General McPherson personally, however, that the object was to threaten Johnston's flank and communications, and the Ninth Illinois Mounted Infantry, supported by the Thirty-ninth Iowa Infantry, went forward through the gap to Sugar-Creek Valley, a portion of the corps without transportation following, and intrenching that night, thus holding its eastern outlet. On the evening of May 8th, instead of May 9th, I was astonished to find this strong position, the side-gate to Johnston's rear, not only undefended but unoccupied, though a few men might have held it long. Having reported the fact to General McPherson, and also that Colonel Phillips reported Resaca occupied by a brigade of the enemy, I received his orders to march at six o'clock next morning, the 9th of May, toward Resaca, and to advance as far as Rome cross-roads in Sugar-Creek Valley, and there await specific orders and instructions. The object of the movement was stated to be a demonstration upon Resaca, while other troops cut the railroad north of that place.

At daylight on the 9th my advance, as before—a regiment of mounted infantry, supported by a regiment of infantry—was attacked by Ferguson's brigade of the enemy's cavalry, and Colonel Phillips was severely wounded. We drove the enemy rapidly before us to Rome cross-roads, where I received orders to advance upon Resaca, to press forward until I should succeed in developing the enemy in line of battle, or in his fortifications, but not to attack him there without orders. I was also ordered to hold the Calhoun and Dalton cross-roads, about two miles west of Resaca, if I became possessed of it, until the Fifteenth Army Corps arrived. These orders were obeyed, my force skirmishing heavily the entire distance to the Calhoun cross-roads.

The enemy was discovered in line of battle on a bald hill, three-quarters of a mile west of Resaca, and also in his works at Resaca.

I placed the Fourth Division at the cross-roads, formed the Second Division in two lines, and carried the hill, and holding there under instructions, awaited my orders from General McPherson, to whom I had promptly reported, sending, I think, my staff-officer, Captain Edward Jonas, telling General McPherson that, if we could make a prompt attack, we could carry Resaca, as the enemy in my front gave way readily, and that though prisoners had reported the arrival of Canty's brigade, the night before, I did not believe it, as no such force as a division showed in our front. General McPherson soon came upon the ground in person; he directed me to send some mounted men up the Dalton road to reconnoitre the country, and find an approach to the railroad, while he would go back and bring up the Fifteenth (Logan's) Corps. Until that corps arrived, I was to hold the bald hill indicated, and the Dalton and Calhoun cross-roads. I sent all the mounted men I had with me at the time, eighteen in number (of the Ninth Illinois), under Captain Hughes. They proceeded toward Dalton, struck the railroad two miles south of Tilton, and found it strongly patrolled by cavalry; they cut the telegraph-wires, burned a wood station, and reported to me again at dark. Meantime the enemy came marching out of Resaca up the Dalton Railroad, and I ordered the Fourth Division to march from Calhoun cross-roads and to intercept them, and to take position on the railroad north of Resaca. This order was reported to General McPherson promptly; he replied that I must hold the cross-roads until relieved. It was about four o'clock when I finally received from one of General McPherson's staff-officers the information that the Fifteenth Army Corps was closing up, and that I was now at liberty to carry out my movement against the railroad. It was intrusted by me to General Veatch, with Fuller's and Sprague's brigades of his division, the Fourth. The Second Division was stationed on the bald hill I had occupied about noon, and the left of this division was now assailed with musketry, while the marching division was fired upon as they advanced in column in full view of the enemy. Fuller, in the advance, moved with spirit across the west fork of Mill Creek, crossed an open field, and the skirmish-line was up to the timber skirting the railroad, when another order came from General McPherson to look well to my right, as the enemy was massing to strike me there. I was with Fuller's advance at this time, and the enemy that had come out of Resaca had opened on Fuller's troops in the open field. Near by was a good cover of woods on the east side of the creek, to attain which I changed the direction of Fuller's column more to the north; his skirmish-line took some prisoners; the morning rumor was confirmed by them that Canty's brigade had arrived. Fuller steadily advanced, however, and as soon as his skirmish-lines debouched from the woods, a regiment of the enemy's infantry and a battery in position opened directly upon his right and front. Another notice had been received from General McPherson, as we got to the roads, that Sprague's brigade was not following us, having been arrested by him to hold the space between the Second and the advance of the Fourth Division. While Fuller was executing the movement to gain the railroad, a final order came to me from General McPherson to halt the column, and to repair in person to him back of the bald hill occupied by the Second Division. There I found General McPherson and General Logan with the advance of Logan's Fifteenth Corps. They were discussing the propriety of an attack upon Resaca. General Logan asked me what I thought of the situation, and if we could carry the place. I replied, I thought we could. Logan responded that he was glad I had so much faith. McPherson appeared to feel the responsibility of his orders from the commander of the army, as well as the responsibility of holding the gap we had already seized. He listened attentively to the conversation, to my description of the position, and to the nature of the orders I had given. He reluctantly gave us orders to immediately return. The Sixteenth Corps withdrew over the eight miles they had already marched that day, reaching the eastern *débouche* of the gap at midnight. I had with the entire corps only seventeen wagons since leaving Chattanooga. My transportation had not yet come up, and the men and the animals had been without other food for a day and a half than what could be afforded by the poor and picked country we had marched over.

A day or two after our return to the gap, General McPherson stated to me the contents of a letter or letters from General Sherman commenting upon the march to Resaca. He seemed to feel that their criticism amounted to censure, but he had assumed the responsibility. He said a part of one of his corps was still west of the gap, guarding trains, that he could not have thrown his whole force across the railroad, as they were situated, and that he looked for his vindication to the successful termination of the campaign. He said: "We had ascertained, from prisoners taken the day of the advance to Resaca, that the enemy knew just what force had passed through the gap, and where the balance of the army was. He made the final decision to return to the gap between five and six o'clock in the afternoon, being satisfied nothing could be accomplished by attacking an intrenched post that late in the day."

At Snake-Creek Gap we waited three days, seeing the whole army move through the pass we had captured "to Johnston's complete surprise," and fortifying Sugar-Creek Valley. May 13th, the Fourth Division of my corps formed on the right of the Fifteenth Corps, resting on the Oostenaula River, and took part in the attack on Resaca. My second division, Sweeney's, May 14th went on to Lay's Ferry, below Resaca, to cross the Oostenaula River and threaten Johnston's communications. General Rice with the advanced brigade crossed in the face of Walker's division. As soon as this movement in the rear was accomplished, Johnston began to retreat from Resaca, which he had defended a second time, and now with his whole army, and which he "only evacuated because his safety demanded it."

Attack of July 4, 1864.

I desire only to refer to the action of July 4th, described in the "Memoirs" as "noisy but not desperate."

The Fourth Division of my corps, under General Fuller, pressed forward on that day, crossing the Nickajack Creek at Ruff's Mill, driving the enemy before us, until, after two miles of skirmishing, we developed him in strong intrenchments, and in very heavy force. The "Memoirs" imply that this was the head of column of the Army of the Cumberland, and unintentionally leave it to be inferred that the storming of the works was General Thomas's performance. It was General McPherson who sent me a message to attack at discretion, or if I thought I could carry the works. Prisoners informed me that Hood's corps was before me, and I proceeded to reconnoitre their works, which I found very strong, but, as I observed a singular confusion there, indicative of retreating, and knew that the 4th of July would be a good day to assault, I formed a charging column of a part of the

Fourth Division, the Thirty-ninth and Twenty-seventh Ohio, and the Sixty-fourth Illinois Infantry of my corps, under command of Colonel E. F. Noyes. A supporting column was made up of the Sixty-sixth Illinois and the Second Iowa infantry, of the Second Division. Noyes moved forward with gallantry, although he fell at the first fire, and lost his leg, but through almost impenetrable abatis and fallen timber, the men went over the intrenchments, and took one hundred prisoners, and they so settled the enemy's confusion, if any there was, that the whole of that line was soon abandoned.

I come, now, to the last subject of my letter, the battle of the 22d of July, where General McPherson lost his life.

Battle of Atlanta.

The movement ordered by General Sherman, of the transfer of the Army of the Tennessee from the right to the extreme left of the combined armies, began June 9th.

Marching from Sand Town, by the rear to the left, on the 9th of July, the Sixteenth Corps bivouacked, at ten o'clock at night, near Marietta, continued on, at three o'clock, in the dark of the morning, and that second day had crossed the Chattahoochee, spanned it with a foot-bridge, seven hundred feet long, covered it with a long *téte-du-pont,* and intrenched on the Atlanta side. The march was thirty-one miles, the heat was intense, yet the men were uncomplaining and ardent, and for nearly three days more they worked in reliefs of one thousand in the mud and water until we completed, July 13th, at Roswell, Georgia, a double-track trestle-bridge, fourteen feet high and seven hundred and ten feet long. The material used was standing timber and some cotton-mills; over this bridge the entire Army of the Tennessee, with trains and artillery, passed.

On the 17th the command moved toward Decatur, cutting a new road so as not to infringe upon the Seventeenth and Twenty-third corps, which took the old roads; keeping its communication with those corps, the Sixteenth advanced behind its pioneers, preceded by the Ninth Illinois mounted infantry, which skirmished with the enemy at Nancy's Creek, and drove them across; and here, one of my scouts, who had left Atlanta that morning, brought the first intelligence of Hood's having superseded Johnston, which was at once sent to Generals Sherman and McPherson. Decatur was occupied July 19th, after a heavy skirmish and artillery-fighting, and Colonel Sprague, with Second Brigade of Fourth Division, was placed there to relieve General Garrard's cavalry division and guard the trains. As we approached Atlanta the converging corps forced the Sixteenth Corps out of line, and a series of transfers began. On the 21st of July General Fuller, with First Brigade, Fourth Division, was put in reserve to the Seventeenth Army Corps, and United States Regular Battery F, of the Fourth Division, was put in front line of General Giles A. Smith's division of the Seventeenth Corps. My second division, under General Sweeny, moved forward three quarters of a mile beyond its old position, to a range of hills, the enemy contesting this advance very sharply, and intrenched there. At four o'clock the next morning General Sweeny reported to me that the enemy had disappeared from his front; whereupon I ordered him to push forward a heavy skirmish-line. He soon found the enemy in force, in works surrounding Atlanta. The Second Division being displaced by the contraction of the lines, and the Fifteenth and Twenty-third Corps closing upon each other, General McPherson ordered me to move to the left of the army, and place Fuller's first brigade on the left of the new position to be assumed by the Seventeenth Corps, and hold the rest of the command in reserve on the extreme left. Before this was done, I rode with General McPherson from his headquarters to the front on the direct Decatur and Atlanta road. It was quite early in the morning, the day of the battle of Atlanta. The sudden evacuation of the enemy was surprising to both of us, and gave General McPherson serious concern. He requested me to return immediately to my command, and get the troops upon the ground they were to occupy, and first to examine that ground myself, and choose a position on the left of the Seventeenth Corps, and also to feel toward the wagon-road running from Atlanta south. I started at once. There was a cross-road leading to the left from the Atlanta road, in the rear of the Fifteenth, and passing through the left of the Seventeenth Army Corps, by which I gave orders for the Sixteenth Corps to march, while I went forward rapidly with my engineers and a part of my staff to select the new position. I rode out beyond the Seventeenth Corps, far in the advance, and within easy musket-range of the works of Atlanta, passing the pioneers of the Seventeenth Corps intrenching the new line. The stillness was oppressive, and, I thought, almost ominous. I could plainly see the enemy's troops working on their fortifications, on the south side of Atlanta, and they allowed myself and staff to approach within easy musket-range, not firing upon us until we turned about to return, after having picked out the ground for the corps. As we retired, the enemy opened on us briskly with musket and artillery. I at once sent word to General Fuller to send out working-parties to intrench his line on the new position, and for the Second Division to move to the rear of the Seventeenth Army Corps and bivouac.

While passing through the Seventeenth Army Corps, I left an order for Murray's Second United States Battery to join its command, and also met General Giles A. Smith, commanding the left division of the Seventeenth Army Corps, who told me that the Seventeenth Corps would not move into their new position until night. Immediately on receiving this information I sent General Sweeny orders to halt and bivouac his division (the Second) where he then was, viz., about three-fourths of a mile in the rear of the Fifteenth Army Corps (General Logan's), and on the right and rear of the Seventeenth (General Blair's). At noon I reached General Fuller's headquarters, in the rear of the Seventeenth Corps, and almost directly on an extension of the line of Sweeny's division, which had halted upon receiving my order, and was resting by the road-side. While at Fuller's headquarters I heard straggling shots fired to the east and to the left of General Sweeny's division, which warned me, and I ordered General Fuller to put his command immediately in position, and spoke to him of the gap that existed of about one-quarter of a mile between him and General Giles A. Smith, and of the exposed condition of the left flank of our army. I called his attention to the position of the ammunition-train of the army on the right of Fuller and in the rear of General Smith, where they were very much exposed; but I had scarcely given General Fuller his orders, when the report came in that the enemy was in force in our rear, and developing far behind General Sweeny. I sent a staff-officer to General Sweeny on the minute, with orders to immediately close on Fuller, and to form to repel an attack. General Sweeny anticipated the order, and had already sent forward skirmishers in the direction of the enemy's fire, and he developed the enemy in large force. The Second Division had just got into position when Hood's army appeared in force, advancing in three columns. I waited until the enemy was fully developed, then dispatched a staff-officer to General Giles A. Smith, telling him that the enemy was attacking in his rear, that he must refuse his left and join with Fuller. My staff-officer came back with the information that

General Smith would comply with the request. Smith had not then been attacked, and the enemy was all developed beyond my right in the timber, covering Fuller's right flank, with their skirmish-line extending around to the left of Sweeny. I observed no movement of General Smith, and became very anxious for the safety of that flank. I sent another staff-officer to General Smith, giving him fully the position of the enemy, and telling him that a very large force was upon our rear. General Smith was by this time apprised of the fact of the enemy's intentions, from the general attack which had been made along my whole line. It afterward was made plain to me by General Smith why he hesitated to comply with my first request. He was in the act of refusing his left, when General McPherson sent him orders to hold his ground, and that reënforcements would be sent to him, or his left protected. General McPherson had evidently sent this order before arriving on the ground, without knowing the position of the enemy as fully as I did. I received no orders from General McPherson during the battle. In moving out of the timber into the open field in my front, now the rear of the army, one of the enemy's columns of attack (the centre column) struck a mill-pond, or some other obstruction, just on the edge of an open field, and became entangled, retarding its progress and exposing the flank of the other column. I saw that something had confused the enemy, and immediately ordered Colonel Mersey's brigade to charge the advance column on the exposed flank, and also sent orders to Fuller to instantly charge the enemy in his front, and to take advantage of their embarrassment. Both commands moved promptly, and fell upon the enemy and drove them back across the field, and I have no doubt saved my command. While this attack was progressing, not hearing from the staff-officer I sent to General Giles A. Smith, and seeing that the enemy was passing to my right in the rear, and far down the line of the Seventeenth Army Corps, I sent another staff-officer to that flank who must have passed up the road a short time before General McPherson, for he found General Giles A. Smith hotly engaged and unable to move. Fortunately, two batteries that were in line were in the centre of Sweeny's division, on a knoll naturally strong and commanding, and giving a sweeping fire across an open field, covering both the right and left of Sweeny's division; this knoll being the apex of the formation of Sweeny, the road bent to the west at that point, and Sweeny followed the direction of the road, forming his line right where his men were resting. These two batteries fired very effectively upon the enemy's advance forces, pouring into them canister at short range. The fire was so destructive and Mersey's charge so furious that the enemy very soon gave way on their front and fell back to the timber. General Fuller advanced rapidly across the field, driving the enemy before him, developed them in the gap between General Smith and his right, and drawing a rapid fire on his right flank, from the body of the enemy that had poured around the left of the Seventeenth Corps, he promptly changed front with a portion of his division, and, under a galling fire, moved on the enemy in the timber, clearing that point. The Sixty-fourth Illinois Infantry pushed in between the main column of the enemy and their advance in the timber, and captured their skirmish-line, the same that had killed General McPherson a few minutes before, and were then in possession of his papers and effects, including his orders, which we obtained. The fighting in General Fuller's front was very severe, and the ground contested inch by inch, his artillery doing very effective service. Finally, the enemy fell back along Fuller's whole line, and I swung my right in order to bring it into line with the brigade that McPherson had ordered up to General Giles A. Smith's aid, which had been forced to take position to the right, and somewhat in rear of Fuller's advance. The Seventeenth Army Corps reformed its left at right angles with the original line, and joined this brigade. This brought the enemy well to our front, and there we kept them the rest of the day. Major-General McPherson arrived on the ground during the attack on me, stood near the ammunition-train on right of my line, watching the result of my counter-charge upon the enemy. As soon as the tide turned in my favor, he followed a road through the timber leading from Fuller's right before his advance to the left of the Seventeenth Army Corps, still unaware of the advance of the enemy into the gap between Fuller's right and the Seventeenth Corps. About half an hour after my first repulse of the enemy I received a report that General McPherson was wounded, and it was about 3 P. M. before I was aware he was dead. About 4 P. M. General Logan called in person for aid to drive back the enemy on the Decatur and Atlanta road, where he had made a sortie and gained a temporary advantage, breaking through General Morgan L. Smith's division of the Fifteenth Army Corps. I sent the Second Brigade of the Second Division under Colonel Mersey, accompanied by Captain Jonas of my staff. Mersey's brigade immediately went into line and moved down the main road, participating in the charge with General Wood's division of the Fifteenth Army Corps, retook the works and batteries that had been lost, Colonel Mersey receiving a wound in his leg, having his horse killed under him. General Morgan L. Smith, who witnessed Colonel Mersey's attack, sent by Captain Jonas a very complimentary message as to Colonel Mersey's charge and its success. When General Logan called for Mersey's brigade, he told me that if the enemy again attacked me and I needed help to call upon General J. D. Cox, of the Twenty-third Corps. At 5 P. M. the enemy made a demonstration on my extreme left, and I requested General Cox to send me a brigade, which he promptly did. The enemy, however, only opened with artillery. Again Mersey's brigade was called into action about midnight, when General Logan ordered two regiments from it to occupy the hill that had been hotly contested in line of the Seventeenth Army Corps and relieve the troops of that command. Mersey's troops promptly executed the request, crawling in on their hands and knees, finding the enemy in the ditches on the outside, and driving them out. The time of Colonel Mersey's brigade had expired; they were exempt from participating in this battle had they chosen to avail themselves of this right, and were awaiting transportation North. They fought successfully on different parts of the field, suffering heavy loss in killed and wounded. General Sprague, who was at Decatur holding that town, covering the trains of the Army of the Tennessee with three regiments of his brigade and six guns of the Chicago Board of Trade Battery and one section of the Eighth Michigan Artillery, was attacked by the enemy in overwhelming numbers. Two divisions of Wheeler's cavalry, dismounted, charged upon Sprague from three different directions. General Sprague concentrated his command, and, after a doubtful and determined contest, held the enemy in check and gained a position north of the town, which he was able to keep. In their charge the enemy twice got possession of Sprague's artillery, but were immediately driven from it. General Sprague, by his good generalship and hard fighting, saved the trains of the Fifteenth, Sixteenth, and Seventeenth Army Corps at Decatur and *en route* from Roswell to the army. The trains on the march were guarded by the Ninth Illinois Infantry and the Forty-third Ohio Infantry, which regiments, upon their arrival at Decatur, went promptly into the action. The Sixteenth Army Corps, at the time of Hood's attack, was in the rear of the Fifteenth and Seventeenth Corps, stretched out upon a common wagon-road. Three brigades disposed in single line, numbering about forty-five hundred men, and not in line with the other corps, had met the attack of the rebel army, staggered it at the first onset, and driven it back with great slaughter, leaving the dead and wounded of the enemy in our hands. Any failure on the part of the Sixteenth Corps to check the enemy's advance when he was already in our rear and certain of success, would have been disastrous to the whole Army of the Tennessee. The fortunate topography of the ground, the intelligence of the commanders, and the alacrity and bravery of the troops, enabled us to take advantage of the confusion created in the enemy's ranks in finding this corps prepared for the attack, and to rout the enemy.

The disparity of forces can be seen from the fact that in the charge made by the two brigades under Fuller and Mersey they took three hundred and fifty-one prisoners, representing forty-nine different regiments, eight brigades, and three divisions. These two brigades brought back eight battle-flags from the enemy.

After the fight, four hundred and twenty-two of the enemy's dead were buried in my front, and large numbers of the wounded were cared for in my hospitals.

The Sixteenth Army Corps suffered terribly in the battle of Atlanta. Their loss in killed and wounded was eight hundred and fifty-four out of fifty-four hundred men engaged, and nearly every field-officer of my command was killed or wounded.

I am, general, very respectfully, your obedient servant,

G. M. Dodge.

Council Bluffs, Iowa, *November* 30, 1875.

Tecumseh, Alabama, *February* 22, 1876.

Mrs. General W. T. Sherman.

My dear Madam: I have read with great interest General Sherman's "Memoirs," and some of the criticisms made upon it, and venture to give my testimony in regard to some of the disputed points falling within my personal knowledge, as of interest possibly to some of my comrades in arms, if not to the general public and history.

The March to the Sea.

On the 5th of May, 1864, I reported to General Sherman at Ringgold, Georgia, for duty as inspector-general on his staff. The general, with his map before him, explained the general course of his proposed campaign against General Johnston, ending with the capture of Atlanta. I remember that he had his coat and hat off, and his slippers on. When he had done his explanations, he began walking the floor of the room, smoking a cigar. I said to him that when he got to Atlanta he would be four hundred and fifty miles from his real base of supplies, with one railroad as his only means of transportation, and every mile of that liable to be broken by the enemy, and that it would absorb the whole of his army to hold Atlanta and protect the road, and asked him what he proposed after the capture of Atlanta. Stopping short in his walk, and snapping the ashes off his cigar in a quick, nervous way, he replied in two words—"Salt water." I did not comprehend his meaning, but after a little further examination of the map I asked him if he meant Savannah or Charleston, and he said, "Yes."

Again, soon after the capture of Atlanta, he called Colonel Beckwith, his chief commissary, and myself into his room in Judge Lyon's house in Atlanta, and, locking the door, laid his map on the floor, and indicated his proposed march to Savannah. Colonel Beckwith's first question naturally was, "How about supplies?" The general replied that there were one million of people in Georgia, and that where they could live his army would not starve.

Snake-Creek Gap.

Before and during the movements against General Johnston, at Rocky Face, General Sherman explained to me and others of his staff that the demonstrations on Johnston's front and right were feints to cover and hide the real movement of attack by General McPherson through Snake-Creek Gap. In speaking of the danger that Johnston might fall on McPherson with his whole force, and crush him before help could be got to him, he said that the twenty-three thousand muskets of the Army of the Tennessee could not "be run over by anybody in a hurry," and that the moment Johnston let go of Rocky Face, Thomas and Schofield would be on his rear, and thus place him between two fires, when ruin would be sure.

On the night of May 9th, as we were at supper at the brick house, by the spring near Tunnel Hill Station, a letter was brought to the general. Reading it, he instantly left the table, and bade me follow him. When we had got a little way from the house, he stopped short, and, with a vehement gesture of his right hand clinched, said: "I have got Joe Johnston dead. This letter is from McPherson. At one o'clock to-day he was within one and a half mile of the railroad. He must be on it now. I want to go over and see 'Tom'"—meaning General Thomas. On his way he said that Johnston would be compelled to abandon the railroad and most of his artillery and trains, and retreat to the east through the mountains (Pigeon Mountains, I think they were called); that we would follow the railroad, and beat Johnston to Atlanta.

Arriving at General Thomas's headquarters, we found him at supper, and General Sherman repeated to him the same expressions he used to me. General Thomas was also greatly pleased, and my recollection is that he said he thought Johnston would fortify and defend the gap. Sherman and Thomas agreed that Johnston must now let go Rocky Face, and that Thomas and Schofield must push him hard in the morning to crush him and prevent his crushing McPherson. This understanding had, we returned to our headquarters, General Sherman being in high spirits.

Late that night word came from McPherson that he had failed to seize the railroad, and had fallen back to the mouth of the gap and fortified. I think that all the members of the staff will remember how disappointed and excited the general was on receipt of this news, and how cross he was the next day, and that we all thought he might relieve McPherson of his command, though the general gave no intimation of such intent—to me, at least. We simply inferred it from McPherson's failure to execute the work expected of him.

I was present when General Sherman and McPherson first met after this, and well remember that General Sherman's manner toward McPherson was one of sadness rather than anger, and that his first remark was, "Well, Mac, you have missed the great opportunity of your life." General Adkins and Colonel Hickenlooper, both of whom were in good position to know the truth, express, I think, the general judgment of the Army of the Tennessee—that if certain other division commanders had been in the lead, the railroad would have been seized and held, and Johnston ruined.

That the failure to do this was by far the most grievous disappointment which General Sherman met with during the Atlanta campaign, will, I think, be admitted by all who participated in it, and were familiar with its history.

The Battle of the 22d of July, or "Atlanta."

Perhaps I cannot better state my knowledge of this battle than by quoting some remarks made by me in the Ohio Senate in 1866, when the facts were all fresh in my memory, and repeated in the United States Senate May 4, 1870. Though not all exactly pertinent to the points in issue about the battle of Atlanta, I will copy the whole of these remarks, as affording the conclusive proof of my high regard and admiration for all three of these true men and great soldiers—Sherman, Thomas, and McPherson—and how incapable I am of seeking to lessen in the slightest degree their well-earned fame. Grant, Sherman, Thomas, McPherson, and Sheridan, are names that will be illustrious throughout the world while the history of our late great war is preserved.

The joint resolution appropriating condemned cannon for the use of the McPherson Monument Association having been taken up, Senator Warner said:

"I claim the indulgence of the Senate for a few minutes.

"Mr. President, I speak on this resolution with feelings of unusual interest, growing out of the remarkable character of the man whom it is intended to honor, and of my long association during the late war with him. I first met him just after we had fought so successfully the battle of Fort Donelson, when he was a lieutenant-colonel on the staff of General Grant; and from that time until the hour of his death I was in the same army, campaigns, and battles, with him. During the ever-memorable and brilliant Atlanta campaign, it was my honor to serve as an inspector-general on the staff of General Sherman, and, as such, was brought much in contact with General McPherson, and had large opportunities of learning his character and services, and the regard in which he was held by the army and by his military peers and superiors. That esteem was in some respects peculiar. General Sherman had, above all others, the supreme confidence of the entire army in his military skill and bold energy, and none stood higher for personal patriotism, purity, and integrity—an integrity of Roman firmness, rigidity, and self-denial. These qualities are well shown in his refusal to accept, in the beginning of the Atlanta campaign, a commission as major-general in the regular army, on the ground that the Government had already sufficiently rewarded and honored him for his services, and that it should be held up as a prize for the most meritorious service during the campaigns then about to be begun, of Atlanta and the Wilderness.

"General Thomas, in his Washingtonian greatness, solidity, and purity, had universal respect and confidence throughout the army.

General Schofield, though less widely known than either Sherman or Thomas, yet had the entire confidence and perfect respect of his own army, and of all who were competent to judge him, as a soldier of skill and courage, and as a pure patriot and just man. But McPherson, added to the utmost confidence in his military skill and personal courage, had such noble beauty of form and countenance, such winning gentleness of expression and manner; his face, which in repose had an expression of almost womanly sweetness, would so light up and blaze with fiercest courage and daring in the moment of battle, that in danger he was worshiped as a hero; in quiet regarded in tenderest love as a man—it seemed as though the love of the beautiful one whom he worshiped, but whom the Fates in blind cruelty decreed he might never wed, so lighted the noble soul which God gave him, as to illuminate his face, and make gentle and true and winning his life, his own love attracting to him the love of all other men.

"And then the circumstances of his life and death were so touching and tragic! At two o'clock of the morning of the memorable 22d of July, 1864, when General Sherman's army was laying close siege to Atlanta, I was called by him and ordered to go to McPherson, some six miles distant on our left, and inform him that the enemy had evacuated his works in front of our centre, and with directions for him to pursue, by certain roads, in case the enemy had abandoned his whole line and Atlanta. I found him at daylight in bed. Waking him up, he gave instantly the necessary orders for a reconnaissance to ascertain the movements of the enemy. We ate breakfast together, mounted our horses, rode to the front, and found the enemy had only retired about a mile to an inner and shorter line. We rode to his skirmish-line and outside of it, and a mile in front of the line on which the great battle was fought later in the day, passing twice over the spot on which he fell a few hours later. Very near this spot we met General G. M. Dodge, and then General McPherson gave him the order to halt his two divisions of the Sixteenth Corps, which were then marching by the flank in a direction at right angles to our line, the head of the column being less than a mile from our extreme left. Neither McPherson nor Dodge nor General Frank P. Blair, who was with us, then comprehended the mighty and happy influence which this order, given only to await the intrenching by working parties of the extended and advanced line on our left, which Dodge was to occupy, was to have on the day's battle, whose stillness was even then upon us. One may well regard it as providential. No one then knew or thought that Hood had, during the night before, contracted his line so as to be able to spare Hardee with a corps of ten to fifteen thousand men, to make by a night march of fifteen miles a circuit round our left to attack us in flank and rear, and who was then, just out of our sight, forming his troops for the attack. We left the field on our left and rode rapidly to the centre to General Sherman, at the Howard House, an abandoned private dwelling near the centre of our line, and within easy reach of the enemy's rifles. On our way we halted for a few moments at the tent of Major-General Frank P. Blair. While there, Blair's surgeon reported that rebel cavalry had been seen near the hospital of the Seventeenth Corps, which held our left. It was also reported to McPherson that rebel cavalry had been seen near his headquarters, located in the rear of our left, on Decatur road. The necessary orders were given by McPherson and Blair to guard against dashes of bands of cavalry, but no importance was attached by any one to the fact of their appearance, as it was so common, though, in fact, it was the first pattering of the great storm of battle which was soon to burst upon the two armies, and prostrate in wounds and death ten thousand brave men. A few moments after dismounting at General Sherman's headquarters, the sharp, rattling fire of musketry was heard in the direction of our left rear. Sherman and McPherson listened to it attentively for a few moments, both detecting in it the decisive sound of coming battle, when McPherson quickly mounted his horse and rode rapidly toward it. In less than two hours his dead body was laid at Sherman's feet on the porch of the Howard House. In riding from the right of General Dodge's line through the interval that separated it from the left of Leggett's division of the Seventeenth Corps by a blind road through the woods, attended only by an orderly, his staff having all been sent away with orders for the conduct of the battle, he was halted by a squad of rebel infantry and ordered to surrender. Raising his hat as if in token of surrender, he essayed to rein his horse quickly away and plunge into the woods and escape. The rebels, instantly detecting his purpose, fired a volley, and the brave and chivalrous McPherson fell to rise no more.

"I can never forget the touching scene at the Howard House as his body lay there, still and beautiful in death. McPherson was betrothed to a girl of rare beauty and worth in Baltimore, and had the promise of a leave of absence in the spring of 1864 to go to Baltimore and be married. The exigencies of the military service, in connection with the grand movements of the Atlanta and Wilderness campaigns, which General Grant directed should be begun simultaneously, compelled General Sherman to the painful necessity of denying this leave. He wrote a kind and touching letter to the girl, taking the whole responsibility, and begging her to consider that General McPherson had no option but obedience or soldierly dishonor, and promising him leave the earliest time the service would allow. As we looked on his face, pale and cold in death, even the remembrance of his virtues, and his value to the army and to the country, was hushed in the thought of the deep love which, but a few hours before, had lent such light to his eyes and such geniality to his manners, and of the irreparable sorrow soon to come to one from whom death had so cruelly snatched her beautiful hero. Sherman slowly paced the floor, frequently stopping short to receive reports of the progress of the fight, or to give orders for its conduct, or to gaze into the lifeless face of his beloved captain, the tears meanwhile rapidly coursing down his war-worn face.

"Mr. President, the tears shed on the battle-field over his dead body by his great chief Tecumseh and his brave men would have made his most fitting monument, had the skill of other than a divine artist been equal to the task of gathering them in the form in which they fell, and of giving them the perpetuity as they had the radiance of diamonds, of fashioning them into 'a form of beauty,' sparkling in God's light, while time shall last, the story of his virtues. But earth caught them, mingled with the blood of those who shed them, and her flowers, nourished by them, will be Nature's sympathetic testimony to his kindred beauty of form and soul.

"The high military renown of General McPherson, together with the possession by him of those gentle qualities which won for him the *sobriquet* of 'the beloved McPherson,' so peculiarly distinguished him as to warrant us in making this contribution, to aid in raising a monument which shall tell to all future ages of his services and fame."

On my way to General McPherson's headquarters, on the morning of the 22d of July, I passed General Logan's quarters at daylight, and seeing him in front of his tent, told him my errand, and my recollection is that he at once proceeded to reconnoitre his front, without waiting for orders from General McPherson, which were sent by a staff-officer on my arrival at General McPherson's, perhaps a mile distant and to the left rear.

When news came of General McPherson's death, and of the partial turning of our left, General Sherman said to me, "Warner, you have been over all this ground to-day; go quickly and see how matters stand, and report to me." I went and saw Generals Dodge, Blair, and Leggett. Blair's left had been turned, but he had reformed it refused from Leggett's Hill, and had made connection, or nearly so, with Dodge's divisions, and the three stood firm and were confident of holding their positions, which they did, and repulsed the enemy with great slaughter. General Blair said to me, on my asking him of the condition of matters, "We have had a d——d hard fight, but we whipped them, and can do it again if they come back at us."

As I returned I had to ride, in order to pass a fence, up the main wagon-road alongside the railroad from Atlanta to Decatur to within one or two hundred yards of our main line on our centre, when it crossed the wagon and rail roads near the brick house. The enemy were just attacking our centre with great energy, and their artillery enfiladed the road up which I was riding—three solid shots or shells striking in the road in front of me and ricochetting over me, in going a distance of half a mile. Just as I passed nearest our line, the enemy issued from the railroad-cut in the rear of our line and captured a part of it belonging to General Morgan L. Smith's division, and not to General Wood's, as General Kilpatrick erroneously states. General Wood's line was nowhere broken, nor seriously attacked, as I remember. The splendid fighting of his division was done later in aiding General Smith's division to recover the lost part of their line.

Reaching General Sherman a few minutes later at the Howard House, I informed him of the condition of affairs on the left, as stated by Generals Blair, Dodge, and Leggett, and as seen by myself, and said to him that Leggett's Hill was the key of our entire left from the railroad, and that it would be held—that, in fact, the enemy were already repulsed and beaten on that part of the field.

General C. R. Wood had just reported the breaking of our line to his left, but General Sherman was incredulous, and sent him back to be sure. I confirmed the report, and presently General Wood returned and again confirmed it. Then it was that General Wood's troops were formed *en échelon* and advanced in such splendid style to the left to the attack of the enemy's left flank, swinging to the right up to the breastworks as the enemy were driven from the opposite side by the enfilading fire of Wood, aided by Schofield's guns on the hill in front of the Howard House trained on the enemy's flank. I directed the fire of one of these guns, by watching with my glass where the shots struck and hinting accordingly to the officer sighting the gun. To understand all this it must be borne in mind that the guns were on a high hill, Wood's troops in a deep hollow, and the enemy on the face of the hill opposite—the line of breastworks crossing the hollow at right angles. All this was done by the orders and under the eye of General Sherman.

The result was that our entire line was speedily recovered, and the day closed with the enemy completely foiled of his object, and everywhere repulsed and beaten with great loss.

The next morning General Sherman, soon followed by General Logan, rode along our entire line to the left of the Howard House, and both were received with the wildest enthusiasm by the troops which had done such severe and splendid fighting the day before.

The sight of the great number of Confederate dead in front of our lines was appalling, and never to be forgotten by those who saw it.

As showing General Sherman's estimate of General McPherson, I will say that, as we rode to our quarters from the battle-field late that night. General Sherman said: "The army and the country have sustained a great loss by the death of McPherson. I had expected him to finish the war. Grant and I are likely to be killed, or set aside after some failure to meet popular expectation, and McPherson would have come into chief command at the right time to end the war. He had no enemies."

Successor to McPherson.

General Sherman talked to me freely about this matter at the time, and the considerations that seemed to influence him were that General Howard was a soldier of education and training, with a larger experience than General Logan, and therefore better fitted for such high command; but he seemed to regret that these reasons compelled him to prefer General Howard to so brave and daring a soldier as General Logan.

Removal of the People of Atlanta.

The following letter, the original of which is in my possession, throws some light on this matter, in regard to which General Sherman was so sharply censured at the South. The fact is, that not more than half the people of Atlanta obeyed the order, and no force was used to compel obedience. I was detailed by the general to attend to the delivery of the people to General Hood at Rough and Ready, where he sent Colonel Clare, of his staff, to receive them. The inhabitants had choice of transportation by rail or wagons—Colonel Le Duc, of General Geary's command, having control of all the transportation of the army for the purpose, and sending as many wagons to each house as were asked for. I had a train of cars standing on the track in Atlanta every day from 8 A. M. to 3 P. M., and the people were allowed to put on what they chose. The only limit to amount of goods to be taken was Hood's ability to transport from Rough and Ready. This letter Colonel Clare handed to me sealed and addressed to myself, when we parted, with request that I would not open it until I reached Atlanta. It illustrates his generous nature.

"ROUGH AND READY, GEORGIA,
September 21, 1864.

"COLONEL: Our official connection is about to cease. You will permit me to bear testimony to the uniform courtesy you have shown on all occasions to me and my people; and the promptness with which you have corrected all irregularities arising in our intercourse.

"Hoping, sir, to be able at some future time to reciprocate your courtesy and in many instances your positive kindness,

"I am, with respect, your obedient servant,

"W. CLARE, *Major and Assistant Inspector-General, General Hood's Staff.*

"*Colonel* WARNER, *Inspector-General, Major-General Sherman's Staff.*"

General Thomas.

General Sherman has been censured for not doing General Thomas justice in his "Memoirs," and particularly for speaking of him as "slow." That General Sherman is rapid and bold, and that Thomas was slow and cautious, in thought and action, in word and deed, in constitutional habit of mind, certainly no sane and honest man acquainted with each will deny.

This is certainly as well known as that General Grant was quicker and bolder than McClellan, and Sheridan than Buell. Which was the better general, on the whole, is a question not here in dispute.

On the 5th of May, 1864, General Thomas came to General Sherman's headquarters at Ringgold, Georgia. I did not then know him, but asked General Sherman if that were not General Thomas. He said, "Yes," and I then asked him if there was any truth in the rumor that Thomas felt aggrieved at having him (Sherman) put in command over him. He replied: "No, not a bit! It don't make much difference which of us commands. I would obey 'Tom's' orders to-morrow as cheerfully as he obeys mine to-day, but I think I can give an army a little more impetus than 'Tom' can." Here was the whole truth and difference in a nut-shell.

Their consultations were frequent, frank, and free, and I never saw any sign of bad feeling between them. After the battle of Nashville, General Thomas complained to me, as I understood he did to others, that injustice was done him in sending General Logan to relieve him of command; that those who gave and allowed the order did not and could not know the facts of his position, and that results had justified and vindicated him.

After the war he complained to me of the treatment of President Grant. I well remember his grand old figure, as he leaned on the little marble pedestal that used to stand in the vestibule of Willard's Hotel, in Washington, at the Fourteenth Street entrance, and said sadly: "I think that I have done the country some service, and something toward the success of the Republican party, and the only thing I have asked of this Administration was the appointment of my old commissary, Paul, as postmaster at Nashville, and that was refused, as the place was needed for some politician. I shall never ask for anything more."

WILLARD WARNER,
Late Brigadier-General of Volunteers,
and late United States Senator of Alabama.

SAVANNAH, GEORGIA, *October* 23, 1875.

General W. T. SHERMAN, *United States Army, St. Louis, Missouri.*

GENERAL: I read in a paper yesterday that you were bringing out a second edition of your "Memoirs." If this be so, permit me to correct a few errors in your first edition in regard to your march through Georgia, which, though of no moment to you in comparison with your grand operations, are pertinent to the truth of history, and to me in connection with it.

Official account of the people sent south, their numbers and luggage, under Special Field Order No. 67, issued by Major General W. T. Sherman, Atlanta, Georgia, September 4, 1864.

DATE.	NO.	NAME.	ADULTS, CHILDREN, AND SERVANTS.	BAGGAGE.
1864.				
Sept. 10.	1	J. M Bryant.	3 adults, 6 children, 1 servant. .	30 packages.
	2	Mrs. B Ogletree.	2 Adults.	27 "
	3	Mrs. Bookout	1 adult and 1 child	18 "
	4	Mrs. M. R Thornton.	1 adult, 5 children, 1 servant. . .	41 "
	5	Mrs. F. Winkfield	1 adult and 1 child	12 "
	6	Mrs. S. Hood	1 adult and 3 children	11 "
	7	Mrs. J. P. Brooks	1 adult and 1 child	14 "
	8	Mrs. L. C. Kent.	1 adult and 1 child	10 "
	9	Mrs. J. W. Thurman	1 adult and 1 child	6 "
	10	Mrs. N. Eason.	1 adult and 1 child	5 "
	11	Mrs. M. F. McDuffie.	1 adult and 4 children	14 "
	12	Mrs. S. E. Bell.	1 adult and 2 children	12 "
	13	Mrs. J. S. Johnson	1 adult.	5 "
	14	Mrs. Blanchard	1 adult, 2 children, 1 servant. . .	40 "
	15	Mrs. C. E. Harris	1 adult.	2 "
	16	Mrs. M. Struce	2 adults and 1 child	11 "
	17	Mrs. G. E. Forrest	2 adults and 2 children	12 "
	18	Mrs. C. Grubbs.	1 adult and 2 children	4 "
	18½	Mrs. M. A. P Jones	1 adult.	4 "
	19	Josiah Kent	2 adults	15 "
	20	Mrs. M. Huggenbottom . .	1 adult and 2 children	11 "
Sept. 11	21	Mrs. Stafford.	2 adults and 1 child	14 "
	22	Mrs. M. Blackburn	2 adults and 3 children.	12 "
	23	B. Evans	1 adult and 1 child	18 "
	24	Mrs. B. Thompson . . . . . . Mrs. E. Lee . . . . Mrs. M. Lee . . . . Mrs. M. Cook.	5 adults and 7 children	44 packages and 1 old horse and wagon.
	25	Mrs. S. Lee	1 adult and 6 children	17 packages.
	26	Mrs. S. Abrams	1 adult.	7 "
	27	Mrs. M. Wright.	1 adult and 1 servant	17 "
	28	Miss J. Combs.	1 adult.	14 "
	29	Mrs. Sims and Davis	2 adults and 1 child	24 "
	30	John Cassen.	2 adults	22 "
	31	Mrs. M. Higgens.	1 adult and 2 children	23 "
	32	Mrs. S. A. Gossett	1 adult.	15 "
	33	Mrs. E. J. Lofton.	1 adult and 1 child	14 "
	34	Mrs. M. Johnson.	1 adult and 5 children	21 "
	35	Mrs. S. McDuffie . . . . Mrs. M. J. Self.	3 adults and 4 children.	20 packages and 1 cow.
	36	Mrs. E. McGriff	1 adult and 1 child	13 packages.
	37	G. M. Lester	1 adult and 2 servants.	26 "
	38	Mrs. A. Patterson	1 adult and 2 children	15 "
	39	Mrs. M. Ballard.	1 adult and 4 children	23 "

(continued)

Official account of the people sent south, etc.—(CONTINUED.)

DATE.	NO.	NAME.	ADULTS, CHILDREN, AND SERVANTS.	BAGGAGE.
1864.				
Sept. 11.	40	Mrs. F. C. House.	1 adult and 2 children	23 packages.
	41	Mrs. C. Johnson	1 adult and 6 children	25 "
	42	Mrs. S. Ellis.	1 adult and 1 child	13 "
	43	Mrs. M. Wilson.	1 adult and 5 children	23 "
	44	Mrs. E. Phillips	4 adults	17 "
	45	Mrs. G. W. Adair	2 adults, 4 children, 2 servants.	53 packages and 2 horses, carriage, cow, and calf.
	46	Mrs. M. Ball . . . . Mrs. Brooks	} 2 adults and 4 children	35 packages
	47	Mrs. C. Johnson	1 adult and 1 child	9 "
	48	Mrs. J. Kramer	1 adult and 3 children	4 "
	49	Miss. L. Miller.	1 adult.	14 "
	50	Mrs. J. Kilby	1 adult and 5 children	35 "
	51	J. M. Blackburn.	2 adults	15 "
	52	Mrs. F. Witcher.	1 adult and 1 child	18 "
	53	Mrs. S. Freeman	1 adult.	7 "
	54	Mrs. E. L. Mill	1 adult, 3 children, 1 servant. . .	27 packages and 1 cow.
	55	Mrs. N. Mayson	1 adult, 1 child, 1 servant	28 packages and a cow and calf.
	56	Mrs. N. McTeer	1 adult.	8 packages.
	57	Mrs. A. M. McTeer	1 adult and 6 children	27 "
	58	Mrs. S. Mayson.	1 adult and 5 children	22 packages, and 1 old horse and dray, cow, and calf.
	59	Mrs. A. J. Mayson	1 adult.	10 packages.
	60	Mrs. S. A. Moss.	2 adults and 1 child	17 "
	61	Mrs. S. Armstrong.	1 adult, 2 children, 1 servant. . .	19 "
	62	J. L. Mayson	2 adults and 1 servant.	34 packages and horse and dray.
	63	Mrs. E. Gilham	1 adult.	10 packages.
	64	A. H. Webb.	2 adults, 2 children, 4 servants.	21 "
	65	Mrs. M. Waier.	1 adult.	17 "
	66	Mrs. E. Harper	1 adult and 5 children	27 "
	67	Mrs. M. Brady.	1 adult and 2 children	17 "
	68	Benjamin Gaum	2 adults and 8 children	31 "
	69	Mrs. N. Ireland	1 adult and 4 children	19 "
	70	Mrs. N. Waddail	2 adults	15 "
	71	Mrs. Preckett.	1 adult, 2 children, 1 servant. . .	18 "
	72	J. Hawkins	1 adult.	4 "
	73	R. W. T. Denham	1 adult and 5 children	12 "
	74	Mrs. M. A. Franklin	1 adult and 2 children	8 "
	75	Mrs. N. M. Franklin	1 adult and 2 children	8 "
	76	Mrs. S. Saul.	1 adult.	7 "
	77	Mrs. S. Clownes	2 adults and 1 servant.	9 "
	78	B. Eustell.	2 adults and 4 children	41 packages and cow and calf.
	79	Mrs. F. Crawford.	1 adult.	7 packages.

DATE.	NO.	NAME.	ADULTS, CHILDREN, AND SERVANTS.	BAGGAGE.
	80	Mrs. Makridge	1 adult and 5 children	23 "
	81	Mrs. R. Corsey	1 adult and 3 children	7 "
	82	Mrs. A. M. Rollo.	1 adult.	10 "
	83	Mrs. L. Smith	1 adult and 4 children	12 "
	84	Mrs. J. Sheppard	1 adult and 5 children	20 "
	85	Mrs. L. Whitmire	1 adult and 2 children	13 "
	86	Mrs. E. Lee	1 adult.	1 package.
	87	Miss C. Powers	1 adult.	1 "
Sept. 12.	88	Mrs. S. Corsey.	1 adult.	11 packages.
	89	Mrs. M. Grubbs	1 adult and 4 children	15 "
	90	S. Robinson.	2 adults and 2 children	14 "
	91	Mrs. E. Hill.	1 adult and 1 child	10 "
	92	Mrs. L. Patterson.	1 adult and 3 children	24 "
	93	Mrs. P. Jones	1 adult.	5 "
	94	Mrs. C. Grubbs.	1 adult and 2 children	11 "
	95	Mrs. E. Cook	1 adult and 1 child	12 "
	96	Mrs. M. H. Atkinson	1 adult and 4 children	16 "
	97	Mrs. T. Harebork	2 adults and 4 children	18 "
	98	Mrs. A. Hall	2 adults and 1 child	1 package.
	99	Mrs. E. Sears.	1 adult and 4 children	7 packages.
	100	Mrs. A. Willard.	1 adult and 3 children	7 "
	101	J. Haslett.	2 adults	22 "
	102	R. McCowan.	2 adults and 1 child	17 "
	103	Mrs. J. Atkins	1 adult and 1 child	16 "
	104	Mrs. M. Wing.	1 adult and 1 child	7 "
	105	B. Knott	2 adults	33 "
1864. Sept.12.	106	Mrs. S. Johnson.	1 adult and 1 child	10 packages.
	107	J. M. Knott	2 adults and 1 child	7 "
	108	Mrs. C. Knott.	1 adult and 1 child	22 "
	109	B. Thrower	2 adults and 2 children	32 "
	110	Mrs. M. E. Sharpe.	1 adult and 4 children	26 "
	111	Mrs. E. Glenn.	1 adult and 3 children	31 packages and cow and calf.
	112	Mrs. L. Wing	1 adult and 1 child	21 packages.
	113	W. H. H. Dorsey.	2 adults and 1 child	16 "
	114	Mrs. M. A. Gober	2 adults	14 packages and cow and calf.
	115	Mrs. J. I. Shaw	2 adults and 3 children.	17 packages.
Sept. 13	116	Mrs. S. Banks	1 adult and 2 children	16 "
	117	Mrs. M. Kelly	2 adults 4 children.	19 "
	118	Mrs. L. Dean.	1 adult and 3 children	7 "
	119	Mrs. M. Kelly	2 adults and 2 children	14 "
	120	Mrs. E. Bellew.	1 adult.	none.
	121	Mrs. J. S. McWaters	1 adult and 4 children	31 packages and 1 cow.
	122	Mrs. N. Reeves	1 adult and 2 children	21 packages.
	123	Mrs. M. L. Holbrook	1 adult and 3 children	33 "
	124	Mrs. S. Hewitt	1 adult.	13 "

(continued)

Official account of the people sent south, etc.—(CONTINUED.)

DATE.	NO.	NAME.	ADULTS, CHILDREN, AND SERVANTS.	BAGGAGE.
	125	Mrs. L. Bowls	1 adult	2 "
	126	Mrs. A. Blackman	2 adults and 1 child	19 "
	127	Mrs. E. Winfield	1 adult and 2 children	15 "
	128	Mrs. D. Defoor	3 adults and 2 children	22 "
	129	Mrs. E. N. Hilton	1 adult and 1 child	12 packages and 1 cow.
	130	J. B. McDaniel	1 adult	2 packages.
	131	Mrs. C. J. Lamb	1 adult and 9 children	21 "
	132	Mrs. P. Campbell	1 adult, 3 children, and 1 servant.	3 "
	133	Miss G. Timmons	1 adult	1 package.
	134	Mrs. M. Richards	1 adult	1 "
	135	Mrs. J. Johns	2 adults and 5 children	15 packages.
	136	Mrs. S. Williams	1 adult and 2 children	1 package.
	137	Mrs. C. Jenkins	1 adult and 2 children	4 packages.
	138	Mrs. M. Kilpatrick	2 adults and 9 children	12 "
	139	Miss M. Teall	3 adults	7 "
	140	Mrs. M. Edwards	1 adult and 1 child	10 "
	141	Mrs. S. Blalock	1 adult	11 "
	142	A. Grist	4 adults and 3 children	34 "
	143	Mrs. N. C. White	1 adult	22 "
	144	Mrs. M. E. Hutchens	1 adult and 2 children	9 "
	145	Mrs. N. Studevent	1 adult and 1 child	19 "
	146	Mrs. M. C. Seale	2 adults and 2 children	20 "
	147	Mrs. S. P. Baggerly	1 adult	4 "
	148	Mrs. P. Rothwell	1 adult	6 "
	149	Mrs. C. McHugh	2 adults	8 "
	150	W. L. White	2 adults	1 package.
	151	Miss E. Taylor	1 adult	5 packages.
	152	Mrs. J. M. Taylor	1 adult and 3 children	15 packages.
	153	Mrs. M. Wooding	1 adult and 2 children	11 "
	154	Thomas Byne	1 adult	1 horse.
	155	W. G. Grist	2 adults and 1 child	28 packages.
	156	J. Thompson	3 adults	13 "
	157	Mrs. M. E. Brace	1 adult and 2 children	16 "
	158	Mrs. E. Brace	1 adult and 3 children	17 "
	159	Mrs. S. P. Wilson	1 adult, 4 children, 2 servants	37 "
	160	Mrs. J. McLaughlin	5 adults and 4 children	7 "
	161	Mrs. L. Loren	1 adult and 2 children	18 "
	162	Mrs. A. Gerrett	1 adult	7 "
	163	Mrs. P. S. Jenkins	1 adult and 7 children	30 "
	164	Joseph Coker	1 adult	10 "
	165	Mrs. Mary Harper	2 adults and 3 children	19 packages and 1 cow.
	166	Mrs. L. Knight	1 adult and 2 children	11 packages.
	167	John Bash W. L. Bash	4 adults and 4 children	40 "
Sept.14.	168	Mrs. E. Robinson	2 adults	18 "
	169	Mrs. J. Williams	2 adults	19 "
	170	Mrs. M. Bell	3 adults and 7 children	38 packages and 1 cow.
	171	Mrs. L. Plummer	3 adults and 3 children	13 packages.

DATE.	NO.	NAME.	ADULTS, CHILDREN, AND SERVANTS.	BAGGAGE.
	172	W. D. Crockett	2 adults	16 "
	173	Mrs. W. D. Mitchell	1 adult, 3 children, and 1 servant.	25 "
1864. Sept. 13.	174	Miss Drum	1 adult and 1 child	8 packages.
	175	Mrs. S. Smith	1 adult and 4 children	26 "
	176	Mrs. N. Johnson	1 adult and 1 child	17 "
	177	Miss L. Buffington	2 adults	5 "
	178	Mrs. M. A. Miner	1 adult and 3 children	25 "
	179	J. G. Mitchell	2 adults, 1 child, and 2 servants.	40 "
	180	T. H. Wilson.	2 adults	21 packages and 1 cow.
	181	Mrs. M. Johnson.	3 adults and 3 children.	18 "
	182	Mrs. E. M. Tweely.	1 adult and 1 child	20 "
	183	Mrs. A. Robinson	1 adult.	4 "
	184	J. Wilson.	2 adults	9 "
	185	Mrs. M. Faulkner	1 adult.	13 "
	186	Mrs. Oslin.	3 adults	49 "
	187	W. C. Parker	2 adults	none.
	188	A. W. Weaver	2 adults, 4 children, 2 servants.	30 packages.
	189	W. Kenodle	2 adults and 5 children.	13 packages and 1 cow.
	190	J. L. Matthews.	1 adult.	2 packages.
	191	Mrs. J. Whaley	1 adult and 3 children	38 "
	192	E. Daniel.	2 adults and 6 children	19 "
	193	Mrs. H. B. Hutchens.	1 adult.	26 "
	194	Mrs. S. Robinson	1 adult.	39 "
	195	Mrs. C. Bell.	1 adult and 2 children	28 "
	196	J. Carmichael	2 adults	31 "
	197	W. Whitaker	3 adults and 5 children.	35 "
	198	George Kidd	2 adults	19 "
	199	Debby Wall.	1 adult, 2 children, 1 servant. . .	19 "
	200	L. L. Bird	1 adult and 2 servants.	10 "
	201	P. W. Carter.	1 adult.	8 "
	202	C. Emmet	1 adult.	25 "
	203	E. D. Graff	3 adults and 1 child	26 "
	204	J. A. Timmons.	2 adults and 3 children.	15 "
	205	Daniel Sanders	2 adults	5 "
	206	Mary Richards.	1 adult and 2 children	16 "
	207	Mrs. M. Shields.	2 adults and 2 children	10 "
	208	Mrs. J. Batterns.	3 adults and 1 child	13 "
	209	T. M. Jones	2 adults, 4 children, 6 servants.	70 "
	210	Mrs. M. Crawford.	1 adult and 1 child	19 "
	211	Mrs. M. C. Morris	1 adult and 6 children	48 "
	212	M. E. Grey	1 adult and 2 children	20 "
	213	E. Carmichael	1 adult and 5 children	12 "
	214	J. W. Rucker	2 adults	20 "
	215	Mrs. L. V. Rucker	2 adults	15 "
Sept. 14	216	S. A. Bridwell	1 adult.	7 "
	217	Mrs. M. Coker	1 adult and 2 children	16 "

(continued)

Official account of the people sent south, etc.—(CONTINUED.)

DATE.	NO.	NAME.	ADULTS, CHILDREN, AND SERVANTS.	BAGGAGE.
	218	Henry Buise	2 adults and 2 children	27 "
	219	Mrs. W. Rushton	1 adult and 7 children	39 "
	220	Mrs. Rose	1 adult, 2 children, 1 servant	4 "
	221	Jos. Herndon	2 adults and 3 children	18 "
	222	Mrs. Zimmerman	2 adults and 1 child	10 "
	223	J. L. Wilson	1 adult	1 package.
	224	W. C. Nelson	2 adults and 1 child	14 packages.
	225	C. Harden	2 adults	20 "
	226	J. C. Reves	3 adults	7 "
	227	Mrs. M. J. Corsey	1 adult and 4 children	6 "
	228	Alfred Lamb	5 adults and 1 child	17 "
	229	Mrs. M. Paine	3 adults and 7 children	19 "
	230	Mrs. T. H. Greyson	1 adult and 4 children	21 "
	231	Mrs. R. Nichols	2 adults	10 "
	232	Mrs. M. G. Wickner	1 adult and 1 child	6 "
	233	S. Hopper	3 adults and 4 children	43 packages and 1 cow.
	234	E. T. Hunnecut	2 adults, 4 children, 2 servants	43 packages.
	235	Mrs. N. Pulient	1 adult and 1 child	17 "
	236	Sarah Fry	1 adult, 2 children, 1 servant	17 "
	237	J. Veals	2 adults, 2 children, 2 servants	22 "
	238	C. A. Martin	1 adult	none.
	239	D. O. Driscoe	3 adults	37 packages.
	240	Jane Lofton	1 adult and 1 child	18 "
	241	Mrs. N. A. Bray	1 adult	29 "
	242	Mrs. E. J. Frederick	2 adults and 4 children	25 "
1864. Sept. 14.	243	Mrs. E. Leach	1 adult and 4 children	23 packages.
	244	H. H. Richards	2 adults, 1 child, 1 servant	18 "
	245	J. A. Rush	2 adults and 4 children	23 "
	246	James Lester	2 adults	22 "
	247	Mrs. N. Christean	1 adult	4 "
	247½	Mrs. W. A. Norris	1 adult	6 "
	248	Mrs. C. P. O'Keefe	1 adult, 2 children, 1 servant	45 "
	249	J. Caldwell	5 adults	50 "
	250	Mrs. B. F. Bennett	2 adults and 2 children	40 "
	251	Mrs. E. C. Smith	1 adult and 4 children	40 "
	252	G. Stewart	3 adults and 6 children	33 "
	253	Mrs. Cook	1 adult, 2 children, 2 servants	47 "
	254	Mrs. N. Simpson	5 adults	22 "
	255	Mrs. A. Smith	2 adults and 3 children	1 package.
	256	Wm. Christean	1 adult	none.
	257	Mrs. E. Adams	2 adults and 1 child	10 packages.
	258	J. C. Rogers	1 adult	2 "
	259	Mrs. S. E. Osborne	1 adult, 4 children, 1 servant	13 "
	260	Mrs. Collins	1 adult and 4 children	13 "
	261	Miss Reeves	1 adult	12 "
	262	J. J. Whitly	1 adult	1 package.
	263	Dr. Biggers	2 adults and 1 child	60 packages.
	264	A. F. Cuming	2 adults and 1 child	10 "

DATE.	NO.	NAME.	ADULTS, CHILDREN, AND SERVANTS.	BAGGAGE.
	265	G. A. Pilgrim.	3 adults and 2 children.	35 "
	266	W. M. Bryant	2 adults and 5 children.	25 "
	267	Jos. Coker	1 adult	10 "
	268	E. B. Bachus	3 adults and 6 children	40 "
	269	Mrs. N. Carroll	1 adult and 3 children	20 "
	270	Mrs. E. Grubb.	2 adults and 1 child	20 "
	271	Mrs. M. Heton	1 adult and 4 children	23 "
	272	Mrs. E. Aiken	1 adult and 1 child	13 "
	273	Mrs. N. A. Williams	1 adult and 4 children	18 "
	274	Mrs. M. Hartman	1 adult	7 "
	275	John Ealeman	2 adults, 1 child, 1 servant	37 "
	276	Mrs. L. Taylor	1 adult	15 "
	277	Mrs. S. A. Trout	3 adults and 4 children.	8 "
	278	W. A. Packett	2 adults, 3 children, 3 servants.	42 "
	279	Mrs. L. Ford	1 adult and 6 children	42 "
	280	N. McPherson.	2 adults and 4 children	17 "
	281	H. Wilson	2 adults and 7 children	10 "
	282			2 "
	283	Mrs. C. C. Rhodes	1 adult and 3 children	23 "
	284	Mrs. M. Combs	1 adult	12 "
	285	James Kile	2 adults and 1 child	19 "
	286	Mrs. A. F. Powers.	1 adult	16 "
	287	S. Hamilton	3 adults and 2 children.	16 "
	288	Henry Gaum.	2 adults and 5 children.	25 "
	289	W. F. Simpson	2 adults and 5 children.	17 "
	290	Mrs. Robinson	1 adult, 2 children, 1 servant. . .	20 "
	291	Mrs. Scruchen.	1 adult, 1 child, 1 servant	40 "
	292	Mrs. C. A. Jett.	2 adults and 4 children	30 "
	293	J. T. Coppage	2 adults and 5 children.	25 "
	294	J. H. Smith	2 adults and 2 children	56 "
	295	Mrs. L. Simpson	1 adult and 5 children	24 "
	296	Mrs. L. Williams	1 adult and 5 children	16 "
	297	Mrs. J. Berry	1 adult and 7 children	20 "
	298	Miss Cole	4 adults	18 "
	299	R. J. Maynard	2 adults and 4 children	41 "
	300	R. Faulkner	2 adults, 1 child, 1 servant	45 packages and 1 cow.
	301	D. Howard	2 adults and 3 children.	30 packages.
	302	A. H. Bramlett	1 adult	1 package.
	303	T. J. London.	2 adults and 4 children	26 packages.
	304	Mrs. E. Green.	2 adults and 2 children	50 "
	305	W. B. Webb	4 adults, 3 children, 1 servant. .	35 "
		J. E. Webb	2 adults	
	307	A. M. Johnson	3 adults	37 "
	308	J. A. Jett	1 adult	10 packages, wagon & horses.
	309	Mrs. R. Otto	2 adults	10 packages.
	310	W. R. Venable.	2 adults and 3 children.	25 "

(continued)

Official account of the people sent south, etc.—(CONTINUED.)

DATE.	NO.	NAME.	ADULTS, CHILDREN, AND SERVANTS.	BAGGAGE.
1864.				
Sept.16.	311	Mrs. L. Pain	1 adult and 1 child	10 packages.
	312	G. W. Croft	2 adults and 6 children	52 "
	313	E. W. Marsh	3 adults, 4 children, 1 servant	67 "
	314	Mrs. H. Ward	1 adult	3 "
	315	Mrs. General Bowen	2 adults, 3 children, 1 servant	26 "
		Mrs. Joyner		
	316	Mrs. Darst	1 adult and 2 children	5 "
	317	J. R. Crew	2 adults and 3 servants	15 "
	318	W. J. Ballard	1 adult	1 "
	319	P. Broadshaw	2 adults	10 packages.
	320	T. E. Jones	1 adult and 1 child	1 package.
	321	Mrs. E. Grey	1 adult	2 packages.
	322	Mrs. M. A. Hoosins	1 adult and 1 child	none.
	323	Mrs. E. Skinner	1 adult and 4 children	20 packages.
	324	G. O. Reed	1 adult	none.
	325	J. C. Johnson	2 adults and 2 children	25 packages.
	326	P. J. McCullough	1 adult	2 "
	327	G. Slaton	2 adults and 4 children	25 "
	328	Mrs. E. Warrick	2 adults and 6 children	32 "
	329	M. Solomen	2 adults	35 "
	330	Mrs. E. Buice	3 adults and 2 children	50 "
	331	Mrs. M. A. Haygood	2 adults	60 "
	332	Mrs. E. Roberts	1 adult	2 "
	333	Mrs. M. E. Martin	1 adult and 5 children	42 "
	334	F. P. Rice	2 adults	3 "
	335	Mrs. M. Denny	1 adult and 4 children	23 "
	336	A. J. Pouder	2 adults and 3 children	18 "
	337	Mrs. E. Leach	1 adult and 4 children	26 "
	338	W. C. Hueghton	3 adults and 5 children	40 "
	339	Sam Farrar	2 adults	17 "
Sept. 16.	340	Mrs. E. Sewell	7 adults and 1 servant	48 packages and 1 cow.
	341	J. J. Hunt	2 adults	2 packages.
	342	Mrs. McCormack	1 adult and 4 children	11 "
	343	Mrs. M. Davis	1 adult and 1 servant	41 "
	344	W. W. Roack	1 adult and 3 children	60 "
	345	T. C. Bradbury	3 adults	25 "
	346	M. E. Smith	1 adult and 2 children	35 "
	347	Mrs. R. P. Reid	1 adult and 3 children	30 "
	348	Mrs. L. Underwood	1 adult	1 package.
	349	Mrs. E. Curtis	1 adult and 6 children	60 packages.
	350	Mrs. J. Winship	1 adult	54 "
	351	J. L. Smith	5 adults and 1 servant	72 "
	352	Mrs. M. J. Johnson	4 adults	39 "
	353	P. Maddox	4 adults	50 "
	354	Miss Born	1 adult	25 "
	355	Mrs. E. C. Trail	4 adults	25 "
	356	Mrs. N. Loveless	1 adult	30 "
	357	Mrs. T. C. Jackson	1 adult and 1 child	39 "

DATE.	NO.	NAME.	ADULTS, CHILDREN, AND SERVANTS.	BAGGAGE.
	358	J. C. Rasboy	2 adults and 6 children	62 "
	359	J. M. Clark	2 adults and 3 servants	10 "
	360	J. M. Bramlett	2 adults, 4 children, 1 servant. .	20 "
	361	W. H. McMillen	1 adult	12 "
	362	C. Rinehart	2 adults and 3 children.	27 "
	363	E. M. Monday	2 adults and 4 children	48 packages and horse & buggy.
	364	Mrs. F. W. Johnson	1 adult, 5 children, 2 servants . .	35 packages.
	365	Mrs. E. Phillips	1 adult and 1 child	23 "
	366	B. Mullegan	3 adults	12 "
	367	Mrs. M. Owens	2 adults and 6 children	30 packages and 1 cow.
	368	Mrs. A. C. Trehelem.	3 adults and 1 child	11 packages.
	369	Wm. Garvin	2 adults and 4 children	15 "
	370	Mrs. C. C. Pain	1 adult and 2 children	11 "
	371	Mrs. M. Tubb.	1 adult and 1 servant	10 "
	372	R. Powens.	1 adult and 3 children	10 packages and "negro."
	373	Mrs. J. Wilson	1 adult	3 packages.
	374	Mrs. E. Farr	1 adult and 5 children	20 "
	375	B. J. Austin.	2 adults, 1 child, 1 servant	40 "
	376	Mrs. J. Hall	1 adult	20 "
	377	Mrs. S. Sumerlin	1 adult and 2 children	25 "
	378	J. E. Buchanan	2 adults and 5 children.	none.
1864. Sept. 16.	379	Mrs. M. Merritt	1 adult	10 packages.
	380	Mrs. Wilson	1 adult	5 "
	381	S. N. Biggers	1 adult	25 "
	382	Miss M. Burke	1 adult	20 "
	383	J. Ormend	1 adult	1 package.
	384	Miss S. Ament	2 adults and 4 children	20 packages.
	385	Mrs. Emma Rince	2 adults and 2 children	10 "
	386	T. P. Fleming	3 adults and 3 servants	30 "
	387	Mrs. N. Ray	1 adult and 5 children	20 "
	388	Mrs. Coleman	1 and 4 children	25 "
	389	Mrs. A. G. Ware.	1 adult	2 "
	390	Mrs. F. Glave	1 adult	1 package.
	391	Mrs. J. R. Wilson	1 adult	2 packages.
	392	Mrs. N. Thompson	2 adults	20 "
	393	T. S. Denney	2 adults and 1 child	30 "
	394	Mrs. A. Manion	1 adult	36 "
	395	J. M. Calhoun	1 adult and 4 servants	30 "
	396	E. J. Clark.	1 adult	1 package.
	397	J. F. Trout	2 adults and 5 children.	60 packages.
	398	Mrs. Solomon	1 adult	2 "
	399	M. A. McCaian	1 adult and 2 children	2 "
	400	Mrs. N. Wilder	2 adults	58 "
	401	Mrs. M. D. Wormack	1 adult and 3 children	22 "
	402	Mrs. C. Kill	1 adult	17 "
	403	Mrs. E. Sheirs.	1 adult and 3 children	18 "

(continued)

Official account of the people sent south, etc.—(CONTINUED.)

DATE.	NO.	NAME.	ADULTS, CHILDREN, AND SERVANTS.	BAGGAGE.
	404	J. Langston	3 adults and 4 children	50 "
	405	J. J. Jenkins	2 adults and 7 children	55 "
	406	Mrs. F. W. Flynn	2 adults, 3 children, 1 servant.	20 "
	407	Mrs. C. Flynn	1 adult	10 "
	408	Mrs. C. M. Winn	1 adult, 2 children, 1 servant	30 "
	409	Mrs. C. Caldwell	4 adults and 9 children	20 packages and 1 cow
	410	W. N. Kirkpatrick	2 adults and 3 children	40 packages.
	411	Mrs. F. Glave	1 adult	1 package.
	412	Mrs. M. Maddox	1 adult, 5 children, 1 servant	20 packages.
	413	A. F. Morrison	2 adults and 4 children	10 "
	414	E. Monday	2 adults and 6 children	50 packages (did not go).
	415	A. J. Blackham	1 adult	50 packages.
	416	Mrs. N. D. Wood	2 adults	25 "
Sept. 18.	417	Mrs. C. Wood	2 adults	20 "
	418	Mrs. L. Cox	1 adult	none.
	419	Frank Berry	2 adults and 2 children	50 packages.
	420	James Turner	1 adult	1 package.
	421	Miss. E. Simpson	1 adult	3 packages.
	422	A. D. Westmoreland	1 adult and 1 servant	20 "
	423	Mrs. L. Ross	1 adult, 3 children, 1 servant	40 "
	424	Mrs. Morgan	2 adults and 10 children	12 "
	425	Mrs. M. Holynd	2 adults	100 "
	426	Mrs. M. E. Clements	1 adult, 8 children, 1 servant	50 "
	427	J. B. Colen	1 adult	1 package.
	428	Mrs. L. L. Grant	1 adult, 2 children, 1 servant	50 packages.
	429	F. M. Jeffrys	1 adult	none.
	430	J. J. Ford	1 adult	none.
	431	Mrs. N. McDaniel	1 adult and 5 children	10 packages.
	432	E. Kennedy	2 adults, 1 child, 2 servants	35 "
	433	Mrs. Kennedy	3 adults	22 "
	434	Mrs. V. Williams	1 adult and 4 children	20 "
	435	W. Terry	1 adult	20 "
	436	Mrs. Dolman	1 adult and 6 children	10 "
	437	Mrs. Robbins	1 adult and 1 child	3 "
	438	Miss. E. Johns	2 adults	10 "
	439	Mrs. Gilmore	1 adult and 2 children	20 "
	440	G. M. Barry	1 adult	none.
Sept. 20.	441	Mrs. F. Carr	1 adult	10 packages.
	442	Mrs. J. Powell	1 adult and 3 children	12 "
	(A)	Mrs. J. Dudley	1 adult	3 "
	(B)	Mrs. A. Knight	1 adult and 3 children	4 "
	(C)	Mrs. K. Bouls Mrs. M. Bouls	2 adults	4
	(D)	R. A. Davis	1 adult	none.

Official account of the people sent south, etc.—(CONCLUDED.)

RECAPITULATION.

Adults	705	Packages of baggage	8,842
Children	860	Horses	9
Servants	86	Cows	19
Total	1,651	Calves	6
		Wagons	2
		Drays	2
		Carriages	1
		Buggies	1

Respectfully submitted:

(Signed) William G. Le Duc,

Lieutenant-Colonel and Chief Quartermaster Twentieth Army Corps.

Statement showing the organizations actually participating in the movement on Atlanta, Georgia, under General W. T. Sherman, in May, 1864.

ARMY OF THE CUMBERLAND.

MAJOR-GENERAL GEORGE H. THOMAS.

Fourth Army Corps.—Major-General O. O. Howard, *commanding.*

FIRST DIVISION.

Major-General D. S. Stanley.

First Brigade.	Second Brigade.	Third Brigade.
Brigadier-General Charles Cruft.	*Brig.-General W. C. Whitaker.*	*Colonel William Grose.*
1st Kentucky Infantry.	96th Illinois Infantry.	59th Illinois Infantry.
2d Kentucky Infantry.	115th Illinois Infantry.	75th Illinois Infantry.
90th Ohio Infantry.	35th Indiana Infantry.	80th Illinois Infantry.
101st Ohio Infantry.	84th Indiana Infantry.	84th Illinois Infantry.
31st Indiana Infantry.	40th Ohio Infantry.	9th Indiana Infantry.
81st Indiana Infantry.	51st Ohio Infantry.	30th Indiana Infantry.
21st Illinois Infantry.	99th Ohio Infantry.	36th Indiana Infantry.
38th Illinois Infantry.	21st Kentucky Infantry.	77th Pennsylvania Infantry.

Artillery.

5th Indiana Battery Light Artillery; Independent Battery B, Pennsylvania Light Artillery.

SECOND DIVISION.

Major-General JOHN NEWTON.

First Brigade.

Brigadier-General N. Kimball.

2d Missouri Infantry.
15th Missouri Infantry.
24th Wisconsin Infantry.
36th Illinois Infantry.
44th Illinois Infantry.
73d Illinois Infantry.
74th Illinois Infantry.
88th Illinois Infantry.

Second Brigade.

Brig.- General G. D. Wagner.

40th Indiana Infantry.
57th Indiana Infantry.
26th Ohio Infantry.
97th Ohio Infantry.
100th Illinois Infantry.
28th Kentucky Infantry.

Third Brigade.

Brig.-General C. G. Harker.

3d Kentucky Infantry.
64th Ohio Infantry.
65th Ohio Infantry.
125th Ohio Infantry.
22d Illinois Infantry.
27th Illinois Infantry.
42d Illinois Infantry.
51st Illinois Infantry.
79th Illinois Infantry.

Artillery.

M, 1st Illinois Light Artillery; A, Ohio Light Artillery.

THIRD DIVISION.

Brigadier-General T. J. WOOD.

First Brigade.

Colonel W. H. Gibson.

8th Kansas Infantry.
15th Wisconsin Infantry.
15th Ohio Infantry.
49th Ohio Infantry.
32d Indiana Infantry.
25th Illinois Infantry.
35th Illinois Infantry.
89th Illinois Infantry.

Second Brigade.

Brig.-General W. B. Hazen

1st Ohio Infantry.
6th Ohio Infantry.
41st Ohio Infantry.
93d Ohio Infantry.
124th Ohio Infantry.
5th Kentucky Infantry.
6th Kentucky Infantry.
23d Kentucky Infantry.
6th Indiana Infantry.

Third Brigade.

Colonel Fred Knefler.

9th Kentucky Infantry.
17th Kentucky Infantry.
13th Ohio Infantry.
19th Ohio Infantry.
59th Ohio Infantry.
79th Indiana Infantry.
86th Indiana Infantry.

Artillery.

6th Battery Ohio Light Artillery; Bridge's Battery, Illinois Light Artillery.

Fourteenth Army Corps.—Major-General JOHN. M. PALMER, commanding.

FIRST DIVISION.

Brigadier-General R. W. JOHNSON.

First Brigade.

Brigadier-General W. P. Carlin.

21st Wisconsin Infantry.
10th Wisconsin Infantry

Second Brigade.

Brigadier-General J. H. King.

1st Bat. 15th U.S. Infantry.
2d Bat. 15th U.S. Infantry.

Third Brigade.

Colonel B. F. Scribner.

78th Pennsylvania Infant'y.
79th Pennsylvania Infant'y.

33d Ohio Infantry.
94th Ohio Infantry.
2d Ohio Infantry.
42d Indiana Infantry.
88th Indiana Infantry.
104th Illinois Infantry.
15th Kentucky Infantry.

1st Bat. 16th U.S. Infantry.
2d Bat. 16th U.S. Infantry.
1st Bat. 18th U.S. Infantry.
2d Bat. 18th U.S. Infantry.
1st Bat. 19th. U.S. Infantry.
69th Ohio Infantry.
11th Michigan Infantry.

21st Ohio Infantry.
74th Ohio Infantry.
37th Indiana Infantry.
1st Wisconsin Infantry.
38th Indiana Infantry.

Artillery.

C, 1st Illinois Light Artillery; I, 1st Ohio Light Artillery.

SECOND DIVISION.

Brigadier-General J. C. DAVIS.

First Brigade.

Brigadier-General J. D. Morgan.

10th Illinois Infantry.
16th Illinois Infantry.
60th Illinois Infantry.
10th Michigan Infantry.
14th Michigan Infantry.

Second Brigade.

Colonel J. G. Mitchell.

121st Ohio Infantry.
113th Ohio Infantry.
98th Ohio Infantry.
108th Ohio Infantry.
3d Ohio Infantry.
78th Illinois Infantry.
34th Illinois Infantry.

Third Brigade.

Colonel Daniel McCook.

52d Ohio Infantry.
85th Illinois Infantry.
86th Illinois Infantry.
110th Illinois Infantry.
125th Illinois Infantry.
22d Indiana Infantry.

Artillery.

I, 2d Illinois Light Artillery; 5th Wisconsin Battery.

THIRD DIVISION.

Brigadier-General ABSALOM BAIRD.

First Brigade.

Brigadier-General J. B. Turchin.

11th Ohio Infantry.
17th Ohio Infantry.
31st Ohio Infantry.
89th Ohio Infantry.
92d Ohio Infantry.
82d Indiana Infantry.
19th Illinois Infantry.
24th Illinois Infantry.

Second Brigade.

Colonel F. Van Derveer.

35th Ohio Infantry.
2d Minnesota Infantry.
9th Ohio Infantry.
87th Indiana Infantry.
105th Ohio Infantry.
101st Indiana Infantry.
75th Indiana Infantry.

Third Brigade.

Colonel George P. Este.

4th Kentucky Infantry.
10th Kentucky Infantry.
18th Kentucky Infantry.
10th Indiana Infantry.
74th Indiana Infantry.
14th Ohio Infantry.
38th Ohio Infantry.

Artillery.

7th Indiana Battery; 19th Indiana Battery.

Twentieth Army Corps.—Major-General JOSEPH HOOKER, *commanding.*

Escort. K, 15th Illinois Cavalry.

FIRST DIVISION.

Brigadier-General A. S. WILLIAMS.

First Brigade.
Brigadier-General J. F. Knipe.
123d New York Infantry.
3d Maryland Infantry (det.)
141st New York Infantry.
5th Connecticut Infantry.
46th Pennsylvania Infantry.

Second Brigade.
Brigadier-General T. H. Ruger.
2d Massachusetts Infantry.
3d Wisconsin Infantry.
107th New York Infantry.
150th New York Infantry.
27th Indiana Infantry.
13th New Jersey Infantry.

Third Brigade.
Colonel J. S. Robinson.
82d Ohio Infantry.
61st Ohio Infantry.
143d New York Infantry.
45th New York Infantry.
82d Illinois Infantry.
101st Illinois Infantry.

Artillery.
I and M, 1st New York Artillery.

SECOND DIVISION.

Brigadier-General JOHN W. GEARY.

First Brigade.
Colonel Charles Candy.
5th Ohio Infantry.
7th Ohio Infantry.
29th Ohio Infantry.
66th Ohio Infantry.
28th Pennsylvania Infantry.
147th Pennsylvania Infan'y.

Second Brigade.
Colonel J. F. Lockman.
73d Pennsylvania Infantry.
109th Pennsylva. Infantry.
33d New Jersey Infantry.
119th New York Infantry.
134th New York Infantry.
154th New York Infantry.

Third Brigade.
Colonel David Ireland.
60th New York Infantry.
78th New York Infantry.
102d New York Infantry.
137th New York Infantry.
149th New York Infantry.
29th Pennsylvania Infant'y.
111th Pennsylvania Infan'y.

Artillery.
13th New York Battery—Independent; E, Pennsylvania Light Artillery.

THIRD DIVISION.

Major-General DANIEL BUTTERFIELD.

First Brigade.
Brigadier-General W. T. Ward.
70th Indiana Infantry.
102d Illinois Infantry.
105th Illinois Infantry.
129th Illinois Infantry.
79th Ohio Infantry.

Second Brigade.
Colonel John Coburn.
33d Indiana Infantry.
85th Indiana Infantry.
19th Michigan Infantry.
22d Wisconsin Infantry.

Third Brigade.
Colonel James Wood, Jr.
136th New York Infantry.
33d Massachusetts Infan'y.
55th Ohio Infantry.
73d Ohio Infantry.
26th Wisconsin Infantry.
20th Connecticut Infantry.

Artillery.

C, 1st Ohio Light Artillery; I, 1st Michigan Light Artillery.

Cavalry Corps.—Brigadier-General W. L. Elliott.

FIRST DIVISION.

Colonel E. M. McCook.

First Brigade.

Colonel Joseph B. Dorr.

2d Michigan Cavalry.
8th Iowa Cavalry.
1st East Tennessee Cavalry.
18th Indiana Battery.

Second Brigade.

Colonel O. H. La Grange.

1st Wisconsin Cavalry.
2d Indiana Cavalry.
4th Indiana Cavalry.

SECOND DIVISION.

Brigadier-General Kenner Garrard.

First Brigade.

Colonel R. H. G. Minty.

4th U.S. Cavalry.
4th Michigan Cavalry.
7th Pennsylvania Cavalry.

Second Brigade.

Colonel Eli Long.

1st Ohio Cavalry.
3d Ohio Cavalry.
4th Ohio Cavalry.

Third Brigade.

Colonel John T. Wilder.

17th Indiana Mounted Infantry.
72d Indiana Mounted Infantry.
98th Illinois Mounted Infantry.
123 Illinois Mounted Infantry.

Chicago Board of Trade Battery.

THIRD DIVISION.

Brigadier-General Judson Kilpatrick.

First Brigade.

Colonel Charles C. Smith.

5th Iowa Cavalry.
3d Indiana Cavalry.
9th Pennsylvania Cavalry.

Second Brigade.

Colonel E. H. Murray.

10th Ohio Cavalry.
2d Kentucky Cavalry.
8th Indiana Cavalry.

Third Brigade.

92d Illinois M'nted Infantry.
3d Kentucky Cavalry.
5th Kentucky Cavalry.

Artillery.

10th Wisconsin Battery.

Reserve Brigade.

Colonel H. Le Favour.
9th Michigan Infantry.
22d Michigan Infantry.

Pioneer Brigade.

Colonel George P. Buell.
58th Indiana Infantry.
Pontoon Battalion.

Unassigned Artillery.

11th Indiana Battery.

ARMY OF THE TENNESEE.

MAJOR-GENERAL JAMES B. MCPHERSON.

Fifteenth Army Corps.—Major-General JOHN A. LOGAN, *commanding.*

FIRST DIVISION.

Brigadier-General P. J. OSTERHAUS.

First Brigade.

Brigadier-General C. R. Woods.

76th Ohio Infantry.
26th Iowa Infantry.
30th Iowa Infantry.
27th Missouri Infantry.

Second Brigade.

Colonel J. A. Williamson.

4th Iowa Infantry.
9th Iowa Infantry.
25th Iowa Infantry.
31st Iowa Infantry.

Third Brigade.

Colonel H. Wangelin.

3d Missouri Infantry.
12th Missouri Infantry.
17th Missouri Infantry.
29th Missouri Infantry.
31st Missouri Infantry.
32d Missouri Infantry.

Artillery.

F, 2d Missouri Light Artillery; 4th Ohio Battery.

SECOND DIVISION.

Brigadier-General MORGAN L. SMITH.

First Brigade.

Brigadier-General Giles A. Smith.

6th Missouri Infantry.
8th Missouri Infantry.
55th Illinois Infantry.
111th Illinois Infantry.
127th Illinois Infantry.
57th Ohio Infantry.

Second Brigade.

Brigadier-General J. A. J. Lightburn.

30th Ohio Infantry.
37th Ohio Infantry.
47th Ohio Infantry.
53d Ohio Infantry.
54th Ohio Infantry.
83d Indiana Infantry.
4th West Virginia Infantry.

Artillery.

A, B, and H, 1st Illinois Light Artillery.

FOURTH DIVISION.

Brigadier-General William Harrow.

First Brigade.

Colonel R. Williams.

12th Indiana Infantry.
100th Indiana Infantry.
26th Illinois Infantry.
90th Illinois Infantry.
97th Indiana Infantry.

Second Brigade.

Brig.-General John M. Corse

46th Ohio Infantry.
6th Iowa Infantry.
40th Illinois Infantry.
103d Illinois Infantry.

Third Brigade.

Colonel John M. Oliver.

15th Michigan Infantry.
70th Ohio Infantry.
48th Illinois Infantry.
99th Indiana Infantry.

Artillery.

1st Iowa Battery; F, 1st Illinois Light Artillery.

Sixteenth Army Corps (Left Wing).—Brigadier-General G. M. Dodge, *commanding.*

SECOND DIVISION.

Brigadier-General T. W. Sweeny.

First Brigade.

Colonel E. W. Rice.

2d Iowa Infantry.
7th Iowa Infantry.
52d Illinois Infantry.
66th Indiana Infantry.

Second Brigade.

Colonel Augustus Mersy.

9th Illinois Infantry.
12th Illinois Infantry.
66th Illinois Infantry.
81st Ohio Infantry.

Third Brigade.

Colonel M. M. Bane.

7th Illinois Infantry.
50th Illinois Infantry.
57th Illinois Infantry.
39th Iowa Infantry.

Artillery.

H, 1st Missouri Light Artillery; B, 1st Michigan Light Artillery.

FOURTH DIVISION.

Brigadier-General James C. Veatch.

First Brigade.

Brigadier-General J. W. Fuller.

18th Missouri Infantry.
27th Ohio Infantry.
39th Ohio Infantry.
64th Illinois Infantry.

Second Brigade.

Colonel John W. Sprague.

25th Wisconsin Infantry.
35th New Jersey Infantry.
43d Ohio Infantry.
63d Ohio Infantry.

Cavalry.

1st Alabama Cavalry.

Artillery.

14th Ohio Battery; C, 1st Michigan, and F, 2d U.S. Artillery.

**Seventeenth Army Corps.—Major-General* F. P. Blair, *Jr., commanding.*

THIRD DIVISION.

Brigadier-General M. D. LEGGETT.

First Brigade.	Second Brigade.	Third Brigade.
Brigadier-General M. F. Force.	*Colonel R. K. Scott.*	*Colonel A. G. Molloy.*
20th Illinois Infantry.	20th Ohio Infantry.	17th Wisconsin Infantry.
30th Illinois Infantry.	32d Ohio Infantry.	14th Wisconsin Infantry.
31st Illinois Infantry.	68th Ohio Infantry. Det's.	81st Illinois Infantry.
45th Illinois Infantry.	78th Ohio Infantry.	95th Illinois Infantry.
16th Wisconsin Infantry.		
* Joined in June, 1864.		

Artillery.

D, 1st Illinois; H, 1st Michigan and 3d Ohio Battery.

FOURTH DIVISION.

Brigadier-General W. Q. GRESHAM.

First Brigade.	Second Brigade.	Third Brigade.
Colonel W. S. Sanderson.	*Colonel J. C. Rogers.*	*Colonel William Hall.*
3d Iowa Infantry.	14th Illinois Infantry.	11th Iowa Infantry.
12th Wisconsin Infantry.	15th Illinois Infantry.	13th Iowa Infantry.
23d Indiana Infantry.	41st Illinois Infantry.	15th Iowa Infantry.
32d Illinois Infantry.	53d Illinois Infantry.	16th Iowa Infantry.
53d Indiana Infantry.	33d Wisconsin Infantry.	

Cavalry.

G, 11th Illinois Cavalry.

Artillery.

10th and 15th Ohio Batteries; 1st Minnesota Battery; C, 1st Missouri, and F 2d

Illinois Batteries.

Army of the Ohio (Twenty-third Army Corps).—Major-General J. M. SCHOFIELD, commanding.

FIRST DIVISION.

Brigadier-General A. P. HOVEY.

First Brigade.	Second Brigade.
Colonel Richard Baxter.	*Colonel J. C. McQuiston.*
120th Indiana Infantry.	123d Indiana Infantry.
124th Indiana Infantry.	129th Indiana Infantry.
128th Indiana Infantry.	130th Indiana Infantry.

Artillery.

23d and 24th Indiana Batteries.

SECOND DIVISION.

Brigadier-General M. S. Hascall.

First Brigade.

Brigadier-General N. C. McLean.

25th Michigan Infantry.
80th Indiana Infantry.
13th Kentucky Infantry.
3d Tennessee Infantry.
6th Tennessee Infantry.

Second Brigade.

Colonel John A. Bond.

23d Michigan Infantry.
111th Ohio Infantry.
107th Illinois Infantry.
118th Ohio Infantry.

Artillery.

19th Ohio Battery, and F, 1st Michigan Light Artillery.

THIRD DIVISION.

Brigadier-General J. D. Cox.

First Brigade.

Colonel J. W. Reilly.

100th Ohio Infantry.
104th Ohio Infantry.
112th Illinois Infantry.
16th Kentucky Infantry.
8th Tennessee Infantry.

Second Brigade.

Brigadier-General M. D. Manson.

65th Indiana Infantry.
63d Indiana Infantry.
24th Kentucky Infantry.
5th Tennessee Infantry.
103d Ohio Infantry.

Artillery.

D, 1st Ohio and 15th Indiana Battery.

CAVALRY DIVISION.

Major-General George Stoneman.

First Brigade.

Colonel C. D. Pannabaker.

1st Kentucky Cavalry.
11th Kentucky Cavalry.
8th Michigan Cavalry.
6th Indiana Cavalry.
12th Kentucky Cavalry.
16th Illinois Cavalry.

Second Brigade.

Colonel Israel Garrard.

7th Ohio Cavalry.
9th Michigan Cavalry.
5th Indiana Cavalry.
16th Kentucky Cavalry.

List of regiments, etc., belonging to the Armies of the Cumberland, Tennessee, and Ohio, left in Tennessee, Kentucky, Alabama, and Mississippi, when General W. T. Sherman commenced his advance on Atlanta, Georgia, in May, 1864.

ARMY OF THE CUMBERLAND.

At Wauhatchie.

Third Brigade, First Cavalry Division—Col. L. D. Watkins, *commanding.*

4th, 5th, and 6th Kentucky Cavalry.

At Nashville, Tullahoma, and Gallatin, Tennessee.

Fourth Cavalry Division—Brigadier-General A. C. Gillem, *commanding.*

First Brigade. *(Nashville.)*	Second Brigade. *(Tullahoma.)*	Third Brigade. *(Gallatin.)*
Lieut.-Col. D. G. Thornburgh.	Lieut.-Colonel George Spalding.	Colonel J. K. Miller.
2d Tennessee Cavalry.	5th Tennessee Cavalry.	8th Tennessee Cavalry.
3d Tennessee Cavalry.	11th Tennessee Cavalry.	9th Tennessee Cavalry.
4th Tennessee Cavalry.	12th Tennessee Cavalry.	13th Tennessee Cavalry.
	A, 1st Tennessee Light Artillery.	

District of Nashville—General L. H. Rousseau, *commanding.*

First Brigade, Fourth Division, Twentieth Corps.

Brigadier-General R. S. Granger.

At Nashville.

18th Michigan Infantry.
102d Ohio Infantry.
13th Wisconsin Infantry.
10th Tennessee Infantry.
73d Indiana Infantry.

Unassigned Regiments, Fourth Division, Twentieth Corps.

At Murfreesboro, Tennessee, 115th Ohio Infantry.
At Duck River Bridge, Tennessee, 31st Wisconsin Infantry.
At McMinnville, Tennessee, 23d Missouri Infantry.
At Clarksville, Tennessee, 83d Illinois Infantry (Right Wing).
At Fort Donelson, Tennessee, 83d Illinois Infantry (Left Wing).
At Elk River Bridge, Tennessee, 71st Ohio Infantry.
At Bridgeport, Alabama, 58th and 68th New York, 75th Pennsylvania and 106th Ohio Infantry, 9th Ohio and 20th Indiana Batteries.

Post Forces, Nashville, Tennessee.

Brigadier-General R. S. Granger.

15th United States Colored Infantry.
17th United States Colored Infantry.
15th Pennsylvania Cavalry.
8th Indiana Cavalry.

Garrison Artillery.

C, 1st Tennessee Light Artillery.
D, 1st Tennessee Light Artillery.
G, 1st Tennessee Light Artillery.
E, 1st Michigan Light Artillery.
I, 4th United States Light Artillery.
12th Indiana Light Artillery.

22d Indiana Battery.
M, 2d Illinois Light Artillery.
I, 1st Missouri Light Artillery.
} Temporarily at post.

Artillery Reserve, D. C.

F, 4th United States Artillery.
G, 4th United States Artillery.
H, 4th United States Artillery.
M, 4th United States Artillery.
H, 5th United States Artillery.
K, 5th United States Artillery.
F, 1st Ohio Artillery.
G, 1st Ohio Artillery.
M, 1st Ohio Artillery.
1st Kentucky Battery.
18th Ohio Battery.

POST FORCES, FORT DONELSON, TENNESSEE.

Lieutenant-Colonel E. C. Brott, *commanding.*

C, 2d Illinois Light Artillery.

POST FORCES, CLARKSVILLE, TENNESSEE.

Colonel A. A. Smith, *commanding.*

H, 2d Illinois Light Artillery.

POST FORCES, GALLATIN, TENNESSEE.

Lieutenant-Colonel A. I. Brown, *commanding.*

13th Indiana Battery.

POST FORCES, COLUMBIA, TENNESSEE.

Colonel — Funkhouser, *commanding.*

21st Indiana Battery.

POST FORCES, MURFREESBORO, TENNESSEE.

Brigadier-General H. P. Van Cleve, *commanding.*

D, 1st Michigan Artillery.
12th Ohio Battery.
8th Wisconsin Battery.

POST FORCES, BRIDGEPORT, ALABAMA.

Colonel W. Krzyzanowski, *commanding.*

133d Indiana Infantry.

TROOPS ON THE NASHVILLE & NORTHWESTERN RAILROAD.

Brigadier-General A. C. Gillem, *commanding.*

12th United States Colored Infantry. 1st Missouri Engineers and Mechanics.
13th United States Colored Infantry. 1st Kansas Battery.

GARRISON ARTILLERY, BRIDGEPORT, ALABAMA.

Major W. Edgarton, *commanding.*

B and E, 1st Ohio Light Artillery.

ENGINEER BRIGADE, CHATTANOOGA, TENNESSEE.

Colonel W. B. McCreery, *commanding.*

18th Ohio Infantry.
13th Michigan Infantry.
21st Michigan Infantry.
22d Michigan Infantry.

PIONEER BRIGADE.

Colonel George P. Buell, *commanding.*

58th Indiana Infantry (with army in the field).
1st Battalion Pioneers (at Chattanooga).
2d Battalion Pioneers (at Chattanooga).
Pontoon Battalion (with army in the field).

POST FORCES, CHATTANOOGA, TENNESSEE.

Brigadier-General J. B. Steedman, *commanding.*

15th Indiana Infantry.
29th Indiana Infantry.
44th Indiana Infantry.
51st Indiana Infantry.
68th Indiana Infantry.
3d Ohio Infantry.
24th Ohio Infantry.
8th Kentucky Infantry.

GARRISON ARTILLERY, CHATTANOOGA, TENNESSEE.

Major C. S. Cotter, *commanding.*

20th Ohio Battery.
K, 1st Michigan Light Artillery.
C, 1st Wisconsin Heavy Artillery.
A, 1st Michigan Light Artillery.
3d Wisconsin Battery.
G, 1st Missouri Light Artillery.
8th Indiana Battery.
4th Indiana Battery.

WESTERN RESERVE CORPS, NASHVILLE, TENNESSEE.

Major A. W. Gazzam, *commanding.*

139th, 148th, 149th, 150th, 151st, 152d, 153d, 154th, 155th, 160th, and 165th Co's.

SIGNAL CORPS.

Captain Charles R. Case, *Chief Signal-Officer.*

ARMY OF THE TENNESSEE.

Third Division, Fifteenth Army Corps—Brigadier-General JOHN E. SMITH, *commanding.*

First Brigade.
(At Huntsville, Alabama).
Colonel J. J. Alexander.
59th Indiana Infantry.
48th Indiana Infantry.
4th Minnesota Infantry.
18th Wisconsin Infantry.
63d Illinois Infantry.
Cavalry.
5th Ohio Cavalry.
F, 4th Missouri Cavalry.

Second Brigade.
(At Larkinsville, Alabama).
Colonel G. B. Raum.
56th Illinois Infantry.
17th Iowa Infantry.
10th Missouri Infantry.
80th Ohio Infantry.
E, 24th Missouri Infantry.

Third Brigade.
(At Decatur, Alabama).
Colonel B. D. Dean.
26th Missouri Infantry.
5th Iowa Infantry.
10th Iowa Infantry.
93d Illinois Infantry.

Artillery.
D, 1st Missouri Light Artillery.
6th Wisconsin Battery.
12th Wisconsin Battery.

Third Brigade, Fourth Division, Sixteenth Army Corps—Colonel JOHN H. HOWE, *commanding.*

AT DECATUR, ALABAMA.

32d Wisconsin Infantry.
17th New York Infantry.
25th Indiana Infantry.
D, 2d Illinois Light Artillery.

First Division, Sixteenth Army Corps—Brigadier-General J. A. MOWER, *commanding.*

First Brigade.
(At Memphis.)
Colonel W. L. McMillen.
72d Ohio Infantry.
95th Ohio Infantry.
114th Illinois Infantry.
93d Indiana Infantry.
E, 1st Illinois Light Art'y.

Second Brigade.
(At Vicksburg.)
Colonel L. B. Hubbard.
11th Missouri Infantry.
47th Illinois Infantry.
8th Wisconsin Infantry.
5th Minnesota Infantry.
2d Iowa Battery.

Third Brigade.
(At Vicksburg.)
Colonel S. G. Hill.
8th Iowa Infantry.
12th Iowa Infantry.
33d Missouri Infantry.
35th Iowa Infantry.
6th Indiana Battery.

Third Division, Sixteenth Army Corps—Colonel DAVID MOORE, *com'ding.*

AT VICKSBURG, MISSISSIPPI.

First Brigade.
Colonel C. D. Murray.
89th Indiana Infantry.

Second Brigade.
Colonel W. T. Shaw.
14th Iowa Infantry.

Third Brigade.
Colonel E. H. Wolfe.
117th Illinois Infantry.

119th Illinois Infantry.
58th Illinois Infantry.
21st Missouri Infantry.
9th Indiana Battery.

27th Iowa Infantry.
32d Iowa Infantry.
24th Missouri Infantry.
3d Indiana Battery.

178th New York Infantry.
52d Indiana Infantry.
49th Illinois Infantry.

District of West Tennessee—Major-General C. C. Washburne, *command'g.*

CAVALRY DIVISION, SIXTEENTH ARMY CORPS.

Brigadier-General B. H. Grierson, *commanding.*

First Brigade.
(At White's Station, Tennessee.)
Colonel George E. Waring
4th Missouri Cavalry.
2d New Jersey Cavalry.
19th Pennsylvania Cavalry.
7th Indiana Cavalry.
6th Tennessee Cavalry.

Second Brigade.
(At Memphis, Tennessee.)
Colonel E. F. Winslow.
4th Iowa Cavalry.
3d Iowa Cavalry.
10th Missouri Cavalry.
K, 1st Illinois Light Art'y.

Third Brigade.
(At Memphis, Tennessee.)
Lieutenant-Colonel H. B. Burgh.
9th Illinois Cavalry.
6th Illinois Cavalry.
3d Illinois Cavalry.

District of Memphis—Brigadier-General R. P. Buckland, *commanding.*

113th Illinois Infantry.
108th Illinois Infantry.
120th Illinois Infantry.
11th Missouri Infantry.
59th U. S. Colored Inf'try.

61st U. S. Colored Inf'try.
55th U. S. Colored Inf'try.
63d U. S. Col'd (det.) Inf'y.
14th Indiana Battery.
F, 2d U. S. Col'd L't Art'y.

3d U. S. Col'd Heavy Art'y.
7th U. S. Col'd Heavy Art'y.
G, 1st Illinois Light Artil'y.
B, 2d Illinois Light Artil'y.
7th Wisconsin Battery.

District of Columbus—Brigadier-General Henry Prince, *commanding.*

122d Illinois Infantry.
34th New Jersey Infantry.
10th Minnesota Infantry.

4th U. S. Col'd Heavy Ar'y.
C, 2d Illinois Light Artil'y.
7th Minnesota Infantry.

8th U. S. Col'd Heavy Art'y.
7th Tennessee Cav'y (det.)

District of Vicksburg—Major-General H. W. Slocum, *commanding.*

FIRST DIVISION, SEVENTEENTH ARMY CORPS.

Brigadier-General E. S. Dennis, *commanding.*

First Brigade.
Colonel F. A. Starring.
30th Missouri Infantry.
58th Ohio Infantry.
72d Illinois Infantry.
1st Kansas Infantry.

Second Brigade.
Colonel J. H. Coates.
11th Illinois Infantry.

Second Brigade (4th Division).
Colonel B. Dornblaser.
46th Illinois Infantry.
76th Illinois Infantry.

Artillery.
7th Ohio Battery.
L, 2d Illinois Light Artillery.
M, 1st Missouri Light Artillery.

First Division, U.S. Colored Troops—Brigadier-General J. P. Hawkins, *commanding.*

First Brigade.	Second Brigade.	United States Forces.
(Vicksburg, Mississippi.)	*(Vicksburg, Mississippi.)*	*(Goodrich's Landing, Louisiana.)*
Brigadier-General J. F. Shepard.	Colonel H. Schofield.	Colonel A. W. Webber.
48th U. S. Colored Inf'y.	47th U. S. Colored Inf'y.	51st U. S. Colored Infantry.
49th U. S. Colored Inf'y.	50th U. S. Colored Inf'y.	66th U. S. Colored Infantry.
53d U. S. Colored Inf'y.	52d U. S. Colored Inf'y.	D, 2d U. S. Col'd Light Ar'y.
46th U. S. Colored Inf'y.	C, 2d U. S. Col'd Light Ar'y.	

5th United States Colored Heavy Artillery. (Garrison of Vicksburg.)

United States Forces at Milliken's Bend, Louisiana—Colonel W. F. Wood, *commanding.*

46TH UNITED STATES COLORED INFANTRY.

Cavalry Brigade—Colonel T. Stephens, *commanding.*

2d Wisconsin Cavalry.
5th Illinois Cavalry.
11th Illinois Cavalry.
10th Missouri Cavalry.
3d U. S. Colored Cavalry.

Garrison of Vicksburg—Brigadier-General J. A. Maltby, *commanding.*

8th Illinois Infantry.
124th Illinois Infantry.
17th Illinois Infantry (det.).
81st Illinois Infantry.
7th Missouri Infantry (det.).
8th Ohio Battery.
26th Ohio Battery.

District of Natchez—Colonel B. G. Farrar, *commanding.*

29th Illinois Infantry.
28th Illinois Infantry.
4th Illinois Cavalry.
K, 2d Illinois Light Artillery.
58th U. S. Colored Infantry.
71st U. S. Colored Infantry.
70th U. S. Colored Infantry.
63d U. S. Colored Infantry.
64th U. S. Colored Infantry.
6th U. S. Colored Heavy Art'y.

Mississippi Marine Brigade—Brigadier-General A. W. Ellet, *com'ding.*

ARMY OF THE OHIO.

Fourth Division, Twenty-third Army Corps—Brigadier-General Jacob Ammen, *commanding.*

First Brigade.	Second Brigade.	Third Brigade.
(Cumberland Gap, Tennessee.)	*(Knoxville, Tennessee.)*	*(Loudon, Tennessee.)*
Colonel W. Y. Dillard.	Brigadier-General D. Tillson.	Colonel B. P. Runkle.

34th Kentucky Infantry.
2d N. C. Mounted Infantry.
9th Indiana Infantry.
L, 1st Michigan Light Ar'y.
M, 1st Michigan Light Ar'y.
B, 1st Tenn'see Light Ar'y.
22d Ohio Battery.
11th Tennessee Cavalry.
2d East Tennessee Inf'y.
1st Ohio Heavy Artillery.
1st U. S. Col'd Heavy Ar'y.
21st Ohio Battery.
Colvin's Illinois Battery.
Elgin's Illinois Battery.
Wilder's Indiana Battery.
10th Michigan Cavalry.
50th Ohio Infantry.
1st Tennessee Infantry.
11th Kentucky Infantry.
27th Kentucky Infantry.
4th Tennessee Infantry.
Henshaw's Illinois Battery.
14th Illinois Cavalry.

NOTE.—The 91st Indiana, 50th Ohio, 1st Tennessee, and the 11th and 27th Kentucky, of this command, were ordered to join the army in the field, May 17, 1864.

District of Kentucky, or Fifth Division, Twenty-third Army Corps—Brigadier-General S. G. BURBRIDGE, *commanding.*

FIRST DIVISION.

Brigadier-General E. H. HOBSON, *commanding.*

First Brigade.
Colonel S. Brown.

39th Kent'y Mounted Inf'y.
11th Michigan Cavalry.
14th Kentucky Infantry.

Second Brigade.
Colonel C. J. True.

40th Kent'y Mounted Inf'y.
12th Ohio Cavalry.
13th Kentucky Cavalry.

Third Brigade.
Colonel C. S. Hanson.

37th Kent'y Mounted Inf'y.
52d Kent'y Mounted Inf'y.

FOURTH BRIGADE.
Colonel J. M. BROWN, *commanding.*

30th Kentucky Mounted Infantry.
45th Kentucky Mounted Infantry.
47th Kentucky Infantry.
49th Kentucky Infantry.
1st Wisconsin Heavy Artillery.

SECOND DIVISION.

Brigadier-General HUGH EWING, *commanding.*

First Brigade.
Lieutenant-Colonel T. B. Fairleigh.

77th Co., 2d Battalion, V. R. C.
56th Co., 2d Battalion, V. R. C.
40th Co., 2d Battalion, V. R. C.
D, 23d Regiment, V. R. C.
48th Kentucky Infantry.
2d Ohio Heavy Artillery (det.).
20th Kentucky Infantry.
27th Kentucky Infantry.

Second Brigade.
Colonel C. Maxwell.

26th Kentucky Infantry.
35th Kentucky Infantry (mounted).
2d Ohio Heavy Artillery (det.).

Newport Barracks, Kentucky—Captain CHARLES SMITH, *commanding.*

Permanent party.

SAVANNAH, GEORGIA, *October* 23, 1875.

General W. T. SHERMAN, *United States Army, St. Louis, Missouri.*

GENERAL: I read in a paper yesterday that you were bringing out a second edition of your "Memoirs." If this be so, permit me to correct a few errors in your first edition in regard to your march through Georgia, which, though of no moment to you in comparison with your grand operations, are pertinent to the truth of history, and to me in connection with it.

On page 188, second volume, you say, "But these hastily retreated east across the Oconee River, leaving a good bridge, which we promptly secured."

I did not cross the Oconee River, as you state, but moved by rail to the support of General Cobb at Macon, with a company of mounted scouts, one battery of field-artillery, and about five hundred men, composed as you have stated. Before leaving Milledgeville, I ordered the bridge you refer to to be burned; but, on the representation to me by leading citizens that the bridge was essential to the town for supplies, and for a way of escape at the last, and knowing that its destruction would offer but a slight impediment to your well-appointed army, in the absence of all opposition, I revoked the order for its destruction. On arrival at Gordon, I learned that the wires between it and Macon had been cut about twenty minutes before, which caused me to halt, as I apprehended you had anticipated me, and that a portion of your command was in my way. Scouts were sent forward, and about midnight I learned from them and from citizens who came in of the repulse at Macon, and of General G. W. Smith's affair at Griswold. I was completely cut off from all communication with Macon I knew, and awaited further information and instructions, intrenching meanwhile. None, however, came to me, and learning from my scouts that a force of the enemy, of between four and five thousand, were close upon me, which my few hundreds could not contend with in the flat, open country, I fell back about sunset to the railroad crossing of the Ogeechee River, where a battalion of Confederate troops and a field-battery of Confederate artillery were stationed under command of Major Alfred L. Hartridge, of the Confederate army. The advance of your troops entered Gordon as I left, but failed in its attempt to head and cut me off. On arriving at the Ogeechee I assumed the command of the mixed troops, and spent Monday and Tuesday in strengthening my position at the bridge and at Ball's Ferry, eight miles below. My force numbered twelve hundred men, all told.

On Wednesday morning, at half-past ten, your advance opened upon me at the bridge, and about 3 P. M. at the ferry below. I held my ground, repulsing every attempt to carry the bridge and the ferry throughout Wednesday, Thursday, and Friday, when at dusk I learned that your left wing was closing my rear. In consequence, I withdrew my troops at the ferry, and abandoning the bridge at 1 A. M. Saturday, I fell back toward Millen, passing at Tenille within three miles of Slocum's advance. While at the bridge I had acquired from my scouts, who examined your columns closely, accurate information of your strength and movements, all of which was telegraphed to General Hardee at Savannah. But so possessed was he with the idea that my reports were exaggerated, and that you were making the best escape you could to the protection of the gunboats at Port Royal or Ossabaw, that my advice with regard to his action was not heeded. He was induced, however, to run up to me at the bridge, arriving Friday evening, but even there and at Tenille, where I had a consultation with him again, he could not comprehend the situation, so prejudiced had his mind become by telegrams from General Bragg at Augusta. At Millen I again halted until a courier from General Wheeler advised me to fall back to the crossing of the Little Ogeechee, as General Kilpatrick was working to get behind me.

At the Little Ogeechee I again took up position until your right wing lapped me, when I fell back. On receiving my telegram to that effect, General Hardee peremptorily ordered me to return to my position at the Little Ogeechee, adding that he would send up four thousand Confederate troops to my assistance. I returned as ordered, although my officers, in a body, protested against it, resumed my abandoned lines, and was reënforced as promised. The troops were disposed to make the best fight against overwhelming odds that could be made, and I grimly awaited the result. Your advance began skirmishing in the morning. In the course of the day General McLaws arrived with orders from General Hardee to relieve me in the command. I rode with McLaws along the lines, explaining my positions and the reasons for them, and the condition of affairs, and, returning to the telegraph station on the line of the railroad, resigned the command and retired to sleep, of which I stood in need. Hardly had I closed my eyes, when a request from General McLaws took me again to the telegraph station. Taking me aside, he told me that he had come up under a total misconception of the state of affairs; that their true condition had not been represented to him, and that under the circumstances he would not take the command, and that I must get out of the scrape. I told him that General Hardee had my telegrams representing Sherman's force at over seventy thousand men, marching leisurely along; that I had got out of the scrape once, but was sent back with increased numbers to complicate the problem, and that I was truly glad to be relieved from such (in my opinion) unwise operations. He positively refused to continue in command, and immediately returned to Savannah. Skirmishing in front was continuing, and from my advanced line I observed your position and movements to flank my right, the river being fordable, about waist-deep, above. Keeping my own counsel, I waited until eleven o'clock at night, when I sent for the generals of divisions and brigades, explained to them the position, and gave orders for withdrawing immediately and silently. The orders were well executed, and by 2 A. M. I had extricated my men and was in retreat; the cavalry, with a battery of field-artillery, covering it. At daybreak I saw my anticipations realized. You had flanked me, ready to close upon my right wing and rear. Escaping from your troops, I found my retreat embarrassed by an unexpected and dangerous obstruction. Civilians had been sent out from Savannah to burn the bridges in your front, and had commenced by destroying them in my rear, instead of waiting for me to pass. This nearly cost me my artillery, which was only saved by the coolness and energy of the officer in command of it. At about fifteen miles from Savannah my retreat was arrested by orders to take position behind a line of rifle-pits that had been dug there, and to occupy the line between the railroad and the Savannah River. Reconnoitring the position, I returned to my command and began my dispositions, when orders came to me to fall back upon the city, and occupy a line between the Augusta road and the river.

On arriving in Savannah I reported in person at headquarters, and found there General Beauregard, who had come over from Charleston. Making my report to him, in which your strength was included, he threw his hands up and exclaimed: "My God, Harry! what has come over you? You did not use to be so nervous! General Bragg telegraphs me from Augusta that Sherman has not more than twenty-one thousand men with him, that he hardly has eighteen thousand muskets, and is making a hasty retreat for his gunboats, either across Sister's Ferry to Port Royal, or to Ossabaw." I replied: "General, I don't know what reliable sources of information General Bragg may have in Augusta, but General Wheeler and I, who are the only general officers who have been in front of the enemy for the past fifteen days, have both reported that General Sherman has with him a force of more than seventy thousand men, well organized and equipped, marching leisurely, and showing no signs of haste. He cannot cross the Savannah River at Sister's Ferry, as there is a freshet, and the South Carolina side is flooded for three miles and more beyond it. Believe me, that Savannah is his objective point, and that on Friday night he will invest the city." My words seemed, unfortunately, to have no weight, and General G. W. Smith recovering from a slight attack of illness, I turned over to him the next day my command, and awaited the inevitable result of your movements.

On Friday morning early, my cousin, Colonel George Gordon, of the Sixtieth Georgia, temporarily attached to headquarters, called upon me in much concern, for he was sincerely attached to me, and expressed great regret at the position I held in the public estimation, saying that scouts had gone seventy miles up the right bank of the Ogeechee without encountering a sign of an enemy, and that I must certainly be mistaken. To which I answered that I was fully aware of the public feeling toward me and was sorry for it, but that I was right and not mistaken, as events would show, and that, though unpleasant, I had to bear like a man present contumely, knowing that I was right; and added: "Mark my words! at 2 P. M. to-day some of Osterhaus's men will break up the little command of North Carolinians at No. 2, and at nine to-night Savannah will be surrounded. I hear that your uncle, Mr. Cuyler, the President of the Central Railroad, intends leaving by a special train this evening on the Gulf Railroad for Macon. Beg him, from me, not to attempt it, for if he does he will run into Sherman's lines." He went, however, and was captured. Learning toward evening that General Beauregard intended to return that night to Charleston by the railroad, I called upon him and urged him not to attempt it, but cross at Screven's Ferry, below Savannah, and take the road at Hardeeville. My advice, however, was rejected, and he left by rail. Fortunately, the conductor thought there might be some danger, and ran slowly, stopping his train within about a mile of Slocum's lines. General Beauregard returned to Savannah and crossed at Screven's Ferry. The next morning revealed to the incredulous that Savannah was invested. The capture of McAllister settled the doubts as to your object completely.

The defense of Savannah should have been made, as I advised at the time, along the line of the Great Ogeechee. There you might have been checked, as my own slight resistance subsequently convinced me. That river passed, however, there was no serious impediment in your way to the sea. And had a strong fight been made there, I question if you could have made your way through the Carolinas unless reënforced strongly at Savannah. At no time was General Hardee in the field with ten thousand men, as you state on page 193, second volume. He was not in the field at all with any troops. And what you state on the same page with regard to McLaws at Ogeechee Church (the Little Ogeechee I call it) I have already explained in this narrative.

In all the incidents of this, my little campaign, I owe whatever merit may attach to them largely to my chief-of-staff, General Capers; and in resistance at the bridge and Ball's Ferry, to him, and to Major Alfred L. Hartridge, an *élève* of the Georgia Military Institute, in immediate command of the Confederate troops under me.

If I have been prolix, attribute it to the necessity for explaining, in justice to myself and my family, that which has not yet been understood, until this the first opportunity for explanation has been properly presented to me. Very respectfully, your obedient servant,

HENRY C. WAYNE.

SAVANNAH, GEORGIA, *January*, 1865.

Hon. GERRIT SMITH, *Peterboro, New York.*

MY DEAR SIR: You have heard, I know, of our occupation of this place, and many of the incidents connected with it must be familiar to you, but there is one which I wish you could have witnessed. I chanced on two or three consecutive days after our arrival to be in General Sherman's rooms when he was receiving the negroes of the place. Poor creatures! they came to him as their deliverer, and one black preacher told him, like Simeon in the Bible, he had prayed for this day, and all he now wanted was to see Mr. Lincoln. Some of them wanted to kneel before him, but the general would not permit it, and told them they must not kneel to any one but their Maker. To the white rebels, particularly those in high official positions, swelling, as they are apt to do, with their own self-importance, Sherman is not conciliatory. He tells them plainly of their crime and of the penalties which they must expect, and his treatment is the same of those who attempt to shield themselves under the garb of foreign allegiance or foreign official position; but to these humble creatures, overflowing with gratitude to God and to him, he was a different person, all kindness and goodness. He detained them with him, and their simple talk seemed to give him a pleasure which I have not seen him display in his intercourse with those of more pretension. While I was with him a negro recruiting officer came in to exhibit his papers. The general did not encourage him, and the other blacks present at once appealed to the general to know whether they were all liable to be conscripted and carried off, as armed parties were then circulating through the city, seizing every one they could, doubtless to speculate upon the bounties offered by the Government. General Sherman at once dispatched his staff-officers to put a stop to this outrage, and told the negroes that they were now free, that they must look for their living, and that, if they chose to enter the army and fight, they could do so, but should not be compelled to enlist or be treated otherwise than white men were; and that, so far as his feelings were concerned, he would rather for some time yet use them as laborers and pioneers than as soldiers.

You and I, who have been abolitionists of the strictest school for so many years—I since 1834, and you longer—may be permitted to be critical respecting the faith of new converts, and I am willing to take this display of General Sherman's feelings before the louder professions of many others. Previous to this interview with the blacks, which I witnessed, I had regarded General Sherman as a pro-slavery man—for most of the men I meet are pro-slavery—but since then I have looked upon him as not simply a great man but a good man as well.

I wish you would let your friend Phillips, and others thinking as we do, know these facts, since a man having the ability to do so much good, and having his heart in the right direction, should have all possible encouragement and support. Most affectionately yours,

A. Baird.

Note.—To this letter Mr. Smith made a prompt reply, expressing great gratification on his part and on that of Mr. Wendell Phillips, to whom he sent the letter, at this exhibition of General Sherman's feelings. I forwarded Mr. Smith's reply to General Sherman, and he promptly sent me the following reply: A. B.

Headquarters Military Division of the Mississippi,
in the field, Goldsboro, North Carolina, *April* 3, 1865.

General A. Baird, *present*.

Dear Baird: I thank you for the perusal of Gerrit Smith's letter. I doubt not he feels the joy he expresses at our progress, because we free the slaves in the same ratio that we manifest the power of our Government.

It seems impossible for citizens to understand us of the *old army.* In our private circles we may be gentle, kind, and forbearing, but when mutiny and war show their horrid heads we may seem very devils. As to the negro, I know I will do as much to ameliorate his political and social condition as Mr. Gerrit Smith, Wendell Phillips, Greeley, and others who seem to me mere theorists and not practical workers. If the people of the South had stood by the Constitution, I for one would have fought for the protection of the slave property, just as much as for any other kind of property, because the Constitution was a contract, signed, sealed, and delivered, and we had no right to go behind it. The right or wrong of slavery in the abstract had nothing to do with the contract made by our forefathers, for reasons good enough for them, and which we were bound in honor and law to abide by. But when the people and States of the South undertook to save their slave property by themselves breaking the Constitution, they themselves released us of our honorary and legal obligation, and we are free to deal with slavery as we please. They were slaves, but are now free, made so by their former owners breaking the bonds by which their slave property alone could be held.

Slavery as of old in this land is, in my judgment, long since determined, but we live in a busy world, and people won't be still. No sooner is one point gained than new ones arise, and we find plenty of people contending to make negroes voters, and even, with the legal right and encouragement, to commingle their blood with ours. On these points I think men may honestly differ very widely, and I for one would be slow in going to such extremes. The negro should, of course, be protected in his industry and encouraged to acquire property, knowledge, trade, and every means possible to better his condition, but I think we should all be rather too slow than too fast in extending political rights. These in time will adjust themselves according to the laws of Nature and experience. "Festina lente" is a good old maxim, and we, who have to catch the buffeting of political factions fighting their battles over our shoulders, ought to have a voice in questions which involve prejudices that influence the actions of men quite as much as pure reason.

I believe you and I have practically done more acts of kindness to the negroes of America than all the philanthropists put together; but our acts are quiet and unknown, whereas theirs have been noisy and demonstrative. I do not say this of Gerrit Smith, but of others who make the negro a hobby, and keep their precious persons well out of harm's way in the bloody struggle they have had their share in making, but not in subduing.

Your friend, W. T. SHERMAN, *Major-General.*

APPENDIX B.

"History of the Civil War in America." Comte de Paris. Translated by Louis F. Tasistro, edited by Professor Coppée, and published by J. H. Coates & Co., Philadelphia, 1876. Vol. III., page 853:

"Let us quote, in short, among our authors, the most illustrious of all, General Sherman, to whom we owe, under the form of 'Memoirs,' the pages the most original, brilliant, and instructive, which have ever been written on the war. General Sherman, who has never been ambitious for any political post, nor solicited the votes of any political party, has had the rare courage to say frankly in these 'Memoirs' what he thought of the officers who served near or under him. Judgments without any reticence, thus expressed by the commander of an army, clash with many feelings of self-love, and sometimes wound legitimate susceptibilities, and excite some manifestations of anger; but they have, in the eyes of the historian, an incomparable value."

"Around the World with General Grant." John Russell Young. Vol. II., pages 290 and 291:

"So far as the war is concerned," said the general, "I think history will more than approve the places given to Sherman and Sheridan. Sherman I have known for thirty-five years. During that time there never was but one cloud over our friendship, and that," said the general, laughing, "lasted about three weeks. When Sherman's book came out, General Boynton, the correspondent, printed some letters about it. In these, Sherman was made to disparage his comrades, and to disparage me especially. I cannot tell you how much I was shocked. But there were the letters and the extracts. I could not believe it in Sherman, the man whom I had always found so true and knightly, more anxious to honor others than win honor for himself. So I sent for the book, and I resolved to read it over, with paper and pencil, and make careful notes, and in justice to my comrades and myself prepare a reply. I do not think I ever ventured upon a more painful duty. I was some time about it. I was moving to Long Branch. I had official duties, and I am a slow reader. Then I missed the books when I reached the Branch, and had to send for them. So it was three weeks before I was through. During these weeks," replied the general, laughing, "I did not see Sherman, and I am glad I did not. My mind was so set by Boynton's extracts that I should certainly have been cold to him. But, when I finished the book, I found that I approved every word; that, apart from a few mistakes that any writer would make in so voluminous a work, it was a true book, an honorable book, creditable to Sherman, just to his companions—to myself particularly so—just such a book as I expected Sherman would write. Then it was accurate, because Sherman keeps a diary, and he compiled the book from notes made at the time. Then he is a very accurate man. You cannot imagine how pleased I was, for my respect and affection for Sherman were so great, that I look on these three weeks as among the most painful in my remembrance. I wrote Sherman my opinion of the book. I told him the only points I objected to were his criticisms upon some of our civil soldiers, like Logan and Blair. As a matter of fact, there were in the army no two men more loyal than John A. Logan and Frank Blair. I knew that Sherman did not mean to disparage either of them, and that he wrote hastily. Logan did a great work for the Union in bringing Egypt out of the Confederacy, which he did; and he was an admirable soldier, and is, as he always has been, an honorable, true man—a perfectly just and fair man, whose record in the army was brilliant. Blair also did a work in the war entitling him to the gratitude of every Northern man, and the respect of every soldier. Sherman did not do justice to Burnside; Burnside's fine character has sustained him in the respect and esteem of all who knew him through the most surprising reverses of fortune. There was a mistake in Sherman's book as to the suggestion of the Fort Henry and Donelson campaign coming from Halleck. But these are mistakes natural to a large book, which Sherman would be the last to commit, and the first to correct. Taking Sherman's book as a whole, it is a sound, true, honest work, and a valuable contribution to the history of the war."

NOTE.—The only allusion to General Burnside in my "Memoirs," to which his friends have ever taken exception, is found on pages 367 and 368, Vol. I., where I describe our reception at Knoxville, December 4, 1863, ending with a handsome "turkey-dinner."[1] This occurred after the Fifteenth Corps had marched about four hundred and fifty miles from Memphis, and fought two or three days from Mission Ridge back to Ringgold, when I was required to march it still another one hundred and twenty miles to Knoxville, Tennessee, by order of General Grant, furnished with copies of dispatches from General Burnside, to the effect that his provisions could only hold out until December 3d, by which time he must have relief, or could not be held responsible for the consequences.

[1] See the relevant section in Chapter 14 "Chattanooga and Knoxville. July to December, 1863."

General Burnside himself never took offense at this, but, on the contrary, many a time since the war we have, at his most hospitable table and mine, in Washington enjoyed "turkey-dinners," at which we have laughed over the "Knoxville affair."

As to Generals Logan and Blair, the newspaper critics quoted, as from the "Memoirs," the offensive words "political generals." Such words never did exist in the "Memoirs," and the simple truth was this:

When General McPherson was killed in battle, July 22, 1864, it was the office of the President to appoint his successor—mine simply to recommend. On pages 84 and 85, Vol. II., I endeavor to describe simply and truthfully the circumstances which influenced *my own action.* I would most gladly change the language if thereby I could purge it of all offense, but find it impossible; and I deny that a fair interpretation of the words used contains any just cause of offense to these most distinguished officers. I indorse fully every word General Grant says in reference to the value of their services before, during the war, and after; and go further, because I had a better opportunity to witness their individual conduct in the field. I have on many a public occasion borne willing testimony to their transcendent courage and ability in actual battle, and insist that the "Memoirs" contain many evidences of the high estimation in which I personally held them.

And where, afterward, I record that these two most prominent commanders of corps went back to take part in the presidential campaign, then at its crisis—General Logan went by President Lincoln's express and positive orders, and General Blair to resume his seat in Congress—I meant no reflection on these officers, but referred to the circumstance to explain *my own* embarrassment in preparing for the final campaign, which was bound to be fatal to the Southern Confederacy, or to me.

Finally, as to the movement of General Grant's army up the Tennessee in January and February, 1862, one of the most skillful and the most fruitful in results of the whole war, I simply describe, on pages 219 and 220, Vol. I., a scene which I personally witnessed in General Halleck's room, at the Planters' House, in St. Louis, and drew from it the only logical inference, that he, General Halleck, then in supreme command, was the author of that movement.[2] I did not and could not know who had suggested it to him; nor do I now attach as much importance to the conception of a plan of military operations as to the execution of the plan. This latter was unquestionably wholly General Grant's.

[2] See the relevant section in Chapter 9 "From the Battle of Bull Run to Paducah—Kentucky and Missouri. 1861–1862."

Acknowledgments

Index

Acknowledgments

This project could not have been completed without the firm support of the membership of the Ulysses S. Grant Association and its board of directors, led by President James A. Bultema and Executive Director Dr. Anne E. Marshall. The tangible support from the Ulysses S. Grant Library and its personnel, including Program Coordinator Eddie Rangel, Director of Research Dr. Ryan P. Semmes, and Office Associate Hannah Krapac, along with material support from Mississippi State University Libraries and Mississippi State University itself, have been invaluable to the editors' work. We thank undergraduates David Sides, Rebecca Woods, Tifanee Mask, Naja Morris, Hallie Greene, Kayleigh Wakefield, Clay Turner, Maggie Ellis, Kayla Crissinger, Margaret Haggerty, Catherine Babb, and Victoria Horton. Special thanks to Ivy Bopp, a student at Mississippi State University with an unmatched work ethic who went above and beyond on this project, putting in a very high number of hours. This project was also completed with assistance from a long list of talented graduate students from Mississippi State University's History Department, including Fraser Livingston, Aaron Thomas, Jeremy Montgomery, Heath Anderson, Ryan "Deadpool" Reynolds, Christy Davenport, Alex Cagle, Rachel Banks, John Scott, Jack Verhayden, David Hatfield, Jake Gabriele, Hunt Spencer, and Robert H. Conway Jr.

Additional thanks to Jeanne A. Marszalek and Regan Plunkett for their helpful comments and suggestions. Thanks also to former dean of the Mississippi State University Libraries, Frances N. Coleman, former interim dean Tommy Anderson, and the current dean of the libraries, Dr. Lis Pankl. The editors would also like to acknowledge Merri Gwin, Dr. Susannah Ural, Josh Nolen, Walt Giesen, Ben Nagel, Rebecca Houston, and Scott Jenkins. The editors would be remiss if they did not acknowledge Mississippi State University's president, Dr. Mark E. Keenum, whose love and passion for history and education have translated into invaluable support for the growth and success of the Ulysses S. Grant Presidential Library.

Index